Lecture Notes in Computer Science 3691

Commenced Publication in 1973
Founding and Former Series Editors:
Gerhard Goos, Juris Hartmanis, and Jan van Leeuwen

Editorial Board

David Hutchison
 Lancaster University, UK
Takeo Kanade
 Carnegie Mellon University, Pittsburgh, PA, USA
Josef Kittler
 University of Surrey, Guildford, UK
Jon M. Kleinberg
 Cornell University, Ithaca, NY, USA
Friedemann Mattern
 ETH Zurich, Switzerland
John C. Mitchell
 Stanford University, CA, USA
Moni Naor
 Weizmann Institute of Science, Rehovot, Israel
Oscar Nierstrasz
 University of Bern, Switzerland
C. Pandu Rangan
 Indian Institute of Technology, Madras, India
Bernhard Steffen
 University of Dortmund, Germany
Madhu Sudan
 Massachusetts Institute of Technology, MA, USA
Demetri Terzopoulos
 New York University, NY, USA
Doug Tygar
 University of California, Berkeley, CA, USA
Moshe Y. Vardi
 Rice University, Houston, TX, USA
Gerhard Weikum
 Max-Planck Institute of Computer Science, Saarbruecken, Germany

André Gagalowicz Wilfried Philips (Eds.)

Computer Analysis of Images and Patterns

11th International Conference, CAIP 2005
Versailles, France, September 5-8, 2005
Proceedings

Springer

Volume Editors

André Gagalowicz
INRIA Rocquencourt Research Unit
Domaine du Voluceau-Rocquencourt, B.P. 105, 78153 Le Chesnay, Cedex, France
E-mail: andre.gagalowicz@inria.fr

Wilfried Philips
TELIN, University of Ghent
Sint-Pietersnieuwstraat 41, 9000 Ghent, Belgium
E-mail: philips@telin.ugent.be

Library of Congress Control Number: 2005932111

CR Subject Classification (1998): I.5, I.4, I.3.5, I.2.10, I.2.6, F.2.2

ISSN   0302-9743
ISBN-10   3-540-28969-0 Springer Berlin Heidelberg New York
ISBN-13   978-3-540-28969-2 Springer Berlin Heidelberg New York

This work is subject to copyright. All rights are reserved, whether the whole or part of the material is concerned, specifically the rights of translation, reprinting, re-use of illustrations, recitation, broadcasting, reproduction on microfilms or in any other way, and storage in data banks. Duplication of this publication or parts thereof is permitted only under the provisions of the German Copyright Law of September 9, 1965, in its current version, and permission for use must always be obtained from Springer. Violations are liable to prosecution under the German Copyright Law.

Springer is a part of Springer Science+Business Media

springeronline.com

© Springer-Verlag Berlin Heidelberg 2005
Printed in Germany

Typesetting: Camera-ready by author, data conversion by Scientific Publishing Services, Chennai, India
Printed on acid-free paper   SPIN: 11556121   06/3142   5 4 3 2 1 0

Preface

This volume presents the proceedings of the 11th International Conference on Computer Analysis of Images and Patterns (CAIP 2005). This conference series started about 20 years ago in Berlin. Initially, the conference served as a forum for meetings between scientists from Western and Eastern-block countries. Nowadays, the conference attracts participants from all over the world. The conference gives equal weight to posters and oral presentations, and the selected presentation mode is based on the most appropriate communication medium. The program follows a single-track format, rather than parallel sessions. Non-overlapping oral and poster sessions ensure that all attendees have the opportunity to interact personally with presenters.

As for the numbers, we received a total of 185 submissions. All papers were reviewed by two to four members of the Program Committee. The final selection was carried out by the Conference Chairs. Out of the 185 papers, 65 were selected for oral presentation and 43 as posters. CAIP is becoming well recognized internationally, and this year's presentations came from 26 different countries. South Korea proved to be the most active scientifically with a total of 16 accepted papers. At this point, we wish to thank the Program Committee and additional referees for their timely and high-quality reviews. The paper submission and review procedure was carried out electronically. We also thank the invited speakers Reinhardt Koch and Thomas Vetter for kindly accepting to present invited papers.

CAIP 2005 was organized by INRIA Rocquencourt and took place at INRIA, close to the Versailles Castle. We hope that the conference proved to be a stimulating experience, and that you had an enjoyable stay in the beautiful town of Versailles.

July 2005 A. Gagalowicz and W. Philips
Editors

Organization

CAIP 2005 was organized by INRIA Rocquencourt and Ghent University.

Steering Committee

André Gagalowicz (INRIA Rocquencourt, France).
Reinhard Klette (The University of Auckland, Auckland, New Zealand).
Nicolai Petkov (University of Groningen, Groningen, The Netherlands).
Wladyslaw Skarbek (Warsaw University of Technology, Warsaw, Poland).
Gerald Sommer (Christian-Albrechts-Universität zu Kiel, Kiel, Germany).

Organizing Committee

André Gagalowicz (INRIA Rocquencourt, France).
Marie-Francoise Loubressac (INRIA-Rocquencourt, France).
Wilfried Philips (Ghent University, Ghent, Belgium).
Dominique Potherat (INRIA Rocquencourt, France).
Richard Roussel (INRIA, Le Chesnay, France).

Sponsors

CAIP 2005 was sponsored by the following organizations:

- INRIA
- Ghent University
- DGA
- IEEE Section France

Program Committee

Patrick Bouthemy (IRISA / INRIA, Rennes, France).
Aurélio Campilho (Universidade do Porto, Portugal).
Dmitry Chetverikov (Computer and Automation
    Research Institute of Budapest, Hungary).
Leszek Chmielewski (Institute of Fundamental Technological
    Research, PAS, Warsaw, Poland).
David Cooper (Brown University, USA).
Patrick De Smet (Ghent University, Ghent, Belgium).
Alberto Del Bimbo (Università degli Studi di Firenze, Italy).
Rachid Deriche (INRIA, Sophia-Antipolis, France).
Vito Di Gesu (University of Palermo, Palermo, Italy).
Jan-Olof Eklundh (Royal Institute of Technology, Sweden).
André Gagalowicz (INRIA Rocquencourt, France).
Sidharta Gautama (Ghent University, Ghent, Belgium).
Georgy Gimel'farb (University of Auckland, Auckland, New Zealand).
Oliver Grau (BBC R&D, Tadworth, UK).
Vaclav Hlavac (Czech Technical University, Prague, Czech Republic).
Atsushi Imiya (Chiba University, Chiba, Japan).
Jean-Michel Jolion (INSA Lyon, Villeurbanne, France).
Wlodzimierz Kasprzak (Warsaw University of Technology, Warsaw, Poland).
Ashraf Kassim (National University of Singapore, Singapore).
Yukiko Kenmochi (CNRS, Marne-la-Vallée, France).
Reinhard Klette (The University of Auckland, Auckland, New Zealand).
Reinhard Koch (Christian-Albrechts-Universität zu Kiel, Kiel, Germany).
Walter Kropatsch (Vienna University of Technology, Austria).
Marek Kurzynski (Technical University of Wroclaw, Poland).
Ales Leonardis (University of Ljubljana, Ljubljana, Slovenia).
Martin Levine (McGill University 1, Montreal, Canada).
Klaus-Eberhard Liedtke (Universität Hannover, Hannover, Germany).
Takashi Matsuyama (Kyoto University, Kyoto, Japan).
Vittorio Murino (University of Verona, Verona, Italy).
Heinrich Niemann (Universität Erlangen-Nürnberg, Erlangen, Germany).
Constantinos Pattichis (University of Cyprus, Cyprus).
Dietrich Paulus (University of Koblenz, Koblenz, Germany).
Peter Peer (CEIT, San Sebastián, Spain).
Shmuel Peleg (The Hebrew University, Jerusalem, Israel).
Nicolai Petkov (University of Groningen, Groningen, The Netherlands).
Maria Petrou (University of Surrey, Guildford, UK).
Wilfried Philips (Ghent University, Ghent, Belgium).
Ioannis Pitas (Aristotle University of Thessaloniki, Thessaloniki, Greece).
Dan Popescu (CSIRO, Sydney, Australia).
Ralf Reulke (Humboldt-Universität zu Berlin, Berlin, Germany).
Alberto Sanfeliu (Polytechnic University of Catalonia, Barcelona, Spain).
Jean Serra (Ecole des Mines de Paris, France).

Wladyslaw Skarbek (Warsaw University of Technology, Warsaw, Poland).
Franc Solina (University of Ljubljana, Ljubljana, Slovenia).
Gerald Sommer (Christian-Albrechts-Universität zu Kiel, Kiel, Germany).
Tele Tan (Curtin University of Technology, Perth, Australia).
Tieniu Tan (Chinese Academy of Sciences, China).
Jean-Philippe Tarel (LCPC, Paris, France).
Emanuele Trucco (Heriot-Watt University, Edinburgh, UK).
Juan José Villanueva (Autonomous University of Barcelona, Barcelona, Spain).
Harry Wechsler (George Mason University, USA).
Michel Westenberg (University of Stuttgart, Stuttgart, Germany).
Konrad Wojciechowski (Institute of Automation, Gliwice, Poland).

Table of Contents

Contour Tracking Using Modified Canny Edge Maps with
Level-of-Detail
    Jihun Park 1

Moment Invariants for Recognizing Symmetric Objects
    Jan Flusser, Tomáš Suk 9

A Linear Algorithm for Polygonal Approximations of Thick Curves
    Trung Nguyen 17

NMF with LogGabor Wavelets for Visualization
    Zhonglong Zheng, Jianmin Zhao, Jie Yang 26

A Study on Fast Iris Image Acquisition Method
    Kang Ryoung Park 33

Automatic Human Model Generation
    Bodo Rosenhahn, Lei He, Reinhard Klette 41

An Illumination Invariant Face Recognition Approach Using
Exemplar-Based Synthesis Technique
    Tele Tan, Thorsten Kühnapfel, Amelyn Wongso, Fee-Lee Lim 49

A Phase Correlation Approach to Active Vision
    Hongchuan Yu, M. Bennamoun 57

A Novel Verification Criterion for Distortion-Free Fingerprints
    Neil Yager, Adnan Amin 65

Nonparametric Fingerprint Deformation Modelling
    Neil Yager, Adnan Amin 73

Outdoor Image Classification Using Artificial Immune Recognition
System (AIRS) with Performance Evaluation by Fuzzy Resource
Allocation Mechanism
    Kemal Polat, Seral Şahan, Halife Kodaz,
    Salih Güneş 81

Statistical Approach to Boar Semen Head Classification Based on
Intracellular Intensity Distribution
    Lidia Sánchez, Nicolai Petkov, Enrique Alegre 88

3D Triangular Mesh Parametrization Using Locally Linear Embedding
  Xianfang Sun, Edwin R. Hancock 96

Variational Analysis of Spherical Images
  *Atsushi Imiya, Hironobu Sugaya, Akihiko Torii,
  Yoshihiko Mochizuki* 104

Iterative Stereo Reconstruction from CCD-Line Scanner Images
  Ralf Reulke, Georgy Gimel'farb, Susanne Becker 112

Content-Based Image Retrieval Using Color and Pattern Histogram
Adaptive to Block Classification Characteristics
  Tae-Su Kim, Seung-Jin Kim, and Kuhn-Il Lee 120

Commute Times for Graph Spectral Clustering
  Huaijun Qiu, Edwin R. Hancock 128

A New Approach to Camera Image Indexing
  Rastislav Lukac, Konstantinos N. Plataniotis 137

Discrete Average of Two-Dimensional Shapes
  Isameddine Boukhriss, Serge Miguet, Laure Tougne 145

Coupled Statistical Face Reconstruction
  William A.P. Smith, Edwin R. Hancock 153

Recovery of Surface Height Using Polarization from Two Views
  Gary Atkinson, Edwin R. Hancock 162

FSVC: A New Fully Scalable Video Codec
  *Manuel F. López, Sebastián G. Rodríguez, Juan P. Ortiz,
  José M. Dana, Vicente G. Ruiz, Inmaculada García* 171

Eigenspaces from Seriated Graphs
  Hang Yu, Edwin R. Hancock 179

A Predictive Direction Guided Fast Motion Estimation Algorithm
  Cheng-Dong Shen, Tie-Jun Li, Si-Kun Li 188

Toward Polygonalisation of Thick Discrete Arcs
  Firas Alhalabi, Laure Tougne 197

A Segmentation Algorithm for Noisy Images
  Soufiane Rital, Hocine Cherifi, Serge Miguet 205

Finding the Number of Clusters for Nonparametric Segmentation
  Nikolaos Nasios, Adrian G. Bors 213

Optical Flow Diffusion with Robustified Kernels
  Ashish Doshi, Adrian G. Bors 222

Stereo Vision Based Localization of Free Parking Site
  Ho Gi Jung, Dong Suk Kim, Pal Joo Yoon, Jai Hie Kim 231

Data Fusion for Photorealistic 3D Models
  Zsolt Jankó, Dmitry Chetverikov 240

Virtualized Real Object Integration and Manipulation in an Augmented Scene
  Brahim Nini, Mohamed Batouche 248

Automatic Detection of Spiculated Masses Using Fractal Analysis in Digital Mammography
  HyungJun Kim, WonHa Kim 256

Hybrid Framework for Medical Image Segmentation
  Chunyan Jiang, Xinhua Zhang, Christoph Meinel 264

Evolving Spanning Trees Using the Heat Equation
  Fan Zhang, Huaijun Qiu, Edwin R. Hancock 272

Design of Statistical Measures for the Assessment of Image Segmentation Schemes
  Marc Van Droogenbroeck, Olivier Barnich 280

Re-lighting and Compensation for Face Images
  Xiaoyue Jiang, Tuo Zhao, Rong Xiao, Rongchun Zhao 288

Shape from Silhouettes in Discrete Space
  Atsushi Imiya, Kosuke Sato 296

Multiple Feature Domains Information Fusion for Computer-Aided Clinical Electromyography
  Hongbo Xie, Hai Huang, Zhizhong Wang 304

Color Transfer Using Motion Estimations and Its Application to Video Compression
  Ritwik K. Kumar, Suman K. Mitra 313

Minimum-Length Polygons of First-Class Simple Cube-Curves
  Fajie Li, Reinhard Klette 321

Combining Character Level Classifier and Probabilistic Lexicons in
Handwritten Word Recognition - Comparative Analysis of Methods
  Marek Kurzynski, Jerzy Sas 330

Preprocessing Convex Polygons Using Range Trees for Recognition
with Few Finger Probes
  Sumanta Guha, Kiêu Trọng Khánh 338

Separable Linear Classifiers for Online Learning in Appearance Based
Object Detection
  Christian Bauckhage, John K. Tsotsos 347

The Randomized Hough Transform for Spherical Images
  Akihiko Torii, Atsushi Imiya 355

Computerized Extraction of Craniofacial Anatomical Structures for
Orthodontic Analysis
  *Weining Yue, Dali Yin, Guoping Wang, Chengjun Li,
  Tianmin Xu* 363

Stability of the Eigenvalues of Graphs
  Ping Zhu, Richard C. Wilson 371

3D Modeling of Humans with Skeletons from Uncalibrated Wide
Baseline Views
  *Chee Kwang Quah, Andre Gagalowicz, Richard Roussel,
  Hock Soon Seah* 379

Magnitude and Phase Spectra of Foot Motion for Gait Recognition
  *Agus Santoso Lie, Shuichi Enokida, Tomohito Wada,
  Toshiaki Ejima* 390

Advances in Background Updating and Shadow Removing for Motion
Detection Algorithms
  Paolo Spagnolo, Tiziana D'Orazio, Marco Leo, Arcangelo Distante .. 398

Sequential Coordinate-Wise Algorithm for the Non-negative Least
Squares Problem
  Vojtěch Franc, Václav Hlaváč, Mirko Navara 407

Recognition of Partially Occluded and Deformed Binary Objects
  Ondřej Horáček, Jan Kamenický, Jan Flusser 415

InfoBoost for Selecting Discriminative Gabor Features
  Li Bai, Linlin Shen 423

Computer Vision Based System for Interactive Cooperation of Multiple Users
  Alberto Del Bimbo, Lea Landucci, Alessandro Valli 433

Supervised Texture Detection in Images
  Branislav Mičušík, Allan Hanbury 441

Filter Selection and Identification Similarity Using Clustering Under Varying Illumination
  Mi Young Nam, Battulga, Phill Kyu Rhee 449

Method for Automatically Segmenting the Spinal Cord and Canal from 3D CT Images
  László G. Nyúl, Judit Kanyó, Eörs Máté, Géza Makay, Emese Balogh, Márta Fidrich, Attila Kuba 456

Vehicle Area Segmentation Using Grid-Based Feature Values
  Nakhoon Baek, Ku-Jin Kim, Manpyo Hong 464

Improvement of a Temporal Video Index Produced by an Object Detector
  Gaël Jaffré, Philippe Joly 472

Multi-camera Person Tracking in a Cluttered Interaction Environment
  Daniel Grest, Reinhard Koch 480

Improvement of a Person Labelling Method Using Extracted Knowledge on Costume
  Gaël Jaffré, Philippe Joly 489

Face Modeling and Adaptive Texture Mapping for Model Based Video Coding
  Kamil Yurtkan, Hamit Soyel, Hasan Demirel, Hüseyin Özkaramanlı, Mustafa Uyguroğlu, Ekrem Varoğlu 498

Multispectral Integration for Segmentation of Chromosome Images
  Shishir Shah 506

Bit-Rate Control Algorithm for ROI Enabled Video Coding
  Adam Pietrowcew, Andrzej Buchowicz, Władysław Skarbek 514

Classification of Moving Humans Using Eigen-Features and Support Vector Machines
  Sijun Lu, Jian Zhang, David Feng 522

A Queue Based Algorithm for Order Independent Anchored
Skeletonisation
   Marcin Iwanowski, Pierre Soille 530

Morphological Refinement of an Image Segmentation
   Marcin Iwanowski, Pierre Soille 538

Pattern Analysis of Movement Behavior of Medaka (*Oryzias latipes*):
A Decision Tree Approach
   *Sengtai Lee, Jeehoon Kim, Jae-Yeon Baek, Man-Wi Han,
   Sungshin Kim, Tae-Soo Chon* 546

Linear Algorithm and Hexagonal Search Based Two-Pass Algorithm for
Motion Estimation
   Yunsong Wu, Graham Megson 554

Designing Mathematical Morphology Algorithms on FPGAs: An
Application to Image Processing
   Damien Baumann, Jacques Tinembart 562

Object Detection in Multi-channel and Multi-scale Images Based on
the Structural Tensor
   Bogusław Cyganek 570

Evaluating Minimum Spanning Tree Based Segmentation Algorithms
   *Yll Haxhimusa, Adrian Ion, Walter G. Kropatsch,
   Thomas Illetschko* 579

Feature Space Reduction for Face Recognition with Dual Linear
Discriminant Analysis
   Krzysztof Kucharski, Władysław Skarbek, Mirosław Bober 587

On the Design of Reliable Graph Matching Techniques for Change
Detection
   Sidharta Gautama, Werner Goeman, Johan D'Haeyer 596

Extraction of 3D Vascular Tree Skeletons Based on the Analysis of
Connected Components Evolution
   Juan F. Carrillo, Maciej Orkisz, Marcela Hernández Hoyos 604

Color-Contrast Landmark Detection and Encoding in Outdoor Images
   Eduardo Todt, Carme Torras 612

Global Color Image Features for Discrete Self–localization of an Indoor
Vehicle
   Włodzimierz Kasprzak, Wojciech Szynkiewicz, Mikołaj Karolczak 620

Application of Automatic Image Registration in a Segmentation
Framework of Pelvic CT Images
  Attila Tanács, Eörs Máté, Attila Kuba 628

A New Snake Model Robust on Overlap and Bias Problems in Tracking
a Moving Target
  Youngjoon Han, Hernsoo Hahn 636

Neighborhood Decomposition of 3D Convex Structuring Elements for
Morphological Operations
  Syng-Yup Ohn 644

Domain Knowledge Extension with Pictorially Enriched Ontologies
  Marco Bertini, Rita Cucchiara, Alberto Del Bimbo, Carlo Torniai ... 652

Segmentation via Graph-Spectral Methods and Riemannian Geometry
  Antonio Robles-Kelly 661

A Practical Guide to Marker Based and Hybrid Visual Registration for
AR Industrial Applications
  *Steve Bourgeois, Hanna Martinsson, Quoc-Cuong Pham,
  Sylvie Naudet* 669

Pattern Selective Image Fusion for Multi-focus Image Reconstruction
  Vivek Maik, Jeongho Shin, Joonki Paik 677

Fast Pixel Classification by SVM Using Vector Quantization, Tabu
Search and Hybrid Color Space
  *Gilles Lebrun, Christophe Charrier, Olivier Lezoray,
  Cyril Meurie, Hubert Cardot* 685

CamShift-Based Tracking in Joint Color-Spatial Spaces
  Bogdan Kwolek 693

A Robust Detector for Distorted Music Staves
  Mariusz Szwoch 701

Illusory Surface Perception Using a Hierarchical Neural Network Model
of the Visual Pathways
  Woobeom Lee, Wookhyun Kim 709

A Robust Digital Watermarking Adopting 2D Barcode
  Su-Young Han, Eui-Hyun Jung, Seong-Yun Cho 717

4D Reconstruction of Coronary Arteries from Monoplane Angiograms
  Sahla Bouattour, Richard Arndt, Dietrich Paulus 724

Temporal Video Indexing Based on Early Vision Using Laguerre Filters
Carlos Joel Rivero-Moreno, Stéphane Bres 732

Comparative Study of 3D Face Acquisition Techniques
Mark Chan, Patrice Delmas, Georgy Gimel'farb, Philippe Leclercq ... 740

A Fuzzy Hierarchical Attributed Graph Approach for Handwritten Hieroglyphs Description
Denis Arrivault, Noël Richard, Philippe Bouyer 748

Adaptive Fuzzy Text Segmentation in Images with Complex Backgrounds Using Color and Texture
Julinda Gllavata, Bernd Freisleben 756

Neighborhood Sequences and Their Applications in the Digital Image Processing
Attila Fazekas, András Hajdu, István Sánta, Tamás Tóth 766

Viseme Classification for Talking Head Application
Mariusz Leszczynski, Władysław Skarbek 773

New Algorithms for Example-Based Super-Resolution
László Czúni, Gergely Császár, Dae-Sung Cho, Hyun Mun Kim 781

Determination of Fabric Viscosity Parameters Using Iterative Minimization
Hatem Charfi, André Gagalowicz, Rémi Brun 789

Efficient Off-Line Verification and Identification of Signatures by Multiclass Support Vector Machines
Emre Özgündüz, Tülin Şentürk, M. Elif Karshgil 799

Motion-Based Hierarchical Active Contour Model for Deformable Object Tracking
Jeongho Shin, Hyunjong Ki, Joonki Paik 806

Multi-modal Face Tracking in Multi-camera Environments
Hang-Bong Kang, Sang-Hyun Cho 814

Facial Features Detection by Coefficient Distribution Map
Daidi Zhong, Irek Defée 822

Region Based Detection of Occluded People for the Tracking in Video Image Sequences
Yongtae Do 829

Virtual Garment Pre-positioning
  Tung Le Thanh, André Gagalowicz 837

Real-Time Topology Modification for Finite Element Models with
Haptic Feedback
  Dan C. Popescu, Bhautik Joshi, Sébastien Ourselin 846

A Hierarchical Face Behavior Model for a 3D Face Tracking Without
Markers
  Richard Roussel, Andre Gagalowicz 854

Author Index 863

Contour Tracking Using Modified Canny Edge Maps with Level-of-Detail

Jihun Park

Department of Computer Engineering,
Hongik University, Seoul, Korea
jhpark@cs.hongik.ac.kr

Abstract. We propose a simple but powerful method for tracking a non-parameterized subject contour in a single video stream with a moving camera and changing background for the purpose of video background removal to capture motion in a scene. Our method is based on level-of-detail (LOD) *modified* Canny edge maps and graph-based routing operations on the LOD maps. We generated modified Canny edge maps by computing intensity derivatives in a normal direction of a previous frame contour to remove irrelevant edges. Computing Canny edge maps in the previous contour normal direction have effects of removing irrelevant edges. LOD Canny edge maps are generated by changing scale parameters for a given image. A *simple (strong)* Canny edge map, *Scanny*, has the smallest number of edge pixels while the most detailed Canny edge map, $Wcanny_N$, has the largest number of edge pixels. To reduce side-effects because of irrelevant edges, we start our basic tracking by using *Scanny* edges generated from large image intensity gradients of an input image. Starting from *Scanny* edges, we get more edge pixels ranging from simple Canny edge maps until the most detailed (weaker) Canny edge maps, called *Wcanny* maps along LOD hierarchy. LOD Canny edge pixels become nodes in routing, and LOD values of adjacent edge pixels determine routing costs between the nodes. We find the *best* route to follow Canny edge pixels favoring stronger Canny edge pixels. If *Scanny* edges are disconnected, routing between disconnected parts are planned using Wcanny edges in LOD hierarchy. Our accurate tracking is based on reducing effects from irrelevant edges by selecting the stronger edge pixels, thereby relying on the current frame edge pixel as much as possible contrary to other approaches of always combining the previous contour. Our experimental results show that this tracking approach is robust enough to handle a complex-textured scene.

1 Introduction and Related Works

This work is an improvement on our previous work in contour tracking[1]. We track a highly textured subject moving in a complex scene compared to a relatively simple subject tracking done by others. We mean *complex* because both tracked subject and background scene leave many edges after the edge detection. We assume our subject is never occluded by any background objects, but it occludes other objects in the background. In tracking a parameterized contour, a subject contour estimating the motion is represented by using parameters. In general, these methods use the Snake model[2]; Kalman Snake[3] and Adaptive Motion Snake[4] are popular Snake models.

In the method of tracking a nonparameterized contour, a subject contour as a subject border is represented. The contour created by these algorithms is represented as a set of pixels. Recently, Nguyen proposed a method[5] for tracking a nonparameterized subject contour in a single video stream with a moving camera and a changing background. Nguyen's approach combined the outputs of two steps: creating a predicted contour and removing background edges. Nguyen's background edge removal method of leaving many irrelevant edges is subject to inaccurate contour tracking in a *complex* scene because removing the background edges is difficult. Nguyen's method[5] of combining the predicted contour computed from the previous frame accumulates tracking error. We remove redundant edges by modifying Canny edge generation, one of major contribution of this paper.

2 Overview of Our System

Figure 1 shows an overview of our system for tracking a single image frame. As inputs, we get a previous image frame, denoted as $frame\ (t-1)$ and the corresponding tracked subject contour of input $frame\ (t-1)$, and a current image frame, denoted as $frame\ (t)$. From $frame\ (t-1)$, contour of $frame\ (t-1)$, and $frame\ (t)$, we compute a predicted contour, $\partial\Omega^{(p,t)}$, for $frame\ (t)$ using subject motion[5]. Then, we generate various detailed levels of modified Canny edge image maps for the input $frame\ (t)$. The *modified* Canny edge maps are generated in terms of the predicted contour normal direction. We select *Scanny* edges from the LOD Canny edge maps. From a *Scanny* edge map, we derive a corresponding distance map. Using the predicted contour, the best matching is then found between the predicted contour and the *Scanny* distance map. *Scanny* edge pixels matching with the predicted contour become the frame of the contour build up. We call these pixels *selected Scanny contour pixels*. Selected *Scanny contour pixels* are the most reliable reference contour pixels to start building a closed tracked contour, and are stored in the *selected Scanny found list*. We then

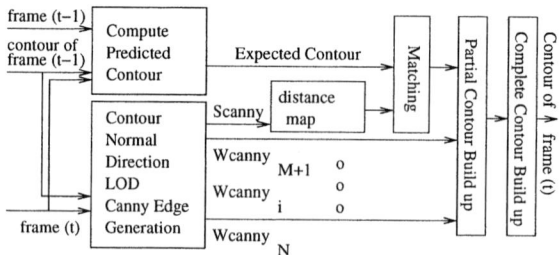

Fig. 1. Overview of our single frame tracking

route a path to connect adjacent *selected Scanny contour pixels* in the found list using LOD Canny edge pixels. If we finish connecting every adjacent *selected Scanny contour pixel* pair, we get a set of *partial contours*. We run a final routing using the computed segments of partial contours and *Scanny* edges around it to find the best contour. The resulting contour becomes the contour of $frame\ (t)$.

3 Modified Canny Edge Generation

To overcome Nguyen's two problems, difficulty in removing noisy background edges and accumulating tracking errors, we propose a new method to increase the subject tracking accuracy by using LOD Canny edge maps in predicted contour normal direction. We use two major approaches. First, in order to reduce side-effects caused by irrelevant edges, we generate Canny edge maps around the predicted contour in the contour normal direction. Second, we start our basic tracking contour using *Scanny* edges, some of them become our reference edge pixels for contour routing.

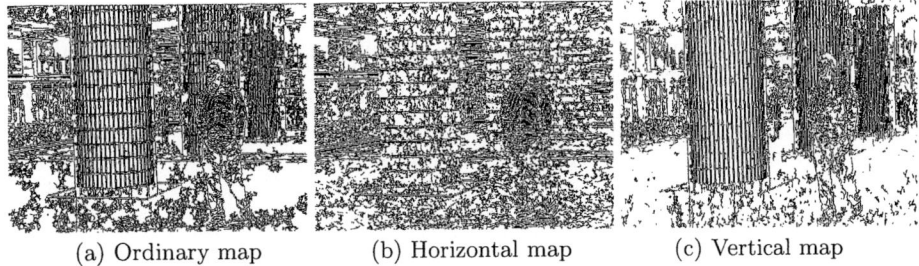

(a) Ordinary map   (b) Horizontal map   (c) Vertical map

Fig. 2. Effect of computing Canny edge maps of the same image according to the contour direction

Figure 2(a) shows an ordinary Canny edge map, and Figure 2(b,c) show modified Canny edge maps generated for the same image assuming horizontal and vertical contour direction respectively. It is generated by computing the image intensity derivatives in the contour normal direction. As can be found from the figures, the contour direction effect on generating Canny edge maps is removing redundant edges generated in an ordinary Canny edge map. The first frame contour is given as an input, as presented in Figure 3(a), and subsequent contours are computed using modified Canny edges as presented in Figure 1.

4 LOD Canny Edge Maps

A *strong Canny edge map* is generated by a pixel-wise union of the simplest Canny edge maps out of various scaled Canny edge maps. Our new method selects only the Canny edges with large image intensity gradient values, *Scanny* edges. A *Scanny* edge map does not have noisy background edges and looks simple. Working on Scanny has an effect of background edge removal. Our accurate tracking is based on reducing the effects from irrelevant edges by only selecting strongest edge pixels, and relying on the current frame edge pixels as much as possible contrary to Nguyen's approach of always combining the previous contour.

For Canny edge maps generated with smaller image intensity gradient values, we call $Wcanny_i$, $i = M+1, \cdots, N$ where N is the number of LOD Canny edge maps, M is the number of Canny edge maps used in computing *Scanny* edge map. $Wcanny_{M+1}$ has the simplest Canny edges among $Wcanny_i$s. $Wcanny_N$ has the most detailed Canny edges generated by an accumulation from largest (*strongest*) till to the smallest (*weakest*) intensity gradient valued edges.

Scanny edge maps are very reliable because they are generated only if there are big intensity changes in the image. We need both simple and detailed Canny edge maps for the best subject tracking. We totally order the resulting Canny edge maps by counting the number of edge pixels in each edge map.

Let $\Phi_i^{(I,t)}$, where $i = 1, \cdots, N$, be a totally ordered set of Canny edge maps of an input image frame (t). $\Phi_1^{(I,t)}$ has the smallest number of edge pixels while $\Phi_N^{(I,t)}$ has the largest number of edge pixels. Then, we take the top 10 percent to 30 percent of the simple Canny edge maps and union into pixel-level to make a *Scanny* edge map, $S\Phi^{(I,t)}$. The rest of the Canny edge maps are used to generate $Wcanny_i$, $W\Phi_i^{(I,t)}$.

$$S\Phi^{(I,t)} = \bigcup_{i=1}^{M} \Phi_i^{(I,t)}$$
$$W\Phi_i^{(I,t)} = S\Phi^{(I,t)} \cup \left(\bigcup_{j=M+1}^{i} \Phi_j^{(I,t)}\right), i = (M+1), \cdots, N \quad (1)$$

where $\bigcup$ is pixel-wise union of bitmaps. Part of Figure 3(e) shows an example of *Scanny*, while Figure 2(a) looks the same as $Wcanny_N$ Canny edge map.

LOD Canny edge map, $L\Phi^{(I,t)}$, is generated using $S\Phi^{(I,t)}$ and $W\Phi_i^{(I,t)}$s edge pixels around $\partial\Omega^{(p,t)}$. $\Gamma(L\Phi^{(I,t)}(x,y))$ is a function returning an LOD value given an edge pixel (x,y) of a LOD edge map, $L\Phi^{(I,t)}$. To build a $L\Phi^{(I,t)}$, we search $S\Phi^{(I,t)}$ and $W\Phi_i^{(I,t)}$s from the simplest edge map to the most detailed edge map.

5 Matching for Selecting Reference Scanny Contour Pixel

Basically, we rely only on a *Scanny* edge map and a predicted contour from the previous frame to find reference pixels, called *selected* Scanny pixels, for building a basic tracked contour frame. Then, we seek additional edge pixels from $Wcanny_i$s following LOD in edge maps. These *selected* Scanny pixels become start nodes and end nodes in routing. LOD Canny edge pixels become nodes in routing, and LOD values of adjacent edge pixels determine routing costs between the nodes. We assign the lowest cost between two adjacent *Scanny* edge pixels to encourage *Scanny*-based routing.

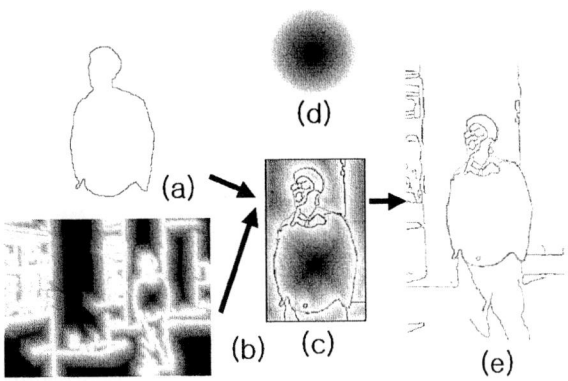

Fig. 3. Predicted contour from frame $(t-1)$ (a), distance map generated from *Scanny* (b), matching between predicted contour and *Scanny* distance map (c), circular distance map used in matching (d), *Scanny* edge map and selected reference pixels(e)

Figure 3 shows a process of computing *selected Scanny pixels*, and the selection result is presented in Figure 3(e). *Selected Scanny pixels* are denoted as green pixels in Figure 3(e), along the predicted contour, while red pixels mean a failure in finding a matching *Scanny* pixel. By using an image matching as used by others[5], we can get a predicted contour, $\partial \Omega^{(p,t)}$, as presented in Figure 3(a). Then, we generate a distance map of *Scanny*, $DS\Phi^{(I,t)}$, as in Figure 3(b).

Figure 3(c) shows an example of the best matching with the reference contour pixel point (marked as red cross). The green contour denotes the predicted contour, while black edge pixels denote *Scanny* edge pixels. Gray levels are shown because of a distance map of *Scanny* edge map. *Selected Scanny contour pixels* are the reference pixels to start building a segment of a tracked contour and are stored in the *selected Scanny found list*.

6 Reference Contour Pixel Connection by LOD Pixel Routing

From a set of adjacent *selected Scanny edge pixels*, reference pixels for routing, we find segments of contours, called *partial contour*. In finding a *partial contour*, we find the *best* route to follow Canny edge pixels favoring stronger Canny edge pixels using Dijkstra's minimum cost routing. We route a minimum cost path to connect *adjacent selected Scanny contour pixels* in the *selected Scanny found list* using LOD Canny edge pixels, $L\Phi^{(I,t)}$. If we finish connecting every adjacent *selected Scanny contour pixel* pairs, we get a set of *partial contours*. Figure 4 shows a close up of a matching result between the predicted contour and the current frame Scanny edge map. The green pixels were stored in the selected Scanny found list. The group of computed partial contours will be the *basic* tracked subject contour for $frame\ (t)$. We take a part of the LOD Canny edge map around two adjacent *selected Scanny contour pixels*. Pixels of the LOD map become

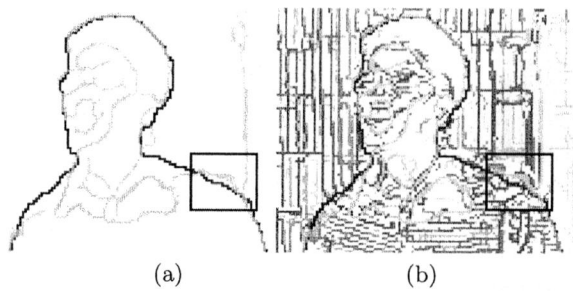

Fig. 4. Close-up of selected Scanny pixels after matching between the predicted contour and the current frame Scanny edge map (a), selected Scanny pixels as well as accumulation from $Wcanny_{M+1}$ until $Wcanny_N$ edge pixels (b)

nodes, and we determine costs between *adjacent* pixels. We assign the lowest cost between two adjacent *Scanny* edge pixels to encourage *Scanny*-based routing.

To build a closed and complete contour for the current frame, we use *Scanny* edge maps around the predicted contour as well as a set of *partial contours* computed from *selected Scanny edge pixels*. The resulting contour becomes the contour of the current frame.

7 Experimental Results

We have experimented with easily available video sequences either available on the Internet or generated with a home camcorder, SONY DCR-PC3. We have generated 64 different LOD Canny edge maps, ordered them according to the number of Canny edge pixels, and union simplest 13 (top 20 percent) Canny edge maps to make *Scanny* Canny edge map. It is not necessary to keep 64 different levels. We may vary the percentage of Canny edge maps in determining a *Scanny* edge map. Figure 5 shows a man walking in a subway hall. The hall tiles as well as a cross stripe shirt generate many complicated Canny edges. The tracked contour shape and color changes as the man with a cross stripe shirt rotates from facing the front to the back as he comes closer to a camera and then moves away from it. There are many edge pixels in the background and the subject has many edges inside the tracked contour. There are other people moving in different directions, in the background. To make tracking more difficult, the face color of the tacked subject is similar to the hall wall color (Figure 5[c,e]) while his shirt color is similar to that of stairs (Figure 5[i,j]), and tracked body black hair is interfered with by a walking woman in Figure 5(f,g) and a man with a black suit in Figure 5(k-r). Stair colors in Figure 5(j-s) are similar to the tracked subject shirt color. Our tracked contour is bothered by these interferences, but recovers as soon as we get *Scanny* edges for the interfered part. Even under this complex circumstance, our boundary edge-based tracking was successful. [1]

---

[1] The input image sequence was provided by Taeyong Kim. Full tracking movies can be downloaded from http://www.cs.hongik.ac.kr/~jhpark

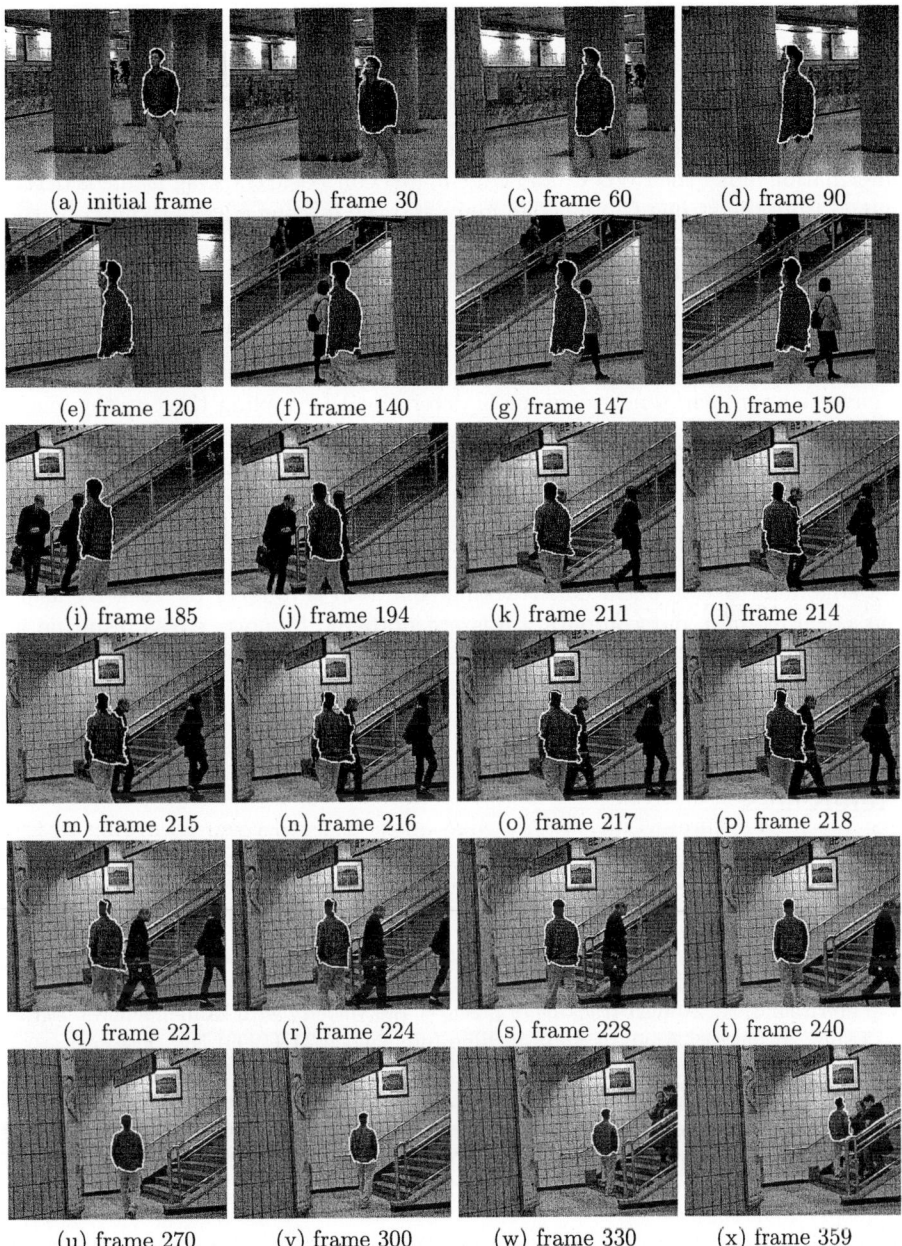

Fig. 5. Input frame with input contour(a), tracking results at frame 30 (b), at frame 60 (c), at frame 90 (d), at frame 120 (e), at frame 140, before occluding a woman (f), at frame 147, after occlusion (g), at frame 150 (h), at frame 185, before occluding a second woman (i), at frame 194, after occluding the second woman (j), at frame 211, before occluding a man (k), at frames from 214 untill 228, after occluding the man (l-s), and tracking contour recovered at frames from 240 untill 359 (t-x)

8 Conclusion

In this paper, we proposed a method of improving accuracy in tracking a highly textured subject. We start by selecting a boundary edge pixel from the *simple (strong) Canny edge map*, referring to the most detailed edge map to get edge information along the LOD Canny edge maps. Our basic tracking frame is determined from the strong Canny edge map, and the missing edges are filled by the detailed Canny edges along the LOD hierarchy. In order to reduce side-effects because of irrelevant edges, we modified Canny edge computation in the normal direction of the previous contour. Even though detailed Canny edges are noisy, our basic tracking frame is determined from the *Scanny* and is not disturbed by noisy edges. This has an effect of Nguyen's background noisy edge removal. In Nguyen's approach, a new contour is determined by mixing the current image edge map with the previous contour. Another major contribution of our work is not accumulating tracking errors. We minimize the possibility of accumulated tracking errors by relying on pixel-routing the *current* Canny edge map only. The problem with our approach is that we need edge information as every other edge-based approach does. But, our tracking performance recovers whenever we get edge information back. Our tracking condition is tougher to track By using our novel method, our computation is not bothered by noisy edges resulting in a robust tracking. Our experimental results show that our tracking approach is reliable enough to handle a sudden change of the tracked subject shape in a complex scene. [2]

References

1. Park, J., Kim, T., Park, S.: Lod canny edge based boundary edge selection for human body tracking. Lecture Notes in Computer Science (ICIAR 2004) **3212** (2004) 528–535
2. Kass, M., Witkin, A., Terzopoulos, D.: Snakes: Active contour models. International Journal of Computer Vision **1** (1987) 321–331
3. Peterfreund, N.: Robust tracking of position and velocity with kalman snakes. IEEE Trans. on Pattern Analysis and Machine Intelligence **21** (1999) 564–569
4. Fu, Y., Erdem, A.T., Tekalp, A.M.: Tracking visible boundary of objects using occlusion adaptive motion snake. IEEE Trans. on Image Processing **9** (2000) 2051–2060
5. Nguyen, H.T., Worring, M., van den Boomgaard, R., Smeulders, A.W.M.: Tracking nonparameterized object contours in video. IEEE Trans. on Image Processing **11** (2002) 1081–1091
6. Roerdink, J.B.T.M., Meijster, A.: The watershed transform: Definition, algorithms and parallelization strategies. Fundamenta Informaticae **41** (2000) 187–228
7. Nguyen, H.T., Worring, M., van den Boomgaard, R.: Watersnakes: energy-driven watershed segmentation. IEEE Trans. on Pattern Analysis and Machine Intelligence **25** (2003) 330–342

---

[2] This work was supported by 2005 IITA basic research fund.

Moment Invariants for Recognizing Symmetric Objects*

Jan Flusser and Tomáš Suk

Institute of Information Theory and Automation,
Academy of Sciences of the Czech Republic,
Pod vodárenskou věží 4, 182 08 Prague 8, Czech Republic
{flusser, suk}@utia.cas.cz
http://www.utia.cas.cz

Abstract. A new kind of rotation moment invariants suitable for recognition of symmetric objects is presented. They are composed of complex moments of the image and their invariance to rotation is achieved by multiplicative phase cancellation. Unlike earlier moment invariants they explicitly consider the degree of symmetry of the objects. Thanks to this, they do not vanish on symmetric objects and are able to recognize them.

1 Introduction

During last forty years, moment invariants have become a classical tool for object recognition and have found numerous applications [1], [2], [3], [4]. The latest results on rotation moment invariants have been recently published by Flusser [5], [6], who presented a general method how to derive independent and complete sets of invariants of any orders. He proposed to construct the invariants from complex moments of the image

$$c_{pq} = \int_{-\infty}^{\infty} \int_{-\infty}^{\infty} (x+iy)^p (x-iy)^q f(x,y) dx dy. \qquad (1)$$

Under rotation of the object by an angle α, each complex moment preserves its magnitude while its phase is shifted by $(p-q)\alpha$

$$c'_{pq} = e^{-i(p-q)\alpha} \cdot c_{pq}. \qquad (2)$$

This property allows us to construct moment invariants by phase cancellation achieved just by multiplying complex moments of appropriate orders and powers (see [5] for details).

It was also shown that there exist relatively small complete and independent basis by means of which all other rotation invariants can be expressed. Such a basis $\mathcal{B}$ is defined as

$$(\forall p,q | p \geq q \bigwedge p+q \leq r)(\Phi(p,q) \equiv c_{pq} c_{q_0 p_0}^{p-q} \in \mathcal{B}),$$

---

* This work has been supported by the grant No. 201/03/0675 of the Grant Agency of the Czech Republic.

where p_0 and q_0 are arbitrary indices such that $p_0 + q_0 \leq r$, $p_0 - q_0 = 1$ and $c_{p_0 q_0} \neq 0$ for all images involved (see [5], [6] for proof and further discussion).

However, this construction of the basis cannot be applied if the objects to be described/recognized exhibit certain degree of symmetry because such nonzero $c_{p_0 q_0}$ need not exist. If we still used it, most of the invariants would vanish.

This "vanishing effect" is not restricted to the invariants introduced in [5]. As many authors have pointed out, it is a common problem of all systems of moment invariants. For example, all odd-order moments of a centrosymmetric object equal identically zero. If an object is circularly symmetric, all its complex moments, whose indices are different, also vanish. Since moment invariants have a form of products of moment powers, many of them became useless.

Let us imagine an illustrative example. We want to recognize three shapes–square, cross, and circle – independently of their orientation. Because of symmetry, all complex moments of the 2nd and 3rd orders except c_{11} are zero. If the shapes are appropriately scaled, c_{11} can be the same for all of them. Consequently, neither the traditional Hu's invariants nor the invariants constructed as described above provide any discrimination power, even if the shapes are easy to recognize visually. Appropriate invariants in this case would be $c_{22}, c_{40}c_{04}, c_{51}c_{04}, c_{33}, c_{80}c_{04}^2, c_{62}c_{04}, c_{44}$, etc.

The above simple example shows the necessity of having different systems of invariants for objects with different types of symmetry. The question on how to construct them has not been resolved yet. In this paper, we present a solution to this problem for objects having so called N–fold rotation symmetry (N-FRS). The proposed solution consists in a modification of the above theory about invariant bases.

2 Invariants for Objects with N–Fold Rotation Symmetry

An object is said to have N-FRS if it repeats itself when it rotates around its centroid by $2\pi j/N$ for all $j = 1, \cdots, N$. Rotation symmetry (or, more precisely, the number of folds) of the object determines the vanishing moments.

Lemma 1: If object $f(x,y)$ has N–fold rotation symmetry, then all its complex moments with non-integer $(p-q)/N$ equal zero.

Proof: Let us rotate the object around its origin by $2\pi/N$. Due to its symmetry, the rotated object must be the same as the original. In particular, it must hold $c'_{pq} = c_{pq}$ for any p and q. On the other hand, it follows from eq. (2) that

$$c'_{pq} = e^{-2\pi i (p-q)/N} \cdot c_{pq}.$$

Since $(p-q)/N$ is assumed not to be an integer, this equation can be fulfilled only if $c_{pq} = 0$. □

Construction of (non-trivial) invariants for recognition of objects with N–fold rotation symmetry is described in the following Theorem.

Theorem 1: Let us consider objects having N-FRS, $N \geq 1$, and their complex moments up to the order $r \geq 2$. Let a set of rotation invariants $\mathcal{B}_N$ be constructed as follows:

$(\forall p,q | p \geq q \bigwedge p+q \leq r \bigwedge k \equiv (p-q)/N$ is integer$)(\Phi(p,q) \equiv c_{pq} c_{q_0 p_0}^k \in \mathcal{B}_N)$,

where p_0 and q_0 are arbitrary indices such that $p_0 + q_0 \leq r$, $p_0 - q_0 = N$, and $c_{p_0 q_0} \neq 0$ for all images involved. Then $\mathcal{B}_N$ is a basis of a set of all rotation invariants for objects with N-FRS, created from the moments up to the order r.

Proof: The invariance of all $\Phi(p,q)$'s with respect to rotation follows directly from eq. (2). The independence of $\mathcal{B}_N$ is a consequence of mutual independence of the complex moments themselves. To prove the completeness of $\mathcal{B}_N$, it is sufficient to show that all complex moments up to the order r can be recovered when knowing the elements of $\mathcal{B}_N$. The proof of this so-called *symmetric inverse problem* is similar to the proof of the general inverse problem published in [6]. The only difference is that only the moments with integer-valued $(p-q)/N$ are recovered. The other complex moments are zero. □

Let us consider some particular values of N. For $N=1$, which means no rotation symmetry, Theorem 1 is reduced exactly to the general case described in [5]. An important case is when $N=2$, which includes all centrosymmetric objects. Then only even-order invariants exist. Another special case is $N=\infty$, which characterizes objects having circular symmetry $f(x,y) = f(\sqrt{x^2+y^2})$. Then the only existing nontrivial invariants are $\Phi(p,p) \equiv c_{pp}$.

Theorem 1 has several interesting consequences. Some of them are summarized in the following Lemma.

Lemma 2: Let us denote all rotation invariants which can be expressed by means of elements of basis $\mathcal{B}$ as $\langle \mathcal{B} \rangle$. Then it holds for any order r

1. If M and N are finite and L is their least common multiple, then

$$\langle \mathcal{B}_M \rangle \cap \langle \mathcal{B}_N \rangle = \langle \mathcal{B}_L \rangle.$$

In particular, if M/N is integer then $\langle \mathcal{B}_M \rangle \subset \langle \mathcal{B}_N \rangle$.

2.
$$\bigcap_{N=1}^{\infty} \langle \mathcal{B}_N \rangle = \langle \mathcal{B}_\infty \rangle.$$

3. The number of elements of $\mathcal{B}_N$ is

$$|\mathcal{B}_N| = \sum_{j=0}^{n} \left[\frac{r - jN + 2}{2}\right],$$

where $n = [r/N]$ and symbol $[a]$ means integer part of a. Particularly,

$$|\mathcal{B}_\infty| = \left[\frac{r+2}{2}\right].$$

3 Recognition of Symmetric Objects

In practical pattern recognition experiments, the number of folds N may not be known beforehand. In that case we can apply a fold detector (see [7], [8], and [9] for algorithms detecting the number of folds) to all elements of the training set before we choose an appropriate system of moment invariants. However, different shape classes may have different numbers of folds. As can be seen from Lemma 2, we cannot simply choose one of the numbers of folds detected (although one could intuitively expect the highest number of folds to be a good choice, it is not that case). Instead, the least common multiple of all finite fold numbers should be taken as the appropriate N for constructing invariant basis according to Theorem 1.

4 Experiments on Artificial Data

In order to illustrate how important is a careful choice of the invariants in particular pattern recognition tasks, we carried out the following experimental study.

In the first experiment we used nine simple binary patterns with various numbers of folds: capitals F and L ($N = 1$), rectangle and diamond ($N = 2$), equilateral triangle and tripod ($N = 3$), cross ($N = 4$), and circle and ring ($N = \infty$) (see Fig. 1). Each pattern was ten times rotated by ten random angles.

First, we applied general rotation invariants [5], which are in fact equivalent to the invariants from Theorem 1 when choosing $p_0 = 2$ and $q_0 = 1$. The positions of our test patterns in the feature space are plotted in Fig. 3. Although only a 2-D subspace showing the invariants $c_{21}c_{12}$ and $\mathrm{Re}(c_{20}c_{12}^2)$ is visualized here, we can easily observe that the patterns form one dense cluster around the origin (the only exception is the tripod, which is slightly biased because of its non-symmetry caused by quantization effect). Two non-symmetric objects – the letters F and L – are far from the origin, out of the displayed area. The only source of non-zero variance of the cluster are spatial quantization errors. All other invariants of the form $c_{pq}c_{12}^{p-q}$ behave in the same way. Thus, according to our theoretical expectation, we cannot discriminate among symmetric objects (even if they are very different) by means of the general invariants.

Secondly, we employed the invariants introduced in Theorem 1 choosing $N = 4$ (the highest finite number of folds among the test objects), $p_0 = 4$, and $q_0 = 0$ to resolve the above recognition experiment. The situation in the feature space looks different from the previous case (see the plot of two simplest invariants $c_{40}c_{04}$ and $\mathrm{Re}(c_{51}c_{04})$ in Fig. 4). Five test patterns formed their own very compact clusters which are well separated from each other. However, the patterns circle, ring, triangle, and tripod still made a mixed cluster around the origin and remained non-separable. This is also fully in accordance with the theory, because the number of folds used here is not optimal for our test set.

Finally, we repeated this experiment again with invariants according to Theorem 1 but selecting N correctly as the least common multiple of all finite fold numbers involved, i.e. $N = 12$. One can learn from Fig. 5 that now all clusters

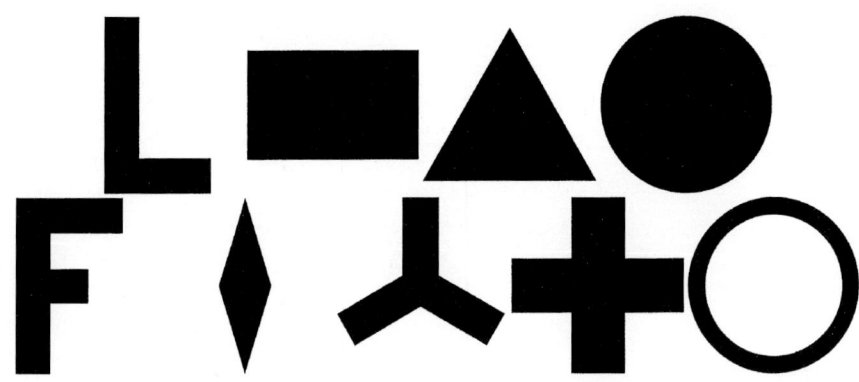

Fig. 1. Test patterns: capital L, rectangle, equilateral triangle, circle, capital F, diamond, tripod, cross, and ring

Fig. 2. The test trademarks (from left to right): Mercedes-Benz, Mitsubishi, Recycling, Fischer, and Woolen Stuff

are well separated (because of high dynamic range, logarithmic scale was used for visualization purposes). The only exception are two patterns having circular symmetry – the circle and the ring – that still made a mixed cluster. If we wanted to separate also these two patterns from one another, we could use the invariants c_{pp}. On the other hand, using *only* these invariants for the whole experiment is not a good choice from the practical point of view – since there is only one such invariant for each order, we would be pushed into using high-order noise-sensitive moments and, moreover, c_{pp}'s may not provide enough discrimination power for the other objects.

In the second experiment, we tested the capability of recognizing objects having *the same* number of folds, particularly $N = 3$. As a test set we took three trademarks of major companies (Mercedes-Benz, Mitsubishi and Fischer) downloaded from the respective web-sites, and two commonly used symbols ("recycling" and "woolen stuff"). We decided to use trademarks as the test objects because most trademarks have certain degree of symmetry and all commercial trademark recognition systems face the problem of symmetry. A comprehensive case study on trademark recognition and retrieval [10] used the Hu's moment invariants as a pre-selector; here we show that Theorem 1 yields more discriminative features.

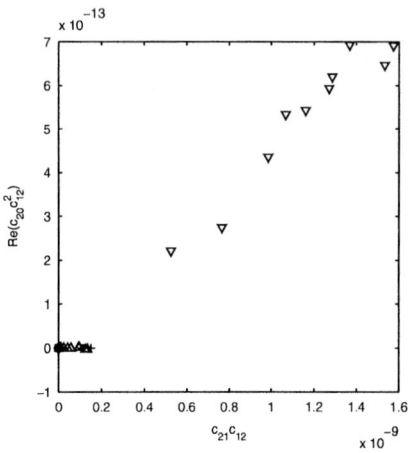

Fig. 3. The space of two general invariants $c_{21}c_{12}$ and $\mathrm{Re}(c_{20}c_{12}^2)$. The symbols: × rectangle, ◇ diamond, △ equilateral triangle, ▽ tripod, + cross, • circle, and ○ ring.

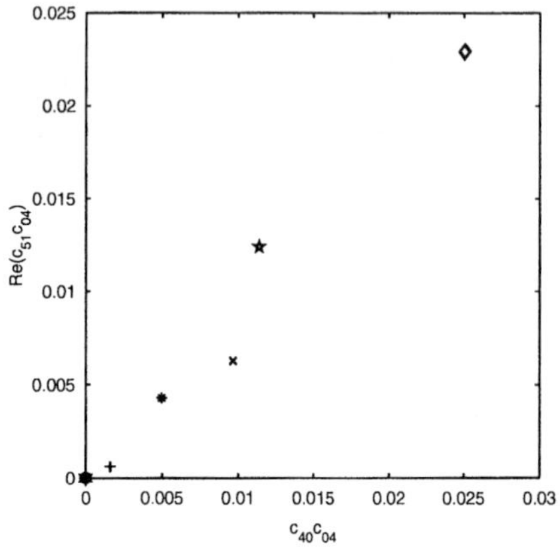

Fig. 4. The space of two invariants $c_{40}c_{04}$ and $\mathrm{Re}(c_{51}c_{04})$ introduced in Theorem 1, $N = 4$. The symbols: × rectangle, ◇ diamond, △ equilateral triangle, ▽ tripod, + cross, • circle, ○ ring, ∗ capital F and, ⋆ capital L.

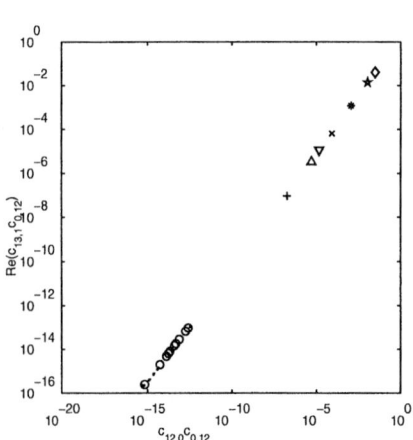

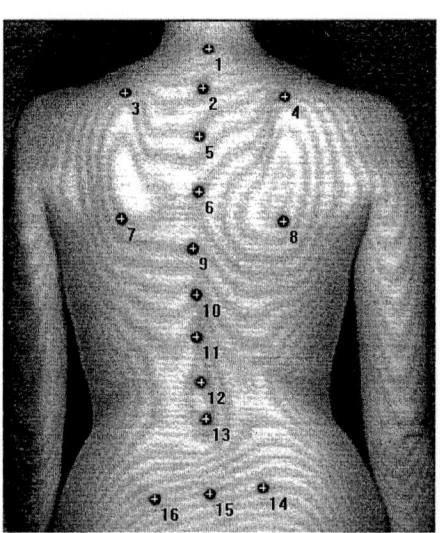

Fig. 5. The space of two invariants $c_{12,0}c_{0,12}$ and $\mathrm{Re}(c_{13,1}c_{0,12})$ introduced in Theorem 1, $N = 12$ (logarithmic scale). The symbols: × rectangle, ◇ diamond, △ equilateral triangle, ▽ tripod, + cross, • circle, ○ ring, ∗ capital F, and ⋆ capital L.

Fig. 6. Moire strips and landmarks for scoliosis measurement. The landmark centers were detected by means of moment invariants.

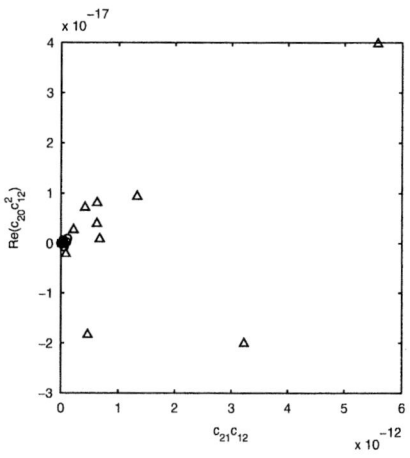
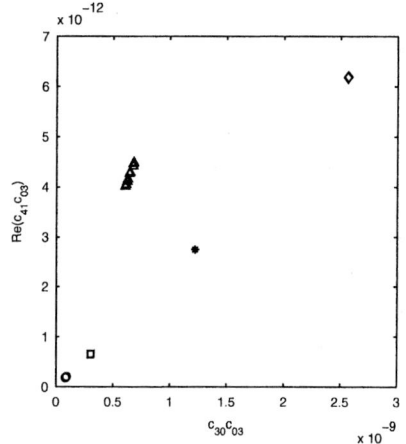

Fig. 7. The trademark positions in the space of two general invariants $c_{21}c_{12}$ and $\text{Re}(c_{20}c_{12}^2)$. These invariants have no discrimination power with respect to this trademark set. The symbols: □ Mercedes-Benz, ◇ Mitsubishi, △ Recycling, * Fischer, and ○ Woolen Stuff.

Fig. 8. The trademark positions in the space of two invariants $c_{30}c_{03}$ and $\text{Re}(c_{41}c_{03})$ showing good discrimination power. The symbols: □ Mercedes-Benz, ◇ Mitsubishi, △ Recycling, * Fischer, and ○ Woolen Stuff.

As can be seen in Fig. 2, all our test marks have three-fold rotation symmetry. Each mark was ten times rotated by randomly generated angles. Moment invariants from Theorem 1 ($N = 3$, $p_0 = 3$, and $q_0 = 0$) provide an excellent discrimination power even if we take only two simplest of them (see Fig. 7), while the general invariants are not able to distinguish the marks at all (see Fig. 8).

4.1 Real Data Experiment

A practical example of application of Theorem 1 in medical imaging is shown in Fig. 6. The goal of this medical project was to measure and to evaluate the changes of the women's back and spine arising from pregnancy (see [11] for the details of this study). All measurements were non-invasive using Moire contourgraphs and specific landmarks attached to the body. This technique allows a 3-D measurement from a sequence of 2-D images.

One of the tasks was to measure the progress of scoliosis. In order to do so, circular black landmarks were glued on the women's back. A template matching algorithm was used for automatic localization of the landmark centers. In each possible position, the values of four moment invariants of even orders were calculated and correlated with the moment invariants of the template. Correlation peaks indicated the matching positions. As one can see in Fig. 6, this method yielded accurate localization of all landmarks and produced no false matches (the crosses denote identified landmark centers). It should be noted that the Hu's invariants failed sometimes because they were not able to distinguish between the landmarks and parts of Moire strips.

5 Conclusion

In this paper, moment invariants suitable for recognizing symmetric objects were proposed. Since most traditional moment invariants vanish on symmetric objects, this problem requires special treatment and has not been appropriately resolved before. Our solution to this problem for objects having N–fold rotation symmetry is given in Theorem 1, where the construction of the invariant basis is described. The new moment invariants explicitly consider the degree of symmetry of the objects. Thanks to this, they are able to recognize both symmetric and non-symmetric objects.

References

1. M. K. Hu, "Visual pattern recognition by moment invariants," *IRE Trans. Information Theory*, vol. 8, pp. 179–187, 1962.
2. J. Flusser and T. Suk, "Pattern recognition by affine moment invariants," *Pattern Recognition*, vol. 26, no. 1, pp. 167–174, 1993.
3. C. H. Teh and R. T. Chin, "On image analysis by the method of moments," *IEEE Trans. Pattern Analysis and Machine Intelligence*, vol. 10, pp. 496–513, 1988.
4. Y. S. Abu-Mostafa and D. Psaltis, "Recognitive aspects of moment invariants," *IEEE Trans. Pattern Analysis and Machine Intelligence*, vol. 6, pp. 698–706, 1984.
5. J. Flusser, "On the independence of rotation moment invariants," *Pattern Recognition*, vol. 33, pp. 1405-1410, 2000.
6. J. Flusser, "On the inverse problem of rotation moment invariants," *Pattern Recognition*, vol. 35, pp. 3015-3017, 2002.
7. J. C. Lin, W. H. Tsai, J. A. Chen, "Detecting number of folds by a simple mathematical property," *Pattern Recognition Letters*, vol. 15, pp. 1081–1088, 1994.
8. J. C. Lin, "A simplified fold number detector for shapes with monotonic radii," *Pattern Recognition*, vol. 29, pp. 997–1005, 1996.
9. D. Shen and H. H. S. Ip, "Symmetry detection by generalized complex (GC) moments: A close-form solution," *IEEE Trans. Pattern Analysis and Machine Intelligence*, vol. 21, pp. 466–476, 1999.
10. A. K. Jain and A. Vailaya, "Shape-based retrieval: A case study with trademark image databases," *Pattern Recognition*, vol. 31, pp. 1369–1390, 1998.
11. K. Jelen and S. Kušová, "Pregnant women: Moire contourgraph and its semiautomatic and automatic evaluation," *Neuroendocrinology Letters*, vol. 25, pp. 52–56, 2004.

A Linear Algorithm for Polygonal Approximations of Thick Curves*

Trung Nguyen

Ecole Normale Superieure, 45 rue d'Ulm, 75005 Paris, France

Abstract. The concept of fuzzy segment was introduced in [2]. In this paper we suggest a notion of strict fuzzy segment and provide a linear algorithm for recognizing it thanks to a simple property of convex hull. A linear method to decompose a thick curve into strict fuzzy segments is also given. The quality of decomposition can be easily controlled by setting two threshold values: the maximum order and the minimum density of the fuzzy segments. The algorithm is fast, practical and multi-purpose.

1 Introduction

Polygonal approximation of curves is an important task in contour analysis, shape recognition, digital cartography, and data compression. The problem can be informally stated as follows: given a digitized curve of $N \geq 2$ ordered vertices[1], find M dominant vertices among them that define a sequence of segments which most closely resemble the original curve. A great deal of algorithms to resolve this problem have been proposed for over forty years. Most of them base on one of two approaches: dynamic programming and heuristics.

One of the best known algorithms using *dynamic programming* was presented by Perez and Vidal [6]. They suggested the sum of the squared Euclidean distance as the global error criterion. The drawback of this algorithm is that its implementation requires $\mathcal{O}(MN^2)$ time and $\mathcal{O}(MN)$ space. Salotti [8] improved this algorithm so that the complexity is close to $\mathcal{O}(N^2)$ by inserting the lower bound and employing the A* search algorithm instead of the dynamic programming one. Keeping the same ideas of Perez and Vidal, Kolesnikov and Fränti [4] introduced a bounding corridor and iterated dynamic programming within it. The complexity has been significantly reduced ranging from $\mathcal{O}(N)$ to $\mathcal{O}(N^2)$ but the solution does not remain optimal.

While dynamic programming tries to give relatively optimal results, many algorithms using the *heuristic approach* are more favorable in real-time applications thanks to their rapidity. Relying on the Diophantine definition of discrete straight line and its arithmetical characteristics in [7], Debled-Rennesson and Reveillès [1] gave a linear method for segmentation of curves into exact discrete lines. Their idea is to grow a segment incrementally as much as possible and the vertex that cannot be added to the

---

* This work is partially supported by the Geometrica project, INRIA Sophia Antipolis, France. Any opinions, findings, or conclusions expressed in this paper are those of the author and do not necessarily reflect the views of the Geometrica.

[1] The terms vertex and point will be used interchangeably through this paper.

segment will be the beginning one of the next segment. This algorithm is distinguished from the others by its lossless data compression: the original curve can be reconstructed exactly from only the set of output segments and its first point. The number of segments unfortunately being large in particularly for irregular curves makes the algorithm less practical. In a slightly similar approach, Debled-Rennesson et al. [2] introduced the concept of fuzzy segment and provided a linear algorithm for decomposition of discrete curves into fuzzy segments. The algorithm is fast but not effective when applied to spiral curves.

To the best of our knowledge, none of the algorithms of either approach reported in the literature have formally resolved the problem of approximation of thick curves as done in this paper. In many areas such as cartography or object recognition, we are interested in detecting the shape of roads, rivers, fingerprints, the jet of wind, etc. whose width is variable and considerable in comparison with their length. Obviously, one can simplify them to thin curves and then apply to them any available algorithm but we are likely to lose a valuable characteristic of curves. Another idea is to find the upper and lower borders of the object and do the approximation on them separately. The shape of the contour is however difficult to analyze. Moreover, no one can assure that the pairs of corresponding segments of the two borders are parallel – an important condition in cartography. In this paper, we extend the concept of fuzzy segment defined in [2] and provide a linear method to detect strict fuzzy segments. The idea we base on is a simple property of convex hull. Further, we present a fast algorithm to decompose a thick curve into thick fuzzy segments. We introduce the density parameter of fuzzy segments which, associated with the order parameter defined in [2], makes the quality of approximation better.

2 Discrete Lines and Strict Fuzzy Segments

Many applications in Computer Vision are based on discrete points in $\mathbb{Z}^2$. The integer set is however not strong enough even for the most basic properties in geometry, e.g. two non parallel discrete lines may intersect at no point or at an infinite number of points. In this paper, we base on the arithmetical definition of discrete line [7] on which many basic operators like translation, rotation, symmetry, calculation of distance from a point can be done in constant time. A great interest of this framework is that one may visit all points of a line in only linear time.

Definition 1. *[7] A discrete line, noted* $\mathcal{D}(a, b, \mu, \omega)$, *is the set of integer points* (x, y) *verifying the inequalities* $\mu \leq ax - by < \mu + \omega$ *where* a, b, μ, ω *are integers. The real value* $\frac{a}{b}$ *with* $b \neq 0$ *and* $\gcd(a, b) = 1$ *is the* slope *of the discrete line,* μ *is named* lower bound *and* ω *arithmetical* thickness.

We call $\mathcal{D}$ the *naive line* if the thickness ω verifies $\omega = max(|a|, |b|)$. $\mathcal{D}$ is the *thick line* if $\omega \geq |a| + |b|$.

Definition 2. *[2] Real straight lines* $ax - by = \mu$ *and* $ax - by = \mu + \omega - 1$ *are named the* leaning lines *of the discrete line* $D(a, b, \mu, \omega)$. *An integer point of these lines is named a* leaning point *(see Fig. 1).*

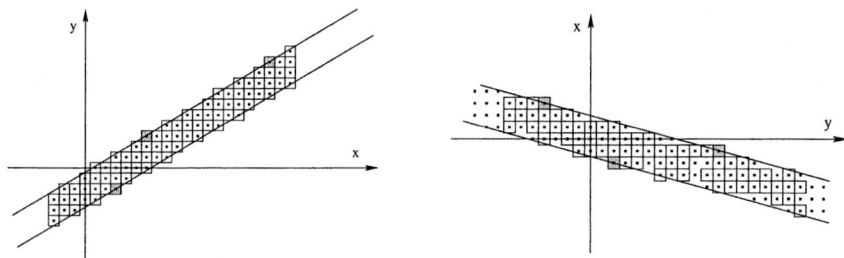

Fig. 1. A segment of the discrete line $D(7, 12, 6, 40)$ whose equation is $6 \leq 7x - 12y < 46$, for $x \in [-3, 20]$. In grey are the leaning points.

Fig. 2. The points in squares constitute a strict fuzzy segment with order $d = \frac{52}{15}$, bounding line $\mathcal{D}(4, -15, -22, 52)$ and density $\varphi \approx 78\%$

We can now state our definitions about strict fuzzy segments which may be independent with those of fuzzy segments in [2].

Definition 3. *A nonempty set $\mathcal{S}_f$ of consecutive points of an object is a strict fuzzy segment with order d if:*

1. *There is a discrete line $\mathcal{D}(a, b, \mu, \omega)$ such that all points of $\mathcal{S}_f$ belong to $\mathcal{D}$ and $d = \frac{\omega}{max(|a|,|b|)}$*
2. *If there exits a discrete line $\mathcal{D}'(a', b', \mu', \omega')$ containing all points of $\mathcal{S}_f$, then $\frac{\omega'}{max(|a'|,|b'|)} \geq d$.*

The line $\mathcal{D}$ is said bounding *for $\mathcal{S}_f$.*

Definition 4. *Let $\mathcal{S}_f$ be a strict fuzzy segment whose order is d, and whose abscissa interval is [0, l - 1], the* density *φ of strict fuzzy segment $\mathcal{S}_f$ is the quotient $\varphi = \frac{n}{ld}$, where n is the number of points of $\mathcal{S}_f$ (see Fig. 2).*

Lemma 1. *A set of points $\mathcal{S}_f$ is a strict fuzzy segment with bounding $\mathcal{D}(a, b, \mu, \omega)$ only if $\mathcal{D}$ possesses at least three leaning points. Among them, at least one is upper leaning point and one is lower leaning point.*

Corollary 1. *Given a set of points $\mathcal{S}_f$ and its upper and lower hull, $\mathcal{S}_f$ is a strict fuzzy segment with bounding $\mathcal{D}$ if $\mathcal{D}$ has on its leaning lines at least two consecutive points of one hull and at least one point of the other hull. Moreover, this point is the farthest point (i.e. the Euclidean distance is maximal) from the leaning line through the two points.*

3 Strict Fuzzy Segment Recognition

From Corollary 1, the problem of detecting a strict fuzzy segment for an object is reduced to the problem of scanning triples of points, two consecutive points of the upper (resp. lower) envelope and one of the other envelope. We adopt the Rotating Caliper Algorithm [3] to calculate the order of the segment. Although width of a set, which is defined as the minimum distance between the parallel lines of its support, is generally not order of the segment since the latter depends on slope of segment, the idea of Rotating Caliper Algorithm works well. Indeed, at each rotating caliper where the slope of segment is fixed, the point of minimum distance to the parallel line has also the smallest order. An algorithm for recognizing strict fuzzy segment is described as below.

Algorithm STRICT FUZZY SEGMENT RECOGNITION
$order \leftarrow \infty$, $F \leftarrow topL$
CONSTRUCT CONVEX HULL
▷ Rotating calipers on the upper envelope
for $i \leftarrow 0$ **to** $topU - 1$ **do**
  $maxLocal \leftarrow$ DISTANCE$(Low[F], Upp[i], Upp[i+1])$
  $d \leftarrow$ DISTANCE$(Low[F-1], Upp[i], Upp[i+1])$
  while $maxLocal < d$ **and** $F > 0$ **do**
    $maxLocal \leftarrow d$
    $F \leftarrow F - 1$
    $d \leftarrow$ DISTANCE$(Low[F-1], Upp[i], Upp[i+1])$
  if $order > maxLocal$ **then**
    $order \leftarrow maxLocal$
    $a \leftarrow Upp[i+1].y - Upp[i].y$
    $b \leftarrow Upp[i+1].x - Upp[i].x$
    $\mu \leftarrow a \times Upp[i].x - b \times Upp[i].y$
    $\omega \leftarrow a \times Low[F].x - b \times Low[F].y - \mu + 1$
    $l \leftarrow Upp[topU].x - Upp[0].x + 1$
    $density = \frac{n}{l \times order}$
▷ Rotating calipers on the lower envelope
(same as the above with Upp and Low exchanged)
return $\mathcal{D}(a, b, \mu, \omega)$, $order$ and $density$

For the construction of convex hull, we can employ any algorithm which computes it correctly. In this paper, we recommend the algorithm of Melkman [5] for its simple implementation. The construction takes $\mathcal{O}(n)$ time when the points of object are in order and $\mathcal{O}(n \log n)$ times when applied to the general case. In order that our paper is self-contained, the pseudo-code of Melkman algorithm is given below with a minor modification that we make use of two stacks to store the upper and lower envelope separately instead of one deque in the author's paper. The function DISTANCE takes three vertices as arguments and returns the distance from the first vertex to the line passing through two last ones. The function ISLEFT in the Melkman algorithm below feeds the same arguments but returns the predicate whether the first point is strictly on the left of the line taking into account its direction.

Correctness. The correctness of our algorithm comes from Corollary 1 and Rotating Caliper Algorithm.

Algorithm MELKMAN'S CONVEX HULL CONSTRUCTION
for each $M \in \mathcal{S}_f$ **do**
    if not (ISLEFT$(M, Low[topL-1], Low[topL])$
    and ISLEFT$(M, Upp[topU], Upp[topU-1])$) **then**
        ▷ Get the rightmost tangent on the upper convex
        while not ISLEFT$(M, Upp[topU], Upp[topU-1])$ **do** $topU \leftarrow topU - 1$
        $topU \leftarrow topU + 1$
        $Upp[topU] \leftarrow M$
        ▷ Get the rightmost tangent on the lower convex
        while not ISLEFT$(M, Low[topL-1], Low[topL])$ **do** $topL \leftarrow topL - 1$
        $topL \leftarrow topL + 1$
        $Low[topL] \leftarrow M$
return Upp and Low

Complexity. The main **for** loop will run $topU$ times which is smaller than N. The assignment operations, the **if** condition and the functions ISLEFT and DISTANCE can be computed in constant time. After each iteration of the **while** loop, the value of F is decreased by one. The number of passes through this loop is therefore smaller than $topL$ in total. For the case where all of the points are ordered, Melkman's construction works in linear time. Hence, the complexity of our algorithm is $\mathcal{O}(N)$ time, where N is the number of vertices. In the implementation, we use two arrays Upp and Low of size N for storing the coordinates of the convex hull. Thus, the total memory requirement of the algorithm is proportional to $2N$, which is linear.

Remark. Rotating Caliper Theorem applies for the computational geometry where the distance is in the Euclidean space. In the discrete geometry, the distance of a point (x_0, y_0) to the discrete line $\mathcal{D}(a, b, \mu, \omega)$ is alternatively defined in [1] as $ax_0 - by_0 - \mu$. This number is only the result of multiplying the distance in the Euclidean space above by $(a^2 + b^2)$. In Algorithm STRICT FUZZY SEGMENT RECOGNITION, we fix the line passing through a couple of convex points, i.e. the value of a and b are unchanged, when compare the distances. Therefore, our algorithm works in the discrete geometry as well. Moreover, it also allows to deal with the sets of disconnected points that do occur in the real-world problems.

4 Strict Fuzzy Segmentation

In this section, we present a technique for approximating an object into strict fuzzy segments. We introduce two thresholds, the maximum order and the minimum density, for all decomposed segments. Increasing the maximum permitted order makes the number of segments reduce but it also decreases the quality of segmentation. This trade-off can be under control by setting the appropriate value for the minimum density threshold. Our idea of segmentation is then very simple: try to prolong the current segment as much as possible until it violates the given thresholds. This idea can be best implemented with the dichotomy algorithm. Fixing the first point of the object of N vertices, we wish to look for the last possible point that the points between them constitute a strict fuzzy segment. This segment must satisfy our thresholds and have the possibly maximal order. Firstly, the algorithm STRICT FUZZY SEGMENT RECOGNITION is applied for the whole object. If it returns the positive answer, we are done; otherwise, the algorithm will check for the first half set $[0, \lceil N/2 \rceil]$.[2] If again this subset is not a satisfying segment, we try for a smaller set $[0, \lceil N/4 \rceil]$; if not, we extend the set to $[0, \lceil 3N/4 \rceil]$. After each step, we divide the interval by two and maintain the segment which satisfies simultaneously the two thresholds and has the maximum order by far. Continue halving the search interval in this way until the order of the segment reaches the threshold or the interval is a unit. In the former case, we report the current segment as result; in the latter case, the output segment is the one that we have recorded before. We repeat this procedure again and the ending point of the current segment will start the next segment.

In the algorithm below, the variables $first$ and $last$ indicate the expected first and last points of the current segment, $maxOrder$ and $minDensity$ are two given thresholds. The function EXTRACT MONOTONE SET takes the argument $first$ and returns the maximal value of $last$ such that the set of points $[first, last]$ is horizontally or vertically monotone. The function STRICT FUZZY SEGMENT RECOGNITION described in the previous section returns the characteristics of the strict fuzzy segment for the subset $[first, last]$ of the object $\mathcal{O}$.

Algorithm STRICT FUZZY SEGMENTATION
$Segs \leftarrow \emptyset, first \leftarrow 0$
while $first < N$ **do**
    $last \leftarrow$ EXTRACT MONOTONE SET$(\mathcal{O}, first)$
    $interval \leftarrow last - first$
    $curOrder \leftarrow 0$
    while $interval > 0$ **and** $curOrder \neq minOrder$ **do**
        STRICT FUZZY SEGMENT RECOGNITION$(\mathcal{O}, first, last)$
        if $curOrder < order \leq maxOrder$ **and** $density \leq minDensity$ **then**
            $curOrder \leftarrow order$
            $cur\mathcal{D} \leftarrow \mathcal{D}(a, b, \mu, \omega)$
            $split \leftarrow last$
        $interval \leftarrow \lceil interval/2 \rceil$
        if $order < minOrder$ **then** $last \leftarrow last + interval$
        else if $order > minOrder$ **then** $last \leftarrow last - interval$
    $Segs \leftarrow Segs \cup \{cur\mathcal{D}\}$
    $first \leftarrow split$
return $Segs$

Correctness. The dichotomy algorithm works well when the orders of segments are sorted, that is verified by the following lemma. The algorithm of segmentation always terminates and returns the correct answer since the unit set of two vertices defines an ideal fuzzy segment whose order is 0 and density is 1.

---

[2] To simplify the writing, we note $[a, b](a \leq b)$ the subset of points from the point numbered a to the point numbered b according to their orders in the set $\mathcal{S}_f$.

Lemma 2. *Let A and B be two nonempty sets of points and $A \subseteq B$. Suppose that A and B are strict fuzzy segments with orders d_A and d_B respectively, then $d_A \leq d_B$.*

Complexity. Let us show that the algorithm STRICT FUZZY SEGMENTATION decomposes an object $\mathcal{O}$ into a set of strict fuzzy segments in linear time. The trick lies in the implementation of two functions EXTRACT MONOTONE SET and STRICT FUZZY SEGMENT RECOGNITION.

For the first function, we make use of four variables for each point P of $\mathcal{O}$. These variables store respectively the maximal lengths that vertically decreased, horizontally decreased, vertically increased and horizontally increased sets starting from P may have. They can be backwards determined in linear time at the initialization of the algorithm. The function EXTRACT MONOTONE SET is only a simple calculation on them, therefore not costly.

For the second function, we make a minor modification to the construction of convex hull thanks to the online property in Melkman algorithm. Instead of computing the new stacks Upp and Low from the first point for each halving of $interval$, we try to reuse them as much as possible. For the first case where $last \leftarrow last + interval$, we keep the old stacks and store them in memory. The construction may be continued at the point in $last + 1$. The reason to store these stacks in memory is that all expected last points in the following steps are on the right of the current last point $last$; so we may reuse them further. For the other case where $last$ is decreased by $interval$, we restore the stacks from memory that we last saved. A simple deduction can show that these stacks in fact stored the subsets $[first, last - 2 \times interval]$. The construction thus may continue from the top point on these stacks. In either case, the number of points needed to be calculated is smaller than $interval$. The function STRICT FUZZY SEGMENT RECOGNITION therefore takes no more than $\mathcal{O}(N)$ time in total. Hence, the complexity of our algorithm is linear. In addition to the memory required by the function STRICT FUZZY SEGMENT RECOGNITION, we only use two stacks of size N for memorizing. Thus the space complexity is $\mathcal{O}(N)$ as well.

Approximation of thick curves into thick segments. Our algorithm may also be performed to decompose thick curves into thick segments. The output segments vary in thickness. Figure 3 illustrate the results of decomposition when we apply the algorithm STRICT FUZZY SEGMENTATION to a digitized route of 55705 vertices with different values of the maximum order and the minimum density. In our examples, the algorithm produces 9 and 12 segments respectively. Thus the compression ratio is about $3-5 \times 10^{-3}\%$, given a segment takes two times as much space in memory as a point does. Along with the fact that one may visit all points of a line in linear time, we have constructed a model of compression/decompression in linear time.

Choice of parameters. The maximum order should not be smaller than the largest thickness of the curve, otherwise no solution will be found. Increasing the value of $maxOrder$ allows to minimize the number of detected segments. In return, it also reduces the quality of segmentation in the sense that many points of the segments do not belong to the object. We call them the *false points*. The parameter $minDensity$ therefore is added to restrict the ratio of false points in each detected segment. The experimental evaluations show that the choice of this parameter does not affect the running

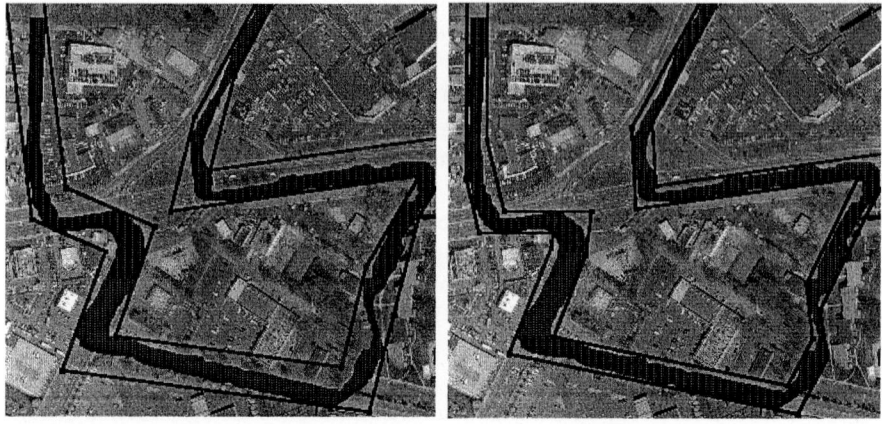

Fig. 3. Results of polygonal approximation of a thick curve of 55708 points. LEFT: max order = 65, min density = 0.4, $\leadsto M = 9$. RIGHT: max order = 60, min density = 0.7 $\leadsto M = 12$.

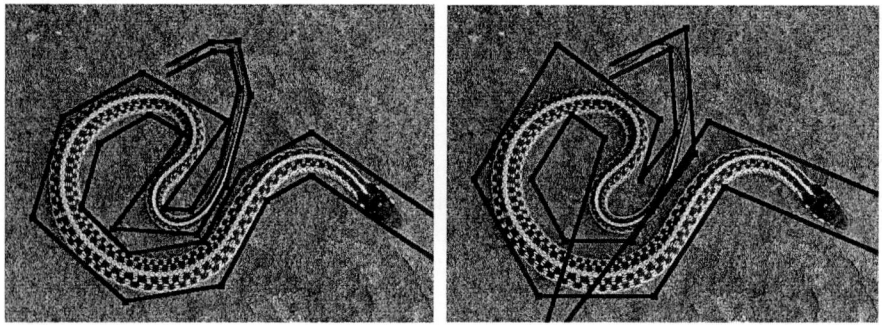

Fig. 4. Results of polygonal approximation of a thick curve on a snake. LEFT: max order = 60, min density = 0.6, $\leadsto M = 14$. RIGHT: max order = 75, min density = 0.4 $\leadsto M = 10$. Photo *Eastern Garter Snake* courtesy of John White and CalPhotos.

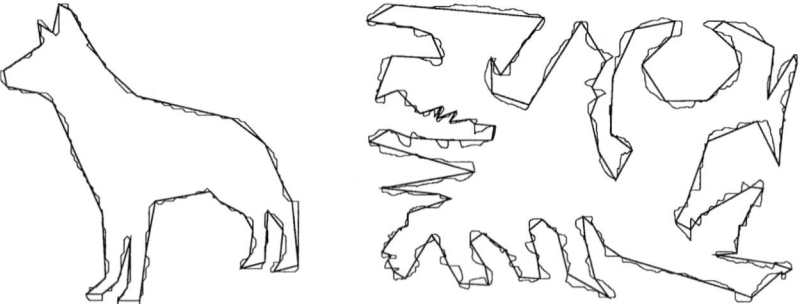

Fig. 5. Results of polygonal approximation of *thin* curves

time. Maintaining a high value of minimum density can lead to a high quality segmentation but a large number of segments will be reported. Too small values of minimum density may change the geometrical structures of output segments (compare in Fig. 4). When the minimum density is set to 0, all fuzzy segments are strict, thus the number of segments is minimal (min-# problem). On the other hand, when $minOrder = 1$, no false point is allowed and the output retains only *exact* segments. In this case, the algorithm has the same property of lossless data compression as [1]. At last, the algorithm may apply for thin curves which is shown in Fig. 5.

5 Conclusion

We have presented a linear algorithm of strict fuzzy segmentation using a simple property of convex hull. The trade-off between the number of segments and the quality of segmentation can be regulated by the selection of the maximum order and the minimum density. Our algorithm is multi-purpose: it can be used to decompose a thick or thin curve into strict fuzzy segments or exact segments. It works in both geometries, computational and discrete. The points may be connected or not making our algorithm more practical. This work opens many perspectives for studying polygonal approximation of noisy thick curves in 3D space.

Acknowledgements

The author wishes to express his gratitude to Isabelle Debled-Rennesson for the helpful discussions in the course of the preparation of this paper. The test sets illustrated in Fig. 5 were provided by her and Pasi Fränti. Many thanks to John White for giving permission to use his nice photo.

References

1. I. Debled-Rennesson and J.-P. Reveillès, A linear algorithm for segmentation of digital curves, *International Journal of Pattern Recognition and Artificial Intelligence*, vol. 9, pp. 635-662, 1995.
2. I. Debled-Rennesson, J.-L. Remy and J. Rouyer, Segmentation of discrete curves into fuzzy segments, *Electronic Notes in Discrete Mathematics*, vol. 12, 2003.
3. M. E. Houle, and G. T. Toussaint, Computing the width of a set, *IEEE Transactions on Pattern Analysis and Machine Intelligence*, vol. 10 , Issue 5 , pp. 761-765, 1988.
4. A. Kolesnikov and P. Fränti, Reduced-search dynamic programming for approximation of polygonal curves, *Pattern Recognition Letters*, 24 (14), 2243-2254, 2003.
5. A. Melkman, On-line construction of the convex hull of a simple polyline, *Information Processing Letters*, vol. 25, pp. 11-12, 1987.
6. J.-C. Perez and E. Vidal, Optimum polygonal approximation of digitized curves, *Pattern Recognition Letters*, vol. 15, pp. 743-750, 1994.
7. J.-P. Reveillès, Géométrie discrète, calcul en nombres entiers et algorithmique, *Thèse d'Etat*, Université Louis Pasteur, Strasbourg, 1991.
8. M. Salotti, An efficient algorithm for the optimal polygonal approximation of digitized curves, *Pattern Recognition Letters*, vol. 22, pp. 215-221, 2001.

NMF with LogGabor Wavelets for Visualization

Zhonglong Zheng[1,2], Jianmin Zhao[1], and Jie Yang[2]

[1] Institute of Information Science and Engineering, Zhejiang Normal University,
Jinhua, China
[2] Institute of Image Processing and Pattern Recognition, Shanghai Jiao Tong University,
Shanghai, China
zhonglong@sjtu.edu.cn

Abstract. Many problems in image representation and classification involve some form of dimensionality reduction. Non-negative matrix factorization (NMF) is a recently proposed unsupervised procedure for learning spatially localized, parts-based subspace representation of objects. Here we present an improvement of the classical NMF by combining with Log-Gabor wavelets to enhance its part-based learning ability. In addition, we compare the new method with principal component analysis (PCA) and locally linear embedding (LLE) proposed recently in Science. Finally, we apply the new method to several real world datasets and achieve good performance in representation and classification.

1 Introduction

Recently, a new approach called non-negative matrix factorization (NMF), is proposed by Lee and Seung [6]. The new one demonstrates how to obtaining a reduced representation of global data in an unsupervised way. Non-negative matrix factorization is different from other methods by adding its non-negative constraints. When applied to image analysis and representation, the obtained NMF basis are localized features that correspond with intuitive notions of the parts of the images. It is supported by psychological and physiological evidence that perception of the whole is based on parts-based representations. And many recent learning strategies focus on the fact that an object can be divided into distinguished parts and only a subset of them are necessary for identification.

In this paper, we combine NMF with Log-Gabor wavelets to improve the performance of learning parts of images of the classical NMF. And then we compare the new method with PCA and LLE. Finally, we apply the new method to several real world datasets to verify its good performance in image representation and classification.

2 NMF vs. PCA and LLE Techniques

2.1 Non-negative Matrix Factorization

Non-negative matrix factorization (NMF), proposed recently by Lee and Sueng, is an outstanding method for obtaining a reduced representation of global data. When applied to images analysis, the obtained NMF basis are localized features that correspond with intuitive notions of the parts of images.

The goal of NMF is to find two new matrices W and H to approximate the whole database V as

$$V_{i\mu} \approx (WH)_{i\mu} = \sum_{a=1}^{r} W_{ia} H_{a\mu} \qquad (1)$$

The r columns of W are the so called basis images. The update rules for W and H are:

$$W_{ia} \leftarrow W_{ia} \sum_{\mu} \frac{V_{i\mu}}{(WH)_{i\mu}} H_{a\mu}$$

$$W_{ia} \leftarrow \frac{W_{ia}}{\sum W_{ja}} \qquad (2)$$

$$H_{a\mu} \leftarrow H_{a\mu} \sum_{i} W_{ia} \frac{V_{i\mu}}{(WH)_{i\mu}} \qquad (3)$$

and all elements in W and H are non-negative.

2.2 Performance Comparison of NMF with PCA and LLE

To illustrate the performance of data representation and dimensionality reduction by NMF, PCA and LLE vividly, we applied these methods to a manifold in 3D space. Fig 1 shows the original data and the results by enforcing those three methods. After mapping the manifold to 2D space, the properties of these methods give rise to deep visual impression on us.

The result (c) in Fig 1, discovered by LLE, demonstrates its neighbor relationship preserving property. Just imagine that using a scissors to cut the manifold into small squares that represent

Locally linear patches of the nonlinear scroll-shape surface, and then put these squares onto a flat tabletop while preserving the angular relationship between neighboring squares. But if the data points in the original space are sparse enough, LLE leads to bad performance.

As shown in Fig 1, PCA demonstrates the maximum projection of the original data in lower dimensional space. It is an optimal representation of the original space. In other words, PCA is the optimal method for dimensionality reduction in the sense of mean-square error.

While the result (e) in Fig 1, discovered by NMF, is a compromise between PCA and LLE to some sense. It preserves the neighbor relationship and also gives a good representation of the original data in some way.

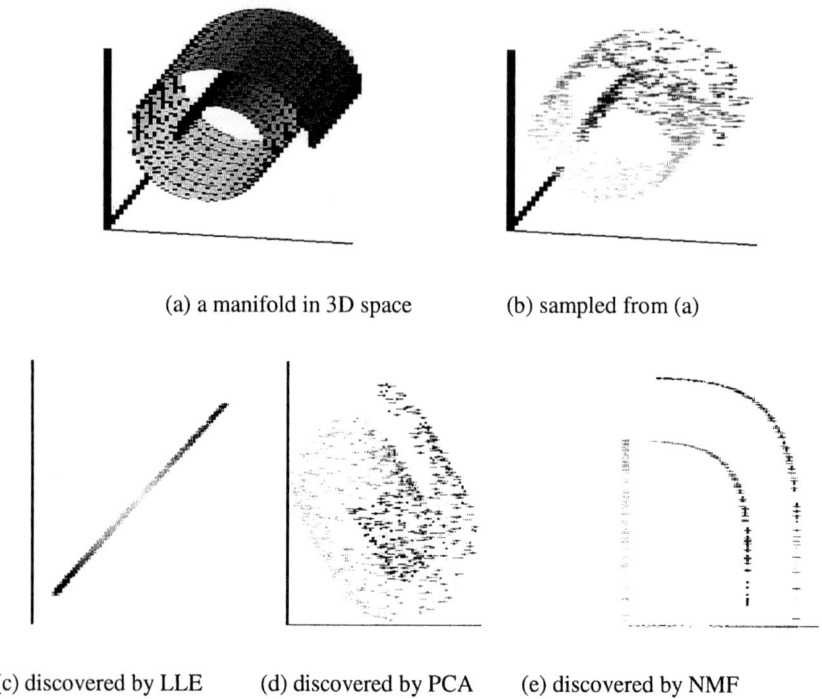

Fig. 1. Mapping a manifold in 3D space to 2D space by LLE, PCA and NMF respectively. The results are shown in (c)(d)(e).

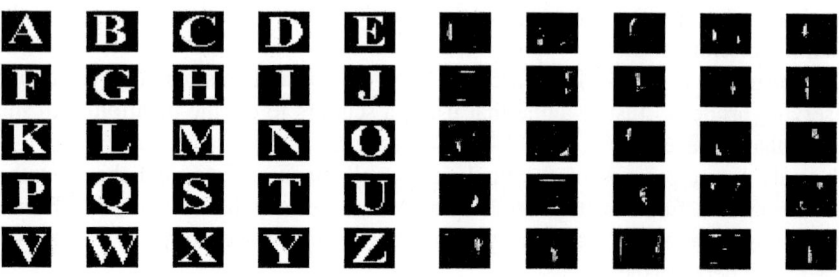

Fig. 2. Some English letters (left) and its basis images discovered by NMF with $r = 25$

After comparison with other methods, NMF is applied to real world datasets such as characters and human ears to demonstrate its parts-based learning ability. The results are shown in Fig 2.

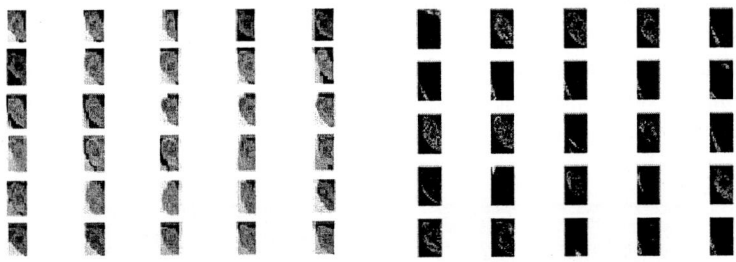

Fig. 3. Images of 30 human ears (left) and its basis images discovered by NMF with $r = 25$

3 LogGabor Wavelets for Image Representation

Here we choose Log-Gabor wavelets because they have no DC response and a better response to high frequency details [10]. The transfer function of Log-Gabor in frequency domain is

$$g(\omega) = e^{\frac{-(\log(\omega/\omega_0))^2}{2(\log(\beta/\omega_0))^2}} \quad (4)$$

where ω is frequency, and ω_0 is the tuning frequency of the filter. β controls the spread of the filter. Fig 4 shows the result of Log-Gabor filter convolving with a face image at five scale and 8 spread. The first block image of (a) in Fig 4 is the original image.

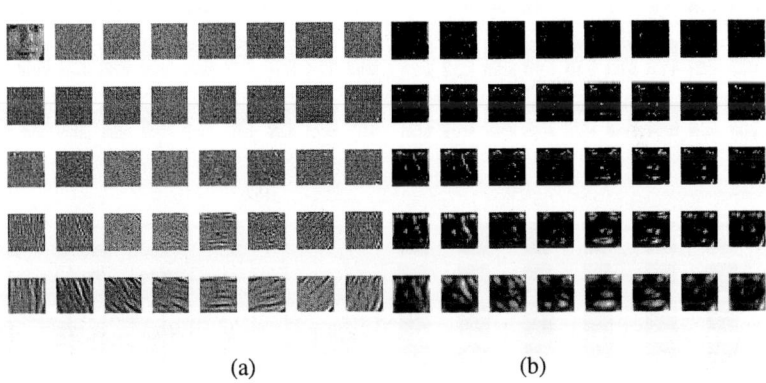

(a)   (b)

Fig. 4. Log-Gabor representation of a face image. (a) real part of the representation and (b) the magnitude of the representation.

4 NMF with Log-Gabor Wavelets for Representation

As mentioned in section 1, NMF takes a longer time to give a desirable result. And for images contained complicated structure, such as face images, the basis images discovered by NMF are not wholly part-based perception. Fig 5 shows the basis images learned by NMF without and with Log-Gabor wavelets. Here, the face image is the same as in Fig 4. When combined with Log-Gabor wavelets, NMF yields powerful performance in learning parts of the images. It is attributed to the non-negative constraints of NMF on the one hand, and the preprocessing the images by Log-Gabor wavelets on the other hand.

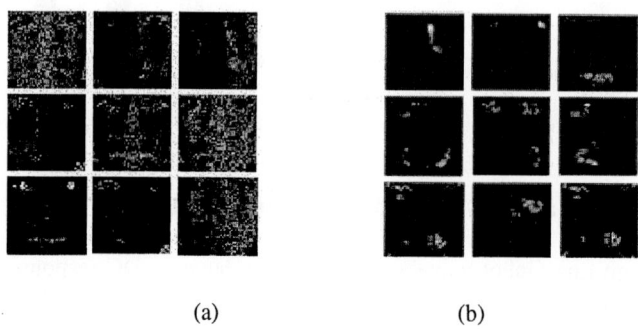

Fig. 5. Basis images learned by NMF (a) without Log-Gabor (b) with Log-Gabor $r = 9$

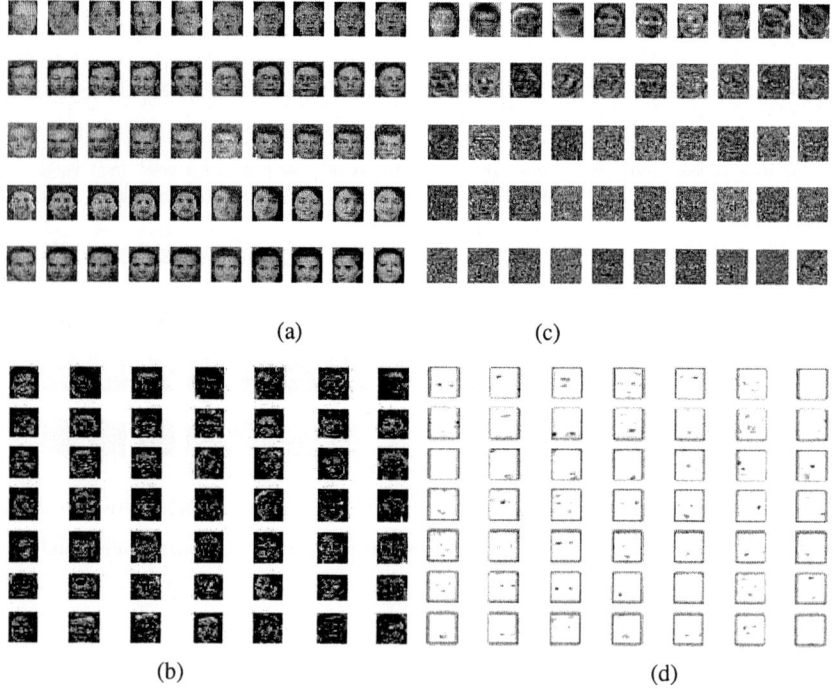

Fig. 6. Comparison of NMF without and with Log-Gabor, PCA eigenfaces. (a) parts of ORL database (b) basis images learned by NMF only (c) PCA eigenfaces (d) basis images learned by NMF with log-Gabor wavelets.

Next, NMF is applied to ORL face database combined with Log-Gabor wavelets. In addition, PCA is also applied to the face database to have a comparison with NMF. Fig 6 shows the results.

The experiments related to NMF (b) (d) in Fig 6 choose $r = 49$. Higher pixel values are in darker color in (d) in order to make it clearer. This is different from the other three. The basis images of learned by NMF only are as holistic as the PCA basis (eigenfaces) for the training set (a) in Fig 6. It is noticed that the result demonstrated in [6] does not appear so probably because the faces used for producing that result are well aligned and processed. The new method, NMF combined with Log-Gabor wavelets, learns basis components which not only lead to non-subtractive representations, but also yields truly localized features and parts-based representations. Also, the features formed in basis components discovered by the new method become more localized as the r increases.

5 Conclusions

We have introduced a new method, original NMF with Log-Gabor wavelets, for image representation and visualization. The new method improves the classical NMF in terms of part-based learning ability largely because of a sparse and informative representation given by Log-Gabor wavelets. It gives a meaningful perceptual representation in image analysis and a high recognition performance in image classification. When compared with other methods such as linear PCA and nonlinear LLE, the new method shows robustness to variations in illumination, occlusion and facial expression.

Our next goal is to further improve the performance of NMF such as accelerating the convergence time, learning the basis r by machine and learning more informative local features.

References

1. A.M. Martinez and R. Benavente, ``The AR face database," CVC Tech. Report #24, 1998.
2. C. Liu, H. Wechsler, "A Gabor feature classifier for face recognition", Proc. 8th IEEE Int. Conf. Computer Vision, Vancouver, BC, Canada, July 9-12, 2001.
3. G. Donato, M. S. Bartlett, J. C. Hager, & al., "Classifying facial actions", IEEE Trans. Pattern Anal. Machine Intell., vol. 21, pp. 974-989, 1999.
4. M. Turk, A. Pentland, "Eigenfaces for recognition", Journal of Cognitive neuroscience, vol. 3, pp. 71-86, 1991.
5. S. T. Roweis, L. K. Saul. "Nonlinear dimensionality reduction by locally linear embedding", Science, 290(5500), pp. 2323-2326, 2000.
6. D. Lee, H. Seung. "Learning the parts of objects by non-negative matrix factorization", Nature, vol.401, pp.788-791, 1999.
7. P. N. Belhumeur, J. P. Hespanha, D. J. Kriegman, "Eigenfaces vs. Fisherfaces: Recognition using class specific linear projection", IEEE Trans. Pattern Anal. Machine Intell., vol. 19, pp. 711-720, July 1997.

8. A. Martinez, A. C. Kak, "PCA versus LDA", IEEE Trans. Pattern Anal. Machine Intell.,vol.23, pp. 228-233, 2001.
9. C. M. Bishop, M. Svensén, C. K. I. Williams, "GTM: The general topographic mapping", Neural Computation. Vol. 10, pp. 215-234, 1998.

A Study on Fast Iris Image Acquisition Method

Kang Ryoung Park

Division of Media Technology,
Sangmyung University,
7 Hongji-Dong, JongRo-Gu,
Seoul, Republic of Korea
parkgr@smu.ac.kr

Abstract. In this paper, we propose a new method to capture user's focused iris image at fast speed based on the corneal specular reflection and the human eye model. Experimental results show that the focused iris image acquisition time for the users with and without glasses is 450 ms on average and our method can be used for a real-time iris recognition camera.

1 Introduction

For iris recognition, it is required to capture a magnified iris image to process fine iris textures [1][5]. Consequently, it is reported that the DOF(Depth of Field: the Z distance range in which focused iris images can be captured) of iris camera is very small and it is very difficult to capture user's focused iris image at fast speed. Slow focusing can cause the increase of the total recognition time and the severe inconvenience to user. In previous researches and systems [2-4][8-15], they use the focusing method which has been used for general scene (landscape or photographic scenes) without considering the characteristics of iris image. However, their method can generate the erroneous focusing value in case of iris image. Especially, in case of users with glasses, even if the lens is positioned for focusing the glass surface or the glass frame, the scratch on the glass surface or the glass frame may make their focusing value the greatest. However, the conventional distance between glasses and iris is more than 1 cm and the input iris image remains blurred consequently unless the focus lens does not move. Due to those problems, the research [16] uses the method of checking the pixel difference in the region of corneal specular reflection. However, they use only one illuminator for checking focus value and iris recognition. In such a case, the focus checking is impossible when the large specular reflection which happens on the surface of glasses hides that on a cornea. In addition, in case that many specular reflections happen from the scratch on the glass surface, it is very difficult to detect the genuine specular reflection on a cornea by that method [16]. To overcome such problems, we propose a new method to capture user's focused iris image at fast speed based on the corneal specular reflection and the human eye model.

2 A Fast Iris Image Acquisition Method

2.1 Auto Zooming and Focusing Based on Corneal Specular Reflection

Due to the limitation of increasing the DOF(Depth of Field) with the single(fixed) focal camera, we use the variable focal camera for iris recognition and propose auto focusing algorithm. For focusing algorithm, we use the corneal specular reflection(SR) generated by IR-LED illuminator. In case that the Z position of user's eye is within the DOF, the size of SR can be minimized. On the other hand, in case that the Z position of user's eye is farther than DOF from camera, the size of SR can be increased and dark gray pixels exist in the edge of SR. And in case that the Z position of user's eye is nearer than DOF from camera, the size of SR can be also increased and dark gray pixels exist in the center of SR. Based on that information, we can determine the lens direction in case of defocusing. After determining the lens direction, the lens movement step should be also determined. Our experiments show that we can determine the amount of lens movement step based on the detected diameter of SR in image. Because our iris camera uses zoom lens, the captured iris diameter in image is maintained almost same size and the change of SR size in image is only caused by the optical defocusing(blurring). So, we can get the experimental relationship between the zoom(focus) lens position and the diameter of detected SR in image. According to our experiments (on 350 persons), such relationship proves to be almost identical to all the users and we can regard it as a standard relation generalized for all the user.

2.2 Lens Position Compensation Considering Human Eye Structure

In general, a human iris is positioned inside the cornea and the aqueous humor as shown in Fig. 1(a) [18]. The cornea and aqueous humor which surround iris

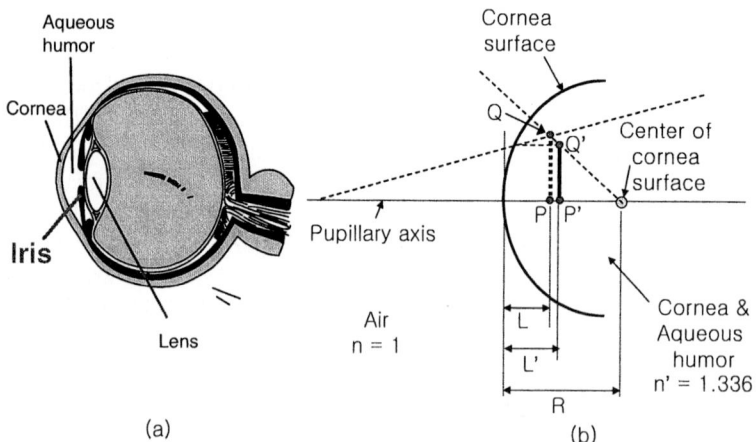

Fig. 1. A human eye structure and an equivalent eye model for obtaining the projected image of iris

and pupil act as a convex lens. As a result, the location and the size of the "projected image(PQ) of genuine iris " are different from those of the "genuine iris(P'Q')". In other words, when we see someone's iris of the eye, we see the refracted image(PQ) of the genuine iris(P'Q'). From that, we can see there exists some distance gap(L) between the position of corneal surface(on which specular reflection happens) and that of the projected iris image(PQ). As explained in section 2.1, we perform auto zooming(focusing) in the direction of making the size of detected SR in image smallest and it means our algorithm is operated by focusing the corneal specular reflection in other words. So, we should compensate the distance gap (L) because the projected iris(PQ) is positioned behind the cornea with the distance gap (L). Now, we explain the method of calculating the distance gap (L) based on a human eye structure and an equivalent eye model as shown in Fig. 1. According to the Gullstrand's eye model [19], the refractive index of cornea and aqueous humor is 1.336(n'), the radius of cornea is 7.8 mm(R) and the iris exists 3.6 mm(L') behind the cornea surface as shown in Fig. 1(b). From that, we can obtain the location(P) of the projected image of the iris from the Gaussian imaging formula[20] written as (n'/L' - n/L = (n'-n)/R). Here, n' and n are the refractive indexes of lens and air, respectively. In addition, L' and L are the locations of the object and the projected image, respectively. R is the radius of lens surface (See Fig. 1(b)). From the Gauss lens formula and Gullstrand's eye model (1.336/3.6 - 1/L = (1.336-1)/7.8), we can obtain the distance gap (L = 3.05 mm) between the position of corneal surface and that of the projected iris image(PQ). So, in order to compensate such distance gap(3.05 mm) and focus actual iris region, we make the zoom(focus) lens be positioned closer to the eye by one more step (one step of lens corresponds to 5mm in our camera) compared to focusing corneal specular reflection.

2.3 Specular Reflection Detection in an Input Image

Now, we explain the method of detecting specular reflection in an input image. In order to detect the SR more easily, we use the method of changing the decoder value of frame grabber board. Due to the limitation of A/D converting range (from 0 to 2^8-1), the camera NTSC signal cannot be fully represented and some signal range may be cut off. In this case, the NTSC signal in high saturated range is represented as 255(2^8-1) gray level in the input image and both the genuine SR on eye (cornea) and the other reflection region on facial skin or glasses surface may be represented as same gray level(255) in the input image. However, the NTSC analog level of SR on eye is higher than that of other region such as the reflection on facial skin. That is because the reflectance rate on cornea is greater than that on facial skin. So, if we change the decoder's brightness setting (making the brightness value lower), then the A-D converting range with decoder can be shifted to the upper range. In such case, there is no high saturated range and it is easy to discriminate the SR on eye and the other reflection. However, when a user wears the glasses, some large SR on glasses surface may still happen. In addition, if the surface of glasses is not smooth, many scratches may make a lot of small imposter SRs. To overcome such problems, we use the successive On/Off scheme for IR-LED illuminators. When the user approaches in the operating range of the iris camera, our iris camera can detect it and notify the user's approach to the micro-controller of camera. Then, the micro-controller turns on the left IR-LED illuminator(during the even field period(16.7ms) of the CCD output signal) and the right one(during the odd field period(16.7ms) of the CCD output signal), alternately and repeatedly. In our iris camera, we use two illuminators, which are positioned at left and right symmetrical to camera axis. So, one SR by left illuminator happens in even field and the other one does in odd field. Because we know the curvature of general human cornea(as explained in section 2.2) and the distance between left and right illuminators, we can estimate the distance between the genuine SRs in even and odd field image. However, the other SRs (that happens on the glasses surface or the scratches of glasses) have the tendencies not to exist with the pair characteristics (or having different size in even and odd field) or the distance between each SR may be greater than that between the genuine SRs on the cornea. That is because the curvature of glasses is much smaller than that of human cornea.

Here, we explain it in details. The Fig. 2 shows the relationship among the user's eye, illuminators and iris camera. In our iris camera, the distance between two illuminators (P_1 and P_2) is 70mm and they are positioned symmetrical to the camera axis (Z_c axis in the Fig. 2). From that, we can get the 3D positions of P_1 and P_2 as (35, 0) and (-35, 0), respectively. In addition, two lights from illuminators are aligned to be intersected at the Z position of 165mm in our camera. The corneal (C_1) radius of the general user is known as about 7.8 mm as shown in Fig. 1(b) and the distance (Z_p) between the camera and the cornea surface is measured by distance measuring sensor. Based on that information, we can obtain two line equations of L_1 ($Z = -4.714X + 165$) and L_2 ($Z = 4.714X + 165$) in the coordinate (X_c, Z_c). In addition, we can get the circle equation of C_1 ($X^2 + (Z - (Z_p + 7.8))^2 = 7.8^2$). With two lines($L_1$, L_2) and circle equations(C_1), we can obtain the X positions(X_1, X_2) of p_1 and p_2 in the coordinate (X_c, Z_c) and obtain the X distance (D) between p_1 and p_2. With the

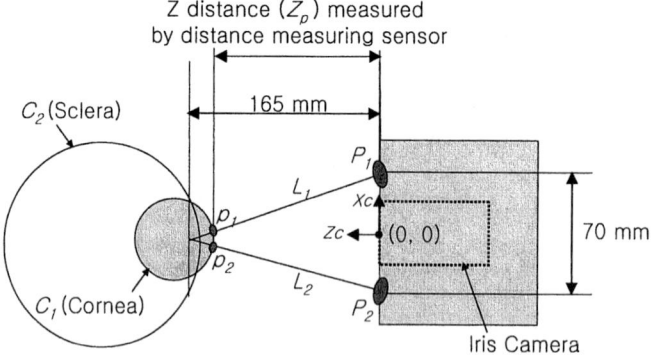

Fig. 2. Estimating the pixel distance between the genuine(corneal) SRs in even and odd field image

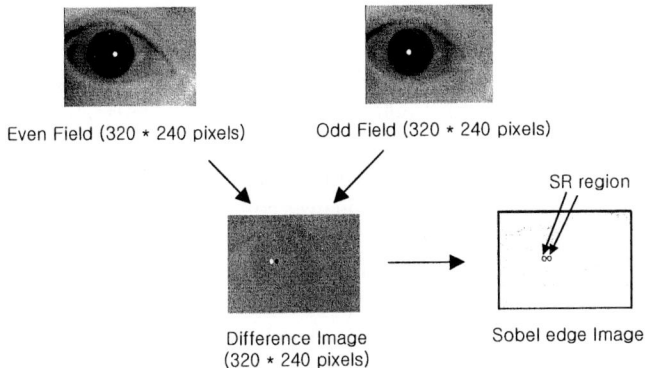

Fig. 3. Detecting SR in difference image

calculated X distance (D) and the perspective transform[6], we can estimate the X distance (d) between two specular reflections in image like Eq. (1)

$$d = (D*f)/Z', \tag{1}$$

where f is camera focal length (we can get the value from camera microcontroller) and Z' is the actual Z distance between the p_1 (or p_2) and the origin (0,0) in the coordinate (X_c, Z_c). With two lines(L_1, L_2) and circle equations(C_1), we can obtain Z' ($Z' = Z_p + (7.8 - 7.8cos(sin^{-1}(D/(2*7.8))))$). Of course, in case that the user does not align his eye into the camera optical axis (Z_c) accurately, there can be some variations for d in Eq. (1). However, such variations are very small according to our experiments (due to large Z distance of operating range of our iris camera (more than 100 mm) compared to small corneal radius (7.8 mm) and perspective transform) and we allow a little margin (+- 3 pixels) for d in Eq. (1) to cover such variations. With the difference image of even and odd field image(in this case, we subsample each field of 640*240 pixels into that of 320*240 pixels in order to reduce processing time), we get an edge image by 3*3 sobel operator as shown in Fig. 3. As mentioned before, the time difference between even and odd field is only 16.7ms and the motion difference of user is very small during that time. So, almost only the edge for SR can be dominant in the edge image. In addition, due to small time difference, we do not need the time consuming procedure of motion compensation in order to reduce the motion difference and we can reduce the processing time consequently [6]. From that, we detect the center and radius of the corneal SR by 2D gradient-based circle Hough transform [7]. With this scheme, we can detect the exact SR regions on cornea and move the zoom(focus) lens to the exact focusing position according to the SR size in image.

From that, we can get the clear and focused eye image for iris recognition at very fast speed. In addition, we can know which illuminator (left or right) makes less specular reflection on glasses surface from the detected SR and select that illuminator for recognition in order to reduce the FRR(False Rejection Rate) caused by the SR on the glasses surface.

3 Experimental Results

The evaluation tests were performed on 350 persons (175 persons without glasses and 175 persons with glasses). Each person tried to recognize 10 times and total 3500 trial data were acquired to measure the performance of our proposed algorithm. The test data includes the persons from 23 to 60 ages, composed of 282 Korean and 68 Occidental. In addition, we collected(rearranged) the test data according to the approaching speed of user; 1000 data at normal speed (from 5cm/sec to 15cm/sec), 1000 data at fast speed (more than 15cm/sec), and 1000 data at slow speed (below 5cm/sec). The remaining 500 data were collected in case that users approached to the camera not from the front but from the side. In the first experiment, we measured the processing time of detecting the SR in an input image and it takes a little processing time as 3 ms in Pentium-IV 1.8Ghz.

In the second experiment, we compared the performance of our focusing algorithm to those [8],[13],[14],[15] as shown in Fig. 4(a)(b). Fig. 4(a)(b) shows the focusing performance by the curve of focus value vs. focus lens position. In general, if the curve is steep near a focusing point and in the blurred region, it is reported that the focusing algorithm shows good performance [15]. That is because if the slope near the focusing point is steep, the focus lens can reach the focused position fast and accurately. In addition, if the slope in the blurred region is also steep, the focus lens can determine its movement direction easily [15]. According to Fig. 4(a), our method shows the best focusing performance. In addition, other methods show the local maximums of focus value curve which make the focusing more difficult as shown in Fig. 4(b), but our method does not show any local maximum in focus value curve. In the third experiment, we compared the average focusing time. The focusing time of users without glasses is shown as 551ms by Tenengrad[8], 434ms by SMD[13], 535ms by SML[14], 425ms by WDOM[15], 328ms and 309ms by our method without and with lens position compensation (as shown in section 2.2), respectively. The focusing time of users with glasses is like these; 1523ms by Tenengrad, 928ms by SMD, 1411ms by SML, 890ms by WDOM, 628ms and 601ms by our method without and with lens position compensation, respectively. Experimental results show the focusing time

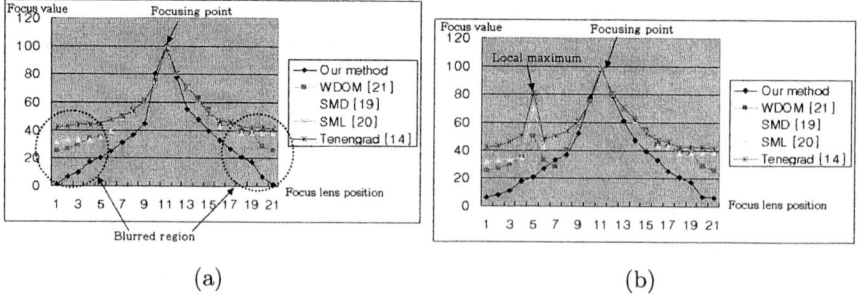

Fig. 4. Focus value vs. focus lens position (a)in case of users without glasses (b)in case of users with glasses

of all users with/without glasses as 1037ms by Tenengrad, 681ms by SMD, 973ms by SML, 658ms by WDOM, 474ms and 450ms by our method without and with lens position compensation, respectively. From that, we can know our focusing method shows the best performance. In the fourth experiment, we measured the performances of our algorithm(with lens position compensation) in terms of recognition speed. The average recognition time (including focusing and iris recognition time) is 698 ms in case of the users without glasses and that is 1201 ms in case of that with glasses. The reason that the recognition time is increased in the latter case is that large SR on glasses surface caused by illuminator hides the whole iris region sometimes. In such case, our system turns on the other illuminator (from left to right or from right to left) and the total recognition time is increased, consequently. In the fifth experiment, we measured the recognition rate and the results show the FAR of 0% and the FRR of 0.8%(28/3500 trials). The FRR is mainly caused by the large SR from glasses and most of them are recognized in second trial. In the sixth experiment, we tested the focusing time, recognition time and recognition rate according to the Z distance between user and the iris camera. The focusing time is like these; 452ms at 10cm, 458ms at 12cm, 457ms at 16cm, 451ms at 20cm, 451ms at 22cm. The recognition time is like these; 946ms at 10cm, 952ms at 12cm, 949ms at 16cm, 954ms at 20cm, 950ms at 22cm. The FAR is 0% at all Z distances. The FRR is like these; 0.7% at 10cm, 0.79% at 12cm, 0.8% at 16cm, 0.79% at 20cm, 0.8% at 22cm. From that, we can know the focusing time, recognition time and recognition rate are almost same irrespective of the Z distance. In the last experiment, we tested the focusing time, recognition time and recognition rate by changing environmental lighting intensity(with fluorescent lamp). The focusing time is like these; 451ms in 250 Lux., 448ms in 500 Lux., 452ms in 750 Lux., 451ms in 1000 Lux., 455ms in 1250 Lux. The recognition time is like these; 1220ms in 250 Lux., 1209ms in 500 Lux., 952ms in 750 Lux., 951ms in 1000 Lux., 948ms in 1250 Lux. The FAR is 0% in all lighting intensity. The FRR is like these; 0.92% in 250 Lux., 0.83% in 500 Lux., 0.8% in 750 Lux., 0.79% in 1000 Lux., 0.8% in 1250 Lux. From that, we can know the focusing time, recognition time and recognition rate are almost same irrespective of the change of lighting intensity. To be notable, in case that the lighting intensity is below 500 Lux., the FRR and the recognition time is increased a little. That is because the pupil is dilated too much due to dark environmental light (iris region is contracted too much) and it causes False Rejection cases.

4 Conclusions

In this paper, we propose a new iris image acquisition method to capture user's focused iris image at very fast speed based on the corneal specular reflection and human eye model. From the experimental results, we can conclude our method can be applicable for the real-time iris recognition camera. In future works, we plan to estimate the user's motion and move the lens in advance to enhance the performance.

References

1. John G. Daugman, "High confidence visual recognition of personals by a test of statistical independence". IEEE Trans. PAMI., Vol. 15, No. 11, pp. 1148-1160, 1993
2. http://www.lgiris.com
3. http://www.iridiantech.com
4. http://www.panasonic.com/cctv/products/biometrics.asp
5. http://www.iris-recognition.org
6. Ramesh Jain, "Machine Vision", McGraw-Hill International Edition, 1995
7. D. Ioammou et al., "Circle Recognition through a 2D Hough transform and Radius Histogramming", Image and Vision Computing, vol. 17, pp. 15-26, 1999
8. Je-Ho Lee et al., "Implementation of a passive automatic focusing algorithm for digital still camera", IEEE Trans. on CE, vol. 41, no. 3, pp. 449-454, Aug. 1995.
9. H. Toyoda et al., "New Automatic Focusing System for Video Camera", IEEE Transactions on Consumer Electronics, vol. CE-32, no. 3, pp. 312-319, Aug. 1986
10. T. Haruki and K. Kikuchi, "Video Camera System Using Fuzzy Logic", IEEE Transactions on Consumer Electronics, vol. 38, no. 3, pp. 624-634, Aug. 1992
11. K. Ooi et al., "An Advanced Auto-focusing System for Video Camera Using Quasi Condition Reasoning", IEEE Trans. on CE, vol. 36, no. 3, pp. 526-529, Aug. 1990
12. K. Hanma et al., "Novel Technologies for Automatic Focusing and White Balancing of SolidState Color Video Camera", IEEE Trans. on CE, vol.CE-29, no. 3, pp.376-381, Aug. 1983
13. R. A. Jarvis, "Focus Optimization Criteria for Computer Image Processing", Microscope, vol. 24(2), pp. 163-180
14. S. K. Nayar and Y. Nakagawa, "Shape from Focus", IEEE Transactions on Pattern Analysis and Machine Intelligence, vol. 16, no. 8, pp. 824-831, Aug. 1994.
15. Kang-Sun Choi et al., "New Auto-focusing Technique Using the Frequency Selective Weight Median Filter for Video Cameras", IEEE Trans. on CE, Vol.45, No.3, pp.820-827, Aug. 1999
16. Y. Park et al., "A Fast Circular Edge Detector for the Iris Region Segmentation", LNCS, Springer Verlag, Vol. 1811, 2000, pp. 417-423
17. Sheng-Wen Shih, "A Novel Approach to 3-D Gaze Tracking Using Stereo Cameras", IEEE Transactions on Systems, Man and Cybernatics-Part B, Vol. 34, No. 1, Feb. 2004
18. Jeong Jun Lee, "Eye Gaze Estimation in Wearble Monitor", Ph.D Thesis, the Graduate School of Yonsei University, Nov. 2004
19. Y.L.Grand, "Light, Color and Vision", New York: Wiley, 1957
20. http://fizz.phys.dal.ca/ hewitt/Web/PHYC3540/Lecture5.ppt

Automatic Human Model Generation

Bodo Rosenhahn*, Lei He, and Reinhard Klette

University of Auckland (CITR), Computer Science Department,
Private Bag 92019 Auckland, New Zealand
rosenhahn@mpi-sb.mpg.de

Abstract. The contribution presents an integrated system for automatic acquisition of a human torso model, using different input images. The output model consists of two free-form surface patches (with texture maps) for the torso and the arms. Also, the positions for the neck joint on the torso, and six joint positions on the arms (for the wrist, elbow and shoulder) are determined automatically. We present reconstruction results, and, as application, a simple tracking system for arm movements.

1 Introduction

Human motion modeling plays an increasingly important role in medical applications, surveillance systems or avatar animation for movies and computer games. This work is part of a human motion analysis project as presented in [16]. For a detailed study of human motions the research project requires an automatic model generation system, so that the pose recovery can be evaluated for different persons (e.g. male, female, small, tall and so forth). Our goal is to present an integrated framework for the automatic generation of human models that consist of free-form surface patches and body segments connected by joints. The input of the algorithm is a set of 4 images and the output is a VRML-model of the torso. The basic structure is given in Figure 1.

In the literature reconstruction techniques can be broadly divided into active and passive methods. Where active methods use a light pattern projected into the scene, or a laser ray emitting from a transmitter, passive techniques use the image data itself. Our approach is a passive reconstruction method due to its greater flexibility in scene capturing and being a low-cost technique. Kakadiaris et al. propose in [7] a system for 3D human body model acquisition by using three cameras in mutually orthogonal views. A subject is requested to perform a set of movements according to a protocol. The body parts are identified and reconstructed incrementally from 2D deformable contours. Hilton et al. [4] propose an approach for modeling a human body from four views. The approach uses extrema to find feature points. It is simple and efficient. However, it is not reliable for finding the neck joint and it does not provide a solution to find elbow or wrist joints. Plänkers et al. [13] model an articulated body by using layers for a skeleton, ellipsoidal meta-balls (to simulate muscles) and a polygonal surface representation (to model the skin). But as discussed in [15] we prefer a non-layered representation, where free-form surface patches are directly assigned to joint indexes. This leads to a

---
* From Nov. 2005: Max Planck Center Saarbrücken.

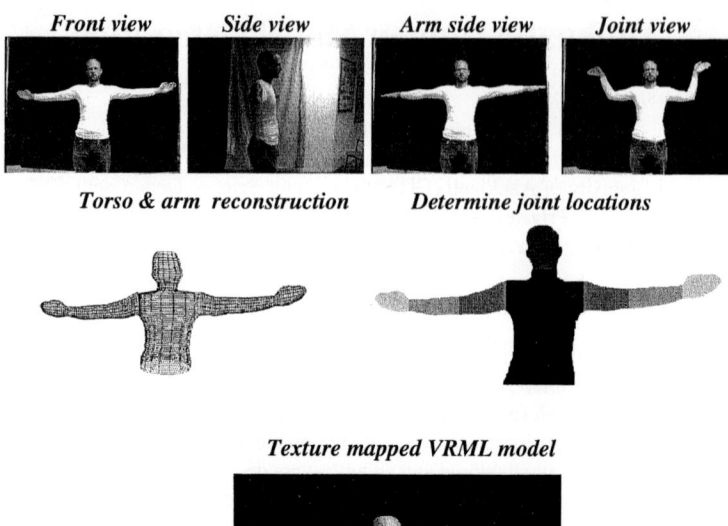

Fig. 1. Steps of the implemented system. Four input images are used for model generation.

more compact representation and allows further freedom for modeling mesh deformations or joint shifts during tracking. Lee et al. [6] build a seamless human model. Their approach obtains robust and efficient results, but it cannot detect joint positions which have to be arranged manually.

The next section presents the implemented modules needed for model reconstruction. Section three presents some reconstruction and tracking results. Section four concludes with a brief discussion.

2 Implemented Modules

This section describes implemented modules and those modifications of existing algorithms which have been necessary to adapt them to our specific tasks.

Segmentation
Segmentation is the process of extracting a region of interest from an image. Accuracy and efficiency of contour detection are crucial for the final outcome. Fortunately, the task is relatively easy to solve, since we assume a person in a lab environment with known static background. Here we use a modified version of [5], which proves to be fast and stable: To decide between object and background pixels, we compare pixels of typical background characteristics with all pixels in the given image. The difference

between two pixels is decomposed in two components, brightness and chromaticity. Thresholds are used to segment the images as shown in Figure 1. Afterwards the images are smoothed using morphological operators [9].

Body Separation
Firstly it is necessary to separate the arms from the torso of the model. Since we only reconstruct the upper torso, the user can define a bottom line of the torso by clicking on the image. Then we detect the arm pits and the neck joint from the *front view* of the input image. The arm pits are simply given by the two lowermost corners of the silhouette which are not at the bottom line. The position of the neck joint can be found when walking along the boundary of the silhouette from an upper shoulder point to the head. The narrowest x-slice of the silhouette gives the neck joint.

Joint Localization
After a rough segmentation of the human torso we detect positions of arm joints. Basically, we use a special reference frame (*joint view*) which allows to extract arm segments. To gain the length of the hands, upper arms, etc. we firstly apply a skeletonization procedure. Skeletonization is a process of reducing object pixels in a binary image to a skeletal remnant that largely preserves the extend and connectivity of the original region while eliminating most of the original object pixels. Two skeletonization approaches are common, those based on thinning and those based on distance transforms. We implemented the thinning approach presented in [8] called iterative thinning algorithm. The left image of Figure 2 shows that the algorithm leads to a connected skeleton, but unfortunately it is not centered. Furthermore, we are interested in detecting corners of the skeleton, but the resulting curve is very smooth which makes it hard to detect, for example, the position of the elbow joint. The middle image of Figure 2 shows the result using the Chamfer distance transform. Here the skeleton is centered, but unfortunately it is not connected. We decided to work with the skeletons based on the Chamfer distance transform and close the skeleton by connecting nearest non-neighboring points. This leads to centered skeletons as shown on the arms in right of Figure 2. We further use the method presented in [2] to detect corners on the skeleton to identify joint positions of the arms.

Furthermore, we would like to point out that the joint localizations need to be refined since the center of the elbow joint is not at the center of the arm, but beneath. For this reason we shift the joint position such that it corresponds to the human anatomy, see

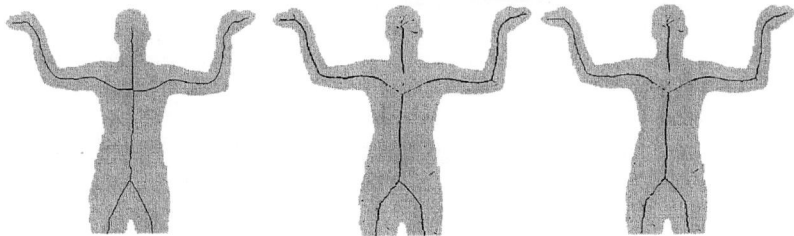

Fig. 2. Skeletonization using iterative thinning (left), Chamfer distance transform (middle), and our modified version (right)

Fig. 3. Left: Adapting elbow joints. Right: Extracted joint segments.

in the left image of Figure 3: Starting from the shoulder joint S and elbow joint E, we use the midpoint C between the right boundary of the silhouette B and E as new elbow position. The result of joint locations is shown at the right image of Figure 3.

Surface Mesh Reconstruction

For surface mesh reconstruction we assume calibrated cameras in nearly orthogonal views. Then a shape-from-silhouettes approach [10] is applied. We attempt to find control points for each slice, and then to interpolate them as a B-spline curve using the DeBoor algorithm. For this we start with one slice of the first image and use its edge points as the first two reference points. Then they are multiplied with the fundamental matrix of the first to the second camera and the resulting epipolar lines are intersected with the second silhouette resulting in two more reference points. The reference points are intersected leading to four control points in 3D space.

For arm reconstruction we use a different scheme for building a model: We use two other reference frames (input images 2 and 3 in Figure 1). Then the arms are aligned such so that they are horizontally and have the same fingertip starting point. This is shown in Figure 4. These silhouettes are sliced vertically to gain the width and height of each arm part. The arm patches are then connected to the mid plane of the torso.

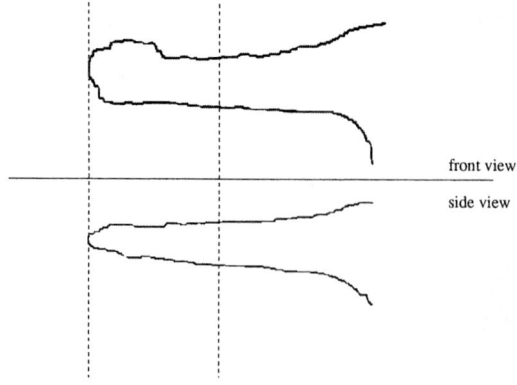

Fig. 4. Alignment of the arm

Fig. 5. Texture fusion: The images from the stereo setup are merged to get a texture map for the head: the left texture gives a good face, whereas the right texture gives a good ear and side view of the face. The fusion of both textures leads to a new texture used for the 3D model.

For texture mapping, we generate a texture file as a combination of the different views: Here we apply the multi-resolution method proposed by Burt et al. [1] for removing boundaries between different image sources. This is achieved by using a weighted average splining technique. For sake of simplicity, we adapt it to a linear weighted function. A texture resulting from a fusion of two different input views is shown on the right of Figure 5.

3 Experiments

We tested the algorithm on four different models. Figure 6 shows in the lower two rows reconstruction results from two persons. One useful application is to animate the models using motion capture data: The top row in Figure 6 shows some capture results

Fig. 6. Pose results of the pose recognition software. Mimicking the arm configurations with the reconstructed models.

Table 1. Example lengths for a test subject (unit: cm)

	Name	real person	reconstructed model	error
	lower arm	25.0	27.0	2.0
Bodo	hand	20.0	19.0	1.0
	width	185.2	187.3	2.0

using a human motion estimation algorithm and below are the pose configurations of the reconstructed model. This allows us to let the "Reinhard" model mimic the actors (Bodo) motion.

For a quantitative error analysis we compare reconstructed body parts with (manually) measured ones. One example is shown in Table 1. A comparison with all (four reconstructed) subjects and 6 body parts (head, upper arm, lower arm, width, etc.) shows a maximum deviation of 2 cm. The average error is 0.88 cm.

3.1 Joint Tracking

In a second experiment we apply the model on a simple joint tracking algorithm. Therefore we assume that the reconstructed model is standing in front of a camera and moving its arms. The images are separated in their arm and body components and a skeletonization is applied to detect the arm joints. This approach is similar to the one described in

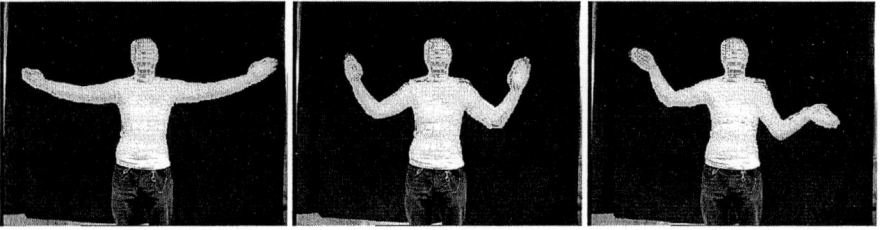

Fig. 7. Joint tracking

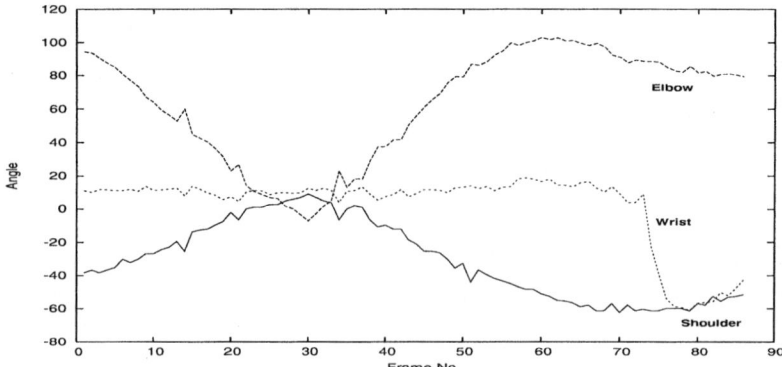

Fig. 8. Joint angles

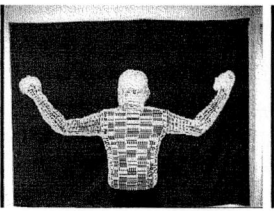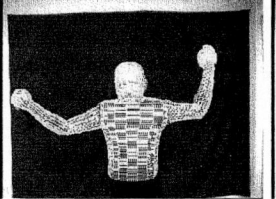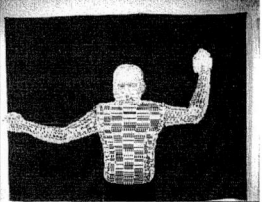

Fig. 9. Arms and head tracking of the "Reinhard"-model

Section 2. If the arm is stretched, the position of the arm is known from the length ratios of the arm components. Tracking results are shown in Figure 7. Some joint angles of the left arm are shown in Figure 8. Though we do not have any ground truth, the angles match with the real motion and the curves are relatively smooth indicating a reasonable stable algorithm.

Figure 9 shows results of the tracked Reinhard model, where also the head angle is estimated. As can be seen, the model fits satisfactory to the image data.

4 Discussion

We present an automatic human model generation system. Several sub tasks are solved and integrated into a system, including a GUI for comfortable interaction of threshold parameters. The algorithm takes a sequence of four images and separates the arms from the torso from a front and a side view. Then a shape-from-silhouettes approach is applied to reconstruct the torso from two views, and the arms from two other views. The joint locations are determined from a fourth image showing a special pose of the arms. Here a skeletonization is applied to detect the joint locations. Finally the model is reconstructed including a texture map from the image data. We apply the reconstruction to a simple joint tracking procedure and show that we are able to track a persons arms with reasonable quality.

The system is developed under a Linux Redhat 9.0 environment. OpenGL is used as the graphics API. The application is written in C/C++. Human models are specified in the format VRML. A scene graph system OpenSG helps to parse and visualize the VRML file. GTK is our GUI development toolkit.

Acknowledgments

This work has been supported by the DFG project RO 2497/1.

References

1. Burt P.J. and Andelson E.H. A multiresolution spline with aplication to image mosaics. *ACM Tarns. on Graphics*, II, No 4, pp. 217-236, 1983.
2. Chetverikov D. A simple and efficient algorithm for detectiopn of high crvature points. *In: Computer Analysis of Images and Patterns*, N. Petkov and M.A. Westenberg (Eds.) Springer-Verlag Berlin, LNCS 2756, pp. 746-753, 2003.

3. Grimson W. E. L. *Object Recognition by Computer.* The MIT Press, Cambridge, Massachusetts, 1990.
4. Hiltion A., Beresford D., Gentils T. Smith R. and Sun W. Vitual people: capturing human models to populate virtual worlds. in *Proc. Computer Animation,* pp. 174-185, 1999.
5. Horprasert T., Harwood D. and Davis L.S. A Statistical Approach for Real-time Robust Background Subtraction and Shadow Detection *In: International Conference on Computer Vision,* FRAME-RATE Workshop, Kerkyra, Greece, 1999. Available at www.vast.uccs.edu/~tboult/FRAME/ Horprasert/HorprasertFRAME99.pdf (Last accessed February 2005).
6. Lee W. Gu J. and Magnenat-Thalmann N. Generating animatable 3D virtual humans from photographs. *Computer Graphics Forum,* Vol. 19, No. 3, pp. 1-10, 2000.
7. Kakadiaris I. and Metaxas D. Three-dimensional human body model acquisition from multiple views. *Internation Journal on Computer Vision,* Vol. 30 No. 3, pp. 191-218, 1998.
8. Klette G. A Comparative Discussion of Distance Transformations and Simple Deformations in Digital Image Processing. *Machine Graphics and Vision* Vol. 12, No. 2, pp. 235-356, 2003.
9. Klette R. and Rosenfeld A. Digital Geometry–Geometric Methods for Digital Picture Analysis *Morgan Kaufmann,*San Francisco, 2004.
10. Klette R., Schlüns K. and Koschan A. Computer Vision. Three-Dimensional Data from Images. *Springer,* Singapore, 1998.
11. Murray R.M., Li Z. and Sastry S.S. *A Mathematical Introduction to Robotic Manipulation.* CRC Press, Inc. Boca Raton, FL, USA, 1994.
12. ORourke J. *Computational Geometry in C.* Cambridge University Press, Cambridge, UK, 1998.
13. Plänkers R. and Fua P. Articulated Soft Objects for Multiview Shape and Motion Capture. *IEEE Trans. on Pattern Analysis and Machine Intelligence,* 25(9), pp.1182-1187, 2003.
14. Rosenhahn B. Pose Estimation Revisited *Technical Report 0308, Christian-Albrechts-Universität zu Kiel, Institut für Informatik und Praktische Mathematik,* 2003. Available at http://www.ks.informatik.uni-kiel.de
15. Rosenhahn B. and Klette R. Geometric algebra for pose estimation and surface morphing in human motion estimation *Tenth International Workshop on Combinatorial Image Analysis (IWCIA),* R. Klette and J. Zunic (Eds.), LNCS 3322, pp. 583-596, 2004, Springer-Verlag Berlin Heidelberg. Auckland, New Zealand,
16. Rosenhahn B., Klette R. and Sommer G. Silhouette based human motion estimation. *In Proc. Pattern Recognition 2004, 26th DAGM-symposium,* Tübingen, Germany, C.E. Rasmussen, H.H. Bülthoff, M.A. Giese, B. Schölkopf (Eds), Springer-Verlag Berlin, LNCS 3175, pp 294-301, 2004.
17. Shi Y. and Sun H. *Image and Video Compression for Multimedia Engineering: Fundamentals, Algorithms, and Standards.* CRC Press, Boca Raton, FL, USA, 1999.

An Illumination Invariant Face Recognition Approach Using Exemplar-Based Synthesis Technique

Tele Tan, Thorsten Kühnapfel, Amelyn Wongso, and Fee-Lee Lim

Department of Computing, Curtin University of Technology,
GPO Box U1987, Perth, Western Australia 6845
{teletan, thorsten, wongsoa, limfl}@cs.curtin.edu.au

Abstract. This paper proposes a new method to solve the problem of face recognition under varying illumination conditions. We introduce an exemplar-based technique to decouple and subsequently recover the canonical face and the illumination functions from the intensity images. The canonical image is equivalent to the reflectance field of the face that is invariant to illumination. We subsequently use the canonical face to synthesize novel face appearances together with a set of lighting models. We then demonstrate the ability of the synthesis approach to improve the performance of the face recognition task.

1 Introduction

The need to further develop robust face recognition techniques to meet real world situations is still an open research challenge. It is widely stated that the two main contributions of poor recognition performances are that caused by variations in face pose and lighting. We will deal with the problem of illumination in this paper. Approaches addressing the illumination-related problems can be broadly classified into two categories; feature-based approach and exemplar- or appearance- based approach. Feature-based approaches aim to define a feature space that exhibits some broad invariance over the lighting variations. Examples of these are [1][10] which uses different image representations like 2D Gabor-like filters, first and second derivatives of the image, and the logarithmic transformation. Although these features may exhibit intensity immunity, none of these are found to be reliable to cope with significantly large variations in illumination changes [9][10].

Exemplar- or appearance- based approaches use a set of sample images taken of a class object (in this case a face) as a basis to compute an intermediary image. The intermediate image can then be used either directly as the probe image or be used to synthesize novel views of the face under different lighting conditions [11]. For example, [2] reported a method to compute the Quotient Image from a small sample of bootstrap images representing a minimum of two class objects. The illumination invariant signature of the Quotient Image enables an analytic generation of the novel image space with varying illumination. However, this technique is highly dependent on the types of bootstrap images used which has the undesirable effect of generating diversely looking Quotient Images even from the same person. Sim and Kanade [3] use a statistical shape-from-shading model to estimate the 3D face shape from a single image. The 3D recovery model is based on the symmetric shape-from-shading algorithm proposed by [4]. They used the 3D face model to synthesize novel faces under new illumination conditions using computer graphics techniques. The approach produce high recognition rate on the illumination subset of the CMU PIE database [5]. However, it was not evident how their synthesis technique can cope with extreme illumination conditions [3]. Debevec in [6] presented a method to acquire the reflectance field of a human face and use these measurements to render the face under arbitrary changes in lighting and viewpoint. However, the need to generate a large sample of images using the light stage is unfeasible for most face recognition systems. A parameter-free method of estimating the bi-directional reflectance distribution of a subject's skin was proposed by Hancock et al in [12]. They estimated the radiance function by exploiting differential geometry and making use of the Gauss map from the surface onto a unit sphere. They demonstrated the approach by applying it to the re-rendering of faces with different skin reflectance models.

As in [2] and [11], we address the problem of class-based image synthesis and recognition with varying illumination conditions. We define an ideal class as a collection of 3D objects that have the same shape but different albedo functions. For recognition purposes, we can broadly assume all human faces to belong to a certain class structure. This assumption was similarly adopted by Shashua [2] and Mariani [11]. Our approach is based on the dual recovery of the canonical face model and lighting models given a set of images taken with varying lighting conditions and from a minimum of two distinct subjects within the class. The canonical image is equivalent to the reflectance field of the face that is invariant to illumination. The lighting model is the image representation of the ambient lighting independent of the face input. We will first formulate the problem with an over-determined set of equations and propose a method in solving them over every pixel location in the image. We will demonstrate the quality of the recovered canonical face for generating novel appearances using both subjective and objective measures.

2 The Simplified Illumination Function

The intensity of reflected light at a point on a surface is the integral over the hemisphere above the surface of a light function L times a reflectance function R. The pixel equation at point (x,y,z) can be expressed as

$$I(x,y,z) = \iiiint_{t\,\lambda\,\theta\,\phi} L(t,x,y,z,\theta,\phi,\lambda) R(t,\theta,\phi,\lambda)\,d\theta\,d\phi\,d\lambda\,dt \tag{1}$$

where
  x,y,z = the co-ordinate of the point on the surface
  ϕ and θ = azimuth and yaw angle from the z axis respectively
  t and λ = time and wavelength of the light source

This equation is computationally too complex to solve in many real-time applications. We need to make further simplification of the equation without significantly affecting the goal of our work. Firstly, z, t and λ can be eliminated because we are dealing with the projected intensity value of a 3D point onto a still frame image with grey scale intensity. Additionally, if one considers fixing the relative location of the camera and the light source, θ and ϕ both become constants and the reflectance function collapses to point (x, y) in the image plane. Therefore, the first-order approximation of equation (1) for a digital image $I(x,y)$ can be further written as:

$$I(x,y) \approx R(x,y) L(x,y) \qquad (2)$$

where $R(x,y)$ is the reflectance and $L(x,y)$ is the illumination at each image sample point (x,y). Our approach is to use exemplar images taken over different fixed lighting directions to recover both the reflectance model and illumination source. It is not the scope of this work to accurately model the skin reflectance property according to specificity like the melanin content of the skin, skin hemoglobin concentration and level of perspirations. These are important for visually accurate skin rendering application but less so for face recognition.

3 The Approach

In our case, only the measured intensity images are available. Therefore, there are twice as many unknown data (RHS) as there are known data (LHS) making equation (2) ill-posed. The reflectance surface essentially comprises the combination of the reflectance property associated with the pigmentation of the skin, mouth, eyes and artifacts like facial hair. We define the reflectance model as the canonical face and represent it as a grey level intensity image. We will discuss in this section an approach that we propose to recover the canonical and illumination information from a set of intensity images $I_{ij}(x,y) \approx R_j(x,y) L_i(x,y)$, where i and j are indices to the collection of bootstrap[1] faces and illumination directions respectively.

3.1 Defining and Solving the Systems of Equations

As explained in the previous section, equation (2) has more unknown terms than known. In order to make the equation solvable in a least square sense, we need to introduce additional measurements thus making the system of equations over *determined*. We further note that the bootstrap image, $I_{ij}(x,y)$ has two variable components. They are the reflectance component which is unique to the individual person and the illumination model which is dependent on the lighting source and direction. Suppose we have M distinct persons which we use in the bootstrap collection (i.e. $R_j, j = 1, ..., M$) and N spatially distributed illumination sources whose direction with respect to the person is fixed at all instances (i.e. $L_i, i = 1, ..., N$), we will have therefore a total of MxN known terms and M+N unknown terms. These *over-determined* systems of equations can be solved by selecting any values of M and N that are greater than 1. For example, if we use M persons from the bootstrap collection, and collect N images for each person by varying the illumination, we get the following system of equations;

---

[1] The bootstrap collection comprises of face sample images taken of various person over multiple illumination directions, the relative location of which are fixed.

$$I_{i1}(x,y) \approx R_1(x,y) L_i(x,y)$$
$$\vdots$$
$$I_{iM}(x,y) \approx R_M(x,y) L_i(x,y)$$
(3)

where $i = 1,...,N$. The terms on the left hand side of these equations are the bootstrap images from the M number of persons. If the illuminations used to generate these bootstrap images are the same, the illumination models, L_i will be common for every person as is reflected in equation (3).

Numerous non-linear minimization algorithms exist and are usually problem dependent [7]. We chose to use the Levenberg-Marquardt non-linear least square fitting algorithm [8] as it is fast and suited to problems of high dimensionality. The solver takes as input the set of equations shown in (3) to minimize, a Jacobian matrix of derivatives, a set of known data (i.e. I_{ij}) and seed values for the unknowns. We chose to set the seed value to 128 since there are 256 possible grey values for both the reflectance and illumination models. The internal functions of the solver are iterated until the change in computed values falls below a threshold. At this point the algorithm is said to have converged, and the current computed values for the unknown data are taken as the solution. The algorithm is extremely fast and can recover the unknown values (for most practical values of M and N) in near real-time.

3.2 Appearance Synthesis

Once the canonical face and the illumination model are recovered, we can proceed to perform the appearance synthesis using the following principles:

1. New illumination models can be generated by the combination of the subset of the recovered illumination models.
2. Novel appearance views for each person can be generated by the combination of an expanded set of illumination models to closely match the actual illumination conditions.

It is not economical and computationally feasible to store specific illumination models for specific faces. To make this approach viable, we need to define a set of generic illumination models that is suitable for a broad cross section of people with different skin types and bone structures. We estimate this generic illumination models using the weighted average models gathered from a genre of subjects.

4 Experiments and Results

4.1 The Database

For our experiments, we make use of the illumination subset of the CMU PIE database [5]. It comprises 63 people taken under 21 different illumination directions (with all ambient lights switched off) in a controlled environment. All the color images are first transformed to grey-level, pre-processed and the faces cropped. The final size for all images is 110 x 90 pixels.

4.2 Canonical Face Recovery

We use equation (3) to recover the canonical faces with different values of M and N and a subset of them are shown in Fig. 1. In order to measure the quality of the recovered canonical face, we define a set of measures that describes the properties of an acceptable canonical face. The measures are; (1) Elimination of lighting effects like specular reflections and cast shadows. (2) Preservation of the visual distinctiveness of the underlying face. (3) Well-balanced intensity distribution. Based on these measures, we can see that in general the recovery of the canonical faces for different values of M and N are very good. This is a significant improvement over the Quotient Image reported in [2]. To further support the significance of the recovered canonical face, we will next describe a face recognition experiment that will quantitatively show the ability of our approach to deal with illumination variation problem.

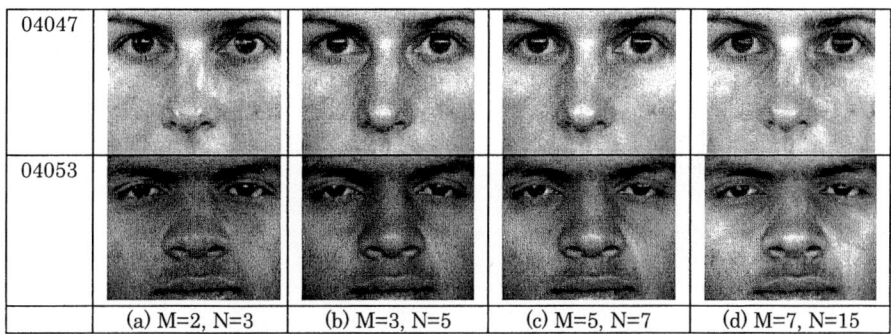

Fig. 1. Canonical faces generated for candidate samples 04047 and 04053 using (a) M=2,N=3, (b) M=3,N=5, (c) M=5,N=7 and (d) M=7,N=15

4.3 Face Appearance Synthesis

For each recovered canonical face, the corresponding set of 21 illumination models can then be computed. We further estimated the generic illumination models as defined in Section 3.2 by using 10 candidate samples from the CMU PIE database. We then use these generic illumination models and the canonical faces from the remaining samples to generate novel appearance faces. Fig. 2a shows the synthesized views of a subject generated using 5 different illumination models. The corresponding images captured by the actual illuminations are shown in Fig. 2b.

4.4 Recognition Experiment

To demonstrate the feasibility of the face appearance synthesis for recognition, we implement a simple classifier based on template matching. This is equivalent to the nearest neighbor classifier reported by Sim and Kanade [3]. We use only frontal pose faces throughout the experiment. The generic illumination models used here is the same as in Section 4.3. To maintain unbiased recognition outcome, the test samples used for recognition does not come from any of the samples used to produce the

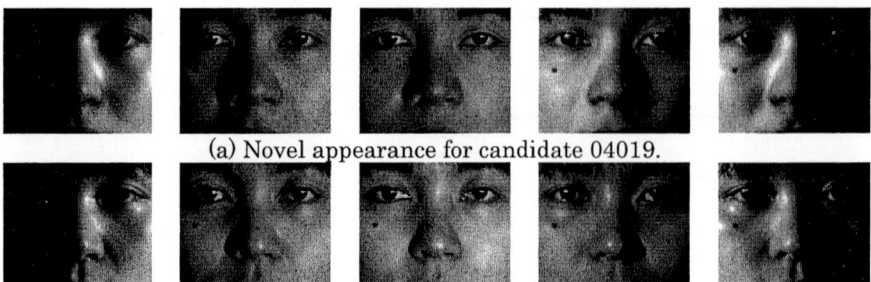

(a) Novel appearance for candidate 04019.

(b) Corresponding actual appearance for candidate 04019 from CMU PIE database.

Fig. 2. Novel appearance synthesis results using a subset of the generic illumination models and its comparison with the actual appearance (derived from camera locations f02, f10, f07, f14 and f17 as defined in the CMU database)

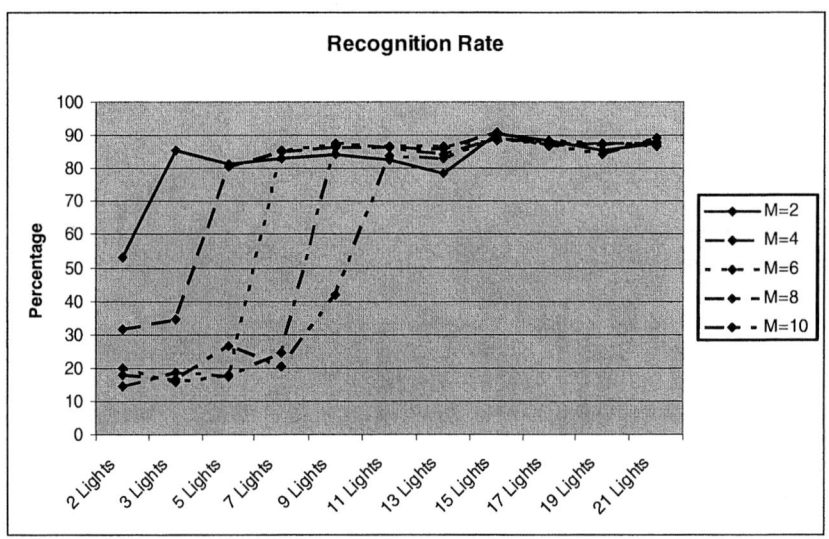

Fig. 3. Recognition rates (in percentage) by varying the values of M and N

generic illumination models. There are 21 persons in the test samples. From each person we compute the canonical representation and use it to synthesize 21 appearances of the person under different lighting conditions. These images collectively form the registry representation of the person in the database. We use actual illumination samples of the PIE database as the test images. There are a total of 441 (i.e. 21x21) test sample images. We construct different registry databases for different combination of M (number of person) and N (number of lighting) values. We then perform the face recognition experiments on the test samples over the different registries. Fig. 3 shows the summary of recognition rate for different values of M and N. We observe several important behaviors. They are:

1. For a fixed value of M, the recognition rate increases monotonically when N increases.
2. However when M increases, N has to consequentially increase for the canonical face to be recovered with reasonable quality. The minimum (M,N) pair needed to establish good recognition rates are (2,3), (4,5), (6,7), (8,9) and (10,11).
3. The recognition rate for N=2 is very poor for all values of M.
4. The range of recognition rates for different values of M and N (ex N=2) are between 83.0% and 90.7%.

As can be seen, the results obtained here is significantly better than [3] which reported an accuracy of 39% with the nearest neighbor classifier on a similar dataset. The general trend of the recognition rates which flatten off as N increases for all values of M suggest a wide perimeter for the choices of these values. However, from the computation, data acquisition and hardware standpoint, it would be effective to keep the M and N values small, without negatively impacting the recognition rate.

5 Discussions

The results obtained using the canonical face recovery algorithm is very encouraging. Besides using the images captured by the lighting module as described here, we can explore shape-from-shading techniques to recover the 3D shape of the face as was done in [4]. The range information together with the canonical face are essential for improving the illumination rendering quality and to deal with pose invariant recognition. Although the illumination models recovered using the CMU PIE database generates 21 different variations they are still inadequate as some crucial lighting directions (i.e. especially those coming from the top) are missing. We will next consider using computer graphics tools to develop a virtual light stage that can produce light rendering from any arbitrary lighting directions. These can then be used to extract finer illumination models. We are also in the process of building a scale-down lighting platform to validate our approach further.

6 Conclusion

We have developed an exemplar-based approach aim at recovering the canonical face of a person. The canonical face can either be use as a probe face for recognition or use as a base image to generate novel appearance models under new illumination conditions. We have shown subjectively that the canonical faces recovered with this approach are very stable and not heavily dependent on the types and numbers of the bootstrap images. The strength of the view synthesis algorithm based on the canonical face was further demonstrated by a series of face recognition tests using the CMU PIE images.

Acknowledgement

We would like to thank the Robotics Institute, Carnegie Mellon University for providing the PIE images.

References

1. Y. Adini and S. Ullman, "Face Recognition: the Problem of Compensating for Changes in Illumination Direction", in Proc. of IEEE Trans. on PAMI. Vol. 19, No. 7, 1997, pp. 721-732.
2. T. Riklin-Raviv and A. Shashua, "The Quotient Image: Class based Re-rendering and Recognition with Varying Illuminations", in Proc. of IEEE Trans. on PAMI. Vol. 23, No. 2, 2001, pp. 129-139.
3. T. Sim and T. Kanade, "Combining Models and Exemplars for Face Recognition: an Illumination Example", in Proc. of Workshop on Models versus Exemplars in Computer Vision, Dec 2001.
4. Zhao and Chellappa, "Robust Face Recognition using Symmetric Shape-from-Shading", Technical Report CARTR-919, Centre for Automation Research, University of Maryland, College Park, MD, 1999.
5. T. Sim, S. Baker and M. Bsat, "The CMU Pose, Illumination and Expression Database", in Proc. of IEEE Trans. on PAMI, Vol. 25, No. 12, 2003, pp. 1615-1618.
6. P. Debevec, T. Hawkins, C. Tchou, W. Sarokin, and M. Sagar, "Acquiring the Reflectance Field of a Human Face", in Proc. of SIGGRAPH 2000, pp. 145-156.
7. A. Yeredor, "The Extended Least Squares Criterion: Minimisation Algorithms and Applications", IEEE Trans. on Signal Processing, Vol. 49, No. 1, Jan 2000, pp. 74-86.
8. J. More, "The Levenberg-Marquardt Algorithm: Implementation and Theory", in G. Watson, Ed, Lecture Notes in Mathematics, Springer Verlag, 1978, pp. 105-116.
9. B. Manjunath, R. Chellappa and C. D. Malsburg, "A feature based approach to face recognition", in Proc. of IEEE Computer Society. Confr. On Computer Vision and Pattern Recognition, 1992, pp. 373-378.
10. P. Yang, S. Shan, W. Gao, S. Li and D. Zhang, "Face recognition using Ada-boosted Gabor features", FG 2004, pp. 356-360.
11. R. Mariani, "A Face Location and Recognition System Based on Tangent Distance", Multimodal Interface for Human-Machine Communication, Vol. 48. Ed. PC Yuen, YY Tang and PSP Wang, World Scientific, pp 3-31.
12. W.A.P Smith, A. Robles-Kelly and E.R. Hancock, "Skin Reflectance Modelling for Face Recognition", in Proc. of the Int'l Confr. on Pattern Recognition, 2004, pp. 210-213.

A Phase Correlation Approach to Active Vision

Hongchuan Yu and M. Bennamoun

School of Computer Science and Software Engineering,
University of Western Australia, Perth, 6009, Australia
{yu, bennamou}@csse.uwa.edu.au

Abstract. In this paper, dealing with the case of large movements in active vision applications, we first develop an algorithm to estimate the motion of an object and its background. Furthermore, with the assumption of small translations between successive frames, we develop an active tracking algorithm. Its main advantage is that an area-based projection method is presented which resorts to an area integral. Thus, it becomes more robust to the translation distortion of the Log-polar image. In addition, the rotation and scaling estimates can be fulfilled in the spatial domain and not in the frequency domain. Thus, the intrinsic drawbacks of the discrete Fourier transform, such as rotationally dependent aliasing and spectral leakages, can be avoided in our case. Our novelty consists in the introduction of the normalized phase correlation approach in our two algorithms. Because this approach does not rely on the smoothness or differentiability of the flow field in a sequence, it makes the large movement estimation possible. The experimental results show that the motions of object and background can be effectively estimated and a moving object can be tracked using our proposed algorithm in an image sequence.

1 Introduction

Motion detection and estimation play an important role in visual tracking. In this paper, we pay attention to the motion estimation based object tracking approach for active vision.

In motion detection and estimation, we focus on the following challenging problems in the context of active vision. The first problem is that an abrupt large movement of an object results in the failure of tracking, such as a discontinuous optical flow field. The second one is the estimation of the background motion. Active vision systems usually seek to dynamically and intelligently gather selective scene information. Hence, the familiar case is that a moving camera is controlled to automatically track a single object. With the knowledge of the background motion, we can effectively recognize an object being tracked, as well as have information to recover a lost object when our other tracking methods fail or have uncertain results. In this paper, the phase correlation technique is introduced to the estimation criterion. Its main advantage is that the phase correlation approach does not require the smoothness or differentiability of the flow field of the image sequence. This is suitable to detect a moving target with a large displacement. From a theoretical viewpoint, 2D similarity motion parameters can be estimated using the phase correlation under the Fourier-Mellin transform framework. In particular, this technique has been widely exploited in the areas of image registration

[1,2] and image watermarking [3] in recent years. The SVD approach presented in [4] improves the accuracy of translation estimates to a sub-pixel level. On the other hand, the frequency-domain criteria had been applied to the estimation of a constant-velocity motion in an image sequence in [5]. Due to the lack of suitable theorems, this kind of approach could not be applied to the non-translational motion model.

Furthermore, with the assumption of small translations between successive frames in a sequence, we further devise an active tracking algorithm. Active tracking is different from the general tracking or motion estimation. In general, only a single object is tracked and encompassed by a higher field of view at a time in active tracking[6,7]. This context is very suitable for the utilization of phase correlation techniques. But then, due to the rotation, we will have to encounter some intrinsic drawbacks from the discrete Fourier transform, such as rotationally dependent aliasing and spectral leakages[8], which result in the failure of the rotation estimate. Thus, improving the robustness of the rotation and scaling estimates will be emphasized in our study.

The rest of this paper is structured as follows. Section 2 shows a brief introduction of the phase correlation techniques. Then, section 3 presents our motion estimation and tracking algorithms. Section 4 presents the experimental results and analysis. Finally, our conclusions and future works are provided in section 5.

2 Phase Correlation Techniques

Consider the images $I_0(x,y)$ and $I_1(x,y)$ are related by $I_1(x,y) = I_0(x+t_x, y+t_y)$, where $(t_x, t_y)^T$ is a translation vector. Taking the Fourier Transform of $I_0(x,y)$ and $I_1(x,y)$ gives $F_1(u,v) = F_0(u,v)e^{-j(ut_x+vt_y)}$. The normalized cross power spectrum of the two images is expressed as, $Corr(u,v) = \frac{F_1(u,v)F_0^*(u,v)}{|F_1(u,v)F_0^*(u,v)|} = e^{-j(ut_x+vt_y)}$, where F^* is the complex conjugate of F. It is clear that the phase of the normalized cross-power spectrum is equivalent to the phase difference between the images I_0 and I_1. By computing the linear phase of $Corr(u,v)$, we can thus determine the translation vector $(t_x, t_y)^T$. Furthermore, by taking the inverse Fourier transform of $Corr(u,v)$, we obtain its spatial representation, $corr(x,y) = IFT(Corr) = \delta(x+t_x, y+t_y)$, where $corr(x,y)$ is a delta function which is zero everywhere except at the displacement, namely the phase correlation peak. This correlation method is usually called the phase correlation approach. Under the Fourier-Mellin transform framework, the rotation and scaling can also be estimated by using it.

3 Motion Estimation and Tracking

3.1 Motion Estimation of an Object and Its Background

In this section, we will focus on the following challenging problems. The first problem is that an abrupt large movement of an object results in the failure of tracking. The second one deals with the estimation of the background motion.

First, consider the translation case $I_1(x,y) = I_0(x+t_x, y+t_y)$. Applying the phase correlation approach, one can obtain the normalized cross power spectrum $Corr(u,v) = e^{-j(ut_x+vt_y)}$, and its spatial representation $corr(x,y) = \delta(x+t_x, y+$

t_y). When the motions of an object and its background are considered simultaneously, there are three cases. The first case is that an object I_b in the successive images is in motion while the background of the images I_0 and I_1 is still, i.e. $I_{1b} = I_{0b}(x + t_x, y + t_y)$, $I_{0b,1b} \subset I_{0,1}$. By computing their cross-correlation spectrum, there are two impulses in $corr(x, y)$, one is at (0,0) which corresponds to the stationary background while the other is at (t_x, t_y) which corresponds to the motion of the object. If the object is still while the background is shifted by a cyclic translation, we have the same explanation. The second case is when the background image is translated and not cyclically shifted (i.e. some new features appear while some others disappear from the scene), and the object is still. This translation can be expressed as a linear phase $e^{-j(ut'_x + vt'_y)}$ in $Corr(u, v)$. Similarly, there are two impulses in $corr(x, y)$, one is at the origin of $corr(x, y)$ which corresponds to the non-shifted object and the other is at (t'_x, t'_y) which corresponds to the background translational shift. However, due to the change of the background information, some noise would be introduced to the linear phase $e^{-j(ut'_x + vt'_y)}$. When the translation is very big, the linear phase will be submerged by noise. However, the phase correlation usually enjoys superior signal-to-noise ratio (SNR). For a tracking task, the background translation between the successive frames is too small to cover the true linear phase. The third case is when an object is moving faster than the background (i.e. both object and background are moving). In this case, there are two linear phases. The first factor $e^{-j(ut_x + vt_y)}$ corresponds to the object translational shift while another factor $e^{-j(ut'_x + vt'_y)}$ corresponds to the background translation respectively. Summarizing the above analysis, we can state the following proposition.

Proposition: Between two successive images related by a translational shift, there are two linear phase components, one is for the object translational shift and the other is for the background translational shift.

It can be noted that the above phase-correlation based motion estimation is unrelated to the smoothness or differentiability of the flow field of an image sequence. Thus, it can be exploited to solve the abrupt large movement problem. Nevertheless, in practice, we have to consider noise which usually causes the phase correlation peak in the spatial domain to spread across neighboring pixels, degrading the accuracy of the translation estimate. For simplicity, let's first illustrate the singular linear phase case, e.g. the background is translated while the object is still in two successive images related by $I_1(x, y) = I_0(x + t_x, y + t_y)$. Their normalized cross-power spectrum can be rewritten in matrix notation as, $\mathbf{Corr} = \mathbf{q}_u \mathbf{q}_v^H$, where $(\cdot)^H$ indicates the complex conjugate transpose and the components of vectors $\mathbf{q}_u$ and $\mathbf{q}_v$ are $q_u(u) = e^{-jut_x}$ and $q_v(v) = e^{jvt_y}$ respectively. It is clear that the normalized phase correlation matrix $\mathbf{Corr}$ should be a rank-one matrix. Due to noise, $rank(\mathbf{Corr}) > 1$. In order to get a rank-one approximation of the correlation matrix $\mathbf{Corr}$, the SVD decomposition is applied $\mathbf{Corr} = \mathbf{U}\Lambda\mathbf{V}^H$. By preserving the left and right dominant singular vectors corresponding to the maximum singular value, we can obtain an optimal rank-one approximation of the matrix $\mathbf{Corr}$ in the least squares sense. Furthermore, it was shown in [4] that the linear phase coefficients t_x and t_y could be estimated independently by linear fitting. Now, let's consider the two linear phase case, in which the translations of the object and the background are taken into account. Our basic idea is to preserve two rank-one approximations of the correlation matrixes corresponding to the object and the background respectively. Since the rank-one approximation of the correlation matrix corresponding to the maximum singular value must indicate the linear phase with the maximum correlation value, while the rank-one approximation of the correlation matrix corresponding to the secondary maximum singular value implies another linear phase with a lesser correlation value.

Furthermore, when considering the rotation, translation and scaling altogether under the Fourier-Mellin transform framework, we unfortunately encounter the rotationally dependent aliasing [8], which usually results in many spurious peaks in the spatial domain and diminishes the value of the phase correlation peak at the correct displacement position. Although using Blackman window in the pixel domain to eliminate the spectral leakage caused by the boundary effects and masking out the central frequencies in the Fourier domain, we can only eliminate the influence of the rotationally dependent aliasing from the background and not the one from the moving object. Our basic idea is that the motion parameters of the background are first estimated, then the background in successive images are rectified and subtracted so that the region of the moving object could be outlined. Finally, the motion estimates of the object are carried out on these cropped regions.

Motion Estimation Algorithm of Object and Background is summarized as follows: **1)** Under the Fourier-Mellin transform framework, compute the normalized cross-power spectrum of the successive images (Blackman window and removal of the central frequencies are adopted); **2)** Determine the rotation and scaling parameters of the background respectively using the SVD approach; **3)** Rectify the original images using the obtained rotation and scaling parameters, and compute the cross-power spectrum of the rectified images; **4)** Determine the translation parameters of the background using the SVD approach; **5)** Rectify the original images according to the obtained motion parameters of the background, and determine the region of the object by computing DFD; **6)** Crop the object regions in the original successive images respectively, and repeat step (1)-(4) to determine the motion parameters of the object.

3.2 Active Tracking Algorithm

In this section, we focus on the case of small translations between successive frames in an image sequence. Using the Log-polar mapping in active tracking, an object occupying the central part of the visual field becomes dominant over the coarsely sampled background elements of the image periphery. This makes it possible to directly estimate the rotation and scaling of an object in the Log-polar image but not in the magnitude spectrum so as to avoid the rotational dependent aliasing.

However, because of translation distortion or noise, projection methods are usually applied to motion estimation in active vision. They can be classified into two kinds, the frequency domain projection and the spatial domain projection. In the former, the radial and angular projections are carried out on the magnitude spectrum under the Fourier-Mellion transform framework [8]. While in the later, the projections are carried out on the spatial Log-polar image [6,7]. Although the frequency domain projection can avoid translations, it usually has to bear the rotationally dependent aliasing. With the assumption of small translations between successive frames, the spatial domain projection method has been exploited to estimate the rotation angle, scaling factor and translation vector respectively. However, the challenging problem of this kind of approach is to overcome the translation distortion in the spatial Log-polar image. From the projection definitions in [6,7], it can be noted that the angular projection is an anisotropic radial summation, while the radial projection is an isotropic circular summation. Indeed, the angular projection is more sensitive to a cartesian translation within the whole Log-polar plane than the radial projection. In this section, we devise an area-based projection method for the rotation and scaling estimates. Due to the use of the area integral, this method is more robust to the translation distortion. It can also be computed in the spatial domain and hence avoids any rotationally dependent aliasing.

In polar coordinates, let's consider the following circular Fourier transforms, $F_u(\rho) = \frac{1}{2\pi} \int_0^{2\pi} I(\rho,\theta) e^{ju\theta} d\theta$ and $F_v(\theta) = \frac{1}{\rho_{max}} \int_1^{\rho_{max}} I(\rho,\theta) e^{jv\rho} d\rho$, where u and v are the coordinates of the spatial-frequency domain respectively defined by, $u = \frac{2k\pi}{M}, k = 0, ..., M-1$ and $v = \frac{2k\pi}{N}, k = 0, ..., N-1$, in the discrete case. Furthermore, we consider the radial projection of $F_u(\rho)$ and angular projection of $F_v(\theta)$ as follows, $A_u = \int_1^{\rho_{max}} F_u(\rho) d\rho$ and $A_v = \int_0^{2\pi} F_v(\theta) d\theta$. For the successive images related by $I_1(\rho,\theta) = I_0(\rho + \rho_0, \theta + \theta_0)$, it is not difficult to see that these two integral quantities hold the translation property, i.e. $A_{1u} = A_{0u} e^{-ju\theta_0}$ and $A_{1v} = A_{0v} e^{-jv\rho_0}$. A_u and A_v are independent of each other. Therefore, we can easily obtain two 1D phase correlation arrays respectively for the rotation and scaling estimates,

$$\begin{cases} Corr(u) = \frac{A_{1u} A_{0u}^*}{|A_{1u} A_{0u}^*|} \\ Corr(v) = \frac{A_{1v} A_{0v}^*}{|A_{1v} A_{0v}^*|} \end{cases} \quad (1)$$

In order to avoid any rotationally dependent aliasing in the frequency domain, we will have to use their spatial representations. Further expanding A_u and A_v and decomposing them into the real and imaginary parts, we have,

$$\begin{cases} Re(A_u) = \frac{1}{2\pi} \iint_D I(x,y) \cos\left(u \cos^{-1}\left(\frac{x}{\sqrt{x^2+y^2}}\right)\right) \frac{dxdy}{\sqrt{x^2+y^2}} \\ Im(A_u) = \frac{1}{2\pi} \iint_D I(x,y) \sin\left(u \sin^{-1}\left(\frac{y}{\sqrt{x^2+y^2}}\right)\right) \frac{dxdy}{\sqrt{x^2+y^2}} \end{cases} \quad (2)$$

and,

$$\begin{cases} Re(A_v) = \frac{1}{\rho_{max}} \iint_D I(x,y) \cos(v\sqrt{x^2+y^2}) \frac{dxdy}{\sqrt{x^2+y^2}} \\ Im(A_v) = \frac{1}{\rho_{max}} \iint_D I(x,y) \sin(v\sqrt{x^2+y^2}) \frac{dxdy}{\sqrt{x^2+y^2}} \end{cases} \quad (3)$$

where $D \subset R^2$ is a sub-domain of the original image frame. It can be noted that A_u and A_v are essentially area integrals in the cartesian image, which are isotropic integrals. Therefore, they are insensitive to small cartesian translations. Using Eq.(2,3), we can efficiently compute A_u and A_v in the spatial domain and not in the frequency domain. Hence, the rotational dependent aliasing can be avoided.

After the rotation and scaling estimations, one can rectify the original successive frames, then apply the translation estimation approach of section 3.1 to estimate the translation. Due to the active tracking, the object can be centered by a window in the previous frame, and slightly translated in the next frame. All the motion estimations of an object can be fulfilled in the sub-images of a window. Thus, estimating the translation, we only need the estimate corresponding to the maximum singular value.

Active Tracking Algorithm is simply summarized as follows:
1) Select appropriate object-centered window in the successive frames as the integral domain D; 2) Use Eq.(2,3) to compute A_u and A_v of the successive frames respectively; 3) Apply Eq.(1) to the rotation and scaling estimates; 4) Rectify the original images using the obtained rotation and scaling estimates; 5) Apply the translation estimation approach of section 3.1 to the translation estimate, and adjust the view field so that the object is centered in the image.

4   Experiments and Analysis

We demonstrate our motion estimation algorithm of object and background presented in section 3.1 on a real image sequence. For comparison, our experiments are carried out on the translation and the rotation cases respectively. In Fig.1a, we illustrate the case of large translation in an image sequence. The initial rectangle is manually drawn in the first frame. This rectangle is tracked from the first frame to the second one using motion estimation and so on. In the first three frames, it can be noted that the moving hand can be tracked without occlusion. While it is occluded by book, the tracking is failed. In the fifth frame, there is no occlusion. We do the phase correlation on the second frame and the fifth one. The result indicates that although there is a large translation between the second frame and the fifth one, the translation can be exactly estimated using our proposed algorithm. In Fig.1b, our algorithm is illustrated on an image sequence with large rotation angles. We choose seven frames from an image sequence of ninety frames, so that the rotation angle between each two successive frames is more than 10 degrees. The rotating arm is marked by eight cross flags. The initial cross flags are manually marked in the first frame, they are tracked from the first frame to the second frame using motion estimation, and so on until the last frame. Compared with the results of Fig.1a, the accuracy of the rotation estimate is less than the accuracy of the translation estimate. Specially, when the rotation angle of the object is small (less than 3 degrees), there is no distinct phase correlation peak corresponding to the rotation angle in the spatial domain. This is because the rotationally dependent aliasing can only be diminished and not removed in our algorithm. When the true peak and false peaks lie close to each other, it is difficult to obtain an accurate estimate. However, the proposed algorithm is suitable for the motion estimates of an object and its background. It can provide accurate motion estimates for large rotations and translations. Thus, this proposed algorithm can also be incorporated with other tracking algorithms to deal with the case of large movements.

In Fig.2, we illustrate the spatial projection method in [6,7] on a still image, which is respectively scaled by 0.75 (Fig.2b), scaled by 0.75 and translated by (-5,5) (Fig.2c), rotated by 15° counter clockwise (Fig.2d), and rotated by 15° counter clockwise and translated by (-5,5) (Fig.2e). Fig.2f shows the radial projections of the original image, the scaled image, and the scaled and translated image. Obviously, there is a distinct phase difference between the projection of the scaled image and the projection of the

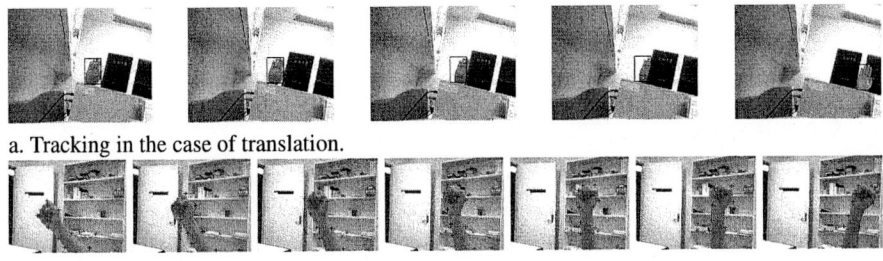

a. Tracking in the case of translation.

b. Tracking in the case of rotation.

Fig. 1. Illustration of motion estimation algorithm

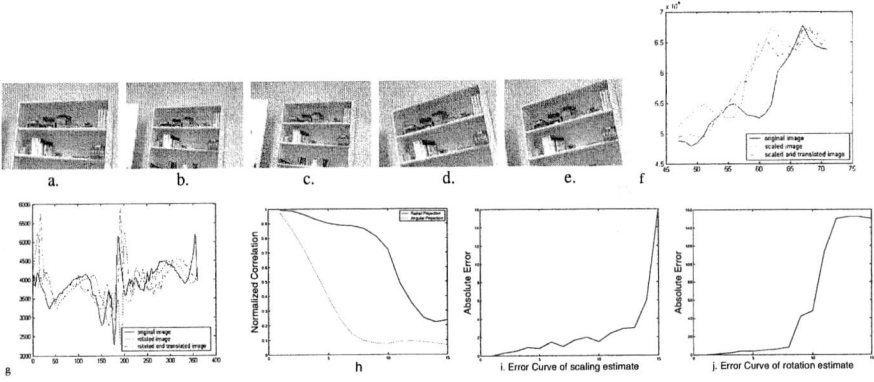

Fig. 2. The comparison between the angular projection and the radial projection. a) original image; b) scaled by 0.75; c) scaled by 0.75 and translated by (-5,5); d) rotated by 15 degrees; e) rotated by 15 degrees and translated by (-5,5); f) radial projection; g) angular projection; h) comparison of radial and angular projection; i-j) area-based projection method.

original image. It can also be noted that the projection of the scaled and translated image is distorted. Translation results in the distortion of the projection of scaled image. Fig.2g shows the angular projections of the original, rotated, and rotated and translated images. It can be noted that the projection of the rotated and translated image is distorted. Compared with Fig.2f, the angular projection is more sensitive to translation than the radial one. In order to compare the influence of translation in the radial and angular projections, the image scaled by 0.75 and the image rotated by 15° counter clockwise are translated from (-1,1) to (-15,15), respectively. We respectively compute the normalized correlation coefficient of the radial projections of the scaled image and the scaled and translated image; and the normalized correlation coefficient of the angular projections of the rotated image and the rotated and translated image. The coefficients at every translation level are depicted in Fig.2h. It is clear that the angular projection is more sensitive to translation than the radial one.

In Fig.2i-2j, we repeat the above experiment in Fig.2a-2e, and respectively estimate the rotation and scaling using our area-based projection method described in the section

3.2. It is clear that the area-based projection can suppress the translation distortion of small translations.

5 Conclusions

In this paper, we focused on the motion estimation based object tracking for active vision, and presented two algorithms. The first algorithm is a motion estimation algorithm of object and background, which can deal with the case of large movements in active vision applications. The second is an active tracking algorithm, which works under the assumption of small translations between successive frames. The novelty of these two proposed algorithms consists in the introduction of the normalized phase correlation approach. Because this approach does not rely on the smoothness or differentiability of the flow field in a sequence, it makes the large movement estimation possible in the first algorithm. Moreover, applying the SVD approach to the linear phase estimation improves the accuracy of motion estimates. The experimental results show that the motions of object and background can be effectively estimated and a moving object can be tracked using our proposed algorithm in an image sequence.

However, some problems need to be further investigated in our future work. The main issue is the constant-intensity assumption. In active vision, because the camera and the object are both moving at all time, this assumption can be violated. Although the background can be reduced using an object-centered window and the Log-polar mapping, the background's disturbance sometimes results in a large error for motion estimation. In our future work, we will introduce the time-frequency analysis techniques to overcome this problem.

References

1. H. Foroosh, J.B. Zerubia, and M. Berthod, Extension of phase correlation to subpixel registration, IEEE Transactions on Image Processing, Vol.11, No.3, pp.188-200, 2002
2. H.S. Stone, M. Orchard, E.C. Chang, and S. Martucci, A fast direct Fourier-based algorithm for subpixel registration of images," IEEE Trans. On Geosci. Remote Sensing, Vol.39, No.10, pp.2235-2243, 2001
3. D. Zheng, J.Y. Zhao, and A.E. Saddik, RST Invariant Digital Image Watermarking Based on Log-Polar Mapping and Phase Correlation, IEEE Transactions on Circuits and Systems for Video Technology, Vol.13, No.8, pp.753-765, 2003
4. W.S. Hoge, Subspace identification extension to the phase correlation method, IEEE Trans. Medical Imaging, Vol.22, No.2, pp.277-280, 2003
5. D.J. Fleet and A.D. Jepson, Computation of component image velocity from local phase information, Int. Journal of Computer Vision, Vol.5, No.1, pp.77-104, 1990
6. V.J. Traver and F. Pla, Similarity motion estimation and active tracking through spatial-domain projections on log-polar images, Computer Vision and Image Understanding, Vol.97, pp.209-241, 2005
7. V.J. Traver and F. Pla, Dealing with 2D translation estimation in log-polar imagery, Image and Vision Computing, Vol.21, pp.145-160, 2003
8. H.S. Stone, B. Tao and M. McGuire, Analysis of image registration noise due to rotationally dependent aliasing, Journal of Visual Communication and Image Representation, Vol.14, No.2, pp.114-135, 2003

A Novel Verification Criterion for Distortion-Free Fingerprints

Neil Yager and Adnan Amin

School of Computer Science and Engineering,
University of New South Wales, Sydney, NSW 2052, Australia
{nyager, amin}@cse.unsw.edu.au

Abstract. An important aspect of fingerprint verification systems is the method used to quantify the similarity between two fingerprints. This involves two key components: choosing fingerprint features that will be used for comparison and selecting a match score function to calculate the degree of correspondence. The choice of features and a match score function can have a significant impact on the performance of a system. This paper presents a novel fingerprint verification criterion based on tabulating ridge intersections between distortion free fingerprints. Several alternative matching criteria have been implemented, and their performance is compared using a publicly available FVC2002 dataset. The novel ridge based approach proves to be highly discriminative, and a strong result is obtained by a hybrid system using a combination of minutiae and ridge based features.

1 Introduction

Biometrics is the automatic identification of an individual based on his or her physiological or behavioural characteristics. Fingerprints have emerged as one of the most researched and trusted biometrics. However, despite decades of study there remains several challenges for the developers of automated fingerprint verification systems. These challenges include the enhancement of noisy fingerprint images, dealing with the nonlinear deformations present in fingerprints, and exploiting the full, rich structure of fingerprints for verification. This last point involves selecting appropriate fingerprint features for comparison and deriving a method to calculate the degree of correspondence. This is an important (and often overlooked) aspect of designing a fingerprint verification system and can have a significant effect on a system's performance.

As fingerprint databases increase in size, it is becoming increasingly important to choose features that are highly discriminative. The majority of algorithms in the literature rely heavily on minutiae information [1]. Minutiae do embody much of a fingerprint's individuality, yet when used in isolation useful discriminatory information is inevitably lost. Therefore, for systems requiring a high degree of accuracy it is important to supplement minutiae information with non-minutiae features.

Several approaches to fingerprint deformation modelling are available in the literature [2,3]. As these techniques become more mature and robust, fingerprint verification algorithms should begin to exploit the discriminative information from the entire fingerprint ridge map. Two approaches to this are explored in this paper. In one approach, correlation techniques are used to compare the pixel intensities between the images. For the second approach, a novel method of fingerprint verification based on tabulating ridge intersections is developed.

Section 2 contains a review of existing approaches to fingerprint verification, and Section 3 presents the proposed ridge based method. The results of the experimental validation can be found in Section 4. Finally, the paper concludes with a discussion of the results in Section 5.

2 Fingerprint Verification

The output of a fingerprint verification systems is a score that quantifies the degree of similarity between two prints. Without loss of generality, we will assume the score is between 0 and 100, with 100 indicating a very strong match. A threshold is determined for verification, above which two prints are labelled a match and below which they are labelled a non-match. Fingerprint verification systems can be broadly categorized by the features they use for matching. The most common feature is minutiae points, however systems incorporation non-minutiae features are becoming more common.

2.1 Minutiae Based Verification

Minutiae are local ridge discontinuities that come in two varieties: ridge endings occur when a ridge terminates, and bifurcations are locations where a single ridge separates into two. Each minutiae has a type, location, and orientation. Match score functions using minutiae features typically involve tabulating minutiae correspondences. A minutiae correspondences is two minutiae (one from each print) that are in close proximity after registration and have similar attributes. The ratio of minutiae correspondences to the total number of minutiae gives a score for the match. An example score function is [4]:

$$\text{Match Score} = \frac{100 N_{\text{pair}}}{\max\{M, N\}} \quad (1)$$

where N_{pair} is the number of correspondences, M is the number of minutiae in the reference set, and N is the number of minutiae in the test set.

There are three main drawbacks of minutiae based matching: (i) Minutiae detection is a very difficult task (especially for low qualities images). This often leads to missing and spurious minutiae, having a detrimental effect on the robustness of the system. (ii) Many of the scanning devices currently being used for biometric systems have a very small capture surface, so the amount of overlap between two prints may be very small. Consequently, there may be few (or even 0) minutiae correspondences. (iii) Finally, minutiae information is only a subset of the information contained by a fingerprint's ridge structure. By using only this information, much of a fingerprint's discriminatory information is lost.

2.2 Non-minutiae Based Verification

One approach to non-minutiae verification is the correlation of fingerprint images. At first glance, this seems like an obvious and powerful approach to fingerprint verification as it uses all of the information from the images. However, there are several obstacles that prevent this from being a common approach. In particular, the presence of nonlinear distortions and varying skin conditions can cause captures of the same fingerprint to appear very different [5]. One approach to overcome the problem of fingerprint deformations is to perform correlation locally rather than globally [6,7].

Other non-minutiae features that can be used for verification can be derived from local textural analysis. In these systems, filters are applied to extract frequency and orientation information from the ridges in a local area [8,9,10]. The main disadvantage of these approaches is that they do not take fingerprint deformations into consideration.

3 A Ridge Based Matching Criterion

Assume that the distortion has been mostly removed from a query fingerprint with respect to a reference print. This deformation modelling can be accomplished using any of the available methods in the literature [2,3]. After aligning the ridge maps, the ridges patterns will appear very similar for genuine matches (assuming the deformations have been modelled accurately). This can be illus-

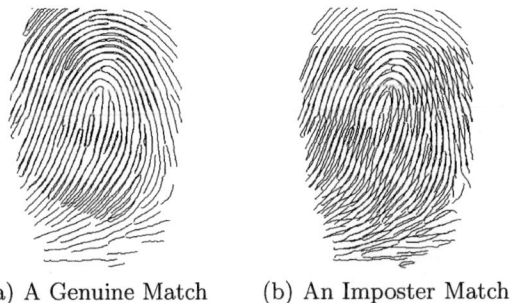

(a) A Genuine Match   (b) An Imposter Match

Fig. 1. Ridge map alignment examples

trated with an example. In Fig. 1 (a), the alignment of a genuine match pair is shown. Although not all ridges align exactly, it is obvious that their patterns are the same. However in Fig. 1 (b), two prints from different fingers are shown. In this case, although the overall curvature and ridge spacing is very similar, it is obvious that the ridge patterns are different. It is this intuitive notion of ridge map similarity that should be captured and quantified.

The approach proposed in this paper is to count ridge crossings between the aligned ridge maps. A crossing is defined as any contact between two ridges.

For each ridge in the query ridge map, it is traced and the number of distinct ridges (after the first) in the reference ridge map that are crossed is tallied. A score for each ridge is computed as $100 - (r \times 100)$, where r is the number of ridge crossings. A global score for the entire match is calculated by averaging the individual ridge scores. Negative global match scores are set to 0. This is a very simple algorithm, but it elegantly captures the notion of ridge map similarity.

There are a few implementation points that should be made. First of all, very short ridges should be ignored. Due to their short length, they are unlikely to cross any other ridges, and therefore give the overall print an artificially high score. Secondly, dealing with bifurcations is a little bit troublesome. We have found that the best approach is to break bifurcations, and treat all of the branches as individual ridges. Finally, there are a few situations in which ridges end prematurely, leading to spurious crossings. Ridges may be broken due to noise or when part of the fingerprint leaves the capture area. When tracing a ridge, if the ridge it last crossed has ended before a new ridge is reached, it should not be counted as a new crossing. For example, in Fig. 2 the upper portion of

Fig. 2. In the reference ridge map, many ridges are broken due to the upper region of the fingerprint not being captured

the reference print has not been captured. Therefore, when tracing ridges in the query print, the ridge will make contact with a reference ridge, the query ridge will loop around above and eventually make contact with a new ridge. This "new" ridge is not actually a new ridge: it is the same reference ridge as before, but has been broken because part of the print was not captured. Therefore, this should not be counted as a new ridge crossing. The best way to handle this situation is to record the remaining length of the reference ridge at each crossing. When a new ridge is reached, it will not be counted as a new crossing if the previous ridge has ended.

There are several advantages of this approach over both minutiae and correlation based methods. One advantage over minutiae based methods is that missing and spurious minutiae will have little effect on the match score. This is because their effect is local and will not cause additional ridge intersections. Furthermore, this method has the potential to be much more discriminative as it is based on information from the entire ridge map. The primary advantage over correlation techniques is that it does not require perfect alignment of the ridge maps. For correlation techniques to be successful it is necessary for the ridges to align exactly, and this is very difficult to achieve. The ridge counting method has some tolerance for misaligned ridges; even if the ridges are not aligned exactly, they will not create false ridge crossings as long as they stay within the boundaries created by the neighbouring ridges. Therefore, the method is robust even if the deformation modelling is not exact.

4 Experimental Results

Several verification methods have been implemented for comparison. All methods use the same preprocessing, registration and deformation modelling. For registration, we have used a two stage optimization algorithm that first finds a coarse registration using orientation field, curvature and frequency information, and then fine tunes this registration using minutiae features [11]. Fingerprint deformation modelling is accomplished using a nonparametric elastic modelling algorithm [3].

The following five verification methods have been implemented for evaluation. (i) Minutiae matching based on the ratio of minutiae correspondences to the maximum number of minutiae from the reference or query fingerprint (see Eq. 1). (ii) The correlation of greyscale fingerprint pixel intensities. The score is based on finding the average absolute difference of corresponding pixel intensities between the registered images. This value is normalized and subtracted from 100 to give a match score. (iii) The correlation of binary ridge maps. Before correlation, the images are processed to extract binary ridge maps with a standard ridge width. These binary ridge maps are then compared using cross-correlation. (iv) The ridge based method presented in Section 3. (v) A hybrid method using both minutiae and ridge crossing information. Assume that a minutiae score s_m and ridge score s_r have been obtained for a given pair of fingerprints. The match score S is defined as follows:

$$S = \begin{cases} 0 & \text{if } s_r < t_1, \\ 100 & \text{if } s_r > t_2, \\ s_m & \text{otherwise.} \end{cases} \quad (2)$$

where t_1 and t_2 are determined empirically. Intuitively, when prints have a very similar (different) ridge map, they are automatically accepted (rejected). When the ridge based match score is midrange, the minutiae matching score is used to discriminate them.

The dataset used for evaluation is the publicly available FVC 2002 database DB1 [12]. The fingerprint images were captured using fingerprint scanners and contain a wide variety of fingerprint image qualities. The database contains 880 fingerprints from 110 different fingers. The competition organizers have selected a set of 2,800 genuinely matching pairs and 4,950 non-matching pairs from the databases for evaluation. A variety of performance measures are calculated, the

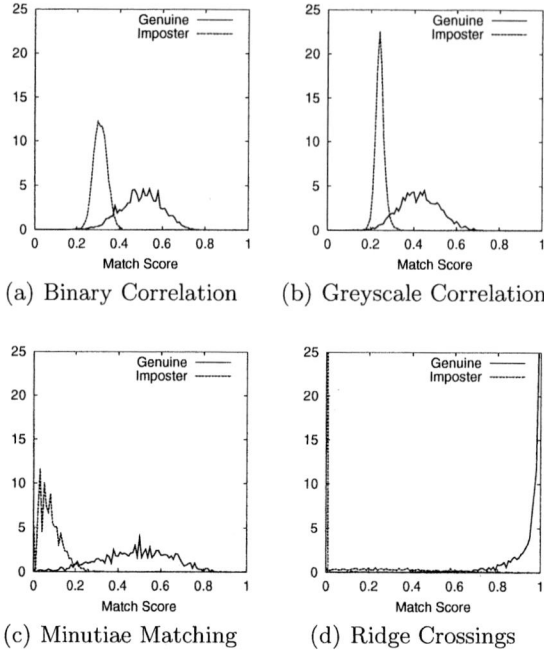

Fig. 3. Match score distributions

Table 1. Match Score EERs

Match Score Method	EER	Run Time (ms)
Binary Correlation	6.21 %	21
Greyscale Correlation	4.52 %	35
Minutiae Matching	4.51 %	6
Ridge Crossing	3.46 %	21
Combination	2.09 %	27

details of which can be found in [12]. One measure in particular is often used to summarize a system's performance. The equal error rate (EER) is the point at which a system's false match rate (FMR) equals its false non-match rate (FNMR).

The EER's and run times for the various match score functions can be found in Table 1, and the match score distributions can be found in Fig. 3. The running times do not include the time taken for preprocessing, registration, and deformation modelling (which is constant for all algorithms).

The error rate for greyscale correlation is lower than for binary correlation. This is surprising as it was expected that the preprocessing applied for binary correlation would remove much of the noise, making correlation more reliable. However, it appears that using the full range of pixel intensities is advantageous despite the presence of noise. The results of both correlation algorithms are not very impressive. There are two main reasons for this. First of all, highly accurate deformation modelling is necessary to obtain high scores for genuine matches. Secondly, there tends to be a lot of ridge overlap between imposter matches with similar ridge patterns. This can lead to relatively high scores. These two factors lead to many midrange genuine and imposter scores. These midrange scores lead to greater overlap of the score distributions, and consequently a higher error rate.

The proposed ridge based method has a lower error rate than both the minutiae and correlation algorithms. Furthermore, there is a significant reduction in error by using a combination of ridge and minutiae information. Using combinations of multiple features has been investigated by several researchers, and shows promise for powerful algorithms [13].

In terms of running time, all methods are roughly in the same range. These running times are almost insignificant compared to the other stages of verification (e.g. preprocessing and deformation modelling).

The match score distributions in Fig. 3 illustrate an important advantage of the ridge based approach developed in this paper. The genuine and imposter distributions are extremely well separated compared to the other distributions. Specifically, over 90% of genuine matches receive a score greater than 80, and almost 80% of imposter matches receive a score of 0. This is highly discriminative. Approximately 2% of genuine matches receive a score below 50, and virtually the only reason for this is when the nonlinear distortions have not been modelled accurately. If improvements to the deformation modelling algorithm are made, it is expected that the EER for the ridge based approach will drop dramatically.

5 Conclusion

The results in this paper show that the choice of features for verification makes a dramatic difference on the accuracy of a system. In our experiments, the exact same registration and deformation modelling was used, yet the EER's varied from 6.21% down to 2.09%.

Traditionally fingerprint deformation algorithms have not been common in verification systems due to the additional computational costs they demand. However, as computational resources increase and become more readily available this will cease to be as much of an issue. Therefore, it is expected that deformation modelling algorithms will be increasingly researched, and become more common and robust in the coming years. As this happens, it will be important for verification systems to select fingerprint features that are able to exploit the full, rich discriminatory power from a fingerprint's ridge pattern. In particular, it will be important to no longer rely strictly on minutiae information. Correlation is one approach that has been explored, but its results are comparatively poor. The novel ridge based approach presented in this paper is very discriminative, and has the potential to be a powerful addition to future verification systems.

References

1. Yager, N., Amin, A.: Fingerprint verification based on minutiae features: a review. Pattern Analysis and Applications **7** (2004) 94-113
2. Bazen A., Gerez, S.: Fingerprint matching by thin-plate spline modelling deformations. Pattern Recognition **36** (2003) 1859-1867
3. Yager, N., Amin, A.: Nonparametric fingerprint deformation modelling. Proceedings of CAIP 2005.
4. Jain, A., Hong, L., Bolle, R.: On-line fingerprint verification. IEEE Trans. Pattern Analysis and Machine Intelligence **19** (1997) 302-314
5. Maltoni, D., Mario, D., Jain, A., Prabhakar, S.: Handbook of Fingerprint Recognition. Springer-Verlag, New York (2003)
6. Bazen, A., Verwaaijen, G., Gerez, S., Veelenturf, L., Zwaag, B.: A correlation-based fingerprint verification system. Proceedings of the Workshop on Circuits Systems and Signal Processing. Veldhoven, The Netherlands (2000) 205-213
7. Kovacs-Vajna, Z.: A fingerprint verification system based on triangular matching and dynamic time warpipng. IEEE Trans. Pattern Analysis and Machine Intelligence **22** (2000) 1266-2000
8. Jain, A., Prabhakar, S., Hong, L., Pankanti, S.: Filterbank-based fingerprint matching. IEEE Trans. Image Processing **9** (2000) 846-859
9. Ross, A., Reisman, J., Jain, A.: Fingerprint matching using feature space correlation. Proceedings of Post-ECCV Workshop in Biometric Authentication. Lecture Notes in Computer Science, Vol. 2359. Springer-Verlag, Berlin Heidelberg New York (2002) 48-57
10. Park, C., Lee, J., Smith, M., Park, S., Park, K.: Directional filter bank-based fingerprint feature extraction and matching. IEEE Trans. Circuits and Systems for Video Technology **14** (2004) 74-85
11. Yager, N., Amin, A.: Fingerprint verification using two stage optimization. Pattern Recognition Letters. In Press.
12. FVC2002: Second International Fingerprint Verification Competition. http://bias.csr.unibo.it/fvc2002/.
13. Prabhakar, S., Jain, A.: Decision-level fusion in fingerprint verification. Pattern Recognition **35** (2002) 861-874

Nonparametric Fingerprint Deformation Modelling

Neil Yager and Adnan Amin

School of Computer Science and Engineering,
University of New South Wales, Sydney, NSW 2052, Australia
{nyager, amin}@cse.unsw.edu.au

Abstract. This paper presents a novel approach to modelling fingerprint deformations. When fingerprints are captured, they undergo a certain amount of distortion due to the application of a three dimensional elastic tissue against a flat surface. This poses a challenge for automated fingerprint verification systems, which are generally based on aligning two fingerprints and comparing their respective features. There are only a few methods reported in the literature for modelling fingerprint distortions. One prominent method is based on using minutiae correspondences as landmarks, and creating a deformation model using thin-plate splines. There are several disadvantages to this approach, and a nonparametric elastic modelling algorithm is developed in this paper to address these issues. Both algorithms have been implemented and are evaluated by incorporating them into a fingerprint verification system. The results show an improvement of the proposed algorithm over the existing method of deformation modelling.

1 Introduction

Fingerprints have been used as a means of personal identification for over a century. Traditionally, the driving force behind advancements in fingerprint technology has been law enforcement agencies and forensic scientists. The administration and querying of massive fingerprint repositories motivated the early research efforts towards automation. An application of fingerprint-based identification that has emerged more recently is biometric systems. Biometrics is the automatic identification of an individual based on his or her physiological or behavioural characteristics. The ability to accurately identify or authenticate an individual based on these characteristics has several advantages over traditional means of authentication such as knowledge-based (e.g., password) or token-based (e.g., key) authentication [1]. Due to its security related applications and the current world political climate, biometrics has become the subject of intense research by both private and academic institutions.

Despite decades of intensive study, there are still many challenges facing developers of automated fingerprint matching systems. Fingerprint image preprocessing continues to be a difficult problem due to the large intraclass variation of fingerprint images. Varying skin and capture conditions often cause images of the same fingerprint to appear very different (see Fig. 1).

Another obstacle to matching is fingerprint deformations. The skin tissue of a finger is elastic, so when a finger is applied against a flat surface the ridge pattern experiences some distortion. This deformation is nonlinear, and the extent of distortion varies with the angle of incidence and the amount of pressure applied. Fingerprint matching algorithms generally work by aligning two prints and comparing their respective features. Deformations are usually accounted for by allowing some tolerance for displacements when matching features. Therefore, the deformation is not explicitly modelled (i.e. a rigid transformation is used). However, if a strong deformation is present the corresponding features will not align closely, causing the match to fail.

This paper addresses the issue of fingerprint deformations and proposes a novel method for modelling them. Section 2 gives some background to the problem and presents a brief review of existing deformation modelling techniques. This is followed by a description of the proposed modelling algorithm in Section 3. An experimental evaluation of the technique is presented in Section 4, and the paper concludes with some final thoughts and possible future directions for the research in Section 5.

2 Deformation Modelling

As mentioned in the introduction, there is an inevitable deformation that occurs when fingerprint images are captured. An example of this deformation is illustrated in Fig. 1. The prints from Figs. 1(a) and 1(b) have been captured from

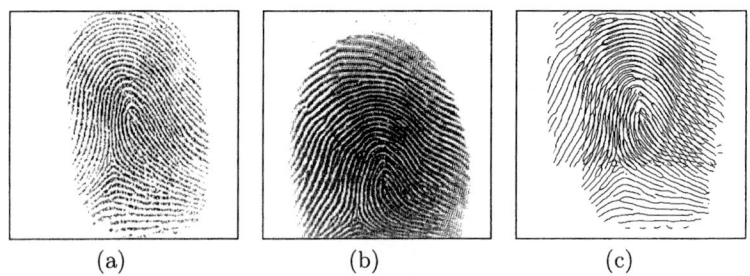

Fig. 1. Two different captures of the same fingerprint and their alignment

the same finger, however the finger in Fig. 1(b) has been pressed against the sensor with greater pressure. This has caused a deformation, as illustrated by the overlapping ridge maps in Fig. 1(c). It is clear that the ridge maps do not align very well, despite originating from the same finger.

We define deformation modelling as creating a mapping function that registers features from a query fingerprint to the corresponding features in a reference fingerprint. Several methods for dealing with fingerprint distortion exist in the literature. Cappelli et al. have developed a theoretical model of the elastic distortion in fingerprints [2]. This model could be used as a basis to analyze and remove distortions from prints. Senior and Bolle propose to remove distortions by normalizing ridge spacing throughout the print [3]. Their system is based on the assumption that the average ridge frequency is close to constant throughout a non-distorted fingerprint.

A common technique for modelling deformations in image processing is using the thin-plate spline (TPS) [4], which is a function that interpolates landmark points. An obvious choice for landmark features in fingerprints are minutiae. Minutiae come in two varieties: ridge endings are places where ridges terminate, and bifurcations are places where a single ridge splits into two. Two sets of researchers appear to have independently applied thin-plate splines to fingerprint deformation modelling using minutiae landmarks. Almansa and Cohen [5] present a two-step iterative minimization algorithm for elastic matching using thin-plate splines. Another application is suggested by Bazen and Gerez [6]. In their system, several iterations are used to refine the initial model by incorporating new minutiae correspondences as they become sufficiently close together. These iterations continue until the model converges to its final state. Ross et al. use thin-plate splines to estimate an "average" distortion model for a fingerprint given several of its prints [7]. This model can be applied to unseen query images during the matching phase, thereby removing typical distortions for that print and improving the accuracy of the system.

3 Nonparametric Elastic Deformation Modelling

There are several disadvantages of the thin-plate spline model when dealing with fingerprints: (i) A minimum of 4 correspondence pairs is necessary to model non-linear distortions (only 3 pairs are necessary for an affine deformation). If the area of overlap between genuinely matching fingerprints is small, very few minutiae correspondences may have been captured. In these cases, the thin-plate spline model can not be used. (ii) The spatial locations of the correspondences is important. If the correspondences are concentrated in a small area of the print or are co-linear, small displacement errors lead to radical global distortions. Ideally, the landmarks are plentiful and evenly distributed throughout the print; however, this is not always the case. (iii) The TPS model aligns landmark correspondences and interpolates the area between them. However, the deformations outside the convex hull of correspondence points are unpredictable. Distortions tend to be amplified in areas far from the correspondences, and therefore are unreliable when matching prints. (iv) Minutiae correspondence errors are difficult to avoid during fingerprint matching. Since TPS's align all pairs of correspondences using one set of parameters, a single correspondence error can cause nonlocal consequences. (v) Finally, TPS's are a parameterized model, meaning the entire global deformation is represented by a finite set of parameters. These parameters are chosen such that the bending energy of the deformation is minimized. Using this model, certain assumptions are being made about the nature of fingerprint distortions. However, the authors are not aware of any studies validating the belief that the elastic properties of skin tissue adhere to the TPS's energy minimization criterion. The same argument applies to all parameterized methods of distortion modelling, such as polynomial transformations, multiquadratics, cubic B-splines, etc..

To deal with the aforementioned challenges, an alternative approach to the parametric paradigm has been investigated. The general idea is to model the distortion as if one was locally deforming an elastic surface. In this case, the deformation function has few constraints and the function space is very large. The deformation is represented using a dense displacement vector field: for each pixel in the query image, a vector indicates its new location after distortion modelling.

The algorithm for calculating the displacement field is as follows. First an initial rigid registration is found. Any method can be used to achieve this: we have employed a two stage optimization algorithm [8]. The first stage of this algorithm finds a coarse registration using non-minutiae features (orientation field, ridge curvature, and ridge frequency) and the second stage fine-tunes this alignment using minutiae information. At this stage we have a robust global registration estimate. Modelling the fingerprint deformations adds a third stage to this algorithm, conforming to the hierarchical philosophy that coarse global features should be used initially, followed by finer localized features as the prints become more closely registered. This is a powerful and effective approach to fingerprint registration.

After the initial rigid registration, minutiae correspondences are found based on similarity of type (ridge ending or bifurcation), location, and orientation. It is these minutiae correspondences that are used to calculate the displacement field. Intuitively, imagine a rubber sheet has been fastened in place by the initial rigid registration. Next, the local regions are stretched and twisted to align the minutiae correspondences. The implementation of this idea is accomplished by using Gaussian fields centered at the minutiae correspondences to weigh how heavily their displacement will affect the surrounding area. The idea is similar to one presented by Burr [9], however there are a few key differences. Burr's algorithm is an iterative model where the strength of the Gaussian varies at each step to dynamically control the cooperation between the correspondences. Conversely, our algorithm is performed in a single stage. Furthermore, our method has been updated to take orientation information into account.

A minutia p is stored using a 3-tuple (p_x, p_y, p_θ) which represents its coordinates and orientation respectively. Assume that n minutiae correspondences $((p^1, q^1)...(p^n, q^n))$ have been found, where correspondence i contains a minutia p^i from the reference print and a minutia q^i from the query print. Each correspondence pair uniquely determines rigid registration parameters for the entire image by translating the minutiae to be in the same location and then rotating to align their orientations. Given a correspondence pair (p^i, q^i), the rigid transformation parameters $(\Delta x^i, \Delta y^i, \theta^i)$ are computed as follows: $\Delta x^i = p_x^i - q_x^i$, $\Delta y^i = p_y^i - q_y^i$, and θ^i is the oreintation difference between p_θ^i and q_θ^i. Using the parameters for the ith correspondence, the new location (x^i, y^i) for any point (x, y) in the query image can be found using:

$$\begin{bmatrix} x^i \\ y^i \end{bmatrix} = \begin{bmatrix} \cos(\theta^i) & \sin(\theta^i) \\ -\sin(\theta^i) & \cos(\theta^i) \end{bmatrix} \begin{bmatrix} x - q_x^i \\ y - q_y^i \end{bmatrix} + \begin{bmatrix} q_x^i \\ q_y^i \end{bmatrix} + \begin{bmatrix} \Delta x^i \\ \Delta y^i \end{bmatrix} \qquad (1)$$

creating the displacement vector:

$$\mathbf{D}_i(x, y) = \begin{bmatrix} x \\ y \end{bmatrix} - \begin{bmatrix} x^i \\ y^i \end{bmatrix} \qquad (2)$$

This displacement is very relevant near the correspondence pair i, but as you move away it is less useful because local distortions and feature extraction inaccuracies will cause translation and rotation errors that are magnified as you move away. Therefore, a Gaussian field is used to determine a given correspondence's influence on the rest of the image. The weight of correspondence i's transformation parameters at the location (x, y) in the query image is determined using the following function:

$$W_i(x, y) = \exp\left(-\frac{\sqrt{(x - q_x^i)^2 + (y - q_y^i)^2}}{\sigma^2}\right) \qquad (3)$$

The weight W_i will be high (close to 1) in the area close to the ith correspondence, but deceases rapidly (towards 0) as the distance increases. The speed of decay is determined by the user defined parameter σ. A displacement vector field for the entire query image is calculated for each correspondence. Therefore, for each pixel in the original query image there are n displacements (one for each correspondence). There is also one additional displacement vector for the "background" rigid registration, which has a constant weight and will dominate in areas distant from all minutiae correspondences. Define this background displacement to be D_0 and its weight to be W_0. There are now $n + 1$ displacement vectors defined for each pixel. These are averaged to determine the pixel's final location:

$$\mathbf{D}'(x, y) = \frac{\sum_{i=0}^{n} W_i(x, y) \mathbf{D}_i(x, y)}{\sum_{i=0}^{n} W_i(x, y)} \qquad (4)$$

The effect of this algorithm is as follows. In areas of the fingerprint close to a single correspondence, its displacement will be strongly determined by aligning that correspondence. In areas close to several correspondences, the displacement will be averaged according to their proximity to the minutiae. Finally, in areas distant from all correspondences, the initial rigid registration will be used. Due to the use of Gaussian weighting, the final displacement vector field is smooth.

4 Experimental Results

To evaluate the effectiveness of the proposed deformation modelling procedure, experiments were conducted to see the influence of the algorithm on the accuracy of a fingerprint verification system. The results of verification using no deformation modelling, TPS deformation modelling, and the nonparametric elastic algorithm are reported. For all three algorithms, the same preprocessing, initial image registration, and minutiae correspondences are used. Therefore the only

Table 1. Verification Results

Distortion Modelling Method	EER	Average Score for Genuine Matches
None	4.59 %	89.6
Thin-Plate Spline	3.99 %	91.3
Nonparametric Elastic	3.46 %	92.3

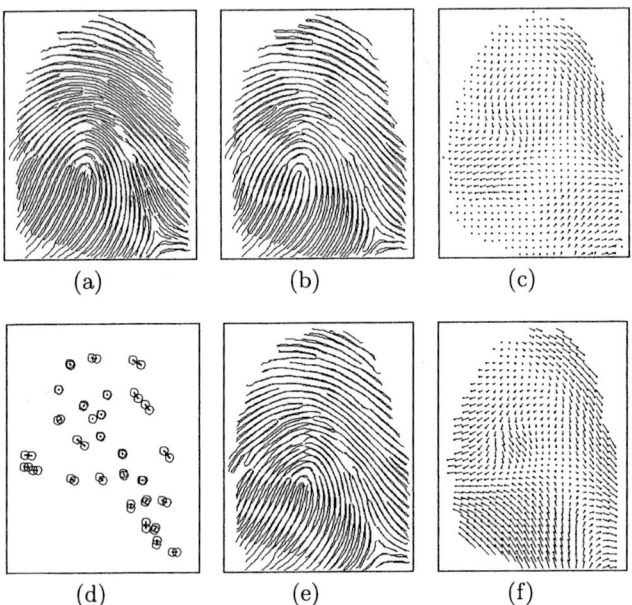

Fig. 2. Deformation modelling examples. (a) No deformation modelling. (b) Nonparametric elastic deformation modelling. (c) Displacement field for (b). (c) Minutiae Correspondences. (d) TPS deformation modelling. (d) Displacement field for (d).

variable is the distortion modelling. It should be noted that an iterative algorithm (such as the one presented by Bazen and Gerez [6]) to find additional minutiae correspondences after each stage of deformation modelling is not being employed.

The dataset used for evaluation is the publicly available FVC 2002 database DB1 [10]. The fingerprint images were captured using fingerprint scanners and contain a wide variety of fingerprint image qualities. The database contains 880 fingerprints from 110 different fingers. The competition organizers have selected a set of 2,800 genuinely matching pairs and 4,950 non-matching pairs from the databases for evaluation. A variety of performance measures are calculated, the details of which can be found in [10]. One measure in particular is often used to summarize a system's performance. The equal error rate (EER) is the point at which a system's false match rate (FMR) equals its false non-match rate (FNMR).

The match score function being used is ridge-based, and operates by counting ridge intersections of the aligned ridge skeletons [11]. The advantage of this method is that it is not only a very discriminative match score function, but also directly measures how well the distortion is being removed from the prints.

The results from the experiments can be found in Table 1. As can be seen, the nonparametric elastic algorithm outperforms the other methods in terms of both lowering the error rate and increasing the mean match score for genuine matches. In terms of running time, both modelling methods take approximately the same amount of time (about 400 ms in our system).

Fig. 2 shows an example of both TPS and nonparametric deformation modelling. This example illustrates an important advantage of the method proposed in this paper. The minutiae correspondences (see Fig. 2(d)) are well distributed throughout most of the print area, except for the lower left quadrant where there are none. Both methods have been successful in aligning the ridges maps in the rest of the print. However, in the lower left quadrant the TPS model has created a strong deformation (see Fig. 2(f)). This has caused the ridges in that region to cross over each other. However, the nonparametric method does not attempt to extrapolate the deformation model to this area (see Fig. 2(c)), creating a much better result.

5 Conclusion and Future Directions

There are several advantages of the proposed algorithm over the TPS deformation modelling algorithm. First of all, there is no minimum number of correspondences necessary (whereas the TPS algorithm requires at least 4 to model nonlinear deformations). Even if only one correspondence is found, this can be used to remove local distortions from the query fingerprint. Secondly, when correspondence errors occur, they only cause local disruptions. Thirdly, unlike the TPS method, the orientation of the minutiae is taken into account when calculating the displacements. Fourthly, the deformation model is not extrapolated to areas distant from the minutiae correspondences. Finally, since the solution is not parameterized all plausible mappings exist within the function space.

The algorithm struggles for prints with very high distortion (such as the example in Fig. 1). The main reason for this is not the deformation modelling algorithm itself, but the difficulty in finding all of the correct minutiae correspondences. In cases of severe distortion there is no initial rigid registration that aligns all of the correspondences closely. One method to deal with this would be to incorporate an iterative scheme for dynamically updating the correspondences as new minutiae pairs become close together (like the approach taken by Bazen and Gerez [6]). This is one possible future direction for the research, and is currently under investigation.

Another possible extension of the research is to incorporate additional fingerprint features into the algorithm. For example, pixel intensities, filterbank responses, and ridge information could be used to supplement the landmark based approach taken in this paper. Approaches along these lines are common for nonrigid registration in the medical imaging domain. However, these methods tend to be very computationally demanding, so the challenge lies in deriving a method that can incorporate these supplementary features while remaining computationally efficient.

References

1. Jain, A., Hong, L., Pankanti, S.: Biometric identification. Comm. ACM. **43** (2000) 90-98
2. Cappelli, R., Maio, D., Maltoni, D.: Modelling plastic distortion in fingerprint images. Proceedings of the Second International Conference on Advances in Pattern Recognition. Rio De Janeiro, Brazil (2001) 369-376
3. Senior, A., Bolle, R.: Improved fingerprint matching by distortion removal. IEICE Transactions on Information and Systems. **E84-D** (2001) 825-831
4. Bookstein, F.: Principal warps: thin-plate splines and the decomposition of deformations. IEEE Trans. Pattern Analysis and Machine Intelligence **11** (1989) 567-585
5. Almansa, A., Cohen, L.: Fingerprint matching by minimization of a thin-plate energy using a two-step algorithm with auxiliary variables. Proceedings of the Fifth IEEE Workshop on Applications of Computer Vision. Palm Springs, USA (2000) 35-40
6. Bazen A., Gerez, S.: Fingerprint matching by thin-plate spline modelling deformations. Pattern Recognition **36** (2003) 1859-1867
7. Ross, A., Dass, S., Jain, A.: A deformable model for fingerprint matching. Pattern Recognition **38** (2005) 95-103
8. Yager, N., Amin, A.: Fingerprint verification using two stage optimization. Pattern Recognition Letters. In Press.
9. Burr, D. J.: A dynamic model for image registration. Computer Graphics and Image Processing **15** (1981) 102-112
10. FVC2002: Second International Fingerprint Verification Competition. http://bias.csr.unibo.it/fvc2002/.
11. Yager, N., Amin, A.: A novel verification criterion for distortion-free fingerprints. Proceedings of CAIP 2005.

Outdoor Image Classification Using Artificial Immune Recognition System (AIRS) with Performance Evaluation by Fuzzy Resource Allocation Mechanism

Kemal Polat[1], Seral Şahan[1], Halife Kodaz[2] and Salih Güneş[1]

[1] Selcuk University, Eng.-Arch. Fac. Electrical & Electronics Eng.,
42031-Konya/Turkey
{kpolat, seral, sgunes}@selcuk.edu.tr
[2] Selcuk University, Eng.-Arch. Fac. Computer Eng.,
42031-Konya/Turkey
hkodaz@selcuk.edu.tr

Abstract. AIRS classification algorithm, which has an important place among classification algorithms in the field of Artificial Immune Systems, has showed an effective and intriguing performance on the problems it was applied. In this study, the resource allocation mechanism of AIRS was changed with a new one determined by Fuzzy-Logic rules. This system, named as Fuzzy-AIRS and AIRS were used as classifiers in the classification of outdoor images. The classification of outdoor dataset taken from UCI repository of machine learning databases was done using 10-fold cross validation method. Both versions of AIRS well performed over other systems reported in UCI website for corresponding dataset. Fuzzy-AIRS reached to the classification accuracy of 90.00 % in the applications whereas AIRS obtained 88.20 %. Besides, Fuzzy-AIRS gained one more advantage over AIRS by means of classification time. In the experiments, it was seen that the classification time in Fuzzy-AIRS was reduced by about 67% of AIRS for dataset. Fuzzy-AIRS classifier proved that it can be used as an effective classifier for image classification by reducing classification time as well as obtaining high classification accuracies.

1 Introduction

While a new artificial intelligence field named as Artificial Immune Systems (AIS) was emerging in late 1990s, performances of proposed methods were not so good especially for classification problems. However, AIRS system proposed in 2001 has changed this situation by taking attention among other classifiers with its performance [1].

Image segmentation is the process of dividing a given image into homogenous regions with respect to certain features, which correspond to real objects in the actual scene. The segmentation process is perhaps the most important step in image analysis since its performance directly affects the performance of the subsequent processing steps in image analysis [2].

In this study, resource allocation of AIRS was changed with its equivalent formed with Fuzzy-Logic to increase its classification accuracy. To see effects of this modification, trials were made wtih an image segmentation problem. Both versions of algorithms were used to classify an outdoor image dataset and they were also compared with other classifiers used for same data set beside of being compared with each other. Fuzzy-AIRS obtained the highest classification accuracy among the classifiers reported in UCI website for related dataset consisting of Outdoor Image taken from UCI database [3]. Fuzzy-AIRS, which proved itself to be used as an effective classifier in image classification field by reaching its goal, has also provided a considerable decrease in the number of resources. In conducted application, Fuzzy-AIRS required less resource than half of required by AIRS and by this way, classification time has reduced by a great rate. The rest of the paper is organized as follows. Section 2 presents Artificial Immune Systems and AIRS (Artificial Immune Recognition System. The results obtained in applications are presented in Section 3 for Image data set. Consequently in Section 4, we conclude the paper with summarization of results by emphasizing the importance of this study.

2 Artificial Immune Systems and AIRS (Artificial Immune Recognition System)

Artificial Immune System (AIS) can be defined as a computational system based upon metaphors of biological immune system [1]. The topics involved in the definition and development of Artificial Immune Systems cover mainly: hybrid structures and algorithms that take into account immune-like mechanisms; computational algorithms based on immunological principles, like distributed processing, clonal selection algorithms, and immune network theory; immune based optimization, learning, self-organization, artificial life, cognitive models, multi-agent systems, design and scheduling, pattern recognition and anomaly detection and lastly immune engineering tools [1], [3].

In unsupervised learning branch of AISs, there are lots of works conducted by researchers Dasgupta, De Castro, Timmis, Watkins, Neal...etc [1], [3], [8]. There are only two studies in supervised AISs. First of these was performed by Carter [8]. The other work is AIRS (Artificial Immune Recognition System), proposed by A.Watkins which is a supervised learning algorithm inspired from the immune system [3].

The used immune metaphors used in AIRS are: antibody-antigen binding, affinity maturation, clonal selection process, resource competition and memory acquisition. AIRS learning algorithm consists of four stages: initialisation, memory cell recognition, resource competition and revision of resulted memory cells.

2.1 AIRS Algorithm

The AIRS algorithm is as follows:

1. Initialization: Create a random base called the memory pool (M) and the pool (P).
2. Antigenic Presentation: for each antigenic pattern do:
    a) Clonal Expansion:
    For each element of M determine their affinity to the antigenic pattern, which resides in the same class. Select highest affinity memory cell (mc)

and clone mc in the proportion to its antigenic
affinity to add to set of ARBs (P).
b) Affinity Maturation:
Mutation each ARB descendant of this highest
affinity mc. Place each mutated ARB into P.
c) Metadynamics of ARBs:
Process each ARB through the resource allocation
mechanism. This will result in some ARB death,
and ultimately controls the population. Calculate
the average stimulation for each ARB, and check
for termination condition.
d) Clonal Expansion and Affinity Maturation:
Clone and mutate a randomly selected subset of
the ARBs left in P based in proportion to their
stimulation level.
e) Cycle:
While the average stimulation value of each ARB
class group is less than a given stimulation
threshold repeat from step 2.c.
f) Metadynamics of Memory Cells:
Select the highest affinity ARB of the same class
as the antigenic from the last antigenic interaction. If the affinity of this ARB with the antigenic pattern is better than that of the previously identified best memory cell mc then add the
candidate (mc-candidate) to memory set M.
Additionally, if the affinity of mc and mc-candidate below the affinity threshold, then remove mc from M.
3. Cycle. Repeat step 2 until all antigenic patterns have been presented.

2.2 Fuzzy Resource Allocation Method

The competition of resources in AIRS allows high-affinity ARBs to improve. According to this resource allocation mechanism, half of resources are allocated to the ARBs in the class of Antigen while the remaining half is distributed to the other classes. The distribution of resources is done according to a number that is found by multiplying stimulation rate with clonal rate. In the study of Baurav Marwah and Lois Boggess, a different resource allocation mechanism was tried [5]. In their mechanism, the Ag classes occurring more frequently get more resources. Both in classical AIRS and the study of Marwah and Boggess, resource allocation is done linearly with affinities. This linearity requires excess resource usage in the system that results long classification time and high number of memory cells.

In this study, to get rid of this problem, resource allocation mechanism was done with fuzzy logic. So there existed a non-linearity because of fuzzy rules. The difference in resource number between high-affinity ARBs and low-affinity ARBs is bigger in this method than in classical approach.

The input variable of Fuzzy resource allocation mechanism is stimulation level of ARB hence the output variable is the number of resources that will be allocated to that ARB. As for the other fuzzy-systems, input membership functions as well as output membership functions were formed. The input membership functions are shown in Fig. 1.

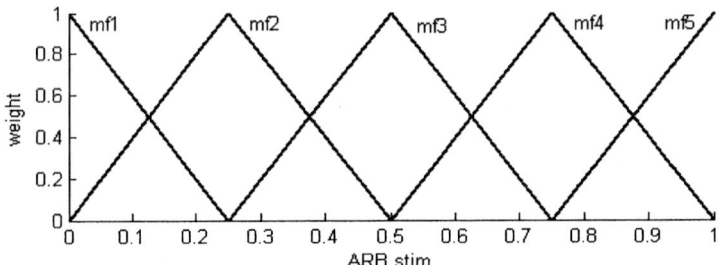

Fig. 1. Input membership functions

The input variable, ARB.stim, varies between 0 and 1. A membership value is calculated according to this value using input membership functions. In this calculation, two points are get which are the cutting points of membership triangles by the input value, ARB.stim. Also these points are named as membership values of input variable for related membership function. The minimum of these points is taken as the membership value of input variable x, ARB.stim (Eq. (1)).

$$\mu_{A \cap B}(x) = \min(\mu_A(x), \mu_B(x)), x \in X. \tag{1}$$

Here in Eq. (1), $\mu_A(x)$ is the membership value of x in A and $\mu_B(x)$ is the membership value of x in B, where A and B are the fuzzy sets in universe X. The calculated input membership value is used to get the output value through output membership functions that are shown in Fig. 2.

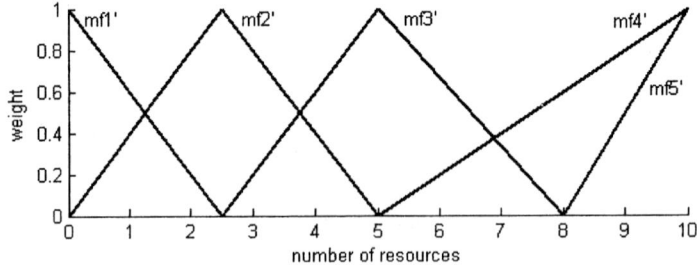

Fig. 2. Output membership functions

In the x-axis of this Figure, allocated resource number that will be calculated using the membership functions for the ARB is shown which changes between 0-10. The weight in the y-axis that is the input membership value get as explained above intersects the membership triangles at several points.

Here mf1, mf2...etc are the labels of input membership triangles and mf1', mf2'...etc are the labels of output membership values. The rules in Table 1 define which points will be taken to average. For example if the input value cuts the triangles mf1 and mf2 among the input membership functions, then the points to be averaged will be only the ones of mf1' and mf2' triangles in the output membership functions.

These linguistic values were determined in such a manner that the allocated resource number for ARBs which have stimulation values between 0 and 0.50 will be less while for ARBs which have stimulation values between 0.50 and 1 will be more.

2.3 Measures for Performance Evaluation in AIRS

In this study, the classification accuracies for the datasets were measured according to the Eq. (2). [1]:

$$accuracy(T) = \frac{\sum_{i=1}^{|T|} assess(t_i)}{|T|}, t_i \in T .\quad (2)$$

$$assess(t) = \begin{cases} 1 & if \quad classify(t) \equiv t.c \\ 0 & otherwise \end{cases} \quad (3)$$

In equation 3, T is the set of data items to be classified (the test set), $t \in T$, $t.c$ is the class of the item t, and classify (t) returns the classification of t by AIRS.

For test results to be more valuable, k-fold cross validation is used among the researchers. It minimizes the bias associated with the random sampling of the training [5]. In this method, whole data is randomly divided to k mutually exclusive and approximately equal size subsets. The classification algorithm trained and tested k times. In each case, one of the data subsets is taken as test data and the remaining folds are added to form training data. Thus k different test results exist for each training-test configuration. The average of these results gives the test accuracy of the algorithm [5]. We used this method as 10-fold cross validation in our applications. But we also conducted our experiments in such a way that there runs, one for each of the possible configurations of the traing versus test data set. The average of these three test results gave us the test result for each fold. So we obtained 30 results in total to average.

3 Fuzzy-AIRS Performance Analysis

The classification performance of Fuzzy-AIRS was analyzed in outdoor image data set.

3.1 Outdoor Image Data Set

The problem to be solved here is classification of outdoor image dataset. This dataset was taken from Vision Group, University of Massachusetts in 1990 with the contributions of Carla Brodley. In image segmentation data set, the instances were drawn randomly from a database of 7 outdoor images. The images were hand segmented to create a classification for every pixel. Each instance is a 3x3 region. In training data there are 210 instances and in test data there are 2100 instances with 19 continuous attributes [2, 3].

In the data set, the third attribute is the same for all inputs therefore while the simulations are being done this attribute is not added to network. The existing seven classes are grass, path, window, cement, foliage, sky, and brickface [2, 3].

Fuzzy-resource allocation mechanism provided Fuzzy-AIRS to classify Outdoor Image data set with 90.00% classification accuracy. The accuracy reached with the use of AIRS was 88.2%.

The results obtained by Fuzzy-AIRS and AIRS for Outdoor Image dataset is presented in Table 1. The values of used resource number and classification time in the table are recorded for the highest classification accuracy.

Table 1. Obtained results by Fuzzy-AIRS and AIRS for Outdoor Image Dataset

Outdoor Image dataset	Classification accuracy (%)	Number of resources used in classification algorithm	Classification Time (Sec)
AIRS	88.20	700	180
FuzzyAIRS	90.00	400	60

The classification accuracy otained by Fuzzy-AIRS for Outdoor Image dataset is the highest one among the classifiers reported in UCI web site. The comparison of Fuzzy-AIRS with these classifiers with respect to the classification accuracy is shown in Table 2.

Table 2. Fuzzy-AIRS's classification accuracy for Outdoor Image dataset problem with classification accuracies obtained by other methods in UCI web site

Author(Year)	Method	Classification Accuracy (%)
Tin and Kwork (1999)	SVM	83.00
Lim et.al. (2000)	Decision Trees	85.01
Tolson (2001)	k-NN	85.2
Çoşkun and Yildirim (2003)	PNN	87.6
Çoşkun and Yildirim (2003)	GRNN	86.7
Our study (2005)	**AIRS**	**88.2**
Our study (2005)	**Fuzzy-AIRS**	**90.00**

The considerable difference between the accuracies of Fuzzy-AIRS and the classifier that reached highest accuracy previously can be seen easily from the table. We don't include AIRS for this comparison because we want to emphasize the classification power of Fuzzy-AIRS over the other classifiers in the table.

4 Conclusions

In this study, the resource allocation mechanism of AIRS that is among the most important classification systems of Artificial Immune Systems was changed with a new one that was formed using fuzzy-logic rules.

In the application phase of this study, Outdoor image dataset data set was used. In the classification of this dataset, the analyses were conducted both for the comparison of reached classification accuracy with other classifiers in UCI web site and to see the effects of the new resource allocation mechanism.

According to the application results, Fuzzy-AIRS showed a considerably high performance with regard to the classification accuracy for Outdoor image dataset. The reached classification accuracy of Fuzzy-AIRS for Outdoor image dataset was 90.00% which was the highest one among the classifiers reported in UCI web site. With this result, it is going clearer that AIRS is ready for real world problems with some improvements possibly done.

Beside of this success, Fuzzy-AIRS reduced the classification time with respect to AIRS approximately by the amount of 66.7% for Outdoor image dataset. This was the result of decrease in resource number done by fuzzy-resource allocation. If we consider the importance of classification time for image data and large data sets, this improvement makes AIRS more applicable. An increase in classification accuracy was also obtained by Fuzzy resource allocation over the AIRS that is 1.8%.

References

1. Watkins, A. *AIRS: A Resource Limited Artificial Immune Classifier*. Master Thesis, Mississippi State University, Mississippi, (2001).
2. Coşkun N., Yıldırım T., Image Segmentation Using Statistical Neural Networks. In *Proceedings of International Conference On Artificial Neural Networks / International Conference on Neural Information Processing (ICANN/ICONIP)*(Istanbul, Turkey, June 26-29,2003). 154-156.
3. ftp://ftp.ics.uci.edu/pub/machine-learning-databases
4. Marwah, G. and Boggess, L. Artificial immune systems for classification: Some issues. In *Proc. First Intl. Conf. Art. ImmuneSystems* (University of Kent at Canterbury, England, Sep. 2002) 149-153.
5. Tin, J. and Kwork, Y. Moderating the Outputs of Support Vector Machine Classifiers. *IEEE Trans. On NN 10,* 5 (1999),1018-1031.
6. Tolson, E. *Machine Learning in the Area of Image Analysis and Pattern Recognition*, Advanced Undergraduate Project Spring 2001.
7. Loh, W., Tim, L. and Shih, Y. A Comparison of Prediction Accuracy, Complexity, and Training Time of Thirty-Three Old and New Classification Algorithms. *Machine Learning 40,* 3 (2002),203-228.
8. De Castro, L.N and Timmis, J., Artificial Immune Systems: A New Computational Intelligence Approach, Springer-Verlag Press (2002)

Statistical Approach to Boar Semen Head Classification Based on Intracellular Intensity Distribution

Lidia Sánchez[1], Nicolai Petkov[2], and Enrique Alegre[1]

[1] Department of Electrical and Electronics Engineering,
University of León,
Campus de Vegazana s/n, 24071 León, Spain
[2] Institute of Mathematics and Computing Science,
University of Groningen,
P.O. Box 800, 9700 AV Groningen, The Netherlands
lidia@unileon.es, petkov@cs.rug.nl, enrique.alegre@unileon.es

Abstract. We propose a technique to compute the fraction of boar spermatozoid heads which present an intracellular density distribution pattern hypothesized as normal by veterinary experts. This approach offers a potential for digital image processing estimation of sperm capacitation which can substitute expensive staining techniques. We extract a model distribution from a training set of heads assumed as normal by veterinary experts. We also consider two other training sets, one with heads similar to the normal pattern and another formed by heads that substantially deviate from that pattern. For each spermatozoid head, a deviation from the model distribution is computed. This produces a conditional probability distribution of that deviation for each set. Using a set of test images, we determine the fraction of normal heads in each image and compare it with the result of expert classification. This yields an absolute error below 0.25 in the 89% of the samples.

1 Introduction

In the last years, digital image processing and analysis are used for computer assisted evaluation of semen quality with therapeutic goals or to estimate its fertility by means of spermatozoid motility and morphology.

Boar artificial insemination presents more advantages than the natural one: reduction of the number of boars in a farm, maximization of genetic improvements, homogeneous production lots, fertility control of males, and also savings in time and work. Sperm quality analysis is the basic means to avoid infertility problems and to identify boars with the best reproductive features. Generally, four factors are considered to evaluate boar sperm quality: concentration, motility, morphology and acrosome integrity [1]. For instance, if a given sample contains more than 30% of abnormal spermatozoa, the fertility will be reduced. Computer programs are essential tools in such an evaluation because of the complexity of sperm quality estimation. Digital image analysis can be used to assess this problem.

Fourier descriptors and neural nets yield classification error rates similar to the results obtained by experts in evaluation of human spermatozoid head morphology [2].

Most of the commercial systems in this area are based on motility measures (Hobson Tracking and Mika Medical) [3] or shape abnormalities (Cell-Morf of Motion Analysis) [4]. Hamilton-Thorn combines both features and has a specific module for boar semen [5]. Several morphometric measures are computed by the Sperm Class Analyzer of Microptic [6]. However, some disadvantages are encountered due to the specific design for human spermatozoa. Also aspects like density distribution or intracellular texture are not considered.

Various features are deployed in spermatozoid assessment with digital images, such as cellular motility [7], head abnormalities and distal or proximal droplets. Acrosome integrity and plasma membrane integrity determine the sperm viability because their enzymes take part in the oocyte penetration process. For instance, a pear shaped head, acrosome lifting or a detached acrosome are abnormalities that cause fertility reduction. Spermatozoid heads present a variety of cellular textures that are determined by their corresponding cytoplasmic densities. New research is directed towards finding a correlation between certain patterns of intracellular density distribution and semen fertility. In this approach, veterinary experts first assume that a certain intracellular density distribution is characteristic of healthy cells. Then the fraction of spermatozoid heads in a sample which have intracellular distributions that are sufficiently similar to the assumed model distribution is determined. Applying traditional techniques as vital and fluorescent stains, experts assess the sperm capacitation of such a sample, and try to find a correlation between the above mentioned fraction and semen fertility. The goal is to find a pattern of intracellular density distribution, such that the fraction of sperm heads that exhibit such a pattern has high correlation with the semen fertility as determined by traditional techniques. If successful, this approach can lead to the substitution of expensive staining techniques for fertility evaluation by inexpensive image analysis techniques.

In the current work, we analyse grey-level images of boar semen samples obtained with a phase-contrast microscope, Fig. 1a. More specifically, we study the intracellular density distributions of the spermatozoid heads. Using a training set of images of heads that have been hypothesized by an expert to be "normal", we create a model intracellular density distribution and use it to estimate the fraction of heads in a sample that are sufficiently similar to the model distribution. The goal is to determine automatically the fraction of heads that match an expert's idea of how a normal healthy cell should look like.

In Section 2, we present the methods we have used and the obtained results. Discussion and conclusions are given in Section 3.

2 Methods and Results

2.1 Image Acquisition, Preprocessing and Head Segmentation

Fresh boar semen sample images of size 1600×1200 pixels were captured using a digital camera connected with a phase-contrast microscope at $\times 40$ magnification. They are converted to grey-level images. Each image presents a variable number of spermatozoa whose heads are in different orientations just as tails without head, agglutinated heads and debris. Using morphological closing, holes in the contours of the heads are filled and the spermatozoid tails are removed. In a next segmentation stage, spermatozoid heads are separated from the background deploying Otsu's method to find a threshold that separates the heads from the background [8]. Heads near the boundary of the image as well as the ones with an area smaller than an experimental obtained value of 45% of the average head area are not considered. Fig. 1b shows a typical image obtained by the above mentioned preprocessing and segmentation.

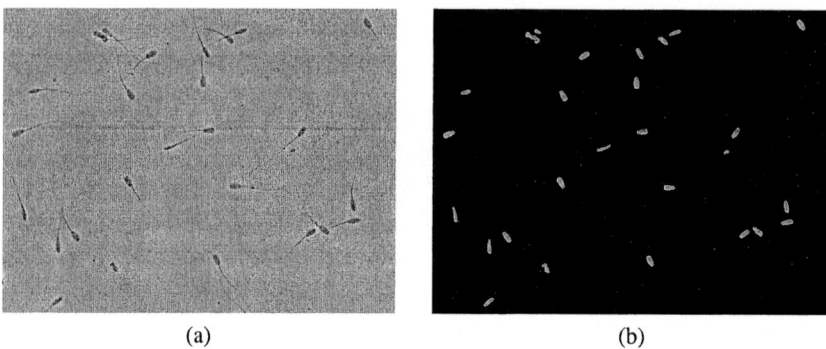

(a) (b)

Fig. 1. (a) Sample image of boar sperm using a phase-contrast microscope. (b) Image obtained after preprocessing and segmentation. The spermatozoid heads are grey-level distributions on a black background.

2.2 Head Orientation and Re-scaling

Taking into consideration that a spermatozoid head presents an oval shape, for each of the spermatozoid heads in an image (Fig. 2a), we determine a major and a minor axis of the ellipse that fits into the head by applying principal component analysis. Subsequently, we consider the grey-level distribution in the head in these (head-specific) principal component coordinates. In practice, we rotate the head image so that the major and minor axes of the concerned ellipse coincide with the x and y axes, respectively, Fig. 2b. According to the empirical measures, a normal boar spermatozoid head takes an oval shape which is from 4 to 5 μm wide and from 7 to 10 μm long. We re-scale all head images to size 19×35 pixels. Next, for each head we consider the 2D function that is defined by the grey levels of those pixels of the head that lie in the fitting ellipse with a minor axis of 19 pixels and a major axis of 35 pixels, Fig. 2c.

2.3 Brightness and Contrast Normalization

Sample images contain heads with diverse intracellular distributions. Three areas can be distinguished in a head image: a darker region which corresponds to the post nucleus cap, an intermediate light area, and the acrosome that covers the nucleus region. However, the contrast between the regions and the average head brightness are not the same

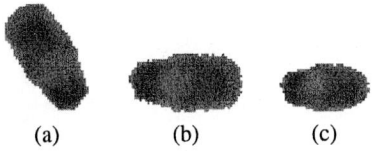

Fig. 2. (a) Image of a spermatozoid head obtained after preprocessing and segmentation. (b) Rotated head image. (c) 2D grey-level distribution defined in an ellipse fitting in a head image re-scaled to a size of 19 × 35.

across different images. To deal with that, we carry out a linear transform on the grey-levels of the 2D function of each head, such that after this transform the 2D functions of all heads have the same mean and standard deviation. More precisely, let $f(x, y)$ be the 2D grey-level function defined on a region S enclosed by an ellipse with main axes 19 and 35 pixels. We transform the function $f(x, y)$ into a function $g(x, y)$ defined on S by:

$$g(x,y) = af(x,y) + b, \qquad (1)$$

where the coefficients a and b are defined as follows:

$$a = \frac{\sigma_g}{\sigma_f}, \quad b = \mu_g - a\mu_f . \qquad (2)$$

The mean μ_f and the standard deviation σ_f of f are computed from f and the mean μ_g and the standard deviation σ_g of g are fixed to $\mu_g = 100$ and $\sigma_g = 8$ since the spermatozoid head images assumed as "potentially normal" by experts take around those values for their means and standard deviations.

2.4 Definition of a Model Head Intensity Distribution

Next, we compute a model 2D intensity distribution function $m(x, y)$ as an average of a given number of 2D intensity distribution functions obtained from the images of heads that have been hypothesized to be "potentially normal" by experts, Fig. 3a. Such heads are characterized by an appropriate intracellular density distribution according to the regions: dark post nucleus cap, light intermediate area and slightly darker acrosome. Let $g_i(x, y)$, $i = 1 \ldots n$, be n such functions that were obtained from images of normal heads by applying the above given pre-processing steps of re-scaling and contrast and brightness normalization. In our experiments we took the images of $n = 34$ such heads that form our *"model" training set M*. We define the model 2D intensity distribution function $m(x, y)$ as a pixel-wise average of these functions (Fig. 4):

$$m(x,y) = \frac{1}{n} \sum_{i=1}^{n} g_i(x,y) . \qquad (3)$$

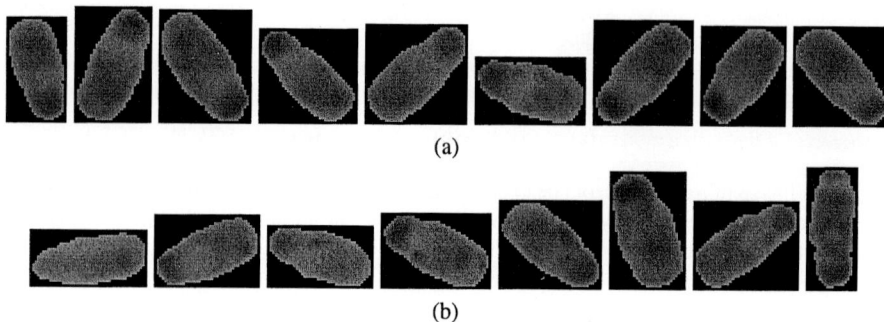

Fig. 3. Examples of heads that were classified by an expert as having distributions that are (a) similar and (b) not similar to an assumed normal density distribution

Fig. 4. Intensity map of the model intensity distribution function obtained as an average of the intensity distributions of a number of heads that were assumed to be "potentially normal" by an expert

We also compute the standard deviation $\sigma(x, y)$ in each pixel inside the ellipse to assess the variability of the grey-levels for each point

$$\sigma(x, y) = \sqrt{\sum_{i=1}^{n} \frac{(g_i(x, y) - m_i(x, y))^2}{n}} . \qquad (4)$$

2.5 Measure of Deviation from the Model Distribution

We now consider a set of microscopic images of boar semen samples and isolate a number of heads according the above described segmentation method. A re-scaled and normalized intensity distribution function can be computed for each segmented head. Let $g(x, y)$ be the function that represents one of the heads observed in the image. We now compute a measure of deviation d of this function from the model function $m(x, y)$ using the L_∞ norm:

$$d = \max \left(\frac{|g(x, y) - m(x, y)|}{\sigma(x, y)} \right) . \qquad (5)$$

We compute the value of this measure of deviation from the model intensity distribution for every head in an image. Different values are computed for different heads. Fig. 5a presents a histogram of the values that were computed for a group of 44 heads that were hypothesized to be normal by an expert from the isolated head images (Fig. 3a). These heads form our *"normal" training set N* and yield values for d from 2 to 5.2. This histogram defines a conditional probability distribution $P(d|n)$ of observing deviation value d for a normal head. Similarly, Fig. 5b presents a histogram of the values that were computed for a group of 82 heads (from a *"not-normal" or "bad" training set B*) that were classified as "not-normal" by an expert (Fig. 3b). The obtained values of d for each head image of such set B fall in the range $[3, 15]$. This histogram defines a conditional probability distribution $P(d|b)$ of observing deviation value d for a not-normal head.

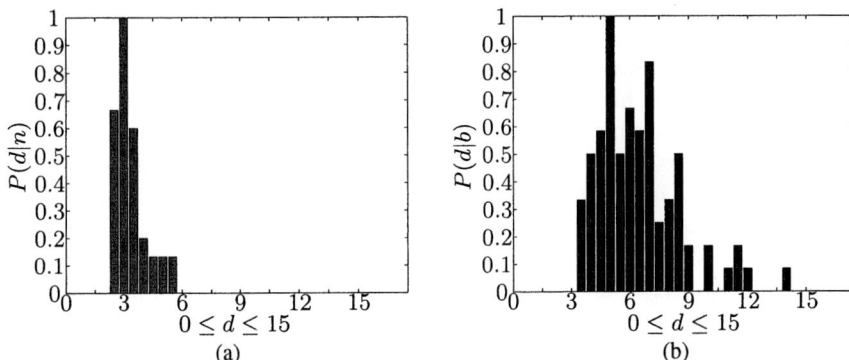

Fig. 5. Histograms of the values of the deviation from the model function for (a) normal and (b) not-normal heads. These histograms can be seen as conditional probability distributions $P(d|n)$ and $P(d|b)$, respectively.

2.6 Estimation of the Fraction of Normal Heads in an Image

Considering a new boar semen sample, we next estimate the fraction of normal heads. For this purpose, a deviation value d is computed for each head in a microscopic image of the semen sample and a histogram of the observed values is built. This histogram defines a distribution $P(d)$ for which in theory holds:

$$P(d) = P(d|n)P_n + P(d|b)(1 - P_n) . \qquad (6)$$

where $P(d|n)$ and $P(d|b)$ are the above defined conditional probabilities of observing deviation value d for a normal and a not-normal head, respectively, and P_n and $1 - P_n$ are the probabilities that a given head is normal or not-normal, respectively. In the above equation, $P(d)$, $P(d|n)$ and $P(d|b)$ are considered as known and P_n as unknown. This equation defines an overdetermined system of linear equations for P_n that contains one equation for each histogram bin of d. The approximate solution to this system according to the least squares method is given by:

$$P_n = \frac{\sum_d (P(d) - P(d|b))(P(d|n) - P(d|b))}{\sum_d (P(d|n) - P(d|b))^2} . \qquad (7)$$

Using the distribution $P(d)$ for the considered sample and the conditional probabilities $P(d|n)$ and $P(d|b)$ pre-computed on the training sets N and B of sample images, the above formula is an effective means to compute the fraction P_n of normal heads in a sample. Note that we estimate this fraction without having to classify each head separately as normal or not normal.

2.7 Experimental Results

A test set T of 100 images of different samples of boar sperm was considered. After preprocessing, segmentation, brightness and contrast normalization, each head was described by a 2D grey level distribution function and a deviation of this function from the model distribution function as defined above was computed. The heads obtained from a given sample yield a histogram $P(d)$ of the deviation from the model for that sample. Then, the fraction P_n of heads with a normal intracellular distribution was evaluated for each test image according to the method described above. The obtained 100 values are illustrated by a box-and-whisker diagram shown in Fig. 6a. These values were compared with the values of the fraction P_e of normal heads in the concerned images as determined by an expert (Fig. 6b). The values of the absolute error $P_n - P_e$ computed for the different test images are illustrated by the box-and-whisker diagram shown in Fig. 6c. The absolute error is below 0.25 for 89 of the 100 test images, between 0.25 and 0.32 for another 8 test images and below 0.47 for the 3 remaining images.

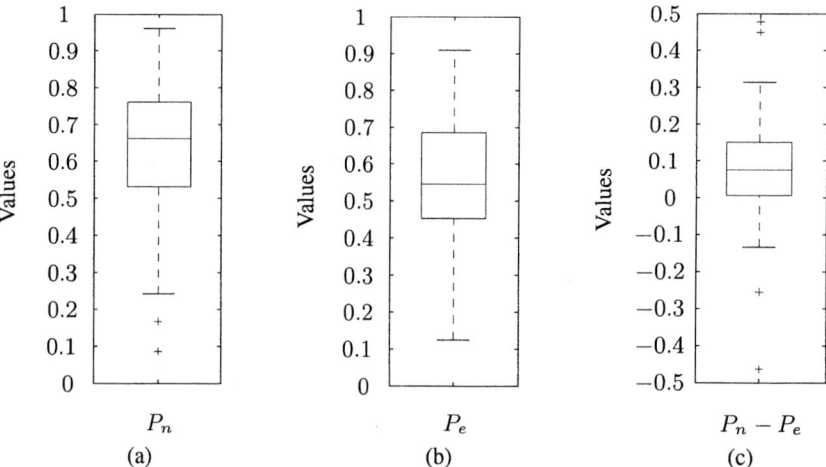

Fig. 6. (a) Box-and whisker diagrams of the values of the fraction of normal heads determined by means of the proposed method, and (b) by veterinary experts and (c) absolute error of the method in comparison with the experts

3 Discussion and Conclusions

We proposed a novel approach to the analysis of images of boar spermatozoid heads in order to describe and classify them by means of their intracellular distribution. Using a training set M of spermatozoid head images that were hypothesized by a veterinary expert as potentially "normal", we compute a model intracellular distribution for such a head. For each head in an image we compute a value of dissimilarity of its intracellular distribution to the model distribution. The histogram of dissimilarity values obtained for the intracellular distributions of normal heads is different from the histogram obtained for the distributions of heads that are considered by an expert as potentially not normal. To build these histograms we use two other training sets (N and B). We use the two histograms to estimate the fraction of heads in a semen sample image that would be classified as "potentially normal" by an expert. The absolute error of our method compared to a human expert is less than 0.25 in 89% of the sample images. That is an encouraging result because this work is the first that uses cellular density information instead of morphological features. Note that our algorithm gives systematically an overestimation of the concerned fraction. Our future work will be directed towards reducing this error. We will also explore the potential of single head classification in which first each head is classified individually as normal or not normal and the results for all heads in a sample image are used to determine the concerned fraction of normal cells.

The absolute error defined above is not the final criterion for the performance of our method because the classification by a human expert can differ from one session to another and across experts. It is more important that, once the algorithm is trained to evaluate the fraction of potentially normal heads in a sample, this fraction is correlated with the sperm vitality of that sample as determined by means of staining techniques. The potential of our approach in that respect will next be tested in veterinary praxis.

References

1. Thurston, L., Holt, W., Watson, P.: Post-thaw functional status of boar spermatozoa cryopreserved using three controlled rate freezers: a comparison. Theriogenology **60** (2003) 101–113
2. Linneberg, C., Salamon, P., Svarer, C., Hansen, L.: Towards semen quality assessment using neural networks. In: Proc. IEEE Neural Networks for Signal Processing IV. (1994) 509–517
3. Verstegen, J., Iguer-Ouada, M., Onclin, K.: Computer assisted semen analyzers in andrology research and veterinary practice. Theriogenology **57** (2002) 149–179
4. Gravance, C., Garner, D., Pitt, C., Vishwanath, R., Sax-Gravance, S., Casey, P.: Replicate and technician variation associated with computer aided bull sperm head morphometry analysis (asma). International Journal of Andrology **22** (1999) 77–82
5. PIC: Artificial insemination: Semen processing and quality control. Artificial Insemination **1** (2003)
6. Quintero, A., Rigaub, T., Rodríguez, J.: Regression analyses and motile sperm subpopulation structure study as improving tools in boar semen quality analysis. Theriogenology **61** (2004) 673 – 690
7. Robles, V., Alegre, E., Sebastián, J.: Tracking algorithms evaluation in feature points image sequences. In Campilho, A., Kamel, M., eds.: Image Analysis and Recognition: International Conference ICIAR 2004, Porto, Portugal, September 29 - October 1, 2004, Proceedings, Part II. Volume 3212 of Lecture Notes in Computer Science. Springer-Verlag Heidelberg (2004) 589–596
8. Alegre, E., Sánchez, L., Aláiz, R., Dominguez, J.: Utilización de momentos estadísticos y redes neuronales en la clasificación de cabezas de espermatozoides de verraco. In: XXV Jornadas de Automática. (2004)

3D Triangular Mesh Parametrization Using Locally Linear Embedding

Xianfang Sun[1,2] and Edwin R. Hancock[2]

[1] School of Automation Science and Electrical Engineering, Beihang University,
Beijing 100083, P.R. China
[2] Department of Computer Science, The University of York, York YO10 5DD, UK
{xfsun, erh}@cs.york.ac.uk

Abstract. In this paper we describe a new mesh parametrization method which combines the mean value coordinates and the Locally Linear Embedding (LLE) method. The mean value method is extended to compute the linearly reconstructing weights of both the interior and the boundary vertices of a 3D triangular mesh, and the weights are further used in the LLE algorithm to compute the vertex coordinates of a 2D planar triangular mesh parametrization. Examples are provided to show the effectiveness of this parametrization method.

1 Introduction

Triangular mesh parametrization aims to determine a 2D triangular mesh with its vertices, edges, and triangles corresponding to that of the original 3D triangular mesh, satisfying an optimality criterion. The technique has been applied in a wide range of problems in computer graphics and image processing, including texture mapping [9], morphing [7], and remeshing [4]. Extensive research has been undertaken into the theoretical issues underpinning the method and its practical application. For a tutorial and survey, the reader is referred to [3].

A well-known parametrization method is that proposed by Floater [1]. It is a generalization of the basic procedure originally proposed by Tutte [8] which was used to draw planar graphs. The basic idea underpinning this method is to use the vertex coordinates of the original 3D triangular mesh to compute reconstructing weights of each interior vertex with respect to its neighbour vertices. These weights are subsequently used together with the boundary vertex coordinates on a plane to compute the interior vertex coordinates of a 2D triangular mesh. A drawback of Floater's parametrization method is that the boundary vertex coordinates must be determined manually beforehand.

There are many methods for computing the reconstructing weights. The simplest one is Tutte's barycentric coordinates [8]. Floater provided a method of computing the weights in his first paper about parametrization [1], which has a so-called shape-preserving property. More recently, Floater computes mean value coordinates as the reconstructing weights[2]. These mean value coordinates perform better than the earlier shape-preserving weights of [1].

The Linearly Local Embedding (LLE) [5] is a method of mapping high dimensional data to a low dimensional Euclidean space. The idea underlying the method is to use the high dimensional data to compute locally linear reconstructing weights for each data point. These weights are then used to compute the point coordinates in a low dimensional data space. It can be used in a natural way to map 3D coordinates to 2D coordinates. Thus it can be used as a parametrization method. However, because for 3D triangular meshes, the dimension of the data (here it is 3) is usually less than the number of neighbours of any data point, the original algorithm does not compute optimal weights. Hence, LLE is not a good parametrization method.

In this paper, we combine the advantages of both the mean value coordinates and LLE to develop a new parametrization method. The paper is organised as follows. Section 2 introduces the basic problem and provides a overview of the proposed algorithm. Sections 3 and 4 describes the mean value coordinates and the LLE method, and their adaptation for use in our algorithm. Section 5 provides some experimental examples of the method. Finally, Section 6 draws some conclusions.

2 Problem and Algorithm Overview

Consider a triangular mesh $T = T(V, E, F, X)$ with vertex set $V = \{i : i = 1, 2, ..., N\}$ and corresponding coordinate set $X = \{x_i : x_i \in R^d, i \in V\}$ ($d = 2$ or 3), edge set $E = \{(i,j) : (i,j) \in V \times V\}$, and triangular face set $F = \{(i,j,k) : (i,j),(i,k),(j,k) \in E\}$. Here an edge (i,j) is represented by a straight line segment between vertices i and j, and a triangular face (i,j,k) is a triangular facet bounded by three edges (i,j), (i,k) and (j,k). When $d = 2$, T is drawn on a plane and represents a planar triangular mesh, while $d = 3$, T is drawn in a 3-dimensional space and represents a 3D triangular mesh. A triangular mesh is called valid if the only intersections between edges are at common end points (vertices) and the only intersections between triangular faces are on the common edges. Hereafter, when a triangular mesh is referred without qualification, it implies that the triangular mesh is valid.

The parametrization is made on a valid 3D triangular mesh. A parametrization of a valid 3D triangular mesh $T = T(V, E, F, X)$ is any valid planar triangular mesh $T_p = T_p(V, E, F, Y)$ with $Y = \{y_i : y_i \in R^2, i \in V\}$ being the corresponding coordinates of V.

The parametrization algorithm proposed here combines the mean co-ordinates of Floater and the LLE method. It consists of the following three steps.

- Based on the algorithm proposed by Floater [2], the mean value coordinates (or the reconstructing weights) are computed for each vertex using the vertex coordinates X.
- Using the LLE algorithm [5], the weights obtained above are used to recover the vertex coordinates Y of the planar triangular mesh.

- If $T_p(V, E, F, Y)$ is not valid, then the coordinates of the boundary vertices are fixed, and the coordinates of the interior vertices are computed using Floater's algorithm [1].

Note that in Step 1 of our algorithm, the reconstructing weights of both the interior and boundary vertices are computed, while only the weights of interior vertices are computed in Floater's algorithm [1,2].

3 Mean Value Coordinates

Given a 3D triangular mesh $T = T(V, E, F, X)$, where the vertex set V is divided into disjoint boundary and interior vertex subsets, i.e. $V = V_I \cup V_B$, where V_I is the interior vertex set, V_B is the boundary vertex set and $V_I \cap V_B = \emptyset$. The parametrization method proposed by Floater [1] is a generalization of Tutte's method of drawing a planar graph [8], which consists of the following steps.

- For each interior vertex $i \in V_I$, assign a non-negative weight $W_{i,j}$ to each of its incident edges $(i,j) \in E$ such that $\sum_{(i,j) \in E} W_{i,j} = 1$, and $W_{i,j} = 0$ for all $(i,j) \notin E$.
- For each boundary vertex $i \in V_B$, determine a coordinate $y_i \in R^2$ in the plane such that the order of the boundary vertices in the plane remains the same as that of the original ones, and they form a closed convex polygon.
- Solve the following linear system for the coordinates of the interior vertices

$$y_i = \sum_{(i,j) \in E} W_{i,j} y_j, \ i \in V_I \ . \tag{1}$$

There are some important features of this algorithm that deserve further comment. In the first step, although Tutte's barycentric coordinates [8] and Floater's early shape-preserving weights [1] can be used here as the reconstructing weights, a better choice are the mean value coordinates recently proposed by Floater [2]. The mean value coordinates are computed using the formula

$$W_{i,j} = \frac{\lambda_{i,j}}{\sum_{(i,k) \in E} \lambda_{i,k}}, \ \lambda_{i,j} = \frac{tan(\alpha_{i,j-1}/2) + tan(\alpha_{i,j}/2)}{\|x_j - x_i\|} \ , \tag{2}$$

where $\alpha_{i,j-1}$ and $\alpha_{i,j}$ are the angles between the edge (i,j) and its two neighbouring edges $(i, j-1)$ and $(i, j+1)$ (see Fig. 1(a)).

Next, we consider the second step. The boundary vertex coordinates are determined manually. This a drawback since if the boundary vertex coordinates are selected inappropriately, the resulting parametrization is poor. In our method, the boundary vertex coordinates are determined by the LLE method. Hence, although we dispense with this step, the weights of boundary vertices must still be computed.

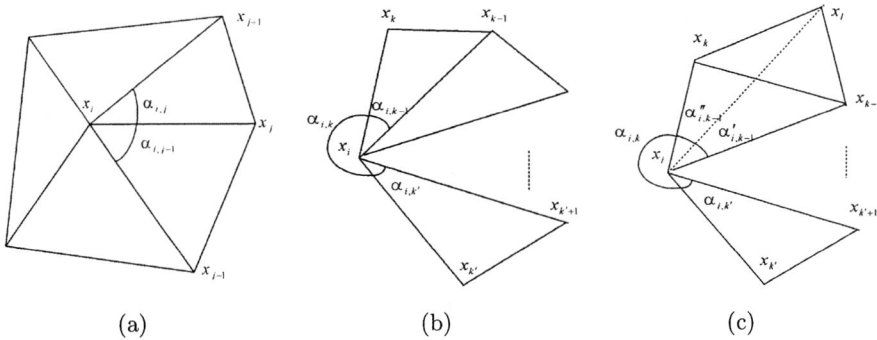

Fig. 1. Elements for the computation of mean value coordinates: (a) interior vertex, (b) general boundary vertex, (c) boundary vertex in case with additional neighbour vertex

Here, we still use the mean value coordinates as the weights of the boundary vertices. For the boundary vertex i, the weights $\lambda_{i,k}$ and $\lambda_{i,k'}$ of its neigbouring boundary vertices k and k' are computed using the formula (refer to Fig. 1(b))

$$\lambda_{i,k} = \frac{\tan(\alpha_{i,k-1}/2) + \tan(\alpha_{i,k}/2)}{\|x_k - x_i\|}, \quad \lambda_{i,k'} = \frac{\tan(\alpha_{i,k}/2) + \tan(\alpha_{i,k'}/2)}{\|x_{k'} - x_i\|}, \quad (3)$$

Because $\alpha_{i,k}$ is not strictly less than π, two problems arise when (2) and (3) are used to compute $W_{i,j}$. The first problem occurs when $\alpha_{i,k} = \pi$, i.e. $\tan(\alpha_{i,k}/2) = \infty$, which causes a computational overflow. The solution of this problem is to simply set $\lambda_{i,k} = 1/\|x_k - x_i\|$, $\lambda_{i,k'} = 1/\|x_{k'} - x_i\|$, and $\lambda_{i,j} = 0$ for all other $j \subset V$. The second problem occurs when $\sum_{(i,j) \in E} \lambda_{i,j} = 0$, which causes a divide-by-zero error when $W_{i,j}$ is computed. In this case, an additional vertex l, which is originally not the neighbour vertex of i, but that of one of i's neighbouring vertices, is now taken as the neighbour vertex of i in computing the mean value coordinates (see Fig. 1(c)).

After computing the reconstructing weights, we depart from Floater's version of Tutte's algorithm. Our idea here is to borrow ideas from LLE algorithm to compute the co-ordinates of the interior vertices.

4 Locally Linear Embedding

In this paper, we only exploit a component part of the LLE method for mesh parametrization. However, for completeness and further analysis of this method, the complete LLE algorithm is described. The LLE algorithm consists of following three steps:

- For each data point x_i, find the K nearest neighbours $\{x_{i1}, \cdots, x_{iK}\}$.
- Compute the weights $W_{i,j}$ that best linearly reconstruct x_i from its neighours through minimizing the cost function

$$E(W) = \sum_i \|x_i - \sum_j W_{i,j} x_j\|^2 \qquad (4)$$

with the additional constraints $\sum_j W_{i,j} = 1$, and $W_{i,j} = 0$ if x_j is not the K nearest neighbour of x_i.
- Compute the low dimensional embedding vector y_i that is best reconstructed by $W_{i,j}$ by minimizing the embedding cost function

$$\Phi(Y) = \sum_i \|y_i - \sum_j W_{i,j} y_j\|^2 \qquad (5)$$

with additional constraints $\sum_i y_i = 0$ and $\frac{1}{N} \sum_i y_i y_i^T = I$.

When the LLE method is directly used for parametrization of a 3D triangular mesh, the first step (i.e. the selection of the K nearest neighbours) may seem superfluous, since the 3D triangular mesh has its own natural neighbourhood. However, the number of neighbours significantly affects the performance of the algorithm. If the number of neighbours is too small, then the reconstructed embedding will be poor. Unfortunately, the numbers of natural neighbours in a triangular mesh are usually small. Hence, better results can be obtained by choosing a suitable value of K.

The second step attempts to locate the best weights that minimize (4). However, because for most of the interior vertices, the valency (the number of neighbour vertices) is greater than 3, the solution of (4) has been conditioned in the original LLE algorithm [5], thus the weights are in fact not optimal. In this paper, the mean value coordinates described in Section 3 are used as alternative weights to obtain a better result.

After the weights are obtained, y_i in Step 3 can be easily obtained by using the eigenvectors of the matrix $M = (I - W)^T(I - W)$.

Let $\Lambda = diag(\lambda_1, \lambda_2, \lambda_3, ...)$ be the matrix with the ordered eigenvalues $0 = \lambda_1 \leq \lambda_2 \leq \lambda_3 ...$ as diagonal elements, and let $\Phi = (\phi_1|\phi_2|\phi_2|...)$ be the matrix with the corresponding eigevalues as columns. The eigendecomposition of the matrix M is $M = \Phi \Lambda \Phi^T$. The eigenvector of this matrix corresponding to eigenvalue $\lambda_1 = 0$ is the unit vector with equal components, and is discarded. The eigenvectors ϕ_2 and ϕ_3 give us the 2D coordinates Y, and $y_i = (\phi_2(i), \phi_3(i))^T$.

Now that Y has been obtained, then $T_p(V, E, F, Y)$ gives us a parametrization of $T(V, E, F, X)$. In most of the cases, $T_p(V, E, F, Y)$ is a valid planar triangular mesh. However, when the original 3D mesh has too high curvatures on some points, the above resulting planar triangular mesh may fold over. In this case, we only need to select the 2D coordinates of the boundary vertices from Y and adjust their order if necessary. Fixing the coordinates of the boundary vertices, the coordinates of the interior vertices can then be computed by solving equation system (1), and finally, a valid planar triangular mesh $T_p(V, E, F, Y)$ is obtained.

5 Examples

In this section, two examples are provided to illustrate some of the properties of the algorithm proposed in this paper. In the first example, we consider an

S-shaped manifold [6]. It is an intrinsically two dimensional manifold. Figure 2(a) shows a regular sample of $N = 600$ data points and its triangulation in the 3D space. Figure 2(b) shows the parametrization using the algorithm proposed here, and Fig. 2(c) shows the result using LLE with $K = 12$ neighbours per data point. It is evident that the algorithm of this paper performs better than the LLE algorithm. In particular, the current algorithm results in a parametrization with an appearance which is closer to the original one than that obtained by the LLE algorithm.

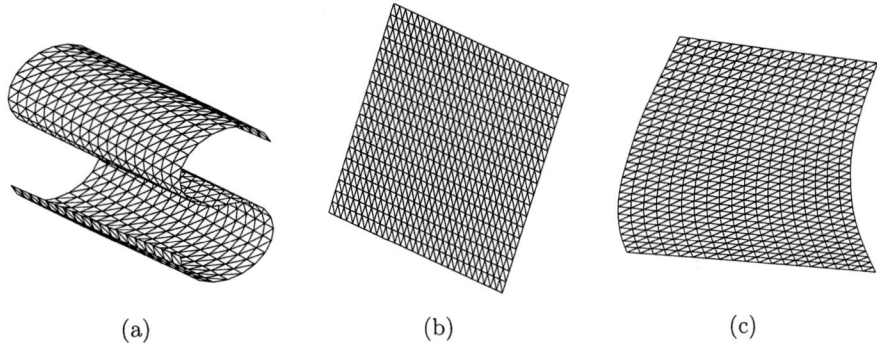

(a) (b) (c)

Fig. 2. Parametrization of S-shape manifold: (a) regular triangulation, (b) parametrization using our algorithm, (c) parametrization using LLE algorithm with $K=12$

Figure 3(a) shows a random sample of $N = 600$ data points on the same S-shape manifold. Figure 3(b) shows the parametrization using the algorithm proposed here, and Fig. 3(c)~(e) shows the result obtained using LLE with $K = 6$, 12, 24 neighbours per data point, respectively. Again, it can be seen that the proposed algorithm results in a parametrization of better appearance. Moreover, the performance of the LLE algorithm is highly dependent on a suitable choice of the parameter K. When K is too small (here, $K = 6$) or too large ($K = 24$), the resulting planar triangular mesh is invalid because some of the interior or boundary edges cross each other (see Fig. 3(c) and 3(e)). The second example uses the *peaks* function of Matlab. Figure 4(a) shows an irregular triangulation of this function. Figure 4(b) shows the result using only the first two steps of the proposed algorithm and Fig. 4(c) shows a local zoom-in part of Fig. 4(b). It can be seen that some triangles are folded over, and the resulting parametrization is invalid. From the other point, however, we can see that the boundary vertices have been self-adjusted on the plane, and thus we can use these coordinates of the boundary vertices and perform Step 3 of the proposed algorithm to obtain a valid parametrization of the original 3D triangular mesh.

We have also scaled down the z-coordinates by 1/3 and directly obtained a valid parametrization using just the first two steps of the proposed algorithm. The result is shown in Fig. 4(d). Figure 4(e) is the result of texture mapping using the parametrization of Fig. 4(d). It can be seen that the resulting parametrization is suitable for the texture mapping application.

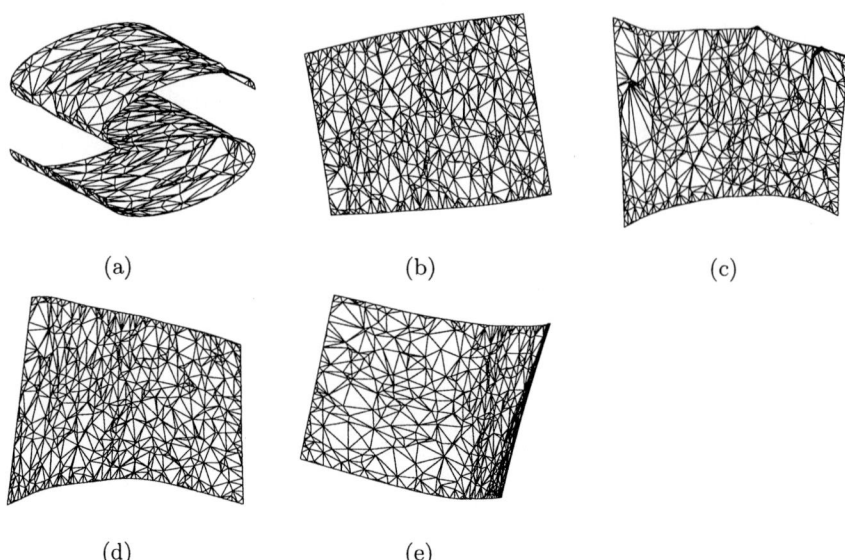

Fig. 3. Parametrization of S-shape manifold with random sample: (a) triangulation, (b) parametrization using our algorithm, (c)~(e) parametrization using LLE algorithm with K=6,12,24, respectively

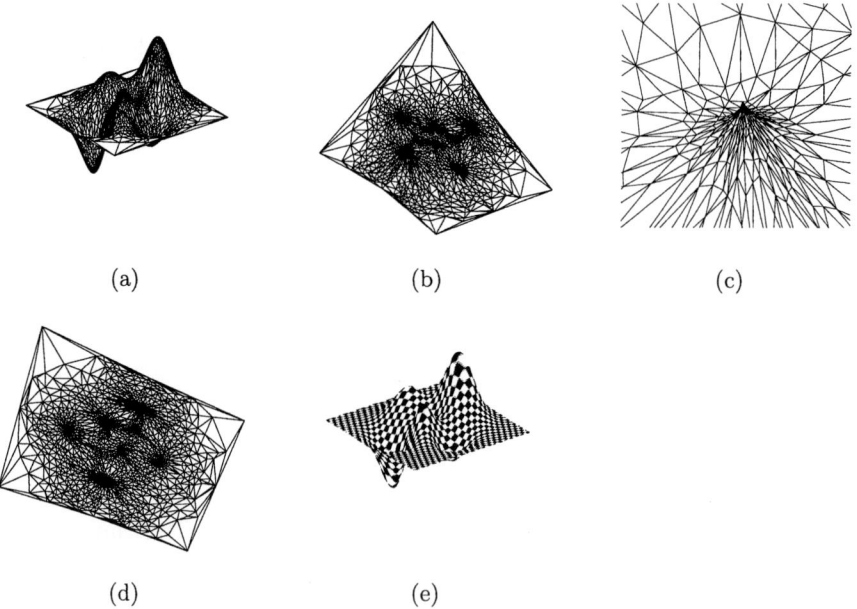

Fig. 4. Parametrization of peaks function: (a) an irregular triangulation, (b) parametrization with only first two steps, (c) zoom-in part of (b), (d) parametrization for z-axis being scaled down by 1/3, (e) texture mapping

6 Conclusion

In this paper, we have combined the mean value coordinates and the LLE method to construct a new parametrization method. Although the parametrization method using mean value coordinates has a drawback of requiring manually determined boundary vertex coordinates and the LLE method has the drawback that reconstructing weights are not optimal, a combination of these two methods have been proved to be reasonable. We have used examples to show that the proposed parametrization method can automatically find good boundary vertex coordinates and it is practically useful.

References

1. Floater, M. S.: Parametrization and smooth approximation of surface triangulations. Comp. Aided. Geom. Design. **14** (1997) 231–250
2. Floater, M. S.: Mean value coordinates. Comp. Aided. Geom. Design. **20** (2003) 19–27
3. Floater, M. S., Hormann, K.: Surface Parameterization: a Tutorial and Survey. in Advances in Multiresolution for Geometric Modelling, N. A. Dodgson, M. S. Floater, and M. A. Sabin (eds.), Springer-Verlag, Heidelberg, 2004, 157–186
4. Praun, E., Hoppe, H.: Spherical parametrization and remeshing. ACM Trans. Graphics. **22** (2003) 340–349
5. Roweis, S. T., Saul, L. K.: Nonlinear dimensionality reduction by locally linear embedding. Science. **290** (2000) 2323–2326
6. Saul, L. K., Roweis, S. T.: An introduction to locally linear embedding. Report at AT & T Labs-Research, 2000.
7. Surazhsky, V., Gotsman, C.: Intrinsic morphing of compatible triangulations. Int. J. Shape Modelling.**9** (2003) 191–201
8. Tutte, W. T.: How to draw a graph. Proc. London Math. Soc. **13** (1963) 743–768
9. Zigelman, G., Kimmel, R., Kiryati N.: Texture mapping using surface flattening via multi-dimensional scaling. IEEE Trans. Visualization Comp. Graphics. **8** (2002) 198–207

Variational Analysis of Spherical Images

Atsushi Imiya[1], Hironobu Sugaya[2], Akihiko Torii[2], and Yoshihiko Mochizuki[2]

[1] Institute of Media and Information Technology, Chiba University,
[2] School of Science and Technology, Chiba University,
Yayoi-cho 1-33, Inage-ku, Chiba 263-8522, Japan

Abstract. This paper focuses on variational image analysis on a sphere. Since a sphere is a closed Riemannian manifold with the positive constant curvature and no holes, a sphere has similar geometrical properties with a plane, whose curvature is zero. Images observed through a catadioptric system with a conic-mirror and a dioptric system with fish-eye lens are transformed to images on the sphere. Therefore, in robot vision, image analysis on the sphere is an essential requirement to the application of the omni-directional imaging system with conic-mirror and fish-eye lens for navigation and control. We introduce algorithms for optical flow computation for images on a sphere.

1 Introduction

In this paper, we deal with image analysis on a sphere. A sphere has mathematically important geometrical properties.

1. A sphere is a closed manifold without any holes.
2. The mean curvature on a sphere is constant and positive. Therfore, a spherical surface and a plane, which is the manifold with zero curvature, have geometrically similar properties [1].
3. Functions on a sphere are periodic.
4. The stereographic projection provides a one-to-one correspondence between points on a plane and on a sphere. Therefore, a function on a plane is bijectively transformed to a function on a sphere.

Since variational method provides a coordinate-free expression of image analysis such as optical flow computation, noise removal, edge detection, in-printing [2,3] and boundary detection and tracking [2,13,14]. We extend the the variational-method-based image-analysis algorithms as fundamental tools for image analysis on a sphere. Spherical motion field on the spherical retina has some advantages for ego-motion estimation of an autonomous mobile observer [4,5]. Furthermore, the spherical retina is interested both from robot vision and biological vision.

- An omni-directional image captured by conic-mirror-based catadioptric system is transformed to images on a sphere [6].
- A view captured by the insect compound eye is modelled as an image on a sphere [8].

Since the omni-directional imaging system is widely used as imaging system of mobile robots, image analysis on a sphere is required in robot vision. Furthermore, in biological vision, spherical views are fundamental tools for studies on ego-motion estimation of insects with compound eyes in environments. Motion analysis and tracking of obstacles and targets are fundamental requirements for robot vision. In this paper, as an application of image analysis on a sphere, we introduce optical flow computation for motion analysis on a sphere and edge detection for tracking of the boundary of a region on a sphere.

2 Optical Flow Computation on the Sphere

Setting $\boldsymbol{x} = (x, y, z)^\top$ to be a point on a space $\mathbf{R}^3$, for $0 \leq \theta \leq \pi$ and $0 \leq \phi < 2\pi$, a point on the unit sphere is parameterised as $x = \cos\phi\sin\theta$, $y = \sin\phi\sin\theta$, and $z = \cos\theta$. Therefore, a function on the unit sphere S^2 is parameterised as $I(\theta, \phi)$. The vector expressions of the spatial and spatio-temporal gradients on the unit sphere are $\nabla_S = \left(\frac{\partial}{\partial\theta}, \frac{1}{\sin\theta}\frac{\partial}{\partial\phi}\right)^\top$ and $\nabla_{St} = \left(\frac{\partial}{\partial\theta}, \frac{1}{\sin\theta}\frac{\partial}{\partial\phi}, \frac{\partial}{\partial t}\right)^\top$, respectively. For temporal image $I(\theta, \phi, t)$ on the unit sphere S^2, the total derivative is

$$\frac{d}{dt}I = \frac{\partial}{\partial\theta}I\frac{d\theta}{dt} + \frac{1}{\sin\theta}\frac{\partial}{\partial\phi}I\frac{d\phi}{dt} + \frac{\partial}{\partial t}I. \tag{1}$$

The solution $\boldsymbol{q} = (\dot{\theta}, \dot{\phi})^\top = \left(\frac{d\theta}{dt}, \frac{d\phi}{dt}\right)^\top$ of the equation

$$\boldsymbol{q}^\top(\nabla_S I) + I_t = \boldsymbol{s}^\top(\nabla_{St} I) = 0, \tag{2}$$

for $\boldsymbol{s} = (\boldsymbol{q}^\top, 1)^\top = (\dot{\theta}, \dot{\phi}, 1)^\top$, is optical flow of image I on the unit sphere S^2.

The computation of optical flow from eq. (2) is an ill-posed problem. Horn-Schunck criterion for the computation of optical flow [9,10] on the unit sphere is expressed as the minimisation of the functional

$$J(\dot{\theta}, \dot{\phi}) = \int_{S^2} \left(|\boldsymbol{s}^\top(\nabla_{St} I)|^2 + \alpha(\|\nabla_S \dot{\theta}\|_2^2 + \|\nabla_S \dot{\phi}\|_2^2)\right) \sin\theta d\theta d\phi, \tag{3}$$

where L_2 norm on the unit sphere is defined by

$$\|f(\theta, \phi)\|_2^2 = \int_{S^2} |f(\theta, \phi)|^2 \sin\theta d\theta d\phi. \tag{4}$$

The Euler-Lagrange equations of this minimisation problem are

$$\begin{aligned}\nabla_S^\top \cdot \nabla_S \dot{\theta} &= \frac{1}{\alpha}\frac{\partial I}{\partial\theta}\left(\frac{\partial I}{\partial\theta}\dot{\theta} + \frac{1}{\sin\theta}\frac{\partial I}{\partial\phi}\dot{\phi} + \frac{\partial I}{\partial t}\right), \\ \nabla_S^\top \cdot \nabla_S \dot{\phi} &= \frac{1}{\alpha\sin\theta}\frac{\partial I}{\partial\phi}\left(\frac{\partial I}{\partial\theta}\dot{\theta} + \frac{1}{\sin\theta}\frac{\partial I}{\partial\phi}\dot{\phi} + \frac{\partial I}{\partial t}\right).\end{aligned} \tag{5}$$

From this system of equations, we have the system of diffusion-reaction equations on the sphere as

$$\frac{\partial}{\partial \tau}\dot{\theta} = \nabla_S^\top \cdot \nabla_S \dot{\theta} - \frac{1}{\alpha}\frac{\partial I}{\partial \theta}\left(\frac{\partial I}{\partial \theta}\dot{\theta} + \frac{1}{\sin\theta}\frac{\partial I}{\partial \phi}\dot{\phi} + \frac{\partial I}{\partial t}\right),$$

$$\frac{\partial}{\partial \tau}\dot{\phi} = \nabla_S^\top \cdot \nabla_S \dot{\phi} - \frac{1}{\alpha\sin\theta}\frac{\partial I}{\partial \phi}\left(\frac{\partial I}{\partial \theta}\dot{\theta} + \frac{1}{\sin\theta}\frac{\partial I}{\partial \phi}\dot{\phi} + \frac{\partial I}{\partial t}\right) \quad (6)$$

for the computation of optical flow. For numerical computation, we adopt backward Euler method.

Since q is a function of the time t, we accept the smoothed function

$$q(t) := \int_{t-\tau}^{t+\tau} w(\tau)q(\tau)d\tau, \quad \int_{t-\tau}^{t+\tau} w(\tau)d\tau = 1, \quad (7)$$

as the solution. Furthermore, we achieve the operation

$$q^* = \text{argument}\left(\text{median}_{\Omega(q)}\left\{|q| \leq T|\text{median}_M(\min J(q))|\right\}\right), \quad (8)$$

which we call the double median operation [11].

The Nagel-Enkelmann criterion [12] for the optical flow computation on the unit sphere is expressed as,

$$J_{NE}(\dot{\theta}, \dot{\phi}) = \int_S \left(|s^\top(\nabla_{St}I)|^2 + \alpha(\nabla_S \dot{\theta}^\top N_S \nabla_S \dot{\theta} + \nabla_S \dot{\phi}^\top N_S \nabla_S \dot{\phi})\right) \sin\theta d\theta d\phi, \quad (9)$$

where

$$N_S = \frac{1}{(\frac{\partial I}{\partial \theta})^2 + \frac{1}{\sin^2\theta}(\frac{\partial I}{\partial \phi})^2 + 2\lambda^2}\begin{pmatrix} \frac{1}{\sin^2\theta}(\frac{\partial I}{\partial \phi})^2 + \lambda^2 & -\frac{1}{\sin\theta}\frac{\partial I}{\partial \theta}\frac{\partial I}{\partial \phi} \\ -\frac{1}{\sin\theta}\frac{\partial I}{\partial \theta}\frac{\partial I}{\partial \phi} & (\frac{\partial I}{\partial \theta})^2 + \lambda^2 \end{pmatrix}. \quad (10)$$

This minimisation criterion derives the Euler-Lagrange equation in the form of system of equations as

$$\nabla_S^\top N_S \cdot \nabla_S \dot{\theta} - \frac{1}{\alpha}\frac{\partial I}{\partial \theta}\left(\frac{\partial I}{\partial \theta}\dot{\theta} + \frac{1}{\sin\theta}\frac{\partial I}{\partial \phi}\dot{\phi} + \frac{\partial I}{\partial t}\right) = 0,$$

$$\nabla_S^\top N_S \nabla_S \dot{\phi} - \frac{1}{\alpha\sin\theta}\frac{\partial I}{\partial \phi}\left(\frac{\partial I}{\partial \theta}\dot{\theta} + \frac{1}{\sin\theta}\frac{\partial I}{\partial \phi}\dot{\phi} + \frac{\partial I}{\partial t}\right) = 0. \quad (11)$$

On the unit sphere, to solve this system of equation, we have a system of diffusion-reaction equations

$$\frac{\partial}{\partial \tau}\dot{\theta} = \nabla_S^\top N_S \cdot \nabla_S \dot{\theta} - \frac{1}{\alpha}\frac{\partial I}{\partial \theta}\left(\frac{\partial I}{\partial \theta}\dot{\theta} + \frac{1}{\sin\theta}\frac{\partial I}{\partial \phi}\dot{\phi} + \frac{\partial I}{\partial t}\right),$$

$$\frac{\partial}{\partial \tau}\dot{\phi} = \nabla_S^\top N_S \nabla_S \dot{\phi} - \frac{1}{\alpha\sin\theta}\frac{\partial I}{\partial \phi}\left(\frac{\partial I}{\partial \theta}\dot{\theta} + \frac{1}{\sin\theta}\frac{\partial I}{\partial \phi}\dot{\phi} + \frac{\partial I}{\partial t}\right). \quad (12)$$

This system of equation is solved with the same scheme which we adopt to solve the Euler-Lagrange equation derived by the Horn-Schunck criterion.

For an image on the sphere and a weight function $w(\theta, \phi) > 0$, the Lucas-Kanade criterion is expressed as the minimisation of the functional

$$J_{LK}(\dot{\theta}, \dot{\phi}) = \int\int_{\Omega \subset S^2} w^2(\theta, \phi, t)|\mathbf{s}^\top \nabla_{St} I|^2 \sin\theta d\theta d\phi dt = \mathbf{s}^\top \mathbf{L}_w \mathbf{s}, \qquad (13)$$

for the smoothed structure tensor on the sphere

$$\mathbf{L}_w = \int\int_{\Omega \subset S^2} (w(\theta, \phi, t) \nabla_{St} I(\theta, \phi, t))(w(\theta, \phi, t) \nabla_{St} I(\theta, \phi, t))^\top \sin\theta d\theta d\phi dt, \qquad (14)$$

assuming that $\mathbf{q} = (\dot{\phi}, \dot{\theta})^\top$ is constant in the finite region Ω. Therefore, setting $\mathbf{v} = (a, b, c)^\top$ to be the eigenvector of the matrix $\mathbf{L}$ associated to the smallest eigenvalue, we have the relation $\mathbf{q} = (\frac{a}{c}, \frac{b}{c})^\top$ for $c \neq 0$. For the achievement of Lucas-Kanade-criterion-based method to the accurate computation of optical flow on a sphere, we are required to design an appropriate weight function and the window-control process based on the domain decomposition on the sphere [?].

Table 1. Discretisation Parameters for Real-World Images

Parameter (H-S, N-E)	α	1000
Parameter (N-E)	λ^2	10000
Parameter (L-K)	T	4
Grid pitch	$\Delta\theta$	0.20°
Grid pitch	$\Delta\phi$	0.20°
Grid size	$(\phi \times \theta)$	1800 × 900
Discretisation pitch	$\Delta\tau$	0.002
Iteration times		2000

In Figure 1 we show the detected optical flow in the spherical representations by the Lucas-Kanade with the unit weight, the Horn-Schunck, and Nagel-Enkelmann criteria from left to right. In these results, flows whose vector length are shorter than 0.5 pixels for the Lucas-Kanade and Horn-Schunck criteria are removed. Furthermore, for the Nagel-Enklemann criterion, flows whose vector length are shorter than 0.01 pixels are removed. These results tell us that as expected the Nagel-Enkelmann method detect the boundary of moving objects, though the method fails to detect small motion. The Lucas-Kanade method requires to design appropriate windows since it assumes the local stationarity on the flow vectors. Furthermore, these results show the validity of the embedding of the Horn-Schunck and Nagel-Enkelmann methods to the system of diffusion-reaction equations. In Figure 1 (j) and (k) show a pair of successive cylindrical images from a sequence of spherical images for the computation of optical flow.

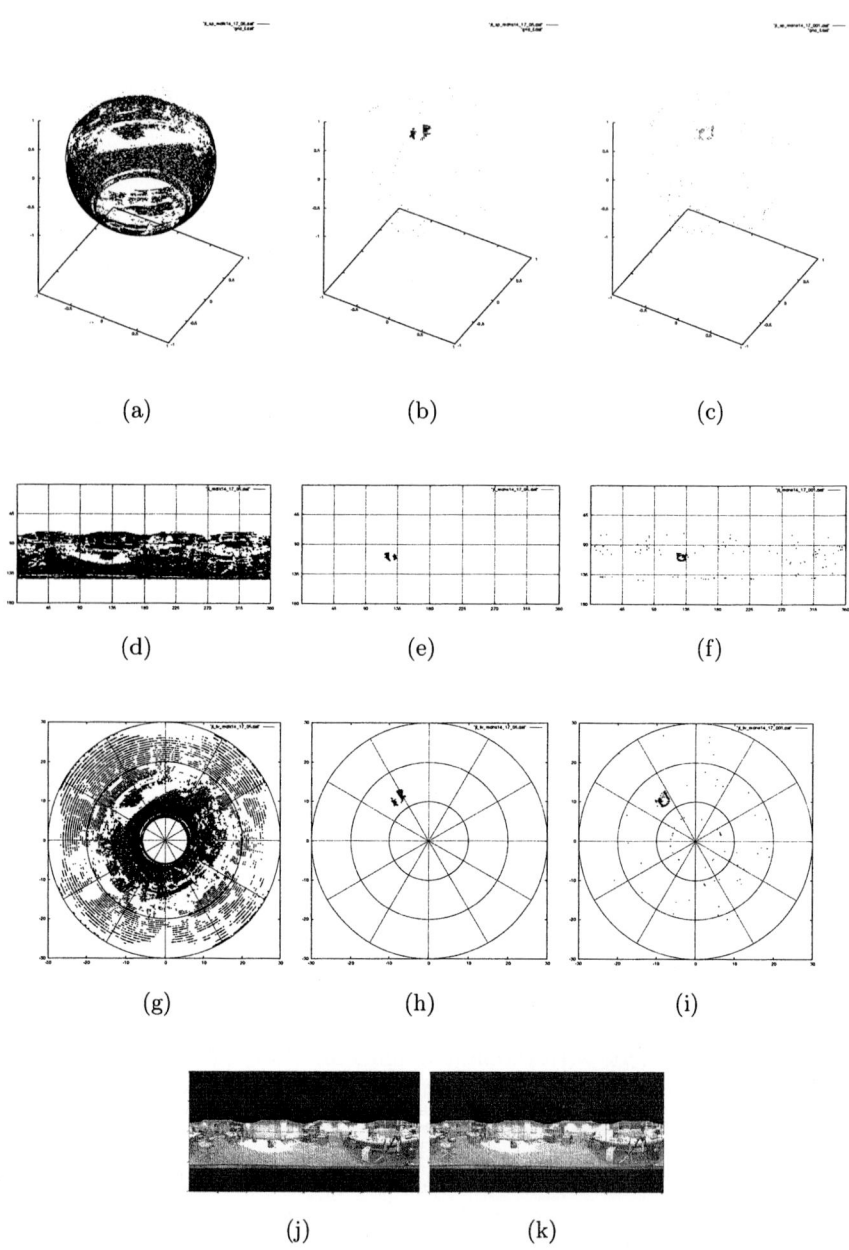

Fig. 1. Results of real world images: (a), (b), and (c) are spherical expressions of computed by the Lucas-Kanade criterion, the Horn-Schunck criterion, and the Nagel-Enkelmann criterion, respectively. The thresholds for (a), (b), and (c) are 0.5, 0.5 and 0.01 pixels, respectively. (d), (e), and (f), and (g), (h), and (i) are cylindrical expressions of (a), (b), and (c), and images observed from the north poles. (j) and (k) are a pair of successive cylindrical images of a sequence of spherical images.

3 Boundary Detection on the Unit Sphere

Setting $v(\theta,\phi) = (\dot\theta(\theta,\phi), \dot\phi(\theta,\phi))^\top$, for an image $I(\theta,\phi)$ on the unit sphere, the minimisation criterion of the gradient vector flow (GVF) [13] is expressed as

$$J_{GVF}(\phi,\theta) = \int_0^\theta \int_0^{2\pi} \mu(|v|_2^2) + |\nabla_S I(\theta,\phi)|^2 |v - \nabla_S I(\theta,\phi)|^2 \sin\theta d\theta d\phi. \quad (15)$$

The GVF allows us to detect the boundary of gray-valued images [13]. Therefore, the criterion of eq. (15) provides a boundary-detection algorithm for images on the unit sphere. The Euler-Lagrange equations which minimise this functional are

$$\mu\nabla_S \cdot \nabla_S \dot\theta - (\dot\theta - I_\theta)(I_\theta^2 + \frac{1}{\sin^2\theta}I_\phi^2) = 0,$$

$$\mu\nabla_S \cdot \nabla_S \dot\phi - (\dot\phi - \frac{1}{\sin\theta}I_\phi)(I_\theta^2 + \frac{1}{\sin^2\theta}I_\phi^2) = 0. \quad (16)$$

The solutions are computed using the system of the diffusion-reaction equations on the sphere,

$$\frac{\partial}{\partial t}\dot\theta = \mu\nabla_S \cdot \nabla_S\dot\theta - (\dot\theta - I_\theta)(I_\theta^2 + \frac{1}{\sin^2\theta}I_\phi^2),$$

$$\frac{\partial}{\partial t}\dot\phi = \mu\nabla_S \cdot \nabla_S\dot\phi, -(\dot\phi - \frac{1}{\sin\theta}I_\phi)(I_\theta^2 + \frac{1}{\sin^2\theta}I_\phi^2). \quad (17)$$

We show numerical examples of the boundary detection for synthetic data on a sphere. In Figure 2 (a) and (b) show the cylindrical expression of synthetic images on the sphere. (c) and (d) are the cylindrical expression of the boundaries extracted using the gradient field flow of images (a) and (b), respectively. (e) and (f) are images observed from north poles and (g) and (h) are boundaries on the spheres. We set the parameters as shown in table 2. These results show that our method extracts the boundary of a binary pattern on a sphere.

Table 2. Discretisation Parameters for the Computation of GVF

Reguralisation parameter	μ	1
Grid pitch	$\Delta\theta$	0.25°
Grid pitch	$\Delta\phi$	0.25°
Grid size	$(\phi \times \theta)$	1440 × 360
Discretisation pitch	$\Delta\tau$	0.002
Iteration time		2000

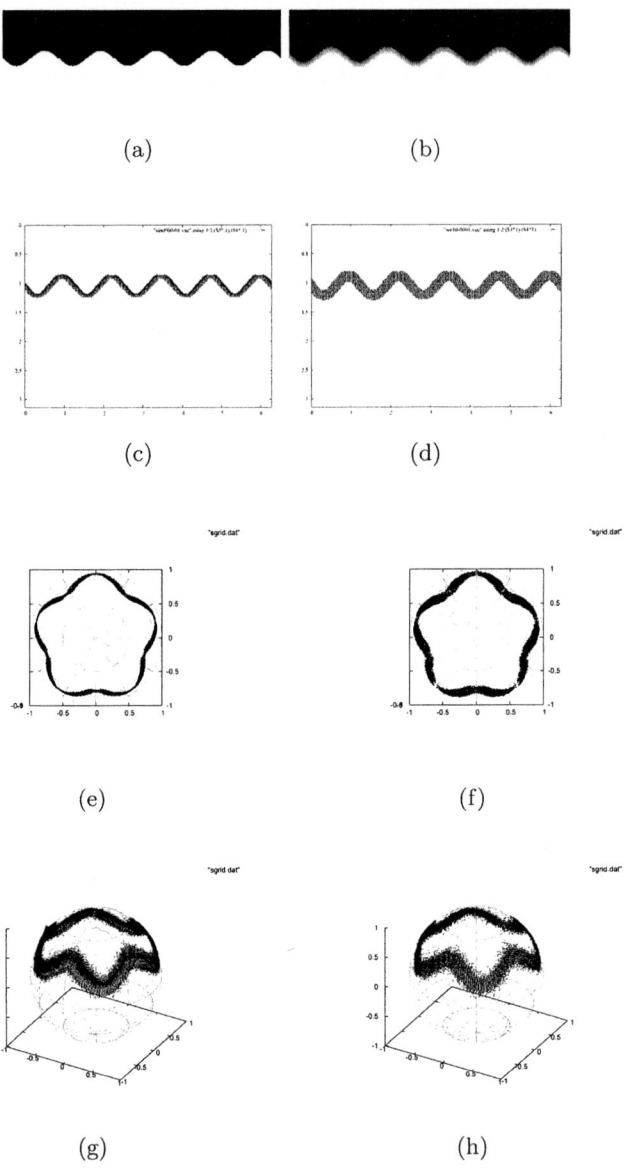

Fig. 2. Numerical results of the boundary extraction by the gradient vector flow. (a) and (b) show the cylindrical expression of synthetic images on the sphere. (c) and (d) are the cylindrical expression of the boundaries extracted the gradient field flow of images (a) and (b), respectively. (e) and (f) are images observed from north poles and (g) and (h) are boundaries on the spheres. (a) and (b) are binary and gray-value images, respectively on the sphere.

4 Conclusions

We have introduced some examples for image analysis on the sphere, which are required from the context of robot vision. Since, the Hamiltonian-minimisation-based variational methods for image analysis provide a coordinate-free expression for the image analysis, our idea and extension of image analysis are applicable to wide ranges of new problems, which would be interested in robot vision and image analysis.

References

1. Zdunkowski, W., Bott, A., *Dynamics of the Atmosphere*, Cambridge University Press, 2003.
2. Morel, J.-M., Solimini,.S., *Variational Methods in Image Segmentation*, Rirkhaäuser, 1995.
3. Osher, S., Paragios, N., eds., *Geometric Level Set Methods in Imaging, Vision, and Graphics*, Springer-Verlag 2003.
4. Nelson, R. C., Aloimonos, J., Finding motion parameters from spherical flow fields (or the advantage of having eyes in the back of your head), Biological Cybernetics, **58**, 261-273, 1988.
5. Fermüller, C., Aloimonos, J., Ambiguity in structure from motion: sphere versus plane, IJCV. **28**, 137-154, 1998.
6. Baker, S. Nayer, S., A theory of single-viewpoint catadioptric image formation International Journal of Computer Vision, **35**, 175-196 1999.
7. Geyer, C., Daniilidis, K., Catadioptric projective geometry, International Journal of Computer Vision, **45**, 223-243, 2001.
8. Neuman, T. R., Modeling insect compound eyes: Space-variant spherical vision LNCS, **2525**, 360-367, 2002.
9. Horn, B. K. P. and Schunck, B. G., Determining optical flow, Artificial Intelligence, **17**, 185-204, 1981.
10. Barron, J. L. Fleet, D. J., Beauchemin, S. S., Performance of optical flow techniques, International Journal of Computer Vision, **12**, 43-77, 1994.
11. Imiya, A., Iwawaki, K., Voting method for subpixel flow detection, Pattern Recognition Letters, **24**, 197-214, 2003.
12. Nagel, H.-H., On the estimation of optical flow:Relations between different approaches and some new results, Artificial Intelligence, **33**, 299-324, 1987.
13. Xu, C., Prince, J. L., Generalized gradient vector flow external forces for active contours, Signal Processing, **71**, 131-139, 1998.
14. Xu, C., Prince, J.L., Gradient vector flow: A new external force for snakes, Proc. CVPR 97, 66-71, 1997.

Iterative Stereo Reconstruction from CCD-Line Scanner Images

Ralf Reulke[1], Georgy Gimel'farb[2], and Susanne Becker[3]

[1] Inst. for Transport Research, German Aerospace Centre (DLR), Berlin, Germany
Ralf.Reulke@dlr.de
[2] Dept. of Computer Science, Tamaki Campus, Univ. of Auckland, New Zealand
g.gimelfarb@auckland.ac.nz
[3] Inst. for Photogrammetry (IFP), University of Stuttgart, Germany
susanne.becker@ifp.uni-stuttgart.de

Abstract. Digital photogrammetric processing of aerial and space stereo images acquired with CCD-line scanners is widely used in today's remote sensing, surveying, and mapping of the Earth's surface. Because of considerable geometric distortions due to movements of a scanner platform, the acquired images have to be corrected before processing. A conventional approach consists of sequential correction and terrain reconstruction stages. Its main drawback is that the former stage loses calibration information for restoring terrain model in a world co-ordinate frame, so that an extra processing is necessary to restore this information. We propose a more flexible approach iteratively combining both the stages. Experiments confirm that such processing holds much promise for photogrammetric processing of the line scanner stereo images.

1 Introduction

Digital photogrammetric terrain reconstruction from space and aerial digital images occupies a prominent place in modern remote sensing, surveying, and mapping of the Earth's surface. At present only scanners with digital CCD-line sensors [5] can compete by spatial resolution and field of view with conventional photogrammetric photocameras. But in contrast to these latter or a CCD frame camera, the line scanner does not form central perspective projections assumed in traditional photogrammetry. Also, scanner attitude disturbances due to continuous movements of an aerial or space platform result in heavy geometric distortions comparing to photographic images. Hence, terrain reconstruction from the line scanner images differs much from traditional photogrammetric stereo, e.g. the distortions have to be eliminated or at least reduced before the further processing. Fortunately, today's inertial and GPS measurements combined with sophisticated signal processing provide precise estimates of dynamics of the sensor platform for correcting the images up to a sub-pixel level.

Conventional stereo processing of line scanner images begins with an attitude correction assuming a mean-altitude flat (horizontal) planar terrain. Then to reconstruct actual terrain, one-to-one correspondence between 3D co-ordinates of each binocularly visible terrain point and 2D co-ordinates of corresponding points in two or more corrected stereo images is established with stereo matching. The matching specifies quantitatively (and visually) similar regions that may represent the same terrain parts under their admissible geometric and photometric distortions. The main disadvantage of such two-stage approach is that the correction stage loses information about spatial camera positions and orientations and an additional processing is necessary later on to restore connections between the original and corrected stereo data.

We propose a more flexible iterative approach to terrain reconstruction from stereo pairs obtained by three-line scanners such as ADS40 [7] or WAOSS / WAAC [8]. It is built upon the common observation that the attitude correction assuming a constant-height planar terrain produces stereo images which become "quasi-epipolar" under low spatial resolution. Epipolar geometry of binocular viewing relates 3D co-ordinates of each visible surface point to differences between 2D x- and y-co-ordinates of two corresponding image points (pixels) called x- and y-disparities, or parallaxes. True epipolar geometry means zero y-disparities, and we call images quasi-epipolar if their y-disparities are relatively small, e.g. less than one pixel. This feature is considerably weaker than the true epipolar geometry but still allows for examining stereo correspondences only along rows with the same y-coordinate of pixels in both the images. A digital x-parallax map (DPM) for computing a digital terrain model (DTM) can be easily found with an appropriate row-by-row stereo matching of the quasi-epipolar images. Stereo matching is an ill-posed mathematical problem because the same stereo images are produced by a large number of different 3D surfaces due to partial occlusions of and homogeneous textures on the surfaces. The matching usually involves regularisation to bring the reconstructed DTM closer to visually perceived terrain. Because the obtained DTM allows for more precise image correction, the quasi-epipolarity persists in the corrected higher-resolution images.

Section 2 below describes a general framework of correcting the line scanner images. Our iterative terrain reconstruction and image correction algorithm based on fast symmetric dynamic programming stereo is presented in Section 3. Experimental results with images obtained by the WAOSS/ WAAC airborne scanner and concluding remarks are given in Section 4.

2 Correction of the Line Scanner Imagery

We assume that interior calibration parameters of a line scanner such as its focal length f and principal image point (x_0, y_0) as well as parameters of optical distortions are determined by classical (laboratory) measurements or directly from image data during the correction process. Spatial attitude of a line scanner (in terms of its optical centre position and optical axis orientation) is changing for each captured scan-line along a flight path in accord with varying roll, pitch, and yaw angles, flight velocity, and acceleration of an aerial or space platform. Thus each initial image formed from the successive scan-lines has considerable geometric distortions comparing to a central projection of the same terrain. With no precise knowledge of the platform movements, it is impossible to calculate geometric relationships for the image points. Typically, spatial positions and attitudes of the scanner are measured with a very precise combined global positioning (GPS) and inertial device like Applanix POS-AV 410 being an integral part of the digital line scanner Leica Geosystems ADS40. After post-processing, its absolute and relative positional error is 5–30 cm, and roll (ψ), pitch (θ), and yaw (ϕ) angular errors are $\delta\phi = \delta\theta = 0.008°$, and $\delta\psi = 0.015°$.

To exclude the distortions, an attitude correction using either accurate onboard measurements or posterior estimates of the scanner attitude for each scanline has to be included into photogrammetric processing of the initial images. Generally, the precise correction can be obtained only by using both the accurate DTM and the accurately measured scanner attitudes. But usually the DTM has to be reconstructed just from these images by stereo matching. Figure 1,a presents an extreme example of how the images acquired by an airborne CCD-line scanner could be distorted by the platform motions. White and black lines along the left side indicate changes of the image roll and pitch, respectively, due to the actual aircraft movements. It is evident that horizontal and vertical image disturbances relate directly to these latter. In this case it is extremely difficult (if at all possible) to perform any traditional photogrammetric image processing, for instance, stereo matching. The same image corrected by assuming terrain is roughly approximated with a horizontal reference plane is shown in Fig. 1,b.

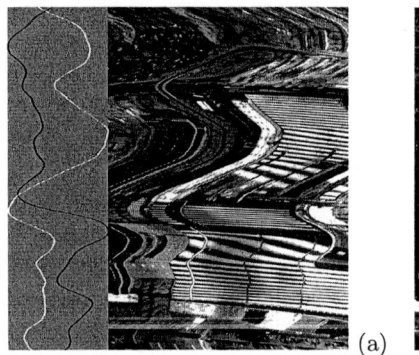
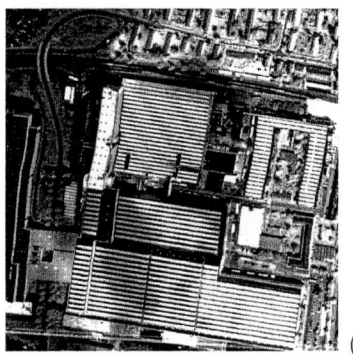

(a) (b)

Fig. 1. Initial distorted image (a) acquired by the line scanner WAAC and its correction (b) by projecting onto the reference plane

Figure 2 illustrates principles of such correction. Pixels of the initial distorted images are back-projected onto an object plane by ray tracing based on the known spatial position and orientation of the scanner for each measured scanline. Each ray represents the line-of-sight of the corresponding sensing element, the ray origin and direction being the optical centre of the scanner and viewing direction of the sensing element, respectively.

Let vectors $\mathbf{X}_n = [X, Y, Z]^\mathsf{T}$ and $\mathbf{X}_0 = [X_0, Y_0, Z_0]^\mathsf{T}$ denote 3D positions of an object point and of the camera (scanner) projection center, respectively, in the world (geographical or navigation) coordinate system. Let $\mathbf{x}_p$ be the point coordinates in the own camera coordinate frame. Let a 3×3 matrix $\mathbf{R}$ with the components $r_{11}...r_{33}$ specify a 3D rotation of the camera coordinate frame into the world coordinate one. The matrix can be expressed in terms of the three photogrammetric orientation, or Euler angles ω, ϕ and κ: $\mathbf{R} = \mathbf{R}_z(\kappa)\mathbf{R}_y(\varphi)\mathbf{R}_x(\omega)$ where each matrix $\mathbf{R}_t(\tau)$ describes the rotation through an angle τ around a co-ordinate axis t. The measured roll, pitch, and yaw platform orientation angles differ from the Euler angles but end up with the same rotation matrix. Generally, a misalignment between the camera and the image coordinate systems have to be corrected, too, in order to accurately relate the 3D image and world coordinates:

$$\mathbf{X}_n = \mathbf{X}_0 + \lambda \mathbf{R}\,(\mathbf{x}_p - \mathbf{x}_0) \qquad (1)$$

where λ is a scaling factor and $\mathbf{x}_0 = [x_0, y_0, f]^\mathsf{T}$ is the projection centre with respect to the image coordinate system. The viewing directions are measured in the camera coordinate system (by calibrating the scanner) and then transformed to the world co-ordinate system using the attitude data. Each ray traces to the position observed by the sensing element in the reference plane. The rays are specified in the world co-ordinate system for the terrain. Let the

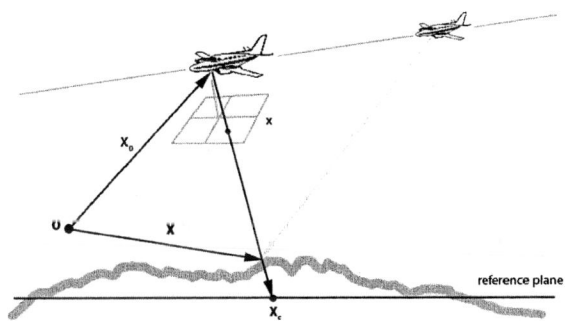

Fig. 2. Projecting an object point onto the reference plane

vector $\mathbf{x}_d = [x, y, z]^\mathsf{T}$ denote the particular image pixel position in the camera coordinate system of the scanner with the focal length f and an offset x_0, y_0 to the perspective center origin. It is easily shown that the position $\mathbf{X}_c = [X_c, Y_c, Z_c]^\mathsf{T}$ of the observed point $\mathbf{r}$ in the horizontal reference plane having a known constant height Z_c is specified with the collinearity equation as follows:

$$X_c = X_0 + (Z_c - Z_0) \frac{r_{11}(x-x_0)+r_{21}(y-y_0)-r_{31}f}{r_{13}(x-x_0)+r_{23}(y-y_0)-r_{33}f}$$
$$Y_c = Y_0 + (Z_c - Z_0) \frac{r_{12}(x-x_0)+r_{22}(y-y_0)-r_{32}f}{r_{13}(x-x_0)+r_{23}(y-y_0)-r_{33}f} \qquad (2)$$

It should be noted that pixel coordinates in the corrected images relate to the 3D object coordinates in a much less straightforward way than in the central image projections. Because of no direct relationships between the corrected and initial coordinates, most of the standard photogrammetric techniques cannot be used for terrain reconstruction, and more adequate techniques taking account of actual intricate links between the image, attitude, and calibration data have to be developed. One possible approach to solve this problem is proposed in [1].

3 Combined Image Correction and DTM Reconstruction

Stereo pairs after the above initial correction procedure differ much from the central-projection images such that acquired by conventional photo cameras or digital matrix cameras. Actually, this procedure is close to a classic orthophoto generation that corrects all relief effects of observed terrain in perspective stereo images to form an orthographic projection superposing the images onto an accurate terrain map. To eliminate geometric deviations of the corrected images from this latter projection, the initial images should be back-projected onto the real terrain model in the world co-ordinate system. Thus to produce the orthoimages, the collinearity relationships of Eq. (2) are inverted for mapping the corresponding grey values from the perspective images onto a raster supporting both terrain and its orthoimage. Because continuous changes of the projection centre in the line scanner images impact heavily the forward terrain-to-image projection, such a backward image-to-terrain projection becomes possible only if image correction and DTM reconstruction are combined.

This suggests an iterative approach to more accurate correction of stereo images acquired by line scanners. It exploits the same pixel-wise backward ray tracing as in Fig. 2 but places each back-projected point on a known DTM. For a true terrain, the process produces an accurate orthoimage. Obviously, its geometric accuracy depends on the accuracy of the DTM and attitude data. Let the initially corrected images forming a stereo pair are represented by two pyramids such that the top-level pair has (almost) no y-disparities in the corresponding image rows. Then a top-level DTM can be reconstructed with an epipolar (i.e. row-to-row) stereo matching. The higher resolution images at the lower pyramids level have also almost no y-disparities of the corresponding pixels after having been corrected by projection onto the higher-level DTM. Thus the same epipolar matching gets a supplementary x-disparity map to refine the current DTM.

The following top-down iterative processing based on the above considerations reconstructs and successively refines the DTM by correcting stereo images at each pyramidal level in accord with the previous-level DTM. It assumes that a stereo pair is converted into two multiple-resolution quadtrees, or bottom-up image pyramids, such that each next pyramid level halves the spatial x- and y-resolution of the preceding level by averaging grey values in non-overlapping 2×2 windows. Each iteration consists of three stages:

1. **Correction:** Images at a current pyramidal level are independently transformed into orthoimages using the current DTM in order to form a stereo pair with only residual x- and y-disparities of the corresponding pixels.
2. **Reconstruction:** A supplementary disparity map is formed by terrain reconstruction from the obtained stereo pair.

3. **DTM refinement:** The supplementary map is combined with the current DTM to refine this latter providing the residual disparity range allows for stereo matching of the higher resolution images from the next pyramid level.

Due to relatively limited (at least, by the current image resolution) geometric distortions, the corrected images are suitable for both visual and computational stereo reconstruction of the supplementary disparity maps. The first stage performs the above attitude correction using the DTM from the previous iteration and the stereo pair of current resolution doubling the resolution at the previous iteration. The corrected pair of the quasi-epipolar higher resolution images is used at the second stage for reconstructing the map of the residual x-disparities. The third stage uses the reconstructed map to refine the higher resolution DTM.

This pyramid-based iterative algorithm for processing large amounts of image data acquired by line scanners assumes that both the images and DTMs at each level can be refined in a relatively small range with respect to the previous level. The attitude correction produces exactly the epipolar images only if the DTM precisely represents the underlying terrain because large height errors disrupt the (quasi)epipolar image structure. Therefore, the first iteration starts with the images of the lowest resolution at the top level of the pyramids ensuring (almost) no y-disparities. Each next iteration doubles the resolution, the number of iterations being equal to the number of the pyramid levels. Each currently reconstructed disparity map refines the DTM in order to correct the higher-resolution images at the next iteration. The iterative refinement of the images and DTM terminates after reaching the initial (bottom-level) image resolution.

Because of the large data volumes to process, our implementation uses the fast symmetric dynamic programming stereo (SDPS) [3] for the row-by-row DTM reconstruction at the first iteration and the like DTM refinement at all other iterations. The implemented SDPS combines the reconstruction of the supplementary x-disparity map and the DTM refinement using the map. At present better reconstruction performance than can be achieved by the SDPS is provided by more sophisticated stereo matching techniques such as graph minimum-cut or belief propagation ones [2,9]. Unfortunately these latter are too computationally complex for typical photogrammetric applications involving large-size stereo pairs. The SDPS comprises a reasonable compromise between the reconstruction quality and rate because it is faster than most of the known techniques and is second only to the best performing ones, e.g., 38.8 s with the mean error of 3.37 pixels and standard deviation of 5.74 pixels with respect to a set of known ground control points for the SDPS comparing to 1320.1 s, 2.79 pixels, and 4.89 pixels, respectively, for the graph minimum-cut algorithm to obtain the DPM of the same urban scene of size 1054×721 under the disparity range $[0, 100]$ [4].

To simplify and accelerate the above DTM reconstruction, the quasi-epipolar lines in the corrected images should be horizontal, i.e. coincide with the image rows, and the overlapping regions should be specified in both the images. To meet the first requirement, the corresponding rows in the images must be oriented along the flight direction. The typical flight path is not straight, but it can be approximated by a straight line using an appropriate coordinate regression.

4 Experimental Results and Conclusions

Figure 3 shows the aerial stereo pair acquired by the line scanner WAAC during the flight in the Rigi region of Switzerland (south of Zurich) on July 23,1996, and the DTM with the linear resolution of 25 m generated with the proposed iterative algorithm. One more example of correcting the backward – nadir stereo pair of images acquired by WAAC is shown in Fig. 4. The ground test objects on these latter images confirm the accuracy of the process.

These and other experiments show that the proposed combined iterative DTM and orthophoto generation from CCD-line scanner stereo images notably improves photogrammetric quality of the reconstructed DTMs. Our approach needs no knowledge about how the attitude corrected images on a plane relate to the original ones in accord with the interior and exterior orientation data which is necessary for their conventional photogrammetric processing. Also it produces very fast a first approximation of the DTM due to the combined image correction and epipolar stereo matching. Therefore this approach is also feasible to mutually register on a very early processing level the spectral and panchromatic channels of a line scanner that have different positions on the focal plane and different view angles.

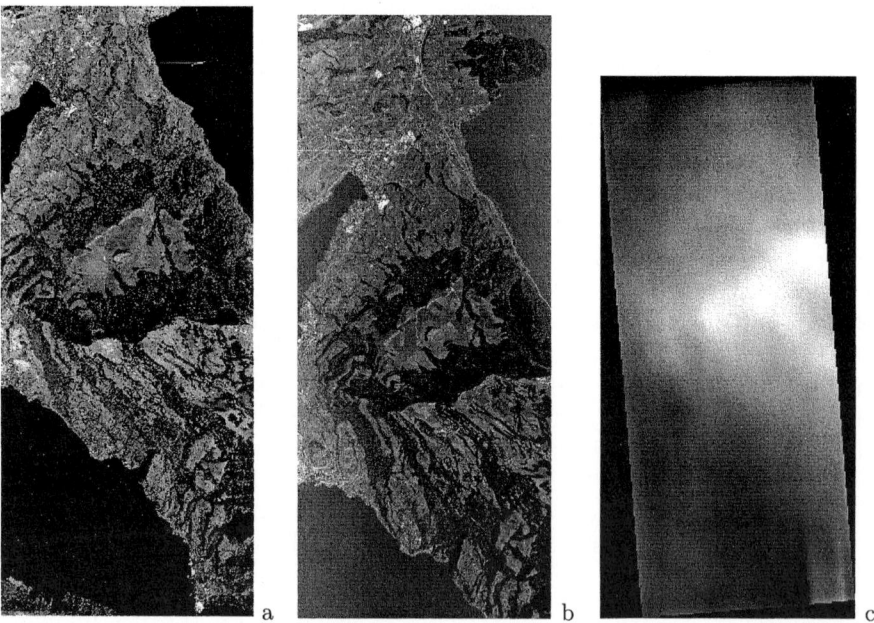

Fig. 3. Backward (a) and nadir (b) images of the flight over the Rigi region (23rd July 1997) and the generated DTM (c)

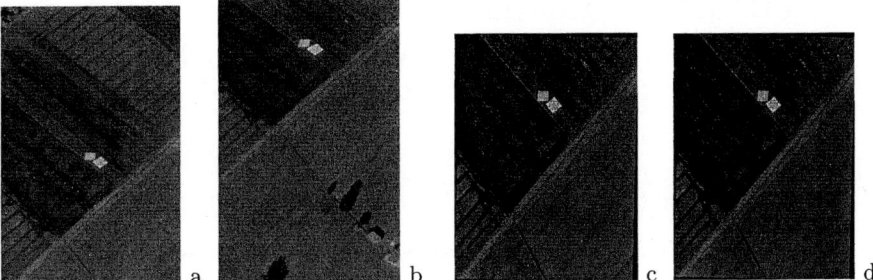

Fig. 4. Uncorrected backward – nadir (a,b) vs corrected (c,d) stereo pair 1239PAN with calibrated rectangular ground test objects

References

1. Börner, A., and Reulke, R., On-line processing of stereo data of a CCD-line scanner, *Int. Archives of Photogrammetry and Remote Sensing*, Vol. 32, Part I, pp. 137–140, 1998.
2. Boykov, Yu., Veksler, O., and Zabih, R., Fast approximate energy minimization via graph cuts, *Proc. 7th Int. Conf. on Computer Vision (ICCV 1999), Kerkyra, Corfu, Greece, Sept. 20–25, 1999*, IEEE Computer Soc. Press: Los Alamitis, pp. 377–384, 1999.
3. Gimel'farb, G., Probabilistic regularisation and symmetry in binocular dynamic programming stereo, *Pattern Recognition Letters*, Vol. 23, pp. 431–442, 2002.
4. Liu, J., and Gimel'farb, G., Accuracy of stereo reconstruction by minimum cut, symmetric dynamic programming, and correlation, *Proc. Image and Vision Computing New Zealand 2004 Conf., The Gaiety Hall, Akaroa, New Zealand, 21–23 Nov. 2004*, Landcare Research: Lincoln, pp. 65–70, 2004.
5. Reulke, R., Film-based and digital sensor - Augmentation or change in paradigm? *Photogrammetric Week '03* (D. Fritsch, ed.), Wichmann: Karlsruhe, p. 41–52, 2003.
6. Reulke, R., and Scheele, M., CCD-line digital imager for photogrammetry in architecture. *Int. Archives of Photogrammetry and Remote Sensing*, Vol. 32, Part 5C1B, pp. 195–201, 1997.
7. Sandau, R., Braunecker, B., Driescher, H., Eckardt, A., Hilbert, S., Hutton, J., Kirchhofer, W., Lithopoulos, E., Reulke, R., and Wicki, S., Design principles of the LH Systems ADS40 airborne digital sensor, *Int. Archives of Photogrammetry and Remote Sensing*, Vol. 33, Part B1, pp. 258–265, 2000.
8. Sandau, R., and Eckardt, A., The stereo camera family WAOSS/WAAC for spaceborne/air-borne applications, *ISPRS*, Vol. 31, Part B1, Commission I, pp. 170-175, 1996.
9. Sun, J., Zheng, N. N., and Dshum, H. Y., Stereo matching using belief propagation, *IEEE Trans. on Pattern Analysis and Machine Intelligence*, Vol. 25, pp. 787–800, 2003.
10. Tempelmann, U., Börner, A., Chaplin, B., Hinsken, L., Mykhalevych, B., Miller, S., Recke, U., Reulke, R., and Uebbing, R., Photogrammetric software for the LH Systems ADS40 Airborne Digital Sensor, *Int. Archives of Photogrammetry and Remote Sensing*, Vol. 33, Part B2, pp. 552–559, 2000.

Content-Based Image Retrieval Using Color and Pattern Histogram Adaptive to Block Classification Characteristics

Tae-Su Kim, Seung-Jin Kim, and Kuhn-Il Lee

School of Electrical Engineering and Computer Science,
Kyungpook National University,
1370, Sankyug-Dong, Buk-Gu, Daegu, 702-701, Korea
{kts1101, starksjin}@ee.knu.ac.kr, kilee@knu.ac.kr

Abstract. We propose a new content-based image retrieval method using the color and pattern histogram that is adaptive to the block classification characteristics. In the proposed method, the color and pattern feature vectors are extracted according to the characteristics of the block classification after dividing an image into the blocks with a fixed size. Specifically, the adaptive representative color histograms are calculated according to the statistical characteristics of the classified block and the directional pattern histograms are extracted by performing the directional pattern classification. Experimental results show that the proposed method can outperform the conventional methods as regards the precision.

1 Introduction

Recent years have seen a rapid increase in the volume of digital media such as image, audio, and video. Also, users that store and transmit such information are on the increase. In particular, efficient searching and retrieval methods for digital image have been proposed due to the spread of digital camera and the growth of the Internet. A general framework of image retrieval is divided into text-based image retrieval system and content-based image retrieval system. Text-based image retrieval system is embodied by representing contents of the image using text such as the keywords or sentences. In this system, the same image can be differently annotated because contents of the image are represented according to the subjective perception of the classifier. Also, this system has difficulties in manual annotation in the case of a vast database. Content-based image retrieval (CBIR) extracts the feature vectors from visual information of the image such as color, texture, and shape. This system is more objective than text-based image retrieval system because the feature vectors are extracted without the subjective perception of the classifier. Also, it is automatic annotation in extracting the feature vectors. Consequently, many CBIR methods have been proposed as efficient retrieval methods [1]-[9].

Swain et al. [1] proposed a CBIR method using a color histogram, which is robust to rotation and a change of image size, as it extracts the global color distribution. However, in the case of a vast database volume, different images can have a similar color histogram because it does not include any spatial correlation. Huang et al. [2] proposed a CBIR method using a color correlogram which is a table indexed by color pairs that combine a color histogram and the spatial correlation. Therefore, this method is superior to the method using only a histogram because it considers the spatial correlation. Recently, many methods that combine color, texture, and shape features have been proposed because color information cannot represent overall visual information of images. Qiu et al. [3] proposed a CBIR method that derived two content description features, one termed a block color co-occurrence matrix and the other block pattern histogram. However, it extracts two representative colors regardless of block statistical characteristics. In addition, it requires many training images and additional storage space for a codebook. Nezamabadi-pour et al. [4] proposed a histogram of uni-color for uniform block, a histogram of bi-color for non-uniform block, and a histogram of directional changes in intensity gradient. However, it does not represent completely the color features for the block with various colors because it extracts two representative colors for even all complex block. Therefore, we propose a new CBIR method using an adaptive representative color histogram and a directional pattern histogram.

We divide an image into the blocks and classify the blocks into three classes, such as the flat blocks, smooth blocks, and complex blocks, according to the block variance. In the classified blocks, the adaptive representative color histogram is calculated as the color feature, according to the block characteristics. Also, a directional pattern feature is extracted by calculating a histogram of maximum direction among intensity directional changes. Simulation results show that the proposed method is superior to conventional methods as regards a precision.

2 Proposed Retrieval Method

A block diagram of the general CBIR system is shown in Fig. 1. When the user selects a query image, the feature vectors are automatically extracted and the retrieved images shown in a descending order of similarity. A block diagram for the proposed feature vector extraction process among the total retrieval system is shown in Fig. 2. In the proposed method, color and pattern features are extracted adaptively according to block classification characteristics.

2.1 Adaptive Color Feature Vector Extraction

The intensity average $I(i,j)$ in the location (i,j) of the RGB color image with the size $N_v \times N_h$ is defined as

$$I(i,j) = \frac{I^r(i,j) + I^g(i,j) + I^b(i,j)}{3} \qquad (1)$$

The intensity average **I** has blocks **B** with the size $(N_v \times N_h)/(N_n \times N_m)$ when an image is divided into a fixed size $N_n \times N_m$. The block $B_{k,l}$ in the block

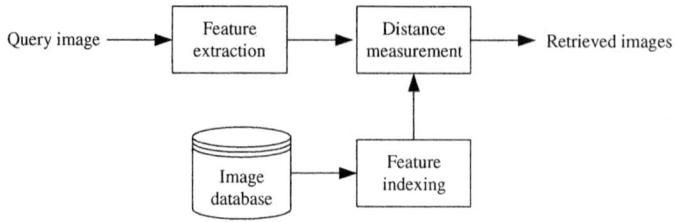

Fig. 1. Block diagram of general content-based image retrieval system

location (k, l), according to the block variance $\sigma_{k,l}$ of $I_{k,l}$, is classified into three classes $\mathbf{C_c} = \{cc_l, cc_m, cc_h\}$ where $cc_l, cc_m,$ and cc_h are classes that represent flat, smooth, and complex blocks which satisfy

$$cc_l = \{\mathbf{B}|\sigma_{k,l} < T_1\} \qquad (2)$$

$$cc_m = \{\mathbf{B}|T_1 \leq \sigma_{k,l} < T_2\} \qquad (3)$$

$$cc_h = \{\mathbf{B}|T_2 \leq \sigma_{k,l}\} \qquad (4)$$

For the cc_l class, as the class has little color change within block, the color feature is represented as one representative color $LM = \{mr, mg, mb\}$ where LM indicates the block average for each RGB image. For the cc_m class, as the class has smooth color change within block, the color feature is represented as one representative color pair $MM_b = \{mr_b, mg_b, mb_b\}$ and $MM_d = \{mr_d, mg_d, mb_d\}$ where MM_b are the average of brighter pixels than the block average LM, while MM_d the average of darker pixels. For the cc_h class, the color feature cannot be represented as one or one color pair, as the class is complex block with various colors. Therefore, the feature vector of two color pairs is extracted. Four representative averages HM_b, HM_d, SM_b, and SM_d are calculated by comparing each pixels with LM, MM_b, and MM_d. HM_b is the average of brighter pixels than MM_b, HM_d the average of pixels between LM and MM_b, SM_b the average of pixels between LM and MM_d, and SM_d is the average of darker pixels than MM_d. After extracting all representative color and color pairs, color quantization is performed and a histogram $\mathbf{H_c}$ is calculated.

2.2 Pattern Feature Vector Extraction

The intensity directional change pattern of each block is classified as six classes to extract the pattern feature as shown in Fig. 3. The pattern class $\mathbf{C_p}$ is defined as $\mathbf{C_p} = \{cp_l, cp_{ch}, cp_{cv}, cp_{d1}, cp_{d2}, cp_{cr}\}$ where cp_l is no directional flat block, cp_{ch} the horizontal directional block, cp_{cv} the vertical directional block, cp_{d1} the 45 degree directional block, cp_{d2} the 135 degree directional block, and cp_{cr} no directional complex random block. Because the cc_l is the flat block, it is automatically classified as no directional flat block. For cc_m and cc_h, the

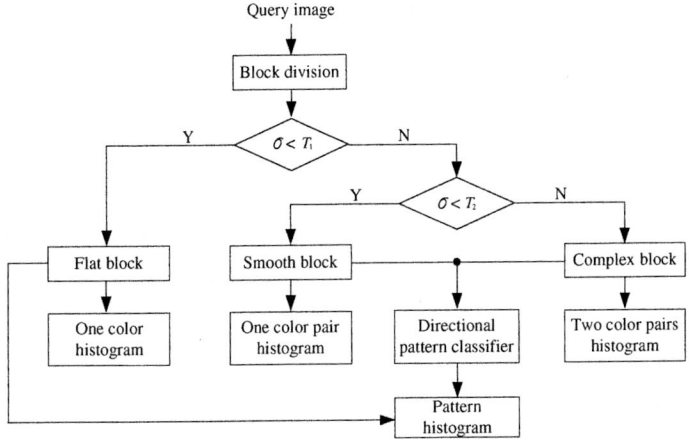

Fig. 2. Block diagram of the proposed feature vector extraction

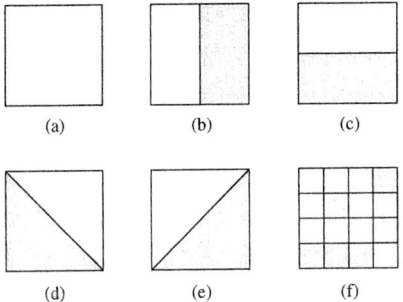

Fig. 3. Directional pattern with (a) non-directional flat block cp$_l$, (b) horizontal directional block cp$_{ch}$, (c) vertical directional block cp$_{cv}$, (d) 45 degree directional block cp$_{d1}$, (e) 135 degree directional block cp$_{d2}$, and (f) no directional complex random block cp$_{cr}$ for pattern feature vector extraction

directional pattern classification is performed by calculating the intensity directional change $G = \{G_h, G_v, G_{d1}, G_{d2}\}$ as shown in Fig. 3. After calculating four directional changes, the directional pattern is decided as the direction with the maximum value among four directional changes. For example, the vertical directional change pattern cp$_{cv}$ is defined as

$$cp_{cv} = \{\mathbf{B}|max(G_h, G_v, G_{d1}, G_{d2}) = G_v\} \tag{5}$$

Meanwhile, cc$_m$ and cc$_h$ are decided as no directional complex random block cp$_{cr}$ when the directional pattern is not dominated as one direction. Finally, the pattern feature vector is extracted by calculating a histogram H_p of the directional pattern.

3 Experimental Results

Experiments were conducted to evaluate the performance of the proposed method. The database included one thousand JPEG encoded color test images sized 384×256 or 256×384 [4], [6]. It consists of ten classes as shown in Table 1. The distance measure $D(q,r)$ between the query images q and the images r in the database were used as

$$D(q,r) = \lambda_1 (H_c(q) - H_c(r)) + \lambda_2 (H_p(q) - H_p(r)) \tag{6}$$

where λ_1 and λ_2 represent weighting factors for the color and pattern respectively. For the equal weighing factor, we determined $\lambda_1 = \lambda_2$. The image was divided into size 4×4 blocks and the thresholds T_1 and T_2 were determined experimentally. The RGB color space was transformed into the HSV (hue, saturation, and value) space and it was quantized into 54 levels with 6 levels of hue, 3 levels of saturation, and 3 levels of value. As an objective measurement for evaluation, the precision P was used. The precision calculates the number of images that is included in the same class with the query images among the retrieved images and it is represented as

$$P_k = \frac{A_k}{A_k + B_k} \tag{7}$$

where A_k and B_k are the number of image included and not included in same class with the query images respectively. The rank k has ten interval ranges from ten to one hundred. The proposed method was compared with two conventional methods, one is block color histogram and the other is [4]. Fig. 4 shows some of query image and retrieved images. The precision of proposed method is 4.50~7.81% higher than block color histogram and 2.80~3.77% higher than [4] as shown in Table 2.

Table 1. Image categories for experiment

Class number	Class name
1	Africa people and villages
2	Beach
3	Buildings
4	Buses
5	Dinosurs
6	Elephants
7	Flowers
8	Horses
9	Mountains and glaciers
10	Food

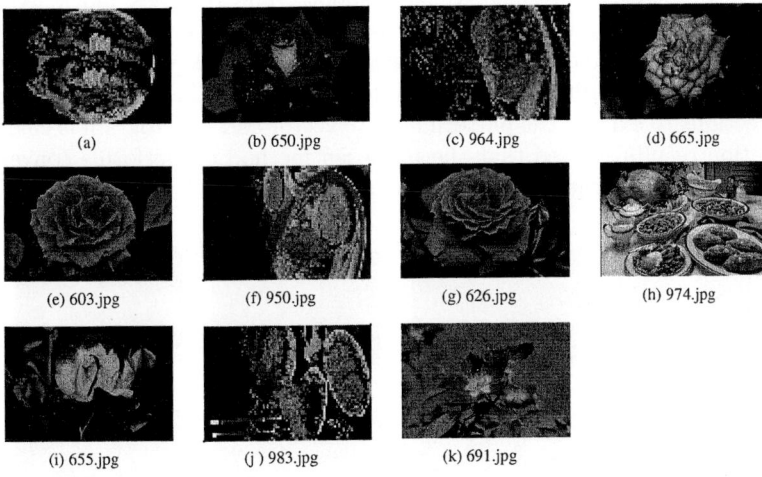

Fig. 4. (a) Query image and retrieved images from (b) 650.jpg of rank 1 to (k) 691.jpg of rank 10 ranked in a descending order of similarity using a Histogram

Table 2. Precision of retrieved images according to rank

Rank	Precision [%]		
	Histogram	Nezamabadi-pour's method [4]	Proposed method
10	67.76	72.63	75.48
20	63.00	68.01	70.81
30	59.69	64.41	67.42
40	57.02	61.07	64.18
50	54.53	58.11	61.46
60	52.18	55.16	58.92
70	50.15	52.68	56.38
80	48.30	50.30	53.93
90	76.64	48.04	51.59
100	44.94	45.97	49.43

4 Conclusions

We proposed a new CBIR method by using the color and pattern histogram that is adaptive to the block classification characteristics. In the proposed method, an image is divided into blocks to exploit local characteristics and then classified blocks into three classes such as flat, smooth, and complex block. After the block classification, a color histogram is calculated by extracting one color for the flat block, one color pair for the smooth block, and two color pairs for the complex block. In addition, the directional pattern classification is performed for six directions to extract the pattern feature vector and a histogram is calculated. Simulation results showed that the proposed method outperforms conventional methods as regards the precision.

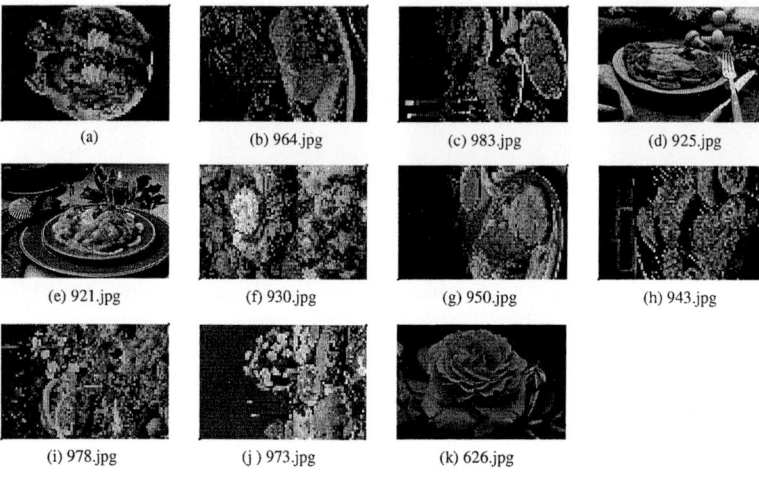

Fig. 5. (a) Query image and retrieved images from (b) 964.jpg of rank 1 to (k) 626.jpg of rank 10 ranked in a descending order of similarity using Nezamabadi-pour's method

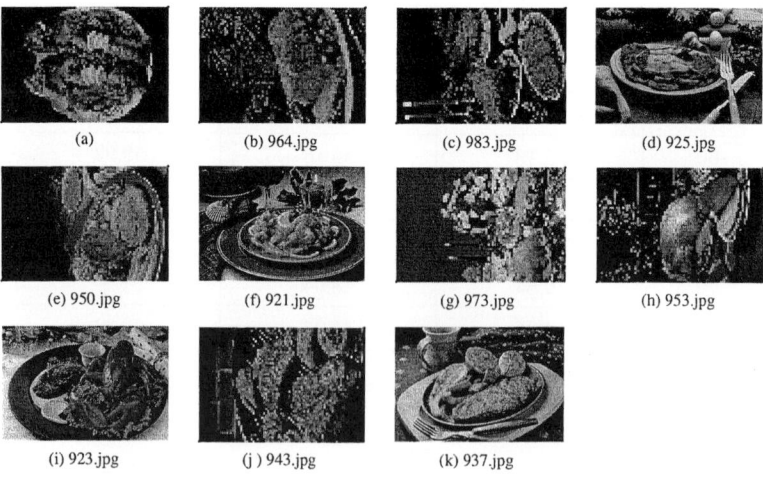

Fig. 6. (a) Query image and retrieved images from (b) 964.jpg of rank 1 to (k) 937.jpg of rank 10 ranked in a descending order of similarity using proposed method

References

[1] Michael J. Swain and Dana H. Ballard: Color indexing. Int. J. Comput. Vis., Vol. 7, No. 1, (1991) 11-32
[2] J. Huang, S. R. Kumar, M. Mitra, Wei-Jing Zhu, and R. Zabih: Image indexing using color correlegram. Proc. CVPR97, (1997) 762-768
[3] Guoping Qiu: Color image indexing using BTC. IEEE Trans. Image Processing, Vol. 12, No. 1, (2003) 93-101
[4] H. Nezamabadi-pour and E. Kabir: Image retrieval using histograms of uni-color and bi-color blocks and directional changes in intensity gradient. Pattern Recogn. Lett., Vol. 25, No. 14, (2004) 1547-1557
[5] Yong Rui, Thomas S. Huang, and Shiu-Fu Chang: Image retrieval: Current techniques, promising directions, and open issues. J. Vis. Commun. Image Represent., Vol. 10, No. 1, (1999) 39-62
[6] J. Z. Wang, Jia Li, and Gio Wiederhold: SIMPLIcity: semantics-integrated matching for picture libraries. IEEE Trans. Pattern Anal. Machine Intell., Vol. 23, No. 9, (2001) 947-963
[7] D. Chen and A. C. Bovik: Visual pattern image coding. IEEE Trans. Commun., Vol. 38, No. 12, (1990) 2137-2146
[8] A. Mojsilovic, H. Hu, and E. Soljanin: Extraction of perceptually important colors and similarity measurement for image matching, retrieval, and analysis. IEEE Trans. Image Processing, Vol. 11, No. 11, (2002) 1238-1248
[9] S. Sural, G. Quin, and S. Pramanik: Segmentation and histogram generation using HSV color space for image retrieval. Proc. of ICIP, Vol. 2, No. 2, (2002) 589-592

Commute Times for Graph Spectral Clustering

Huaijun Qiu and Edwin R. Hancock

Department of Computer Science, University of York, York, YO10 5DD, UK

Abstract. This paper exploits the properties of the commute time to develop a graph-spectral method for image segmentation. Our starting point is the lazy random walk on the graph, which is determined by the heat-kernel of the graph and can be computed from the spectrum of the graph Laplacian. We characterise the random walk using the commute time between nodes, and show how this quantity may be computed from the Laplacian spectrum using the discrete Green's function. We explore the application of the commute time for image segmentation using the eigenvector corresponding to the smallest eigenvalue of the commute time matrix.

1 Introduction

Spectral graph theory [2] is concerned with characterising the structural properties of graphs using information conveyed by the eigenvalues and eigenvectors of the Laplacian matrix (the degree matrix minus the adjacency matrix). One of the most important tasks that arises in the analysis of graphs is that of how information flows with time across the edges connecting nodes. This process can be characterised using the heat equation [5]. The solution of the heat equation, or heat kernel, can be found by exponentiating the Laplacian eigensystem over time. The heat kernel contains a considerable amount of information concerning the distribution of paths on the graph. For instance, it can be used to compute the lazy random walk on the nodes of the graph. It may also be used to determine commute times under the random walk between pairs of nodes. An alternative, but closely related, characterisation of the graph is the discrete Green's function which captures the distribution of sources in the heat flow process. Not surprisingly, there is a direct link between commute times and the Green's function [3].

Random walks [14] have found widespread use in information retrieval and structural pattern analysis. For instance, the random walk is the basis of the Page-Rank algorithm which is used by the Googlebot search engine [1]. In computer vision random walks have been used for image segmentation [7] and clustering [10]. More recently both Gori, Maggini and Sarti [4], and, Robles-Kelly and Hancock [9] have used random walks to sort the nodes of graphs for the purposes of graph-matching. However, most of these methods use a simple approximate characterisation of the random walk based either on the leading eigenvector of the transition probability matrix, or equivalently the Fiedler vector of the Laplacian matrix [6]. However, a single eigenvector can not be used to determine more detailed information concerning the random walk such as the distribution of commute times. The aim in this paper is to draw on more detailed information contained within the Laplacian spectrum, and to use the commute time as means of grouping.

A. Gagalowicz and W. Philips (Eds.): CAIP 2005, LNCS 3691, pp. 128–136, 2005.
© Springer-Verlag Berlin Heidelberg 2005

There are two quantities that are commonly used to define the utility in graph-theoretic methods for grouping and clustering. The first of these is the association, which is a measure of total edge linkage within a cluster and is useful in defining clump structure. The second is the cut, which is a measure of linkage between different clusters and can be used to split extraneous nodes from a cluster. Several methods use eigenvectors to extract clusters using the utility measure. Some of the earliest work was done by Scott and Longuet-Higgins [12] who developed a method for refining the block-structure of the affinity matrix by relocating its eigenvectors. At the level of image segmentation, several authors have used algorithms based on the eigenmodes of an affinity matrix to iteratively segment image data. For instance, Sarkar and Boyer [11] have a method which uses the leading eigenvector of the affinity matrix, and this locates clusters that maximise the average association. This method is applied to locating line-segment groupings. The method of Shi and Malik [13], on the other hand, uses the normalized cut which balances the cut and the association. Clusters are located by performing a recursive bisection using the eigenvector associated with the second smallest eigenvalue of the Laplacian (the degree matrix minus the adjacency matrix), i.e. the Fiedler vector. Recently Pavan and Pelillo [8] have shown how the concept of a dominant set can lead to better defined clusters, and can give results that are superior to those delivered by the Shi and Malik algorithm for image segmentation. The dominant set provides a more subtle definition of cluster membership that draws on the mutual affinity of nodes. The method does not rely simply on the affinity between pairs of nodes alone. Here argue that commute time can also capture the affinity properties of nodes in a way that extends beyond the use of pairwise weights.

Graph theoretic methods aim to locate clusters of nodes that minimize the cut or disassociation, while maximizing the association. The commute time has properties that can lead to clusters of nodes that increase both the dissociation and the association. A pair of nodes in the graph will have a small commute time value if one of three conditions is satisfied. The first of these is that they are close together, i.e. the length of the path between them is small. The second case is if the sum of the weights on the edges connecting the nodes is small. Finally, the commute time is small if the pair of nodes are connected by many paths. Hence, the commute time can lead to a finer measure of cluster cohesion than the simple use of edge-weight which underpins algorithms such as the normalized cut [13]. In this respect it is more akin with the method of Pavan and Pelillo [8].

2 Heat Kernel, Lazy Random Walks and Green's Function

Let the weighted graph Γ be the quadruple (V, E, Ω, ω), where V is the set of nodes, E is the set of arcs, $\Omega = \{W_u, \forall u \in V\}$ is a set of weights associated with the nodes and $\omega = \{w_{u,v}, \forall (u,v) \in E\}$ is a set of weights associated with the edges. Further let $T = diag(d_v; v \in V(\Gamma))$ be the diagonal weighted degree matrix with $T_u = \sum_{v=1}^{n} w_{u,v}$. The un-normalized weighted Laplacian matrix is given by $L = T - A$ and the normalized weighted Laplacian matrix is defined to be $\mathcal{L} = T^{-1/2} L T^{-1/2}$, and has elements

$$\mathcal{L}_{uv}(\Gamma) = \begin{cases} 1 & \text{if } u = v \\ -\frac{w_{u,v}}{\sqrt{d_u d_v}} & \text{if } u \neq v \text{ and } (u,v) \in E \\ 0 & \text{otherwise} \end{cases}$$

The spectral decomposition of the normalized Laplacian is $\mathcal{L} = \Phi \Lambda \Phi^T$, where $\Lambda = diag(\lambda_1, \lambda_2, ..., \lambda_{|V|})$ is the diagonal matrix with the ordered eigenvalues as elements satisfying: $0 = \lambda_1 \leq \lambda_2 ... \leq \lambda_{|V|}$ and $\Phi = (\phi_1|\phi_2|....|\phi_{|V|})$ is the matrix with the ordered eigenvectors as columns.

In the paper we are interested in the heat equation associated with the graph Laplacian, i.e. $\frac{\partial \mathcal{H}_t}{\partial t} = -\mathcal{L}\mathcal{H}_t$ where $\mathcal{H}_t$ is the heat kernel and t is time. The solution of the heat-equation is found by exponentiating the Laplacian eigenspectrum i.e. $\mathcal{H}_t = \exp[-t\mathcal{L}] = \Phi \exp[-t\Lambda]\Phi^T$. The heat kernel is a $|V| \times |V|$ matrix, and for the nodes u and v of the graph Γ the element of the matrix is $\mathcal{H}_t(u,v) = \sum_{i=1}^{|V|} \exp[-\lambda_i t]\phi_i(u)\phi_i(v)$.

Now consider the discrete Laplace operator $\Delta = T^{-1/2}\mathcal{L}T^{1/2}$. The Green's function is the left inverse operator of the Laplace operator Δ, defined by $G\Delta(u,v) = I(u,v) - \frac{d_v}{vol}$, where $vol = \sum_{v \in V(\Gamma)} d_v$ is the volume of the graph. A physical interpretation of the Green's function is the temperature at a node in the graph due to a unit heat source applied to the external node. It is related with the heat kernel $\mathcal{H}_t$ in the following manner

$$G(u,v) = \int_0^\infty d_u^{1/2} \left(\mathcal{H}_t(u,v) - \phi_1(u)\phi_1(v)\right) d_v^{-1/2} dt \qquad (1)$$

Here ϕ_1 is the eigenvector associated with eigenvalue 0 and its k-th entry is $\sqrt{d_k/vol}$. Furthermore, the normalized Green's function $\mathcal{G} = T^{-1/2}GT^{1/2}$ is defined as (see [3] page 6(10)),

$$\mathcal{G}(u,v) = \sum_{i=2}^{|V|} \frac{1}{\lambda_i} \phi_i(u)\phi_i(v) \qquad (2)$$

where λ and ϕ are the eigenvalue and eigenvectors of the normalized Laplacian $\mathcal{L}$.

The normalized Green's function is hence the generalized inverse of the normalized Laplacian $\mathcal{L}$. Moreover, it is straightforward to show that $\mathcal{G}\mathcal{L} = \mathcal{L}\mathcal{G} = I - \phi_1 \phi_1^*$, and as a result $(\mathcal{L}\mathcal{G})_{uv} = \delta_{uv} - \frac{\sqrt{d_u d_v}}{vol}$. From equation 2, the eigenvalues of $\mathcal{L}$ and $\mathcal{G}$ have the same sign and $\mathcal{L}$ is positive semidefinite, and so $\mathcal{G}$ is also positive semidefinite. Since $\mathcal{G}$ is also symmetric(see [3] page 4), it follows that $\mathcal{G}$ is a kernel.

3 Commute Time

We note that the *hitting time* $Q(u,v)$ of a random walk on a graph is defined as the expected number of steps before node v is visited, commencing from node u. The *commute time* $CT(u,v)$, on the other hand, is the expected time for the random walk to travel from node u to reach node v and then return. As a result $CT(u,v) = Q(u,v) + Q(v,u)$. The hitting time $Q(u,v)$ is given by [3]

$$Q(u,v) = \frac{vol}{d_v} G(v,v) - \frac{vol}{d_u} G(u,v)$$

where G is the Green's function given in equation 1. So, the commute time is given by

$$CT_{uv} = Q_{uv} + Q_{vu} = \frac{vol}{d_u}G_{uu} + \frac{vol}{d_v}G_{vv} - \frac{vol}{d_u}G_{uv} - \frac{vol}{d_v}G_{vu} \quad (3)$$

As a consequence of (3) the commute time is a metric on the graph. The reason for this is that if we take the elements of G as inner products defined in a Euclidean space, CT will become the norm satisfying: $\|x_i - x_j\|^2 = <x_i - x_j, x_i - x_j> = <x_i, x_i> + <x_j, x_j> - <x_i, x_j> - <x_j, x_i>$.

Substituting the spectral expression for the Green's function into the definition of the commute time, it is straightforward to show that

$$CT(u,v) = vol \sum_{i=2}^{|V|} \frac{1}{\lambda_i} \left(\frac{\phi_i(u)}{\sqrt{d_u}} - \frac{\phi_i(v)}{\sqrt{d_v}} \right)^2 \quad (4)$$

For a regular graph with $d_u = d_v = d$, and the commute time satisfies:

$$CT(u,v) = \frac{vol}{d} \sum_{i=2}^{|V|} \frac{1}{\lambda_i} (\phi_i(u) - \phi_i(v))^2 \quad (5)$$

This expression is important, since in the data clustering and image segmentation literature it is usual to work with an affinity matrix, and the underlying graph is therefore regular for the clustering problem and almost regular for the segmentation problem (boundary pixels have smaller degrees). As a result, the commute time can be taken as a generalisation of the normalized cut since from Equation 5, for a pair of node u and v the commute time depends on the difference of the components of the successive eigenvectors of $\mathcal{L}$. Of the eigenvectors, the Fiedler vector is the most significant since its corresponding eigenvalue λ_2 is the smallest.

4 Commute Times for Grouping

The idea of our segmentation algorithm is to use the spectrum of the commute time matrix for the purposes of grouping. We do this by using the eigenvector corresponding to the smallest eigenvalue to bipartition the graphs recursively.

Our commute time algorithm consists of the following steps:

1. Given an image, or a point set, set up a weighted graph $\Gamma = (V, E)$ where each pixel, or point, is taken as a node and each pair of nodes is connected by an edge. The weight on the edge is assigned according to the similarity between the two node as follows
   – a) for a point-set, the weight between node i and j is set to be $w(i,j) = exp(-d(i,j)/\delta_x)$, where $d(i,j)$ is the Euclidean distance between two points and δ_x controls the scale of the spatial proximity of the points.
   – b) for an image, the weight is:

$$w(i,j) = exp\left(\frac{-\|\mathbf{F}_i - \mathbf{F}_j\|_2}{\delta_I}\right) * \begin{cases} exp\left(\frac{-\|\mathbf{X}_i - \mathbf{X}_j\|_2}{\delta_X}\right) & \text{if } \|\mathbf{X}_i - \mathbf{X}_j\|_2 < r \\ 0 & \text{otherwise} \end{cases} \quad (6)$$

where $\mathbf{F}_i$ is the intensity value at pixel i for a brightness image or the RGB value for a color image.
2. From the weight matrix W we compute the Laplacian $L = T - W$.
3. Then we compute the normalized Green's function using Equation 2 and the eigenspectrum of the normalized Laplacian $\mathcal{L}$.
4. From Equation 3, we compute the commute time matrix CT whose elements are the commute times between each pair of nodes in the graph Γ.
5. Use the eigenvector corresponding to the smallest eigenvalue of the commute time matrix to bipartition th weighted graph.
6. Decide if the current partition should be sub-divided, and recursively repartition the component parts if necessary.

5 Experiments

In this section we experiment with our new spectral clustering method. We commence with examples on synthetic images aimed at evaluating the noise sensitivity of the method. We then provide examples on real world images and compare the performance of our method with that of Shi and Malik.

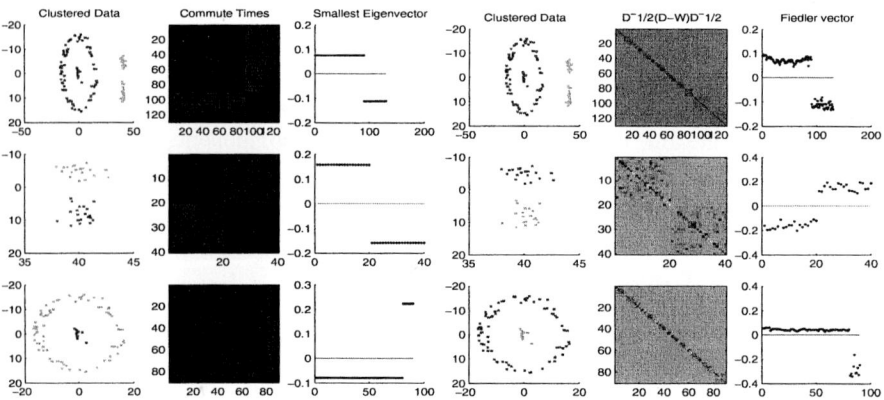

Fig. 1. Clustering examples

Point-set clustering examples: In Figure 1(a) and 1(b) we compare the results for point-set clustering using commute-times and the normalized cut. Here we set $\delta = 1.5$. The sub-figures in both figures are organised as follows. The left-hand column shows the point-sets, the middle column the affinity matrices and right-most column the components of the smallest eigenvector. The first row shows the first bipartition and the successive two rows show the bipartition based on the first partitions. From the figures it is clear that both methods succeeded in grouping the data. However, the commute time method outperforms the normalized cut since its affinity matrix is more block like and the distribution of the smallest eigenvector components is more stable, and its jumps corresponding to the different clusters in the data are larger.

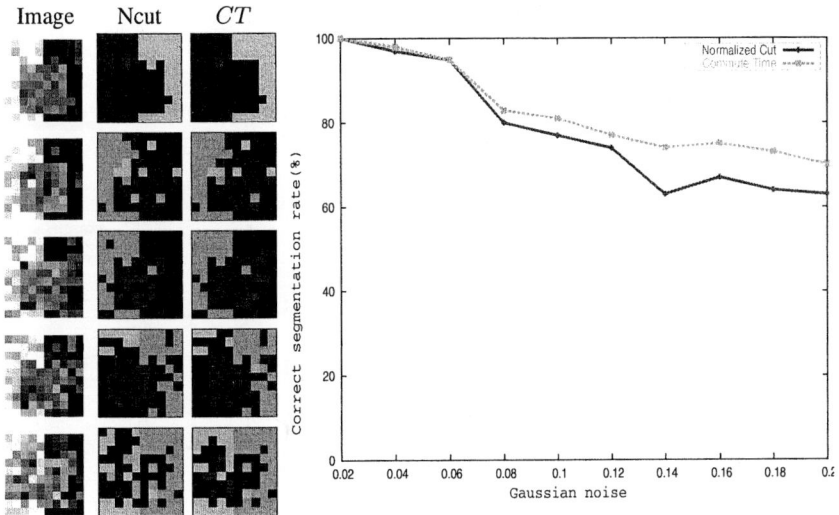

Fig. 2. Method comparison for synthetic image with increasing Gaussian noise

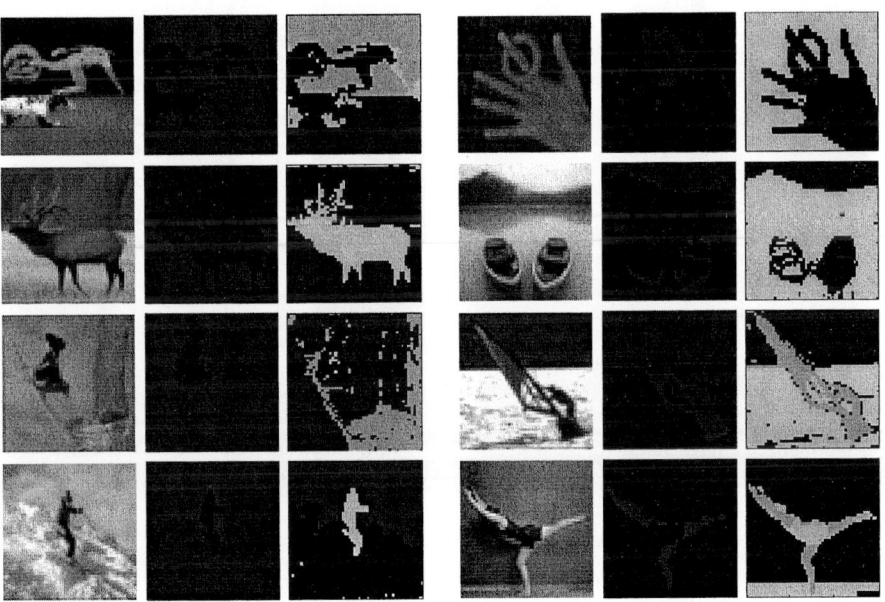

Fig. 3. Real world segmentation examples

Image segmentation: We have compared our new method with that of Shi and Malik [13] on synthetic images subject to additive Gaussian noise. On the left-hand side of Figure 2, we show the results of using these two methods for segmenting a synthetic

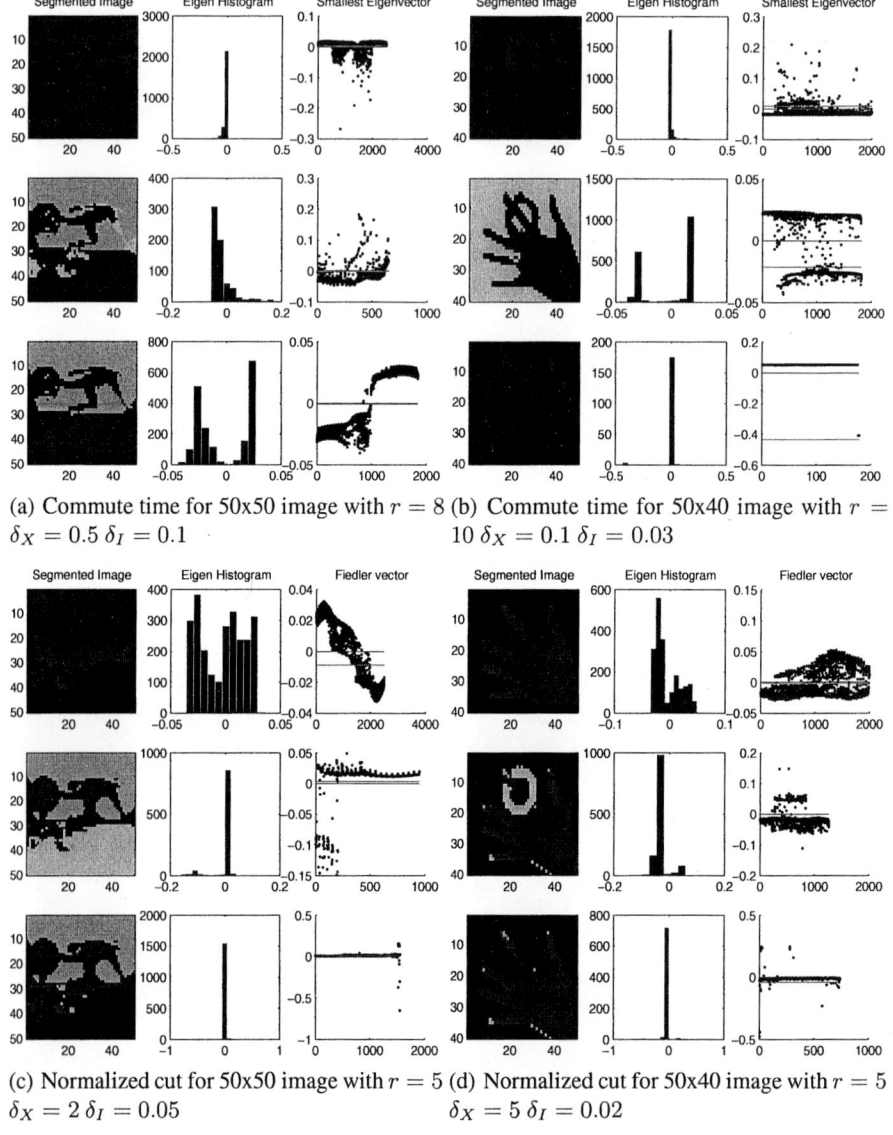

Fig. 4. Detailed segmentation process in comparasion

image composed of 3 rectangular regions with additive Gaussian noise increasing from 0.04 to 0.20 with width 0.04. On the right hand side of Figure 2 we show the fraction of pixels correctly assigned as a function of the noise standard derivation. At the highest noise levels our method outperforms the Shi and Malik method by about 10%.

In Figure 3, we show eight real world images (from the Berkeley image database) with the corresponding segmentation results. The images are scaled to be 50x50 in size and the parameters used for producing the results are $r = 5$, $\delta_I = 0.02$ and $\delta_X = 0.2$.

In each set of the images, the left-most one shows the original image. The middle and right panels show the results from two successive bipartitions.

For two of the real images in Figure 3, we compare our method with the normalized cut in the following sub-figures 4(a),4(b),4(c) and 4(d). The first column of each sub-figure shows the first, second and third bipartitions of the images. The second column shows the histogram of the components of the smallest eigenvector, and the right-hand column the distribution of the eigenvector components. The blue and red lines in the right-hand column respectively correspond to zero and the eigenvector component threshold.

Comparing the results of using the commute time and the normalized cut, it is clear that commute time out performs the normalized cut in both maintaining region integrity and continuity. Another important feature is that once again our eigenvector distribution is more stable and discriminates more strongly between clusters.

6 Conclusion

In this paper we have described how commute time can be computed from the Laplacian spectrum. This analysis relies on the discrete Green's function of the graph, and we have reviewed the properties of Green's function. Two of the most important of these are that the Green's function is a kernel and that the commute time is a metric. We show how commute time can be used for clustering and segmentation. Our future plans involve using the commute times to embed the nodes of the graph in a low dimensional space, and to use the characteristics of the embedded node points for the purposes of graph-clustering.

References

1. S. Brin and L.Page. The anatomy of a large-scale hypertextual Web search engine. *Computer Networks and ISDN Systems*, 30(1–7):107–117, 1998.
2. F.R.K. Chung. *Spectral Graph Theory*. CBMS series 92. American Mathmatical Society Ed., 1997.
3. F.R.K. Chung and S.-T. Yau. Discrete green's functions. In *J. Combin. Theory Ser.*, pages 191–214, 2000.
4. M. Gori, M. Maggini, and L. Sarti. Graph matching using random walks. In *ICPR04*, pages III: 394–397, 2004.
5. R. Kondor and J. Lafferty. Diffusion kernels on graphs and other discrete structures. *19th Intl. Conf. on Machine Learning (ICML) [ICM02].*, 2002.
6. L. Lovász. Random walks on graphs: A survey.
7. M. Meila and J. Shi. A random walks view of spectral segmentation, 2001.
8. M. Pavan and M. Pelillo. A new graph-theoretic approach to clustering and segmentation. In *CVPR03*, pages I: 145–152, 2003.
9. A. Robles-Kelly and E. R. Hancock. String edit distance, random walks and graph matching. *PAMI to appear*, 2005.
10. M. Saerens, F. Fouss, L. Yen, and P. Dupont. The principal components analysis of a graph, and its relationships to spectral clustering. In *LN-AI*, 2004.
11. S. Sarkar and K. L. Boyer. Quantitative measures of change based on feature organization: Eigenvalues and eigenvectors. In *CVPR*, page 478, 1996.

12. G. Scott and H. Longuet-Higgins. Feature grouping by relicalisation of eigenvectors of the proximity matrix. In *BMVC.*, pages 103–108, 1990.
13. J. Shi and J. Malik. Normalized cuts and image segmentation. *IEEE PAMI*, 22(8):888–905, 2000.
14. V. Sood, S. Redner, and D. ben Avraham. First-passage properties of the erdoscrenyi random graph. *J. Phys. A: Math. Gen.*, pages 109–123, 2005.

A New Approach to Camera Image Indexing

Rastislav Lukac and Konstantinos N. Plataniotis

The Edward S. Rogers Sr. Dept. of Electrical and Computer Engineering,
University of Toronto, 10 King's College Road, Toronto, M5S 3G4, Canada
{lukacr, kostas}@dsp.utoronto.ca
http://www.dsp.utoronto.ca/~lukacr

Abstract. This paper presents a color filter array (CFA) image indexing approach. To enhance the functionality of single-sensor consumer electronics such as digital cameras, imaging-enabled mobile phones and wireless personal digital assistants (PDAs), the proposed solution embeds the metadata information to a CFA image using a common discrete cosine transform (DCT) based watermarking scheme. Depending on a consumer electronic device employed, the metadata information can be used to indicate ownership, capturing device identification numbers, time and location information. The metadata information can be extracted from the gray-scale, mosaic-like CFA image or the full-color, demosaicked image using PC software commonly available by camera manufacturers or with conventional public image database tools. Simulation studies reported in the paper indicate that the proposed CFA indexing approach does not affect the performance of the demosaicking methods which produce full-color images that are visually identical to those obtained by demosaicking of the non-indexed CFA data.

1 Introduction

Cost-effective imaging devices use a single image sensor, usually a charge-coupled device (CCD) or complementary metal oxide semiconductor (CMOS) sensor, to capture a visual scene [1]-[5]. Due to the monochromatic nature of the sensor, a color filter array (CFA) is placed at the top of the sensor to capture the Red-Green-Blue (RGB) primary colors at the same time [3]. Since each sensor cell has its own spectrally selective filter, the CFA sensor values constitute a mosaic-like gray-scale image (*Fig.1a*) [4]. The full-color RGB image (*Fig.1c*) is obtained by estimating the two missing color components at each spatial location of the CFA image using a process called demosaicking [5]-[9].

Single-sensor devices store a captured image either in CFA or demosaicked formats. To organize and retrieve the captured images in personal databases, and authenticate the visual material available to public, a single-sensor captured image should be naturally connected to digital databases using metadata [10],[11] embedded in the CFA domain. The metadata information can be extracted from either the CFA images or their demosaicked variants in both personal and public image databases using the processing routines to be built in PC software commonly available by camera manufacturers and public database programmers.

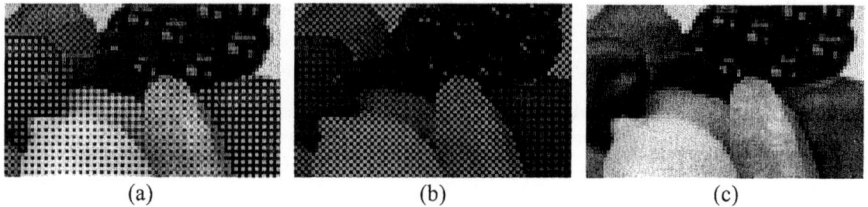

Fig. 1. Single-sensor imaging: (a) raw sensor data, (b) CFA data arranged as a color image, (c) reconstructed, full-color, demosaicked image

2 Bayer CFA Based Single-Sensor Imaging

Let us consider a single-sensor imaging pipeline equipped with a Bayer CFA (*Fig.2*) [12]. The captured sensor data constitute a $K_1 \times K_2$ gray-scale, mosaic-like, CFA image $z : Z^2 \to Z$ (*Fig.1a*) of integer samples $z_{(r,s)}$, with $r = 1, 2, ..., K_1$ and $s = 1, 2, ..., K_2$ denoting the image rows and columns, respectively. This CFA image z can be transformed to a $K_1 \times K_2$ color (RGB) image $\mathbf{x} : Z^2 \to Z^3$ (*Fig.1b*) of RGB vectors $\mathbf{x}_{(r,s)} = [x_{(r,s)1}, x_{(r,s)2}, x_{(r,s)3}]$ with $x_{(r,s)k}$ indicating the R ($k = 1$), G ($k = 2$) and B ($k = 3$) component. Similarly to z, the vector field $\mathbf{x}$ have a mosaic-like structure due to the fact that the vector $\mathbf{x}_{(r,s)}$, such as $\mathbf{x}_{(r,s)} = [z_{(r,s)}, 0, 0]$ for (odd r, even s), $\mathbf{x}_{(r,s)} = [0, 0, z_{(r,s)}]$ for (even r, odd s), and $\mathbf{x}_{(r,s)} = [0, z_{(r,s)}, 0]$ for (odd r, odd s) and (even r, even s), contains the values which correspond to different spectral bands [4],[6].

The full-color image (*Fig.1c*) is recovered from the CFA image using the so-called demosaicking process which calculates the missing color components from the adjacent CFA data [4],[9]. Depending on the device and the demosaicking solution employed, the quality of the demosaicked image as well as the computational complexity can vary significantly [4],[6]. Since the demosaicked images often suffer from zipper effects, reduced sharpness, and false coloration which result in various visual impairments, the postprocessing steps should be used to complete the demosaicking process [13],[14].

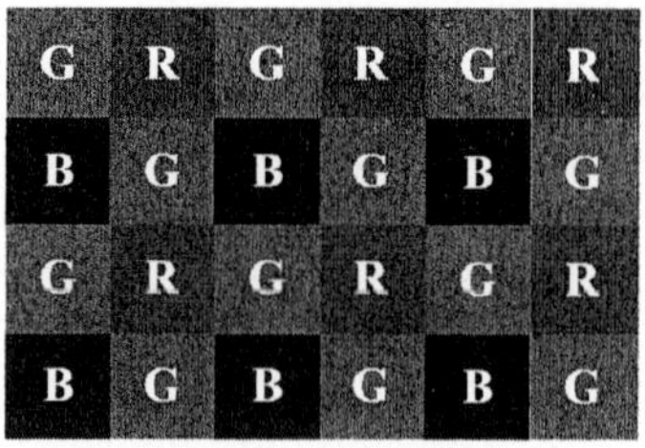

Fig. 2. Bayer CFA pattern with a GRGR phase in the first row [12]

3 Proposed CFA Image Indexing Approach

The demosaicking solutions are conventionally implemented in a digital camera which stores the demosaicked output. Alternatively, demosaicking is performed in a companion personal computer (PC) which interfaces with the digital camera that stores the images in the raw CFA format. Therefore, a single-sensor captured image should be naturally connected to digital databases using metadata embedded in the CFA domain [10]. As it is shown in *Fig.3*, the metadata can vary in the type and amount of the information to be processed, for example: i) digital cameras can automatically use their identification number, ownership information and a time stamp, ii) imaging enabled phones can complete the camera's metadata information by adding location stamps, and iii) semantic content can be optionally added using the mobile phone's or pocket device's keyboard.

The solution in [10] processes the metadata information using image sharing concepts [15]-[21] and encrypts the metadata information into two shares. In the sequence, the highest perceptual quality of the captured image is obtained by embedding the metadata share information at the least significant bits (LSB) of R and B CFA samples.

By embedding the metadata information in the frequency domain of the CFA image through digital watermarking (DW) concepts, the proposed here approach enhances efficiency of the CFA indexing approach and increases the robustness against signal processing operations. In addition, it twice reduces the amount of the embedded information compared to the information embedded through the secret sharing concept in [10]. Note that the proposed solution can employ any DW scheme operating in the frequency domain. To demonstrate the concept, the conventional discrete cosine transform (DCT) based DW solution [22]-[24] is used in the sequence.

Following the dominance of G values (50%) in the Bayer CFA which greatly contribute to the perceived sharpness of the demosaicked image [8],[9], our solution embeds the metadata information to the spatial locations corresponding to the R or B CFA components. It will be shown that by operating on the indexed CFA image, the subsequent demosaicking procedure produces a demosaicked image which is visually identical to the one reconstructed using the non-indexed, original CFA data.

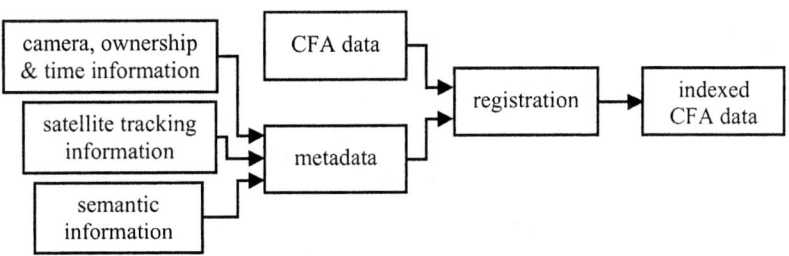

Fig. 3. A CFA image indexing concept

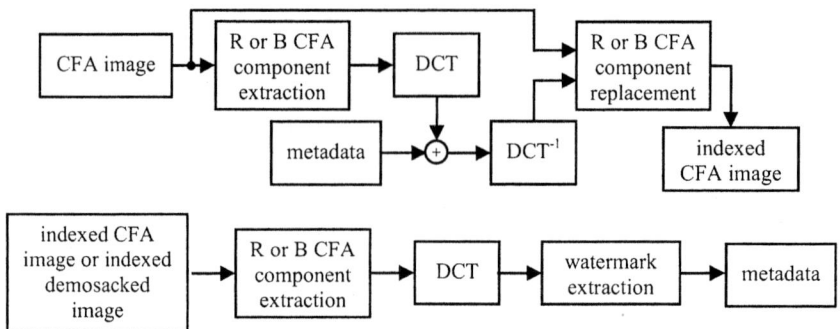

Fig. 4. Simplified block scheme representation of the proposed CFA image indexing solution: (top) metadata embedding, (bottom) metadata extraction

Using the conventional DCT based DW framework [22]-[24], the metadata information is considered here as a binary image. As it is shown in *Fig.4*, the highest perceptual quality of the captured image is ensured by performing the indexing operations over the R or B components of the captured data. To demonstrate the concept, only the R CFA locations were considered in this paper to be affected by the indexing operations and thus, the proposed solution firsts extracts all the R CFA components. Following the conventional practice, the DCT is applied in blocks of 8×8 pixels. The metadata information is embedded in the DCT transform domain of the image constituted by the R CFA components. The metadata embedding process was controlled by global parameter α used to amplify or attenuate the watermark at each DCT coefficient. By tuning the value of α, the tradeoff between the maximization of watermark energy (and robustness of the watermark) and imperceptibility of the changes introduced by watermarking is controlled. In this paper we used the value $\alpha = 3$.

Based on the extracted metadata information, the indexed single-sensor captured images (both CFA images and demosaicked images) can be archived, uniquely organized, and retrieved in digital databases [10]. The original CFA components, as described in Section 2, are not affected by the demosaicking procedure and thus, they are present in both CFA and demosaicked images. The database tools are used to extract the R CFA components in order to recover the original metadata information (*Fig.4*).

4 Experimental Results

To demonstrate the performance of the proposed method, a number of color and binary (metadata) test images have been used. The test color images, such as those shown in *Figs.5a-d* have been captured using three-sensor devices and normalized to 8-bit per channel RGB representation. The example of a binary metadata image is shown in *Fig.5e*.

Fig. 5. Test images: (a-d) 512 × 512 color images Parrots, Lighthouse, Bikes and Rafting, (e) 64 × 64 binary metadata image

Table 1. Demosaicking performance using the BI scheme

Input CFA image	non-indexed			indexed		
Image / Criterion	MAE	MSE	NCD	MAE	MSE	NCD
Parrots	2.087	29.5	0.0265	2.149	29.7	0.0268
Lighthouse	4.555	129.5	0.0579	4.612	129.7	0.0579
Bikes	6.060	155.5	0.1205	6.114	155.7	0.1208
Rafting	4.711	89.4	0.0750	4.746	89.6	0.0752

Following the conventional practice, the mosaic versions of the original color images were created by discarding color information in a GRGR phased Bayer CFA filter shown in *Fig.2*. The indexed version of the CFA image was produced via the proposed CFA image indexing solution (*Fig.4*). The demosaicked and indexed demosaicked images were respectively obtained from non-indexed and indexed images by applying the bilinear demosaicking (BI) solution of [25] and the color-correlation demosaicking approach (CCA) of [1]. Note that the BI scheme is commonly accepted as an industry standard whereas the CCA scheme is one of the most powerful demosaicking solutions.

The difference between the original images and the demosaicked images, as well as the original images and the indexed demosaicked images was evaluated using the mean absolute error (MAE), the mean square error (MSE) and the normalized color difference criterion (NCD). The interesting reader can find the definition of the above criteria in [1],[9]. Demosaicking results reported in *Tables 1-2* indicate that the demosaicked images obtained using both non-indexed and indexed CFA data are of similar quality. The comparison of the results also reveals the qualitative difference between the simple BI scheme and the sophisticated CCA solution. In both cases, demosaicking of the non-indexed data led to slightly better results.

Since the demosaicked images are intended for human inspection, visual comparisons are provided in *Fig.6*. As it can be seen, visual inspection does not reveals any difference by comparing the non-indexed BI demosaicked (*Fig.6b*)

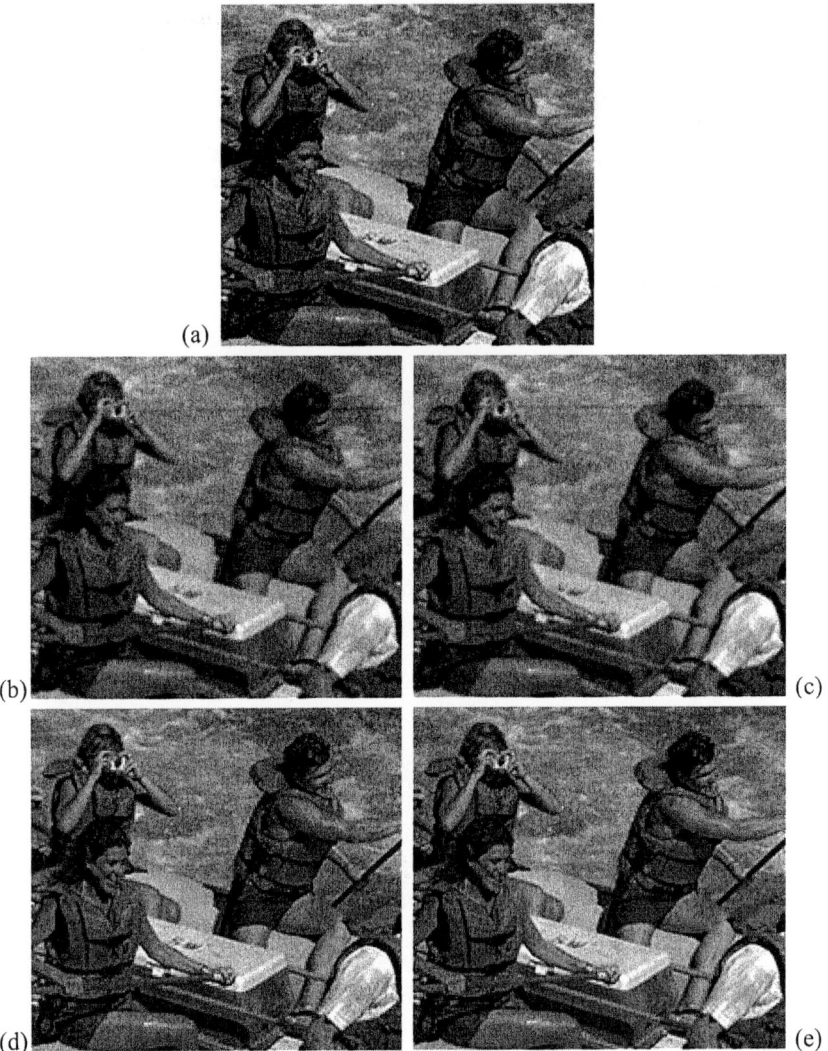

Fig. 6. Detailed parts of the obtained results: (a) original image, (b,c) BI demosaicking, (d,e) CCA demosaicking, (b,d) demosaicking using non-indexed CFA data, (c,e) demosaicking using indexed CFA data

and indexed BI demosaicked (*Fig. 6c*) images. Similarly, no difference between non-indexed and indexed demosaicked images can be observed by inspecting the images produced using the CCA demosaicking method (*Figs. 6d,e*). It should be noted that the various visual impairments present in the BI demosaicked images are caused by the lack of spatial and spectral information during the BI demosaicking process. In the summary, it can be said that the proposed solution

Table 2. Demosaicking performance using the CCA scheme

Input CFA image	non-indexed			indexed		
Image / Criterion	MAE	MSE	NCD	MAE	MSE	NCD
Parrots	1.062	4.2	0.0151	1.123	4.4	0.0154
Lighthouse	1.455	9.3	0.0193	1.513	9.5	0.0195
Bikes	1.772	12.2	0.0428	1.829	12.3	0.0432
Rafting	1.725	14.1	0.0308	1.783	14.2	0.0311

preserves the perceptual quality of both the CFA and demosaicked images. In addition, it does not introduce any side effect nor decrease the measured and/or visual quality of the captured image.

5 Conclusion

A new CFA image indexing approach was presented. Digital watermarking concepts were used to embed metadata into the single-sensor captured image in an imperceivable way. The extraction procedure recovers the original metadata from either indexed CFA or demosaicked image.

References

1. Lukac, R., Plataniotis, K.N., Hatzinakos, D., Aleksic, M.: A novel cost effective demosaicing approach. IEEE Transactions on Consumer Electronics **50** (2004) 256–261
2. Lukac, R., Martin, K., Plataniotis, K.N.: Digital camera zooming based on unified CFA image processing steps. IEEE Transactions on Consumer Electronics **50** (2004) 15–24
3. Adams, J., Parulski, K., Spaulding, K.: Color processing in digital cameras. IEEE Micro **18** (1998) 20–30
4. Lukac, R., Plataniotis, K.N.: Normalized color-ratio modelling for CFA interpolation. IEEE Transactions on Consumer Electronics **50** (2004) 737–745
5. Lu, W., Tang, Y.P.: Color filter array demosaicking: new method and performance measures. IEEE Transactions on Image Processing **12** (2003) 1194–1210
6. Lukac, R., Plataniotis, K.N.: Data-adaptive filters for demosaicking: a framework. IEEE Transactions on Consumer Electronics, **51** (2005)
7. Pei, S.C., Tam, I.K.: Effective color interpolation in CCD color filter arrays using signal correlation. IEEE Trans. Circuits and Systems for Video Technology **13** (2003) 503–513
8. Gunturk, B., Altunbasak, Y., Mersereau, R.: Color plane interpolation using alternating projections. IEEE Transactions on Image Processing **11** (2002) 997–1013
9. Lukac, R., Plataniotis, K.N., Hatzinakos, D.: Color image zooming on the Bayer pattern. IEEE Trans. on Circuit and Systems for Video Technology **15** (2005)

10. Lukac, R., Plataniotis, K.N.: Digital image indexing using secret sharing schemes: a unified framework for single-sensor consumer electronics. IEEE Trans. Consumer Electronics, submitted (2004)
11. Toyama, K., Logan, R., Roseway, A., Anandan, P.: Geographic location tags on digital images. Proc. ACM International Conference on Multimedia in Berkeley, USA, (2003) 156–166.
12. Bayer, B.E.: Color imaging array. U.S. Patent 3 971 065 (1976)
13. Lukac, R., Martin, K., Plataniotis, K.N.: Demosaicked image postprocessing using local color ratios. IEEE Transactions on Circuit and Systems for Video Technology **14** (2004) 914–920
14. Lukac, R., Plataniotis, K.N.: A robust, cost-effective postprocessor for enhancing demosaicked camera images. Real-Time Imaging, Special Issue on Spectral Imaging II, **11** (2005)
15. Naor, M., Shamir, A.: Visual Cryptography. Lectore Notes in Computer Science **950** (1994) 1–12
16. Yang, C.N.: New visual secret sharing schemes using probabilistic method. Pattern Recognition Letters, **25** (2004) 481–494
17. Yang, C.N., Chen, T.S: Aspect ratio invariant visual secret sharing schemes with minimum pixel expansion. Pattern Recognition Letters, **26** (2005) 193–206
18. Ateniese, G., Blundo, C, de Santis, A., Stinson, D.G.: Visual cryptography for general access structures. Information and Computation **129** (1996) 86–106
19. Lukac, R., Plataniotis, K.N.: Bit-level based secret sharing for image encryption. Pattern Recognition **38** (2005) 767–772
20. Lukac, R., Plataniotis, K.N.: Colour image secret sharing. IEE Electronics Letters **40** (2004) 529–530
21. Lukac, R., Plataniotis, K.N.: Image representation based secret sharing. Communications of the CCISA, Special Issue on Visual Secret Sharing **11** (2005) 103–114
22. Hernandez, J.R., Amado, M., Perez-Gonzalez, F., DCT-domain watermarking techniques for still images: detector performance analysis and a new structure. IEEE Transactions on Image Processing **9** (2000) 55–68.
23. Kejariwal, A.: Watermarking. IEEE Potentials **22** (2003) 37–40
24. Barni, M., Bartolini, F., Piva, A.: Multichannel watermarking of color images. IEEE Transactions on Circuits and Systems for Video Technology **12** (2002) 142–156
25. Sakamoto, T., Nakanishi, C., Hase, T.: Software pixel interpolation for digital still cameras suitable for a 32-bit MCU. IEEE Transactions on Consumer Electronics **44** (1998) 1342–1352

Discrete Average of Two-Dimensional Shapes[*]

Isameddine Boukhriss, Serge Miguet, and Laure Tougne

Laboratoire LIRIS, Université Lyon 2,
5 avenue Pierre Mendès 69500 , France
isameddine.boukhriss@liris.cnrs.fr
http://liris.cnrs.fr

Abstract. In this article we present an algorithm for computing discrete average of n two-dimensional shapes. Our previous work was limited to two shapes, we generalize it to an arbitrary number of objects with consideration of increasing inter-individual variability. The first step of our approach performs a rigid transformation that aligns the shapes as best as possible. The next step consists in searching the progressive metamorphosis of one object toward the other one, that iteratively adds or suppresses pixels. This process is then iterated between the last average shape obtained and the new object from the set according to weighting consideration. It considers the rank in which each shape is added and gives criteria of optimization in variability and global topology preservation. The basic operations are based on geodesic distance transformations and lead to an optimal (linear) algorithm.

1 Introduction

Electronic devices produce a lot of images in medical, multimedia and physics domains. These images are produced every moment and their interpretation is a very hard and heavy task. It would be of great interest to concentrate all the data in a flexible representative.

Morphing techniques allow the creation of an image starting from an initial image under particular constraints and permit also the generation of a sequence of images starting from given images. This later functionality interests us in this study. An average shape could be among the images in this sequence. In this paper, our goal is to generalize an already developed study of progressive deformation, from one object to another one, to a set of shapes. By considering pair wise shapes, our method is decomposed into two steps: the first one consists in making a rigid registration of the two objects and the second one in computing the deformation. The new obtained average shape is then updated with another shape from the hole set by repeating the same process with proportionality considerations.

---

[*] This work is supported by the Ragtime project of the Rhone Alpes region and Medigrid project of ACI GRID Program.

2 State of the Art

Morphing techniques allow the transformation of a source into a target object. They generate a sequence of images starting from two given images. It is very interesting to investigate this sequence to extract an average shape. Many approaches for morphing are studied.

One of the oldest technique [1] called mesh morphing consists in superimposing a deformable grid on the image source, and to deform this grid so that its intersections indicate particular features of the image. The operation is applied to the image destination, and the transformation of the passage of a grid deformed with the other is calculated by interpolation. Another approach was later introduced [2], based on the mapping of segments, defined in each image by the user. Physical studies gave also another technique based on deformation of a model according to laws of rigidity and elasticity [5]. The best results were observed with point-based morphing. It operates directly on vertices, their interpolation can be done with different methods based on thin plate splines or Gaussian [3] or elastic splines [4]. Our technique consists in adding pixels to one shape and deletion of others from the second with a control technique which makes it possible to generate a sequence of transitions from shapes.

A recent study [6] computes the average shape between two continuous shapes. First, it makes the registration of the two images and it computes the skeleton of the difference between the two shapes. Using an elimination process, it only keeps the points of the skeleton that are equidistant of two borders of two different objects. The method we present in this paper is a generalized discrete version of the previous one. The generalization we propose allows to compute not only a median shape but also the different intermediate shapes.

3 Preliminaries

Let us give the formal context of our study and recall some basic notions concerning the inertia moments and neighborhood properties.

3.1 Neighborhood, Connectivity and Distance

We consider 2D shapes in the Z^2 space. The pixels of the shape have the value 1 and the pixels that belong to the background have the value 0. The object is considered as 8-connected and background is considered as 4-connected. We work in 3×3 neighborhood. Let a and b denote two binary shapes, we denote the symmetric difference by $a \Delta b = \{a \cup b\} \setminus \{a \cap b\}$.

In our study, we will use the chamfer distance 3-4 which is a good approximation of the Euclidean distance.

3.2 Inertia Moments: Eigen Values and Vectors

In order to make the registration, we will use the moments associated to the shapes. Such descriptors are especially interesting in order to determine the position, the orientation and scale of an object. Moreover, one of their main advantages is their small sensitivity to noise. With these moments, we deduce the eigenvectors V_1 and V_2 and the associated eigenvalues λ_1 and λ_2 for each shape. Let us suppose $\lambda_1 > \lambda_2$. V_1 represents the maximal elongation axis of the object. These data will be used to apply the different transformations in the morphing process.

4 Discrete Average Shape

4.1 Previous Work

The overall system structure of the proposed approach is similar to our previous work [7]. The method is based on aligning rigidly the two considered input shapes and then applying the morphing. The first step is directly deduced from the computation of the inertia moments and consists in a translation and a rotation.

The scaling and re-sampling operations are very important. We have chosen a compromise which aligns the principal vectors on a new system of coordinates and which chooses an intermediate scale between the two shapes (it reduces the biggest and increases the smallest). Lets suppose that our first two shapes are a and b. λ_a^1 and λ_b^1 are the eigenvalues corresponding to the two maximal elongation of shapes V_a^1 and V_b^1. The factor of scaling of the first shape is:

$$F_1 = \sqrt{(\lambda_1^a + \lambda_1^b)/2\lambda_1^a} \qquad (1)$$

The factor of scaling of the second shape is similar and proportional to its maximal elongation:

$$F_2 = \sqrt{(\lambda_1^a + \lambda_1^b)/2\lambda_1^b} \qquad (2)$$

Once the two input shapes are superimposed, we deformate one into the other to make morphing. This process is based on two operations: adding and deletion of pixels.

We construct first of all, two kinds of geodesic waves as shown in figure 3. We denote by d_1 the 3-4 distance from $a \cap b$ to $a \Delta b$, and d_2 the 3-4 distance from the complement of $a \cup b$ to $a \Delta b$. Consequently, to each pixel of the difference we associate two distances d_1 and d_2. The next step consists in labeling each connected component of $a \Delta b$ in order to permit proportionality considerations between each other.

Let us denote by β a parameter, varying between 0 and 1, that gives the degree of progression of the morphing. To obtain exactly the median shape, the parameter β must be equal to $\frac{1}{2}$. Suppose we deform a into b.

A pixel of $a \backslash b$ in the ith connected component of $a \Delta b$ is removed from a if it is labeled with distances d_1 and d_2 verifying:

$$d_1 \geq d_{1i}(1-\beta) \text{ or } d_2 \leq d_{2i}\beta \qquad (3)$$

A pixel of $b \backslash a$ in the ith connected component of $a \Delta b$ is added to a if it is labeled with distances d_1 and d_2 verifying:

$$d_1 \leq d_{1i}\beta \text{ and } d_2 \geq d_{2i}(1-\beta) \tag{4}$$

where d_{ji} is the biggest distance value in the ith connected component according to the jth propagation. These equations should be modified if we have more than two shapes to average. These considerations will be explained in the following section.

4.2 N Shapes Generalization

The important part previously described makes possible the deformation of a shape into another one and to generate their average. This section is about the extension to n objects. At this level, this extension can be done according at least to two possibilities:

- Dichotomic approach: it consists in subdividing the set of n objects in $n/2$ pairs and then applying the same process between each couple. The new $n/2$ average shapes are then treated to get $n/4$ other average objects. If the starting whole is odd, we can consider one of the shapes as a first average one.
- Unilateral approach: this approach consists in always keeping the average shape active in all the transformations. That is to say every new object, according to its rank, will directly affect the average form until the last one. We have chosen this approach because it allows to add *a posteriori* a new shape easily. Suppose we denote $\bar{x}$ the $(n-1)^{th}$ average shape created from $(n-1)$ objects, let x_{n+1} be a new form. Suppose we readjusted, scaled and re-sampled the two shapes as best as possible. We suppose that we deform $\bar{x}$ into x_{n+1}. Adding or deletion of pixels will depends on these conditions:
  - If we add pixels to $\bar{x}$ and remove pixels from x_{n+1}:
    a pixel of $x_{n+1} \backslash \bar{x}$ in the ith connected component of $\bar{x} \Delta x_{n+1}$ is added to $\bar{x}$ if it is labeled with distances d_1 and d_2 verifying:

    $$d_1 \leq d_{1i}\beta \frac{n+1}{n} \text{ and } d_2 \geq d_{2i}(1-\beta)\frac{n}{n+1} \tag{5}$$

    According to equation 4, we should add more pixels to $\bar{x}$, so increasing d_{1i} will be tolerant to accept more pixels. The same reason for decreasing d_{2i}.
  - If we add pixels to x_{n+1} and remove pixels from $\bar{x}$:
    a pixel of $\bar{x} \backslash x_{n+1}$ in the ith connected component of $\bar{x} \Delta x_{n+1}$ is removed from $\bar{x}$ if it is labeled with distances d_1 and d_2 verifying:

    $$d_1 \geq d_{1i}(1-\beta)\frac{n}{n+1} \text{ or } d_2 \leq d_{2i}\beta\frac{n+1}{n} \tag{6}$$

    According to equation 3, we should remove less pixels from $\bar{x}$, so decreasing d_{1i} will be less tolerant to remove pixels. The same reason for increasing d_{2i}.

One of the important points also, which is in the two approaches, is the order in which the forms are taken. This is closely related to the first phase concerning the scaling. Let us suppose that we have an average form, if the next form which will update it is too small or too large compared to it, we would risk to have a considerable modification on the size of the new average form.

What we have done is according to the maximum elongations of the two forms, we add matter to small shape and remove matter from the biggest. We can also use the same technique based on weighting according to at least two different techniques:

- If there is a sufficient knowledge of the set of forms, we can order them in a growing or decreasing way of variation according to the maximum elongation. This will enable us to have a direction balanced of the growth of our average form each time that a form is selected to update it.
- If the unilateral approach is chosen, which is our case, we use the same factor of weight of the form (its rank in the cycle) which will update the average form like factor loading in the phase of scaling. That is to say, if there is an average form created starting from n forms, the scaling process will be $(n/n+1)$ more attracted towards it than towards the $(n+1)^{th}$ form. The equations 1 and 2 should be changed. What we did before is equivalent to compute an average between λ_1^a and λ_1^b, if we suppose that λ_1^a is now the big eigenvalue of our recent average shape, we should give more weight to its value. So instead of having $\frac{\lambda_1^a + \lambda_1^b}{2}$, we will get:

$$coef = \lambda_1^a + |\frac{\lambda_1^a - \lambda_1^b}{n+1}| \qquad (7)$$

Thus, the factors of scaling will attract the two shapes, according to maximal elongation, to a shape closer to the recent average one.

$$F_1 = \sqrt{coef}/\sqrt{\lambda_1^a} \qquad F_2 = \sqrt{coef}/\sqrt{\lambda_1^b} \qquad (8)$$

Figure 1 gives the result of each average shape obtained during the whole process. It indicates that we can have a considerable size modification if we have important inter-individuality. This not the case in figure 2 where we apply our

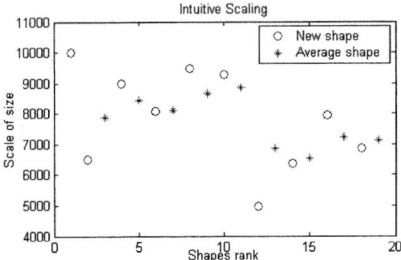

Fig. 1. Scaling with intuitive coefficients(1/2)

modified coefficients F_1 and F_2. Each average shape is more attracted by the previous one even if we introduce a shape with important variation of size.

In order to preserve topology, we adopted a technique which consists in adding only pixels from the difference of the shapes to their intersection. By considering each layer of propagation as a source, we compute the next layer which is connected to the previous one.

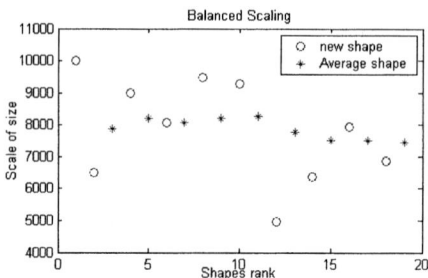

Fig. 2. Scaling with weighting considerations

5 Results

In order to validate our approach, we made tests on a set of fishes. They have an important inter-individual variability concerning scale and shape. We begin with two arbitrary shapes that we registrate and scale. We propagate then the two geodesic waves. By fixing the parameter $\beta=1/2$ we generate our first average fish. This process was then iterated by considering:

- The order in which each shape is added to update the recent average one.
- The proportionality of adding and deletion of pixels depend on the rank of the new added shape.

We made tests on ten shapes as shown in figure 3. The order in which they were treated was arbitrary chosen. For best check of the whole process, we extracted the two last average shapes obtained as shown in figure 5. We remark, according to the order in which the shapes are treated, that results seem to be satisfying. The variations are small due to the fact that starting from a certain rank, average shape is less influenced by new shapes. It should be noted that an anti-aliasing filter could be applied to improve the results. Figure 4 gives the distance propagation results between the 8th average shape and the last shape to get the 9th one. These results are used to decide about adding or deletion of pixels. Shaded zones of the difference of the two shapes in the figure indicate, according to the final result, that we have small number of added/deleted pixels in connected components where the maximum values due to the propagations are important. However, this number is almost null in the other connected components. It is obvious that the result should be $\frac{1}{10} * \beta$ proportional to the maximum values. The final result is so more attracted to the 8th average shape.

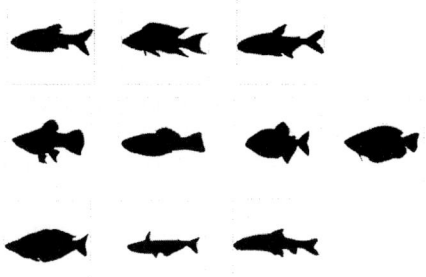

Fig. 3. Sample of our fish data base

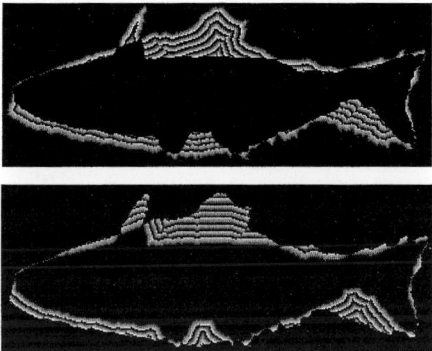

Fig. 4. Distance propagation in the 9th average shape generation process

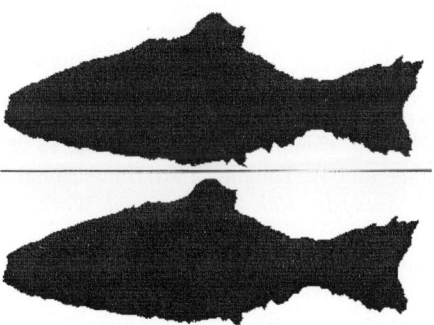

Fig. 5. The 8th and 9th average shape

6 Conclusion

The proposed approach gives a linear solution for computing an intermediate shape between arbitrary input set of binary objects. This average shape could be updated easily. We give also a solution to inter-individual variability by balancing the scaling process in the first step of registration between shapes. This permits less influence of size difference which can affect clearly the average shape even between two iterations. A progression parameter β ranging from 0 to 1 allows to control the influence of each input shape.

In this paper we have used the chamfer distance as a good integer approximation of Euclidian distance. An improvement in precision could be the use of the Euclidian distance itself which can also be computed in linear time as shown in [8] at least for 2D domains. With our approach, the topology of intermediate shapes is "globally" preserved, due to the continuous propagation from the intersection of shapes to their difference. An heuristic for reaching better results could be to use thinning or thickening operators, allowing to ensure that the removal or adding of a point does not change the topology of intermediate. These topics and other problems related to noise and segmentation errors should be the subject of further studies.

References

1. Smythe DB, A two-pass mesh warping algorithm for object transformation and image interpolation, *Technical Report 1030, Calif*, 1990.
2. T. Beier and S. Neely, Feature-based image metamorphosis, In: *Computer Graphics and Interactive Techniques*, 1992, pp. 35-42.
3. N. Arad, N. Dyn, D. Reisfeld, and Y. Yeshurin, Image warping by radial basis functions: application to facial expressions. In: *CVGIP 56(2)*, 1994, pp. 161-172.
4. A. Hassanien and M. Nakajima. Image morphing of facial images transformation based on navier elastic body splines. In Computer Animation, volume 7, pages 3-23, 1998.
5. T. Sederberg and E. Greenwood. A physically-based approach to 2-D shape blending. Computer Graphics, vol 26, July 1992,35-42.
6. R. Blanding, G. Turkiyyah, D. Storti, and M. Ganter, Skeleton-based Three Dimensional Geometric Morphing. *Computational Geometry*, 15, 2000, pp. 129-148.
7. I. Boukhriss, S. Miguet and L. Tougne, Two Dimensional discrete morphing, In: *Combinatorial Image Analysis: 10th International Workshop*, december 2004, pp. 409-420.
8. D. Coeurjolly, S. Miguet and L. Tougne, 2D and 3D Visibility in Discrete Geometry: An Application to Discrete Geodesic Paths, Pattern Recognition Letters, 2004, vol 25, pp. 561-570.

Coupled Statistical Face Reconstruction

William A.P. Smith and Edwin R. Hancock

Department of Computer Science, The University of York
{wsmith, erh}@cs.york.ac.uk

Abstract. We present a coupled statistical model that can be used to accurately recover facial surfaces from single images by jointly capturing variations in surface normal direction and surface height. The model is trained on range data. By fitting the model to surface normal data, the surface height function is implicitly recovered without having to integrate the recovered field of surface normals. We show how the coupled model can be fitted to image brightness data using geometric constraints on surface normal direction furnished by Lambert's law.

1 Introduction

One of the most alluring ways to recover 3D facial shape from a 2D image, is to use shape-from-shading is to extract a field of surface normals. Surface height can then be recovered by integrating the surface normals. Unfortunately, there are a number of obstacles that are encountered when this simple strategy is applied to real-world data. The first of these is that when integrated, the concave/convex ambiguities in the needle-map can lead to the distortion of the topography of the reconstructed face. One of the most serious instances of this problem is that the nose can become imploded. The second problem encountered is how to accommodate variations in facial albedo.

One way of overcoming these problems is to use domain specific constraints. Several authors [1,2,3] have shown that, at the expense of generality, the accuracy of recovered shape information can be greatly enhanced by restricting a shape-from-shading algorithm to a particular class of objects. For instance, Prados and Faugeras [3] use the location of singular points to enforce convexity on the recovered surface. Zhao and Chellappa [2], on the other hand, have introduced a geometric constraint which exploited the approximate bilateral symmetry of faces. Atick et al. [1] proposed a statistical shape-from-shading framework based on a low dimensional parameterisation of facial surfaces. Principal components analysis was used to derive a set of 'eigenheads' which compactly captures 3D facial shape. Unfortunately, it is surface orientation and not depth which is conveyed by image intensity. Therefore, fitting the model to an image equates to a computationally expensive parameter search which attempts to minimise the error between the rendered surface and the observed intensity. Dovgard and Basri [4] combined the statistical constraint of Atick et al. and the geometric constraint of Zhao and Chellappa into a single shape-from-shading framework. However, asymmetry in real face images results in errors in the recovered surfaces. Nandy and Ben-Arie [5] attempt to learn the relationship between 3D shape and image intensity for a number of face parts. Their shape-from-recognition framework helps constrain the space of solutions to the image irradiance equation, but relies on statistical methods to learn the effects of illumination variations.

The aim in this paper is to present a coupled statistical model that can be used to overcome these difficulties by jointly describing variations in surface normal direction and height over the surface of a face. The coupled model is inspired by the active appearance model developed by Cootes, Edwards and Taylor [6], which simultaneously models 2D shape and texture. The model is trained on range images of faces. We construct separate eigenspaces for the surface normal and height variations from the covariance matrices of the training data. To overcome problems associated with constructing a statistical model over the surface normals, we convert to a Cartesian representation using the azimuthal equidistant projection.

2 A Coupled Surface Normal and Depth Model

Shape-from-shading is concerned with recovering surface shape information from single images of shaded surfaces. Ultimately, the aim is to recover the surface height function $z(x,y)$ from the image intensity $I(x,y)$, where x,y are the orthographic projections onto the image plane of the 3D coordinates (x,y,z) in which the surface, $z(x,y)$, is embedded. Assuming Lambertian reflectance and a single known light source, $\mathbf{s}$, the measured brightness $I(x,y)$ is uniquely determined by the orientation of the surface at the coordinates (x,y). This relationship is captured by the image irradiance equation: $I(x,y) = \mathbf{n}(x,y).\mathbf{s}$, where $\mathbf{n}(x,y)$ is the local surface normal at the coordinates (x,y). The surface height function may be related to image intensity by expressing the local surface normal in terms of the surface gradients: $\mathbf{n} = (-p, -q, 1)$, where $p = \partial_x z$ and $q = \partial_y z$.

The aim in this paper is to construct a generic statistical model that can be used to simultaneously capture the modes of variation in surface normal direction and surface height. Our ultimate goal is to develop a model that can be used to recover surface height by fitting the surface normal component to image brightness using Lambert's law. We train the model on range data. Here the surface normals and height are both available. The model used is a linear eigenspace method, in which the eigenvectors of the covariance matrices for the surface normals and height, or depth, data are used to represent statistical variations in the data. The parameters of the model are the weights associated with the eigenmodes. We demonstrate how the parameters may be estimated by fitting the model to surface normal data. The parameters may then be used to recover the surface height using a simple matrix multiplication operation.

Statistical Representation of Surface Normals: To overcome problems associated with modelling the statistics of directional data we represent the surface normals as points on a unit sphere, and then convert them to Cartesian point data by using the *azimuthal equidistant* or Postel projection from the unit sphere onto a tangent plane. This projection has the important property that it preserves the distances between locations on the sphere.

Let $\mathbf{n}_k(i,j) = (n_k^x(i,j), n_k^y(i,j), n_k^z(i,j))^T$ be the unit surface normal at the pixel indexed (i,j) in the kth training image. At the location (i,j), the mean-surface normal direction is $\hat{\mathbf{n}}(i,j) = \bar{\mathbf{n}}(i,j)/||\bar{\mathbf{n}}(i,j)||$ where $\bar{\mathbf{n}}(i,j) = (1/K)\sum_{k=1}^{K} \mathbf{n}_k(i,j)$.

On the unit sphere, the surface normal $\mathbf{n}_k(i,j)$ has elevation angle $\theta_k(i,j) = \frac{\pi}{2} - \arcsin n_k^z(i,j)$ and azimuth angle $\phi_k(i,j) = \arctan n_k^y(i,j)/n_k^x(i,j)$, while the mean surface normal at the location (i,j) has elevation angles $\hat{\theta}(i,j) = \frac{\pi}{2} - \arcsin \hat{n}^z(i,j)$ and azimuth angle $\hat{\phi}(i,j) = \arctan \hat{n}^y(i,j)/\hat{n}^x(i,j)$.

To construct the azimuthal equidistant projection we proceed as follows. We commence by constructing the tangent plane to the unit-sphere at the location corresponding to the mean-surface normal. We establish a local co-ordinate system on this tangent plane. The origin is at the point of contact between the tangent plane and the unit sphere. The x-axis is aligned parallel to the local circle of latitude on the unit-sphere.

Under the azimuthal equidistant projection at the location (i,j), the surface normal $\mathbf{n}_k(i,j)$ maps to the point with coordinates $\mathbf{v}_k(i,j) = (x_k(i,j), y_k(i,j))^T$. The transformation equations between the unit-sphere and the tangent-plane co-ordinate systems are

$$x_k(i,j) = k' \cos \theta_k(i,j) \sin[\phi_k(i,j) - \hat{\phi}(i,j)]$$

$$y_k(i,j) = k' \left\{ \cos \hat{\theta}(i,j) \sin \phi_k(i,j) - \sin \hat{\theta}(i,j) \cos \theta_k(i,j) \cos[\phi_k(i,j) - \hat{\phi}(i,j)] \right\}$$

where $\cos c = \sin \hat{\theta}(i,j) \sin \theta_k(i,j) + \cos \hat{\theta}(i,j) \cos \theta_k(i,j) \cos[\phi_k(i,j) - \hat{\phi}(i,j)]$ and $k' = \frac{c}{\sin c}$.

Surface Normal Model: Suppose that each training example is a range image which consists of an array of depth data. For the pixel indexed (i,j) in the kth training sample the depth is $z_{i,j}^k$. Using the range data we estimate the surface normal directions, and the surface normal at the pixel location (i,j) for the kth training image is $\mathbf{n}_{i,j}^k$. The components of the vector are transformed into the coordinates $(x_k(i,j), y_k(i,j))$ using the azimuthal equidistant projection. If the range images have M rows and N columns the surface normal coordinates of each training sample may be represented by the long vector $\mathbf{U}^k = [x_k(1,1), \ldots, x_k(M,N), y_k(1,1), \ldots, x_k(M,N)]^T$ which is length $2MN$ and contains the x and y coordinates obtained by applying the azimuthal equidistant projection to the surface normals. Since the azimuthal equidistant projection involves centering the local co-ordinate system, the coordinates corresponding to the mean direction are $(0,0)$ at each image location. Hence, the long-vector corresponding to the mean direction at each image location is zero.

The K training samples can be used to form the $(2MN) \times K$ data-matrix $\mathbf{D}_s = [\mathbf{U}^1| \ldots |\mathbf{U}^K]$. The $(2MN) \times (2MN)$ covariance matrix is therefore given by $\mathbf{L} = \frac{1}{K}\mathbf{D}_s\mathbf{D}_s^T$. We use the numerically efficient *snap-shot* method of Sirovich [7] to compute the eigenvectors of $\mathbf{L}$. Accordingly, we construct the matrix $\hat{\mathbf{L}} =$

$\frac{1}{K}\mathbf{D}_s^T\mathbf{D}_s$. The eigenvectors $\hat{\mathbf{e}}_i$ of $\hat{\mathbf{L}}$ can be used to find the eigenvectors $\mathbf{e}_i$ of $\mathbf{L}$ using $\mathbf{e}_i = \mathbf{D}_s\hat{\mathbf{e}}_i$. We deform the azimuthal equidistant point projections in the directions defined by the matrix $\mathbf{P}_s = (\mathbf{e}_1|\mathbf{e}_2|\ldots|\mathbf{e}_K)$ formed from the leading K principal eigenvectors. As a result, the long-vector $\mathbf{U}$ may be projected onto the eigenvectors and represented by a vector of model parameters $\mathbf{b}_s = \mathbf{P}_s^T\mathbf{U}$.

Depth Model: Each of the K range images in the training set may be represented by the vector of depth values ordered according to the raster scan: $\mathbf{z}^k = [z_{1,1}^k, z_{1,2}^k, \ldots, z_{M,N}^k]^T$. The mean depth vector $\hat{\mathbf{z}}$ is given by $\hat{\mathbf{z}} = \frac{1}{K}\sum_{i=1}^K \mathbf{z}^i$. We form the $MN \times K$ data matrix of depth values using: $\mathbf{D}_d = [(\mathbf{z}^1 - \hat{\mathbf{z}})|(\mathbf{z}^2 - \hat{\mathbf{z}})|\ldots|(\mathbf{z}^K - \hat{\mathbf{z}})]$. Once again we use principal components analysis to extract the set of orthogonal modes of variation $\mathbf{P}_d$. Again, a long-vector of depth values $\mathbf{z}^k$ can be projected onto the eigenvectors and represented using the vector of model parameters $\mathbf{b}_d = \mathbf{P}_d^T(\mathbf{z}^k - \hat{\mathbf{z}})$.

Combining the Depth and Surface Normal Models: We now show how the depth and surface normal models described above can be combined into a single coupled model. Each training sample can be summarised by the parameter vectors $\mathbf{b}_s$ and $\mathbf{b}_d$, representing the needle-map and depth map of the sample respectively. Since depth and surface normal direction are closely related (recall that $\mathbf{n} = (-\partial_x z, -\partial_y z, 1)$) the two sets of parameters will contain strong correlations.

In both models, we may consider small scale variation as noise. Hence, if the ith eigenvalue for the surface normal model is λ_{si}, we need only retain S eigenmodes to retain p percent of the model variance. We choose S using $\sum_{i=1}^S \lambda_{si} \geq \frac{p}{100}\sum_{i=1}^K \lambda_{si}$. Similarly for the depth model we retain D eigenmodes to capture p percent of the variance.

For the kth training sample we can generate the concatenated vector of length $S + D$:

$$\mathbf{b}^k \begin{pmatrix} \mathbf{W}_s \mathbf{b}_s^k \\ \mathbf{b}_d^k \end{pmatrix} = \begin{pmatrix} \mathbf{W}_s \mathbf{P}_s^T \mathbf{U}^k \\ \mathbf{P}_d^T(\mathbf{z}^k - \hat{\mathbf{z}}) \end{pmatrix} \qquad (1)$$

where $\mathbf{W}_s$ is a diagonal matrix of weights for each surface normal model parameter, allowing for the different relative weighting of the surface normal and depth models. The reason for performing this weighting is that the elements of $\mathbf{b}_s$ have units of radians, $\mathbf{b}_d$ have units of distance, so they cannot be compared directly. We set $\mathbf{W}_s = r\mathbf{I}$ where r^2 is the ratio of the total depth variance to the total surface normal variance. The coupled model data matrix is $\mathbf{D}_d = [\mathbf{b}^1|\ldots|\mathbf{b}^K]$, where $\mathbf{b}^k$ represents the concatenated vector for the kth training sample. We apply a final PCA to this data to give the coupled model

$$\mathbf{b} = \mathbf{P}_c \mathbf{c} = \begin{pmatrix} \mathbf{P}_{cs} \\ \mathbf{P}_{cd} \end{pmatrix} \mathbf{c} \qquad (2)$$

where $\mathbf{P}_c$ are the eigenvectors and $\mathbf{c}$ is a vector of coupled parameters controlling both the surface normal model and depth model simultaneously. The matrix $\mathbf{P}_{cs}$ has S rows, and represents the first S eigenvectors, corresponding to the surface normal subspace of the model. The matrix $\mathbf{P}_{cd}$ has D rows, and represents the final D eigenvectors, corresponding to the depth subspace of the model.

The vectors of projected surface normal directions $\mathbf{U} = \mathbf{P}_s\mathbf{W}_s^{-1}\mathbf{P}_{cs}\mathbf{c}$ and depth values $\mathbf{z} = \hat{\mathbf{z}} + \mathbf{P}_d\mathbf{P}_{cd}\mathbf{c}$ are given in terms of the parameter vector $\mathbf{c}$. For compactness we write $\mathbf{Q}_s = \mathbf{P}_s\mathbf{W}_s^{-1}\mathbf{P}_{cs}$ and $\mathbf{Q}_d = \mathbf{P}_d\mathbf{P}_{cd}$.

We aim to recover the coupled model parameters which minimise the error between the observed and reconstructed field of surface normals. Suppose that $\mathbf{U}$ is a vector of length $2MN$ that represents a field of surface normals obtained by applying shape-from-shading to the brightness image of a face. We fit the model to data seeking the vector $\mathbf{c}^*$ of length $S + D$ that satisfies the condition

$$\mathbf{c}^* = \arg\min_{\mathbf{c}}(\mathbf{U} - \mathbf{Q}_s\mathbf{c})^\mathrm{T}(\mathbf{U} - \mathbf{Q}_s\mathbf{c}) \tag{3}$$

The corresponding best-fit vector of depth values is given by $\mathbf{z} = \hat{\mathbf{z}} + \mathbf{Q}_d\mathbf{c}^*$.

3 Fitting the Model to Image Brightness Data

The overall aim in this paper is to fit the model to image brightness data rather than surface normal data. To do this we exploit the constraint that according to Lambert's law the surface normal must fall on a cone whose axis is the light source direction and whose opening angle is the inverse cosine of the normalised image brightness. If I is the measured image brightness, then according to Lambert's law $I = \mathbf{n}.\mathbf{s}$, where $\mathbf{s}$ is the light source direction. The recovered surface normal lies on the reflectance cone whose axis is aligned with the light-source vector $\mathbf{s}$ and whose opening angle is $\arccos I$. Suppose that $(\mathbf{n}')^l(i,j)$ is an off-cone surface normal estimate at iteration l of the algorithm, then the update equation is $\mathbf{n}^{l+1}(i,j) = \Theta(\mathbf{n}')^l(i,j)$, where Θ is a rotation matrix computed from the apex angle α and the angle between $(\mathbf{n}')^l(i,j)$ and the light source direction $\mathbf{s}$. To restore the surface normal to the closest on-cone position it must be rotated by an angle $\theta = \alpha - \arccos\left[(\mathbf{n}')^l(i,j).\mathbf{s}\right]$ about the axis $(u, v, w)^T = (\mathbf{n}')^l(i,j) \times \mathbf{s}$.

To iteratively fit our model to brightness data using the geometric constraints on surface normal direction, we make use of the following algorithm:

1. Calculate an initial estimate of the field of surface normals $\mathbf{n}$ by placing each normal on its reflectance cone at the point closest to the local average normal direction. Each normal in the estimated field $\mathbf{n}$ undergoes an azimuthal equidistant projection to give a vector of transformed coordinates $\mathbf{U}$.
2. The vector of surface normal model parameters representing the best fit to $\mathbf{U}$ is given by $\mathbf{b}_s = \mathbf{P}_s^T\mathbf{U}$. The vector of transformed coordinates corresponding to the best-fit parameters is given by $\mathbf{U}' = \mathbf{P}_s\mathbf{P}_s^T\mathbf{U}$
3. Using the inverse azimuthal equidistant projection find the off-cone best fit field of surface normals $\mathbf{n}'$ from $\mathbf{U}'$. Find the on-cone surface normals $\mathbf{n}''$ by rotating the off-cone surface normals in $\mathbf{n}'$.
4. Test for convergence. If $\sum_{i,j} \cos^{-1}\left[\mathbf{n}(i,j).\mathbf{n}''(i,j)\right] < \epsilon$, where ϵ is a predetermined threshold, then proceed to step 6.
5. Make $\mathbf{n} = \mathbf{n}''$ and return to step 1.
6. Find the coupled model parameters $\mathbf{c}^*$ corresponding to the best fit field of normals $\mathbf{U}'$ using Eq. 3. Return $\mathbf{z} = \hat{\mathbf{z}} + \mathbf{Q}_d\mathbf{c}^*$ as the recovered depth map.

4 Experiments

We begin by examining the effect of the number of eigenmodes used on the surface normal, depth and coupled models. The models were trained on a set of high resolution 3D scans of 100 male and 100 female subjects with a neutral expression. The scans were collected using a *Cyberware*[TM] 3030PS laser scanner.

In Figure 1 we plot cumulative variance against the number of eigenmodes used. It is evident that fewer eigenmodes are required to capture variance in facial depth than in facial needle maps. This is because the surface normal at each point has two degrees of freedom whereas the depth value has only one. We retained 63 dimensions of the depth model and 142 dimensions of the surface normal model (each accounting for 95% of the variance). As would be expected, the coupled model lies between the two and requires 95 dimensions to capture 95% of the variance.

We now compare the surfaces recovered using the coupled model with the surfaces recovered using the technique of Frankot and Chellappa [8] on ground truth data. We use a leave-one-out validation strategy, in which we train the coupled model with all but one of the range scans. We render an intensity image of the out-of-sample subject to which we fit the coupled model using the technique described in Section 3. We use a Matlab implementation of a quasi-Newton minimisation procedure to solve Equation 3, constrained such that each coupled parameter lies within ±3 standard deviations of the mean. Let $z^k_{frankot}$ be the surface for the kth subject recovered by integrating the best fit needle-map ($\mathbf{n}'$) using the method of Frankot and Chellappa, and let $z^k_{coupled}$ be the surface for the kth subject given by the best-fit surface in the coupled model. We found that

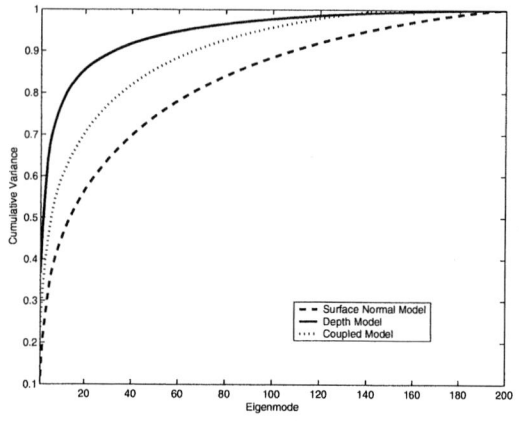

Fig. 1. Plot of cumulative variance versus number of eigenmodes used for depth model (solid line), surface normal model (dashed line) and coupled model (dotted line)

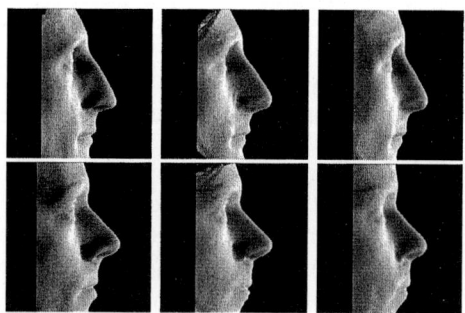

Fig. 2. Ground truth profile view (left), surface recovered from best fit needle-map using coupled model (middle) and using Frankot and Chellappa's method (right)

the average absolute error of the surfaces recovered using the coupled model was 2.3mm with a standard deviation of 0.7mm. Using the Frankot and Chellappa method this error was 3.2mm with a standard deviation of 1.1mm. Hence using the coupled model for surface recovery offers both improved accuracy and stability over integrating the recovered field of normals.

In Figure 2 we show two typical sets of recovered surfaces as described above. On the left of the figure the ground truth profile view is shown. In the middle column the surface recovered using the coupled model is shown, while on the right the surface using the Frankot and Chellappa method are shown. In both cases the Frankot and Chellappa method has reduced the size of the nose and brought the forehead forwards.

The results on ground truth data suggest fitting the coupled model to an image in a frontal view allows surfaces to be recovered of sufficient quality to synthesise accurate profile views. We now test whether this performance can be transferred to real world images which contain noise and albedo variations. We use images from the Yale B [9] database of subjects in a frontal pose illuminated by a single light source situated close to the view point. As a preprocessing step we remap Lambertian reflectance onto the faces using an image-based re-

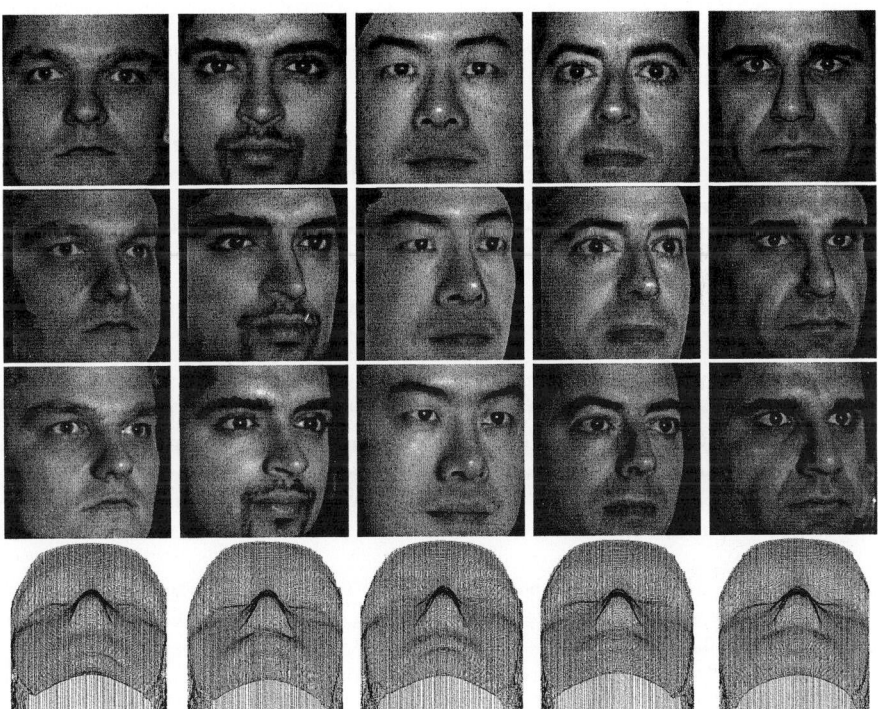

Fig. 3. Top row: Input frontal view, second row: synthesised view rotated 24° from frontal, third row: corresponding actual view, fourth row: recovered surface mesh

flectance estimation process [10]. Figure 3 shows the results of fitting the coupled model to images of five subjects. The first row shows the input images prior to reflectance correction. The second row shows a synthesised view in which the input image has been texture mapped onto the estimated surface and rotated 24° about the vertical axis. The third row contains a real image of the subject in approximately the same pose and frontal illumination for comparison. In all cases the synthesis is convincing under a fairly large change in viewpoint, recovering the size and relative height of the features accurately. Note that the placement of specularities is inconsistent because their position is dependent on viewpoint, an effect which is not captured by texture mapping a frontal view onto the recovered mesh. In the fourth row we show the recovered surface meshes rotated 40° about the horizontal axis to allow inspection of the shape alone.

5 Conclusions

In this paper, we have shown how variations in surface normal direction can be coupled to variation in height using a global statistical model inspired by the active appearance model. Effectively the method allows us to overcome the problems of concave-convex ambiguity associated with recovering surface height from brightness alone and avoids an explicit height-from-gradient step. The face model is represented by separate subspaces that represent the modes of variation in the covariance matrices for surface normal direction and relative depth. The model is trained on range data, and fitted to image brightness data using a simple geometric algorithm. We experiment with the method on frontal brightness images of faces and demonstrate that synthesised views are well reconstructed by the fitted surfaces.

References

1. Atick, J.J., Griffin, P.A., Redlich, A.N.: Statistical approach to SFS: Reconstruction of 3D face surfaces from single 2D images. Neural Comp. **8** (1996) 1321–1340
2. Zhao, W.Y., Chellappa, R.: Illumination-insensitive face recognition using symmetric SFS. In: Proc. CVPR. (2000) 286–293
3. Prados, E., Faugeras, O.D.: Unifying approaches and removing unrealistic assumptions in shape from shading: Mathematics can help. In: Proc. ECCV. (2004) 141–154
4. Dovgard, R., Basri, R.: Statistical symmetric shape from shading for 3D structure recovery of faces. In: Proc. 8th European Conference on Computer Vision. Volume 2. (2004) 99–113
5. Nandy, D., Ben-Arie, J.: Shape from recognition: A novel approach for 3-D face shape recovery. IEEE Trans. Image Processing **10** (2001) 206–217
6. Cootes, T.F., Edwards, G.J., Taylor, C.J.: Active appearance models. In: Proc. ECCV. (1998) 484–498
7. Sirovich, L.: Turbulence and the dynamics of coherent structures. Quart. Applied Mathematics **XLV** (1987) 561–590

8. Frankot, R.T., Chellappa, R.: A method for enforcing integrability in shape from shading algorithms. IEEE Trans. PAMI **10** (1988) 439–451
9. Georghiades, A., Belhumeur, P., Kriegman, D.: From few to many: Illumination cone models for face recognition under variable lighting and pose. IEEE Trans. PAMI **23** (2001) 643–660
10. Smith, W., Robles-Kelly, A., Hancock, E.R.: Reflectance correction for perspiring faces. In: Proc. ICIP. (2004) 1389–1392

Recovery of Surface Height Using Polarization from Two Views

Gary Atkinson and Edwin R. Hancock

Department of Computer Science,
University of York, York, YO1 5DD, UK
{atkinson, erh}@cs.york.ac.uk

Abstract. This paper describes a method for establishing stereo correspondences using diffuse polarization information. To do this we exploit the spontaneous polarization of light caused by reflection from dielectric surfaces to recover surface normals. The normals recovered from two different views are used to locally reconstruct surface height. The similarity between reconstructed surface regions determines whether or not a pair of points correspond to each other. The technique is able to overcome the convex/concave ambiguity found in many single view techniques. As the technique relies on smooth surface regions to detect correspondences it is applicable to objects that normally cause difficulty for stereo vision algorithms.

1 Introduction

Multiple view techniques have proved to be highly effective in recovering models of surface shape [1]. The basic principle behind most computational stereo is that with two known views of an object it is possible to calculate the three-dimensional location of a point that is visible in both images. One major difficulty with stereo is deciding which points in one image correspond to which other points in the second. Most existing methods are largely geometric in nature and rely on the availability of salient surface features to establish correspondence.

Unfortunately, these methods are not particularly effective in the recovery of surface shape for smooth featureless surfaces. A different approach, photometric stereo, involves the object under study being kept static with respect to the camera, and the direction of the light source being varied [8]. However, such methods implicitly assume correspondence is known since they rely on the capture of a relatively large number of images under fixed object position and varying light source direction.

One source of information that has not been widely used on the photometric recovery of surface shape from multiple views is polarization. The aim in this paper is therefore to explore whether information provided by the polarization of light caused by diffuse surface reflection can be used to establish correspondences on featureless surfaces for the purposes of stereoscopic depth recovery.

Polarization has been extensively exploited for many decades now [6] and has recently been used in computer vision [7]. Analysis of the polarization of light caused by surface reflection has been used in the past as a means to provide constraints on surface geometry. The underlying principle is that when initially unpolarized light is reflected from a surface, it becomes partially polarized [7]. This applies to both specular reflection (which we refer to as specular polarization) and diffuse reflection (diffuse polarization) and is due to the directionality of the molecular electron charge density interacting with the electromagnetic field of the incident light [3].

Most research aimed at extracting and interpreting information from polarization data, involves placing a linear polarizer in front of a camera and taking images of an object or a scene with the polarizer oriented at different angles [5,7]. Ikeuchi and colleagues have used specular polarization in shape recovery, where there is a need for specular reflections across the whole surface. This was achieved by placing the object under investigation inside a spherical diffuser, with several light sources outside and a hole for the camera [4]. *Diffuse* polarization [5] can also be used in shape recovery. In this case the polarizing effects are weaker but the global specular reflection is not required.

The aim of this paper is to describe a new method for shape recovery that uses polarization data from images of an object taken from different viewpoints. The views of the object are found by rotating the object on a turn-table. Our method obtains a set of correspondences, a field of surface normals and a depth map. To do this, we make use of Fresnel Theory, which relates the reflected and incident wave amplitudes and provides a route to estimating the surface normals from polarization data. The available information is the phase and degree of polarization of the reflected light. The phase ambiguously defines azimuth angle, while the degree of polarization determines the zenith angle. Surface normal determination is most reliable when the degree of polarization, and therefore the zenith angle, are large, that is close to the occluding boundary.

A number of features make this work distinct from other stereo methods. Firstly, the height is reconstructed via surface integration, not triangulation, hence the need for a highly detailed geometric calibration is diminished. Secondly, the new method is applicable to surfaces that have no distinctive albedo or curvature features. Results presented here show that some albedo variations or specularities do not severely affect correspondence detection. The method is applicable to smooth dielectric objects that do not have excessive albedo variations. For slightly rough surfaces, results are degraded but still of use (the surface azimuth angle can still be very accurately estimated). Illumination conditions do not need to be known, but results are most reliable when fewer light sources are used since this reduces specularities.

2 Polarization and Reflection

The Fresnel equations [3] give the ratios of the reflected wave amplitude to the incident wave amplitude for incident light that is linearly polarized perpendicular to, or parallel to, the plane of specular incidence. These ratios depend upon the angle of incidence and the refractive index, n, of the reflecting medium. Since

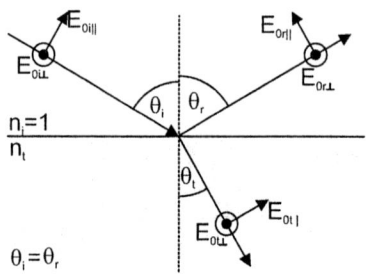
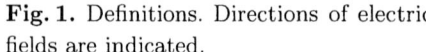
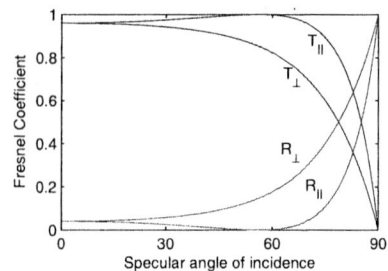

Fig. 1. Definitions. Directions of electric fields are indicated.

Fig. 2. Reflection and transmission coefficients for a dielectric ($n = 1.5$)

the incident light can always be resolved into two perpendicular components, the Fresnel equations are applicable to all incident polarization states. Indeed, throughout this work, we assume that the incident light is unpolarized.

For the geometry of Fig. 1, the Fresnel reflection coefficients are

$$r_\perp(n_i, n_t, \theta_i) \equiv \frac{E_{0r\perp}}{E_{0i\perp}} = \frac{n_i \cos\theta_i - n_t \cos\theta_t}{n_i \cos\theta_i + n_t \cos\theta_t} \tag{1}$$

$$r_\parallel(n_i, n_t, \theta_i) \equiv \frac{E_{0r\parallel}}{E_{0i\parallel}} = \frac{n_t \cos\theta_i - n_i \cos\theta_t}{n_t \cos\theta_i + n_i \cos\theta_t} \tag{2}$$

where (1) gives the reflection ratio for light polarized perpendicular to the plane of incidence and (2) is for light polarized parallel to the plane of incidence. The angle θ_t can be obtained from the well-known Snell's Law: $n_i \sin\theta_i = n_t \sin\theta_t$. Cameras do not measure the amplitude of a wave but the square of the amplitude, or *intensity*. With this in mind, it is possible to show that the *intensity coefficients*, which relate the reflected power to the incident power, are $R_\perp = r_\perp^2$ and $R_\parallel = r_\parallel^2$ [3].

Figure 2 shows the Fresnel intensity coefficients for a typical dielectric as a function of the angle of the incident light. Both reflection and transmission coefficients are shown, where the latter refers to the ratio of transmitted to incident power (the transmission coefficients are simply $T_\perp = 1 - R_\perp$ and $T_\parallel = 1 - R_\parallel$).

The work reported here relies on taking a succession of images of objects with a polarizer mounted on the camera at different angles. As the polarizer is rotated, the measured pixel brightness at a given point varies according to the *Transmitted Radiance Sinusoid* (TRS):

$$I(\theta_{pol}, \phi) = \frac{I_{max} + I_{min}}{2} + \frac{I_{max} - I_{min}}{2} \cos(2\theta_{pol} - 2\phi) \tag{3}$$

Let I_{max} and I_{min} be the maximum and minimum intensities in this sinusoid respectively. The *degree of polarization* is defined to be

$$\rho = \frac{I_{max} - I_{min}}{I_{max} + I_{min}} \tag{4}$$

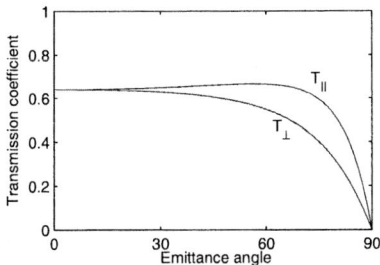
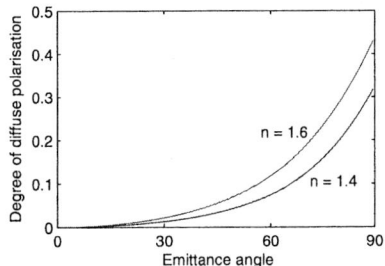

Fig. 3. Fresnel coefficients for light leaving a medium ($n = 1.5$)

Fig. 4. Degree of polarization for diffuse reflection for two different refractive indices

Careful consideration of Fig. 2 and the Fresnel equations leads to an expression for the degree of polarization in terms of the refractive index and the zenith angle, the angle between the surface normal and the viewing direction. Unfortunately, this equation is only applicable to specular reflection since the process that causes diffuse polarization is different, as explained below.

Diffuse polarization is a result of the following process [7]: A portion of the incident light penetrates the surface and is scattered internally. Due to the random nature of internal scattering, the light becomes depolarized. Some of the light is then refracted back into the air, being refracted and partially polarized in the process. Snell's Law and the Fresnel equations can be used to predict the degree of polarization of light emerging from the surface at a given angle. Figure 3 shows the Fresnel coefficients for light being refracted from within the medium back into air.

Using a similar method to that used for specular polarization, an equation for the degree of polarization in terms of the zenith angle and refractive index can be derived:

$$\rho = \frac{(n - 1/n)^2 \sin^2 \theta}{2 - 2n^2 - (n + 1/n)^2 \sin^2 \theta + 4 \cos \theta \sqrt{n^2 - \sin^2 \theta}} \tag{5}$$

The dependence of the diffuse polarization ρ on the zenith angle θ is shown in Fig. 4. The azimuth angle of the surface normal, i.e. the angle of the projection of the surface normal onto the image plane, is also intimately related to the Fresnel equations. As Fig. 3 shows, diffusely reflected light is reflected most efficiently when polarized parallel to the plane containing the surface normal and the ray reflected towards the camera. The orientation of this plane is determined by the surface normal azimuth angle.

3 Method and Algorithm

In this section we discuss the experimental set-up used to acquire the images for processing and the structure of the new algorithm. The inputs to the algorithm are polarization images of the object being studied. For this paper, the images were obtained by mounting a Nikon D70 digital SLR camera with a linear polarizer and taking images of the object with the polarizer at 10° increments. A single point light source was used, placed near the camera. Different views were obtained by rotating the object on a turn-table. The table and walls of the laboratory are matte black to minimise reflections from the environment. For each view, the phase ϕ and degree of polarization ρ were calculated at each pixel by fitting the TRS (3) to measured pixel brightnesses.

The novel contribution of this paper, namely the *unambiguous* conversion of these polarization images to needle maps can be divided into three main sections:

1. Selection of *potential* correspondences directly from polarization images.
2. Calculation of most likely correspondences from this selection.
3. Disambiguation of azimuth angles.

In addition to these steps, we have used the Frankot-Chellappa needle map integration algorithm [2] to recover depth from the field of surface normals.

3.1 Locating Potential Correspondences

The purpose of this stage is to select pixels from each image that have similar surface normals and to form a list of potential correspondences. Before the initial selection of points is made, an angle is calculated from which the algorithm derives all correspondences. This angle, θ_D, is defined to be that between the viewing direction and the projection of the surface normal onto the horizontal plane. Note that θ_D falls in the interval $[-90°, +90°]$, where negative values indicate that the surface normal is directed to the left. At this stage however, the sign of θ_D is unknown since ϕ falls within the interval $[0, 180°)$. θ_D allows reconstruction of the depth of any single slice of the object and is given by

$$\theta_D = \arctan\left(\sin\left(\phi\right)\tan\left(\theta\right)\right) \quad (6)$$

After θ_D has been calculated for each pixel, a search is performed for points with certain values and listed as potential correspondences. For example, if the angle by which the object was rotated was $\theta_{rot} = 20°$, then it would be reasonable to search for $\theta_D = 70°$ (call this θ_0) in the unrotated image, and $\theta_D = \theta_0 - \theta_{rot} = 50°$ in the rotated image. Because the rotation is about a vertical axis, we know that points on the object move about a horizontal plane. This means that the two points in any correspondence lie in the same horizontal line in the images. More correspondences can be then found using other values of θ_0.

Figure 5a shows points on a (simulated) sphere that have $\theta_D = 70°$. In Fig. 5b, which shows the sphere rotated by 20° (obviously with an identical intensity image) points are highlighted where $\theta_D = 50°$. Without prior knowledge of surface geometry, we know that some of the highlighted points from Fig. 5a are likely to correspond to those in Fig. 5b, but it is not yet clear, for example, whether point A corresponds to A' or B'. Indeed, it may be that A is occluded in the second image so no correspondence exists for that point.

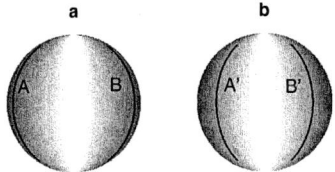

Fig. 5. a) Simulated $|\theta_D|$ image for a sphere. Darker areas have higher values. The highlighted regions have $|\theta_D| = \theta_0$, in this case 70°. b) Same sphere rotated by 20°. Here points with $|\theta_D| = 50°$ are highlighted.

Moderate smoothing is applied at this stage of the algorithm to the featureless areas. Since these areas have no features, the problem of over-smoothing, which is frequently encountered in computer vision, is not an issue. The unsmoothed images can be used again later for needle map integration, after correspondences have been found.

Consider an object rotating clockwise if viewed from above. Now imagine the object viewed horizontally. Most, and on many occasions all, of the points on the visible surface of the object will be moving away from the occluding contour that is to left of the point, and toward the contour to its right. This fact is used to reduce the number of potential correspondences for a given point.

3.2 Final Estimates of Correspondences

The algorithm takes the remaining correspondence possibilities and decides which are genuine and which to discard. This is done by locally reconstructing the height of parts of surfaces near the selected points and comparing the results from each view.

The surface height, z is calculated in the vicinity of each selected point for both views using standard integration methods [9]:

$$p_x = \tan(\theta_D) \qquad z_n = \sum^{n} p_{x_n} - c \qquad (7)$$

where p_x is the x-component of the surface normal (in 2D) and c is an unimportant constant. The surface is not reconstructed where θ_D is close to zero since the diffuse polarization theory is less accurate here. Reconstructed surface segments from the rotated image are then rotated in the opposite direction by θ_{rot} and aligned with the point's potential correspondence in the unrotated image. The root-mean-square (RMS) difference, ε, between the two surfaces is calculated.

The final list of correspondences are then found by using the combination of correspondences that gives the least total RMS error while remaining valid (i.e. does not cause the surface to overlap on itself).

3.3 Disambiguation

After correspondences have been located using a range of θ_0, many points on the surface are unambiguous since the sign of θ_D for the two points of any detected correspondence is the same. For the remaining points the following procedure was used:

Correspondences are sorted according to reliability by introducing the following confidence measure: $f_c = l\theta_0/\varepsilon$, where l is the length of the reconstructed slice. A more meaningful measure will be derived for future work.

The algorithm then propagates away from the correspondences in order of confidence and sets the surface azimuth angle to whichever is closest to the local mean, either ϕ or $\phi+180°$. This process continues until an area is reached where $\theta_D < \theta_{min}$, (where θ_{min} is taken to be about 20° although the exact figure is not important), at which point, the next correspondence is used. A few areas, mainly where $\theta_0 < \theta_{min}$, still remain ambiguous. These regions are simply "closed" by aligning with the local mean azimuth angle. Such regions are unimportant, since the surface height changes only slightly across these areas.

4 Results

To demonstrate the usefulness of the method, we have analysed the shape of the porcelain bear shown in Fig. 6. The bear is made of a smooth featureless white dielectric so is well suited to the technique. The overall geometry however, is complex and specular inter-reflections are present, where the incident light is reflected twice or more without absorption. For these areas the theory for specular reflection is obeyed. The phase images show the results that one would expect apart from a few small areas (near arms, legs and ears) where the phase has deviated by 90° from the expected value. This is due to the inter-reflections.

With a few exceptions, the correspondences have been accurately located. The addition of the constraint that corresponding points move away from the left occluding contour clearly plays an important (and computationally inexpensive) role. The disambiguation routine appears to work well except for areas where θ_D is near zero. This is due to the unsophisticated final stage of processing, which attempts to disambiguate these areas.

Figure 7 shows the result of applying the Frankot-Chellappa algorithm to recovered needle maps. The first depth map shows the frontal view (let the angle of the turn-table here be $\theta_{turn} = 0$) of the bear obtained using $\theta_{turn} = 0$ and 20°. The other depth maps were found using $\theta_{turn} = 120°$ and 140° and $\theta_{turn} = 240°$ and 260°. This combination of six different θ_{turn} allows for a compromise between keeping the two views used to disambiguate azimuth angles close (which allows a greater density of correspondences to be obtained since there is less occlusion) and the acquisition of 360° of the object. Zippering the segments together will be the focus of future work. Figure 8 shows a reconstruction of a partly painted porcelain cat. This shows that even in the presence of some textured regions accurate correspondence detection and height reconstruction are still possible. The figure also shows the original colours mapped back onto the surface.

5 Conclusion

A new method for height reconstruction has been presented that makes use of diffuse polarization information from two views. The polarization data is used

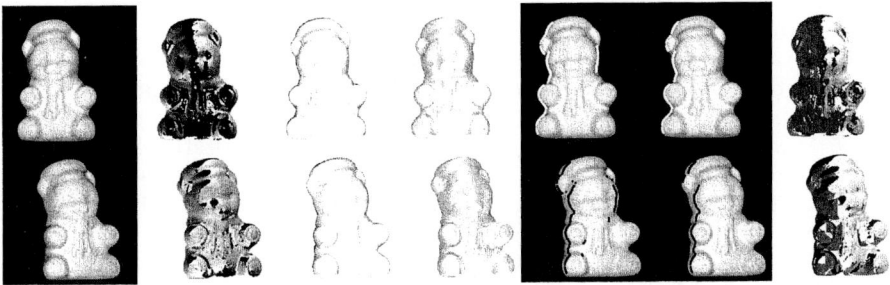

Fig. 6. Various stages in the processing of a porcelain bear. From left: greyscale images from the original view and after a 20° rotation; phase image; degree of polarization (dark areas are highest); $|\theta_D|$, (the sign of θ_D is unknown at this stage and, again, dark areas are higher); potential correspondences (where the $|\theta_D|$ condition is met); final estimates of correspondences (for a single value of θ_0); disambiguated azimuth angles.

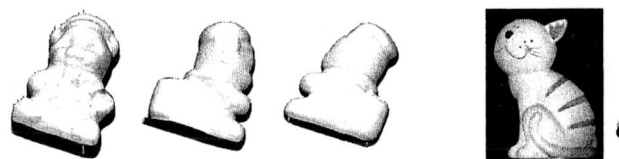

Fig. 7. Reconstruction of the porcelain bear from different views separated by 120°

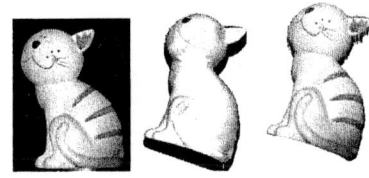

Fig. 8. Left: original image of porcelain cat with a small amount of paint added. Centre: recovered depth map. Right: mapping of original colours onto the surface.

both to find correspondences and to recover surface normals. The results are promising, with the majority of azimuth angles correctly disambiguated and the surface height accurately recovered. There are nevertheless several possible improvements to the technique. For example, including the detection of surface features (for objects with one or more textured regions), as in previous stereo methods, would provide a greater density of correspondences for some objects. Accuracy in surface height would be improved by the use of normals from both views when applying the Frankot-Chellappa algorithm. We also intend to compare and possibly combine this method with intensity-based methods such as shape from shading [10].

References

1. M. Z. Brown and G. D. Hager. Advances in computational stereo. *IEEE Trans. Patt. Anal. Mach. Intell.*, 25:993–1008, 2003.
2. R. T. Frankot and R. Chellappa. A method for enforcing integrability in shape from shading algorithms. *IEEE Trans. Patt. Anal. Mach. Intell.*, 10:439–451, 1988.

3. E. Hecht. *Optics*. Addison Wesley Longman, third edition, 1998.
4. D. Miyazaki, M. Kagesawa, and K. Ikeuchi. Transparent surface modelling from a pair of polarization images. *IEEE Trans. Patt. Anal. Mach. Intell.*, 26:73–82, 2004.
5. D. Miyazaki, R. T. Tan, K. Hara, and K. Ikeuchi. Polarization-based inverse rendering from a single view. In *Proc. ICCV*, volume 2, pages 982–987, 2003.
6. W.A. Shurcliff. *Polarized Light: Production and Use*. Harvard University Press, 1962.
7. L. B. Wolff and T. E. Boult. Constraining object features using a polarisation reflectance model. *IEEE Trans. Pattern Anal. Mach. Intell*, 13:635–657, 1991.
8. R. J. Woodham. Photometric method for determining surface orientation from multiple images. *Optical Engineering*, 19:139–144, 1980.
9. Z. Wu and L. Li. A line-integration based method for depth recovery from surface normals. In *CVGIP(43)*, pages 53–66, 1988.
10. R. Zhang, P. Tsai, J.E. Cryer, and M. Shah. Shape from shading: A survey. *IEEE Trans. Pattern Anal. Mach. Intell*, 21:690–706, 1999.

FSVC: A New Fully Scalable Video Codec

M.F. López, S.G. Rodríguez, J.P. Ortiz, J.M. Dana, V.G. Ruiz, and I. García

Computer Architecture and Electronics Dept.
University of Almería, Almería, Spain

Abstract. This work describes FSVC (Fully Scalable Video Codec), a scalable video compression system which is able to generate temporal-, spatial- and quality-scalable video streams. FSVC is very suitable for video-on-demand applications where a single version of the compressed video sequence is used. A video server can provide video streams to several clients with different visualization and band-width requirements using a single copy of the stream which is organized as a set of packets (as in Motion JPEG 2000). The server is able to accommodate to a large variety of clients just selecting which packets will be transmitted. The simplicity of this transcoding operation makes possible a low-power server to provide service to a large number of clients.

1 Introduction

Scalable video coding is a technique which allows a compressed video stream to be decoded in several different ways. Users can adaptively recover a specific version of a video just selecting which parts of the compressed sequence will be decoded depending on its own requirements: (1) frame-rate, (2) spatial resolution, (3) image quality and (4) data-rate. Frame-rate (or image-rate) is obtained by means of the *Temporal Scalability*. *Spatial Scalability* provides a set of spatial resolutions for each image. The progressive minimization of the distortion of the reconstructed video at the decoder is obtained by the *Quality Scalability*. These types of scalabilities can be combined together to achieve some target bit-rate that can be limited by the capabilities of the decoder or the transmission link. Therefore, it is possible to generalize the scalability idea to the concept of a *Data-rate Scalability*. Video scalable coding is a major feature for video storage and transmission systems. For example, in Video on Demand (VoD) applications a server sends a video stream to a set of clients thorough a number of transmission links. For most of the cases, the quality, resolution, and frame-rate of the visualizations must be adapted to the requirements of the decoder and/or the band-width available for each link. In this context, the computational requirements of the servers are proportional to the number of clients. For non-scalable video coding, there are two alternatives to minimize one of these requirements (not both): (1) the creation of a specific copy of each sequence for each possible client or (2) the use of CPU-intensive real-time transcoding processes to re-encode on-the-fly the sequences. A scalable video coding can address both problems at the same time because only a copy of each sequence is stored in the server and the transcoding task is simplified. In the worst case, the transcoding will consist of a re-ordering of the compressed data at the transmission time. This action is so simple that it can be carried out by the clients retrieving the adequate portions of the stream.

2 The Video Codec

Our proposed video compressor FSVC (Fully Scalable Video Codec), as shown in Figure 1, is a differential coding system that reduces the temporal redundancy of the video sequence I and the spatial redundancy of each image (frame) of the video sequence. FSVC produces a compressed stream that is highly scalable. The FSVC decompressor recovers the original input video I when the full stream of the compressed data is available.

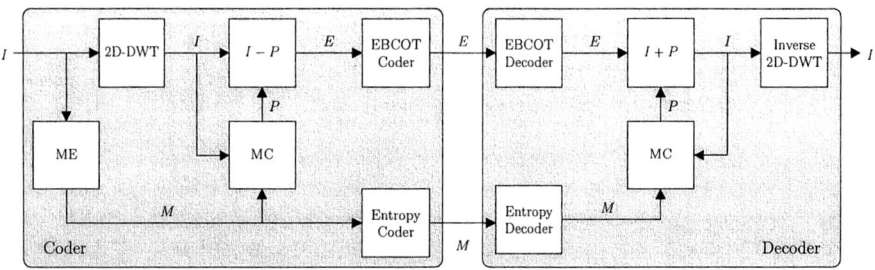

Fig. 1. A block diagram of FSVC

The input sequence of frames is first divided in GOFs (Group of Frames) and each GOF is encoded separately. This allows the decoder: (1) to access any GOF of the compressed video without decoding the rest and (2) to avoid the error propagation when real-time transmissions are carried out over error-prune transmission links.

A differential prediction scheme (MCTF Motion Compensated Temporal Filtering [1]) is used to reduce the temporal redundancy of the video. For each frame $I[i]$, a prediction image $P[i]$ is generated by the Motion Compensation (MC) module. This module uses the motion vectors $M[i]$ that have been produced by the Motion Estimation (ME) module. The motion estimation is performed in the image domain. Each motion field $M[i]$ indicates the spatial displacements of a set of blocks in a set of previously encoded images (reference images, see Figure 2) in order to create the prediction image $P[i]$ that approximates the current frame $I[i]$. The differential coding is carried out in the wavelet domain in order to (1) minimize the disgraceful blocking artifacts that are visible at low bit-rates when it is carried out in the image domain and (2) avoid spatial scalability drift errors [2]. For this reason, each image $I[i]$ is transformed using the 2-D Discrete Wavelet Transform (DWT). The compensated blocks are also in the wavelet domain, but using the correct phase to avoid the shift variability of the DWT [3]. The same motion field is used at each resolution level. Thus, the resulting sequence of residues E has smaller entropy than the original I.

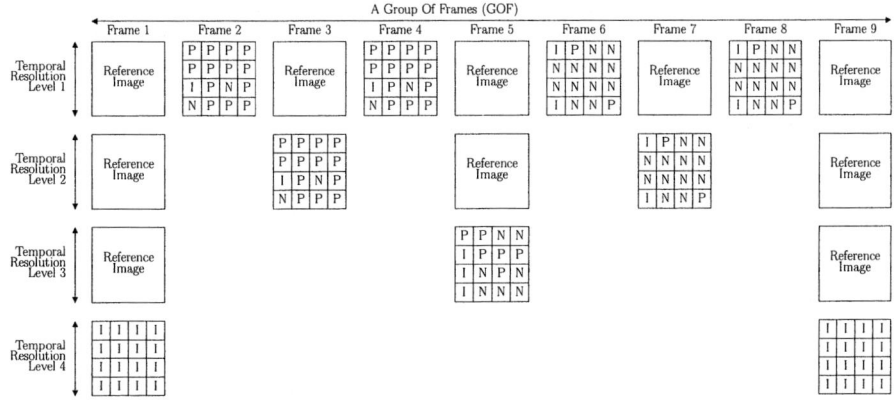

Fig. 2. An example of a motion-compensated prediction for a 8-frames GOF (only one sub-band is shown). Frame 9 is shared with tne next GOF.

The MCTF is performed in the wavelet domain. The prediction image is composed by blocks of a previous frame (P-blocks) and by blocks of a future frame (N-blocks) as shown in Figure 2. When no prediction can be generated, an I-block (intra) is used. Figure 2 shows also the relationship between the images of the GOF to obtain dyadic temporal scalability. For instance, frame 5 is predicted with frames 1 and 9; frame 3 is predicted with frames 1 and 5, and so on. Every block of a predicted frame can be backward or forward predicted. The choice between forward or backward prediction is made according to the MSE (Mean Square Error) and minimizing drift errors. Drift errors accumulate over dependencies between predicted frames. Therefore, for predicted frame 2, forward predictions have higher priority than backward, because at the decoder, frame 1 (whose every block is intra coded) will be reconstructed with more or less quality but with no drift errors.

Notice that the frames of every GOF are predicted with two intra coded frames (in Figure 2, frames 1 and 9). This feature is not possible in conventional MPEG standards, but for scalable video frameworks it allows better reconstructions at the decoder because the intra-frames are shared by two GOFs.

Each residue $E[i]$ is compressed using EBCOT [4], generating a collection of packets. Each packet is the contribution of a precinct P (a spatial region of the image) to a quality layer L (a level of distortion), for a spatial resolution R, for a colour component C and for a GOF G. The packet-stream can be easily reorganized because information about the location of each packet is also stored in it.

The motion data M is entropy compressed. An static 0-order probabilistic model and Huffman coding are used to remove the statistical redundancy. For future work we should include techniques for scalable coding of the motion information.

3 The Use of FSVC on VoD Systems

Most VoD systems are implemented using a client-server architecture. The compressed video data is stored in the server and several clients retrieve the data (or a part of it) in order to visualize the video sequence. Scalable video coding is extremely useful in these applications because usually it is impossible to decode all the data. Therefore, the server or the clients must select which packets are going to be transmitted.

In FSVC, the output is a sequence of packets that are placed in the stream using some ordering. This ordering is important because it determines the way the video sequence will be displayed when only a partial decoding of the compressed stream is carried out. In our system the coder selects the ordering (also called progression) depending on the requirements of the visualization:

1. **Progressive by quality** is used when most of the clients need to preserve the original frame-rate and spatial resolution, but allowing a variation of the quality (in a SNR sense) of the GOF. Any GL-subordinated ordering can be used for this proposal because packets are organized in the stream first by GOF and second by quality layer.
2. **Progressive by resolution** is provided by any GR-subordinated ordering. Using these progressions clients preserve the original frame-rate of the GOF but the spatial resolution is controlled by the bit-rate.
3. **Progressive by frame-rate** is used when most of the clients need to preserve the maximal spatial resolution of the GOF. GT-subordinated orderings should be used.

All the proposed progressions are G-subordinated. These progressions have two advantages in VoD applications: (1) for a simple configuration, the control of the data-flow between a client and the server is produced once for each GOF and can be done using reliable protocols such as the TCP (Transmission Control Protocol); (2) it is easy to access randomly to any GOF of the video sequence because each GOF can be independently decompressed.

As it has been explained before, the default packet ordering can be modified in real-time by the clients depending on their own requirements. For example, if the number of precincts used is large enough, a client could retrieve the packets that improve (with respect to the rest of the image) the quality of a moving Region Of Interest (ROI) [5].

4 Experimental Results

In this section, results on coding efficiency and visual quality in a "progressive by quality scenario" are presented. This scenario is the most interesting for VoD applications because its excellent bit-rate scalability. A comparison has been performed between our codec and the RWMH codec proposed by Cui et al. [6]. Table 1 describes the FSVC and RWMH codecs used in the experiments.

Table 1. Summary of FSVC and RWMH: SF = Spatial Filters, SRL = Spatial Resolution Levels, TF = Temporal Filters, TRL = Temporal Resolution Levels, MC = Motion Compensation, MC-PA = MC Pixel Accuracy, EoR = Encoding of Residuals, EoMI = Encoding of Motion Information

	FSVC	RWMH
SF	Biorthogonal 9/7	Biorthogonal 9/7
SRL	4	1
TF	Bidirectional 1/1	IPPP...
TRL	5	-
MC	Fixed block-size	Fixed block-size
MC-PA	1/1	1/8
EoR	EBCOT	SPIHT
EoMI	Huffman coding	Huffman coding

In the experiments described in this section, we have compressed the luminance component of the *flower garden* and *tempete* sequences. The GLTRPC progression has been selected for FSVC. Each GOF is composed of 16 frames (4 TRLs). Each image is encoded using 16 quality layers and 4 SRLs. Coding only the luminance component implies that $C = 1$ in GLTRPC. Finally, 1 precinct per subband has been used. Therefore, each quality layer is composed of $16 \times 4 \times 1 \times 1 = 64$ packets and each GOF has $16 \times 64 = 1024$ packets. Using the GLTRPC progression, the first n packets of each GOF will be decoded, depending on the available bit-rate and the size of the packets.

4.1 Rate-Distortion Evaluations

The results for FSVC have been obtained compressing at high bit-rates and decoding at the desired bit-rate. Thus, the images reconstructed by the decoder are expected to show drift errors (these errors are minimized due to the temporal filtering we have used). Nevertheless, the bit-rate is a parameter only available at the RWMH coder (due to the RWMH implementation provided by the author; it can not be set at the decoder) and the decoded images are artificially free of drift errors. In spite of this, as can be seen in Figures 3 and 4 FSVC performs between 0.5 and 1.0 dB better than RWMH. FSVC is specially superior at low bit-rates. We think that these results are due mainly to (1) the coding efficiency of EBCOT compared to SPIHT (which is the coding algorithm used by RWMH) and (2) the sharing of intra frames between GOFs.

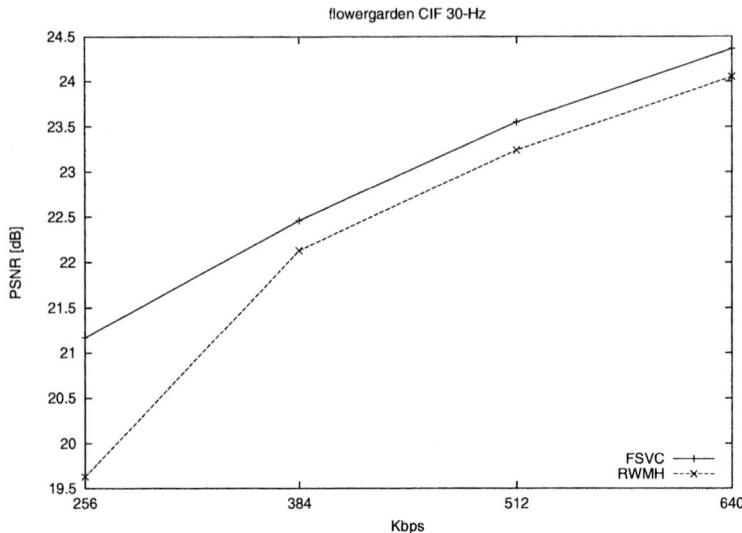

Fig. 3. Luminance PSNRs for *flower garden* sequence

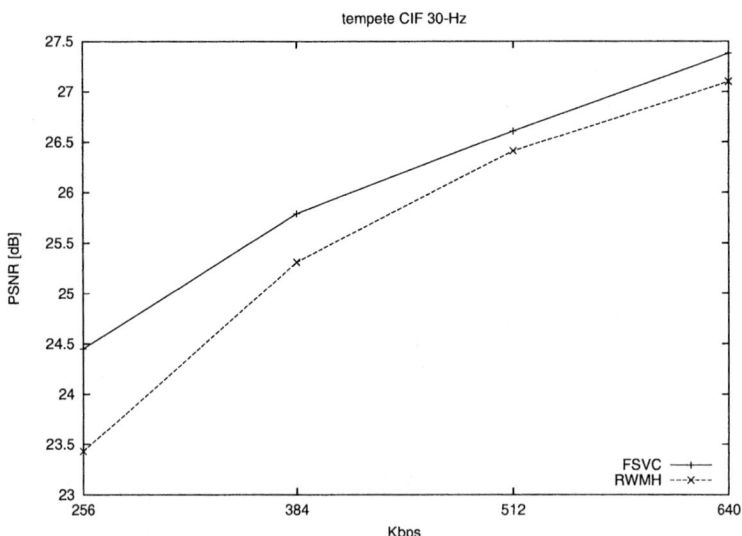

Fig. 4. Luminance PSNRs for *tempete* sequence

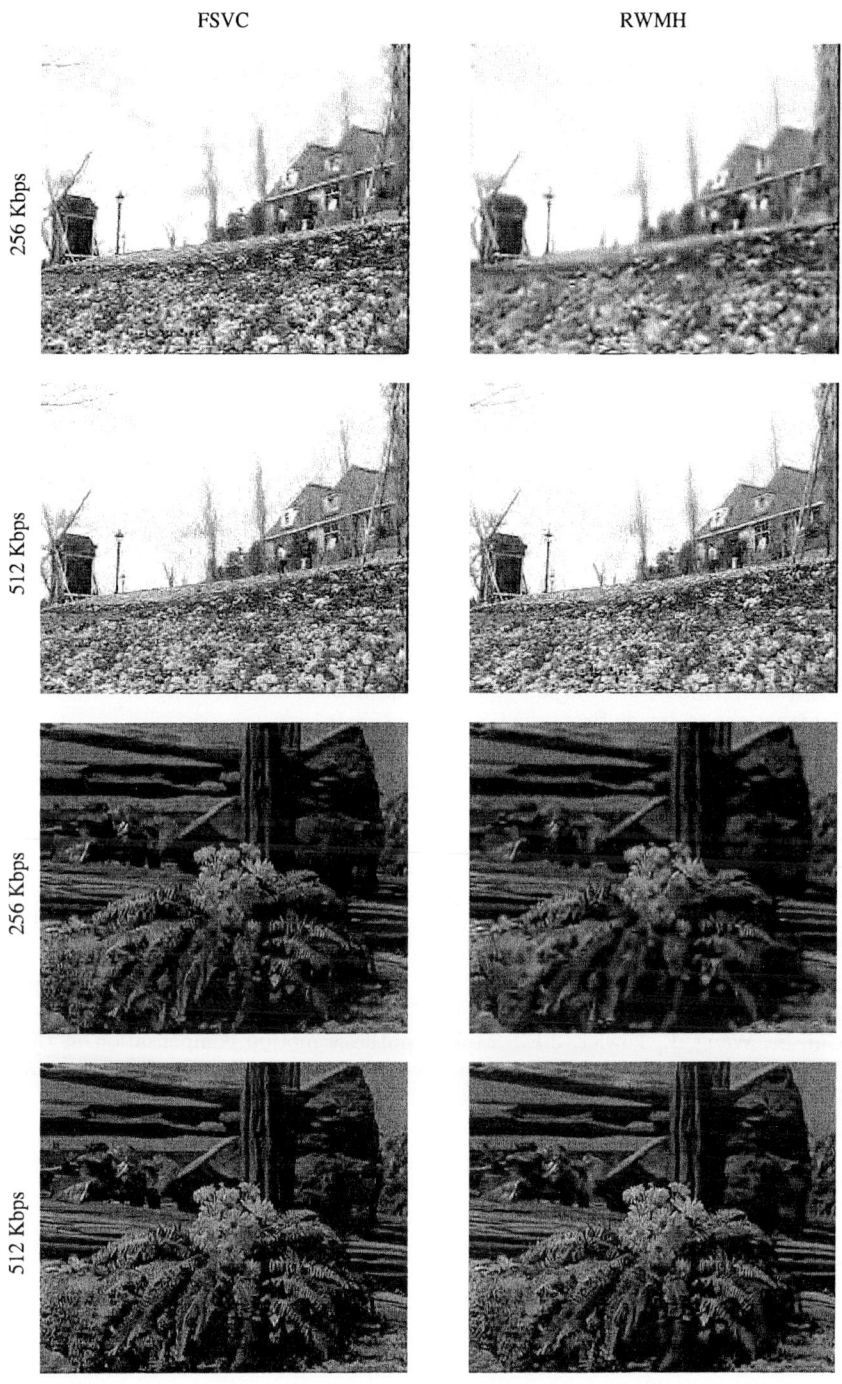

Fig. 5. Visual comparison between FSVC and RWMH

4.2 Visual Evaluations

Figure 5 shows a visual comparison between FSVC and RWMH. At the left, images from *flower garden* and *tempete* reconstructed with the FSVC decoder at different bit-rates; at the right, RWMH's. At 256 Kbps FSVC is clearly better. At 512 Kbps both codecs perform quite similar; however paying attention, some elements as the street lamp of *flower garden* and the vertical trunk of *tempete* are more detailed in FVSC decompressions.

5 Conclusions

A new fully scalable video codec FSVC based on MCTF and JPEG 2000 has been described. Our codec provides fine granularity on temporal, quality and spatial/ROI scalabilities. Moreover it exhibits higher performance than others scalable video coders, such as RWMH, on both objective and subjective comparison carried out in our experiments. Our future work involves the optimization of the parameters of our coder in order to improve its coding efficiency, and the study of techniques for the scalable coding of the motion information.

References

1. Choi, S.J., Woods, J.: Motion compensated 3-D subband coding of video. IEEE Transactions of Image Processing **8** (1999) 155–167
2. Andreopoulos, Y., van der Schaar, M., Munteanu, A., Barbarien, J., Schelkens, P., Cornelis, J.: Fully-scalable wavelet video coding using in-band motion compensated temporal filtering. In: Proceedings of the IEEE International Conference on Acoustics, Speech, and Signal Processing. Volume 3. (2003) 417–420
3. Shensa, M.: The discrete wavelet transform: weeding the Á Trous and Mallat algorithms. IEEE Transactions on Signal Processing **40** (1992) 2464–2482
4. Taubman, D.: High performance scalable image compression with EBCOT. IEEE Transactions on Image Processing **9** (2000) 1158–1170
5. Skodras, A., Christopoulos, C., Ebrahimi, T.: The jpeg 2000 still image compression standard. Signal Processing Magazine, IEEE **18** (2001) 36–58
6. Cui, S., Wang, I., Fowler, J.E.: Multihypothesis motion compensation in the redundant wavelet domain. In: Proceedings of the International Conference on Image Processing. (2003) 53–56

Eigenspaces from Seriated Graphs

Hang Yu and Edwin R. Hancock

Department of Computer Science, University of York, York Y01 5DD, UK

Abstract. The aim in this paper is to show how the problem of learning the modes of structural variation in sets of graphs can be solved by converting the graphs to strings. We commence by showing how the problem of converting graphs to strings, or seriation, can be solved using semi-definite programming (SDP). This is a convex optimisation procedure that has recently found widespread use in computer vision for problems including image segmentation and relaxation labelling. We detail the representation needed to cast the graph-seriation problem in a matrix setting so that it can be solved using SDP. We show how to perform PCA on the strings delivered by our method. By projecting the seriated graphs on to the leading eigenvectors of the sample covariance matrix, we pattern spaces suitable for graph clustering.

1 Introduction

The literature describes a number of attempts at developing probabilistic models for variations in graph-structure that can be used for shape recognition. Some of the earliest work was that of Wong, Constant and You [2], who capture the variation in graph-structure using a discretely defined probability distribution. Bagdanov and Worring [1] have overcome some of the computational difficulties associated with this method by using continuous Gaussian distributions. For problems of graph matching Christmas, Kittler and Petrou [5] and Wilson and Hancock [14] have used simple probability distributions to measure the similarity of graphs. However, despite this effort the methods fall well short of constructing genuine generative models from which explicit graph structures can be sampled. In this respect the study of graph-structures is less advanced than the study of pattern-vector or shape spaces. The reasons for limited progress are two-fold. First, graphs are not vectorial by nature. While conventional pattern recognition techniques construct shape-spaces from vectors, it is not straightforward to convert graphs into vectors. Second, in practice there usually exists structural noise or disturbance, and graphs are of different size.

To solve these problems, in this paper we turn to graph-seriation as a means of placing the nodes of a graph in a serial order. Theoretically, the graph-seriation is a challenging one since the task of locating optimal paths on graphs is one that is thought to be NP-hard [12]. The problem is known under a number of different names including "the minimum linear arrangement problem" (MLA) [15] and "graph-seriation"[9]. Stated formally, graph seriation involves finding a permutation of the nodes of a graph that satisfies constraints provided by the edges of the graph. The recovery of the permutation order can be posed as an optimisation problem. It has been shown that when the cost-function is harmonic, then an approximate solution is given by the Fiedler vector of the Laplacian matrix for the graph under study [9]. In a recent paper, Robles-Kelly and Hancock [3] have reformulated the problem as that of recovering the node permutation order subject to edge connectivity constraints, and have provided an approximate spectral solution to the problem. Although spectral methods are elegant and convenient, they are only guaranteed to locate solutions that are locally optimal. Recently, semidefinite programming (SDP) [11] has been developed as an alternative method for locating optimal solutions couched in terms of a matrix representation. Broadly speaking, the advantage of the method is that it has improved convexity properties, and is less likely to locate a local optimum. The method has been applied to a number of graph-based problems in pattern recognition including graph partitioning [7], segmentation [8][16] and the subgraph isomorphism problem [6].

The aim in this paper is hence to investigate whether SDP can be applied to the graph-seriation problem and whether the resulting strings can be used for learning a generative model of graph structure. We commence by illustrating how the cost-function can be encoded in a matrix form to which SDP can be applied. With this representation to hand, then standard SDP methods can be applied to extract the optimal serial ordering. To do this we lift the cost function to a higher-dimensional space. Here the optimization problem is relaxed to one of convex optimization, and the solution recovered by using a small set of random hyperplanes.

We explore how the resulting strings delivered by the seriation method can be used for the purposes of constructing eigenspaces for sets of graphs. To do this we use an optimisation method to construct a reference string, and bring each of the set of graphs under study into correspondence with this reference string. Using this permuted order, we construct a covariance matrix for the set of graphs. We then perform principal components analysis by projecting the graphs onto the leading eigenvectors of the covariance matrix. We demonstrate that provided sufficient eigenvectors are used, then the Euclidean distance in the eigenspace approximates well the edit distance between the strings.

2 Graph Seriation

We are concerned with the undirected graph $G = (V, E)$ with node index-set V and edge-set $E = \subseteq V \times V$. The adjacency matrix A for the graph is the $V \times V$ matrix with elements

$$A(i,j) = \begin{cases} 1 & \text{if}(i,j) \in E \\ 0 & \text{otherwise} \end{cases} \tag{1}$$

The graph seriation problem has been formally posed as one of optimisation in the work of Atkins *et al* [9]. Formally, the problem can be stated as finding a path sequence for the nodes in the graph using a permutation π which will minimize the penalty function

$$g(\pi) = \sum_{i=1}^{|V|} \sum_{j=1}^{|V|} A(i,j)(\pi(i) - \pi(j))^2 \tag{2}$$

Since the task of minimizing g is NP-hard due to the discrete nature of the permutation, a relaxed solution is sought using a function h of continuous variables x_i. The relaxed problem can be posed as seeking the solution of the constrained optmisation problem

$x = \arg\min_{x^*} h(x^*)$ where $h(x) = \sum_{(i,j)} f(i,j)(x_i - x_j)^2$ subject to the constraints $\sum_i x_i = 0$ and $\sum_i x_i^2 = 1$. Using graph-spectral methods, Atkins and his coworkers showed that the solution to the above problem can be obtained from the Laplacian matrix of the graph. The Laplacian matrix is defined to be $L_A = D_A - A$ where D_A is a diagonal matrix with $d_{i,i} = \sum_{j=1}^{n} A_{i,j}$. The solution to the relaxed seriation problem equation (2) is given by the Fiedler vector, i.e. the vector associated with the smallest non-zero eigenvalue of L_A. The required serial ordering is found by sorting the elements of the Fiedler vector into rank-order. Recently, Robles-Kelly and Hancock [3] have extended the graph seriation problem by adding edge connectivity constraints. The graph seriation problem is restated as that of minimising the cost-function

$$h_E(x) = \sum_{i=1}^{|V|-1} \sum_{k=1}^{|V|} (A(i,k) + A(i+1,k))x_k^2 \qquad (3)$$

By introducing the matrix

$$\Omega = \begin{bmatrix} 1 & 0 & 0 & 0 \cdots 0 & 0 \\ 0 & 2 & 0 & 0 \cdots 0 & 0 \\ \vdots & & & & \\ 0 & 0 & 0 & 0 \cdots 2 & 0 \\ 0 & 0 & 0 & 0 \cdots 0 & 1 \end{bmatrix}$$

the path connectivity requirement is made more explicit. The minimiser of $h_E(x)$ satisfies the condition

$$\lambda = \arg\min_{x_*} \frac{x_*^T \Omega A x_*}{x_*^T \Omega x_*} \qquad (4)$$

Although elegant and convenient, spectral methods are only guaranteed to find a locally optimal solution to the problem. For this reason in this paper we turn to the more general method of semidefinite programming to locate an optimal solution which utilizes the convexity properties of the matrix representation.

3 Semidefinite Programming

Semidefinite programming (SDP) is an area of intense current topical interest in optimization. Generally speaking, the technique is one of convex optimisation that is efficient since it uses interior-point methods. The method has been applied to a variety of optimisation tasks in combinatorial optimization, matrix completion and dual Lagrangian relaxation on quadratic models. Semidefinite programming is essentially an extension of ordinary linear programming, where the vector variables are replaced by matrix variables and the nonnegativity elementwise constraints are replaced by positive semidefiniteness. The standard form for the problem is: $X = \arg\min_{X^*} traceCX^*$, such that $traceF_iX = b_i$, $i = 1...m$, $X \succeq 0$. Here C, F_i and X are real symmetric $n \times n$ matrices and b_i is a scalar. The constraint $X \succeq 0$ means that the variable matrix must lie on the closed convex cone of positive semidefinite solutions. To solve the graph seriation problem using semidefinite programming, we denote the quantity $\Omega^{1/2} A \Omega^{-1/2}$ appearing in equation (4) by B and $\Omega^{1/2} x_*$ by y. With this notation the optimisation problem can be restated as $\lambda = \arg\min_{y^T y=1} y^T B y$. Noting that $y^T B y = trace(B y y^T)$ by letting $Y = y y^T$ in the semidefinite programming setting the seriation problem becomes $Y = \arg\min_{Y^*} trace B Y^*$ such that $trace E Y^* = 1$, where the matrix E is the unit matrix, with the diagonal elements set to 1 and all the off-diagonal set to 0. Note that $Y = y y^T$ is positive semidefinite and has rank one. As a result it is convex and we can add the positive semidefinite condition $Y \in S_n^+$ where S_n^+ denotes the set of symmetric $n \times n$ matrices which are positive semidefinite.

Interior Point Algorithm: To compute the optimal solution Y^*, a variety of iterative interior point methods can be used. By using the SDP solver developed by Fujisawa et.al [10], a primal solution matrix Y^* can be obtained. Using the solution Y^* to the convex optimization problem, we must find an ordered solution y to the original problem. To do this we use the randomized-hyperplane technique proposed by Goemans and Williamson [13].

Since $Y^* \in S_n^+$, by using the Cholesky decomposition we have that $Y = V^T V, V = (v_1, ...v_n)$. Recalling the constraint $y^T y = 1$, the vector y must lie on the unit sphere in a high dimensional space. This means that we can use the randomized hyperplanes approximation. This involves choosing a random vector r from the unit sphere. An ordered solution can then be calculated from $Y^* = V^T V$ by ordering the value of $v_i^T r$. We repeat this procedure multiple times for different random vectors. The final solution y_* is the one that yields the minimum value for the objective function $y^T B y$. This technique can be interpreted as selecting different hyperplanes through the origin, identified by their normal r, which partition the vectors $v_i, i = 1....n$.

The solution vector x_* can be obtained using the equation $\Omega^{1/2} x_* = y$, and the elements of the vector x_* then can be used to construct the serial ordering of the nodes in the graph. Commencing from the node associated with the largest component of x_*, we sort the nodes in so that the nodes are ordered so that the components of x_* are of decreasing magnitude and also satisfy edge connectivity constraints on the graph. We iteratively proceed in the following. Let us denote the list of the visited nodes by S_k at the kth iteration. Initially $S_1 = i_1 = \arg\max_i x_*(i)$. We proceed by searching the set of the first neighbours of i_1, i.e. $N_{i_1} = \{j | (i_1, j) \in E\}$, to locate the node which is associated with the largest remaining component of x_*. This node is then appended to the list of nodes visited list and satisfies the condition $i_2 = \arg\max_{l \in N_{i_1}} x_*(l)$. This process is repeated until every node in the graph is visited. At termination the sorted list of nodes is the string S_G.

4 Graph Matching

With the converted strings at hand, we are able to pose the graph matching problem as that of aligning the strings so as to minimise the transition cost on a string edit matrix. We denote the seriations of the data graph $G_D = (V_D, E_D)$ and model graph $G_M = (V_M, E_M)$ by $X = \{x_1, x_2, ..., x_m\}$ and $Y = \{y_1, y_2, ..., y_n\}$ respectively. Here m and n represent the number of nodes in the two graphs. These two strings can be used to index the rows and columns of an edit lattice. Since the graphs may have different sizes, we introduce a null symbol ϵ which can be used to pad the strings. The graph matching problem can be stated as finding a path $\Gamma =< p_1, p_2, ... p_k ..., p_L >$ through the lattice which generates the minimum transition cost. Each element $p_k \in (V_D \cup \epsilon) \times (V_M \cup \epsilon)$ of the edit path is a Cartesian pair. We constrain the path to be connected on the edit lattice, and also the transition from the state p_k to the state p_{k+1} is constrained to move in a direction on the lattice, which is increasing and connected in the horizontal, vertical or diagonal directions on the lattice. The diagonal transition corresponds to the match of an edge of the data graph to an edge of the model graph. A horizontal transition implies that the traversed nodes of the model graph are null-matched. Similarly, the visited nodes of the data graph are null-matched when a vertical transition is made.

By representing the adjacent states on the path by p_k and p_{k+1}, the cost function of the edit path can be given as follows:

$$d(X,Y) = \sum_{p_k \in \Gamma} \eta(p_k \to p_{k+1}) \quad (5)$$

where $\eta(p_k \to p_{k+1})$ is the transition cost between the adjacent states. The optimal edit path is the one that minimises the edit distance between string and satisfies the condition $\Gamma^* = arg\,min_\Gamma\, d(X,Y)$. The optimal edit sequence may be found using Dijkstra's algorithm and the matching results are obtained from the optimal transition path on the edit lattice.

5 Computing a Reference String

We are interested in whether the strings delivered by our graph seriation method can be used for the purposes of graph clustering and constructing eigenspaces for graphs. To do this a reference string is required, since this can be used as a class prototype, and also allows the covariance matrix for a set of strings (i.e. seriated graphs) to be computed. To construct the reference string, we proceed as follows. After converting the set of M graphs $\{G_1, G_2, .., G_k, ..G_M\}$ into a set of strings $\{S_{G_1}, S_{G_2}, .., S_{G_k}, .., S_{G_M}\}$, we compute the pair-wise edit distances of the strings using the correspondences between graphs obtained using graph matching technique. We denote the edit distance matrix by ED_G. We then select the reference string $S_{\{r\}}$ so as to satisfy the condition $r = arg\,min_{r^*}\sum_{j\in|M|} ED_G(r^*, j)$.

This reference string can be used to capture the statistical properties of the set of graphs. In order to create a meaningful pattern-space for graph clustering, we construct permuted graph adjacency matrices by making use of the matching results between the individual string $S_{G-\{r\}}$ and the reference string S_r. For the graph indexed k, the permuted adjacency matrix is given by

$$\mathcal{A}_k(i,j) = \begin{cases} 1 & \text{if } (C(i), C(j)) \in E \\ 0 & \text{otherwise} \end{cases} \quad (6)$$

where the $C(i)$ and $C(j)$ represent the node correspondences of nodes i and j in the reference string. Next we convert the permuted adjacency matrices into long-vectors by stacking the columns of the permuted adjacency matrices. For the graph indexed k, the long vector is $H_k = (\mathcal{A}_k(1,1), \mathcal{A}_k(2,1), \mathcal{A}_k(3,1), ...)^T$.

6 Graph Eigenspaces

Our aim is to construct an eigenspace which can be used to capture the modes of variations is graph edge-structure. To do this, we represent the variations present in the set of graphs using the mean long-vector and the covariance matrix for the long-vectors. The eigenspace is constructed by projecting the individual graph long-vectors onto the directions spanned by the principal eigenvectors of the covariance matrix.

To be more formal, we commence by calculating the mean long-vector ($\hat{z}$) and the long-vector covariance matrix (σ) for the set of permuted adjacency matrices using the following formulae

$$\hat{H} = \frac{1}{M} \sum_{k=1}^{M} H_k \qquad \Sigma = \frac{1}{M} \sum_{k=1}^{M} (H_k - \hat{H})(H_k - \hat{H})^T. \qquad (7)$$

To construct the eigenspace we commence by computing the eigenvalues and eigenvectors for the covariance matrix Σ. The eigenvalues $\lambda_1, \lambda_2, \ldots, \lambda_N$ are found by solving the polynomial equations $|\Sigma - \lambda I| = 0$, where I is the identity matrix. The associated eigenvectors $\phi_1, \phi_2, \ldots, \phi_N$ are found by solving the linear eigenvector equation $\Sigma \phi_k = \lambda_k \phi_k$. From the eigenvectors we construct a modal matrix. The eigenvectors are ordered in decreasing eigenvalue order to form the columns of the modal matrix, denoted by $\Phi = (\phi_1|\phi_2|\ldots|\phi_N)$. If eigenspace is taken over the leading K eigenvectors, then the projection matrix is $\Phi_K = (\phi_1|\phi_2|\ldots|\phi_K)$. The projection of the long-vector H_k onto the eigenspace is given by $\mathcal{H}_k = \Phi_K^T H_k$. In the eigenspace the distance between the graphs indexed k_1 and k_2 is $SD(k_1, k_2) = (\mathcal{H}_{k_1} - \mathcal{H}_{k_2})^T (\mathcal{H}_{k_1} - \mathcal{H}_{k_2})$.

7 Experiments

For our experimental evaluation we use the COIL image database. To extract graphs from the images, we detect feature points using the Harris corner detector[4]. The graphs used in our study are the Delaunay triangulations of the point sets. The reason for using Delaunay graph is that it incorporates important structural information from the original image. In the images studied there are rotation, scaling and perspective distortions present. Example images from the sequences are shown in Fig 1 and correspond to different camera viewing directions of the objects. The detected feature points and their Delaunay triangulations are overlayed on the images.

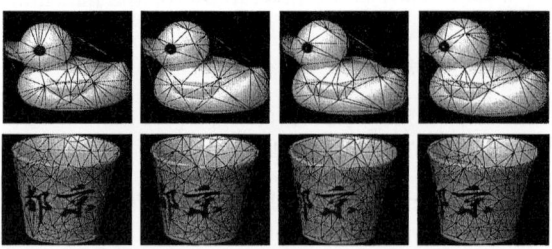

Fig. 1. Delaunay graphs overlayed on COIL data

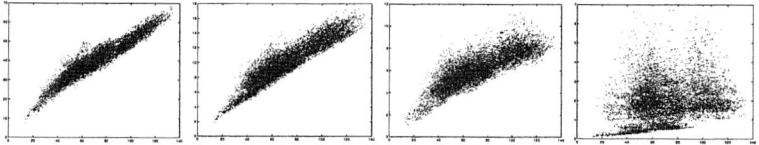

Fig. 2. Scatter Plot of SD versus ED for k=81,k=30,k=10,k=1

Table 1. Value of dispersion about the best-fit regression line

No. of eigenvectors	Value of dispersion
1	7.0718
10	3.587
30	2.3337
81	0.6914

We have selected six objects from the COIL database. For each object there are 20 different views. For the 120 graphs in the data-set, we have computed the complete set of distances between each pair of graphs.

We commence by exploring the relationship between the string edit distance ED and the Euclidean distance between the graphs in the eigenspace SD. In Figure 2, we show scatter plots of SD versus ED as the number of leading eigenvectors is decreased. The main feature to note is that for large numbers of eigenvectors, there is a clear regression trend in the plots. Hence, the distance in the eigenspace reflects well the true edit distance. However, as the number of eigenvectors decreases then so the regression trend weakens and the eigenspace distance is a poor approximation of the edit distance. In Table 1 we list the value of the dispersion about the best-fit regression line as a function of number of eigenvectors.

Finally, we consider the distribution of the graphs in the eigenspace. In Figure 4 we show the projections of the graphs onto the leading eigenvectors of the sample covariance matrix. The different objects form well defined clusters.

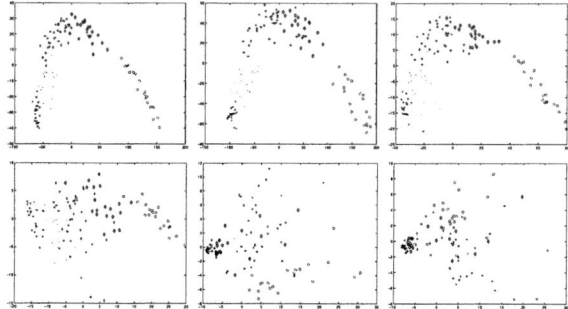

Fig. 3. MDS on graph distance. First panel shows result for edit distance. The remaining panels show the results with SD when k=81,k=30,k=10,k=2,k=1.

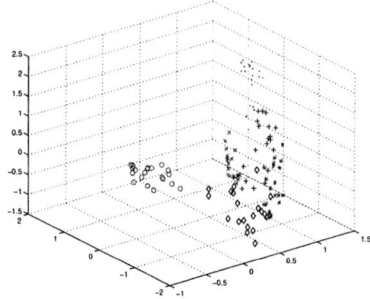

Fig. 4. Projections of graphs on eigenspace

In Figure 3 we take this analysis one step further. Here we show the result of applying multidimensional scaling to the Euclidean distances computed in the eigenspace and the edit distances. In each plot we show the result of projecting the graphs into a two dimensional space spanned by the leading two eigenvectors of the distance matrix for the graphs. The graphs extracted from the different views of the same object are shown as points of the same symbol . The first panel shows the embedding obtained from the edit distances, and the remaining panels show the results obtained using the Euclidean distances as the number of eigenvectors is decreased. Initially, both the edit distances give good separations of the the different object-views, but as the number of eigenvectors is decreased then so the results obtained using Euclidean distance degrades badly.

8 Conclusions

In this paper we have shown how graphs can be projected into an eigenspace using strings extracted using semi-definite programming. SDP is a convex optimisation procedure that uses randomised hyperplanes to locate the solution. By applying PCA to the resulting strings we have constructed an eigenspace for the sample of graphs. We have demonstrated that provided a sufficiently large number of eigenvectors are used, then the Euclidean distances in the eigenspace approximate well the edit distance between graphs.

References

1. A.D.Bagdanov and M.Worring. First order Gaussian graphs for efficient structure classification. *Pattern Recognition*, 36(6):1311–1324, 2003.
2. A.K.C.Wong, J.Constant,and M.You. Random graphs. *Syntactic and Structural Pattern Recognition-Fundamentals, Advances, and Applications*, 1990.
3. A.Robles-Kelly and E.R.Hancock. Graph Edit Distance from Spectral Seriation. *IEEE Transactions on Pattern Analysis and Machine Intelligence*, To appear, 2004.
4. C.Harris and M.Stephens. A combined corner and edge detector. *Fourth Alvey Vision Conference*, pages 147–151, 1988.

5. William J. Christmas, Josef Kittler, and Maria Petrou. Structural matching in computer vision using probabilistic relaxation. *IEEE Transactions on Pattern Analysis and Machine Intelligence*, 17(8):749–764, 1995.
6. C.Schellewald and C.Schnörr. Subgraph Matching with Semidefinite Programming . *Proceedings IWCIA (International Workshop on Combinatorial Image Analysis), Palermo, Italy*, 2003.
7. Henry Wolkowicz and Qing Zhao. Semidefinite Programming relaxation for the graph partitioning problem. *Discrete Appl. Math*, pages 461–479, 1999.
8. J.Keuchel,C.Schnörr,C.Schellewald,and D.Cremers. Binary Partitioning, Perceptual Grouping, and Restoration with Semidefinite Programming. *IEEE Trans. Pattern Analysis and Machine Intelligence*, 25(11):1364–1379, 2003.
9. Jonathan E. Atkins, Erik G. Boman and Bruce Hendrickson. A Spectral Algorithm for Seriation and the Consecutive Ones Problem. *SIAM Journal on Computing*, 28(1):297–310, 1998.
10. K.Fujisawa,Y.Futakata,M.Kojima,K.Nakata and M.Yamashita. Sdpa-m user's manual. *http://sdpa.is.titech.ac.jp/SDPA-M*.
11. L.Vandenberghe and S.Boyd. Semidefinite Programming. *SIAM Review*, 38(1):49–95, 1996.
12. M.Veldhorst. Approximation of the consecutive one matrix augmentation problem. *J.Comput.*, 14:709–729, 1985.
13. M.X.Goemans and D.P.WIlliamson. Improved Approximation Algorithms for Maximum Cut and Satisfiability Problems Using Semidefinite Programming. *J.ACM*, 42(6):1115–1145, 1995.
14. R.C.Wilson and E.R.Hancock. Structural Matching by Discrete Relaxation. *IEEE Transactions on Pattern Analysis and Machine Intelligence*, 19(6):634–648, 1997.
15. W Satish Rao, Andrea and Richa. New approximation techniques for some ordering problems. *ACM-SIAM Symposium on Discrete Algorithms*, pages 211–218, 1998.
16. Yuri Boykov, Olga Veksler, Ramin Zabih. Fast Approximate Energy Minimization via Graph Cuts. *IEEE transactions on Pattern Analysis and Machine Intelligence*, 23(11):1222–1239, 2001.

A Predictive Direction Guided Fast Motion Estimation Algorithm

Cheng-Dong Shen, Tie-Jun Li, and Si-Kun Li

Office 621, School of Computer Science, National University of Defense Technology,
410073 ChangSha, China
shencd@163.com

Abstract. A set of predictive-direction-oriented quadrangle search patterns is proposed in this paper. Based on these patterns, a new fast motion estimation algorithm is developed. In this new algorithm, the search process is guided by the predictive direction and adaptively selects the appropriate search pattern from predictive-direction-oriented quadrangle search patterns, thus significantly reduces the number of search steps and search points of every search step. Simulation results demonstrate the effectiveness of this algorithm by considerably reducing encoding complexity while incurring little if any loss in quality.

1 Introduction

The rapid growth of wireless communication and access, together with the success of the Internet, has brought a new era of mobile/wireless multimedia applications and services. Motion estimation (ME) and compensation are critical components for digital video compression and coding systems especially in wireless video applications, where the bandwidth is limited and precious. BMA (Block-Matching ME Algorithm) has been widely adopted by international standards such as MPEG4 and h.264 [1, 2], aiming at exploiting the strong temporal redundancy between successive frames. BMA method attempts to find a block from a reference frame within the predefined search window that best matches the co-located block in the current frame. Matching is performed by minimizing a matching criterion, which in most cases is the SAD (Sum of Absolute Difference) between this pair of blocks. However, the motion estimation is quite computationally intensive and can consume up to 80% of the computational power of the encoder if the full search (FS) is used by exhaustively evaluating all possible candidate blocks within the search window. Therefore, fast algorithms are highly desired to significantly speed up the process without sacrificing the distortion seriously.

Many computationally efficient BMAs were developed, among which are typically the three-step search (TSS), new three-step search (NTSS) [3], four step search (4SS) [4], block-based gradient descent search (BBGDS) [5], diamond search (DS)[6], Hexagon-Based Search(HEXBS)[7] and Context-Adaptive Parallelogram Search(CAPS) [8] algorithms. The methods in [3]-[8] use the different special search pattern respectively during the search process, can remarkably reduce the number of search points thus lead to very low encoding complexity and high efficiency compared to the brute force Full Search (FS) algorithm. But these algorithms do not consider selecting the appropriate start search point so that they maybe result in too much pattern search iteration steps or can be easily trapped into local minima areas. The literature [8] takes into account the initial search point selection and using different search pattern according to the predictive motion vector (MV)'s direction. But it only compute the median MV of the three spatial adjacent points (left, top and top-right) as the initial predictor and does not exploit the temporal correlations such as the co-located and it's surrounding blocks. Also the consideration of the predictive direction in this method is not adequate.

In this paper we propose a set of predictive-direction-oriented quadrangle search patterns (PDQS), each of which responds to a special prediction direction. Based on the patterns proposed, we develop a new fast motion estimation algorithm. Simulation results demonstrate the efficacy of our algorithm.

The remainder of the paper is organized as follows. In Section 2, we introduce the proposed search patterns. The developed ME algorithm are described in Section 3. Experiment results are presented in Section 4. Section 5 is conclusion of this paper.

2 Predictive-Direction-Oriented Quadrangle Search Patterns

A set of predictive-direction-oriented quadrangle search patterns is depicted in Fig. 1, which consists of seven patterns. Among them, patterns in Fig .1(a)-(f) indicate different prediction direction respectively, namely horizontal, horizontal-right, horizontal-left, vertical, vertical-right, and vertical-left. The direction of the quadrangle pattern can also be indicated by the direction of the vector $\overrightarrow{AB}$. They are used in the predictive direction guided search procedure according to some special rules described in section 3.2. The pattern illustrated in Fig. 1(g) is the small search pattern, which used in the final refinement search step.

3 ME Algorithm Development

Based on the PDQS search patterns proposed, we have developed a new motion estimation algorithm, which mainly includes two parts: initial search point selection and predictive direction guided search.

3.1 Initial Search Point and Search Pattern Selection

In contrast with the CAPS [8] where the median MV of the three spatial adjacent points is used as the predictor and the end point of this MV selected as the initial search point, here we select the MV of co-located point in reference frame in addition to the median MV as the candidates. The MV with the minimal SAD value is used as the predictor named as $pred\_mv$ and the end point of the $pred\_mv$ selected as the initial search point.

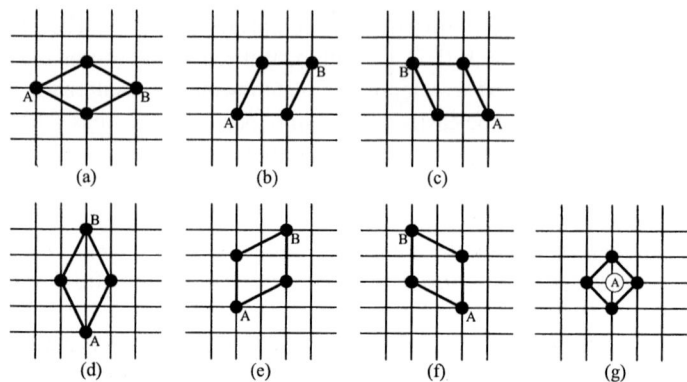

Fig. 1. PDQS patterns: (a) horizontal pattern; (b) horizontal-right pattern; (c) horizontal –left pattern; (d) vertical pattern; (e) vertical-right pattern; (f) vertical-left pattern; and (g) final refinement pattern

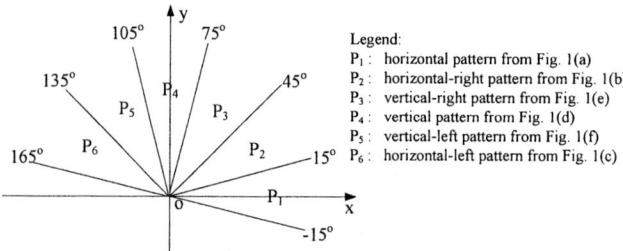

Fig. 2. Initial search pattern selection method

After selecting the initial search point, we choose the appropriate start search pattern from that the Fig. 1(a)-(f) illustrated according to the direction of $pred\_mv$. There are six direction used responding to the direction of the pattern: horizontal, horizontal-right, horizontal-left, vertical, vertical-right and vertical-left. The detailed search pattern selection method is illustrated as Fig. 2. The value of the angle between $pred\_mv$ and the horizontal x axial is defined as α, and the selected search pattern named as p_s. The following formula defined the start search pattern selection rules:

$$P_s = \begin{cases} P_1 & \text{if } \alpha \in [-15°, 15°) \\ P_2 & \text{if } \alpha \in [15°, 45°) \\ P_3 & \text{if } \alpha \in [45°, 75°) \\ P_4 & \text{if } \alpha \in [75°, 105°) \\ P_5 & \text{if } \alpha \in [105°, 135°) \\ P_6 & \text{if } \alpha \in [135°, 165°) \end{cases} \quad (1)$$

The Above formula considers the situation that $\alpha \in [-15^0, 165^0)$. In this situation, the point "A" in the Fig. 1. (a)-(f) is the start search point. If $\alpha \notin [-15^0, 165^0)$, the same pattern is selected as that of the opposite direction and the point "B" in Fig. 1. (a)-(f) is regarded as the start search point.

3.2 Predictive Direction Guided Search

During the search procedure, the ME algorithm compute the candidate points' SAD value and find the best matched point with the minimal SAD. At the first step of the search, there are seven candidate points to be considered including an initial search point and other six points located at the vertex of two same search patterns which are connected by the initial search point and toward the same direction. This can be depicted by Fig. 3, which is just an example of six cases (patterns from Fig. 1(a)-(f)). The solid dots in Fig. 3 refer to the seven points, among which the "A" is the initial search point.

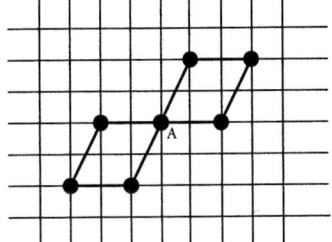

Fig. 3. First step of the predictive direction guided search

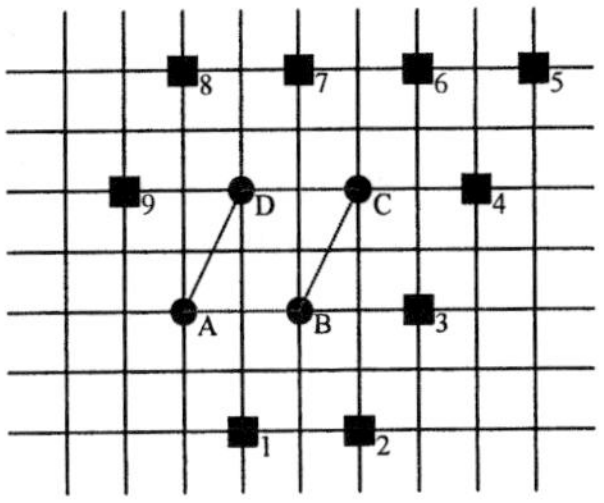

Fig. 4. Predictive direction guided search (pattern last step used as Fig. 1.(b) for example)

In the flowing search steps, the point with minimum block distortion (MBD) and the point with second MBD (SMBD) of the last search step are used to decide the prediction direction and the corresponding PDQS search pattern. There are two situations: the two points belong to the same edge of quadrangle pattern or are diagonal. If it is the former, two additional points are selected as the candidate points to be computed. The four points including these two additional points, the MBD point and the SMBD construct the new search pattern. At the same time, if the latter situation exists, three additional points will be selected and together with the MBD point they form the new search pattern same as the last step used. For simplicity, below is the detailed description of the search method in case of that the pattern in Fig. 1(b) is taken as that of the last search step. The other alterations from Fig. 1(a) and Fig. 1(c)-(f) are similar. Fig. 4 depicts this method.

The point A is taken as the start point of the current search step, if A is the MBD point, then the search will complete the final refinement search step using the pattern in Fig .1(g) and finish the entire search process. If not, then combination of the MBD and SMBD points and the new search points will be the following possibility: BA(1,2), BC(2,3), CB(3,4), CD(6,7), DC(7,8), DA(8,9), BD(1,2,3), and DB(7,8,9), where the former capital letter refers to the MBD point and the latter one refers to the SMBD, followed by which is the new search points. The MBD and(or) SMBD, together with the new quadrangle search pattern, such as Q(A, B, 1, 2), Q(A, 1, 2, 3) and etc.

Fig. 5 illustrates two more alternations: Fig. 5(a) for the horizontal search pattern as the last search step used depicted in Fig. 1(a); Fig. 5(b) for the vertical-left one in Fig. 1(f). From Fig. 4 and Fig. 5 we can observe that: (1) there are nine candidate points around the quadrangle search pattern, and the figure formed by these points is similar to a taper which direction is corresponding the direction of the surrounded quadrangle search pattern; (2) the quadrangle search patterns can be divided into two groups: one is composed of the vertical, horizontal-right, and horizontal-left pattern (as Fig. 1(d)(b)(c) refers); the other consists of the horizontal, vertical-right, and vertical-left pattern(as Fig. 1(a)(e)(f) refers), the search pattern is adaptively selected from one special group according to the distribution of the MBD and SMBD points.

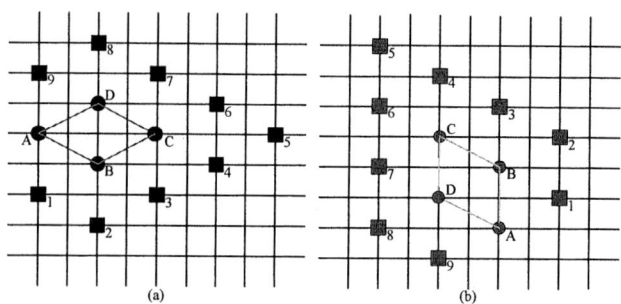

Fig. 5. Predictive direction guided search. (a) horizontal pattern as last step used; and (b) vertical-left one as last step used.

3.3 Detailed ME Algorithm Description

The proposed algorithm can be summarized in the following detailed steps.

Step 1) Select the median MV of the three spatial adjacent points and the MV of the co-located in the reference frame as the predictor MVs. By computing the two predictor's SAD, picking out the predictor with the minimal SAD as the initial prediction MV and the end point of it as the initial search point.

Step 2) Perform the first search step according to the search rules as Section3.1 described, and find out the MBD and SMBD points. If the MBD point is the initial search point, then proceed to Step 4) (Ending); otherwise, proceed to Step 3) (Searching).

Step 3) Go on searching guided by the predictive direction which decided by the pre-used pattern and the relative location of the MBD and SMBD points last search step found, which is detailed described in Section3.2. Three or two new candidate points are checked, and the MBD point is again identified. If the MBD point is still the MBD point of the last search step, then proceed to Step 4) (Ending); otherwise, repeat this step continuously.

Step 4) Switch the large search pattern (illustrated in Fig. 1 (a)-(f)) to the small refinement search pattern as in Fig. 1(g). The four points covered by the small quadrangle are evaluated to compare with the current MBD point. The new MBD point is the final solution of the motion vector.

The above process applies to each block in the current frame for block motion estimation. From the procedure, it can be easily derived that the total number of search points per block will be

$$N_{PDQS}(m_x, m_y) = 7 + 2 \times m + 3 \times n + 4 \quad (2)$$

where (m_x, m_y) is the final motion vector found, m is the number of execution of Step 3) where the MBD and SMBD points are diagonal, and n is the number of execution of Step 3) where the MBD and SMBD points are on the same edge.

3.4 Analysis of the Proposed Algorithm

In contrast to the DS algorithm [6], the HEXBS algorithm [7], and other non-predictive ME algorithms, the proposed algorithm uses predictive-direction-oriented quadrangle search patterns and predicts the initial motion vector, thus can substantially reduce the search step. Compare with the CAPS algorithm [8], this algorithm can predict the initial motion vector more accurately with additional predictor checked and use more search patterns which cover the predictive motion direction more elaborate.

Compare with the proposed algorithm by which the number of search points used is indicated in (2), the DS method requires the following number of search points per block:

$$N_{DS}(m_x, m_y) = 9 + M \times n + 4 \quad (3)$$

where M is either 5 or 3, depending on the search direction, and n depends on the search distance which is always greater than or equal to the sum of m and n in (2). The number of search points required for the HEXBS method is:

$$N_{HEXBS}(m_x, m_y) = 7 + 3 \times n + 4 \quad (4)$$

where n is the number of search steps, it is easily know that n is always greater or equal to the sum of m and n in (2). For the CAPS method, the number of search points as below:

$$N_{CAPS}(m_x, m_y) = 7 + 2 \times p + 3 \times q + 3 \quad (5)$$

where p and q is the number of search step corresponding to different search pattern. For the improvement of the prediction technology, we can conclude that the sum of p and q in (5) is always greater than or equal to the sum of m and n in (2). The speed improvement rate (SIR) of HEXBS over DS for locating a motion vector is obtained by

$$SIR = \frac{N_{PDQS} - N_{DS,HEXBS,CAPS}}{N_{DS,HEXBS,CAPS}} \times 100\% \quad (6)$$

From the aforementioned analysis, it can be concluded that SIR is always greater than zero.

4 Experimental Results

Our proposed algorithm was integrated within version 7.6 of the H.264 software [9], and it is compared versus FS, the DS algorithm [6], the HEXBS algorithm [7], and the CAPS algorithm [8]. The experimental setup is as follows. The distortion measurement of sum of absolute difference (SAD) used, CAVLC entropy coder used, with quantizer values of 28, 32, 36, and 40, a search range of ±32, and 5 references. Even though we have examined several different resolution sequences, we have selected to only present four relatively difficult sequences in this paper. These are CIF sequences Foreman, Stefan, Bus, and Garden. To make the estimation even more difficult, we have also selected to encode the sequences at 10fps, thus reducing temporal correlation even further. The average SIR results of the proposed algorithm versus the other algorithms are shown in Table 1. Also we show average PSNR gain and bitrate reduction results, while also we show speed up results for the entire encoding versus the overlapped FS. The results are shown in Table 2. As an example, The RD-plot of the Foreman 10fps is shown in Fig. 6.

Table 1. Average SIR results for the proposed algorithm versus DS, HEXBS, and CAPS

Sequence Versus.	Forman	Stefan	Bus	Garden
DS	45.12	50.35	47.76	51.64
HEXBS	27.06	31.48	33.15	34.53
CAPS	18.32	22.98	20.72	24.08

Table 2. RD performance of the proposed algorithm

	Sequence	Forman	Stefan	Bus	Garden
DS	△bitrate%	15.09	32.18	2.63	4.24
	△PSNR	-0.9	-2.08	-2.42	-0.12
	SpeedUp	5.28	4.99	5.08	5.33
HEXBS	△bitrate%	9.33	17.24	1.32	2.56
	△PSNR	-0.82	-0.97	-0.16	-0.13
	SpeedUp	5.33	5.22	5.37	5.64
CAPS	△bitrate%	7.05	15.16	1.75	2.88
	△PSNR	-0.81	-0.79	-0.67	-0.53
	SpeedUp	5.59	5.37	5.65	5.78
PROP.	△bitrate%	3.68	2.13	0.97	1.46
	△PSNR	-0.06	-0.06	-0.12	-0.07
	SpeedUp	6.43	6.78	6.43	7.36

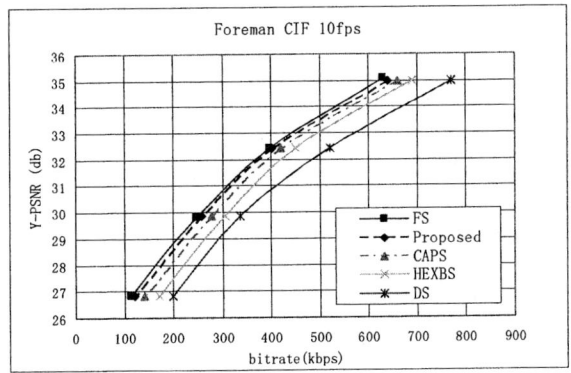

Fig. 6. RD performance plot for sequence Foreman CIF at 10fps

From these results we observe that our proposed algorithm is considerably better than the DS, HEXBS, and CAPS algorithm. Table1 shows that the proposed algorithm checks the least check points. From Table2, it can be observed that this algorithm can significantly speed up the encoding process while losing a little video quality. Fig. 6 demonstrates that the proposed algorithm can achieve better RD performance than other fast ME algorithms while keeping similar video quality as compared to FS algorithm.

5 Conclusions

In this paper we developed a novel fast algorithm using a set of predictive-direction-oriented search patterns in block motion estimation. Our results demonstrate that our scheme can produce similar and in some cases better results compared to even the FS algorithm while having considerably lower complexity.

References

1. "Information Technology—Generic Coding of Audio-Visual Objects" Part 2: Visual, ISO/IEC 14 496-2 (MPEG-4 Video), 1999.
2. ITU-T Ree.H.264/ISO/IEC 11496-10,"Advanced Video Coding",Final Committee Draft, Document JVT-G050, March 2003
3. R. Li, B. Zeng, and M. L. Liou, "A new three-step search algorithm for block motion estimation" IEEE Trans. Circuits Syst. Video Technol., vol. 4, pp. 438–442, Aug. 1994.
4. L. M. Po and W. C. Ma, "A novel four-step search algorithm for fast block motion estimation" IEEE Trans. Circuits Syst. Video Technol., vol. 6, pp. 313–317, June 1996.
5. L. K. Liu and E. Feig, "A block-based gradient descent search algorithm for block motion estimation in video coding" IEEE Trans. Circuits Syst. Video Technol., vol. 6, pp. 419–423, Aug. 1996.
6. S. Zhu and K.-K. Ma, "A new diamond search algorithm for fast block matching motion estimation," IEEE Trans. Image Processing, vol. 9, pp. 287–290, Feb. 2000.

7. Ce Zhu, Xiao Lin and Lap-Pui Chau,"Hexagon-Based Search Pattern for Fast Block Motion Estimation", IEEE Trans. Circuits Syst. Video Technol., Vol.12, NO.5 ,may 2002
8. Chuanyan Tian, Chendong Shen, Sikun Li, "A Fast Motion Algorithm Based on Context-Adaptive Parallelogram Search Pattern" MIPS 2004,LNCS 3311, pp.175-186, 2004
9. http://bs.hhi.de/~suehring/tml/download/Unofficial/. JVT Reference Software unofficial version 7.6.

Toward Polygonalisation of Thick Discrete Arcs*

Firas Alhalabi and Laure Tougne

Laboratoire LIRIS, Université Lyon 2, France
ltougne@liris.cnrs.fr
http://liris.cnrs.fr

Abstract. All the polygonalisation algorithms we can find in the literature proceed on 4-connected or 8-connected discrete arcs. In this article, we aim to polygonalise "thick arcs". A first step consists in giving a definition of such arcs based on morphological properties. In a second step, we propose two methods in order to polygonalise such arcs. The first one is based on a squelettisation of the arc and uses the fuzzy arc polygonalisation. The second one is based on a grouping of the cells in order to obtain heterogeneous pixels and then, the polygonalisation of heterogeneous arcs is applied.

1 Introduction

Within the framework of image analysis, one step consists in representing and describing the shapes. Hence, on the basis of the objects identified during the segmentation, the goal of this step is to extract characteristics, also called descriptors. These are informations that can be computed on the shape. These characteristics can be the perimeter, the area, the compactness, the curvature, the inertia center, the orientation for examples. The computation of such characteristics can be done directly on the frontier of the object such as the inertia center or the principal axis. Others, on the contrary, need before the extraction of primitives. A primitive is an elementary component such as straight lines or circular arcs. This article deals with the second ones and more precisely its goal is to give an approximation of the contour.

Many approaches are available in the literature in order the approximate the contour of an object. We can cite for example methods based on Minimum Length Polygon [SZ96, KKY99, KB00] or on Euclidean path [Via96]. However, a basic approach that consists in decomposing the contour of the object into polygonal arc offers a good approximation of if [CDRT01] and allows efficient computation of global estimators. This is the reason why we are interested in the polygonalisation of discrete curves or arcs.

We can find in the literature many articles dealing with polygonalisation of discrete arcs or recognition of segments. As a matter of fact, many equivalent or quasi-equivalent characterizations of a discrete segment have been proposed [Fre74,

---

* This work is supported by the french ACI GeomDiGIT (http://liris.cnrs.fr/geodigit/)

Ros74, LDW82, DS84, Kov90, Rev91] for example, and have been at the origin of recognition algorithms more or less powerful [Kov90, DR95, Buz02]. But all these works deal with 4−connected or 8−connected arcs in which we have an intrinsic way to traverse the pixels. But, such arcs are restrictive. I. Debled introduced in [DRRD03] the notion of fuzzy segment in order to be more tolerant with the noise but her algorithm also took in entry 4−connected or 8−connected arcs. In this article, we present two methods that take in entry *thick arcs*.

In the section 2, we remember existing definitions and existing algorithms that allow to polygonalise 4−connected or 8−connected arcs [DRR95, DRRD03] and heterogeneous arcs [CT04]. All these elements are then used in the sections 3 and 4 in which we respectively propose a definition of thick arcs and describe two methods to polygonalise them.

2 Existing Definitions and Algorithms

In this paragraph, we recall the definitions of an arithmetical discrete line, of a fuzzy segment with order d and of an heterogeneous digital straight line that all lead to polygonalisation algorithms.

First, let us remember the definition of arithmetical discrete line [Rev91].

Definition 1 (Arithmetical discrete line). *A $k-arc$ $\mathbb{A}$ belongs to the arithmetical line of slope $\frac{a}{b}$, of inferior bound μ and of thickness ω (with a, b, μ, ω integers, $b \neq 0$ and $pgcd(a,b) = 1$), if and only if all the pixels (x_i, y_i) of $\mathbb{A}$ satisfy : $\mu \leq ax_i - by_i < \mu + \omega$.*

Associated to this definition, I. Debled and J.P. Reveillès have proposed an algorithm that allows to recognize arithmetical 4− or 8−connected segments in linear time [DRR95]. An optimal time algorithm that give the polygonalisation of a 4- or 8-arc has also been proposed by the same authors. Just remark that this definition is not tolerant with the noise. As a matter of fact, if only one pixel is not exactly between the real lines $ax - by = \mu$ and $ax - by = \mu + \omega - 1$, named leaning lines, the recognition stops. Hence, in order to be more tolerant with the noise, I. Debled introduced the notion of fuzzy segment [DRRD03].

Definition 2 (Fuzzy segment with order d). *A $k-arc$ $\mathbb{A}$ is a fuzzy segment with order d if and only if there is an arithmetical discrete line $\mathbb{D}(a, b, \mu, \omega)$ such that all the points of $\mathbb{A}$ belong to $\mathbb{D}$ and $\frac{\omega}{max(|a|,|b|)} \leq d$. The line $\mathbb{D}$ is said bounding for $\mathbb{A}$.*

Associated to this definition, a segmentation algorithm of 8-connected arcs into fuzzy segments has been proposed. Let us called it *Polygonalisation Algorithm based on Fuzzy Segments* in the following. Such an algorithm takes in entries a 8-arc and a real number d. Each point of the 8-arc is sequentially added and tested to the current segment and the characteristics a, b, μ and ω of a strictly bounded line of this new segment are computed. More precisely, at each step, the value $\frac{\omega}{b}$ is evaluated and if it is greater than d, the recognition stops : we don't have a fuzzy segment. Otherwise, we proceed with the next point of the

8-arc. For more details, the reader can refer to [DRRD03]. Such an algorithm allows to decompose a 8-arc or a 4-arc into segments, in fact "fuzzy segments", which length depends on the order d fixed *a priori*.

On other side, works have been done on heterogeneous grid [CT04]. In this context, a polygonalisation algorithm based on heterogeneous segments has been proposed. In this context, a discretisation process is considered. For example, an extension of the Closed Discrete Naive Model [And00, CA02] denoted by $\tilde{N}(F)$ for the object F $\mathbb{R}^2$. Using this discretisation process, the notion of heterogeneous digital straight line can be defined as follows.

Definition 3 (Heterogeneous digital straight line). *Let S be a set of pixels in $\mathbb{H}$, S is called a piece of* heterogeneous digital straight line *(HDSL for short) iff there exists an Euclidean straight line l such that: $S \subseteq \tilde{N}(l)$.*

Using a conversion in the dual space, we can propose an algorithm that segment a *ve*-arc into *heterogeneous segment*. Such an algorithm is relatively simple. It consists on one hand to verify that the current piece of *ve*-arc is monotonic and in other hand, that the two associated pre-images are not empty. If they are empty or if the monotonic constraint is not satisfied, a new segment begins.

Just remark that in all the previous works, the starting arc is either *ve*− or *e*−connected (8−connected or 4−connected). In order to be more tolerant, we propose in this article to study "thick arcs" such that the one presented in figure 1. In other words, we want to decompose such arcs into "thick segments", segments we can easily see on the example and which are marked by rectangles.

Fig. 1. Example of decomposition we would have of a "thick arc"

Just remark that the notion of "thick segment", we want here, is different from the notion of "arithmetical thick segment" proposed by J.P. Reveillès [Rev91] where the parameter $\omega > a + b$. Indeed, in the "arithmetical thick segment" case, if one pixel is missing or if one pixel is adding, it is not an "arithmetical thick segment". In this article, we want to be more flexible. This is the reason why, in the following section, we introduce the notion of "thick arcs". Let's notice that polygonalising such arcs will be more difficult than polygonalising *ve*− or *e*−arcs in the way where we don't have, in this case, an intrinsic circuit to scan the pixels.

Just before introducing such "thick arcs", let us remember the problem of polygonalisation.

Problem 1. Let $\mathbb{E} = \{P_1, ..., P_n\}$ be a k-arc. What is the polygonalisation of $\mathbb{E}$ from P_1? In other words, what are the segments S_j of the polygonalisation of $\mathbb{E}$ from P_1, denoted $P_{P_1}^{\mathbb{E}}$, such that $P_{P_1}^{\mathbb{E}} = \{S_j, \; j \in [1, k]\}$, with

1. $\pi_1(S_1) = P_1$,
2. $\forall j \in [1, k], \quad S_j$ is a segment,
3. $\forall j \in [1, k-1], \quad S_j \cap S_{j+1} = \pi_2(S_j) = \pi_1(S_{j+1})$,
4. in the k-curve case, $S_k \cap S_1 = \pi_2(S_k) = \pi_1(S_1)$.

where $\pi_1(S)$ and $\pi_2(S)$ denote respectively the left and the right extremities of the segment S.

In theory, the polygonalisation which we want is the one the segments of which have maximal length even if in the arc case, the last segment is seldom maximal.

3 Definition of Thick Discrete Arcs

The definition of thick discrete arcs (thick arcs in short) we propose, and by extension of thick discrete arc (thick arc in short) is a morphological definition based on the dilation operation using a circular structuring element.

Definition 4 (Thick discrete arc). *Let l be an Euclidean arc in $\mathbb{R}^2$ and B_x a circular structuring element centered on x. Let $\mathbb{L}$ be the set of points of $\mathbb{R}^2$ defined by : $\mathbb{L} = l \oplus B_x = \{x \in \mathbb{R}^2, B_x \cap L \neq 0\}$. The thick arc $L(l, B_x)$ associated to the Euclidean arc l and the structuring element B_x is defined by $B_x = D(\mathbb{L})$ where D is a discretisation process.*

As the object "thick arc" is now mathematically well-defined, we are going to describe two methods to decompose such an arc into "thick segments". Just remark that the definition of "thick segment" will be algorithmic.

4 Polygonalisation of Thick Discrete Arcs

As polygonalising such arc is not easy due to the fact that we don't have an intrinsic way to scan the pixels, we will propose two different methods to transform the thick arc in order to obtain a simple way to go through the pixels. The first one is very intuitive and is based on a squelettisation of the arc. It then uses the polygonalisation based on fuzzy segments. This basic method presents some advantages, as we will see in the following and in particular, it is easy to implement and very rapid. But, it takes in entry a parameter, the order d used in the polygonalisation based on fuzzy segments. Such a parameter is not easy to fix and it is very dependent of the arc we work on. This is the reason why we propose a second method which transforms the thick arc into an heterogeneous arc, grouping the pixels, and which then uses the polygonalisation based on heterogeneous segments. The figure 2 resume the two methods and their different steps.

Let us now detail more precisely these two methods.

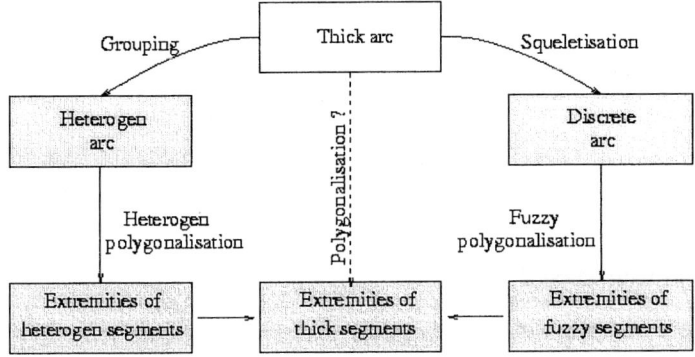

Fig. 2. Diagram which recapitulates the two proposed methods

4.1 Squelettisation Based Method

This first method is very basic as it is founded on the squelettisation of the thick arc. This squelettisation is obtained by intersection of wave frontiers initialized on the borders of the thick arc. The so obtained skeleton is then "clean up": it is transformed into a 8−arc and the simple points are suppressed.

The second step of this method consists in polygonalising the so obtained 8−arc using the polygonalisation algorithm based on fuzzy segments previously described. The extremity pixels of the thick segments are then marked using the extremity fuzzy segments. In order to observable, we mark them with large squares as we can see on the figure 3.

Fig. 3. Examples of obtained polygonalisation for the arc of the figure 1: (right) d=2,5 and (left) d=9. The large squares mark the segment extremities.

As it is based on the fuzzy polygonalisation, the number of obtained thick segments depends on the fixed parameter d. On a given arc, it is possible, by blind searching, to find the value of d that extracts the segments that seems correct that is to say visible to the naked eye. Meanwhile this value would not be necessarily available for another arc. This is the main drawback of the fuzzy polygonalisation that is transmitted here. Then, even if this method is easy to implement and is efficient, because the fuzzy polygonalisation as a linear complexity, the parameter d is a problem.

This is the reason why we have look for an other method that not requires to fix a parameter. Such a method is based on the grouping of cells. This is the purpose of the next subsection.

4.2 Grouping Based Method

In order to relieve the previous problem, we propose a second method which, in a first step, extracts from the thick arc an heterogeneous arc and in a second step, proceeds to the polygonalisation of the heterogeneous arc.

The extraction of the heterogeneous arc is based on the previous skeleton and uses the distance transform, based on the distance d_8, associated to the image that contains the thick arc. Indeed, it allows to extract successively the largest heterogeneous pixels contained in the thick arc. More precisely, we first browse all the pixels of the skeleton and keep the maximal distance associated, by the distance transform, to each pixel. Let us denote this distance d_{max}. Then, we extract as soon as possible heterogeneous pixels of length d_{max} from the thick arc taking into account that two pixels may not overlap. When we can extract no more pixels of length d_{max}, we try with (d_{max}-1) and so on until pixels of length 1.

The previous heterogeneous polygonalisation algorithm is then applied to mark the extremity of heterogeneous segment which coincide here with the extremity of thick segments.

The figure 4 shows the heterogeneous arc extracted from the thick arc of the figure 1 and the obtained segment extremities. These ones are the grey pixels on the figure.

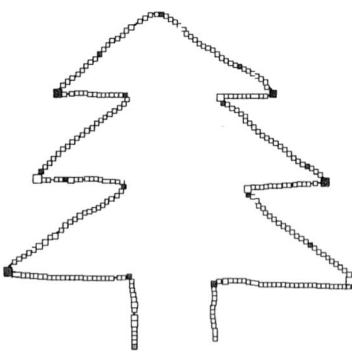

Fig. 4. Heterogeneous arc extracted from the thick arc of the figure 1 and its polygonalisation

4.3 Discussion

The first proposed algorithm based on a skeletisation of the arc and that uses the fuzzy polygonalisation algorithm has some advantages such as its complexity, its simplicity to implement. In the meantime, it takes in entry a parameter d which is not easy to fix and which is very dependent on the arc we study.

The second method is a little more complex to implement particularly concerning the extraction of heterogeneous pixels. But, it does not need such parameter. We can remark that, on the presented example, the obtained result with the second method is better than the ones obtained with the first one. One can say that for a given arc, we could adjust the parameter d in order to obtain a better result. But, even if we manage it, such parameter would not be available for another arc. So, it seems that the second method is better than the first, even if it is not perfect. In fact, we can see some extremities that are not well situated and some of them that are not expected.

In the following section, we conclude about this work and give some possible extensions in order to improve the second method that seems to be a sound idea.

5 Conclusion and Future Works

In this article, on the one hand we have proposed a definition of thick arc and on the other hand we have presented two algorithms that allow to polygonalise such thick arcs. All the works that exist in the literature until now focus on $e-$ or $ve-$arcs. The notion of thick arc is then new and the proposed algorithms use recent works in the domain, combining them in order to obtain interesting results.

Obviously these are first results on a new problem and many extensions are possible to improve the results. In particular, we could try other methods to extract heterogeneous pixels in order to limit the small ones for example or try to work with non square pixels [Coe05] which could also reduce small ones. Another direct extension should be the study of curves instead of arcs. Some results exist in the literature about minimal number of segments extracted by polygonalisation of the 4− or 8−arc [FT03].

Finally, such a work is included in a more general project that consists in obtaining algorithms more tolerant with the noise in discrete geometry.

References

[And00]   E. Andrès. Modélisation analytique discrète d'objets géométriques. Master's thesis, Laboratoire IRCOM-SIC, Université de Poitiers, 2000.

[Buz02]   L. Buzer. An incremental linear algorithm for digital line and plane recognition using a linear incremental feasibility problem. In *10th International Conference on Discrete Geometry for Computer Imagery*, number 2301 in LNCS, pages 372–381. Springer, 2002.

[CA02]   Philippe Carré and Eric Andrès. Ridgelet transform based on reveillès discrete lines. In *10th International Conference on Discrete Geometry for Computer Imagery*, number 2301 in LNCS, pages 313–325, 2002.

[CDRT01] D. Coeurjolly, I. Debled-Rennesson, and O. Teytaud. Segmentation and length estimation of 3d discrete curves. *Digital and Image Geometry*, pages 295–313, 2001.

[Coe05] David Coeurjolly. Supercover model and digital straight line recognition on irregular isothetic grids. In Berlin Springer-Verlag, editor, *LNCS 3429. Discrete Geometry for Computer Imagery*, 2005. To appear.

[CT04] D. Coeurjolly and L. Tougne. Digital straight line recognition on heterogeneous grids. In *Vision Geometry*, pages 283–294. SPIE, 2004.

[DR95] I Debled-Rennesson. *Etude et reconnaissance des droites et plans discrets.* PhD thesis, Université Louis Pasteur, Strasbourg, 1995.

[DRR95] I Debled-Rennesson and J P Reveillès. A linear algorithm for segmention of digital curves. *International Journal of Pattern Recognition and Artificial Intelligence*, 9:635–662, december 1995.

[DRRD03] I. Debled, J.L. Rémy, and J. Rouyer-Degli. Segmentation of discrete curves into fuzzy segments. International Workshop on Combinatorial Image Analysis (IWCIA'03), 2003.

[DS84] L Dorst and A W M Smeulders. Discrete representation of straight lines. *IEEE Transaction on Pattern Analysis and Machine Intelligence*, 6:450–463, 1984.

[Fre74] H. Freeman. Computer processing of line-drawing images. *ACM Computing Surveys*, 6(1):57–497, 1974.

[FT03] F. Feschet and L. Tougne. On the min dss problem of the closed discrete curves. International Workshop on Combinatorial Image Analysis (IWCIA'03), 2003.

[KB00] R. Klette and T. Bulow. Minimum-length polygons in simple cube-curves. In Springer-Verlag, editor, *Discrete Geometry for Computer Imagery*, Lecture Notes in Computer Science, Vol. 1953, pages 467–478, 2000.

[KKY99] R. Klette, V.A. Kovalevsky, and B. YIP. Length estimation of digital curves. pages 117–129. SPIE, 1999.

[Kov90] V.A. Kovalevsky. New definition and fast recognition of digital straight segments and arcs. In *Proceedings of the tenth international conference on Pattern Analysis and Machine Intelligence*, 1990.

[LDW82] Li-De-Wu. On the chain code of a line. *IEEE Transaction on Pattern Analysis and Machine Intelligence*, 4:347–353, 1982.

[Rev91] J.-P. Reveillès. *Géométrie discrète, calcul en nombres entiers et algorithmique.* Thèse d'etat, Université Louis Pasteur, Strasbourg, 1991.

[Ros74] A. Rosenfeld. Digital straight line segments. *IEEE Transaction on Computers*, 23(12):1264–1269, 1974.

[SZ96] F. Slobada and B. Zatko. On one-dimensional grid continua in $\mathbb{R}^2$. Technical report, Institute of Control Theory and Robotics, Bratislava, 1996.

[Via96] A. Vialard. Geometrical parameters extraction from discrete paths. In *Discrete Geometry and Computer Imagery*, Lecture Notes in Computer Science 1176, pages 24–35. Springer Verlag, 1996.

A Segmentation Algorithm for Noisy Images

Soufiane Rital[1], Hocine Cherifi[2], and Serge Miguet[1]

[1] LIRIS CNRS, Lyon II University, Lyon, France
{Soufiane.Rital, Serge.Miguet}@liris.cnrs.fr
[2] LIRSIA, University of Bourgogne, Dijon, France
Hocine.Cherifi@u-bourgogne.fr

Abstract. This paper presents a segmentation algorithm for gray-level images and addresses issues related to its performance on noisy images. It formulates an image segmentation problem as a partition of a weighted image neighborhood hypergraph. To overcome the computational difficulty of directly solving this problem, a multilevel hypergraph partitioning has been used. To evaluate the algorithm, we have studied how noise affects the performance of the algorithm. The α-stable noise is considered and its effects on the algorithm are studied.

Keywords: graph, hypergraph, neighborhood hypergraph, multilevel hypergraph partitioning, image segmentation and noise removal.

1 Introduction

Image segmentation is an important step in computer vision. Several algorithms have been introduced to tackle this problem. Among them are approaches based on graph partitioning [1,2,3]. Their common point is the building of a weighted graph. This graph is partitioned into components in a way that minimizes a specified cost function of the vertices in the components and/or the boundary between those components. One of the most frequently used techniques to partition a graph is by means of the cut cost function. Several alternatives to the cut criterion have been proposed [1,2,3]. Of particular note is the normalized cut criterion (Ncut) of Shi and Malik [1], which attempts to rectify the tendency of the cut algorithm to favor isolated nodes of the graph. Also, like graphs, hypergraphs may be partitioned such that a cut metric is minimized. However, hypergraph cut metrics provide a more accurate model than graph partitioning in many cases of practical interest [4]. It has been shown that, in general, there does not exist a graph model that correctly represents the cut properties of the corresponding hypergraph [5]. Recently, several serial and parallel hypergraph partitioning techniques have been extensively studied [6,7] and tools support exists (e.g. hMETIS [8], PaToH [4] and Parkway [9]). These partitioning techniques showed a great efficiency in distributed databases and VLSI circuits fields.

In practice, the images are often corrupted by a noise. Indeed, the noise influences considerably the segmentation quality. To solve this problem, many methods integrate a pre-filtering step. The segmentation quality is conditioned by this step, and more precisely by preserving the useful information. The latter one can be assured by using conditional filters. Only the noisy pixels are filtered. Our goal in this paper is to create a hybrid method between a conditional noise removal algorithm and an image segmentation algorithm. The two algorithms use a combinatorial model of the hypergraph theory. The hybrid method integrates three goals: (1) the use of a combinatorial model which adapts perfectly to the image. This model can be used to model a variety of systems, where the relations between objects in a system play a dominant role. (2) The implementation of a multilevel hypergraph partitioning algorithm. (3) The use of a structural noise model. These objectives are gathered in an algorithm which processes in three steps. In the first step, we generate the weighted hypergraph of an image, while in the second step we remove the noise. Only the noisy pixels are filtered. In the last step, we partition the weighted hypergraph into k regions.

The remainder of this paper is organized as follows: in section 2, we introduce the weighted image neighborhood hypergraph. In section 3, we define the structural model of noise. The hypergraph partitioning is introduced in section 4. In section 5, we illustrate the performance of the proposed segmentation approach. The paper ends with a conclusion in section 6.

2 Weighted Image Neighborhood Hypergraph (WINH)

A hypergraph H on a set X is a family $(E_i)_{i \in I}$ of non-empty subsets of X called *hyperedges* with : $\cup_{i \in I} E_i = X, I = \{1, 2, \ldots, n\}, n \in \mathbb{N}$. Given a graph $G(X; e)$, where X is a set of vertices, and e is a set of unordered pairs of members of X called edges. The hypergraph having the vertices of G as vertices and the neighborhood of these vertices as hyperedges (including these vertices) is called the *neighborhood hypergraph* of graph G. To each G we can associate a neighborhood hypergraph: $H_G = (X, (E_x = \{x\} \cup \Gamma(x)))$ where $\Gamma(x) = \{y \in X, (x, y) \in e\}$.

Let $H_G = (X; (E_i)_{i \in I})$ be a hypergraph. A chain is a sequence of hyperedges E_x. It is disjoined if the hyperedges E_x are not connected two by two. An hyperedge E_i is *isolated* if and only if : $\forall j \in I, j \neq i$ if $E_i \cap E_j \neq \emptyset$ then $E_j \subseteq E_i$.

The image will be represented by the following mapping : $I : X \subseteq \mathbb{Z}^2 \longrightarrow C \subseteq \mathbb{Z}^n$. Vertices of X are called pixels, elements of C are called colors. A distance d on X defines a grid (a connected, regular graph, without both loop and multi-edge). Let d' be a distance on C, we have a neighborhood relation on an image defined by: $\Gamma_{\lambda,\beta}(x) = \{x' \in X, |d'(I(x), I(x')) \leq \lambda$ and $d(x, x') \leq \beta)$.

The neighborhood of x on the grid will be denoted by $\Gamma_{\lambda,\beta}(x)$. To each image we can associate a hypergraph called *Image Neighborhood Hypergraph* (INH): $H_{\Gamma_{\lambda,\beta}} = (X, (\{x\} \cup \Gamma_{\lambda,\beta}(x))_{x \in X})$.

On a grid Γ_β, to each pixel x we can associate a neighborhood $\Gamma_{\lambda,\beta}(x)$, according to a predicate λ. The threshold λ can be carried out in two ways. In the first way, the λ is given for all the pixels of the image. In the second way, the λ is generated locally and applied in an adaptive way to the unit of the pixels.

From $H_{\lambda,\beta}$, we define a Weighted Image Neighborhood Hypergraph (WINH) according to the two maps functions f_{w_v} and f_{w_h}. The first map f_{w_v}, associates an integer weight w_{xi} with every vertex $x_i \in X$. The weight is defined by the color in each pixel. The map function f_{w_h} associates to each hyperedge a weight w_{hi} defined by the mean color in hyperedge. According to λ, we generate two representations: WINH and WAINH using respectively global and local thresholds. The last one is named: Weighted Adaptive Image Neighborhood Hypergraph.

3 Noise Model Definition

In this section, we define a structural noise model. This model exploits a lack of homogeneity criterion. We consider that the non-homogeneity characterizes noise. The isolated hyperedge can be used to model this non-homogeneity in an image. It is a hyperedge which does not have any information shared with its open neighborhood in the image. We call open neighborhood of the hyperedge E noted $\Gamma^o(E)$, the set $\Gamma(E)\backslash E$.

By using this property, we propose the following noise definition: $E_{\lambda,\beta}(x)$ is a *noise hyperedge* if it verifies one of the two conditions : (1) The cardinality of $E_{\lambda,\beta}(x)$ is equal to 1 and $E_{\lambda,\beta}(x)$ is not contained in disjoined thin chain having ω elements at least. (2) $E_{\lambda,\beta}(x)$ is an isolated hyperedge and there exists an element y belonging to the open neighborhood of $E_{\lambda,\beta}(x)$ on the grid, such that $E_{\lambda,\beta}(y)$ is isolated.

4 Multilevel WINH Partitioning

The formal definition of the k-way hypergraph partitioning technique is as follows: find k disjoint subsets X_i, $(i = 0,\ldots,k-1)$ of the vertex set X with part (region) weights W_i $(i = 0,\ldots,k-1)$(given by the sum of the constituent vertex weights), such that, given a prescribed balance criterion $0 < \epsilon < 1$, $W_i < (1+\epsilon)W_{avg}$ holds $\forall i = 0,\ldots,k-1$ and an objective function over the hyperedges is minimized. The W_{avg} denotes the average part weight.

If the objective function is the hyperedge cut metric, then the partition cost (or cut-size) is given by the sum of the costs of hyperedges that span more than one part.

Computing the optimal bisection or k-section of a hypergraph under the hyperedge cut metric is known to be NP-complete [10]. Thus, researches have

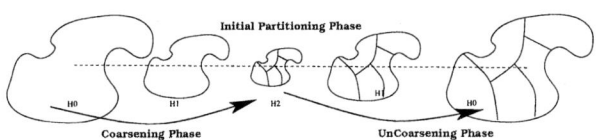

Fig. 1. Multilevel Hypergraph Partitioning

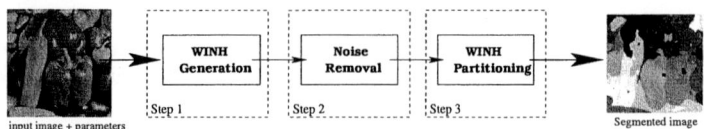

Fig. 2. The three steps of the proposed segmentation algorithm. The input parameters are: λ, β, ω and k desired regions.

focused on developing polynomial time heuristic algorithms resulting in good sub-optimal solutions. Because it scales well in terms of run time and solution quality with increasing problem size, the multilevel paradigm is preferred to direct solution approaches. Below, we describe the main steps of the multilevel paradigm (figure. 1):

- Coarsening phase: $H_{\lambda,\beta}$ is approximated via a succession of smaller hypergraphs that maintain its structure as accurately as possible. Many approaches have been proposed for finding the groups of vertices to be merged [7].
- Initial partitioning phase: During the initial partitioning phase, a partitioning of the coarsest hypergraph $H_{\lambda,\beta}^{coarse}$ is computed, such that it minimizes the cut.
- Uncoarsening phase: During the uncoarsening phase, a partitioning of the coarser hypergraph is successively projected to the next level finer hypergraph, and a partitioning refinement algorithm is used to reduce the cut-set.

Figure 2 illustrates the proposed algorithm. It starts with a WINH generation, noise removal using structural noise model followed by a multilevel hypergraph partitioning.

5 Experimental Results

We shall present a set of experiments in order to assess the performance of the segmentation approach we have discussed so far. The experimental results contain two steps. In the first step, we evaluate only the segmentation method in non-corrupted images. The algorithm is carried out in two stages: weighted image neighborhood generation followed by a multilevel hypergraph partitioning. In the second step, we evaluate the segmentation method in corrupted images. In this step, the algorithm is carried out in three stages. We start with an evaluation of noise model, then we evaluate the segmentation algorithm in noisy images. For all experiments: In WINH generation, we use the parameters values β, λ and k adjusted in experiments . In the case of WAINH generation, we use an adaptive threshold λ estimated using: $\lambda = Median\ \{I(y) - Median(F(x))\}_{\forall y \in F}$. F is the window centered in x with the size $[2\beta + 1 \times 2\beta + 1]$. In WINH partitioning, and in the coarsening phase, we use the hyperedge coarsening approach (figure 3). In the initial partitioning phase, we compute the k-way partitioning

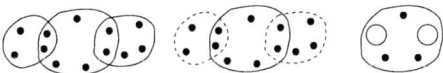

Fig. 3. Hyperedge coarsening method

of the coarsest hypergraph using the multilevel hypergraph bisection algorithm [7]. In the uncoarsening phase, we use the F.M. refinement algorithm [6].

For the coarsening, initial partitioning and uncoarsening phases we use the Hmetis package [8].

We will now show the effect of the weighted hypergraph generation on the quality of the image segmentation results. For this study, we implement two weighted neighborhood hypergraph representation : WINH and WAINH. Figure 4 shows the segmentation results of Peppers image. From this figure, we can see that using the WAINH, we obtain significant and better results. Indeed, using WAINH, we detect more significant regions compared to segmentation approach using WINH representation.

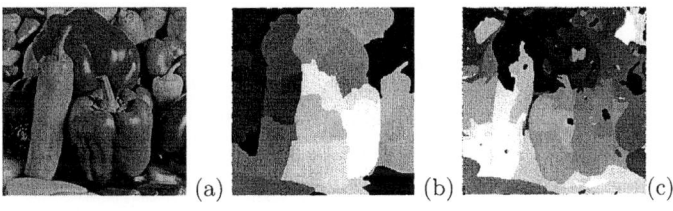

Fig. 4. WINH and WAINH comparison. (a) the original image of size 256×256. Outputs of our algorithm : (b) using WINH with $(\lambda, \beta, k) = (10, 1, 51)$ and (c) using WAINH with $(\beta, k) = (1, 51)$.

In order to compare our method with an existing one, we have chosen the technique of Shi and Malik (Normalized Cuts detection - Ncut) [1]. We have processed a group of images with our segmentation method and compared the results to Ncut algorithm. The Ncut algorithm used the same parameters for all images, namely, the optimal parameters given by authors. Figure 5 shows a comparison between the proposed and Ncut algorithms on Peppers and Medical images. According to the segmentation results on these images, we note that our algorithm make a better localization of the regions in the processed image compared to the Ncut method. The strength of this algorithm is that it better detects the regions containing many details. In addition, it results in shorter computing times faster than Ncut algorithm. The computing times of these two algorithms have been implemented using C++ language in a notebook with the following characteristics: Pentium Centrino, 1.5GHz, 512 Mo RAM.

Using the noise model illustrated in section 3, we develop a conditional noise removal algorithm. It is conditional because only the noisy hyperedges are filtered. The noise removal algorithm starts with AINH representation followed

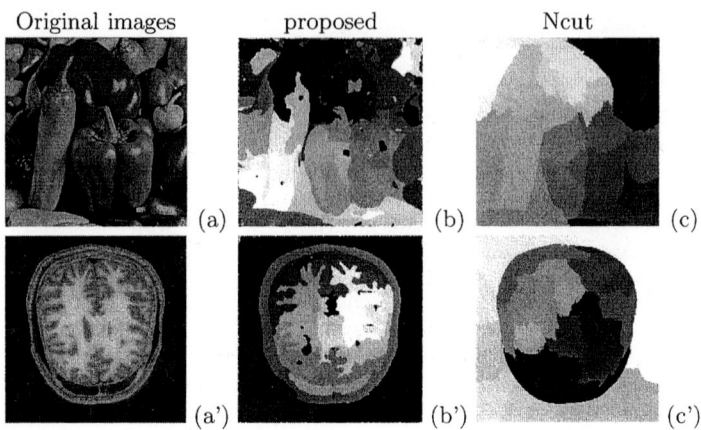

Fig. 5. A comparison between the proposed and Ncut algorithms. (b,b') The outputs processed in 32,23s and 29,06s respectively. (c,c') The outputs processed in 402,75s with $k = 51$ and 463,64s $k = 40$ respectively. The parameters of (b,b') are $((\beta, k) = (1, 51))$ and $((\beta, k) = (1, 39))$ respectively.

by noisy hyperedge detection and followed by noisy hyperedge estimation. We tested the performance of noise removal algorithm in the presence of α-stable noise. This distribution is a useful model of noise distribution. For a symmetrical distribution, the characteristic function is given by: $\varphi(t) = e^{\{jat - \gamma |t|^\alpha\}}$, where: (1) α is the characteristic exponent satisfying $0 < \alpha \leq 2$. The characteristic exponent controls the heaviness of the tails of the density function. The tails are heavier, and thus the noise more impulsive, for low values of α while for a larger α the distribution has a less impulsive behavior. (2) a is the location parameter $(-\infty < a < +\infty)$. (3) γ is the dispersion parameter $(\gamma > 0)$, which determines the spread of the density around its location parameter.

The objective of the filtering is to remove the noisy hyperedges while preserving the noise-free patterns. In figure 6, we present the results of the noise detection in Peppers and Medical images corrupted by α-stable noise with two parameters: $\alpha = 0.5$ and $\alpha = 1, 5$ representing respectively a impulsive and Gaussian distribution noise. These two results are compared with the Median Filter. It operates using 3×3 square processing windows. From the error images 6(e,e') between the filtered image and the original image, we note that the proposed algorithm preserves better the edge of the corrupted image than the Median filter.

Segmentation results of Peppers and Medical images corrupted by the same parameters of α-stable noise are illustrated in figure 7. This figure shows the segmentation results with and without the integration of the noise model in the proposed algorithm. In the case of non-integration of noise model in the proposed algorithm, we note that this last one detects the noise like regions (figures 7(c,c')). This noise influences the segmentation result considerably. The figures 7 (b,b') justify the absence of this drawback in the case of use of noise

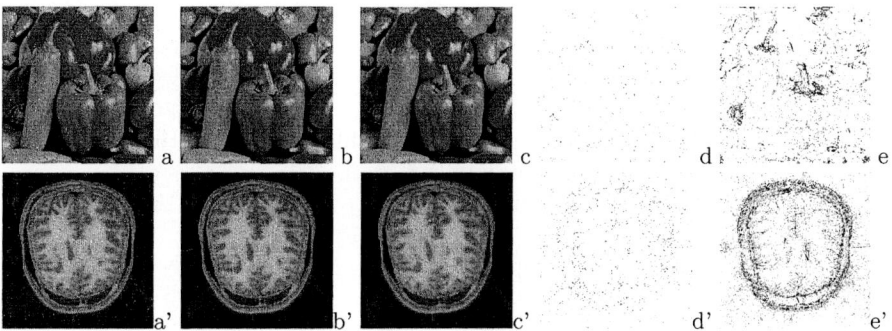

Fig. 6. Noise model evaluation. (a,a') corrupted images by α-stable noise. The α-stable noise parameters are ($\alpha = 0.5, \gamma = 1$, $a = 0$, percentage = 10%) and ($\alpha = 1, 5, \gamma = 20$, $a = 0$ and percentage = 10%) for images a,a' respectively. (b,b') filtered image by our noise model ($\beta = 1, \omega = 5$). (c,c') output of median 3×3 filter. (d,d') error $\times 10$ between the orginal images and b,b' images respectively. (e,e') error $\times 10$ between the original images and c,c' images respectively.

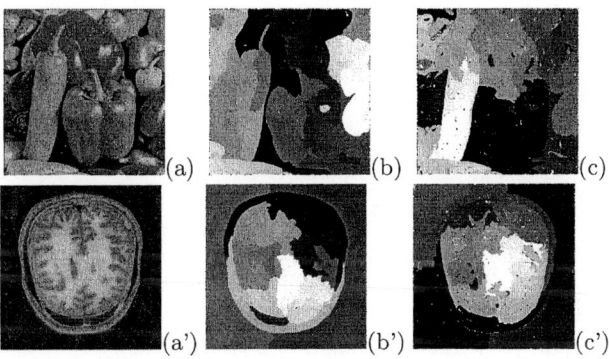

Fig. 7. Robustness evaluation of the proposed algorithm to noise effect. (a,a') corrupted images with $\alpha = 0.5$, $\gamma = 1$ and $\alpha = 1.5$, $\gamma = 20$ respectively with 10% of α-stable noise. (b,b') The output of the proposed algorithm after noise removal with proposed noise model. (c,c') the output of the proposed algorithm without noise removal. The Peppers image was processed by $\beta = 2$ and $k = 56$ parameters, while the Medical image used $\beta = 2$ and $k = 37$ parameters.

model. According to this figure and to several simulations on several image types we note that the use of both noise model and hypergraph partitioning in WAINH representation constitutes a robust segmentation algorithm to the noise effect.

6 Conclusions

We have presented a segmentation algorithm for noisy images. The segmentation is accomplished in three steps. In the first step, a weighted adaptive image neighborhood hypergraph is generated. In the second stage, a conditional noisy hyperedge removal algorithm is computed. In the last stage, a hypergraph partitioning method is computed using a multilevel technique . Experimental results demonstrate that our approach performs better than Ncut algorithm. It can be improved in several ways (parameters: the function maps, the colorimetric threshold, the unsupervised region number, etc.).

References

1. Shi, J., Malik, J.: Normalized cuts and image segmentation. IEEE Transactions on Pattern Analysis and Machine Intellignece **22** (2000)
2. Martinez, A.M., Mittrapiyanuruk, P., Kak, A.C.: On combining graph-partitioning with non-parametric clustering for image segmentation. Computer Vision and Image Understanding **95** (2004) 72–85
3. Wang, S., Siskind, J.M.: Image segmentation with ratio cut - supplemental material. IEEE Trans. Pattern Anal. Mach. Intell. **25** (2003)
4. Catalyurek, U., Aykanat, C.: Hypergraph-partitioning-based decomposition for parallel sparse-matrix vector multiplication. IEEE Trans. Parallel Distrib. Syst. **10** (1999) 673–693
5. Ihler, E., Wagner, D., Wagner, F.: Modeling hypergraphs by graphs with the same mincut properties. Inf. Process. Lett. **45** (1993) 171–175
6. Sanchis, L.A.: Multiple-way network partitioning. IEEE Transactions on Computers (1989) 6281
7. Karypis, G., Aggarwal, R., Kumar, V., Shekhar, S.: Multilevel hypergraph partitioning: applications in vlsi domain. IEEE Trans. Very Large Scale Integr. Syst. **7** (1999) 69–79
8. Karypis, G., Kumar, V.: hmetis 1.5: A hypergraph partitioning package. Technical report, University of Minnesota, Available on http://www.cs.umn.edu/hmetis (1998)
9. Trifunovic, A., Knottenbelt, W.: Parkway 2.0: A parallel multilevel hypergraph partitioning tool. In: Proceedings of 19th International Symposium on Computer and Information Sciences (ISCIS 2004). Volume 3280. (2004) 789–800
10. Garey, M., Johnson, D.: Computers and Intractability: A Guide to the Theory of NP-Completeness. W.H. Freeman and Co. (1979)

Finding the Number of Clusters for Nonparametric Segmentation

Nikolaos Nasios and Adrian G. Bors

Dept. of Computer Science, University of York,
York YO10 5DD, United Kingdom
{nn, adrian.bors}@cs.york.ac.uk

Abstract. Non-parametric data representation can be done by means of a potential function. This paper introduces a methodology for finding modes of the potential function. Two different methods are considered for the potential function representation: by using summations of Gaussian kernels, and by employing quantum clustering. In the second case each data sample is associated with a quantum physics particle that has a radial energy field around its location. Both methods use a scaling parameter (bandwidth) to model the strength of the influence around each data sample. We estimate the scaling parameter as the mean of the Gamma distribution that models the variances of K-nearest data samples to any given data. The local Hessian is used afterwards to find the modes of the resulting potential function. Each mode is associated with a cluster. We apply the proposed algorithm for blind signal separation and for the topographic segmentation of radar images of terrain.

1 Introduction

There are two main data modelling approaches in pattern recognition: parametric and non-parametric. The second approach aims to achieve a good estimate of the density function without any underlying model assumption [1]. A non-parametric technique is unsupervised and can model any probability density function [2]. The nonparametric methods can be classified into histogram-based and kernel-based approaches [2,3,4,5,6]. While histogram based approaches require a large data set, kernel methods usually result in smooth, continuous and differentiable density estimates [1,6].

Most nonparametric approaches associate a function to each data sample [2]. Such a function is usually assumed to be Gaussian. The cumulating effect of the influence of several such functions, each associated with a data sample, creates a potential function [2]. The way how the activation function is defined can be assimilated with the electro-magnetic field that develops around a particle.

Recently, a new approach was considered, where the potential of a data set is modelled by the Shrödinger partial differential equation [7]. In quantum mechanics, orbits of particles and their corresponding energy can be found by solving this equation. Horn and Gottlieb, considered the reverse problem [8]. The eigenfunction (ground state) is considered as a sum of Gaussians, each centred at a data sample, and depending on a scale parameter. The corresponding Shrödinger potential is calculated for the given eigenfunction [8]. The minima of the resulting potential corresponds to data clusters.

The number of modes in any nonparametric representation, modelling either minima or maxima of a potential function, depends on the scaling parameter, also known as the bandwidth [5,6,8]. In this paper we propose a statistical approach for estimating the scale parameter of a potential function. The average Euclidean distance to a set of neighbours is evaluated for each data sample. The resulting histogram of such local variances is modelled as a Gamma distribution and the scale parameter is estimated as the mean of this Gamma distribution [9]. Horn and Gottlieb have chosen the minima in the potential landscape provided by the Shrödinger equation by using gradient descent after appropriate thresholding [8]. However, there is no rule about selecting the threshold while gradient descent is prone to getting stuck in local minima and failing to find all the modes. In this study we employ the Hessian of the potential function for finding the modes. The data set is split into regions according to the sign of the local Hessian eigenvalues. The proposed approach is applied in blind detection of modulated signals [10] and for segmenting vector fields. In the second case, the vector fields represent surface orientations in a Synthetic Aperture Radar (SAR) image of terrain [11].

Data modelling using nonparametric clustering is described in Section 2. The estimation of the scale parameter is presented in Section 3, while the identification of cluster modes is explained in Section 4. Experimental results are provided in Section 5 and the conclusions of this study are drawn in Section 6.

2 Nonparametric Methods

A major problem in data modeling is that of defining clusters [1]. The advantage in nonparametric clustering is that we can use a very simple model to represent any data set. By assigning a kernel function to each data sample, usually considered Gaussian, we can model the potential function as [2]:

$$\psi(\mathbf{X}) = \sum_{i=1}^{N} K\left(\frac{\mathbf{X} - \mathbf{X}_i}{\sigma}\right) = \sum_{i=1}^{N} \exp\left[-\frac{(\mathbf{X} - \mathbf{X}_i)^2}{2\sigma^2}\right] \quad (1)$$

where there are N data samples $\mathbf{X}_i$, $K(\cdot)$ is the kernel function, and σ corresponds to the scale parameter (bandwidth). Maxima of $\psi(\mathbf{X})$ from (1) have been considered as cluster centers in a nonparametric approach in [3].

More recently, Horn and Gottlieb introduced a new nonparametric algorithm called quantum clustering [8]. Their method was derived based on the analogy between the quantum potential and data representation. Each data sample is associated with a particle that is part of a quantum mechanical system. The state of a quantum mechanical system is completely specified by a function that depends on the coordinates $\mathbf{X}$ of that particle at time t and can be described using $\psi(\mathbf{X}, t)$, similar to the potential function used for (1). According to the first postulate of quantum mechanics, the probability that a particle lies in a volume element $d\mathbf{X}$, located at $\mathbf{X}$, at time t, is given by $|\psi(\mathbf{X}, t)|^2 d\mathbf{X}$, [7].

According to the fifth postulate of quantum mechanics, a quantum system evolves according to the Schrödinger differential equation [7]. The time-independent Schrödinger equation is given by:

$$H \cdot \psi(\mathbf{X}) \equiv \left(-\frac{\sigma^2}{2}\nabla^2 + V(\mathbf{X})\right) \cdot \psi(\mathbf{X}) = E \cdot \psi(\mathbf{X}) \qquad (2)$$

where H is the Hamiltonian operator, E is the energy, $\psi(\mathbf{X})$ corresponds to the state of the given quantum system, $V(\mathbf{X})$ is the Shrödinger potential and ∇^2 is the Laplacian. In Quantum mechanics the potential $V(\mathbf{X})$ is given and the equation is solved to find solutions $\psi(\mathbf{X})$ [7]. The solutions of this equation describe orbits of electrons and other particles. However, in nonparametrical clustering we consider the inverse problem where we assume known the location of data samples and their state as given by equation (1). This equation is considered as a solution for (2). We want to calculate the resulting potential $V(\mathbf{X})$ created by the quantum mechanical system assimilated with the given data.

We assume that the potential is always positive, $V(\mathbf{X}) > 0$. After replacing $\psi(\mathbf{X})$ from (1) into (2), we calculate the Shrödinger potential as, [8] :

$$V(\mathbf{X}) = E - \frac{d}{2} + \frac{1}{2\sigma^2 \psi(\mathbf{X})} \sum_{i=1}^{N} (\mathbf{X} - \mathbf{X}_i)^2 \exp\left[-\frac{(\mathbf{X} - \mathbf{X}_i)^2}{2\sigma^2}\right] \qquad (3)$$

The modes of a potential function are associated with data clusters. The modes are indicated by the local minima in the potential function given by (3).

3 The Estimation of the Scale Parameter

It can be observed that both the function $\psi(\mathbf{X})$ from (1) and the quantum potential $V(\mathbf{X})$ from (3) depend on the scale parameter (bandwidth), σ. The number of modes of a potential function are determined by σ. In [8] σ was initialized to arbitrary values, while in [5,6] various test hypotheses were considered. In this paper we propose a statistical approach for estimating the bandwidth σ. For a given data sample $\mathbf{X}_i$ we consider the ranking of all the other data samples, according to their squared Euclidean distance to $\mathbf{X}_i$:

$$\mathcal{R}_K(\mathbf{X}_i) = \{\, \mathbf{X}_{(k)} \mid \|\mathbf{X}_{(k-1)} - \mathbf{X}_i\|^2 < \|\mathbf{X}_{(k)} - \mathbf{X}_i\|^2 \,\} \qquad (4)$$

for $k = 1, \ldots, K$, where $\mathbf{X}_{(k)}$ represent the K nearest neighbours of $\mathbf{X}_i$ [1], and $\|\cdot\|$ denotes the Euclidean distance between a data sample and $\mathbf{X}_i$. The variance in the local neighbourhood is calculated as :

$$s_i = \frac{\sum_{k=1}^{K} \|\mathbf{X}_{(k)} - \mathbf{X}_i\|^2}{K} \qquad (5)$$

for $i = 1, \ldots, N$, where $K < N$, is the neighbourhood set cardinality. An empirical distribution of local variance estimates from (5) is formed by considering several data samples $\mathbf{X}_i$ and their neighbourhoods $\mathcal{R}_K(\mathbf{X}_i)$.

The probability density function characterizing the empirical local variance is modelled with the Gamma distribution [9] :

$$p(s) = \frac{s^{\alpha-1}}{\beta^\alpha \Gamma(\alpha)} e^{-s/\beta} \qquad (6)$$

where $\alpha > 0$ is the shape parameter, and $\beta > 0$ is the scale parameter of the Gamma distribution. $\Gamma(\cdot)$ represents the Gamma function:

$$\Gamma(t) = \int_0^\infty r^{t-1} e^{-r} dr \qquad (7)$$

By modeling distributions of variances of K-nearest neighbours we have a statistical description of the local variance in the given data set.

The parameters α and β are estimated from the empirical distribution of random variables calculated as (5), modelled by equation (6). A well known method to calculate the parameters of the Gamma distribution is the moments method [9]. This method calculates first the sample mean and standard deviation of the distribution, denoted as $\bar{s}$ and l, respectively. The parameters are estimated as :

$$\hat{\alpha} = \left(\frac{\bar{s}}{l}\right)^2 \; ; \; \hat{\beta} = \frac{l^2}{\bar{s}} \qquad (8)$$

After inferring the parameters of the Gamma probability density function we take the estimate of $\hat{\sigma}$ as the mean of the Gamma distribution, [9] :

$$\hat{\sigma} = \hat{\alpha}\hat{\beta} \qquad (9)$$

where $\hat{\alpha}$ and $\hat{\beta}$ are calculated in (8).

4 Finding the Modes of the Potential Function

After estimating an appropriate bandwidth $\hat{\sigma}$, we define a potential function such as $\psi(\mathbf{X})$ from (1), or $V(\mathbf{X})$ resulting from applying the Schrödinger equation (3). Such a function can be interpreted as a landscape in the $(d+1)$th dimension, where d is data dimension. Let us assume a regular orthogonal lattice $\mathbf{Z}$ that is defined by sampling at regular intervals between extreme data entries along each dimension. The inter-lattice distance is considered equal along each axis and depends on the scale as $\|\mathbf{z}_{i,j} - \mathbf{z}_{i,j-1}\| = \hat{\sigma}/2$, where $\mathbf{z}_{i,j} \in \mathbf{Z}$ is a lattice knot and $\hat{\sigma}$ is estimated in (9). Data clusters will correspond to local maxima in the potential function when using (1), or to local minima for (3).

In order to determine the relative extremes in the potential function we use the local Hessian. The Hessian is calculated at each lattice knot as:

$$\mathbf{H}[F(\mathbf{Z})] = \left(\frac{\partial^2 F(\mathbf{Z})}{\partial x \partial y}\right) \qquad (10)$$

where $F(\mathbf{Z})$ is either $\psi(\mathbf{Z})$ or $V(\mathbf{Z})$. The evaluation of a potential function on a regular lattice facilitates the calculation of the local discrete Hessian. The eigendecomposition of the Hessian matrix provides :

$$\mathbf{H} = \mathbf{T} \cdot \mathbf{\Lambda} \cdot \mathbf{T}^{-1} \qquad (11)$$

where $|\cdot|$ denotes matrix multiplication, $\mathbf{T}$ is a matrix whose columns represent the eigenvectors, while $\Lambda = \{\lambda_i | i = 1, \ldots, d\}$ is a diagonal matrix that contains the eigenvalues λ_i. We can identify local minima, maxima and saddle points according to the signs of the local Hessian eigenvalues :

$$\begin{aligned} &\lambda_i(\mathbf{Z}) > 0, \ \forall \ i = 1, \ldots, d \ \text{then local minimum} \\ &\lambda_i(\mathbf{Z}) < 0, \ \forall \ i = 1, \ldots, d \ \text{then local maximum} \\ &\exists \lambda_j(\mathbf{Z}) > 0, \ \wedge \ \exists \lambda_i(\mathbf{Z}) < 0, \ i \neq j \ \text{then saddle point} \end{aligned} \quad (12)$$

A common sense assumption is that either local minima or local maxima are surrounded by saddle points.

In the case when considering the potential as defined by (1) we assume that clusters are represented as compact areas of local maxima that are surrounded by local minima and saddle points. Conversely, when using (3) we consider that clusters are defined in the regions of local minima that are surrounded by maxima and saddle points. Let us assume eight-knots neighbourhoods denoted as $\mathcal{N}_8(\mathbf{Z})$ on the given lattice $\mathbf{Z}$. The resulting regions will correspond, when the potential is modelled by (1), to local clusters defined as:

$$\mathcal{C}(k) = \{\mathbf{z}_k | \ \lambda_i(\mathbf{z}_k) < 0, \ \forall \ i = 1, \ldots, d \ \ \mathbf{z}_k \in \mathcal{N}_8(\mathbf{z}_k), \mathbf{z}_k \notin \mathcal{N}_8(\mathbf{z}_j), j \neq k\} \quad (13)$$

where k and j are two different local modes that are separated by saddle points and have no connectivity to each other. To each mode we assign a factor F_k, calculated as the ratio of its potential from the potential of all modes :

$$F_k = \frac{\int_{\mathcal{C}(k)} F(\mathbf{Z}) d\mathbf{Z}}{\sum_j \int_{\mathcal{C}(j)} F(\mathbf{Z}) d\mathbf{Z}} \quad (14)$$

where $F(\mathbf{Z})$ is the potential function defined as $\psi(\mathbf{Z})$ from (1), or as $V(\mathbf{Z})$ from (3). The integrals from (14) are calculated using Riemman additions. The factors F_k corresponding to the local extrema are ordered according to their decreasing importance in the total potential. Consequently, the entire lattice is split into clusters according to a region growing process that works on labelled regions employing Markov Random Fields (MRF) propagation. At each iteration a layer of lattice points are added simultaneously to each cluster. This process continues until lattice areas assigned to two different clusters become adjoint.

5 Experimental Results

Nonparametric clustering algorithms are considered for blind detection of modulated signals. We consider quadrature amplitude (QAM) and phase-shifting-key (PSK) modulated signals. The modulated signals are corrupted assuming inter-symbol interference and noise, identically with the model used in [10]. We have generated $N = 960$ signals, by assuming equal probabilities for all inter-symbol combinations. The resulting signal constellations are displayed in Figures 1a and 1d, where each signal is represented by a point.

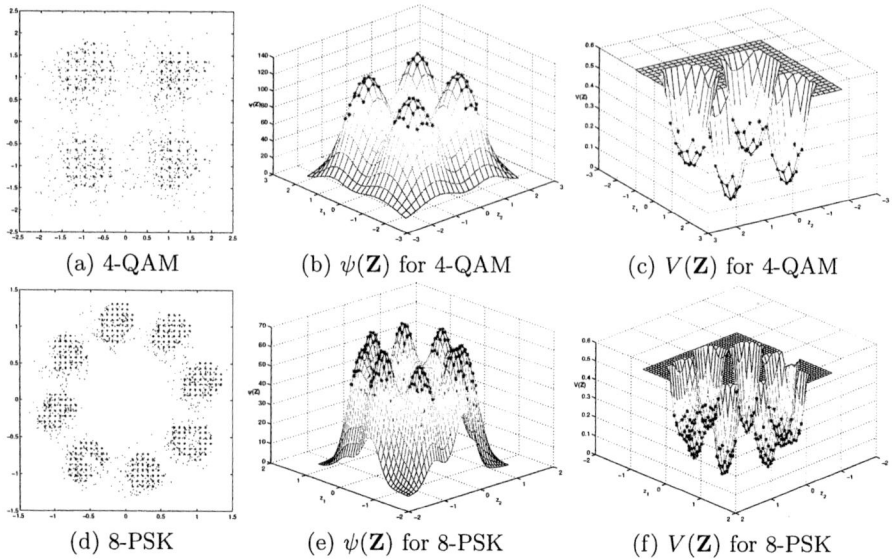

Fig. 1. Modulated signals and their potential surfaces

K-nearest neighbours for $K = N/4$ are considered and $\hat{\sigma}$ is estimated from the resulting empirical distribution of the local variance as described in Section 3. We evaluate the potential $\psi(\mathbf{Z})$ from (1) and the quantum potential $V(\mathbf{Z})$ according to (3) on a lattice. In Figures 1b and 1c the two potentials are shown for 4-QAM, while in Figures 1e and 1f they are calculated for 8-PSK. The lattice knots assigned to each mode, according to the quantum potential, are marked with '*' in Figures 1a and 1d. Correctly, 4 clusters have been identified for 4-QAM and 8 for 8-PSK when using the estimated bandwidth.

We consider several values for the scale parameter $\hat{\sigma}$. We evaluate the number of clusters and the misclassification error, by comparing the data sets that are

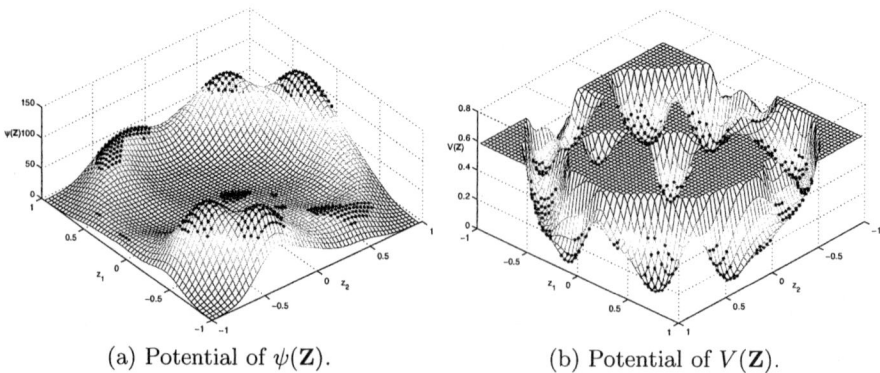

Fig. 2. Potential corresponding to the surface normal vectorial data

Table 1. Misclassification error and the number of clusters when varying the scale $\hat{\sigma}$ for 4-QAM and 8-PSK. The results that correspond to the chosen scale are highlighted.

	4-QAM					8-PSK			
	$\psi(\mathbf{X})$		$V(\mathbf{X})$			$\psi(\mathbf{X})$		$V(\mathbf{X})$	
σ	Misclas. Error (%)	No. of cluster	Misclas. Error (%)	No. of cluster	σ	Misclas. Error (%)	No. of cluster	Misclas. Error (%)	No. of cluster
0.3	-	8	-	36	0.10	-	48	-	84
0.4	3.54	4	-	9	0.15	-	15	-	37
0.5	4.37	4	4.79	4	0.20	2.29	8	-	20
0.6	4.58	4	5.10	4	0.25	1.98	8	1.46	8
0.63	**6.56**	**4**	**6.15**	**4**	**0.27**	**2.71**	**8**	**2.50**	**8**
0.7	6.04	4	8.13	4	0.30	3.02	8	2.71	8
0.8	10.00	4	9.69	4	0.35	9.17	8	6.67	8
0.9	16.56	4	15.21	4	0.50	-	7	-	7
1.0	11.35	4	11.46	4	0.55	-	4	-	5
1.1	-	2	-	3	0.60	-	2	-	4

assigned to each potential function mode with those that have been generated. The results obtained for both potential functions and for both data sets are displayed in Table 1. From this table it can be observed that the procedure of estimating $\hat{\sigma}$ proved to be reliable, even though suboptimal. The estimation of the scale parameter $\hat{\sigma}$ is more important for the quantum potential $V(\mathbf{Z})$ from (3), which without a proper scale parameter it can miss to find the right number of clusters. The misclassification error is better when using the quantum potential $V(\mathbf{X})$ from (3) when compared to $\psi(\mathbf{X})$ from (1).

In another application we consider a Synthetic Aperture Radar (SAR) image of terrain shown in Figure 3a. We want to identify various topographic regions in this image according to the clustering of local surface orientation. In [11] the surface normals have been estimated by adapting shape-from-shading techniques to radar images. The resulting local surface normals depicted as needle maps are shown in Figure 3b. The x and y coordinates of 1518 local surface normal vectors are used for nonparametric clustering. The resulting potentials corresponding to the given data set are shown for $\psi(\mathbf{Z})$, calculated as in (1), in Figure 2a, and for $V(\mathbf{Z})$, calculated as in (3), in Figure 2b. The ratio of the total energy F_k associated with each mode is calculated for both potentials according to (14). The segmentation in topographic regions for the SAR image from Figure 3a, when using the potential $\psi(\mathbf{X})$, is shown in Figure 3c for 4 clusters and in Figure 3e for 7 clusters. The SAR image segmentation when considering the quantum potential $V(\mathbf{X})$ is displayed in Figure 3d for 4 clusters and in Figure 3f for 7 clusters. In the segmented representations we can identify several compact topographical areas that correspond to the actual terrain features. From Figure 3 it can be observed that the segmentation of the potential modelled by $V(\mathbf{Z})$ provides more compact regions than when using $\psi(\mathbf{Z})$. When considering 7 modes we can see from Figures 3e and 3f that a cluster is assigned for the top of ridges and bottom of valleys, both characterized by vector normals parallel with z axis.

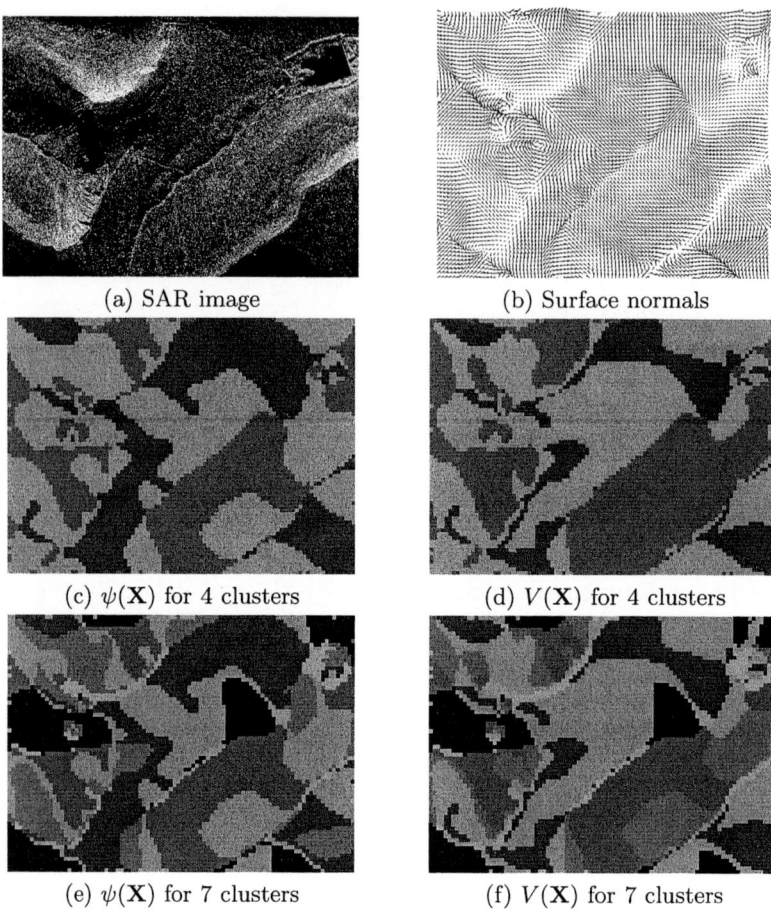

Fig. 3. Topographical segmentation of a SAR image of terrain

6 Conclusions

This paper proposes a new methodology for nonparametric segmentation. Two different approaches are considered for generating a potential function from a given data set. The first approach assumes simple additions of Gaussian kernels. The second approach considers an algorithm, called quantum clustering, that employs the Shrödinger partial differential equation. Two important interrelated problems in nonparametric clustering are analysed. The first one is the selection of the scale parameter and the second one consists of finding the appropriate number of modes in the potential function. The local data variance is modelled with a Gamma distribution. The scale parameter is considered as the mean of this distribution. The resulting potential function is interpreted using the local Hessian on a lattice. From the signs of the eigenvalues of the local Hessian we identify the modes of the potential function and the data are segmented accordingly. The proposed algorithm is applied in blind detection of modulated signals and in segmenting vector fields of surface normals extracted from a synthetic aperture radar image of terrain. The segmented areas can be used in a graph-based representation of the local topographical information.

References

1. R. O. Duda, P. E. Hart, D. G. Stork, *Pattern Classification*. Wiley, 2000.
2. E. Parzen, "On estimation of a probability density function and mode," *Annals Mathematical Statistics*, vol. 33, pp. 1065–1076, 1962.
3. S. J. Roberts, "Parametric and non-parametric unsupervised cluster analysis," *Pattern Recognition*, vol. 30, no. 2, pp. 261–272, 1997.
4. N. N. Schraudolph, "Gradient-based manipulation of nonparametric entropy estimates," *IEEE Trans. on Neural Networks*, vol. 15, no. 4, pp. 828-837, Jul. 2004.
5. S.J. Sheather, "Density estimation," *Stat. Science*, vol. 19, no. 4, pp. 588-597, 2004.
6. B. W. Silverman, *Density estimation for statistics and data analysis*. Chapman and Hall, 1986.
7. S. Gasiorowicz, *Quantum Physics*. Wiley, 1996.
8. D. Horn, A. Gottlieb, "The method of quantum clustering," *Proc. of Advances in Neural Infor. Proc. Systems (NIPS) 14*, 2001, pp. 769–776.
9. A. Gelman, J. B. Carlin, H. S. Stern, and D. B. Rubin, *Bayesian Data Analysis*, Chapman & Hall, 1995.
10. N. Nasios, A. G. Bors, "Blind source separation using variational expectation-maximization algorithm," *Proc. 10th Inter. Conf. on Computer Analysis of Images and Patterns, LNCS 2756*, Groningen, Netherlands, 25-27 Aug. 2003, pp. 442-450.
11. A. G. Bors, E. R. Hancock, R. C. Wilson, "Terrain analysis using radar shape-from-shading," *IEEE Trans. on Pattern Analysis and Machine Intelligence*, vol. 25, no. 8, pp. 974-992, 2003.

Optical Flow Diffusion with Robustified Kernels

Ashish Doshi and Adrian G. Bors

Dept. of Computer Science,
University of York, York YO10 5DD, United Kingdom
{adoshi, adrian.bors}@cs.york.ac.uk

Abstract. This paper provides a comparison study among a set of robust diffusion algorithms for processing optical flows. The proposed algorithms combine the smoothing ability of the heat kernel, modelled by the local Hessian, and the outlier rejection mechanisms of robust statistics algorithms. Smooth optical flow variation can be modelled very well using heat kernels. The diffusion kernel is considered Gaussian, where the covariance matrix implements the inverse of the local Hessian. Robust statistics operators improve the results provided by the heat kernel based diffusion, by rejecting outliers and by avoiding optical flow oversmoothing. Alpha-trimmed mean and median statistics are considered for robustifying diffusion kernels. The robust diffusion smoothing is applied onto multiple frames and is extended to 3D lattices.

1 Introduction

Analyzing motion patterns is essential for understanding visual surroundings [1]. When estimating motion, the common assumption is that the intensity of a moving pixel in the image plane is constant along its trajectory, in time [2]. This condition represents the main assumption for the optical flow constraint equation. However, in many cases, for example when representing the motion of fluids, the optical flow becomes very complex. Outlier vectors could affect the optical flow estimation in such situations.

Optical flow estimation algorithms can be classified as gradient-based and feature-based methods. A widely used local motion detection method is the block matching algorithm (BMA) [1]. BMA estimates the optical flow based on the correlation between a block of pixels in one frame and the corresponding block from within a search region in another frame and is used in the MPEG-2 motion compression standard. However, lack of contrast can lead to erroneous estimations. In order to overcome such problems, regularization terms have been used. Other approaches employ robust statistics algorithms [3,4].

This paper develops a methodology that combines the advantages of two different approaches: diffusion with heat kernels and robust statistics. This methodology is applied for smoothing vector fields. Perona and Malik introduced anisotropic diffusion for multiscale image segmentation [5]. Their proposed method uses partial differential equations (PDE) [6] to smooth grey-level images while preserving edges. Black et al. proposed *Tukey's biweight* function for obtaining sharper boundaries [7]. Field regularization of orthonormal vector sets, using constraint-preserving anisotropic diffusion kernels was used by Tschumperlé and Deriche for denoising color images and for inpainting [8,9]. Their method introduces the use of tensor and Hessian matrices that are calculated from the local statistics. Important image structure such as edges and features are preserved while noise and smaller features are smoothed out in directions that are parallel with those of edges. Burgi [10] uses an optical flow constraint equation that includes diffusion terms and considers gradient directions. PDE's have been used in inpainting [9,11] and for various other applications [12].

The concept behind the approach presented in this paper is to enable the smoothing process with an outlier rejection mechanism. Diffused outliers can cause undesirable effects. The proposed algorithms aim to remove outliers without affecting structural data. When using local Hessian diffusion kernels, as in the case of the heat equation, the diffusion occurs along the direction of the edges, thus preserving the structure of objects. Section 2 introduces the application of diffusion kernels on vector fields and its extentions for 3D lattices. Section 3 introduces robust statistical diffusion kernels. Section 4 provides the experimental results of this study, while the conclusions are drawn in Section 5.

2 Hessian Diffusion Kernels

The heat equation of a geometric manifold can be described as [6]:

$$\frac{\partial I(x,t)}{\partial t} - \nabla^2 I(x,t) = 0 \tag{1}$$

where $I(x,t)$ represents the heat at location x and time t, starting with the initial conditions $I(x,0) = I(x)$ and ∇^2 denotes the Laplacian. The solution to the heat equation is [6]:

$$I(x,t) = \int_M K_t(x,y) I(y) dy \tag{2}$$

where $K_t(x,y)$ is the heat kernel (diffusion kernel) and $x, y \in M$. When $M \equiv \mathbb{R}$, the heat kernel becomes the Gaussian function :

$$I(x,t) = \frac{1}{\sqrt{4\pi d}} \int_{\mathbb{R}} \exp\left[-(\mathbf{x} - \mathbf{z}_c)^T \Sigma^{-1} (\mathbf{x} - \mathbf{z}_c)/4d\right] I(y) dy \tag{3}$$

where Σ represents the covariance matrix, $\mathbf{z}_c$ the kernel center and d is a normalization coefficient.

Differential techniques compute velocity from spatio-temporal derivatives of image intensities. After considering the Taylor series expansion, we obtain, [2]:

$$I(\mathbf{x} + \delta\mathbf{x}, t + \delta t) \approx I(\mathbf{x}, t+1) = I(\mathbf{x},t) + \nabla I \cdot \delta\mathbf{x} + \delta t g_t \tag{4}$$

where $\nabla I = (\frac{\partial I}{\partial x}, \frac{\partial I}{\partial y})$ and g_t represent first order partial spatial and temporal derivatives, respectively. Rearranging equation (4), we obtain :

$$\nabla I \cdot \mathbf{V} + g_t = 0 \tag{5}$$

where $\mathbf{V} = (V_x, V_y)$ denotes the motion vector and ∇I is the local intensity gradient. Equation (5) is known as the constrained optical flow equation. The optical flow is represented as a vector field on a 3D lattice. Each plane of the lattice corresponds to the motion between two consecutive frames [4]. Motion vectors can be calculated using the block matching algorithm. Block matching uses the correlation of a given image block from the frame $I(t)$ with blocks of the same size inside a search region in the next frame $I(t + 1)$ [1]. Matching is performed by minimizing the displaced frame difference (DFD) for a particular block of pixels. Matching blocks in image areas that have constant grey-levels or similar texture patterns can lead to erroneous motion vectors [4]. The challenge is to achieve high robustness against strong assumption violations, commonly met in real sequences. In such cases, vector field smoothing is necessary. In order to obtain well defined moving objects and to maintain the optical flow constraints, second order differential methods are needed [2]. The local Hessian can be used as a detector of change in the direction of the optical flow.

The Hessian for the optical flow is represented as a matrix, $\mathbf{H}_{2D}$:

$$\mathbf{H}_{2D} = \begin{bmatrix} \psi_{xx} & \psi_{xy} \\ \psi_{yx} & \psi_{yy} \end{bmatrix} \tag{6}$$

whose entries ψ_{xx}, ψ_{xy}, ψ_{yx} and ψ_{yy} are second order partial spatial derivatives, $\psi_{xx} = \dfrac{\partial^2 V}{\partial x^2}$, $\psi_{yy} = \dfrac{\partial^2 V}{\partial y^2}$, $\psi_{xy} = \dfrac{\partial^2 V}{\partial x \partial y}$, $\psi_{yx} = \dfrac{\partial^2 V}{\partial y \partial x}$.

2.1 Smoothing Using 2D Hessian Kernel

The Hessian detects major changes in the direction of the optical flow. Optical flow associated with complex motion such as that of rotation, zooming or created by turbulent fluids can be accurately represented after being smoothed with a Hessian kernel. Hessians have been employed as kernels for diffusion smoothing in various applications [8,9]. The discretization of (3) is given by :

$$\hat{\mathbf{V}}_{kc}^{t+1} = \frac{\sum_{\mathbf{x}_i \in \eta(\mathbf{z}_c)} \exp[-(\mathbf{x}_i - \mathbf{z}_c)^T \mathbf{H}_{2D,c}^{-1}(\mathbf{x}_i - \mathbf{z}_c)/4d] \cdot \mathbf{V}_{ki}^t}{\sum_{\mathbf{x}_i \in \eta(\mathbf{z}_c)} \exp[-(\mathbf{x}_i - \mathbf{z}_c)^T \mathbf{H}_{2D,c}^{-1}(\mathbf{x}_i - \mathbf{z}_c)/4d]} \tag{7}$$

where $\mathbf{V}_{ki}^t$ is the vector at location i within a neighborhood $\eta(\mathbf{z}_c) = 3 \times 3$ around the central location $\mathbf{z}_c$, t denotes iteration number and k is the frame number.

2.2 Smoothing Using Multiple Frame 2D Hessian Kernel

The 2D Hessian kernel applies smoothing on pairs of 2 frames. This can be extended to include data from multiple frames, thus considering the temporal influence in smoothing. In this case the Hessian is calculated in each vector field, individually, as in (6), and the diffused vector takes into account all these Hessians assuming the temporal continuity. The resulting smoothed vector is :

$$\hat{\mathbf{V}}_{kc}^{t+1} = \frac{\sum_{j=k-K}^{j=k+K} \sum_{\mathbf{x}_i \in \eta(\mathbf{z}_{j,c})} \exp[-(\mathbf{x}_i - \mathbf{z}_{j,c})^T \mathbf{H}_{2D,jc}^{-1} (\mathbf{x}_i - \mathbf{z}_{j,c})/4d] \cdot \mathbf{V}_{ji}^t}{\sum_{j=k-K}^{j=k+K} \sum_{\mathbf{x}_i \in \eta(\mathbf{z}_{j,c})} \exp[-(\mathbf{x}_i - \mathbf{z}_{j,c})^T \mathbf{H}_{2D,jc}^{-1} (\mathbf{x}_i - \mathbf{z}_{j,c})/4d]} \quad (8)$$

where $j \neq k$ and $2K$ represents the number of frames considered.

2.3 Smoothing Using 3D Hessian Kernels

In the following the diffusion kernel is extended to 3D lattices :

$$\hat{\mathbf{V}}_{kc}^{t+1} = \frac{\sum_{\mathbf{x}_i \in \eta_{3D}(\mathbf{z}_c)} \exp[-(\mathbf{x}_i - \mathbf{z}_c)^T \mathbf{H}_{3D,c}^{-1} (\mathbf{x}_i - \mathbf{z}_c)/4d] \cdot \mathbf{V}_{ki}^t}{\sum_{\mathbf{x}_i \in \eta_{3D}(\mathbf{z}_c)} \exp[-(\mathbf{x}_i - \mathbf{z}_c)^T \mathbf{H}_{3D,c}^{-1} (\mathbf{x}_i - \mathbf{z}_c)/4d]} \quad (9)$$

where the neighbourhood is defined in 3D as $\eta_{3D}(\mathbf{z}_c) = 3 \times 3 \times 4$, and j is the central frame. In (9) the 2D Hessian kernel is extended to 3D to accommodate the spatio-temporal variation in the optical flow. By processing a larger amount of data, the optical flow transitions and moving object boundaries will be better preserved, whilst diffusing the vector field. The 3D Hessian matrix is given by :

$$\mathbf{H}_{3D} = \begin{bmatrix} \psi_{xx} & \psi_{xy} & \psi_{xt} \\ \psi_{yx} & \psi_{yy} & \psi_{yt} \\ \psi_{tx} & \psi_{ty} & \psi_{tt} \end{bmatrix} \quad (10)$$

where $\psi_{xx} = \frac{\partial^2 V}{\partial x^2}$, $\psi_{yy} = \frac{\partial^2 V}{\partial y^2}$, $\psi_{xt} = \frac{\partial^2 V}{\partial x \partial t}$, $\psi_{yt} = \frac{\partial^2 V}{\partial y \partial t}$, $\psi_{tx} = \frac{\partial^2 V}{\partial t \partial x}$, $\psi_{ty} = \frac{\partial^2 V}{\partial t \partial y}$ and $\psi_{tt} = \frac{\partial^2 V}{\partial t^2}$, where t denotes the frame index.

3 Robust Statistics Diffusion Kernels

3.1 Alpha-Trimmed Mean of Hessians Kernel

We integrate robust statistics into diffusion kernels. The alpha-trimmed mean algorithm, called also interquartile range averaging, ranks the given data and excludes from further computation a certain percentage of data at both extremes of the ranked array. The aim of this method is to remove outliers and to apply the diffusion algorithm only onto data that are statistically consistent. The updating equation is :

$$\hat{\mathbf{V}}_{kc}^{t+1} = \frac{\sum_{i=\alpha N}^{N-\alpha N} \exp[-(\mathbf{x}_i - \mathbf{z}_c)^T \mathbf{H}_c^{-1} (\mathbf{x}_i - \mathbf{z}_c)/4d] \cdot \mathbf{V}_{(i)}^t}{\sum_{i=\alpha N}^{N-\alpha N} \exp[-(\mathbf{x}_i - \mathbf{z}_c)^T \mathbf{H}_c^{-1} (\mathbf{x}_i - \mathbf{z}_c)/4d]} \quad (11)$$

where the motion vectors have been ranked according to their length, $\|\mathbf{V}_{(0)}\| < \|\mathbf{V}_{(1)}\| < \cdots < \|\mathbf{V}_{(N)}\|$, where $\|\mathbf{V}\|$ represents the length of the vector $\mathbf{V}$, N is the total number of vectors in the neighbourhood $\eta(\mathbf{z}_c)$, $\alpha \in (0,1)$ is the trimming percentage from a ranked array. The Hessian can be either $\mathbf{H}_{2D}$, multiple frame $\mathbf{H}_{2D}$ or $\mathbf{H}_{3D}$.

3.2 The Median of Directional Hessians Kernel

Another robust statistics approach consists of combining the use of median statistics with the diffusion kernel. Median algorithms have the ability to eliminate up to 50 % outliers and have been successfully used with radial basis function networks for moving object segmentation and motion estimation [4]. We first apply the Hessian-based diffusion algorithm as in (7) but calculated directionally, instead of centrally, with respect to the window location. We obtain directional smoothing for all the vectors from a certain neighbourhood. In this case we take into account extended neighbourhoods and we aim to reduce overlaps among local estimates. The total number of vectors considered in the smoothing process is extended from 3×3 vectors to 5×5 vectors. The median operator is applied onto the results produced by directional diffusions:

$$\mathbf{V}_{kc}^{t+1} = Median(\mathbf{V}_{kc}^{t+1}, \eta_{\text{med}(\mathbf{z}_c)}) \qquad (12)$$

where $\eta_{\text{med}(\mathbf{z}_c)}$ is the window of the median operator centered at the location $\mathbf{z}_c$ that contains ranked diffused vectors. The influence of outliers will be diffused during the first operation. During the second processing operation any biased influence is eliminated. This operator can be applied with 2D Hessian (7), multiple frame 2D Hessian (8), or 3D Hessian (9) kernels.

4 Experimental Results

The proposed robust diffusion algorithms have been applied onto artificial vector fields as well as on optical flows extracted from image sequences. The vectorial field, entitled "Synthetic-1" is given by:

$$\begin{bmatrix} V_x \\ V_y \end{bmatrix} = \begin{bmatrix} c & -s \\ s & c \end{bmatrix} \begin{bmatrix} D+S & -R \\ R & D-S \end{bmatrix} \begin{bmatrix} c & s \\ -s & c \end{bmatrix} \begin{bmatrix} x-\mu \\ y-\mu \end{bmatrix} \qquad (13)$$

where V_x and V_y are velocity components in the x and y direction, $c = \cos(\theta)$ and $s = \sin(\theta)$, respectively, where $\theta = 0$, $D = 0.8$ is the dilation coefficient, $S = 0.05$ is the shear coefficient, $R = 0.1$ is the rotation coefficient, and $\mu = 31$ is the center position of the resultant flow. The vector field, entitled "Synthetic-2," is created by differentiating the expression :

$$Z(x,y) = 3(1-x)^2 \exp^{-(x^2)-(y+1)^2} -10(\frac{x}{5}-x^3-y^5)\exp^{-x^2-y^2} -\frac{1}{3}\exp^{-(x+1)^2-y^2}$$

The velocity components are obtained as $\mathbf{V} = (\partial Z/\partial x, \partial Z/\partial y)$.

Table 1. MSE and MCE for synthetic vector fields after one iteration of diffusion

Data	Noise	σ^2	Perona-Malik		Black		2DH		ATM-2DH		MED-2DH	
			MSE	MCE	MSE	MCE	MSE	MCE	MSE	MCE	MSE	MCE
Synthetic-1	Gaussian	0.01	**0.007**	0.991	**0.007**	0.991	0.016	0.982	0.017	0.973	**0.007**	**0.995**
		0.10	0.063	0.933	0.063	0.933	0.097	0.931	0.154	0.860	**0.059**	**0.973**
		0.25	0.180	0.872	0.180	0.871	0.237	0.887	0.444	0.740	**0.126**	**0.952**
		0.30	0.229	0.855	0.229	0.854	0.276	0.873	0.528	0.721	**0.158**	**0.947**
		0.40	0.287	0.819	0.286	0.818	0.327	0.852	0.680	0.690	**0.186**	**0.933**
	Poisson	0.01	0.015	0.993	0.015	0.993	0.009	0.998	**0.001**	0.998	0.002	**0.999**
		0.05	0.309	0.963	0.309	0.963	0.182	0.978	**0.005**	**0.995**	0.094	0.987
		0.10	1.053	0.934	1.052	0.934	0.728	0.959	**0.036**	**0.985**	0.501	0.975
		0.25	7.594	0.797	7.594	0.797	7.091	0.830	**1.627**	**0.867**	6.454	0.851
		0.40	20.874	0.649	20.873	0.649	20.767	0.668	**10.629**	**0.712**	19.470	0.692
Synthetic-2	Gaussian	0.01	**0.011**	0.722	**0.011**	0.722	0.019	0.682	0.023	0.626	0.012	**0.776**
		0.10	0.061	0.532	0.061	0.532	0.088	0.531	0.239	0.428	**0.043**	**0.612**
		0.25	0.156	0.435	0.156	0.435	0.195	0.473	0.473	0.350	**0.108**	**0.554**
		0.30	0.214	0.469	0.213	0.469	0.253	0.493	0.482	0.362	**0.146**	**0.572**
		0.40	0.425	0.415	0.425	0.414	0.522	0.443	0.658	0.320	**0.342**	**0.546**
	Poisson	0.01	0.021	0.961	0.021	0.961	0.027	0.956	**0.007**	0.974	0.008	**0.985**
		0.05	0.291	0.803	0.291	0.805	0.338	0.800	**0.013**	**0.969**	0.113	0.889
		0.10	1.364	0.631	1.364	0.633	1.482	0.633	**0.070**	**0.923**	0.832	0.703
		0.25	8.008	0.374	8.008	0.376	8.106	0.372	**2.427**	**0.623**	6.883	0.359
		0.40	19.592	0.239	19.591	0.240	20.073	0.237	**10.871**	**0.359**	17.994	0.219

We consider Gaussian and Poisson noise distributions, each with five different variances, corrupting the given vector fields. The algorithms described in this paper and two well know diffusion algorithms, respectively Perona-Malik (PM) [5], and Black [7], that have been adapted for the use on vectorial data, are applied for smoothing the noisy vector fields with the aim of trying to reconstruct the original vectorial fields. The numerical results obtained after smoothing the synthetic vectorial fields corrupted by noise after one iteration by the given algorithms are provided in Table 1. The algorithms are denoted according to the type of kernel and the algorithm that has been used for smoothing as: 2DH - 2D Hessian, ATM-2DH - alpha trimmed mean using 2D Hessian, M2DH - multiple 2D Hessian, ATM-M2DH - alpha trimmed mean of multiple 2D Hessian, 3DH - 3D Hessian, ATM-3DH - alpha trimmed mean of 3D Hessian, MED-2DH - median of 2D Hessian, MED-M2DH - median of multiple 2D Hessian, MED-3DH - median of 3D Hessian. For the alpha-trimmed mean smoothing algorithm in the case of the H_{2D} kernel we consider $N = 9$, while $\alpha N = 3$ and so 6 vectors are eliminated from the diffusion process. The results are assessed numerically in terms of mean square error (MSE) and mean cosine error (MCE). The second measure calculates the average cosines of the angle between the ground truth vector and its smoothed version. In Table 1 the best results are highlighted. MED-2DH proved to be better in the case when removing the Gaussian noise, while ATM-2DH is better in the case of Poisson noise.

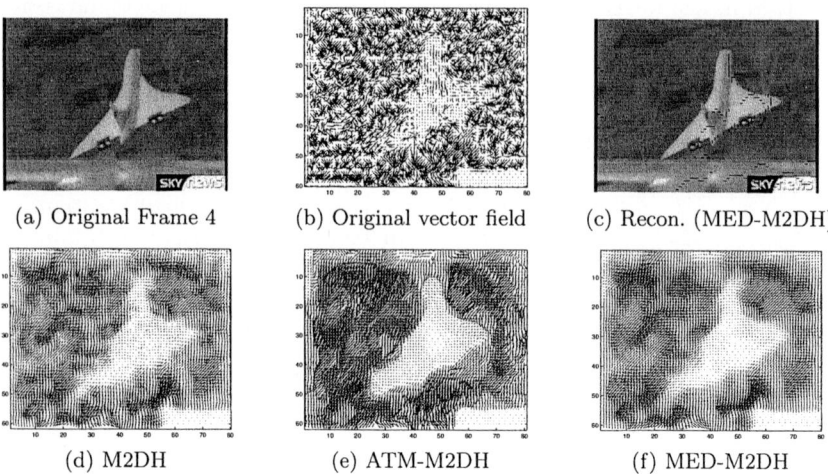

Fig. 1. Results obtained for "Concorde" sequence

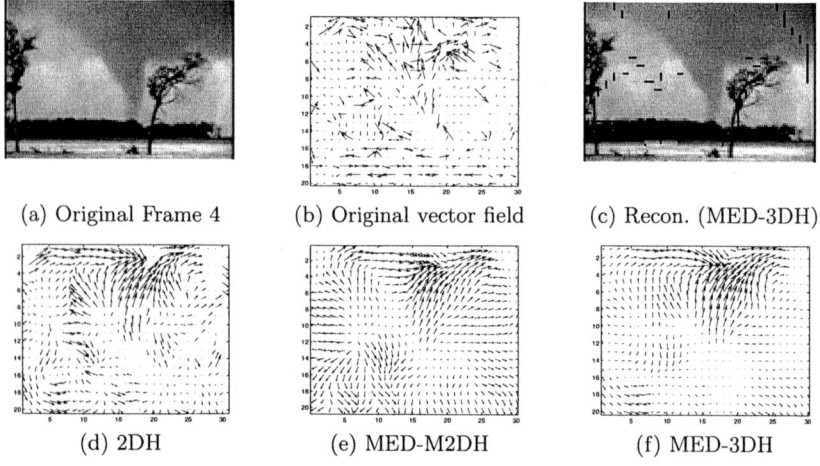

Fig. 2. Results obtained for "Tornado" sequence

The second set of experiments provides a comparison when diffusion algorithms are applied on optical flows estimated from image sequences. The block matching algorithm (BMA) has been used to estimate motion vector fields in a set of image sequences. The image sequences considered are listed in Table 2. Fig. 1 shows the results obtained when applying diffusion algorithms on "Concorde take-off" sequence, while Fig. 2 shows the results when processing the "Tornado" sequence. Fig. 1a displays frame 4 of the "Concorde" sequence, Fig. 1b shows the vector field extracted between frames 4 and 6, using BMA. This sequence was chosen for its complex motion characteristics such as rotational move-

Table 2. PSNR between the predicted frame based on smoothed optical flow after 1 iteration and the actual frame

Method	PSNR(dB)					
	Taxi	Concorde	Fighter	Clouds	Tornado	Traffic
PM	18.15	17.40	16.65	16.93	21.14	12.97
Black	18.05	17.39	16.68	16.99	21.21	13.00
2DH	19.10	17.83	17.32	17.57	21.72	13.90
M2DH	19.43	19.03	18.23	16.91	21.75	13.67
ATM-2DH	20.40	16.81	16.62	16.85	22.32	14.05
MED-2DH	20.99	19.04	19.13	20.29	22.95	15.84
ATM-M2DH	20.12	18.59	16.20	16.86	23.33	13.56
MED-M2DH	20.88	**20.40**	**20.07**	**20.31**	**23.71**	**16.10**
3DH	18.96	17.77	17.29	17.76	21.64	13.86
ATM-3DH	19.84	18.31	16.05	16.54	23.40	13.30
MED-3DH	**21.07**	19.00	19.10	20.28	23.09	15.83

ment, turbulent air from jet thrusters, blocky artifacts from compression and camera movement combined with a rigid moving object. In order to assess the efficiency of the smoothed optical flows we calculate the PSNR (peak signal-to-noise ratio) between the next frame and the corresponding frame reconstructed using the smoothed optical flow. Fig. 1c shows the reconstructed frame 6, obtained by translating individually each block of the frame with its corresponding smoothed vector by MED-M2DH. Figs. 1d-1f show the smoothed vector fields after 5 iterations when using M2DH, ATM-M2DH and MED-M2DH, respectively. The corresponding results are displayed in Fig. 2 for the "Tornado" sequence. The movement and the area affected by the twister can be easily identified after employing the robust diffusion algorithms and their multi frame extensions, as it can be seen in Figs. 2d-2f. In the case of the 3D Hessian kernel the total number of vectors considered in smoothing is $N = 36$.

Table 2 provides the PSNR calculated between the actual frame and the predicted frame for six different image sequences. From this table as well as from Figs. 1 and 2 it can be observed that robust kernels such as MED-M2DH and MED-3DH, have better performance than Perona-Malik, Black or 2DH algorithms. Methods that use data from the 3D lattice such as those based on ATM-3DH and MED-3DH kernels smooth better than 2DH kernels.

5 Conclusions

A set of robust diffusion algorithms is proposed for optical flow smoothing. The diffusion kernel ensures that smoothing occurs along the optical flow structure. The extention of 2D Hessian to the 3D Hessian kernel considers the temporal information from multiple frames. Robust statistics algorithms such as alpha trimmed-mean and marginal median are employed on diffusion kernels for removing the outliers and for enhancing vector smoothing. The improvements provided by the robust algorithms are particularly evident when dealing with complex optical flows such as those that describe the motion of fluids. Optical flow smoothing algorithms represent a core processing module for motion estimation, segmentation, tracking of moving objects as well as in video compression.

References

1. A. M. Tekalp, *Digital Video Processing*. Prentice Hall, 1995.
2. J. L. Barron, D. J. Fleet, S. Beauchemin, "Performance of optical flow techniques," *International Journal of Computer Vision*, vol. 12, no. 1, pp. 43-77, 1994.
3. M. Black, P. Anandan, "The robust estimation of multiple motions: parametric and piecewise-smooth flow fields," *Computer Vision and Image Understanding*, Vol. 63, No. 1, pp. 75-104, 1996.
4. A. G. Bors, I. Pitas, "Optical Flow Estimation and Moving Object Segmentation Based on Median Radial Basis Function Network," *IEEE Trans. on Image Processing*, vol. 7, no. 5, pp. 693-702, 1998.
5. P. Perona, J. Malik, "Scale-Space and Edge Detection Using Anisotropic Diffusion," *IEEE Trans. on Pattern Anal. and Machine Intell.*, vol. 12, no. 7, pp. 629-639, 1990.
6. S.-T. Yau, ed., *Surveys in Differential Geometry: Differential Geometry inspired by String Theory*. American Mathematical Society, 1999.
7. M. J. Black, G. Sapiro, D. H. Marimont, David Heeger, "Robust Anisotropic Diffusion," *IEEE Trans. on Image Processing*, vol. 7, no. 3, pp. 421-432, 1998.
8. D. Tschumperlé, R. Deriche, "Orthonormal vector sets regularization with PDE's and Applications," *Inter. Jour. on Computer Vision*, vol. 50, no. 3, pp. 237-252, 2002.
9. D. Tschumperlé, R Deriche, "Vector-Valued Image Regularization with PDE's: A Common Framework for Different Applications," *Proc. IEEE Computer Vision and Pattern Recognition*, Madison, USA, 2003, vol. I, pp. 651-656.
10. P.-Y. Burgi, "Motion estimation based on the direction of intensity gradient," *Image and Vision Computing*, vol. 22, no. 8, pp. 637-653, 2004.
11. M. Bertalmio, L. Vese, G. Sapiro, S. Osher, "Simultaneous Structure and Texture Image Inpainting," *IEEE Trans. on Image Proces.*, vol. 12, no. 8, pp. 882-889, 2003.
12. M. Irani, "Multi-Frame Optical Flow Estimation Using Subspace Constraints," *Proc. IEEE Int. Conf. on Computer Vision*, Corfu, Greece, 1999, vol. I, pp. 626-633.

Stereo Vision Based Localization of Free Parking Site

Ho Gi Jung[1], Dong Suk Kim[1], Pal Joo Yoon[1], and Jai Hie Kim[2]

[1] MANDO Corporation Central R&D Center, Advanced Electronic System Team,
413-5, Gomae-Ri, Giheung-Eub, Yongin-Si, Kyonggi-Do 449-901, South Korea
{hgjung, greenhupa, pjyoon}@mando.com
http://www.mando.com/eng/main.asp
[2] Yonsei University, Department of Electrical and Electronic Engineering,
134, Sinchon-Dong, Seodaemun-Gu, Seoul 120-749, South Korea
jhkim@yonsei.ac.kr
http://cherup.yonsei.ac.kr

Abstract. This paper describes a novel stereo vision based localization of free parking site, which recognizes the target position of automatic parking system. Pixel structure classification and feature based stereo matching extracts the 3D information of parking site in real time. Parking site marking is separated by plane surface constraint and is transformed into bird's eye view, on which template matching is performed to determine the location of parking site. Obstacle depth map, which is generated from the disparity of adjacent vehicles, can be used as the guideline of the template matching by limiting search range and orientation. Proposed method using both the obstacle depth map and the bird's eye view of parking site marking increases operation speed and robustness to visual noise by effectively limiting the search range.

1 Introduction

Generally novice, female and old driver feels constraint in parking backward between vehicles. J. D. Power's 2001 Emerging Technology Study, which found that 66% of consumers were likely to purchase parking aid, is a good proof [1]. Many upper class cars adopt ultrasonic parking assist system, which warns the driver of close distance to obstacle. Recently, car and component manufacturers started to provide vision based parking assist system. Toyota and Aisin Seiki introduced Back Guide Monitor, which helps the driver by projecting predicted driving course on the image of a rear view camera [2,3]. Aisin Seiki's next generation is expected to include circumstance recognition function to provide an optimistic view to the driver [4]. They use wheel speed sensor, structure from motion technology and virtual camera, i.e. IVR (Intermediate View Reconstruction) technology, to make a virtual rendered image from an optimistic viewpoint.

Automatic parking system automates parking operation with automatic steering control and automatic braking control. Automatic parking system consists of three components : path planning including the localization of target position, automatic steering and braking system used to implement the planned trajectory, HMI (Human

Machine Interface) used to receive driver's input and provide the visual information of ongoing parking process. The localization of target position can be implemented by various methods, e.g. fully manual designation [2], GPS infrastructure [5] and the vision based localization of free parking site [6,7]. Toyota's IPA (Intelligent Parking Assist) is a semiautomatic parking system, which leaves the braking control as driver's responsibility. Toyota's IPA developed the localization of target position by HMI, which shows a potential target position on the image from rear view camera and enables the driver to change the target position with direction control buttons such as up, down, left, right and rotation [2].

Although semiautomatic parking system becomes commercialized, fully manual designation is too tedious and complicated for daily usage. Therefore, it is natural that the need of the vision based localization of free parking site is increasing rapidly. Nico Kaempchen developed a stereo vision based pose estimation of parking lots, which uses feature based stereo algorithm, template matching algorithm on a depth map and 3D fitting to the planar surface model of vehicle by ICP (Iterative Closest Point) algorithm [6]. The vision system uses the disparity of vehicles but ignores all the information of parking site marking. Jin Xu developed a color vision based localization of parking site marking, which uses color segmentation based on RCE neural network, contour extraction based on least square method and inverse perspective transformation [7]. Because the system depends only on parking site marking, it can be degraded by poor visual conditions such as stain on marking, shadow and occlusion by adjacent vehicles.

This paper proposes a novel vision system to localize free parking site for automatic parking system. Proposed method is based on feature based stereo matching and separates parking site marking by plane surface constraint. The location of parking site is determined by template matching on the bird's eye view of parking site marking, which is generated by inverse perspective transformation on the separated parking site marking. Obstacle depth map, which is generated by the disparity information of adjacent vehicles, can be used to narrow the search range of parking site center and the orientation. Because the template matching is fulfilled within the limited range, the speed of searching effectively increases and the result of searching is robust to noise including previously mentioned poor visual conditions. Using both obstacle depth map and parking site marking can be justified because typical parking site in urban area is constructed by nation-wide standards.

2 Stereo Vision System

2.1 Pixel Classification

In the case of automotive vision, it is known that vertical edges are sufficient to detect noticeable objects [9]. Consequently, stereo matching using only vertical edges drastically reduces computational load [10,11]. Pixel classification investigates the intensity differences between a pixel and 4 directly connected neighbors so as to assign the pixel a class reflecting the intensity configuration. It is known that the feature based stereo matching with pixel class is fast and robust to noise [11]. Equation (1) shows that a pixel of smooth surface will be classified as zero class and a pixel of edge will be classified as non-zero class. To reduce the effect of threshold T, histogram equalization or adaptive threshold can be used.

$$d(i) = \begin{cases} 1, & \text{if } g(i)-g(x) > +T \\ 2, & \text{if } g(i)-g(x) < -T \\ 0, & \text{else} \end{cases} \qquad (1)$$

4 neighbors   g(.) : grey value   pixel class

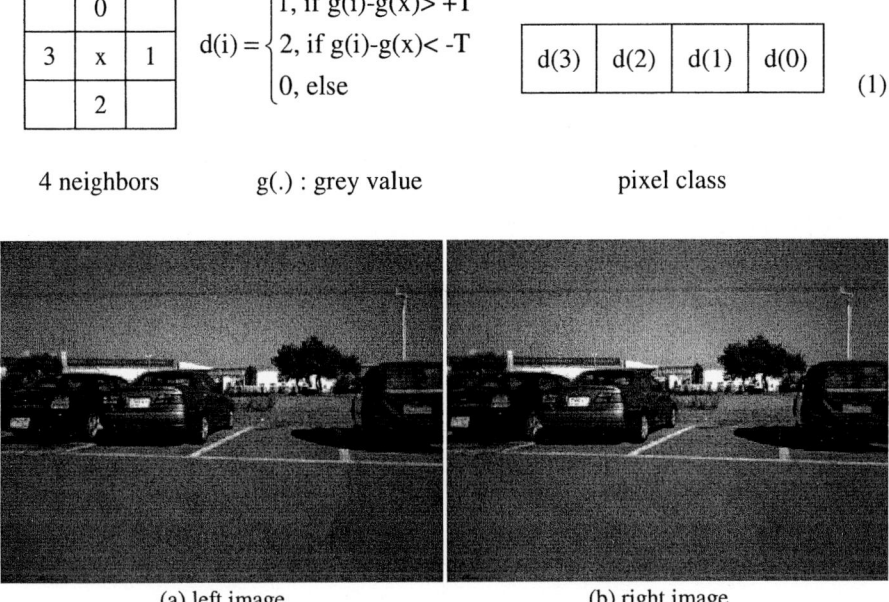

(a) left image   (b) right image

Fig. 1. Stereo image of typical parking site. Parking site marking is drawn according to corresponding standards. Some portion of parking site marking is occluded by adjacent vehicle and trash. Some portion of parking site marking is invisible because of shadow.

Fig.1 is the stereo image of typical parking site, which is acquired with Point Grey Research's Bumblebee camera installed on the backend of test vehicle. Each image has 640x480 resolution and 24 bits color information. The images are rectified with

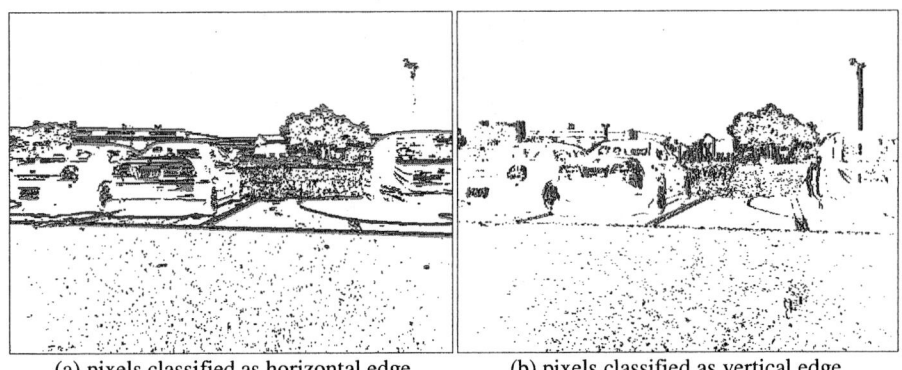

(a) pixels classified as horizontal edge   (b) pixels classified as vertical edge

Fig. 2. Pixel classification result

Point Grey Research's Triclops rectification library [8]. Fig.2 shows the result of the pixel classification. 13.7% of total pixels are classified as horizontal edge and 7.8% are classified as vertical edge.

2.2 Feature Based Stereo Matching

Stereo matching is performed only on pixels classified as vertical edge. Furthermore, stereo matching is composed of step-by-step test sequences through class comparison, class similarity, color similarity and maximum similarity detection. Only correspondence candidates passing previous test step successfully will be investigated in the next test step.

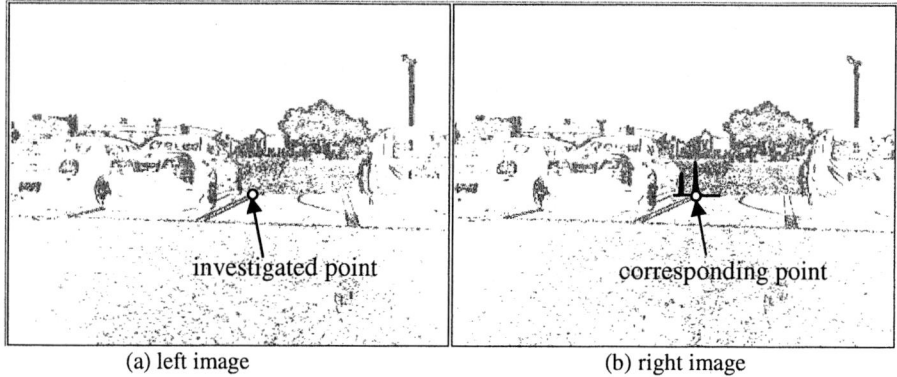

(a) left image   (b) right image

Fig. 3. Stereo matching result of a pixel. Graph on the right image shows the total similarity of pixels within search range. A pixel with highest total similarity becomes corresponding point.

Assuming that the vertical alignment of Bumblebee is correct, the search range of a pixel is limited to a horizontal line with $-35 \sim 35$ displacement. First, correspondence test is performed on pixels with the same class as the investigated pixel. Class similarity is the measure of how the candidate pixel is similar to the investigated pixel in the sense of 3x3 class window. Color similarity is the measure of how the candidate pixel is similar to the investigated pixel in the sense of 5x5 color window. Total similarity is the product of the class similarity and the color similarity. If highest total similarity is lower than a certain threshold, the investigated pixel fails to find corresponding point and is ignored.

$$\text{ClassSimilarity}(x,y,s) = \frac{1}{3 \times 3} \sum_{u=-1}^{1} \sum_{v=-1}^{1} f(\text{Class}_{\text{left}}(x+u,y+v), \text{Class}_{\text{right}}(x+u+s,y+v))$$

$$\text{where } f(\text{Class}_{\text{left}}, \text{Class}_{\text{right}}) = \begin{cases} 0, & \text{Class}_{\text{left}} \neq \text{Class}_{\text{right}} \\ 1, & \text{Class}_{\text{left}} = \text{Class}_{\text{right}} \end{cases}$$

(2)

$$\text{ColorSimilarity}(x,y,s) = 1 - \frac{1}{256}\sqrt{\frac{\text{ColorSSD}(x,y,s)}{5 \times 5}}$$

$$\text{where ColorSSD}(x,y,s) = \sum_{u=-2}^{2}\sum_{v=-2}^{2}\begin{Bmatrix}(R_{\text{left}}(x+u,y+v)-R_{\text{right}}(x+u+s,y+v))^2 + \\ (G_{\text{left}}(x+u,y+v)-G_{\text{right}}(x+u+s,y+v))^2 + \\ (B_{\text{left}}(x+u,y+v)-B_{\text{right}}(x+u+s,y+v))^2\end{Bmatrix} \quad (3)$$

$$\text{Similarity}(x,y,s) = \text{ClassSimilarity}(x,y,s) \times \text{ColorSimilarity}(x,y,s) \quad (4)$$

2.3 Road / Object Separation

Generally, pixels on the road surface satisfy plane surface constraint, i.e. the y coordinate of a pixel is in linear relationship with the disparity of the pixel, d(x,y), like equation (5) [11]. Consecutively, the pixels of obstacles, e.g. adjacent vehicles, do not follow the constraint. Therefore, the disparity map which is the result of stereo matching can be separated into two disparity maps : the disparity map of parking site marking and the disparity map of obstacle.

$$d(x,y) = \frac{B}{H}f_x(\frac{y}{f_y}\cos\alpha + \sin\alpha), \text{ with } y \rangle f_y \tan\alpha \quad (5)$$

where B : baseline, H : Height, f_x, f_y : focal length, α : tilt angle

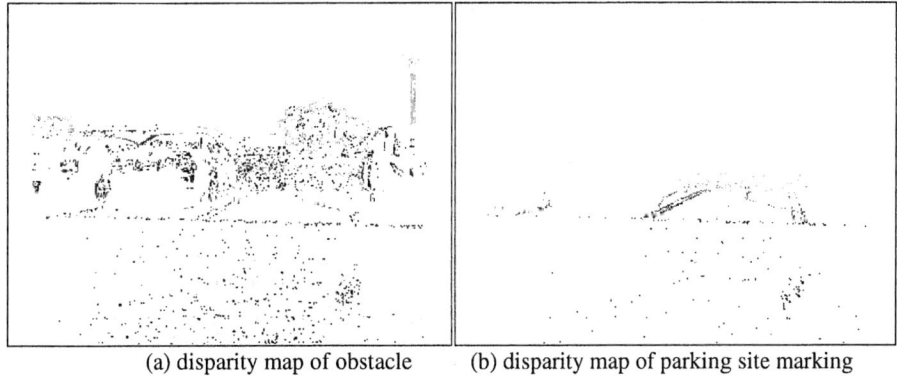

(a) disparity map of obstacle   (b) disparity map of parking site marking

Fig. 4. Road / Object separation result

The distance between camera and object, Z_{world}, is inverse proportional to the disparity like equation (6-1). Previously mentioned plane surface constraint can be simplified like equation (6-2). P_1 and P_2 is the constant parameter of camera configuration. Consequently, the relationship between the y coordinate of a pixel on road surface and Z_{world} can be summarized like equation (6-3), (6-4). The relationship between X_{world} and the x coordinate of a pixel can be defined like (6-5) by triangulation. Using the relationship, the disparity map of parking site marking is transformed into the bird's eye view of parking site marking. The bird's eye view is constructed by copying values from the disparity map to the ROI (Region Of Interest) of X_{world} and Z_{world}. Pixels with different color from parking site marking are ignored to remove the noise of textures such as asphalt and grass.

$$Z_{world} = \frac{B \cdot f}{d(x,y)} \quad (6\text{-}1)$$

$$d(x,y) = P_1 y + P_2, \text{ where } P_1 = \frac{B\,f_x}{H\,f_y}\cos\alpha,\; P_2 = \frac{B\,f_x}{H\,f_y}\sin\alpha \quad (6\text{-}2)$$

$$Z_{world} = \frac{B \cdot f}{P_1 \cdot y + P_2} \quad (6\text{-}3)$$

$$y = \frac{1}{P_1}\left(\frac{B \cdot f}{Z_{world}} - P_2\right) \quad (6\text{-}4)$$

$$X_{world} : Z_{world} = x : f \;\Rightarrow\; x = \frac{f \cdot X_{world}}{Z_{world}} \quad (6\text{-}5)$$

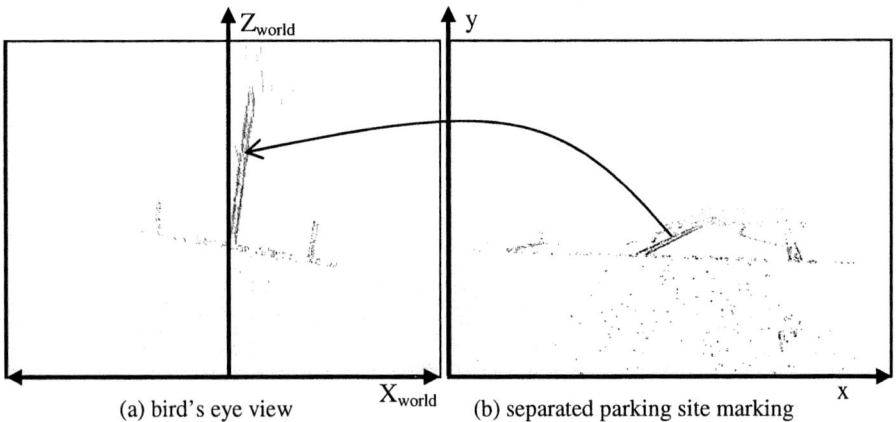

Fig. 5. Bird's eye view of parking site marking

Obstacle depth map is constructed by projecting the disparity information of pixels unsatisfying the plane surface constraint. World coordinate point (X_{world}, Z_{world}) corresponding to a pixel in the obstacle disparity map can be determined by equation (6-1) and (6-5) [10]. Because the stereo matching does not implement sub-pixel resolution for real time performance, a pixel in the disparity map contributes to a vertical array in the depth map. The element of depth map accumulates the contributions of corresponding disparity map pixels. By eliminating the elements of depth map under a certain threshold, noise on the disparity map can be removed. In general, the noise of the disparity map does not make a peak on the depth map.

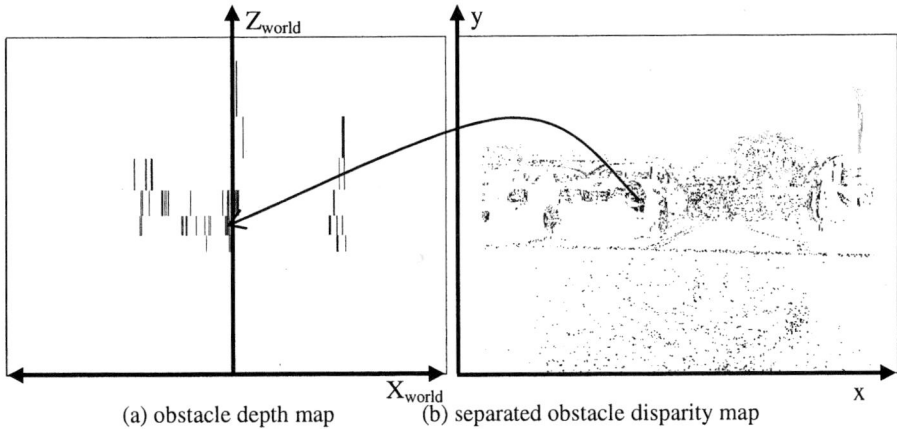

(a) obstacle depth map (b) separated obstacle disparity map

Fig. 6. Obstacle depth map

3 Localization of Parking Site

Free parking site is localized using both the depth map of obstacle and the bird's eye view of parking site marking. Localization algorithm consists of 3 steps : 1) finding the guideline, which is the front line of parking area, by the Hough transform of the bird's eye view of parking site marking, 2) obstacle histogram which is generated by projecting the obstacle depth map onto the guideline, 3) template matching within the search range limited by the obstacle histogram.

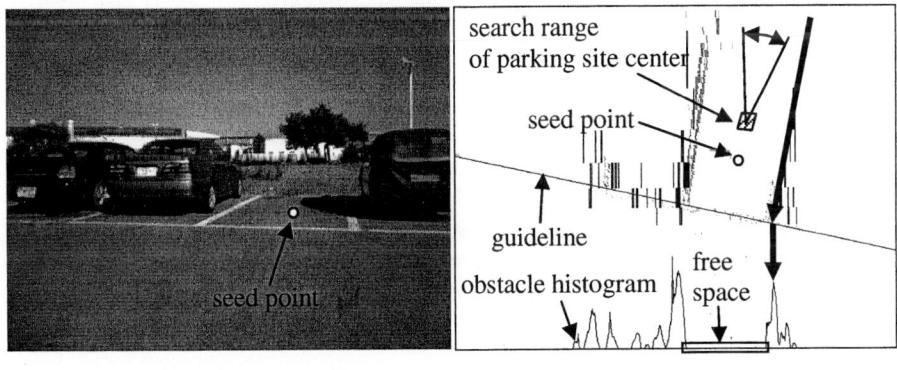

(a) seed point for localization   (b) guideline and obstacle histogram

Fig. 7. Search range reduction by guideline and obstacle histogram. HMI displays the image of rear view camera during parking process and user can set target position by clicking on touch screen. User's input is seed point and is used to restrict initial search range.

The pose of ego-vehicle is limited to –40~40 degrees with respect to the longitudinal direction of parking area. Therefore, the peak of Hough transform in this angular range is the guideline depicted in Fig. 7(b). Free space is the continuous portion of the obstacle histogram under a certain threshold and is determined by bi-directional search from the seed point. The search range of parking site center in the guideline direction is central 20% of the free space. The initial guess of parking site center in another direction, i.e. orthogonal to the guideline direction, is the position distant from the guideline by the half size of template length. Search range in the orthogonal direction is 10 pixels and angular search range is 10 degrees.

Final template matching uses a template consisting of 2 rectangles derived from standards about parking site drawing. The template matching measures how many pixels of parking site marking exist between 2 rectangles, i.e. between inner and outer rectangle. Fig. 8(a) shows the result on the bird's eye view of parking site marking and Fig. 8(b) projects the result on the bird's eye view of input image. Because the search range is narrowed by the obstacle depth map, template matching successfully detects correct position in spite of stain, blurring and shadow. Furthermore, template matching, which is the bottleneck of localization process, consumes little time. Total computational time on 1GHz PC is about 400~500 msec. Once the initial position is detected successfully, the next scene needs only template matching with little variation around the previous result.

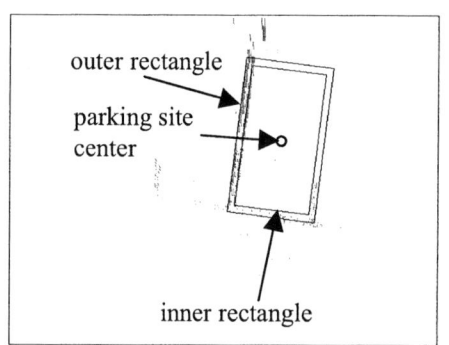 

(a) result on parking site marking   (b) result on input image

Fig. 8. Detected parking site

4 Conclusion

This paper proposes a stereo vision based 3D localization of the target position of automatic parking system. Obstacle depth map establishes the search range of free parking site and simple template matching finds the exact location of free parking site. By using both parking site marking and obstacle depth map, the search range of template matching is drastically reduced and the result is robust to noise such as stain, waste and shadow. Hereafter, to make practical system, research on the variation of parking site marking is needed.

References

1. Randy Frank : Sensing in the ultimately safe vehicle. SAE Paper No. : 2004-21-0055, Society of Automotive Engineers (2004)
2. Masayuki Furutani : Obstacle detection systems for vehicle safety. SAE Paper No. : 2004-21-0057, Society of Automotive Engineers (2004)
3. Shoji Hiramatsu, etc. : Rearview Camera based parking assist system with voice guidance. SAE Paper No. : 2002-01-0759, Society of Automotive Engineers (2002)
4. K. Fintzel, etc. : 3D vision system for vehicles. In : Proceedings of IEEE Intelligent Vehicle Symposium 2003 (2003) 174-179
5. Massaki Wada, etc. : Development of advanced parking assistance system. IEEE Transaction on Industrial Electronics, Volume 50, No. 1, February 2003 (2003) 4-17
6. Nico Kaempchen, etc. : Stereo vision based pose estimation of parking lots using 3D vehicle models. In : Proceedings of IEEE Intelligent Vehicle Symposium 2002 (2002) 459-464
7. Jin Xu, Guang Chen, Ming Xie : Vision-guided automatic parking for smart car. In : Proceedings of IEEE Intelligent Vehicle Symposium 2000 (2000) 725-730
8. Point Grey Research http://www.ptgrey.com
9. Dariu M. Gavrila, etc. : Real-time vision for intelligent vehicles. IEEE Instrumentation & Measurement Magazine, Volume 4, Issue 2, June 2001 (2001) 22-27
10. U. Franke, A. Joos : Real-time stereo vision for urban traffic scene understanding. In : Proceedings of IEEE Intelligent Vehicle Symposium 2000 (2000) 273-278
11. U. Franke, I. Kutzbach : Fast stereo based object detection for stop&go traffic. In : Proceedings of IEEE Intelligent Vehicle Symposium 1996 (1996) 339-344

Data Fusion for Photorealistic 3D Models

Zsolt Jankó and Dmitry Chetverikov

Computer and Automation Research Institute and
Eötvös Loránd University, Budapest, Hungary
{janko, csetverikov}@sztaki.hu

Abstract. This study aims at building photorealistic 3D models of real-world objects. We discuss the problem of combining a 3D textureless model obtained by 3D scanner, with optical images that provide textural information of the object. Recently, we have proposed a novel method to register an uncalibrated image pair to a 3D surface model. After registration, the images are mapped to the surface. However, as the images show different parts of the objects, partial overlapping textures can only be extracted from them. Combining the images into a complete texture map that covers the entire object is not trivial. We present a method to build photorealistic 3D models that includes algorithms for data registration and for merging multiple texture maps using surface flattening. Experimental results on real and synthetic data are shown.

1 Introduction

Thousands of cultural heritage objects around the world are in the danger of being lost. During the last years a number of ambitious projects have been started to preserve these objects by digitalising them. Such projects are: the Michelangelo Project [13], the Pieta Project [2] and the Great Buddha Project [4].

There exist different techniques to reconstruct the object surface and to build photorealistic 3D models. Active and passive methods are discussed in [18]. Although the geometry can be measured by various methods of computer vision, for precise measurements laser scanners are usually used. However, most of laser scanners do not provide texture and colour information, or if they do, the data is not accurate enough. (See [18] for a detailed discussion.)

We address the problem of combining geometric and textural information of the object. We consider the case when the two sources are independent, namely the 3D model is obtained by 3D scanner and is combined with high quality optical images. In [8] and [9] we introduced a novel method based on photo-consistency. The novelty of our method consists in using uncalibrated cameras – in contrast to Clarkson et al. [5] who need a calibrated setup – and applying a genetic algorithm.

Textures extracted from the images can cover only parts of the object. Merging multiple texture maps is not trivial. Mayer et al. [3] paste multiresolution textures to objects with large flat surfaces, for instance to buildings. They split rectangular surfaces until each portion can uniquely be related to a texture map, which shows it in the highest resolution. However their method handles polyhedrons only, while we look for solution for arbitrary surfaces.

Yemez et al. [18] use triangulated 3D mesh and subdivide each triangle into particles. For each particle the best colour is determined from the full set of images from which the particle is visible. Their method could not guarantee the continuity of the neighbouring texture maps; in addition, it assumes that the triangles have very similar sizes, which is a strong constraint. Papers [2] and [15] present similar techniques for combining multiple texture mappings.

Surface flattening is popular technique to support texture mapping. Zigelman et al. [19] discuss how to flatten arbitrary surfaces preserving the structure and having minimal distortions, which properties are of crucial importance from the point of view of texture mapping. Papers [6,11,14,16] also examine surface parameterisation, although none of them discusses the problem of merging multiple texture mappings.

In this paper we present our technique to build photorealistic 3D models. In section 2 a photo-consistency based registration method with genetic algorithm based optimisation is discussed. In section 3 we analyse the problem of fusion of multiple texture mappings, and present a novel method which combines the techniques of surface flattening and texture merging. Test results on synthetic and real data are shown for the methods.

2 Registration

In this section the registration of images to a 3D model is discussed based on our previous papers [8,9]. We give a mathematical formulation of the registration problem and show a possible solution for it.

2.1 Problem Formulation

The input data consists of two colour images, I_1 and I_2, and a 3D surface model. They represent the same object. (See figure 1 for an example.) The images are acquired under fixed lighting conditions and with the same camera sensitivity. All other camera parameters may differ and are unknown. The raw data is acquired by a hand-held 3D scanner, then processed by the triangulator of Kós [10]. The 3D model obtained consists of a triangulated 3D point set $\mathcal{P}$ with normal vectors assigned.

The finite projective camera model [7] is used to project the object surface to the image plane: $\mathbf{u} \simeq P\mathbf{X}$, where $\mathbf{u}$ is an image point, P the 3×4 **projection matrix** and $\mathbf{X}$ a surface point. ($\simeq$ means that the projection is defined up to an unknown scale.)

The task of registration is to determine the precise projection matrices, P_1 and P_2, for both images. Since the projection matrix is up to a scale factor, it has only 11 degrees of freedom in spite of having 12 elements. The collection of the 11 unknown parameters can be denoted by p, which represents the projection matrix P as an 11-dimensional parameter vector.

Values of the two parameter vectors p_1 and p_2 are sought such that the images are *consistent* in the sense that the corresponding points – different projections of the same 3D point – have the same colour value. Note that the precise mathematical definition is valid only when the surface is Lambertian. The formal definition is the following: We say that images I_1 and I_2 are consistent by P_1 and P_2 (or p_1 and p_2) if for each $X \in \mathcal{P}$: $\mathbf{u}_1 = P_1\mathbf{X}$, $\mathbf{u}_2 = P_2\mathbf{X}$ and $I_1(\mathbf{u}_1) = I_2(\mathbf{u}_2)$. (Here $I_i(\mathbf{u}_i)$ is the colour value in point $\mathbf{u}_i$ of image I_i.) This type of consistency is called **photo-consistency** [5,12].

The photo-consistency holds for accurate estimates for p_1 and p_2. Inversely, misregistered projection matrices mean much less photo-consistent images. The cost function introduced in [9] is the following:

$$C_\phi(p_1, p_2) = \frac{1}{|\mathcal{P}|} \sum_{\mathbf{X} \in \mathcal{P}} \|I_1(P_1\mathbf{X}) - I_2(P_2\mathbf{X})\|^2. \tag{1}$$

Here ϕ stands for *photo-inconsistency* while $|\mathcal{P}|$ is the number of points in $\mathcal{P}$. Difference of the colour values $\|I_1 - I_2\|$ can be defined by a number of different colour models: CIE XYZ ITU, HSI, CIE LUV [8]. The minimum of the cost function (1) gives a good estimation for the projection matrices.

The problem of occlusion and wrong measurements requires the cost function to be robustified. Occluded points are eliminated by using the surface normals, and the outliers by rejecting a certain amount of the smallest and largest squares (α-trimmed mean technique). Finally we note that although the problem is formulated with two images, it can be easily extended to the case of more images.

2.2 Optimisation Method

Although the cost function $C_\phi(p_1, p_2)$ is simple, it has unpredictable shape in the 22-dimensional parameter space, thus the standard local nonlinear minimisation techniques we have tested (such as the Levenberg-Marquardt algorithm [7]) failed to provide reliable results. A global nonlinear optimisation technique has also been tested. However, the stochastic optimisation method by Csendes [1] did not yield acceptable results either. The randomness of a stochastic method is excessive, and it does not save nearly good solutions. Finally, we decided to apply a genetic algorithm, as a time-honoured global search strategy. Note that in contrast to the stochastic optimisation, genetic algorithms preserve the most promising results and try to improve them. Running a GA without elitism yields also unstable and imprecise results.

We pre-register the images and the 3D model manually. This yields a good initial state for the search, which narrows the search domain and accelerates the method. Manual pre-registration is reasonable since this operation is simple and fast compared to the 3D scanning, which is also done manually. The photo-consistency based registration makes the result more accurate.

The genetic algorithm starts by creating the initial population. The individuals of the population are chosen from the neighbourhood of the parameter vector obtained by the manual pre-registration. The values of the genes are from the intervals defined by the pre-registered values plus a margin of $\pm\epsilon$. In our experiments ϵ was set to values between 1% and 3%, depending on the meaning and the importance of the corresponding parameter. The individual that encodes the pre-registered parameter vector is also inserted in the initial population to avoid losing it.

We have tested the method with a number of different genetic settings to check their influence on registration. Different settings can lead to significantly different results, but choosing the best settings the projection error of registration can be decreased from 18–20 pixels, which is the average error of the manual pre-registration, to 5–6 pixels[1]. After preliminary testing with semi-synthetic data, the following genetic setting has been selected: Steady state algorithm with Tournament selector, Swap mutator and Arithmetic crossover, with 250 individuals in the population, with mutation probability of 0.1 and crossover probability of 0.7. The typical running time with a 3D model containing 1000 points was 5–6 minutes on a 2.40 GHz PC with 1 GB memory.

We applied the method to different real data. Due to the paper size limitations, only the Bear Dataset is shown here (figure 1). (Papers [8] and [9] present other results.) The precision of the registration can be best judged at the mouth, the eyes, the hand and the feet of the Bear. Figure 2 visualises the difference between the manual pre-registration and the photo-consistency based registration. The areas of the mouth, the eyes and the ears show the improvement of the quality.

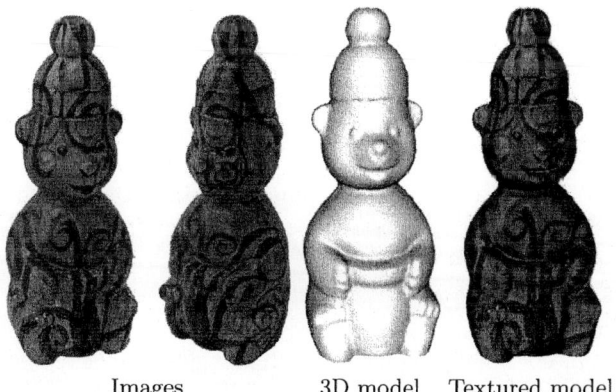

Images   3D model   Textured model

Fig. 1. The Bear Dataset and the result of the registration

---

[1] Here the projection error is measured, which means that the 3D point set $\mathcal{P}$ is projected onto the image planes by both the ground truth and the estimated projection matrices, and then the average distance between the corresponding image points is calculated.

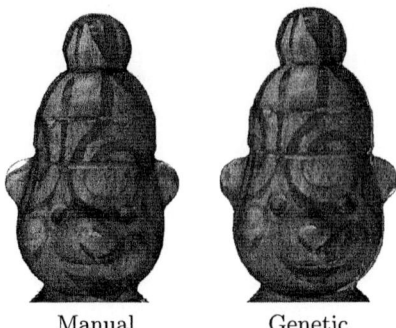

Manual   Genetic

Fig. 2. Difference between manual pre-registration and genetic registration

3 Merging Multiple Textures

After registering the images to the 3D model, they can be mapped to the surface. Usually one image can show only one part of the model, but a number of images of the same object taken from different viewpoints can cover the whole. This section discusses the problem of combining partial overlapping textures and shows a novel method for it.

To paste texture to the surface of an object we need two pieces of information: a *texture map* and *texture coordinates*. The former is the image we paste, while the latter specify where it is mapped to. Texture coordinates can be determined by a texture mapping function, for instance, by applying projection matrix P to 3D point $\mathbf{X}$.

Figure 3a shows two images of the globe, which can be considered as texture maps. Merging the two texture maps to one is not obvious. Creating an image by appending the second image to the first one and modifying the second projection matrix with a translation yields gap between the border of the textures.

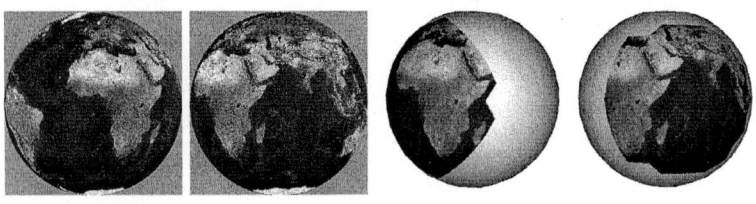

a. Input Images   b. Partially Textured Model

Fig. 3. Textures cover only parts of the model

There exists an other way to create a texture map based on the images. Flattening the surface of the object yields also a two-dimensional parameterisation. The advantage of this parameterisation is that it preserves the topology of the three-dimensional mesh. A texture that covers entirely the flattened 2D surface

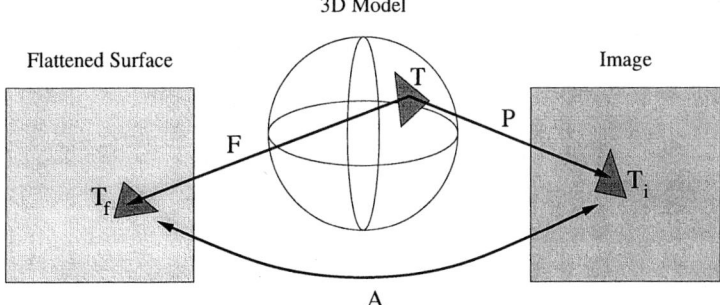

Fig. 4. Relation between 3D model, optical image and flattened surface

covers also the original 3D surface. Figure 4 illustrates the relation between the 3D surface, the optical image and the flattened surface. Converting optical images to flattened surfaces yields partially textured meshes, but since flattening preserves the structure of the 3D mesh, these texture maps can be merged, in contrast to the optical images.

We use the algorithm of Kós and Várady [11] to flatten and parameterise triangular meshes. After this one needs to convert the optical images to flattened texture maps. Since the transformation of flattening cannot be represented by a matrix, we have to use the mesh representation for conversion. Given a triangle of the mesh, denote by T_i and T_f the known corresponding triangles in the optical image and on the flattened surface, respectively. (See figure 4.) The affine transformation between T_i and T_f can be easily determined. This transformation gives the correspondence between the points of the triangles. Note that the affine transformation is unique for each triangle pair.

Conversion of optical images yields partially textured flattened surfaces. (See figure 5.) Merging these partial texture maps may cause problem only at the overlapping areas. To eliminate the seams appearing at the borders of the texture maps, we blend the views as follows. For each triangle all the views are collected which the given triangle is entirely visible from. A measure of visibility of a 3D point is the scalar product of the normal vector and the unit vector pointing towards the camera. This measure is used to set a weight for each view: If the point is better visible from the view, the weight is greater. To set the colour of a point, all of these views with their weights are combined.

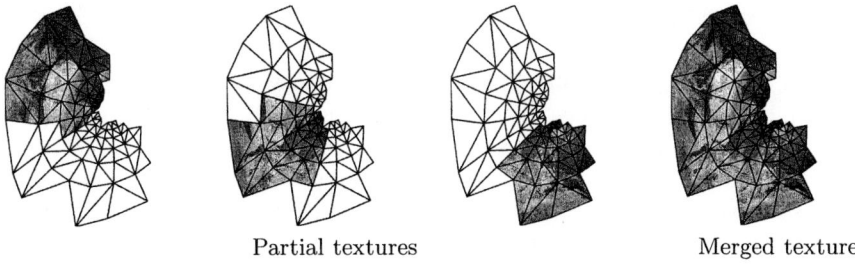

Partial textures   Merged texture

Fig. 5. Partial and merged texture maps

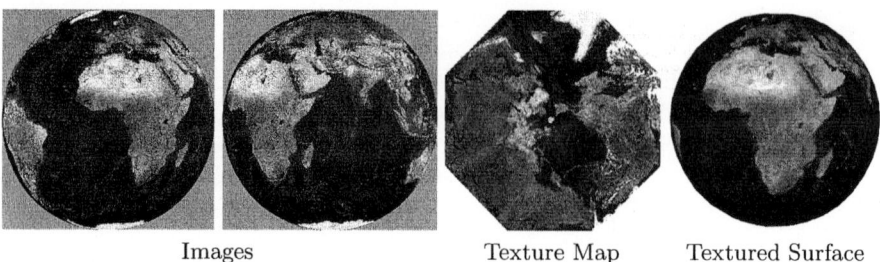

Images   Texture Map   Textured Surface

Fig. 6. Result for the Earth

The method has been tested both on synthetic and real data. The Earth Dataset consists of 8 images of the globe and a synthetic 3D model. The images were obtained by the script of John Walker [17], which also gives the precise projection matrices. Figure 6 shows two of the input images, the merged texture map and a snapshot of the textured 3D model.

Applying the method to real data is illustrated by figure 7. The projection matrices of the images of the Bear Dataset were obtained by our photo-consistency based registration method described in section 2.

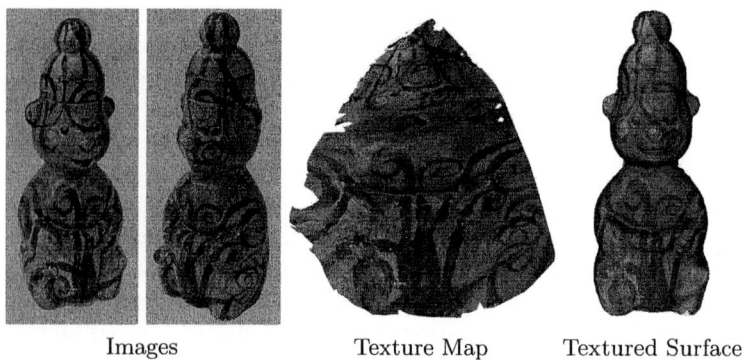

Images   Texture Map   Textured Surface

Fig. 7. Result for the Bear

4 Conclusion

We have discussed the problem of building photorealistic 3D models. Our technique assumes having accurate 3D model measured by laser scanner and high quality images of the object. The images are registered to the 3D model by minimising a photo-consistency based cost function using a genetic algorithm. Since textures extracted from images can only cover parts of the 3D model, they should be merged to a complete texture map. We have presented a novel method to combine partial texture mappings using surface flattening. Test results with synthetic and real data demonstrate the efficiency of the proposed methods.

Acknowledgement

This work was supported by the Hungarian Scientific Research Fund (OTKA) under grants T038355 and M28078 and the EU Network of Excellence MUSCLE (FP6-507752).

References

1. T. Csendes. Nonlinear parameter estimation by global optimization – Efficiency and Reliability. *Acta Cybernetica*, 8:361–370, 1988.
2. F. Bernardini et al. Building a digital model of Michelangelo's Florentine Pietà. *IEEE Comp. Graphics & Applications*, 22(1):59–67, 2002.
3. H. Mayer et al. Multiresolution texture for photorealistic rendering. In *Proc. 17th Spring Conference on Computer Graphics*, page 109. IEEE Comp. Soc., 2001.
4. K. Ikeuchi et al. The great Buddha project: Modeling cultural heritage for VR systems through observation. In *Proc. IEEE ISMAR03*, 2003.
5. M.J. Clarkson et al. Using photo-consistency to register 2D optical images of the human face to a 3D surface model. *IEEE Tr. on PAMI*, 23:1266–1280, 2001.
6. S. Haker et al. Conformal surface parameterization for texture mapping. *IEEE Tr. on Visualization and Comp. Graphics*, 6(2):181–189, 2000.
7. R. Hartley and A. Zisserman. *Multiple View Geometry in Computer Vision*. Cambridge Univ. Press, 2000.
8. Z. Jankó and D. Chetverikov. Photo-consistency based registration of an uncalibrated image pair to a 3D surface model using genetic algorithm. In *Proc. 2nd Int. Symp. on 3D Data Processing, Visualization & Transmission*, pages 616–622, 2004.
9. Z. Jankó and D. Chetverikov. Registration of an uncalibrated image pair to a 3D surface model. In *Proc. 17th Int. Conf. on Pattern Recognition*, volume 2, pages 208–211, 2004.
10. G. Kós. An algorithm to triangulate surfaces in 3D using unorganised point clouds. *Computing Suppl.*, 14:219–232, 2001.
11. G. Kós and T. Várady. Parameterizing complex triangular meshes. In *Proc. 5th International Conf. on Curves and Surfaces*, pages 265–274, 2003.
12. K.N. Kutulakos and S.M. Seitz. *A Theory of Shape by Space Carving*. Prentice Hall, 1993.
13. M. Levoy et al. The digital Michelangelo project. *ACM Computer Graphics Proceedings*, pages 131–144, 2000.
14. D. Piponi and G. Borshukov. Seamless texture mapping of subdivision surfaces by model pelting and texture blending. In *Proc. 27th Annual Conf. on Comp. Graphics and Interactive Techniques*, pages 471–478. ACM Press, 2000.
15. V. Sequeira and J.G.M. Gonçalves. 3D reality modelling: Photo-realistic 3D models of real world scenes. In *Proc. 1st Int. Symp. on 3D Data Processing, Visualization & Transmission*, pages 776–783, 2002.
16. A. Sheffer and E. de Sturler. Smoothing an overlay grid to minimize linear distortion in texture mapping. *ACM Tr. Graphics*, 21(4):874–890, 2002.
17. J. Walker. Satellite data. URL: http://www.fourmilab.ch/cgi-bin/uncgi/Earth.
18. Y. Yemez and F. Schmitt. 3D reconstruction of real objects with high resolution shape and texture. *Image and Vision Computing*, 22:1137–1153, 2004.
19. G. Zigelman, R. Kimmel, and N. Kiryati. Texture mapping using surface flattening via multi-dimensional scaling. *IEEE Tr. on Visualization and Comp. Graphics*, 8(2):198–207, 2002.

Virtualized Real Object Integration and Manipulation in an Augmented Scene

Brahim Nini and Mohamed Batouche

Faculty of Engineering, LIRE laboratory, Vision and Computer Graphics Group,
Mentouri University, 25000 Constantine, Algeria. Tel & Fax: 213 31 61 43 46 / 63 90 10
Brahim_nini@yahoo.fr

Abstract. This paper presents a new technique of a scene augmentation using images of real objects' views that are not generated using a graphical library. We call them 'Virtualized Real Objects' (VRO). The idea may be used, for example, for art objects of a commercial organization wanting to deploy its trade by Internet. VRO are important for cases where real objects 3D models availability is not obvious. This orientation is equally useful for adaptation tests of heavy or big real objects with respect to their expected places. This article outlines our developed prototype for this realization. In the occurrence, how real objects' images can be integrated in a sequence and how they are manipulated for a visual disposition.

1 Introduction

The augmentation of a real scene is the addition, in real time, of one or several virtual objects to the related video sequence. The objects are assumed virtual because of their computer-generated nature which limits their existence to the video flow. They may accurately register to searched and located real-world marks. These marks may be explicitly added to the real-world or deduced from its 3D depth study. The foremost augmentation techniques used without explicit marks suffer from computation time-consuming and do not allow real time augmentations [2]. As opposed to the formers ones, the use of explicit indices inevitably denaturalize the scene and the augmentation techniques become typical patterns constrained [11], [12].

To reach an accurate augmentation process, a set of problems must be solved. There are algorithmic problems related to static and dynamic parameters errors cited in [10] and others related to semantic nature of the scene. The type of problems we are concerned by is how to maintain the real aspect of a generated scene. Ideally, the virtual and real objects appear to co-exist in the same space and merge together seamlessly. The possible manipulation of virtual objects improves the realism sensation and facilitates the reaching of some user's objectives in the achievement of particular tasks [4], [6], [9]. More over, it may become a new means of communication for the user to convey her or his ideas.

This work reports the manipulation of inserted virtual objects in a collaborative environment. According to her or his objectives, the user will be able to adjust them into the scene. Adjustments consist of a set of geometrical transformations to apply for virtual objects. According to our objectives, the system uses the simple means of manipulation: the mouse and the keyboard [7], [9]. To do so, we use a visual augmentation implemented using a video system [11]. This consists of a 2D pattern added to a filmed scene in order to serve as a mark for the registration of virtual elements. Initially, inserted objects are supposed to be superimposed on the top of the pattern in the augmented scene.

These objects can be constructed by using a graphical library [4], [5], [6], [7] or inserting different images corresponding to different views of real objects. The aim of our work is that augmentation may use the latter objects category. We call them 'virtualized real objects'. The challenge to insert images of real captured objects is important. For example, it is difficult to have underlying graphical models for some art objects. Our objective is to show real objects for a customer as if she or he owns them and has not to displace them.

To present the underlying theory and to evaluate the obtained results, the work is divided into three more sections. The second one presents an overview of the augmentation process using a planar pattern where the third section shows the theoretical framework used for overlaying VRO, the realized prototype through its advantages and limits, and makes a tour of manipulation laws. The last section includes points that are not yet covered, insufficiencies and future work orientations.

2 Overview of Video Augmentation Using 2D Patterns

Two systems are used for augmentation: optic and video [11]. The optical system uses transparent glasses. They allow the perceiving of the view of the real-world above which virtual objects are projected. The video system consists of an ordinary screen or an opaque helmet (HMD) that totally occludes the user's eyes, and in which a small screen exists. The grabbed scene by HMD's cameras or independent ones is projected on the screen after having been augmented by virtual objects.

A video augmentation begins by analyzing the generated numerical scene to find its correspondence with the real world and to insert virtual objects in it. A great number of techniques are applied according to the environment whether it is prepared or not [4], [6], [8]. The prepared environment consists of adding explicitly indices or markers (2D or 3D patterns) whose form and size are known and searching for them in each frame of the generated sequence. Once found, they should allow to calibrate the camera [11], [12], and to deduce the scene's geometry that allows its augmentation. This technique is characterized by its simplicity, accuracy and its adaptation to real time processing.

The calibration of the camera determines its intrinsic and extrinsic parameters. Intrinsic parameters reflect the camera characteristics as M_{int} matrix. They are the focal length, the generated image centre in pixel units and its horizontal and vertical directions scale factors. Extrinsic parameters are related to the quantified position and orientation of the camera relatively to real world system coordinates.

To achieve augmentation, a perspective transformation is required in order to determine analytic relations that allow the projection of virtual elements. The pin-hole camera model is the simplest and largest used one (Fig. 1). It allows finding three transformations (T_o, T_c, T_i) that respectively express the Object-to-World, World-to-Camera and Camera-to-Image plane transformations.

Firstly, a virtual object is positioned in the real world using 'T_o'. Its position is either computed following located marks disposition or fixed explicitly by a user. Extrinsic parameters reflect the transformation 'T_c' as M_{ext} matrix, that is a rotation R and a translation T to apply on each point $p_o(x_o, y_o, z_o)$ of any real or virtual object, known as camera viewpoint. Intrinsic parameters reflect the 'T_i' transformation. It transforms each point $p(x, y, z)$ in the camera system by projecting it to $p'(x', y')$ in the image plane. It is then possible to compute a 3D object homogeneous coordinates in the image plane system from those in its proper system by using the relationship (1). The projective projection matrix is defined as $M_{int} \cdot M_{ext}$ [11], [12].

$$\begin{bmatrix} x_1 \\ x_2 \\ x_3 \end{bmatrix} = M_{int} M_{ext} \begin{bmatrix} x_o \\ y_o \\ z_o \\ 1 \end{bmatrix} \quad where \quad x_1/x_3 = x' \quad and \quad x_2/x_3 = y' \tag{1}$$

The application of these principles begins by searching for the pattern in each current image of the sequence. This starts by its binarisation using a dynamic threshold based on lighting scene conditions. It is chosen as the average of pixels' values of each image after its transformation to grey level. The transformed image is then prospected for connected black regions having four corners. By a simple binary difference with the real image of the pattern and according to a given threshold value, the region that presents a minimal value will be considered as being the pattern. This allows us to calculate the terms of the homography matrix H. Using it, it would be possible to proceed directly with 2D augmentation or to deduce the projection matrix for 3D augmentation. For the following frames of the sequence, a simple tracking of pattern's corners is made in order to update the homography matrix for each frame.

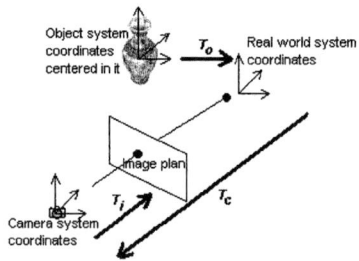

Fig. 1. Correspondence pin-hole camera model used for augmentation

3 Virtualized Real Object Incarnation

A virtual object can be drawn by using two different manners. Most researchers make use of graphical library such as OpenGL in order to draw virtual entities at runtime. They are known as synthetics. They are designed and projected in the sequence according to the computed camera's viewpoint [1]. The second used way about virtual entities' kinds is where they are captured as 2D images. They can be projected by using the computed homography. Images will then appear mapped on the desired plan in the scene. Following this way, our work's idea is to map images of 3D real objects as if they are designed by using a graphical library. Various object's views are projected by using its different captured images from various viewpoints. Thus, the image that shows the object in the current computed camera's viewpoint is used. The projected image is what we call virtualized real object.

A lot of object's images must be grabbed according to different viewpoints in order to allow object projection in different visual oriented positions. They can be acquired from sphere-shaped view space where object background is dark or light (Fig. 2). Finally, the number of images to use is variable and is associated to user's needs. The alone important aspect is that the expected perceptible realism of object's motion is related to the number of captured images and to their qualities.

Fig. 2. Images of real objects associated to different views

3.1 Size Constraint in Augmentation Realism

The used method which uses the pine-hole model allows a good approximation. It gives the possibility to compute the homography matrix to use for projection, but it does not give any information to use directly about the scene's real objects dimensions. The metrics information is included automatically in computed terms as camera auto calibration. Thus, the information about object's size is insufficient to adapt it visually to the scene's real size. The solution that we used for is the respect of relative sizes of the real object and the printed pattern. This constraint is applied to images' sizes in order to deduce their proportion. Fig. 3 shows this problem.

Let us assume that S_o and S_p symbolise respectively the measurement vectors of an object and the pattern. The object's size is related to a chosen reference direction view which is pictured as a reference image. S_o as well as S_p must either be given as an input session in order to calculate the proportion real size $P_r = S_o/S_p$. Similarly, let us also assume that the extracted object's region from the reference image has its size vector equal to S_{io} and the image's size vector is S_i, the proportion of the object in its image is $P_i = S_{io}/S_i$. This hypothesis remains true for similar images' size of object's views even if the sizes of object's views in images are different. Thus, by using the matrix notation and a detail of width (W) and height (H), we obtain:

$$P_r = \begin{bmatrix} W_{P_r} \\ H_{P_r} \end{bmatrix} = \begin{bmatrix} W_o/W_p \\ H_o/H_p \end{bmatrix} \text{ and } P_i = \begin{bmatrix} W_{P_i} \\ H_{P_i} \end{bmatrix} = \begin{bmatrix} W_{io}/W_i \\ H_{io}/H_i \end{bmatrix} \quad (2)$$

In addition, the proportion of the object's region size in the reference image and the detected pattern's size remains constant. So, it is right to write $S_{o_s} = P_r \cdot S_{p_d}$,

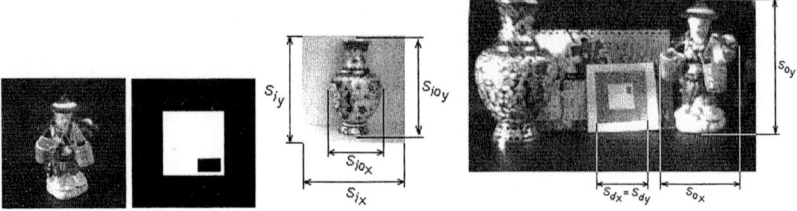

Fig. 3. On the left, the two images equal in size. On the right, the real proportion of the pattern and real objects (not projected) and measurement principles.

where S_{o_s} re-presents the scaled object's size vector to use in current frame relatively to the detected pattern's size vector S_{p_d}. Likewise, knowing that the object's region in the reference image preserves its proportion after scaling (Fig. 6), it would have as size $S_{i_s} = S_{o_s}/P_i = P_r \cdot S_{p_d}/P_i$. The current scale proportion to apply to object's image is then expressed as $P_s = S_{i_s}/S_{p_d} = P_r/P_i$. Using matrix notation, we obtain:

$$P_s = \begin{bmatrix} W_s \\ H_s \end{bmatrix} = \begin{bmatrix} W_{p_r}/W_{p_i} \\ H_{p_r}/H_{p_i} \end{bmatrix} \quad (3)$$

Thus, after having been expressed relatively to the pattern's detected centre, each detected corner $p_{io}(x_o, y_o)$ among the four will be translated to $p_{io_s}(x_{o_s}, y_{o_s})$:

$$p_{io_s} = \begin{bmatrix} x_{o_s} \\ y_{o_s} \end{bmatrix} = \begin{bmatrix} W_s & 0 \\ 0 & H_s \end{bmatrix} \cdot \begin{bmatrix} x_o \\ y_o \end{bmatrix} \quad (4)$$

These expressions must be used to compute the homography matrix for each frame. We note equally that they are all established under supposition of the pattern's plane is always parallel to the camera's image plane. If this is not the case, the size of at least one side decreases under the effect of the geometrical projection. As a primary solution, we impose to the pattern to be a square form. After its detection, the lengths of the four lines connecting the detected points are evaluated. Then, the longest one is the closest to the camera and will be used to calculate the projection scale. Generally, the associated error has no effect on the visual aspect.

3.2 Objects Manipulation

For a synthetic 3D object, the theoretical detail is explained in [1]. For virtualized real objects, translations following x and y axes and rotation following z axis are similar to synthetic objects. On the other hand, rotations following x and y axes are used in order to search for the images that reflect related views of rotated object. Their values serve as index value search which expresses the current camera viewpoint. If the search could not match any image, the first one linked to the nearest coordinates is used. For example, in the acquisition of only six views, the angle between each consecutive two views is $\pi/2$ and all searches for intermediary rotations will fail.

The visual aspect after z translations is controlled as the current image's size change which would make enlarge or narrow its appearance. So, we have to compute a simulated pattern's displacement in order to simulate the visual object's displacement 'm' to the front or to the back (Fig. 4). We have then to compute the estimated size SS'_s, where the found pattern's size in a frame is $2SS_s$. It is easy to see that $SS'_s = f.p'p'_s/(op+m)$ where m is an algebraic value, f is the calculated camera's focal length and $p'p'_s$ and op are the correspondent vectors' modules. In the same way, we can write $op = f.pp_s/SS_s = f.h/2SS_s$; h is the size of the image pattern's side.

By using the same laws, it is simple to evaluate the expression of $p'p'_s = p'p_r.tg\alpha = (pp_r - m)tg\alpha = ((h/2.tg\alpha) - m).tg\alpha$. Hence, by the replacement of all these expressions, we obtain:

$$SS'_s = \frac{f(h - 2m.tg\alpha)}{\left(\dfrac{f.h}{SS_s} + 2m\right)} \quad (5)$$

For our primary solution the angle 2α, that expresses the field of view, is given as an input of the augmentation session as for the OpenGL principle.

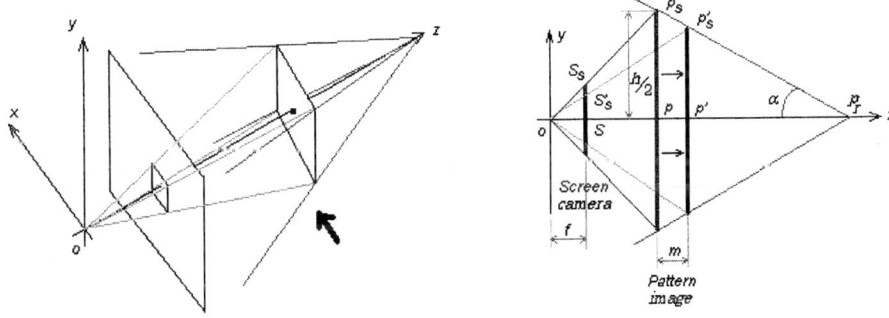

Fig. 4. Geometrical basis used when object is displaced along the z axis. The used principle supposes a displacement 'm' of the pattern which size is controlled by 2α field of view and projects the object's image on the calculated position.

The projection of each image of a virtualized real object is done relatively to the computed gravity centre of the found pattern's region. To do so, a virtual square frame is built firstly around it and rearranged in order to have its sides parallel to image's sides and faced to the camera's image plane. This simulates the object's image sits in front of the camera. Each side's size is scaled to SS'_s and multiplied by the factor P_s. Hence, the selected object's image projection can be done after application of other user's actions.

3.3 Chosen Image Projection

Images of the different views of an object are captured from a spherical equidistant positions 'd', around and in direction of its gravity centre. The adopted principle consists of sweeping the object by fixed angles from the low towards the upper, following its horizontal axes and picturing consequent views. Each captured image constitutes a different view identified by the polar coordinates of the camera's position during its grab. The reference view should have $(d, 0, 0)$ as coordinates (Fig. 5). We notice that as small is the angle of sweeping as great is the obtained realism during augmentation. However, the augmentation performance would be lost. For example, for an angle of $\pi/18$, the total number of images to take for all views is 36 (horizontally) x 19 (vertically) = 684. If each image size is 43.200 bytes, as a RGB bitmap 24 bits and has a dimension of 120x120, the total images' size is 29.548.800 bytes, which is a lot. On other side, a great angle loses the realism. After some tests, we have found out that a step of $\pi/9$ is an optimal value for object's images access to do not degrade the augmentation process time.

Fig. 5. Objects' views sample. After segmentation and internal region extraction, transprent regions surrounding the objects are colored white. For the left object, polar coordinates from left to right are: $(d, 0, 0)$, $(d, -\pi/4, \pi/9)$, for the right one: $(d, 0, 0)$.

Each pictured object's image is pre-processed before its storage. The pre-processing consists of declaring object's surrounding region as transparent in order to do not be projected. To do so, it assumes the external region uniform and tries to delimit it from the internal one by its segmentation. The internal region is assumed to be the object form. The object's surrounding region is set to black or white, according to whether it is respectively clear or dark (Fig. 5, Fig. 6).

Fig. 6. Virtual object disposed visually by the user on a chair

4 Conclusion and Perspectives

In this paper, we have presented a method for the implementation of an augmented reality application allowing the incrustation of real objects. We have shown how it is possible to augment a video sequence in real time, using images of a real object views. We call it 'virtualized real object'. We have equally shown how it is also possible to manipulate it in augmented scene and how to obtain an acceptable realism in relation to user's different actions.

The major problems related to scene augmentation with virtualized real objects are not yet solved and demand more researches to be fulfilled: the proportion size of the real object and the printed pattern, the searching for the current image view, the number of object views images taken, database views images organisation to allow real time augmentation constraint, and so on.

In our work, a number of points have not been covered. The most important is related to visual aspect. It is associated to the change of the camera viewpoint; the view of the object does not change when the camera is moved around the scene. We have not studied the occlusion of real objects by virtual ones and their lighting. Our future work will mainly include opened problems. In addition, our works will improve current results.

References

1. Brahim Nini and Mohamed Chaouki Batouche: Virtual Object Manipulation in Collaborative Augmented Reality Environment. IEEE-ICIT, December 8-10 (2004). Tunis. ISBN: 0-7803-8663-9
2. Gilles Simon, Andrew Fitzgibbon, Andrew Zisserma: Markerless Tracking Using Planar Structures in the Scene. Proceedings of the IEEE International symposium on Augmented Reality (ISAR), 2000. pp. 120-128.
3. Henrik Tramberend: Avocado: A Distributed Virtual Environment Framework. Bielefeld University, Doctoral thesis, Mars (2003)
4. Holger T. Regenbrecht, Michael T. Wagner: Interaction in a Collaborative Augmented Reality Environment. CHI 2002, April 20-25 (2002), Minneapolis, Minnesota, USA. ACM 1-58113-454-1/02/0004
5. Marcio S. Pinho, Doug A. Bowman, Carla M.D.S. Freitas: Cooperative Object Manipulation in Immersive Virtual Environments: Framework and Techniques. VRST'02, November 11-13 (2002), Hong Kong. ACM 1-58113 530-0/02/0011
6. Norbert Braun: Storytelling in Collaborative Augmented Reality Environments. WSGS'(2003), February 3-7. Pizen. CZech Republic
7. Oliver G. Staadt, Martin Näf, Edouard Lamboray, Stephan Würmlin: JAPE: A Prototyping System for Collaborative Virtual Environments. EUROGRAPHICS 2001 / A. Chalmers and T.-M. Rhyne. Volume 20 (2001), Number 3, pp. C-8–C-16
8. Peter Franz STRUM: Vision 3D non calibrée : Contribution à la reconstruction projective et étude des mouvements critiques pour l'auto-calibration. INPG Doctoral Theses, (1997)
9. Raphaël Grasset, Xavier Decoret and Jean-Dominique Gascuel: Augmented Reality Collaborative Environment: Calibration and Interactive Scene Editing. VRIC, Virtual Reality International Conference, Laval Virtual (2001), May 16-18
10. R. Azuma: Recent advances in Augmented Reality. 0272-1716/01/ IEEE Nov-dec (2001)
11. Shahzad Malik, Gerhard Roth, Chris McDonald: Robust 2D Tracking for Real-time Augmented Reality. In Proceedings of Vision Interface (2002), Calgary, Alberta, Canada
12. Zonglei Huang, Boubakeur Boufama: A Semi Automatic Camera Calibration Method for Augmented Reality. Systems, Man and Cybernetics Society (2002) IEEE International Conference. 6 pp. Volume: 4, ISSN: 1062-922X

Automatic Detection of Spiculated Masses Using Fractal Analysis in Digital Mammography

HyungJun Kim[1] and WonHa Kim[2]

[1] Graduate School of Information Security, Korea University
[2] School of Electronics & Information Engineering, Kyung Hee University

Abstract. This paper describes the development of a system for the automatic detection of spiculated masses in digital mammography. We have adopted the lattice space as an image domain model and a distance measure to describe image shapes precisely in pixel scale. Based on the model, we have developed a method to automatically determine binary mass shapes. The method is robust against noise and background brightness of mass region. We also have proposed a novel method in mapping a mass shape into a one-dimensional profile, and then quantified the irregularity of the mass shape by calculating the fractal dimension of the profile. Preliminary experimental results support the hypothesis of the spiculation detection performance of the proposed method would show a possible solution for finding spiculated masses.

1 Introduction

Breast cancer has been a leading cause of fatality among all cancers for women. Mass lesion in mammogram can be described as more or less compact areas that appear brighter than the tissue in which they are embedded because of a higher attenuation of x-rays. The detection of mass lesions in mammogram can be a difficult task for human observers or machines. Especially, spiculation is a stellate distortion caused by the intrusion of breast cancer into surrounding tissue. Its existence is an important clue to characterizing malignant tumors. Incorporation of spiculation measures is an important strategy in the detection of breast cancer with CAD(computer-aided detection).

Due to the reason of the complexity of normal glandular patterns in the breast and the variability in appearance of mass lesions, a straightforward and simple approach to detect mass lesions in mammogram does not exist[1]. A great variety of approaches have been proposed in the literature, but it seems that for a successful approach a number of techniques need to be combined. Karssemeijer studied detecting stellate patterns based on statistical analysis of a map of pixel orientation[2]. Brake further developed the statistical analysis method at different scales in a multi-scale scheme[3]. Recently, Huang and *et al.* proposed a method to identify spiculation from 3-D ultrasonic volume data[4]. They used the modified rotating structure element operation to find the central region, and used stick algorithm to estimate the direction of edge around the central region. Pohlman and *et al.* estimated the fractal dimension of the one-dimensional signature using the ruler method for quantitative classification of breast tumors[5].

We have utilized the fact that the mass lesion in mammogram appears brighter than the tissue around because of a higher attenuation of x-rays. If the region of interest has irregular property based on fractal analysis, they are marked as a potential spiculated mass. The proposed algorithm is designed to identify the location and to mark regions of interest that manifest features associated with spiculation.

2 Automatic Detection of Mass Area

Although the area of mass has a brighter contrast comparing with normal tissue area, each mass area has a different brightness and it has very much diverse contrast even in a small local area. Thus, there are many local maxima even in one mass area. It is very difficult to determine one threshold value for the detection of mass centers or the discrimination of mass areas. In this section, we propose algorithms for the detection of mass center and areas without any prior knowledge.

2.1 Detection of Mass Center

In order to decide the area of mass, we first determine the center of mass. We adopted an iteration of adaptive histogram equalization to detect the centers of masses. When we apply the adaptive histogram equalization, the local contrast is increased and therefore the relatively brighter areas, which are the possible center of mass eventually, can be discriminated from the relatively darker area which are unimportant background. The contrast between the candidate center of mass and unimportant area are getting shaper, therefore, we can determine easily one threshold value for the detection of center of mass. If we apply the above algorithm iteratively, the neighbor areas near the centers of mass are fading away while the center areas are surviving. Fig. 1 shows an example of iterative mass center detection process using the adaptive histogram equalization. The center position can be determined from the center of intensity of the mass area. The following is the iterative histogram equalization algorithm to detect the center of mass.

Let $I^0(i,j)$ be the brightness of a pixel at the position (i,j) of an image.

1. Apply the adaptive histogram equalization process to the image I^k, where $k = 0, 1, 2, \ldots$.
2. Update $I^{k+1}(i,j)$ after removing non-important areas from $I^k(i,j)$ according to the following decision rule:

$$I^{k+1}(i,j) = \begin{cases} I^k(i,j) & \text{for } I^k(i,j) \geq T_c \\ 0 & \text{for } I^k(i,j) < T_c \end{cases} \quad (1)$$

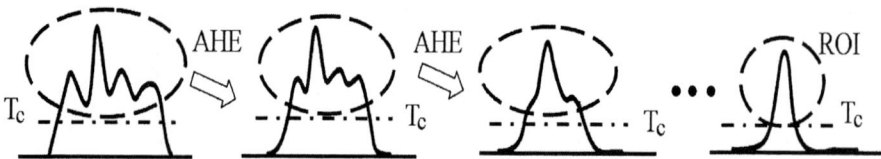

Fig. 1. An example of iterative mass center detection process using the adaptive histogram equalization. AHE means adaptive histogram equalization.

where the threshold value, T_c, is set to be the 50 % of the maximum brightness of an image, i.e. $T_c = 0.5 \times \max\{I^k(i,j)\}$.

3. Iterate the step 1 and 2 for a certain time. We have iterated it for 20 times for the experiment.
4. Apply a labelling algorithm to $I^{k+1}(i,j)$ for discriminating areas. Assume small areas as noise, and then remove them from the list of candidate centers.
5. Provide the detected areas with an index using ROI(Region-of-Interest), i.e., if there exists N numbers of detected areas, those $ROIs$ are labelled such as $ROI_1, ROI_2, \ldots, ROI_N$.
6. Calculate the center of intensity as a center of mass for each ROI, i.e., the n-th ROI's center of mass, (C_i^n, C_j^n), can be calculated as follows,

$$C_i^n = \frac{\sum_{i \in ROI_n} i \cdot I(i,j)}{\sum_{i \in ROI_n} I(i,j)}, \quad C_j^n = \frac{\sum_{j \in ROI_n} j \cdot I(i,j)}{\sum_{j \in ROI_n} I(i,j)} \quad (2)$$

Fig. 2 shows the original mammo image, the candidate areas for the centers of masses which have dominant gray values, and the detected centers of masses. We have applied the proposed algorithm to diverse mammo images, and we can detect the center of mass correctly.

2.2 Adaptive Mass Size Decision

Karssemeijer et al. determined the orientation of line of stellate patterns using gradient operation[1,2,3,4]. However, they should use binomial statistics to calculate the features because of the sensitivity of the operation. Fig. 3 shows one example of spiculated mass, its 3D-image, and its gradient of average contour, respectively, where we can find that application of gradient method is not a good approach because the image itself contains high frequency information.

To prevent the sensitivity against high frequency information we propose a new method which utilizes the gradient of contour rather than the gradient-orientation toward the center of spiculation. The outward gradient of average contour of a specific region of interest can be defined as Eq.(3). The gradient $C(r)$ of average contour of image $I(i,j)$ is determined

$$C(r) = \frac{1}{N_r} \sum_{(i,j) \in C_r} I(i,j), \quad r = 1, 2, \ldots \quad (3)$$

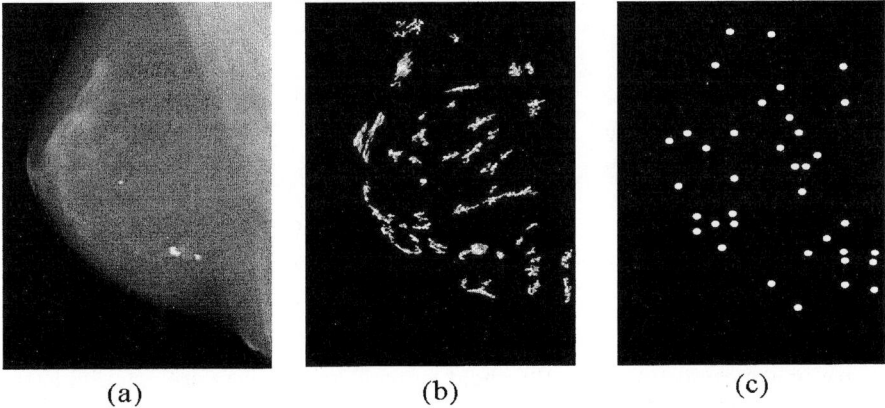

Fig. 2. (a) the original mammo image, (b) the candidate areas for the centers of masses which have dominant gray values, and (c) the detected centers of masses. (The centers are exaggerated for display purpose).

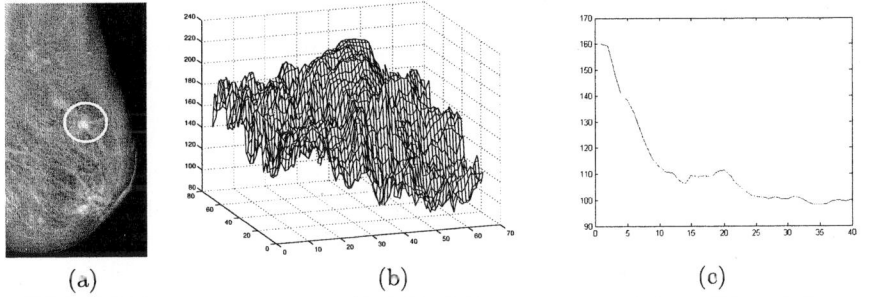

Fig. 3. (a) a mass image, (b) its 3D-image, and (c) its average contour graph

where $C_r = \{(i,j) | \ |i| + |j| = r \ \}$ and N_r is the number of pixels on the contour at the radius r, that is $N_r = |C_r| = 4 \cdot r$. Using this relation we can calculate the orientation and gradient of a stellate pattern.

3 Analysis of Mass Shape

In this section we describe how to detect a binary mass shape using a regional thresholding method, and we propose a new scanning method which can check every degree along the counter-clockwise to estimate the direction of the edge of each pixel around the central region.

3.1 Binary Mass Shape Detection

Sometimes mammogram can vary its contrast rapidly even in a small area and the signal-to-noise ratio is poor, so the region of interest can not convert to

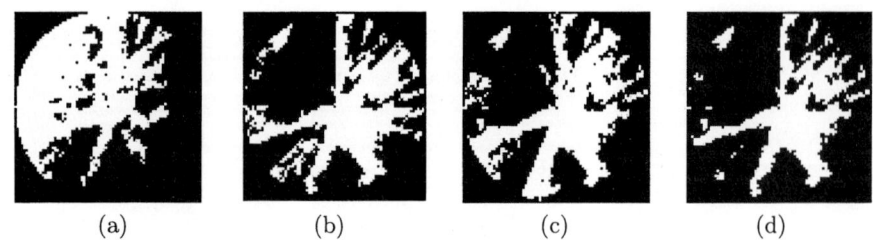

Fig. 4. Binary images: (a) one threshold value, (b) 8 divisions, (c) twisted 8 divisions, and (d) logical AND result of (b) and (c)

binary image correctly if one threshold value is used. Therefore, we divide the region of interest into 8 sections for 45° each ,and use a different threshold value for each section. To prevent a wrong division in case, another 22.5° twisted version of 8 divisions are used for double checking. Those two binary images can be combined using logical AND operation.

An individual threshold value should be selected for each sections using the gradient of average gray values along the contours which are outwards from the center. First, find out the maximum and minimum values of the average contours and calculate the slope of those two points. Using the straight line from the maximum point to the minimum point and the line of the average contour graph, we can determine the maximum distance point between those two graphs which can be used for the threshold value of the section. The above thresholding method is also known as 'Shoulder thresholding'. This method has been applied to each section of 8 divisions to find 8 threshold values. Through these values, we can generate a binary image from 8 sections.

Fig. 4(a) shows that the case of one threshold value is used. The suspect region might lose a stellate pattern since the selected threshold value is too low for the bright region on one side, but too high for the dark region. On the other hand, Fig. 4(b) and (c) show that individual thresholding for each section may not lose the local information, and as a result, a better binary image can be achieved, compared to one threshold value case as shown in Fig. 4(a). Fig. 4(d) is the result of logical AND operation of the outputs of Fig. 4(b) and Fig. 4(c).

3.2 Radar Scanning of Mass Shape

If we divide the region into several sections like a fan-shape, we may interpret incorrectly if we just count on number of pixels in a section. Therefore, we propose a new scanning method like a radar scanning which can check every degree along the counter-clockwise as shown in Fig. 5.

To implement the scanning process on discrete image domain, we should find all lattice points which are the closest pixels to a certain scanning angle as shown in Fig.5. The scanning angle varies from 0° to 360° and the length of the probe is the diamond radius of a mass, r_{max}. If an angle θ of radar scanning and the L^1-norm radius, i.e., the diamond radius r of a mass are given, we should find

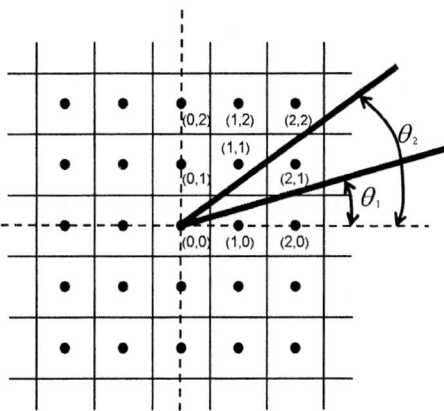

Fig. 5. Example of radar scanning

the closest pixel index, (m_r^θ, n_r^θ) to the scanning angle θ among a set of points, $\{(m_r, n_r) \mid |m_r| + |n_r| = r\}$. For a given scanning angle θ at a certain radius r_{max}, we can find a set of pixels (m_r^θ, n_r^θ) which are on the scanning probe as follows:

$$P(x) = \{(m_r^\theta, n_r^\theta), \; r = 0, 1, \ldots, r_{max}\} \quad (4)$$

After finding the lattice points (m_r^θ, n_r^θ) in the first quadrant, we can achieve a set of pixels (m_r^θ, n_r^θ) for other quadrants using the symmetrical property.

If we define that $p_r = |m_r|$ and $q_r = |n_r|$, then (m_r^θ, n_r^θ) can be found as follows.

$$q_r^\theta = \arg\min_{0 < q_r < r}\left\{\left|\frac{q_r}{p_r} - |\tan\theta|\right|\right\} = \arg\min_{0 < q_r < r}\left\{\left|\frac{q_r}{r - q_r} - |\tan\theta|\right|\right\} \quad (5)$$

$$(m_r^\theta, n_r^\theta) = \begin{cases} (r - q_r^\theta, q_r^\theta) & \text{for } 0° \leq \theta < 90° \\ (-r + q_r^\theta, q_r^\theta) & \text{for } 90° \leq \theta < 180° \\ (-r + q_r^\theta, -q_r^\theta) & \text{for } 180° \leq \theta < 270° \\ (r + q_r^\theta, -q_r^\theta) & \text{for } 270° \leq \theta < 360° \end{cases} \quad (6)$$

Thus, we should check all the pixels of which indices are (m_r^θ, n_r^θ) at each diamond radius r and a certain scanning angle θ. To find those indices, we only need to find q_r^θ. Let $\mathcal{D}(y)$ be the difference of two slopes; a slope of certain point y and the slope of a certain scanning angle θ

$$\mathcal{D}(y) = \frac{y}{r - y} - |\tan\theta| \quad (7)$$

where y is a real number and $y \in [0, r)$. Since the $\mathcal{D}(y)$ is a monotonously increasing function and $\mathcal{D}(0) < 0$, $\mathcal{D}(r^-) > 0$, a solution x_0 which satisfies $\mathcal{D}(y_0) = 0$ must be existed as

$$y_0 = \frac{r \cdot |\tan\theta|}{1 + |\tan\theta|} \quad (8)$$

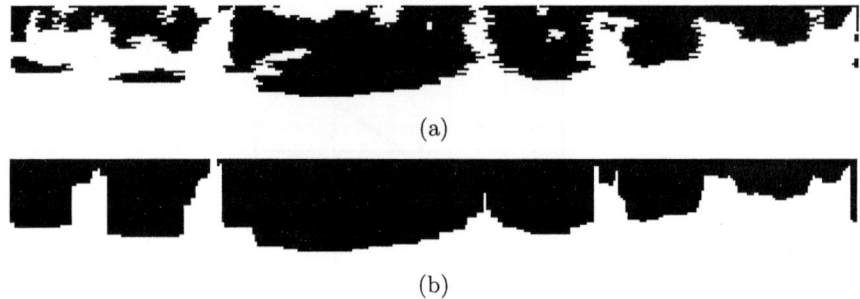

Fig. 6. (a) original binary image and (b) a cleaned binary image

As shown in Fig.5, if $x_0 = r - y_0$, the coordinate (x_0, y_0) in real form should be the intersection of the scanning probe at a certain angle θ and a diamond radius r. Since the closest lattice coordinate to (x_0, y_0) is the closest integer coordinate to (x_0, y_0), q_r^θ is the closest integer to y_0. Therefore, we can get q_r^θ as

$$q_r^\theta = \arg\min_{0 < q_r < r} \left\{ \left| \frac{q_r}{p_r} - |\tan\theta| \right| \right\} = \mathcal{R}\left(\frac{r \cdot |\tan\theta|}{1 + |\tan\theta|} \right) \qquad (9)$$

where $\mathcal{R}(\cdot)$ represents a round operation.

The binary image of a suspect region is converted to 2-D image using radar scanning method, where x-axis represents the degree from 0 to 359 and y-axis represents the number of pixels as shown in Fig. 6. The binary image is very noisy, and therefore the disconnected part from center should be removed to process further. After the disconnected part is removed, the binary image showed sharp edges.

3.3 Fractal Analysis of Mass Irregularity

The fractal dimension of the one-dimensional profile was estimated by using the ruler method[5]. Malignant tumors generally have a higher fractal dimension than benign masses because they are more spiculated. If a high fractal dimension is found, this should increase the likelihood of a stellate pattern presence.

The proposed method is applied to 50 cases for the preliminary test. One radiologist has tested and described all of the test images. The images were analyzed with the proposed method, and the resultant output which is the location of spiculated masses was compared with the standard overlays created by the radiologist. Overall false negative error rate is 10% and false positive error rate is about 30 %.

4 Conclusions

We have presented the development of a system for the automatic detection of spiculated masses in digital mammogram. We have adopted the lattice space as an image domain model and a distance measure to describe image shapes precisely in pixel scale. Based on the model, we have developed a method to automatically detect sizes and centers of various masses. We devised a regional binarization that is robust against noise and background brightness of mass region. We also have proposed a novel method mapping a mass shape into one-dimensional profile that enable to analyze and parameterize the irregularity of mass shapes, and then quantified the irregularity of the mass shape by calculating the fractal dimension of the profile. The proposed system has merits such as no sensitive to noise, adaptive tumor size processing, and fast processing time compared to other approaches. Preliminary experimental results support that the proposed system can accurately discriminate a spiculated mass from glandular patterns or adipose tissues.

Acknowledgement

This work was supported in part by the Ministry of Information & Communications, Korea, under the Information Technology Research Center(ITRC) Support Program.

References

1. Karssemeijer, N.: Detection of masses in mammogram. Image Processing Techniques for Tumor Detection (ed. Strickland, R. N.) Marcel Dekker, Inc., New York (2002) 187–212
2. Karssemeijer, N., Brake, G. M.: Detection of stellate distortions in mammogram. IEEE Trans. Medical Imaging, vol. 15, no. 5, **Oct.** (1996) 611–619
3. Drake, G. M., Karssemeijer, N.: Single and multiscale detection of masses in digital mammograms. IEEE Trans. Medical Imaging, vol. 18, no. 7, **July** (1999) 628–639
4. Huang, S., Chang, R., Chen, D., Moon, W.: Characterization of spiculation on ultrasound lesions. IEEE Trans. Medical Imaging, vol. 23, no. 1, **Jan.** (2004) 111–121
5. Pohlman, S., Powell, K., Obuchowski, N., Chilcote, W., Grundfest-Broniatowski, S.: Quantitative classification of breast tumors in digitized mammograms. Med. Phys., vol. 23, no. 8, **Aug.** (1996) 1337–1345
6. Otsu, N.: A threshold selection method from gray-level histograms IEEE Trans. Syst. Man Cybern., vol. SMC-9, **Jan.** (1979) 62–66

Hybrid Framework for Medical Image Segmentation

Chunyan Jiang[1], Xinhua Zhang[2], and Christoph Meinel[1]

[1] Hasso-Plattner-Institut, University of Potsdam, Postfach 900460,
D-14440, Potsdam, Germany
chunyan.jiang@hpi.uni-potsdam.de
[2] LIASIT, Luxemburg
zhang_xinhua@hotmail.com

Abstract. Medical image segmentation is essential step for many image processing applications. In this paper, we present a hybrid framework designed for automated segmentation of radiological image, to get the organ or interested area from the image. This approach integrates region-based method and boundary-based method. Such integration reduces the drawbacks of both methods and enlarges the advantages of them. Firstly, we use fuzzy connectedness method to get an initial segmentation result and homogeneity classifier. Then we use Voronoi Diagram-based to refine the last step's result. Finally we use level set method to handle some vague or missed boundary, and get smooth and accurate segmentation. This hybrid approach is automated, since the whole segmentation procedure doesn't need much manual intervention, except the initial seed position selection for fuzzy connectedness segmentation.

1 Introduction

Internal organ segmentation from different kinds of image modalities is an essential step for many anatomy and pathology studies. A variety of segmentation methods have been developed over past several years. There are two main sorts of segmentation techniques, region-based and edge-based. Region-based method tries to divide the image into regions and classify the pixels as inside, outside or on the boundary according to its position and surrounding structure. Edge-based method uses a numerical test for image gradient or curvature, or other properties to classify pixels.

The fuzzy connectedness-based method [1] is one kind of region-based techniques. Medical image is considered fuzzy. It is composed by signal intensities specific to different tissue types, noise, blurring, background variation, partial voluming, and certain acquisition-specific effects. The fuzzy connectedness-based method assigns fuzzy affinities to the target object. The affinity is computed as the weight sum of some characters. They are the intensity, the intensity gradient in the neighborhood of the pixel to capture the intensity features and patterns of intensity variations. The weight can also be dynamically adaptive for the homogeneity and the gradient energy functions [2]. The adaptive weights introduce shift-variance to the definition of fuzzy connectedness, and decrease user interaction. The other region-based segmentation algorithm is to divide an image into regions, classify each region as either inside or outside the target object. For the boundary region between two classifications, the dividing and classifying procedure will be repeated till the boundary is satisfied the segmentation of target. [3] describes such a region-based method. It makes use of Voronoi diagrams to perform the division on the image. And [4] improves this method so that the final result can be produced in a few iterations.

Snake method [5] is one kind of boundary-based techniques. In this method, there is an energy function to qualify the difference between the model and the edge in the image. The model starts with a coarse initialization, by minimizing the energy function with smoothness constraints, and attempts to align this boundary to the edge in the image. To avoid the propagation of the model sticking locally, the initial model should be set near the solution. Prior model [6] adapts an "average shape" as a prior term in active contour model. A statistical model of shape variation can be constructed by finding corresponding points across a set of training images [7]. The prior information can combine the shape of an object and its neighbors [8]. However, for the energy function model, it is difficult to handle the situation, when the topological of the contour changes during the evolution. Level set method [9] solves this problem by computing the evolution in one higher dimension. This method is combined in active contour methods in [10], [11]. Level set evolution with fixed propagation direction is either initialized inside or outside sought objects, and the propagation force is opposed by a strong gradient magnitude at image discontinuities. The internal force is strong enough to act against to global smoothness and leaks through gaps when the boundary is miss or fuzzy. This is the region competition, where two adjacent regions compete for the common boundary.

We have developed a new method to segment the organ from image. It integrates region-based techniques and edge-based techniques. The hybrid framework amplifies the strengths of both region-based and edge-based techniques but reduces the weaknesses of them.

2 Hybrid Framework

We present a hybrid approach for medical image segmentation. This approach requires minimum user interactions. It starts with fuzzy connectedness method to get the region, which contains the target object. Then with automatically homogeneity statistics, the VD-based algorithm will generate an estimation of boundary in a few iterations. After that, the level-set method will find the accurate boundary for the segmentation procedure. In the following sections, we will introduce the each algorithm that composes our hybrid approach, and how we use them in our hybrid segmentation framework.

2.1 Fuzzy Connectedness Algorithm

Medical image captured by devices is inherent fuzzy. The fuzzy property is caused by both the capture procedure and the anatomical objects hang together. The fuzzy setting notion is developed by J. K. Udupa in [1]. It is considered that the object should be defined formally in the fuzzy setting so that the data inaccuracies can be handled beyond mere visualization to object segmentation, manipulation, and analysis. The fuzzy affinities are defined to the target object during classification. The affinity between two elements in an image (e.g. pixels, voxels, spels) is defined via a degree of adjacency and the similarity of their intensity values. The aim of fuzzy connectedness is to capture the specific intensity patterns related to the target object.

We define a scene over a fuzzy digital space (Z^n, α) as a pair $\varsigma = (C, f)$, where C is a n-dimensional array of spels (spatial elements – pixels or voxels) and f is a function in the domain C. Its range is a subset of the closed interval [0, 1], $f : C \rightarrow [0,1]$. Fuzzy affinity k is any reflexive and symmetric fuzzy relation in C, that is:

$$k = \{((c,d), \mu_\kappa(c,d))|(c,d) \in C\}$$
$$\mu_\kappa : C \times C \rightarrow [0,1]$$
$$\mu_\kappa(c,c) = 1, \forall c \in C$$
$$\mu_\kappa(c,d) = \mu_\kappa(d,c), \forall (c,d) \in C$$
(1)

μ_κ can be written as follows generally:

$$\mu_\kappa(c,d) = h(\mu_\alpha(c,d), \mu_\varphi(c,d), \mu_\phi(c,d), c, d) \forall (c,d) \in C,$$

where: $\mu_\alpha(c,d)$ represents the degree of coordinate space adjacency of c and d; μ_φ represents the degree of intensity space adjacency of c and d; and μ_ϕ represents the degree of intensity gradient space adjacency of c and d to the corresponding target object features. Fuzzy k-connectedness K is a fuzzy relationship in C, where $\mu_\kappa(c,d)$ is the strength of a path is the strongest path between c and d, and the strength of a path is the smallest affinity along the path. The hard binary relation K_θ based on the fuzzy relation K is used to define the notion of a fuzzy connected component.

$$\mu_\kappa(c,d) = \begin{cases} 1 & \text{iff } \mu_\kappa(c,d) \geq \theta \in [0,1] \\ 0 & \text{otherwise} \end{cases}$$
(2)

In a generic implementation of fuzzy connectedness for $c, d \in C : \mu_\kappa(c,d) = h(\mu_\alpha(c,d), f(c), f(d), c, d)$ where c, d are the image locations of the two pixels, $\mu_\alpha(c,d)$ is an adjacency function based on the distance of the two pixels, and $f(c)$ and $f(d)$ are the intensity of pixels c and d, respectively. In this general form, $\mu_\kappa(c,d)$ is shift-variant. A more specific and shift-variant definition for a fuzzy affinity was introduced in [1]. The weight values can be captured by some improved methods [2] so that the only manual work is to select the seed pixel.

2.2 Voronoi Diagram-Based Algorithm

The second part in our hybrid approach is Voronoi diagram (VD)-based segmentation algorithm. This algorithm divides the Voronoi regions repeatedly according to the homogeneity classifier for the medical image segmentation. And the classifier for different tissue type is generated from the regions that segmented by the fuzzy connectedness based method mentioned above.

The definition of the Voronoi Diagram is detailed described in [12]. We give a brief review here. Let S be a set of N points in the plane, indexed by $i \in \{1,\ldots,N\}$. The Voronoi region associated to one point $p_i \in S$ denoted by $Vor_S(p_i)$ is the set of the points closer to p_i than to any other points of S. Let us denote $H(p_i, p_j)$ the half-plane containing p_i that is defined by the perpendicular bisector of $\overline{p_i p_j}$. It is written as below:

$$Vor_S(p_i) = \bigcap_{i \neq j} H(p_i, p_j) \tag{3}$$

The Voronoi diagram is defined by the set of all Voronoi polygons.

An interesting property is that the dual graph of the Voronoi diagram is the Delaunay graph with the following properties: the Delaunay graph is a triangulation such that each circle C circumscribed by every triangle $\overline{p_i p_j, p_k}$ does not contain any point of S in its interior. The proof is that assume there exists a point p_i of S in the interior of C. Then the distance between the center c of C and p_l is smaller than the distance between c and any $p_n \in S, n \neq l$. According to the definition of a Voronoi polygon, c belongs to the interior of $Vor_S(p_l)$, which is contradictory.

As the continue step in our hybrid approach, the Voronoi diagram-based segmentation method processes the image based on the result of last step, fuzzy connectedness-based segmentation. The former step has got the initial segmented area of the target object. It offers the following step the statistic homogeneity classifier for the exterior part, interior part and boundary. By adding some seed points, the image will be divided into some regions as Voronoi diagram. For each region, the homogeneity classifier will reclassify it to exterior, interior or boundary. For the boundary region, connecting the seed points as Delaunay triangulation, the boundary outline is formed. This procedure can be repeated in a number of iterations till the boundary is accurate enough. The pseudocode for the algorithm is shown as Figure 1.

This algorithm is quite robust. Normally in a few iterations, the accuracy of the boundary outline computed by this method is acceptable. Since it is region-based algorithm, the search procedure can only be concentrated on the specified area by the result of last step. It improves the algorithm both in speed and in accuracy.

> 1. Input some points in the image
> 2. Compute Voronoi Diagram of those points
> 3. Classify each region as interior, exterior or boundary
> 4. Compute Delaunay triangulation and show the connection of the boundary regions
> 5. Add seeds to the edges and inside of boundary regions
> 6. Goto 2 until a specified number of iterations procedures are processed or user quits

Fig. 1. Pseudocode for VD-based Segmentation Algorithm

2.3 Level Set Method

The third part of our hybrid framework is level set method. Level set method solves the topology modified problem that snake method is difficult to handle. Level set front evolution with fixed propagation direction is either initialized inside or outside sought objects, and the propagation force is opposed by a strong gradient magnitude at image discontinuities. At location of missing or fuzzy boundaries, the internal force is often strong enough to counteract global smoothness and leaks through these gaps.

A level set model specifies a surface as a level set (iso-surface) of a scalar volumetric function, $\phi: U \mapsto \Re$, where $U \subset \Re^3$ is the range of the surface model. Thus, a surface S is

$$S = \{s | \phi(s) = k\}, \qquad (4)$$

and k is the isovalue. In other words, S is the set of points s in $\Re^3$ that compose the k th iso-surface of ϕ. The embedding ϕ can be specified as a regular sampling on a rectilinear grid. Level set methods provide the mathematical and numerical mechanisms for computing surface deformations as isovalues of ϕ by solving a partial differential equation (PDE) on the 3D grid.

One approach to define a deformable surface from a level set of a volumetric function as described in equation (4) is to think of $\phi(s)$ as a static function and fix k and let the volumetric function dynamically change in time, i.e. $\phi(s,t)$. The dynamic model is expressed mathematically as

$$\phi(s,t) = k. \qquad (5)$$

To transform this definition into PDE that can easily be solved by standard numerical techniques, we differentiate both sides of equation (5) with respect to time t, and apply the chain rule:

$$\frac{\partial \phi(s,t)}{\partial t} + \nabla \phi(s,t) \cdot \frac{ds}{dt} = 0. \qquad (6)$$

Equation (6) is sometimes referred to as a "Hamilton-Jacobi-type" equation and defines an initial value problem for the time-dependent ϕ. Let ds/dt be the movement of a point on a surface as it deforms, such that it can be expressed in terms of the position of $s \subset U$ and the geometry of the surface at that point, which is, in turn, a differential expression of the implicit function, ϕ. This gives a PDE on $\phi : s \equiv s(t)$

$$\frac{\partial \phi}{\partial t} = -\nabla \phi \cdot \frac{ds}{dt} \equiv -\nabla \phi \cdot F(s, D\phi, D^2\phi, \cdots), \qquad (7)$$

where F is user-defined "speed" term which generally depends on a set of order-n derivatives of ϕ, $D^n \phi$ evaluated at s, as well as other functions of s. $F(x)$ can combine the attraction term with smooth term as weighting factors. So that the surface can be attracted following the gradient of grey scale features, at the same time kept its smoothness.

Level set models have a number of practical and theoretical advantages over conventional surface models. They are topologically flexible, and easily represent complicated surface shapes that can, form holes, split to form multiple objects, or merge with other objects to form a single structure. These models can incorporate many of degrees of freedom, and therefore they can accommodate complex shapes.

3 Implementation of Hybrid Framework

The framework consists of three methods, fuzzy-connectedness, VD-based algorithm and level set method. The concept of each algorithm has been described above. The fuzzy connectedness algorithm is used to find the broad outline of the target tissue. It might be not so precise. The segment result offers a set of statistics automatically to define the homogeneity operator. The homogeneity operator is used in the next step, VD-based algorithm as classifier. The second step enhances the result of the first step since fuzzy-connectedness algorithm will stick locally. The VD-based algorithm improves the boundary to the target. The third step is level-set method. This deformable surface model refines the output from the second step. It extracts boundary data to fill in the missing boundary data and to override the spurious boundary data due to image noise. So it keeps the boundary preciseness and smoothness also.

For the first step, the fuzzy connectedness algorithm segments a sample of the target tissue, and generates statistics, average and variance. To initialize the fuzzy connectedness algorithm, the user clicks on the image and selects one small square region inside the target tissue. From the segmented sample of the tissue, the homogeneity operator is generated. It classifies the internal and external region.

For the second step, the VD-based algorithm computes an initial VD by adding random points in the image. Then every region in VD is classified to as internal or external region by homogeneity operator. Those external regions having at least one internal region neighbour are identified as boundary region. The boundary region is processed iteratively by the VD-based algorithm until the boundary is precise enough or user chooses quit.

For the third step, the output of the second step is the coarse segmentation of the target issue. The boundary separates the region of interest and its background during last two steps. However, the boundary is not smooth enough. Level set model makes use of its two kinds of forces to get smooth and accurate boundary. The level set model works on the output of the second step. It needs a small number of iterations to converge.

4 Result of Hybrid approach

In this section, we present the result from experiments of the hybrid approach. As shown in figure 2, we segment the MRI proton density brain image to get the light part. As the first step, fuzzy connectedness method gets sample of target object. But it is not the whole object. The segmentation procedure stops locally since the grey level variance. The second step improves the segmentation result of the first step. The segmented area covers the whole target tissue. However, the boundary is quite rough since the image might contain some noise. The third step refines the rough boundary of the last step. The final segmentation result gets both precise and smooth property of the boundary of the target tissue.

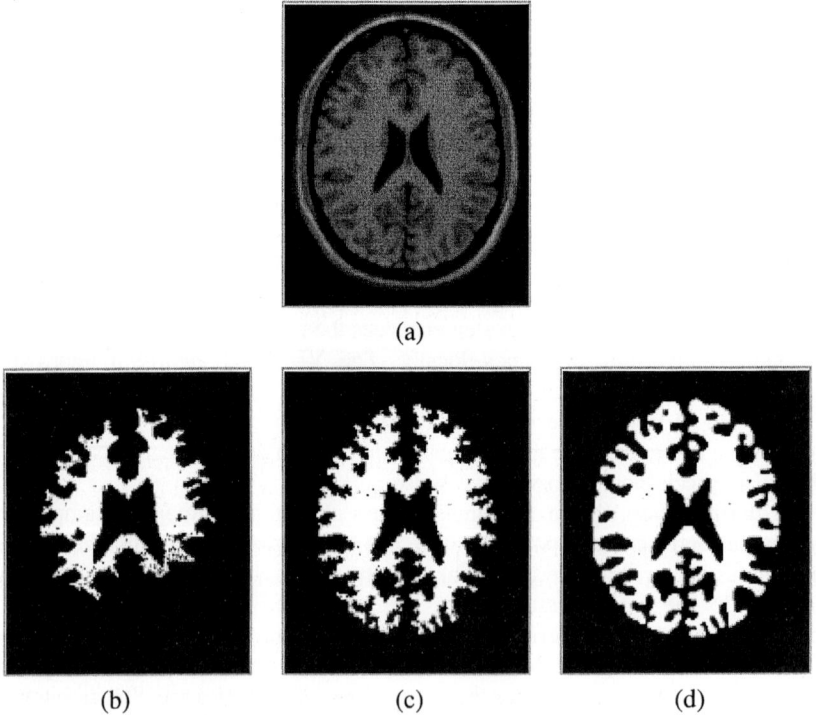

Fig. 2. This figure shows one example of our hybrid approach. The image (a) is one MRI proton density brain image. The following images (b), (c), (d) are the result of three segmentation steps, respectively.

5 Conclusions and Future Work

In this paper, we report a hybrid framework for medical image segmentation. This approach integrates region-based and edge-based segmentation method. There are three components in this hybrid approach, fuzzy connectedness method, VD-based method, and level set model. The hybrid approach offers the greater robustness than either technique alone.

In the current system, only 2D image is segmented. We would expend it to 3D segmentation. However, the complexity of each method for 3D increases largely, and robustness decreases at meanwhile. We will find a good strategy to overcome it.

Reference

1. J. K. Udupa, S. Samarasekera, "Fuzzy connectedness and object definition: theory, algorithms, and applications in image segmentation," Graphical Models and Image Processing, Volume 58, Issue 3, Pages: 246 – 261, 1996
2. A. Pednekar, I. A. Kakadiaris, U. Kurkure, "Adaptive fuzzy connectedness-based medical image segmentation," Proc. of the Indian Conf. on Computer Vision, Graphics, and Image Processing (ICVGIP'02), pp.457-462, 2002.
3. Bertin E, Parazza F, Chassery JM. "Segmentation and measurement based on 3D Voronoi diagram: application to confocal microscopy." Computerized Medical Imaging Graphics, 17(3):175-82, 1993
4. Imielińska, C.; Downes, M; and Yuan, W., "Semi-Automated Color Segmentation of Anatomical Tissue", Journal of Computerized Medical Imaging and Graphics, 24(2000), 173-180, April, 2000.
5. M. Kass, A. Witkin, and D. Terzopoulos, ``Snakes - Active Contour Models" International Journal of Computer Vision, 1(4): pp. 321-331, 1987
6. Chen, YM, Tagare, HD., Thiruvenkadam, S., Huang, F., Wilson, D., Gopinath, KS, Briggs, RW, and Geiser, EA, "Using prior shapes in geometric active contours in a variational framework," International Journal of Computer Vision, vol. 50, pp. 315 -328, 2002
7. Y. Wang and L. H. Staib, "Boundary finding with correspondence using statistical shape models," IEEE Conference on Computer Vision and Pattern Recognition (CVPR'98), pp. 338-345, Santa Barbara, CA, USA, June 1998
8. J. Yang, L. H. Staib, and J. S. Duncan, "Neighbour-Constrained Segmentation with Level Set Based 3D Deformable Models," IEEE Transactions on Medical Imaging, Vol. 23, No. 8, 940-948, August 2004
9. Osher, S., Sethian, J.A., "Fronts propagating with curvature-dependent speed: algorithms based on Hamilton-Jacobi formulation." Journal of Computational Physics 79 (1988) 12-49
10. C. Jiang, X. Zhang, W. Huang, Ch. Meinel, "Segmentation and Quantification of a Brain Tumor," Proc. IEEE VECIMS 2004 Boston/MA (USA), pp. 61-66, 2004
11. R. Whitaker, D. Breen, K. Museth, and N. Soni. "Segmentation of Biological Volume Datasets Using a Level-Set Framework" Volume Graphics 2001, Springer, pp. 249-263, 2001
12. F. P. Preparata and M. I. S. Shamos, Computational Geometry, an Introduction. Springer Verlag, NewYork, 1988

Evolving Spanning Trees Using the Heat Equation

Fan Zhang, Huaijun Qiu, and Edwin R. Hancock

Department of Computer Science,
University of York, York, YO10 5DD, UK

Abstract. This paper explores how to use the heat kernel to evolve the minimum spanning tree of a graph with time. We use the heat kernel to weight the edges of the graph, and these weights can be computed by exponentiating the Laplacian eigensystem of the graph with time. The resulting spanning trees exhibit an interesting behaviour as time increases. Initially, they are bushy and rooted near the centre of graph, but as time evolves they become string-like and hug the boundary of the graph. We characterise this behaviour using the distribution of terminal nodes with time, and use this distribution for the purposes of graph clustering and image segmentation.

1 Introduction

Graphs play a pivotal role in structural pattern analysis. However, they are not as easily manipulated as pattern vectors since there is no canonical ordering of the nodes of a graph. Instead, they must be labelled or a correspondence order established before their statistical properties can be easily analysed. However, frequently the modes of variation in a population or sample of graphs correspond to changes in node or edge structure. Establishing correspondence under these circumstances can prove computationally restrictive, since the subgraph isomorphism problem is suspected to be NP complete.

An alternative to explicitly establishing a correspondence order is to extract a simpler structure from the graph which imposes a natural order on its nodes. There are a number of ways of doing this. One approach is to compute the spanning tree of the graph. Here the distance of the nodes from the root provides a way of sorting them into order, and this can be used to characterise the graph. An alternative is to use the random walk on the graph. This can be used to convert the graphs into a string order.

Random walks [1] have found widespread use in information retrieval and structural pattern analysis. For instance, the random walk is the basis of the Page-Rank algorithm which is used by the Googlebot search engine [2]. In computer vision random walks have been used for image segmentation [3] and clustering [4]. More recently both Gori, Maggini and Sarti [5], and, Robles-Kelly and Hancock [6] have used random walks to sort the nodes of graphs for the purposes of graph-matching. Most of these methods use a simple approximate characterisation of the random walk based either on the leading eigenvector of the transition probability matrix, or equivalently the Fiedler vector of the Laplacian matrix [7]. In general though, the random walk is not edge-connected on the graph. Hence, it may not preserve the edge structure and can prove to be an ineffective way of capturing the structural properties of the graph. In an attempt to overcome this problem Robles-Kelly and Hancock [6] explore two approaches. The first of these is to use a postpocessing step to recover an edge connected path from the components of the leading eigenvector. The second refinement is to pose the recovery of an edge-ordered path as one of graph seriation using a utility function and to recover an approximate solution to this problem using graph-spectral (i.e. eigenvector) methods.

In this paper we aim to take a different approach to the problem of extracting a simplified ordered structure from the graph. It is well known that the random walk on a graph is the limit of the heat kernel in the continuous time limit. The heat kernel [8] is the solution of the heat-equation on the graph and is found by exponentiating the normalised Laplacian of the graph (the identity matrix minus the degree normalised adjacency matrix) with time. As a result, the heat kernel can be computed efficiently by exponentiating the Laplacian eigensystem [9]. The heat kernel can be viewed as capturing the way in which information flows with time across the edges of the graph. For large times the heat kernel is dominated by the Fiedler vector, and so it is equivalent to the random walk.

Our idea in this paper is to study the minimum spanning tree associated with the heat kernel as time evolves, and to use the time dependance of the spanning tree as a way of characterising the graph. We associate with each edge in the graph a weight that is determined by the heat kernel. We then use Prim's method to locate the spanning tree that minimises the sum of weights. The spanning trees evolve in a rather interesting way with time. For small time, they are rooted near the centre of the graph, and branches connect to terminal nodes that are on the boundary of the graph. As time increases, the tree becomes string like, and winds itself from the centre of the graph to the perimeter. As it does so, the number of terminal nodes decreases, i.e. the large time tree has the appearance of a string to which a small number of short branches or ligatures are attached. Based on these observations, we explore whether the distribution of the number of terminal nodes with time can be used as a signature of the graph. Experiments show that this signature can be used for the purposes of graph clustering. We also show how the spanning trees can be used for image segmentation.

2 Heat Kernels and Lazy Random Walks

In this section, we review some of the properties of the heat kernel and explain its relationship with the lazy random walk on a graph. To commence, suppose that the graph under study is denoted by $G = (V, E, W)$ where V is the set of nodes, $E \subseteq V \times V$ is the set of edges and $W : E \to [0,1]$ is the weight function. Since we wish to adopt a graph-spectral approach we introduce the adjacency matrix A for the graph where the elements are

$$A(u,v) = \begin{cases} 1 & \text{if } (u,v) \in E \\ 0 & \text{otherwise} \end{cases} \tag{1}$$

We also construct the diagonal degree matrix D, whose elements are given by $D(u,u) = deg(u) = \sum_{v \in V} A(u,v)$. From the degree matrix and the adjacency matrix we construct the Laplacian matrix $L = D - A$, i.e. the degree matrix minus the adjacency matrix. The normalised Laplacian is given by $\hat{L} = D^{-\frac{1}{2}} L D^{-\frac{1}{2}}$. The spectral decomposition of the normalised Laplacian matrix is $\hat{L} = \Phi \Lambda \Phi^T$ where $\Lambda = diag(\lambda_1, \lambda_2, ..., \lambda_{|V|})$ is the diagonal matrix with the ordered eigenvalues $(0 = \lambda_1 < \lambda_2 \leq \lambda_3...)$ as elements and $\Phi = (\phi_1|\phi_2|....|\phi_{|V|})$ is the matrix with the correspondingly ordered eigenvectors as columns. Since $\hat{L}$ is symmetric and positive semi-definite, the eigenvalues of the normalised Laplacian are all positive. The eigenvector ϕ_2 associated with the smallest non-zero eigenvalue λ_2 is referred to as the Fiedler-vector. We are interested in the heat equation associated with the Laplacian, i.e. $\frac{\partial h_t}{\partial t} = -\hat{L} h_t$ where h_t is the heat kernel and t is time. The heat kernel can hence be viewed as describing the flow of information across the edges of the graph with time. The rate of flow is determined by the Laplacian of the graph. The solution to the heat equation is found by exponentiating the Laplacian eigenspectrum, i.e. $h_t = \exp[-\hat{L}t] = \Phi \exp[-t\Lambda] \Phi^T$. The heat kernel is a $|V| \times |V|$ matrix, and for the nodes u and v of the graph G the resulting element is

$$h_t(u,v) = \sum_{i=1}^{|V|} \exp[-\lambda_i t] \phi_i(u) \phi_i(v) \qquad (2)$$

When t tends to zero, then $h_t \simeq I - \hat{L}t$, i.e. the kernel depends on the local connectivity structure or topology of the graph. If, on the other hand, t is large, then $h_t \simeq \exp[-\lambda_2] \phi_2 \phi_2^T$, where λ_2 is the smallest non-zero eigenvalue and ϕ_2 is the associated eigenvector, i.e. the Fiedler vector. Hence, the large time behavior is governed by the global structure of the graph.

2.1 Path Length Distribution

It is interesting to note that the heat kernel is also related to the path length distribution on the graph. To show this, consider the matrix $P = D^{-1/2} A D^{-1/2} = I - \hat{L}$, where I is the identity matrix. The heat kernel can be rewritten as $h_t = e^{-t(I-P)}$. We can perform a McLaurin expansion [10] on the heat-kernel to re-express it as a polynomial in t. The result of this expansion is

$$h_t = e^{-t}\left(I + tP + \frac{(tP)^2}{2!} + \frac{(tP)^3}{3!} + \cdots\right) = e^{-t} \sum_{k=0}^{\infty} P^k \frac{t^k}{k!} \qquad (3)$$

The matrix P has elements

$$P(u,v) = \begin{cases} 1 & \text{if } u = v \\ \frac{1}{\sqrt{deg(u)deg(v)}} & \text{if } u \neq v \text{ and } (u,v) \in E \\ 0 & \text{otherwise} \end{cases} \qquad (4)$$

As a result, we have that

$$P^k(u,v) = \sum_{S_k} \prod_{i=1}^{k} \frac{1}{\sqrt{deg(u_i)deg(u_{i+1})}} \qquad (5)$$

where the walk S_k is a sequence of vertices $u_0, \cdots, u_k$ of length k such that $u_i = u_{i+1}$ or $(u_i, u_{i+1}) \in E$. Hence, $P^k(u, v)$ is the sum of weights of all walks of length k joining nodes u and v. The spectral expression for the matrix is $P^k = (I - \hat{L})^k = \Phi(I - \Lambda)^k \Phi^T$.

2.2 Lazy Random Walk

The heat kernel is the continuous time limit of the lazy random walk. Consider a lazy random walk with transition matrix $T = (1-\alpha)I + \alpha D^{-1}A$ which migrates between different nodes with probability α and remains static at a node with probability $1 - \alpha$. When $\alpha = 1$, then $T = D^{-1}A = D^{1/2}PD^{1/2}$. Let $\Delta = D^{-1}L$, $\alpha = \alpha_0 \Delta t$ and $\Delta t = \frac{1}{N}$. In the continuous time limit, i.e. $N \to \infty$

$$\lim_{N \to \infty} T^N = \lim_{N \to \infty} \left(I + \alpha_0 \frac{1}{N}(D^{-1}A - I) \right)^N = \exp[-\alpha_0 D^{-1}L] \quad (6)$$

Another way of viewing the contininuous time ramdom walk. Let $\boldsymbol{p}_t$ be the vector whose element $p_t(i)$ is the probability of visiting node i of the graph under the random walk. The probability vector evolves under the equation $\frac{\partial \boldsymbol{p}_t}{\partial t} = -\hat{L}\boldsymbol{p}_t$, which has the solution $\boldsymbol{p}_t = \exp[-\hat{L}t]\boldsymbol{p}_0$. As a result $\boldsymbol{p}_t = h_t \boldsymbol{p}_0$. Consequently the heat kernel determines the random walk. The aim in this paper is to explore how the heat kernel of the graph evolves with time and to use this as a means of constructing spanning trees on the graph.

3 Prim's Minimum Spanning Tree Algorithm

We use the elements of the heat kernel as edge-weights and seek the minimum spanning tree on the weighted graph. A spanning tree T of a connected weighted graph $G = (V, E, W)$ is a connected subgraph of G which contains every vertex of G and contains no cycles. A minimum spanning tree is a spanning tree of G with a minimum total weight.

There are two classical algorithms that efficiently construct a minimum spanning tree of a general weighted graph G, namely the algorihms of Prim and Kruskal. Here, we choose Prim's algorithm which uses Dijkstra's method to find a shortest path between two nodes. Prim's algorithm commences with a tree T that contains an arbitrary vertex r, and then repeatedly locates the lowest weight edge connecting T to $G - T$ and then adds it to T. The minimum spanning tree can be constructed in $0(|E| + |V|log|V|))$ time by using a Fibonacci heap.

We use the heat kernel as the edge weight function of the graph, i.e. $W(u, v) = h_t(u, v)$. Then using Prim's algorithm to find the minimum spanning tree of the graph. Since the heat kernel varies with time, so does the minimum spanning tree of the graph.

In order to extract a feature vector that can efficiently characterize the graph, we use the number of terminal nodes $N_T(t)$ of the minimum spanning tree at different times t. The idea is a simple one. At each time t we count the number of terminal nodes. The distribution of terminal nodes is sampled at a number of equally spaced times and normalised (so that the area under the distribution is unity). If C_t is value of the normalised distribution and $t_1, t_2, ..., t_M$ are the sampling times, then our graph feature vector is $F = (C_{t_1}, ..., C_{t_M})^T$. We embed the graph feature vectors in a low dimensional pattern space using PCA [11].

4 Experiments

Graph Clustering: We applied our method to images from the COIL database. The database contains images of 3D objects under controlled camera direction and lighting conditions. For each object in the database there are 72 equally spaced views, which are obtained as the camera circumscribes the object. We used six example objects and for each object we used a subsample of 15 equally spaced views. For each image of each object we computed the Voronoi tessellations of feature points [12] extracted using a corner detector and constructed the Delaunay graph from the Voronoi regions. A sample view of each object and its Delaunay graph is shown in Fig 1. In our experiment, we investigated the time interval from $t = 0.1$ to $t = 10$, which we sampled at $M = 25$ equally spaced intervals. At each of the sample times we constructed the minimum spanning tree using the value of heat kernel to computer edge weights, and recorded the frequency of the terminal nodes.

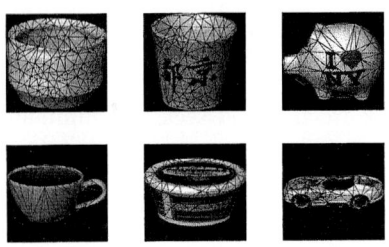

Fig. 1. Delaunay graphs of six objects

In Fig 2 for one of the graphs used in our experiments, we illustrate the evolution of the spanning tree with time. The first image in the sequence shows the input graph, and the remaining images show the recovered spanning trees as time elapses. Initially, the tree is rooted near the centre of the graph with terminal nodes on the boundary. The recovered tree has many branches and is very "bushy". As time evolves, the pattern changes. The tree becomes rather string-like and wraps itself around the boundary, with branches extending it to the centre of the original graph.

Fig 3 shows the normalised distributions of terminal node numbers. Each plot in the figure is for a different object. The different plots shows the distributions stacked in view order. Hence, the axis pointing to upper left is time, and that pointing to the upper right is view number. There are a number of features to note from this plot. First, the distributions are rather different in shape for the different objects. Second, the distributions for images of the same object are stable with view number. This suggests that they could form the basis of a stable object characterisation.

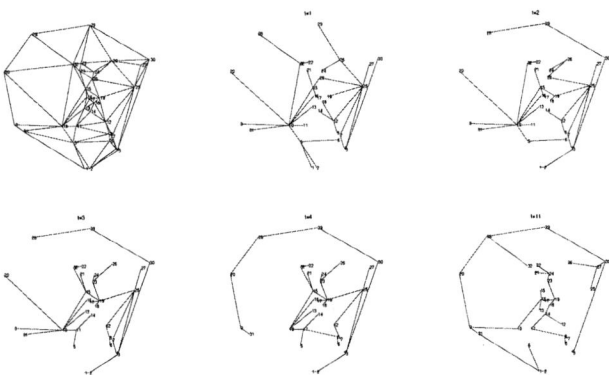

Fig. 2. A Delauney graph and its minimum spanning trees with varying t

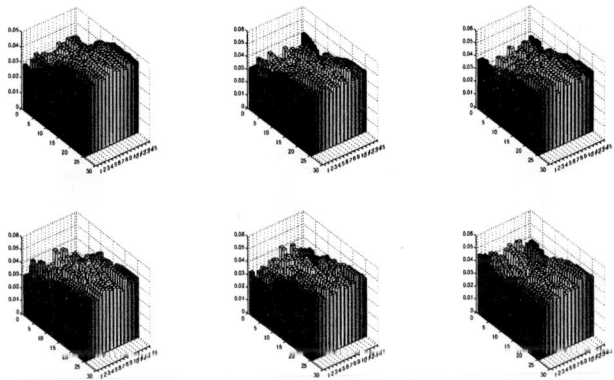

Fig. 3. Terminal node distributions for six objects with varying view number

Figure 4 shows the result of applying PCA to the feature vectors for the graphs. This involves first computing the covariance matrix for the feature vectors. Next we compute the eigenvectors of the covariance matrix. The graph feature vectors are projected into the space spanned by the leading two eigenvectors. In the figure the different symbols correspond to different objects. The object-views are well separated by the projection and can be separated by linear boundaries.

Image Segmentation: We have also applied our method to the problem of image segmentation[13]. To do this we have commenced by constructing an affinity matrix from the measured pixel brightness I_i. The matrix has elements $A(i,j) = \|I_i - I_j\|_2$ if the image pixels i and j are separated by a distance less than r, and $A(i,j) = 0$ otherwise. From the affinity matrix A we construct the normalised Laplacian matrix $\hat{L}$. Using the heat kernel and Prim's algorithm we construct the minimum spanning tree, so all the pixels from the same region are

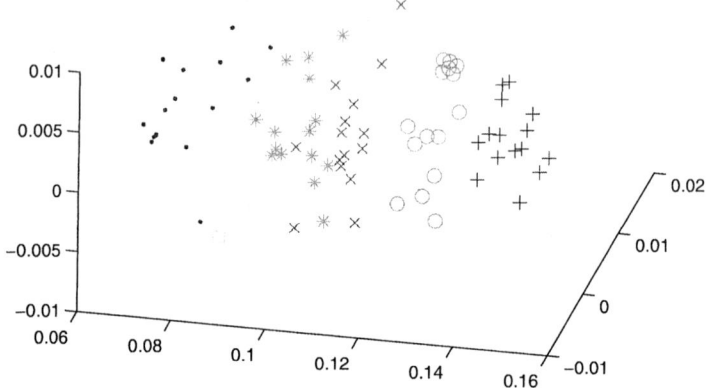

Fig. 4. PCA embedding result

Fig. 5. Four image segmentation sequences of t=0.01, 0.1, 0.5, 1, 2, 3 respectively from column 2 to column 7. Row 1: imagesize 50×50 $r=5$ $\sigma=0.03$ Row 2: imagesize 60×40 $r=9$ $\sigma=0.03$ Row 3: imagesize 55×53 $r=6$ $\sigma=0.04$ Row 4: imagesize 60×40 r=6 $\sigma=0.04$.

the nodes of a subtree in it. To segment the image into regions, we recursively partition the spanning tree into two subtrees by removing an edge. Suppose that the spanning tree is partitioned into two subtrees T_i and T_j by removing the edge (i,j), where T_i is the sub-tree rooted at the node i and T_j is the sub-tree with node j as its root. This "tree cut" method is based on the criterion $CT(T_i, T_j) = A_{i,j} \exp[-(1-B_{i,j})/\sigma]$ where $B_{i,j} = \min(|T_i|, |T_j|)/\max(|T_i|, |T_j|)$. We cut the tree at the edge with the maximum value of $CT(T_i, T_j)$.

In Figure 5 we show four sequences of segmentations obtained for different values of t. The main features to note from these results are as follows. First, for low values of t we detect a larger number of regions, and the method tends to oversegment the images. For larger values of t a smaller number of regions are detected. However, these larger regions preserve fine boundary detail. Hence, the effect of using the heat kernel is different to that of image smoothing.

5 Conclusions

In this paper we have explored how the minimum spanning tree of a graph can be evolved with time using the heat-equation. The spanning trees formed at different times have different structural properties and probe the structure of the original graph in different ways. At small time the tree is "bushy" and rooted near the centre of the graph. At large times the tree becomes string like and clings to the boundary of the graph. We capture this behaviour using the distribution of terminal nodes with time. This distribution is shown to be useful for the purposes of graph-clustering. We also demonstrate that the spanning trees can be used for image segmentation.

References

1. Sood, V., Redner, S., ben Avraham, D.: First-passage properties of the erdoscrenyi random graph. J. Phys. A: Math. Gen. (2005) 109–123
2. Brin, S., L.Page: The anatomy of a large-scale hypertextual Web search engine. Computer Networks and ISDN Systems **30** (1998) 107–117
3. M.Meila, J.Shi: A random walks view of spectral segmentation. In proceedings of AI and STATISTICS (AISTATS) (2001)
4. Saerens, M., Fouss, F., Yen, L., Dupont, P.: The principal components analysis of a graph, and its relationships to spectral clustering. In: 15th European Conference on Machine Learning. (2004)
5. Gori, M., Maggini, M., Sarti, L.: Graph matching using random walks. In: ICPR04. (2004) III: 394–397
6. Robles-Kelly, A., Hancock, E.R.: Graph edit distance from spectral seriation. PAMI **27** (2005) 365–378
7. Lovsz, L.: Random walks on graphs: A survey. Combinatorics, Bolyai Society for Mathematical Studies, Budapest **2** (1996) 353–397
8. Kondor, R., Lafferty, J.: Diffusion kernels on graphs and other discrete structures. 19th Intl. Conf. on Machine Learning (ICML) [ICM02]. (2002)
9. Chung, F.: Spectral Graph Theory. CBMS series 92. American Mathmatical Society Ed. (1997)
10. Chung, F., Yau, S.T.: Discrete green's functions. In: J. Combin. Theory Ser. (2000) 191–214
11. Chatfield, C., A.J.Collins: Introduction to Multivariate Analysis. Chapman and Hall (1980)
12. Harris, C., Stephens, M.: A combined corner and edge detector. Proceedings Fourth Alvey Vision Conference (1988) 147–151
13. Shi, J., Malik, J.: Normalized cuts and image segmentation. IEEE PAMI **22** (2000) 888–905

Design of Statistical Measures for the Assessment of Image Segmentation Schemes

Marc Van Droogenbroeck and Olivier Barnich*

University of Lige, Department of Electricity, Electronics and Computer Science,
Institut Montefiore B-28, Sart Tilman, B-4000 Liège, Belgium

Abstract. Image segmentation is discussed for years in numerous papers, but assessing its quality is mainly dealt with in recent works. Quality assessment is a primary concern for anyone working towards better segmentation tools. It both helps to objectively improve segmentation techniques and to compare performances with respect to other similar algorithms.

In this paper we use a statistical framework to propose statistical measures capable to describe the performances of a segmentation scheme. All the measures rely on a ground-truth segmentation map that is supposed to be known and that serves as a reference when qualifying the results of any segmentation tool. We derive the analytical expression of several transition probabilities and show how to calculate them. An important conclusion from our study, often overlooked, is that performances can be content dependent, which means that one should adapt a measure to the content of an image.

1 Introduction

Segmentation is one the most difficult task in automatic image analysis. It consists in partitioning an image into objects (segments) homogeneous with respect to a specific property. Many algorithms for segmentation have been proposed over the years and this number still continues to raise. One of the reasons for this proliferation of techniques is that no segmentation technique offer enough universality to meet the requirements of a broad family of applications.

While the development of new segmentation techniques has attracted significant attention, fewer efforts have been spent on their evaluation. Some could also argue that no satisfactory evaluation measure has been proposed so far and that the discipline is still in its infancy.

In [1] ZHANG reviews some methods for segmentation evaluation. He divides the family of evaluation methods into two categories:

1. the *analytical* methods, which evaluates the properties and the principles of segmentation algorithms,

---

* This work was supported by the Belgian Walloon Region (http://www.wallonie.be), under the CINEMA project. The second author is supported by a FRIA grant.

2. and the *empirical* methods, that judge algorithms by applying them to test images and by measuring the results.

According to ZHANG [1], empirical methods can been further divided into two types: *goodness* methods and *discrepancy* methods. In the first category results are qualified according to human intuition and judged by the values of goodness measures. In the second category some segmentation references, called *ground-truth* maps, that represent expected results are given, and results are compared with these references by counting the difference.

In the following we investigate the statistical significance of a discrepancy method. In Section 2 we develop a framework for describing a segmentation result. This model leads to statistical measures that are defined and discussed in Section 3. From our study it appears that evaluating the quality of segmentation depends on the data and that one has to adapt the measures to the size of the segmentation maps. These conclusions are presented in Section 4.

2 Statistical Model for Assessing Segmentation Techniques

Let x be the location of a pixel inside the image that can be of any type (a 2D flat image, a volumetric 3D image, or an image flow like a video). Generally speaking image segmentation produces a region map, in which each pixel is labeled with a number designating the region to which it was assigned. In the following we restrict the number of regions to a single object, that might be composed of several disconnected parts, and a background.

There are various ways to generate segmentation references. Ideally a reference is specified on the base of a perfect segmentation process. If this last is available the need to measure the quality of segmentation techniques is rather low. One possible alternation is to use synthetic images made by the superposition of an object (the blue screen technique can help producing a realistic object) on a real background.

In the following we assume that there exists perfect segmentation maps. The known background is denoted by $b[x]$, and $f[x]$ is the image captured by the camera. If no object is superimposed on the background then $b[x] = f[x]$ for any x. To the contrary, when an object is added to the scene, the previous equality holds for some pixels but not all of them anymore. In this case, the background is masked by a function denoted $m[x]$. We define $m[x] = 0$ when the background is visible and $m[x] = 1$ when an object in the foreground hides the background. If per coincidence the color of the object is identical to the background color, i.e. $b[x] = f[x]$, we still consider that the background is masked and therefore that $m[x] = 1$. Note that this simple model does not discard transparent objects like windows.

With the aforementioned model and notations the segmentation algorithm has to process

$$f[x] = m[x]f[x] + (1 - m[x])b[x] \tag{1}$$

where $m[x]f[x] = o[x]$ denotes the superimposed object. From all the functions, $b[x]$ is known and $f[x]$ is observed. If we choose a non-cooperative design scheme, the algorithm has no prior knowledge of $o[x]$, nor of $m[x]$. Despite that relation (1) holds for any x, there is not enough information for the algorithm to recover $o[x]$ or $m[x]$.

One of the key techniques to segment an image is *background substraction* [2,3]. A background is first estimated, by time integration for example, and then the estimated background $\widehat{b}[x]$ is compared to $f[x]$. If one assumes that noise has been filtered out, a simple decision rule states that if $f[x] \neq \widehat{b}[x]$ then $m[x] = 1$ and $f[x] = o[x]$. Clearly this technique does not suffice as $f[x] = \widehat{b}[x]$ does not imply that $m[x] = 0$. In order words background substraction produces underestimated object surfaces. Therefore background substraction is usually combined to an object tracking algorithm. This avoids the two main drawbacks of background substraction techniques : the progressive inclusion in the background of static objects and the non-detection of objects that have the same color than the background (like transparent objects).

2.1 A Statistical Interpretation of the Segmentation Process

Regardless of whether the background is known or not the segmentation process may be seen as a stochastic process. Let us consider image segmentation as a two states pixel classification process $M[x]$. For any location x, $M[x]$ is a random variable equal to

- 1 when x belongs to a foreground object $\mathcal{O}$, and
- 0 when x is included in the background $\mathcal{B}$.

When the ground-truth segmentation map is not available, $M[x]$ can only be described in terms of probabilities characterizing two possible outcomes: $M[x] = 1$ or $M[x] = 0$. Let the probabilities of these events be $p(x \in \mathcal{O})$ and $p(x \notin \mathcal{O}) = p(x \in \mathcal{B})$. For simplicity these probabilities are denoted $p(o)$ and $p(b)$ respectively. Obviously $x \in O$ or $x \in B$, so that $p(o) = 1 - p(b)$.

The role of segmentation is to estimate the masking function $M[x]$, hopefully as close as possible to the real segmentation mask. In practical terms we have to estimate the function $\widehat{M}[x]$ which should be equal to $M[x]$ almost everywhere. Since a perfect match is not achievable, we have to model the segmentation process with some probabilities. Let $p_s(o)$ and $p_s(b)$ be the probabilities for a pixel to be classified as a foreground object or as a background respectively. The probability $p_s(o)$ sums the probability of two cases: x belongs to the object or, although x is in the background, it has been assigned to the object.

Figure 1 shows the model used in the following. Let us consider a given location x. The input, drawn on the left-hand side, represents the original two possible states (and probabilities) for the mask. A referenceless segmentation produces an estimated binary value $\widehat{M}[x]$; it is drawn on the right-hand side of Figure 1.

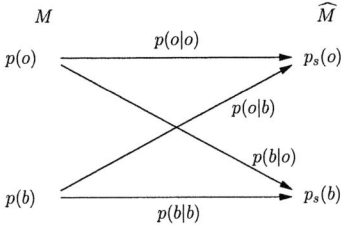

Fig. 1. Binary model for segmentation

As suggested by MARTIN [4], we could compute the mutual information I between $\widehat{M}$ and the ground-truth map M which is a global measure. Our model puts the focus on several probabilities rather than on a global measure. The model is characterized by the set of possible original states, the set of possible outcomes, and a set of conditional probabilities also called transition probabilities. For example, $p(o|b)$ is the probability of an error for a background pixel to be labelled as an object.

As a consequence

$$p_s(o) = p(o|o)p(o) + p(o|b)p(b) . \tag{2}$$

A similar relation yields for $p_s(b)$:

$$p_s(b) = p(b|b)p(b) + p(b|o)p(o) . \tag{3}$$

Segmentation errors originate from the diagonal probabilities $p(b|o)$ and $p(o|b)$. The larger these probabilities, the larger the segmentation error rate will be. The probability of error p_e for a two-class problem can be defined by

$$p_e = p(b|o)p(o) + p(o|b)p(b) \tag{4}$$

where $p(o)$ and $p(b)$ are viewed as *a priori* probabilities. An extension of p_e for multi-class problems can be found in [5].

3 Statistical Discrepancy Measures

3.1 Statistical Assumptions

The statistical segmentation model summarized in Figure 1 is location-dependent. Indeed classification probabilities as well as transition probabilities are related to the position of a pixel in the image. We will nevertheless suppose that $M[x]$ is spatially stationary in the wide sense, which implies that its mean is constant. This assumption is debatable but if an object moves equally over the image plane or inside a 3D volume, wide-sense stationarity is acceptable.

Additionally we assume that $M[x]$ is *mean-ergodic*. As a consequence the constant local mean theoretically equals the average over the observation volume. In order words, if x is observed over $\mathcal{D} \in \mathbb{R}^n$ then

$$\mu_M = E\{M\} = \frac{1}{\sharp(\mathcal{D})} \int_{\mathcal{D}} m(x)\, dx \qquad (5)$$

where $\sharp(\mathcal{D})$ is the cardinality of $\mathcal{D}$. Again this is acceptable if $\mathcal{D}$ is large enough, which is the case for a usual image size, like a 640×480 VGA image.

3.2 Estimation of the Means

Assuming wide-sense stationarity and ergodicity in the mean it is possible to compute the means of M and $\widehat{M}$. The statistical mean of M is equal to

$$\mu_M = E\{M\} = 1 \times p(o) + 0 \times p(b) = p(o). \qquad (6)$$

If the ground-truth segmentation map is known, the cardinality of the objects by $\sharp(o)$ is easily computed so that $\mu_M = p(o)$ is nothing but the ratio of $\sharp(o)$ to the image size $\sharp(\mathcal{D})$:

$$\mu_M = \frac{\sharp(o)}{\sharp(\mathcal{D})}. \qquad (7)$$

Computing the mean of $\widehat{M}$ is not as straightforward. Analytically,

$$\mu_{\widehat{M}} = E\{\widehat{M}\} = 1 \times p_s(o) + 0 \times p_s(b) = p_s(o). \qquad (8)$$

Using equation (2) this yields

$$\mu_{\widehat{M}} = p(o)p(o|o) + p(b)p(o|b). \qquad (9)$$

Because of segmentation inaccuracies, $\mu_M \neq \mu_{\widehat{M}}$.

3.3 Probabilistic Quality Measures

Basically all four transition probabilities drawn on Figure 1 are interesting measures but for different reasons:

- $p(o|o)$ directly relates to the aim of segmentation,
- $p(b|b)$ is a useful measure for gauging the quality of any background detection tool, and
- $p(o|b)$ and $p(b|o)$ determine the overall segmentation errors.

Like for relation (7), the mean of $\widehat{M}$ can be estimated by counting the number of object pixels divided by the image size:

$$\mu_{\widehat{M}} = \frac{\sharp(o_s)}{\sharp(\mathcal{D})} \qquad (10)$$

where o_s represents the objects after segmentation. Accordingly we can easily compute a valid statistical estimate of $\mu_{\widehat{M}}$, and its value is assumed to be known hereafter.

Let us now reconsider equation (9). A substitution of $p(o)$ and $p(b)$ by their values yields

$$\mu_{\widehat{M}} = \frac{\#(o)}{\#(\mathcal{D})} p(o|o) + \left(1 - \frac{\#(o)}{\#(\mathcal{D})}\right) p(o|b) . \qquad (11)$$

Further simplifications are needed to isolate $p(o|o)$ and $p(o|b)$. We will first consider the case of large objects and then the case of small objects as the number of samples impact of the statistical significance of the estimates.

First Case: Large Objects. If the objects occupy a large portion of the image and the segmentation performs relatively well —it would be pointless to address the performances of a poor segmentation technique!—, $p(o|b) \ll p(o|o)$. Consequently $\mu_{\widehat{M}}$ reduces to

$$\mu_{\widehat{M}} \simeq \frac{\#(o)}{\#(\mathcal{D})} p(o|o) . \qquad (12)$$

This provides the value of $p(o|o)$:

$$p(o|o) \simeq \mu_{\widehat{M}} \frac{\#(\mathcal{D})}{\#(o)} = \frac{\#(o_s)}{\#(o)} . \qquad (13)$$

So two simple counting processes on the segmentation reference and on the real segmentation are sufficient to compute a criterion capable to estimate the object segmentation quality. Note that $p(o|o)$ might be superior to 1 which is theoretically impossible. Therefore we should use a modified criterion, like the absolute value of $1 - p(o|o)$, to evaluate the segmentation performances.

To compute $p(b|b)$ we start with the complementary probability of $p_s(o)$, $1 - p_s(b)$, and replace $p_s(b)$ by its value (see relation 3):

$$p_s(o) = 1 - p(b)p(b|b) - p(o)p(b|o) = 1 - \left(1 - \frac{\#(o)}{\#(\mathcal{D})}\right) p(b|b) - \frac{\#(o)}{\#(\mathcal{D})} p(b|o) . \qquad (14)$$

Remember that $\mu_{\widehat{M}} = p_s(o)$ and considering that the large objects hypothesis also implies that $p(b|o) \ll p(b|b)$, we get after some simplifications,

$$p(b|b) = \frac{\#(\mathcal{D}) - \#(o_s)}{\#(\mathcal{D}) - \#(o)} . \qquad (15)$$

To determine the missing diagonal transition probabilities we use the coherence relationship between probabilities originated from the same original event: $p(b|o) + p(o|o) = 1$. Therefore

$$p(b|o) = 1 - p(o|o) = \frac{\#(o) - \#(o_s)}{\#(o)} . \qquad (16)$$

Likewise,
$$p(o|b) = 1 - p(b|b) = \frac{\#(o_s) - \#(o)}{\#(\mathcal{D}) - \#(o)} . \tag{17}$$

Second Case: Small Objects. Expression (13) is inadequate when the objects occupy a negligible part of the image. More precisely, if $\#(o) \ll \#(\mathcal{D})$, then
$$\mu_{\widehat{M}} \simeq \frac{\#(o)}{\#(\mathcal{D})} p(o|o) + p(o|b) . \tag{18}$$

We now consider that the segmentation is symmetric, i.e. that $p(b|o) = p(o|b)$; a non-symmetric segmentation would otherwise be biased towards the foreground or the background and would lead to unacceptable results in the case of small objects. As $p(o|o) = 1 - p(b|o)$,
$$\mu_{\widehat{M}} \simeq 1 + \left(\frac{\#(o)}{\#(\mathcal{D})} - 1 \right) p(o|o) \tag{19}$$

so that, after further simplifications,
$$p(o|o) \simeq \frac{1 - \mu_{\widehat{M}}}{\left(1 - \frac{\#(o)}{\#(\mathcal{D})} \right)} \simeq (1 - \mu_{\widehat{M}}) \left(1 + \frac{\#(o)}{\#(\mathcal{D})} \right) = 1 + \frac{\#(o) - \#(o_s)}{\#(\mathcal{D})} + \frac{\#(o)\#(o_s)}{\#(\mathcal{D})} . \tag{20}$$

$\#(o_s)$ and $\#(o)$ are small compared to $\#(\mathcal{D})$, so that the quadratic term is negligible and therefore
$$p(o|o) \simeq 1 + \frac{\#(o) - \#(o_s)}{\#(\mathcal{D})} . \tag{21}$$

This probability gets very close to 1 as $\#(o_s)$ tends to 0. We then obtain $p(b|o)$ on the spot:
$$p(b|o) = 1 - p(o|o) = \frac{\#(o_s) - \#(o)}{\#(\mathcal{D})} , \tag{22}$$

which is also the value of $p(o|b)$. Again, by symmetry, $p(b|b) = p(o|o)$. The probability of error is then
$$p_e = \frac{\#(o_s) - \#(o)}{\#(\mathcal{D})} . \tag{23}$$

Discussion. In [1] ZHANG concludes that evaluation methods based on discrepancy measures are more powerful than evaluation methods using other measures. Moreover he compared several discrepancy measures to rank their ability to discriminate the overall quality. While there are many discrepancy measures, it appears that p_e is one of the best quality measure. Subsequently we can rely on this conclusion and do not have to validate p_e as a useful measure.

In the meanwhile we have computed additional probabilities that can have their relevance for certain segmentation purposes. A possible measure could be any weighted summation of $p(o|o)$, $p(b|b)$, $p(o|b)$, and $p(b|o)$. But one has to be careful with the interpretation of such a criteria because its statistical suitability is questionable. A sounder approach consists in comparing the probabilities separately, but then one has to cope with multiple criteria.

All four transition probabilities offer different insights on the quality of the segmentation but we can notice that the transition probabilities, in particular $p(o|b)$, seem less sensitive to the object size. They are also analytically very close to p_e. Therefore, if one is looking for a measure independent of the size of the object, we recommend $p(o|b)$. On the other hand $p(o|o)$ and $p(b|b)$ can also be useful if one wants a measure that changes its discriminating power with the foreground size.

4 Conclusions

In this paper we have derived several statistical measures to assess the quality of a segmentation algorithm with respect to a ground-truth reference. These measures are expressed in terms of transition probabilities.

From these values we can conclude that:

- appropriate estimates of transition probabilities depend on the data content.
- the statistical relevance of these estimates varies with the size of the object in the foreground. Analytical expressions show that $\sharp(o)$ and $\sharp(o_s)$ appears in all the transition probabilities. Since $\sharp(o_s)$ is an estimate, it would be interesting to investigate the impact of the variability of $\sharp(o_s)$ on the probabilities.
- we recommend $p(o|b)$ as a assessment criterion insensitive to the size of the object.

Further works are needed to examine the influence of several parameters of the model. Still we have established the unsuitability to trust a single criterion all over the foreground object size range.

References

1. Zhang, Y.: A survey on evaluation methods for image segmentation. Pattern Recognition **29** (1996) 1335–1346
2. Li, L., Huang, W., Gu, Y.H., Tian, Q.: Statistical modeling of complex backgrounds for foreground object detection. IEEE Transactions on Image Processing **13** (2004) 1459–1472
3. Radke, R., Andra, S., Al-Kofahi, O., Roysam, B.: Image change detection algorithms: a systematic survey. IEEE Transactions on Image Processing **14** (2005) 294–307
4. Martin, D.: An Empirical Approach to Grouping and Segmentation. PhD thesis, University of California, Berkeley (2002)
5. Lim, Y., Lee, S.: On the color image segmentation algorithm based on the thresholding and the fuzzy C-means techniques. Pattern Recognition **23** (1990) 935–952

Re-lighting and Compensation for Face Images

Xiaoyue Jiang[1], Tuo Zhao[2], Rong Xiao[3], and Rongchun Zhao[1]

[1] College of Computer Science, Northwestern Polytechnical University,
Xi'an, China, 710072
xiaoyuejiang@mail.nwpu.edu.cn
[2] School of Mechatronic Engineering, Northwestern Polytechnical University,
Xi'an, China, 710072
[3] Microsoft Research Asia, Beijing, China, 10080

Abstract. The illumination variance makes the robust face detection a challenging problem. Although there are some methods focusing on the de-lighting problem, the requirement for testing set or the 3D information limits the application for the detection tasks. According to the reflection function, the illumination takes the role of amplification for the reflective character of the surface. The shadows will make the features of the object attenuated or diminished. We introduce the radiance map ratio to adjust the image to a new illumination condition and apply the original image to compensate the adjusted image. The re-lighting and compensation makes the illumination condition uniform and keeps the original smooth changed information. As a pre-filter in the detector, the re-lighting and compensation method facilitates the performance of the detector. [1]

1 Introduction

The image is the projection of 3D objects on a 2D plane. When the same object appears in different poses under different illumination conditions, the image will be very different. Therefore the pose and illumination variance make the robust recognition and detection challenging tasks. Under the uniform and suitable illumination condition, the details of the object can be shown out clearly. However, under the non-uniform illumination condition, some part of the object is under brighter lighting and some under dimmer lighting. Then the details in the darker region cannot be shown out clearly in the image. It is because that the dim lighting suppresses the information while the bright lighting expands the information.

Histogram equalization (HE) is the most used method to adjust the illumination condition through making the intensity distribution more uniform. It is a global adjustment and always there is some abrupt noise left. Belhumeur [1, 2] proposes the illumination cone theory. He points out that the face images with the same pose under different illumination conditions compose a convex cone, which is called illumination cone. The requirement for a set of test images limits the illumination cone's application in the detection task. Ramamoorith

---
[1] This work was performed in Microsoft Research Asia.

[3, 4] and Baris [5] prove the first nine spherical harmonic bases can span the lighting space. The spherical harmonic theory provides a good framework for object rendering and inverse rendering. However, its application range is limited by the requirement for the 3D information of the object.

An image can be considered as the product of incident illumination and the reflective properties of the surface, i.e. the reflectance, in general. Land presents the Retinex theory [6]. He estimates the reflectance as the ratio of the image to its illumination condition that is approximated by the low pass version of the image. However at large discontinue part of the image, the halo effects are obvious. Jobson [7] gives an isotropic filter to extract the low pass information, Gross [8] applies anisotropic filter. But their methods still cannot resolve the halo problem. And always too much low frequency information of the image is lost.

Based on the reflection theory, we propose a method to do re-lighting. The re-lighting method is not to remove the illumination but adjust the illumination condition of the image to be more uniform. In the rest part of the paper, we first introduce the method to estimate the radiance map and the method to do re-lighting and compensation for images with the radiance map in Sec. 2. The experiments are given in Sec. 3. And the conclusion is drawn in Sec. 4.

2 Illumination Adjustment for Images

The image is the result of the surface reflectance and the lighting irradiating on it. For a certain object, the reflectance is considered as a constant. But with the changing of lighting as well as object's pose, the images will be greatly different. To remove the illumination from the image is an ill-posed problem. Therefore we aim to re-lighting images, i.e. to adjust the image to another illumination condition.

2.1 Reflection Function

The intensity of every point in the image is decided by the reflective character (including the surface normal of that point and the reflectance of the material) and the incident lighting from the up sphere of the point. Then we have

$$I(\boldsymbol{n}) = \int_{\Omega(\boldsymbol{n})} L(\omega)(\boldsymbol{n} \cdot \omega)\rho d\omega \qquad (1)$$

where $\Omega(\boldsymbol{n})$ is the up sphere of the point that is with surface normal $\boldsymbol{n}$. $L(\omega)$ is the incident lighting. ρ is the reflectance of the point. $(\boldsymbol{n} \cdot \omega)$ is the inner product of $\boldsymbol{n}$ and ω. That inner product represents the incident angle of the lighting. To every point its reflectance is always a constant. Then the reflection function can be rewritten as

$$\begin{aligned} I(\boldsymbol{n}) &= \rho \int_{\Omega(\boldsymbol{n})} L(\omega)(\boldsymbol{n} \cdot \omega) d\omega \\ &= \rho E(\boldsymbol{n}) \end{aligned} \qquad (2)$$

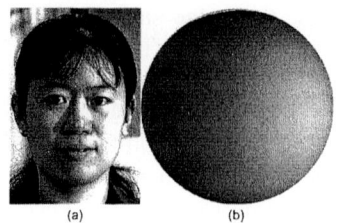

Fig. 1. The sample of the radiance environment map (a) a sample image (b) the radiance environment map of image (a)

$E(n)$ is the radiance environment map. According to formula 2, given the radiance environment map, we can look up the intensity of every point according to the surface normal in the radiance environment map. Fig.1 gives an example of the radiance environment map. The map describes the intensity of the points on a ball under the same illumination condition of the test image (Fig.1(a)). Then with another radiance environment map , we can render the object to a new lighting condition.That is

$$I'(n) = \rho E'(n) \qquad (3)$$

This method is very efficient and can produce photorealistic results. However the requirement for the 3D information limits its application range.

2.2 Estimation of the Radiance Map

Without 3D information the exact description of the environment illumination will be very difficult. Furthermore without the knowledge of the reflectance, the separation of the illumination from intensity is an ill-posed problem. In order to solve the ill-posed problem we need to put some constrains on it.

From the viewpoint of convolution, the reflection function can be considered as the rotational convolution in the angular space. Then similar to the Fourier basis on the line, the spherical harmonics are the bases on the sphere. Therefore the illumination can be represented through linear combination of spherical harmonic bases $Y_{lm}(\theta, \phi)$ as,

$$L(\theta, \phi) = \sum_{l,m} L_{lm} Y_{lm}(\theta, \phi) \qquad (4)$$

where bases $Y_{lm}(\theta, \phi) = N_{lm} P_l^m(\cos\theta) e^{Im\phi}$ and $N_{lm} = \sqrt{\frac{2l+1}{4\pi} \frac{(l-m)!}{(l+m)!}}$. Ramamoorith [3] points out that the first nine spherical harmonic bases can approximate the radiance map well enough. The average error rate of all the point in the estimated radiance map can be under 3%. In Fig. 2, we give a sample image (a) and its illumination condition estimated by the first nine spherical harmonic bases (b). The estimated lighting map describes the slowly changed information

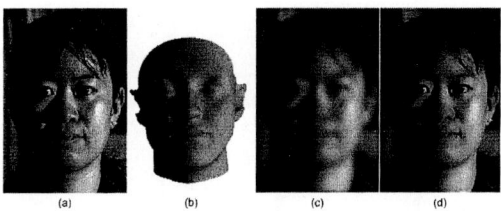

Fig. 2. Estimated radiance maps (a) a sample image (b) estimated radiance map for the sample image by spherical harmonic bases (c) Gauss radiance map (d) Wiener radiance map

of illumination condition but not the abruptly changed information. Therefore the low-frequency part of the illumination condition can account for the radiance map.

Then the radiance map can be estimated from the local information of every point with a proper low-pass filter. And also we should consider of the abrupt changes of the image. When the local variance is larger, the filter should perform little smoothing. When the local variance is small, the filter should perform more smoothing. The Wiener filter is just the filter that can filter out the noise while keeping the signal's original changes. Fig.2 (d) is the result of Wiener filter for the sample image (a). Compared with the Gauss filter result (c), Wiener filter can do the smooth work adaptively to the local variance. Wiener filter also keeps the abrupt changes in original images, which can help to alleviate the halo effect.

2.3 Re-lighting and Compensation

According to the reflection function, the intensity of every point is only decided by the reflectance and the incident lighting. Then when two of these three factors are known, the third one should be calculated out in theory. For example when we know the intensity and radiance map, the reflectance can be represented as,

$$\rho = \frac{I(n)}{E(n)} \qquad (5)$$

Formula (5) describes the basic idea of quotient image (QI) methods [6~8]. In practice, the radiance map is always estimated from image, i.e. $E(n) \approx I(n)$. Then in the smooth region, the estimated reflectance $\hat{\rho} \approx 1$; in the region with changes, the changes will be enlarged. Therefore some bigger changes in original images will be more obvious in the quotient images. Those changes contain the character of the object itself as well the noises caused by non-uniform illumination. Fig.3 gives a sample of face image and their re-lighting results. From the histogram of QI we can see that the dynamic range of the image is suppressed greatly. In a face the skin is very smooth and the local variance is small. But in the QI, the skin will be suppressed to be a same value and the local variance is enlarged. However these low frequency information that describes the

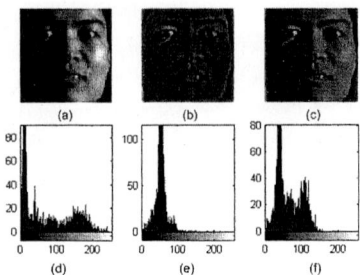

Fig. 3. Face image and re-lighting results. (a) original image, (b) quotient image of (a), (c) the re-lighting and compensation result of (a).(d)∼(f) is the histogram of (a)∼(c), respectively.

slowly changes of the skin also takes its role in representing object and can do help to the detection or recognition tasks.The suppression of that low-frequency information will make the facial features diminished.

From the viewpoint of signal processing, illumination is the amplification for the reflectance. In order to alleviate the illumination influence, we can make the reflectance expressed in a uniform illumination condition. According to the reflection function, we have

$$\rho = \frac{I(n)}{E(n)} = \frac{I'(n)}{E'(n)} \quad (6)$$

Then the image under new illumination condition is

$$I'(n) = \frac{I(n)}{E(n)} E'(n) \quad (7)$$

To avoid doing the direct division of image to radiance map, formula (7) can be rewritten in another form

$$I'(n) = I(n) r_E(n)$$
$$= I(n) \frac{E'(n)}{E(n)} \quad (8)$$

According to formula (8), the image under new illumination condition can be gotten from the product of the original image and the radiance map ratio $r_E(n)$, which is the ratio of new radiance map to original one. The ratio describes the changes of the illumination condition. Intuitively for the information in the shadow region, we want to enlarge absolute value of every point as well the local contrast. And for the highlight region, we want to reduce the brightness and suppress the local contrast. Then the radiance map ratio $r_E(n)$ should enhance the shadow part while suppress the highlight part. The new radiance map can be the inverse of the original one. The inverse lighting will make the shadow part brighter while the highlight part dimmer. Then the new image $I'(n)$ expresses the situation that the object under the inverse illumination environment. With the aim to make the object under uniform illumination condition, we combine the new inverse image $I'(n)$ and original image to alleviate the influence of non-uniform illumination. And these two images should be in the same scale. Therefore the new image should be normalized to the range of [0,255]. The re-lighting and compensated image $I_r(n)$ is

$$I_r(n) = I_{inverse}(n) + I_{original}(n)$$
$$= N(I_{original}(n)\frac{E_{inverse}(n)}{E_{original}(n)}) + I_{original}(n) \qquad (9)$$

where $N(\cdot)$ is the normalizing method that can make the image in the range of [0,255]. In Fig. 3(c), we also give a re-lighting and compensated face image sample. Compared with the quotient image, the compensated image reduces the dynamic range of the original signal but also keeps the original low frequency information.

3 Experiments and Discussions

Before evaluating the proposed re-lighting method, we give out some samples of the illumination adjustment results. In Fig.4(a), we give the results of histogram equalization (HE), quotient image (QI) and the proposed re-lighting and compensation (RC). HE method adjusts the intensity value according to the global intensity distribution. It does not consider the local information, and as a result there is some abrupt noises left in the HE result images. QI methods makes most part of the face same value. In the QI result images, only the great changes are left and much low frequency information is lost. RC method suppresses the dynamic range of the images, i.e. alleviates the influence of non-uniform illumination. RC method can enhance the shadow part and suppress the highlight part as well. Also it can keep the low frequency information.

We evaluate these re-lighting methods as the pre-filter for face detector. The detector is based on Gabor features. We first extract the Gabor features from every test images which are labeled as face and non-face. The boosting method is applied to choose the most discriminative features. Based on these selected features we decide whether the test image contains face or not.

In order to train the face detector, we collect images from more than 12000 images without faces and 10000 faces images. These images were collected by cropping from various sources, such as AR, Rockfeller, FERET, BioID and from WEB [9, 10]. Most faces in the training set have the variation of pose and lighting. A total number of about 80000 face samples with the size of are generated from the 10000 face images by random transformation: mirroring, four-direction shift with 1 pixels, in-plane rotation within 15 degrees and scaling within 20% variations. 20000 face and 20000 non-face samples are chosen randomly to train the face detectors.

The test image is a part of the PIE dataset (C27 series) [11]. According to the illumination condition, we separate it into four subsets. The detail of the

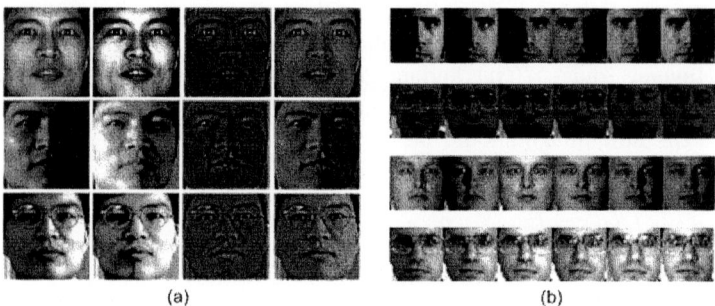

Fig. 4. (a)For every row from left to right, they are the original image and HE, QI, RC results of the original image, respectively; (b)From top to bottom, every row are the sample images of PIE subset 1 to 4, respectively

Table 1. Illumination condition of every PIE subset

	Ambient Light	Flash No.
Subset1	Yes	2,3
	No	2~4 and 19~22
Subset2	Yes	None
Subset3	No	5~18
Subset4	Yes	4~22

Table 2. Detection rate on the PIE datasets

	Subset1	Subset2	Subset3	Subset4
HE	510/88	365/73	821/94	1129/163
QI	553/45	433/5	902/13	1273/19
RC	538/15	438/0	906/9	1278/14

illumination condition is shown in Table 1. Fig.4(b) gives the example images of every subset. In the test procedure, we first apply the re-lighting methods to adjust the lighting condition of the images. Then the adjusted images are sent to the face detector to decide whether it is a face or not. The detection results of face detectors with the HE, QI and RC methods as the pre-filter are shown in Table 2(the value X/Y in the table means true positive/false negative). Compared with HE and QI methods, RC method alleviates the influence of illumination variance, keeps the appearance of the faces which is lost in the QI method and does not bring the abrupt noises that is introduced in HE method. Therefore with the RC method as the pre-filter, the face detector can reduce the number of false negative much more. Especially in the extreme lighting condition, the performance of RC method is much better.

4 Conclusion

Illumination makes the appearance of a same object greatly different. That makes the robust detection a challenging problem. Illumination is too complicated to describe it completely. Due to the reason that the low frequency part of the illumination takes over 90% energy of the overall illumination, the low frequency part can be applied to describe the illumination condition. According to the reflection function, illumination can be considered as the amplification for the reflectance. Given a new radiance map we can re-lighting the image to a new illumination condition with the radiance map ratio. Additionally with the compensation of the original image, the adjusted image can keep the smooth changes of the original image, which will do help to the detection task. In the experiments, we introduce some different illumination correction methods as the pre-filter of the detector. Compared with other methods, the proposed re-lighting and compensation method improve the performance of detector more greatly.

References

1. Belhumeur, P.N. and Kriegman, D. J.: What is the set of images of an object under all possible lighting conditions? IEEE Conference on Computer Vision and Pattern Recognition, (1996)
2. Georghiades, A.S., Kriegman, D.J. and Belhumeur P.N.: Illumination cones for recognition under variable lighting: faces, IEEE conf. Computer Vision and Pattern Recognition, (1998)
3. Ramamoorthi, R. and Hanrahan P.: A Signal-Processing Framework for Inverse Rendering, Proceedings of the 28th annual conference on Computer graphics and interactive techniques, (2001)117-128
4. Ramamoorthi, R. and Hanrahan, P.: On the relationship between radiance and irradiance: determine the illumination from images of a convex Lambertian object, J. Opt. Soc. Am. A, vol. 18, no. 10, (2001)2448-2459
5. Basri, R. and Jacobs, D.: Lambertian reflectance and linear subspaces, IEEE Trans. On Pattern Recognition and Machine Intelligence, vol.25, no. 2, (2003) 218-233
6. Land, E.: The retinex theory of color vision. Sci. Amer. 237,(1977) 10-128
7. Jobson, D. J., Rahman, Z., and Woodell, G.A.: A multiscale retinex of bridging the gap between color images and the human observation of scenes. IEEE Tran. On Images Processing, vol.6, No. 7, (1997)965-976
8. Gross, R. and Brajovic, V.: An image preprocessing algorithm for illumination invariant face recognition. 4th international conference on Audio and Video based Biometric Person Authentication, (2003)10-18
9. Martinez, A.M. and Benavente, R: The AR Face Database. CVC Technical Report #24, (1998)
10. Phillips, P.J., Wechsler, H., Huang, J., and Rauss, P.J.: The FERET database and evaluation procedure for face-recognition algorithms. Image and Vision Computing, 16(5), (1998) 295-306
11. Sim, T., Baker, S., and Bsat, M.: The CMU Pose, Illumination, and expression (PIE) database. Processing of the IEEE International Conference on Automatic Face and Gesture Recognition, (2002)

Shape from Silhouettes in Discrete Space

Atsushi Imiya and Kosuke Sato

Institute of Media and Information Technology, Chiba University,
Yayoi-cho 1-33, Inage-ku, 263-8522, Chiba, Japan

Abstract. Shape from silhouettes is a problem in binary geometric tomography since both objects and projections, which are measured as silhouettes, are binary. In this paper, we formulate shape from silhouettes in two- and three- dimensional discrete spaces. This treatment of the problem implies an ambiguity theorem for the reconstruction of objects in a discrete space. Furthermore, we show that, in the three-dimensional Euclidean space, it is possible to reconstruct a class of non-convex objects from a collection of silhouettes although on a plane non-convex object is unreconstractable from projections.

1 Introduction

Shape reconstruction from silhouette is a conventional technique for the detection of shape models and shape reconstruction in computer graphics, computer vision [1], and robotics [2,3,4,5,6]. Shape reconstruction from silhouette is achieved by visible voting [7], shape carving [1] and so on. Though these reconstruction methods are mathematically formulated in the continuous framework [5,8], the reconstruction is achieved in a discrete space. In this paper, we deal with the shape-from-silhouette problem in a discrete space and describe the problem as a discrete binary geometric tomography since both objects and projections, which are measured as silhouettes, are binary.

In two- and three- dimensional Euclidean space $\mathbf{R}^n$ for $n = 2$ and $n = 3$, respectively, for a finite closed region $\mathbf{O}$, we define the silhouette from a source $s \in \mathbf{R}^n$ as

$$\Omega(s) = \{\omega | l(s) \cap \mathbf{O} \neq \emptyset\}, \tag{1}$$

for the half line

$$l(s) = \{x | x = s + t\omega, \omega \in S^{n-1}, t \geq 0\}, \tag{2}$$

where S^{n-1} is the unit sphere in $\mathbf{R}^n$, that is, S^1 and S^2 are the unit circle and the unit sphere on $\mathbf{R}^2$ and in $\mathbf{R}^3$, respectively. Therefore, the collection of $\Omega(s)$ corresponds to the measurements of ray summations. The cross section of cone $l(s)$, $s \in \Omega(s)$ with hyperplane $s^\top x = d$ is geometrically defined as the silhouette from source s. In this paper, we define the direction of the rays which yield silhouettes as the silhouettes.

If for all s in $\mathbf{R}^n \setminus K$, where K is a finite convex region in $\mathbf{R}^n$, $\Omega(s)$ are measured, we can reconstruct K as

$$K = \bigcap_{s \in \mathbf{R}^n \setminus K} \left(\bigcap_{\omega \in \Omega(s)} \{x | x = s + t\omega\} \right). \tag{3}$$

This is the inversion formula for the reconstruction of an object from silhouettes.

On two-dimensional Euclidean plane, the method is equivalent to the reconstruction of K from support lines as the intersection of half planes. In three-dimensional Euclidean space, for a source s, a set $\Omega(s)$ in S^2 defines a convex cone. This convex cone defines a set of tangent plane to the cone. Then, using these planes, the reconstruction of K in $\mathbf{R}^3$ is also achieved by support planes as the intersection of half spaces.

For a finite convex object K in $\mathbf{R}^3$, if we can detect all planes which intersect with K, we can obtain all rays which pass through K as the intersections of pairs of planes. These rays defines silhouettes. Therefore, this geometrical property implies that we can reconstruct a finite convex object in three-dimensional Euclidean space from the collection of all planes which intersect with this object. In this paper we, deal with the reconstruction problem in two- and three-dimensional discrete spaces $\mathbf{Z}^2$ and $\mathbf{Z}^3$, respectively.

2 Shape Reconstruction on Discrete Plane

On the discrete plane $\mathbf{Z}^2$, three types of discrete lines, for $\gcd(a,b) = 1$,

$$\{(x,y)^\top | 0 \leq a^\top x + \mu < |a|_\infty\}, \tag{4}$$

$$\{(x,y)^\top | 0 \leq a^\top x + \mu < |a|_1\}, \tag{5}$$

$$\{(x,y)^\top | |a^\top x + \mu| \leq \frac{1}{2}|a|_1\}, \tag{6}$$

are dealt with, where for vectors $x = (x,y)^\top$ and $a = (a,b)^\top$, $|a|_\infty = \max(|a|,|b|)$ and $|a|_1 = (|a| + |b|)$. These lines are called naive, standard, and supercover lines on $\mathbf{Z}^2$. For the reconstruction of objects as the intersection of digital half planes, we adopt modified naive and standard lines, which are defined as

$$\{(x,y)^\top | -\frac{1}{2}|a|_\infty \leq a^\top x + \mu < \frac{1}{2}|a|_\infty\}, \tag{7}$$

$$\{(x,y)^\top | -\frac{1}{2}|a|_1 \leq a^\top x + \mu < \frac{1}{2}|a|_1\}, \tag{8}$$

since these modified lines have symmetry for the thickness of discrete lines.

In $\mathbf{Z}^n$ for $n = 2$, instead of the pair of s and $\Omega(s)$, for a line, we detect the pair of s and d, where d lies on the detector. We assume that detector pixels lie on the edges E of the square D^2 whose four vertices are

$$(-3n, -3n)^\top, (3n, -3n)^\top, (3n, 3n)^\top, (-3n, 3n)^\top,$$

and that a discrete object exists in the square R whose four vertices are

$$(-n, n)^\top, (n, -n)^\top, (n, n)^\top, (-n, n)^\top.$$

We assume that our object is a 4-connected simple object. Furthermore, the source pixel moves on the square D^2. Therefore, we can detect collection of discrete half-planes which are separated by line segments connecting two pixels, namely the source s and the detector d on D^2.

Setting $l(s, d)$ to be the line segment in D^2 connecting s and d, for a fixed s, we classify l into three classes

$$l(s,d) \cap R = \emptyset, \ l(s,d) \cap R \neq \partial R, \ l(s,d) \cap R \neq R \setminus \partial R. \tag{9}$$

Following pixels on E from the source s in the counter-clock-wise direction, we set pixels which satisfy the relation

$$l(s,d) \cap R \neq \emptyset \tag{10}$$

as $d = \{d_\perp(s), d_1(s), d_2(s), \cdots, d_\top(s)\}$. We affix the labels for pixels on lines as

$$L(s,d) = \begin{cases} 1, & \text{if } d_i \in l(s,d), \\ 2, & \text{if } d_\perp, d_\top \in l(s,d), \\ 3, & \text{otherwise}. \end{cases} \tag{11}$$

For these labels, we apply the operation

$$L(p) = \max_{s \in D^2} (L(s,d)). \tag{12}$$

This operation classifies the pixels in D^2 as

$$\hat{R} = \{p | L(p) = 1, 2\}, \ \partial \hat{R} = \{p | L(p) = 2\}, \ D \setminus \hat{R} = \{p | L(p) = 3\}. \tag{13}$$

For these pixels, we have the next theorem.

Theorem 1. *If K is the discretisation of a finite convex region in $\mathbf{R}^2$, $\hat{K}$ satisfies the relation*

$$\hat{K} \setminus K \subset (K \oplus N_8 \oplus N_8) \setminus K, \tag{14}$$

where N_8 is the eight-neighbourhood of the origin and $\oplus$ is the Minkowski addition of point sets on $\mathbf{R}^n$.

Since the right-hand-side of eq. (14) is the collection of pixels whose 8-connected distance to K is at most two, this theorem implies that the object $\hat{K}$ reconstructed from the silhouettes encircles the original object K and the difference is the collection of pixels which lie on the discrete closed curve with width two with respect to 8-connected neighbourhood.

From this theorem, in shape carving and visible voting, smoothing and weighting, respectively, are considered as operations to yield K' such that

$$|\hat{K} \Delta K| > |K' \Delta K|, \ K \subseteq K' \subset \hat{K}, \tag{15}$$

where
$$A \Delta B = (A \cap \overline{B}) \cup (\overline{A} \cap B) \tag{16}$$
and $|A|$ is the number of elements in set A. Modified naive and standard lines for the reconstruction eliminate some pixels in $(K \oplus N_8 \oplus N_8) \setminus K$ since these lines have symmetry for the thickness of lines.

3 Reconstruction of Non-convex Object

In this section, we summarise the results in reference [9] on the reconstruction of non-convex object from silhouettes.

Lemma 1. *From the collection of silhouettes which observed from vertices which lie on a sphere encircling this object, we can obtain the collection of 2-dimensional perspective projections of a slice from a point which moves on a circle encircling this object.*

For any points on the boundary, if there exists at least one unique convex slice curve which contains this point, we call this object a slice convex object. A convex closed object is slice convex. This geometric property and Lemma 1 derive the following theorem.

Theorem 2. *A slice convex object is uniquely reconstructible from the collection of silhouettes observed from vertices which lie on the whole sphere encircling this object.*

This theorem permits us for the reconstruction of a class of non-convex objects from silhouettes. Furthermore, in this expression, the axis for the reconstruction is not required to be a straight line.

For a slice convex object V with respect to axis λv_0 for $|v_0| = 1$ and $\lambda \neq 0$, setting $A[v]$ to be a reconstructed object with respect to the axis λv, for $\lambda \neq 0$, we have the following theorem

Theorem 3. *For an object V the relation $V = \cap_{v \in S^2} A[v]$ is satisfied if V is slice convex with respect to axis λv_0.*

If an object is defined as the common region of a finite number of slice convex objects, that is, object V is expressed as $V = \cap_{\alpha=1}^n A[a_\alpha]$, such that $|a_\alpha| = 1$, for $\lambda \neq 0$, where λa_α is the axis with respect to which slices of an object is convex, we have the relation

$$V = \cap_{\alpha=1}^n A[a_\alpha] \supseteq \cap_{v \in S^2} A[\lambda v] \supseteq V. \tag{17}$$

This relation leads to the following theorem.

Theorem 4. *Object V is reconstructed as*

$$V = \cap_{v \in S^2} A[v]. \tag{18}$$

These theorems show that it is possible to reconstruct a slice convex object from silhouettes using the equation

$$\mathbf{O} = \cap_{s \in A} l(s, \mathbf{O}), \tag{19}$$

where A is a closed convex manifold encircles an object $\mathbf{O}$ and $l(s, \mathbf{O})$ is a line which passes through s and satisfies the property $l(s, \mathbf{O}) \cap \mathbf{O} \neq \emptyset$, if we do not detect the axe of a slice convex object. Furthermore, if we can pre-detect axes of slice convex object, we can reconstruct a three-dimensional non-convex object. This property show the difference between shape from silhouettes in 2D and 3D, since, in 2D, the collection of silhouettes does not allow us the reconstruction of non-convex objects.

4 Shape Reconstruction in Discrete Space

In $\mathbf{Z}^3$, we adopt the supercover

$$\begin{aligned}
|ax + bz + \mu_1| &\leq \frac{1}{2}(|a| + |c|), \\
|ay + cz + \mu_2| &\leq \frac{1}{2}(|a| + |b|), \\
|cx - by + \mu_3| &\leq \frac{1}{2}(|b| + |c|),
\end{aligned} \tag{20}$$

and the modified standard

$$\begin{aligned}
-\frac{1}{2}(|a| + |c|) &\leq ax + bz + \mu_1 < \frac{1}{2}(|a| + |c|), \\
-\frac{1}{2}(|a| + |b|) &\leq ay + cz + \mu_2 < \frac{1}{2}(|a| + |b|), \\
-\frac{1}{2}(|b| + |c|) &\leq cx - by + \mu_3 < \frac{1}{2}(|b| + |c|),
\end{aligned} \tag{21}$$

of line in $\mathbf{R}^3$,

$$ax + bz + \mu_1 = 0, \; ay + cz + \mu_2 = 0, \; cx - by + \mu_3 = 0. \tag{22}$$

In $\mathbf{Z}^3$, we assume that detectors are voxels on a cube D^3 whose vertices are

$$(-3n, -3n, -3n)^\top, (-3n, 3n, -3n)^\top, (3n, 3n, -3n)^\top, (3n, -3n, -3n)^\top,$$
$$(-3n, -3n, 3n)^\top, (-3n, 3n, 3n)^\top, (3n, 3n, 3n)^\top, (3n, -3n, 3n)^\top,$$

and an object exits in a cubic region R whose vertices are

$$(-n, -n, -n)^\top, (-n, n, -n)^\top, (n, n, -n)^\top, (n, -n, -n)^\top,$$
$$(-n, -n, n)^\top, (-n, n, n)^\top, (n, n, n)^\top, (n, -n, n)^\top.$$

Source s moves on the faces F of D^3. We assume that our object is 6-connected simple object.

Setting $l(\boldsymbol{s}, \boldsymbol{d})$ to be a line which passes through a fixed source $\boldsymbol{s}$ and a voxel $\boldsymbol{d}$ on D^3, we define a collection of voxels $\boldsymbol{d}$ on D^3 such that

$$\boldsymbol{S} = \{\boldsymbol{d}|l(\boldsymbol{s}, \boldsymbol{d}) \cap \mathbf{O} = \emptyset\} \tag{23}$$

for an object $\mathbf{O}$. A collection of voxels $\boldsymbol{d}$ is the silhouette of object $\mathbf{O}$ with respect to the source $\boldsymbol{s}$.

The boundary voxels of silhouettes on the detector is computed as

$$\partial \boldsymbol{S} = \{\boldsymbol{S} \setminus (\boldsymbol{S} \ominus N_{26})\} \cap D^3, \tag{24}$$

where $\ominus$ expresses the Minkwoski subtraction operation.

In D^3, for voxels on a line $l(\boldsymbol{s}, \boldsymbol{d})$ with respect to a source $\boldsymbol{s}$, we affix the labels as

$$L(\boldsymbol{s}, \boldsymbol{x}) = \begin{cases} 1, \text{ if } \boldsymbol{x} \in \boldsymbol{S} \setminus \partial \boldsymbol{S} \\ 2, \text{ if } \boldsymbol{x} \in \partial \boldsymbol{S} \\ 3, \text{ otherwise.} \end{cases} \tag{25}$$

Same as the two-dimensional case, for these labels, we apply the operation

$$L(\boldsymbol{p}) = \max_{\boldsymbol{s} \in D^3}(L(\boldsymbol{s}, \boldsymbol{x})). \tag{26}$$

This operation classifies the voxels in D^3 as

$$\hat{R} = \{\boldsymbol{p}|L(\boldsymbol{p}) = 1, 2\}, \ \partial \hat{R} = \{\boldsymbol{p}|L(\boldsymbol{p}) = 2\}, \ D^3 \setminus \hat{R} = \{\boldsymbol{p}|L(\boldsymbol{p}) = 3\}. \tag{27}$$

For these voxels, we have the next theorem.

Theorem 5. *If K is the discretisation of a finite convex region in $\mathbf{R}^2$, $\hat{K}$ satisfies the relation*

$$\hat{K} \setminus K \subset (K \oplus N_{26} \oplus N_{26}) \setminus K, \tag{28}$$

where N_{26} is the 26-neighbourhood of the origin.

Furthermore, the labelling operation in $\mathbf{Z}^3$ allows us to reconstruct a class of non-convex objects as discussed in the previous section.

5 Examples

In this section, we show four examples.

1. Reconstruction of a convex object on a plane, which shows ambiguity properties. The results are shown in Figure 1.
2. Reconstruction of a slice convex object from rays, without pre-detecting axes. The results are shown in Figure 2.
3. Reconstruction of a slice convex object as the intersection of objects reconstructed using 2D method in each slice. The results are shown Figure 3.
4. Comparison of 3D reconstructed objects using supercover, standard, and naive lines. The results are shown in Figure 4.

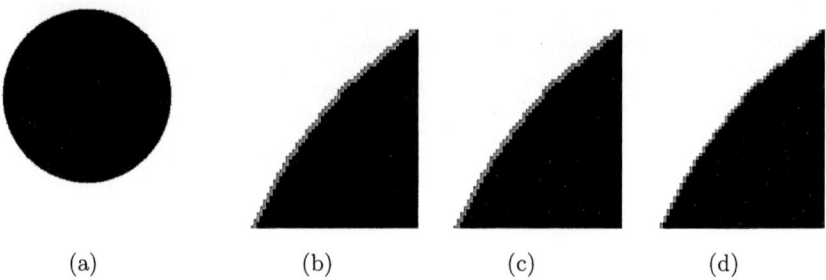

Fig. 1. Reconstruction of Convex Object in 2D. (a) Reconstructed object by supercover. (b) Expanded part of the reconstructed object by supercovers. (c) Expanded part of the reconstructed object by standard lines. (d) Expanded part of the reconstructed object by naive lines.

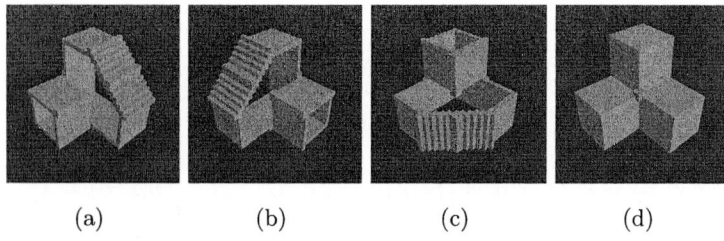

Fig. 2. Reconstruction of Non-Convex Object as the Intersection of Slice Convex Objects. (d) is the intersection of (a)(b),and (c)

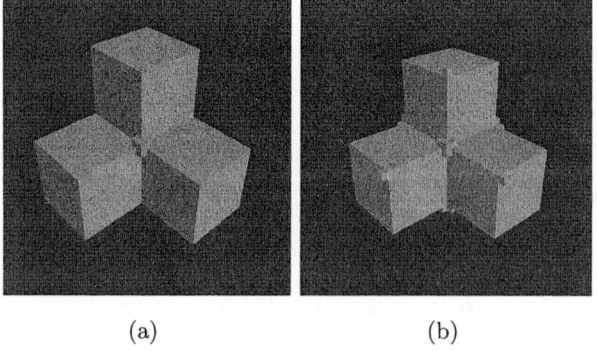

Fig. 3. Reconstruction of Non-Convex Object. (a) Multi-slice Method and (b) Line Voting.

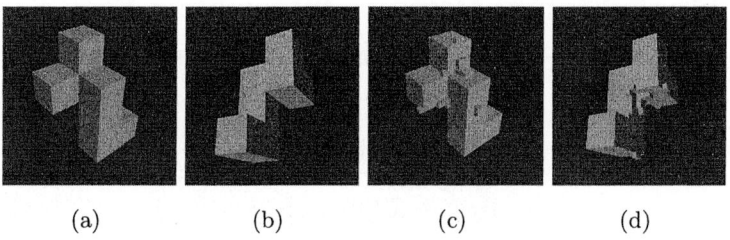

Fig. 4. Reconstruction of Non-Convex Object by Line Voting. (a) and (b) are views of the original object. (c) and (d) are the corresponding views of the reconstructed object.

6 Conclusions

In this paper, we formulated shape from silhouettes in two- and three- dimensional discrete space. This treatment of the problem implied an ambiguity theorem for the reconstruction of objects in discrete space. To reduce the ambiguity of the reconstructed shapes, we introduced a modified naive and standard models discrete lines in both two- and three- dimensional spaces.

References

1. Kutulakos, K., Seitz,S. M., A theory of shape by space carving, Proceedings of 7th ICCV, **1**, 307-314, 1999.
2. Skiena, S. S., Interactive reconstruction via geometric probing, IEEE Proceedings, **80**, 1364-1383, 1992.
3. Skiena, S. S., Probing convex polygon with half-planes, Journal of Algorithms, **12**, 359-374, 1991.
4. Li, R. S.-Y. Reconstruction of polygons from projections, Information Processing Letters, **28**, 235-240, 1988.
5. Prince, J. L., Willsky, A.S., Reconstructing convex sets from support line measurements, IEEE Trans. PAMI, **12**, 377-389, 1990.
6. Rao A. S., Goldberg, Y. K., Shape from diameter: Recognizing polygonal parts with parallel-jaw gripper, International Journal of Robotics Research, **13**, 16-37, 1994.
7. Kawamoto, K., Imiya, K., Detection of spatial points and lines by random samping and voting process, Pattern Recognition Letters, **22**, 199-207, 2001.
8. Imiya, A., Kawamoto, K., Shape reconstruction from an image sequences, Lecture Notes in Computer Sceince, **2059**, 677-686, 2001.
9. Imiya, A., Kawamoto, K., Mathematical aspects of shape reconstruction from an image sequence, Proc. 1st Int'l. Symp. 3D data Processing Visualization and Transformations, 632-635, 2002.

Multiple Feature Domains Information Fusion for Computer-Aided Clinical Electromyography

Hongbo Xie[1,2], Hai Huang[2], and Zhizhong Wang[2]

[1] Department of Computation Science, Huaiyin Institute of Technology, Huaian,
223300, PR of China
[2] Department of Biomedical Engineering, Shanghai Jiao Tong University,
200030, PR of China
xiehb2008@hotmail.com

Abstract. The conventional neural networks methods of motor unit action potential analysis in clinical Electromyography are mainly based on single feature set model, the diagnosis accuracy of which is not always satisfactory. In order to utilize multiple feature sets to improve diagnosis accuracy, a hybrid decision support system based on fusion of multiple feature sets classification outputs is presented. Back-propagation (BP) neural network is used as single diagnosis model in every feature set, i.e. i) time domain morphological measures, ii) frequency parameters, and iii) time-frequency domain wavelet transform feature set. Then these outputs are combined by a modified fuzzy integral method to obtain the consensus diagnosis result. More excellent diagnosis yield indicates the potential of the proposed multiple feature domain strategies for aiding the neurophysiologist in the early and accurate diagnosis of neuromuscular disorders. The method is also compared with the majority vote combination scheme.

1 Introduction

The motor unit is the smallest functional unit of the muscle. The motor unit action potential (MUAP) is recorded that reflects the electrical activity of a single anatomical motor unit, the procedure known as electromyography (EMG). The MUAP findings are used to detect and describe different neuromuscular disease [1]. With the development of quantitative EMG techniques, some automated decision making system of neuromuscular disorder diagnosis have emerged. Neural network based MUAPs classification system has been used to give a more standardized, sensitive and specific evaluation of the neurophysio-logical findings. The networks used include back-propagation, the radial basis function network, and the self-organizing feature map network [2-4]. The feature sets used as network input include time domain parameters, frequency domain parameters, AR coefficients, cepstral coefficients, wavelet transform coefficients. However, the MUAP is a complicated physiological electric action with low amplitude. Moreover, the different force, muscles, and difference of the number of activated fibers render different MUAP from person to person. It is very difficult to extract one feature domain parameters which reflect the unique feature of the complicated neuromuscular action for all persons. The problem is currently solved with not very satisfactory accuracy by using these single neural networks classifiers of different architectures and based on different sets of features. So, it is desirable to utilize multiple domain information from different points to represent and analysis MUAPs in clinical electromyography.

On the other hand, it is well known that in many situations combination the outputs of several neural network classifiers with different feature inputs lead to an improved classification result. This happens because each network makes errors on a different region of the input space. Till now, many methods to combine the outputs of several individual neural networks have been developed, such as majority vote, Borda count, and Dempster-Shafer (D-S) evidence accumulation, etc [5].

In this paper, we propose to utilize the multiple MUAPs feature domain information, for improving the diagnostic performance in computer-aid clinical electromyography. A modified fuzzy integral combination scheme, which considers the difference of performance of each feature domain classification network in combination, is adopted in the system. The paper is organized as follows. Section 2 presents the modified fuzzy integral fusion method that considers the difference of performance of each network in combining the networks in detail. Section 3 describes MUAP feature sets used as neural networks inputs and Section 4 covers the experimental results for the assessment of normal subjects (NOR) and subjects suffering with myopathy (MYO) and motor neuron disease (MND) with the fuzzy integral fusion method, and the results are also compared with the majority vote. At last, section 5 the discussion and concluding remarks.

2 Combination Scheme Based on Modified Fuzzy Integral Theory

2.1 The Fuzzy Integral Theory

A set function $g: 2^Y \rightarrow [0,1]$ with $g(\phi) = 0$, $g(Y) = 1$ and $g(A) < g(B)$ if $A \subset B$, is said a fuzzy measure. From this definition, Sugeno [6] introduced the so-called g_λ-fuzzy measure which comes with an additional property

$$g(A \cup B) = g(A) + g(B) + \lambda_g g(A) g(B) \quad (1)$$

for all $A, B \subset X$ and $A \cap B = \phi$, and for some $\lambda > -1$.

Let $Y = \{y_1, y_2, \cdots, y_n\}$ be a finite set and let $g^i = g(\{y_i\})$. The values g^i are called the densities of measure. λ is given by solving the equation

$$\lambda + 1 = \prod_{i=1}^{n}(1 + \lambda g^i) \quad (2)$$

where $\lambda \in (-1, +\infty)$ and $\lambda \neq 0$.

It affords that the measure of the union of two disjoint subsets can be computed from the component measures.

Let Y be a finite set and $h: Y \rightarrow [0,1]$ a fuzzy set of Y. The fuzzy integral over Y of the function h with respect to a fuzzy measure g is defined by

$$h(y) \circ g(\cdot) = \max_{E \subseteq Y}[\min(\min_{y \in E} h(y), g(E))]$$
$$= \max_{\alpha \in [0,1]}[\min(\alpha, g(F_\alpha))] \qquad (3)$$

where $F_\alpha = \{y \mid h(y) \geq \alpha\}$

When Y is a finite set, the calculation of the fuzzy integral is easily given. Let $Y = \{y_1, y_2, \cdots, y_n\}$ and $h: Y \to [0,1]$ be a function. Suppose $h(y_1) \geq h(y_2) \geq \cdots \geq h(y_n)$, (if not, Y is rearranged so that this relation holds). Then a fuzzy integral e, with respect to a fuzzy measure g over Y can be computed by

$$e = \max_{i=1}^{n}\{\min(h(y_i), g(A_i))\} \qquad (4)$$

where $A_i = \{y_1, y_2, \cdots, y_i\}$.

When g is a g_λ-fuzzy measure, the values of $g(A_i)$ can be calculated recursively as

$$g(A_1) = g(\{y_1\}) = g^1 \qquad (5)$$

$$g(A_i) = g^i + g(A_{i-1}) + \lambda g^i g(A_{i-1}) \qquad (6)$$

where $1 < i < n$

In terms of multiple evidences combination, a more explicit understanding over the fuzzy integral is given as following [7]:

When Y is a set of evidence sources, $h(y_i)$ could be interpreted as an evaluation of how certain we are about decision proposition of the evidence toward the final evaluation. If an evidence subset $A \subset Y$ is considered, $\min_{y \in A} h(y)$ may be regard as the most conservative evaluation that this subset gives about decision proposition. $g(A)$ indicates the degree of importance of the subset A toward the final evaluation. The fuzzy integral could be interpreted as searching for the maximal grade of agreement between the objective evidence and the expectation.

2.2 Modified Combination Algorithm by Fuzzy Integral

Given K diagnosis propositions by $\Theta = \{A_1, A_2, \cdots, A_K\}$, $A_j = X \in C_j$, $\forall j \in \Lambda$, which respectively denote that the input sample X belongs to the category C_j. For the input sample X, M neural networks are considered and each of them will produce a confidence value for each class. These networks are represented by the integral set Y above. Those confidence values are represented by the function h about the decision proposition. On the other hand, the output of each network in corresponding feature domain will present an evidence about the final diagnosis evaluation. The output, O_{ij}, $(i = 1, 2, \cdots, M; j = 1, 2, \cdots K)$ is just an appropriate evaluation that the evidence in domain i about proposition A_j. So, it is reasonable to take O_{ij} as $h_j(x_i)$ [7].

The fuzzy density is an important parameter in the algorithm and fluctuates by the influence of parameter λ. It indicates the worth of various 'expert' for the diagnosis proposition. The conventional methods often take the diagnosis accuracy of each network as this degree of importance, i.e. the fuzzy densities, $\{g^i : i = 1,2,\cdots,M\}$, could be obtained by network test in various feature domains. However, in many situations, even for on features domains, its classification power to different classes is also various. So, in the present work, we propose a modified method to determine parameter λ. We utilize the diagnosis accuracy of each network for each class to determine λ_{ji}, not simply using the diagnosis accuracy of each network to obtain parameter λ_i ($i = 1,2,\cdots,M; j = 1,2,\cdots K$). Then λ_{ji} is applied to Eq.(5) and Eq.(6) to calculate the fuzzy measure. Given the fuzzy densities, the parameter λ could be determined by Eq. (4).

Now, we can calculate the fuzzy integral e_j over Y of the functions, $\{h_j : j = 1,2,\cdots,K\}$, with respect to the fuzzy densities, $\{g^i : i = 1,2,\cdots,M\}$ by

$$e_j = \sum_{i=1}^{M}[\min(h_j(x_i), g(A_i))] \tag{7}$$

The overall confidence for the class is the fuzzy integral. The class with the largest integral value can be taken as the final diagnosis result.

3 MUAP Features Sets

Motor Neuron Disease (MND) is a disease causing selective degeneration of the upper and lower motor neuron. This disease affects middle to old-aged people, with progressive widespread loss of motor neurons usually leading to death within three to five years. In the advanced stages of this disease, large motor units also denervate. Motor unit potentials with duration values that are longer than normal and with increased amplitude are typical findings in MND. Their occurrence reflects an increase in the number or density of fibers in motor units, or increased temporal dispersion of the activity picked up by the recording electrode.

Myopathy (MYO) is a group of diseases that affect primarily skeletal muscle fibers and are divided into two groups, according to whether they are inherited or acquired. Most muscular dystrophies are hereditary, causing severe degenerative changes in the muscle fibers. They show a progressive clinical course from birth or after a variable period of apparently normal infancy. MUAP's with short duration and reduced amplitude are typical findings in patients suffering from myopathy. These findings are attributed to fiber loss within the motor unit, with the degree of reduction of these parameters reflecting the amount of fiber loss.

In this study, the EMG signal is acquired from the biceps brachii muscle using a concentric needle electrode. The template matching method was used to identify twenty MUAPs recorded from the motor unit. Three various MUAP feature set parameters are considered as neural network inputs.

3.1 Time Domain Morphological Parameters

As shown in Figure.1, the features measured from each MUAP in time domain include [4, 8]:

1) Duration: (*Dur*), beginning and ending of the MUAP are identified by sliding a measuring window of 3ms in length and 10uV in width;
2) Spike duration: (SpDur), measured from the first to the last positive peak;
3) Amplitude: (*Amp*), maximum peak to peak measure of the MUAP;
4) Area: sum of the rectified MUAP integrated over the duration;
5) Spike area: (*SpArea*), sum of the rectified MUAP integrated over the spike duration;
6) Phase: (*Ph*), number of the baseline crossings that exceed $25\mu V$, plus one;
7) Turns: (*T*), number of positive and negative peaks separated from the preceding and following peak by $25\mu V$.

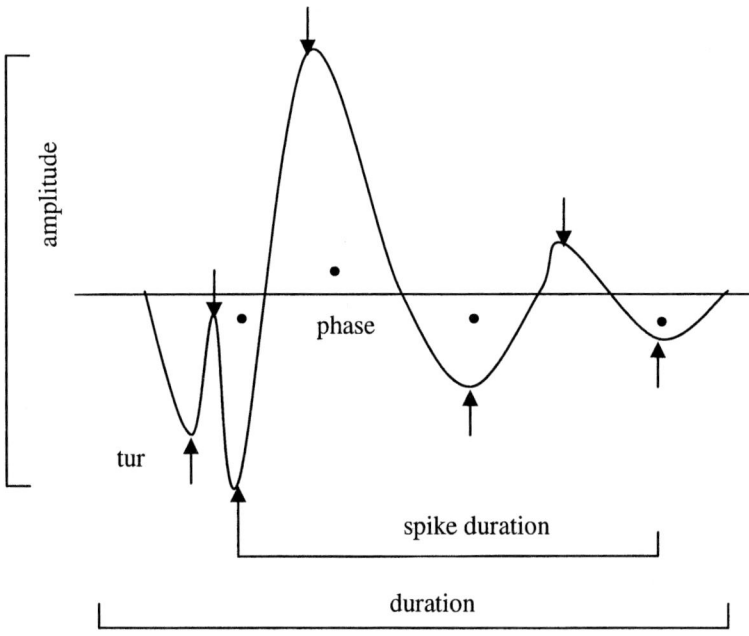

Fig. 1. MUAP morphological parameters

3.2 Frequency Domain Parameters

The frequency parameters of MUAP are derived from its autoregressive (AR) model. The AR model of a signal is given by:

$$x(k) = \sum_{i=1}^{M} a_i x(k-i) + e(k) \qquad (8)$$

where $x(k)$ is the signal we want to model, a_i are the coefficients of the AR model signal, M is the order of the AR model of the signal, and $e(k)$ is the white noise. According to the Akaike's information criterion, the AR model of order 11 is usually used for MUAP processing. Several techniques are available for estimating the parameters of an autoregressive random process. We use the Fast Transversal Filters (FTF) algorithm, which presents highly desirable characteristics in terms of numerical stability and time of convergence [9]. After the AR coefficients a_i of each MUAP are estimated, then it was normalized with its maximum power value. The following frequency domain spectral parameters are computed from the AR power spectrum curve [10].

1) Bandwidth (*BW*) is the difference of frequencies at the upper (F_2) and lower (F_1), 3dB points of the power spectrum and is given as:

$$BW = F_2 - F_1 \qquad (9)$$

2) Quality factor (*Q*) is the ratio of the dominant peak frequency F_0 divided by *BW* and is expressed as:

$$Q = \frac{F_0}{BW} \qquad (10)$$

3) Moments of order 0, 1 and 2: A moment M_j of order j is defined as given by Lindstrom and Petersen [7]:

$$M_j = \frac{2}{(2\pi)^{j+1}} \sum_{n=0}^{N-1} f(n)^j P_{AR}(f(n)) \qquad (11)$$

4) Median frequency (*FMED*) is the frequency at which the power spectrum is divided into two regions with equal power defined as:

$$\sum_{n=0}^{FMED} P_{AR}(f(n)) = \sum_{FMED}^{N-1} P_{AR}(f(n)) \qquad (12)$$

5) Maximum frequency (*FMAX*) is the frequency with the maximum power.

3.3 Time-Frequency Domain Wavelet Transform Energy Coefficients

Wavelet transform gives the information of the signal localized in both time and frequency domain. The wavelet transform of the signal $x(t)$ is defined as:

$$W(s,\tau) = \frac{1}{\sqrt{s}} \int x(t) \psi(\frac{t-\tau}{s}) dt \qquad (13)$$

where mother wavelet ψ is scaled by parameter s and translated by τ. The result of such decomposition is a series of "*detail*" coefficients d_j and approximation coefficients a_j. Here, the index j represents the decomposition level. In our study, Daubechies 4 mother wavelet is selected and the energy in each frequency band, i.e. d_1 to d_6 and a_6 is computed by summing the coefficients square of each frequency band. Then, the normalized percentage wavelet energy of each frequency band is used as time-frequency domain feature set.

4 Experiment and Results

There was a total of 80 subjects corresponding to 3 situations, 20 normal, 30 suffering motor neuron disease and 30 myopathy, involving in the experiment. Informed consents were provided by all subjects. The data are recorded from the biceps brachii of each subject at Hua Shan Hospital, Shanghai. Three back-propagation neural networks are chosen as the single model classifier of corresponding feature set. For each single network, the average vector of 20 MUAPs per subject for each feature set is computed as input. The conjugate gradient method is used in training to improve the convergence. Training and testing of the neural network are all completed using the Matlab neural network toolbox. The architecture of the networks is determined as follows:

1) NN1-network: $7\times7\times3$. The inputs are the aforementioned time domain morphological parameters' means of 20 MUAP per subject.
2) NN2-network: $7\times7\times3$. Frequency domain seven parameters.
3) NN3-network. $7\times7\times3$. Normalized percentage value of wavelet energy coefficients d_1 to d_6 and a_6

15 subjects of each category are extracted randomly to compose the training set. The mean value of there feature domain for the NOR, MND, and MYO groups of the train set are given in Table 1, Table 2, and Table 3. The others are used as testing set. In order to verify the effectiveness and robustness of the multiple neural networks diagnosis approach, bootstrap resample technique is used to obtain 6 different training and testing samples [11]. The output in each network of corresponding feature set presents an evidence about the final diagnosis evaluation. After training the three neural networks, we obtain the diagnosis performance of the various neural networks. The mean diagnosis accuracy of various feature parameters is shown in table 4. Then, utilizing the outputs and diagnosis accuracy of each neural network for each class, the consensus diagnosis result could be calculated. The diagnosis yields based on fuzzy integral and majority vote are also shown in Table 4.

Table 1. The mean value of morphological parameters for the train sets of three groups

	Duration ms	Spike Duration ms	Amplitude mV	Area mVms	Spike Area mVms	Phases	Turns
NOR	8.73	4.92	0.342	0.337	0.221	2.5	2.9
MND	12.27	6.25	0.568	0.758	0.475	4.1	4.5
MYO	6.58	3.96	0.301	0.223	0.149	2.6	3.3

Table 2. The mean value of frequency domain parameters for the train sets of three groups

	M_0 mV^2	M_1 $mV^2/s *10^3$	M_2 $mV^2/s^2 *10^6$	FMED Hz	FMAX Hz	Bandwidth Hz	Quality factor
NOR	9.24	13.95	22.46	399	202	507	0.44
MND	14.97	8.92	12.84	305	197	388	0.80
MYO	27.15	26.01	40.28	622	423	778	0.66

5 Discussion and Conclusions

The multiple feature domains consensus diagnosis based on fuzzy integral is investigated in this study for the assessment of MUAPs recorded from NOR, MND, and MYO subjects. When the single feature set is used, the morphological feature gives the highest diagnostic yield, followed by time-frequency parameters. Frequency domain feature gives the worst classification performance. There has been no one feature set has performed consistently highly for all trails and none of them is good enough to be employed in practice. This may due to the fact that MUAPs are modified by various neural, physiological and physical factors. It is difficult to extract the feature domain parameters which reflect the unique feature of the measured MUAPs. So, one can hardly say that a specific MUAP feature sets will give high discriminant power consistently. Compared to the above single domain method, the proposed multiple feature domains consensus diagnosis strategy based on fuzzy integral achieves a highly accurate and more consistent diagnosis result. This happens for the hybrid system utilizing the multiple domain information of the initial data.

For comparison, majority vote is also investigated in the experiment. It gives slight higher accuracy than time domain parameters but lower than fuzzy integral. For the majority vote, the class label assigned to the sample is the one that is most represented in the set of the crisp class labels obtained from all networks. The deficiency is that all networks are treated equally. However, the recognition ability of each feature set in each network is not the same. The fuzzy integral considers the difference of performance of each network in combination. More excellent diagnosis yield indicates the potential of the proposed multiple feature domain strategies for aiding the neurophysiologist in the early and accurate diagnosis of neuromuscular disorders.

Table 3. The mean value of normalized percentage wavelet energy distribution for the train sets of three groups

	d_1	d_2	d_3	d_4	d_5	d_6	a_6
NOR	0.52	1.75	5.95	26.7	18.4	17.7	28.9
MND	0.33	1.27	4.04	15.29	16.56	23.71	38.80
MYO	0.83	3.31	9.77	38.86	22.78	11.48	12.97

In the future work, we will investigate the results of combination some other feature domain parameters, such as cepstral coefficient, short-time Fourier transform coefficient, and wavelet packet transform coefficient of MUAPs. Also, in order to improve the fusion performance, different approach to determine the fuzzy density should be considered.

Table 4. MUAPs diagnosis results based on single network and multiple networks fusion

Network	Accuracy (%)
Time domain feature set	72.38 ± 7.8
Frequency domain feature set	60.48 ± 10.6
Time-frequency domain feature set	65.24 ± 7.1
Fuzzy integral fusion	80.95 ± 6.6
Majority vote	75.22 ± 7.6

References

[1] Stalberg, E., Nandedkar, S.D., Sanders, D.B.: Quantitative Motor unit potential analysis. Clinical Neurophysiology. 13(1996) 401-422
[2] Andreassen, S., Andreassen, S.K., Jensen, F. V.: MUNIN—An expert system for EMG. Electroence Clinical Neurophysiol. 66(1987) S4
[3] Coatrieux, J.L., Toulouse, P., Rouvrais, B: Automatic classification of electromyographic signals. Electroence Clin Neurophysiol. 55(1983) 333-341
[4] Pattichis, C. S., Elia, A.C.: Autoregressive and cepstral analyses of motor unit action potentials. Med Eng Physi. 21(1999) 405-419
[5] Shipp, C.A., Kuncheva, L.I.: Relationships between combination methods and measures of diversity in combining classifiers. Information Fusion. 3(2002) 135-148
[6] Sugeno, M.: Fuzzy measures and fuzzy integrals: a survey. Fuzzy Automata and Decision Processes. Amsterdam. North Holland. (1977)
[7] He, Y.Y., Chu, F.L., Zhong, B.L.: A study on group decision-make based fault multi-symptom- domain consensus diagnosis. Reliability Engineering & System Safety. 74(2001) 43-52
[8] Stalberg, E., Andreassen, S., Falck, B.: Quantitative analysis of individual motor unit potentials: A proposition for standardized terminology and criteria for measurement. Clinl Neurophysiol. 3(1986) 313-348
[9] Cioffi, J.M., Kailath, T.: Fast recursive least-squares traversal filters for adaptive filtering. IEEE Trans Acoust Speech Sig Process. 32(1984) 304-337
[10] Lindsotrm, L., Petersen, I.: Power spectrum analysis of EMG signals and its application. In Desmedt, J.E., eds.: Computer-Aided Electromyography Prog Clin Neurophysiol. Basel, Karger. 10(1983) 1-51
[11] Breiman, L.: Bagging predictors. Machine Learning. 24(1996): 123-140

Color Transfer Using Motion Estimations and Its Application to Video Compression

Ritwik K. Kumar and Suman K. Mitra

Dhirubhai Ambani Institute of Information and Communication Technology,
Gandhinagar – 382009, Gujarat, India
{ritwik_kumar, suman_mitra}@da-iict.org

Abstract. In this paper a novel scheme for colored video compression using color transfer techniques is proposed. Color transfer for video sequences is made more accurate by incorporation of motion information in the transfer mechanism. Encoder and decoder architectures for the proposed compression scheme are also presented. Compression is achieved by firstly discarding chrominance information for all but selected reference frames and then using motion prediction and DCT based quantization techniques. While decoding, luminance-only frames are colored using chrominance information from the reference frames using the proposed color transfer technique. Furthermore, this strategy is such that it can be seamlessly integrated with traditional hybrid compression schemes like MPEG1 and H.263.

1 Introduction

Colorization is generally used for increasing visual appeal of grayscale images and perceptually enhancing various single band medical and scientific images. For this, traditional approach is to segment an image into some regions and manually or semi-automatically color it region by region. Obtaining high quality colorization using traditional techniques is extremely time consuming and thus, grossly inefficient for time constrained applications like compression. An attempt to minimize human intervention in colorization process to speed it up was presented by Welsh et al. [1] where they used luminance statistics to colorize grayscale images (target) using some reference color images (source). Unfortunately, empirical evidence suggests that the degree of similarity between the color source and target image has a strong influence on the quality of the results obtained. Thus, obtaining reasonably high quality coloring with the techniques developed in [1] is, in principle, still strongly dependent on human selection of an appropriate source color image for each given grayscale (target) image.

This very property of dependence of results on appropriate source color image can be exploited for video compression as proposed by Rao et al. [2]. The idea is to remove color from all but selected reference frames at the encoder and transfer color (using luminance statistics) to chrominance-less frames using color reference frame at the decoder. The compression is obtained by the fact that chrominance information need not be transferred for all frames between encoder and decoder. They propose retaining color every eighth frame and encoding rest of the frames as luminance only. The quality of color transfer is relatively better in case of video frames because the color source image is generally only a motion displaced version of the target image.

Colorization using color transfer, as proposed in [1], does not produce results of acceptable quality when used as it is for video compression (as proposed in [2]). In this work we propose a novel method of color transfer designed specifically for video sequences using motion information. Also the method proposed by Rao et al. [2] does not exploit temporal and spatial redundancies to achieve higher compression. We present an approach that integrates color transfer, motion prediction and DCT based quantization. The proposed architecture is such that it can be easily integrated with various popular hybrid compression schemes like MPEG1 and H.263, in certain cases without even modifying the file formats.

2 Colorization

2.1 Colorization Technique

Mathematically the coloring problem amounts to replacing each scalar values stored in the grayscale image by a color vector (e.g. mapping from g to RGB or g → [R, G, B], where g is luminance or intensity of a grayscale image and RGB is a three dimensional vector). This is, in general, a severely under-constrained problem with no inherently correct solution. In an attempt to tackle this problem, Reinhard et al. [3] proposed a general scheme for color transfer between two images focusing on "color mood" transfer (e.g. giving a day time image a night time look) between images. Their remarkable achievement was the use of target pixel's luminance value and neighborhood luminance variance to find matching source pixel for color transfer, using $l\alpha\beta$ color space (originally defined by Ruderman et al. in [4]). This technique was adapted by Welsh et al. [1] to transfer color from a color image to a grayscale image. Although before the actual color transfer, Welsh et al. [1] used luminance remapping to linearly shift and scale the luminance histogram of the source image to fit the histogram of the target image. This helped create better correspondence in luminance range between the two images. They also defined the *color-transfer-metric*, weighted average of luminance (50%) and standard deviation (50%), to find the best source pixel for color transfer.

Our approach for color transfer exploits motion information from video to enhance the quality of color transfer. We explore the use of YCbCr color space instead of $l\alpha\beta$ space so as to enable better integration of this technique with existing compression mechanisms which are largely YCbCr based. Exploiting the spatial redundancy in images, we propose transferring color for 2 x 2 pixel block (called pixel-group hereon) at a time instead of pixel-by-pixel. This speeds up the transfer without much loss in quality. Further, as the transfer of color is between two (similar) frames, for each pixel-group in the target image, best match can be found (using *color-transfer-metric*) by searching only a small neighborhood (3 x 3 pixel-groups) in the source image (exploiting the temporal redundancy in videos sequences). The color is transferred pixel-to-pixel from the selected pixel-group to target pixel-group. The luminance value of the target pixel-group is retained. The crucial part of our proposal, which significantly improves the quality of color transfer, is the use of motion estimations in color transfer. We effectively expand the search area for the best match by incorporating the motion flow information. As motion estimates are generally calculated anyway in hybrid compression schemes, no extra overhead is added by incorporating this proposal.

2.2 Color Spaces

$l\alpha\beta$ color space was defined by Ruderman et al. [4] and is such that, all the three channels are uncorrelated to each other unlike RGB and YCbCr. Reinhard et al. [3] and Welsh et al. [1] adapted this color space because in color transfer, chrominance is transferred based on luminance statistics and this demands uncorrelated luminance and chrominance channels so as to avoid cross channel artifacts from creeping in when luminance-chrominance channels are converted back to RGB.

In case of video sequences the source frame and the target frame are similar (assuming same shot) and thus the nature of correlation between luminance and chrominance channels is also similar in both source and target frames. This property in video sequences, by virtue of temporal redundancy, allows correlated color spaces like YCbCr to be used for color transfer because though the cross channels artifacts are induced, these not undesirable artifacts and infact were always present in original image. Further, as our color transfer technique is developed to be used with video compression, in order to keep the encoder and decoder efficient, it is better not to introduce extra transforms to new color spaces.

2.3 Integration with Motion Estimations

Our proposal is independent of the method used for motion estimation and only assumes existence of motion vectors. The quality of color transfer degrades or improves with the quality of motion prediction. In cases where motion is nil, *color-transfer-metric* for the current pixel-group in the target image is matched against corresponding (same pixel row and column) 3 x 3 pixel-groups search space in the source image to find the best pixel-group for color transfer. In cases where motion estimation algorithm detects motion and renders motion vectors to non-zero values, we propose displacement of search space in accordance with motion vectors and then searching for the best match. Note that motion is generally estimated for a larger pixel block size (16 x 16) as compared to our smaller pixel-group size of 2 x 2. Thus the motion vectors need to be appropriately mapped for smaller size pixel-groups. This process effectively pushes the search domain in the direction where the best match is most likely to be found and thus produces better results.

While estimating motion, there exists a possibility that for a given block (16 x 16) no good match can be found in the reference image. This can arise due to various camera movements like panning, zooming out etc. In many popular video compression algorithms such block are intra-coded or stored as it is without using any motion estimates. We propose to adopt this practice for color transfer as well. For blocks that are designated to be intra-coded by the motion estimation process, all color is stored as it is and these blocks are excluded from participating in color transfer process. This was not necessary for works presented in [1] and [3] because there is no "correct" color transfer in color-mood transfers while in case of video, the transfer needs to be near exact. The number of blocks that need to be intra-coded generally increases as the motion between the source and the target frames increases but can be forcibly increased or decreased on cost of quality of color transfer.

Fig. 1. Use of motion estimates in color transfer: First image is the first frame of the 'tennis' video sequence. Second and third images are the eighth frames of this sequence and have been colored using first frame as color source. Second image is colored without using any motion information while third image has been colored using motion information. White boxes in second image shows the color spilling out.

3 Video Compression

3.1 Basic Approach

Though a simple approach for video compression using color transfer was proposed by Rao et al. [2], it does not take advantage of various redundancies present in video sequences. Here we propose an integrated approach towards video compression on lines of hybrid compression mechanism by bringing together color transfer technique, motion prediction and DCT based quantization.

In a typical hybrid video compression scheme, most of the compression is obtained in the last stage – entropy encoding. Stages before this try to render the data to entropy encoder in a form that can be compressed to the maximum. The primary job for these initial stages is to identify and remove redundancies and lesser important components (in case of lossy compression) from the data. Three kinds of redundancies are taken care of in our design. Firstly, the redundant chrominance information is removed at encoder and regenerated at decoder using color transfer technique. Secondly, spatial redundancy is removed at encoder using Discrete Cosine Transform based quantization scheme. Finally, temporal redundancies from the video sequence are removed at encoder using motion prediction. Infact, we use motion vectors generated form motion prediction to our advantage by using them in color transfer.

3.2 Encoder Design

To design the encoder, we borrow the concept of Group of Pictures (GOP) as defined for MPEG1 [5] and extend it to encompass color transfer mechanism. GOP refers to a sequence of frames such that their luminance and chrominance is coded independent of any frame not in GOP. Within a GOP there are three kinds of frames, Intra-coded frames (I), Predicted frames (P) and Bi-directionally predicted or interpolated frames (B). I frames are coded independently of any other frame in GOP. P frames are predicted from previous I or P frames. B frames are predicted from both previous and next I or P frames. Unlike MPEG1, the term prediction here is not limited to luminance based motion prediction but it also include chrominance transfer. For I frames all color information is preserved, for P frames color is transferred from previous I or P frames and for B frames color is transferred from both previous and next I or P frame. The blocks that need to be intra-coded (cannot be predicted) are identified during the prediction of P and B frames. Number of such blocks for P frames tends to be higher than those for B frames as later uses two reference frames.

It must be noted that though luminance based motion prediction from a single I frame may work for up to 16 frames or more but this is not necessarily true for chrominance transfer. Every time color is transferred from one frame to another certain amount of error is induced into the target frame. In present scheme, error is accumulated and passed on from frame to frame. This limits the number of frames to which color can be transferred from a single color source. To handle this, we propose an overlay structure for color transfer which is fully compatible with luminance based GOP structure. For luminance based motion prediction we use I B B P B B P B B P B B P B B P GOP structure while for chrominance transfer we define a new structure **I** B B P B B P B B **P** B B P B B P. The highlighted frames in chrominance GOP represent those frames which have all color information intact (although in highlighted **P** frames chrominance can still be motion predicted from previous I frames) while other P frames are colored from previous (towards left) I or P frame and B frames are colored using previous and next I or P frames. This structure can be changed in application specific manner, even from one GOP to another within a single video sequence.

Compression by virtue of color transfer is obtained as only minimal (for intra-coded blocks) chrominance information is being encoded for all but highlighted **I** and **P** frames. Out of three kind of frames, I frames provide the least amount of compression, followed by P and B frames respectively. Encoder's first stage down-samples chrominance channel for I frames and removes chrominance completely for P and B frames. Then error frames are computed using luminance based motion estimation. After computing error frames (output of prediction stage) the next step is to exploit spatial redundancy to obtain more compression. Two-dimensional frequency decomposition of elementary (8 x 8) pixel blocks is carried out and all but the most prominent frequency coefficients are removed by the process of quantization depending on *quantization scale factor* (QSF). QSF is an integer (1-31) defined for each frame type by which the quantization matrix is scaled. After quantization the blocks are scanned in the 'zig-zag' [5] manner and then entropy coding is used. Fig. 2 shows the encoder architecture.

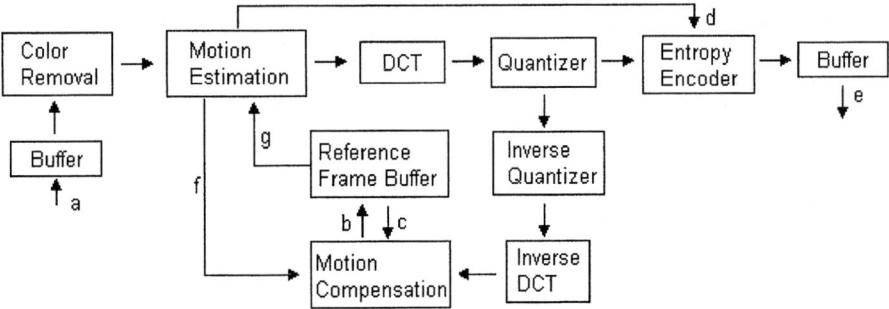

Fig. 2. Encoder Design [a: Uncompressed video, b: Reconstructed frames, c: Reference frame, d: Motion vectors, e: Compressed video stream, f: Motion vectors, g: Reference frame]. Buffers are provided at input and output to handle variable bit rates

3.3 Decoder Design

The decoder is almost a reverse of the encoder except for the fact that this is where the actual color transfer takes place. First of all, entropy encoding is decoded and Inverse Quantization followed by Inverse Discrete Cosine Transform is applied to obtain intra coded frames (I) and error frames (B, P). Then from I frames P frames are derived using motion compensation and then colored using the algorithm described in the section 2. Then all the B frames between the decoded I and P frames are predicted and colored using bi-directional compensation.

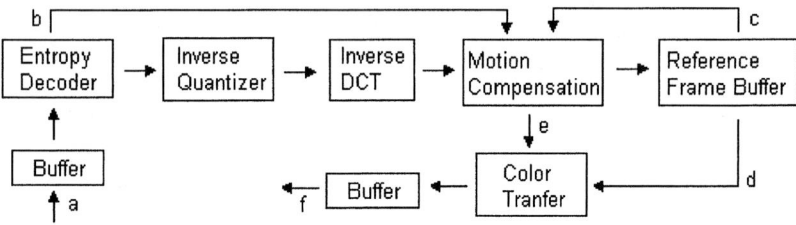

Fig. 3. Video Decoder [a: Compressed video stream, b: Motion vectors, c: Reference frame, d: Color reference frame, e: Luminance-only frame, f: Uncompressed video]. Buffers are provided at input and output to handle variable bit rates

The advantage of this decoder architecture (Fig. 3) is that it can be easily integrated with existing popular video compression schemes. In case of MPEG1, all that is required at encoder is to save no chrominance information for appropriate frames (as described above) and the decoder can be plugged in with a module for color transfer keeping other functionalities intact.

4 Experimental Results

The methodology has been implemented and tested on a set of benchmark video sequences. For the experiments, quantization matrices as defined in [5] and exhaustive block search method for motion estimation were used. For a typical QSF setting (IQSF = 1, PQSF=8, BQSF=16), quality loss (PSNR) for Y channel is 0 db, for Cb channels 0.65 db and for Cr channel 0.47 db as compared to MPEG1 with almost no visually detectable difference in quality. Our approach outperforms MPEG1 for typical settings by 1 to 14 percent in terms of compression as shown in Fig. 4. Fig. 5 shows compression across different frame types for various test video sequences. Chrominance bearing I (frame 1) and P (frame 10) frames are coded exactly as in MPEG1 and thus they show no improvement in compression over MPEG1. B frames show more compression than P frames both in absolute terms and relative to MPEG1 due to the fact that they use two reference frames.

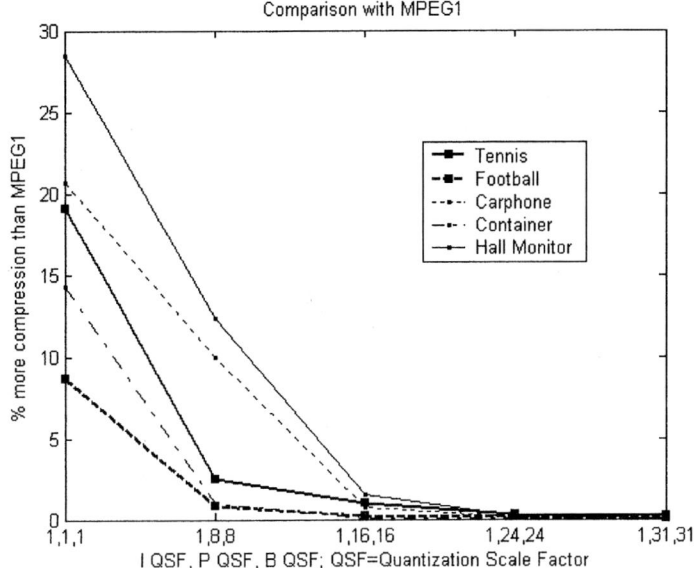

Fig. 4. Performance comparison of proposed scheme with MPEG1 for various video sequences

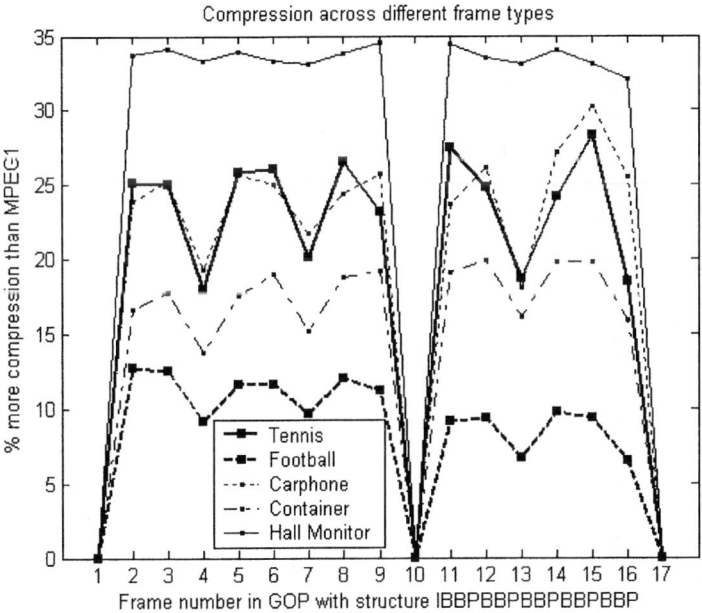

Fig. 5. Performance comparison of proposed method with MPEG1 for all frame types in GOP

5 Conclusion

In this paper we have presented a novel mechanism of color transfer for video frames and there by using it for video compression. We have adapted and evolved the color transfer technique described in [1] for video sequences and have improved the compression mechanism described in [2] to achieve better quality and compression. It has been shown that integration of color transfer with video compression schemes can produce significant improvement in compression without much loss in quality. We proposed an architecture which can easily be integrated with popular hybrid compression schemes, but for this, we had to compromise at certain stages which could have improved compression and quality of color transfer but at loss of execution efficiency e.g. use of YCbCr color space, use of intra-coded blocks, and use of overlay GOP for chrominance transfer. Besides integration with MPEG1, the proposed scheme can be easily extended to be integrated with MPEG2 also.

References

1. Tomihisa Welsh, Michael Ashikhmin and Klaus Mueller, "Transferring color to grayscale images", In proceedings of ACM SIGGRAPH 2003.
2. K. Madhu Sudhana Rao and Suman K. Mitra, "A study of the application of color transfer technique for video compression", In proceedings of 12th International Conference of Advanced Computing and Communication 2004.
3. E. Reinhard, M. Ashikhmin, B. Gooch and P. Shirley, "Color transfer between images", IEEE Computer Graphics and Applications, September/October 2001, 34-40.
4. D. L. Ruderman, T. W. Cronin and C. C. Chiao, "Statistics of Cone Response to Natural images: Implications of Visual Coding", J. Optical Society of America, 1998, vol 15, no. 8, 2036-2045.
5. ISO-IEC/JTV1/SC2/WG11, "MPEG video Committee Draft 11172.2".

Minimum-Length Polygons of First-Class Simple Cube-Curves

Fajie Li and Reinhard Klette

CITR, The University of Auckland, Tamaki Campus, Building 731,
Auckland, New Zealand

Abstract. We consider simple cube-curves in the orthogonal 3D grid. The union of all cells contained in such a curve (also called the tube of this curve) is a polyhedrally bounded set. The curve's length is defined to be that of the minimum-length polygonal curve (MLP) fully contained and complete in the tube of the curve. So far only one general algorithm called rubber-band algorithm was known for the approximative calculation of such an MLP. A proof that this algorithm always converges to the correct curve, is still an open problem. This paper proves that the rubber-band algorithm is correct for the family of first-class simple cube-curves.

1 Introduction

The analysis of cube-curves is related to 3D image data analysis. A cube-curve is, for example, the result of a digitization process which maps a curve-like object into a union S of face-connected closed cubes. The definition of length of a simple cube-curve in 3D Euclidean space can be based on the calculation of the minimal length polygonal curve (MLP) in a polyhedrally bounded compact set [3,4].

The computation of the length of a simple cube-curve in 3D Euclidean space was a subject in [5]. But the method may fail for specific curves. [1] presents an algorithm (rubber-band algorithm) for computing the approximating MLP in S with measured time $O(n)$, where n is the number of grid cubes of the given cube-curve.

The difficulty of the computation of the MLP in 3D may be illustrated by the fact that the Euclidean shortest path problem (i.e., find a shortest obstacle-avoiding path from source point to target point, for a given finite collection of polyhedral obstacles in 3D space and a given source and a target point) is known to be NP-complete [8]. However, there are some algorithms solving the approximate Euclidean shortest path problem in 3D with polynomial-time, see [9]. The rubber-band algorithm is not yet proved to be always convergent to the correct 3D-MLP.

Recently, [6] developed of algorithm for calculation of the correct MLP (with proof) for a special class cube-curves. The main idea is to decompose a cube-curve into arcs by finding "end angles" (see Definition 3 below).

More recently, [7] constructed an example of a (special - see title of reference) simple cube-curve, and generalized this by characterizing the class of all of those cube-curves. In particular, it is true that these cube-curves do not have any end angle; and this means that we cannot use the MLP algorithm proposed in [6] which is provable correct. This was the basic importance of the result in [7]: we showed the existence of cube-curves which require further algorithmic studies.

Both [6] and [7] focus on a special class of simple cube-curves which are called first-class simple cube-curves (defined below). This paper proves that the rubber-band algorithm is correct for first-class simple cube-curves.

The paper is organized as follows: Section 2 defines the notations used in this paper. Section 3 describes theoretical proofs of our results. Section 3 discusses the computational complexity. Section 4 gives the conclusions.

2 Definitions

Following [1], a grid point $(i, j, k) \in \mathbb{Z}^3$ is assumed to be the center point of a *grid cube* with *faces* parallel to the coordinate planes, with *edges* of length 1, and *vertices* as its corners. *Cells* are either cubes, faces, edges, or vertices. The intersection of two cells is either empty or a joint *side* of both cells. A *cube-curve* is an alternating sequence $g = (f_0, c_0, f_1, c_1, \ldots, f_n, c_n)$ of faces f_i and cubes c_i, for $0 \leq i \leq n$, such that faces f_i and f_{i+1} are sides of cube c_i, for $0 \leq i \leq n$ and $f_{n+1} = f_0$. It is *simple* iff $n \geq 4$ and for any two cubes $c_i, c_k \in g$ with $|i - k| \geq 2$ (mod $n + 1$), if $c_i \cap c_k \neq \phi$ then either $|i - k| = 2$ (mod $n + 1$) and $c_i \cap c_k$ is an edge, or $|i - k| \geq 3$ (mod $n + 1$) and $c_i \cap c_k$ is a vertex.

A *tube* **g** is the union of all cubes contained in a cube-curve g. A tube is a compact set in $\mathbb{R}^3$, its frontier defines a polyhedron, and it is homeomorphic with a torus in case of a simple cube-curve. A curve in $\mathbb{R}^3$ is *complete* in **g** iff it has a nonempty intersection with every cube contained in g. Following [3,4], we define:

Definition 1. *A minimum-length polygon (MLP) of a simple cube-curve g is a shortest simple curve P which is contained and complete in tube **g**. The length of a simple cube-curve g is defined to be the length $l(P)$ of an MLP P of g.*

It turns out that such a shortest simple curve P is always a polygonal curve, and it is uniquely defined if the cube-curve is not only contained in a single layer of cubes of the 3D grid (see [3,4]). If it is contained in one layer, then the MLP is uniquely defined up to a translation orthogonal to that layer. We speak about *the* MLP of a simple cube-curve.

A *critical edge* of a cube-curve g is such a grid edge which is incident with exactly three different cubes contained in g.

Definition 2. *If e is a critical edge of g and l is a straight line such that $e \subset l$, then l is called a* critical line *of e in g or critical line for short.*

Definition 3. *Assume a simple cube-curve g and a triple of consecutive critical edges e_1, e_2, and e_3 such that $e_i \perp e_j$, for all $i, j = 1, 2, 3$ with $i \neq j$. If e_2 is parallel to the x-axis (y-axis, or z-axis) implies that the x-coordinates (y-coordinates, or z-coordinates) of two vertices (i.e., end points) of e_1 and e_3 are* equal, then we say that e_1, e_2 and e_3 form an end angle, and g has an end angle, denoted by $\angle(e_1, e_2, e_3)$; otherwise we say that e_1, e_2 and e_3 form a middle angle, and g has a middle angle.

Definition 4. *A simple cube-curve g is called* first-class *iff each critical edge of g contains exactly one vertex of the MLP of g.*

Figure 1 shows a first-class simple cube-curve (left) and a non-first-class simple cube-curve (right). Because the vertices of the MLP must be in e_0, e_1, e_3, e_4, e_5, e_6 and e_7. In other words, the critical edge e_2 does not contain any vertice of the MLP of this simple cube-curve.

The rubber-band algorithm is published in [1].

Definition 5. *One iteration of rubber-band algorithm is a complete pass through the main loop of the algorithm.*

Let g be a simple cube-curve. Let $AMLP_n(g)$ be an n-polygon of g, where $n = 1, 2, \ldots$. Let $AMLP = \lim_{n \to \infty} AMLP_n(g)$. Let $p_i(t_{i_0})$ be the i-th vertex of $AMLP$, where $i = 0, 1, \ldots,$ or $m+1$. Let $d_i = d_e(p_{i-1}, p_i) + d_e(p_i, p_{i+1})$, where $i = 1, 2, \ldots,$ or m. Let $d(t_0, t_1, \ldots, t_m, t_{m+1}) = \sum_1^m d_i$.

Definition 6. *Let e_0, e_1, e_2, ... e_m and e_{m+1} be all consecutive critical edges of g and $p_i \in e_i$, where $i = 0, 1, 2, \ldots, m$ or $m+1$. We call the $m+2$ tuple $(p_0, p_1, p_2, \ldots, p_m, p_{m+1})$ a critical point tuple of g. We call it an AMLP critical point tuple of g if it is the set of the vertices of an AMLP of g.*

Definition 7. *Let $P = (p_0, p_1, p_2, \ldots, p_m, p_{m+1})$ be a critical point tuple of g. Using P as an initial point set, and n iterations of the rubber-band algorithm, we get another critical point tuple of g, say $P' = (p'_0, p'_1, p'_2, \ldots, p'_m, p'_{m+1})$. The polygon with vertice set $\{p'_0, p'_1, p'_2, \ldots, p'_m, p'_{m+1}\}$ is called an n-polygon of g, denoted by $AMLP_n(g)$, or $AMLP_n$ for short, where $n = 1, 2, \ldots$.*

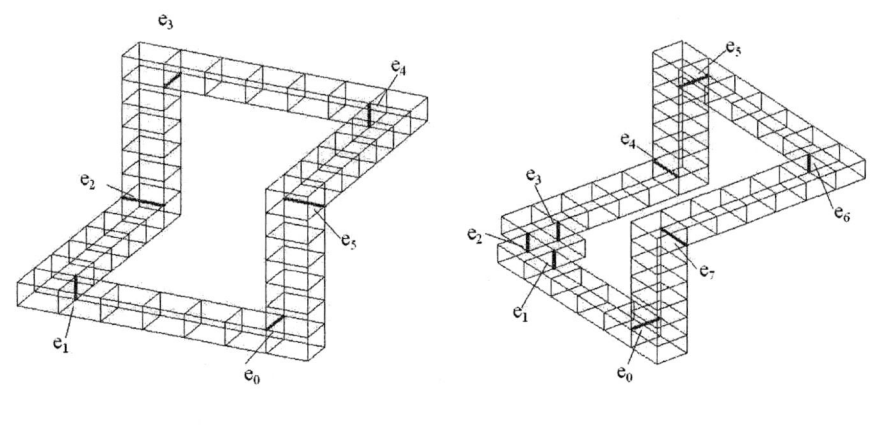

Fig. 1. (1) A first-class simple cube-curve. (2) A non-first-class simple cube-curve.

Definition 8. Let $\frac{\partial d(t_0, t_1, \ldots, t_m, t_{m+1})}{\partial t_i}|_{t_{i0}} = 0$, where $i = 0, 1, \ldots,$ or $m+1$. Then we say that $(t_{00}, t_{10}, \ldots, t_{m0}, t_{m+10})$ is a critical point of $d(t_0, t_1, \ldots, t_m, t_{m+1})$.

Definition 9. Let $P = (p_0, p_1, p_2, \ldots, p_m, p_{m+1})$ be a critical point tuple of g. Using P as an initial point set, n iterations of the rubber-band algorithm, we calculate an n-rubber-band transform of P, denoted by $P\overrightarrow{(r-b)_n}Q$, or $P \to Q$ for short, where Q is the resulting critical point tuple of g, and n is an positive integer.

Definition 10. Let $P = (p_0, p_1, p_2, \ldots, p_m, p_{m+1})$ be a critical point tuple of g. For sufficiently small real $\epsilon > 0$,
 the set
$\{ (p'_0, p'_1, p'_2, \ldots, p'_m, p'_{m+1}) : x'_i \in (x_i - \epsilon, x_i + \epsilon) $ and $y'_i \in (y_i - \epsilon, y_i + \epsilon)$ and $z'_i \in (z_i - \epsilon, z_i + \epsilon)$ and $p'_i = (x'_i, y'_i, z'_i)$ and $p_i = (x_i, y_i, z_i)$, where $i = 0, 1, 2, \ldots, m, m+1 \}$
 is called P's ϵ-Neighborhood, denoted by $U(P, \epsilon)$.

Definition 11. Let n be a positive integer. Let $x = (x_1, x_2, \ldots, x_n)$. Let T be the family of subsets of $\mathbb{R}^n$ defined by : A subset K of $\mathbb{R}^n$ belongs to T iff for each $r = (r_1, r_2, \ldots, r_n)$ in K there are real numbers a_i, b_i such that $a_i < r_i < b_i$ and
$$\{x : x \in \mathbb{R}^n, a_i < x_i < b_i, i = 1, \ldots, n\} \subset K.$$
The topological space $(\mathbb{R}^n, T)$ is called n dimensional usual topology.

Definition 12. ([12], Definition 4.1) Let $Y \subset X$, where (X, T) is a topological space. Let T' be the family of sets defined as follows: A set W belongs to T' iff there is a member U in T such that $W = Y \cap U$. The family T' is called the relativization of T to Y, denoted by $T|_Y$.

3 Proofs

We provide mathematical fundamentals to prove that the rubber-band algorithm is correct for any first-class simple cube-curve. We start with citing a basic theorem from [1]:

Theorem 1. Let g be a simple cube-curve. Critical edges are the only possible locations of vertices of the MLP of g.

Let $d_e(p, q)$ be the Euclidean distance between points p and q.
 Let $e_0, e_1, e_2, \ldots, e_m$ and e_{m+1} be $m+2$ consecutive critical edges in a simple cube-curve, and let $l_0, l_1, l_2, \ldots, l_m$ and l_{m+1} be the corresponding critical lines. We express a point $p_i(t_i) = (x_i + k_{x_i} t_i, y_i + k_{y_i} t_i, z_i + k_{z_i} t_i)$ on l_i in general form, with $t_i \in \mathbb{R}$, where $i = 0, 1, \ldots,$ or $m+1$.
 In the following, $p_i(t_i)$ will be denoted by p_i for short, where $i = 0, 1, \ldots,$ or $m+1$.

Theorem 2. *([10], Theorem 8.8.1) Let $f = f(t_1, t_2, \ldots, t_k)$ be a real-valued function defined on an open set U in $\mathbb{R}^k$. Let $C = (t_{10}, t_{20}, \ldots, t_{k0})$ be a point of U. Suppose that f is differentiable at C. If f has a local extremum at C, then $\frac{\partial f}{\partial t_i} = 0$, where $i = 1, 2, \ldots, k$.*

Lemma 1. *$(t_{0_0}, t_{1_0}, \ldots, t_{m_0}, t_{m+1_0})$ is a critical point of $d(t_0, t_1, \ldots, t_m, t_{m+1})$.*

Proof. $d(t_0, t_1, \ldots, t_m, t_{m+1})$ is differentiable at each point $(t_0, t_1, \ldots, t_m, t_{m+1}) \in [0,1]^{m+2}$. Because $AMLP_n(g)$ is a n-polygon of g, where $n = 1, 2, \ldots$ and $AMLP = \lim_{n \to \infty} AMLP_n(g)$, so $d(t_{0_0}, t_{1_0}, \ldots, t_{m_0}, t_{m+1_0})$ is a local minimum of $d(t_0, t_1, \ldots, t_m, t_{m+1})$. By Theorem 2, $\frac{\partial d}{\partial t_i} = 0$, where $i = 0, 1, 2, \ldots, m+1$. □

Theorem 3. *([7], Theorem 2) If $e_i \perp e_j$, where $i, j = 1, 2, 3$ and $i \neq j$, then e_1, e_2 and e_3 form an end angle iff the equation $\frac{\partial(d_e(p_1,p_2)+d_e(p_2,p_3))}{\partial t_2} = 0$ has a unique root 0 or 1.*

Theorem 4. *([7], Theorem 3) If $e_i \perp e_j$, where $i, j = 1, 2, 3$ and $i \neq j$, then e_1, e_2 and e_3 form a middle angle iff the equation $\frac{\partial(d_e(p_1,p_2)+d_e(p_2,p_3))}{\partial t_2} = 0$ has a root t_{2_0} such that $0 < t_{2_0} < 1$.*

Theorem 5. *([7], Theorem 4) e_0 and e_{m+1} are on different grid plane iff $0 < t_{1_0} < t_{2_0} < \ldots < t_{m_0} < 1$.*

Let $p_i(t_{i_0})$ be i-th vertex of an $AMLP$, where $i = 0, 1, \ldots,$ or $m+1$.
By Lemma 1 and Theorems 3, 4 and 5, we immediately prove the following theorem.

Theorem 6. *If e_{i-1}, e_i and e_{i+1} form an end angle, then $t_{i_0} = 0$ or 1; otherwise, $0 < t_{i_0} < 1$, where $i = 1, 2, \ldots,$ or m.*

By the proofs of the two lemmas (Lemmas 1 and 2) of [7], we have

Lemma 2. *If $e_1 \perp e_2$, then $\frac{\partial d_e(p_1,p_2)}{\partial t_2}$ can be written as $\frac{t_2-\alpha}{\sqrt{(t_2-\alpha)^2+(t_1-\beta)^2+\gamma}}$, where $\alpha, \beta,$ and γ are reals.*

Lemma 3. *If $e_1 \parallel e_2$, then $\frac{\partial d_e(p_1,p_2)}{\partial t_2}$ can be written as $\frac{t_2-t_1}{\sqrt{(t_2-t_1)^2+\alpha}}$, where α is a real.*

Theorem 7. *([6], Theorem 4) $\frac{\partial d_2}{\partial t_2} = 0$ implies that we have one of the following representations for t_3: we can have*

$$t_3 = \frac{-c_2 t_1 + (c_1 + c_2)t_2}{c_1}$$

if $c_1 > 0$; we can also have

$$t_3 = 1 - \sqrt{\frac{c_1^2(t_2 - a_2)^2}{(t_2 - t_1)^2} - c_2^2}$$

or

$$t_3 = \sqrt{\frac{c_1^2(t_2-a_2)^2}{(t_2-t_1)^2} - c_2^2}$$

if a_2 is either 0 or 1, and c_1 and c_2 are positive; and we can also have

$$t_3 = 1 - \sqrt{\frac{(t_2-a_2)^2[(t_1-a_1)^2+c_1^2]}{(t_2-b_1)^2} - c_2^2}$$

or

$$t_3 = \sqrt{\frac{(t_2-a_2)^2[(t_1-a_1)^2+c_1^2]}{(t_2-b_1)^2} - c_2^2}$$

if a_1, a_2, and b_1 are either 0 or 1, and c_1 and c_2 are positive reals.

Lemma 4. *The number of critical points of $d(t_0, t_1, \ldots, t_m, t_{m+1})$ in $[0,1]^{m+2}$ is finite.*

Proof. Let $d = d(t_0, t_1, \ldots, t_m, t_{m+1})$.

Case 1. The simple cube-curve g has some end angles.

Assume that e_i, e_{i+1}, and e_{i+2} form an end angle, and also e_j, e_{j+1}, and e_{j+2}, and no other three consecutive critical edges between e_{i+2} and e_j form an end angle, where $i \leq j$ and $i, j = 0, 1, 2, \ldots, m-2$. By Theorem 6 we have $t_{i+3} = f_{i+3}(t_{i+1}, t_{i+2}), t_{i+4} = f_{i+4}(t_{i+2}, t_{i+3}), t_{i+5} = f_{i+5}(t_{i+3}, t_{i+4}), \ldots, t_j$, and $t_{j+1} = f_{j+1}(t_{j-1}, t_j)$. This shows that $t_{i+3}, t_{i+4}, t_{i+5}, \ldots, t_j$, and t_{j+1} can be represented by t_{i+1}, and t_{i+2}. In particular, we obtain an equation $t_{j+1} = f(t_{i+1}, t_{i+2})$, or

$$g(t_{j+1}, t_{i+1}, t_{i+2}) = 0,$$

where t_{j+1}, and t_{i+1} are already known, or

$$g_1(t_{i+2}) = 0. \qquad (1)$$

By Lemmas 2 and 3, function $g_1(t_{i+2})$ can be decomposed into finitely many monotonous functions. Therefore, Equation (1) has finite solutions. This implies that the system formed by $\frac{\partial d}{\partial t_i} = 0$ (where $i = 0, 1, \ldots,$ and $m+1$.) has finite solutions.

Case 2. The simple cube-curve g does not have any end angle.

Analogous to Case 1, the system formed by $\frac{\partial d}{\partial t_i} = 0$ (where $i = 0, 1, \ldots,$ and $m+1$.) implies a two variables system formed by

$$h_1(t_0, t_1) = 0 \qquad (2)$$
$$h_2(t_0, t_1) = 0 \qquad (3)$$

Again by Lemmas 2 and 3, Equations (2) and (3) can be decomposed into finite monotonous functions, so the system formed by Equations (2) and (3) has finite solutions. This implies that the system formed by $\frac{\partial d}{\partial t_i} = 0$ (where $i = 0, 1, \ldots,$ and $m+1$.) has finitely many solutions. □

By Lemmas 4 and 1, we have

Lemma 5. *g has only a finite number of AMLP critical point tuples.*

Let e_0, e_1 and e_2 be three consecutive critical edges. Let $p_i(p_{i_1}, p_{i_2}, p_{i_3}) \in e_i$, where $i = 0, 1, 2$. Let the two endpoints of e_i be $a_i(a_{i_1}, a_{i_2}, a_{i_3})$ and $b_i(b_{i_1}, b_{i_2}, b_{i_3})$, where $i = 0, 1, 2$.

Lemma 6. *There is an algorithm such that its computing complexity of finding a point $p_1 \in e_1$ with $d_e(p_1, p_0) + d_e(p_1, p_2) = \min\{p_1 | d_e(p_1, p_0) + d_e(p_1, p_2), p_1 \in e_2\}$ is $O(1)$.*

Proof. p_1 can be written as $(a_{1_1} + (b_{1_1} - a_{1_1})t, a_{1_2} + (b_{1_2} - a_{1_2})t, a_{1_3} + (b_{1_3} - a_{1_3})t)$. Note that
$$d_e(p_1, p_0) = \sqrt{\sum_{i=1}^{3} ((a_{1_i} - p_{1_i}) + (b_{1_i} - a_{1_i})t)^2}$$
can be simplified. In fact, the straight line $a_1 b_1$ is parallel to one coordinate axis (x, y or z axis) So, only one element of the set $\{b_{1_i} - a_{1_i} : i = 1,2,3\}$ is 1 and the other two should be 0. Without loss of generality, we can assume that $d_e(p_1, p_0) = \sqrt{(t + A_1)^2 + B_1}$, where A_1 and B_1 are functions of a_{1_i}, b_{1_i} and p_{1_i}, where $i = 0, 1, 2$. Analogously, $d_e(p_1, p_2) = \sqrt{(t + A_2)^2 + B_2}$, where A_2 and B_2 are functions of a_{1_i}, b_{1_i} and p_{2_i}, where $i = 0, 1, 2$. In order to find a point $p_1 \in e_1$ such that $d_e(p_1, p_0) + d_e(p_1, p_2) = \min\{p_1 | d_e(p_1, p_0) + d_e(p_1, p_2), p_1 \in e_1\}$, we can solve the equation $\frac{\partial(d_e(p_1, p_0) + d_e(p_1, p_2))}{\partial t} = 0$: the unique solution is $t = -(A_1 B_2 + A_2 B_1)/(B_2 + B_1)$. □

By the proof of Lemma 6, and if we represent p_i as $(a_{i_1} + (b_{i_1} - a_{i_1})t_i, a_{i_2} + (b_{i_2} - a_{i_2})t_i, a_{i_3} + (b_{i_3} - a_{i_3})t_i)$, then we have

Lemma 7. *$t_2 = t_2(t_1, t_3)$ is a continous function at each tuple $(t_1, t_3) \in [0, 1]^2$.*

Lemma 8. *If $\overrightarrow{P(r-b)_1 Q}$, then for every sufficient small real $\epsilon > 0$, there is a sufficient small real $\delta > 0$ such that $P' \in U(P, \delta)$ and $\overrightarrow{P'(r-b)_1 Q'}$ implies $Q' \in U(Q, \epsilon)$.*

Proof. By Lemma 6 and note that g has $m + 2$ critical edges, so by using Lemmas 1 repeatedly $m + 2$ times we prove this lemma. □

By Lemma 8, we have

Lemma 9. *If $\overrightarrow{P(r-b)_n Q}$, then for every sufficiently small real $\epsilon > 0$, there is a sufficiently small real $\delta_\epsilon > 0$ and a sufficiently large integer N_ϵ such that $P' \in U(P, \delta_\epsilon)$ and $\overrightarrow{P'(r-b)_{n'} Q'}$ implies $Q' \in U(Q, \epsilon)$, where n' is an integer and $n' > N_\epsilon$.*

By Lemma 5, let $Q_1, Q_2, \ldots, Q_N$ with $N \geq 1$ be the set of all $AMLP$ critical point tuples of g. Let ϵ be a sufficiently small positive real such that $U(Q_i, \epsilon) \cap U(Q_j, \epsilon) = \emptyset$, where $i, j = 1, 2, \ldots, N$ and $i \neq j$. Let $D_i = \{P : P \to Q', Q' \in U(Q_i, \epsilon), P \in [0, 1]^{m+2}\}$, where $i = 1, 2, \ldots, N$.

The following two lemmas are straightforward.

Lemma 10. *If $N > 1$ then $D_i \cap D_j = \emptyset$, where $i, j = 1, 2, \ldots, N$ and $i \neq j$.*

Lemma 11. $\cup_{i=1}^{N} D_i = [0,1]^{m+2}$.

We consider usual topology $T = R^{m+2}|_{[0,1]^{m+2}}$.

Lemma 12. *D_i is an open set of T, where $i = 1, 2, \ldots, N$ with $N \geq 1$.*

Proof. By Lemma 9, for each $P \in D_i$, there is a sufficiently small real $\delta_P > 0$ such that $U(P, \delta_P) \subseteq D_i$. So we have $\cup_{P \in D_i} U(P, \delta_P) \subseteq D_i$.

On the other hand, for $P \in U(P, \delta_P)$, we have $D_i = \cup P \subseteq \cup_{P \in D_i} U(P, \delta_P)$. Note that $U(P, \delta_P)$ is an open set of T. So $D_i = \cup_{P \in D_i} U(P, \delta_P)$ is an open set of T.

□

Lemma 13. *([11], Proposition 5.1.4) Let $U \subset R$ be an arbitrary open set. Then there are countably many pairwise disjoint open intervals U_n such that $U = \cup U_n$.*

Lemma 14. *g has a unique AMLP critical point tuple.*

Proof. By contradiction. Suppose that $Q_1, Q_2, \ldots, Q_N$ with $N > 1$ are all $AMLP$ critical point tuples of g. Then there exists $i \in \{1, 2, \ldots, N\}$ such that $D_i|_{e_j} \subset [0,1]$, where e_j is a critical edge of g, $i, j = 1, 2, \ldots, N$. Otherwise we have $D_1 = D_2 = \cdots = D_N$. This is a contradiction to Lemma 10.

Let $E = \{e_j | D_i |_{e_j} \subset [0,1]\}$, where e_j is a critical edge of g. We can select a critical point tuple of g as follows: go through each $e \in \{e_0, e_1, \ldots, e_m, e_{m+1}\}$. If $e \in E$, by Lemmas 12 and 13, select the minimum left endpoint of the open intervals whose union is $D_i|_e$. Otherwise select the midpoint of e. We denote the resulting critical point tuple as $P = (p_0, p_1, p_2, \ldots, p_{m+1})$. By the selection of P, we know that P is not in D_i. By Lemma 11 there is $j \in \{1, 2, \ldots, N\} - \{i\}$ such that $P \in D_j$. Therefore there is a sufficiently small real $\delta > 0$ such that $U(P, \delta) \subset D_j$. Again by the selection of P, there is a sufficiently small real $\delta' > 0$ such that $U(P, \delta') \cap D_i \neq \emptyset$. Let $\delta'' = \min\{\delta, \delta'\}$. Then we have $U(P, \delta'') \subset D_j$ and $U(P, \delta'') \cap D_i \neq \emptyset$. This implies that $D_i \cap D_j \neq \emptyset$, and it is a condtradiction to Lemma 10.

□

Let g be a simple cube-curve. Let $AMLP_n(g)$ be an n-polygon of g, where $n = 1, 2, \ldots$. $AMLP = \lim_{n \to \infty} AMLP_n(g)$.

Theorem 8. *The AMLP of g is the MLP of g.*

Proof. By Lemma 14 and the proof of Lemma 1, $d(t_0, t_1, \ldots, t_m, t_{m+1})$ has a unique local minimal value. This implies that the $AMLP$ of g is the MLP of g.

□

4 Computational Complexity

Assume that a simple cube-curve g has m critical edges. By Lemma 6, the computational complexity of each iteration of running the rubber-band algorithm is $O(m)$. Let $AMLP_n(g)$ be an n-polygon of g, where $n = 1, 2, \ldots$. Then the computational complexity of finding $AMLP_n(g)$ is $nO(m)$. Suppose $\lim_{n \to \infty} AMLP_n(g) = AMLP$. By Theorem 8, we can use $AMLP_{N(\epsilon)}(g)$ as an approximate MLP of g, where ϵ is the error between the length of $AMLP_{N(\epsilon)}(g)$ and that of MLP. The computational complexity is $N(\epsilon)O(m)$.

5 Conclusions

We have proved that the rubber-band algorithm is correct for the family of first-class simple cube-curves and that the algorithm's computational complexity of finding an approximate MLP of a simple cube-curve is linear for this family of curves.

Acknowledgements. The CAIP reviewers' comments have been very helpful for revising an earlier version of this paper.

References

1. T. Bülow and R. Klette. Digital curves in 3D space and a linear-time length estimation algorithm. *IEEE Trans. Pattern Analysis Machine Intelligence*, **24**:962–970, 2002.
2. R. Klette and A. Rosenfeld. *Digital Geometery: Geometric Methods for Digital Picture Analysis.* Morgan Kaufmann, San Francisco, 2004.
3. F. Sloboda, B. Zaťko, and R. Klette. On the topology of grid continua. *SPIE Vision Geometry VII*, **3454**:52–63, 1998.
4. F. Sloboda, B. Zaťko, and J. Stoer. On approximation of planar one-dimensional grid continua. In R. Klette, A. Rosenfeld, and F. Sloboda, editors, *Advances in Digital and Computational Geometry*, pages 113–160. Springer, Singapore, 1998.
5. A. Jonas and N. Kiryati. Length estimation in 3-D using cube quantization, *J. Math. Imaging and Vision*, **8**: 215–238, 1998.
6. F. Li and R. Klette. Minimum-length polygon of a simple cube-curve in 3D space. In Proceedings IWCIA2004, LNCS3322: 502-511.
7. F. Li and R. Klette. The class of simple cube-curves whose MLPs cannot have vertices at grid points. In Proceedings DGCI2005, LNCS3429: 183-194.
8. J. Canny and J.H. Reif. New lower bound techniques for robot motion planning problems. Proc. *IEEE Conf. Foundations Computer Science*, pages 49–60, 1987.
9. J. Choi, J. Sellen, and C.-K. Yap. Approximate Euclidean shortest path in 3-space. Proc. *ACM Conf. Computational Geometry*, ACM Press, pages 41–48, 1994.
10. S. A. Douglass. *Introduction to Mathematical Analysis.* Addison-Wesley Publishing Company, 1996.
11. B. G. Wachsmuth. *Interactive Real Analysis.* http://www.shu.edu/projects/reals/index.html, 2000.
12. T. O. Moore. *Elementary General Topology.* PRENTICE-HALL, INC., Englewood Cliffs, N.J., 1964.

Combining Character Level Classifier and Probabilistic Lexicons in Handwritten Word Recognition - Comparative Analysis of Methods

Marek Kurzynski[1] and Jerzy Sas[2]

[1] Wroclaw University of Technology, Faculty of Electronics, Chair of Systems and Computer Networks, Wyb. Wyspianskiego 27, 50-370 Wroclaw, Poland
marek.kurzynski@pwr.wroc.pl
[2] Wroclaw University of Technology, Institute of Applied Informatics, Wyb. Wyspianskiego 27, 50-370 Wroclaw, Poland
jerzy.sas@pwr.wroc.pl

Abstract. In this paper the probabilistic aproach to handwritten words recognition is described. The decision is performed using results of character classification based on a character image analysis and probabilistic lexicon treated as a special kind of soft classifier. The novel approach to combining these both classifiers is proposed, where fusion procedure interleaves soft outcomes of both classifiers so as to obtain the best recognition quality. The proposed algorithms were experimentally investigated and results of recognition of polish handwritten surnames and names are given.

1 Introduction

Handwritten character recognition has attracted enormous scientific interest due to its evident practical utility. To achieve high recognition accuraccy, many different classification algorithms have been proposed here, which are based on a variety of theories and methodologies. For several years, the concept of combining multiple classifiers is considered as a method for the development of highly reliable character recognition system (e.g. [12]).

In this paper, adopting the probabilistic model, we discuss the handwritten word recognition method which uses character classifier supported with probabilistic lexicon. Probabilistic properties of lexicon and character classifier are typically used to build Hidden Markov Model (HMM) of the language (e.g. [11]). We propose another approach to the word recognition, in which probabilistic lexicon is treated as a special kind of classifier based on a word length, and next result of its activity is combined with soft outcomes of character classifier based on recognition of character image. Different algorihms of fusion of both classifiers lead to the several word classifiers which differ in procedures and - as it results from experimental investigations - also in recognition quality.

This paper is a sequel to the authors earlier publications ([4], [5], [6], [7]) and it yields an essential extension of the results included therein.

The contents of the work are as follows. In section 2 necessary background is introduced and a task of combining character and lexicon classifiers is formulated as an appropriate optimization problem. In section 3 we present the novel method of fusion of both classifiers. Its idea consists in original so-called interleaving procedure, in which successive characters in a word are recognized using either character classifier or lexicon classifier, so as to achieve the best result of a whole word recognition. The proposed algorithms were experimentally investigated in the computer-aided recognition of handwritten polish surnames and names and results of classification accuracy on real data are given in section 4.

2 Preliminaries and the Problem Statement

Let us consider a paper form designed to be filled by handwritten characters. The form consists of data fields. Each data field contains a sequence of characters of limited length coming from the alphabet $\mathcal{A} = \{c_1, c_2, ..., c_L\}$. Data fields do not have to be filled completely - only the leading part of each field must be filled with characters. We assume that the actual length of filled part of data field can be faultlessly determined. The set $\mathcal{A}$ can be different for each field. Typically we deal with fields that can contain only digits, letters or both of them.

We assume next that on character (alphabetical) level classifier Ψ_C is given which gets character image x as its input and assigns it to a class (character label) c from $\mathcal{A}$, i.e., $\Psi_C(x) = c$. Alternatively, we may define the classifier output to be a L-dimensional vector with supports for the characters from $\mathcal{A}$ ([3]), i.e.

$$\Psi_C(x) = [d_1(x), d_2(x), ..., d_L(x)]^T. \qquad (1)$$

Without loss of generality we can restrict $d_i(x)$ within the interval $[0, 1]$ and additionally $\sum_i d_i(x) = 1$. Thus, $d_i(x)$ is the degree of support given by classifier Ψ_C to the hypothesis that image x represents character $c_i \in \mathcal{A}$. If a crisp decision is needed we can use the maximum membership rule for soft outputs (1), viz.

$$\Psi_C(x) = arg\,(\max_i\, d_i(x)). \qquad (2)$$

There are different possibilities to determine the output vector of classifier (1) on character level. Generally, the nature of extracted features, classification criteria (discriminant functions of classifier) or classifier statistical properties can suggest some solutions. Some proposals of support vector for MLP and dissimilarity-based methods applied to the character classifier Ψ_C can be found in [5].

Any classifier can be used on character level. In further experiments we have applied MLP-based classifier using a vector of directional features ([1]). The vector of support values $[d_1(x), d_2(x), ..., d_L(x)]^T$ in (1) is the normalized output of MLP obtained by clipping network output values to $[0, 1]$ range and by normalizing their sum to 1.0.

Independently of nature of classifier Ψ_C, support vector (1) is usually interpreted as an estimate of posterior probabilities of classes (characters) provided that observation x is given ([3], [8], [9]), i.e. in next considerations we adopt:

$$d_i(x) = P(c_i \mid x), \quad c_i \in \mathcal{A}. \tag{3}$$

For each data field there exists a probabilistic lexicon $\mathcal{L}$. Lexicon contains words that can appear in the data field and their probabilities:

$$\mathcal{L} = \{(W_1, p_1), (W_2, p_2), ..., (W_N, p_N)\}, \tag{4}$$

where W_j is the word consisting of characters from $\mathcal{A}$, p_j is its probability and N is the number of words in the lexicon.

Let the length $\mid W \mid$ of currently recognized word $W \in \mathcal{L}$ be equal to n. This fact defines the probabilistic sublexicon $\mathcal{L}_n$

$$\mathcal{L}_n = \{(W_k, q_k)_{k=1}^{N_n} : W_k \in \mathcal{L}, \mid W_k \mid = n\}, \tag{5}$$

i.e. the subset of $\mathcal{L}$ with modified probabilities of words:

$$q_k = P(W_k / \mid W_k \mid = n) = \frac{p_k}{\sum_{j:|W_j|=n} p_j}. \tag{6}$$

The sublexicon (5) can be also considered as a soft classifier Ψ_L which maps feature space $\{\mid W_k \mid : W_k \in \mathcal{L}\}$ into the product $[0,1]^{N_n}$, i.e. for each word length n produces the vector of supports to words from $\mathcal{L}_n$, namely

$$\Psi_L(n) = [q_1, q_2, ..., q_{N_n}]^T. \tag{7}$$

Let suppose next, that classifier Ψ_C, applied n times on the character level, on the base of character images $X_n = (x_1, x_2, ..., x_n)$, has produced the sequence of character supports (1) for the whole recognized word, which can be organized into the following matrix of supports, or matrix of posterior probabilities (3):

$$D_n(X_n) = \begin{pmatrix} d_{11}(x_1) & d_{12}(x_1) & ... & d_{1L}(x_1) \\ d_{21}(x_2) & d_{22}(x_2) & ... & d_{2L}(x_2) \\ \vdots & \vdots & ... & \vdots \\ d_{n1}(x_n) & d_{n2}(x_n) & ... & d_{nL}(x_n) \end{pmatrix}. \tag{8}$$

Now our purpose is to built soft classifier Ψ_W for word recognition as a fusion of activity of both lexicon-based Ψ_L and character-based classifier Ψ_C:

$$\Psi_W(\Psi_C, \Psi_L) = \Psi_W(D_n, \mathcal{L}_n) = [s_1, s_2, ..., s_{N_n}]^T, \tag{9}$$

which will produce support vector for all words from sublexicon $\mathcal{L}_n$. In the next chapters a method of combination of Ψ_C and Ψ_L will be proposed and discussed.

3 Method of Combining Classifiers

Let $\mathcal{N} = \{1, 2, ..., n\}$ be the set of numbers of character positions in a word $W \in \mathcal{L}_n$ and $\mathcal{I}$ denotes a subset of $\mathcal{N}$. In the proposed fusion method with "interleaving" first the algorithm Ψ_C applied for recognition of characters on positions $\mathcal{I}$ on the base of set of images $X^\mathcal{I} = \{x_k : k \in \mathcal{I}\}$, produces matrix of supports $D^\mathcal{I}$ and next - using these results of classification - the lexicon $\mathcal{L}_n$ (or algorithm Ψ_L) is applied for recognition of a whole word W.

The main problem of proposed method consists in an appriopriate division of $\mathcal{N}$ into sets $\mathcal{I}$ and $\bar{\mathcal{I}}$ (complement of $\mathcal{I}$). Intuitively, subset $\mathcal{I}$ should contain these positions for which character recognition algorithm gives the most reliable results. In other words division of $\mathcal{N}$ should lead to the best result of classification accuracy of a whole word. Thus, subset $\mathcal{I}$ can be determined as a solution of an appropriate optimization problem.

Let $W^\mathcal{I} = \{c_{i_k} : k \in \mathcal{I}, c_{i_k} \in \mathcal{A}\}$ be any set of characters on positions $\mathcal{I}$. Then we have following posterior probability:

$$P(W^\mathcal{I} \mid X^\mathcal{I}) = \prod_{k \in \mathcal{I}} d_{k\ i_k}(x_k). \tag{10}$$

The formula (10) gives conditional probability of hypothesis that on positions $\mathcal{I}$ of word to be recognized are characters $W^\mathcal{I}$ provided that set of character images $X^\mathcal{I}$ has been observed.

Applying for remaining part of the word sublexicon $\mathcal{L}_n$, we can calculate conditional probability of the whole word $W_j \in \mathcal{L}_n$, which constitutes the support (9) for word W_j of soft classifier Ψ_W:

$$s_j = P(W_j \mid X^\mathcal{I}) = P(W^\mathcal{I} \mid X^\mathcal{I}) P(W_j \mid W^\mathcal{I}). \tag{11}$$

The first factor in (11) is given by (10) whereas the second one can be calculated as follows:

$$P(W_j \mid W^\mathcal{I}) = \frac{q_j}{\sum_{j: W_j contains W^\mathcal{I}} q_j}. \tag{12}$$

Since the support vector (11) of the rule Ψ_W strongly depends on the set $\mathcal{I}$ hence we can formulate the following optimization problem:

It is neccesary to find such a subset $\mathcal{I}^*$ of $\mathcal{N}$ and such a set of charcters $W^{\mathcal{I}^*}$ which maximize some criterion $Q(\Psi_W)$ of word classifier quality (or classifiers Ψ_C and Ψ_L fusion quality), namely

$$Q(\Psi_W^*) = \max_{\mathcal{I}, W^\mathcal{I}} Q(\Psi_W). \tag{13}$$

The following two criteria of soft classifier quality Ψ_W producing vector of supports (9), seem to be intuitively substantiated:

- the maximum value of decision supports dependent on sets $\mathcal{I}$ and $W^\mathcal{I}$:

$$Q_1(\Psi_W = (s_1(\mathcal{I}, W^\mathcal{I}), s_2(\mathcal{I}, W^\mathcal{I}), ..., s_{N_n}(\mathcal{I}, W^\mathcal{I})) = \max_{j=1,2,...,N_n} s_j(\mathcal{I}, W^\mathcal{I}), \tag{14}$$

- the normalized entropy of the support vector (9):

$$Q_2(\Psi_W = (s_1(\mathcal{I}, W^{\mathcal{I}}), ..., s_{N_n}(\mathcal{I}, W^{\mathcal{I}}))) =$$
$$= 1 - \frac{\sum_{j=1}^{N_n} s_j(\mathcal{I}, W^{\mathcal{I}}) log_2(s_j(\mathcal{I}, W^{\mathcal{I}}))}{log_2 \frac{1}{N_n}}, \quad (15)$$

which is frequently used as a measure of discriminative power of a classifier ([13]).

It should be noted, that both criteria (14) and(15) may be also used in the fusion methods as a quality measure of character classifier Ψ_C with support values (1), i.e. $Q(\Psi_C = (d_1(x), d_2(x), ..., d_L(x))$.

The number of solutions of discrete optimization problem (13) is equal to $(L+1)^n - 1$, hence - except the case of very short words - the exhaustive search is rather infeasible method. Therefore we suggest the following suboptimal procedure which was applied in the further experimental investigations.

```
Initial data: D_n(X_n), L_n, I_0 = ∅
for i = 1 to n do
  Find k* : Q(d_{k*1}(x_{k*}), d_{k*2}(x_{k*}), ..., d_{k*L}(x_{k*}) =
  = max_{k∉I_{i-1}} Q(d_{k1}(x_k), d_{k2}(x_k), ..., d_{kL}(x_k))
  I_i ← I_{i-1} ∪ k*
  For j = 1 to N_n calculate s_j(I_i) according to (10), (11) and (12)
  Calculate Q(I_i) = Q(s_1(I_i), s_2(I_i), ..., s_{N_n}(I_i))
end i
Find I* for which Q(I*) = max_{i=1,2,...,n} Q(I_i)
```

4 Experimental Comparative Analysis of Algorithms

In order to study the performance of the proposed word recognition concept and evaluate their usefulness to the practical structured handwritten forms recognition, several computer experiments were made, in which polish names and surnames were applied as recognized words.

In experiments six words classifiers were tested:

- **C1W1** - algorithm with criterion Q_1 for Ψ_C and Ψ_W evaluation,
- **C2W2** - algorithm with criterion Q_2 for Ψ_C and Ψ_W evaluation,
- **C1W2** - algorithm with criterion Q_1 for Ψ_C and Q_2 for Ψ_W evaluation,
- **C2W1** - algorithm with criterion Q_2 for Ψ_C and Q_1 for Ψ_W evaluation,
- **C** - classifier based merely on classification of isolated characters,
- **CL** - classifier based on character level recognizer results where lexicon is used merely to restrict the set of word recognition results (probabilistic lexicon properties not used).

On the character level, MLP recognizer was applied based on gradient features set extracted according to the procedure described in [1]. MLP with L outputs (each one corresponding to single element of alphabet) was trained in

"1 of L" manner. It means that when presenting to the net the feature vector extracted from the image of character c, the expected MLP response consists of 0.0 on all net outputs except the one corresponding to character c, where the value 1.0 is expected. The training set consists of 354 character prototypes prepared manually in such way that they imitate typical writing styles of characters from the alphabet. The average accuracy of MLP character recognizer was equal to 90.1%. Relatively weak quality of MLP classifier results from the specific properties of the polish alphabet - it contains 35 characters which have special diacritical marks. The name and surname lexicons containing 818 and 17,440 items, respectively, were created on the base of hospital information database system containing 47,845 patient records. In order to test how the method performance depends on the lexicon size, the subsets of surnames consisting of 5,000, 1,000 and 17,440 most frequently appearing words were used.

The experiments were performed using simulated data according to the following scheme. First, the word to be recognized is randomly selected from the lexicon, taking into account its probabilistic properties. Then, for each character field of the selected word, appropriate letter image is randomly drawn from the set of 5,040 letter images other than images used to train MLP-based character classifier Ψ_C. The word images obtained in this way are subject of recognition. Results are presented in Table 1. It includes the frequency of misclassifications (in percent) for the investigated algorithms. The first row contains results obtained in names recognition with 818 elements lexicon. Successive rows contain results of surnames recognition based on lexicon subsets containing 5,000, 10,000 and 17,440 elements.

Table 1. Error rates comparison - names and surnames recognition

Test set	C	CL	C1W1	C1W2	C2W1	C2W2
818 names	42.3%	10.2%	3.6%	3.6%	3.5%	3.2%
5,000 surnames	48.1%	9.4%	6.0%	5.8%	5.8%	4.9%
10,000 surnames	48.0%	11.0%	6.5%	6.2%	6.1%	5.3%
17,440 surnames	48.3%	12.2%	8.3%	7.9%	7.7%	6.5%

For some applications it is not extremely important that the actual word has the highest support s_i. Instead, it is expected that the actual word is among k words with highest s_i. Hence, we can consider the recognition as successful if the word being recognized is among k ones highestly evaluated by the classifier, and as failure otherwise. Tables 2. and 3. present the failure rate for compared algorithms for $k=3$ and $k=5$.

These results imply the following conclusions:

1. Word classification based merely on isolated character recognition gives very poor results, even for best currently available letter classifiers for which error rate is lower that 10%. In practical applications, the lexicon is necessary at least to reduce the set of admissible words by applying CL algorithm.

Table 2. Failure rates comparison for $k=3$

Test set	C	CL	C1W1	C1W2	C2W1	C2W2
818 names	37.0%	7.7%	2.4%	2.4%	2.3%	2.3%
5,000 surnames	41.7%	8.7%	4.4%	4.2%	4.6%	3.7%
10,000 surnames	41.9%	10.2%	4.8%	4.6%	4.6%	4.2%
17,440 surnames	41.7%	12.1%	6.2%	5.9%	5.8%	5.0%

Table 3. Failure rates comparison for $k=5$

Test set	C	CL	C1W1	C1W2	C2W1	C2W2
818 names	34.9%	7.4%	2.1%	2.2%	2.1%	2.0%
5,000 surnames	39.3%	8.3%	3.9%	3.7%	3.8%	3.2%
10,000 surnames	39.4%	10.4%	4.4%	4.2%	4.3%	4.0%
17,440 surnames	39.2%	11.2%	5.7%	5.5%	5.4%	4.8%

2. Combining character level classification with probabilistic lexicon always gives better results than classifier which does not utilize the lexicon probabilistic properties (CL vs. C1W1, C1W2, C2W1, C2W2). In our experiments it resulted in reduction of error rate by 50-60% (from 10% to 4% on average). This confirms the effectiveness and usefulness of the concepts and algorithms presented above.
3. Selection of criteria (14), (15) used to assess character classification and partial word classification seems to have only minor influence on final recognition quality. Combinations C1W1, C1W2, C2W1 result in approximately equal recognition quality. Application of entropy on both levels (C2W2) gives slightly better result (further reduction of error rate by about 5% in relation to C1W1).

5 Conclusions

In this paper we have focused our attention on the combined words recognition in structured handwritten documents via fusion of results of character classifier on lower level and probabilistic lexicon treated as a special classifier. Taking the probabilistic model of classification task, we have proposed the novel concept of fusion of both classifiers which leads to the soft word classifier producing vector of support values for all words from the lexicon. Soft outcomes of a word classifier can be used next as data for semantic level classifier, which recognize the object described by the whole form ([7]).

Presented algorithms have been experimentally tested on the real data containing a set of polish names and surnames. Their results, especially comparison with recognition quality of separated character image recognition algorithm, demonstrate the effectiveness of the proposed word recognition concept and yield some recommendation for a wide range of practical applications which deal with problem of structured handwritten text recognition.

Acknowledgement. This work was financed from the State Committee for Scientific Research (KBN) resources in 2005 - 2007 years as a research project No 3 T11E 005 28.

References

1. Liu C., Nakashima K., Sako H., Fujisawa H.: Handwritten Digit Recognition: Benchmarking of State-of-the-Art Techniques, Pattern Recognition, Vol. 36 (2003) 2271-2285
2. Lu Y., Gader P. Tan C.: Combination of Multiple Classifiers Using Probabilistic Dictionary and its Application to Postcode Generation, Pattern Recognition, Vol. 35 (2002) 2823-2832
3. Kuncheva L.: Combining Classifiers: Soft Computing Solutions, [in.] Pattern Recognition: from Classical to Modern Approaches, Pal S., Pal A. [eds.], World Scientific (2001) 427-451
4. Sas J., Kurzynski M.: Multilevel Recognition of Structured Handwritten Documents - Probabilistic Approach, Proc. 4th Int. Conf. on Computer Recognition Systems, Springer Verlag (2005) 723-730
5. Sas J., Kurzynski M.: Application of Statistic Properties of Letter Succession in Polish Language to Handprint Recognition, Proc. 4th Int. Conf. on Computer Recognition Systems, Springer Verlag 731-739
6. Sas J.: Handwritten Laboratory Test Order Form Recognition Module for Distributed Clinic, J. of Medical Informatics and Technologies, Vol. 8 (2004) 59-68
7. Sas J.: Three-Level Lexicon Based Handwritten Form Recognition Method, In: Klopotek M., Tchorzewski J. (eds), Proc. VI Int. Conf. on Artificial Intelligence, Vol. 1 (2004) 113-124
8. Devroye L., Gyorfi P., Lugossi G.: A Probabilistic Theory of Pattern Recognition, Springer Verlag, New York (1996)
9. Duda R., Hart P., Stork D.: Pattern Classification, John Wiley and Sons (2001)
10. Woods K., Kegelmeyer W.:, Combination of Multiple Classifiers Using Local Accuracy Estimates, IEEE Trans. on PAMI, Vol. 19 (1997) 405-410
11. Vinciarelli A. et al.: Offline Recognition of Unconstrained Handwritten Text Using HMMs and Statistical Language Models, IEEE Trans. on PAMI, Vol. 26 (2004) 709-720
12. Xu L., Krzyzak A., Suen C.: Methods of Combining of Multiple Classifiers and Their Applications to Handwriting Recognition, IEEE Trans. on SMC, vol. 22 (1992) 418-435
13. Kapur J., Kesavan H.: Entropy Optimization Principles with Applications, Academic Press (1992)

Preprocessing Convex Polygons Using Range Trees for Recognition with Few Finger Probes

Sumanta Guha and Kiêu Trọng Khánh

Computer Science & Information Management Program,
Asian Institute of Technology,
P.O. Box 4, Klong Luang,
Pathumthani 12120,
Thailand
{guha, kieutrong.khanh}@ait.ac.th

Abstract. The problem considered is that of recognizing if a given convex polygon comes from a known collection by applying probes. Existing approaches use a number of probes that is linear in the number of sides of the polygon. The current premise is that probing is expensive, while computing is cheap. Accordingly, a method is proposed that recognizes a polygon from the collection, with high probability, using only a constant number of probes, at the cost of fairly large computing resources, particularly, in setting up and applying a range tree data structure.

1 Introduction

The problem of recognizing an object by means of probes has application in domains ranging from robotics to security. Because of its significance the problem has been studied extensively (see [10,11,12] for surveys of methodologies). In this paper we consider finger probes which are probes of an object by directed rays, the outcome of each probe being the co-ordinates of the point of contact of the ray with the object. Finger probes model existing devices that shoot laser or sonar beams.

Cole and Yap [4] initiated the theoretical study of finger probes. Research since then has focused primarily on determining the shape of an object given that it belongs to some restricted class – often, convex polygons or polytopes, e.g., [4,6,11] – or recognizing an object given that it belongs to a known finite collection – called model-based probing, again, often, for collections of convex polygons, e.g., [1,2,8,11]. Results proved require, typically, $O(n)$ probes, where n is the number of sides of the convex polygon(s).

Our premise for this paper is the following: the process of physical probing itself is expensive relative to the computing power available to process the outcome of the probes. This is justified by real scenarios. For example, consider airport surveillance where laser or sonar beams are aimed at individuals streaming through a checkpoint. An individual is in the checkpoint area for a short duration and within that time some number of beams are fired at him (or her), and, subsequently, the outcome transmitted over a network to a central computer. The constraints on the size of the checkpoint area, the number and location of the probing devices, the turnaround time of the physical beams, and network delay imply the desirability of being able to recognize a suspect with *very few probes*. On the other hand, it is equally reasonable to assume that the central computer that processes probe outcomes, once they arrive, is extremely powerful with massive RAM and processor speed.

Accordingly, we propose a method where an object from a given finite collection – we restrict to collections of convex polygons in this paper – can be detected with *very high probability* using $O(1)$ finger probes. Our method is based on the observation (proved partially in this version) that the probability that the outcome of four finger probes, from one convex polygon in a random collection, will match another, is zero. We preprocess the collection, therefore, that, given four probe outcomes, we can determine possible matches: as we allow for noise and computational error, our method, typically, picks up a few possible matches, even though the theoretical probability of more than one is zero. With additional probes, that we process in groups of four, the number of possible matches drops rapidly to one.

Our primary search structure is a range tree – for a given set P of points in n-dimensional space, a range tree is a geometric data structure that allows efficient orthogonal range searching, i.e., reporting of points of P that lie in some query box B with axes-parallel sides. Owing to the size of the parameters involved our particular range tree requires a large amount of time to construct and space to store, which is acceptable given our assumption on available computing resources. Our theoretical analysis is mostly heuristic, so we have performed extensive experiments to assess our method. The results are encouraging.

We feel that primary significance of our contribution is in initiating the study of this very practical problem of model-based recognition using few probes – we are not aware of any earlier papers – and formulating a practical solution.

2 Problem and Solution Plan

We are given a collection $\mathcal{C} = \{C_0, \ldots, C_{m-1}\}$ of m mutually disjoint convex polygons on a plane. Our problem is to determine if some target polygon C, assumed to lie on the same plane as the collection $\mathcal{C}$, can be obtained by a 2D rigid transformation t (i.e., by translation and rotation on the plane) of some $C_i \in \mathcal{C}$ – if it can then we say that C_i is a *match* for C. We are only allowed finger probes on C. Now, r finger probes on C yield r points $q_0, q_1, \ldots, q_{r-1}$ on the boundary of C (say, the points lie in the given order, either clockwise or counterclockwise, on the boundary). We first formalize a trivial necessary condition for a polygon $C_i \in \mathcal{C}$ to be a match for C based on the results of the r probes.

Lemma 1. *A necessary condition for $C_i \in \mathcal{C}$ to be a match for target polygon C is if the polygon P, with vertices at the r probed points $q_0, q_1, \ldots, q_r$, can be inscribed in C_i by rigid transformation.*

Proof. If C_i is a match for C, then there exists a rigid transformation t such that $t(C_i) = C$, so that $t^{-1}(C) = C_i$, which implies that the vertices of $t^{-1}(P)$ lie on the boundary of C_i.

This leads to the following proposition in case of three finger probes:

Proposition 1. *Say that the target polygon C has been probed at three points q_0, q_1, q_2 on its boundary. A necessary condition for $C_i \in \mathcal{C}$ to be a match for C is that there exist three points p_0, p_1, p_2 on the boundary of C_i such that $d(q_i, q_{i+1}) = d(p_i, p_{i+1})$, $0 \leq i \leq 2$ (addition in the subscripts being modulo 3), and so that the order q_0, q_1, q_2 and p_0, p_1, p_2 on the plane is the same (either both counterclockwise or clockwise).*

Proof. The proposition follows from the preceding lemma and that a rigid transformation is an orientation-preserving Euclidean transformation.

For example, see Figure 1(a), where the triangle T gives a match between the target polygon C and the polygon C_0 of a collection of three polygons.

For a pair of straight-line segments s_0, s_1 define (see Figure 1(b)):

$$\max(s_0, s_1) = \sup\{d(p, q) : p \in s_0, q \in s_1\} \text{ and}$$
$$\min(s_0, s_1) = \inf\{d(p, q) : p \in s_0, q \in s_1\}$$

Assume the result of probing a target polygon C are three non-collinear points q_0, q_1, q_2 on the plane such that the order q_0, q_1, q_2 is counterclockwise. Let $d_0 = d(q_0, q_1)$, $d_1 = d(q_1, q_2)$, $d_2 = d(q_2, q_0)$. By Proposition 1, a necessary condition for $C_i \in \mathcal{C}$ to be a match for C is that there exist points p_0, p_1 and p_2 on the boundary of C_i such that $d(p_i, p_{i+1}) = d_i$, $0 \leq i \leq 2$, and so that the order p_0, p_1, p_2 is counterclockwise as well. If the points p_0, p_1, p_2 are assumed to lie on the edges e_0, e_1, e_2 of C_i, respectively, this in turn implies the following necessary condition for C_i to be a match for C:

There exist exist edges e_0, e_1, e_2 of C_i (not necessarily distinct) so that:

(1) The order e_0, e_1, e_2 around C_i is counterclockwise (if at least two of e_0, e_1 and e_2 are identical then the order can be assumed to be either of counterclockwise or clockwise).
(2) Not all three of e_0, e_1, e_2 are identical (for, otherwise, p_0, p_1, p_2 are collinear).
(3) $\min(e_i, e_{i+1}) \leq d_i \leq \max(e_i, e_{i+1})$, $0 \leq i \leq 2$.

Physical probing is never exact as noise cannot be fully eliminated from the process, and, moreover, exact arithmetic is computationally infeasible as well. Therefore, we heuristically relax condition (3) to:

(3') $\min(e_i, e_{i+1}) - \epsilon \leq d_i \leq \max(e_i, e_{i+1}) + \epsilon$, $0 \leq i \leq 2$

where ϵ is a user-specified small constant.

Call a triple of edges (e_0, e_1, e_2) from C_i satisfying these conditions (1), (2) and (3') a *candidate triple of edges* from C_i w.r.t. q_0, q_1, q_2. Note that conditions

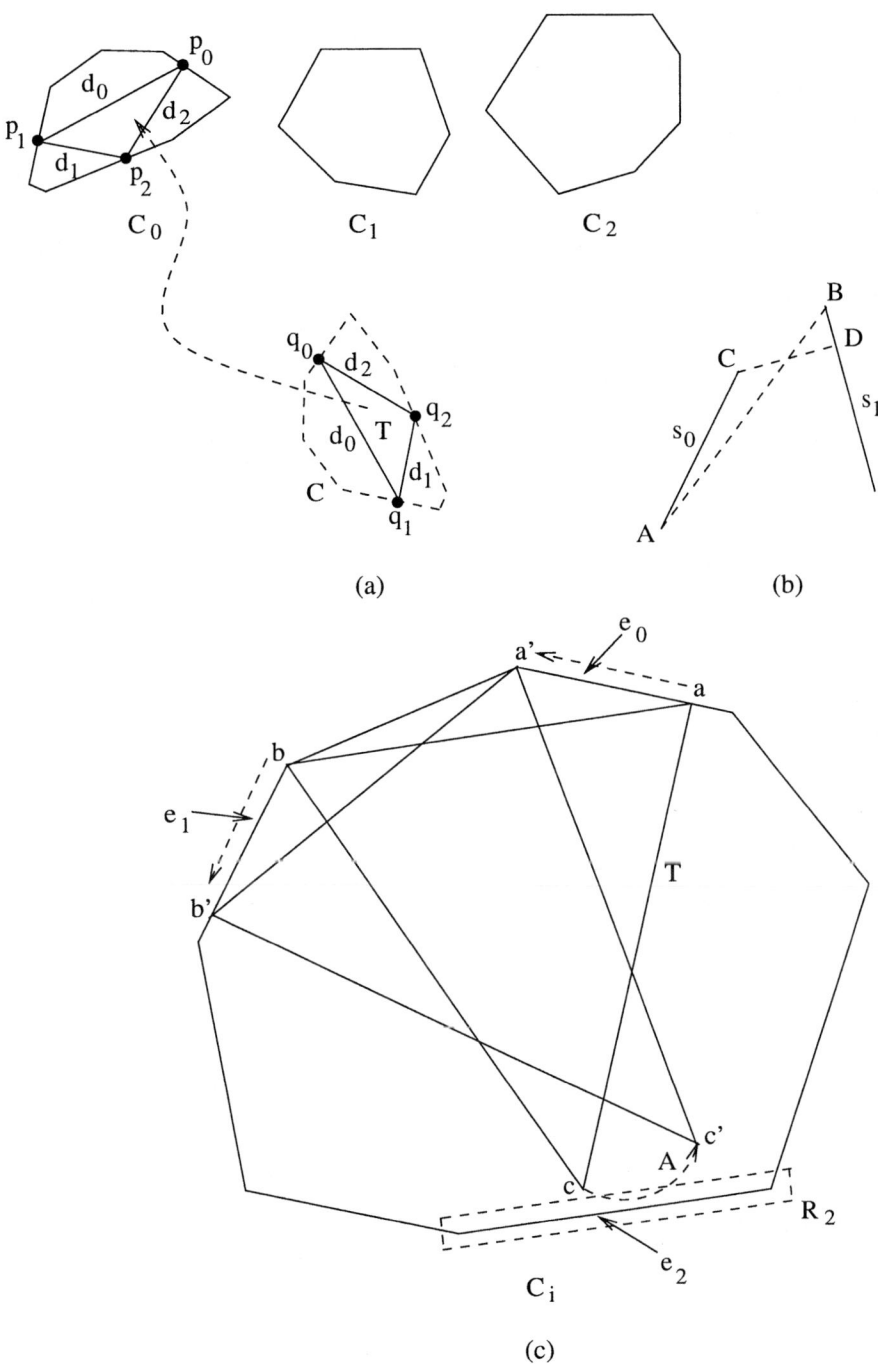

Fig. 1. (a) Target polygon C probed to find triangle T which can be inscribed in C_0 (b) Two straight-segments s_0 and s_1 with $|AB| = \max(s_0, s_1)$ and $|CD| = \min(s_0, s_1)$ (c) Sliding triangle T with its base on two edges of the polygon C_i

(1) and (2) are independent of the results of probes, while (3') depends on the knowing the results.

With the above in mind, our plan is simple. First, preprocess to construct a data structure such that, given the result q_0, q_1, q_2 of three finger probes, one can rapidly find all candidate triples of edges w.r.t. q_0, q_1, q_2 from each polygon in the collection $\mathcal{C}$. Subsequently, apply this data structure to determine matches given sets of four probes.

3 Implementation

3.1 Preprocessing and Data Structures

For $0 \leq i \leq m-1$, let

$$E_i^2 = \{(e_0, e_1) : e_0, e_1 \text{ are edges of } C_i\}$$

Let

$$E^2 = \cup \{E_i^2 : 0 \leq i \leq m-1\}$$

For each $(e_0, e_1) \in E^2$, define the point

$$P(e_0, e_1) = (\min(e_0, e_1), \max(e_0, e_1))$$

in $\mathbb{R}^2$.

Construct a 2-dimensional *range tree* (see [5]) $\mathcal{R}$ on the set of points

$$\{P(e_0, e_1) : (e_0, e_1) \in E^2\}$$

which is allowed to contain duplicates, that arise in case $P(e_0, e_1) = P(e'_0, e'_1)$, for distinct pairs (e_0, e_1) and (e'_0, e'_1) from E^2.

At each point $P(e_0, e_1) \in \mathcal{R}$ put a pointer back to (e_0, e_1). Since the polygons in $\mathcal{C}$ are mutually disjoint, so that a straight-line segment can be an edge of at most one member of $\mathcal{C}$, this pointer identifies, as well, the polygon C_i amongst whose edges are e_0 and e_1.

Given $(e_0, e_1) \in E_i^2$, let

$$E(e_0, e_1) = \{e_2 : e_2 \text{ is an edge of } C_i \text{ and } e_0, e_1, e_2 \text{ is counterclockwise around}$$
$$C_i \text{ and } e_0, e_1, e_2 \text{ are not all identical}\}$$

In other words, $E(e_0, e_1)$ consists of the edges e_2 of C_i such that the triple (e_0, e_1, e_2) satisfy conditions (1) and (2) above.

For each $e_2 \in E(e_0, e_1)$, define the point

$$Q(e_2) = (\min(e_0, e_2), \max(e_0, e_2), \min(e_1, e_2), \max(e_1, e_2))$$

in $\mathbb{R}^4$.

For each $(e_0, e_1) \in E_i^2$, construct a 4-dimensional range tree $\mathcal{R}(e_0, e_1)$ on the set of points

$$\{Q(e_2) : e_2 \in E(e_0, e_1)\}$$

which again is allowed to contain duplicates, that arise if $Q(e_2) = Q(e'_2)$, for distinct edges e_2 and e'_2.

At each point $P(e_0, e_1)$ of $\mathcal{R}$ place a pointer to $\mathcal{R}(e_0, e_1)$. The entire structure $\mathcal{R}'$ consisting of $\mathcal{R}$ with $\mathcal{R}(e_0, e_1)$, for all $(e_0, e_1) \in E^2$, is equivalent to a 6-dimensional range tree on the set of points

$$(\min(e_0, e_1), \max(e_0, e_1), \min(e_0, e_2), \max(e_0, e_2), \min(e_1, e_2), \max(e_1, e_2))$$

for all triples (e_0, e_1, e_2), such that $(e_0, e_1) \in E^2$ and $e_2 \in E(e_0, e_1)$.

3.2 Algorithm

Given the result q_0, q_1, q_2, q_3 of four finger probes – we assume that they are no three collinear and that the given order is counterclockwise – we proceed as follows:

Step 1: Search $\mathcal{R}'$ to report the points that lie in the 6-dimensional box

$$\begin{aligned} B = &[-\infty,\ d(q_0, q_1) + \epsilon] \times [d(q_0, q_1) - \epsilon,\ \infty] \times \\ &[-\infty,\ d(q_0, q_2) + \epsilon] \times [d(q_0, q_2) - \epsilon,\ \infty] \times \\ &[-\infty,\ d(q_1, q_2) + \epsilon] \times [d(q_1, q_2) - \epsilon,\ \infty] \end{aligned}$$

which determines the set S of triples (e_0, e_1, e_2) such that (e_0, e_1, e_2) is a candidate triple of edges from some C_i w.r.t. q_0, q_1, q_2, as membership in B verifies condition (3') above.

In other words, S consists of those triples (e_0, e_1, e_2) of edges from some polygon $C_i \in \mathcal{C}$ such that the image $p_j = t(q_j)$, by some rigid transformation t, *may approximately* lie on e_j, for $j = 0, 1, 2$.

Step 2: For each $(e_0, e_1, e_2) \in S$, search $\mathcal{R}(e_0, e_1)$ to report the points that lie in the 4-dimensional box

$$\begin{aligned} B(e_0, e_1) = &[-\infty,\ d(q_0, q_3) + \epsilon] \times [d(q_0, q_3) - \epsilon,\ \infty] \times \\ &[-\infty,\ d(q_1, q_3) + \epsilon] \times [d(q_1, q_3) - \epsilon,\ \infty] \end{aligned}$$

which determines the set $S(e_0, e_1)$ of edges e_3 such that (e_0, e_1, e_3) is a candidate triple of edges from C_i (the polygon amongst whose edges are e_0 and e_1) w.r.t. q_0, q_1, q_3.

Let $\overline{S}$ denote the set of quadruples (e_0, e_1, e_2, e_3) such that $(e_0, e_1, e_2) \in S$ and $e_3 \in S(e_0, e_1)$. Then $\overline{S}$ contains precisely those quadruples (e_0, e_1, e_2, e_3) of edges from some polygon $C_i \in \mathcal{C}$ such that the image $p_j = t(q_j)$, by some rigid transformation t, *may approximately* lie on e_j, for $j = 0, 1, 2, 3$.

Step 3: For each quadruple $(e_0, e_1, e_2, e_3) \in \overline{S}$ we must now verify if *indeed* the image $p_j = t(q_j)$, by some rigid transformation t, lies approximately on the edge e_j, $0 \leq j \leq 3$.

a: We first verify as follows if the triangle with vertices at q_0, q_1, q_2 can be mapped by some rigid transformation t so that the image of q_j lies on e_j, $j = 0, 1, 2$:

Imagine placing the triangle $T = q_0 q_1 q_2$ so that q_0 lies on e_0 and q_1 on e_1, then "sliding" the base $q_0 q_1$ of T so that q_0 travels along e_0 and q_1 along e_1, and determining if there is (approximately) an intersection with e_2 of the locus of the top q_2 of T by the sliding motion. In fact, to allow for approximation, we first construct a rectangle R_2 of length $l_2 + 2\epsilon$ and width 2ϵ, where l_2 is the length of edge e_2 and ϵ is the earlier user-specified constant, and place it centered about e_2; next, we determine if the locus A of q_2, which is an arc of an ellipse (see, e.g., [7] for the *trammel construction* of an ellipse), intersects R.

For example, Figure 1(c) shows q_0 sliding along e_0 from the position a to a', q_1 sliding along e_1 from b to b', and q_2 traveling along the arc A of an ellipse from c to c'.

If A does not intersect R_2, then the quadruple (e_0, e_1, e_2, e_3) is *rejected*; if it does intersect R_2, in say the arc A', then we proceed to the next stage.

b: Again, to allow for approximation, construct a rectangle R_3 of length $l_3 + 2\epsilon$ and width 2ϵ, where l_3 is the length of edge e_3, and place it centered about e_2. Next, exactly as in the previous step, slide the base, but this time precisely in the range so that the locus of q_2 is is A', and determine if the locus of q_3 for this range, which is again an elliptical arc, say A'', intersects R_3.

If A does not intersect R_3, then the quadruple (e_0, e_1, e_2, e_3) is *rejected*; if it does intersect R_3, then (e_0, e_1, e_2, e_3) is *accepted*, and the polygon C_i, amongst whose edges are e_j, $0 \leq j \leq 3$, is a possible match for the target polygon C.

Let $\mathcal{C}'$ be the subset of polygons of $\mathcal{C}$ that are declared as possible matches for C by the preceding procedure.

We shall prove in the next section that if $C_i \in \mathcal{C}$ is, in fact, a match for C, then, after the preceding procedure, with high likelihood, $\mathcal{C}'$ will contain *precisely* C_i.

4 Analysis

Our analysis is fairly heuristic, and we back it up with experiments reported in the next section.

Proposition 2. *Given a random triangle T and a random convex polygon C, the number of different inscriptions of T in C (equivalently, the number of different rigid-body transformations that inscribe T in C) is $O(1)$ with probability 1.*

Proof. Omitted in this version.

Corollary 1. *Given a random convex quadrilateral Q and a random convex polygon C, the the probability that Q can be inscribed in C (equivalently, that there exists a rigid-body transformations that inscribes Q in C) is 0.*

Proof. Let the $Q = p_0 p_1 p_2 p_3$ and consider the triangle $p_0 p_1 p_2$. Let F be the set of distinct rigid-body transformations that inscribe triangle $p_0 p_1 p_2$ in C. Clearly, Q can be inscribed in C if and only if $t(p_3)$ lies on C for some $t \in F$. However, by Proposition 2, the set F, and so also $\{t(p_3) : t \in F\}$, is of cardinality $O(1)$ with probability 1. That the set $\{t(p_3) : t \in F\}$ of size $O(1)$ intersects a random convex polygon C is 0. The result follows.

Corollary 2. *Given a random collection $\mathcal{C}$ of convex polygons, the probability that a quadrilateral $p_0 p_1 p_2 p_3$, inscribed in a $C_i \in \mathcal{C}$, can be inscribed by rigid transformation in another polygon $C_j \in \mathcal{C}$ ($j \neq i$) is 0.*

Proof. Follows easily from Corollary 1.

Proposition 3. *A range tree on a set of N points in $\mathbb{R}^d$ (i.e., a d-dimensional range tree) can be constructed in $O(N \log^{d-1} N)$ and it uses $O(N \log^{d-1} N)$ space. Such a range tree can be queried to report the points in a d-dimensional box in $O(\log^d N + K)$ time, where K is the number of reported points.*

Proof. Refer to [5].

Assume the number of edges in each polygon of $\mathcal{C}$ is $O(n)$.

Proposition 4. *The time to construct and space to store the data structures required for the algorithm of Section 3.2 are both $O(mn^3 \log^5(mn^3))$. The time to the query the structure and report a match, if there is one, is $O(m \log^4 n)$ with high probability.*

Proof. The time to construct, as well as space to store $\mathcal{R}'$, is $O(mn^3 \log^5(mn^3))$, by Proposition 3, as $\mathcal{R}'$ is a 6-dimensional range tree containing $O(mn^3)$ points. This proves the claim for the construction time and space for our data structures.

As the cardinality of $\mathcal{C}$ is m, it follows, by Proposition 2, that the number of points reported in Step 1 of the procedure is $O(m)$ with high probability. How close the probability actually is to 1 depends on two items (we omit details):

(i) The smallness of the user-specified constant ϵ.
(ii) The smallness of the length of each edge of the polygons in $\mathcal{C}$ relative to the length of the boundary of the polygon to which the edge belongs.

Accordingly, the cardinality of the set S of triples created in Step 1 is $O(m)$ with high probability. Therefore, by Proposition 3, the time spent in Step 1 is $O(\log^6(mn^3) + m)$ with high probability.

Arguing similarly (we omit details), with high probability, the time spent in Step 2 is $O(m(\log^4 n + O(1))) = O(m \log^4 n)$. Each verification in Step 3 takes $O(1)$ time, as it involves $O(1)$ tests to detect the intersection between the arc of an ellipse and a rectangle.

Totaling the time for Steps 1-3, the claim for the query time follows.

5 Experimental Results and Conclusion

We wrote the data structures, as described in Section 3.1, in Java, using range tree code from CGAL [3], and, as well, using kd-trees (another data structure for orthogonal range searching [5], code from [9]), in place of range trees. In our experiments the kd-tree, even though theoretically less efficient, was actually quicker than the range tree.

We tested our algorithm on batches of 50 randomly-generated convex polygons by randomly choosing one from each batch, probing it, and then using our method to determine matches based on the probe outcomes. We started with four probes, and, if this did not yield a unique match, increased the number of probes, each time taking the intersection of the matches for each subset of four, until we were left with a single polygon.

Owing to lack of space we summarize briefly our experimental results: 4 probes almost invariably resulted in a large number of matches – often nearly 20 out of 50 polygons – which we attribute to our method allowing for noise; 8 probes almost always resulted in a unique match.

We conclude that initial results are encouraging for our proposed approach to the extremely practical problem of recognizing objects from a collection of "suspects" using few probes. Obviously, much remains to done. Possibly, data structures, other than for orthogonal range searching, can be applied. Most importantly, methods must be extended to 3-dimensional objects for the majority of practical applications.

References

1. P. Belleville, T. C. Shermer, Probing Polygons Minimally is Hard, *Computational Geometry: Theory and Applications* **2** (1993), 255-265.
2. H. J. Bernstein, Determining the Shape of a Convex n-sided Polygon using $2n+k$ Tactile Probes, *Information Processing Letters* **22** (1986), 255-260.
3. CGAL, Computational Geometry Algorithms Library, http://www.cgal.org.
4. R. Cole, C. K. Yap, Shape from Probing, *Journal of Algorithms* **8** (1987), 19-38.
5. M. de Berg, M. van Kreveld, M. Overmars, O. Schwarzkopf, *Computational Geometry: Algorithms and Applications*, Second Edition, Springer-Verlag, 2000.
6. D. P. Dobkin, H. Edelsbrunner, C. K. Yap, Probing Convex Polytopes, *Proc. 18th ACM Symposium on the Theory of Computing*, 1988, 424-432.
7. H. W. Eves, *A Survey of Geometry*, Revised Edition, Allyn and Bacon, 1965.
8. E. Joseph, S. S. Skiena, Model-Based Probing Strategies for Convex Polygons, *Computational Geometry: Theory and Applications* **2** (1992), 209-221.
9. S. D. Levy, KDTree - A Java class for KD-tree search (exact and nearest-neighbor), http://www.cs.wlu.edu/~levy.
10. K. Romanik, Geometric Probing and Testing - A Survey, DIMACS Technical Report 95-42, 1995.
11. S. S. Skiena, *Geometric Probing*, Ph.D. Thesis, Dept. of Computer Science, University of Illinois at Urbana-Champaign, 1998.
12. S. S. Skiena, Interactive Reconstruction via Geometric Probing, *Proceedings of the IEEE* **80** (1992), 1364-1383

Separable Linear Classifiers for Online Learning in Appearance Based Object Detection

Christian Bauckhage and John K. Tsotsos

Centre for Vision Research, York University, Toronto, ON, M3J 1P3
http://cs.yorku.ca/LAAV

Abstract. Online learning for object detection is an important requirement for many computer vision applications. In this paper, we present an iterative optimization algorithm that learns separable linear classifiers from a sample of positive and negative example images. We demonstrate that separability not only leads to rapid runtime behavior but enables very fast training. Experimental results underline that the approach even allows for real time online learning for tracking of articulated objects in real world environments.

1 Motivation and Scientific Context

A general trend in present day computer vision research appears to be the integration of machine learning techniques into visual processing. Especially in the case of object detection in real world environments, the entanglement of vision and learning has led to stunning results. Cascaded weak classifiers rapidly detect objects of constraint shape and texture [1]. Taking aim at varying shape and texture, recent contributions simultaneously learn lexica of salient object parts as well as global structures [2,3,4]. Cognitive approaches integrate reasoning and learning across and within several levels of processing [5].

Robust as they are, the above techniques all require extensive training times. This hampers their use in scenarios where online learning is mandatory, as in the case of vision systems that assist their users in real world tasks. Among the few current proposals for such a scenario is a system that applies the Winnow algorithm for learning linear classifiers to motion data [6]. Others propose the use of sequential principal component analysis (PCA) and probabilistic tracking [7], or apply VPL classification, a technique that combines vector quantization, PCA and locally linear maps [8]. However, although they are fast, none of these methods reaches real time performance in online learning for object recognition.

In this paper, we present a simple approach to very fast object learning which, nevertheless, provides rapid runtime behavior and reliable detection. Based on positive and negative example images, we propose an iterative least mean squares technique of learning separable linear classifiers. The method accomplishes input processing as rapidly as the popular cascaded weak classifiers. Moreover, it copes with objects of considerably varying shape and texture and is characterized by very short training times. Our classifiers therefore enable real time online learning in object recognition.

The next section first discusses the benefits of linear classifiers for visual object detection and then introduces our algorithm for learning separable classifiers. Section 3 presents experimental results in online learning for object detection. Finally, a discussion ends this contribution.

2 Separable Linear Classifiers for Object Detection

In their most basic form, binary linear classifiers compute the scalar product $\boldsymbol{w}^T\boldsymbol{x}$ of a parameter vector $\boldsymbol{w}$ and a feature vector $\boldsymbol{x}$. Their appeal for visual object detection lies in the fact that they may be implemented as two-dimensional linear filters. This requires writing parameters and features as matrices $\boldsymbol{W}$ and $\boldsymbol{X}$ and considering the Frobenius product of matrices $\boldsymbol{W} \star \boldsymbol{X} = \sum_{i,j} W_{ij} X_{ij}$. If $\boldsymbol{X}$ denotes a digital image and $\boldsymbol{W}$ a suitable finite impulse response filter matrix of size $m \times n$, a label y_{ij} characterizing the visual content in the vicinity of each pixel (i,j) can be computed from the convolution $\boldsymbol{W} \ast \boldsymbol{X}$

$$y_{ij} = \sum_{k=-m/2}^{m/2} \sum_{l=-n/2}^{n/2} W_{m-k,n-l} X_{i-k,j-l} = \boldsymbol{W} \star \boldsymbol{X}_{ij} \quad (1)$$

where $\boldsymbol{X}_{ij}$ denotes an image patch of size $m \times n$ centered at (i,j).

Note that if $\boldsymbol{W}$ is a $m \times n$ matrix, convolution requires $O(mn)$ operations per pixel. This may result in prohibitive computational costs even if m and n are set to moderate values. However, if $\boldsymbol{W}$ was a separable matrix, i.e. $\boldsymbol{W} = \boldsymbol{u}\boldsymbol{v}^T$ where $\boldsymbol{u} \in \mathbb{R}^m$ and $\boldsymbol{v} \in \mathbb{R}^n$, the two-dimensional convolution could be computed as a sequence of two one-dimensional convolutions $(\boldsymbol{X} \ast \boldsymbol{u}) \ast \boldsymbol{v}^T$. This would reduce the effort to $O(m+n)$ and therefore provide a fast linear approach to object detection. Next, we discuss how to obtain separable classifiers from training examples.

2.1 Iterative Least Mean Square Learning of Separable Classifiers

Our approach to classifier training modifies an algorithm introduced by Venkatachalam and Aravena [9]. In contrast to their work, we consider spatial convolutions instead of frequency domain filter design. However, for proofs of some of the assumptions applied below, the reader is referred to [9].

A convenient approach to binary classifier training applies the well-known method of least mean squares (LMS) optimization. If we require the parameter matrix to be a *one term separable filter* $\boldsymbol{W} = \boldsymbol{u}\boldsymbol{v}^T$ and if we consider the equivalence

$$\boldsymbol{u}\boldsymbol{v}^T \star \boldsymbol{X} = \sum_{k,l}(\boldsymbol{u}\boldsymbol{v}^T)_{kl} X_{kl} = \sum_{k,l} u_k v_l X_{kl} = \boldsymbol{u}^T \boldsymbol{X} \boldsymbol{v}, \quad (2)$$

then we can write the LMS error function as:

$$E(\boldsymbol{u},\boldsymbol{v}) = \frac{1}{2} \sum_\alpha (y^\alpha - \boldsymbol{u}^T \boldsymbol{X}^\alpha \boldsymbol{v})^2 \quad (3)$$

where $\{\boldsymbol{X}^\alpha, y^\alpha\}_{\alpha=1,\ldots,N}$ is a sample of image patches of size $m \times n$ with corresponding class labels. A solution for $\boldsymbol{u}$ and $\boldsymbol{v}$ can be determined as follows: Given an arbitrary vector $\boldsymbol{u} \in \mathbb{R}^m$, we can compute $\boldsymbol{x}_{\boldsymbol{u}}^{\alpha^T} = \boldsymbol{u}^T \boldsymbol{X}^\alpha$ and then rewrite equation (3):

$$E(u, v) = \frac{1}{2} \sum_\alpha (y^\alpha - x_u^{\alpha T} v)^2 \qquad (4)$$

which is of the form usually encountered in LMS optimization. Consequently, we can determine the optimal set of weights $v^*(u)$ by means of the usual approach of setting $\nabla_v E(u, v) = 0$. A closed form solution for v^* exists if the correlation matrix $C = \sum_\alpha x_u^\alpha x_u^{\alpha T}$ is non singular. In this case, $v^* = C^{-1} \tilde{y}$ where $\tilde{y}$ denotes the cross correlation vector between inputs and labels.

Given v^*, we can compute $\nabla_u E(u, v^*)$ and hence determine u^*. As we started with an arbitrary u, these two steps have to be iterated until a convergence criterion is met. It can be shown that the solution does not depend on the length of u. Therefore, we constrain the vector u to be of unit length $\|u\| = 1$. On the one hand, this introduces additional effort, because it requires normalizing u after each iteration. On the other hand, as $E(u, v^*)$ becomes a continuous, convex function over the unit ball in $\mathbb{R}^m$, which is a compact set, normalization guarantees the convergence of the procedure. Moreover, the unit length constraint provides a simple convergence criterion. In our implementation, we use $\|u_t - u_{t-1}\| \leq \epsilon$, which proved to converge quickly.

```
for i = 1, ..., k
    randomly initialize u_i
    normalize u_i ← u_i / ||u_i||
    orthogonalize u_i ← u_i − ∑_{j=1}^{i−1} (u_j^T u_i)/(u_j^T u_j) u_j
    repeat
        u_i^old ← u_i
        solve E(u_i, v_i) = (1/2) ∑_α (y^α − u_i^T X^α v_i)^2 for v_i
        orthogonalize v_i ← v_i − ∑_{j=1}^{i−1} (v_j^T v_i)/(v_j^T v_j) v_j
        solve E(u_i, v_i) = (1/2) ∑_α (y^α − u_i^T X^α v_i)^2 for u_i
        normalize u_i ← u_i / ||u_i||
        orthogonalize u_i ← u_i − ∑_{j=1}^{i−1} (u_j^T u_i)/(u_j^T u_j) u_j
    until ||u_i^old − u_i|| ≤ ε
endfor
```

Fig. 1. Iterative algorithm to learn the parameter vectors u_i and v_i of a k term separable linear classifier

Note that the classifier that results from this procedure only comes along with $m+n$ coefficients, whereas, in the non-separable case, one would have learned $m \cdot n$ parameters. In its current form, the separable classifier therefore seems less flexible than the usual solution. However, having derived a solution for a one-term separable classifier, we can construct a separable classifier such that its weight matrix is the sum of k rank 1 separable matrices: $W = \sum_{i=1}^{k} u_i v_i^T$.

One can show that, if $W_k = \sum_{i=1}^{k} u_i v_i^T$ is a *k-term* representation of the coefficient matrix of a classifier, a $(k + 1)$-term solution can be found by minimizing $E(u_{k+1}, v_{k+1})$, if, for $i \neq j$, the parameter vectors obey $u_i^T u_j = 0$ and $v_i^T v_j = 0$.

Given the one-term solution, a binary classifier with an arbitrary $k > 1$ can be generated using recursion. The above optimization method simply has to be extended, such that, after *each* iteration, the vectors $\boldsymbol{v}_{k+1}$ and $\boldsymbol{u}_{k+1}$ are orthogonalized with respect to $\{\boldsymbol{v}_i\}_{i=1,\ldots,k}$ and $\{\boldsymbol{u}_i\}_{i=1,\ldots,k}$, respectively. Orthogonalization can be done by applying the Gram-Schmidt procedure.

Figure 1 summarizes the iterative algorithm for training a k-term separable linear classifier. Next, we point out favorable characteristics of this approach, and then, we present results obtained with our separable object detectors.

2.2 Benefits of the Separable Approach

It is interesting to note that any matrix $\boldsymbol{W}$ can be written as a sum of separable matrices. This immediately results from the singular value decomposition $\boldsymbol{W} = \sum_{i=1}^{r} \sigma_i \boldsymbol{u}_i \boldsymbol{v}_i^T$, where r is the rank of $\boldsymbol{W}$, the σ_i are its singular values, and $\boldsymbol{u}_i$ and $\boldsymbol{u}_i$ denote the left and right singular vectors, respectively. Although the proof is omitted here, the orthogonality of the singular vectors actually establishes why, in our iterative approach, we must orthogonalize the coefficient vectors. However, this analytical, SVD-based approach to classifier design has little appeal for practical application.

For a separable classifier resulting from the SVD of a given coefficient matrix, convolving an image will require $O(r(m + n))$ operations per pixel. As the gain in speed depends on the rank r of $\boldsymbol{W}$, there will be no speed benefit in many practical cases. Dealing with the detection of elongated objects (see Fig. 2), $\boldsymbol{W}$ will be of rectangular form so that its rank will most likely be $r = \min\{m, n\}$. If, w.l.o.g, $r = m$, the convolution effort will amount to $m(m + n) = m^2 + mn > mn$ and separated classification will be even more expensive. Of course, the number of terms in the SVD representation of $\boldsymbol{W}$ can be reduced to $k < r$. However, although SVD yields the minimal Frobenius norm $\|\boldsymbol{W} - \sum_{i=1}^{k} \sigma_i \boldsymbol{u}_i \boldsymbol{v}_i^T\|_F$ for any k, practical experience shows that the corresponding classifiers perform worse than the original one. Using our learning algorithm, both of these drawbacks can be avoided. As the separable classifier is derived directly from data rather than from the optimal non-separable version, our algorithm guarantees reasonable results, even in the case where $k \ll r = rank(\boldsymbol{W})$. Of course, choosing a small k results in classifiers having fast runtimes.

Furthermore, the SVD approach requires knowledge of the $m \times n$ coefficient matrix $\boldsymbol{W}$ of a given classifier. Training this classifier using least mean squares requires the computation and inversion of a covariance matrix $\boldsymbol{C}$ with dimensions $mn \times mn$. For larger values of m and n and many training examples $\alpha = 1, \ldots, N$, this will be very time consuming—even on modern computers. Therefore, in addition to the speed benefit during runtime, our technique also significantly speeds up the training phase: The covariance matrices $\boldsymbol{C}_u$ and $\boldsymbol{C}_v$ that appear in the learning algorithm for separable classifiers are of considerably reduced sizes $m \times m$ and $n \times n$, respectively.

Finally, note that fast training and operation times allow us to consider fairly large values for m and n. The resulting linear classifiers thus can process data from very high dimensional feature spaces. This actually guarantees reasonable reliability in object detection. According to Cover's theorem [10], the probability of finding a suitable hyperplane that separates data of any class distribution increases with the dimension of

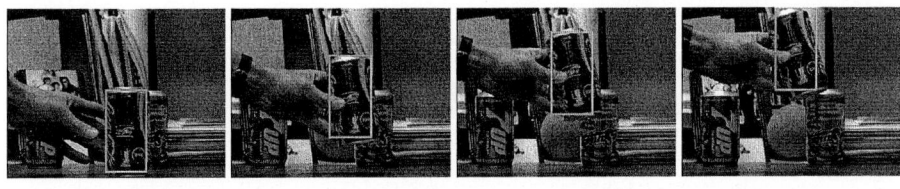

Fig. 2. Exemplary detection results on the *Coke* sequence provided by Black and Jepson [11]

Fig. 3. Exemplary detection results on the desk sequence provided by Gorges et al. [12]

the embedding space. Even if our approach only considers linear discriminance between classes, it can generally be expected to yield good performance.

The experimental results presented in the next section stress that these properties of separable linear classifiers provide an auspicious avenue to online learning for object detection.

3 Experiments in Online Object Learning

In our experiments, we considered several video sequences known from the literature on tracking or scene reconstruction. All sequences show various moving objects in real-world office environments.

In each experiment, the intended object was manually specified in the first frame of a sequence. Then, 30 image patches were randomly selected from the neighborhood of the object and were used as positive training examples (class label +1); 240 image patches randomly selected from outside the neighborhood served as counter examples (class label -1). Training and classification were carried out on simple grey-value intensity information. The activation threshold θ was set to the minimum value resulting from projecting the positive examples onto the normal of the hyperplane learned in the training phase.

After training on the first frame of a sequence, the subsequent frames were convolved with the resulting classifiers. This was done in a brute force manner, where the whole image was convolved and not merely the regions of interest. The intended object was said to be detected where the resulting filter response exceeded the activation threshold θ. Note that we applied a non-maximum suppression to the response map, which reduced the number of false positives. After λ frames, the classifier was retrained using the current image; we experimented with $\lambda \in \{3, 6, 9, \ldots, 30\}$.

Next, we discuss our findings for two of our test cases in more detail.

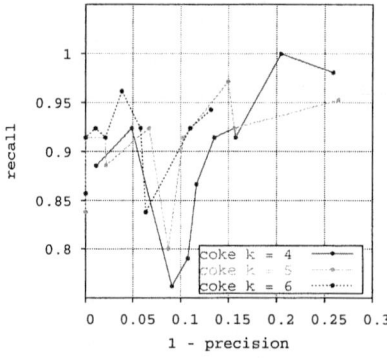 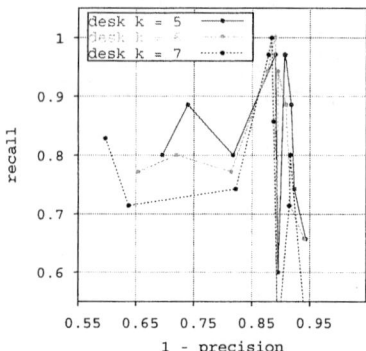

Fig. 4. Precision recall curves for the Coke sequence (left) and the desk sequence (right). The diagrams show the performance of different k term separable classifiers; the free parameter that was varied to generate the curves was the online update rate λ.

3.1 Coke Sequence

In the Coke sequence recorded by Black and Jepson [11], a tin can is moved in front of a static camera (see Fig. 2). We used 115×59 images patches to learn an appearance based model of the can. The diagram on the left in Fig. 4 shows precision recall curves obtained for separable classifiers of different ranks k. The highest recall (100%) resulted from a rank 4 classifier retrained every 21 frames. This classifier detected every instance of the moving can, however, the rate of false positives was 20%. The best performance was reached by a rank 6 classifier that was also retrained every 21 frames. Note that we measure performance quality in terms of equal error rate (EER), which characterizes the point where recall and precision are equal; for our best performing classifier we obtained an EER of 96%. Therefore, updating the classifier every 21 frames best captures the appearance variation due the the can's movement. The poorer performance for more frequent retraining appears to be an over-fitting phenomenon.

The diagram on the left in Fig. 5 plots recall and precision against operation frequency of the tested classifiers. As one would expect, the 4-term classifiers perform fastest. On a 3GHz Intel Xenon PC, the 155 frames, each of size 320×240, were processed at a frequency of approximately 10.5Hz, including file I/O *and* retraining. The most reliable 6-term classifier was measured to operate at 7.4Hz.

3.2 Desk Sequence

Though the results obtained on the Coke sequence are encouraging and representative for most of our experiments, a caveat remains concerning the feature space we considered for classification. The 86 frames of a resolution of 640×480 of the desk sequence provided by Gorges et al. [12] were recorded by a mobile camera panning across an office desk (see Fig. 3). To detect the CD on the left of the scene, we used 121×121 windows. Since the image sizes are four times as large as those in the Coke sequence, the operation frequencies of the resulting classifiers dropped to about a fourth of the

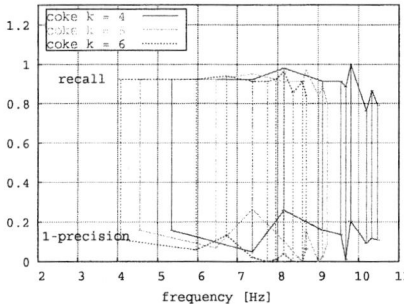
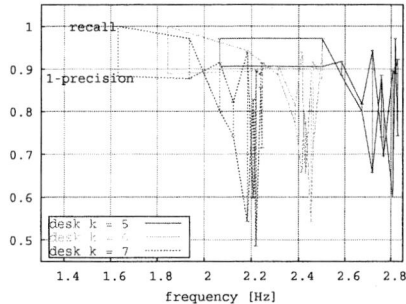

Fig. 5. Precision and recall and corresponding operation frequencies measured for the 320 × 240 images of the Coke sequence (left) and for the 640 × 480 images of the desk sequence (right). Again, the performance of different k term separable classifiers is shown for varying online update rates λ.

ones in the experiments above (see right hand side of Fig. 5). As shown in the digram on the right in Fig. 4, for all rank k classifiers considered in our tests, an update rate λ could be found that yielded high recall rates and reliable CD detection. However, the problem with this sequence is that there are many false positives because the cover of the magazine that is located behind the box becomes visible in the middle of the sequence. As it is very similar to shape and color of the intended object, the cover was frequently classified to depict the CD. The exemplary results in Fig. 3 were obtained with a 7 term separable classifier that was retrained every 18 frames and showed a recall of 83% and a false positive rate of about 59%.

Obviously, online learning did not provide a remedy in this pathological case. However, the problems encountered here do not constitute an inherent shortcoming of our technique. Rather, they are due to the type of features we considered in our experiments. Although simple intensity values yielded satisfactory results in many cases, the desk sequence shows that, depending on the application scenario, other features might have to be considered. To further improve our results, we are currently experimenting with an image representation framework recently proposed by Koenderink [13].

4 Conclusion and Outlook

This paper presented a fast and conceptually simple approach to visual object detection. We described an iterative, two-step optimization method for learning a binary, one-term separable linear classifier from a set of positive and negative example images. Given the optimal one-term classifier, classifiers of arbitrary higher ranks can be obtained from a recursive scheme. By design, the resulting classifiers correspond to linear filters. The classification process itself thus consists of convolving an input image. Since the detectors are separable, their runtime is fast—even for large filter masks. Nevertheless, the required training times are very short. While other recent contributions dealing with online learning report update times of slightly more than a second [6,7,8], our approach reaches several Hz. Experimental results on image sequences known from literature show that this allows for real online learning and adaption of the classifiers.

There are numerous promising directions for further research on our rapid appearance-based approach to object learning. We will especially consider the following ideas: it would be interesting to see if separable classifier matrices can be subjected to affine transformations in order to reduce online update rates but nevertheless detect objects while the camera zooms or rotates. Moreover, integrating separable classifiers into tracking applications seems auspicious. One can imagine a particle filter for robust tracking, where the object models are given as separable classifiers. The adaption step of the filter would correspond to classifier retraining as in our current implementation. Also, if, in the verification step of the particle filter, the classifiers are only applied to small areas of the whole image, the resulting tracker should be fast and accurate.

References

1. Viola, P., Jones, M.: Rapid Object Detection using a Boosted Cascade of Simple Features. In: Proc. CVPR. Volume I. (2001) 511–518
2. Agarwal, S., Awan, A., Roth, D.: Learning to detect objects in images via a sparse, part-based representation. IEEE Trans. on Pattern Analysis and Machine Intelligence **26** (2004) 1475–1490
3. Fergus, R., Perona, P., Zisserman, A.: Object class recognition by unsupervised scale-invariant learning. In: Proc. CVPR. Volume II. (2003) 264–272
4. Leibe, B., Leonardis, A., Schiele, B.: Combined object categorization and segmentation with an implicit shape model. In: Proc. ECCV Workshop on Statistical Learning in Computer Vision, Prague (2004)
5. Bauckhage, C., Hanheide, M., Wrede, S., Sagerer, G.: A Cognitive Vision System for Action Recognition in Office Environments. In: Proc. CVPR. Volume II. (2004) 827–833
6. Nair, V., Clark, J.: An Unsupervised Online Learning Framework for Moving Object Detection. In: Proc. CVPR. Volume II. (2004) 317–324
7. Ross, D., Lim, J., Yang, M.H.: Adaptive Probabilistic Visual Tracking with Incremental Subspace Updat. In: Proc. ECCV. LNCS, Springer (2004) 470–482
8. Heidemann, G., Bekel, H., Bax, I., Ritter, H.: Interactive online learning. Pattern Recognition and Image Analysis **15** (2005) 55–58
9. Venkatachalam, V., Aravena, J.: Optimal Parallel 2-D FIR Digital Filter with Separable Terms. IEEE Trans. on Signal Processing **45** (1997) 1393–1369
10. Cover, T.: Geometrical and Statistical Properties of Systems of Linear Inequalities with Applications to Pattern Recognition. IEEE Trans. on Electronic Computers **14** (1965) 326–334
11. Black, M., Jepson, A.: Eigentracking: Robust matching and tracking of articulated objects using a view-based reprenstation. Int. J. of Computer Vision **26** (1998) 63–84
12. Gorges, N., Hanheide, M., Christmas, W., Bauckhage, C., Sagerer, G., Kittler, J.: Mosaics from Arbitrary Stereo Video Sequences. In: Pattern Recognition. Volume 3175 of LNCS., Springer (2004) 342–349
13. Koenderink, J.J., van Doorn, A.J.: Image Processing Done Right. In: Proc. ECCV. Volume 2350 of LNCS., Springer (2002) 158–172

The Randomized Hough Transform for Spherical Images

Akihiko Torii[1] and Atsushi Imiya[2]

[1] Graduate School of Science and Technology, Chiba University, Japan
akit@graduate.chiba-u.jp
[2] Institute of Media and Information Technology, Chiba University, Japan
imiya@faculty.chiba-u.jp

Abstract. We propose the algorithm for detecting great circles on images on a sphere using the Hough transform. Since our Hough transform on images on a sphere is derived on the basis of the duality, the Hough transform employs a dual sphere as the accumulator of the voting procedure. Furthermore, we propose a robust algorithm based on three-point Hough transform and the segmentation of points on the dual sphere using the metric defined on a sphere.

1 Introduction

In this paper, we propose the detection of great circles on images on a sphere, that is, spherical images, using the Hough transform. Images acquired using an all-central omnidirectional camera system are transformed to spherical images [1,2,3] when the appropriate camera factors of the camera systems, which are generally given in the design phase, are known. Therefore, it is possible to adopt the detection of lines by Hough transform as a preprocess to three-dimensional scene reconstruction from omnidirectional images. It is also possible to analyze the omnidirectional images directly and to develop algorithms based on it [3,4]. However, it is required to modify the developed algorithms depending on the omnidirectional camera systems. For the establishment of unified theory to the omnidirectional systems, we propose the image analysis on spherical images.

Lines in a space, for instance, edges of walls in a man-made environment, are transformed to great circle arcs on a spherical images. The detection of edges in a space from a spherical image is achieved by detection of great circle arcs. The great circles and great arcs correspond to lines and line segments on a plane. This geometrical correspondence implies that great circles on S^2 are geometrically and practically fundamental features for image analysis on a sphere. Therefore, the aim of this study is to derive an algorithm for the detection of many great circles on a sphere.

2 Hough Transform for Great Circle Detection

As illustrated in Fig. 1 (a), since a great circle on the unit sphere $S^2 \in \mathbb{R}^3$ centered at the origin is the intersection of S^2 and a plane passing through

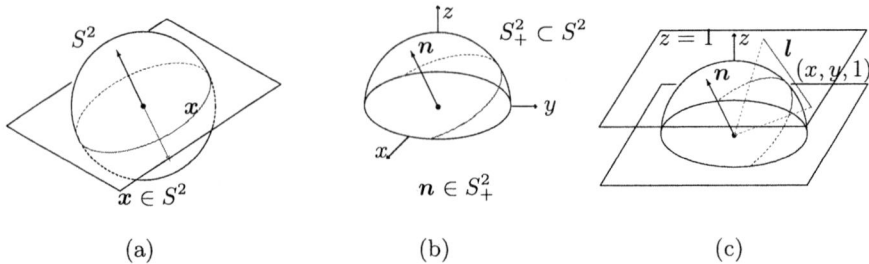

Fig. 1. (a) and (b) Duality of a great circle and a point on S_+^2. (c) Duality of a line on a plane and a point on S_+^2.

the origin, a great circle defines a pair of antidirectional unit normal vectors. Furthermore, as illustrated in Fig. 1 (b), the antidirectional unit normal vectors define the same plane that passes through the origin. Therefore, a great circle corresponds to a vector on the positive unit hemisphere which is defined as $S_+^0 = [1]$, $S_+^1 = S^1 \cap H_+^2 \cup \{s^2\}$, $s^2 = (s, 0)^\top$, $s \in S_+^0$, $H_+^2 = \{(x,y)|y > 0\}$, $S_+^2 = S^2 \cap H_+^3 \cup \{s^3\}$, $s^3 = (S_+^1, 0)^\top$ and $H_+^3 = \{(x,y,z)|z > 0\}$. We set $x \in \mathbb{R}^n$ and $\xi \in \mathbb{P}^{n-1}$. For $n \in S_+^2$ and $x \in \mathbb{R}^3$, a great circle C is given as

$$C = \{x | n^\top x = 0, |x| = 1\}. \tag{1}$$

Therefore, formally the transformation from C to S_+^2 is expressed as

$$f(C) = \lambda \frac{x \times y}{|x \times y|}, \quad f^{-1}(n) = \{x | n^\top x = 0, |x| = 1, n \in S_+^2\}, \tag{2}$$

where $x, y \in S^2$ and $\lambda \in \{-1, 1\}$ is selected so that vector $f(C)$ lies on S_+^2. This transformation allows us to adopt the Hough transform for the detection of great circles. As illustrated in Fig. 1 (c), there exist correspondences between a line l on a plane and a point on S_+^2,

$$g(l) = \lambda \frac{\xi \times \eta}{|\xi \times \eta|}, \quad g^{-1}(n) = \{x | n^\top \xi = 0, \xi = (x^\top, 1)^\top, n \in S_+^2\}, \tag{3}$$

where $\xi = (x^\top, 1)^\top$, $\eta = (y^\top, 1)^\top$ and $x, y \in l$. The transformation is based on the embedding of projective plane P^2 into a unit sphere S^2 in Euclidean space $\mathbb{R}^3$. This duality provides the theoretical background of the traditional Hough transform on the plane. We call this relation the Hough duality. As shown in Eq. (2), the duality of great circles and points on the sphere has the same property as the Hough duality. For a planar line and a point in the projective plane, the function $f(C)$ transforms points lying on a great circle to a point n. Using the transformation $f(C)$ and S_+^2 as the voting operation and the accumulator, respectively, we can design the Hough transform for great circle detection based on these duality.

Considering these geometrical properties, our task is described as follows.

Task 1. *Extract n great circles from a collection of digitized sample points $\boldsymbol{P} = \{\boldsymbol{x}_i = (x_i, y_i, z_i)\}_{i=1}^m$ on the unit sphere, that is, $|\boldsymbol{x}_i| = 1$, assuming that*

1. $n \ll m$,
2. *a collection of samples $\boldsymbol{P}$ contains samples from background and*
3. *elements of $\boldsymbol{P}$ involve noise.*

For a unit vector $\boldsymbol{a} = (a,b,c)^\top$ on S^2, a great circle on S^2 is defined as

$$l = S^2 \bigcup \{\boldsymbol{x} | \boldsymbol{x}^\top \boldsymbol{a} = 0, \boldsymbol{x} \in \mathbb{R}^3\}. \tag{4}$$

Therefore, setting

$$u(\boldsymbol{a}) = \begin{cases} 1, & \boldsymbol{a} = 0, \\ 0, & \text{otherwise}, \end{cases} \tag{5}$$

the classical Hough transform detects the peaks of the function [5,6], as illustrated in Figs. 2 (a) and (b).

$$v(\boldsymbol{a} \in S_+^2) = \sum_{\boldsymbol{x}_i \in P} u(\boldsymbol{a}^\top \boldsymbol{x}_i). \tag{6}$$

It is possible to use the dual sphere S_+^2, as the accumulator of detecting the peaks of Eq. (6). The randomized Hough transform [5,7,8] detects the peaks of the function, as illustrated in Figs. 2 (c) and (d),

$$v(\boldsymbol{a} \in S_+^2) = \sum_{\boldsymbol{x}_i, \boldsymbol{x}_j \in P} u(\boldsymbol{a} - \boldsymbol{a}_{ij}), \quad \boldsymbol{a}_{ij} = \lambda \frac{\boldsymbol{x}_i \times \boldsymbol{x}_j}{|\boldsymbol{x}_i \times \boldsymbol{x}_j|}, \quad \lambda \in \{-1, 1\}, \tag{7}$$

for a randomly selected pair of vectors $\boldsymbol{x}_i$ and $\boldsymbol{x}_j$ on a sphere. λ is selected so that vector $\boldsymbol{a}_{ij}$ lies on S_+^2.

Next, we can evaluate the robustness of Hough transform on a sphere which employs S_+^2 as the voting space of a great circle $l \in S^2$. Setting $\hat{\boldsymbol{x}}_i = \boldsymbol{x}_i + \varepsilon$ and $\hat{\boldsymbol{x}}_j = \boldsymbol{x}_j + \varepsilon$ to be the points on a sphere that includes noise ε, the possibility of a normal vector is computed as $\hat{\boldsymbol{a}}_{ij} = \lambda \frac{\hat{\boldsymbol{x}}_i \times \hat{\boldsymbol{x}}_j}{|\hat{\boldsymbol{x}}_i \times \hat{\boldsymbol{x}}_j|} = \boldsymbol{a}_{ij} + \varepsilon \bar{\boldsymbol{a}}_{ij} + O(\varepsilon^2)$. If $\hat{\boldsymbol{a}}_{ij}$ is voted to the accumulator with finite resolution, the noise definitively affects the result of estimation of the normal vector through the voting procedure. Our Hough transform employs S_+^2 as the voting space of a great circle $l \in S^2$. Therefore, we estimate the normal vector from the collection of points on S^2. The estimation from the collection of points $\{\hat{\boldsymbol{a}}_{ij}\}$ enables us to reduce the noise influence, as described in Section 3. Therefore, it is possible to compute the normal vector $\boldsymbol{a}_{ij}$ robustly.

In both classical and randomized Hough transforms, the detection of peaks $\{\boldsymbol{a}_t^*\}_{t=1}^n$ enables to classify the sample points into clusters, respectively, using

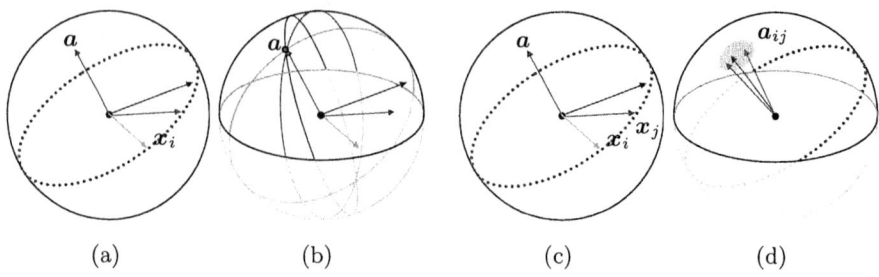

Fig. 2. (a) and (b) The classical Hough transform on a spherical image. (c) and (d) The randomized Hough transform on a spherical image.

the relation $\boldsymbol{x}_\alpha \sim \boldsymbol{x}_\beta$, if $\boldsymbol{x}_\alpha, \boldsymbol{x}_\beta \in P_t$ for $P_t = \{\boldsymbol{x}_\gamma \,|\, |\boldsymbol{x}_\gamma^\top \boldsymbol{a}_t^*| \leq \tau\}$, since the peaks $\{\boldsymbol{a}_t^*\}_{t=1}^n$ on S_+^2 yield lines

$$\boldsymbol{x}^\top \boldsymbol{a}_t^* = 0, \ t = 1, 2, \cdots, n. \tag{8}$$

3 Robust Algorithms for Hough Transform on a Sphere

3.1 Three-Point Hough Transform on a Sphere

In this study, we employ the randomized Hough transform in Eq. (7) for the great circle detection in a spherical image. Since practical implementation of the equi-grid on a sphere [9,10,11] is technically difficult and computationally expensive, we directly use the geometrically defined sphere, which is the dual space of the image on a sphere, as the voting space. This means all $\boldsymbol{a}_{ij}$ in Eq. (7), which are the possible lines, are voted to the dual space, that is, the sphere of the dual space.

Problem 1. Classify the mismatched selection in $\boldsymbol{a}_{ij}$ during the voting procedure.

Since $\boldsymbol{a}_{ij}$ is voted from all combinations of points on the spherical image, $\boldsymbol{a}_{ij}$ implies noise resulting from mismatched selection of the points for great circle detection. Solving this problem, we use the Hough transform using three points [8]. We vote $\boldsymbol{n}_p$ to the voting space, that is, a sphere as the dual space, using the following algorithm.

Algorithm 1. *Three-Point Hough Transform on a Sphere*

1. Set $\boldsymbol{a}_{ij} = \lambda \frac{\boldsymbol{x}_i \times \boldsymbol{x}_j}{|\boldsymbol{x}_i \times \boldsymbol{x}_j|}$ as a possible normal vector which denotes a great circle on a sphere.
2. If $u(\sum_{k=1}^m \boldsymbol{a}_{ij}^\top \boldsymbol{x}_k) \geq 3$, then select $\boldsymbol{n}_p = \boldsymbol{a}_{ij}$ and vote $\{\boldsymbol{n}_p\}_{p=1}^q$ to the voting space.

This voting procedure also removes the points of background as outliers.

3.2 Point Cloud Segmentation on a Sphere

The points $\{n_p\}_{p=1}^{q}$ on the dual sphere detected using **Algorithm 1** described in the previous section still includes the noise yielded by the sampling and discretization process. Therefore, the points $\{n_p\}_{p=1}^{q}$ are expressed as point clouds on the dual sphere. We are required to segment point clouds to $\{\bar{P}_t\}_{t=1}^{n}$ and to select the centroid of $\bar{P}_t$. For the collection of points segmented to $\{\bar{P}_t\}_{t=1}^{n}$, we give the following definition.

Definition 1. *The axis of the cone, which includes a collection of points $\bar{P}_t$, is the centroid of $\bar{P}_t$.*

The centroid of $\bar{P}_t$ express the normal vector which denotes the great circle in S^2. Assuming that we have the cone axis as illustrated in Fig. 3 (a), which is the centroid of $\bar{P}_t$, it is possible to extract $\bar{P}_t$ from the point clouds $\{n_p\}_{p=1}^{q}$. We define that θ, $0 \leq \theta \leq \pi/2$, is an opening angle which is the apex angle of the cone. Setting

$$u^*(a) = \begin{cases} 1, & a \geq 0, \\ 0, & \text{otherwise}, \end{cases} \quad (9)$$

we have the function $d_p(\theta) = \sum_{j=1}^{q} u^*(\frac{\theta}{2} - |\cos^{-1}(n_p^\top n_j)|)$. This function $d_p(\theta)$ evaluates the number of points in the cone, whose axis is n_p, with respect to the changes of θ. As illustrated in Fig. 3 (b), when the opening angle of a cone is large and small, the cone includes other collections of points and does not include a collection of points $\bar{P}_t$, respectively. As illustrated in Fig. 3 (a), if we select the first peak of the function $d_p(\theta)$ with respect to n_p, it is possible to define the opening angle of the cone which extracts a collection of points $\bar{P}_t$ from the point clouds $\{n_p\}_{p=1}^{q}$. We give the following definition.

Definition 2. *The minimum opening angle θ_p of a cone, whose axis is n_p, is derived by selecting the first peak of the function $d_p(\theta)$.*

Since we have no criterion for selecting n_p as the cone axis, we must select the centroid n_p from $\{n_p\}_{p=1}^{q}$ and segment $\{n_p\}_{p=1}^{q}$ to $\{\bar{P}_t\}_{t=1}^{n}$ simultaneously.

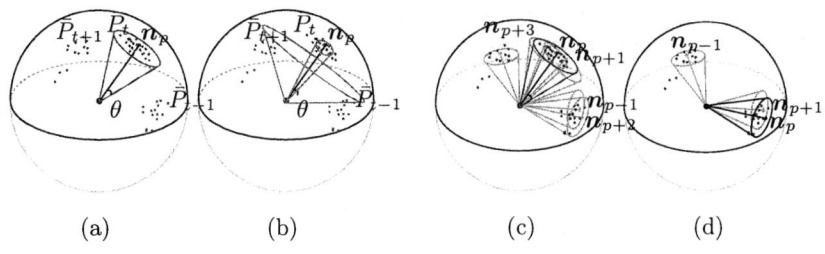

(a) (b) (c) (d)

Fig. 3. (a) and (b) Estimation of minimum opening angle. (c) and (d) Iterative selection of a cone which includes the maximum number of points w.r.t the minimum opening angle and removal of the points.

For $p = 1, 2, \cdots, q$, we compute the minimum opening angle θ_p with respect to $\boldsymbol{n}_p$, as illustrated in Fig. 3 (c). If the cone, whose axis is $\boldsymbol{n}_p$, with the minimum opening angle θ_p includes maximum numbers of points in the point clouds $\{\boldsymbol{n}_p\}_{p=1}^q$, we select the axis $\boldsymbol{n}_p$ as the center of a collection of points. For selecting other axes, that is, other great circles, the collection of points in this cone is removed from $\{\boldsymbol{n}_p\}_{p=1}^q$ as illustrated in Fig. 3 (d). If we iterate this procedure, it is possible to segment the point clouds and, simultaneously, to select the centroid of the point clouds. We summarize this algorithm as follows.

Algorithm 2. *Segmentation of Point Clouds in the Voting Space*

1. Set $t := 1$.
2. For $\{\boldsymbol{n}_p\}_{p=1}^q$, compute the minimum opening angles $\{\theta_p\}_{p=1}^q$.
3. For $p = 1, 2, \cdots, q$, search the cone that includes the maximum numbers of points, employing the minimum opening angles θ_p.
4. Set the points included in the cone as $\bar{P}_t$ and set the cone axis $\boldsymbol{n}_p$ as a great circle $\boldsymbol{a}_t$.
5. Eliminate the points in $\bar{P}_t$ from $\{\boldsymbol{n}_p\}_{p=1}^q$ and update the numbers of points q.
6. Set $t := t + 1$.
7. If $t < t_{max}$, then go to step 2, else exit.

In this algorithm, t_{max} is the number of great circles in the sphere. These processes enable us to detect great circles on a image on a sphere robustly beyond the resolution of the accumulator.

4 Numerical Examples

Figs. 4 (a) and (b) show the results of numerical experiments for the synthetic data from two view angles. The blue dots are the input-data points on a unit sphere. Our Hough transform detected small and large triangles colored in red on a sphere from noisy input samples. For the numerical evaluation, we compute the angles between each normal vector which denotes a line and the normal vector of the grand truth obtained for generating the input data. Table 1 shows the normal vectors and the angles for each line.

Applying our Hough transform to real omnidirectional images, we extract the edges on an input original image using the standard image processing technique

Table 1. Numerical evaluation of synthetic data in Figs. 4 (a) and (b)

	Grand Truth	Detected Line	Angles (rad)
1	(0.00578, 0.315, 0.949)	(0.0157, 0.324, 0.946)	0.0139
2	(0.707, 0.707, 0.000)	(0.713, 0.701, 0.0171)	0.0190
3	(-0.200, -0.194, 0.960)	(-0.241, -0.146, 0.960)	0.0640
4	(0.316, 0.000, 0.949)	(0.310, 0.0268, 0.950)	0.0276
5	(0.000, -0.500, 0.866)	(-0.0107, -0.490, 0.872)	0.0156
6	(-0.866, 0.500, 0.000)	(-0.861, 0.508, -0.0369)	0.0382

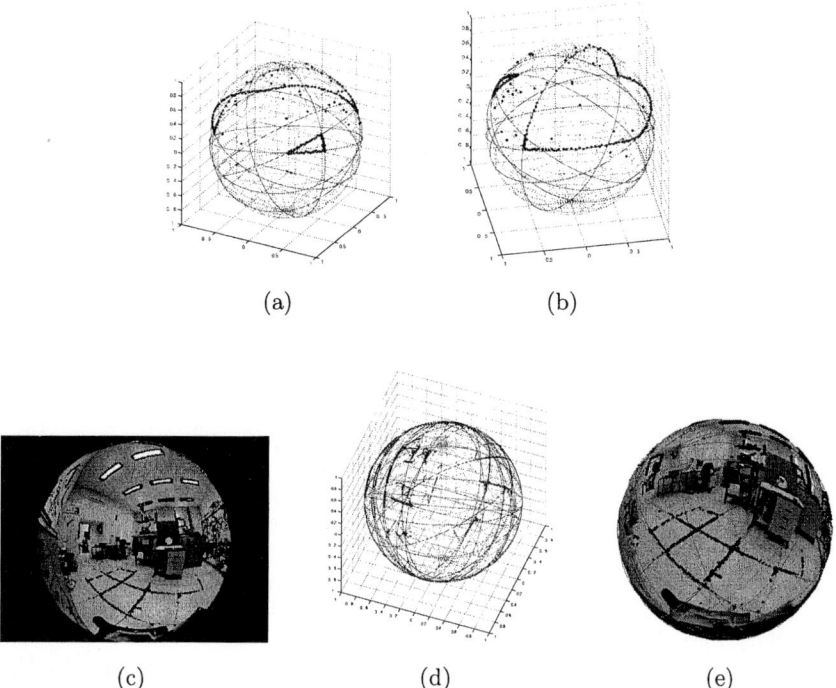

(a)　　　　　　　　(b)

(c)　　　　　　　(d)　　　　　　　(e)

Fig. 4. (a) and (b) Results of great circle detection for synthetic data from different view angles. (c), (d) and (e) Results of great circle detection for the 1600 × 1200-resolution fish-eye-lens camera image. (c) Input image and points, which are colored blue, extracted by Canny operator [12]. (d) Blue points projected onto a sphere and the 17 great circles, which are colored red, detected by our Hough transform. (e) The extracted points using Canny operator and the 17 great circles detected by our Hough transform in (d) are mapped to an image on a sphere.

[12] and then map the extracted points to a sphere. Fig. 4 (c) shows an input image captured by a fish-eye-lens camera, which is Nikon Coolpix 950 and Nikon Fisheye converter FC-E8, and extracted points which are colored blue. 3818 points are extracted as input samples from the 1600 × 1200-resolution fish-eye image. Our Hough transform detected 17 great circles on a sphere. Figs. 4 (d) and (e) show the sample points projected onto a sphere and the detected lines colored in red, and the 17 detected great circles mapped to an image on a sphere, respectively.

5 Conclusions

We introduced the Hough transform on a sphere as a practical application of image analysis on a sphere. We showed the numerical accuracy and robustness of the proposed algorithm through numerical experiments. Since we can detect sufficient numbers of lines in a spherical image, it is possible to employ our Hough transform as a preprocessing for the three-dimensional scene reconstruction of a wide field of view.

Acknowledgment

The images in Section 4 were prepared while the first author was at Center for Machine Perception (CMP) in Czech Technical University. He expresses great thanks to Prof. V. Hlaváč and Assistant Prof. T. Pajdla at CMP for their hospitality.

References

1. B. Mičušík and T. Pajdla. Para-catadioptric camera auto-calibration from epipolar geometry. In *Proc. ACCV*, vol. 2, pp. 748–753, Seoul, South Korea, January 2004.
2. P. Sturm and S. Ramalingam. A generic concept for camera calibration. In LNCS 3021-3024, In *Proc. ECCV*, vol. 2, pp. 1–13, Prague, Czech Republic, Springer, May 2004.
3. T. Svoboda, T. Pajdla and V. Hlaváč. Epipolar geometry for panoramic cameras. In *Czech Technical University Workshop 98*, pp. 177–178, Prague, Czech Republic, February 1998. Czech Technical University.
4. K. Yamazawa, Y. Yagi, M. Yachida. 3D Line Segment Reconstruction by Using HyperOmni Vision and Omnidirectional Hough Transforming. In *Proc. ICPR*, vol.3, pp. 487-490, 2000.
5. H. Kalviainen, P. Hirvonen, L. Xu and E. Oja. Probabilistic and nonprobabilistic hough transforms: Overview and comparisons. *IVC*, vol. 13, no. 4, pp. 239–252, May 1995.
6. E. Aguado, A.S. Montiel and M.S. Nixon. On the intimate relationship between the principle of duality and the hough transform. *Proceedings of the Royal Society A: Mathematical, Physical and Engineering Sciences*, vol. 456, pp. 503–526, 2000.
7. L. Xu and E. Oja. Randomized hough transform (rht): Basic mechanism, algorithm, and computational complexities. *CVGIP: Image Understanding*, vol. 57, pp. 131–154, 1995.
8. T.C. Chen and K.L. Chung. A new randomized algorithm for detecting lines. *Real-Time Imaging* , vol. 7, no. 6, pp. 473–481, 2001.
9. M. Berger. *Geometry I & II*. Springer-Verlag, 1987.
10. F. Pearson. *Map Projections: Theory and Applications*. CRC Press, 1990.
11. J. P. Yang, Q. Snyder and W. R. Tobler. *Map Projection Transformation: Principles and Applications*. Taylor & Francis, 2000.
12. Intel Corporation. *http://www.intel.com/research/mrl/research/opencv/* Open source computer vision library.

Computerized Extraction of Craniofacial Anatomical Structures for Orthodontic Analysis

Weining Yue[1], Dali Yin[1], Guoping Wang[1], Tianmin Xu[2], and Chengjun Li[1]

[1] Department of Computer Science & Technology,
Peking University, Beijing 100871, China
ywn@graphics.pku.edu.cn
[2] School of Stomatology, Peking University,
Beijing 100081, China
tmxu@vip.sina.com

Abstract. Extraction of craniofacial anatomical structures on cephalometric radiographs is important for observing and predicting the growth changes and evaluating the curative effect in orthodontic analysis. Due to the natural of cephalograms, it is difficult for simplex image processing approaches to exactly track both the soft tissue contours and the structure outlines of internal skull. In this paper, we address this problem by recognizing 262 landmark points and then connecting them according to the prior knowledge. Image processing, pattern matching, and modified active shape model are combined to realize the landmark recognition; subdivision curves are used to obtain the structure rendering.

1 Introduction

In orthodontic diagnosis and treatment, some advanced cephalometric analysis (e.g., *superimposition*) are strongly dependent on the extraction of craniofacial anatomical structures. Such structure based analysis allows orthodontists to observe and predict the overview of growth changes and evaluate the curative effect. Since manual operation is time consuming and some subjective errors are inevitable with human vision, computerized the structures extraction is significant for automated orthodontic analysis.

However, as Romaniuk indicated [1], the detection of structure contour edges by classical image processing techniques inevitably fails for some local configurations where gradients are low or inverted. Moreover, these methods need the fine tuning of numerous thresholds for a good detection result. To solve these problems, a regional approach of type shortest path was proposed in [1] to combine robustness and low algorithmic cost, but only the external cranial contour (dome of the skull limited by the nose and the lowest point of the cranium) was extracted. Actually, due to the nature of cephalograms, it is difficult for simplex image processing approaches to extract both the soft tissue edges and the structure outlines of internal skull exactly.

In this paper, we address this problem from a different point of view. Instead of detecting the structure edges directly, we start with recognizing 262 landmark points situated on the structure contours, some of which are cephalometric landmarks [2] and the others are selected according to the prior knowledge of structures. Subdivision curves are used to connect the located landmarks to trace out *all* craniofacial structures. The structures and landmarks to be identified are shown in Fig. 1.

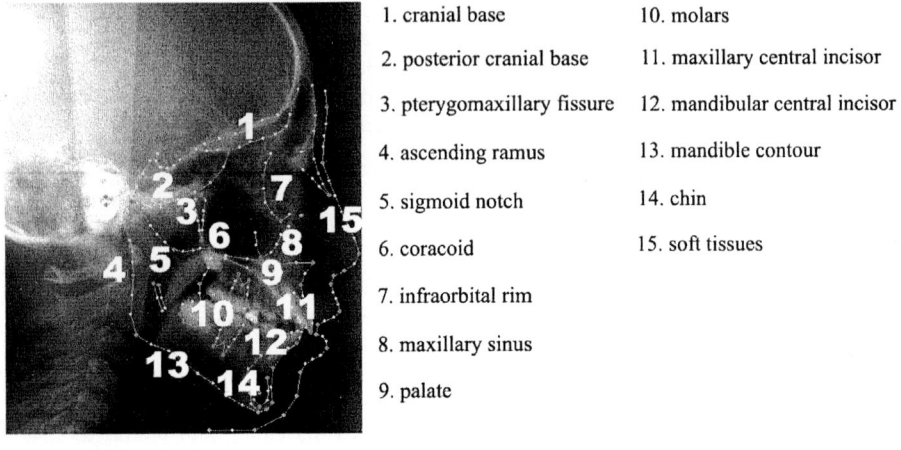

1. cranial base
2. posterior cranial base
3. pterygomaxillary fissure
4. ascending ramus
5. sigmoid notch
6. coracoid
7. infraorbital rim
8. maxillary sinus
9. palate
10. molars
11. maxillary central incisor
12. mandibular central incisor
13. mandible contour
14. chin
15. soft tissues

Fig. 1. Craniofacial structures and landmarks to be recognized

2 Landmark Recognition

2.1 Method Overview

Early works [3][4][5] usually locate commonly-used cephalometric landmarks based on edge detection techniques. After extracting relevant edges, landmarks are located based on a set of pre-defined geometrical properties. Differing from this strategy, our objective requires the recognition algorithm independent on edge information. The statistical model approaches are applicable. Romaniuk [6][7] and Sid-Ahmed [8][9] made substantial contribution in this field. In designing our algorithm, we were also greatly influenced by Hutton's work [10] in which the active shape model (ASM) [11], being widely used in statistical pattern recognition, was employed.

Classical ASM method consists of two steps. First, the mean shape model of a training set and the gray models of landmarks are trained. Then, every landmark in the mean shape is iteratively searched to its best matched position according to the statistical gray profile. However, the number of located landmarks by this method or any other existing work is no more than thirty, which is much less than that in this study. Our previous work [12] has shown that the large-scale point set poses great challenge. In the standard ASM search, the shape model is transformed between model space and input space by affine transformations similar to

$$T\begin{pmatrix}x\\y\end{pmatrix} = \begin{pmatrix}s_x & 0\\0 & s_y\end{pmatrix}\begin{pmatrix}\cos\theta & \sin\theta\\-\sin\theta & \cos\theta\end{pmatrix}\begin{pmatrix}x\\y\end{pmatrix} + \begin{pmatrix}t_x\\t_y\end{pmatrix}. \quad (1)$$

Only the global optimization can be obtained in this way and there are still some points which will be placed far from their matched ones. Meanwhile, lots of landmarks have similar gray profiles because of the dense distribution and the nature of cephalograms. The gray search, therefore, is error-prone or even not convergent. The misplacement will also increasingly occur when the shape similarity between the shape model and the input shape is low since (1) is a similarity transformation.

To solve such problems, we select twelve landmarks as reference points and use them to divide every training shape to ten independent regions according to the anatomical knowledge. For each region, principal component analysis (PCA) is applied to build its shape model and to extract the gray statistics of landmarks. When an image is input, the reference landmarks are detected by edge detection techniques and a pattern matching algorithm. Then each region is exactly located by a modified ASM. In our method, the shape partition will decrease the granularity of modeling and search, and the transformations could be extended to more general form so that the majority of landmarks can be placed more closely to their matched ones and avoid the interference with others.

2.2 Training

170 cephalograms, digitalized with a resolution of 600dpi and sized to 600×700 pixels, are provided by Peking University School of Stomatology as the training materials. They have been located manually by human experts.

Craniofacial Shape Partition. Twelve landmarks are selected as *Reference Landmarks* (see Fig.2). Based on them, every training shape is divided to ten independent regions according to the anatomical knowledge of craniofacial structures, with each region being determined by three reference landmarks (see Table

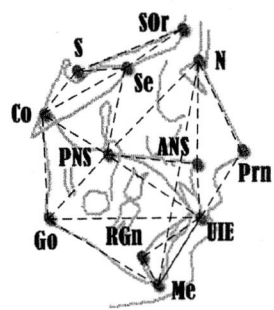

Fig. 2. Reference Landmarks

1). We can see that each craniofacial structure belongs to and only belongs to one certain region.

Table 1. Craniofacial shape partition

Reference landmarks	Associated structures
SOr, S, Se	cranial base
S, Co, Se	posterior cranial base
Co, Se, PNS	pterygomaxillary fissure
Co, Go, PNS	ascending ramus, sigmoid notch, coracoid
N, ANS, PNS	infraorbital rim, maxillary sinus
PNS, ANS, UIE	palate, maxillary central incisor
PNS, Go, UIE	molars
Go, UIE, Me	mandible
UIE, RGn, Me	mandibular central incisor, chin
N, Prn, Me	soft tissues

Shape Modeling. For each region, its training shapes are aligned by *Procrustes analysis* [13]. Then PCA is employed to extract their common features. Representing the ith training shape by its corresponding landmark vector x_i, the covariance matrix of the shape set is given by

$$C = \frac{1}{n}\sum_{i=1}^{n}(x_i - \bar{x}) \cdot (x_i - \bar{x})^T. \qquad (2)$$

Its normalized eigenvectors, explaining the most principal variations of the shape space, compose an orthonormal basis of the pattern $\Phi = (p_1 p_2 \ldots p_n)$. Thus, the difference between any shape x with the mean shape can be represented as a linear combination of Φ. Then we have

$$x = \bar{x} + \Phi \cdot b. \qquad (3)$$

It means x can be regarded as the result of a series of transformations, determined by shape parameter b, on $\bar{x}$. Ordering the eigenvectors in terms of nonincreasing eigenvalues, the dimension of Φ is set to the number of first t eigenvectors that sufficiently explain 95% of the total variance ($\sum_{i=1}^{t}\lambda_i \geq 95\% \cdot \sum_{i=1}^{n}\lambda_i$). By this the shape variations of the region can be represented by $\bar{x}$ and Φ.

Landmark Gray Profile. We sample every landmark to characterize its gray profiles. Assume A is a landmark on image i, we sample the gray values of k points along its normal on each side of A, including its own. In order to reduce the effects of global intensity changes, r derivative points are sampled for each sample point $A_{ij}(j \in [1, 2k+1])$ along the tangent direction of A on each side of the normal (see Fig. 3).

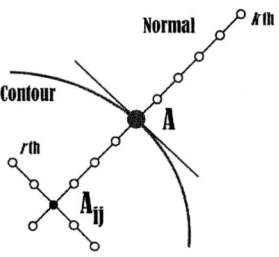

Fig. 3. Gray sampling of landmark A

The weighted average of these $2r + 1$ points, noted as g_{Aij}, is recorded as sample result of A_{ij}. Obtaining $2k + 1$ sample values $(g_{Ai1}, g_{Ai2}, \ldots, g_{Ai(2k+1)})$, we define the normalized gray profile of A as

$$y_{Ai} = \frac{dg_{Ai(2k)}}{\sum_{j=1}^{2k} dg_{Aij}} \quad (4)$$

where

$$dg_{Aij} = (g_{Ai2} - g_{Ai1}, g_{Ai3} - g_{Ai2}, \ldots, g_{Ai(j+1)} - g_{Aij}). \quad (5)$$

This is repeated on every image and we can obtain a set of normalized profiles of A: $(y_{A1}, y_{A2}, \ldots, y_{An})$. Applying PCA, the gray profile of A is built into $\bar{y}_A$ and Φ_A.

2.3 Recognition

Reference Landmark Detection. As an image is input, Gaussian blurring is applied to remove fine image detail and noise leaving only larger scale changes. The Sobel operator is used to extract cranial contours edges. Then the rough edges are thinned and traced. Reference landmarks *UIE*, *Me*, *N*, *Go* and *Prn* can be located according to their geometrical properties.

A pattern matching algorithm is proposed to locate the other reference landmarks. As shown in Fig.4, lines are drawn to connect the detected landmarks and the centroid of polygon. Taking the direction of *UIE-Go* as x-axis, eighteen features are extracted (see Fig.4), and each x-ray image can be represented by a 18-dimension *Feature Vector* $(l_1, \ldots, l_{10}, c_1, \ldots, c_5, \theta_1 \ldots \theta_3)$. We normalize the feature vector with l_1 as the unit length. Then the training images whose distances to the input image are less than a pre-defined threshold are selected. The distance between two images is given by the Euclidean distance between their feature vectors. We can see that the matching process is insensitive to the difference of reference frames because of the selection of x-axis and the normalization.

For every remaining reference landmark, we project its positions on the selected images to the input space and calculate their mean as the detection result. While all reference landmarks are detected, the shape partition is carried out on the input image according to Table 1.

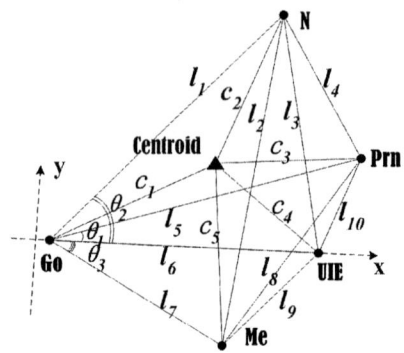

Fig. 4. Pattern extracted from *UIE, Me, N, Go* and *Prn*

ASM Recognition. For each region, we first project its mean shape from the model space to the input image space by an affine transformation $X = T(x)$. T is given by

$$T\begin{pmatrix} x \\ y \end{pmatrix} = \begin{pmatrix} x \cdot a_1 + y \cdot b_1 + c_1 \\ y \cdot a_2 + y \cdot b_2 + c_2 \end{pmatrix}. \tag{6}$$

Since the positions of three reference landmarks associated with this region are known both in the model space and the image space, we can obtain the parameters $(a_1, b_1, c_1, a_2, b_2, c_2)$.

Assume A is a landmark in the region, we search its best matched point A' on the image along the normal, and update A to A'. Here A' means the point whose normalized gray profile $y_{A'}$ has the minimal Mahalanobis distance to the one obtained from training. The Mahalanobis distance is calculated as

$$M = (y_{A'} - \bar{y}_A)^T \cdot S_A^{-1} \cdot (y_{A'} - \bar{y}_A) \tag{7}$$

where S_A is the covariance matrix of the gray profiles of A. Then the reversed transformation T^{-1} is used to map the new matching point set Y back to y in the model space. The shape parameter b of y is updated by

$$b = \Phi^T (y - \bar{x}). \tag{8}$$

The constraint of $|b_i| \leq 3\sqrt{\lambda_i}$ is applied to b_i since it is assumed the variations of shapes are distributed as a multivariate Gaussian on p_i, where λ_i is the ith largest eigenvalue. With the newly obtained shape parameter, the shape x in the model space is updated according to (3), and the shape X in the image space is updated by (6). The procedure of gray search and parameter update is iterated until X is converged. The recognition of the input sample comes to an end when this procedure is performed on all regions.

2.4 Experimental Results

The method was tested on fifty-four x-rays which were not used for training. The mean difference between the results obtained by the algorithm and those given by the human experts was 1.98 mm. It was primarily acceptable in clinical treatment since the mean error of manual landmarking is about 1.26 mm [14].

3 Structure Rendering

An interpolation subdivision scheme is utilized to trace out the craniofacial structures. First, the located landmarks are connected by lines according to the prior knowledge of structures. Then for a series of landmarks $P_0, P_1, \ldots, P_n$, new points are interpolated in accordance with the following rules:

$$\begin{cases} P_{2i}^{k+1} = P_i^k & i \in [-1, 2^k n + 1] \\ P_{2i+1}^{k+1} = (\frac{1}{2} + w)(P_i^k + P_{i+1}^k) - w(P_{i-1}^k + P_{i+2}^k) & i \in [-1, 2^k n] \end{cases} \quad (9)$$

where w is a weight factor.

The interpolation process keeps all the original points and inserts new ones in between. If the contour is not closed, we use each ending point twice at each end; otherwise, point indices are circular. In order to generate smooth contours, we apply this scheme twice or more according to the geometric properties of the structures. Fig.5 shows two examples.

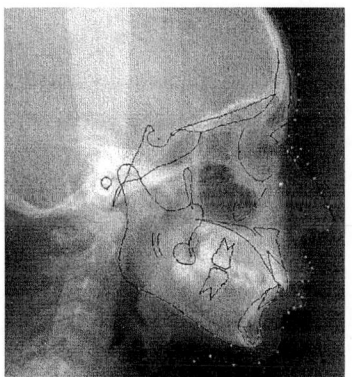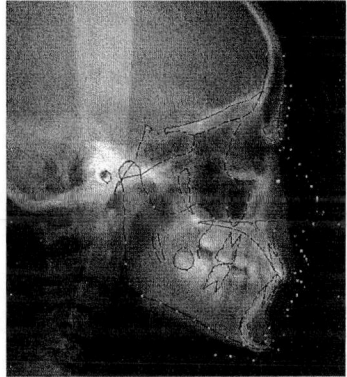

Fig. 5. Examples of structure extraction

4 Conclusion

In this paper we propose a two-level method to locate 262 landmarks on cephalometric radiographs so that the extraction of all craniofacial structures can be obtained. It is useful for automating the structure based advanced orthodontic analysis such as superimposition. Experimental results preliminarily proves that the method is applicable in orthodontic treatment. In the experiment we also notice that the final results somewhat depend on the localization accuracy of the reference landmarks. We will study this influence quantitatively in the future.

Acknowledgment

This study was supported by China 973 Program Grant No.2004CB719403, and China 863 Program Grant No.2001AA114153.

References

1. Romaniuk, B., Desvignes, M., Revenu, M., et al,: Contour tracking by minimal cost path approach. IEEE Int'l Conf. Image Processing. (2004)
2. Rakosi, T.: An Atlas and Manual of Cephalometric Radiology. London: Wolfe Medical Publications. (1982).
3. A. Levy-Mandel, A. Venetsanopoulos, J. Tsotsos: Knowledge-based landmarking of cephalograms. Comput. Bio. Med. Res. **19** (1986) 282–309.
4. Tong, W., Nugent, S.T., Gregson, P.G., et al,: Landmarking of cephalogams using a microcomputer system. Comput. Bio. Med. Res. **23** (1990) 358–397.
5. Ren, J.C., Liu, D., Shao, J.L.: A knowledge-based automatic cephalometric analysis method. 20th Annu. Int'l Conf. the IEEE Eng. Med. Bio. Soc. (1998) 723–727.
6. Romaniuk, B., Desvignes, M., Revenu, M., et al,: Linear and non-linear model for statistical localization of landmarks. 16th Int'l Conf. Pattern Recogn. (2002) 393–396.
7. Romaniuk, B., Desvignes, M., Revenu, M., et al,: Shape variability and spatial relationships modeling in statistical pattern recognition. Pattern Recgon. Lett. **25** (2004) 239–247.
8. Cardillo, J., Sid-Ahmed, M.A.: An image processing system for locating craniofacial landmarks. IEEE T. Med. Imaging. **13** (1994) 275–289.
9. El-Feghi, I., Sid-Ahmed, M.A., Ahmadi, M.: Automatic localization of craniofacial landmarks for assisted cephalometry. Pattern Recogn. **37** (2004) 609–621.
10. Hutton, T.J., Cunningham, S., Hamrnond, P.: An evaluation of active shape models for the automatic identification of cephalometric landmarks. Eur. J. Orthodont. **22** (2000) 499–508.
11. Cootes, T.F., Taylor, C.J., Cooper, D.H., et al,: Active shape modelstheir training and application. Comput. Vis. Image Und. **61** (1995) 38–59.
12. Geng, J.: Study on active shape model and its application in cephalometric landmarks recognition. M.S. Thesis, Peking University, Beijing, China. (2002).
13. Goodal, C.: Procrustes methods in the statistical analysis of shape. J. Roy. Stat. Soc. B. **53** (1991) 285–339.
14. Liu, J.K., Chen, Y.T., Cheng, K.S.: Accuracy of computerized automatic identification of cephalometric landmarks. Am. J. Orthod. Dentofac. **118** (2000) 535–540.

Stability of the Eigenvalues of Graphs

Ping Zhu and Richard C. Wilson

Computer Science Department,
University of York, UK

Abstract. The spectra of graphs has been widely used to characterise and extract information from their structures. Applications include matching, segmentation and indexing. One of the key questions about this approach is the stability and representational power of the spectrum under changes in the graphs. There is also a wide variety of graph matrix representations from which the spectrum can be extracted. In this paper we discuss the issue of stability of various graph representation methods and compare five main graph representations; the adjacency matrix, combinatorial Laplacian, normalized Laplacian matrix, heat kernel and path length distribution matrix. We show that the Euclidean distance between spectra tracks the edit distance over a wide range of edit costs, and we analyse the stability of this relationship. We then use the spectra to match and classify the graphs and demonstrate the effect of the graph matrix formulation on error rates.

1 Introduction

Graph structures have been used to represent structural and relational arrangements of entities in many vision problems. The key problem in utilising graph representations lies in measuring their structural similarity. The nodes of a graph are not ordered or labelled, and therefore the node correspondence problem must be solved before structural similarity can be assessed. Many authors have employed the concept of graph edit distance. The idea here is to perform elementary editing operations on a graph, such as edge or node insertion and deletion, to make pairs of graphs isomorphic. Each operation has an associated 'cost', and the minimum total cost of the set of edit operations can be used to gauge the similarity of the graphs. For example, Fu et al[7,11] have computed similarities using separate edit costs for relabeling, insertion and deletion on both nodes and edges. A search is necessary to locate the set of operations which have minimal cost. More recently, Bunke[2,3] has established a relationship between the minimum graph edit distance and the size of the maximum common subgraph. Torsello and Hancock[1] have exploited this relationship to cast the problem into a continuous optimisation framework.

In recent work[12,13,6], we have shown how spectral features can be found which can characterise a graph and which can be used for graph comparison. This approach is based on spectral graph theory, which is a branch of mathematics that is concerned with characterising the structural properties of graphs using the eigenvectors of the adjacency matrix or the closely related Laplacian matrix (the degree matrix minus the adjacency matrix) [4]. One of the well known successes of spectral graph theory in computer vision is the use eigenvector methods for grouping via pairwise clustering. Examples include Shi and Malik's [9] iterative normalised cut method which uses the Fiedler (i.e. second) eigenvector for image segmentation and Sarkar and Boyer's use of the leading eigenvector of the weighted adjacency matrix [8]. Graph spectral methods have also been used to correspondence analysis. Kosinov and Caelli[5] have used properties of the spectral decomposition to represent graphs and Shokoufandeh et al[10] has used eigenvalues of shock graphs to index shapes. We have previously shown[12,13] how permutation invariant polynomials can be used to derive features which describe graphs and make full use of the available spectral information.

A number of alternative matrix representations have been proposed in the literature. These include the adjacency matrix, Laplacian and normalised Laplacian. More recently, variations of the heat kernel on the graph have also been used. The spectrum of all of these representations may be used to characterise the graph, and each may reveal different graph properties. Some of these representations may be more stable to perturbations in the graph. In this paper we analyse these matrices and quantify the effect the matrix representation has on the stability and representational power of the eigenvalues of the graph. In section 2, we review the standard graph representations. In section 3, we describe more recent graph matrices based on the heat kernel and path length distributions. Section 4 describes how we measure the stability and representative power of the eigenvalues. Finally, section 5 details the experiments aimed at measuring the utility of these representations.

2 Standard Graph Representations

In this section, we review the properties of some standard graph representations and their relationships with each other. The graphs under consideration here are undirected graphs. Whilst we do not consider weighted graphs here, these ideas are straightforwardly extended to such graphs. We denote a graph by $G = (V, E)$ where V is the set of nodes and $E \subseteq V \times V$ is the set of edges. The degree of a vertex u is the number of edges leaving the vertex u and is denoted d_u.

2.1 Adjacency Matrix

The most basic matrix representation of a graph is using the adjacency matrix A for the graph. This matrix is given by

$$A(u,v) = \begin{cases} 1 & \text{if } (u,v) \in E \\ 0 & \text{otherwise} \end{cases} \quad (1)$$

Clearly if the graph is undirected, the matrix A is symmetric. As a consequence, the eigenvalues of A are real. These eigenvalues may be positive, negative or zero and the sum of the eigenvalues is zero. The eigenvalues may be ordered by their magnitude and collected into a vector which describes the graph spectrum.

2.2 Combinatorial Laplacian Matrix

In some applications, it is useful to have a positive semidefinite matrix representation of the graph. This may be achieved by using the Laplacian. We first construct the diagonal degree matrix D, whose diagonal elements are given by the node degrees $D(u,u) = d_u$. From the degree matrix and the adjacency matrix we then can construct the standard Laplacian matrix

$$L = D - A \qquad (2)$$

i.e. the degree matrix minus the adjacency matrix. The Laplacian has at least one zero eigenvalue, and the number of such eigenvalues is equal to the number of disjoint parts in the graph.

2.3 Normalized Laplacian Matrix

The normalized Laplacian matrix is defined to be the matrix

$$\hat{L} = \begin{cases} 1 & \text{if } u = v \\ -\frac{1}{\sqrt{d_u d_v}} & \text{if } u \text{ and } v \text{ are adjacent} \\ 0 & \text{otherwise} \end{cases} \qquad (3)$$

We can also write it as $\hat{L} = D^{-\frac{1}{2}} L D^{-\frac{1}{2}}$. As with the Laplacian of the graph, this matrix is positive semidefinite and so has positive or zero eigenvalues. The normalisation factor means that the largest eigenvalue less than or equal to 2, with equality only when G is bipartite. Again, the matrix has at least one zero eigenvalue. Hence all the eigenvalues are in the range $0 \leq \lambda \leq 2$.

2.4 Spectral Decomposition of Representation Matrix

The spectral properties, which embody all the information of the graph, can be obtained from the eigendecomposition of the representation matrix. Take Laplacian matrix as an example, the spectral decomposition of the Laplacian matrix is $L = \Phi \Lambda \Phi^T$ where $\Lambda = \text{diag}(\lambda_1, \lambda_2, ..., \lambda_{|V|})$ is the diagonal matrix with the ordered eigenvalues as elements and $\Phi = (\phi_1|\phi_2|....|\phi_{|V|})$ is the matrix with the ordered eigenvectors as columns. The spectrum is particularly useful as a graph representation because it is invariant under the similarity transform PLP^T, where P is a permutation matrix. In other words, if we relabel the graph, the spectrum is unchanged.

3 The Heat Kernel and Path Length Distribution

3.1 Heat Kernel

The heat kernel is based on the diffusion of heat across the graph. It is a representation which as attracted recent interest in the literature. We are interested in the heat equation associated with the Laplacian, i.e. $\frac{\partial h_t}{\partial t} = -L h_t$ where h_t

is the heat kernel and t is time. The solution is found by exponentiating the Laplacian eigenspectrum, i.e. $h_t = \Phi \exp[-t\Lambda]\Phi^T$. The heat kernel is a $|V| \times |V|$ matrix, and for the nodes u and v of the graph G the resulting component is

$$h_t(u,v) = \sum_{i=1}^{|V|} \exp[-\lambda_i t]\phi_i(u)\phi_i(v) \qquad (4)$$

When t tends to zero, then $h_t \simeq I - Lt$, i.e. the kernel depends on the local connectivity structure or topology of the graph. If, on the other hand, t is large, then $h_t \simeq \exp[-t\lambda_m]\phi_m\phi_m^T$, where λ_m is the smallest non-zero eigenvalue and ϕ_m is the associated eigenvector, i.e. the Fiedler vector. Hence, the large time behavior is governed by the global structure of the graph. By controlling t, we can obtain representations of varying degrees of locality.

3.2 Path Length Distribution

It is interesting to note that the heat kernel is also related to the path length distribution on the graph. If $D_k(u,v)$ is the number of paths of length k between nodes u and v then

$$h_t(u,v) = \exp[-t] \sum_{k=1}^{|V|^2} D_k(u,v) \frac{t^k}{k!} \qquad (5)$$

The path length distribution is itself related to the eigenspectrum of the Laplacian. By equating the derivatives of the spectral and the path-length forms of the heat kernel it is straightforward to show that

$$D_k(u,v) = \sum_{i=1}^{|V|} (1-\lambda_i)^k \phi_i(u)\phi_i(v) \qquad (6)$$

Hence, $D_k(u,v)$ can be interpreted as the sum of weights of all walks of length k joining nodes u and v.

4 Measuring the Stability and Representational Power of Eigenvalues

Our aim in this paper is to assess the usefulness of the eigenvalues for representing the differences between graphs. In addition, we aim to determine which matrix representation is most appropriate for this task.

4.1 Graph Distance

The fundamental structure of a pattern space can be determined purely from the distances between patterns in the space. There are a number of ways to measure the distance between two graphs, but the most appropriate in this case is the edit distance[7,2]. The edit distance is defined by a sequence of operations, including edge and vertex deletion and insertion, which transform one graph into another. Each of these operations has an associated cost, and the total cost of a sequence of edits is the sum of the individual costs. The sequence of minimal cost which transforms one graph into another is the edit distance between the graphs. In the examples here, we have assigned a cost of 1 to edge insertions and deletions.

Clearly, if the spectrum is to be a good representation in this sense, then the requirement is that the distance between spectra should be proportional to the edit distance between the graphs. In this context, the stability of the spectrum is also an issue which we need to consider. Whilst it may be true on average that the edit and spectral distances are related, the variation in individual graphs may be very large. As a consequence we also need to consider the variance of the spectral distance over large sets of graphs.

4.2 Classification

Classifying a large number of different kinds of graphs is also a common and important task. Any representation which fails to do this well is not a particularly good or practical one. Therefore, as well as determining the distance between graphs, it is also important to be able to classify them using the representation. If the spectrum is a good representation, then we should be able to identify the class of a graph even under noisy conditions. In our second set of experiments, we therefore investigate the classification of graphs when the graphs to be classified are perturbed by edge deletion operations.

5 Experiments

In this section, we provide some experimental evaluation of the five graph representation methods given in the previous sections. There are two aspects of this study; first, we show that the more similar the two graphs are, the smaller the Euclidean distance of the eigenvalues will become. We use both Delaunay graphs and random graphs to demonstrate this. We also compute the relative deviation of the Euclidean distance to assess the accuracy of this relationship. Second, we compute the error rate for classification using random graph matching.

In the first experiment we compute the Euclidean distance between the vector of eigenvalues of the Delaunay graph with thirty vertices and its altered graph, modified by edge deletion from one to thirty edges, using five graph representation methods mentioned before. The edge to be deleted is chosen at random. For each level of editing, we perform 100 trials in order to obtain an average and deviation in the distance. The t in heat kernel equation is set to 3.5 and the length of path is path length distribution is 2. We can obtain the mean Euclidean distance and the standard deviation at each edge deletion of these matrix representations. The results are shown in Figure 1

The second experiment is much the same as the first one. The only difference is that this time we use random graphs. In this experiment, we generate random graph with thirty vertices and seventy edges. The other parameters are identical to the previous experiment.

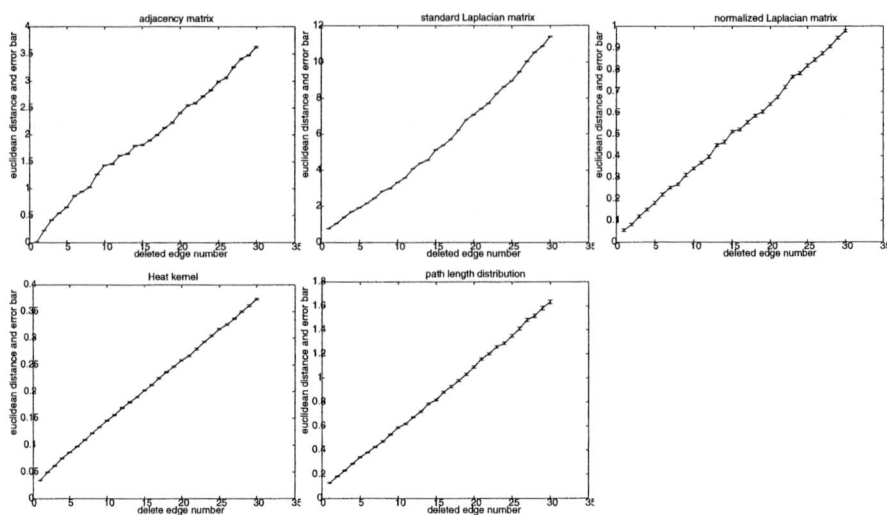

Fig. 1. Five kinds of matrix Euclidean distance of Delaunay graphs

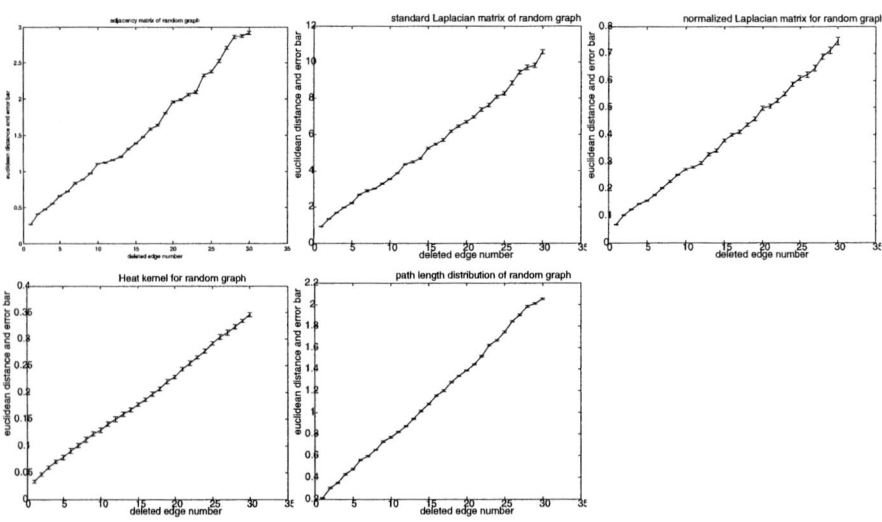

Fig. 2. Five kinds of matrix euclidean distance of random graphs

These plots show that all these representations give a spectrum which follows the edit distance closely, although the adjacency and Laplacian matrices seem marginally less linear. In Tables 1 and 2 we give the relative deviation of the samples for 5, 10, 20 and 30 edit operations. The relative deviation is the standard deviation of the samples divided by the mean. This value gives an indication of how reliably the spectrum predicts the edit distance. In this regard, the heat kernel matrix is clearly superior to the other methods.

Table 1. Relative deviation of Delaunay graphs

Methods	5 edge deletion	10 edge deletion	20 edge deletion	30 edge deletion
adjacency matrix	0.0918	0.0827	0.0716	0.0530
standard Laplacian matrix	0.0802	0.0727	0.0619	0.0498
normalized Laplacian matrix	0.0753	0.0676	0.0571	0.0414
heat kernel matrix	0.0358	0.0287	0.0193	0.0105
path length distribution matrix	0.0420	0.0313	0.0252	0.0127

Table 2. Relative deviation of random graphs

Methods	5 edge deletion	10 edge deletion	20 edge deletion	30 edge deletion
adjacency matrix	0.1164	0.1023	0.0805	0.0657
standard Laplacian matrix	0.1042	0.0930	0.0771	0.0592
normalized Laplacian matrix	0.0947	0.0830	0.0651	0.0558
heat kernel matrix	0.0582	0.0494	0.0299	0.0175
path length distribution matrix	0.0607	0.0523	0.0385	0.0225

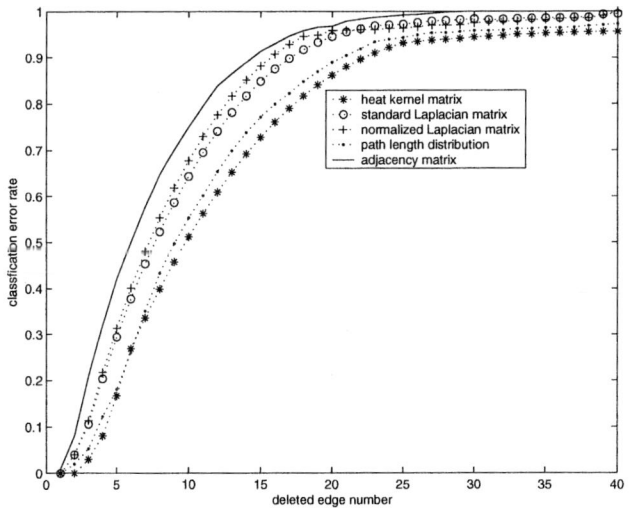

Fig. 3. Error rate of five methods of matrix for random graphs

We now construct a classification experiment using 50 graph classes. Each class is represented by a single graph. We create graphs to be classified by performing random edit operations on the class graphs. The graphs are classified using a simple 1-NN classifier and the Euclidean distance between the spectra; the aim here is to investigate the efficacy of the representation rather than the classifier. Figure 3 shows the classification error rates over a range of numbers of edit operations. Here the heat kernel matrix is the best method followed by the path length distribution. The adjacency matrix is a poor representation whereas the combinatorial and normalized Laplacian have the same performance.

6 Conclusions

In this paper we have compared five main graph representation matrices respectively by computing both the relationship to edit distance between graphs and classification error rate for the spectra of these matrices. Our results show that the heat kernel and path length distribution matrices are superior to the other methods, with the heat kernel being slightly better than the path length distribution.

References

1. A.Torsello and E.R.Hancock. Efficiently computing weighted tree edit distance using relaxation labeling. *Lecture Notes in Computer Science*, 2134:438–453, 2001.
2. H. Bunke. On a relation between graph edit distance and maximum common subgraph. *Pattern Recognition Letters*, 18:689–694, 1997.
3. H. Bunke. Error correcting graph matching: On the influence of the underlying cost function. *IEEE Transactions on Pattern Analysis and Machine Intelligence*, 21:917–922, 1999.
4. F. R. K. Chung. *Spectral Graph Theory*. AMS, 1997.
5. S. Kosinov and T. Caelli. Inexact multisubgraph matching using graph eigenspace and clustering models. *Structural, Syntatic and Statistical Pattern Recognition, LNCS*, 2396:133–142, 2002.
6. B. Luo, R. C. Wilson, and E. R. Hancock. Graph manifolds from spectral polynomials. In 17th *International Conference on Pattern Recognition*, volume III, pages 402–405, 2004.
7. A. Sanfeliu and K. S. Fu. A distance measure between attributed relational graphs for pattern-recognition. *IEEE Transactions on Systems, Man and Cybernetics*, 13(3):353–362, 1983.
8. S. Sarkar and K. L. Boyer. Preceptual organization in computer vision. *IEEE Trans. Systems, Man and Cybernetics*, 23:382–399, 1993.
9. J. Shi and J. Malik. Normalized cuts and image segmentation. *CVPR*, pages 731–737, 1997.
10. A. Shokoufandeh, S. Dickinson, K. Siddiqi, and S. Zucker. Indexing using a spectral coding of topological structure. In *Proceedings IEEE Conference on Computer Vision and Pattern Recognition*, number 491–497, 1999.
11. W. H. Tsai and K. S. Fu. Subgraph error-correcting isomorphisms for syntactic pattern-recognition. *IEEE Transations on Systems, Man and Cybernetics*, 13(1):48–62, 1983.
12. R. C. Wilson and E. R. Hancock. Pattern spaces from graph polynomials. In 12th *International Conference on Image Analysis and Processing*, pages 480–485, 2003.
13. R. C. Wilson and E. R. Hancock. Contour segments from spline interpolation. In *Syntactic and Structural Pattern Recognition Workshop*, volume LNCS 3138, pages 57–65. Springer, 2004.

3D Modeling of Humans with Skeletons from Uncalibrated Wide Baseline Views

Chee Kwang Quah[1], Andre Gagalowicz[2], Richard Roussel[2], and Hock Soon Seah[3]

[1] Nanyang Technological University, School of Computer Engineering, Singapore
quah_ck@pmail.ntu.edu.sg
[2] INRIA, Domaine de Voluceau, BP105 78153 Le Chesnay, France
{andre.gagalowicz, richard.roussel}@inria.fr
[3] Nanyang Technological University, School of Computer Engineering, Singapore
ashsseah@ntu.edu.sg

Abstract. In order to achieve precise, accurate and reliable tracking of human movement, a 3D human model that is very similar to the subject is essential. In this paper, we present a new system to (1) precisely construct the surface shape of the whole human body, and (2) estimate the underlying skeleton. In this work we make use of a set of images of the subject in collaboration with a generic anthropometrical 3D model made up of regular surfaces and skeletons to adapt to the specific subject. We developed a three-stage technique that uses the human shape feature points and limb outlines that work together with the generic 3D model to yield our final customized 3D model. The first stage is an iterative camera pose calibration and 3D characteristic point reconstruction-deformation algorithm that gives us an initial customized 3D model. The second stage refines the initial customized 3D model by deformation via the silhouette limbs information, thus obtaining the surface skin model. In the final stage, we make use of the results of skin deformation to estimate the underlying skeleton. From our final results, we demonstrate that our system is able to construct quality human model, where the skeleton is constructed and positioned automatically.

1 Introduction

In the context of sports science, augmented reality and toward the future for free-viewpoint video [2], 3D television and media production, precise and accurate tracking of the human's movements are needed. To date many computer vision based human tracking systems had been proposed e.g. [5], [13], [19], [23]. However, all these methods employed a too generic model e.g. stick-figures, cylinders.

The process of tracking is very sensitive to the shape model and animation used, with considerable amount of effort spent to tune these parameters [7]. In the work by [6], [9], they also stressed the importance in the quality of the 3D model used for tracking. Thus, it is inappropriate to use, for example, a generic "averaging human" model for accurate and precise tracking of human that come in different shapes and sizes.

In this paper, we focus our attention on building a good customized model, since it is crucial to track the human subject using a very similar 3D human model. The surface skin and the underlying skeleton will be built and fitted to our subject. The key challenge to our system is to accomplish its task from a set of limited images acquired from the various wide baseline viewpoints. For reconstruction we use a maximum of 6 images. The resultant model will maintain the correct object modeling topology, as this is important for future usage e.g. character skinning. In addition, our method does not need any special calibration tools.

In section 2, we review some of the existing modeling systems. In section 3, we propose our modeling system framework, and in sections 4, 5 and 6 we describe our modeling system in detail. Finally we show our results in section 7.

2 Existing Modeling Systems

The existing vision-based reconstruction systems that mainly deal with constructing the surface skin model fall into the 2 categories: (1) 3D laser-scanner systems, and (2) passive multi-camera systems.

The 3D laser-scanner systems [26], [27] capture the entire surface of the human body in about 15 to 20 seconds with resolution of 1 to 2mm. However the drawbacks of such a device are (1) highly priced at about few hundred thousands of dollars, and (2) require the subject to stay still and rigid for the whole duration of scanning (about 15 seconds for full body coverage) which is quite constrictive in practice.

On the other hand the passive multi-camera systems are much cheaper and video cameras are more easily available. Most of the existing methods e.g. [8], [22] make use of shape-from-silhouette related approaches requiring (1) the subject to be segmented from the image background, and (2) the cameras to be calibrated beforehand using calibration tools. Shape-from-silhouette approaches also give rise to 'blocky' results if there are insufficient views (this can be seen from the theoretical proof in [12]). More recent approaches e.g. [16] propose 3D reconstruction from un-calibrated views, which uses feature correspondents, requires the subject to remain still and rigid for about 40 seconds during the video capturing of the whole body. Moreover, the reconstructed model could contain non-manifold problems e.g. holes and open edges.

There are research that attempt to estimate more precisely the joint locations. They are usually done using optical, magnetic or mechanical motion capture system e.g. [14], [15], [20]. However, all these methods require tedious post-processing to clean up the motion capture data. More recent approach [21] attempted to estimate the skeleton from sequence of volume data of rigid bodies. However, the resultant skeleton is an estimated stick-figure-like structure. These structures do not contain sufficient anatomical details for realistic character animation and skinning.

Another alternative to acquire the human skeleton is via X-ray. However X-ray devices are not easily available. In addition, tedious post-processing may be required to integrate the data from both the cameras and X-rays.

3 Our Modeling System

Our proposed human model construction starts from a generic human model in a stanza position (fig. 1). The generic 3D human model that we used is *Ergoman*, provided by MIRAGES, INRIA, France. The surface of our model is made up of about

17000 vertices and 34000 triangular faces. Inside this surface is the underlying generic skeleton. The anatomic measurement of the subject is used for deforming this generic model to produce a specific model. The strategy of our framework is motivated by the method in [17], which was used for the construction of human faces.

In our system, the subject's body is used as the calibration tool. The 3D generic model guides the camera calibration, which, in turn, allows 3D point reconstruction to yield the camera poses and produces the customized 3D model. Our image acquisition for all the views is instantaneous. The inputs to the system are:

1) 2D images from different views (ideally we should have good view coverage of the subject) i.e. wide baseline. This acquisition will be done at a single time instance (using several gen-locked cameras).
2) Generic 3D human model (i.e. surface and skeleton) and its 32 selected surface characteristic points (fig. 2).
3) 2D/3D feature point matches in the image views and 3D human model points.

The outputs of the system are:

1) Calibrated camera poses of the different views.
2) Customized 3D surface model with regular surface that will overlay nicely onto the images of the subject's silhouette limb in all the views. This customized model has the geometry of the shape and size of our subject.
3) Estimated position and reconstruction of the customized skeleton of the subject.

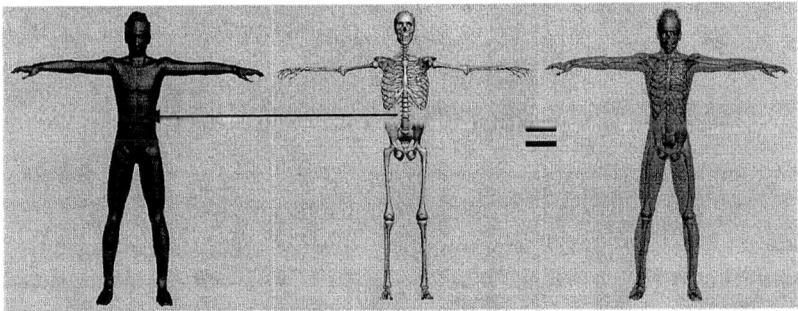

Fig. 1. (a) Generic surface model, (b) generic skeleton, (c) overall generic model

The block diagram of our model construction system is shown in fig. 3. This task can be realized on an off-line basis, comprised the three main stages: (1) camera calibration and reconstruction of model characteristic points (section 4), (2) refinement of model via silhouette limbs deformation, as described in section 5, and (3) skeleton estimation (section 6).

The testing data are the images acquired from different camera views provided by MIRAGES, INRIA, France. Fig. 2 shows the example of the selected feature points on the 2D images corresponding to the 3D points. These correspondences can be established via an interactive point-matching tool that we have developed. This ensures that the correspondences are 100% correct, so that the calibration is always stable. Although automatic body-part recognition had been studied in e.g. [24], however in our wide-baseline and cluttered environment, automatic feature detection becomes highly ill posed. In our set-up, we utilized a set of 32 surface characteristic points. These characteristic points will provide an over-determined set of information and sufficient view coverage for camera calibration and reconstruction of points.

Fig. 2. Example of features points on 3D generic model corresponding on the 2D image

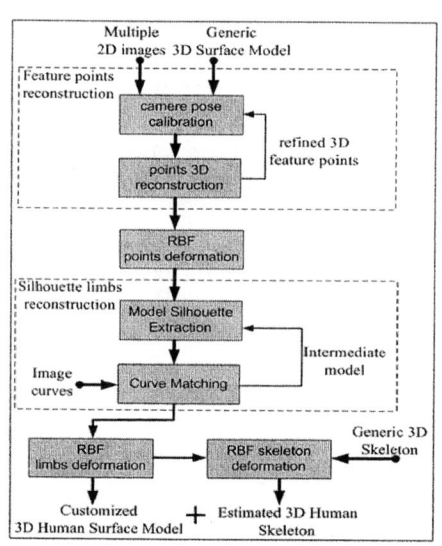

Fig. 3. Block diagram for model construction

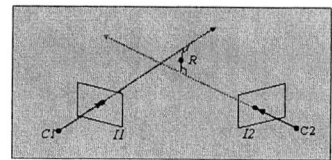

Fig. 4. Triangulation of projected rays, when the rays do not intersect images (R is the reconstructed point)

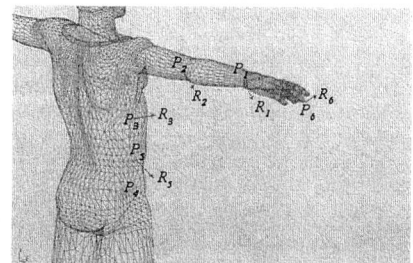

Fig. 5. Example showing some of the deformation vectors

4 Camera Calibration and Feature Reconstruction

This section describes the first stage of our model adaptation system (first 3 blocks of fig. 3). Using the subject's 2D characteristic points from the images in collaboration with their respective correspondents on the 3D generic model (Fig. 3), we iterate the process comprising the camera calibration and 3D generic model point deformation (3D reconstruction) until convergence is attained. At the start the 3D characteristic points of the generic model do not project correctly during the early iterations. As the process iterates, these 3D characteristic points will converge together with the camera poses. We will obtain a set of sparse deformed 3D model points and calibrated camera poses. By using the sparse deformed model points, we complete our initial customized 3D model by interpolating the deformations using radial basis function (RBF).

4.1 Camera Calibration

In this module, we use the POSIT (pose iteration) algorithm [3] to calibrate the camera extrinsic parameters. The intrinsic parameters can be obtained using simple camera calibration software such as [25]. Another alternative that we study is to add an addition layer above POSIT in order to search for the intrinsic parameters. This is done by regarding POSIT as a function of the intrinsic parameters, which we will minimize using simplex minimization.

4.2 Feature Points Reconstruction

By using the calibrated camera parameters and the 3D/2D correspondences, we perform 3D point reconstruction to deform the 3D characteristic points toward the new positions. The 3D point reconstruction is achieved by triangulating the projected rays from the characteristic image points (fig. 4). This algorithm takes into account that the rays will not intersect when the calibration is not perfect by minimizing the sum of square of distances to the projected rays from all the possible views. We only reconstruct the respective points seen in more than one image.

When the process converges, we obtained a final set of reconstructed 3D points R_i. We also have the original set of 3D points from the initial generic model P_i. Using P_i and R_i we form a set of deformation vectors $\overrightarrow{P_i R_i}$ (see fig. 5 for example).

4.3 Interpolating the Deformation

Considering the deformed characteristic 3D model points, they are very sparsely distributed. These sparse points are not sufficient to represent the complete 3D model. Therefore, we make use of the sparse points in collaboration with the generic 3D model to complete the 3D model deformation via interpolation. The interpolation is done by using radial basis functions (RBF). Using RBF for data interpolation had been researched and used successfully in e.g. [4], [18].

We can write the equation of a linear system as:

$$\begin{bmatrix} \sigma(|P_1-P_1|) & \sigma(|P_1-P_2|) & \cdots\cdots & \sigma(|P_1-P_N|) \\ \sigma(|P_2-P_1|) & \ddots & & \vdots \\ \vdots & & \ddots & \vdots \\ \sigma(|P_N-P_1|) & \cdots\cdots & \cdots\cdots & \sigma(|P_N-P_N|) \end{bmatrix} \begin{bmatrix} A_{x1} & A_{y1} & A_{z1} \\ A_{x2} & A_{y2} & A_{z2} \\ \vdots & & \vdots \\ A_{xN} & A_{yN} & A_{zN} \end{bmatrix} = \begin{bmatrix} \overrightarrow{PR}_{x1} & \overrightarrow{PR}_{y1} & \overrightarrow{PR}_{z1} \\ \overrightarrow{PR}_{x2} & \overrightarrow{PR}_{y2} & \overrightarrow{PR}_{z2} \\ \vdots & & \vdots \\ \overrightarrow{PR}_{xN} & \overrightarrow{PR}_{yN} & \overrightarrow{PR}_{zN} \end{bmatrix} \quad (1)$$

where:

1) $\overrightarrow{PR}$ are the set of deformation vectors computed via 3D reconstruction of characteristic points. P, R are the original and reconstructed characteristic points.
2) $\sigma(|P_i - P_j|)$ are the radial basis function. Here we use $\sigma(|P_i - P_j|) = |P_i - P_j|$.
3) A (i.e. A_{xi}, A_{yi}, A_{zi}) are the weights that we are seeking for.

The weights A can be obtained by solving equation (1) using simple linear algebra method like the LU decomposition. After having obtained the deformation weights A, we can then use them to deform the rest of the model points using the equation (2):

$$F_{x,y,z}(P) = \sum_{i=1}^{N} A_{xi, yi, zi} \bullet \sigma(|P - P_i|) \qquad ...(2)$$

where P is the set of 3D points from the generic model that we need to deform.

4.4 Initial Results of Customized Surface Model

Up to this point, we have an initial customized surface model (fig. 6). We can notice from the results that projected local model silhouette limbs of the initial customized model do not overlay exactly onto the images e.g. on the inner legs of the subject.

Fig. 7 shows the results of the feature point reprojection error in pixels plotted against the number of iterations. It can be observed that the process converges after about 30 iterations. The reprojection mean-square error at convergence is about 1.1 pixels with a standard deviation of 0.9 pixels.

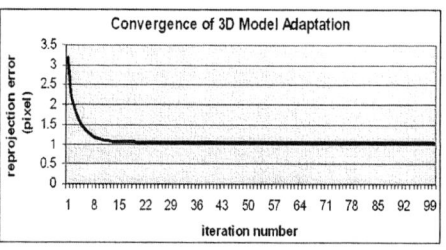

Fig. 6. Initial model – not precisely fitted   **Fig. 7.** Plotting reprojection error vs number of iterations

5 Surface Model Refinement

The deformation based on points enables us to restore the global surface geometry of the human subject. However, the more local elements such as the curves on the shoulders and legs of the subject are not precisely reconstructed. To act on this set of local elements we design an algorithm to deform the human body based on his silhouette contours, called the limbs. For this stage, we will automatically extract the silhouette edges of the model from various views and will deform them so that they correspond exactly to the respective silhouette curves of images (fig. 8).

5.1 Silhouette Extraction

5.1.1 Silhouette from Initial Model

This process deals with the extraction of silhouette curve from the initial surface model from section 4. We follow the method as in [17] to extract the silhouette. We have sped up the process by (1) finding the contour edges [11] via an XOR operation, and (2) checking for the possibility of intersections between the contour edges as we traveling along the bounding silhouette (because our subject is highly concave).

5.1.2 Silhouette from Images

The segmentation and extraction of silhouette pixels from static 2D images may be done either in an (1) automatic way using edge detection, or (2) interactive way. Many edge detection algorithms for image segmentation had been proposed over the last decades e.g. [1]. However, using edge detection to segment out a continuous close

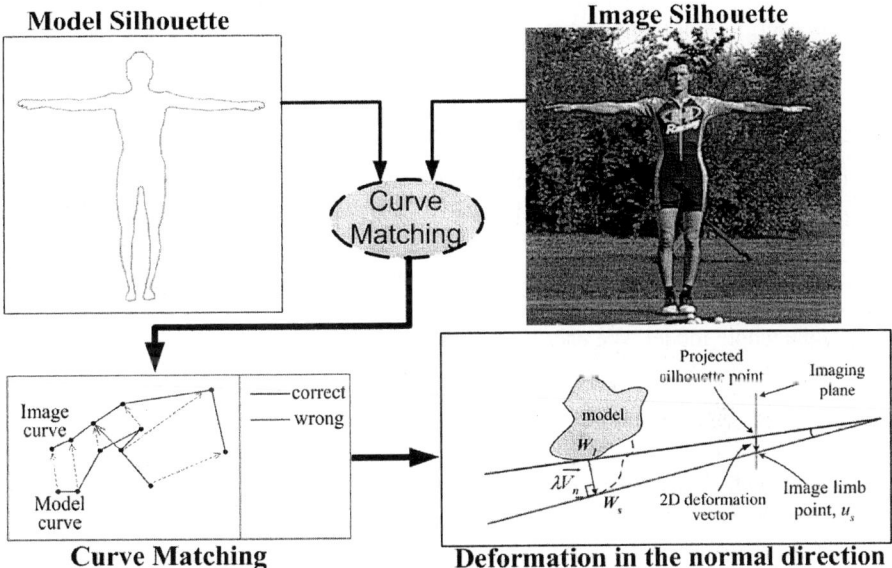

Fig. 8. Model refinement via deformation of silhouette curves

contour from any noisy image is very difficult. The only way to achieve this is to acquire the images in a very well controlled environment e.g. making the subject wear special colored cloth.

If the well-controlled environment is unlikely, then we have to bring out the silhouette features interactively. We can make use of the curve digitizing tools (e.g. Bezier curves drawing) available from common commercial software like the Photoshop.

We perform edge-linking after we have obtained the digitized contours using any one of the above-mentioned methods. This ensures that topological information is maintained when we have to match the two sets of silhouette curves.

5.2 Silhouette Curve Matching

The aim of this module is to find a good correspondence for all projected silhouette vertices with respect to the image curves. We also have to make sure that the matching takes place in a correct order. The bottom-left diagram of fig. 8 shows an example whereby if we simply search for the nearest point, the matching topology will be wrong.

We will proceed with the matching by sub-dividing the model curve at half curve length and seek for the closest point on the image curve. When finding the closest point, we may impose some simple constraint e.g. maximum angle different in the curve directions. The sub-division and seeking for the closest points go on recursively until there are no more points left for matching.

Since our curve matching is a one-pass algorithm, the outcomes may not minimize the energy between the 2 curves. However, we found that the matching is sufficient for us to complete the final deformation (for the next section). If one is not satisfied with the energy minimization between the 2 curves, one may use the active contours [10] to refine the registration.

5.3 Reconstrction of Model via Silhouette Curves

The matching of the correspondences between the model and image curves enables us to compute the refinements needed for the model. For each correspondence in the 2D matching, we are able to calculate its deformation vector in 3D (bottom-left diagram of fig. 8). Once we have computed all the deformation vectors from the curves matching, we use them in addition with the reconstructed feature points (from section 4) to deform the whole model. We use RBF to complete the whole model as before.

6 Skeleton Estimation

Up till now we have constructed the surface of our subject. Here we will estimate the underlying skeleton of the subject. Once again we make use of the deformation vectors of (1) the feature points (from section 4), and (2) silhouette points (from section 5). These respective deformations from the generic model to the customized model were used to compute the RBF function. Finally, we used the RBF weight to deform the generic skeleton (fig. 1b) to yield the customized skeleton. We used the RBF so that the transition from the generic skeleton will give us a smooth customized skeleton.

7 Results and Discussion

In our system, we used at least 4 images for reconstruction. Our algorithm was implemented using C++ (without optimization) running on a Pentium 4. The whole reconstruction process takes about 5 minutes. We had noticed that the bulk of the computation time is due to the silhouette computation because we are processing a fairly dense 3D model of about 50000 edges.

Fig. 9 shows the results of the final surface model. They are reprojected and overlaid onto the testing images. As we can see from the results, refining the initial model by using silhouette curve improved the results tremendously. This is because the feature points alone are too sparse, hence they do not provide enough local information.

Fig. 11 shows the visual results of the estimated skeleton inside the surface model.

Fig. 10 shows the silhouette curve reprojection error in pixels plotted against the number of iterations. It took about 20 iterations to converge. The mean reprojection error of the final model reprojected onto the testing images is about 0.5 pixel.

Fig. 9. Results for reconstruction of model surface

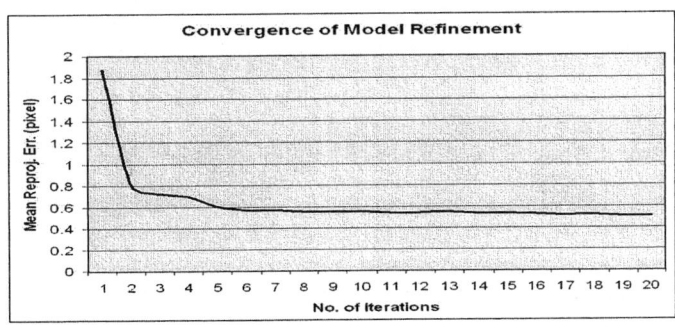

Fig. 10. Result of mean reprojection vs number of iterations

8 Conclusions

In this article, we proposed a new method to (1) construct the skin surface model, and (2) estimate the skeleton of the human from a set of limited images acquired from different views with wide baseline. We execute a 3-stages algorithm using a set of images in collaboration with a generic human model. In the first stage, we establish an initial model by a camera calibration/feature-point reconstruction loop and interpolating the sparsely reconstructed points. The second stage consists of matching the silhouette edges of the initial model with the image silhouette to obtain a refinement for the final deformation. Finally, we combine the deformation results from stages 1 and 2 to estimate the underlying skeleton. The final result is a regular-surface customized model incorporating its skeleton. In our future work, we will use this customized model to track the targeted subject.

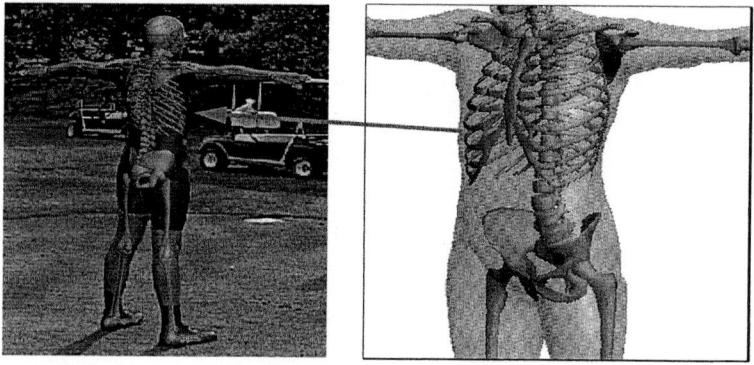

Fig. 11. Visual results of the estimated skeleton inside the surface model

References

1. J Canny, A Computational Approach to edge detection, *IEEE Trans. PAMI*, 8(6), pp 679-698, 1986.
2. J Carranza, C Theobalt, M A Magnor, H Seidel, Free-Viewpoint Video of Human Actors, *Proceedings of the SIGGRAPH2003 Conference*, pp 569-577, 2003.
3. D F Dementhon and L S Davis, Model-based object pose in 25 lines of code, *International Journal of Computer Vision*, 15, pp 123-141, 1995.
4. S Fang, R Raghavan and J Richtsmeier, Volume morphing methods for landmark based 3D image deformation, *SPIE Int. Symp. on Medical Imaging*, CA, 1996.
5. D M Garvrila and L S Davis, 3-D model-based tracking of humans in action: a multi-view approach, In *CVPR*, San Franscisco, USA, pp 73-80, 1996.
6. P Gérard and A Gagalowicz, Human Body Tracking using a 3D Generic Model applied to Golf Swing Analysis, *MIRAGE 2003 Conf.*, INRIA Rocquencourt, France, March, 2003.
7. L Goncalves, E Di Bernardom, E Ursella and P Perona, Monocular tracking of the human arm in 3D, *Proc. of ICCV 1995*, Boston, USA, pp 764-770, 1995.

8. A Hilton, D Beresford, T Gentils, R Smith, W Sun, J Illingworth, Whole-body modelling of people from multi-view images to populate virtual worlds, *The Visual Computer*, 16(7), pp 411-436, 2000.
9. I A Kakadiaris and D Metaxas, Three-dimensional human body model acquisition from multiple views, *International Journal of Computer Vision*, 30, pp 191-218, 1998.
10. M Kass, A. Watkin and D Terzopoulos, Snake: Active contour models, International *Journal of Computger Vision*, 1, pp 321-331, 1988.
11. L Kettner and E Welzl, Contour edge analysis for polyhedral analysis, *Geometric Modeling: Theory and Practice*, Springer, pp 379-394, 1997.
12. A Laurentini, How far 3D shapes can be understood from 2D silhouettes, *IEEE Trans. PAMI*, 17, pp 188-195, 1995.
13. T B Moeslund and E Granum, A survey of computer vision-based human motion capture, *Computer Vision and Image Understanding*, 81, pp 231-268, 2001.
14. J F O'Brien, R E Bodenheimer Jr, G J Brostow and J K Hodgins, Joint parameter estimation from magnetic motion capture data, *Proceedings of Graphics Interface 2000*, Montreal, Canada, pp. 53-60, May 2000.
15. M M Panjabi, V K Goel, S D Walter, Errors in the centre and angle of rotation of a joint: An experimental study. *Journal of Biomechanics*, 15(7), pp 537-544, 1982.
16. F Remondino, 3-D reconstruction of static human body shape from an image sequence, *Computer Vision and Image Understanding*, 93, pp 65-85, 2004.
17. R Roussel, A Gagalowicz, Morphological adaptation of a 3D model of face from images, *MIRAGE 2003 Conf.*, INRIA Rocquencort, France, March, 2003.
18. D Ruprecht and H Muller, Free form deformation with scattering data interpolation methods, *Geometric Modeling (Computing Suppl. 8)*, Springer Verlag, editor G. Farin, H. Hagen and H. Noltemeier, pp 267-281, 1993.
19. H Sidenbladh, M J Black and Leonid Sigal, Implicit Probablistic Models of Human Motion for Synthesis and Tracking, *Proc. of ECCV*, pp 784-800, Copenhagen, 2002.
20. M-C Silaghi, R Plankers, R Boulic, P Fua and D Thalmann. Local and global skeleton fitting techniques for optical motion capture, *Modeling and Motion Capture Techniques for Virtual Environments, Lecture notes in artificial intelligence*, editor N Thalmann and D Thalmann , pp 26-40, 1998.
21. C Theobalt, E Aguiar, M Magnor, H Theisel and H-P Seidel, Marker-free kinematic skeleton estimation from sequence of volume data, *Proc. ACM Virtual Reality Software and Technology,* Hong Kong, pp.57-64, November 2004.
22. S Weik, A passive full body scan using shape from silhouette, *Proc. ICPR 2000*, Barcelona, Spain, pp 99-105.
23. C Wren, A Azarbayejani, T Darrell and A Pentland, Pfinder: real-time tracking of the human body, *IEEE Trans. PAMI*, 19(7), pp 780-785, 1997.
24. C Yaniz, J Rocha and F Perales, 3D Part Recognition Method for Human Motion Analysis, *Proceedings of the International Workshop on Modelling and Motion Capture Techniques for Virtual Environments*, pp 41-55, 1998.
25. Camera calibration toolkit for Matlab, J Bouguet. http://www.vision.caltech.edu/bouguetj/calib_doc
26. Cyberware. http://www.cyberware.com
27. Hamamatsu. http://usa.hamamatsu.com

Magnitude and Phase Spectra of Foot Motion for Gait Recognition

Agus Santoso Lie[1], Shuichi Enokida[1], Tomohito Wada[2], and Toshiaki Ejima[1]

[1] Department of Artificial Intelligence, Kyushu Institute of Technology,
Iizuka City, Fukuoka Pref., 820-8502 Japan
[2] National Institute of Fitness and Sports in Kanoya, Kanoya City,
Kagoshima Pref., 891-2393 Japan

Abstract. Magnitude and phase spectra of horizontal and vertical movement of ankles in a normal walk are effective and efficient signatures in gait recognition. An approach to use these spectra as phase-weighted magnitude spectra is also widely known. In this paper, we propose an integration of magnitude and phase spectra for gait recognition using AdaBoost classifier. At each round, a weak classifier evaluates each magnitude and phase spectra of a motion signal as dependent sub-features, then classification results of each sub-feature are normalized and summed for the final hypothesis output. Experimental results in same-day and cross-month tests with nine subjects show that using both magnitude and phase spectra improves the recognition results.

1 Introduction

Gait recognition is a task to identify or verify the identity of an individual from the person's gait. Compared to biometrics using other modalities, it has the advantages of being unobtrusive, non-contact and executable from a distance. It is a pattern recognition problem that deals with spatio-temporal patterns of gait which are related to physiological and behavioral characteristics of individuals.

Studies on human gait perception using Moving Light Displays(MLDs) showed that human can classify human motion [1], as well as identify their friends from gaits [2]. However, there are several challenges to be overcome in automatic gait recognition: (i)acquisition of gait, (ii)extraction of compact gait signatures and (iii)the effects of covariates. This paper focuses on the extraction of compact frequency domain gait signatures from foot motion dynamics, and evaluates the recognition results under the effects of time covariates. It has been shown that time, footwear type, walking surface type, briefcase carrying condition and viewing angle are important covariates that affect gait and its observations, and that time covariate has the largest impact to gait recognition [3].

There are two prominent methods for gait recognition: model- and appearance-based. In model-based approaches [4,5,6], the observation at each frame is fitted into an explicit structural model of human body, and recognition is achieved from the analysis of the trajectories of high-level body parts. Appearance-based approaches [7,8,9,10,11,3] mostly use silhouette features, and are more sensitive to changes in clothing styles and noises from human segmentation process.

We contend that foot motion are the primary artifacts of gait, and foot holds individual specific characteristics. Furthermore, as a model-based approach, it is not sensitive to changes in clothing style. In our investigation of the effectiveness of foot motion at its best for gait recognition, we relied on a marker-based data acquisition. This way, we can exclude the effects of other covariates as well as possible noises introduced in gait acquisition by image processing. Gait signatures are formed by concatenating the spectral features derived from foot motion, without incorporating direct interrelationship between the signals. Gait signatures in frequency domain facilitate efficient matching of periodic gaits, and have been shown to be effective for classification of human periodic motion [12].

2 Previous Work

In our previous work [13], we proposed a gait recognition using spectral features of foot motion, assuming that the horizontal and vertical trajectories of left and right feet are accessible by a sensor system. The trajectories provide four motion signals $\{h_i(t), v_i(t)\}$, $i = 1, 2$, which corresponds to the horizontal and vertical displacement of left and right feet during a gait. By using Discrete Fourier Transform(DFT), we can obtain the frequency domain representation of the signals $F = \{H_i(\omega), V_i(\omega)\}$, $i = 1, 2$.

2.1 Spectral Features of Foot Motion

The spectral features from $X(\omega) \in F$ are defined as follows:

$$S_1(X(\omega)) = ||\bar{X}(\omega)||, \qquad (1)$$
$$S_2(X(\omega)) = e^{j \arg(\bar{X}(\omega))}, \qquad (2)$$
$$S_3(X(\omega)) = S_1(X(\omega)) \cdot S_2(X(\omega)), \qquad (3)$$

where $\bar{X}(\omega)$ is the normalized Fourier coefficient:

$$\bar{X}(\omega) = \frac{1}{\int ||X(\omega)|| d\omega} X(\omega). \qquad (4)$$

Normalization of scale eliminates the need for depth compensation in different gait acquisition setups. S_1 is the magnitude spectrum, S_2 is the phase spectrum and S_3 is known as the phase-weighted magnitude(PWM) spectrum [5]. Figure 1 shows the average and standard deviation of each spectra of an individual over 20 sequences.

For the phase spectra to be time shift invariant, we set a uniform phase for the fundamental frequency component, which equals to shifting in time-space domain. In other words, the phase spectra are defined as the relative phase of the fundamental frequency component.

The spectral features do not incorporate direct interrelationships between motion signals. For example, the magnitude relationship(the ratio of total power to motion signals) and the timing relationship(the phase difference of the fundamental frequency of two motion signals) are not represented in the spectral features. However, our experiments showed that even by extracting only features related to the dynamics of gait and excluding the shape structures of gait, we can achieve a reliable recognition rate.

2.2 Spectral Features from Two Motion Signals

We also proposed the use of the geometrical mean of two spectra to extract a more compact spectral feature for gait recognition. Using geometrical mean based spectral features offers another simplification in that we do not need to have strict correspondence between signals and their origins, such as signals from left and right feet.

The following spectral features(binary *T-operators*) are defined as a function of spectra of two signals:

$$T_1(X(\omega), Y(\omega)) = \sqrt{||\bar{X}(\omega)|| \, ||\bar{Y}(\omega)||}, \tag{5}$$

$$T_2(X(\omega), Y(\omega)) = (e^{j \arg(\bar{X}(\omega)\bar{Y}(\omega))})^{1/2}, \tag{6}$$

$$T_3(X(\omega), Y(\omega)) = T_1(X(\omega), Y(\omega)) \cdot T_2(X(\omega), Y(\omega)). \tag{7}$$

2.3 Kyutech Foot Motion Gait Database

We evaluate the discriminatory capability of the proposed spectral features using a gait database acquired using Vicon optical motion capture system. Experiments are based on gaits of 9 subjects (22–30 years old, 160–182 cm, 54–130kg), which are captured at 60 Hz in four separate sessions. The first two sessions were taken on the same day(*same-day* dataset), and the rest are taken in two separate days three month after the first two(*cross-month* dataset). A part of the database used in the experiments consists of 357 gait sequences, whose average length is 150 frames.

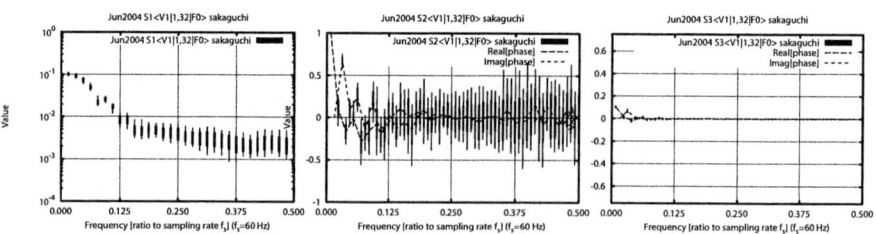

Fig. 1. Plot of average and standard deviation of magnitude, phase and phase-weighted magnitude (PWM) spectra of an individual over 20 sequences taken on the same day

2.4 Spectral Features in Logarithmic Scale

Gait recognition share the common properties with speech processing in that gait is a spatial *temporal* pattern. In speech processing, the power spectra in logarithmic scale are often used. Similarly, we can express spectra in logarithmic scale:

$$S_1^{(L)}(X(\omega)) = \log S_1(X(\omega)), \tag{8}$$

$$S_3^{(L)}(X(\omega)) = S_1^{(L)}(X(\omega)) \cdot S_2(X(\omega)). \tag{9}$$

Improvement in correct classification rates(CCRs) has been observed when magnitude and PWM spectra are in logarithmic scale, especially when magnitude spectra is used.

3 Integration of Magnitude and Phase Spectra

Previous experimental results suggested that both magnitude and phase spectra of foot motion are effective gait signatures. In phase-weighted magnitude(PWM) ($S_1 \odot S_2$) spectra, both spectra are integrated as their products at each frequency components. Instead of taking the product, we can also use information of both spectra as phase-magnitude concatenation(PMC) ($S_1 \otimes S_2 \triangleq (S_1, S_2)$) spectra. However, since the concatenation consists of spectra of different metrics, we cannot directly use it as a gait signature and examine its performance for gait recognition using k-NN rule.

3.1 An AdaBoost Classifier for Multimodal Gait Signatures

We integrate the phase and magnitude spectra of motion signals using an AdaBoost classifier [14] of a summation-type weak classifier with a simple extension for multi-class classification. A summation-type weak classifier consists of weak sub-classifiers, each of which is based on a sub-feature. At each round in AdaBoost, all of weak sub-classifiers are trained simultaneously based on probability density of features, which is calculated at the previous round. After this training phase, summation of outputs of these sub-classifiers makes a weak classifier at the round. This summation-type weak classifier contributes to a normalization of sub-feature metric for classification since output of each weak sub-classifier is normalized by the class-separation degree at corresponding sub-features. In addition to that, created weak sub-classifiers are dependent each other because they are trained on the same set of sample data (as each of them is trained on different sub-feature of the sample data), which leads to promotion of classification accuracy.

The approach was originally proposed for robust face detection of partially occluded face [15], by integrating results from sub-classifiers, each of which is based on a local face region at each round of AdaBoost. In our case, the spectral feature of different type corresponds to the feature of a different local face region.

For each identity in the training data set, we create a two-class AdaBoost classifier that separates samples belonging to the identity and samples belonging to the other identities. In classifying a test sample, first we collect the similarity scores from all the weak classifiers, each of which shows the similarity of the test sample to the training samples of a certain identity in training data set. Finally, the identity of the test sample is set to the identity represented by the classifier with the highest similarity score. As the similarity scores for each identity may not be of the same metric scale, choosing the identity of the highest similarity score may not be the optimal approach, but it is shown to be sufficiently close to results of k-NN rule classification.

Using the Adaboost classifier, we can also integrate the magnitude spectra of vertical motion signals and the phase spectra of horizontal motion signals.

4 Experimental Results

Experiments on nine subjects showed that for the same-day test, in which the grain data set includes the samples taken on the same day as the test sample, a recognition rate over 95% can be achieved using only the concatenation of magnitude spectra of motion signals as the gait signature. However, for cross-month test, where there is a time gap of 3 months between the capture time of training and test samples, the recognition rate dropped to 60%. In the following, we will describe the recognition results of AdaBoost classifiers for cross-month test.

4.1 Integration of Phase and Magnitude Spectra for Gait Recognition

The following results are based on spectra in logarithmic scale. Figure 3 shows the CCRs of recognition using magnitude(S_1), phase(S_2), PWM(magnitude⊙phase) spectra, as well as PMC(magnitude⊗phase). Recognition results for spectra derived from geometrical mean of two spectra in terms of T_1, T_2, $T_3 = T_1 \odot T_2$, and $T_1 \otimes T_2$ are shown in Figure 2.

– The integration of magnitude and phase spectra as PMC($S_1 \otimes S_2$) gives better performance than integrating the spectra into PWM($S_1 \odot S_2$). This also shows that the AdaBoost classifier works well in integration various gait modalities, and that the simple extension to multiple-class classification is also effective.
– Although both phase and magnitude spectra discriminates the gaits of individuals, for motion signals of different directions (h or v), the degree of discriminatory capability is different. The difference may be dataset-dependent, but for a personal identification in a known dataset, we should select the optimal combination of spectra for gait signature. The experimental results on our dataset shown that integration of magnitude spectra of vertical foot motion and phase spectra of horizontal foot motion provides the best recognition rates.

Magnitude and Phase Spectra of Foot Motion for Gait Recognition 395

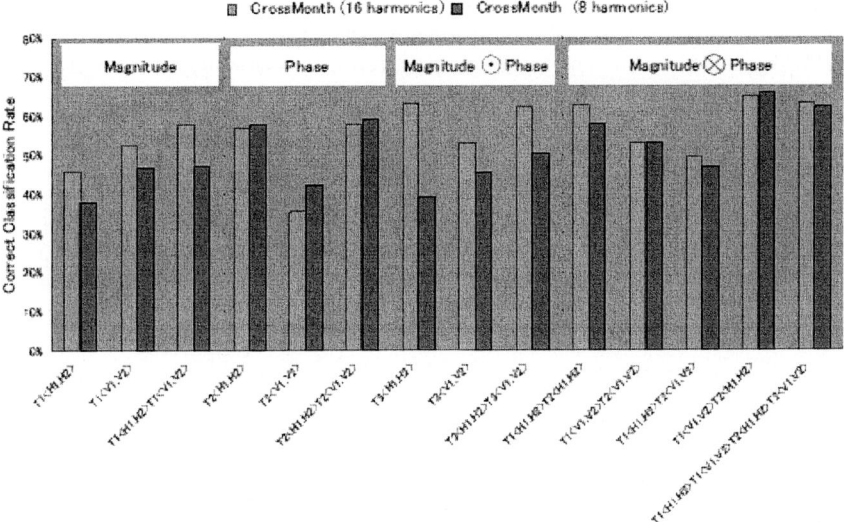

Fig. 2. Recognition results for spectra derived from geometrical mean of two spectra in terms of magnitude(T_1), phase(T_2), PWM($T_3 = T_1 \odot T_2$), and PMC ($T_1 \otimes T_2$)

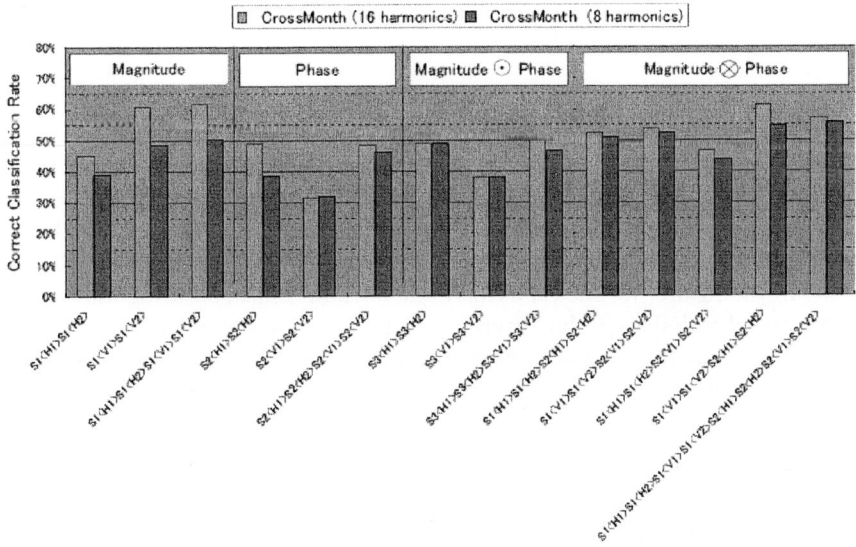

Fig. 3. CCRs of recognition using magnitude(S_1), phase(S_2), PWM (magnitude$\odot$phase) spectra, as well as PMC (magnitude$\otimes$phase)

– Under the effect of time covariate, spectra derived from geometrical mean of two spectra (by the T-operators) shows significant advantages of using PMC gait signature. The more compact representation of gait using $T_j\langle X,Y\rangle$ spectra even shows better performance than $S_j\langle X\rangle S_j\langle Y\rangle$.

5 Conclusion

Magnitude and phase spectra derived from foot motion during a normal walk has been shown to be effective cues to induce the identity of a person. This paper proposed the use of both magnitude and phase spectra together in phase-magnitude concatenation for gait signatures. For gait recognition, we use a summation-type AdaBoost classifier that evaluates magnitude and phase spectra of a motion signal as dependent sub-features. In recognition phase, each of weak classifiers sum up the normalized classification output at each sub-features(spectra).

Experiments on nine subjects showed that using phase-magnitude concatenation spectra in gait signatures is better than using the product of phase and magnitude spectra. Furthermore, it is shown that a motion signal is often best represented by either the phase or magnitude spectra. For example, integrating the magnitude spectra of vertical motion signals and the phase spectra of horizontal motion signals creates the best gait signature in our dataset.

The number of subjects in our experiment is only nine. We don't think this number is enough to evaluate effect of time covariate and to compare fitness of features combinations for gait recognition. Although our result should be verified under large database like GaitChallenge [3], we don't think outline of our result will change so much.

Time covariate has been shown to have the largest impact on accuracy of gate recognition [3]. In our cross-month experiments, recognition accuracy is about 65%. Accordingly, update of feature template should be done frequently in case of using only gait signature as identification, or incorporation with face signatures will be necessary to compensate degrade of each feature(gait and/or face feature).

The spectral features of gait we defined represents the transitional (dynamics) of gait. In the future, we should extend our work into incorporating information on gait structural(shape) characteristics into the gait signatures as well. Furthermore, a method to acquire foot motion trajectories during a gait, especially from video input is necessary for a practical gait recognition system.

Acknowledgment

This work was supported by fund from the MEXT via Kitakyushu innovative cluster project.

References

1. Johansson, G.: Visual motion perception. Scientific American **232** (1975) 76–88
2. Cutting, J., Kozlowski, L.: Recognizing friends by their walk: Gait perception without familiarity cues. Bulletin of the Psychonomic Society **9** (1977) 353–356

3. Sarkar, S., Phillips, P., Liu, Z., Vega, I.R., Grother, P., Bowyer, K.W.: The humanid gait challenge problem: Data sets, performance and analysis. IEEE Trans. Pattern Analysis and Machine Intelligence **27** (2005) 162–177
4. Niyogi, S.A., Adelson, E.H.: Analyzing and recognizing walking figures in xyt. In: IEEE Proceedings of Computer vision and Pattern Recognition. (1994) 467–474
5. Cunado, D., Nixon, M.S., Carter, J.N.: Using gait as a biometric via phase-weighted magnitude spectra. In: Proc. of 1st Int'l Conf. on Audio- and Video-Based Biometric Person Authentication. (1997) 95–105
6. Chew Yean Yam, M.S.N., Carter, J.N.: Automated person recognition by walking and running via model-based approaches. Pattern Recognition **37** (2004) 1057–1072
7. Murase, H., Sakai, R.: Moving object recognition in eigenspace representation: Gait analysis and lip reading. Pattern Recognition Letters **17** (1997) 155–162
8. He, Q., Debrunner, C.: Individual recognition from periodic activity using hidden markov models. In: IEEE Workshop on Human Motion. (2000)
9. Lee, L., Grimson, W.E.L.: Gait appearance for recognition. In: ECCV Workshop on Biometric Authentication. (2002) 143–154
10. Wang, L., Tan, T., Ning, H., Hu, W.: Silhouette analysis-based gait recognition for human identification. IEEE Transactions on Pattern Analysis and Machine Intelligence **25** (2003) 1505–1518
11. Mowbray, S.D., Nixon, M.S.: Automatic gait recognition via fourier descriptors of deformable objects. In: Proceedings of Audio Visual Biometric Person Authentication. (2003) 566–573
12. Li, B., Holstein, H.: Perception of human periodic motion in moving light displays - a motion-based frequency domain approach. Interdisciplinary Journal of Artificial Intelligence and the Simulation of Behaviour (AISBJ) **1** (2004) 403–416
13. Lie, A.S., Shimomoto, R., Sakaguchi, S., Ishimura, T., Enokida, S., Wada, T., Ejima, T.: Gait recognition using spectral features of foot motion. In: Proceedings of the 5th International Conference on Audio- and Video-based Person Authentication. (2005) to appear.
14. Schapire, R.E., Singer, Y.: Improved boosting algorithms using confidence-rated predictions. Machine Learning **37** (1999) 297–336
15. Sato, T., Minami, K., Asao, T., Enokida, S., Ejima, T.: A robust adaboost classifier for partially hidden faces. In: Proceedings of 11th Symposium on Sensing via Image Information. (2005) in Japanese.

Advances in Background Updating and Shadow Removing for Motion Detection Algorithms

Paolo Spagnolo, Tiziana D'Orazio, Marco Leo, and Arcangelo Distante

Istituto di Studi sui Sistemi Intelligenti per l'Automazione - C.N.R.,
Via Amendola 166/5, 70126 Bari, Italy
{spagnolo,dorazio,leo,distante}@ba.issia.cnr.it

Abstract. The problem of detecting moving objects is very important in many application contexts such as people detection and recognition, visual surveillance both in indoor and outdoor environments, and so on. In this paper we propose two additional modules for a generic motion detection algorithm. The first one regards the background updating procedure: the novelty of the proposed algorithm is its capability, unlike traditional similar algorithms, to efficiently update each point of the reference model, even if covered by a foreground object. The second one is a reliable algorithm for shadow removing: it is based on the correlation between regions selected from the reference image and the current one. In addition, with our approach, the artifacts detected in presence of sudden light changes are removed. The experiments have been performed on real image sequences acquired both in indoor and outdoor environments with natural and artificial lights.

1 Introduction

In the last years, motion detection has attracted great interest from computer vision researchers due to its promising applications in many areas, firstly visual surveillance. The most used approach in presence of still cameras is background subtraction [1,2,3,4]. These works implement a model of the background and compare the current image with this reference one. In this way the foreground objects present in the scene are detected.

Background modeling is an active area of research and is not the focus of the work here. Any system capable of reliable detection of moving pixels can be used for the foreground detection phase. Here we introduce two additional modules that can be easily added to a generic motion detection system. The first one is able to correctly update the background model, even for the pixels covered by moving objects. The second one is a shadow removing algorithm that can also remove the artifacts due to the presence of sudden light changes.

Some interesting works about shadows are presented in [10] (it works only on color images), [11] (similarly, it works on color images, but it uses HSV space) and [12] (it is based on a series of assumptions, some of them not applicable in indoor environments). A good review and comparison of shadow removing algorithms is proposed in [13]. The problem of handle sudden changes in light conditions has been treated in [5]. Some solutions are proposed in [7] (it uses many different background models, acquired in different light conditions), [6] and [8] (they are based on the presence of discontinuities in the training set). A good treatment of this problem can be found in [9], where an interesting solution based on HMM is proposed.

Another problem affecting the traditional background subtraction approaches is the updating of the background model. With standard updating procedures only the pixels corresponding to static points in the scene are correctly updated. If there are slowly moving objects in the scene, the intensity variation in correspondence with foreground points is not exactly estimated, so in those regions the background model could lacking in consistency.

In this paper we focus our attention on background updating and shadow removing algorithms. There are some new interesting points that will be introduced. First of all the background updating is carried out on all the pixels in the image, also the ones that are temporarily covered by foreground objects. The basic idea is that the intensity variation of each pixel is estimated by integrating all the variations exhibited by other pixels with the same intensity value, labeled as 'static' in the last frame. Then, a shadow removing algorithm based on the comparison of the correlation exhibited between regions selected from the reference image and the current one is proposed. In addition, the same algorithm permits to cope with the problems due to light switches: when there are sudden changes, the large number of false alarms is eliminated by comparing correlation between background and current regions in the same way of shadows removing.

In the rest of the paper, after a brief presentation of the background model used (section 2), two innovative approaches for background updating (section 3) and shadow removing (section 4) are presented. Finally, the experimental results obtained on real image sequences are reported (section 5).

2 Background Subtraction

Foreground object segmentation is a primary and fundamental step of visual surveillance systems. In order to correctly extract the moving objects it's necessary to develop very reliable motion detection algorithms, that should be adaptive to luminance variations and able to reduce the number of false alarms. In literature many background modeling algorithms have been proposed: our opinion is that they work well in standard conditions, but have same problems in particular situations, such as in presence of shadows and light switches. In addition, updating algorithm is crucial to assure good performance for long period of time. For these reasons, we have chosen to implement a standard background subtraction algorithm; then, we have improved it by our updating and shadow removing algorithms.

The algorithm we have implemented is detailed explained in [3]; for each pixel value at time t, a running average $B^t(x, y)$ and a form of standard deviation $V^t(x, y)$ are evaluated and maintained. A pixel (x, y) is considered a foreground pixel if its intensity value differs from $B^t(x, y)$ more than 2 times $V^t(x, y)$. Formally,

$$\left| I^{t+1}(x, y) - B^t(x, y) \right| > 2 * V^t(x, y) \qquad (1)$$

A higher-level paradigm, based, for example, on the tracking information, or frame difference, is necessary to validate the results of this step, in order to avoid to detect as moving object any variation in the background objects.

3 Background Updating

Any background subtraction approach is sensitive to variations of the illumination, so each algorithm needs an updating procedure of the background model. In most of previous works, only the static pixels of the background model are correctly updated, while all other background points, masked by foreground regions, remain unchanged or are incorrectly updated. This is particularly evident in presence of slow moving objects, as a person staying in a certain region for a certain period of time. The novelty of the proposed approach is that it allows all the pixels of the background to be correctly updated, even if they correspond to points that at time t are masked by foreground objects: every background pixel can be updated even if currently invisible.

The main idea of our approach is that the intensity variation of each pixel of the background model is not estimated by referring only to the corresponding pixel on the current image (as previous methods do), but considering the variations exhibited by all the pixels with the same intensity value. In other words, even if a pixel is covered by foreground object, it can be updated, accordingly to the variations observed at the other background pixels with the same intensity value.

To validate this assumption, we have observed a scene for a period of time (about 40 sec.), and we have registered the photometric gain average exhibited by all image pixels during this period, and their relative variances (fig. 1). For each gray level the value of the variance is very low, i.e. the pixels with the same intensity are varying in the same way. Then, we can generalize this trend, using the average photometric gain for updating of all the image pixels. If the registered values for the variances were not so low, this generalization will be not meaningful, and the corresponding updating could be incorrect. So, the updating value relative to each background model pixel $B^t(x, y)$ is not estimated on the basis of the corresponding pixel value $I^t(x, y)$ on the current image alone, but by averaging all the photometric gains:

$$\Lambda^t(x, y) = \frac{I^{t+1}(x, y)}{B^t(x, y)} \qquad (2)$$

measured on the static pixels having the same intensity value $B^t(x, y) = b_i$:

$$\mu(b_i) = \frac{1}{N(b_i)} \sum_{\{(x,y) \in I^{t+1} | B^t(x,y) = b_i\}} \Lambda^t(x, y) \qquad (3)$$

where $\{b_i\}_{i=1...n}$ are the n different intensity values that a pixel can assume, and $N(b_i)$ is the number of pixels in the background image $B^t(x, y)$ with intensity value b_i. The iterative updating rule becomes:

$$B^{t+1}(x, y) = \alpha * B^t(x, y) \mu(B^t(x, y)) + (1 - \alpha) * B^t(x, y) \qquad (4)$$

In an analogous way the standard deviation is updated. With the proposed approach, all the pixels in the image are updated: this is a great advantage in presence of slowly moving objects, or objects that stay in a certain position for a great period of time.

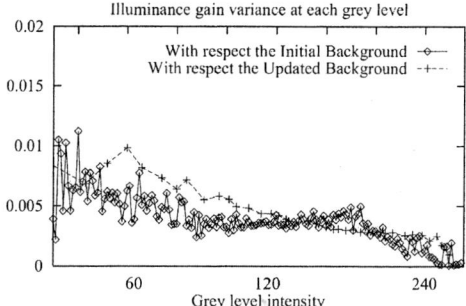

Fig. 1. The photometric gain variance exhibited by each intensity value over the whole current image with respect to an initial background model (i.e. 30 seconds ago) and with respect to the background model updated with the previous image

4 Shadow Removing

After the background subtraction, the resulting binary image contains only foreground objects, each of them with its own shadow. The presence of shadows is a great problem for a motion detection system: they drastically change the topological characteristics of the objects in an unpredictable way. This problem is mostly remarked in indoor contexts, where shadows are emphasized by the presence of many reflective objects; in addition shadows can be detected in every direction, on the floor, on the walls but also on the ceiling, so typical shadow removing algorithms, that assume shadows in a plane orthogonal with the human plane, cannot be used.

The shadow removing approach here described starts from the assumption that a shadow is an abnormal illumination of a part of an image due to the interposition of an opaque object with respect to a bright point-like illumination source. From this assumption, we can note that shadows have not a fixed texture, as real objects: they are half-transparent regions which retain the representation of the underlying background surface pattern. Therefore, our aim is to examine the parts of the image that have been detected as moving regions from the previous segmentation step but with a texture substantially unchanged with respect to the corresponding background. A segmentation procedure has been applied to recover large regions characterized by a constant photometric gain (2); then, for each region previously detected, the correlation between pixels is calculated, and it is compared with the same value calculated in the background image: regions whose correlation is not substantially changed are marked as shadow regions and removed. In fig. 2 we can see the result of segmentation step: as evident, the shadow region is separated from the true shape of the human person.

 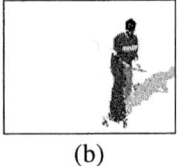

(a)   (b)

Fig. 2. (a) Original image; (b) output of segmentation process

At this point a further step is required to discriminate the real shadow regions, and remove them. All candidate shadow pixels are labeled and the regions with a notable percentage of these candidate shadow-pixels are removed. Candidate shadow pixels are detected as follows: their photometric gain has to be lower than unit; their correlation values with neighbouring points are compared with the corresponding one obtained at the same location on the reference background image; finally if the observed difference is too small, then the pixel is labelled as candidate shadow point. The reliability of this approach improves by increasing the number of neighbouring points that are correlated with every pixel. However, a satisfying trade-off must be found with the computational time constraint. We have proved as the simple correlation between only two adjacent pixels belonging to the same region, i.e. their ratio, is sufficient for an efficient shadow detection. Formally, for each region F_S:

$$D = \begin{cases} \left| \dfrac{I(i,j)}{I(i,j+1)} - \dfrac{B(i,j)}{B(i,j+1)} \right| & \text{if } j < \#\text{col} \\ \left| \dfrac{I(i,j)}{I(i+1,j)} - \dfrac{B(i,j)}{B(i+1,j)} \right| & \text{if } j = \#\text{col} \end{cases} \quad (5)$$

If D is greater then a threshold experimentally selected, the pixel (i,j) is strictly correlated with its neighbour one, so they can be considered as shadow points. Otherwise, they probably will be foreground points. All the regions containing a great number of shadow points are removed. The proposed method works very well both on indoor and on outdoor sequences. The two pixels ratio is a very fast shadow elimination algorithm, but in theory it could have problems removing not only the shadows, but also some points of people whose texture is similar to the background model. In practice, in our experiments on different situations, these cases have not been encountered.

4.1 Sudden Light Changes

The approach we propose for the shadow removing starts from the assumption that a shadow region presents about the same texture with respect to the reference image. In other words, the absolute intensity values change, but the relation between them remains the same. This observation can be used to reduce the effects of light switches in indoor context. In this case, traditional motion detection algorithms, as explained in detail in section 1, fail due to the sudden and unpredictable illumination changes. The background updating rules (3) and (4) are able to adapt the background model to standard light changes, but cannot work in presence of a sudden variation of such conditions. So, the resulting images seem totally unusable. However the successive application of the shadow removing algorithm produces surprising results, making the complete motion detection system more robust and reliable compared to similar approaches proposed in literature. Some works have tried to use supervised approaches including different background images acquired in several light conditions in the reference model. Their main drawback is that in indoor environments there are unpredictable light variations for the simultaneous presence of both natural and artificial light sources. The possibility to cope with these sudden illumination changes in an unsupervised way make the proposed system very general and robust.

5 Experimental Results and Future Works

The experiments have been performed on real image sequences acquired with a static TV camera Dalsa CA-D6 with 528 X 512 pixels. We have chosen to test algorithms both in outdoor and indoor conditions; in particular, three sequences have been acquired in a laboratory, in different light conditions, and in presence of sudden changes, due to light switches. The fourth test sequence has been acquired in an archeological site. In the follow, firstly results of shadow removing will be proposed, then the advantages obtained with the proposed updating procedure will be explained.

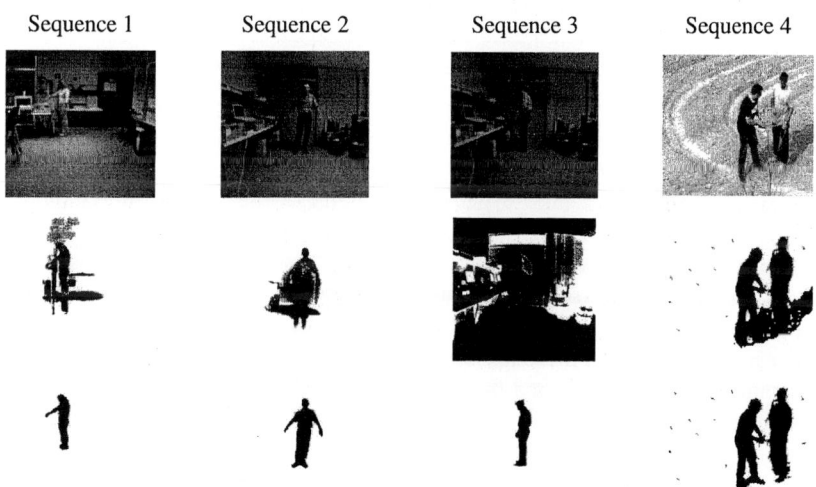

Fig. 3. The results obtained on the test sequences

In fig. 3 a qualitative evaluation of the shadow removing algorithm is represented. We have chosen to report an image for each sequence, so each column shows the original image, the result of background subtraction, and the results of shadow removing algorithm. The aforementioned problem of multiple shadows is evident in first two images. Shadow regions are projected on the floor, on the near desks, and also on the wall above the person. In the third column the image has been taken from a sequence after a sudden light change due to a light switched off. The image obtained after the background subtraction step is not meaningful since a large number of background pixels have not been removed. The final images produced after the shadow removing step become completely clear in every condition. The test sequences together with the corresponding sequences obtained with the proposed algorithm can be seen at the site "http://www.tnl.it/cnr".

In order to have a quantitative estimation of the error, we have characterized the Detection Rate (DR) and the False Alarm Rate (FAR), as proposed in [14]:

$$DR = \frac{TP}{TP+FN} \qquad FAR = \frac{FP}{TP+FP} \qquad (6)$$

where TP (true positive) are the detected regions that correspond to moving objects; FP (false positive) are the detected regions that do not correspond to a moving object; and FN (false negative) are moving objects not detected. In table 1 we can se the results obtained on the four test sequences.

We can note that the FAR parameter is always under 6% in the first three test sequences (indoor environments, more sensitive to effects of shadows) and even under 4% in the fourth test sequence (outdoor context, standard shadows).

Table 1. Rates to measure the confidence

Test sequence	DR (%)	FAR (%)
1	87,46	5,72
2	93,81	4,16
3	89,12	5,83
4	94,31	3,26

In order to compare our algorithm with other consolidate approaches, we have tested it on the same sequences proposed in [13], available at the website http://cvrr.ucsd.edu/aton/shadow. In table 2 the results we have obtained are reported. It can be note that even on these test sequences, the results we have obtained appear to be acceptable. It should be noted that in [13] a modified version of (6) has been used for testing algorithms.

Table 2. Experimental results obtained on the test sequences proposed in [13]

Test sequence	DR (%)	FAR (%)
Highway I	93,65	3,25
Highway II	89,43	4,63
Campus	88,91	6,36
Laboratory	91,77	3,96
Intelligent room	96,54	3,43

Finally, we have compared the results obtained with our background updating algorithm with the one proposed in [3]. In order to correctly compare the results we have applied on all the resulting images our second step of shadow removing. It is important to note that the only goal of this comparison is to emphasize the goodness of the proposed updating algorithm: it can be seen that in region covered by persons, our results are lightly better with respect to the other ones. In fig. 4 the results are shown on two images of outdoor scenes.

Fig. 4. The results obtained applying to a pair of images a traditional statistical background modelling [3] (2nd column) and the proposed algorithm (3th column)

Now we are effecting intensive tests on other test sequences; in particular we are testing our algorithms on the PETS video sets. Future work will investigate the effective real time implementation of our algorithms in a motion detection system for visual surveillance.

References

1. I.Haritaoglu, D.Harwood, L.Davis, A Fast Background Scene Modeling and Maintenance for Outdoor Surveillance, ICPR, pp.179-183, Barcelona,2000.
2. C.Wren, A.Azarbayejani, T.Darrell, A.Pentland, Pfinder: Real-time tracking of the human body, IEEE Trans. on Patt. An. and Mach. Intell. 19(7): pp.780-785, 1997.
3. T.Kanade, T.Collins, A.Lipton, Advances in Cooperative Multi-Sensor Video Surveillance, Darpa Image Underst. Work., Morgan Kaufmann, Nov. 1998, pp. 3-24.
4. H. Fujiyoshi, A. J. Lipton, Real-time human motion analysis by image skeletonisation, IEEE WACV, Princeton NJ, October 1998, pp.15-21.
5. B. Xie, V. Ramesh, T. Boult, Sudden Illumination Change Detection Using Order Consistency, Workshop on Statistical Methods in Video Processing (conj.ECCV2002),June 2002.
6. K. Toyama, J. Krumm, B. Brumitt, B. Meyers, Wallflower: Principles and Practice of Background Maintenance, ICCV, September 1999, Corfu, Greece.
7. O. Javed, Z. Rasheed, O. Alatas and M. S., KNIGHTM:A Real Time Surveillance System for Multiple Overlapping and Non-Overlapping Cameras, The 4th ICME 2003, Baltimore.
8. R.Hamid, A.Baloch, A.Bilal, N.Zaffar Object segmentation Using Feature Based Conditional Morphology- IEEE ICIAP 2003, Mantova, Italy.
9. B. Stenger, V. Ramesh, N. Paragios, F. Coetzee, and J. Bouhman, "Topology free hidden markov models: Application to background modeling," Proc. IEEE ICCV,2001,pp.294-301.

10. A. Elgammal, D. Harwood, & L.S. Davis, Non-parametric model for background subtraction, Proc. ICCV'99 Frame-Rate Workshop, 1999.
11. R. Cucchiara, C. Grana, M. Piccardi, & A. Prati, Detecting objects, shadows and ghosts in video streams by exploiting color and motion information, Proc. ICIAP 2001, pp.360-365.
12. J. Stauder, R. Mech, & J. Ostermann, Detection of moving cast shadows for object segmentation, IEEE Trans. On Multimedia, Vol. 1, N.1, pp. 65-76, 1999.
13. A. Prati, I. Mikic, M.M. Trivedi, R. Cucchiara, "Detecting Moving Shadows: Algorithms and Evaluation", in IEEE Transaction on PAMI, vol. 25, n.7, pp. 918-923, July, 2003
14. E.H.Jaraba, C.Urunuela, J.Senar, Detected motion classification with a double-background and a Neighborhood-based difference, *Pat. Recogn. Letter*,pp.2079-82, 2003(24).

Sequential Coordinate-Wise Algorithm for the Non-negative Least Squares Problem

Vojtěch Franc, Václav Hlaváč, and Mirko Navara

Center for Machine Perception, Department of Cybernetics,
Faculty of Electrical Engineering, Czech Technical University
{xfrancv,hlavac,navara}@cmp.felk.cvut.cz
http://cmp.felk.cvut.cz

Abstract. This paper contributes to the solution of the non-negative least squares problem (NNLS). The NNLS problem constitutes a substantial part of many computer vision methods and methods in other fields, too. We propose a novel sequential coordinate-wise algorithm which is easy to implement and it is able to cope with large scale problems. We also derive stopping conditions which allow to control the distance of the solution found to the optimal one in terms of the optimized objective function. The proposed algorithm showed promising performance in comparison to the projected Landweber method.

1 Introduction

A common approach of fitting model parameters to data is formalized as the least squares problem. There are situations in which additional constraints forcing the fitted parameters to be non-negative are useful. This leads to the non-negative least squares problem (NNLS). The non-negativity constraints are beneficial for the problems in which the negative values of the fitted parameters do not correspond to the physical reality, e.g., the problems dealing with pixel values in image modeling. The non-negativity constraints can also be used to introduce regularization for ill-posed problems. Examples of using NNLS in computer vision include, for instance, object recognition with unknown lighting conditions [1], image restoration [2] or tracking [3]. Learning of associative neural networks [5,6] is another task which can be expressed as the NNLS problem. This work has been motivated by the project COgnitive Systems using Perception-Action Learning (COSPAL http:\\www.cospal.org) in which associative networks play a substantial role in modeling low-level signals of the designed robotic system.

The NNLS problem becomes challenging if a large amount of data is to be processed, which makes standard optimization methods infeasible, e.g., the method by Lawson and Hanson [7]. The projected Landweber method was proposed to deal with large NNLS problems [6]. The projected Landweber method is a gradient-based iterative algorithm which produces a sequence of solutions converging to the optimal one. This paper proposes two contributions to the solution of the NNLS problem: (i) stopping conditions for iterative algorithms which allow to control the precision of the found solution in terms of the optimized objective function and (ii) a novel sequential coordinate-wise algorithm which is easy to implement and has promising performance on synthetical data.

The paper is organized as follows. The NNLS problem is defined in Section 2. The stopping conditions suitable for iterative algorithms solving the NNLS problem are derived in Section 3. A novel sequential coordinate-wise algorithm which solves the NNLS problem is proposed in Section 4. Section 5 describes an experiment comparing the proposed sequential coordinate-wise algorithm to the projected Landweber method. Conclusions are given in Section 6.

Notation used:
Upper-case bold letters denote matrices. Vectors are implicitly columns. Vectors are denoted by lower-case bold italic letters. For instance, $\mathbf{A} = [\mathbf{a}_1, \ldots, \mathbf{a}_n]$ is a matrix made of n column vectors $\mathbf{a}_i$, $i \in \mathcal{I}$, where $\mathcal{I} = \{1, \ldots, n\}$ is a set of entries. The non-bolded letters are used to denote indices of vectors and matrices. For instance, $\mathbf{x} = [x_1, \ldots, x_n]^T$ is a column vector with n entries (coordinates). The notation $[\mathbf{Hx} + \mathbf{f}]_i$ stands for the ith entry of the vector defined by the term $\mathbf{Hx} + \mathbf{f}$. The term $\mathbf{x} \geq \mathbf{0}$ is a shortcut for a set of inequalities $x_i \geq 0$, $\forall i \in \mathcal{I}$. The expression $\langle \mathbf{x}, \mathbf{f} \rangle$ stands for the dot (inner) product of vectors $\mathbf{x}$ and $\mathbf{f}$.

2 Non-negative Least Squares Problem

Let $\mathbf{A} \in \mathbb{R}^{m \times n}$ be a matrix and $\mathbf{b} \in \mathbb{R}^m$ a column vector. The non-negative least squares (NNLS) problem is defined as

$$\mathbf{x}^* = \underset{\mathbf{x} \geq \mathbf{0}}{\operatorname{argmin}} \frac{1}{2} \|\mathbf{A}\mathbf{x} - \mathbf{b}\|^2 . \qquad (1)$$

Without loss of generality, we may assume that all columns $\mathbf{a}_i$, $i \in \mathcal{I} = \{1, \ldots, n\}$ of the matrix $\mathbf{A} = [\mathbf{a}_1, \ldots, \mathbf{a}_n]$ are non-zero. A particular instance of the NNLS problem (1) arises when all entries of $\mathbf{A}$ are non-negative. This case matches the problem of learning of associative networks. In this formulation, we are searching for the optimum within an unbounded positive cone in $\mathbb{R}^n$. It is important to restrict the search to a bounded set by finding also an upper estimate of the optimal solution $\mathbf{x}^*$. In our case $\mathbf{x}^* \leq \mathbf{x}^o = [x_1^o, \ldots, x_n^o]^T$, where

$$x_i^o = \max\left(0, \frac{\langle \mathbf{a}_i, \mathbf{b} \rangle}{\langle \mathbf{a}_i, \mathbf{a}_i \rangle}\right), \quad \forall i \in \mathcal{I} .$$

This condition is a result of [6, Theorem 7], where the maximum with 0 has been omitted in [6, formula (41)]; however, the original proof works after this correction. By $\mathbf{e} \in \mathbb{R}^n$ we denote the vector with all coordinates equal to 1. We have an upper bound of the sum of entries of $\mathbf{x}^*$:

$$\langle \mathbf{x}^*, \mathbf{e} \rangle = \sum_{i=1}^{n} x_i^* \leq \sum_{i=1}^{n} x_i^o = \langle \mathbf{x}^o, \mathbf{e} \rangle . \qquad (2)$$

Inequality (2) will be important for stopping conditions of an iterative algorithm introduced below.

It can be seen that the NNLS problem (1) is a special instance of a more general quadratic programming (QP) task with non-negativity constrains. The quadratic objective function is

$$F(\boldsymbol{x}) = \frac{1}{2}\langle \boldsymbol{x}, \mathbf{H}\boldsymbol{x}\rangle + \langle \boldsymbol{x}, \boldsymbol{f}\rangle \,. \tag{3}$$

The QP task with the non-negativity constraints reads

$$\boldsymbol{x}^* = \operatorname*{argmin}_{\boldsymbol{x}\geq 0} F(\boldsymbol{x}) = \operatorname*{argmin}_{\boldsymbol{x}\geq 0}\left(\frac{1}{2}\langle \boldsymbol{x}, \mathbf{H}\boldsymbol{x}\rangle + \langle \boldsymbol{x}, \boldsymbol{f}\rangle\right)\,. \tag{4}$$

The solution of the QP task (4) coincides with the solution of the NNLS problem (1) if the matrix $\mathbf{H} = \mathbf{A}^T\mathbf{A} \in \mathbb{R}^{n\times n}$ and the vector $\boldsymbol{f} = -\mathbf{A}^T\boldsymbol{b} \in \mathbb{R}^n$.

The form of task (4) cannot be arbitrary; due to the formulation of the original task (1), $\mathbf{H}$ and $\boldsymbol{f}$ satisfy some special properties:

1. $\mathbf{H} = \mathbf{A}^T\mathbf{A}$ is symmetric and positive semidefinite.
2. $\mathbf{H}_{k,k} = \langle \boldsymbol{a}_k, \boldsymbol{a}_k\rangle > 0$ for all k.
3. The task may have multiple solutions if 0 is an eigenvalue of $\mathbf{H}$; however, the positive solutions are bounded.

The rest of this paper deals with this special form of task (4).

3 Stopping Conditions

The QP task (4) can be solved by iterative algorithms which produce a sequence of solutions $\boldsymbol{x}^{(1)}, \boldsymbol{x}^{(2)}, \ldots, \boldsymbol{x}^{(t)}$ converging to the optimal solution $\boldsymbol{x}^*$. There is a need to stop the algorithm when the current solution $\boldsymbol{x}^{(t)}$ is sufficiently close to the optimal $\boldsymbol{x}^*$. Two possible stopping conditions will be introduced. First, the stopping conditions based on the Karush-Kuhn-Tucker (KKT) conditions will be described in Section 3.1. Second, the stopping conditions based on lower and upper bounds of the optimal value $F(\boldsymbol{x}^*)$ will be derived in Section 3.2.

3.1 Karush-Kuhn-Tucker Conditions

The objective function (3) is convex as the matrix $\mathbf{H} = \mathbf{A}^T\mathbf{A}$ is symmetric and positive semidefinite. The constraints $\boldsymbol{x} \geq \mathbf{0}$ define a convex feasible set. As both the objective function and the feasible set are convex, the QP task (4) is convex as well. In the case of a convex optimization task, the Karush-Kuhn-Tucker (KKT) conditions are necessary and sufficient for the optimal solution (see [4]). The KKT conditions for the QP task (4) have a particularly simple form introduced below.

The Lagrange function for task (4) reads

$$L(\boldsymbol{x}, \boldsymbol{\mu}) = \frac{1}{2}\langle \boldsymbol{x}, \mathbf{H}\boldsymbol{x}\rangle + \langle \boldsymbol{x}, \boldsymbol{f}\rangle - \langle \boldsymbol{x}, \boldsymbol{\mu}\rangle\,, \tag{5}$$

where $\boldsymbol{\mu} \in \mathbb{R}^n$ are Lagrange multipliers (or dual variables). We obtain conditions

$$\frac{\partial L(\boldsymbol{x}, \boldsymbol{\mu})}{\partial \boldsymbol{x}} = \mathbf{H}\boldsymbol{x} + \boldsymbol{f} - \boldsymbol{\mu} = \mathbf{0}\,, \quad \boldsymbol{x} \geq \mathbf{0}\,, \quad \boldsymbol{\mu} \geq \mathbf{0}\,, \quad \langle \boldsymbol{x}, \boldsymbol{\mu}\rangle = 0\,. \tag{6}$$

Any vector x which satisfies the KKT conditions (6) is an optimal solution of the QP task (4) and vice versa.

Let $\mathcal{X}^* \subset \mathbb{R}^n$ denote the set of vectors which satisfy (6), i.e., any $x^* \in \mathcal{X}^*$ is the solution of the task (4) for some μ. Notice that the set $\mathcal{X}^*$ is convex and it contains just one vector if the matrix $\mathbf{H}$ is positive definite. Reasonable stopping conditions for an iterative algorithm can be derived by introducing a relaxed version of the KKT conditions. The ε-KKT conditions are defined as a set of linear inequalities

$$x \geq 0,$$
$$[\mathbf{H}x + f]_i \geq -\varepsilon, \quad \text{for} \quad i \in \mathcal{I} = \{1, \ldots, n\},$$
$$[\mathbf{H}x + f]_i \leq \varepsilon, \quad \text{for} \quad i \in \mathcal{I}_\emptyset = \{i \in \mathcal{I} : x_i > 0\}, \quad (7)$$

where $\varepsilon > 0$ is a constant defining the precision of the solution. Let $\mathcal{X}^\varepsilon \subset \mathbb{R}^n$ be the set of vectors which satisfy conditions (7). It is easy to show that $\mathcal{X}^* \subseteq \mathcal{X}^\varepsilon$ holds in general and $\mathcal{X}^* = \mathcal{X}^\varepsilon$ holds for $\varepsilon = 0$.

The ε-KKT conditions are easy to evaluate and they can be used as an indicator that the current solution is close to the optimal one. It is not immediately seen, however, how the solution satisfying the ε-KKT conditions corresponds to the optimal x^* in terms of the optimized function $F(x)$. This drawback is removed after introducing a lower bound $LB(x)$ of the optimal value $F(x^*)$ derived in the sequel.

3.2 Bounds of the Optimal Solution

In this section, we exclude the (possible) trivial solution $x^* = 0$. If the optimum is obtained at 0, we find it easily by a test of the inputs or after the first step (starting from 0 as the initial estimate, we obtain it as the next approximation and a fixed point).

Let the vector $\nabla F(x^*)$ be the gradient of the function F evaluated at x^*. It follows from the convexity of the function F that

$$F(x^*) + \langle (x - x^*), \nabla F(x^*) \rangle \leq F(x),$$
$$\frac{1}{2}\langle x^*, \mathbf{H}x^* \rangle + \langle x^*, f \rangle + \langle (x - x^*), (\mathbf{H}x^* + f) \rangle \leq \frac{1}{2}\langle x, \mathbf{H}x \rangle + \langle x, f \rangle,$$

which can be further rearranged to

$$\langle x^*, \mathbf{H}x + f \rangle - \frac{1}{2}\langle x, \mathbf{H}x \rangle \leq \frac{1}{2}\langle x^*, \mathbf{H}x^* \rangle + \langle x^*, f \rangle. \quad (8)$$

Since the entries of the optimal vector x^* are non-negative, the following inequality holds

$$\langle x^*, \mathbf{H}x + f \rangle \geq \langle x^*, e \rangle \min_{i \in \mathcal{I}} [\mathbf{H}x + f]_i. \quad (9)$$

Inequalities (8) and (9) give a lower bound

$$\underbrace{\langle x^*, e \rangle \min_{i \in \mathcal{I}} [\mathbf{H}x + f]_i - \frac{1}{2}\langle x, \mathbf{H}x \rangle}_{LB(x)} \leq \underbrace{\frac{1}{2}\langle x^*, \mathbf{H}x^* \rangle + \langle x^*, f \rangle}_{F(x^*)}. \quad (10)$$

Equality in (10) is obtained for the optimal solution vector x^*, i.e., $LB(x^*) = F(x^*)$ holds true which follows from the equalities

$$\min_{i \in \mathcal{I}}[\mathbf{H}x^* + f]_i = 0 \quad \text{and} \quad \langle x^*, \mathbf{H}x^* \rangle + \langle x^*, f \rangle = 0,$$

derived directly from the KKT conditions (6). (The former equality is based on the fact that there is at least one $i \in \mathcal{I}$ such that $[\mathbf{H}x^* + f]_i = 0$. Otherwise, $x^* = 0$; this case has been excluded by our assumption.)

The lower bound (10) is valid for an arbitrary optimization task (4). The bound depends on a generally unknown term $\langle x^*, e \rangle$. However, the upper bound of $\langle x^*, e \rangle$ can be derived for a special instance of task (4) which was specified in Section 2. Provided the term $\langle x^*, e \rangle$ (or its upper bound) is known the lower bound $LB(x)$ can be evaluated and used as a stopping condition of an iterative algorithm. A reasonable stopping condition reads

$$F(x) - F(x^*) \leq \delta, \tag{11}$$

where $\delta > 0$ is a constant which limits the distance between vectors x and x^* in terms of the optimized criterion. The stopping condition (11) is satisfied if the inequality

$$F(x) - LB(x) \leq \delta, \tag{12}$$

holds which could be evaluated provided the lower bound (10) is known.

4 Sequential Coordinate-Wise Algorithm

This section describes a novel (according to the authors' knowledge) sequential coordinate-wise algorithm for optimization of the task (4). Without the positivity constraint, our method coincides with the Gauss-Seidel method which is known to converge if $\mathbf{H}$ is positive definite. The algorithm produces a sequence of solutions $x^{(0)}, x^{(1)}, \ldots, x^{(t)}$ which converges to the optimal x^*. The idea is to optimize in each iteration with respect to a single coordinate while the remaining coordinates are fixed. The optimization with respect to a single coordinate has an analytical solution, thus it can be computed efficiently.

Let $x_k \in \mathbb{R}$ be the k-th coordinate of the vector $x = [x_1, \ldots, x_n]^T \in \mathbb{R}^n$ and $\mathcal{I}_k = \mathcal{I} \setminus \{k\}$. The objective function $F(x)$ can be equivalently rewritten as

$$\begin{aligned}
F(x) &= \frac{1}{2} \sum_{i \in \mathcal{I}} \sum_{j \in \mathcal{I}} x_i x_j H_{i,j} + \sum_{i \in \mathcal{I}} x_i f_i \\
&= \frac{1}{2} x_k^2 H_{k,k} + x_k f_k + x_k \sum_{i \in \mathcal{I}_k} x_i H_{i,k} + \sum_{i \in \mathcal{I}_k} x_i f_i + \frac{1}{2} \sum_{i \in \mathcal{I}_k} \sum_{j \in \mathcal{I}_k} x_i x_j H_{i,j} \\
&= \frac{1}{2} x_k^2 \alpha + x_k \beta + \gamma,
\end{aligned}$$

where

$$\alpha = H_{k,k},$$
$$\beta = f_k + \sum_{i \in \mathcal{I}_k} x_i H_{i,k} = [\mathbf{H}\mathbf{x} + \mathbf{f}]_k - H_{k,k} x_k,$$
$$\gamma = \sum_{i \in \mathcal{I}_k} x_i f_i + \frac{1}{2} \sum_{i \in \mathcal{I}_k} \sum_{j \in \mathcal{I}_k} x_i x_j H_{i,j}.$$

The optimization of $F(\mathbf{x})$ with respect to a selected x_k has an analytical solution

$$\begin{aligned} x_k^* &= \operatorname*{argmin}_{x_k \geq 0} \frac{1}{2} x_k^2 \alpha + x_k \beta + \gamma \\ &= \max\left(0, -\frac{\beta}{\alpha}\right) \\ &= \max\left(0, x_k - \frac{[\mathbf{H}\mathbf{x} + \mathbf{f}]_k}{H_{k,k}}\right). \end{aligned}$$

The iterative algorithm derived in the sequel updates a single variable x_k in each iteration, i.e.,

$$x_i^{(t+1)} = x_i^{(t)}, \forall i \in \mathcal{I}_k. \tag{13}$$

The formula for the update requires the gradient $\boldsymbol{\mu}^{(t)} = \mathbf{H}\mathbf{x}^{(t)} + \mathbf{f}$. We recommend to update the vector $\boldsymbol{\mu}^{(t)}$ in each iteration instead of computing it from the scratch. Thanks to (13) the update can be written as

$$\boldsymbol{\mu}^{(t+1)} = \boldsymbol{\mu}^{(t)} + \left(x_k^{(t+1)} - x_k^{(t)}\right) \mathbf{h}_k, \tag{14}$$

where $\mathbf{h}_k$ is the kth column of the matrix $\mathbf{H} = [\mathbf{h}_1, \ldots, \mathbf{h}_n]$. (In fact, the original formula for β has the same order of complexity, because we need only one coordinate of the gradient. However, the latter formula allows to compute the whole gradient which is needed for stopping conditions.) The proposed iterative algorithm to solve task (4) is the following:

Algorithm 1: Sequential Coordinate-wise Algorithm for NNLS (abbrev. SCA)

1. Initialization. Set $\mathbf{x}^{(0)} = \mathbf{0}$ and $\boldsymbol{\mu}^{(0)} = \mathbf{f}$.
2. Repeat until the stopping condition is satisfied:
   For $k = 1$ to n

$$x_k^{(t+1)} = \max\left(0, x_k^{(t)} - \frac{\mu_k^{(t)}}{H_{k,k}}\right) \quad \text{and} \quad x_i^{(t+1)} = x_i^{(t)}, \forall i \in \mathcal{I}_k,$$

$$\boldsymbol{\mu}^{(t+1)} = \boldsymbol{\mu}^{(t)} + \left(x_k^{(t+1)} - x_k^{(t)}\right) \mathbf{h}_k.$$

Algorithm 1 requires $O(n)$ computations for each update from $\boldsymbol{x}^{(t)}$ to $\boldsymbol{x}^{(t+1)}$. The gradient vector $\boldsymbol{\mu}^{(t)}$ is known in each iteration, which can be employed for the evaluation of the stopping conditions. The stopping conditions are evaluated after all n coordinates were updated. Section 3 describes two different stopping conditions which can be used to halt the algorithm. It is obvious that the objective function $F(\boldsymbol{x}^{(t)})$ decreases or remains unchanged in Algorithm 1, however, we have not found a proof of its convergence yet. We have the following observation at least:

Proposition 1. *All fixed points of Algorithm 1 are optimal solutions of task* (4).

PROOF: Suppose that $\boldsymbol{x}^{(t)}$ is a fixed point of Algorithm 1, i.e., $\boldsymbol{x}^{(t+1)} = \boldsymbol{x}^{(t)}$. This means that for each $k \in \mathcal{I}$ either $\mu_k^{(t)} = 0$ or $(\mu_k^{(t)} > 0$ and $x_k^{(t)} = 0)$ hold. Thus the KKT conditions are satisfied for $\boldsymbol{x}^{(t)}, \boldsymbol{\mu}^{(t)}$. ∎

5 Experiments

This section outlines an experiment carried out on synthetical data. The problem selected is to train an associative network with channel-based representation of input and output signals. We refer to [5,6] for more information about associative networks. The adopted setting results into 10 training problems of the form (4) with the number of $n = 2500$ variables.

The proposed sequential coordinate-wise Algorithm 1 (SCA) is compared to the projected Landweber Algorithm [6] (LA). The Matlab implementation was used in all experiments. The data matrix contains only positive entries, which allows to evaluate the lower bound on $F(\boldsymbol{x}^*)$ and to use the stopping condition (12). The stopping condition $F(\boldsymbol{x}^{(t)}) - F(\boldsymbol{x}^*) \leq 10^{-6}$ was used. We measured the speed of convergence in terms of (i) the number of updates required for convergence and (ii) an estimate of the required CPU time on the common PC with Intel Pentium IV 2.80GHz processor.

The comparison of the convergence speed can be seen in terms of the number of iterations and the required CPU time can be seen in Figure 1. These values are measured for all 10 problems separately. The SCA turned out to be on average more than ten times faster compared to the LA.

6 Conclusions

This paper describes two contributions to the problem of solving the non-negative least squares (NNLS) problem. First, stopping conditions suitable for iterative algorithms solving the NNLS problem were proposed. The stopping conditions allow to control the precision of the solution found in terms of the optimized objective function. Second, a sequential coordinate-wise algorithm to solve the NNLS problem was proposed. The algorithm is easy to implement and showed promising performance. The proposed algorithm outperformed the projected Landweber method which has been used to solve the NNLS problem. The methods were benchmarked on synthetical data.

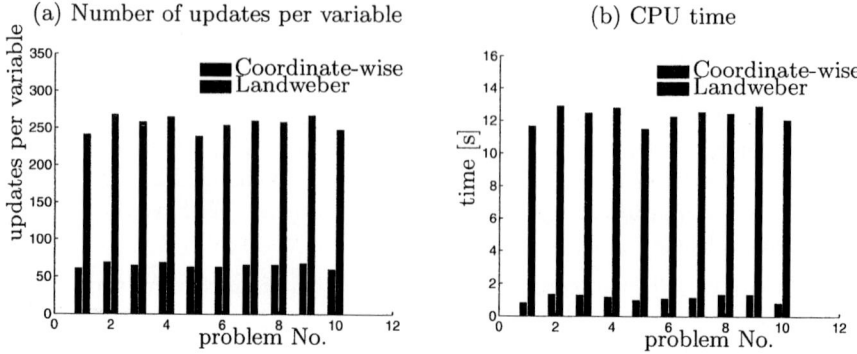

Fig. 1. Comparison between the projected Landweber method and the sequential coordinate-wise algorithm on 10 different NNLS problems having 2500 variables each

Acknowledgments

The authors would like to thank Gösta Granlund, Michael Felsberg, Per-Erik Forssén, and Erik Jonsson for introducing to the problem and for fruitful discussions. The authors were supported by the projects IST-004176 COSPAL, CONEX GZ 45.535. The first author was also supported by MSM 6840770013. The second author was also supported by INTAS 04-77-7347 (PRINCESS).

References

1. R. Basri and D.W. Jacobs. Lambertian reflectance and linear subspaces. *IEEE Transactions on Pattern Analysis and Machine Inteligence*, 25(2):218–233, 2003.
2. M. Bertero and P. Boccacci. *Introduction to Inverse Problems in Imaging*. Institute of Physics Publishing, Bristol, Great Britain, 1998.
3. J.E. Boyd and J. Meloche. Evaluation of statistical and multiple-hypothesis tracking for video surveillance. *Machine Vision and Applications*, 13(5-6):244–351, 2003.
4. R. Fletcher. *Practical Methods of Optimization*. John Wiley & Sons, New York, USA, 2nd edition, 1990.
5. G. Granlund. An associative perception-action structure using a localized space variant information representation. In *Proceedings of Algebraic Frames for the Perception-Action cycle (AFPAC)*, Kiel, Germany, September 2000.
6. B. Johansson, T. Elfving, V. Kozlov, T. Censor, and G. Granlund. The application of an oblique-projected Landweber method to a model of supervised learning. Technical Report LiTH-ISY-R-2623, Dept. EE, Linköping University, SE-581 83 Linköping, Sweden, September 2004.
7. C.L. Lawson and R.J. Hanson. *Solving Least Squares Problems*. Prentice-Hall, Englewood Cliffs, New Jersey, 1995.

Recognition of Partially Occluded and Deformed Binary Objects

Ondřej Horáček, Jan Kamenický, and Jan Flusser [*]

Institute of Information Theory and Automation,
Academy of Sciences of the Czech Republic,
Pod vodárenskou věží 4, 182 08 Prague 8, Czech Republic
{horacek,kamenik,flusser}@utia.cas.cz

Abstract. A method dealing with recognition of partially occluded and affine transformed binary objects is presented. The method is designed for objects with smooth curved boundary. It divides an object into affine-invariant parts and uses modified radial vector for the parts description. Object recognition is performed via string matching in the space of radial vectors.

1 Introduction

Recognition of objects under partial occlusions and deformations caused by imaging geometry is one of the most difficult problems in computer vision. It is required always when analyzing 2-D images of a 3-D scene. Although many methods trying to solve this task have been published, it still remains open. Clearly, there is no universal algorithm which would be "optimal" in all cases. Different methods should be designed for different class of objects and for different groups of assumed deformations. In this paper we assume the objects are deformed by an unknown affine deformation. This assumption approximates real photos with a week perspective deformation.

We introduce a method developed for the recognition of smooth curved objects. First, the shape is divided into parts which are defined by means of inflection points of the object boundary. Then the shape of each part is described by a special kind of radial vector. Finally, the parameters of the affine deformation are estimated and classification is performed by string matching in the space of radial vectors. The performance of the method is demonstrated by experiments.

2 Overview of Current Methods

Current methods can be classified into two major categories. The methods of the first group divide the object into affine-invariant parts. Each part is described

---

[*] Ondřej Horáček and Jan Kamenický were supported by the Czech Ministry of Education under the project No. 1M6798555601 (Research Center DAR). Jan Flusser was supported by the Grant Agency of the Czech Republic under the project No. 102/04/0155.

by some kind of "standard" global invariants, and the whole object is then characterized by a string of vectors of invariants. Recognition under occlusion is performed by maximum substring matching. Since inflection points of the boundary are invariant to affine (and even projective) deformation of a shape, they become a popular tool for the definition of the affine-invariant parts. This approach was used by Ibrahim and Cohen [3], who described the object by area ratios of two neighboring parts. As a modification which does not use inflection points, concave residua of convex hull can be used. For polygon-like shapes, however, inflection points cannot be used. Instead, one can construct "cuts" defined by three or four neighboring vertices. Yang and Cohen [11] used area ratios of the cuts to construct affine invariants. Flusser [2] further developed their approach by finding more powerful invariant description of the cuts. Similar method was successfully tested for perspective projection by Rothwell et al. [6].

Lamdan [4] used mutual position of four "interesting" points for the recognition. To verify the received match, normalized concave areas were described by radial vector.

The methods of the second group are "intrinsically local" – they describe the boundary in every point by means of its small neighborhood. In that way they transform the boundary to so-called signature curve which is invariant to affine/projective transform. Typical representatives of this group are differential invariants. They were probably discovered by Wilczynski [10] and furthermore developed by Weiss [9], [8]. These invariants are based on derivatives of orders from four to eight. They have been experimentally proven to be extremely sensitive to inaccurate segmentation of the boundary, discretization errors and noise.

Mokhtarian and Abbasi [5] used inflection points themselves to characterize the boundary. They constructed so-called Curvature Scale Space and traced the position of inflection points on different levels of image pyramid. The trajectories of the inflection points then served as object descriptors. There have been also methods based on wavelet transform of the boundary. E.g., Tieng and Boles [7] introduced wavelet-based boundary representation, where affine invariance was achieved by enclosed area contour parameterization. However, the use of the wavelet-based methods in case of partial occlusions is questionable.

3 Definition of Affine-Invariant Parts

Both inflection points and central points of straight lines are affine invariant, i.e. the properties "to be an inflection point" and "to be a central point of a straight line" are preserved under arbitrary nonsingular affine transform. Thus, we use these points for the construction of affine-invariant parts. We connect each couple of neighboring cut points by a line. This line and the corresponding part of the object boundary form a convex region which may or may not lie inside the original object (in Fig. 1c). A sequence of such parts carry efficient information about the object.

Detection of inflection points of discrete curves has been discussed in numerous papers. Let us recall that, in the continuous domain, an inflection point is defined by a constraint $\ddot{x}(t)\dot{y}(t) - \dot{x}(t)\ddot{y}(t) = 0$, where $x(t), y(t)$ is a parameterization of the curve and the dots denote derivatives with respect to t. When this definition is directly converted to the discrete domain, it becomes very sensitive to sampling and noise. Thus, we propose a new robust method of curvature estimation.

A circle with fixed radius is placed on each boundary point (in Fig. 1a). Ratio of the whole circle area to its area being inside the object serves for estimation of the curvature. When this ratio equals 0.5, the boundary has zero curvature and the corresponding point is either an inflection point or it lies inside a straight segment. We construct a curvature graph (in Fig. 1b), smooth it and define cut points as zero-crossing points and middle points of approximately zero-value segments. Furthermore, a request of sufficient part size is considered: the segment of the curvature graph between two cut points should have sum of values above some threshold, otherwise it is treated as a part of zero curvature.

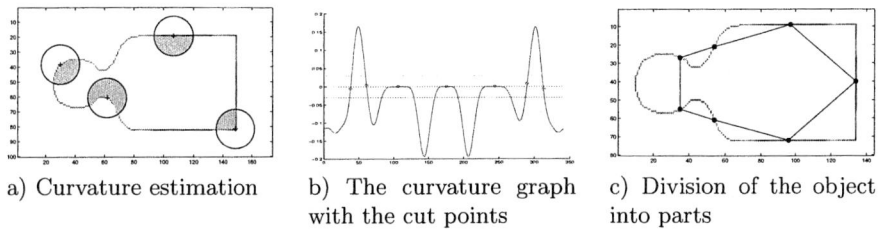

a) Curvature estimation   b) The curvature graph with the cut points   c) Division of the object into parts

Fig. 1. Definition of affine-invariant parts

4 Description of the Parts

The object is represented by the parts, construction of which has been described above. Describing the shape of the parts we get a description of the whole object which is robust to occlusion. Robustness to occlusion means that if some part of the object boundary is missing or changed, only few elements of the feature vector are changed. This is an important attribute. Note that traditional global methods, for instance description of the object by moment invariants or Fourier descriptors, do not have this property.

It would be possible to describe each part individually and eliminate the impact of the deformation by using proper affine invariants (moment invariants or Fourier descriptors for instance). In such a case, however, we do not employ important information that all the parts were deformed by *the same* transformation. Including this consistency information in the object description can significantly increase the recognition performance. Thus, we propose the following description of the parts by a modified radial vector, with included position of critical points. See complete demo object description in Fig. 2a.

The spokes of the radial vector come from the middle of the cutting line and they divide the part into subparts of equal area. For each part, they are constructed as follows.

1. Define the desired number n of the spokes (i.e. the length of the radial vector).
2. Go through the outer boundary of the part.
3. For each step calculate the area of the triangle between the neighbor boundary points and the midpoint of the cutting line.
4. If the cumulated area just steps over $k/(n-1)$ fraction of the total part area, the k-th spoke ends in the current boundary point.

The introduced modified radial vector divides the part invariantly under affine transformation. Note that a classical radial vector with constant-angle spokes distribution or constant-boundary length spokes distribution has not such a favorable property.

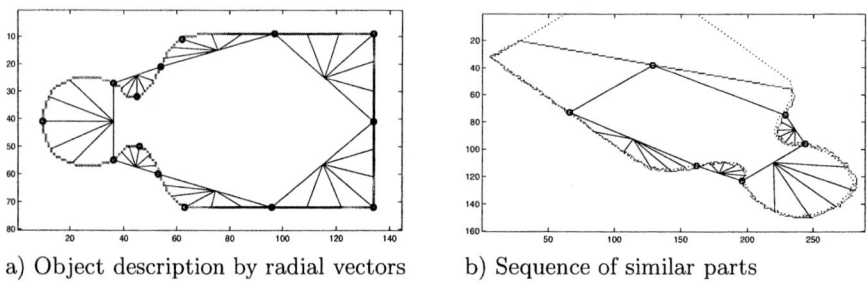

a) Object description by radial vectors   b) Sequence of similar parts

Fig. 2. Description and matching of the demo object

5 Matching

The image is classified by finding the longest and best matching part of the boundary (in Fig. 2b). This is realized by comparing a parts sequences of the image with a parts sequences of the database objects.

1. For each part of the database object and each part of the image do the following:
2. Take a sequence of parts starting from the current part. A length of this sequence is gradually incremented, it begins with the length of the previous longest successful match (or equals one in case of the first trial).
3. Recover the affine transformation T between the database and sensed objects. Use the least square fit of the control points of all parts involved in the sequence. Each part has three control points: two cut points and the middle-spoke end-point.
4. Transform the database radial vectors by transformation T.
5. Compare the transformed database radial vector sequence with the current one from the image. Similarity measure S is evaluated for this purpose – see below. If S is smaller than required similarity threshold, this sequences are considered not to match, and a start of next sequence is taken on the step 1.

6. The current sequence of radial vectors was successfully tested for a match in the previous step. If this sequence is longer than the previous best match, or is equal and the similarity level S is higher, select this match as the best one. Now try to make the matching sequence even longer – continue with the step 2.

Similarity measure S is introduced for suitable comparison of the radial vectors u, v. $S = 1$ only if $u = v$, S approaches zero for growing vector difference. The single similarity measure s_i of the i-th spoke lengths u_i, v_i is a Gaussian quantity of the $u_i - v_i$ difference

$$s_i = e^{-\frac{1}{\sigma_i^2}\left(\frac{u_i-v_i}{2}\right)^2}, \qquad \sigma_i = k_1 + k_2 \left|\frac{u_i+v_i}{2}\right|.$$

The Gaussian dispersion σ_i absolute component k_1 realizes a noise tolerance, the constant k_2 determines a tolerance relative to the value size.

We have the following requirements for combining single component s_i to overall similarity measure S: $S = s_i$ if all s_i are equal; $S = 0$ if some $s_i = 0$; S needs to be sensitive to all s_i; moreover, we require S to be 0.75 if all but one s_i equal 1 and one s_i equals 0.5. All these criteria are met for example by weighted average with weights w_i inversely proportional to s_i

$$S = \frac{\sum_{i=1}^{n} w_i \cdot s_i}{\sum_{i=1}^{n} w_i}, \qquad w_i = \frac{n-2}{s_i} - (n-3).$$

6 Experimental results

The proposed method was tested on a set of 24 binary objects, which had been previously segmented from color images. The objects were successively deformed by various affine transforms, their various regions were occluded and then the objects were matched against the database of the 24 originals. As a matching criterion which should be maximized we took the number of those parts (cuts) of the test object which match with the parts of the database object. This is in fact a well-known principle of string matching.

For illustration, two examples are shown in Fig. 3. On the left-hand side, one can see partially occluded and transformed objects. The corresponding database objects (which were successfully found in both cases) are shown on the right-hand side. The critical (inflection) points are highlighted, their connecting lines define the division into parts. The spokes of the corresponding radial vectors are drown inside the matched parts of the image.

The modified radial vector describes the boundary with a good precision, the tolerance to a shape perturbations is controlled by user-defined parameters/thresholds. This enables an optimization for various types of shapes. Interestingly, the boundary does not need to be a smooth curve with well-defined inflection points. The method finds critical points even on polygonal parts (see

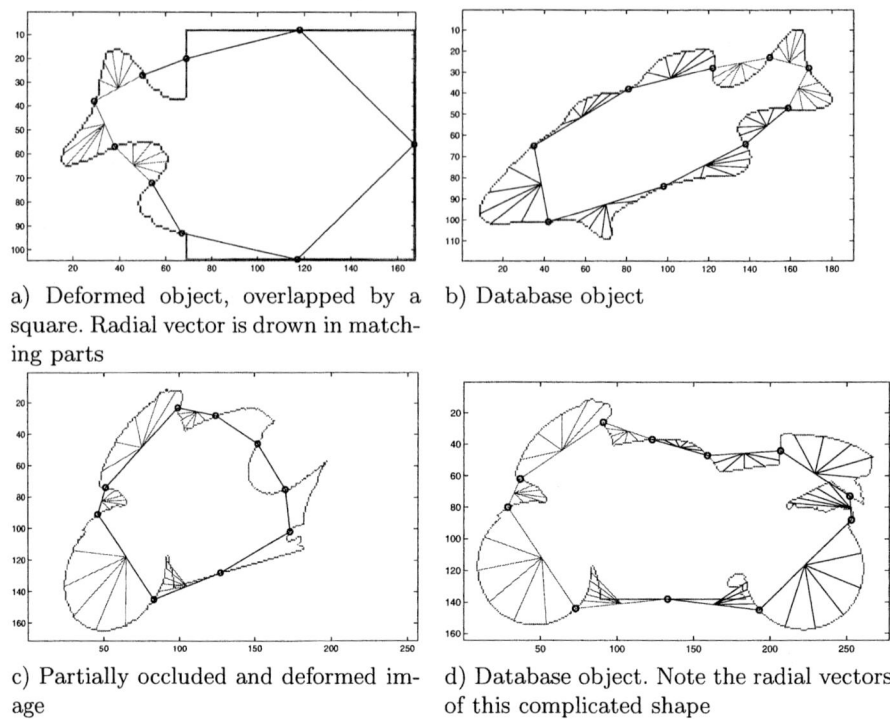

a) Deformed object, overlapped by a square. Radial vector is drown in matching parts

b) Database object

c) Partially occluded and deformed image

d) Database object. Note the radial vectors of this complicated shape

Fig. 3. Recognition samples and description of recognized database objects

Fig. 3a) and is able to construct radial vector even for non-convex parts (see Fig. 3d).

The most problematic part of the presented method is the critical point detection. Different positions of the critical points lead to different descriptions and of course affect the matching. Instability of the critical points can be caused by unsuitable shapes (without clear inflection points), affine transformation (affects the curvature), or occlusion (inflection points originally ignored can become significant). This situation is shown in Fig. 4. Although the database object (Fig. 4 top) was identified correctly in both cases (Fig. 4 bottom) one can see worse match on the right when overlaying the test and the database objects (the overlayed database object is drown by dotted line).

The results of our experiment depends on the object shapes, on the size of the occlusion, on the deformation, and other conditions. The summary is in Table 1. "Image area" denotes the size of the visible part of the test object (in per cent), "Constant scale of details" indicates whether or not the same thresholds were used for database and test objects when detecting inflection points, and "Transformation" means the significance of the deformation measured by skewing. The table itself shows the maximum number of matching parts over all database objects. In all instances where the maximum number of matching parts is greater than 2 the test objects were recognized correctly. One or two matching

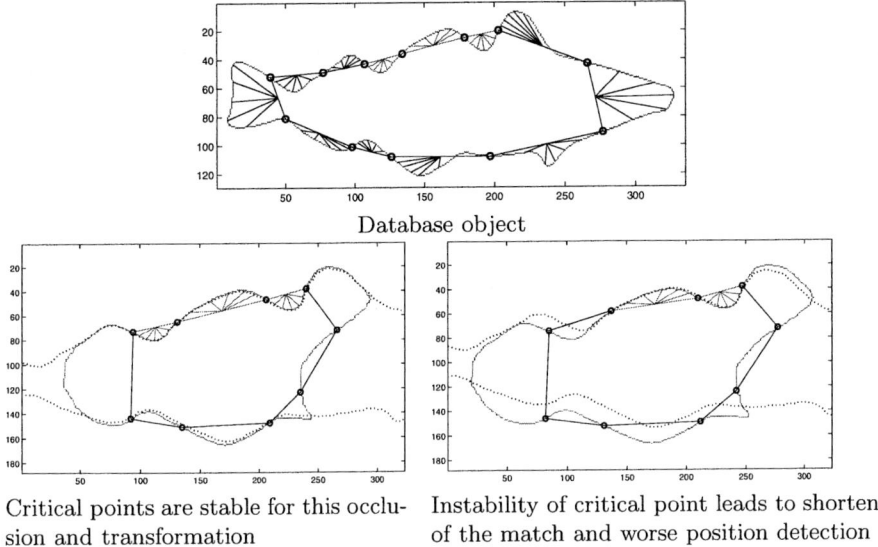

Critical points are stable for this occlusion and transformation — Instability of critical point leads to shorten of the match and worse position detection

Fig. 4. The impact of instability of the critical points

Table 1. Object recognition experiment. The number of matched boundary parts for various occlusion and transformation. All numbers greater than 2 lead to correct match.

Image area	100%	90%	50%	50%	100%	100%	50%
Constant scale of details	yes	yes	no	yes	yes	yes	yes
Transformation	none	none	none	none	medium	strong	medium
Image 1	12	7	4	3	8	5	3
Image 2	11	8	1	4	4	6	2
Image 3	11	8	3	4	4	5	4
Image 4	11	9	3	4	2	1	3
Image 5	7	4	2	2	7	3	2
Image 6	13	8	2	2	2	1	1
Image 7	10	7	2	6	8	1	4
Image 8	9	6	4	4	9	1	4

parts does not ensure unique correct match, the classification can be wrong in such cases. These bad situations were caused mostly by strong deformation or big occlusion which lead to instability of critical points.

7 Conclusion

We presented a method for recognition of partially occluded binary objects deformed by affine transformation. The method uses local affine-invariant description of object boundary by means inflection points and radial vectors. When working with digital boundary, the major limitation of the method is stability of inflection points. As the experiments demonstrated, if the curve has "prominent" inflection points, they are usually very stable under affine transformation and the method works perfectly. On the other hand, in case of obscure boundary the inflection points may be detected at different positions depending on the particular transformation and/or occlusion and the recognition may fail.

Our experiment proved a good discrimination power of the method on a given test set. We discovered that if the maximum number of matched boundary parts between the unknown object and the database is greater than 2, it always indicated a correct match. Thus, this threshold can be recommended for prospective real experiments too.

References

1. Guggenheimer, H.W.: Differential Geometry. New York. McGraw-Hill (1963)
2. Flusser, J.: Affine Invariants of Convex Polygons. IEEE Transactions on Image Processing **11**(9) (September 2002)
3. Ibrahim Ali W.S., Cohen, F.S.: Registering Coronal Histological 2-D Sections of a Rat Brain with Coronal Sections of a 3-D Brain Atlas Using Geometric Curve Invariants and B-spline Representanion. IEEE Transaction on Medial Imaging **17**(6) (December 1998)
4. Lamdan, Y., Schwartz, J.T., Wolfson, H.J.: Object Recognition by Affine Invariant Matching. Computer Vision and Pattern Recognition, (June 1988) 335–344
5. Mokhtarian, F., Abbasi, S.: Shape Similarity Under Affine Transform. Pattern Recognition **35** (2002) 31–41
6. Rothwell, C.A., Zisserman, A., Forsyth, D.A., Mundy, J.L.: Fast Recognition Using Algebraic Invariants. Geometric Invariants in Computer Vision. Cambridge, MIT Press (1992) 398–407
7. Tieng, Q.M., Boles W.W.: An Application of Wavelet-based Affine-invariant Representation. Patern Recognition Letters **16** (1995) 1287–1296
8. Weiss, I.: Noise Resistant Invariants of Curves. Geometric Invariance in Computer Vision. Cambridge, MIT Press (1992) 135–156
9. Weiss, I.: Projective Invariants of Shapes. Proc. Image Understanding Workshop (1988) 1125–1134
10. Wilczynski, E.J.: Projective Differential Geometry of Curves and Ruled Surfaces. B. G. Teubner, Leipzig (1906)
11. Yang, Z., Cohen, F.S.: Image Registration and Object Recognition Using Affine Invariants and Convex Hulls. IEEE Transitional on Image Processing **8**(7) (June 1999)

InfoBoost for Selecting Discriminative Gabor Features

Li Bai and Linlin Shen

School of Computer Science & IT, University of Nottingham, UK
bai@cs.nott.ac.uk

Abstract. We proposed a novel boosting algorithm - InfoBoost. Though AdaBoost has been widely used for feature selection and classifier learning, many of the selected features are redundant. By incorporating mutual information into AdaBoost, InfoBoost fully examines the redundancy between candidate classifiers and selected classifiers. The classifiers thus selected are both accurate and non-redundant. Experimental results show that InfoBoost learned strong classifier has lower training error than AdaBoost. InfoBoost learning has also been applied to selecting discriminative Gabor features for face recognition. Even with the simple correlation distance measure and 1-NN classifier, the selected Gabor features achieve quite high recognition accuracy on the FERET database, where both expression and illumination variance are present. When only 140 features are used, InfoBoost selected features achieve 95.5% accuracy, about 2.5% higher than that achieved by AdaBoost.

1 Introduction

Proposed by Freud and Schapire [1], AdaBoost has been successfully applied to object detection [2;3] and face recognition [4]. The essence of AdaBoost is to learn a number of very simple weak classifiers, which are then linearly combined into a single strong classifier. When the weak classifiers could perform just slightly better than random guessing, AdaBoost learning minimizes the upper bound on both training and generalization errors [5]. AdaBoost has been applied to select Haar-like features [3] for face detection, recognition [4] and select Gabor features [6] for classification. Since minimum error rate is the ultimate objective of AdaBoost learning, the weak learner with smallest weighted error is selected at each iteration. As a result, the learned classifiers are basically "individually" best. The strong classifier thus combined may not necessary to be best [7]. For feature selection, classifiers using similar features are more likely to be selected and redundancy will exist among some selected features. Stanz. Li etc. [7] proposed a floating search based algorithm, named FloatBoost, to eliminate those non-effective weak classifiers. A backtracking mechanism is applied to identify those unfavourable weak classifiers in terms of the error rate. The learned strong classifier thus consists of fewer weak classifiers and has better classification performance. During the learning process, each of the previously selected classifiers is investigated (removed) for possible improvement in terms of the error rate. As a result, FloatBoost requires about 5 times longer training time than AdaBoost. When the number of features is huge, e.g., 163,840, which is normal when using Gabor features, the training process could be unmanageable. A boosting algorithm, which is both effective in eliminating the non-effective classifiers and computationally efficient, is required.

We propose a novel method, namely InfoBoost, to address these issues. InfoBoost uses mutual information to eliminate redundancy. During the learning process, mutual information between the candidate weak classifiers and the selected weak classifiers is examined. As a result, the non-effective classifiers carrying information already captured by the selected feature/classifiers will be excluded. Since the process is forward based, and the mutual information is checked for those candidate classifiers with small errors only, extra computation required is very low. In addition, mutual information is statistically calculated, which enables our method classifier or decision method independent. The experimental results show that InfoBoost achieves lower training error rate with fewer classifiers. Better performance has also been observed when the selected Gabor features are used for face recognition.

2 AdaBoost Learning

For a two-class problem, a set of N labeled training samples is given as $(x_i, y_i), i=1,2,..,N$, where $y_i \in \{0,1\}$ is the class label associated with sample $x_i \in R^n$. A large number of weak classifiers $h(x) \in \{0,1\}$ can be generated. A weak classifier could be very simple, e.g., a threshold function on the kth coordinate axis of x in the n-dimensional space. The algorithm focuses on difficult training patterns, increasing their representation in successive training sets. Over a number of T rounds, T weak classifiers are selected to form the final strong classifier. In each of the iterations, the space of all possible weak classifiers is searched exhaustively to find the one with the lowest weighted classification error. The error is then used to update the weights such that the wrongly classified samples get their weights increased. The resulting strong classifier is a weighted linear combination of all T selected weak classifiers. Variants of the AdaBoost algorithm have been proposed. RealBoost is proposed to boost weak classifiers with real value outputs [8], AdaBoost.M1 and AdaBoost.MH [5] are developed to address the multi-class problem.

3 InfoBoost Learning

3.1 Entropy and Mutual Information (MI)

As a basic concept in information theory, entropy $H(X)$ is used to measure the uncertainty of a random variable (r.v.) X. If X is a discrete r.v., $H(X)$ can be defined as below:

$$H(X) = -\sum_{x} p(X=x) \lg(p(X=x)) \tag{1}$$

Mutual information $I(Y;X)$ is a measure of general interdependency between two random variables X and Y:

$$I(Y;X) = H(X) + H(Y) - H(X,Y) \tag{2}$$

Using Bayes rule on conditional probabilities, Equation 2 can be rewritten as:
$$I(Y;X) = H(X) - H(X|Y) = H(Y) - H(Y|X) \qquad (3)$$

Since $H(Y)$ measures the priori uncertainty of Y and $H(Y|X)$ measures the conditional posteriori uncertainty of Y after X is observed, the mutual information $I(Y;X)$ measure how much the uncertainty of Y is reduced if X has been observed. It can be easily shown that if X and Y are independent, $H(X,Y) = H(X) + H(Y)$, consequently their mutual information is zero.

The estimate of MI requires the value of marginal distribution $p(X)$, $p(Y)$ and the joint probability distribution $p(Y,X)$. For a r.v. with discrete values, the probability could be estimated by simply counting the number of possible cases and dividing that number with the total number of training samples. For a continuous r.v., its pdf could either be discretized by histograms estimation, or be approximated by Gaussian distribution.

3.2 The Proposed Algorithm

```
1) Input: N Training samples (x_i, y_i), i=1,2,.., N with m positive
   (y_i = 1) and l negative (y_i = 0) samples
```
Initialization: weights $w_{1,i} = \begin{cases} 1/2m, & \text{if } i \text{ is a positive sample} \\ 1/2l, & \text{if } i \text{ is a negative sample} \end{cases}$

```
For t=1, ..., T
a) Normalize all weights
b) Classifier selection and redundancy checking:
For each candidate weak classifier h_j, calculate classification error
```
$$\varepsilon_j = \sum_i w_{t,i} |h_j(x_i) - y_i|$$

```
For (;;)
Choose h_{t'} with lowest error ε_{t'} from the candidate classifiers
Calculate the MI R(h_{t'}) according to Eq. (4)
If R(h_{t'}) < TMI
The classifier found, h_t = h_{t'}, ε_t = ε_{t'}
Go to c) Else
Remove h_{t'} from the candidate list
End loop
```
c) Update weights: $w_{t+1,i} = w_{t,i}\beta_t^{1-e_i}$ with $e_i = \begin{cases} 1: x_i \text{ correctly classified} \\ 0: \text{ otherwise} \end{cases}$

and $\beta_t = \varepsilon_t/(1-\varepsilon_t)$

4) Final strong classifier: $H(x) = \begin{cases} 1 & \text{if } \sum_{t=1}^{T} \alpha_t h_t(x) > 1/2 \sum_{t=1}^{T} \alpha_t \\ 0 & \text{otherwise} \end{cases}$ with

$\alpha_t = \log(1/\beta_t)$

Fig. 1. The InfoBoost algorithm

InfoBoost incorporates the idea of MI to eliminate those non-effective weak classifiers. Each weak classifier $h(x) \in \{0,1\}$ is now considered as a r.v.. Before a new weak classifier is added, the MI between the new classifier and each of the selected ones are examined to make sure that the information carried by the new classifier has not been captured before. Given stage T where $T-1$ weak classifiers $\{h_{v(1)}, h_{v(2)}, \cdots h_{v(T-1)}\}$ have been selected, the function to measure the MI $R(h_j)$ between a candidate classifier h_j and the selected classifiers can be defined as:

$$R(h_j) = \max_t I(h_j, h_{v(t)}), t = 1, 2, \cdots T-1 \qquad (4)$$

The value of $R(h_j)$ can be directly used to decide whether the new classifier is redundant or not. The value is compared with a pre-defined Threshold Mutual Information (TMI), if it is larger than TMI, we say that the information carried by the classifier is already captured. Apart from MI, the error of the weak classifier is also taken into consideration, i.e., only those classifiers with small errors are selected. The classifiers thus selected will be both accurate and informative. When those non-redundant classifiers are combined to form a strong classifier, better performance will be achieved.

4 Application to Gabor Feature Selection

Daugman presented evidence that such visual neurons could optimize the general uncertainty relations for resolution in space, spatial frequency and orientation [9]. From an information theoretic viewpoint, Okajima [10] derivedGabor functions as solutions for a certain mutual-information maximization problem. The work shows that the Gabor-type receptive field can extract the maximum information from local image regions. Researchers have also shown that Gabor features, when appropriately designed, are invariant against translation, rotation and scale [11]. Successful applications of Gabor filters in face recognition can be found in the FERET evaluation [12], where Elastic Bunch Graph Matching method [13] gave the best performance. More recent face verification competition 2004 [14] also demonstrates the success of Gabor filters: both of the top two approaches apply Gabor filters for feature extraction. For face recognition applications, the number of Gabor filters used to convolve face images varies with applications, but usually 40 filters (5 scales and 8 orientations) are used [13;15;16]. However, due to the large number of convolution operations, the computation cost is quite high. Even a parallel computer system has been used, it was reported in [15] that the convolution of a 128×128 pixel image with 40 Gabor filters took about 7 seconds. For global methods, the dimension of the feature vectors extracted is also incredibly large, e.g., 163,840 for image with size 64×64. Similar to the work of Viola and Jones [2], where AdaBoost was used to select Haar-like features for face detection, the task here is to select the most discriminative Gabor features for face recognition.

4.1 Gabor Features and the Personal Difference Space

Given a bank of 40 Gabor filters $\{\varphi_{u,v}(x,y), u=0,...,4, v=0,...7\}$, image features at different location, frequency and orientation can be extracted by convolving the image $I(x,y)$ with the filters:

$$O_{u,v}(x,y) = |I(x,y) * \varphi_{u,v}(x,y)| \tag{5}$$

The resultant Gabor feature set thus consists of the convolution results of an input image $I(x,y)$ with all of the 40 Gabor filters:

$$S = \{O_{u,v}(x,y) : u \in \{0,...,4\}, v \in \{0,...,7\}\} \tag{6}$$

Fig. shows the magnitudes of Gabor representations of a face image with 5 scales and 8 orientations. A series of row vectors $\mathbf{O}_{u,v}$ could be converted out of $O_{u,v}(x,y)$ by concatenating its rows or columns, which are then concatenated together to generate a discriminative Gabor feature vector:

$$G(I) = \mathbf{O} = (\mathbf{O}_{0,0}\ \mathbf{O}_{0,1}\cdots \mathbf{O}_{4,7}) \tag{7}$$

Take an image with size 64×64 for example, the convolution result will give 64×64×5×8=163,840 features. Since the parameters of Gabor filters are chosen empirically, we believe a lot of redundant information is included, and therefore a feature selection mechanism should be used to choose the most useful features for classification.

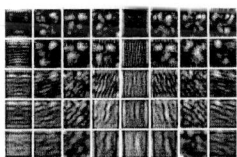 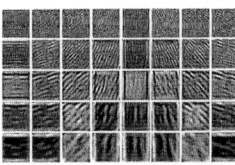

Fig. 2. Convolution with 40 Gabor filters (magnitude and real parts)

To apply InfoBoost algorithm, the difference space proposed in [17] is used here to convert the face recognition problem into a two classes problem. Two classes, dissimilarities between faces of the same person (intra-personal space) and dissimilarities between faces of the different people (extra-personal space) are defined. The two Gabor feature difference sets: CI (intra-personal difference) and CE (extra-personal difference) can be defined as:

$$\begin{aligned} CI &= \{\|G(I_p) - G(I_q)\|, p = q\} \\ CE &= \{\|G(I_p) - G(I_q)\|, p \neq q\} \end{aligned} \tag{8}$$

where I_p and I_q are the facial images from people p and q respectively, and $G(\cdot)$ is the Gabor feature extraction operation as defined in (7). A set of M training samples in the difference space can now be described as $\{(g_1, y_1), \cdots (g_i, y_i), \cdots, g_M, y_M)\}$, $g_i = [x_1 x_2 \cdots x_n \cdots x_N]$, $y_i \in \{0,1\}$, where y_i is the class label (intra-personal or extra-personal) associated with sample g_i, N is the dimension of extracted Gabor features and $x_n = (g)_n = \|G(I_p) - G(I_q)\|_n = \|O_p - O_q\|_n$.

4.2 Weak Classifiers and Estimation of MI

Since we are focusing on weak classifiers with discrete output only, a simple threshold function is used here. The performance of learned strong classifier will be improved if more sophisticated weak classifiers are designed, however we are more interested in feature selection here. The simple threshold function seems to be enough in this particular case. Given a sample $g = [x_1 x_2 \cdots x_n \cdots x_N], g \in R^N$, a weak classifier $h_j(g)$ simply compares the j-th coordinate of g with a threshold t_j, i.e.:

$$h_j(g) = \begin{cases} 1, & \text{if } x_j < t_j \\ 0, & \text{if } x_j \geq t_j \end{cases} \quad (9)$$

As a result, totally N weak classifiers are available. Each of them takes the difference of one of the Gabor features as input, while the output is decided by comparison of the difference against a threshold. As a result, the weak classifier selection process is equivalent with the feature selection process. In this paper, the threshold t_j is simply determined by the centre of intra-personal samples mean and extra-personal samples mean:

$$t_j = \frac{1}{2}\left(\frac{1}{m}\sum_{p=1}^{m}((g_p))_j | y_p = 1\right) + \frac{1}{l}\sum_{q=1}^{l}((g_q))_j | y_p = 0\right) \quad (10)$$

The estimate of MI between two classifiers h_i and h_j requires information about the marginal distribution $p(h_i), p(h_j)$ and the joint probability distribution $p(h_i, h_j)$. Since the output of weak classifiers in this paper are restricted to discrete values only, i.e., $h(g) \in \{0,1\}$, the probability could be estimated by simply counting the number of possible cases and dividing that number with the total number of training samples. For example, the possible cases will be $\{(0,0),(0,1),(1,0),(1,1)\}$ for the joint probability of two binary r.v. $p(h_i, h_j)$.

5 Experimental Results

5.1 Datasets

We analyse the performance of our algorithm using a subset of FERET database, which is a standard testbed for face recognition technologies [12]. 600 frontal face images corresponding to 200 subjects are extracted from the database for the experiments - each subject has three images of size 256×384 with 256 gray levels. The images were captured at different photo sessions so that they display different illumination and facial expressions. Two images of each subject are randomly chosen for training, and the remaining one is used for testing. We select the most discriminative Gabor features using the 400 (2 images each subject) training images, and use 200 test images. As a result, 200 intra-personal and 1600 extra-personal Gabor feature difference samples are randomly generated. Once a small set of discriminative Gabor features are learned by applying AdaBoost or InfoBoost on the training samples, they are used for face recognition.

5.2 Selected Gabor Features

We firstly use AdaBoost on the training samples to select 200 Gabor features for intra-personal and extra-personal difference classification. To show the existence of redundancy among AdaBoost selected features (weak classifiers), the MIs $R(h_j)$ for each selected feature are shown in Fig. 3a. It can be observed from the figure that some of the features are highly redundant, e.g., the MI of features with number 149, 177 and 180 are even bigger than 0.99. The redundancy among selected features increase with the number of features. The larger the number of features, the higher redundancy introduced. We have also shown the MI for InfoBoost selected features in Fig. 3b (with TMI=0.1). Due to the introduction of TMI, all of them are less than 0.1, we can conclude that the features are informative and non-redundant.

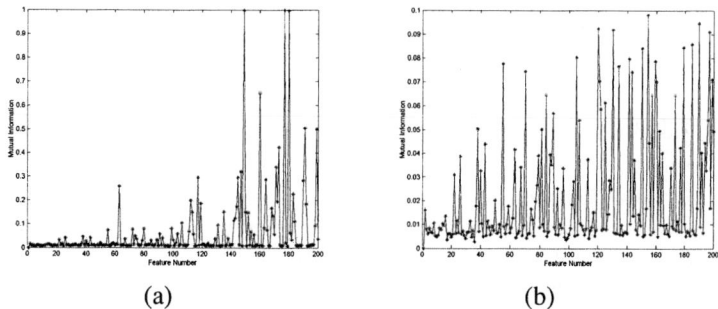

Fig. 3. MI of features selected by AdaBoost a); InfoBoost b)

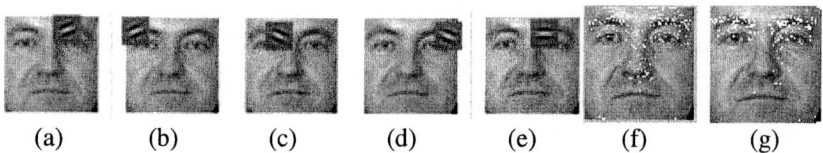

Fig. 4. First five selected Gabor features (a)-(e); and the 200 feature points selected by InfoBoost (f); and AdaBoost (g)

Fig. 4 (a)-(e) show the first five Gabor features selected by InfoBoost, with locations of the first 200 Gabor features selected by InfoBoost and AdaBoost shown in (f) and (g) respectively. The features are superimposed on a typical face image in the database. It is interesting to see that most of the selected Gabor features are located around the prominent facial features such as eye brows, eyes, noses and chins, which indicates that these regions are more robust against the variance of expression and illumination. When almost all of the AdaBoost selected Gabor features are located in the eye region, InfoBoost selected features are more widely distributed. Some features located around the nose are also included.

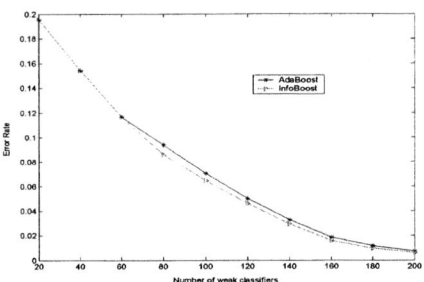

Fig. 5. Classification error rates on the training set

To show the advantage of InfoBoost over AdaBoost, we also compared the performance of the strong classifiers learned by AdaBoost and InfoBoost, which is measured by the classification error on the training set (200 intra-personal and 1600 extra-personal difference samples). As seen from Fig. 5, InfoBoost achieves lower error rates than AdaBoost on the same training set.

5.3 Performance Comparison

Once the most discriminant Gabor features are selected, we are now able to apply them for face recognition. In this experiment, 200 Gabor features selected by AdaBoost and InfoBoost (TMI=0.1) are directly used for similarity comparison, without any further processing. Normalized correlation distance measure and the nearest neighbour classifier are used. Fig. 6 shows the recognition performance of both AdaBoost and InfoBoost selected Gabor features on the 200 test images. When 140 features are used, the highest accuracy achieved by AdaBoost and InfoBoost are 93% and 95.5% respectively. Since the MIs of all the first 60 features are quite small, InfoBoost starts picking up the same features as AdaBoost. However, when the number of feature increases, AdaBoost start to pick up redundant features. The improved accuracy of InfoBoost selected features over AdaBoost proved the usefulness of InfoBoost in eliminating redundancy.

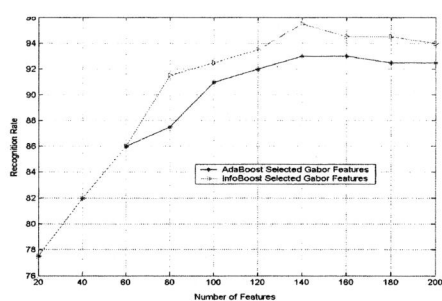

Fig. 6. Performance comparison

References

[1] Y. Freund and R. Schapire, "A decision-theoretic generalization of on-line learning and an application to boosting," *Journal of Computer and System Sciences*, vol. 55, no. 1, pp. 119-139, 2000.
[2] P. Viola and M. Jones, "Rapid object detection using a boosted cascade of simple features," in *Proc. of IEEE Conf. on Computer Vision and Pattern Recognition* Kauai, Hawaii: 2001.
[3] R. Lienhart and J. Maydt, "An extended set of Haar-like features for rapid object detection," in *Proc. IEEE Conference on Image Processing* 2002, pp. 900-903.
[4] J. Michael and P. Viola, "Face recognition using boosted local features," in *Proc. of International Conference on Computer Vision (ICCV)* 2003.
[5] Y. Freund and R. Schapire, "A short introduction to boosting," *Journal of Japanese Society for Artifical Intelligence*, vol. 14, no. 5, pp. 771-780, 1999.
[6] L. Shen and L. Bai, "AdaBoost Gabor Feature Selection for Classification," in *Proc. of Image and Vision Computing NewZealand* 2004, pp. 77-83.
[7] S. Z. Li and Z. Q. Zhang, "FloatBoost learning and statistical face detection," *Ieee Transactions on Pattern Analysis and Machine Intelligence*, vol. 26, no. 9, pp. 1112-1123, 2004.
[8] R. E. Schapire and Y. Singer, "Improved boosting algorithms using confidence-rated predictions," *Machine Learning*, vol. 37, no. 3, pp. 297-336, 1999.
[9] J. G. Daugman, "Uncertainty Relation for Resolution in Space, Spatial- Frequency, and Orientation Optimized by Two-Dimensional Visual Cortical Filters," *Journal of the Optical Society of America A-Optics Image Science and Vision*, vol. 2, no. 7, pp. 1160-1169, 1985.
[10] K. Okajima, "Two-dimensional Gabor-type receptive field as derived by mutual information maximization," *Neural Networks*, vol. 11, no. 3, pp. 441-447, 1998.
[11] V. Kyrki, J. K. Kamarainen, and H. Kalviainen, "Simple Gabor feature space for invariant object recognition," *Pattern Recognition Letters*, vol. 25, no. 3, pp. 311-318, 2004.
[12] P. J. Phillips, H. Moon, S. A. Rizvi, and P. J. Rauss, "The FERET evaluation methodology for face-recognition algorithms," *IEEE Transactions on Pattern Analysis and Machine Intelligence*, vol. 22, no. 10, pp. 1090-1104, 2000.
[13] L. Wiskott, J. M. Fellous, N. Kruger, and C. von derMalsburg, "Face recognition by elastic bunch graph matching," *Ieee Transactions on Pattern Analysis and Machine Intelligence*, vol. 19, no. 7, pp. 775-779, 1997.

[14] K. Messer, J. Kittler, M. Sadeghi, M. Hamouz, A. Kostin, F. Cardinaux, S. Marcel, S. Bengio, C. Sanderson, N. Poh, Y. Rondriguez, J. Czyz, L. Vandendorpe, C. McCool, S. Lowther, S. Sridharan, V. Chandran, R. P. Palacios, E. Vidal, L. Bai, L. Shen, Y. Wang, Y. H. Chiang, H. C. Liu, Y. P. Huang, A. Heinrichs, M. Miiller, A. Tewes, C. v. d. Malsburg, R. Wiirtz, Z. G. Wang, F. Xue, Y. Ma, Q. Yang, C. Fang, X. Q. Ding, S. Lucey, R. Goss, and H. Schneiderman, "Face authentication test on the BANCA database," in *Proc. of International Conference on Pattern Recognition* Cambridge, UK: 2004.

[15] M. Lades, J. C. Vorbruggen, J. Buhmann, J. Lange, C. Vandermalsburg, R. P. Wurtz, and W. Konen, "Distortion invariant object recognition in the Dynamic Link Architecture," *IEEE Transactions on Computers*, vol. 42, no. 3, pp. 300-311, 1993.

[16] C. J. Liu and H. Wechsler, "Gabor feature based classification using the enhanced Fisher linear discriminant model for face recognition," *Ieee Transactions on Image Processing*, vol. 11, no. 4, pp. 467-476, 2002.

[17] P. J. Phillips, "Support vector machines applied to face recognition," in *Proceedings of the 1998 conference on Advances in neural information processing systems II* MIT press, 1999, pp. 803-809.

Computer Vision Based System for Interactive Cooperation of Multiple Users

Alberto Del Bimbo, Lea Landucci, and Alessandro Valli

Universita' degli studi di Firenze, Dipartimento di Sistemi e Informatica,
I-50139 Firenze, Italy
alberto.delbimbo@unifi.it
lea.landucci@unifi.it
valli@micc.unifi.it

Abstract. Natural Human-Computer Interaction (NHCI) was hypothesized in the nineties as a solution to close the gap between computers and systems. It claims for interfaces that can be used in a natural and intuitive way through non intrusive and invisible input sensors, exploiting advances and results of pattern recognition, and image and speech understanding. This paper presents a multiuser natural interaction system that supports cooperative interaction in the manipulation and management of multimedia objects. The system uses a computer vision module to recognize and analyze hand gestures made by several users over a shared large display table.

1 Introduction

New technologies fling open a door on a world made of high-tech devices that *should* make our life more agreeable, safe and pleasant. Some of the most important cognitive psychologist, such as Donald Norman, beware us of *technology paradox* [9] asserting that innovation technology makes our life every day more complex: a warning to make us conscious about the importance of the "human centered design", first of all when we talk about Human-Computer Interaction. The real aim of NHCI research is to create new interactive systems that integrate human language into tech applications, focusing on the way we live, work, play and interact each other. Such systems have to be easy to use, intuitive, entertaining and non intrusive.

Recent examples of human-computer interfaces use integration of speech understanding, or computer vision-based solutions for eye tracking, lip reading or gesture recognition [7], all overworking on natural and human communication ways. Since hands are the most communicative part of human body [8], several works address hand gesture commanded interfaces developing the basic functions of defining and recognizing natural and human-like gestures, associating them to appropriate interaction features. Several interaction methods are employed, based on different Gesture Recognition techniques. 3D data have been used in systems where robust recognition of complex hand postures [1] is needed (such as human-robot interfaces [3], Virtual 3D Environments [10], 3D objects manipulating [6]). While accurate, 3D techniques have high price in terms of computational complexity and need several calibrated cameras or special additional sensors to be worn. Cheaper solutions work with 2D data and use vision based methods to perform colour or motion detection [5], and recognize gestures through neural networks [4], or Hidden Markov models [11], or other techniques. Natural interaction systems are particularly interesting and challenging when several users take part simultaneously in the interaction as in real contexts: in this case real-time processing gets duller, users can interfere each other and actions have to be recognized as independent.

In this paper we present a prototype system that supports a cooperative environment in which people can interact together with an intuitive graphical user interface (GUI) through their own hand gestures (see sec.4).

Using 2D vision based techniques, we created a real-time system based on a single PC station able to track users' hands, recognize their position, shape and motion and make the interface react to them. The gesture recognition method developed, using simple background subtraction technique combining with the use of a near-infrared webcam that solves problems of changing background's shape or color, allows the system to have enough computing resources to be controlled by two or more users.

This paper is organized as follows. In Section 2, we describe the system architecture and the methods used for recognizing and tracking human hands. In Section 3, we explain our solving methods in order to develop a real-time multiuser system and in section 4 we present our experimental results. Finally, in Section 5, we present our conclusions.

2 Hands Recognition and Tracking

We built a collaborative table with an horizontal mat glass surface on which a graphical user interface is projected from behind the table using an inclined mirror placed as in fig.1.

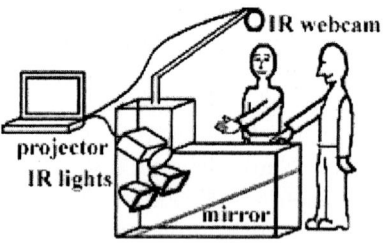

Fig. 1. Structural system scheme

We placed a fixed standard webcam to watch the desk surface at 20 fps, provided with an IR filter to make it impervious to visible light and projected images. Two infrared illuminators next to the projector flood the surface of the desk with infrared light that is reflected by the mirror.

A 2.3 GHz computer is connected to acquire images from a webcam and to visualize the real-time updated interface through the projector.

The processing chain develops from video processing phase that consists in a segmentation done through background subtraction using a dynamic model of the scene in order to cluster pixels into blobs through a connected components algorithm [2]. Each blob (corresponding to one hand) is described with a collection of statistical and morphological measures, including moments (up to the third), bounding box, and color histogram.

In the second processing step, blobs' shapes are discriminated as *poses* by a recognition module that uses blob's related information such as direction, size, and perimeter length. In order to get that, once defined two different circular *finding windows* sized in accordance with standard human-hand size, we developed the following algorithm.

1. Let **O** be the outmost point of blob **A** (according to the arm's direction) and let W_1 and W_2 be two circular finding windows respectively sized 20 and 3 cm in ray, both centered in **A**.
2. Let us consider set $\mathbf{C}(W) = \{(x,y)|(x,y) \in \partial \mathbf{A} \cap W\}$, and let $\mathbf{N}(\mathbf{C}(W))$ be the number of elements in $\mathbf{C}(W)$;
   - if $\mathbf{N}(\mathbf{C}(W_1)) \geq \hat{N}$, where $\hat{N}$ is a fixed bound empirically determined, then we consider the shape of **A** as an *open hand pose*.
   - otherwise, let us denote by $\mathbf{D}(p_1, p_2)$ the distance between p_1 and p_2, where $p_1, p_2 = \{\mathbf{C}(W_2) \cap \partial W_2\}$;
     - if $\mathbf{D}(p_1, p_2) \leq \hat{M}$, where $\hat{M}$ is a fixed bound empirically determined, then the shape of **A** is recognized as a *pointing pose*;
     - otherwise the shape of **A** is recognized as an *hybrid pose*.

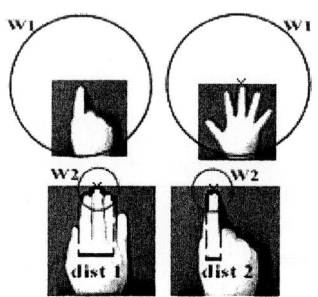

Fig. 2. Recognizing poses

Once recognized the pose, we associate to it a *sensible point* and a *steady time*, both useful data for the interaction dynamics (see sec.4). We define the sensible point of a pose as the fingertip in case of pointing pose and as the center of the palm in case of open hand.

The last processing step includes hand tracking in order to recognize and analyze gestures of each individual user. In order to track all the hands of people who are interacting on the table, in every frame we have to find for each blob its sensible point position. First of all we define a circular *tracking window* within which a point can reasonably move in 1/20 second (that is the time gap between two different frames acquired at 20 fps). Considering a generic blob **A**, the tracking window associated is centered in its *centroid*, defined as follow.

Firstable let us take into consideration the expression of the statistic moments referred to **A**:

$$m_{pq} = \sum_x \sum_y x^p y^q \rho(x,y) \qquad (1)$$

where $\rho(x,y) = \begin{cases} 1 \text{ if } (x,y) \text{ are into } \mathbf{A} \\ 0 \text{ otherwise} \end{cases}$

Then, the centroid coordinates are defined by the first order moments as follow:

$$\bar{x} = \frac{m_{10}}{m_{00}} \quad \bar{y} = \frac{m_{01}}{m_{00}}. \qquad (2)$$

The tracking algorithm proceeds as follow.
In every frame:

1. Let $\mathbf{P}_A(\hat{f})$ correspond to the centroid of blob **A** at frame $\hat{f}$ and let $\mathbf{W}_A$ be the circular tracking window centered in $\mathbf{P}_A(\hat{f})$.
2. For every point $\mathbf{S}(\hat{f}+1)$ s.t. $\mathbf{S}(\hat{f}+1) \in \mathbf{W}_A$
   - if $\mathbf{S}(\hat{f}+1)$ is the centroid of a blob,
     then $\mathbf{S}(\hat{f}+1) \equiv \mathbf{P}_A(\hat{f}+1)$
   - otherwise blob **A** got out of the scenario.

Larger tracking windows allow faster gestures but increase risk of mistakes in multiuser mode. In order to obtain an effective hands tracking in such situations, after several testing sessions, we fixed the tracking window ray at 8 cm.

3 Multi-user System

Management of simultaneous activities of multiple users is made possible according with specific solutions for hands identification (labelling) and for interference between different users' gestures.

To make different hands independent we associate to each of them their own centroid 'id' as their label: choosing a proper tracking window we avoid the risk of wrong label assignments. This labelling technique works as long as there are no total or partial blob overlaps, or rather when we assist to a blob *merging*. In fact, in case of temporary overlapping, the blobs involved in the bump merge into one blob and the system can be subjected to errors in hands tracking and therefore in the association of the observed gestures to the right users.

In order to obtain good results, we have employed some heuristics to detect such cases. We define the following *accidental bump model*:

- there are two blobs involved;
- bump is an occasional accident;
- minimal portions of each blobs are merged.

Once defined the blob surface as the zero order statistic moments (m_{00}, according with def. 1), the system detects a merging case as follow:
- blobs in the current frame are less than them in the previous one;
- the larger one of them has a surface equal to at least 1.5 times the bigger one in the previous frame.

Once such merging is detected, frames are not processed until the two involved blobs detach so that there are no restrictions about the duration of the overlapping. The system predicts the positions of the sensible points associated to the involved blobs using a linear one-step-ahead predictor of the following form:

$$\hat{x}(f) = x(f-1), \hat{y}(f) = y(f-1).$$

where (x(f),y(f)) are the coordinates of the sensible point at frame f (detach frame). Under the reasonable hypothesis made in our accidental bump model, a one step ahead predictor is enough to solve merging cases according with the following three step algorithm.

1. Predict the two blobs' sensible point positions they will have at the frame in which they detach;
2. evaluate the prediction error associated to each blobs in term of distance between predicted and real sensible points (see fig.3);
3. associate to each blob the 'id' of that one which minimizes the prediction error.

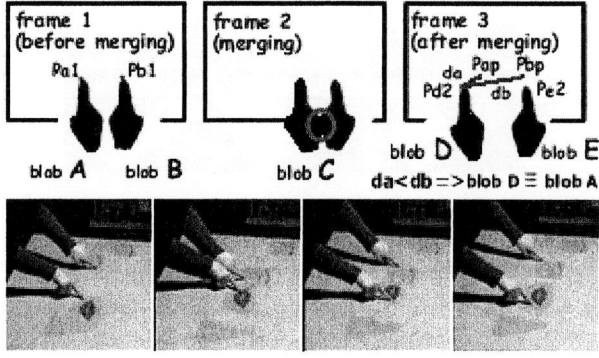

Fig. 3. Merging management and testing

4 Experimental Results

This experimental system is part of the project **VICOM** (Virtual Immersive COMmunications), co-financed by the Italian Ministry of Education, Universities and Research (MIUR).

We created a particular gesture grammar in which hand gestures correspond to actions through which users can interact simultaneously with some multimedia objects (videos, images and sounds). We have developed an interface prototype through which such objects can be manipulated in terms of visualization features. This interface is designed for professor tutorship to students that interact with the collaborative table asking questions about some didactic materials: the professor answers them through a remote computer able to command the interface as well. The associations chosen between gestures and actions are the following:

Static actions.
selection/deselection: persistence of pointing pose on the object chosen (steady time at least of 700 milliseconds) (see fig.4, a));
play/pause/stop: persistence of open hand on the video object chosen (steady time at least of 500 milliseconds).
Dynamic actions.
drag & drop: pointing pose moving through the interactive scenario after an object selection (see fig.4, a)) ;
roto-translation/resizing: two different pointing poses on the object chosen (steady time at least of 800 milliseconds)(see fig.4, b));
clear: open hand pose moving from one side to the opposite side of the table.

Dynamic actions are realized by attaching the multimedia object to the sensible point of the particular involved pose and making it move in a consistent way with the hand that selected it (see fig.4, a)). Roto-translation with resizing

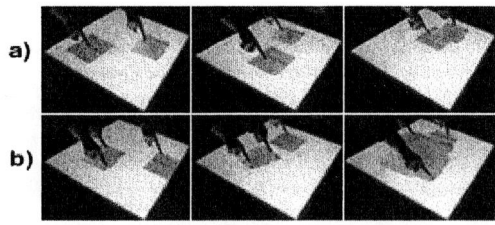

Fig. 4. Testing phases: in a) drag & drop and in b) roto-translation with resizing

is a particular action in which the visualization features of multimedia objects are involved (see fig.4,b)). To achieve this function, the visualization system use the following algorithm.

1. Referring to frame $\hat{f}$, let us consider the roto-translation with resizing of the multimedia object **M**, with the following notations:

M.scale($\hat{f}$) → visualizing scale of **M**;
M.rot($\hat{f}$) → inclination degree of **M** referred to the table;
M.x($\hat{f}$), **M.y**($\hat{f}$) → visualization coordinates of **M**;
$\mathbf{P_1}(\hat{f})=(x_1(\hat{f}),y_1(\hat{f}))$, $\mathbf{P_2}(\hat{f})=(x_2(\hat{f}),y_2(\hat{f}))$ → sensible points of the involved blobs **A** and **B**;
$\bar{x}(\hat{f})$, $\bar{y}(\hat{f})$ → sensible point of blob **A** referred to **M**.

2. Let us consider the motion vector $\mathbf{V}=P_1(\hat{f})$-$P_2(\hat{f})$ characterized by:

   modulus $\rho(\hat{f}) = \sqrt{(x_1(\hat{f}) - x_2(\hat{f}))^2 + (y_1(\hat{f}) - y_2(\hat{f}))^2}$

   inclination $\theta(\hat{f}) = \arcsin(\frac{y_2(\hat{f})-y_1(\hat{f})}{\rho(\hat{f})})$.

3. In every frame $\hat{f}$, we have (see fig.5):
   - **M.scale**($\hat{\mathbf{f}}$) = $M.scale(\hat{f} - 1) \cdot (\frac{\rho(\hat{f})}{\rho(\hat{f}-1)})$;
   - **M.rot**($\hat{\mathbf{f}}$) = $M.rot(\hat{f} - 1) + (correct \cdot \Delta\theta(\hat{f}))$
     where $\Delta\theta(\hat{f}) = \frac{180}{\pi} \cdot (\theta(\hat{f}) - \theta(\hat{f} - 1))$ and *correct* is a moltiplicative factor depending on the position of the blobs **A** and **B**;
   - **M.x**($\hat{\mathbf{f}}$) = $M.x(\hat{f} - 1) + x_1(\hat{f}) - \bar{x}(\hat{f})$;
     M.y($\hat{\mathbf{f}}$) = $M.y(\hat{f} - 1) + y_1(\hat{f}) - \bar{y}(\hat{f})$;

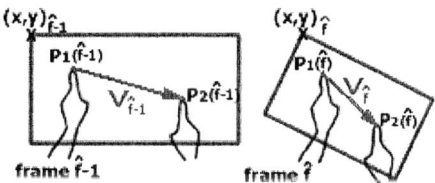

Fig. 5. Roto-translation with resizing

We tested our system with several users and the results reached are very satisfactory.

Trascuring the edge effects that are easily solved by considering a cornice of the table as a no-interaction zone, a good calibration lets the system to rightly recognize poses with a precision of 99% (see fig.6).

PURPOSE	failure %	success %
Recognizing poses	1	99
Solving overlapping	6	94
Recognizing cleaning gestrure	25	75

Fig. 6. Testing Results table

Overlapping problems are solved in the 94% of accidental bump cases tested whatever are the moving directions of the two hands involved, before and after the bump. Cleaning gesture has a precision of almost 75% due to different users' hand speeds.

All the experimental testing data refer to almost 15 full testing days.

The system works in real-time with up to 3 persons. In case of more users, that interact simultaneously, more computing power than that available on a single PC station is needed to support real-time image processing and interface updating.

5 Conclusions

This work addresses a working implementation of a 2D hand gesture recognizing system based on images segmentation through background subtraction. We have developed an interactive environment in which more users can interact simultaneously with multimedia objects by performing object drag & drop, resizing, roto-translating and video management. For hand tracking, in order to solve problems due to overlapping of hands' shapes, we have employed a predictor based method that is able to discriminate (under reasonable hypotheses) between two hands of distinct users even when they accidentally bump. Finally we have tested the system with an interface prototype, and observed very good results.

References

1. S. Aifanti, N. Strintzis, "A gesture recognition system using 3D data", Thessaloniki Univ., Greece, 2002.
2. C. Colombo, A. Del Bimbo and A. Valli, "A real-time full body tracking and humanoid animation system", Parallel Computing, North-Holland 2004.
3. M. Frigola, J. Fernandez, J. Aranda, "Visual human machine interface by gestures", Universitat Politcnica de Catalunya, Barcelona, Spain, 2003.
4. J. Isaacs, S. Foo, "Hand pose estimation for American sign language recognition", FAMU-FSU, Tallahassee, FL, 2004.
5. T. Kapuscinski, M.Wysocki, "Hand gesture recognition for man-machine interaction", Rzeszow Univ., Poland, 2001.
6. B. Leibe, T. Starner, W. Ribarsky, Z. Wartell, D. Kru, B. Singletary and L. Hidges, "The Perceptive Workbench: Toward Spontaneous and Natural Interaction in Semi-Immersive Virtual Environments", Georgia Inst.of Tech., USA, 2000.
7. I. Marsic, A. Medl, J. Flanagan, "Natural communication with information systems",Rutgers Univ., Piscataway,USA,2000.
8. A. Mulder, "Hand Gestures for HCI - Research on human movement behaviour reviewed in the context of hand centred input", Simon Fraser University, Canada, 1996.
9. D. A. Norman, *Psychology of Everyday Things*, 1998.
10. R. O'Hagan, A. Zelinsky, "Visual gesture interfaces for virtual environments", Australian Nat. Univ., Australia, 2000.
11. T. Starner, J. Auxier, D. Ashbrook, M.Gandy, "The gesture pendant: a self-illuminating, wearable, infrared computer vision system for home automation control and medical monitoring", Georgia Inst. of Technol., Atlanta, USA, 2000.

Supervised Texture Detection in Images*

Branislav Mičušík and Allan Hanbury

Pattern Recognition and Image Processing Group, Institute of Computer
Aided Automation, Vienna University of Technology,
Favoritenstraße 9/1832, A-1040 Vienna, Austria
{micusik, hanbury}@prip.tuwien.ac.at

Abstract. This paper presents a technique for texture segmentation in images. Providing a small template of a texture of interest results in the image being segmented into regions with similar properties and background (non-similar) regions. The core of the segmentation engine is based on the minimal cut/maximal flow algorithm in the graph representing an image. The main contribution lies in incorporating the template information (colour, texture) into the whole graph used for segmentation. The method brings the possibility to locate textured regions in the image having same property as the template patch and not only one-colored regions (as in much existing work). The method is supervised since the user provides a representative template of an object being searched for. The object may consist of several isolated parts. Experimental results are presented on some images from the Berkeley database.

1 Introduction

Fully automatic image segmentation is still an open research problem in computer vision. An ideal algorithm would take a single image as input and give the image segmented into semantically meaningful, non-overlapping regions as the output. However, the usual problem is over-segmentation or under-segmentation. Moreover, measuring the goodness of segmentations in general is an unsolved problem and obtaining absolute ground truth is difficult since different people produce different manual segmentations of the same scene.

There are many papers dealing with automatic segmentation. We mention only the work of Shi & Malik [12] based on normalized cuts which segments the image into many non-overlapping regions. They introduced a modification of graph cuts, namely normalized graph cuts, and provided an approximate closed-form solution. However, the boundaries of detected regions often do not follow the true boundaries of the objects. The work [13] is a follow-up to [12] where the segmentation is done at various scales. The final segmentation is then glued together from partial ones.

One possibility to partially avoid the ill-posed problem of image segmentation is to use additional constraints. Such constraints can be *i)* motion in the image caused either by camera motion or by motion of objects in the scene [11,14,1], or *ii)* specifying the foreground object properties [3,10,2].

---

* This work was supported by the Austrian Science Foundation (FWF) under grant SESAME (P17189-N04), and the European Union Network of Excellence MUSCLE (FP6-507752).

Fig. 1. Supervised segmentation. (a) Original image. Top image shows marked place from which the template was cut. (b) The enlarged template patch. (c) binary segmentation with masked original image.

In this paper we concentrate on an easier task than fully automatic segmentation. We constrain the segmentation by using a small user-provided template patch. We search for the segments of the image coherent in terms of colour with the provided template. The texture of an input image is taken into account to correctly detect boundaries of textured regions.

The proposed technique could be useful for segmentation and for detecting the objects in images with a characteristic a priori known property defined through a template patch. Fig. 1 (top row) shows how a tiger can be detected in the image using a small template patch from the same image. The same template patch can be used to detect the tiger in another image even though lighting conditions are slightly different, see Fig. 1 (bottom row).

In this paper we follow the idea given in [3] of interactive segmentation where the user has to specify some pixels belonging to the foreground and to the background. Such labeled pixels give a strong constraint for further segmentation based on the min-cut/max-flow algorithm given in [4]. However, the method [3] was designed for grayscale images and thus most of the information is thrown away. We improved the method in [8] to cope with colour and texture images. However, both seeds for background and foreground objects were still needed. In this work we avoid the need of background seeds and only seeds for the foreground object need to be specified.

In [15] the spatial coherence of the pixels together with standard local measurements (intensity, colour) is handled. They propose an energy function that operates simultaneously in feature space and in image space. Some forms of such an energy function are studied in [5]. In our work we follow a similar strategy. However, we define the neighborhood relation through brightness, colour and texture gradients introduced in [6,7].

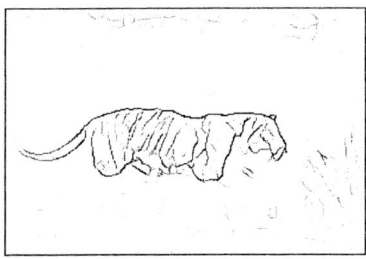

Fig. 2. Combined boundary probability using colour+texture gradient of the tiger image. Black points stand for high, white for low boundary probability.

In the paper [10] a similar idea to ours has been treated. In principle, the result is the same, but the strategy to obtain it differs. The boundary of a textured foreground object is achieved by minimization (through the evolution of the region contour) of energies inside and outside the region. The Geodetic Active Region framework is used to propagate the region contour. However, the texture information for the foreground has to be specified by the user. In [9] the user interaction is omitted. At first number of regions is estimated by fitting a mixture of Gaussians on intensity histogram and then used to drive the region evolution. However, such technique cannot be used for textured images. One textured region can be composed of many colours and therefore Gaussian components say nothing about number of dominant textures.

The main contribution of this paper lies in incorporating the information included in the template patch into the graph representing the image, leading to a reasonable binary image segmentation. Our method does not need seeds for both foreground and the background as in [3,8]. Only some representative template patch of the object being searched for is required, see Fig. 1. Moreover, texture information is taken into account.

The structure of the paper is as follows. First, segmentation based on the graph cut algorithm is outlined together with energy functions. Second, non-parametric computation of probabilities of points being foreground/background through histograms and incorporating template patch information is described. Finally, the results and summary conclude the work.

2 Segmentation

We used a segmentation technique based on the interactive graph cut method first introduced in [3]. There exists a very efficient algorithm for finding min-cut/max-flow in a graph [4]. At first we very briefly outline the boundary detection and then focus in more detail on the construction of the graph representing the image.

2.1 Boundary Detection

Boundary detection is a difficult task, as it should work for a wide range of images, i.e. for images of human-made environments and for natural images. Our main emphasis

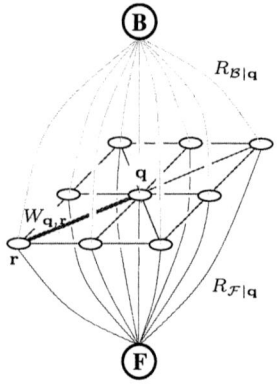

edge	cost	region
$\{\mathbf{q},\mathbf{r}\}$	$W_{\mathbf{q},\mathbf{r}}$	$\{\mathbf{q},\mathbf{r}\} \in \mathcal{N}$
$\{\mathbf{q},F\}$	$\lambda R_{\mathcal{F}|\mathbf{q}}$	$\forall \mathbf{q}$
$\{\mathbf{q},B\}$	$\lambda R_{\mathcal{B}|\mathbf{q}}$	$\forall \mathbf{q}$

Fig. 3. Left: Graph representation for 9 pixel image. Right: Table defining the costs of graph edges. λ is a constant described in the text.

is put on boundaries at the changes of different textured regions and not local changes inside one texture. This is complicated since there are usually large responses of edge detectors inside the texture. To detect boundaries in images correctly, the colour changes and texturedness of the regions have to be taken into account like in work [6,7]. In this paper we use as a cue the brightness, colour, and texture gradients introduced in [6,7] to produce the combined boundary probability, see Fig. 2. For more details see also [8].

2.2 Graph Representing the Image

We introduced new penalties on edges in a graph based on a combined boundary probability image. The general framework for building the graph is depicted in Fig. 3. The graph is shown for a 9 pixel image and an 8-point neighborhood $\mathcal{N}$. For general images, the graph has as many nodes as pixels plus two extra nodes labeled F, B. In addition, the pixel neighborhood is larger.

Neighboring Pixel Relation

The edge weights of neighborhood $\mathcal{N}$ are encoded in the matrix $W_{\mathbf{q},\mathbf{r}}$, which is not necessarily symmetric. The size and density of the neighborhood are controlled through two parameters. We used a neighborhood window of size 21×21 with sample rate 0.3, i.e. only a randomly selected 30% of all pixels in the window are used. Using only a fraction of pixels in the window reduces the computational demand and thus allows the use of larger windows while preserving the spatial relations.

The neighborhood penalty of two pixels is defined as follows

$$W_{\mathbf{q},\mathbf{r}} = \left(e^{-\frac{g(\mathbf{q},\mathbf{r})^2}{\sigma_2}}\right)^2, \tag{1}$$

where σ_2 is a parameter (we used $\sigma_2 = 0.08$ in all our experiments) and

$$g(\mathbf{q},\mathbf{r}) = p_b(\mathbf{q}) + \max_{\mathbf{s} \in \mathcal{L}_{\mathbf{q},\mathbf{r}}} p_b(\mathbf{s}), \tag{2}$$

where $p_b(\mathbf{q})$ is the combined boundary probability mentioned in Sec. 2.1 and

$$\mathcal{L}_{\mathbf{q},\mathbf{r}} = \{\mathbf{x} \in \mathbb{R}^2 \colon \mathbf{x} = \mathbf{q} + k(\mathbf{r}-\mathbf{q}), k \in (0,1)\}$$

is a set of points on a line from the point $\mathbf{q}$ (exclusive) to the point $\mathbf{r}$ (inclusive). We used the DDA line algorithm to discretize the line. The penalty in Eq. (2) follows the idea that there is a large weight if the line connecting two points crosses the edge in the combined boundary probability image. The value of the weight corresponds to the strength of the edge. If there is no edge between the points the weight is zero.

Foreground/Background Nodes

Each node in the graph is connected to the two extra nodes F, B. This allows the incorporation of the information provided by the template and a penalty for each pixel being foreground or background to be set.

The regional penalty of a point as being foreground $\mathcal{F}$ or background $\mathcal{B}$ is defined as follows

$$R_{\mathcal{F}|\mathbf{q}} = -\ln p(\mathcal{B}|\mathbf{c_q})$$
$$R_{\mathcal{B}|\mathbf{q}} = -\ln p(\mathcal{F}|\mathbf{c_q}), \qquad (3)$$

where $\mathbf{c_q} = (c_L, c_a, c_b)^\top$ stands for a vector in $\mathbb{R}^3$ of L*a*b* values at the pixel $\mathbf{q}$. We use the L*a*b* colour space as this results in better performance. This color space is approximately perceptually uniform and Euclidean distances in this space are perceptually meaningful. To compute the posterior probabilities in Eq. (3) we used Bayes' theorem as follows

$$p(\mathcal{B}|\mathbf{c_q}) = \frac{p(\mathbf{c_q}|\mathcal{B})\,p(\mathcal{B})}{p(\mathbf{c_q})} = \frac{p(\mathbf{c_q}|\mathcal{B})\,p(\mathcal{B})}{p(\mathcal{B})\,p(\mathbf{c_q}|\mathcal{B}) + p(\mathcal{F})\,p(\mathbf{c_q}|\mathcal{F})}. \qquad (4)$$

We demonstrate it on $p(\mathcal{B}|\mathbf{c_q})$, for $p(\mathcal{F}|\mathbf{c_q})$ it is analogical.

We do not know a priori the probabilities $p(\mathcal{F})$ and $p(\mathcal{B})$ of the foreground and background regions, i.e. how large the foreground region is compared to the background one. Thus, we fixed them to $p(\mathcal{F}) = p(\mathcal{B}) = 0.5$ and Eq. (4) reduces to

$$p(\mathcal{B}|\mathbf{c_q}) = \frac{p(\mathbf{c_q}|\mathcal{B})}{p(\mathbf{c_q}|\mathcal{B}) + p(\mathbf{c_q}|\mathcal{F})}, \qquad (5)$$

where the prior probabilities are

$$p(\mathbf{c_q}|\mathcal{F}) = f_{c_L}^L \cdot f_{c_a}^a \cdot f_{c_b}^b, \quad \text{and} \quad p(\mathbf{c_q}|\mathcal{B}) = b_{c_L}^L \cdot b_{c_a}^a \cdot b_{c_b}^b,$$

where $f_i^{\{L,a,b\}}$, resp. $b_i^{\{L,a,b\}}$, represents the foreground, resp. the background histogram of each colour channel separately at the ith bin.

All histogram channels are smoothed using one-dimensional Gaussians, i.e. $\bar{f}_i = \frac{1}{G}\sum_{j=1}^{N} f_j e^{-\frac{(j-i)^2}{2\sigma^2}}$, where G is the normalization factor enforcing $\sum_{i=1}^{N} \bar{f}_i = 1$. In our case, the number of histogram bins, $N = 64$. We used $\sigma = 1$ since experiments showed that it is a reasonable value. λ from the table in Fig. 3 was set to 1000.

In an implementation one should take into account the possibility of a zero value of $p(\mathcal{B}|\mathbf{c_q})$ in Eq. (3) and thus avoid an overflow. In such a case $R_{\mathcal{F}|\mathbf{q}} = K$, where K is some "big" number (we use 10000).

The foreground histogram is computed from all pixels in the template patch. To compute the background histogram is a little bit tricky. We know a priori neither the colours nor a template patch of the background. We suggest to compute the background histogram from all image pixels. The basic idea behind this is the assumption that the histogram computed from all points includes information on all colours (the background and the foreground) in the image. Therefore, since $\sum_{i=1}^{N} \bar{b}_i = 1$, the probability $p(\mathbf{c_q}|\mathcal{B})$ gives smaller values than $p(\mathbf{c_q}|\mathcal{F})$ for the colours present in the template. Thus, points more similar to the template are assigned in the graph more strongly to the foreground than to the background node.

3 Experiments

The segmentation method was implemented in MATLAB. Some of the most time consuming operations (such as creating the graph edge weights) were implemented in C and interfaced with MATLAB through mex-files. We used with advantage the sparse matrices directly offered by MATLAB. We used the online available C++ implementations of the min-cut algorithm [4] and some MATLAB code for colour and texture gradient computation [6].

The most time consuming part of the segmentation process is creating the weight matrix W. It takes 50 seconds on a 250×375 image running on a Pentium 4@2.8 GHz. The implementation of the texture gradient in C would dramatically speed up the computation time. Once the graph is built, finding the min-cut takes 2 – 8 seconds.

In all our experiments we used images from the Berkeley database. We marked a small "representative" part of the image and used it for further image segmentation of the image. See Fig. 4 for the results. From the results it can be seen that very good segmentation can be obtained even though only the colour histogram of the template patch is taken into account.

It is also possible to apply the template patch obtained from one image for segmenting another one. In the case depicted in Fig. 1 small tiger patch encoding the tiger's colours obtained from one image is used for finding the tiger in another image. It can be seen that most of the tiger's body was captured but also some pixels belonging to the background were segmented. Such "non-tiger" regions could be pruned using some further procedure, which is not discussed in this paper.

It opens new possibilities for the use of the method, e.g., for image retrieval applications. Since some representative image template is available, images from large databases coherent in colour and texture can be found.

4 Discussion

In the method presented in this paper, only colour histograms are used for description of the texture of the template. Hence there are some limitations. First of all there is a problem in the change of lighting conditions and the presence of shadows. Every

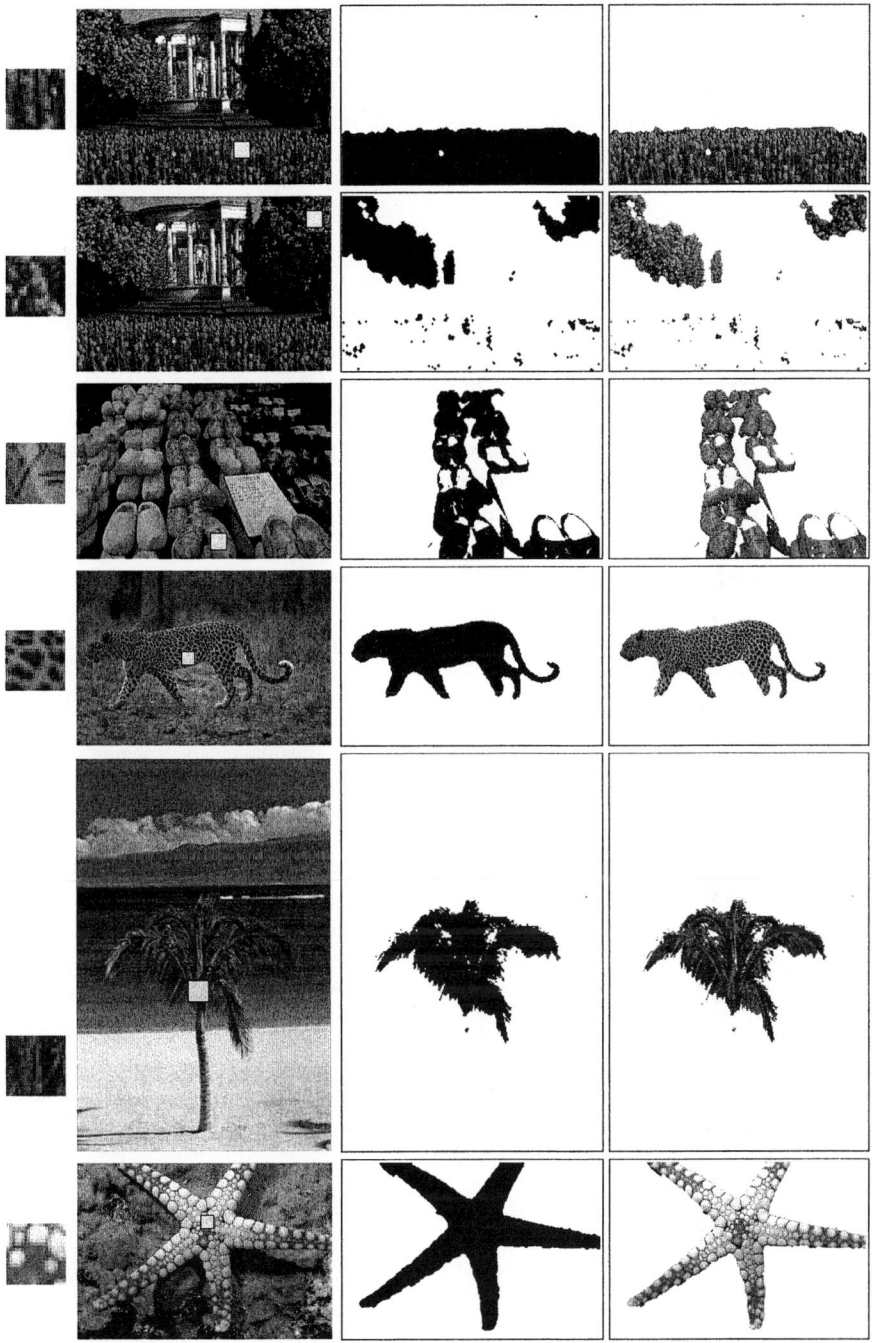

Fig. 4. Results (we recommend to see a colour version of this Figure). 1st column: enlarged image template patch. 2nd column: input image with marked area used as the template. 3rd column: binary segmentation. 4th column: segmentation with masked original image.

image is usually captured under different conditions and to find one universal template capturing all such changes is almost impossible.

However, other properties of the texture, e.g. inner texture structure, topology of texture elements, should be taken into account to improve the robustness of the algorithm to the change of lighting conditions and shadows. We are currently working on this.

5 Conclusion

We suggested a method for supervised texture segmentation in images. The method is based on finding the min-cut/max-flow in a graph representing the image to be segmented. The paper described how to set the weights of graph edges to handle the information present in a small representative template patch provided by the user. We proposed a new strategy to avoid the need for a background template or for a priori information of the background. Experiments presented on some images from the Berkeley database show that the method gives reasonable results.

References

1. N. Apostoloff and A. Fitzgibbon. Bayesian estimation of layers from multiple images. In *Proc. CVPR*, volume 1, pages 407–414, 2004.
2. A. Blake, C. Rother, M. Brown, P. Prez, and P. H. S. Torr. Interactive image segmentation using an adaptive GMMRF model. In *Proc. ECCV*, volume 1, pages 428–441, 2004.
3. Y. Boykov and M.-P. Jolly. Interactive graph cuts for optimal boundary & region segmentation of objects in N-D images. In *Proc. ICCV*, pages 105–112, 2001.
4. Y. Boykov and V. Kolmogorov. An experimental comparison of min-cut/max-flow algorithms for energy minimization in vision. *PAMI*, 26(9):1124–1137, 2004.
5. V. Kolmogorov and R. Zabih. What energy functions can be minimized via graph cuts? *PAMI*, 26(2):147–159, 2004.
6. J. Malik, S. Belongie, T. Leung, and J. Shi. Contour and texture analysis for image segmentation. *IJCV*, 43(1):7–27, 2001.
7. D. R. Martin, C. C. Fowlkes, and J. Malik. Learning to detect natural image boundaries using local brightness, color, and texture cues. *PAMI*, 26(5):530–549, 2004.
8. B. Micusik and A. Hanbury. Steerable semi-automatic segmentation of textured images. In *Proc. Scandinavian Conference on Image Analysis (SCIA)*, 2005.
9. N. Paragios and R. Deriche. Coupled geodesic active regions for image segmentation: A level set approach. In *Proc. ECCV*, volume II, pages 224–240, 2000.
10. N. Paragios and R. Deriche. Geodesic active regions and level set methods for supervised texture segmentation. *IJCV*, 46(3):223–247, 2002.
11. M. Ruzon and C. Tomasi. Alpha estimation in natural images. In *Proc. CVPR*, volume 1, pages 18–25, 2000.
12. J. Shi and J. Malik. Normalized cuts and image segmentation. *PAMI*, 22(8):888–905, 2000.
13. X. Y. Stella. Segmentation using multiscale cues. In *Proc. CVPR*, volume 1, pages 247–254, 2004.
14. Y. Wexler, A. Fitzgibbon, and A. Zisserman. Bayesian estimation of layers from multiple images. In *Proc. ECCV*, volume 3, pages 487–501, 2002.
15. R. Zabih and V. Kolmogorov. Spatially coherent clustering using graph cuts. In *Proc. CVPR*, volume 2, pages 437–444, 2004.

Filter Selection and Identification Similarity Using Clustering Under Varying Illumination

Mi Young Nam, Battulga, and Phill Kyu Rhee

Dept. of Computer Science & Engineering, Inha University,
253, Yong-Hyun Dong, Incheon, South Korea
rera@im.inha.ac.kr, b_battulga_hm@hotmail.com
pkrhee@inha.ac.kr

Abstract. In this paper investigate how to preprocess method from input images for robust face recognition varying illumination environments. By training the different classifiers with different clusters of training data and adopting fusion method considering fitness correlation between clusters we found out better recognition performance than combining classifiers fed with same data. The proposed method tries to provide adaptive preprocessing as well as by exploring the filter selection and fusion based on illumination cluster. Illuminant based clustering is enhanced face recognition ratio. Face image is clustered several cluster unsupervised or statistical method and we adopt adaptive filter each cluster. In this paper, some cluster is preprocessed by single filter others and some cluster adopted preprocessing by filter fusion. We found that the performance of individual filtering methods for image enhancement is highly depending upon face image cluster. Also, in this paper we present the recognition system using the table of fitness correlations between clusters for combining the results from the individual clusters. We present examples from real applications for bad illuminant face images.

1 Introduction

Face recognition technologies have been motivated from the application area of physical access, face image surveillance, people activity awareness, visual interaction for human computer interaction, and humanized vision. Even though many algorithms and techniques are invented, the task of face recognition still remains a difficult problem yet, and existing technologies are not sufficiently reliable. Dynamically changing illumination in a real world application poses one of the most challenging problem in face recognition systems.

There are many general algorithms for classifier fusion such as Bagging and Boosting [1]. In contrast to the huge amount of research in this active area [2, 3, 4], little work has been done on combining the specific classifier: the k nearest neighbor classifier (kNN) [4].

First, the filter fusion guided by an evolutionary approach has been employed to adapt the system for variations in illumination. The proposed approach employs filter fusion.

Second, Classifier fusion methods for identification are illustrated their better reliance on recognition than single classifier and implemented in various ways. Clustering the data set into different regions is added value to recognition systems by finding specific sophisticated system for particular region in ways as selection and fusion of classifiers [5].

In section 2, we present the previous illumination filter fusion methods. In section 3, we present the proposed classifier fusion for identification using fitness correlations between clusters for clustered image and the architecture of the proposed face recognition. We give experimental results in section 4. Finally, we give concluding remarks.

2   GA Based Filter Fusion in Preprocessing

As discussed in session 2, adaptive preprocessing and identification is required for robust face recognition under uneven environments. We employ the method of context-awareness in order to provide the capability of adaptation in preprocessing and feature representation stages. The proposed context-aware preprocessing together with adaptive Gabor feature space can perform well under uneven environments. We use three preprocessing, histogram equalization, contrast stretching and retinex algorithm [6, 7] for filter fusion.

Clustering is researched many peoples [1, 2, 3]. In constrast to the huge amount of research in this active area [1], little work has been done on combining the specific classfifier: the k nearest neighbor classifier(kNN) [4].

In this paper, we generate the method filter fusion as Bayesian based method. The system learns changing environments in the context-awareness stage, and adapts itself

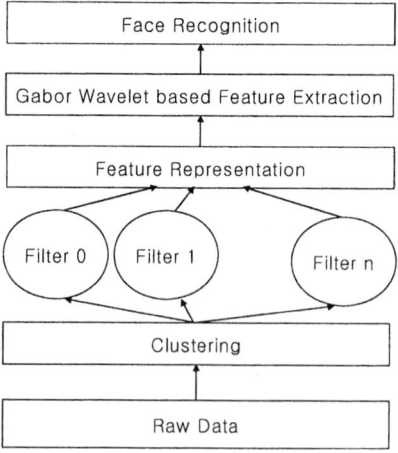

Fig. 1. Face recognition architecture based on the context-aware preprocessing

by restructuring its structure and/or parameters. The adaptation is guided by evolutionary computing module, genetic algorithm here. We adopt Fuzzy ART [8] for achieving an optimal illumination clustering architecture. In this paper, the clustering performance is improved by iterative learning method. Fig. 7shows the clustering result of face images by Fuzzy ART.

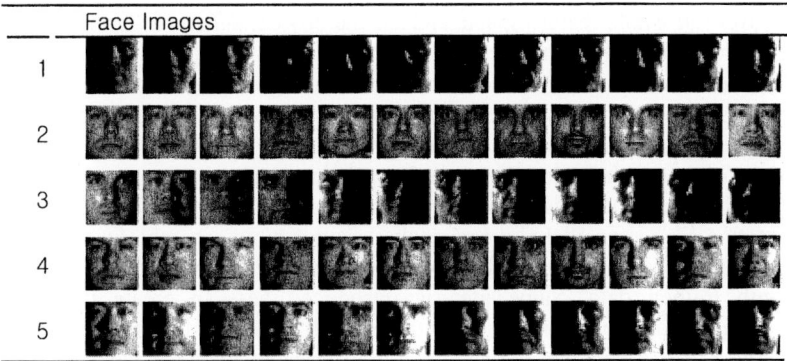

Fig. 2. Examples of face image clustered

The system learns changing environments in the context-awareness stage, and adapts itself by restructuring its structure and/or parameters. The adaptation is guided by evolutionary computing module, genetic algorithm here. Filter fusion maded following figure.

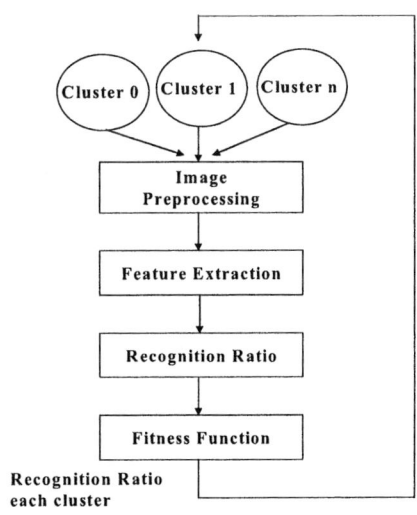

Fig. 3. GA based Filter fusion Architecture

3 The Proposed Classifier Fusion

Classifier outputs are usually made comparable by scaling to interval [0,1]. We assumed the outputs are also measurable as similarity of feature to classes. By the Fig1 the features in same cluster are measured more similar by classifiers.. In this paper, it is assumed that combination of Classifiers, each fed by data in one cluster is more steady in recognition rate. Classifier fusion assumes that all classifiers are trained over the whole feature space, and are thereby considered as competitive rather than complementary. But some methods as bagging, boosting and adaboosting made the classifiers individual from each other by selecting different training data sets [9, 10]. Thus, some solutions considered individualism between classifiers by correlation between them for making final decision.

The assumption that classifiers perform independent of each other might be invulnerable. But methods related to Boosting as Bagging [4], Boosting [2], AdaBoosting [2, 3] considered create each classifier in an ensemble independently of the other classifiers. We can look in way the classifier is simply compares the Test data with trained data. Same idea is introduced here to create the classifiers independent from each other and make the ensemble method fitness correlation more considerable and reasonable. Fig 4 show the difference of independency of classifiers trained by different data set or whole.

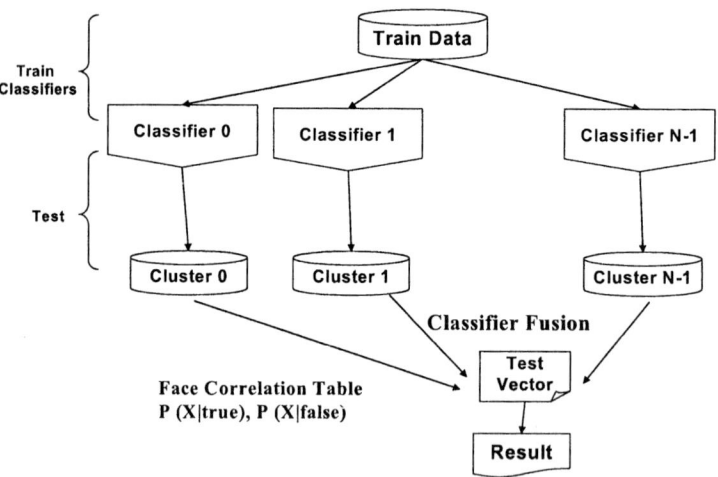

Fig. 4. Classifier Decision Architecture

3.1 Training Fitness Correlation Table

Let $R_0, R_1 \ldots R_N$ are regions clustering the feature vector $x \in R^n$ data sets and $D = \{D_{ij}\}$, $i,j \in \{1,2,3,\ldots,N\}$ are the classifiers. Call a classifier the mapping $D: R^n \rightarrow \{h, y\}$, y is one of $\{1,2,\ldots,c\}$ c classes and h, $h \in [0,1]$ is fitness between x and y measured by classifier. We can look in way the classifier simply compares the Test data set X with trained data set T. Dij is expert on comparing feature vector x, x∈Ri, x with training data t, t∈Rj.

3.2 Classifying Method

Simply combining method is making final decision when we received number of result from different classifiers. Addition information that we need is trueness of that result and fitness correlation table would help us to find them. The trueness of the classifiers's result derivate next figure and equation..

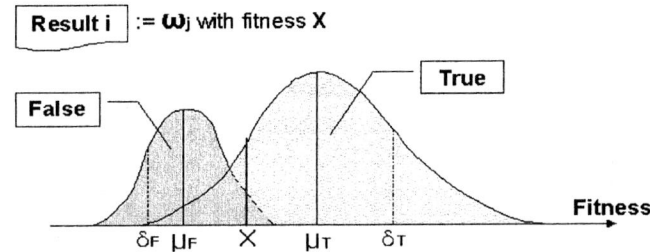

Fig. 5. Decision result

$$\alpha_i = P(True | \omega_j) = P(True | X) = P(X | True) * P(True) / P(X) \quad (1)$$

$$P(X) = (P(X | True) * P(True) + P(X | False) * P(False)) \quad (2)$$

$$P(X | True) = \exp(-0.5 * ((x - \mu_T)/\delta_T)^2) / (\sqrt{2\pi} * \delta_T) \quad (3)$$

4 Experimental Results

The feasibility of the proposed method has been tested using Inha, FERET[9], and Yale [10] database. Experiments have been carried out to compare the recognition performance of the filter fusion and identification based face recognition scheme and that of other methods. We used 1000 images of 100 persons from Inha DB, 60 images of 15 persons from Yale Face DB, and 2418 images of 1196 persons from FERET DB.

As shown in Fig6 and 7, the proposed method based on adaptive feature space outperforms the performance of the non-adaptive methods for the integrated data set. Even though Retnix based method shows the highest performance using FERET fafc, it can not be used under normal illumination. Histogram equalization based method shows the highest performance under normal illumination, i.e. FERET fafb. If the working environment of the system can be controlled well, non-adaptive method may perform better than the proposed adaptive method. However, in general we can not predict or control the system working environment. Thus, we can say that the proposed method is better choice than the non-adaptive methods.

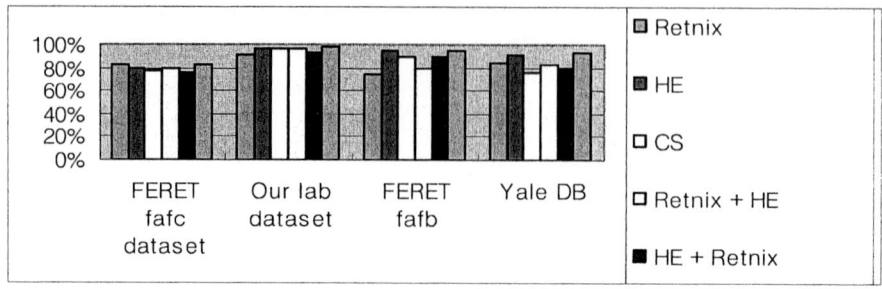

Fig. 6. Comparison of face recognition rates of the proposed adaptive method to those of non-adaptive methods

Table 1. Performance evaluation of the proposed system comparing with other approaches

Algorithm/Method	FERET fafc	FERET fafb	FERET fafb + fafc
arl_cor	0.052	0.827	0.4395
ef_hist_dev_ml1	0.392	0.733	0.5625
ef_hist_dev_ml2	0.309	0.772	0.5405
Excalibur	0.216	0.794	0.505
mit_mar_95	0.155	0.834	0.4945
mit_sep_96	0.32	0.948	0.634
umd_mar_97	0.588	0.962	0.775
usc_mar_97	0.82	0.95	0.885
Proposed method	0.83	0.95	0.89

Table 2. Comparison results between classifier fusion (cluster number 5)

		Ferret	Yale	Our Lab
Single Classifier	Eigenface	60.35	58.91	94.2
	Gabor3	59.59	68.99	93.72
	Gabor13	64.96	77.83	94.44
	Gabor28	82.06	80.46	95.79
	Gabor30	82.06	80.46	95.79
Fusion Method	MV	84.58	82.17	98.41
	MX	84.66	80.46	97.14
	MN	8.38	10.07	8.73
	NB	85.16	83.1	97.77
	Product	78.62	82.63	90.94
	Avarage	83.74	84.03	97.22
	Proposed method	95.25	94.03	99.20

Table 1 and 2 show the comparison of the proposed method to other previous approaches. It becomes apparent that the proposed adaptive method not only shows the highest recognition performance, especially under bad illumination (FERET fafc), but also it shows good performance under normal illumination (FERET fafb). The proposed method shows the highest performance using the integrated data set of FERET fafb and fafc. We can conclude that the proposed adaptive method can operate best under uneven illumination environment.

5 Concluding Remarks

In this paper, we proposed a filter fusion and identification similarity methods for efficient face recognition varying illuminant face images. By training the different classifiers with different clusters of training data and adopting fusion method considering fitness correlation between clusters we found out better recognition performance than combining classifiers fed with same data. From extensive experiment, we found that the performance of individual filtering methods for image enhancement is highly depending upon application environments. The proposed method image preprocessing and feature representation based on context-awareness performs well especially in changing illumination environments due to its adaptability. The proposed method can decide an optimal configuration of filter fusion and cluster's correlation. We enhancement the performance,.

References

1. L.Lim and C.Y.Suen. optimal combination of pattern classifiers. Pattern Recognition Letters, vol.16 (1995) pp.945-954
2. J.Kittler, M.Hatef, R.P.W. Duin, and J.Matas : On combining classifiers. IEEE Trans. Pattern Analysis and Machine Intelligence, vol.20, no.3 , (1998) pp.226-239
3. Bay, SD.: Nearest neighbor classification from multiple feature subsets. Intelligent Data Analysis. vol.3, no.3 (1999) pp.191-209
4. Piotr Indyk. : Approximate nearest neighbor algorithm for frechet distance via product metrics. In Proc. Of Symposium on Computational Geometry, (2002) pp.27
5. L. Kuncheva: Switching Between Selection and Fusion in Combining Classifiers. AnExperiment, IEEE Transaction on Systems, Man and Cybernetics—PARTB, vol.32, no.2, APRIL (2002) pp.146-156
6. Daniel J. Jobson, Zia-ur Rahman, Glenn A. Woodell : The Spatial Aspect of Color and Scientific Implications of Retinex Image Processing. Proc. SPIE, vol. 4388, (2001) pp. 117-128,
7. Brian Funt, Kobus Barnard : Luminance-Based Multi-Scale Retinex. rmalize proceedings AIC Colour 97 8th Congress of the International Colour Association,(1997).
8. Ramuhalli, P., Polikar, R., Udpa L., Udpa S. : Fuzzy ARTMAP network with evolutionary learning. Proc. of IEEE 25th Int. Conf. On Acoustics, Speech and Signal Processing (ICASSP 2000), Vol. 6. Istanbul, Turkey, (2000) pp.3466-3469
9. P.Phillips: The FERET database and evoluation procedure for face recognition algorithms. Image and Vision Computing, vol.16, no.5, (1999) pp.295-306
10. http://cvc.yale.edu/projects/yalefaces/yalefaces.html

Method for Automatically Segmenting the Spinal Cord and Canal from 3D CT Images[*]

László G. Nyúl[1], Judit Kanyó[2], Eörs Máté[1], Géza Makay[3], Emese Balogh[1], Márta Fidrich[2], and Attila Kuba[1]

[1] Department of Image Processing and Computer Graphics, University of Szeged,
Árpád tér 2, H–6720 Szeged, Hungary
{nyul, kuba, mate}@inf.u-szeged.hu
[2] Clinical Software Engineering, GE Medical Systems,
Lajos u. 48-66, H–1036 Budapest, Hungary
{marta.fidrich, judit.kanyo}@med.ge.com
[3] Institute of Mathematics, University of Szeged,
Aradi vértanuk tere 1, H–6720 Szeged, Hungary
makayg@math.u-szeged.hu

Abstract. We present two approaches for automatically segmenting the spinal cord/canal from native CT images of the thorax region containing the spine. Different strategies are included to handle images where only part of the spinal column is visible. The algorithms require one seed point given on a slice located in the middle region of the spine, and the rest is automatic. The spatial extent of the spinal cord/canal is determined automatically. An extended region-growing technique is suggested for segmenting the spinal canal while active contours are applied if the spinal cord is to be segmented. Both methods work in 2D and use propagated information from neighboring slices. They are also very rapid in execution, that means an efficient, user-friendly workflow. The methods were evaluated by radiologists and were found to be useful (in reducing/eliminating contouring labor and time) and met the accuracy and repeatability requirements for the particular task.

1 Introduction

In case of radiation treatment (RT) planning, CT imaging is generally used because image voxel gray values (Hounsfield Units) are in direct function of radiation absorption and therefore can be used directly in dose calculation. In RT planning, clinicians (radiologists, dosimetrists or radiotherapists) must trace the outline of a few critical structures on a large number of images. The time and labor increases significantly with the number of image slices, and the number and sizes of the organs in the anatomical area of interest. The quality of the contouring and then the produced 3D objects depend on the resolution and contrast of the 2D images, and on the knowledge and judgment of the clinician performing the segmentation. Using automated image segmentation could

---
[*] This work was supported by GE Medical Systems.

save tremendous time and effort. Also, automated segmentation could increase precision by eliminating subjectivity of the clinician.

One of the key regions that must be protected during the irradiation treatment is the spinal cord/canal. The difficulty of the automatic segmentation is caused partly by vertebrae that have open cross-sections in the image, partly by the fact that below the level of pelvic bones the cord is no longer situated in the spine.

There are several approaches in the literature to the segmentation of the spinal cord from CT images. The segmentation approach of [1] is based on 2D boundary tracking. It requires an initial point to start tracing the edge. The initial point travels to the vertical or horizontal direction until an edge is reached. Then the algorithm starts to examine the surrounding pixels of that edge and check whether they belong to the current edge or not. The algorithm uses a constant threshold selection which is hard to find (due to the partial volume avaraging effect).

Another approach [2] relies on a knowledge-base which consists of an Anatomical Structures Map and a task-oriented architecture, the Plan Solver. The anatomical structures map contains a frame-like knowledge representation of the macro-anatomy in the human thorax. The plan solver is responsible for determining the position, orientation and size of the structures of interest to radiation therapy. The plan solver relies on a number of image processing operators. However, a general decision making system like the Plan Solver, a method using artificial intelligence could be far from being efficient.

2 Methods

The segmentation procedure described in this paper was devised to work on native CT images of the thorax region containing the spine. Different strategies are included to handle images where only part of the spinal column is visible. The method comprises the following main steps:

1. *Initialization:* The purpose of seed point selection is to determine the starting slice and to provide some localization hint for the segmentation algorithm.
2. *Pre-processing:* Determination of the extent of the cord in the spine between the head and the pelvic bones yields a transaxial slice range, the region of interest (ROI).
3. *2D segmentation on the starting slice:* Cross-section of the spinal cord/canal at the starting slice is segmented by either an active contour or a region growing type algorithm.
4. *Segmentation on other slices:* Repeating propagation and constrain of the 2D segmented region onto the subsequent slice and segmentation on that slice by active contour or region growing, slice-to-slice in upward (toward the head) and downward (toward the feet) directions within the extent yields the final 3D result.

2.1 Determining the Extent of the Cord in the Spine

Seed point is given on a slice located in the middle region of the spine. The slice should contain a 'nice' vertebra, i.e., consisting totally of bone and no cartilage at all. Effectively this assures that the contour of the vertebra is sharp. The extent of the spinal cord/canal is determined by finding the 'upper' end (in the neck region) and the 'lower' end (in the pelvic region) if visible in the image volume. Automatic recognition of the extent is reasonable. Different strategies are used for the two ends.

Extent Towards the Head. Although in many images only the lower part, the pelvic region of the spinal cord is visible there are situations when the upper end is present in the image volume. Here the task is basically the separation of the spinal cord from the brain. This can be reliably done using the bony structures within the region as guides. The region contains the shoulder blades and the collarbone, which are relatively large volumes of bone tissue. The neck contains only a few vertebrae (small bone volume). The skull and jaw are again of relatively large volume. The spinal cord is present in the shoulder and neck region but is not present inside the skull; therefore the extent should be limited to the level below the skull. This can be determined by computing the volume of the bone tissue in each transaxial slice (e.g., by simple thresholding) starting at the seed point level and proceeding toward the head. The level where the bone volume starts to increase considerably after the major decrease indicates the skull base.

Extent Towards the Pelvic Bones. One of the main problems in the automatic segmentation of the spinal cord is to recognize the lower (inferior) end of the spinal canal, where segmentation should be terminated to avoid undesired behavior (e.g., leakage). The main idea of the method is to use the shape of the spine to determine the extent of the cord in the pelvic region. First the apexes of the vertebrae are located on each slice by using the image intensities and some anatomical knowledge of the spine curve. The algorithm seeks for the location of a specific curvature pattern in the spine to determine the lower end of the cord. (see Fig. 1)

2.2 Active Contour Based Segmentation with Propagation

The idea of the active contour or 'snake' algorithm is that a closed curve will best separate the object of interest from its surroundings when its placement and shape is such that an energy function, defined over the boundary, is minimized. [3,4] The contour is described parametrically by $\mathbf{v}(s), s \in [0, 1]$. The snake energy is

$$E_{\text{snake}}(\mathbf{v}(s)) = \int_{s=0}^{1} E_{\text{internal}}(\mathbf{v}(s)) + E_{\text{image}}(\mathbf{v}(s)) + E_{\text{constraint}}(\mathbf{v}(s))\, ds,$$

where internal, the *internal energy* imposes curvature (smoothness) constraints, E_{image}, the *image energy* attracts the contour to the desired features (edges)

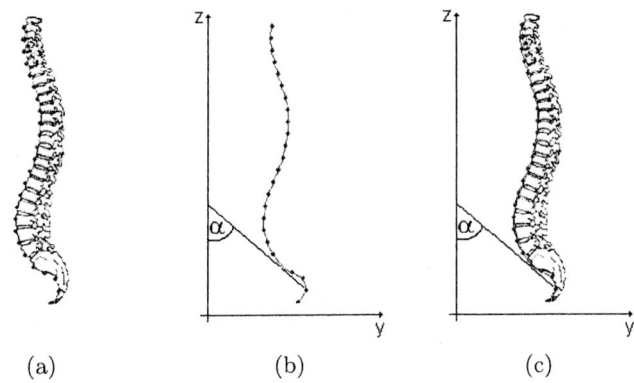

Fig. 1. Spinal cord with marked apexes of the vertebrae (a) and determination of the stopping angle (b), and the spine image superimposed on the curve function (c)

of the image, and $E_{\text{constraint}}$, the *constraint energy* allows other geometric constraints to be applied.

We chose to solve the discrete problem using a more or less discrete method following some ideas of [5]. Instead of energy minimization, we prefer working with the effects of the energies, i.e., we apply discrete forces on each boundary point and look for equilibrium of these forces.

To obtain the segmented 3D object, first, the user selects a seed point in one of the slices and 2D segmentation is performed on that particular slice. The centroid of the enclosed shape is propagated to adjacent slices and the 2D segmentation is performed on those slices also starting from the propagated seed point.

Forces Used for the Active Contour. At each iteration step, various forces are applied to each contour point p, until points stop moving considerably or maximum number of iteration is reached:

$$\mathbf{F}(p) = \mathbf{F}_{\text{image}}(p) + \mathbf{F}_{\text{constraint}}(p) + \mathbf{F}_{\text{inflation}}(p) + \mathbf{F}_{\text{angle}}(p) + \mathbf{F}_{\text{distance}}(p).$$

Image force is used to attract the contour to edges. We compute the image force as a smoothed gradient from the negative gradient norm of the image. *Constraint force* is used to constrain the size and the shape (circular) of the segmented region. The farther the current point is from the centroid of the enclosed polygon, the larger force is applied to pull it back. *Local inflation force* pushes the contour outwards. When a point does not move considerably (i.e., it is stuck in a local minimum), this force pushes the point outward with a small constant. *Angle force* is used to smooth the contour. We compute the deviation from 180 degrees of the angle at each contour point and penalize large deviations and concavities. *Distance force* aims at evenly distributing contour points. We compute the deviation of the distance of two adjacent points from the average distance of the nearby (or all) adjacent points. This pulls the actual point into its tentative middle position between the neighbors.

Cut and merge operations also aim at evenly distributing contour points and at the same time refining the contour. If the length of an edge is too large, the edge is cut and a new contour point is created. If the length of an edge is too small, it is removed by merging its two endpoints.

Propagation to Other Slices. Since the method works in 2D and it requires a seed point within the slice to start with, we need to provide seed points for the object on each slice. To reduce the user interaction and facilitate automation, user-defined seed point is required only on the initializing slice. For subsequent slices the method automatically generates seed points based on the segmented regions from neighboring slices. The centroid of the enclosed region is propagated to adjacent slices. If it is detected to fall out of the spinal cord (by using image intensity measures), the algorithm will correct for the bending of the spine by extrapolation from the positions of the centroid on the actual slice and on the previous slice.

2.3 Region Growing Based Segmentation with Propagation

This technique uses the standard 'textbook' region-growing algorithm with a stopping criterion that combines local and global differences between gray values of voxels, as well as a technique to add geometrical constraints based on the anatomical knowledge about the organ being segmented.

The region growing method is prone to 'leaking out' if object boundaries are not well defined in the image data. Also, since segmentation is done slice by slice and subsequent iterations are initialized using results on preceding slices, one bad slice could ruin all subsequent results. Our algorithm will mostly prevent these failures.

Segmenting the First Slice. The user is required to select an initial slice where the spinal cord is totally enclosed by a vertebra, thus guaranteeing that the initial segmentation of this slice will not leak out. The object is roughly segmented on the initializing slice, starting from the seed point, and following a conservative thresholding strategy where the thresholds depend on the intensity value of the seed point.

The criterion that is used to stop the region-growing algorithm depends on local and global features, which describe the homogeneity of the segmented region. These are represented by parameters m and M:

$$m = \max_{v \in R} |I(S) - I(v)| \qquad M = \max_{v_1, v_2 \in R} |I(v_1) - I(v_2)|,$$

where R is the segmented region, S is the seed point, and $I(v)$ denotes the gray value at voxel v.

Segmenting the Other Slices. Although this variant of region growing operates in 2D, it can be used to extract a whole 3D volume by slice by slice starting off at the slice containing the initial seed point, and traversing every transaxial slice above and below the initial slice. This is realized by propagating a point to be the new seed point, utilizing the statistical features of the initial slice, and applying several constraints to the new region.

Seed propagation is performed analogously to that used with the active contour method described above. The region growing criterion is set up that a voxel v that is neighbor of a region boundary voxel b is included if

$$\alpha \frac{D}{M} + \beta \frac{d}{m} < T,$$

where $D = |I(v) - I(b)|$ and $d = |I(v) - I(S)|$, α and β are weights and T is a pre-specified threshold.

Before the iteration continues, every segmented region must be evaluated to detect leakage and to embed some a priori information about the organ in question. The spinal canal has a tubular structure and in each slice it appears almost circular, therefore, a circular mask of the approximate size of the spinal canal is applied to the segmented region to reduce false positives.

3 Results

Note that the segmented 'spinal canal' is on average 18–20% larger than the segmented 'spinal cord'. Therefore, the two segmentations cannot be directly compared. For radiotherapy planning, any segmented region falling between the borders of cord and canal can be accepted as accurate. Figure 2 shows a few transaxial cross-sections and a sagittal slice with the segmented spinal cord indicated over the original CT images.

There were 27 image volumes included in our studies and three operators performed manual contouring for producing the 'gold standard'. The measure for accuracy was computed by means of true positive volume fraction (TPVF), false positive volume fraction (FPVF), and false negative volume fraction (FNVF) using the 'gold standard' as the true volume.

Operator A performed the same segmentation task 3 times (A1, A2, A3). For each pair (A1-A2, A1-A3, A2-A3), an overlap measure was computed. The measure for intra-operator reproducibility was computed as the mean and the standard deviation of the computed overlap measure among all performed tasks. Inter-operator reproducibility was computed similarly. Three different operators (A, B, C) performed the same segmentation task. Measures are computed for each pair (A-B, A-C, B-C) and for each task and are pooled for statistics. Table 1 shows the results for accuracy and reproducibility.

Accuracy of the active contour method is approximately the same as that of the manual outlining for the spinal cord. This automatic method also shows higher intra- and inter-operator reproducibility. Accuracy and reproducibility of

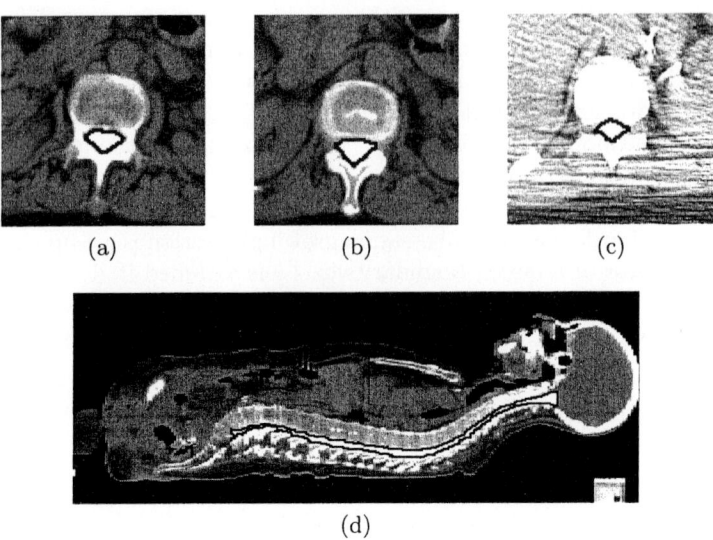

Fig. 2. Segmentation on the initial slice (a), on an additional slice with open vertebra (b), and sagittal view of the entire segmented spinal canal (d). Segmentation on a slice from a very noisy dataset (c).

Table 1. Accuracy, intra- and inter-operator reproducibility measures for the methods. Mean values and standarad deviation of the measures are expressed in percents.

Region	Method	TPVF	FPVF	FNVF	Intra-operator	Inter-operator
Spinal cord	Manual	97.94 (1.49)	2.06 (1.31)	2.06 (1.49)	93.35 (1.75)	91.90 (2.63)
	Auto (AC)	97.59 (2.59)	2.62 (2.01)	2.41 (2.59)	94.77 (1.94)	94.53 (1.72)
Spinal canal	Manual	97.27 (1.53)	2.73 (1.66)	2.73 (1.53)	Not tested	89.62 (2.54)
	Auto (RG)	95.83 (3.85)	8.79 (6.12)	4.17 (3.85)	Not tested	86.69 (7.20)

the region growing based method is somewhat lower than that of the manual outlining due to leakage in a few cases.

Selecting the initial slice and the seed point can be done in a few seconds per data set. Running time for the semi-automatic segmentations was found to be 25 seconds per study on average for the active contour method and a few seconds per study less for the region growing method. This is much less than the time needed for manual contouring.

4 Discussion

The simple method published in [1] has several drawbacks, which limit its accuracy and usability. It can be very sensitive to where the starting point is placed in a slice image. Also, often images show cross-sections in which the vertebra is not closed, therefore the initial traverse to find a boundary point may fail. Due to the partial volume averaging effect the contour of the spinal canal may not be sharp and clearly identifiable in a slice image at all. It is hard to find proper threshold of general use. Our method requires the selection of a reliable initial section but afterwards it automatically propagates size, shape and intensity constraints.

The size and shape of organs, even the spine, vary a lot and their boundary is not always visible. Thus detection is only possible with some prior information. Instead of using probabilistic approaches (which are known to be not only erroneous but also slow, even in case of a very simplistic model), we incorporate anatomical knowledge into our method. After understanding how radiologists work when they analyze images, we built the radiologists decision making procedure directly into our method.

Since our principal aim was to develop a real-time method that can be used in daily routine work, we optimized on speed instead of generality, unlike the Plan Solver [2]. Also, we use initial human interaction to guarantee the correct starting off of the iterative, propagating procedure, in contrast with [2], where the authors use fully automatic initialization and then try to determine failure of initialization.

5 Conclusions

Both of our algorithms to segment the spinal cord/canal require only one point to start, after that the segmentation is fully automatic and fast. This means a highly efficient, user-friendly workflow (no need to trace a contour on a starting slice, no need for initial model fitting, no need for ROI or slice range selection). The methods were evaluated by radiologists and were found to be useful (in reducing/eliminating contouring labor and time) and met the accuracy and repeatability requirements for the particular task. Since the active contour version performed better of the two in terms of reproducibility and accuracy, that one is currently incorporated into the product.

References

1. G. Karangelis and S. Zimeras. A 3D segmentation method of the spinal cord applied on CT data. *Computer Graphics Topics*, 14(1):28–29, 2002.
2. N. Archip, P. J. Erard, M. Egmont-Petersen, J. M. Haefliger, and J. F. Germond. A knowledge-based approach to automatic detection of the spinal cord in CT images. *IEEE Trans. Med. Imaging*, 21(12):1504–1516, 2002.
3. L. D. Cohen. On active contour models and balloons. *CVGIP: Image Understanding*, 53(2):211–218, 1991.
4. L. D. Cohen and I. Cohen. Finite element methods for contour models and balloons for 2D and 3D images. *IEEE Trans. PAMI*, 15(11):1131–1147, 1993.
5. J. V. Miller, D. E. Breen, W. E. Lorensen, R. M. O'Bara, and M. J. Wozny. Geometrically deformed models: A method for extracting closed geometric models from volume data. In *Computer Graphics (SIGGRAPH'91 Proc.)*, volume 25, pages 217–226, 1991.

Vehicle Area Segmentation Using Grid-Based Feature Values*

Nakhoon Baek[1], Ku-Jin Kim[2], and Manpyo Hong[3]

[1] Dept. of Comp. Sci., Kyungpook National Univ., Daegu 702-701, Korea
[2] Dept. of Comp. Eng., Kyungpook National Univ., Daegu 702-701, Korea
[3] Grad. School of Info. and Comm., Ajou Univ., Suwon 443-749, Korea
nbaek@knu.ac.kr, kujinkim@yahoo.com, mphong@ajou.ac.kr

Abstract. We present a vehicle segmentation method for still images captured from outdoor CCD cameras. Our preprocessing process partitions the background images into a set of two-dimensional grids, and then calculates the statistical feature values of the edges in each grid. For a given vehicle image, we compare its feature values of each grid to the statistical values of the background images to finally decide whether the grid belongs to the vehicle area or not. To find the optimal rectangular grid area containing the vehicle, we use a dynamic programming technique. Based on the statistics analysis and the global search technique, our method is more systematic compared to the previous heuristic methods, and achieves high reliability against noises, shadows, illumination changes, and camera tremors. Our prototype implementation performs vehicle segmentation in average of 0.150 second, for each of 1280 × 960 vehicle images. It shows 97.03 % of successful cases from 270 images with various kinds of noises.

1 Introduction

In this paper, we present a method of segmenting the vehicle area from the road images. This vehicle segmentation problem actually removes unnecessary visual information such as lanes, shadows and other noises from road images, and enables other processes to concentrate on the vehicle area. As an example, the license plate recognition and vehicle classification, which are used in various applications including automatic toll fee collection systems, traffic monitoring systems, and Intelligent Transportation Systems (ITS), use the vehicle segmentation as one of their fundamental operations.

The background subtraction method is one of the most widely used one for the vehicle segmentation. It compares a background and a vehicle image in a pixel-by-pixel manner, to report a set of altered pixels as the vehicle area.

---
* Prof. Kim was supported by the Korea Research Foundation Grant funded by Korean Government (MOEHRD) (R04-2004-000-10099-0). Prof. Hong was supported by the Ubiquitous Autonomic Computing and Network Project, the Ministry of Information and Communication (MIC) 21st Century Frontier R&D Program in Korea (05A3-B2-50).

Although it is intuitive and straightforward, it is sensitive to the illumination changes, camera tremors, shadows and other noises. For the cases where the vehicle color is similar to the background color or where shadows of the target vehicle itself or other vehicles exist, it may fail to find the vehicle area. It also has drawbacks that background images and threshold values should be dynamically updated for deriving correct results[1,2,3,4].

To complement the drawbacks of the background subtraction, several researchers combined edge detection techniques with it[2,3,5,6]. Fathy and Siyal[2,3] developed a system that counts the number of vehicles using background subtraction and edge detection techniques. By restricting the vehicle detection to a predefined window area, they could achieve high performance. Yu et al.[6] applied the background subtraction method to the edge detected images rather than the original ones.

Fathy and Siyal[2,3] and Yu et al.[6] attempt to apply their results to collect traffic parameters such as the number of vehicles passed, so they focused on detecting vehicles, rather than precisely finding the vehicle area. Compared to their results, Lee and Kweon[5] find the vehicle area more precisely from the background subtracted results, using symmetries in detected edges and intensity values. Though it shows better performance, it has the limitation of assuming the whole vehicle is neatly captured in the image, to use its symmetry.

In spite of various attempts at the vehicle segmentation, we have no general-case solution yet. In some cases, previous vehicle segmentation methods may be confused by various circumstances including unexpected shadows, irregular illumination changes, and/or camera tremors. In this paper, we present a vehicle segmentation method, aiming to an integrated vehicle recognition system with the capability of license plate recognition, vehicle classification, and so on. Thus, we use input images with comparatively high resolution of 1280 × 960, and the final result of vehicle area segmentation will be used as the input of those post-processing processes.

To reduce the influence from various noises in the outdoor CCD camera images, we use a grid-based approach: the input image is partitioned into a set of grids, for more efficiency and more robustness, as explained in the following sections. After calculating the statistical values of our feature metrics from a set of background images, we use these statistical values to decide whether each grid area is a candidate for the vehicle area or not. Compared to the previous ones, our method has the following strong points:

Robustness to noises: our approach is more suitable for noisy images.
No assumption on the vehicle location: our method can handle the rapid lane changes and/or partially captured vehicles.
Efficiency: our prototype implementation shows average of 0.150 second for each vehicle image of 1280 × 960 resolution. Considering relatively high resolution, its processing speed is acceptable for practical applications.

In Sect. 2, details of our vehicle segmentation method will be presented. Sect. 3 contains the experimental results from the prototype implementation. Conclusions and closing remarks will be followed in Sect. 4.

2 Vehicle Segmentation Algorithm

To define our feature values for the vehicle segmentation, we start from converting the color images into grayscale ones for ease of edge detection process. Then, we detect the edges in the grayscale image. In our prototype implementation, we use Sobel's edge detection value $Edge(\mathbf{p}_{xy})$ for each pixel $\mathbf{p}_{xy} = (x,y)$.

We use the images captured from CCD cameras mounted on poles or other tall structures, looking down on the traffic scene. Including these ones, outdoor cameras almost always move slightly due to winds, shocks, etc. The images additionally show different exposure and/or contrast due to the weather and other circumstances. To overcome these derangements, we use a grid-based approach rather than a pixel-based one.

A given image I would be partitioned into $w \times h$ grids, each of which can be expressed as a set of pixels as follows:

$$I_{ij} = \{\mathbf{p}_{xy} | iw \leq x < (i+1)w \quad \text{and} \quad jh \leq y < (j+1)h\} .$$

We will finally decide that which grid areas belong to the vehicle area. Since the pixels may be slightly moved and/or have different pixel values for the same object under different circumstances, the set of pixels in a grid area will be treated as a unit. This grid-based approach, we think, would be a reasonable way of overcoming the derangements in outdoor captured images.

For each grid area I_{ij}, we need to summarize the $Edge(\mathbf{p}_{xy})$ values over the whole grid area, as feature values. Since the grid area covers a two-dimensional rectangular region, we accumulated $Edge(\mathbf{p}_{xy})$ values along the horizontal and vertical directions. The sum of $Edge(\mathbf{p}_{xy})$'s for each x- and y-coordinate can be calculated as follows:

$$S_{ij}(x) = \sum_{y \in I_{ij}} Edge(\mathbf{p}_{xy}) \quad \text{for each } x \in I_{ij} \quad \text{and}$$

$$S_{ij}(y) = \sum_{x \in I_{ij}} Edge(\mathbf{p}_{xy}) \quad \text{for each } y \in I_{ij} ,$$

where $x \in I_{ij}$ and $y \in I_{ij}$ mean all the x- and y-coordinates suitable for the rectangular area of I_{ij}.

As an example, Fig. 1(d) is the edge-detection result of a grid are in the original image of Fig. 1(a). Its vertical and horizontal accumulation of $Edge(\mathbf{p}_{xy})$ values for the grid area can be expressed as the graphs in Fig. 1(b) and 1(c), respectively. These $S_{ij}(x)$ and $S_{ij}(y)$ graphs have peaks around the x- and y-coordinates corresponding to the vertical and horizontal edges. The vehicle boundaries and interior areas usually have clusters of vertical and horizontal edges, and thus, we derive our feature values from these peak shapes.

To reduce the influence of various derangements, we use the idea of the histogram normalization and use $S_{ij}(x) / \max S_{ij}(x)$ and $S_{ij}(y) / \max S_{ij}(y)$ rather than $S_{ij}(x)$ and $S_{ij}(y)$. Additionally, we focus on the ratio of maximum and minimum values in the graph, and these ratio values are calculated as follows:

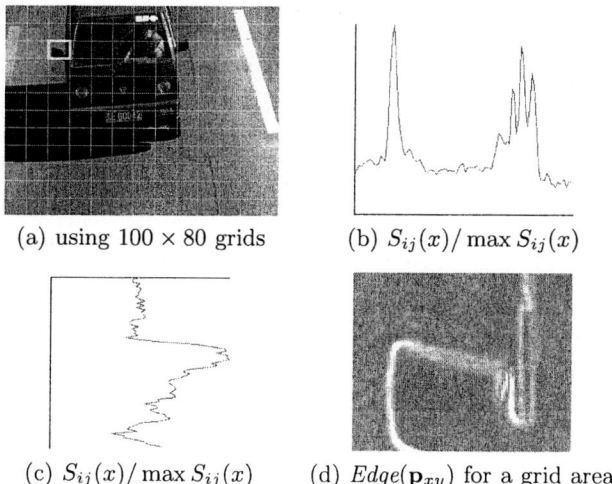

(a) using 100 × 80 grids   (b) $S_{ij}(x)/\max S_{ij}(x)$

(c) $S_{ij}(x)/\max S_{ij}(x)$ (d) $Edge(\mathbf{p}_{xy})$ for a grid area

Fig. 1. Results of our vehicle area segmentation method

$$R_{ij}^x = \max_{x \in I_{ij}}(S_{ij}(x)/\max S_{ij}(x)) - \min_{x \in I_{ij}}(S_{ij}(x)/\max S_{ij}(x)) \quad \text{and}$$
$$R_{ij}^y = \max_{y \in I_{ij}}(S_{ij}(y)/\max S_{ij}(y)) - \min_{y \in I_{ij}}(S_{ij}(y)/\max S_{ij}(y)) \;,$$

where both $\max(S_{ij}(x)/\max S_{ij}(x))$ and $\max(S_{ij}(y)/\max S_{ij}(y))$ are actually evaluated to 1. These R_{ij}^x and R_{ij}^y can be representative values for the $S_{ij}(x)$ and $S_{ij}(y)$ graphs for each grid area I_{ij}, and we use these ratios as the major feature values.

The vehicle segmentation can also be achieved through removing background areas, in an opposite manner. The background subtraction method is a typical example and it removes corresponding pixels with the same color. Although we have some previous works in this approach, they may show unacceptable results due to unexpected shadows, camera tremor, etc. as shown in Fig. 2.

In this paper, the feature values R_{ij}^x and R_{ij}^y are used to decide whether its corresponding grid area I_{ij} may belong to the background region or not. Our basic idea is considering the grid as the background region when it has similar feature values comparing to the background images. Letting $\mathcal{I}_{\text{bg}}$ be the set of background images, it has only the images captured when no vehicle is detected on the loop sensor at the image capturing time.

Actually, most of background images in $\mathcal{I}_{\text{bg}}$ are somewhat defective due to over-exposure, unexpected shadows, camera tremors, etc., as shown in Fig. 3. To remove these defects, we use a statistical approach. We calculate the averages of R_{ij}^x's and R_{ij}^y's over the whole background images in $\mathcal{I}_{\text{bg}}$, and denote them as $\mu_{ij}^x(\mathcal{I}_{\text{bg}})$ and $\mu_{ij}^y(\mathcal{I}_{\text{bg}})$, respectively. Similarly, we calculate $\sigma_{ij}^x(\mathcal{I}_{\text{bg}})$ and $\sigma_{ij}^y(\mathcal{I}_{\text{bg}})$ as the standard deviations of R_{ij}^x's and R_{ij}^y's, respectively.

(a) a background image   (b) a vehicle image   (c) the result

Fig. 2. An example of background subtraction with the unexpected shadow

Assuming that R_{ij}^x's and R_{ij}^y's for $\mathcal{I}_{\text{bg}}$ are normally distributed, the R_{ij}^x and R_{ij}^y for the grid I_{ij} in a vehicle image may be a candidate for the background region when the following conditions are satisfied:

$$\kappa_x = \left| \frac{R_{ij}^x - \mu_{ij}^x(\mathcal{I}_{\text{bg}})}{\sigma_{ij}^x(\mathcal{I}_{\text{bg}})} \right| \leq \alpha_x \quad \text{and} \quad \kappa_y = \left| \frac{R_{ij}^y - \mu_{ij}^y(\mathcal{I}_{\text{bg}})}{\sigma_{ij}^y(\mathcal{I}_{\text{bg}})} \right| \leq \alpha_y , \quad (1)$$

where α_x and α_y are parameters to estimate the confidence interval. For example, $\alpha_x = 2$ and $\alpha_y = 2$ can be used for the confidence rate of 95.5%[7]. In this paper, we use the conditions in Eq. (1) to discriminate candidates for the background and vehicle region, after pre-calculating $\mu_{ij}^x(\mathcal{I}_{\text{bg}})$, $\sigma_{ij}^x(\mathcal{I}_{\text{bg}})$, $\mu_{ij}^y(\mathcal{I}_{\text{bg}})$ and $\sigma_{ij}^y(\mathcal{I}_{\text{bg}})$ for $\mathcal{I}_{\text{bg}}$. Our prototype implementation shows that this statistical approach outperforms the previous background subtraction methods.

For given α_x and α_y values, each grid I_{ij} can be classified into the following four cases:

case A: $\kappa_x > \alpha_x$ and $\kappa_y > \alpha_y$. The grid I_{ij} has abnormally many vertical and horizontal edges compared to the background and may belong to the vehicle region with very high probability.
case B: $\kappa_x > \alpha_x$ and $\kappa_y \leq \alpha_y$.
case C: $\kappa_x \leq \alpha_x$ and $\kappa_y > \alpha_y$. Both cases B and C indicate high probability for being contained in a vehicle region, due to abnormally many vertical or horizontal edges, respectively.
case D: $\kappa_x \leq \alpha_x$ and $\kappa_y \leq \alpha_y$. It may belong to the background region.

After this classification, we can expect that grids around the vehicle region boundary will be classified into cases A, B or C. Almost all remaining grids would be in case D, except some noisy ones. Notice that certain grids corresponding to the interior of the vehicle region may be classified into case D, since they may show wide flat areas without any particular edges.

Our strategy is to find the minimal area enclosing as many grids of cases A, B and C, as possible, to finally report the area as the vehicle region. More precisely, we will report a rectangular region, since most segmentation-related applications usually start with rectangular areas.

Our sample data show that some vehicle images are captured even when the vehicle only passes the boundary of the loop sensor, as shown in the top-middle

(a) normal case (b) over-exposed (c) including shadows

Fig. 3. Background images used for our experiment

image of Fig. 4. Additionally, the vehicles can rapidly change the traffic lane, so the direction of the vehicle can be slanted as shown in the bottom-left image of Fig. 4. As the result, we removed any assumption for the vehicle location or direction, and aim to find the rectangular area for the vehicle (or the partially captured vehicle).

We use a dynamic programming approach to find out the most acceptable candidate vehicle region. Letting W_A, W_B, W_C and W_D be the weights for cases A, B, C and D, respectively, we find the minimum-size rectangular area with a maximum sum of weights for the grid areas in it. Considering the characteristics of our case classification, the weight values would have the relationship of $W_A \geq W_B, W_C > W_D$. Additionally, we can suppress the inclusion of a case D grid areas, through letting $W_D < 0$.

Letting the weight value of I_{ij} be w_{ij}, it will be one of W_A, W_B, W_C and W_D, and the total weight of an $m \times n$ rectangular area with its top left grid area I_{pq} can be expressed as follows:

$$w_{pqmn} = \sum_{i=p}^{p+m-1} \sum_{j=q}^{q+n-1} w_{ij} = \begin{cases} 0, & \text{if } m = 0 \text{ or } n = 0 \\ w_{pq}, & \text{if } m = 1 \text{ and } n = 1 \\ w_{pq} + w_{(p+1)q(m-1)1} + w_{p(q+1)1(n-1)} \\ + w_{(p+1)(q+1)(m-1)(n-1)}, & \text{if } m > 1 \text{ or } n > 1 \end{cases}.$$

Now, we evaluate all the possible w_{pqmn}'s and report the $m \times n$ rectangular region $\{I_{ij} | p \leq i < p+m, q \leq j < q+n\}$ with a maximum weight. The results of our prototype implementation will be presented in the following section.

3 Experimental Results

To verify our method, we implemented our prototype system on a PC platform with C++ programming language and Qt graphics library. We use 1280×960 resolution color images captured in various circumstances from outdoor CCD cameras. Total of 197 images captured without loop sensor responses are selected as background images in $\mathcal{I}_{bg}$. Using the grid size of 100×80, the statistics values of $\mu_{ij}^x(\mathcal{I}_{bg})$, $\sigma_{ij}^x(\mathcal{I}_{bg})$, $\mu_{ij}^y(\mathcal{I}_{bg})$ and $\sigma_{ij}^y(\mathcal{I}_{bg})$ are calculated in the preprocessing stage.

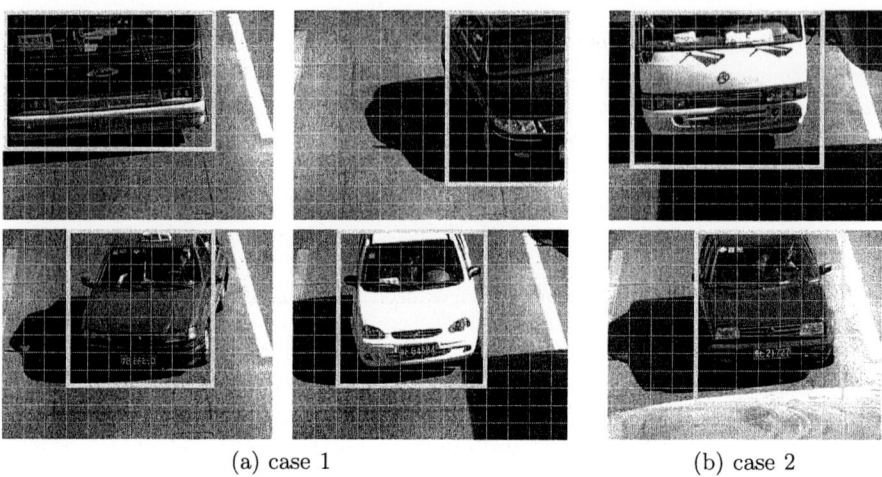

Fig. 4. Results of our vehicle area segmentation method

We use 270 images for the verification of our vehicle segmentation method. Some of them have only partially captured vehicles, and/or various noises such as over exposures. Since almost all background and vehicle images contain various noises, we use large values for the parameters α_x and α_y: $\alpha_x = 6$ and $\alpha_y = 6$. Although these values are extremely high for usual normal distributions, it shows reasonable behavior for our sample images. Additionally, we use $W_A = 1$, $W_B = 2/3$, $W_C = 1/3$ and $W_D = -1/2$ for the weight values. Our prototype implementation shows 0.150 second of average processing time for vehicle images, with Pentium4 3.0 GHz CPU and 1 GB RAM.

The final vehicle segmentation results are manually classified into two cases:

case 1: The segmentation result and the manually-chosen minimum rectangular region coincide, or the difference is within one row or one column width.
case 2: The difference is more than one row or one column width.

Fig. 4 shows some typical examples of each case. From 270 vehicle images, our implementation scored 262 images for case 1. To check the validity of our method seriously, our sample images include various noised ones: some images have very dark areas around the vehicle boundaries mainly due to shades, and actually they are hard to find the vehicle area even with human eyes. Thus, we treat the difference of one row or one column as the successful cases. Additionally, we originally aim to use the vehicle segmentation result as the input of the next stage license plate identification and/or vehicle classification, and they usually endure one row or one column differences.

Conclusively, our implementation finds the correct vehicle area with 97.03 % of success, even with various derangements. Notice that we used many abnormal images as shown in Fig. 4, which are seldom used for the test of previous vehicle segmentation methods. Considering these abnormal sample images, we expect that our methods will be used as a practically stable system.

4 Conclusions

In this paper, we presented a vehicle segmentation method from road images. We partitioned the input images into a set of two-dimensional grids, and then calculated feature values for each grid area. By using the statistical values derived from sample background images, we could determine whether a grid area may belong to the vehicle area or not. Based on the statistical approach and a global search technique, our method has the following advantages:

More systematic: Our method is based on the statistical analysis, so it is more systematic than the previous heuristic approaches.

Robust to noises: By using the grid-based feature values, our method is robust to various noises.

Reliable shadow removal: Experiments show that our method successfully recognizes the vehicle area from the images even with somewhat serious shadows.

Less constraints for input images: Our method can be applied to the input images with various illumination and weather conditions. Even for the cases where the vehicle is partially captured in the image or the vehicle rapidly changes the lane, it shows a good performance.

For the vehicle images from outdoor CCD cameras, our method shows 97.03 % of successful results which are confirmed by human eyes. The average processing time for the vehicle segmentation is 0.150 second per image. When some grid area in the actual vehicle region shows no statistical difference to background images, our method may fail. We will try to overcome this drawback by introducing more powerful feature values, as a future work. We also plan to apply the proposed method for other image processing applications.

References

1. Michalopoulos, P.G.: Vehicle detection video through image processing: The AUTOSCOPE system. IEEE Trans. Vehicular Technol. **40** (1991) 21–29
2. Fathy, M., Siyal, M.: An image detection technique based on morphological edge detection and background differencing for real-time traffic analysis. Pat. Recog. Letters **16** (1995) 1321–1330
3. Fathy, M., Siyal, M.: A window-based image processing technique for quantitative and qualitative analysis of road traffic parameters. IEEE Trans. Vehicular Technol. **47** (1998) 1342–1349
4. Gupte, S., Masoud, O., Papanikolopoulos, N.: Detection and classification of vehicles. IEEE Trans. Intell. Transport. Syst. **3** (2002) 37–47
5. Lee, J.W., Kweon, I.S.: MAP-based probabilistic reasoning to vehicle segmentation. Pat. Recog. **31** (1998) 2017–2026
6. Yu, M., Jiang, G., Yu, B.: An integrative method for video based traffic parameter extraction in ITS. In: Proc. IEEE Asia-Pac. Conf. Circ. and Syst. (2000) 136–139
7. Ross, S.: Introduction to probability and statistics for engineers and scientists, 2nd Ed. Wiley (2000)

Improvement of a Temporal Video Index Produced by an Object Detector

Gaël Jaffré and Philippe Joly

Université Paul Sabatier,
IRIT - Équipe SAMOVA,
31062 Toulouse Cedex 09,
France
{jaffre, joly}@irit.fr

Abstract. The goal of the works described in this paper is to improve results produced by an object detector operating independently on each frame of a video document in order to generate a more robust index. Results of the object detector are "smoothed" along the time dimension using a temporal window. For a given frame, we count the number of occurrences of each object in the previous and next frames, and then only the objects whose number of appearance is above a threshold are validated. In this paper, we present a probabilistic approach for theoretically computing these thresholds. This approach is well suited to limit the number of false alarms provided by the static detector, and its principle of detection generalization also allows some detections that can be missed by the detector.

1 Introduction

In the context of video indexing and retrieval [1], object detection is an important task. Many methods developed for still images could be used [2], by carrying out the detection independently in each frame, without tracking nor propagation of results. However, frame by frame detection produces many false alarms, which can be avoided using the temporal information of the video documents. The use of temporal information was proposed in [3] for robust face tracking, with the CONDENSATION algorithm [4] for prediction over time, and compared to frame by frame methods. A similar approach is presented in [5], where static object detections are computed in each frame, but each candidate detection is tracked in subsequent frames, and validated only if the detection "survives".

This topic is key issue in the domain of automatic video content indexing when the goal is to identify temporal segments where a given object can be seen. Most of evaluation campaigns evaluate the efficiency of an indexing tool in terms of recall and precision rates [6]. In this paper, we propose a temporal "smoothing" of object detection using a temporal window as a postprocessing step in order to obtain higher rates.

In one hand, isolated detections are considered as false alarms (cf Fig. 1); in the other one, when an object is detected in every frame excepted in an isolated one, a

Fig. 1. Some examples of frame by frame face localization (first row), and frame by frame player localization (second row). Each box represents a result of a detection. In these sequences, the false alarms and the non-detections only occurs in one or two single frames. This situation often occurs with noisy images.

miss-detection is inferred. This approach has been applied in [7] for costume detection, but the number of frames to validate a candidate was empirically chosen. In this paper, we propose a generalization for this approach and a theoretical solution to compute the number of frames, using probability computing.

In section 2, we present the temporal smoothing algorithm, and introduce the probability law to be maximized in order to compute the optimal thresholds: a way to solve this maximization is then presented in section 3. Section 4 presents another probability law, combining the notions of precision and recall, and shows that in a particular case, results are nearly the same. Finally, practical results are presented in section 5.

2 Addition of Temporal Information

Object detection methods on still images are widespread in literature for different kinds of objects, such as soccer players [2], faces [8], ... Those methods can be applied on video sequences, but a direct application will provide many false alarms, and some miss-detections in a same shot, due to the noise or some local variations of shooting conditions, as presented in Fig. 1.

In order to reduce these false detections, we propose to exploit persistence properties of objects in a video sequence using a rather simple heuristic: in each frame, all objects are detected using a static approach. Then, we consider a temporal window (subsequence) of N frames. The number of each candidate object occurrences in the $N/2$ previous frames, and in the $N/2$ next frames is computed. Then, a candidate object is considered as an actual one if it appears at least N_2 times in this subsequence.

2.1 Hypothesis

This approach can be carried out under some hypothesis. First, we suppose that objects we are looking for are present in N successive frames at least. Our framework is the analysis of TV broadcasts, and especially talk-shows and TV games. On that kind of content, video cameras are quasi-static, and characters appearing in a frame generally also appear in all the frames of the shot [6]. In this case, the hypothesis of object persistence is always verified. We also suppose that N is lower than the number of frames in a shot. On that kind of content, each shot has a duration greater than 1.5 seconds, and so is composed of at least 30 frames.

Moreover, due to the noise variation from a frame to another one, we suppose that all the detections are also independent inside a same shot.

2.2 Maximization

Let X be the variable which represents the number of correct detections in N frames, and Y the one which represents the number of false alarms. As we want to validate all the correct detections, and reject all the false alarms, then we search N and N_2 so as to maximize

$$\arg\max_{N,N_2} P[(X \geqslant N_2) \cap (Y < N_2)] \quad (1)$$

We can note that the term N does not appear directly in the expression (1). However the probability distributions of X and Y depends on N, and so the term N will indirectly appear in the expression (1).

We can suppose that in each frame the object detection is a Bernouilli trial [9, p. 146], because there are only two possible outcomes: success (detection) or failure (non-detection), and the probabilities remain the same throughout the trials. As we suppose that all the detections are made independently from a frame to another, then the variable X represents the number of successes produced in a succession of N independent Bernouilli trials. So, the probability distribution of X is a Binomial distribution $B(N, p_d)$ where N is the number of trials and p_d is the probability of success. Then, for an integer i in $0..N$ we have

$$P(X = i) = C_N^i p_d^i q_d^{N-i} \quad (2)$$

where $C_N^i = \frac{N!}{i!(N-i)!}$ is the binomial coefficient, and $q_d = 1 - p_d$ is the probability of failure. In the same way, we can show that the probability distribution of Y is a Binomial distribution $B(N, p_f)$, where p_f is the probability to have a false alarm in a frame. If we note $q_f = 1 - p_f$, then the probability of the event $Y = i$ can be computed by

$$P(Y = i) = C_N^i p_f^i q_f^{N-i} \quad (3)$$

If we suppose that the variables X and Y are independent, which is realistic since the probability of correct detections and the probability of false alarms are independent, then using the equations (2) and (3) the expression (1) becomes

$$P[(X \geqslant N_2) \cap (Y < N_2)] = P(X \geqslant N_2)P(Y < N_2) \quad (4a)$$

$$= \left(\sum_{i=N_2}^{N} P(X = i)\right)\left(\sum_{i=0}^{N_2-1} P(Y = i)\right) \quad (4b)$$

$$= \left(\sum_{i=N_2}^{N} C_N^i p_d^i q_d^{N-i}\right)\left(\sum_{i=0}^{N_2-1} C_N^i p_f^i q_f^{N-i}\right) \quad (4c)$$

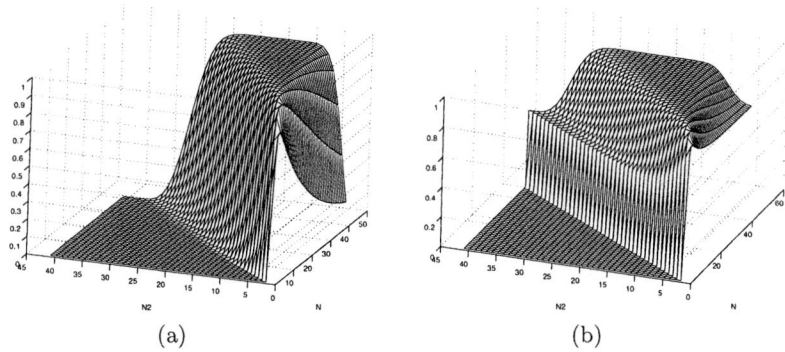

Fig. 2. (a) Graphical representation of probability (1), with $p_d = 0.7$ and $p_f = 0.05$. (b) Graphical representation of probability (10), with $p_d = 0.7$, $p_f = 0.05$ and $\alpha = 0.5$.

3 Optimal Values for N and N_2

The maximization of expression (4c) would be too complex to be analytically solved, because of the binomial expression presence: a derivation using N and N_2 as variables would lead to a very complex expression. A good way to easily solve it would be an approximation of the binomial distribution by a normal distribution, using the central limit theorem [9, p. 174]. However, in our case the number of samples would be too small for the approximation: for a binomial law $B(N,p)$, where N is the number of samples and p is the probability of appearance, approximations are practically used when $Np(1-p) > 10$, which would lead to a value $N > 40$ (because $p(1-p) \leq \frac{1}{4}$), whereas in our problem the value of N can be much lower.

So, we propose a numerical resolution for the maximization of the expression (4c). As N and N_2 can take discrete values in a limited range, we can find the maximum by an exhaustive search, for fixed p_d and p_f estimations. Fig. 2 gives a graphical example of produced results.

We can see on Fig. 2 that we do not have a global maximum, but a set of solutions, represented by a plateau of the distribution. In fact, all the points on the plateau correspond to different probabilities, but the difference is insignificant (less than 10^{-4} for the given parameters). So, we can consider that any of those points can be considered as a good approximation of the solution to the maximization of expression (1).

As far as we made the hypothesis that N has to be lower than the number of frames in a shot, the lower is N, the greater are the chances to verify this hypothesis. Moreover, the larger will be N, the longer will be the computational time. For those reasons, the minimal value of N on the plateau has to be preferred.

As the optimal solution relies on p_d and p_f, we could think that every application has its own optimal values for N and N_2. However, as the set of solutions is a plateau, we can find a solution which can be shared by various applications. In fact, we can note that when p_d decreases and p_f increases, the optimal values for N and N_2 increase. But this new solution is still on the plateau of detectors with highest p_d and lowest p_f. So, if we can find "critical" probabilities for p_d and p_f, i.e. probabilities p_{d_c} and p_{f_c} such as for all the considered detectors $p_d \geqslant p_{d_c}$ and $p_f \leqslant p_{f_c}$, then we can determine a single couple (N, N_2) for all the applications.

We made many experiments with face detectors (some of them are described in section 5), and we took $p_{d_c} = 0.8$ and $p_{f_c} = 0.1$ as limits for p_d and p_f, which provide $N = 11$ and $N_2 = 5$. The experiments description (cf section 5) will show how these values yield correct results for all the tested applications.

4 Recall Versus Precision

The maximization of expression (1) is motivated by the suppression of both false alarms and non-detections. However, in some applications, the importance associated to false alarms and non-detections can differ [6]. For instance, in video surveillance, some false alarms can be tolerated if no detection is missed. In order to reach a compromise between these two parameters, we propose another approach which uses the notions of *precision* and *recall*, in order to weight their influence. These notions are defined by

$$\text{recall} = \frac{\text{number of correct detected objects}}{\text{number of objects to find}} \tag{5}$$

$$\text{precision} = \frac{\text{number of correct detected objects}}{\text{number of detected objects}} \tag{6}$$

Then, a natural way to find the optimal values N and N_2 is, for a given α, to maximize the expression

$$\alpha \times \text{recall} + (1 - \alpha) \times \text{precision} \tag{7}$$

As we suppose that a given object is present in all the frames of the shot, then n frames of the shot infer n occurrences of the object. So, the recall can be computed by

$$\text{recall} = \frac{nP(X \geqslant N_2)}{n} \tag{8a}$$

$$= P(X \geqslant N_2) \tag{8b}$$

The detected objects are the correct detections plus the false alarms. So the precision is

$$\text{precision} = \frac{nP(X \geqslant N_2)}{n\left(P(X \geqslant N_2) + P(Y \geqslant N_2)\right)} \tag{9a}$$

$$= \frac{P(X \geqslant N_2)}{P(X \geqslant N_2) + P(Y \geqslant N_2)} \tag{9b}$$

$$= \frac{P(X \geqslant N_2)}{1 + P(X \geqslant N_2) - P(Y < N_2)} \tag{9c}$$

Table 1. Results with frame by frame detection ($N = 1$, $N_2 = 1$)

	p_d	p_f	Frames	Recall	Precision
Video 1	0.987	0.008	1409	0.987	0.983
Video 2	0.975	0.025	5845	0.975	0.975
Video 3	0.961	0.011	5276	0.961	0.989

The expansions for $P(X \geqslant N_2)$ and $P(Y < N_2)$ were given in equation (4). The maximization of expression (7) becomes

$$\arg\max_{N,N_2} \quad \alpha P(X \geqslant N_2) + (1 - \alpha)\frac{P(X \geqslant N_2)}{1 + P(X \geqslant N_2) - P(Y < N_2)} \qquad (10)$$

This expression is well suited to change the influence of recall or precision. We can note that for $\alpha = 0.5$, the results are nearly the same than with the maximization of expression (1). An example is given in Fig. 2, which shows that the set of solutions is similar for both expressions.

5 Experiments

In order to test the validity of those theoretical results, we made several tests on actual video data with a face detection algorithm. We took three video sequences of TV broadcasts, with contents providing different probabilities for p_d and p_f for the same detector. We only took sequences with exactly one face per frame. For our experiments, we consider that two faces are identical if they are roughly at the same location, with the same scale. The face detector that we used is the one proposed by Viola and Jones [10], freely available in the OpenCV library [11].

The first video sequence is extracted from a TV talk-show, the second one is extracted from a CNN news program, from the TRECVID 2004 corpus [12], and the third one from a televised debate. The results with a frame-by-frame detection are given in table 1.

Results with different values for N and N_2 are presented in Fig. 2. We can notice an improvement with the temporal smoothing on each video. The values $N = 11$ and $N_2 = 5$ computed in section 3 provide good results, that seem to be usable in a really general case. Fig. 4 shows the variation of expression (10) with N_2, for N fixed to 11: we verified that for both videos, $N_2 = 5$ is an optimal value when $N = 11$.

Both the number of false alarms and the number of non detections decrease when N and N_2 grow. Recall that we search the minimum values for N and N_2 such as the number of false alarms and non-detections stalls, as explained in section 3.

In order to have an exhaustive vision of the results with all the possible values for N and N_2, we ran the detection on the video 1 with all the possible values, with $N \leqslant 41$ (we made the hypothesis that we will never keep a value for N greater than 41). The comparison with theoretical values is illustrated by Fig. 3.

Table 2. Results with temporal smoothing, with various scales

Video	N	N_2	Non detection	False alarms	Recall	Precision
	1	1	18	24	0.987	0.983
1	3	2	16	7	0.987	0.995
	7	3	7	5	0.995	0.996
	11	5	2	2	0.998	0.998
	1	1	148	148	0.975	0.975
2	3	2	156	132	0.973	0.977
	7	3	125	150	0.978	0.974
	11	5	139	128	0.976	0.977
	1	1	204	58	0.961	0.989
3	3	2	167	32	0.968	0.993
	7	3	90	31	0.982	0.994
	11	5	85	27	0.983	0.995

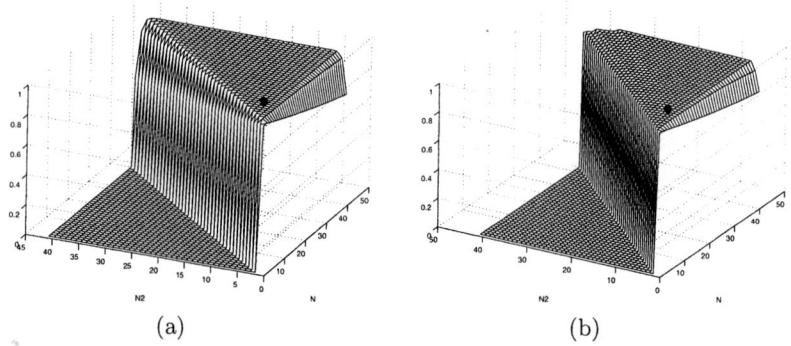

Fig. 3. Graphical representation of probability (1), for the video 1. (a) is the theoretical density, (b) is the true density computed with the data. The big black point represents the value of probability for $N = 11$ and $N_2 = 5$.

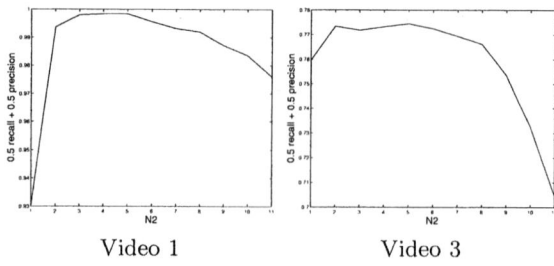

Fig. 4. Values of expression (10) with variation of N_2, with $N = 11$ and $\alpha = 0.5$

6 Conclusion

We proposed in this paper a system for improving results of a frame-by-frame detection of objects in video sequences. The thresholds are theoretically fixed for given probabilities of correct detection and false alarms of the static detector.

In this paper, we only dealt with the case where there is exactly one object per frame. The expression (1) remains correct for more than one object, or for zero object, but the expression related with the precision leads to a more complex expression, which then depends on the number of frames. Future works will lead to take into account in the model empty frames as well as frames with many objects.

References

1. Snoek, C., Worring, M.: Multimodal Video Indexing: A Review of the State-of-the-art. Multimedia Tools and Applications **25** (2005) 5–35
2. Jaffré, G., Crouzil, A.: Non-Rigid Object Localization from Color Model using Mean Shift. In: Proceedings of the IEEE International Conference on Image Processing. Volume 3., Barcelona, Spain(2003) 317–320
3. Mikolajczyk, K., Choudhury, R., Schmid, C.: Face detection in a video sequence - a temporal approach. In: Proceedings of the IEEE Conference on Computer Vision and Pattern Recognition. Volume 2., Kauai, Hawaii, USA(2001) 96–101
4. Isard, M., Blake, A.: CONDENSATION–Conditional Density Propagation for Visual Tracking. International Journal of Computer Vision **29** (1998) 5–28
5. Sivic, J., Schaffalitzky, F., Zisserman, A.: Efficient Object Retrieval From Videos. In: Proceedings of the 12th European Signal Processing Conference, Vienna, Austria(2004)
6. Ruiloba, R., Joly, P., Marchand-Maillet, S., Quénot, G.: Towards a Standard Protocol for the Evaluation of Video-to-Shots Segmentation Algorithms. In: Proceedings of the 1st Content-Based Multimedia Indexing Workshop, Toulouse, France (1999) 41–48
7. Jaffré, G., Joly, P.: Costume: A New Feature for Automatic Video Content Indexing. In: Proceedings of RIAO - Coupling approaches, coupling media and coupling languages for information retrieval, Avignon, France (2004) 314–325
8. Yang, M.H., Kriegman, D., Ahuja, N.: Detecting faces in images: A survey. IEEE Transactions on Pattern Analysis and Machine Intelligence **24** (2002) 34–58
9. Feller, W.: An Introduction to Probability Theory and Its Applications. Third edn. Volume 1. John Wiley & Sons (1968)
10. Viola, P., Jones, M.: Rapid Object Detection using a Boosted Cascade of Simple Features. In: Proceedings of the IEEE Conference on Computer Vision and Pattern Recognition, Kauai, Hawaii, USA(2001) 511–518
11. (OpenCV) http://www.intel.com/research/mrl/research/opencv/
12. Kraaij, W., Smeaton, A., Over, P., Arlandis, J.: TRECVID 2004 - an Introduction. In: Proceedings of the TRECVID 2004 Workshop, Gaithersburg, Maryland, USA(2004) 1–13

Multi-camera Person Tracking in a Cluttered Interaction Environment

Daniel Grest and Reinhard Koch

Multimedia Information Processing,
Christian-Albrechts-University Kiel, Germany
{grest, rk}@mip.informatik.uni-kiel.de

Abstract. Tracking the head and hand in real-time are important tasks for developing an intuitive interaction system. We present a system for robust probabilistic tracking that integrates face detection, face and hand color tracking and foot tracking in a uniform way by using particle filters. The advantages of different cues like motion, color and face detection are combined to yield robust 2D and 3D position estimates in spite of difficult varying lighting conditions and cluttered background. The system enables a user to navigate in the virtual scene by walking around and pointing towards objects by a simple hand gesture. The environment is a 3-sided CAVE with 1-sided stereo back projection.

1 Introduction

Interacting with virtual environments is becoming increasingly important. Spatially immersive displays offer a comprehensive way to visualize and surround a person with a virtual environment, e.g. the *blue-c* system [4]. For a correct perspective visualization the user's head position must be known at all times. The goal in our environment is to give the user the possibility to interact with the vir-

Fig. 1. The interaction area

tual environment in an intuitive way without the need to wear special hardware, but simply by hand gestures or by walking around. Tracking the user's head and hand positions in real-time is therefore a necessary task for developing an intuitive interaction system. We present a system which enables the user to navigate in a scene simply by walking around, allowing other persons to stand in the cluttered background. The image processing and the position estimation of the person's head and hand is based on probabilistic methods using Bayesian estimation. In addition we rely on standard hardware, i.e. low cost pan-tilt-zoom cameras. A general problem in interaction environments is, that the interaction area should be well lighted for better camera images with less noise, while the display screens should not receive any additional light. The compromise between both is usually a rather dimly lighted environment, as shown in figure (1), where the displayed scene is clearly visible in spite of the light from the ceiling.

Another problem to deal with is, that the lighting varies rapidly in our environment as a certain amount of light is reflected from the displays and changes when the displayed scene changes. A three sided cave gives the opportunity for spectators to observe the scene from the background. However, this gives another problem to deal with as the background becomes cluttered and incorporates additional persons, who may distract the face tracking.

A lot of work is devoted to tracking peoples' faces and hands in image sequences. Color cues are often used to localize or detect faces by their skin color. In [12] an overview of face detection methods is given, which also includes a part about skin color. Face tracking methods can basically be divided in Bayesian approaches and non-Bayesian. Bayesian approaches often include particle systems or Monte Carlo methods like [6,8]. A recent work on non-Bayesian face and hand tracking [1] uses hysteresis like thresholding of skin color to detect and track both hands and the face by assuming ellipsoidal projections in monocular images.

The main contribution of this work is the presentation of the system and the integration of different sensors within a unifying probabilistic framework. Due to the integration of multiple cues and the stochastic nature of the sensor fusion we achieve very robust position estimates. The system is designed to be easily extendable to increase the accuracy and robustness with more cameras or other cues.

2 System Overview

The interaction environment consists of a twelve square meters area, which is surrounded by 3 displays, as shown in figure 1. The central display is used for stereo visualization with polarized filters. The area is observed by three cameras, one static camera at the ceiling and two cameras able to pan, tilt and zoom, which are mounted at the left and right side of the center display. The data flow and the connections of all parts of the system are shown in figure 2. On the right side are the face and foot tracking modules for the image processing. The results are fused by the sensor fusion module. On the left and bottom side are the rendering and audio modules. The interaction server receives the head position and adapts the scene view accordingly. The scene data is sent to the display servers, which are connected to one projector each. The scene graph and the correct perspective visualization for a multi-display environment is part of the OpenSG library [9].

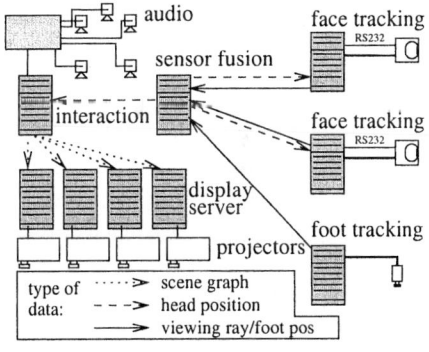

Fig. 2. Data transmission in the system

3 Foot Tracking

The user's foot positions are estimated based on a difference image algorithm with an adaptive threshold. This approach was already described in [3]. The camera mounted at the ceiling views the planar floor, therefore we can use four known points on the floor to compute a homography H_{floor} that relates ground floor scene coordinates and image coordinates. A segmented image with the user as foreground is computed by thresholding a difference image. To deal with the varying lighting conditions the threshold is adapted to the noise and the mean in the difference image. Therefore the segmentation is invariant to small changes in the image brightness. It can be assumed that the feet move on a plane, namely the floor, so the above mentioned homography H_{floor} from the camera coordinates to the floor coordinates is applied to get the position of the user's feet on the floor.

4 Probabilistic Combination of Measurements

Particle filters are used in this work for face tracking and in the sensor fusion module. For details we refer to Isard [6], who introduced particle filters to computer vision tracking tasks in 1998, or to [2] for an introduction. Particle filters estimate the conditional probability $p(\theta_t|M_t)$ that a system is in a specific state θ_t at time t given measurements M_t. The posterior $p(\theta_t|M_t)$ is calculated from the likelihood probability $p(M_t|\theta_t)$, which is the probability to make measurement M_t given that the system is in state θ_t, this probability will be called the measurement probability in this work. When applying a particle filter to a specific problem the sensible task is how to model the measurement probability and the transition probability (prediction), which reflects the system's motion model and the increase in uncertainty without measurements.

Combining different sensor measurements. In this work the probability that the system is in a specific state is assumed to be proportional to the probability that this position in the state space is occupied by the object of interest. Also we derive the inverse measurement model instead of directly taking $p(M|\theta_i)$. The inverse model gives the probability, that a specific state space belongs to the object or is occupied by that object. The measurement probabilities of our sensors are therefore designed to give a probability that the specific state space is occupied. That means if a sensor's measurement does not give any information for one position the probability should be 50%, while a probability of 95% indicates a very likely occupied state space and 10% means it is very likely unoccupied. For the probability that a specific state space is occupied we write $p(\phi[\theta])$ and that it is not occupied $p(n\phi[\theta])$. By definition $p(\phi[\theta]) + p(n\phi[\theta]) = 1$. In the latter $p(\phi)$ is written instead of $p(\phi[\theta])$ as only one position θ is discussed in this section.

To combine two measurements at the same position $p(M_t^1|\phi)$ and $p(M_t^2|\phi)$, we take the joint probability $p(\phi|M_t^1 \wedge M_t^2)$. We will give here only the resulting combining formula. For the derivation see the work about occupancy grids of Moravec, e.g. [7]. If we assume M_t^1 and M_t^2 to be statistically independent, the combining formula can be derived from Bayes' law:

$$f(\phi) = \frac{p(M_t^1|\phi)}{p(M_t^1|n\phi)} \frac{p(M_t^2|\phi)}{p(M_t^2|n\phi)} \frac{p(n\phi)}{p(\phi)} \quad \text{and} \quad p(\phi|M_t^1 \wedge M_t^2) = \frac{f(\phi)}{1 + f(\phi)} \quad (1)$$

where $p(\phi)$ is a possible known prior probability that ϕ is occupied by the object, in our work 50% for all states.

Modeling sensor characteristics. When combining different sensor measurements, whose measurement probabilities where designed separately, it was seen to be very practical to alter them in the following way. To model a sensor's ability of how well it can detect the object of interest in comparison to other competing sensors, the original measurement probability $p(M_t^i|\phi[\boldsymbol{\theta}_t]) \in [0..1]$ of sensor i is shifted and scaled:

$$\tilde{p}(M_t^i|\phi[\boldsymbol{\theta}_t]) = (1 - r_{fp}^i - r_{fn}^i)p(M_t^i|\phi[\boldsymbol{\theta}_t]) + r_{fn}^i \qquad (2)$$

The probability $\tilde{p}(M_t^i|\phi[\boldsymbol{\theta}_t])$ is in $[r_{fn}^i..(1 - r_{fp}^i)]$. The values r_{fn}^i, r_{fp}^i may be interpreted like the false positive and false negative detection rates of the specific sensor. If a sensor is more important or there is more belief into the measurements of a sensor these values will be lower than for a less important sensor.

5 Face Tracking

Face tracking in our system utilizes two separate methods, namely face detection [10] and a color histogram tracking algorithm [8]. The detection part is robust against lighting changes in brightness and color, but detects faces more reliably if seen directly from the front. To track the user's face, when he doesn't look in the direction of the camera, the detection part is combined with a color histogram tracking approach.

To detect faces we use an implementation from the OpenCV library [5], which comes with a trained classifier for faces and worked well within our environment. We optimized the detection method for the special application of tracking by applying the classifier not to the whole image in different sizes, but only to the particles' image position and sizes. This way we achieve a reduction in computation time of 50% while keeping the detection rate at the same level.

The color histogram tracking is similar to that of Perez [8]. We optimized the histogram calculations by the use of an integral histogram image.

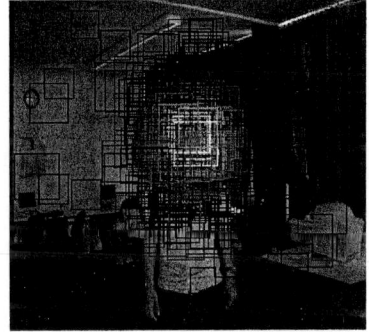

Fig. 3. Particle distribution

The integral histogram image holds at each pixel position the complete histogram from the top left corner of the image up to the pixel position. That way a histogram from (tlx, tly) to (brx, bry) can be computed by only for lookups in the integral histogram image. Also the integral histogram can be computed very efficiently by incrementally adding new pixels. See [11] for more details. The integral histogram image makes the computation almost invariant with respect to the number of particles. Without the integral histogram more than 500 particles will slow the computation down too much for real-time purposes. In [8] about 200 particles were used, while we can calculate 2000 histograms each frame and achieve more than 20 fps on a 3Ghz Pentium 4.

The combination of the color tracking and the face detection is just a matter of calculating the joint probability $p(\boldsymbol{\theta}_t|M_t^c \wedge M_t^d)$, where M_t^f is the color histogram measurement and M_t^d the detection. The false positive rate and the detection rate of the face detection method is principally known from the training of the cascade. However in our environment the detection quality is different, therefore we chose $r_{fp}^d = 0.02$

and $r_{fn}^d = 0.2$, the false negative rate, significantly higher. For the color histogram probabilities we estimated from experiments $r_{fp}^c = 0.1$ and $r_{fn}^c = 0.001$. The false positive rate is rather high, because all objects that have a skin color like appearance give significant responses. Comparing the detection and the color histogram values, it can be seen, that the detection method is given more importance for the ability to measure where the face is, while the the color histogram method is given more importance for the ability to measure where the face *not* is. The transition probability used in face tracking is a second order motion model, which involves the position and velocity of the object. The final estimate of the face's position is calculated as the weighted mean of the particles' positions. Using the known projection matrix of the camera a viewing ray is calculated and a distance to the face is derived from the face size in the image. Together with the weighted variance this is transmitted to the sensor fusion module.

The cameras follow the user by panning and tilting, such that the user is always visible in the middle part of the image. The cameras can not be moved constantly, as their response time is too high. It takes up to 250ms from sending a movement command until the cameras start moving. Therefore the cameras only move if the localized face leaves the innermost central image area, which is set to be half the image size.

Each time a camera moves, the particles have to be moved accordingly. To change the particles' positions, the camera's movement is predicted for each frame, calculated from the response time and the rotation speed of the camera.

6 Sensor Fusion and 3D Position Estimation

The basic idea of the sensor fusion is to combine different sensor data dependent on their certainties. For example a camera that views the face from the side, may be very likely distracted by the background clutter. To achieve this it is necessary to detect situations where one cue, e.g. the color histogram in the face tracking, gives no or multiple position estimates. Instead of explicitly describing these situations, we handle the advantages and disadvantages of different cues implicitly by the probabilistic approach described here. As the face trackers use a particle filter to evaluate the face position in the image, a value for the certainty of each face tracker is given by the weighted variance, that is transmitted together with the viewing ray to the fusion module.

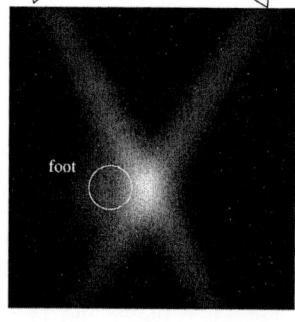

Fig. 4. 3D position probability

In the sensor fusion module the final 3D head position of the user is estimated by taking into account the measurements from the foot and face trackers. Again a particle filter is used to fuse the different measurements and evaluate a 3D position, which has following advantages:

- The accuracy of sensor readings is taken into account.
- The history of previous measurement's is accumulated over time by the Bayesian nature of the particle filter.
- Different sensors with arbitrary probability functions can be easily combined.
- Multiple hypotheses are tracked if sensors do not agree.

The sensor fusion module estimates a new 3D position each time new 2D estimates arrive. The viewing rays from the face trackers are modeled as a Gaussian distribution, that is extended very far in depth and has a variance perpendicular to the depth direction equal to the weighted variance estimated in the 2D face tracking module. The Gaussians for the viewing rays as seen from the top are visible in figure (4), which shows a slice of the probabilities space in 1.70m height, not a projection. The user's head was in about that height, therefore the rays are visible in the slice. Based on the 2D foot position it can be assumed, that the head is somewhere above it, so we model this measurement as a Gaussian that is extended in height and extended parallel to the floor according to the known inaccuracy of the foot tracker. The blob on the left in figure (4) is a slice of the Gaussian representing the foot position, which means that the left foot was detected by the foot tracker.

Additionally, the Gaussians, which model the single measurement probabilities from the face and foot trackers, are scaled and shifted to take the different characteristics of the sensors into account. The normalization factor of the Gaussian is altered, such that the resulting values are in $[0..1]$ for a user defined minimum variance. For higher variances, that reflect larger uncertainties, the Gaussian is shifted and scaled, such that the resulting values are centered around 0.5. This way we can apply the modeling of the sensor characteristics from section 4. We know from experiments, that the head position derived from the foot position is not very accurate, but it is very robust, that means the false positive and false negative rate is very low $r_f p = r_f n = 0.001$. This is basically because there is no clutter for the overhead camera to distract it, as it views the floor from the top. The face trackers' estimates are much more accurate, which is modeled by a very narrow Gaussian. On the other hand they sometimes get distracted by other objects in the background, therefore we set their $r_f p = r_f n = 0.1$.

7 Hand Tracking

An estimate of the user's hand position is necessary for interaction tasks like pointing gesture detection or arm movement. In addition to the face we track one of the user's hands by similar techniques. The hand is assumed to have the same skin color as the face. Therefore the median hue value of the detected face is taken for color blob tracking with a particle system.

The movement of people always includes movement of their hands (with regard to the world coordinate system). Therefore we also take into account motion cues, which stabilizes the tracking for cluttered background with skin colored objects. Both cues are scale and rotation invariant and are therefore well suited for fast and robust tracking.

The size of the projected hand in the image is assumed to be approximately half the size of the face in width and height. Therefore the state for the particle system is just the image position $\theta = (x, y)$. This assumption reduces the necessary amount of particles significantly in contrast to a histogram tracking method with variable sizes. The blob size is updated in each frame, depending on the detected face size. As the position of the face is known, it is omitted for the hand tracking. The measurement probability for the hand color blob tracking is the sum of similar colors over the assumed hand size in the image, while the similarity is a sigmoidal weighted Gaussian difference between the

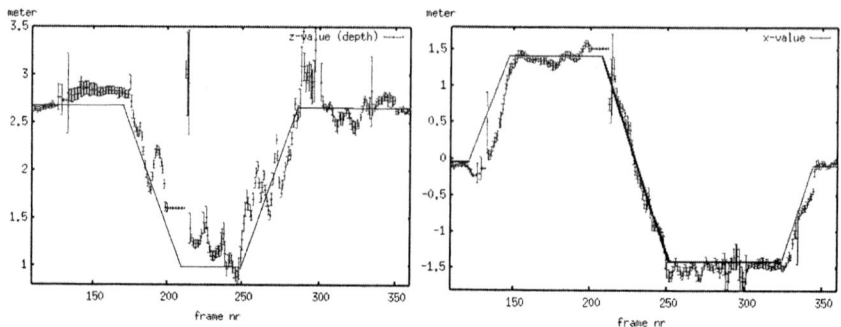

Fig. 5. Left:Measured z-position of the head (depth)   Right: Measured x-position

current pixel's hue value and the mean hue value of the skin color. The variance of the Gaussian is the assumed variance of the skin color and the sigmoid function is centered at an assumed minimum saturation.

The motion cue is computed as the difference of the current image with the mean of the last n images and summed over the expected hand size. Both probabilities are combined by calculating the joint probability as above.

The final 2D estimate of the hand's position is calculated as the weighted mean and is transmitted together with the weighted variance to the 3D position estimation module. The 3D position estimate is performed in the same way as for the head, but only from two sensors.

8 Results

The processing of the head position requires sensor data from the face and the foot tracker. New estimates arrive in about 20-25Hz, such that each 50ms a new 3D position can be estimated. The used image size is 320x240 for all modules. The rendering part is running asynchronously and its speed depends only on the scene complexity.

The user can move around in the virtual scene by walking to the edges of the interaction area. Standing at the front means moving forward, at the left side means rotating left etc. with a center area in the middle, which causes no movement. In our experiments we had about 20 persons, who didn't know the system, didn't know the system, navigating in the scene, while the other 19 were sitting in the background watching. Most of them understood the way of moving very fast without much explanation.

To measure the accuracy of the head position estimates a person had to place its head at three known positions in space. The first was standing straight, with the eyes at 1.78m, the second at 1.27m and the third at 0.98m. Figure (6) shows the estimated height with the weighted variance of the particle system,

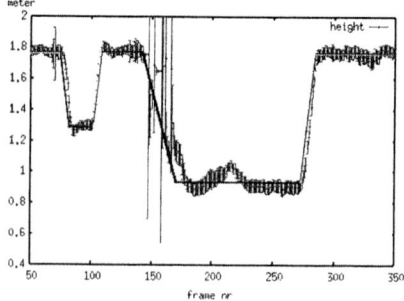

Fig. 6. Measured height (y-position)

which reflects the certainty of the estimated height. The ground truth was measured by hand, therefore an uncertainty of 3cm must be assumed. The height estimated by the system is within that uncertainty. Around frame 150, the variance gets very high, due to lost tracking of the face. About 30 frames later the system recovers and measures the height of 0.98m correctly.

Figure (5) shows the estimated distance to the front display and the estimated position parallel to the display. The head's position was measured during a sequence where the user followed a rectangular path beginning at 2.6m distance (frame 0-150), walking to the display up to one meter (frame 170-210), walking parallel to it (frame 210-250), back to 2.6m distance (frame 250-330) and finally to the center before the display at 2.6m distance. As can be seen in the figures, the depth estimation is not as accurate as in the other directions. This is due to the setup of the 3 cameras, which are all looking from the front into the interaction space.

In addition to the user's head position the position of one hand is estimated, while the other hand should not be visible. A pointing ray is computed as the difference between head and hand position and is projected into the virtual scene. The point where the ray is hitting the scene is marked with a yellow ball as shown in figure (1). Please note, that the pointing ray is not the extension of the arm, but the line of sight over the fingertip. However, due to the nature of the blob tracking method and the small number of 2D hand estimates (two) the estimated 3D hand position was seen to be too noisy and not accurate enough, while the hand was tracked very robustly in the images. Because the 3D position is triangulated only from two rays, small inaccuracies in a single estimate have large effects on the 3D estimate. For manipulation of small objects in the scene, the accuracy of the hand estimation is not good enough. An estimation of the fingertip position as seen from the top would overcome this problem.

9 Conclusion and Outlook

We presented a system for immersive exploration of a virtual scene, which tracks the user's feet, head and one hand by the use of standard cameras and standard lighting in real-time. The combination of different tracking and detection methods within a probabilistic sensor fusion framework leads to robust and accurate head estimation even under difficult lighting conditions and cluttered background, where other persons are allowed to watch the user, who can point towards specific objects in the scene by a simple hand gesture. Future work has to increase the accuracy of the depth estimation and of the hand position estimate, which can be easily achieved by adding additional cameras. For example an additional camera at the ceiling could provide such an estimate. The hand tracking should also be supported by at least one additional camera to increase the accuracy, such that object manipulation gets possible.

References

1. Antonis A. Argyros and Manolis I.A. Lourakis. Real time tracking of multiple skin-colored objects with a possibly moving camera. In *Proc. ECCV*, volume 3, pages 368–379, Prague, Czech Republic, May 2004. Springer-Verlag.

2. M. S. Arulampalam, S. Maskell, N. Gordon, and T. Clapp. A tutorial on particle filters for on-line nonlinear/non-gaussian bayesian tracking. In *IEEE Transactions on Signal Processing*, volume 50(2), pages 174–188, Feb. 2002.
3. Daniel Grest, Jan-Michael Frahm, and Reinhard Koch. A color similarity measure for robust shadow removal in real time. In *Proc. of VMV*, Munich, Germany, Nov. 2003.
4. Markus Gross and al. blue-c: A spatially immersive display and 3d video portal for telepresence. In *Proc. of SIGGRAPH*, pages 819–827, San Diego, USA, July 2003.
5. Intel. openCV: Open source Computer Vision library. http://www.sourceforge.net/opencv/.
6. Michael Isard and Andrew Blake. ICONDENSATION: Unifying low-level and high-level tracking in a stochastic framework. *Lecture Notes in Computer Science*, 1998.
7. Hans P. Moravec. Certainty grids for sensor fusion in mobile robots. In *Nato Asi Series F: Sensor Devices and Systems for Robotics*, volume 52. Springer Verlag, 1989.
8. P. Perez, C. Hue, J. Vermaak, and M. Gangnet. Color-based probabilistic tracking. In A. Heyden et al., editor, *Proc. of ECCV*, LNCS 2350, pages 661–675, 2002.
9. D. Reiners, G. Voss, M. Roth, and al. OpenSceneGraph library (OpenSG). www.opensg.org.
10. Paul Viola and Michael Jones. Rapid object detection using a boosted cascade of simple features. In *Proceedings IEEE Conf. on Computer Vision and Pattern Recognition*, 2001.
11. F. Woelk, I. Schiller, and R. Koch. An airborne bayesian color tracking system. Las Vegas, USA, June 2005.
12. Ming-Hsuan Yang, David J. Kriegman, and Narendra Ahuja. Detecting faces in images: A survey. *IEEE Transactions on Pattern Analysis and Machine Intelligence*, 24(1), Jan. 2002.

Improvement of a Person Labelling Method Using Extracted Knowledge on Costume

Gaël Jaffré and Philippe Joly

Université Paul Sabatier,
IRIT - Équipe SAMOVA,
31062 Toulouse Cedex 09,
France
{jaffre, joly}@irit.fr

Abstract. This paper presents a novel approach for automatic person labelling in video sequences using costumes. The person recognition is carried out by extracting the costumes of all the persons who appear in the video. Then, their reappearance in subsequent frames is performed by searching the reappearance of their costume. Our contribution in this paper is a new approach for costume detection, without face detection, that allows the localization of costumes even if persons are not facing the camera. Actually face detection is also used because it presents a very accurate heuristic for costume detection, but in addition in each shot mean shift costume localization is carried out with the most relevant costume when face detection fails. Results are presented with TV broadcasts.

1 Introduction

Our framework is the analysis of costume as a feature for video content indexing, and especially its automatic extraction. Some experiments made on automatic video summarization showed that the costume feature is one of the most significant clue for the identification of keyframes belonging to some given excerpt [1]. Authors justify this property by the fact that costumes are attached to character function in the video document. Costume is already used as an entity for audiovisual production description scheme [2,3], but only for a theoretical point of view, without automatic detection. Only recently an automatic application using costume was introduced [4].

However, the costume detection remains a problem, because at the moment it is only based on face detection, and so is dependant of the face detector and fails when the faces are too small in the frame. We can find papers in literature where clothes are used to help the recognition [5,6], but in each of them the costume detection is based on face detection. Our contribution in this paper is a new approach for costume detection, without face detection, that allows the localization of costumes even if persons are not facing the camera. Actually face detection is also used because it presents a very accurate heuristic for costume

Fig. 1. Classification of character framings

detection, but in addition in each shot, when face detection fails, mean shift costume localization is carried out with the most relevant costume.

In section 2 we introduce the application of person labelling using costumes. Section 3 presents the costume detection algorithm. Results are presented in section 4.

2 Person Labelling Using Costume

The goal of this application is to automatically create an index which gives, for each frame, all the persons who are present. The application described in this paper is automatic: the first time a character appears, it is added in a costume database with an automatic label. At the end of the processing, the user can update the index by giving a real name to each label.

2.1 Concepts of Shot and Character Framing

In this application, we use the notion of shot. It roughly corresponds to a set of continuous frames taken with an uninterrupted recording of a video camera. As we work on video sequences extracted from TV talk shows, there are only slight camera motions during a same shot, and no person appear or disappear during a shot, the number of persons remains constant. So, in a same shot we can run the costume detection only with some frames, and generalize the results with the remaining frames. Fig. 2 presents examples of propagations.

We call "character framing" the significance of the person according to his position and size in the frame. We considered three classes of framing: the first one corresponds to a character who is centered, and has a sufficient size to be the most important visual interest in the frame. The second one corresponds to characters who are important components of the frame, among several others. The third one corresponds to background characters, or characters who are not easily identifiable. Fig. 1 shows an example. This classification will be significant for the shot propagation (section 2.2), and for the experiment part (section 4).

Fig. 2. Propagation of person detections. The white and black boxes represent the automatic detection provided by the face detector. For each color, the dark box represents the validated faces, the others are the propagated faces. Actually the faces are not directly propagated, this example is only here to better understand the principle, in our real application we only propagate the labels of the detected characters.

2.2 Algorithm of the Application

The goal of the application is to detect and recognize all the persons that appear in each frame. The following algorithm is applied in each shot of the video.

The first step is the detection of faces in the first frames of the shot. Character framing have here an interest: if a first class face is detected (at the moment we consider a centered face as a first class face), then we consider that we have detected the only useful information, so we stop the detection, and propagate (backward and forward) the results to all the frames of the shot. If no face is detected, or only second or third class faces, the search goes on within next frames, because we consider that we could have missed some faces. If this new search does not provide any face, then we consider that the face detector failed.

If faces are detected at any step, then the costume of each person is extracted (from the frame where the face was detected) according to the face locations. The features of each costume are extracted, and compared to the ones of the database. If a costume corresponds, then the person wearing it is recognized. Else, the new costume is added in the database with an automatic label. In both cases this person is considered as present in all the frames of the shot.

When the face detector fails, we add a new step, which is costume localization without face detection. This step will be detailed in section 3.3. With this additional step we can deal with the frames where the face is not detected. Due to computational time, this detection will be carried out in only one frame. If no costume is detected in spite of this step, we finally consider that no character is present in the shot.

2.3 Shot Boundary Detection

Shot boundary detection can be a challenging task, if the boundaries are gradual. However as our application process only TV talk-shows, we do not have the problem of gradual transitions, because the transitions have at most two frames, so a very simple detector is sufficient. Moreover, we need a very fast preprocessing tool, providing exploitable results with a minimum cost of the system resources, in order to keep some for the costume processing, and be able to have real-time processing on a modest computer.

We subsample the frame with a ratio of eight (for both rows and columns), and we take only one channel out of three. Then, we compare each pixel to the same pixel in the previous frame. We consider that the two frames belong to different shots if the mean difference is over a threshold. Under this threshold we consider that the two frames are in the same shot. This algorithm allows exploitable results on our kind of contents, with a very fast processing.

3 Costume Detection

We can find many methods in literature to detect people presence in images, however there are all focused on some special content. First, pedestrian detection focuses on detecting persons, but the context of the applications is often for future driving assistance systems [7], with specific conditions. Some applications dedicated to surveillance allow the detection of persons with different scales [8], but under restricting hypothesis, like fixed video cameras. These methods would not be usable for our application, because our video corpus contains various framings, such as close shots, as well as global views, with mobile cameras. Moreover, it is very common that the whole body does not appear in the frame, just the upper part, which is problematic for these methods.

3.1 Face-Based Costume Detection

Recently, face was used as a visual clue for person detection [4,6]. The main idea is the use of face detection algorithms to detect human presence. Nowadays, face detection is not yet a solved problem, but the existing algorithms produce good results when the input images are not very complex, which is often the case in our corpus of TV broadcasts.

Thus, the first step of our costume detection is the run of a face detection algorithm, so as to detect the different possible characters who are present in the current frame, and their approximate position and scale. Then, the costume of each character is extracted from the image according to the location and the scale of his face.

There are many methods for face detection in literature (see [9] for a recent review), but we do not use a specific one. We intend to make an application which is independent of the face detector, when this one is able to produce some results of at least a given minimal quality. We used the method presented in [10], because a fast implementation is available in the Intel library OpenCV [11].

The costumes are extracted according to the localization and the scale of the detected faces. At the moment, we estimate the costume by the area under the face. The size of this area is proportional to the one of the face. In our examples, we used a width size of 2.3 times the one of the face, and for the height size a ratio of 2.6. We chose experimentally these coefficients by taking the ones which give the best fitting of the box in our learning images.

3.2 Face Detection Improvement

The algorithm of costume localization is based upon face detection. However, frame by frame face localization introduce many false alarms, due to some noise present in the data. Only one false detection in a frame is enough to involve a false alarm on costume detection.

In order to reduce these false detections, we must exploit the properties of a video sequence by using a temporal approach. For each frame, we detect all the faces using a static approach. Then, we take a temporal window (subsequence) of $2N+1$ frames. For each candidate face, we count its number of occurrences in the N previous frames, and in the N next frames. Recall that all these detections are made independently. Then, we keep a candidate face if it appears at least N_2 times in this subsequence. In our application, we took $N = 2$ (which leads to a subsequence of 5 frames) and $N_2 = 4$.

We consider that two detected faces correspond to the same face if there are roughly at the same location. The position parameters may slightly vary considering camera works or character motions. So, a small variation of these parameters is borne to take into account these effects. Moreover, to avoid the detection of faces in dissolves we consider that two faces correspond to the same face if the costumes detected from these faces are also identical (in terms of features, cf section 3.4).

3.3 When the Face Detector Fails

Even if face detection is robustified (cf. section 3.2), there are many frames where the face is occluded, where the person is shot from behind, or where the face detection fails. In order to deal with the case where the persons are not detected using face detection, we added a costume detection step which is not based on face detection.

Costume Classification. Unlike face-based costume detection, we do not have any prior information about the costume location in the frame. So, searching for each model of costume can be very computationally expensive. In order to reduce this cost, we will only search for the costume which is the most likely to be in the frame.

We suppose that if a costume is present in a frame with the same scale, then its histogram h_c is included in the histogram of the frame h_f. So, the histogram intersection [12] with non-normalized histograms would provide as a result the costume histogram h_c

$$\sum_{i=1}^{n} \min\left(h_c^i, h_f^i\right) = \sum_{i=1}^{n} h_c^i \qquad (1)$$

So as to deal with the case where the costume does not have the same scale in the frame, and to obtain a fractional match value between 0 and 1, the intersection is normalized by the number of pixels in the model histogram, and compared to the sum of the costume histogram. So for each costume the coefficient $C_{h_f}(h_c)$ is computed by

$$C_{h_f}(h_c) = \frac{\sum_{i=1}^{n} h_c^i - \sum_{i=1}^{n} \min\left(h_c^i, h_f^i\right)}{\sum_{i=1}^{n} h_c^i} \qquad (2)$$

Each costume is tested to see if its colors are present in the frame, and then the costumes of the database are sorted by relevant color. Then, we only search in the frame the localization of the most relevant costume.

Costume Localization. Now we have a unique model of costume to find in the frame, the problem reduces to detect its presence or not in the frame, and if so to find its location. To quickly find its location using only its color histogram, we use the object detection approach presented in [13]: using the costume histogram, an image of weights is created from the frame, which represents the repartition of the most probable pixels to be part of the object. This image of weights is called backprojected image, and is based on the ratio histogram [12] $r_k = \min\left(\frac{h_c}{h_f}, 1\right)$.

Since the ratio histogram emphasizes the predominant colors of the costume while diminishing the presence of clutter and background colors, the backprojected image represents a spatial measure of the costume presence.

From this image of weights, the problem is to find if there is a "group" of likely pixels, and if so to detect it. Considering this image as a cluster in $\mathbb{R}^2$, the "group" of pixels can be considered as the cluster global mode. Then, a statistical method, the mean shift procedure [14], is used to detect it.

If we note $\{\mathbf{x}_i\}_{i=1...n}$ the set of points of the cluster, and $w(\mathbf{x}_i)$ the weight associated to pixel $\mathbf{x}_i$, then the mean shift vector for the point $\mathbf{x}$ is computed by

$$M_h(\mathbf{x}) = \frac{\sum_{\mathbf{x}_i \in S_h(\mathbf{x})} w(\mathbf{x}_i) \mathbf{x}_i}{\sum_{\mathbf{x}_i \in S_h(\mathbf{x})} w(\mathbf{x}_i)} - \mathbf{x} \qquad (3)$$

where $S_h(\mathbf{x})$ is the sphere centered on $\mathbf{x}$, of radius h and containing $n_\mathbf{x}$ data points. More information about the mean shift procedure and mean shift vector can be found in [14]. The mean shift vector has the direction of the gradient of the density estimate at $\mathbf{x}$. The mean shift procedure is obtained by successive computations of the mean shift vector $M_h(\mathbf{x})$, and translation of the sphere $S_h(\mathbf{x})$ by $M_h(\mathbf{x})$. The procedure is guaranteed to converge [14] to a local mode. Actually, as costumes do not have the same size for height and width, we use a scale $h = (h_x, h_y)$, with $h_x > h_y$, as presented in Fig. 3.

Mean shift iterations guarantee convergence to a local mode, but we are only interested in the global mode. In order to find the global mode, we take many initializations in the frame (cf Fig. 3), and then we only keep the convergence point which brings the largest density. The density is estimated using the Parzen window [15, ch. 4]

$$\hat{f}(\mathbf{x}) = \frac{1}{nh^2} \sum_{i=1}^{n} K\left(\frac{\mathbf{x} - \mathbf{x}_i}{h}\right) \qquad (4)$$

with an Epanechnikov kernel [14]

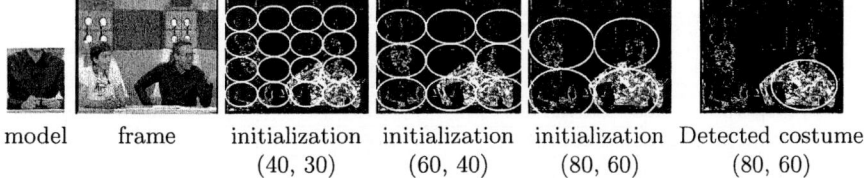

| model | frame | initialization (40, 30) | initialization (60, 40) | initialization (80, 60) | Detected costume (80, 60) |

Fig. 3. Mean shift costume detection. The two first frames are the input data. The two next represent the initialization of the mean shift procedure, with the corresponding scale (h_x, h_y). The last frame is the detected costume, with the optimal scale.

$$K_E(\mathbf{x}) = \begin{cases} \frac{2}{\pi}(1 - \|\mathbf{x}\|^2) & \text{if } \|\mathbf{x}\| < 1 \\ 0 & \text{otherwise} \end{cases} \quad (5)$$

The Epanechnikov kernel was chosen because it was used to derivate the mean shift vector in equation 3 (justifications can be found in [13]).

To give up this prior information about the scale h of the costume, we run the detector many times with various scales, as shown in Fig. 3. Then, we keep the scale that provides the largest density.

Use of this Blind Approach. Using mean shift detection in addition to face-based detection can be computationally expensive if these two approaches are used in each frame, because it is carried out with various scales and several initializations. As we need mean shift detection only when the face detector fails, we apply it only one time in each shot, when the face detector provides no face in the whole shot. Thus, the processing time for blind detection is insignificant relatively to the processing time of a whole shot.

Table 1. Recognition rates for both videos

Video	Class	Number of characters	Face-based approach	+ Blind approach
1	1	19 692	18 587 (94.39%)	18 659 (94.75 %)
	2	34 978	2 226 (6.34%)	2 865 (8.19 %)
	3	56 857	3 755 (6.60 %)	3 755 (6.60 %)
2	1	5 588	4 897 (87.63%)	5 005 (89.57 %)
	2	14 797	6 529 (44.12%)	6 529 (44.12 %)
	3	21 539	1 129 (5.24 %)	1 129 (5.24 %)

3.4 Similarity Measure

The feature that we use is a three-dimensional RGB color histogram. The similarity measure used to compare histograms is the Bhattacharyya coefficient, which is closely related to the Bayes error [16, p. 38]. If we note $\hat{q} = \{\hat{q}_u\}_{u=1...m}$ and $\hat{p} = \{\hat{p}_u\}_{u=1...m}$ the color histograms of the two costumes (m is the number of bins) the Bhattacharyya coefficient can be estimated by [17] $\rho(\hat{p}, \hat{q}) = \sum_{u=1}^{m} \sqrt{\hat{p}_u \hat{q}_u}$. The coefficient interval is the real interval $[0, 1]$. A value of 1 means a perfect match, whereas a value of 0 means a mismatch.

Table 2. Recognition errors for the first video. For the number of miss-classified characters, the percentage is relative to the total number of detected persons.

		Face-based approach	+ Blind approach
Video 1	false alarms	329	329
	misclassified characters	0.56%	0.54%
Video 2	false alarms	514	593
	misclassified characters	1.44%	1.43%

4 Experiments

Experiments have been carried out on different video sequences extracted from TV programs, especially TV talk-shows. We present here numerical results for two different TV talk-shows. The format of the videos is MPEG1, with a frame size of 352 × 288. The first video has a duration of thirty minutes, and contains 46 680 frames. The second one lasts twelve minutes, and has 18 243 frames. We manually indexed these video sequences: for each frame, we noted all the persons that appear as well as their character framing.

We compared the results for the traditional approach, only based on face detection, with our blind approach. Computational time are roughly the same for both methods: the frames were processed at a mean rate of 37 fps for the first video and 30 fps for the second one. Results are summed up in tables 1 and 2.

5 Conclusion

We proposed in this paper an approach for automatic person labelling in video sequences using costumes. We showed that on our kind of content the clothes of a person are relevant for recognition. This approach for costume detection, which is not based on face detection, allows a fast localization of the costumes when the face detector fails. We showed that results are improved when this blind approach is used in addition to face-based costume detection. However, the face-based detector is still essential, because the blind approach can only find costumes of the database, it cannot find new ones.

Moreover, we would like to significantly improve the results for the second and third class characters. A separation of the clothes in different parts (tie, jacket, hat, trousers,...) would perform a better description of the costumes, and could be used to improve the detection.

References

1. Yahiaoui, I.: Construction automatique de résumés vidéos. Thèse de doctorat, Télécom Paris, France (2003)
2. Nack, F.: AUTEUR: The Application of Video Semantics and Theme Representation for Automated Film Editing. PhD thesis, Lancaster University, UK(1996)

3. Bui Thi, M.P., Joly, P.: Describing video contents: the semiotic approach. In: Proceedings of the 2nd Content-Based Multimedia Indexing Workshop, Brescia, Italy(2001) 259–266
4. Jaffré, G., Joly, P.: Costume: A New Feature for Automatic Video Content Indexing. In: Proceedings of RIAO - Coupling approaches, coupling media and coupling languages for information retrieval, Avignon, France (2004) 314–325
5. Lerdsudwichai, C., Abdel-Mottaleb, M.: Algorithm for Multiple Faces Tracking. In: IEEE International Conference on Multimedia & Expo, Baltimore, Maryland, USA(2003)
6. Zhai, Y., Chao, X., Zhang, Y., Javed, O., Yilmaz, A., Rafi, F., Ali, S., alatas, O., Khan, S., Shah, M.: University of Central Florida at TRECVID 2004. In: Proceedings of the TRECVID 2004 Workshop, Gaithersburg, Maryland, USA(2004) 217–224
7. Broggi, A., Bertozzi, M., Chapuis, R., Chausse, F., Fascioli, A., Tibaldi, A.: Pedestrian Localization and Tracking System with Kalman Filtering. In: Proceedings of the IEEE Intelligent Vehicles Symposium, Parma, Italy(2004) 584–589
8. Yang, H.D., Lee, S.W.: Multiple Pedestrian Detection and Tracking based on Weighted Temporal Texture Features. In: Proceedings of the 17th International Conference on Pattern Recognition. Volume 4., Cambridge, UK(2004) 248–251
9. Yang, M.H., Kriegman, D., Ahuja, N.: Detecting faces in images: A survey. IEEE Transactions on Pattern Analysis and Machine Intelligence **24** (2002) 34–58
10. Lienhart, R., Maydt, J.: An Extended Set of Haar-like Features for Rapid Object Detection. In: Proceedings of the IEEE International Conference on Image Processing. Volume 1., Rochester, New York, USA(2002) 900–903
11. (OpenCV) http://www.intel.com/research/mrl/research/opencv/
12. Swain, M., Ballard, D.: Color Indexing. International Journal of Computer Vision **7** (1991) 11–32
13. Jaffré, G., Crouzil, A.: Non-Rigid Object Localization from Color Model using Mean Shift. In: Proceedings of the IEEE International Conference on Image Processing. Volume 3., Barcelona, Spain(2003) 317–320
14. Comaniciu, D., Meer, P.: Mean Shift: A Robust Approach Toward Feature Space Analysis. IEEE Transactions on Pattern Analysis and Machine Intelligence **24** (2002) 603–619
15. Duda, R., Hart, P., Stork, D.: Pattern Classification. Second edn. Wiley-Interscience (2001)
16. Andrews, H.: Introduction to Mathematical Techniques in Pattern Recognition. Wiley-Interscience (1972)
17. Aherne, F., Thacker, N., Rockett, P.: The Bhattacharyya Metric as an Absolute Similarity Measure for Frequency Coded Data. Kybernetika **32** (1997) 1–7

Face Modeling and Adaptive Texture Mapping for Model Based Video Coding

Kamil Yurtkan[1], Hamit Soyel[1], Hasan Demirel[1], Hüseyin Özkaramanlı[1], Mustafa Uyguroğlu[1], and Ekrem Varoğlu[2]

[1] Advanced Technologies Research and Development Institute,
Eastern Mediterranean University, Gazimağusa, Mersin 10 Turkey
[2] Computer Engineering Department, Eastern Mediterranean University,
Gazimağusa, Mersin 10 Turkey
{kamil.yurtkan, hamit.soyel}@emu.edu.tr

Abstract. 3D facial synthesis has been frequently used in model based video coding applications and became popular in various multimedia applications. In this paper a 3D face model, its adaptation algorithm and a texture mapping method using two orthogonal photos are presented to solve several 3D estimation problems in model based video coding. We are successfully estimating the frames between the front and the side views of the face. The experimental results show that the proposed Rotation Adaptive Texture Mapping (RATM) technique increases the visual quality of the synthesized face during rotations of the head, while achieving a PSNR value up to 33dB.

Keywords: 3D face model, model adaptation, texture mapping, facial synthesis, model based video coding, video compression.

1 Introduction

Model based video coding techniques have attracted considerable interest in multimedia applications such as teleconferencing and videophones where bandwidth considerations are of utmost importance. Very low bit rate coding is achieved by first generating the 3D model of the face to be coded in image sequences, and then coding the model parameters for the rest of the image sequence. Thus, 3D face synthesis plays a crucial role in the visual quality of the system.

In 1983, Forchheiner proposed a model-based videophone system that uses a computer-animated head model for the transmission of head and shoulder scenes [1],[2]. Since then, many researches have worked on this concept [3-6]. One of the most important works done is the face model created by Stromberg. This model, named CANDIDE, and its versions are very popular in many research labs [8]. But the problem of estimating 3D information from 2D images still remains to be solved.

This paper presents a new face model proposed for the model based video coding. The proposed face model is compatible with MPEG-4 and consists of about 8000 vertices. In addition, an algorithm is presented for the adaptation of face model to a given face. Finally, a texturing method, Rotation Adaptive Texture Mapping

(RATM), is proposed to solve the problem of estimating 3D information from two orthogonal 2D face images. The developed model along with the proposed RATM approach produces encouraging results by achieving PSNR values up to 33dB.

2 The Generic Model

It is a well known fact that, different people have the same basic face structure, such as the eyes, nose and mouth. Each decoder under MPEG-4 has its own face model called "generic model". However, everyone has different facial features that distinguish one from the others. A generic model should be a structural one for facial animation.

According to MPEG-4 standard specifications, a human head is a synthetic visual object whose representation is based on VRML standard [7]. Our generic model shown in Fig. 1 was implemented using 3DMAX and modified to conform to MPEG-4. Currently, the Face Model includes a group of five standard-conforming objects (skin, eyes, pupils, teeth, tongue) up to 8,000 vertices and 13,500 triangles in total. In MPEG-4 Calibration profile generic model adaptation to the prototype person is required. According to MPEG-4, there are 84 feature points defined on a neutral face that provide referenced space for defining facial animation parameters (FAPs). These points are sufficient for identifying the proper shape of a facial model. Feature points are divided into several groups such as lips, eyes, mouth and so on.

The human face possesses specific regions that are dedicated for communication of information and expression on emotions obviously these regions need to be well defined. In this study we concentrated our efforts on giving a great level of detail in the most expressive regions of the generic model. In order to have more control on the polygonal structure, we subdivided the generic model surface into specific areas which corresponds to the feature points affected by the FAPs. This subdivision was necessary to define and control the displacements of polygonal vertexes induced by the FAPs applied in various feature points. Subdivision into specific areas and their classification are shown in Fig. 2.

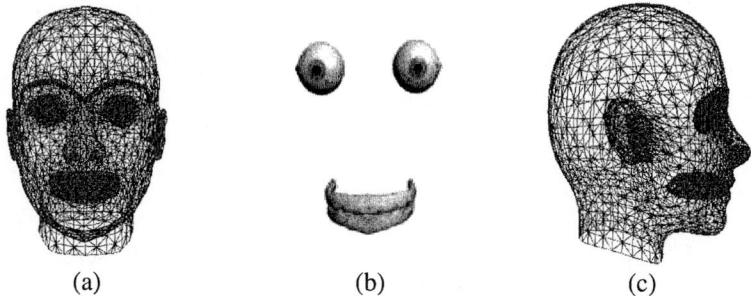

Fig. 1. (a) Generic model, front grid view (b) internal anatomic components and (c) generic model, side grid view

Fig. 2. Subdivision of generic model into specific areas, front and side views

3 Image-Based Model Adaptation

The generic model undergoes a model matching procedure to adapt the 3D model parameters according to the input images. Our adaptation algorithm takes 22 facial features from the two orthogonal pictures and is based on the transformation of distances between feature points, from the neutral model domain to image domain. As expected the number of facial feature points improves the adaptation greatly in terms of the exactness of the face shape. However, increasing the number of feature points also increases the computational complexity of feature points' edition. Therefore there is a tradeoff between the number of feature points and editing time. The 22 feature points chosen from the feature points defined in MPEG-4 are shown in Fig. 3.

To make the head size of side and front views equal, we measure the heights of the face in two views. Then we use scale transformation to normalize the two pictures.

After editing the feature points, the whole size of the individual head is estimated. The height and the width are determined by the front view using points 1, 2 and 3, 4 Fig. 3a respectively, and the depth is determined by the side view using points 20,22 Fig. 3b. Then the corresponding distances on the neutral face model are transformed in to the image domain and the necessary coefficients are calculated to match the input image features accordingly. The adaptation process continues with the updates

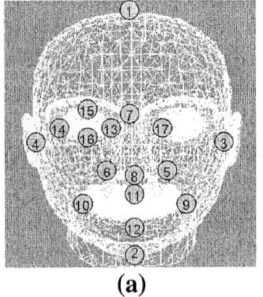 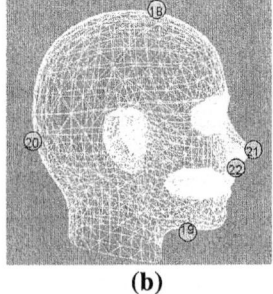

Fig. 3. (a) Feature points from front view (b) Feature points from side view

of the coordinates for the critical regions of the face, which are the nose, mouth and eyes. The width and the height of the nose are estimated from the front view using points 5, 6 and 7, 8 respectively; the depth of the nose is estimated from the side view using points 21,22 . The position of the nose with respect to the eyes is calculated using points 8 and 17. The vertices are shifted along y-axis to place the nose properly on the face. A similar approach is followed for the adaptation of mouth and eyes except the calculation of the depth and displacement of eyes as they are fixed in the face position.

Let the 3D wire frame model be represented by triangles, $T_m(V_{m,1}, V_{m,2}, V_{m,3})$, $m = 1...n$, where $V_{m,1}, V_{m,2}, V_{m,3}$ are the vectors representing three vertices of the triangle T_m, and n indicates the total number of triangles in Eqs. (1-2).

$$3D\_M = \sum_{m=0}^{n} T_m(V_{m,1}, V_{m,2}, V_{m,3}) \tag{1}$$

$$V_{m,i} = [\ V_{m,i_x} \quad V_{m,i_y} \quad V_{m,i_z}\ ]^T \tag{2}$$

For the regional adaptation, consider the overall 3D model as in four parts consisting of triangles: Silhouette, nose, mouth and eyes. After subdivision, Eq. (1) takes the form in Eq. (3), where Ts_i, Tn_i, To_i and Te_i stands for triangles of silhouette, nose, mouth and eyes respectively. The number of triangles for silhouette, nose, mouth and eyes are represented by n1, n2, n3 and n4 respectively.

$$\sum_{i=0}^{n} T_i = \sum_{i=0}^{n1} Ts_i + \sum_{i=0}^{n2} Tn_i + \sum_{i=0}^{n3} To_i + \sum_{i=0}^{n4} Te_i \tag{3}$$

$$n = n1 + n2 + n3 + n4 \tag{4}$$

$$V'_{m,i} = \begin{bmatrix} V'_{m,i_x} \\ V'_{m,i_y} \\ V'_{m,i_z} \end{bmatrix} = \begin{bmatrix} \alpha & 0 & 0 \\ 0 & \beta & 0 \\ 0 & 0 & \gamma \end{bmatrix} \begin{bmatrix} V_{m,i_x} \\ V_{m,i_y} \\ V_{m,i_z} \end{bmatrix} + \begin{bmatrix} 0 \\ I_m \\ 0 \end{bmatrix} \tag{5}$$

While transforming the model feature points into image domain, the coefficients, α, β, γ and I_m are calculated for adapting silhouette, nose, mouth and eyes explicitly. α, β and γ are used to scale the regions of the model to match the input image features and I_m is used to shift the y-axis positions of the mouth and nose relative to eyes as shown in Eq. (5). The overall transformation algorithm used is described below.

```
READ facial feature point coordinates

NORMALIZE two orthogonal images

TRANSFORM model feature points into image domain

CALCULATE error between model feature points and image feature
points, generate coefficients for silhouette adaptation and adapt
silhouette

CALCULATE error between model feature points and image feature
points, generate coefficients for nose adaptation and adapt nose

CALCULATE error between model feature points and image feature
points, generate coefficients for mouth adaptation and adapt mouth

CALCULATE error between model feature points and image feature
points, generate coefficients for the adaptation of the eyes and
adapt eyes

FIX nose position according to the position of the eyes

FIX mouth position according to the position of the eyes

FIX the position of frontal texture frame according to the position
of the eyes on the adapted frame

FIX the position of side texture frame according to the position of
the chin position on the adapted frame

SCALE the resultant textured frame
```

Fig. 4. Adaptation algorithm used to modify 3D model to fit the facial features extracted

4 Rotation Adaptive Texture Mapping (RATM)

As discussed in the previous section, the generic mapping of the face model results in the 3D wire frame model representing the shape of a head. Texture mapping should be applied to the model in order to give a more realistic view. Otherwise it can be a synthetic texture for a talking head application. Alternatively, a texture map obtained by two orthogonal images can be used to give more realistic appearance to the rendered frame.

The Proposed RATM method overcomes the deformations in the texture due to rotations of the head by moving the side image texture along the whole textured frame as illustrated in Fig. 5. For the rotation adaptation, the two orthogonal texture maps, which are the frontal and side images, are combined dynamically. Here the aim is to estimate the face textures during the rotations. This is done by starting with the frontal image and moving the side image across the whole frame until the side image captures the whole texture.

RATM method results in very realistic face images for the front and side views since the information used at these views for texture mapping is obtained from the original front and side images.

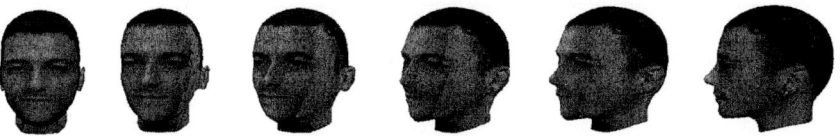

Fig. 5. A half rotation and the corresponding texture maps of the 3D face model

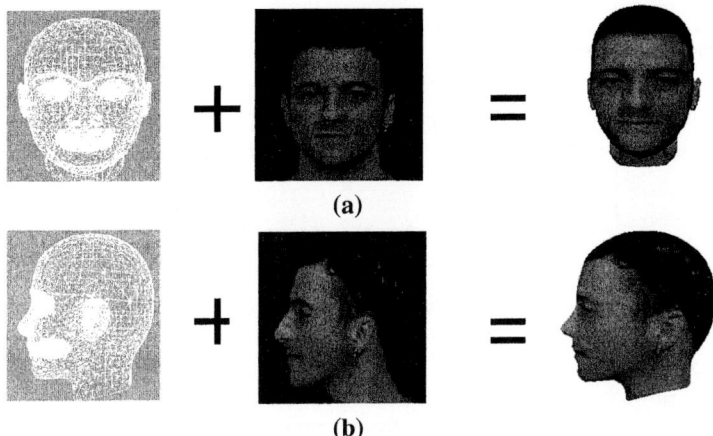

Fig. 6. Front and side profile views of the Rotation Adaptive textured frame

5 Performance Analysis

The performance of our approach is analyzed and the results are shown for a given person's facial orthogonal images with resolution of 256 by 256 pixels per view. The resolution of the generic facial model is about 8000 vertices in the whole 3D wire frame model. Fig. 6 shows the results of the matching from the generic model to the individual orthogonal photos. Fig. 7 shows the generated 3D individual face in different views of a half rotation. It can be clearly observed that the appearance of the generated individual 3D model looks natural and has a good visual effect on the human eyes. Corresponding Peak Signal to Noise Ratio (PSNR) values calculated for a half rotation are given in Fig. 8.

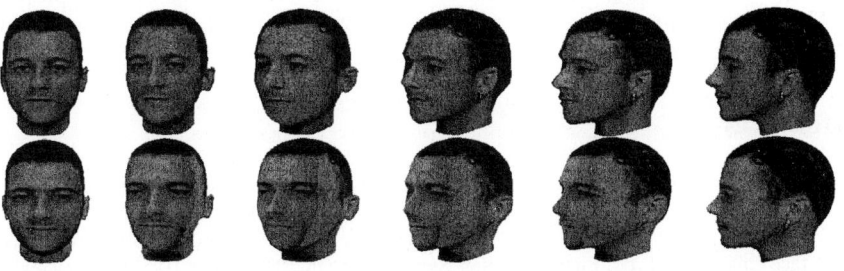

Fig. 7. The real image sequence (1st row) and the resultant adapted frames (2nd row)

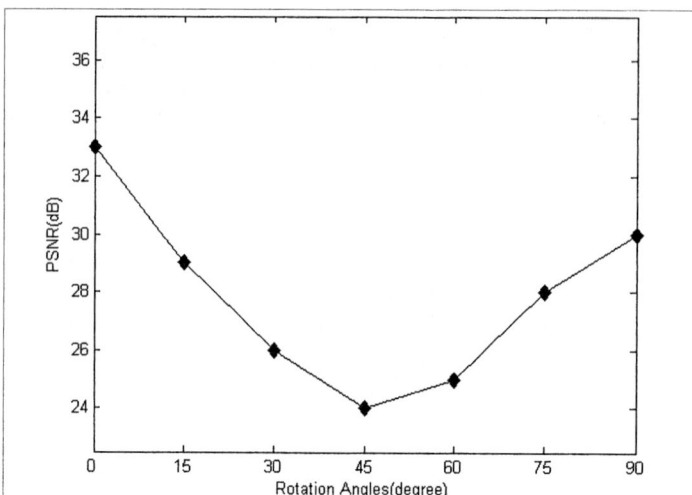

Fig. 8. PSNR graph illustrating the visual quality of our approach for half rotation

The maximum PSNR quality of 33dB is achieved for the front view. The PSNR value is still quite high at 30dB for the side view. The slightly lower PSNR value for the side image compared to that of the frontal image can be explained by the fact that the number of facial feature pointes used for the latter is less, as explained before. The lowest visual quality is obtained for 45 degree of rotation where almost half of the face is covered with the frontal image and the remaining half is covered with the profile image texture. This degradation is expected as it is obvious that the frontal and profile images contain illumination differences due to the changing direction of illumination. The overall visual quality of the synthesized face at varying degrees of rotation is within the acceptable quality of 27dB on the average.

6 Conclusion

In this paper we proposed a new face model, its adaptation and a texture mapping method (RATM) for model based video coding. Our experimental results show that the visual quality of the synthesized face image is within the acceptable quality. The average PSNR is around 27 dB for the rotations between the front and the side views and higher values for front and side views support our visual results. The quantitative and visual results clearly suggest that the developed model along with the proposed RATM approach produces encouraging results and opens a new direction for high quality 3D face synthesis.

References

1. R. Forchheimer, O. Fahlander, and T. Kronander. Low bit-rate coding through animation. In *Proc. Picture Coding Symposium* (PCS), pages 113-114, Davis, California, Mar. 1983.
2. R. Forchheimer, O. Fahlander, and T. Kronander. A semantic approach to the transmission of face images. In Proc. Picture Coding Symposium (PCS), number 10.5, Cesson-Sevigne, France, Jul. 1984.

3. Horace H.S. Ip, and Lijin Yin, "Constructing a 3D Individual Head Model from two Orthogonal Views", the Visual Computer, Springer-Verlag, 1996, pp.254-266.
4. Chia-Ming Cheng, and Shang-Hong Lai. "An Integrated Approach to 3D Face Model Reconstruction from Video", Proceedings of the IEEE ICCV Workshop on Recognition, Analysis, Tracking of Faces and Gestures in Real-Time Systems (RATFG-RTS'01), July 2001.
5. Xu G., et al., "Three-dimension Face Modeling for virtual space teleconferencing systems", Trans. IEICE, E73. Oct.1990
6. Y. Sheng, A.H. Sadka and A.M. Kondoz, Automatic 3D face synthesis using single 2D video frame, ELECTRONICS LETTERS 2004 Vol. 40 No. 19, 16th September.
7. Jie Yan, and Hongjiang Zhang. "Realistic Virtual Face and Body Synthesis", MVA2000 (International Workshop on Machine Vision Applications), Tokyo, Japan, November 28-30, 2000.
8. Ahlberg, J.: 'Candide-3: an updated parameterised face'. Report No. LiTH-ISY-R-2326, 2001 (Linkoping University, Sweden)

Multispectral Integration for Segmentation of Chromosome Images

Shishir Shah

Quantitative Imaging Laboratory,
University of Houston,
Department of Computer Science,
Houston, TX, USA
shah@cs.uh.edu

Abstract. This paper presents a methodology and results for multispectral integration in chromosome images by learning disparate models from each channel for pixel classification. The objective is the classification of pixels to identify each of the individual chromosomes. The methodology is based on a modular structure consisting of multiple classifiers, each of which solves the problem independently based on its input observations. Each classifier module is trained to detect distinct regions and a higher order decision integrator collects evidence from each of the modules to delineate a final region. A Bayesian realization of the framework is developed, where each classifier module represents the conditional probability density function. Results of classification on a public database are presented.

1 Introduction

Chromosomal aberrations are a variation from the normal, either in structure or number of chromosomes, which result from an exchange of genetic material between two or more chromosomes or from a rearrangement of genetic sequences contained in a single chromosome. The analysis of such aberrations can be useful both in a clinical and in a toxicological context. In the former, it serves to carry out pre-natal diagnoses, tumor diagnoses and treatment monitoring. In the latter, it helps to determine the biologically significant dose of specific genotoxic agents to which an individual is exposed. In order for chromosomes to be visualized and for aberrations to be identified and analyzed, chromosomes need to be stained. Different staining techniques allow analysis of different kinds of abnormalities. A particularly useful cytogenetic technique for the analysis of aberrations is *Fluorescence in situ Hybridization* (FISH)[1]. FISH technique is used to achieve a direct visualization of specific chromosomes or nonchromosomal regions in metaphase cells. Moreover, FISH allows us to analyze only those aberrations in which exchanges between hybridized chromosomes are involved. Over the years, many attempts have been made to automate chromosome image analysis. Successful automated systems for segmentation of grayscale chromosome images have been developed that can decompose about 80-90% of touching and

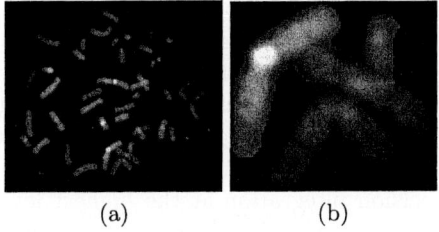

Fig. 1. (a)Example M-FISH Image and (b)Overlapped Chromosomes in M-FISH Image

overlapping chromosomes[2,3]. Most automated procedures rely on chromosome shape and texture.

In the 1990's, new techniques were developed to dye chromosomes with multiple colors so that each chromosome class appears to be a distinct color. This makes analysis of chromosome images easier, not only for human inspection, but also for computer analysis. One such dying technique is M-FISH (multiplex fluorescence in-situ hybridization). M-FISH uses five color dyes that attach to various chromosomes differently to produce a multi-spectral image[4,5], and a sixth dye that attaches to all chromosomes to produce a grayscale image. An example of an M-FISH image is shown in figure 1(a). Segmentation techniques for M-FISH images range from entropy based estimators[6] to probabilistic nave classifiers[7]. While having access to multispectral source of information for each pixel simplifies the task of segmentation, inherent problems still exist in overlapped chromosome within the images. If one observes the example in figure 1(b), it is not clear what the proper segmentation of the cluster is. It is not apparent, even to many human observers, whether there is an overlap involved or even how many chromosomes are included in this cluster. In practice, fluorophore absorption is not binary and there is significant overlap between each of the fluorophore absorptions along with variability in signal strength. This leads to a non-trivial classification problem, especially in the context of overlapping regions. Since chromosomes are somewhat opaque, each pixel will include information from all overlapping chromosomes. This could lead to a pixel being classified as the same type as any of the overlapped chromosomes.

The increased dimensionality of such multispectral data greatly enhances the data information content, but provides a challenge to the current techniques for analyzing such data. The complexity of high dimensional data has been known for many years and its impact varies from one field to another. In order to build a system that can succeed in a realistic environment, certain simplifications and assumptions about the environment and the problem domain are generally made. The use of a priori information is critical. Sensor fusion techniques which alleviate the limitations of a single sensing modality also need to be developed. Good representations of objects and background are needed that provide descriptive and robust signatures to environmental variations. Further, the ability of the system to dynamically adapt to the changing environment is also important.

This paper present a Bayesian methodology in which each mapping between local pixel statistics to the pixel's class is characterized by the probability density function of the image statistics/features. Individual class statistics are used to design the classifiers and the distribution of the class region is modeled as a mixture of Gaussians. An adaptive Expectation-Maximization (EM) algorithm is used to find the parameters of the normal distribution and a supra-Bayesian scheme is used for decision integration at the highest level. Rest of the paper is organized as follows: Section 2 describes our proposed data model and the maximum likelihood framework for characterizing class signatures. Section 3 presents the design of Bayesian classifiers, along with the final stage decision integration. Results of the developed methodology on publicly available database of M-FISH images are presented in section 4. Finally, conclusions and a summary of this study are presented in section 5.

2 Data Modeling

To achieve optimum performance from any classification/clustering system, it is essential that its design exploits the specific characteristics of the data. Given that, the simplest model would be a two-class discrimination where the class region is easily separable from rest of the classes. In realistic situations, due to the complexity of the sample, simple models would not suffice in classifying the region of interest and identifying all the segments across each chromosome. Further, due to varying fluorescence intensities and the presence of noise, the data characteristics may change drastically.

We propose to model the class signatures by using a bank of features computed for each pixel in the multispectral image. Rather than using the direct color values for each of the images, the color space is transformed by the non-linear diffeomorphism to the (H,S,V) representation. A texture measure is also obtained by computing a simple cooccurence matrix in a three-by-three window. A measure of structural entropy is also computed by analyzing the spatial difference in four orientations, thereby characterizing the presence of regularized boundaries. Principal components of the aggregated features are examined and the first five values used to represent each of the classes. Each of the images in the multispectral dataset is examined separately and used as input to individual classifiers. Due to the complex and non-Gaussian distribution of the object features, we model the data using a mixture of Gaussians. Modeling of data is an important consideration in designing statistical classifiers. The simplest way to model non-Gaussian data is to use the histograms of the training data. However, classification based on this method does not generalize well from the training data to the test data. The Parzen density estimate[8] is a well established method to establish density estimates for multivariate models. However, the Parzen windows approach is computationally expensive and has problems when the data is large and sparsely distributed. Maximum likelihood estimators[9] compute piecewise estimates of one-dimensional density functions. This approach can be regularized by introducing a penalty term. Such methods are attractive, but rely on a predefined model of the density function. They also do not generalize well in the case of mixture models unless coupled with other optimization techniques

We use the Expectation-Maximization (EM) algorithm[10] to determine the parameters for the mixture of Gaussians model to estimate the density function. Considering Y to be the data, we pose the parameter estimation as a maximum likelihood problem. The general form of the density function for the measured feature can be given as:

$$P(Y|t) = P(Y|\theta) = \sum_{i=1}^{c} p(Y|t,\theta_i)\alpha_i \qquad (1)$$

where, t is the conditioning variable (class signature), c represents the number of component density functions $p(Y|t,\theta_i)$ that make up the mixture, α_i represents the weight associated with each of the density functions (also called mixing parameter), and θ_i represents the parameter vectors for each component density function. θ, α, and c are unknown, and have to be estimated from the data. We assume the component densities to be normal distributed. That is $p(Y|t,\theta_i) \approx N(\mu_i, \Sigma_i)$, and $\theta_i = (\mu_i, \Sigma_i)$, where μ_i and Σ_i represent the multivariate mean and covariance matrix of the normal distribution. To model each cluster, the values of μ_i, Σ_i, and α_i have to be estimated. At the start of the process, the number of components densities (c), the density means (μ_i), covariance matrices (Σ_i), and the mixing weights (α_i) have to be known. In doing so, we use the K-Means algorithm iteratively with the EM algorithm to determine all the parameters. A stagewise K-Means procedure is used, where the initial guess for the cluster centroids is obtained by splitting the centroids resulting from the previous stage. Given a set of features $Y_m = [Y_{m,1}, Y_{m,2}, \ldots, Y_{m,d}]$ for $m = 1, \ldots, c$, the number of kernels or components is set to one. The centroid of all training points is computed and a measure of the mean and in-class deviation is computed as:

$$\mu = \frac{1}{M} \sum_{u=1}^{n} \sum_{v=1}^{n} Y(u,v) \qquad (2)$$

$$s^2 = \frac{1}{M} \sum_{u=1}^{n} \sum_{v=1}^{n} (Y(u,v) - \mu)^2 \qquad (3)$$

Now, for each cluster, a normalized index is computed as:

$$I = (\frac{1}{M} \sum_{u=1}^{n} \sum_{v=1}^{n} (Y(u,v) - \mu))/s \qquad (4)$$

The normalized index gives a point measure of deviation from the cluster center. The component weights α_i are computed as a ratio of the number of data points in the corresponding component and the total points. Denoting Y_{ik} as the k-th feature sample belonging to cluster i and using the EM approach, the following equations are obtained for the estimates of μ_i, Σ_i, and α_i:

$$\alpha_i = \frac{1}{n} \sum_{k=1}^{n} P(t|Y_{ik}, \theta_i) \qquad (5)$$

$$\mu_i = \frac{\sum_{k=1}^{n} P(t|Y_{ik}, \theta_i) Y_{ik}}{\sum_{k=1}^{n} P(t|Y_{ik}, \theta_i)} \qquad (6)$$

$$\Sigma_i = \frac{\sum_{k=1}^{n} P(t|Y_{ik}, \theta_i)(Y_{ik} - \mu_i)(Y_{ik} - \mu_i)^T}{\sum_{k=1}^{n} P(t|Y_{ik}, \theta_i)} \qquad (7)$$

If the normalized index is greater than a set threshold, a new mean is initialized and the nearest neighbor partition is computed. A new estimate of the means, variances, and the distortion are computed. These equations are iteratively solved until convergence of the parameter values is achieved.

3 Bayesian Classifiers

It is a well known result from decision theory that Bayesian classifiers are optimal due to minimization of the error probability[11]. Given the extracted features from the image, we design a classifier for each band. For simplicity, we discuss the design for a single classifier, as the rest follow the same principles. The transformed feature space is denoted by Y, where each pixel y is sampled from the space of features S. As we are interested in modeling the class signatures, a set of training features are used that are extracted from known classes in the image. Thus the distribution of the features is given as the class conditional density function $p(y|t)$, where t comes from the true class space T, with a priori distribution $p(t)$.

In the Bayesian framework, the decisions are made by evaluating the a posteriori probability for each class and choosing the one with the highest probability as the true class. We are interested in a two class formulation, where each classifier discriminates one region from the background. Given the a priori probability of any class pixel $P(t)$ and the conditional density $p(y|t)$, we can compute the posterior probability of the observed feature being a particular class pixel using the Bayes rule. We are interested in distinguishing a region from the background, and we have modeled the class signature. Thus, in a two case discrimination the posterior probability given by the classifier is:

$$P(t|y) = \frac{p(y|t)P(t)}{p(y|t)P(t) + p(y|b)P(b)} \qquad (8)$$

where, $p(y|b)$ is the conditional density function of the background distribution and $P(b)$ is the prior probability of observing the background feature. Now, as each of the conditional densities are computed as a mixture of Gaussians, the likelihood is

$$p(y|t) = \sum_{i=1}^{c} p(y|\theta_i)\alpha_i \qquad (9)$$

where each component is a multivariate Gaussian. The only remaining unknown parameter is the prior probability of observing a class region. This is calculated from the training set of sites. As we are performing detection based on individual pixels, the prior probability is computed by:

$$P(t) = \frac{\#\ of\ object\ pixels}{total\ \#\ of\ image\ pixels} \qquad (10)$$

A single classifier is designed for each of the object features. Given the posterior estimates from the individual classifiers, the goal of the combining stage is to produce a single estimate that maximizes the probability for localized object detection while reducing clutter and false alarms. Various integration methods have been proposed in the past[12]. We formulate a supra-Bayesian integration in which the posterior estimates from each classifier are assumed to have a probability distribution and, based on the means and variances of the outputs, we can formulate an optimal decision scheme. Strictly speaking, Bayesian theory holds true only for individual decision makers, but if the group decision is viewed as a collaborative effort, the effect is externally Bayesian. As in the case of individual classifiers, the integration module is estimating the probability of observing an object pixel. So, given n individual classifiers, where each $P(t|y)$ is providing a measure of subjective probability of observing a particular class pixel, and that the posteriors are Gaussian distributed, then the integrated posterior decision simplifies to:

$$P_I(t|y_1, y_2, \ldots, y_n) = \frac{[\prod_{i=1}^{n} \frac{P(t|y_i)}{P(t)}^{w_i}]P(t)}{[\prod_{i=1}^{n} \frac{P(t|y_i)}{P(t)}^{w_i}]P(t) + [\prod_{i=1}^{n} \frac{P(b|y_i)}{P(b)}^{w_i}]P(b)} \quad (11)$$

where, w_i weights the contribution of each of the features. As each of the classifiers is designed to identify single class pixels, we know that there is sufficient diversity and complementarity within the estimates. Thus the weight associated with each of the classifiers plays an important role in deciding the contribution from each estimate. This is mainly due to the fact that the integrator module does not have the same information that is seen by each of the classifiers. Evaluating the log likelihood of equation 11 and assuming that the combined probability ratios provide the final probability as

$$P(\ln(\frac{P(t|y_1)}{1 - P(t|y_1)}), \ldots, \ln(\frac{P(t|y_n)}{1 - P(t|y_n)})|t) \quad (12)$$

and

$$P(\ln(\frac{P(b|y_1)}{1 - P(b|y_1)}), \ldots, \ln(\frac{P(b|y_n)}{1 - P(b|y_n)})|b) \quad (13)$$

and, if the joint distributions are multivariate normal densities with mean μ_t and μ_b and covariance Σ_{tb}, then the weights for the individual classifiers can be computed by:

$$w = \Sigma_{tb}^{-1}(\mu_t - \mu_b) \quad (14)$$

This result provides an intuitive insight to the integration of decisions. In general, when all the classifiers provide similar estimates, the combining results in the peaking of that estimate. On the other hand, and more importantly, when the classifiers do not agree on an estimate, their reliability has to be considered. According to the weight assignment in equation 14, the reliability associated with each of the classifiers will depend on how different its estimate is from rest of the classifiers, and how much diversity exists within the estimates.

4 Results

We tested our approach on selected images from a public database of 200 hand-segmented M-FISH images. The database is available from Advanced Digital Imaging Research at http://www.adires.com/05/Project/MFISH_DB/MFISH_DB.shtml. On an individual chromosome basis, the database contains over 9000 individual chromosomes. We divided the dataset into training and testing where 100 images were used to estimate all the parameters of the proposed classifier and the remaining 100 images were used for testing. Images used for test resulted in pixel accuracy rates of 96%. These results were based on applying a threshold of 0.7 on the assessed probabilities. In a parallel experiment, the lower level of individual classifiers was merged into one classifier and the decision integration module was removed. Thus, the features were concatenated to give just a single feature vector. The same experiments were then repeated. This was done to verify the advantage of the proposed methodology. Results of the same test data resulted in pixel classification accuracy of 88%. Figure 2(a) shows an example M-FISH image that contains several overlapping chromosomes and the results of the aggregated classification scheme and the integrated classifier is seen in figures 2(b) and 2(c), respectively.

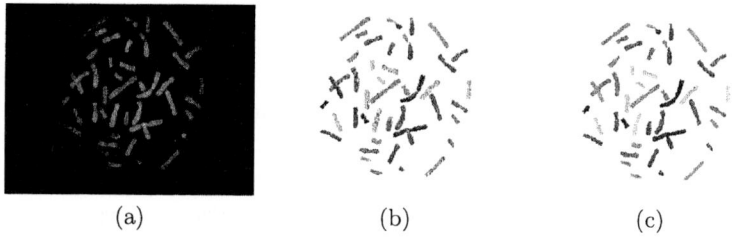

Fig. 2. (a)Example M-FISH Image with Several Overlapping Chromosomes, (b)Corresponding Result of Aggregated Pixel Classifier, and (c)Corresponding Result of Integrated Classifier showing Improved Pixel Classification

5 Summary and Conclusions

In this paper we have presented a methodology for chromosome segmentation in M-FISH images. Image attributes from all the available spectral bands is used independently based on local pixel characteristics. A modular computational structure consisting of multiple classifiers, each trying to solve the global problem based on its input observations is introduced and applied to the problem of classification. A higher level decision integrator oversees and collects evidence from each of the individual modules and combines it to provide a final decision while considering the redundancy and diversity of individual classifiers. A Bayesian realization of the methodology is presented. Each classifier module models the class signature probability density function based on the computed image statistics and the final integration is achieved in a supra-Bayesian scheme.

Results obtained are also compared with classification obtained using a single classifier and the advantage of integration is demonstrated.

References

1. Pinkel, D., Straume, T., Gray, J.: Cytogenetic analysis using quantitative high sensitivity fluorescence hybridization. Proc. National Academy of Science **83** (1986) 2934–2938
2. Lundsteen, C., Piper, J.: Automation of Cytogenetics. Springer-Verlag, Berlin (1989)
3. Liang, J.: Intelligent splitting in the chromosome domain. Pattern Recognition **22** (1989) 519–532
4. Speicher, M.R., Ballard, S.G., Ward, D.C.: Karyotyping human chromosomes by combinatorial multifluor fish. Nature Genetics **12** (1996) 368–375
5. Beau, M.M.L.: One fish, two fish, red fish, blue fish. Nature Genetics **12** (1996) 341–344
6. Schwartzkopf, W., Evans, B.L., Bovik, A.C.: Minimum entropy segmentation applied to multi-spectral chromosome images. In: Proceeding of the IEEE International Conference on Image Processing. Volume 2., Thessaloniki, Greece (2001) 865–868
7. Sampat, M.P., Castleman, K., Bovik, A.C.: Pixel-by-pixel classification of m-fish images. In: 2nd Joint Conference of the IEEE Engineering in Medicine and Biology Society and the Biomedical Engineering Society, Houston, TX (2002)
8. Fukunaga, K.: Introduction to Statistical Pattern Recognition. Academic Press, New York (1972)
9. Silverman, B.W.: Density Estimation for Statistics and Data Analysis. Chapman and Hall, London (1986)
10. Dempster, A.P., Laird, N.M., Rubin, D.B.: Maximum likelihood from incomplete data via the EM algorithm. Journal of the Royal Statistical Society **39-B** (1977) 1–38
11. Duda, R.O., Hart, P.E.: Pattern Classification and Scene Analysis. Wiley-Interscience Publication (1973)
12. Kittler, J., Hatef, M., Duin, R.P.W.: Combining classifiers. In: Proceeding of International Conference on Pattern Recognition. (1996) 897–901

Bit-Rate Control Algorithm for ROI Enabled Video Coding

Adam Pietrowcew, Andrzej Buchowicz, and Władysław Skarbek

Institute of Radioelectronics, Warsaw University of Technology,
ul. Nowowiejska 15/19, 00-665 Warszawa, Poland
{A.Pietrowcew, A.Buchowicz, W.Skarbek}@ire.pw.edu.pl

Abstract. The bit-rate control algorithm allowing ROI encoding in a video sequence has been presented in this paper. The algorithm distributes available bit budget among image layers taking into consideration both the distance from ROI and the local image complexity. It improves the image quality in ROI by lowering the image quality outside ROI with the preservation of the global constraint of the encoded stream bit-rate and the gradual quality degradation outside ROI.

1 Introduction

The trade-off between compression ratio and the quality of the reconstructed signal is the main issue in a video coding. It is obvious that better quality can be achieved with smaller compression ratio and higher encoded stream bit-rate. The optimal coder control, that is the selection of appropriate set of coding parameters, that will guarantee the demanded bit-rate with minimal loss in fidelity of the reconstructed video sequence requires the knowledge of the rate-distortion (R-D) model for the particular coding scheme. The R-D model is usually build in such a way that the quality of the whole frames in a video sequence is taken into account. However in many applications, e.g. video monitoring and surveillance, telemedicine, some areas in the consecutive frames of the video sequence are more important than the others. It is desirable to encode those areas, called region of interest (ROI) with smaller distortion than the rest of the sequence (background).

The algorithm presented in this paper is based on the linear rate-distortion (R-D) model in ρ-domain [1]. It distributes the available bit budget among level sets in the encoded frame taking into consideration both their distance from ROI and local image complexity. ROI is encoded with higher bit-rate ensuring better image quality and the image quality gradually decreases outside ROI. The algorithm has been integrated and tested with the H.264/MPEG-4 AVC [2] reference software JM 8.2 [3].

2 R-D Model in ρ-Domain

In a typical transform image/video coding both rate R and distortion D depend on the quantization parameter denoted here by q. The main task in designing a

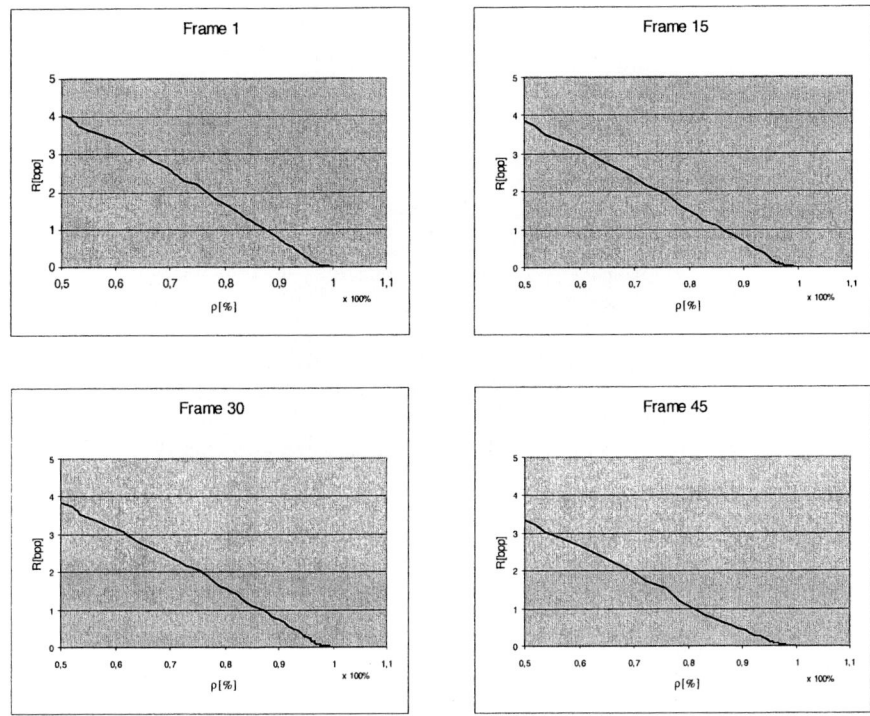

Fig. 1. $R_Y(\rho)$ functions for selected frames of the *Carphone* sequence

rate control algorithm is to find functions $R(q)$, $D(q)$, called R-D functions, for the particular coding scheme.

Methodology of our ROI bit budget allocation technique is based on the ρ-domain algorithm [1], which in turn is running on a top of the JVT-G012 proposal [4]. It has been shown [5,6] that for typical coding algorithms the R-D functions can be expressed by linear equations in the new domain of parameter ρ, which is the percentage of insignificant (quantized to zero) transform coefficients.

We assume that generated bit count values for intra and non-intra frames in encoded sequence satisfy the linear model in ρ-domain:

$$R(\rho) = \theta(1 - \rho) \qquad (1)$$

Context in which ρ is computed depends on data source encoding options. It can be defined for frames or basic units of type I, P and B in one dimension or in color components Y, C_b, C_r respectively. In presented method such context was defined for P frames and Y color component. Linear character of the $R(\rho)$ function is clearly visible in Fig. 1 showing $R_Y(\rho)$ functions obtained for four selected frames of the *Carphone* sequence.

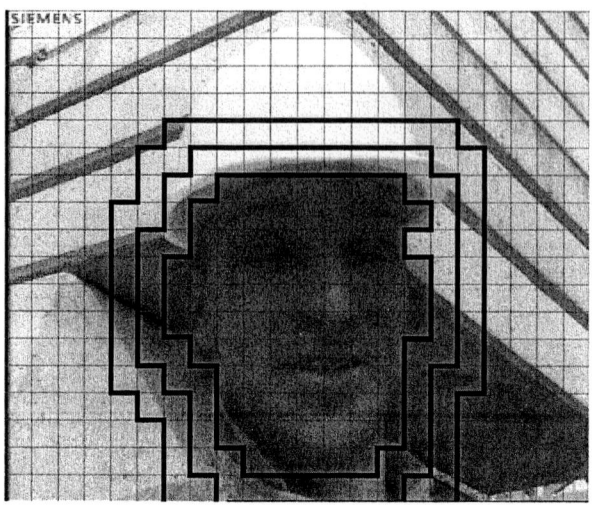

Fig. 2. Level sets in the first frame of the *Foreman* sequence

The slope θ is modeled on the base of the previous context and is given by the formula:

$$\theta = \frac{r_{prev}}{1 - \rho_{prev}} \qquad (2)$$

Parameters r_{prev} and ρ_{prev} denote the bit-rate and zero fraction in the previous context, accordingly.

Such modeling scheme makes application of ρ-domain methodology impractical for I type frames since time interval between them is large. Thus the scene view can change drastically during this period and the slope θ calculated for the previous frame of this type can be inadequate for the current frame encoding.

The mapping from ρ to quantization index q is straightforward, having a lookup table build on the basis of a histogram for zero quantized coefficients obtained for all possible indices q. While model parameter θ depends strongly on the local data, the relationship between ρ and q is less dependent on the data prediction errors.

2.1 ROI Bit-Rate Control

ROI in encoded sequence can be defined as one connected area or a set of connected components [6]. It is composed of macroblocks for which at least one pixel intersects with ROI (Fig. 2). Let us denote all such macroblocks by L_1. Then we can define level sets L_i (for $i > 1$) as sets of macroblocks which are 8-neighbors of macroblocks in L_{i-1} and are not included in L_j for all $j < i$. All such level sets defined in a frame based on its ROI structure are further characterized by $N_i = |L_i|$ - number of macroblocks on the given level set, ρ_i - zero fraction on L_i and r_i - bit-rate for L_i.

In order to distribute bit budget, allocated for the frame by ρ-domain algorithm, we decided to increase the fraction of zeros in consecutive level sets L_i by $\Delta\rho\,\gamma_i$ such that:

$$\rho_i = \rho_{i-1} + \Delta\rho\,\gamma_i \qquad i = 2, \ldots, i_{max} \tag{3}$$

where

$$\gamma_i = \begin{cases} \sqrt{1 + \frac{var_a - var_i}{var_a}} & \text{if } var_1 > var_a \\ 1.0 & \text{if } var_1 \leq var_a \end{cases} \tag{4}$$

In the above equations i_{max} is the number of level sets, var_i denotes image signal variance on ROI level set L_i and var_a is the whole frame variance. Variance is calculated on a motion compensated image and gives us information about an image complexity on consecutive level sets.

Assuming that global frame bit-rate is distributed to level sets L_i proportionally to their sizes we have:

$$r = \sum_{i=1}^{i_{max}} w_i r_i \tag{5}$$

$$\rho_1 = 1 - \frac{r}{\theta} - \Delta\rho \sum_{i=2}^{i_{max}} \left(w_i \sum_{j=2}^{i} \gamma_j \right) \tag{6}$$

where $w_i = \frac{N_i}{N}$, N is the number of all macroblocks in a frame and r denotes the bit-rate (in bits per pixel) for the frame.

Hence for the fixed $\Delta\rho$ we compute ρ_1 by the formula (6) and next ρ_i for all $i > 1$ using (3). Having ρ_i we can use further steps of ρ-domain algorithm, i.e. getting the quantization index q_i from lookup table $\rho[q]$, establishing the encoding mode for each macroblock in L_i and model updating.

Value of ρ_i on all level sets except ROI is modified by γ_i, which is equal to 1.0 when variance of ROI signal is below or equal to variance of the whole frame and is greater than 1.0 in other cases. Such formulation causes that quantization index q_i on level set L_i ($i > 1$) increases more if the ROI is more complex then the rest of the image. We can cut more bits from outside ROI and allocate more to ROI as less complex signal generates lower error during reconstruction, in PSNR sense.

Proposed ROI bit allocation scheme works well on P frames. For I frames similar technique as in JVT-G012 proposal was applied. On each level set L_i we calculate a sum S_{pq}^i of quantization indices q_i for all P frames in a group of pictures (GOP). Then quantization indices for ROI level sets on I frame in given GOP were calculated using the formula:

$$q_i = \frac{S_{pq}^i}{N_p} - \min\left(2, \frac{N_{gop}}{15}\right) \tag{7}$$

where N_p denotes the number of P frames in the previous GOP and N_{gop} is the size of GOP. Also the change between current I type frame quantization index and previous one on appropriate level set should not be greater then 2.

The same methodology as for P frames can be applied to B type frames. However, our experiments showed its drawbacks. In B type frames vast amount of macroblocks is encoded using motion vectors where resulting coefficients are all equal to zero after DCT transform and quantization. Sometimes, B frames occur with all coefficients equal to zero, and these extreme results cause ρ-domain model inconsistency. Therefore for B frames the solution inspired by the JVT-G012 algorithm is proposed in this work. For consecutive B frames in a sequence ROI level sets L_i are defined in similar way as for P frames. Values of quantization indices on ROI level sets L_i are then determined on the basis of corresponding quantization indices for level sets on surrounding P frames. One of the surrounding frames could be of type I at the GOP start, so in such case quantization indices from ROI level sets on this frame are used instead.

The formula for determining quantization indices values on B frames is as follows:

$$q_{B,i}^k = \begin{cases} \frac{1}{2}\left(q_i^{k_{prev}} + q_i^{k_{next}} + 2\right) & \text{if } q_i^{k_{prev}} \neq q_i^{k_{next}} \\ q_{P,i}^{k_{prev}} & \text{otherwise} \end{cases} \quad (8)$$

where k is the B frame index, k_{prev}, k_{next} are indices of the closest two P/I frames and i is the level set number.

In the proposed schema there is no direct allocation of bits for B frames. Bit-rate control algorithm is based mainly on P frames complexity and estimations of supposed bit budget for the following B frames.

The described ROI bit budged allocation scheme based on consecutive increase of zero fraction by $\Delta\rho\gamma_i$ takes into account an image complexity measured as frame pixels variance after motion compensation. It gives much better results for images in which ROI is more complex than the rest of the image. However, in images in which ROI is less complex than background this assumption led to equalization on PSNR on all level sets. Therefore, in such case we decided to increase ρ_i by constant $\Delta\rho$ in order to preserve a higher image quality in the ROI and gradually lower it on level sets with increased distance from the ROI.

3 Experimental Results

The proposed algorithm was evaluated on several standard test sequences. The ROI definitions were loaded to the encoder from external files. These files were created manually by test sequence browsing. The GOP composed of 30 frames with 2 B frames between I/P frames were used. The algorithm works correctly on all sequences recorded with CIF and QCIF resolutions and at different bit-rates. The required bit-rate is preserved with very high accuracy for all GOPs in test videos while at the same time quality of the ROI is better with respect to the original JVT-G012 implementation in JM 8.2.

Figure 3 presents PSNR measures for the *Foreman* sequence encoded with the proposed bit allocation algorithm and the JM 8.2 with JVT-G012 algorithm. The PSNR values for the JM 8.2 were calculated in the same macroblock sets as level sets defined for the proposed ρ-domain algorithm. Comparing two diagrams figures, we can observe, that PSNR measure on ROI is more stable for bit allocation method working in ρ-domain. Also quality of the ROI is better for almost all frames by more than 1,5 dB. The periodicity visible on this two diagrams is typical for sequences encoded with B-frames, which have slightly lower quality than surrounding I/P-frames.

Quality on level sets L_1 and L_2 is comparable in both implementations. Only on the last level set quality in JM 8.2 is better than in ROI ρ-domain algorithm, where more bits were allocated to the area of interest.

We proposed to divide all frame macroblocks into level sets in our bit allocation algorithm to avoid strong quality change on the border between the ROI and the rest of the image. Such solution allows to gradually decrease the image quality on consecutive level sets lying farther from ROI.

Table 1 compares the performance of the proposed algorithm with the performance of the original JM 8.2. It contains values averaged over the whole test sequences PSNR values on level sets. Results for *Foreman*, *News* and *Mobile & Calendar* are presented. Each sequence contained 90 frames. For all sequences quality on ROI - level set L_1, is better by more then 1 dB compared to the original JM 8.2/JVT-G012 proposal. This quality improvement in ROI is controlled by the value of $\Delta\rho$ parameter. Greater $\Delta\rho$ values give better quality in ROI, which decreases smoothly on macroblocks laying farther from defined area of interest.

The PSNR at L_1 level set (ROI) was slightly lower than on level set L_2 on almost all frames in the *News* test sequence. This was a result of the video sequence content, which presents a scene with two speakers in the foreground, a dancing pair in the middle distance and a very dark background.

On the *Mobile & Calendar* sequence the quality difference between proposed method and the original JVT implementation is most visible in the defined ROI

Table 1. Averaged PSNR (in dB) on level sets in the proposed ρ-domain algorithm and the original JM 8.2

Sequence	Level set	ρ-domain	JM-8.2
Foreman	L1	39.07	37.75
	L2	38.62	38.07
	L3	38.10	38.40
	L4	36.69	37.93
News	L1	40.40	39.13
	L2	41.44	41.83
	L3	39.88	42.66
	L4	37.40	42.75
Mobile & Calendar	L1	32.70	31.38
	L2	31.88	31.40
	L3	30.66	31.06
	L4	28.08	30.34

a)

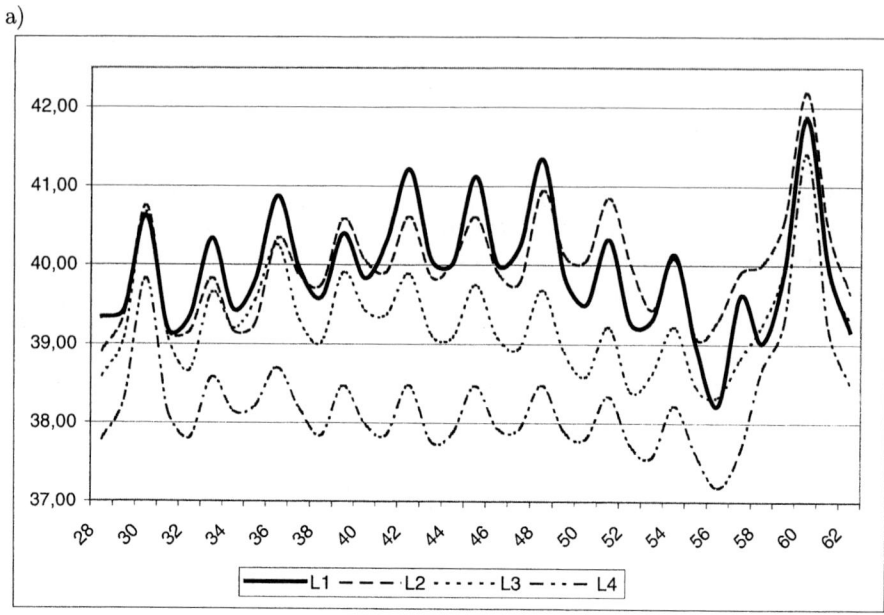

b)

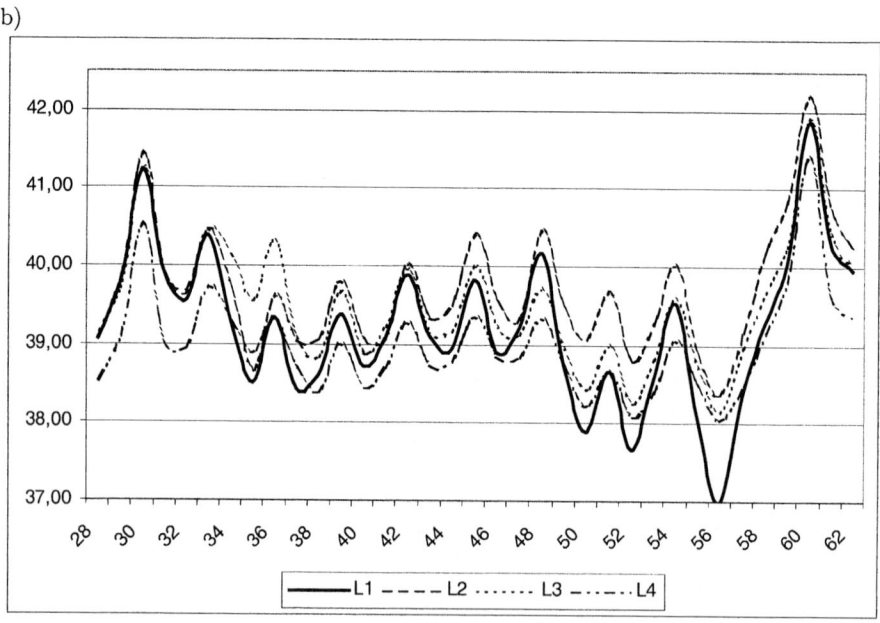

Fig. 3. PSNR for the *Foreman* CIF sequence a) in the proposed algorithm with $\Delta\rho = 1/80$, b) for the original JM 8.2; bit-rate 270 kbit/s. The PSNR values were calculated in both cases for macroblock collections $L_1,\ldots,L_4$ used as level sets in the proposed ρ-domain algorithm.

when we encoded it at a low bit-rate. The ROI which was defined on the calendar stays readable even at a bit-rate of 180 kbit/s, which is not possible to achieve for the whole frame encoding implemented in JM 8.2. Average bit-rate for all GOPs (309,30 kbit/s) is below the desired value (312 kbit/s) in the ρ-domain method, while it is slightly above (313,87 kbit/s) in the case of the JM 8.2.

The algorithm described in this paper has also better performance than the algorithm presented in our previous paper [7]. The increase of the PSNR in the ROI for the *News* video sequence was improved by approximately 1 dB by taking into consideration the local image complexity.

4 Conclusions

The modified version of the bit-rate control algorithm presented in [7] for video sequence with ROI has been presented in this paper. The algorithm guarantees higher quality of the reconstructed video in the ROI and gradual video quality degradation outside the ROI. The available bit budget was distributed among level sets in the consecutive frames by increasing the fraction of zero quantized coefficients by a constant value multiplied by the factor depending on the local image complexity. The algorithm performance was improved when the complexity of ROI is higher than the complexity of the background by taking into consideration the image complexity in the bit budget distribution.

Acknowledgement. The work presented was developed within VISNET, a European Network of Excellence (http://www.visnet-noe.org), funded under the European Commission IST FP6 programme.

References

1. Z.He, S.K.Mitra: A unified rate-distortion analysis framework for transform coding. IEEE Trans. on Circuits and Systems for Video Technology **11** (2001) 1221–1236
2. ISO/IEC: Generic Coding of Audiovisual Objects Part 10: Advanced Video Coding (MPEG-4 AVC). (2003) ISO/IEC 14496-10.
3. H.264/AVC: Software coordination. http://iphome.hhi.de/suehring/tml/ (2004)
4. Z.Li, F.Pan, K.P.Lim, G.Feng, X.Lin, S.Rahardja: Adaptive basic unit layer rate control for JVT. In: JVT-G012-r1, Pattaya, Thailand (2003)
5. P.Bobinski, W.Skarbek: Analysis of rd models for coding efficiency in h.264 standard. In: International Workshop on Image Analysis for Multimedia Interactive Services WIAMIS 2004, Lisboa, Portugal (2004)
6. W.Skarbek, A.Buchowicz, A.Pietrowcew, F.Pereira: Bit-rate control for compression of video with ROI. In: International Conference on Computer Vision and Graphics ICCVG 2004, Warszawa, Poland (2004)
7. A.Pietrowcew, A.Buchowicz, W.Skarbek: Bit-rate control for video coding with ROI. In: International Workshop on Image Analysis for Multimedia Interactive Services WIAMIS 2005, Montreux, Switzerland (2005)

Classification of Moving Humans Using Eigen-Features and Support Vector Machines

Sijun Lu[1,*], Jian Zhang[1], and David Feng[2]

[1] National ICT Australia
{Sijun.lu, Jian, Zhang}@nicta.com.au
[2] School of Information Technology, The University of Sydney, Australia
feng@it.usyd.edu.au

Abstract. This paper describes a method of categorizing the moving objects using eigen-features and support vector machines. Eigen-features, generally used in face recognition and static image classification, are applied to classify the moving objects detected from the surveillance video sequences. Through experiments on a large set of data, it has been found out that in such an application the binary image instead of the normally used grey image is the more suitable format for the feature extraction. Different SVM kernels have been compared and the RBF kernel is selected as the optimal one. A voting mechanism is employed to utilize the tracking information to further improve the classification accuracy. The resulting labeled object trajectories provide important hints for understanding human activities in the surveillance video.

1 Introduction

Video surveillance technology is gaining more and more interest from both the government and industrial institutes as an effective way of protecting public security. The research efforts on object classification in video surveillance can be reviewed from two perspectives: what features are extracted for classification and how to discriminate between these features.

In [2], two object classification algorithms were developed. The first one used the features like dispersedness and area, and a three-layer neural network to categorize the image blobs into three object classes: human, vehicle, and human group. The second one used the shape and color moment features and the linear discriminant analysis to distinguish the vehicles into finer types like van, truck, and sedan. The algorithms in [3] [4] combined the motion feature and the appearance feature such as the silhouette similarity to generate the categories of vehicle, animal, human, human group, and others. The support vector machine was used as the classifier. In [5], Fourier descriptors for the object shapes and a feed-forward neural network were used to determine the object classes among human, vehicle and background clutters.

In this paper, we present an algorithm to categorize the moving objects detected from the surveillance video into three classes: human with a bag, human without a

---

* National ICT Australia is funded through the Australian Government's *Backing Australia's Ability* initiative, in part through the Australian Research Council.

bag and the unknown class. The purpose of choosing these classes is for further research in the future on detecting unattended objects from surveillance video. Instead of using the features as those in the above references, the eigen-features, which are often used in the face and static image recognition applications [6] [7] [8], are exploited and the SVM classifier is chosen because of its proved performance in many papers. Different image formats for feature extraction and different SVM kernels are compared to select the most appropriate ones for the classification. Furthermore, the tracking information is taken into account to reduce the random misclassification of moving objects in consecutive frames.

The structure of this paper is arranged as follows: section 2 describes the process of the proposed object classification algorithm, including the moving object detection, the eigen-feature extraction, and the support-vector classification; section 3 explains the combination of the object tracking with on-line classification through a voting mechanism; section 4 describes the experiment results; and section 5 summarizes the findings and describes some further work in the future.

2 Moving Object Classification

Our framework of the moving object classification, Figure 1, has two parts: one is performed off-line to collect and label the training and test object images, extract eigen-features and train the support vector machine classifier; the other part is performed continuously on-line to detect the individual moving object, extract its eigen-feature, and categorize into the predefined classes. A large set of video sequences was recorded to collect training and test data. In total we used 37 sequences for training and 13 video sequences for testing, which were produced in different dates with different groups of people.

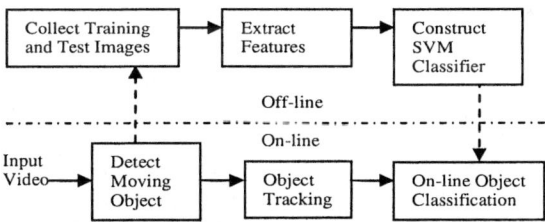

Fig. 1. Framework of the proposed moving object classification algorithm

2.1 Moving Object Detection

For detecting the moving objects in the surveillance video, background subtraction and temporal differencing are two popular and efficient approaches [2]. By gradually updating the pixel values in the background, the impact of lighting changes can be significantly reduced. For a more dynamic environment, the Gaussian mixture model (GMM) has been proposed to model the background changes [9]. In this paper, since the video sequences are generated in an indoor environment with a relatively static background, an adaptive background modeling method similar to that in [2] is used, instead of the computation-intensive GMM method. The motion detection result achieved (see figure 2 as an example) is reliable and satisfactory. In the face recognition, the grey images are used to extract the eigen-features. Here both grey and binary images in the bounding boxes are taken as candidates. The comparison result in section 4 shows that the binary image is actually more suitable for such an application as moving object classification, because the grey image contains extra unwanted information.

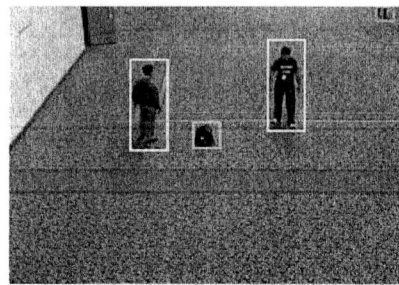 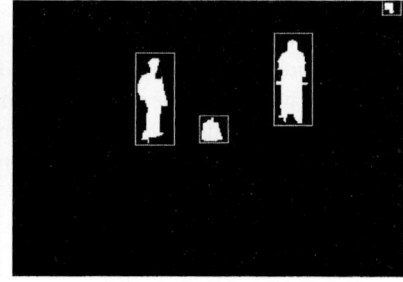

Fig. 2. Example of moving object detection using adaptive background modeling

2.2 Eigen-Feature Generation

The eigen-feature is generated by projecting the image of a moving object into the eigenspace using the principal component analysis (PCA) [6] [7]. Here is the brief description of the feature extraction method we use in the paper. First, the average image Ψ is calculated:

$$\Psi = \frac{1}{M}\sum_{i=1}^{M}\Gamma_i \text{, where } M \text{ is the number of training images.}$$

Then, the difference between the average and each object image is calculated $\Phi_i = \Gamma_i - \Psi$, and the difference images form a matrix $A = [\Phi_1\ \Phi_2\ ...\ \Phi_M]$. Then the covariance matrix C is computed as:

$$C = AA^T = \frac{1}{M}\sum_{i=1}^{M}\Phi_i\Phi_i^T$$

Next, the eigen-vectors of this matrix are calculated and ranked according to their associated eigen-values. An eigen subspace is constructed by selecting a subset of K eigen-vectors with the largest eigen-values. Finally, for a new object image, we calculate the difference image Φ and project it to the eigen subspace. The resulting vector, that is the so-called "eigen-feature", provides a compact representation of the original image in a much lower dimensional space.

In the face recognition, grey-scale images are generally used to extract the eigen-feature rather than the binary images, because the grey-scale images contain more information about the human face. When used to classify the moving objects in the

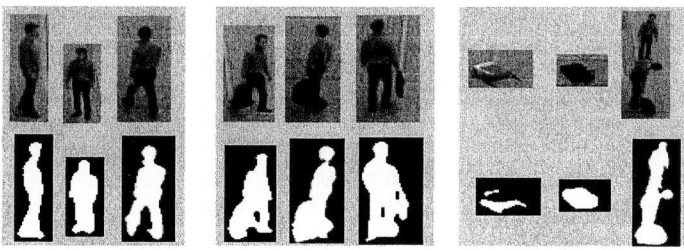

Fig. 3. Example grey-scale and binary images in three classes: a human without a bag, a human with a bag, and the unknown class

surveillance video, the grey-images may possibly introduce some unwanted disturbance due to the additional background information and the variety of the human's clothes. To compare the performance, we collected object images in both formats and performed the classification. In total, we collected and labeled 1724 grey-scale and 1745 binary images for training data, and 1505 grey-scale and 1333 binary images for test data. Figure 3 shows some examples.

2.3 Support Vector Classification

The basic idea of the SVM classification [10][11] is to find an optimal hyperplane to separate the feature vectors that belong to two classes, so that on either side of this plane there are the largest possible portion of vector points of the same class, while the distance from the hyperplane to either class is maximized.

Because different kernel functions have different performance for a specific feature, three SVM kernels have been tested and compared in this paper:

- Dot product: $k(x_i, x_j) = x_i^T x_j$
- Radial basis function (RBF): $k(x_i, x_j) = exp(-\gamma \|x_i - x_j\|^2)$, $\gamma > 0$
- Polynomial: $k(x_i, x_j) = (\gamma x_i^T x_j + r)^d$, $\gamma > 0$

The SVM library LIBSVM [1], provided by Chang and Lin, is used in the paper to perform the SVM classification. To achieve a better classification result, several useful techniques have been adopted. The first one is to normalize the input feature vectors before the classification. The purpose is to reduce the computation difficulty caused by the arbitrary vector value in a large data set. The second one is to perform the n-fold cross-validation on training data, where the training data are divided into n subsets and each subset is used as test data to test the classifier trained by the rest of the data. This method reduces the risk of the overfitting problem. The third one is to perform a grid-search on the parameter(s) in the kernel function. For example, instead of using a fixed value for the parameter γ in the RBF kernel, a series of values increased exponentially, such as $2^{-5}, 2^{-3}, 2^{-1}, ..., 2^{11}$, are tested.

3 On-Line Tracking and Labeling

The SVM classifier trained in section 2 is applied to the moving objects detected and tracked by the motion detection and tracking models in the system (figure 1). Here a region-based tracking algorithm with the Kalman-filtering is used in the tracking model. In most indoor surveillance video sequences, we can assume the status of the moving human will not change frequently within a few frames, which means in most cases the object class for a moving object should be the same in neighboring frames. A voting mechanism, utilizing this status consistency and the object tracking information, is applied to further improve the accuracy of the moving object classification. As illustrated in Figure 4, the classification is applied on a tracked object, one vote is cast for the resulting object class; votes are counted after five on-line classifications; the object class receiving the largest number of votes decides the object's class in this period. If there is a tie for first place, the human with a bag is given the highest priority, then the human without a bag, then the unknown class. This voting mechanism reduces the number of the random misclassifications in the video sequence caused by the temporal occlusion of a bag by its carrying people or other reasons such as imperfection in motion detection.

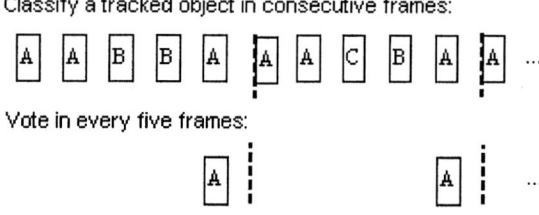

Fig. 4. Voting on the tracked and classified object

4 Experimental Results

The proposed algorithm has been tested on a 2.4 GHz Intel Xeon[TM] based PC using the RedHat Linux operating system. The algorithm, without specific optimization, is able to run 5 frames per second at size of 320x240. Figure 5 shows the significant difference in the classification accuracy of the binary motion images and the grey-scale ones. The RBF kernel is used in both groups of tests. This suggests that, although the grey-scale images contain more information about the target objects, such as the complete shapes, than the binary images, some unwanted information are also included, like the background and human clothing details. Unless a very big library of grey-scale object images has been collected from a large number of scenes under varying illumination conditions and different environments, the property of being insensitive to background and object details makes the binary image a better choice for the purpose of moving human classification in this paper.

Figure 6 shows the classification results using three different SVM kernels: the RBF, the dot product, and the polynomial kernel. The binary images are used here. The ranking of the best classification accuracies are 89.65% with the RBF kernel, 89.35% using the polynomial kernel, and 86.42% with the dot product kernel. As the number of eigen-vectors increases, the classification accuracy using the polynomial kernel drops more noticeably than those using the RBF and the dot product kernel.

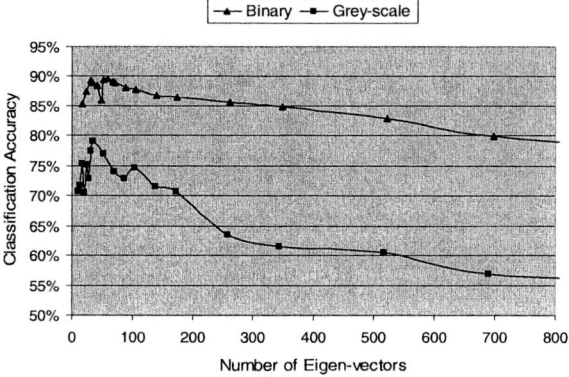

Fig. 5. Classification accuracies using binary and grey-scale images

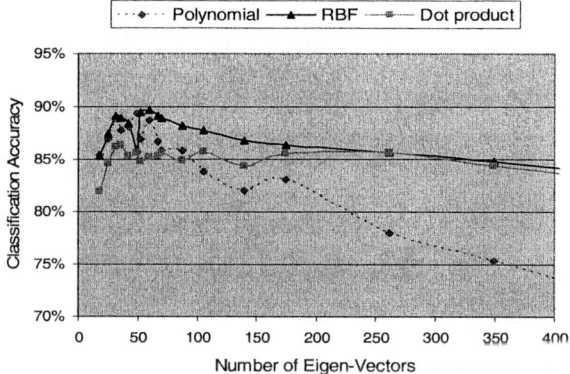

Fig. 6. Classification accuracies with different SVM kernels

Table 1 shows one classification result on the three pre-defined classes using binary images and the RBF kernel. The table reveals the classification accuracy for a human with a bag is much lower than other classes. This reflects the same difficulty experienced by the human eye: due to the partial occlusion on the bag, sometime it is hard to tell whether a person is carrying a bag or not. Similar classification accuracy was achieved in additional experiments performed on five pre-defined classes.

Table 1. One classification result for three pre-defined classes

Target class	Human w. a bag	Human w.o. a bag	Unknown Class	Total
Test Images	431	646	256	1333
Misclass.	80	38	20	138
Correct	351	608	236	1195
Accuracy	81.44%	94.12%	92.19%	89.65%

Figure 7 shows the labeled object trajectories. First, as shown by the right trajectory (red), object A appeared from the bottom as a human with a bag, moved to the center of the image, where it changed to a human without a bag. At this moment, an unknown object (green) appeared. After that, object A wandered around in the middle-right of the scene. Then, as shown by the left (blue) trajectory, object B appeared as a human without a bag from the bottom left, moved to the center, changed to a human with a bag and walked out of the scene. From these labeled trajectories, we can get some understanding about the activities in this video: a bag was dropped down by person A and was then picked up and taken away by person B. Note that during the entering and exiting periods, person A and B were classified as the unknown class, because only part of the body was detected. During the pick-up and drop-down periods, person A and B were also labeled as "x", because we include a bending-person as the unknown class. In the future, extra classes like a bending or crouching person will be added to understand more details about the human activities.

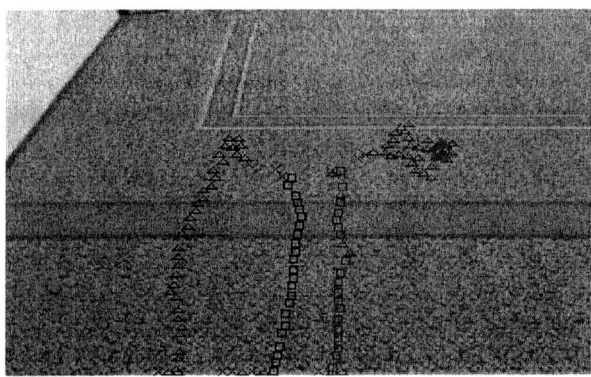

Fig. 7. Labeled object trajectories, where a square "□", triangle "Δ", and cross "x" represent a human with a bag, without a bag and the unknown class respectively

5 Conclusion

In this paper, we describe a method to classify the moving humans in the surveillance video using the eigen-feature and the support vector machine classification. The performance of different image formats for feature extraction and different SVM kernels are compared and analyzed. The result shows that when using the binary images and the RBF kernel, an accuracy of almost 90% can be achieved in a large set of test images. A voting method is introduced to utilize the tracking information to further improve the classification accuracy and generate the labeled tracking trajectories, which can help understand the human activities in a surveillance sequence. Further efforts are being carried out to improve the motion detection and object tracking algorithms, in order to detect moving objects from a dynamic outdoor environment and track the objects under heavy occlusions. The final goal is to automatically understand the human activities and detect various meaningful events from the surveillance video.

Acknowledgment

The authors thank Yu Z., Mathew R., and Vishwanathan S. from NICTA, Mustafa A. and Swords C. from the University of Sydney, for their valuable suggestions and assistance in preparing this paper.

References

1. Chang C. and Lin C.: LIBSVM: a Library for Support Vector Machines, http://www.csie.ntu.edu.tw/~cjlin, August 12, 2004.
2. Collins R. T., Lipton A. J., Kanade T., Fujiyoshi H., Duggins D., Tsin Y., Tolliver D., Enomoto N., Hasegawa O., Burt P., and Wixson L.: A System for Video Surveillance and Monitoring. CMU-RI-TR-00-12, Carnegie Mellon University, 2000.
3. Bogomolov Y., Dror G., Lapchev S., Rivlin E., Rudzsky M.: Classification of Moving Targets Based on Motion and Appearance. British Machine Vision Conference, 2003.
4. Rivlin E., Rudzsky M., Goldenberg R., Bogomolov U., Lapchev S.: A Real-Time System for Classification of Moving Objects. IEEE Conference on Computer Vision and Pattern Recognition, 2002.
5. Toth D. and Aach T.: Detection and Recognition of Moving Objects Using Statistical Motion Detection and Fourier Descriptors. International Conference on Image Analysis and Processing, 2003.
6. Turk M. A. and Pentland A. P.: Face Recognition Using Eigenfaces. IEEE Conference on Computer Vision and Pattern Recognition, 1991.
7. Sun Z., Bebis G., and Miller R.: Boosting Object Detection Using Feature Selection. Proceedings of the IEEE Conference on Advanced Video and Signal Based Surveillance, 2003.
8. Leibe B. and Schiele B.: Analyzing Appearance and Contour Based Methods for Object Categorization. IEEE Conference on Computer Vision and Pattern Recognition, 2003.
9. Stauffer C. and Grimson W.: Adaptive Background Mixture Models for Real-time Tracking. IEEE Conference of Computer Vision and Pattern Recognition, 1999.
10. Boser B., Guyon I., and Vapnik V.: A Training Algorithm for Optimal Margin Classifier. In Proceedings of the Fifth Annual Workshop on Computational Learning Theory, 1992.
11. Scholkopf B. and Smola A. J.: A Short Introduction to Learning with Kernels. Advanced Lectures on Machine Learning, Springer-Verlag Berlin Heidelberg 2003.

A Queue Based Algorithm for Order Independent Anchored Skeletonisation

Marcin Iwanowski and Pierre Soille

Joint Research Centre of the European Commission,
T.P. 262, I-21020 Ispra (VA), Italy
{Marcin.Iwanowski, Pierre.Soille}@jrc.it

Abstract. In this paper, we propose an efficient implementation of order independent anchored skeletons. It is based on a series of queue data structures and enables the processing of large images. An application to the reduction of thick river networks to their medial axis is briefly described.

1 Introduction

A widely used approach for computing discrete skeletons consists in iteratively thinning the input pattern with a series of homotopic structuring elements until no further pixels can be removed. However, an issue which has not been often investigated when developing thinning algorithms is *order independence*. When this property is satisfied, the computed skeleton is the same no matter the order in which the image pixels are processed. Recently, Ranwez and Soille [1,2] have introduced the concept of order independent homotopic thinning and shown that it leads to order independent skeletonisation when iterated until no more pixels are modified. In this paper, we propose an efficient implementation based on a series of queue data structures.

The paper is organised as follows. Section 2 details background notions about skeletonisation while emphasising issues related to order independence. The proposed algorithm is described in Sec. 3 and its extension to grey tone images is presented in Sec. 4. Finally, results and conclusions are given in Sec. 5.

2 Background Notions

Except for coding applications where skeletons defined by the centre of maximal discs are of interest, a desired property of a skeletonisation procedure is the preservation of the homotopy of the original image. Two binary images are *homotopic* if and only if they have the same *homotopy tree* [3]. This tree is defined as a graph whose vertices correspond to the foreground and background connected components and whose edges represent the adjacency relations between these components. Usually, it is assumed that the image is surrounded by a background connected component which uniquely defines the root of the tree.

One of the most popular approaches to skeletonisation is based on sequential *thinning* [4] which removes pixels iteratively until the input image is reduced to its own skeleton. In case of homotopic thinning, only *simple* pixels are removed. A simple pixel is defined as a pixel which can be removed without changing the homotopy of the image. Rosenfeld [5] has shown that a pixel p is simple if and only if the following two conditions hold (in this paper, 8-connectivity is used for the foreground and 4-connectivity for the background):

1. the set of 8-connected foreground neighbours of p is non-empty and 8-connected;
2. the set of 4-connected background neighbours of p is non-empty.

A skeleton resulting from the iterative deletion of all simple pixels does not reflect all structures of the input pattern. For example, an object without holes (a simply connected set) is reduced to a single pixel while the block letter 'R' has the same skeleton as the letter 'P', i.e. the closed loop surrounding the hole of these letters. In order to get more control on skeletonisation, *anchor skeletons* [6,7,8,9] have been introduced so that a series of pre-defined points, called anchor points, are flagged as non deletable during the thinning process. Anchor points are usually defined by the maxima of the distance function which are greater than a given threshold value.

Typical order dependent thinning algorithms for anchored homotopic skeletons proceed as follows:

Algorithm 1 Order dependent binary anchor skeleton

call: *OrderDependentSkel(I, A)*
I input binary image
A anchor image: $A(p) = 1$ if p is an anchor pixel, $A(p) = 0$ otherwise
S temporary image for marking the simple pixels

1. **do**
2. $deleted \leftarrow$ **false**
3.   **for** each pixel p of I **do**
4.   **if** $IsSimple(p, I) =$ **true** and $A(p) = 0$ **then**
5. $S(p) \leftarrow 1$ **else** $S(p) \leftarrow 0$
6.   **for** each pixel p of I **do** (arbitrary sequential scanning order)
7.   **if** $S(p) = 1$ and $IsSimple(p, I) =$ **true then**
8. $I(p) \leftarrow 0$; $deleted \leftarrow$ **true**
9. **while** $deleted =$ **true**

The function $IsSimple$ (lines 4 and 7) indicates whether a pixel p of an image I is simple or not according to Rosenfeld's conditions. To accelerate this test, an indicator look-up-table with 256 entries is used to determine once for all whether any given neighbourhood configuration is homotopic or not.

The skeleton resulting from Alg. 1 depends on the scanning order of the image pixels (line 6). When computing an order independent skeleton only those simple pixels which would be removed by Alg. 1, no matter the chosen arbitrary sequential scanning order, should be removed. Such pixels are called order independent simple pixels [2]. They are detected by a detailed analysis of the dependence relationships between each simple pixel and its simple neighbours. A simple pixel not adjacent to any other simple pixel is a trivial example of an order independent simple pixel. Figure 1 shows a small pattern containing configurations of order dependent and independent pixels.

Fig. 1. Order dependent (dark grey) versus order independent (light grey) simple pixels. Black pixels are the non-simple pixels.

We present hereafter a condensed version of the developments proposed in [2,10]. Let p an q be two simple neighbour pixels. Then, p is *independent* from q if and only if there is another foreground pixel within the intersection of the 8-neighbourhoods of p and q and, in addition, if p and q are 4-adjacent, p has a 4-adjacent background neighbour which is 4-adjacent to a 4-adjacent background neighbour of q. If these conditions are not satisfied, p is dependent on q, which means that p will be deleted or not depending on the selected scanning order. Consequently, it should not be removed by an order independent algorithm. Independence of p from q is not a sufficient condition for asserting that p will be removed by all scanning orders. This happens however, when p is *strictly independent* from all of its simple neighbours. A simple pixel p is strictly independent from a simple pixel q if and only if they are independent and there exists a non simple foreground pixel in the intersection of their 8-neighbourhoods. If pixels are independent, but not strictly (p has only background foreground simple or background neighbours) further neighbourhood analysis is necessary. It is then checked whether there are any foreground pixels among the 8-neighbours of p which are not 8-neighbours of q. If this is the case, p cannot be removed. Otherwise, the whole connected component of foreground pixels to which p belongs, denoted by $CC_8(p)$, must be tested. If $CC_8(p)$ is *strongly 8-deletable* [11,12], there exists a scanning order where p is not removed. Therefore p should only be removed by an order independent algorithm if $CC_8(p)$ is *not* strongly 8-deletable. A connected component is strongly 8-deletable if and only if two conditions are fulfilled: all its pixels are simple *and* there exists a sequential scanning order such that all scanned pixels can be removed without modifying the homotopy of the connected component. This latter condition is fulfilled if and only if the connected component is simply connected.

3 Queue-Based Implementation

3.1 The Main Body

The main body of the algorithm for binary anchored order independent skeletonisation (Alg. 2) consists of two parts. The first part (lines 1–4) initialises the queue Q_{main} by inserting all simple pixels of the input image I which are not anchor points. These pixels are simultaneously flagged in an auxiliary image S to indicate that they are potentially deletable. To mark the end of the insertion of simple pixels in the queue, a control value '−1' is inserted since a negative value cannot correspond to the position index of a pixel.

The second part (lines 5–21) is executed while pixels are deleted. Initially, a flag named *deleted* is set to false (line 6). Then (lines 7–10), simple pixels previously inserted in the queue Q_{main} are retrieved and passed on to the function *IsDeletable* which returns true if they are order independent simple pixels (this function is described in Sec. 3.2). In this latter case (see line 9), they are inserted in the queue Q_{del} while the flag *deleted* is reset to true. Order independent simple pixels are inserted in the Q_{del} queue because their deletion on the fly could influence the result of the *IsSimple* test performed on the subsequent simple pixels. Then (lines 11–20), all order independent simple pixels are set to 0 (lines 13–14) and their simple neighbours are inserted on the queue Q_{main} (lines 15–19). Again, to mark the end of the insertion of simple pixels, a control value '−1' is inserted (line 20). If no pixel was deleted, the algorithm stops (line 21) otherwise it starts again from line 5.

Algorithm 2 Binary order independent anchored skeletonisation

call: *OrderIndependentSkel(I, A)*
I input image
A anchor image: $A(p) = 1$ if p is an anchor pixel, $A(p) = 0$ otherwise
S temporary image for flagging simple pixels
p, q pixels
$I(p)$ value of p on the input image I
$N_8(p)$ a set of 8-neighbours of p
Q_{main} the main FIFO queue
Q_{del} the supplementary FIFO queue used for deleting pixels
deleted flag indicating that at least one point is qualified for deletion

1. for each pixel p do
2.   if $IsSimple(p, I)$ = true and $A(p) = 0$ then
3.   fifo_add(Q_{main}, p) ; $S(p) \leftarrow 1$ else $S(p) \leftarrow 0$
4. fifo_add($Q_{main}, -1$)
5. do
6.   *deleted* $\leftarrow$ false
7.   while $(p \leftarrow$ fifo_retrieve$(Q_{main})) \neq -1$ do
8.   if $IsDeletable(p, I, S)$ = true then
9.   fifo_add(Q_{del}, p) ; *deleted* $\leftarrow$ true
10.   else fifo_add(Q_{main}, p)
11.   if *deleted* = true then
12.   fifo_add($Q_{del}, -1$)
13.   while $(p \leftarrow$ fifo_retrieve$(Q_{del})) \neq -1$ do
14.   fifo_add(Q_{del}, p) ; $I(p) \leftarrow 0$; $S(p) \leftarrow 0$
15.   while fifo_empty(Q_{del}) = false do
16. $p \leftarrow$ fifo_retrieve(Q_{del})
17.   for all $q \in N_8(p)$ do
18.   if $IsSimple(q, I)$ and $A(q) = 0$ and $S(q) = 0$ then
19.   fifo_add(Q_{main}, q) ; $S(q) \leftarrow 1$
20.   fifo_add($Q_{main}, -1$)
21. while *deleted* = true

3.2 To Remove or Not to Remove?

Algorithm 3 describes the deletability test (in the sense of order independent deletability) of a pixel p of a binary image I and given a binary image S where all simple pixels of I are set to 1, all other pixels being set to 0. The function implementing this algorithm is called *IsDeletable* and is called from line 8 of Alg. 2. For an input pixel p the algorithm investigates all its simple neighbours (lines 1–2). For every simple neighbour q the following tests are performed. At first, the property of being independent simple is investigated (lines 3–4). If pixels p and q are not independent simple, p cannot be deleted and `false` is returned without investigating other neighbours. In case the pixel p is independent from its currently analysed neighbour q, non-strict independence between p and q is tested for at line 6. If the test is positive, the last two tests (lines 7–8) are performed. The test on line 7 checks whether pixel p has within its 8-connected neighbourhood a pixel of value 1 which does not belong to the 8-neighbours of q. If true, p cannot be removed. The final connected component test ($CCtest$) returns `true` if and only if the connected component p belongs to ($CC_8(p)$) is strongly 8-deletable. This test is described in the next section.

Algorithm 3 Deletability test

call: $IsDeletable(p,I,S)$
         description of variables used: see Alg. 2

1. for all $q \in N_8(p)$ do
2.   if $S(q) = 1$ then
3.   if $\forall r \in N_8(p) \cap N_8(q) : I(r) = 0$ then return false
4.   if $\exists r, s \in N_8(p) \cap N_8(q) : I(r) = I(s) = 1$ and $r \notin N_8(s)$ then
5.   return false
6.   if $\forall r \in N_8(p) \cap N_8(q) : I(r) = 0$ or $S(r) = 1$ then
7.   if $\exists r \in N_8(p) \setminus N_8(q) : I(r) = 1$ then return false
8.   if $CCtest(p, I, S) = $ true then return false
9. return true

3.3 Connected Component Test

The connected component test described by Alg. 4 investigates a connected component to which a given pixel p belongs, in order to check its strong 8-deletability. The algorithm consists of three parts. In the first part (lines 1–9) all the pixels of a given connected component are analysed using the queue propagation. All pixels belonging to this component are scanned to check whether they are simple (i.e. have the value 1 in the auxiliary image S). If a non-simple pixel is found, it means that the connected component is not strongly 8-deletable and therefore `false` is returned (line 5). During the simpleness checking all the simple pixels belonging to the current connected component are marked with a value 1 in the auxiliary image B.

In the second part (lines 10–14) the external border marking is performed. Marking begins from the first external border point detected in the first part of the algorithm (stored in $firstex$ variable) and propagates along the boundary using the 4-connected neighbourhood propagation. Finally a 4-connected path containing $firstex$ is considered to be the external boundary of the given connected component. This boundary is marked by the value 2 in the auxiliary image B.

The third part of the algorithm (lines 15–23) processes again all the pixels belonging to the currently analysed connected component (similar to the first part). This time however another feature is investigated: the existence of a non-marked external boundary points. If such a pixel is found, it indicates that the connected component contains at least one hole and therefore is not simply connected. In such a case, it is not strongly 8-deletable and `false` is returned at line 20. Otherwise, the algorithm returns `true`.

Since the property of strong 8-deletability is a property of a whole connected component to which the pixel belongs (not a property of a single pixel), *CCtest* can be performed only once for each component (alternative implementation not shown in pseudo-code). To make the result of this test accessible for the other pixels of the connected component, a supplementary connected component marking must be performed. Depending on the result of the test, all pixels belonging to the currently analysed component are set to *'deletable'* or *'not-deletable'*. When the next pixel belonging to the already marked component is tested, instead of going through all steps of *CCtest*, `true` or `false` is directly returned depending on whether the pixel was flagged *'deletable'* or *'not-deletable'*.

Algorithm 4 Connected component test

call:	*CCtest(p,I,S)*
B	supplementary image used for marking (all pixels initially set to 0)
bnm	"border not marked" - a flag indicating marking the external borders
$firstex$	first external border pixel found
Q_{cc}	FIFO queue used in this algorithm
$N_4(p)$	a set of 4-neighbours of p
	for the other variables - see Alg. 2

1. $bnm \leftarrow$ true
2. fifo_add(Q_{cc}, p) ; $B(p) \leftarrow 1$
3. while fifo_empty(Q_{cc}) = false do
4. $r \leftarrow$ fifo_retrieve(Q_{cc})
5.   if $S(r) = 0$ then return false
6.   for all $q \in N_8(r)$ do
7.   if $I(q) = 1$ then
8.   if $B(q) = 0$ then fifo_add(Q_{cc}, q) ; $B(q) \leftarrow 1$
9.   else if $bnm =$ true then $bnm \leftarrow$ false ; $firstex \leftarrow q$
10. fifo_add$(Q_{cc}, firstex)$; $B(s) \leftarrow 2$
11. while fifo_empty(Q_{cc}) = false do
12. $s \leftarrow$ fifo_retrieve(Q_{cc})
13.   for all $t \in N_4(s)$ do
14.   if $B(t) = 0$ and $\exists u \in N_4(t) : B(u) = 1$ then fifo_add(Q_{cc}, t) ; $B(t) \leftarrow 2$
15. fifo_add(Q_{cc}, p) ; $B(p) \leftarrow 3$
16. while fifo_empty(Q_{cc}) = false do
17. $r \leftarrow$ fifo_retrieve(Q_{cc})
18.   for all $q \in N_8(r)$ do
19.   if $I(q) = 0$ then
20.   if $B(q) = 0$ then return false
21.   else if $B(q) = 1$ then
22.   fifo_add(Q_{cc}, q) ; $B(q) \leftarrow 3$
23. return true

4 Extension to Grey Tone Images

To extend the order independent homotopic thinning to grey tone images, one has to consider a definition of homotopy suitable to these images. Serra [3] proposed the following definition based on the image cross-sections (binary images obtained by thresholding the grey tone image for each successive grey level): two grey tone images are homotopic if and only if their corresponding cross-sections are homotopic. A transformation applied to a grey tone image is then homotopic if the homotopy of input and output images are the same. We assume that grey tone levels correspond to nonnegative integer numbers. As for the binary case, we consider here 8-connectivity for the foreground and 4-connectivity for the background. A set of background (resp. foreground) neighbours of a given pixel p, denoted by $N^<(p)$ (resp. $N^\geq(p)$) consists of its neighbours with lower (resp. higher or equal) grey value. A pixel p of a grey tone image I is *simple* if and only if its set of background 4-adjacent neighbours is nonempty and if, in addition, the image obtained by decreasing the value of this pixel from its original value $I(p)$ to the maximum value of its background 8-adjacent neighbours, i.e. $\max\{I(p') \mid p' \in N_8^<(p)\}$, is homotopic to the original image. In other words, a pixel p of an image I is simple if and only if the two following conditions hold:

1. the set of foreground 8-neighbours of p, $N_8^\geq(p)$, is nonempty and 8-connected;
2. the set of background 4-neighbours of p, $N_4^<(p)$, is nonempty.

The pseudo-code for an order dependent grey tone anchored skeletonisation algorithm is similar to that presented in the binary case. One just needs to substitute $I(p) \leftarrow 0$ in line 8 of Alg. 1 with $I(p) \leftarrow \max\{I(p') \mid p' \in N_8^<(p)\}$.

An order independent algorithm requires the detection of order independent simple pixels. They are detected like in the binary case by considering the pixels with a lower value as background pixels, those with a greater value as anchor foreground pixels, and those with the same value as additional foreground pixels while some of them may belong to the set of predefined anchor points. Similarly to the algorithm proposed for binary images (Alg. 2), grey tone order independent skeletonisation is performed in two main steps, repeated until stability. During the first step, order independent simple pixels are detected. In the second step, the detected pixels are set to the maximal value of their lower 8-neighbours.

5 Results and Conclusions

Figure 2 illustrates the use of the proposed skeletonisation algorithm for the extraction of the medial axis of river networks. The graytone skeletonisation has been applied to the Euclidean distance function of the binary mask of the rivers using its maxima as anchor points. In contrast to the developments detailed in [2] and which required numerous scans of the whole image definition domain, the proposed queue based algorithm allows for the fast computation of order independent skeletons with or without anchor points. We are currently using it for extracting relevant morphological information from geospatial raster data such as satellite images and digital elevation models. Its extension to the computation of order independent watersheds will be detailed in a forthcoming paper.

References

1. Ranwez, V., Soille, P.: Order independent homotopic thinning. Lecture Notes in Computer Science **1568** (1999) 337–346
2. Ranwez, V., Soille, P.: Order independent homotopic thinning for binary and grey tone anchored skeletons. Pattern Recognition Letters **23** (2002) 687–702

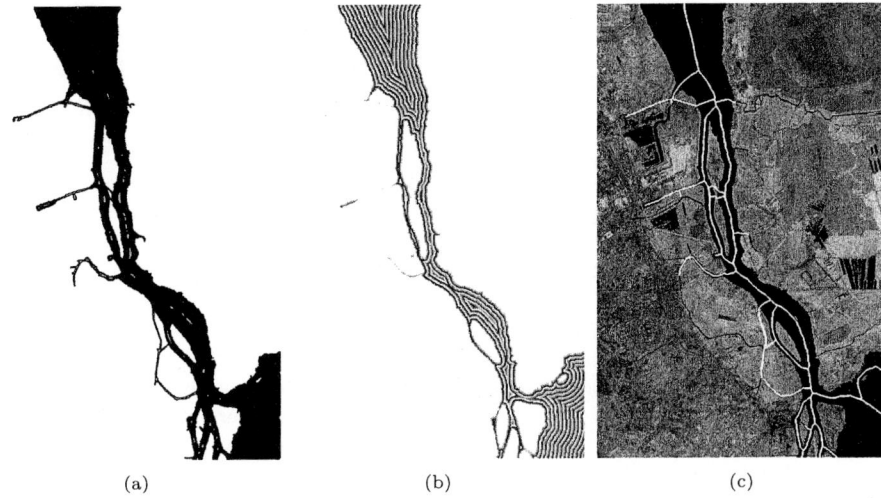

(a) (b) (c)

Fig. 2. Application of the proposed algorithm to the computation of the medial axis of a river network. (a) Binary image of river silouhette with anchor points superimposed in grey. (b) Euclidean distance function of binary mask. (c) Skeleton (white) superimposed on the original image used for extracting the river silhouette.

3. Serra, J.: Image analysis and mathematical morphology. Academic Press, London (1982)
4. Lam, L., Lee, S.W., Suen, C.: Thinning methodologies: a comprehensive survey. IEEE Transactions on Pattern Analysis and Machine Intelligence **14** (1992) 869–885
5. Rosenfeld, A.: Connectivity in digital pictures. Journal of the ACM **17** (1970) 146–160
6. Vincent, L.: Efficient computation of various types of skeletons. In Loew, M., ed.: Medical Imaging V: Image Processing. Volume SPIE-1445. (1991) 297–311
7. Pudney, C.: Distance-ordered homotopic thinning: a skeletonization algorithm for 3D digital images. Computer Vision and Image Understanding **72** (1998) 404–413
8. Davies, E., Plummer, A.: Thinning algorithms: a critique and a new methodology. Pattern Recognition **14** (1981) 53–63
9. Mazanzera, A., Bernard, T., Preteux, F., Longuet, B.: n-dimensional skeletonization: a unified mathematical framework. Journal of Electronic Imaging **11** (2002) 25–37
10. Soille, P.: Morphological Image Analysis. 2nd edn. Springer-Verlag, Heidelberg (2003)
11. Ronse, C.: A topological characterization of thinning. Theoretical Computer Science **43** (1986) 31–41
12. Ronse, C.: Minimal test patterns for connectivity preservation in parallel thinning algorithms for binary digital images. Discrete Applied Mathematics **21** (1988) 67–79

Morphological Refinement of an Image Segmentation

Marcin Iwanowski and Pierre Soille

Joint Research Centre of the European Commission,
T.P. 262, I-21020 Ispra (VA), Italy
{Marcin.Iwanowski, Pierre.Soille}@jrc.it

Abstract. This paper describes a method to improve a given segmentation result in order to produce a new, refined and more accurate segmented image. The method consists of three phases: shrinking of the input partitions, filtering of the input imagery leading to a mask image, and expansion of the shrunk partitions within the filtered image. The concept is illustrated for the enhancement of a land cover data set using multispectral satellite imagery.

1 Introduction

Segmentation is one of the key tasks of digital image processing. Its goal is to detect and mark uniform areas visible in the input image. There are however situations where a segmentation result is *a priori* known but must be *improved* so as to exactly match the object boundaries. For example, geographic information systems often contain vector data sets representing objects derived by manual photo-interpretation means. Therefore, boundaries following precisely the image objects could be obtained by using the knowledge stored in this data when processing imagery representing the same area. The proposed method requires two input images: given segmentation result (partition, labeled image) and an image which is segmented referred to as underlying image. The approach consists of three principal steps: shrinking of a given partition (e.g. areas of a rasterised vector data set), mask preparation which transforms the underlying image, and expansion which reconstructs the regions of the input partition while precisely following the image boundaries. All are based on mathematical morphology [1,2]. The results of segmentation improvement are validated using the modified gradient measurement which is also described in the paper.

In remote sensing where image objects are often marked manually by a photo-interpreter, the quality of the contours depends strongly on non-measurable factors, like interpretation skills of a human operator. An example of manual segmentation is a pan-European land cover map (known as CORINE Land Cover or CLC) which was produced using various sources, the main one being Landsat satellite imagery. By means of the proposed method, the shape of the regions occurring in the CLC map is refined so that they precisely follow the boundaries of the image objects.

The paper is organised as follows. Section 2 describes three principal steps of the method: shrinking, mask preparation, and expansion. Section 3 presents a method of validating the improvement. In section 4, an application of the method to improve the CORINE land cover map is presented. Conclusions are given in Section 5.

2   Methodology

The approach consists of three principal steps: shrinking, mask preparation, and expansion. The aim of the first step is to process the labeled image (input segmentation result) by transforming it into the markers which are later used as the seeds in the region growing segmentation process. The mask preparation deals with the underlying image (to be segmented) and is based on filtering techniques which simplify the image. Images created in the first two steps become the input for the third, expansion phase, which is a segmentation process that produces the final result. All three steps are described in the following sections.

2.1   Shrinking Phase

The shrinking phase reduces the size of the partitions of a given segmentation in order to generate an 'empty space' between regions, which can be further used in the expansion phase. The input segmentation is an image where pixel values refer to labels describing the class to which a particular point belongs. This labeled partition is obtained e.g. by rasterising a vector data set representing the same area as the input image. We assume that label values are represented by positive integer values ≥ 1 so that the value 0 can be used as background value in the sequel. We also denote by l the largest label value. Shrinking operators process the given labeled partition by processing it label value by label value. The set of pixels with the same label is considered as a separate binary image and treated by an anti-extensive operator of shrinking. Finally, the results of this treatment are merged in a single output image. The thresholding operator T for the label i is defined as a function which sets to 0 all pixels which are not equal to i:

$$T_i(F)[p] = \begin{cases} i & \text{if } F(p) = i, \\ 0 & \text{otherwise.} \end{cases} \quad (1)$$

where F stands for the labeled image. The shrinking of F based on an anti-extensive flat operator S is then defined as the point-wise maximum of the output of the operator S applied to the successive thresholds of the labeled image:

$$\bigvee_{i=1}^{l} S(T_i(F)) \quad (2)$$

The choice of the operator S depends on the features of the input image F which should be preserved. In the simplest case, an erosion of a given size can be used. However, if there exist regions relatively small compared to the size of

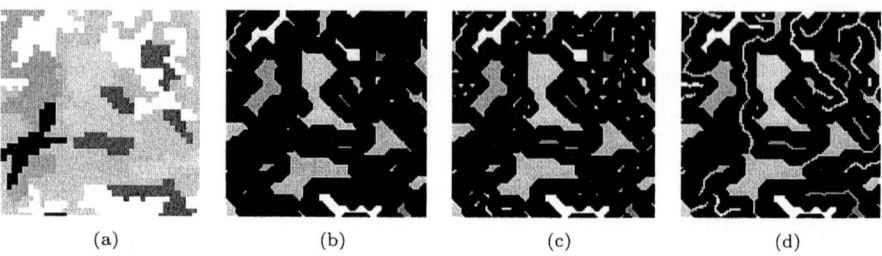

Fig. 1. Shrinking phase: (a) original labeled image, (b) erosion, (c) ultimate eroded set of a given size, and (d) homotopic shrinking. The same size has been considered for three all operations.

the selected structuring element, some regions would disappear in the output partition. This problem can be solved by considering the ultimate eroded set of each threshold:

$$ULT(X) = \bigcup_{i=1}^{\infty} \left\{ \varepsilon^{(i)}(X) \setminus R_{\varepsilon^{(i)}}^{\delta} \left[\varepsilon^{(i+1)}(X) \right] \right\} \quad (3)$$

where $\varepsilon^{(i)}(X)$ stands for erosion of size i of X, R^{δ} is the morphological reconstruction by dilation of its argument while the subscript indicates the considered geodesic mask. It can be shown [2] that the ultimate eroded set is equivalent to a set containing the maxima of a distance function: $ULT(X) = RMAX[D(X)]$. In case of shrinking the goal is to shrink the partitions not until idempotence as in the Eq. 3 but within the required extent only. In order to reach this goal, successive erosions in Eq. 3 should be stopped at a given level, which defines an ultimate eroded set of a given size n:

$$ULT^{(n)}(X) = \bigcup_{i=1}^{n} \left\{ \varepsilon^{(i)}(X) \setminus R_{\varepsilon^{(i)}}^{\delta} \left[\varepsilon^{(i+1)}(X) \right] \right\} = \varepsilon^{(n)}(X) \cup ULT(X) \quad (4)$$

It may also be required, that the homotopy of the labeled regions should be preserved. In such a case, the ultimate eroded set of a given size is not the desired solution because it can change the homotopy of segments. Homotopic transformations such as skeletonisation based on homotopic thinning and anchor points [3,4] should be considered. Anchor points are the points which cannot be removed during the thinning process. For defining the skeletonisation based shrinking operator, the set of anchor points is equal to the ultimate eroded set. Hence, the resulting shrinking operator can be written as follows:

$$S^{(n)}(X) = \varepsilon^{(n)}(X) \cup Skel(X, ULT(X)) = Skel(X, ULT^{(n)}(X)) \quad (5)$$

where $Skel(X,Y)$ stands for the anchored skeleton of image X with anchor points defined by Y. Since the operation defined by Eq. 5 preserves homotopy of the input set, we call it *homotopic shrinking*. Results of shrinking using all three proposed approaches are shown in Fig. 1.

2.2 Mask Preparation

The refinement of the input partition (labeled image) is based on the propagation of the shrunk labeled regions within an underlying input image so as to improve the position of the boundaries of each labeled region that was present in the input partition. Since the propagation may be sensitive to the presence of structures that are smaller than the smallest segment of the input partition, as well as small variations of pixel values (noise), which can result in disturbances in the final region boundaries, the underlying image should be filtered before starting the propagation. Filtering must be applied while preserving boundaries on the filtered image because accuracy in the segmentation result is of utmost importance. Mathematical morphology offers a range of tools for efficient filtering suitable for this purpose: reconstruction filtering [5], self-dual filtering [6], area filters [7], or area flat-zone filters [8,9]. Filtered underlying image is a mask used during the expansion phase as a reference image for propagation.

2.3 Expansion Phase

In this step, labels stored in the marker image are propagated inside non-labeled areas ('gaps') created during the shrinking phase. The propagations are performed using the priority queue: pixels with higher priority are removed before those with lower priority. Pixels with the same priority are removed using the FIFO rule. In the propagation algorithm the priority of any pixel put into the queue depends on the value of this pixel on the underlying mask image. A generic region growing algorithm is described by Algorithm 1.

Algorithm 1 Generic region growing algorithm

call:	$grow(M, U)$
M	input marker image and output (result of segmentation)
U	input underlying mask image
p, q	image pixels
$N(p)$	neighborhood of pixel p
$bglabel$	background label (for pixels not belonging to any of partitions, set to 0)
$inqueue$	pseudo-label indicating that a pixel is in the queue (set e.g. to -1)
pq-$add(p,v)$	adding a pixel p into the priority queue with priority v
pq-$remove$	removing a pixel from the priority queue
pq-$empty$	boolean test returning $TRUE$ if the queue is empty and $FALSE$ otherwise

1. for all p do
2.   if $M(p) = bglabel$ and $\exists q \in N(p) : M(q) \neq bglabel \wedge M(q) \neq inqueue$ then
3. $M(p) \leftarrow inqueue$
4. $v \leftarrow priority(p, U)$
5. pq-$add(p, v)$
6. while pq-$empty = FALSE$ do
7. $p \leftarrow pq$-$remove$
8. $M(p) \leftarrow get$-$label(p, M)$
9.   for all $q \in N(p)$ do
10.   if $M(q) = bglabel$ then
11. $v \leftarrow priority(q, U)$
12. $M(q) \leftarrow inqueue$
13. pq-$add(q, v)$

The choice of functions *priority* and *get-label* depend on a type of propagation which is performed. In particular, the first of these two functions influences the propagation itself. In case of morphological watershed operation [10], the priority is inversely proportional to the gradient of the underlying image. This simulates the flooding starting from markers. In case of seeded region growing approach [11], the priority depends on the measure indicating the difference between the pixel value and the average value of pixels belonging to the region. The priority is inversely proportional to this measure. The second function *getlabel(p,M)* returns a label which should be assigned to pixel p on image M. The label is chosen after the analysis of the neighborhood of p in M.

3 Validation of Improvement Results

In order to validate the improvement, the statistical measure of modified gradient is used. The idea is based on an assumption that the better segmentation result is, the more homogenous are the grayvalues of pixels from the underlying image within the regions from the segmented one. The homogenity of image pixels can be measured by means of image gradient. The morphological gradient G of underlying image U is defined as a difference between image dilation and erosion, both of a minimal size 1: $G = \delta^{(1)}(U) - \varepsilon^{(1)}(U)$.

When using the gradient to measure the quality of segmentation, the high gradient values along the boundaries of segmented image should not be considered. In order to exclude them, the following procedure is applied. First, a region mask is computed in two steps. Initially, the segmentation image M is being shrunk using the erosion operator of a given size k. Finally, this image is thresholded in such a way that boundary areas are set to 0, while the inner regions to a maximal image value (usually equal to 255):

$$R = \begin{cases} 0 & \text{if } \bigvee_{i=1}^{l} \varepsilon^{(k)}(T_i(M)) = 0 \\ 255 & \text{otherwise} \end{cases} \quad (6)$$

The image R is, in the next step, applied to hide (set to 0) all the parts on the gradient image, which refer to boundary areas of the segmented image. This is done by point-wise minimum (inf) of the gradient image G and region mask R so that a modified gradient is obtained: $G' = inf\{G, R\}$. Final image G' contains only gradient values of underlying image inside regions from the segmented one. Image G' is then computed for different segmentation result (different images M). Better segmentation results, which fits better the boundaries, will result in lower number of pixels with high values of gradient on image G'. This is due to the fact that high boundary gradient values are masked by R and therefore set to 0 on image G'. In case of a segmentation which doesn't follow precisely the borders of objects on the underlying image, the image G' will contain more high valued pixels, since some of high boundary gradient pixels will not be hidden by R. The variability is measured using statistical parameters of mean value μ and standard deviation σ of the image G':

$$\mu = \frac{1}{m} \sum_{\forall p} G'(p) \;;\; \sigma = \sqrt{\frac{1}{m} \sum_{\forall p} (G'(p) - \mu)^2} \quad (7)$$

where m stands for the number of pixels of the image. Improvement of a given segmentation will be reflected in above parameters: improved segmentation will result in lower values comparing to the initial segmentation.

4 Application to CORINE Land Cover Improvement

The proposed methodology was motivated by the need to improve the the CORINE Land cover Map of year 2000 (CLC 2000) [12] so as to match it with the images from the Image 2000 database of Landsat 7 imagery [13]. CLC 2000 is a digital land cover map produced based on a variety sources, including satellite multispectral images. The resulting manual segmentation is a mosaic of land cover classes (44 in total) describing the land use. The CLC 2000 project was supported by most European countries (including all the EU members). The manually marked regions refer to real entities on the terrain, being somewhat generalised. According to the project specifications, only the objects having a surface larger than 25 ha were mapped. Most region boundaries were simplified, especially for more complex shapes so that they do not precisely follow the content of the satellite image. The mask was prepared from the original multispectral image (a part of it, of size 502x424 pixels, is shown on Fig. 2a) using the flat-zone area filter [6,9]. This filter removes quasi-flat zones of an area smaller than the given value (in this example the area value was set to 10 pixels). The contrast of quasi flat-zones was equal to 1 which means that the difference between two adjacent pixels of a flat-zone was equal to 1 (in all 7 channels). The filtered image is shown in Fig. 2b. This color picture was created from channels 1,2, and 3 by considering them as color components B,G, and R respectively.

Table 1. Validation of improvement - mean values (standard deviations in brackets)

band	original segm. - original U	improved segm. - original U	original segm. - filtered U	improved segm. - filtered U
1	27.53 (30.08)	13.26 (26.55)	23.15 (28.24)	9.15 (21.45)
2	27.31 (27.37)	14.34 (27.16)	22.16 (24.78)	9.35 (19.89)
3	32.15 (28.54)	12.17 (22.99)	27.77 (28.04)	8.54 (18.69)

The initial segmentation shown in Fig. 2c was subjected to homotopic shrinking of size 5 in 4-connected grid. Owing to that, the regions shrunk without loosing their homotopy. Shrunk particles were used as the markers for the region growing segmentation of the reference, mask image (shown in Fig. 2b). The propagation of the labels was done using the seeded region growing method. The priority of pixels added to the queue was computed as a difference between the (vector) value of the currently considered pixel and the average value of the closest adjacent region. The *get-label* function (sec. 2.3) was based on the rule, according to which the label assigned to a pixel was set to the label value of

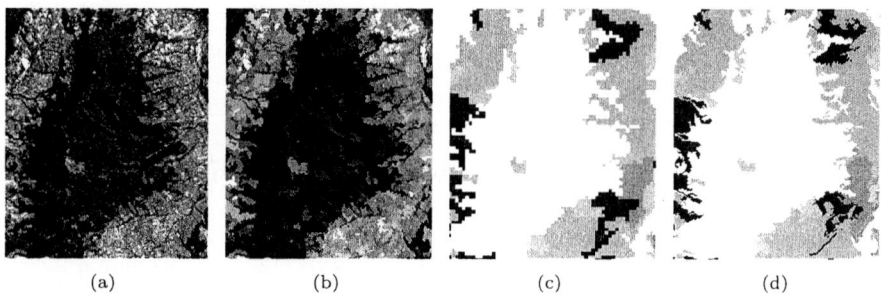

Fig. 2. The original underlying image (a), the image filtered using flat-zone area filtering, the mask (b), the original rasterised CLC map - initial segmentation (c), the improved CLC segmentation (d)

the preceeding pixel. Processing results are shown in Fig. 2. Compared to the original segmentation (Fig. 2c) the computed new one (Fig. 2d) matches much better to the underlying image (Fig. 2a). The results of improvement has been validated using the method described in section 3 (the k parameter was set to 2). The mean value and standard deviations (see Table 1) has been computed for both initial and improved segmentation (M) using two underlying images U as a reference - original one, and filtered one (with the same filter as the one used in mask preparation step). The mean values computed for improved segmentation are much lower than those for original one. The decrease is visible even better for filtered image used as a reference one. Standard deviation values are decreasing as well, but the difference is not as remarkable as the one of mean values. All these values confirm that the proposed method improves the segmentation results and regions on the improved segmented image fits better the boundaries of object on the underlying image[1].

5 Conclusions

This paper presented the generic schema for the improvement of existing segmentation results which consists of three steps: shrinking, mask preparation and expansion. The first phase aims at preparing the markers necessary in the expansion phase and consists in shrinking the regions of an existing segmentation. Three tools capable of reaching this goal were proposed: erosion, ultimate eroded set of given size and homotopic shrinking. The second step transforms the underlying image by removing trivial details which can influence the final segmentation result. The expansion phase performs region growing from the markers obtained by shrinking, using a mask produced from the underlying imagery. The method was applied to improve the CORINE land cover map, which is a required step for obtaining an improved pan-european information layer. The improvements

---

[1] Due to space limitations, in Table 1 only values of visible bands are given. Similar results are also measurable on the rest of bands.

was measured using the method based of modified gradient also described in the paper. The proposed schema can also be applied to improve other kinds of segmentation results, also when a given segmentation does not cover the whole underlying image (i.e. there are some unsegmented regions). For example, in medical imaging, the position and shape of some organs or structures may be approximately known so that their actual outline can be inferred using this a priori knowledge.

References

1. Serra, J.: Image analysis and mathematical morphology. Academic Press, London (1982)
2. Soille, P.: Morphological Image Analysis: Principles and Applications. 2nd edn. Springer-Verlag, Berlin Heidelberg New York (2003)
3. Vincent, L.: Efficient computation of various types of skeletons. In Loew, M., ed.: Medical Imaging V: Image Processing. Volume SPIE-1445. (1991) 297–311
4. Ranwez, V., Soille, P.: Order independent homotopic thinning for binary and grey tone anchored skeletons. Pattern Recognition Letters **23** (2002) 687–702
5. Vincent, L.: Morphological grayscale reconstruction in image analysis: applications and efficient algorithms. IEEE Transactions on Image Processing **2** (1993) 176–201
6. Soille, P.: Beyond self-duality in morphological image analysis. Image and Vision Computing **23** (2005) 249–257
7. Vincent, L.: Morphological area openings and closings for greyscale images. In: Proc. Shape in Picture '92, NATO Workshop, Driebergen, The Netherlands, Springer-Verlag (1992)
8. Salembier, P., Serra, J.: Flat zones filtering, connected operators, and filters by reconstruction. IEEE Transactions on Image Processing **4** (1995) 1153–1160
9. Brunner, D., Soille, P.: Iterative area seeded region growing for multichannel image simplification. In Ronse, C., Najman, L., Decencire, E., eds.: Mathematical Morphology: 40 Years On. Volume 30 of Computational Imaging and Vision. Kluwer Academic Publishers, Dordrecht (2005) 397–406
10. Beucher, S., Meyer, F.: The morphological approach to segmentation: the watershed transformation. In Dougherty, E., ed.: Mathematical morphology in image processing. Volume 34 of Optical Engineering. Marcel Dekker, New York (1993) 433–481
11. Adams, R., Bischof, L.: Seeded region growing. IEEE Transactions on Pattern Analysis and Machine Intelligence **16** (1994) 641–647
12. Buetner, G., Feranec, J., G., J.: Corine land cover update 2000, technical guidelines. Technical Report 89, European Environmental Agency, Copenhagen (2000)
13. Nunes de Lima, V., Peedell, S.: Image2000 - the European spatial reference. In: Proc. of 10th EC-GI & GIS Workshop, Warsaw, 23–25 June, European Commission, Joint Research Centre (2004)

Pattern Analysis of Movement Behavior of Medaka (*Oryzias latipes*): A Decision Tree Approach

Sengtai Lee[1], Jeehoon Kim[2], Jae-Yeon Baek[2], Man-Wi Han[2],
Sungshin Kim[1], and Tae-Soo Chon[3]

[1] School of Electrical Engineering, Pusan National University,
Jangjeon-dong, Geumjeong-gu, 609-735 Busan, Korea
{youandi, sskim}@pusan.ac.kr
[2] Korea Minjok Leadership Academy,
Sosa-ri, Anheung-myeon, Heongseong-gun, Gangwon-do, 225-823, Korea
{fantasy002, mrswoolf}@hanmail.net, manwihan@chol.com
[3] Division of Biological Sciences, Pusan National University,
Jangjeon-dong, Geumjeong-gu, 609-735 Busan, Korea
tschon@pusan.ac.kr

Abstract. The medaka, *Oryzias latipes*, is a small, egg-laying, freshwater, bony fish which is native to Asian countries. We were continuously investigated behavioral sequences of the medaka through an automatic image recognition system in increasing temperature from 25°C to 35°C. The observation of behavior through the movement tracking program showed many patterns of the medaka. Behavioral patterns could be divided into basically 5 patterns: 'active-smooth', 'active-shaking', 'inactive-smooth', 'inactive-shaking', and 'not determined'. These patterns were analyzed by 3 features: 'high-speed Ratio', 'FFT to angle transition', and 'product of projections to x-axis and y-axis'. Each pattern was classified using a devised decision tree after the feature choice. The main focus of this study was to determine whether the decision tree could be useful in interpreting and classifying behavior patterns of the medaka.

1 Introduction

Ecological data are very complex, unbalanced, and contained missing values. Relationships among variables may be strongly nonlinear and involving high-order interactions. The commonly used exploratory and statistical modeling techniques often fail to find meaningful ecological patterns from such data [1], [2], [3]. The behavioral or ecological monitoring of water quality is important regarding bio-monitoring and risk assessment [4], [5]. An adaptive computational method was utilized to analyze behavioral data in this study. Decision tree is modern statistical techniques ideally suited for both exploring and modeling such data. It is constructed by repeatedly splitting the data, defined by a simple rule based on a single explanatory variable.

The observation of the movement tracks of small sized animals has been separately initiated in the field of searching behavior in chemical ecology [6] and computational behavior [7], [8]. For searching behavior, the servometer and other tools were used for investigating the continuous movement tracks of insects including cockroaches, in characterizing the effects of wind [9], pheromone [10], [11], relative humidity [12], and sucrose feeding [13]. These computational methods convey useful mathematical information regarding similarities presented in data of the movement tracks, for instance, correlation coefficients or fractal dimensions.

The medaka, Oryzias latipes, is a small, egg-laying, freshwater, bony fish which is native to Asian countries (primarily Japan, Korea, China). It is a eurythermal fish, and can survive in outdoor containers (ponds) even under unfavorable environmental conditions [14]. In this paper, we utilized the decision tree for the classification of response behaviors of medaka and attempted to explain the shapes of the movement tracks through feature extraction in increasing temperature. Realizing there is a limit to observing with the naked eye, computational methods were used to conduct our research more effectively. This research can help the biosensor field in detecting defects in fish, or in finding out chemical toxicants that exist in the water by observing specific behavior patterns of fish.

2 Experimental Conditions

The specimens of medaka (*Oryzias latipes*) used in our experiment were obtained from the Toxicology Research Center, Korea Research Institute of Chemical Technology (KRICT; Taejon, Korea). Only the specimens six to twelve months from birth were used. The medaka is about 4cm long and lives for about 1-2 years.

A day before experimentation, the medaka was put into the observation tank and was given approximately twelve hours to adjust. In order to achieve image processing and pattern recognition effectively, stable conditions were maintained in the monitoring system. Any disturbances to observation tanks and changes in experimental conditions were minimized. Aeration, water exchange and food were not provided to test specimens during the observation period and the light regime was kept consistent.

The observed aquarium size was 40cm×20cm×10cm in volume. The temperature was adjusted by using the circulator. The heated water from the circulator flows into the tank and then flows back into the circulator. The analog data captured by the camera set in front of the aquarium were digitized by using the video overlay board every 0.25 seconds and were sent to the image recognition system to locate the target in spatial time domains.

After giving the experimenting specimen approximately twelve hours to adjust to the observation aquarium, the experiment was started. The initial temperature was 25°C. After 2 hours, the setting temperature was increased to 35°C using the water circulatory system. Depending on the day and external temperature, the time it took for the aquarium to elevate to 35°C varied. 90 minutes for the temperature of 25°C and 35°C, 30~60 minutes for the transition period were used as data. Each data from a movement pattern had an interval of a minute, and were overlapped every 30 seconds for analysis. The main focus was whether the medaka would be able to adapt quickly to the changing temperatures and show little or none or whether the increase in temperature would serve as a stress factor and change movement patterns.

548   S. Lee et al.

3 Feature Choice

In this paper, the movement patterns of the medaka were classified into shaking and smooth patterns as shown in Fig. 1. The behavior of the medaka in a minute period of time was used to classify them into 5 patterns: active-smooth, active-shaking, inactive-smooth, inactive-shaking, and not determined in each case. "Not determined" are patterns that were not classified into any one of these four categories. By the observation of an expert in fish behavior to initiate pattern isolation, the features were observed and the following three feature variables could be defined: high-speed ratio, FFT (Fast Fourier transformation) to angle transition, and projection to x- and y-axes. Fig. 2 shows the schematic diagram of the movement analysis in one minute for the process of extracting three distinctive characteristics from the data we acquired and classifying 5 patterns based on this information.

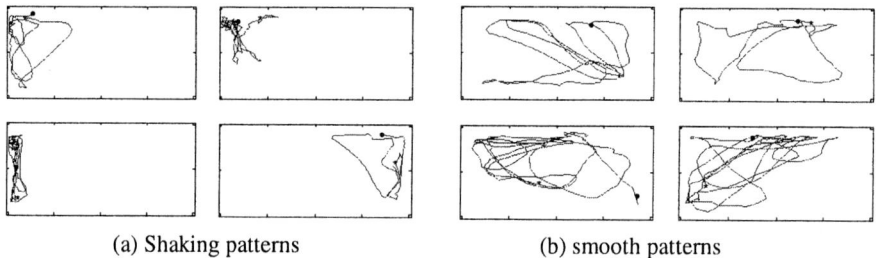

(a) Shaking patterns   (b) smooth patterns

Fig. 1. Example of shaking and smooth patterns in one minute (•: start, *: end)

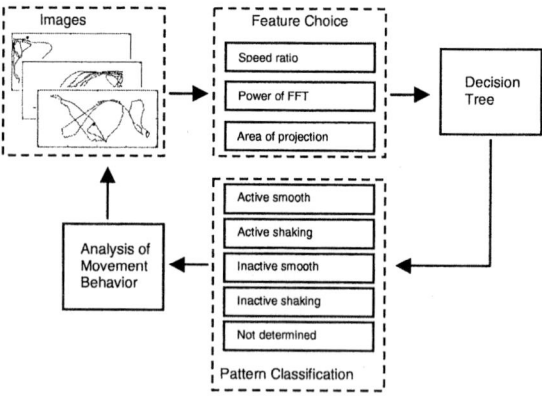

Fig. 2. Schematic diagram for automatic pattern isolation

In order to know the activeness of a medaka, speed information was used to define high-speed ratio. Speed of the medaka shows whether an active movement or inactive movement occured. The formula of speed is as following:

$$S = \sqrt{(x_{n+1} - x_n)^2 + (y_{n+1} - y_n)^2} \quad n = 1, 2, 3, \cdots \tag{1}$$

Where, x_n and y_n are the position values of the medaka in a sampled time. The ratio that exceeded the calculated average speed of the overall 7 data sets, 21mm/sec, was used as the first feature variable. High-speed ratio is calculated as the following equation.

$$S_{ratio} = \frac{\text{Number of samples above A2}}{\text{Number of samples in one minute}} \times 100(\%) \quad (2)$$

The change of direction is represented as an angle transition to classify the movement behavior of medaka. Angle transition between two sampled times denoted as H is calculated in the following equation. Where x_n and y_n shows the coordinate value for the x and y axes.

$$H = \arctan(\frac{y_{n+1} - y_n}{x_{n+1} - x_n}), \quad n = 1, 2, \ldots \quad (3)$$

Fourier transformation is used to transform signals in the time domain to signals in the frequency domain [19]. We apply the Fast Fourier transform (FFT) to the signal of angle transition to calculate energy. The FFT for a given discrete signal $x[n]$ is calculated through the following equation:

$$X[k] = \sum_{n=0}^{N-1} x[n] \cdot e^{-j(2\pi kn/N)}, \quad k = 0, 1, \cdots, N-1. \quad (4)$$

After applying the FFT to angle transition, the power of FFT (PF) is calculated in the following equation for the amplitudes above a median.

$$P = \sqrt{\sum_{i=1}^{k} x_i^2} \quad (5)$$

Where x_i is the amplitudes above a median. We use all sets to find median in experiments. We are used to FFT power because of the calculation in qualified angle transition. The PF is employed as a second feature variable for pattern isolation.

In this paper, the method of projection was used to observe and understand the movement route of the medaka in a two-dimensional space. The projection to the x-axis and the projection of the y-axis were calculated and then multiplied to figure out the area of the movement track of the medaka. The calculated area tells whether the medaka moved broadly all over the tank or in a restricted area of the tank. The area calculated was used as the third variable to classify smooth and shaking patterns.

4 Pattern Classification Based on Decision Tree

A decision tree is a graph of decisions and their possible consequences, used to create a plan to reach a goal. It has interpretability in its own tree structure. Such interpretability has manifestations which can easily interpret the decision for any particular test pattern as the conjunction of decisions along the path to its corresponding leaf node [3], [18].

Many people related to artificial intelligence research has developed a number of algorithms that automatically construct decision tree out of a given number of cases, e.g. CART [1], ID3 [15], C4.5 [16], [17]. The C4.5 algorithm, the successor and refinement of ID3, is the most popular in a series of "classification" tree methods. In it, real-valued variables are treated the same as in CART.

A decision tree consists of nodes(N) and queries(T). The fundamental principle underlying tree creation is that of simplicity. During the process of building the decision tree, we seek a property query T at each node N that makes the data reaching the immediate descendent nodes as "pure" as possible. It turns out to be more convenient to define the impurity, than to define the purity of a node. Several different mathematical measures of impurity have been proposed, i.e. entropy impurity (or occasionally information impurity), variance impurity, *Gini* impurity, misclassification impurity in equation (6), (7), (8), (9) respectively.

$$i(N) = -\sum_j P(\omega_j) \log_2 P(\omega_j) \tag{6}$$

Where $i(N)$ denote the impurity of a node and $P(w_i)$ is the fraction of patterns at node N that are in category w_j.

$$i(N) = P(\omega_1) P(\omega_2) \tag{7}$$

$$i(N) = \sum_{i \neq j} P(\omega_i) P(\omega_j) = 1 - \sum_j P^2(\omega_j) \tag{8}$$

$$i(N) = 1 - \max_j P(\omega_j) \tag{9}$$

All of them have basically the same behaviors. By the well-known properties of entropy, if all the patterns are of the same category, the entropy impurity is 0. A variance impurity is particularly useful in the two-category case. A generalization of the variance impurity is the *Gini* impurity in equation (8). This is just the expected error rate at node N if the category label is selected randomly from the class distribution present at N. The misclassification impurity measures the minimum probability that a training pattern would be misclassified at N. Of the impurity measures typically considered, this measure is the most strongly peaked at equal probabilities. In order to drop in impurity, we used the equation (10)

$$\Delta i(N) = i(N) - P_L i(N_L) - (1 - P_L) i(N_R) \tag{10}$$

Where N_L and N_R are the left and right descendent nodes, $i(N_L)$ and $i(N_R)$ are their impurities, and P_L is the fraction of patterns at node N that will go to N_L when property query T is used. Then the "best" query value s is the choice for T that maximizes $\Delta i(T)$.

If we continue to grow the tree fully until each leaf node corresponds to the lowest impurity, then the data have been typically overfitted. Conversely, if splitting is stopped too early, then the error on the training data is not sufficiently low and hence performance may suffer. To search sufficient splitting value, we used cross-validation (hold-out method).

The decision tree is employed and programmed to express the classification in the form of a tree and as a set of *IF-THEN* rules. In order to classify the patterns into active smooth, active shaking, inactive smooth, and inactive shaking divided by experts in fish behavior, the following features were used: high speed ratio (HSR), power of FFT (PF), and area of projection product (APP). These 3 features were used as input variables to decision tree. The training data for the decision tree are consisted of 30 data in each patterns. The decision tree gives a rough picture of the relative importance of the features influencing movement tracks of the medaka. We continue splitting nodes in successive layers until the error on the validation data is minimized. The principal alternative approach to stopped splitting is pruning. Fig. 6 shows the decision tree applied to evaluated pruning.

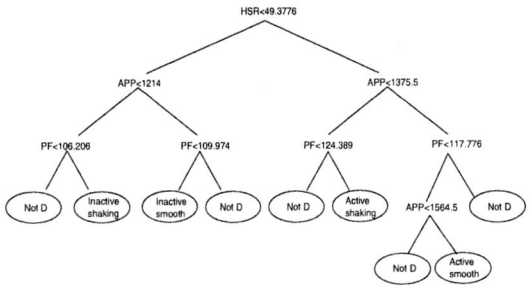

Fig. 3. The decision logic for pattern classification generated by decision tree applied to pruning. (HSR: high-speed ratio, APP: area of projection product, PF: power of FFT)

5 Pattern Analysis and Discussion

We developed models based on the classification and regression tree (CART) in order to classify and recognize movement tracks of medaka in different temperatures. Results were calculated for the decision logic for 90 minutes at a temperature of 25°C. This was the same for the temperature at 35°C. Also, a time period of 30~60 minutes was calculated for the transition period, in which the temperature was raised from 25°C to 35°C. The total number of specimens used in the experiment was 7. The recognition is calculated by 4 patterns over 5 patterns that includes "not determined." "Smooth" means that "active smooth" patterns and "inactive smooth" patterns appeared in the decision tree logic. "Shaking" means that "active shaking" patterns and "inactive shaking" patterns appeared in the decision tree logic. "Not determined" means that neither "smooth" nor "shaking" appeared in the decision tree logic.

Fig. 4 shows the ratio of smooth and shaking patterns. Each specimen is represented by bar graphs. The first bar graph shows the ratio of smooth and shaking patterns in 25°C, and the second bar graph shows the ratio in 35°C. Most specimens showed an increase in smooth patterns detected by the decision tree logic in 35°C.

The problem that arouses from this experiment is that biological specimens such as the medaka show too many different types of movement patterns. This makes selecting certain characteristics for a certain pattern difficult. This is why so many artificial systems such as neural networks and fuzzy are being used [20], [21]. However, although neural networks are sufficiently able to differentiate patterns, it is impossible to interpret exactly how much a certain pattern that the specimen shows.

The results revealed that after differentiating smooth and shaking patterns through a decision tree, temperature increase caused the smooth ratio to increase. This can be seen as a pattern that appears in response to a new environment, such as change of temperature, and is a process of adaptation. Shaking patterns show many changes of angle and can be seen as a pattern right before adaptation, and it can be said that it appears the most frequently. Speed ratio of the medaka shows whether it is an active movement or inactive movement as shown in Fig. 3. Also, the area of projection product interprets smooth or shaking pattern. Power of FFT distinguishes specific patterns from unknown patterns.

Though this research, decision tree logic was devised using 4 characteristic patterns and "not determined" for the patterns that could not be defined, based on the knowledge of experts. The decision tree was able to differentiate the 4 patterns based on the observation of three variables. However, more research must be done in order to define the patterns that were "not determined." Also, in order to better observe the many movement patterns of the medaka, more data sets should be examined and studied.

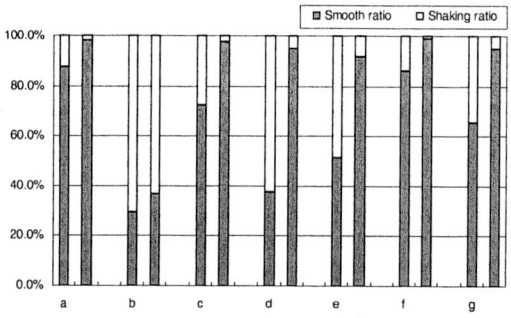

Fig. 4. Smooth ratio vs shaking ratio

6 Conclusions

The complex movement data were used to construct a decision tree with 3 features that could represent movement tracks of medaka: speed ratio, power of FFT, and x- and y-axes projection product. As new input data were given to the decision logic, it was possible to recognize the changes of pattern in increasing temperature. It is possible that for medaka treated with sub-lethal chemicals, there might be patterns that cannot be classified. However, in these cases, a new analysis can be done to add new patterns and update the decision tree. The results of the decision tree revealed that medaka was interpretable in different temperature as speed, angle, area of projection to x- and y-axes. If this is applied to more sets of data, it is thought that more distinctive and accurate methods of differentiating the behavior patterns can be created. Also, this research in differentiating patterns may help in the field of research for the special characteristics of living organisms. This research can help the biosensor field in detecting defects in fish, or in finding out chemical toxicants that exist in the water by observing specific behavior patterns of fish.

References

1. Breiman, L., J. H. Friedman, R. A. Olshen, and C.G.Stone.: Classification and Regression Trees, Wadsworth International Group, Belmont, California. USA (1984)
2. Ripley, B. D.: Pattern recognition and neural networks. Cambridge University Press, Cambridge, UK (1996)
3. Richard, O. D., Peter, E.H., David, G.S.: Pattern Classification 2nd edn. Wiley Interscience, USA (2001)
4. Dutta, H., Marcelino, J., Richmonds, Ch.: Brain acetylcholinesterase activity and optomotor behavior in bluefills, Lepomis macrochirus exposed to different concentrations of diazinon. Arch. Intern. Physiol. Biochim. Biophys., 100(5) (1993) 331-334
5. Lemly, A. D., Smith, R. J.: A behavioral assay for assessing effects of pollutants of fish chemoreception. Ecotoxicology and Enviornmental Safety 11(2) (1986) 210-218
6. Bell, W. J.: Searching behavior patterns in insects. Annual Review of Entomology 35, (1990) 447-467
7. Alt, W., Hoffman, G. (Eds): Biological Motion. Lecture notes in Biomathematics 89. Springer-Verlag, Berlin (1989)
8. Tourtellot, M. K., Collins, R. D., Bell, W. J.: the problem of movelength and turn definition in analysis of orientation data. Journal of Theoretical Biology 150 (1991) 287-297
9. Bell, W. J., Kramer, E.: Search and anemotactic orientation of cockroach. Journal of Insect Physiology 25 (1975) 631-640
10. Bell, W. J., Kramer, E.: Sex pheromone-stimulated orientation of the American cockroach on a servosphere apparatus. Journal of Chemical Ecology 6 (1980) 287-295
11. Bell, W. J., Tobin, R. T.: Orientation to sex pheromone in the American cockroach: analysis of chemo-orientation mechanisms. Journal of Insect Physiology 27 (1981) 501-508
12. Sorensen, K. A., Bell, W. J.: Orientation responses of an isopod to temporal changes in relative humidity simulation of a "humid patch" in a "dry habitat," Journal of Insect Physiology 32 (1986) 51-57
13. White, J., Tobin, T. R., Bell, W. J., 1984. Local search in the house fly Musca domestica after feeding on sucrose. Journal of Insect Physiology 30 (1984) 477-487
14. Nelson, J. S.: Fishes of the World. Willey, New York, (1994)
15. Quinlan, J. R.: Induction of decision trees. Machine Learning, 1(1) (1986) 81-106
16. Quinlan, J. R.: C4.5: programs for machine Learning. Morgan Kaufmann, San Francisco, CA, (1993)
17. Quinlan, J. R.: Improved use of continuous attributes in C4.5, Journal of Artificial Intelligence, 4. (1996) 77-90
18. Tom M. Mitchell.: Machine Learning. McGraw-Hill, New York. (1997)
19. Kreyszig, Erwin: Advanced Engineering Mathematics, 8th Ed, Wiley. (1999)
20. Chon, T.-S., Park, Y. S., Moon, K. H., Cha, E. Y.: Patternizing communities by using an artificial neural network, Ecological Modeling 90 (1996) 69-78
21. I. S. Kwak, T. S. Chon, H. M. Kang, N. I. Chung, J. S. Kim, S. C. Koh, S. K. Lee, Y. S. Kim.: Pattern recognition of the movement tracks of medaka (*Oryzias latipes*) in response to sub-lethal treatments of an insecticide by using artificial neural networks. Environmental Pollution, 120 (2002) 671-681

Linear Algorithm and Hexagonal Search Based Two-Pass Algorithm for Motion Estimation

Yunsong Wu and Graham Megson

School of Systems Engineering, Reading University,
Reading, UK, RG6 6AA
{sir02yw,m.megson}@rdg.ac.uk

Abstract. This paper presents a novel two-pass algorithm constituted by Linear Hashtable Motion Estimation Algorithm (LHMEA) and Hexagonal Search (HEXBS) for block base motion compensation. On the basis of research from previous algorithms, especially an on-the-edge motion estimation algorithm called hexagonal search (HEXBS), we propose the LHMEA and the Two-Pass Algorithm (TPA). We introduced hashtable into video compression. In this paper we employ LHMEA for the first-pass search in all the Macroblocks (MB) in the picture. Motion Vectors (MV) are then generated from the first-pass and are used as predictors for second-pass HEXBS motion estimation, which only searches a small number of MBs. The evaluation of the algorithm considers the three important metrics being time, compression rate and PSNR. The performance of the algorithm is evaluated by using standard video sequences and the results are compared to current algorithms. Experimental results show that the proposed algorithm can offer the same compression rate as the Full Search. LHMEA with TPA has significant improvement on HEXBS and shows a direction for improving other fast motion estimation algorithms, for example Diamond Search.

1 Introduction

In this paper, we propose a Linear Hashtable Motion Estimation Algorithm (LHMEA) and a Two-Pass Algorithm constituted by LHMEA and Hexagonal Search (HEXBS) to predict motion vectors for inter-coding. The objective of our motion estimation scheme is to achieve good quality video with very low computational complexity. There are a large number of motion prediction algorithms in the literature. This paper is only concerned with one class of such algorithms, the Block Matching Algorithms (BMA), which is widely used in MPEG2, MPEG4, and H.263. In BMA, each block of the current video frame is compared to blocks in reference frame in the vicinity of its corresponding position. The one with the least Mean Square Error (MSE) is considered as a match, and the difference of their positions is the motion vector of the block in the current frame to be saved in the corresponding position on the motion map. Motion estimation is quite computationally intensive and can consume up to 80% of the computational power of the encoder if the full search (FS) is used. It is highly desired to speed up the process without introducing serious distortion.

In the last 20 years, many fast algorithms have been proposed to reduce the exhaustive checking of candidate motion vectors (MV). Fast block-matching algorithms (BMA) use different block-matching strategies and search patterns with various sizes and shapes. Such as Two Level Search (TS), Two Dimensional Logarithmic Search (DLS) and Subsample Search (SS) [1], the Three-Step search (TSS), Four-Step Search (4SS) [2], Block-Based Gradient Descent Search (BBGDS) [3], and Diamond Search (DS) [4], [5] algorithms. A very interesting method called HEXBS has been proposed by Ce Zhu, Xiao Lin, and Lap-Pui Chau [6]. There are some variant HEXBS methods, such as Enhanced Hexagonal method [7], Hexagonal method with Fast Inner Search [8] and Cross-Diamond-Hexagonal Search Algorithms [9]. The fast BMA increases the search speed by taking the nature of most real-world sequences into account while also maintain a prediction quality comparable to Full Search. Most algorithms suffer from being easily trapped in a non-optimum solution.

Our LHMEA method attempts to predict the motion vectors using a linear algorithm and Hashtable [10]. In this paper we propose the LHMEA and the TPA. In the first-pass coding, we employ LHMEA to search all Macroblocks (MB) in picture. Motion Vectors (MV) generated from first pass will be used as predictors for second-pass HEXBS motion estimation, which only searches a small number of the MBs. Because LHMEA is based on a linear algorithm, which fully utilizes optimized computer's structure based on addition, its computation time is relatively small. Meanwhile HEXBS is one of best motion estimation methods to date. The new method proposed in this paper achieves the best results so far among all the algorithms investigated.

Contributions from this paper are:

(1) It achieves the best results among all investigated BMA algorithms. (2)First time, hashtable concept is used in the search for motion vectors in video compression. (3) Linear algorithm is used in video compression to improve speed and allow for future parallel coding. (4) The Two Pass Algorithm (TPA) is proposed. LHMEA is used for the first pass while HEXBS is used for a second pass. MVs produced by the first pass will be used as predictors for the second pass and this makes up for the drawback of the coarse search in the hexagonal search. This can also be used and leave space for research of nearly all kinds of similar fast algorithms for example Diamond Search etc. (5) Invariant moments are added into hashtable to check how many coefficients work best for hashtable. We also prove that the more information hashtable has the better result the table will have. (6) Spatially related MB information is used not only in coarse search but also inner fine search.

The rest of the paper is organized as follows. Section I continues with a brief introduction to HEXBS and varieties. The proposed LHMEA and LAHSBTPA are discussed in Section II. Experiments conducted based on the proposed algorithm are presented in Section III. We conclude in Section IV with some remarks and discussions about the proposed scheme.

1.1 Hexagonal Search Algorithm

The Hexagonal Search Method is an improved method based on the DS (Diamond Search). HEXBS has shown significant improvement over other fast algorithms such as DS. In contrast with the DS that uses a diamond search pattern, the HEXBS adopts a hexagonal search pattern to achieve faster processing due to fewer search points being evaluated. The motion estimation process normally comprises of two steps. First is a low-resolution coarse search to identify a small area where the best motion vector is expected to lie, followed by fine-resolution inner search to select the best motion vector in the located small region. The large central 5x5 search pattern used in HEXBS, can provide fast searching speed. It gives consistently better motion estimates and directions due to larger size. Another relief of reducing checking points is to have successive search patterns can be overlapped. HEXBS requires only three extra points to be evaluated in each step. Most fast algorithms focus on speeding up the coarse search by taking various smart ways to reduce the number of search points to identify a small area for inner search. There are two main directions to improve the coarse search:

usage of predictors [8], [11]

early termination [11]

A new algorithm [11] was introduced on HEXBS, which is similar as Motion Vector Field Adaptive Search Technique (MVFAST) [12] based on DS. The algorithm has significantly improved the preexisting HEXBS both in image quality and speed up by initially considering a small set of predictors as possible motion vector predictor candidates. Then a modified Hexagonal pattern uses the best motion vector predictor candidate as the center of search. Another prediction set is proposed in the literature [13], [14]. In general, Search blocks correlated with the current one can be divided into three categories as in Figure.1.:

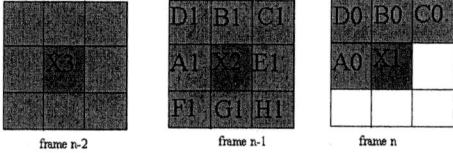

Fig. 1. Blocks correlated with the current one

(1) Spatially correlated blocks (A0, B0, C0, D0),
(2) Neighboring blocks in the previous frame (A1, B1, C1, D1, E1, F1, G1, H1)
(3) Co-located blocks in the previous two frames (X2 and X3), which provide the Acceleration motion vector (MV).

Except for coarse search improvement, Inner search improvement includes:
4 points [8]; 8 points [9]; Inner group search [9]

2 Linear Algorithm and Hexagonal Search Based Two-Pass Algorithm (LAHSBTPA)

Most of the current Hexagonal search algorithms are predictive methods that focus on relations between current frame and previous frames. They approach the global minimum on assumption that local minimum is global minimum which may not always be the case. What we want to do is to find a fast method which discovers the predictor from the current frame information by using spatially related MB or pixel information. The method can avoid trapping in local minimum, fast, accurate and independent on finding right predictors. So we have designed a vector hashtable lookup and block matching algorithm. It is more efficient method to perform an exhaustive search. It uses global information in the reference block. The block-matching algorithm calculates each block to set up a hashtable. By definition hashtable is a dictionary in which keys are mapped to array positions by a hash function.

We try to find as few as possible variables to represent the whole macroblock. Through some preprocessing steps, "integral projections" are calculated for each macroblock. These projections are different according to each algorithm. The aim of these algorithms is to find the best projection function. The algorithms we present here have two projections, one of them is the massive projection, which is a scalar denoting the sum of all pixels in the macroblock. It is also DC coefficient of macroblock. Another is A of Y=Ax+B (y is luminance, x is the location.) Each of these projections is mathematically related to the error metric. Under certain conditions, the value of the projection indicates whether the candidate macroblock will do better than the best-so-far match. The major algorithm we discuss here is linear algorithm.

2.1 Linear Hashtable Motion Estimation Algorithm (LHMEA)

In previous research methods, when people try to find a block that best matches a predefined block in the current frame, matching was performed by SAD (calculating difference between current block and reference block). In Linear Hashtable Motion Estimation Algorithm (LHMEA), we only need to compare two coefficients of two blocks. In the current existing methods, the MB moves inside a search window centered on the position of the current block in the current frame. In LHMEA, the coefficients move inside the hashtable to find the matched blocks. If coefficients are powerful enough to hold enough information of the MB, motion estimators should be accurate. So LHMEA increases accuracy, reduces computation time and may allow for a new era of video encoding. The Linear Algorithm is the easiest and fastest way to calculate on a computer because the constructions of computer arithmetic units are based on additions. So if most of calculations of video compression are done on linear algorithm, we can save lots of time on compression. It is also very easy to put on parallel machines in the future, which will benefit real time encoding. In the program, we try to use polynomial approximation to get such result y=mx+c; y is luminance value of all pixels, x is the location of pixel in macroblocks. The way of scan y is from left to right, from top to buttom. Coefficients m and c are what we are looking for to put into hashtable.

$$m = \frac{N*\sum_{i=0}^{N}(x_i*y_i) - \sum_{i=0}^{N}x_i*\sum_{i=0}^{N}y_i}{1000}; \quad c = \frac{\sum_{i=0}^{N}y_i*\sum_{i=0}^{N}x_i^2 - \sum_{i=0}^{N}x_i*\sum_{i=0}^{N}x_i*y_i}{N*\sum_{i=0}^{N}x_i^2 - \sum_{i=0}^{N}x_i*\sum_{i=0}^{N}x_i} \quad (1)$$

According to experience of our research in the encoder, we changed m to keep its value around 100-1000. This improves a lot on previous research result whose m is always zero in hashtable, in which case there is only c in hashtable. In this way, we initially realized the way to calculate the hashtable.

2.2 The Proposed Two-Pass Algorithm

In order to take advantages of the two different schemes of LHMEA and HEXBS, meanwhile, in order to strike a compromise between efficiency of LHMEA and performance of HEXBS in the estimation, we develop an efficient TPA [15], where HEXBS's problem is solved by LHMEA. Within the TPA, first-pass, LHMEA will generate a set of MVs. The second-pass, which is the HEXBS, will use MVs from first-pass for coarsely search as predictors, thereby further improving the efficiency of HEXBS while these predictors are different from all previous predictors. They are based on full search and current frame only. Because LHMEA is linear algorithm, it is fast. Because the predictors generated are accurate, it improves HEXBS without too much delay.

The original HEXBS is moved step by step, maximum two pixels per step, but in our proposed method, in second-pass, the LHMEA motion vectors are used to move hexagon pattern directly to the area close to the pixel whose MB distortion is smallest. This saved computation in the low-resolution coarse search and improved accuracy.

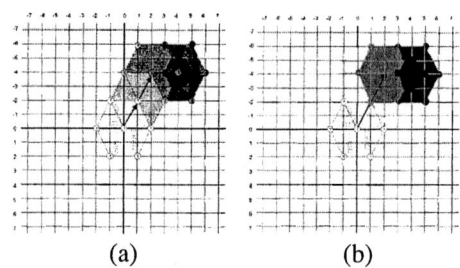

(a)   (b)

Fig. 2. Original HEXBS Coarse Search [6](a) and proposed HEXBS Coarse Search(b)

3 Experimental Result

In the Fig.4 we compare our method to other method. The method listed are Full Search (FS), Linear Hashtable Motion Estimation Algorithm (LHMEA), Subsample Search (SS), Two Level Search (TLS), Logarithmic Search (LS), Hexagonal Search (HEXBS) and Linear Algorithm and Hexagonal Search Based Two-Pass Algorithm (LAHSBTPA). LAHSBTPA used 6-side-based fast inner search [11] and early termination criteria [12] mentioned in this paper. The reason of choice of other algorithms is that they are most famous algorithms in the field. The video data are common video data, and the experimental results are average case. The LAHSBTPA was found to be the fastest of all the current algorithms tested when compression rate and PSNR remain a priority. In Fig.4, LAHSBTPA is fastest algorithm when compression rate is best and PSNR is high being 23% faster than the Logarithmic Search. In the tables of Football, LAHSBTPA is the fastest algorithm when compression rate is near same as

Linear Algorithm and Hexagonal Search Based Two-Pass Algorithm 559

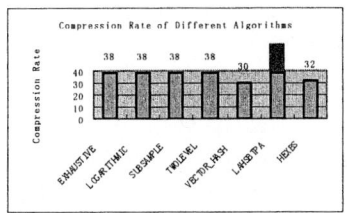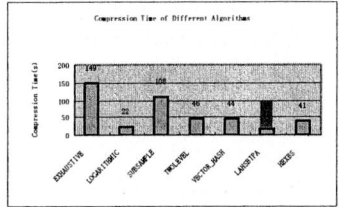

Fig. 3. Comparison of compression rate and time among FS, LS, SS, TLS, LHMEA, LAHSBTPA, HEXBS (based on 150 frames of Flower Garden)

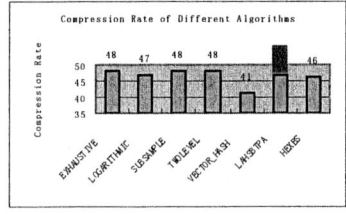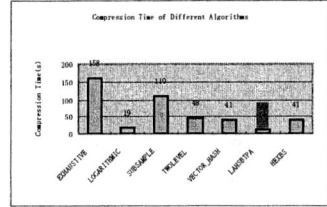

Fig. 4. Comparison of compression rate and time among FS, LS, SS, TLS, LHMEA, LAHSBTPA, HEXBS (based on 125 frames of Football)

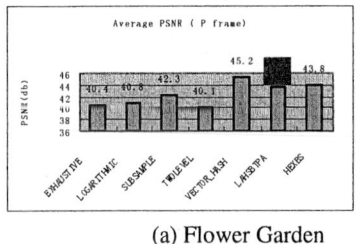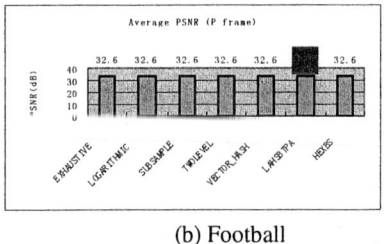

(a) Flower Garden   (b) Football

Fig. 5. Comparison of PSNR among FS, LS, SS, TLS, LHMEA, LAHSBTPA, HEXBS (based on 150 frames of Flower Garden and Football)

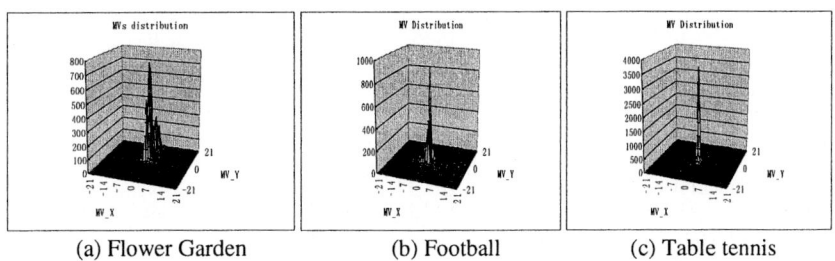

(a) Flower Garden   (b) Football   (c) Table tennis

Fig. 6. MVs distribution of different video steams: Flower Garden (a), Football (b), Table tennis (c). (based on P frames)

Fig. 7. Motion vectors and MB analysis in frames from Table Tennis, Football and Flower Garden by LAHSBTPA

the Full Search while the PSNR is same and is 27% faster than the Logarithmic Search. LAHSBTPA is better than HEXBS on compression rate, time and PSNR. If we can find better coefficients in the hashtable to represent MB, the hashtable may show great promise.

The FS, HEXBS, LAHSBTPA are certain center biased algorithms. This is also basis of several other algorithms. It means that most of MVs are equal to each other as demonstrated in the figures below. As the center-biased global minimum motion vector distribution characteristics, more than 80% of the blocks can be regarded as stationary or quasi-stationary blocks and most of the motion vectors are enclosed in the central area (as depicted in Fig. 8). Based on the fact that for most sequences motion vectors were concentrated in a small area around the center of the search, it suggests that, instead of initially examining the (0,0) position, we could achieve better results if the LHMEA predictor is examined first and given higher priority with the use of early termination threshold. It avoids to be trapped in local optimum around the central point of the search window which is also the problem of most fast algorithms as previously mentioned. It also avoids producing wrong motion vectors for the blocks undergoing large motion.

In Fig. 8. we randomly picked frames from Flower Garden, Football and Table Tennis MPEG clips generated by LAHSBTPA. We analyzed MB types and displayed value of MVs in the pictures. These pictures show our method made excellent decision on MB types.

3 Summary

In the paper we proposed a new two-pass algorithm called Linear Algorithm and Hexagonal Search Based Two-Pass Algorithm (LAHSBTPA) in video compression. In our algorithm, a preprocessing pass uses linear algorithm to set up hashtable. The algorithm searches in hashtable to find motion estimator instead of by FS. Then the motion estimator it generated will be sent to second-pass HEXBS, which is best motion estimation algorithm, as predictor. So TPA is obtained by applying motion estimation twice, which we call two-pass algorithm. The result of LAHSBTPA is much better than LHMEA or HEXBS used alone in motion estimation and also best in all survey algorithms. No matter in coarse search or fine inner search, new method used lots of spatial related MB or pixels' information. In this way, it is improved both in quality and speed of motion estimation. The key point in the method is to find suitable coefficients to represent whole MB. The more information the coefficients in hashtable hold about pictures, the better result LAHSBTPA will get. At the same time, this TVP will improve other similar fast motion estimations. This leaves space for future development.

Acknowledgment

Thanks to Dr. Simon Sherratt for his advice and comments

References

[1] Ze-Nian li Lecture Note of Computer Vision on personal website (2000)
[2] L. M. Po and W. C. Ma: A novel four-step search algorithm for fast block motion estimation," IEEE and systems for video technology, vol. 6, pp. 313–317, (June 1996.)
[3] L. K. Liu and E. Feig: A block-based gradient descent search algorithm for block motion estimation in video coding," IEEE Trans. Circuits Syst. Video Technol., vol. 6, pp. 419–423, (Aug. 1996.)
[4] S. Zhu and K.-K. Ma: A new diamond search algorithm for fast blockmatching motion estimation: IEEE Trans. Image Processing, vol. 9, pp. 287–290, (Feb. 2000.)
[5] J. Y. Tham, S. Ranganath, M. Ranganath, and A. A. Kassim: A novel unrestricted center-biased diamond search algorithm for block motion estimation: IEEE Trans. Circuits and systems for video technology, vol. 8, pp. 369–377, (Aug. 1998)
[6] Ce Zhu, Xiao Lin, and Lap-Pui Chau: Hexagon-Based Search Pattern for Fast Block Motion Estimation: IEEE Trans on circuits and systems for video technology, Vol. 12, No. 5, (May 2002)
[7] Ce. Zhu, X. Lin and L.P. Chau: An Enhanced Hexagonal Search Algorithm for Block Motion Estimation: IEEE International Symposium on Circuits and Systems, ISCAS2003, Bangkok, Thailand, (May 2003)
[8] Ce Zhu, Senior Member, IEEE, Xiao Lin, Lappui Chau, and Lai-Man Po: Enhanced Hexagonal Search for Fast Block Motion Estimation: IEEE Trans on circuits and systems for video technology, Vol. 14, No. 10, (Oct 2004)
[9] Chun-Ho Cheung, Lai-Man Po:Novel Cross-Diamond-Hexagonal Search Algorithms for Fast Block Motion Estimation:IEEE Trans on Multimedia, Vol. 7, No. 1, (Feb. 2005)
[10] Graham Megson & F.N.Alavi Patent 0111627.6 -- for SALGEN Systems Ltd
[11] Paolo De Pascalis, Luca Pezzoni, Gian Antonio Mian and Daniele Bagni: Fast Motion Estimation With Size-Based Predictors Selection Hexagon Search In H.264/AVC encoding: EUSIPCO (2004)
[12] Alexis M. Tourapis, Oscar C. Au, Ming L. Liou: Predictive Motion Vector Field Adaptive Search Technique (PMVFAST) Enhancing Block Based Motion Estimation: proceedings of Visual Communications and Image Processing, San Jose, CA, January (2001)
[13] A. M. Tourapis, O. C. Au and M. L. Liou: Highly Efficient Predictive Zonal Algorithms for Fast Block. Matching Motion Estimation: IEEE Transactions on Circuits and Systems for Video Technology, vol. 12, No.10, pp 934-947, (October 2002)
[14] H-Y C. Tourapis, A. M. Tourapis: Fast Motion Estimation within the JVT codec: Joint Video Team (JVT) of ISO/IEC MPEG and ITU-T VCEG 5th meeting, Geneva, Switzerland: (09-17 October 2002)
[15] Jie Wei and Ze-Nian Li: An Efficient Two-Pass MAP-MRF Algorithm for Motion Estimation Based on Mean Field Theory: IEEE Transactions on Circuits and Systems for Video Technology, vol. 9, No. 6, (Sep. 1999)

Designing Mathematical Morphology Algorithms on FPGAs: An Application to Image Processing

Damien Baumann and Jacques Tinembart

Ecole d'Ingénieurs de Genève, HES-SO, 1202 Geneva, Switzerland

Abstract. Mathematical morphology is a well-known image and signal processing technique. However, most morphological tools such as Matlab are not suited for strong real-time constraints. We address this problem through hardware implementation on FPGAs. A library of VHDL basic modules was built to allow the implementation of complex algorithms. We also propose an environment for generating VHDL code from a high-level description of a user-defined algorithm. We then integrate morphological algorithms in more complex applications: vision-based robots or real-time processing and displaying of video flows. In order to facilitate this integration, a development board as well as an interface between a FPGA and Matlab were realized.

1 Introduction

Mathematical morphology (see [3]) is an image processing technique based on shape criteria within the framework of set theory. Unlike traditional approaches which consider an image as a set of pixels, mathematical morphology analyses images in terms of objects. Applications of mathematical morphology are found mostly in image/signal processing and analysis. Most morphological algorithms can be solved on a PC, typically with Matlab. However, when including strong real-time constraints, such an approach becomes ineffective.

In this paper, we aim at optimizing performances of morphological algorithms with respect to high throughput real-time execution. We address this problem through hardware implementation on highly parallel reconfigurable chips, namely FPGAs. To this end, we built a library of VHDL basic modules implementing morphological operators and auxiliary modules for combining them. We also propose an environment for developing morphological algorithms with this library and thereon generating FPGA configuration files. We actually integrated these algorithms in more complex systems. In order to facilitate this integration, a development board as well as a FPGA / Matlab interface were realized.

This article is an extended version of [1]. In particular, the previous results are improved using different techniques such as multiple pixel per clock cycle.

2 Designing Morphological Algorithms on a FPGA

Here the main idea for designing morphological algorithms consists in the selection, according to morphological theory, of some basic modules. These modules can be combined into morphological operators. Complex algorithms are then built using these operators. Two basic blocks were thus developed. Both can use structuring elements of any size.

2.1 Type 1 Basic Block: Dilation

Basic Concept and Architecture. The type 1 basic block implements a fundamental morphological operation, known as dilation, defined by

$$\delta(F)(\mathbf{x}) := [\delta(F, SE)](\mathbf{x}) = \max_{\mathbf{b} \in SE} F(\mathbf{x} + \mathbf{b}) ,$$

where F represents the processed image, $\mathbf{x}$ a pixel, and SE the structuring element, i.e. the shape used for the analysis. Traditional processor approaches successively centre SE on each pixel of the image and replace the pixel at the centre with the maximum value of the image in the window defined by SE. To compute a single pixel, processors must therefore read many nonadjacent pixels from the memory. This method is not adapted to high throughput real-time execution, because several clock cycles are needed. Conversely, FPGA approaches move the processed image (not the structuring element) in such a way that SE is centred on a new pixel at each clock cycle. This can be realized using shift registers and a maximum detection unit. Figure 1(a) depicts the type 1 basic block for a 3-pixel-wide cross-shaped structuring element. Three shift registers[1] align the image on SE, while another one propagates a second image G required for some morphological operators such as geodesic dilation:

$$[\delta_G(F)](\mathbf{x}) = [\delta(F) \wedge G](\mathbf{x}) = \min\{\delta(F)(\mathbf{x}), G(\mathbf{x})\} .$$

Figure 1(b) shows the state of the shift registers at time t and $t+1$ for a 3 x 3

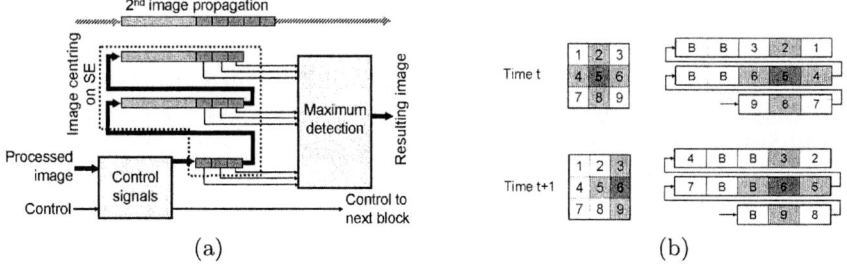

Fig. 1. Type 1 basic block

image and the same structuring element as above. To ensure an identical treatment of every pixel, we add an external zero-valued border to the original image. The border values are designated by B. With this technique and considering a one-pixel-per-clock cycle flow, the process has the following features:

---

[1] This number depends on the SE height.

- Pixel-by-pixel processing.
- The same incoming and outgoing rate. However, the first resulting pixel will come after a short latency time[2]. It is thus possible to achieve a one-pixel-per-clock cycle throughput no matter what the algorithmic complexity is, as long as only type 1 basic blocks are used.
- High operating frequency, limited by the maximum detection unit.
- Ability to easily combine modules into more complex operators.
- No need to store the whole image.
- FPGA independent architecture.

Multiple Pixel per Clock Cycle. To reduce computing time, we subdivide the original image into M regions, each subimage being processed in parallel, but in a totally interdependent way. Thus, the type 1 basic block has been modified. It is now able to compute M pixels per clock cycle. Let P_1 to P_N be the N successive pixels of the source image. At time t, P_{tM+1} to $P_{(t+1)M}$ enters the block in parallel. P_{tM+1} will be computed by the first processing unit, P_{tM+2} by the second and so on.

Estimation of the Computing Time. Let A be a morphological algorithm composed of K successive type 1 basic blocks, named B_1 to B_K. Let L_i be the latency of block B_i when processed with one pixel per clock cycle, L_{tot} the latency of A, T_i the computation time[3] of B_i and T_{tot} the computation time of A. For L_{tot}, T_i and T_{tot}, M pixels are processed at each clock cycle. The following relations are satisfied:

$$L_{tot} = \frac{1}{M} \sum_{j=1}^{K} L_j \quad \text{and} \quad T_{tot} \cong L_{tot} + \frac{1}{\nu_{max} \cdot M} \cdot N_{pix} ,$$

where N_{pix} represents the number of pixels in the processed image and ν_{max} the maximum frequency at which FPGA can operate. Since the computation is pipelined, T_{tot} is much smaller than $\sum_{j=1}^{K} T_j$, because B_i ($i = 2, ..., K$) does not have to wait until the completion of B_{i-1}. Therefore, the K successive blocks form a huge pipeline.

2.2 Type 2 Basic Block: Reconstruction by Dilation

Basic Concept and Architecture. Some operators, often used in practice, perform iterations until a stability criterion is reached. Reconstruction by dilation is one of them:

$$R_G(F) = \delta_G^{(i)}(F) ,$$

---

[2] Latency is the time difference between the moment the first pixel enters the block and the moment where it leaves it.
[3] Including first pixel latency.

where i, not known a priori, is such that $\delta_G^{(i)}(F) = \delta_G^{(i+1)}(F)$ and $\delta_G^{(0)}(F) = \delta(F) \wedge G$. The image F (resp. G) is called the marker (resp. mask) image.

In order to implement this kind of operators, named operators with reconstruction, a new basic block, more complex because it includes iteration mechanisms, was developed. Figure 2 depicts this basic block for the same structuring element as in Fig. 1. Two datapaths must be considered:

1. F image (black arrows): Image centring on SE, maximum computation, minimum computation ($[\delta(F) \wedge G](\mathbf{x})$), idempotence detection (module '=' in Fig. 2), storage of the iteration being computed and resynchronisation of the last iteration in order to use it in the current iteration computation.
2. G image (grey patterned arrows): propagation, minimum computation, storage and resynchronisation.

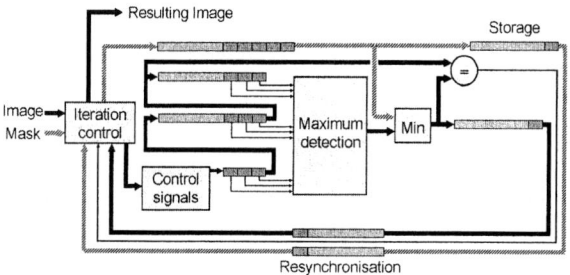

Fig. 2. Type 2 basic block

Different ν and M for the Source and the Processing Unit. The computation time of a reconstruction by dilation depends on the number of iterations. Let T_{max} be the theoretical maximum computation time:

$$T_{max} \cong \frac{1}{M \cdot \nu_{max}} \cdot S \cdot N_{it} \cong \frac{1}{2 \cdot M \cdot \nu_{max}} \cdot S^2 ,$$

where M represents the number of pixels processed per clock cycle, S the image size, N_{it} the maximum number of iterations and ν_{max} as above. Assuming $M = 1$ and a reasonable ν_{max} of 50 MHz, T_{max} is therefore equal to 3.68 s for a 160 x 120 image: this is clearly unacceptable. Beware that N_{it} has been replaced by $\frac{S}{2}$ which corresponds to the theoretical worst case. In practice, the average number of iterations is much smaller.

In order to improve the throughput of our type 2 basic block, we will assume that ν_{max} and M are different for the source and the processing unit (i.e. the basic block). Let ν_S and M_S characterize the source, ν_T and M_T the processing unit. The following relations are, most of the time, satisfied: $M_S = 1$, $M_T > 1$ and $\nu_T > \nu_S$. Therefore, considering a 160 x 120 image with $M_T = 40$ and $\nu_T = 100$ MHz, T_{max} is equal to 46 ms which is 80 times faster than before. In order to implement this concept in VHDL, we have to bufferize data from the source in order to change ν and M.

2.3 Morphological Compiler and Development Environment

The combination of both basic blocks together with auxiliary modules leads to the realization of most morphological operators defined in [3], e.g. gradients, opening, top-hats, hit-or-miss transformations, thinning, top-hats by reconstruction, regional extrema, extended extrema and double threshold.

So as to design morphological algorithms by combining operators, we built a compiler. It generates FPGA-independent optimized VHDL code from a script language providing more than 40 morphological operators. This compiler is included in a specific Win32-like development environment, named BTMorph, within which it is possible to develop morphological algorithms and thereon generate FPGA configuration files by calling a VHDL simulator as well as synthesis and place-and-route (PAR) tools. A program consists of an incoming flow, expressions and an outgoing flow. An expression corresponds to either a structuring element or a morphological operator. In its current version, the compiler syntax does not include any control statements such as `if`, `for` or `while`.

3 Results

The test environment, unless otherwise specified, was the following:

- **PC**   Pentium IV 1.4 GHz with 768 MB RDRAM (400 MHz) running Windows 2000 with Matlab Release 13.
- **Matlab**   SDC morphology toolbox compiled for x86.
- **FPGA tools** Synplify Pro 7.7.1 and Xilinx ISE 6.3.03i.
- **FPGA**   Xilinx Virtex II XC2V2000-BG575-6.
- **Image**   160 × 120 with 8 bits per pixel.
- **SE**   3-pixel-wide cross-shaped structuring element.
- **M**   One-pixel-per-clock cycle.

Basic Blocks. Both basic blocks (with $M = 1, 10$) were synthesized, then placed and routed. The results are shown in Table 1. The maximum frequency decreases as M grows because of design complexity and maximum combinatorial path.

Table 1. Results for the PAR of the two basic blocks ($M = 1$ and $M = 10$)

	Type 1		Type 2	
	$M = 1$	$M = 10$	$M = 1$	$M = 10$
f_{max}	283 MHz	220 MHz	216 MHz	210 MHz
LUTs	344 (1.6%)	1289 (6%)	643 (3%)	1903 (9%)
Flip Flops	133 (0.6%)	981 (4.5%)	256 (1.2%)	1495 (7%)
RAM blocks	0	0	20 (35%)	24 (43%)

Algorithms without Reconstruction. In order to illustrate results obtained with algorithms using only type 1 basic blocks, we implemented a multi-scale gradient operator (see [3] p. 127). After PAR, it occupies 2740 LUTs (12.7%) and 1144 (5.3%) flip-flops when $N = 2$, where the parameter N is related to the size of the structuring element used. For example, considering a basic 3-pixel-wide cross-shaped structuring element, the structuring element used for multi-scale gradient will be a cross-shaped structuring element of width $2N + 1$.

A multi-scale gradient combines $2N$ dilations, $3N-1$ erosions[4], 2 subtractions and 1 threshold. Figure 3 gives an example of a multi-scale gradient application.

Fig. 3. Example of a multi-scale gradient application

We will now compare our results with Matlab. First of all, we assume ν_{max} is constant no matter what the parameter values are. However, beware that this is not true. In fact, a larger design will normally run with a lower frequency. Let TH_{Matlab} and TH_{FPGA} be the throughputs of a multi-scale gradient execution respectively with Matlab and the FPGA. In Fig. 4(a-b), we plot the throughputs as a function of N. As mentioned in section 2.1, the throughput of an algorithm without reconstruction is constant independently of its complexity and is equal to ν_{max}. A 160 x 120 image will be therefore processed at 14'000 frames per second. Conversely, Matlab is not able to process images in parallel. It has to compute them one after the other. Thus, Fig. 4(a) shows the throughput decreasing with algorithmic complexity. Figure 4(c-d) shows the same throughputs for different image sizes. Images are in 4/3 format and $N = 2$. FPGA throughput is linear relative to image size and therefore quadratic relative to image line length as for Matlab. Figure 4(e-f) shows ratio between FPGA and Matlab throughputs first as a function of N and then as a function of the image size. The ratio grows with N and reaches 400 for $N = 20$. When increasing the image size, the ratio remains constant near 125 except for small images where it is bigger.

All these results assume that only one pixel is processed per clock cycle. With M pixels per clock cycle, assuming ν_{max} is constant, FPGA throughput has to be multiplied by M.

Algorithms with Reconstruction. It would also be interesting to compare our results with Matlab as we did for algorithms without reconstruction. However, up to now, no comparison was performed for the following reasons:
- Algorithms used by Matlab [5] are totally different from our FPGA approach and no information was found about morphological algorithm complexity in Matlab.

---
[4] Defined as $[\varepsilon(F, SE)](\mathbf{x}) = \min_{\mathbf{b} \in SE} F(\mathbf{x} + \mathbf{b})$.

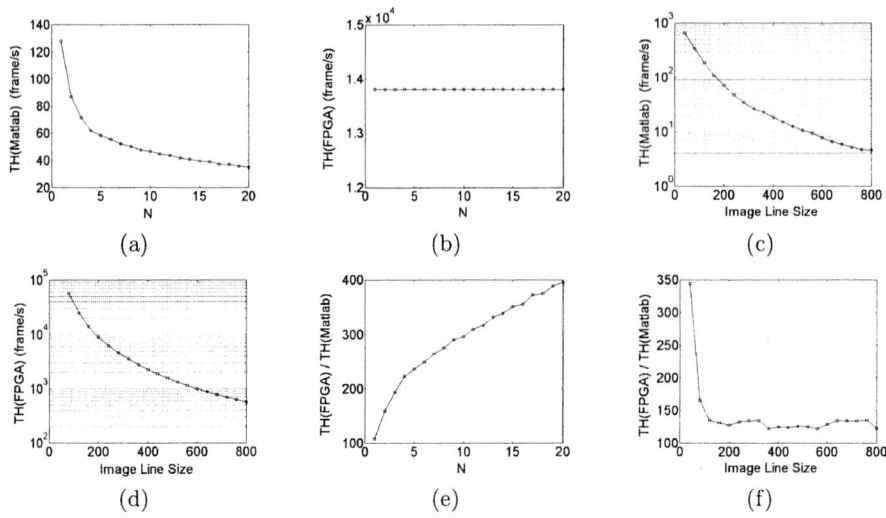

Fig. 4. Throughput of a multi-scale gradient

- Finding average iterations number is really hard for FPGA algorithms.
- Worst case, average case and best case are totally different for Matlab and our FPGA approach.

4 Validation

A development board, named *ezPC104*, was designed to implement morphological algorithms. PC104-Plus[5] compliant, it includes a Xilinx Virtex II XC2V2000-BG575 FPGA, static, dynamic and flash memories, as well as many interfaces: ethernet, USB, serial, camera, JTAG and LCD. Moreover, in order to validate the results obtained with the FPGA, a communication interface between Matlab and the *ezPC104* board, which uses JTAG Boundary-Scan, was developed. Matlab emulates this protocol by calling C functions. These routines communicate with the JTAG port on the *ezPC104* through the parallel port of the PC. Via this interface, Matlab is then able to load algorithms into the FPGA as well as provide test images, read the results and verify them.

5 Integration in Complex Systems

Our mathematical morphology implementations in VHDL can easily be integrated in more complex systems, such as video preprocessing. After preprocessing, data should often be transmitted to the PC. We therefore developed a VHDL USB 2.0 core which can be combined in the FPGA with the morphological algorithm in order to transmit data via the USB bus.

---

[5] PCI standard for embedded systems.

Some morphological algorithms were implemented on the *ezPC104* board in order to illustrate integration capabilities. A demonstration application was also realized. A 160 x 120 camera provides monochrome images with 8 bits per pixel. This flow is processed by an FPGA. The resulting flow is stored in a framebuffer which is then continuously read by the FPGA and displayed on a LCD. The camera has to be configured using the I^2C protocol. This is achieved using an embedded Leon2 processor. Mathematical morphology algorithms were also integrated on a FPGA-based robot in our research lab.

6 Conclusion

In this work, we built a VHDL morphological library and an environment named BTMorph. In combination with Matlab, these tools allow us to implement morphological algorithms without writing a single line of VHDL. More precisely, BTMorph is able to generate VHDL code from a morphological script and to create a configuration file which can be loaded using Matlab into a FPGA. In addition, we developed a FPGA-based board as well as an interface with Matlab in order to validate our methodology. A demonstration application using a camera and a LCD was also realized.

Mathematical morphology finds many applications to image analysis and pattern recognition. Nowadays, much attention is given to real-time image and video processing. This raises the problem of performance in terms of throughput to which the intrinsic parallelism of FPGAs can offer a solution. However, programming morphological or signal processing algorithms on a FPGA still remains a tedious task. Hence, we plan to further develop our framework and methodology by using the synchronous programming language Esterel.

Finally, the authors would like to thank Paul Albuquerque for his help.

References

1. D. Baumann, J. Tinembart. *Mathematical Morphology Image Analysis on FPGA*, IEEE Int. Conf. on Advances in Intelligent Systems Theory and Applications, 2004.
2. R. Peyrard. *Conception et mise en oeuvre d'un ASIC de morphologie mathématique à architecture programmable,* PhD Thesis, Ecole des Mines de Paris, France, 1992.
3. P. Soille. *Morphological Image Analysis*, 2nd ed. Springer, Berlin, 2003.
4. M. Van Droogenbroeck, H. Talbot. *Fast Computation of Morphological Operations with Arbitrary Structuring Elements.* Patt. Recogn. Lett., 17(14):1451-1460, 1996.
5. L. Vincent. *Morphological Grayscale Reconstruction in Image Analysis: Applications and Efficient Algorithms,* IEEE Trans. on Image Processing, 2:176-201, 1993.

Object Detection in Multi-channel and Multi-scale Images Based on the Structural Tensor

Bogusław Cyganek

AGH – University of Science and Technology,
Al. Mickiewicza 30, 30-059 Kraków, Poland
cyganek@uci.agh.edu.pl

Abstract. The paper presents theory and practical aspects of the detectors of characteristic objects in multi-channel images. It is based on the scale-space version of the structural tensor, adapted to operate on multi-channel signals. The method allows for object detection in $N \times 2D$ signal space with additional respect to the scale-space. Responses of the structural tensor are composed in a linear weighted sum that allows for better signal discrimination. In such a unified tensor framework different feature detectors were defined for detection of lines, corners, lines in the Hough space, structural places, etc. Although the presented method was developed for road sing recognition is can be also used for detection of other regular shapes. The sought objects are defined by a syntactical description of building line segments and their connection type. The paper presents also experimental results and implementation details.

1 Introduction

Detection of objects in images is one of the fundamental tasks of image processing. However, the variety of objects and image acquisition parameters makes this process not trivial. There are many types of filter based feature detectors for lines and corners [14] model based, such as the Hough transform [12], or statistical [1][16], just to name a few. The task gets even more troublesome in a case of noise, distortion, and multi channel signals. There are many attempts to overcome these problems and define a general framework for multi channel and scale processing. An original idea of such a framework comes from Sochen et al. [15]. They propose to treat multi channel and scale images as surfaces in a coordinate-value space. The derived metric of such a space has very similar properties (i.e. the same eigenvalues) to the structural tensor which modifications and applications are presented in this paper.

The paper begins with a short description of the multi channel and scale space structural tensor with some further propositions of its modifications, as well as discrete realizations. Then we present an overview of a class of feature detectors that all operate in the multi tensor domain. These are: line, corner, and Hough detectors, as well as image structural segmentation. The detectors can be further joined to work together for detection of more complex objects. In our case we were interested in detection of road signs. The presented grammar rules allow for syntactical description of such compounds. The paper ends with experimental results and conclusions.

2 The Multi-channel Scale Space Structural Tensor

The concept of the structural tensor was proposed by Bigün et al. [3], then investigated by many authors [2][13][14]. It allows for analysis of local structures, as well as their strength and orientations in local neighborhoods of pixels. In such a neighborhood $U(x_0)$ centered at a point x_0, a *dominant directional* vector w is sought that would represent all other directional vectors q_i in this neighborhood. The vectors q_i usually are local intensity gradients. Vectors are compared by computation of their inner product. Thus, the vector w at a point x_0 is an estimator of an average orientation in a neighborhood $U(x_0)$ that maximizes a certain functional Ω, given as follows:

$$\max_{w}(\Omega) = \max_{w}\left(\int_{U(x_0)} \left(\mathbf{q}^T(\vec{x})\mathbf{w}(\vec{x_0}) \right)^2 d\vec{x} \right) = \max_{w}(\vec{w}^T \mathbf{T}\vec{w}), \quad (1)$$

where the structural tensor $\mathbf{T}$ is defined by the following formula:

$$\mathbf{T}(\vec{x_0}) = \int_{U(x_0)} \mathbf{q}(\vec{x})\mathbf{q}^T(\vec{x}) d\vec{x}. \quad (2)$$

The square of the inner product in (1) fulfils the invariant assumption on rotation of π radians. Otherwise parallel and anti-parallel configurations of vectors would cancel out. In turn, the outer product $q(x)q^T(x)$ in (2) determines dimension of the tensor $\mathbf{T}$.

In a case of multi-channel images, such as color images, the question arises on definition of the gradient vector $q(x)$. In this paper we follow an approach proposed by Di Zenzo [10][8], used also in a work by Sochen et al. [15]. It assumes summation of the partial gradient components throughout image channels. To find the structural tensor for images with M channels we employ this idea to (2), as follows:

$$\mathbf{T}(\vec{x_0}) = \int_{U(x_0)} \sum_{k=1}^{M} \left(\mathbf{q}_k(\vec{x})\mathbf{q}_k^T(\vec{x}) \right) d\vec{x} = \sum_{k=1}^{M} \int_{U(x_0)} \left(\mathbf{q}_k(\vec{x})\mathbf{q}_k^T(\vec{x}) \right) d\vec{x} = \sum_{k=1}^{M} \mathbf{T}_k(\vec{x_0}). \quad (3)$$

Thus the summation in (3) spans all gradient fields, each computed independently for every intensity channel of a given image. This important extension allows for computation of local structures in multi dimensional images such as multi-spectral (e.g. color) images. It is also possible to employ (1) and (3) to analyze structures in other physical data than images.

In this paper we propose a further extension of the multi channel structural tensor (3) and form a linear combination of the component tensors $\mathbf{T_k}$, as follows:

$$\mathbf{T}(\vec{x_0}) = \sum_{k=1}^{M} c_k \mathbf{T}_k(\vec{x_0}), \quad (4)$$

where c_k are multiplicative constants. This way we can control an influence of each channel separately. We can go even further and propose a general function as follows:

$$\mathbf{T}(\vec{x_0}) = \Gamma\left(\mathbf{T}_k(\vec{x_0})\right), \quad (5)$$

where Γ is a function operating in a space of component tensors $\mathbf{T_k}$.

There are also at least two different space dimensions involved in (1) and (3)-(5). The first dimension is connected with a dimension of **T** which comes directly from dimension of the gradient vector: It is 2D for single images (**T** is 2×2) or 3D for video sequences (3×3). The second dimension follows the number of image channels; given by M in (3) and (4). There are also two scale-spaces involved in (3)-(5):

1. The scale associated with the input images (computation of tensors q_i).
2. The scale imposed by the averaging (computation of components T_{ij}).

Discrete realization of (3) was presented in [13]. In this paper we extend this concept to comprise the aforementioned scale-space parameters as follows:

$$\hat{T}_{ij}(\rho,\xi) = F_\rho(R_i^{(\xi)} R_j^{(\xi)}), \qquad (6)$$

where $R_i^{(\xi)}$ is a ξ-tap discrete directional operator (i.e. an order the corresponding filter is ξ-1), F_ρ is a smoothing kernel of scale ρ (this is a second discussed type of a scale).

3 Multi Structural Tensor for Object Detection

There are many ways to employ the structural tensor for feature detection. For example it can be used for detection of corners and oriented structures [8], image partitioning into structural regions, feature and area stereo matching [7][9], motion analysis [13], optical flow [3][4], or direct computation of the Hough transform [14]. In this paper we propose to apply the extended multi channel and scale structural tensor, given by (4) and(5), to the aforementioned and many other object detectors.

To find a local phase φ of features in local neighborhoods of an image we need to find a phase of the vector **w** in (1), which corresponds to an eigenvector of the greatest eigenvalue of **T**. In 2D case **w** can be found analytically [13]:

$$\mathbf{w} = [w_1 \quad w_2]^T = [T_{xx} - T_{yy} \quad 2T_{xy}]^T. \qquad (7)$$

For corner detection the eigenvalues of **T** can be analyzed [2][8]. They are as follows:

$$\lambda_{1,2} = \tfrac{1}{2}\left((T_{xx}+T_{yy}) \pm \sqrt{(T_{xx}-T_{yy})^2 + 4T_{xy}^2}\right). \qquad (8)$$

It was shown [2][8] that the structure analysis can be based solely on the analysis of the local eigenvalues (8). However, the two eigenvalues can be joined together in a form of the coherence component $c=(\lambda_1-\lambda_2)^2/(\lambda_1+\lambda_2)^2$ [3]. Coefficient c takes on 0 for ideal isotropic areas or structures with constant intensity value, and up to 1 for ideally directional structure. An analysis of the coefficient c and magnitude of w by non-linear operators can be used for image partitioning into structural and quasi-constant intensity places [7]. Similarly, the local phase φ of w (7) can be used for more *efficient* than classical computation of the Hough transform, as follows [14]:

$$\mathbf{nx} = p \Rightarrow x_1 \cos\varphi + x_2 \cos\varphi = p, \qquad (9)$$

where $x=(x_1,x_2)$, **n** is a normal vector to the line, φ is an angle of this line to the x axis (a slope of w), p is a (scalar) distance from the center of the image coordinate system.

For detection of more complex objects the simple feature detectors can be joined and their binary output can serve as a space for fast template matching [12]. Formal specification of such a compound detector that describes a sought object can be done e.g. with trees or simple LR-grammars [5]. In our implementation of the road sign detection the latter approach was used. The productions describe expected local structure configurations that can form a sign. For example the S_A and $S_{D,E,F,T}$ productions define silhouettes of the "A" and "D", "E", "F", or "T" groups of road signs, respectively: They are made of concatenations of line segment L_i, as follows:

$$S_A \to L_1 L_2 L_3 \, , \qquad S_{D,E,F,T} \to L_3 L_4 \, . \tag{10}$$

The line segments L_i are defined by the following productions:

$$L_i \to L(\eta_i \pi, p_i, \kappa_i), \qquad L \to L_S \mid L_H \, , \tag{11}$$

where L_i defines a local structure segment with a slope $\pi/\eta_i \pm p_i$ which is returned by the detector L controlled by a set of specific parameters κ_i. The segment detector L, described by the second production in (11), can be either an oriented structure (7) or a Hough detector (9) build upon (4). The parameters η_i are as follows: $\eta_1=1/3$, $\eta_2=2/3$, $\eta_3=0$, and $\eta_4=1/2$; Parameter p_i describing slope variation was set to $p_i=5\%$.

4 Experimental Results

The discrete realization of the multi channel and scale structural tensor requires computation of its components from (6) which are then composed according to (4) or (5). Choice of gradient and smoothing filters in (6) influences precision of feature detection. Many filters were tested [7] and the best results were obtained with the Simoncelli directional filters with $\xi=5$ taps [11], followed by the Gaussian smoothing filter of size determined by scale ρ. Moreover, the both filters have separable masks. The directional filter is composed of the smoothing prefilter p_5 and differentiating d_5:

$$\begin{aligned} p_5 &= [0.035697 \quad 0.248874 \quad 0.430855 \quad 0.248874 \quad 0.035697] \\ d_5 &= [0.107663 \quad -0.282671 \quad 0 \quad 0.282671 \quad -0.107663] \end{aligned} \tag{12}$$

The computational platform was composed from the IBM PC with Pentium 4, 3.4 GHz, 2GB RAM, implementation was done in C++ Microsoft Visual 6.0. The implementation directly follows (4), (6), and (12).

The experiments were performed on color images with six channels available (RGB and HSI). However, the presented technique allows for many other signal channels to be used in computation of the structural tensor (e.g. infrared, etc.). Influence of each channel is controlled by a pertinent parameter c_k in (4). Different scales of the structural tensor, as described by (6), were also applied and tested. Simultaneously, with each of the presented detectors, the segmentation detector was used as well. This allowed for feature detection only in areas with rich texture (not addressed in this paper, see [7][9] and Fig. 5b). Presented experimental results show variety of detection techniques in the multi tensor domain which are harnessed to the road signs detection.

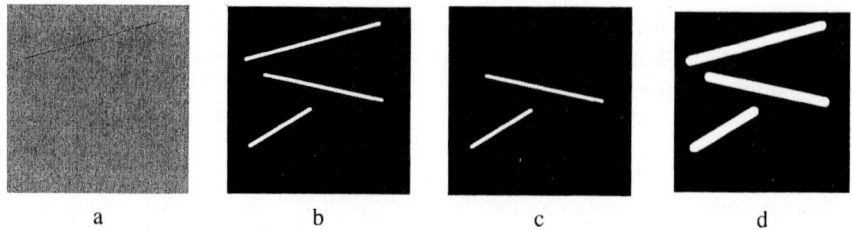

Fig. 1. Discriminating properties of the multi channel structural tensor: original RGB color lines (a), detected lines with $c_i=\{1,1,1\}$ (b), detected lines for $c_i=\{1,0,0\}$ (c), detection in larger scale ρ in (6)

The discriminating search of regular structures (lines) was tested in a three-channel colour image in Fig. 1a (i.e. 3×300×300). The RGB coordinates of the lines are: {5,62,165}, {252,66,228}, {248,121,104}. Detection of structural places [7][9] was performed with the tensor (4) with 3-tap directional filters [11] and Gaussian smoothing in (6). Fig. 1b presents results of detection with all channels equivalent, i.e. $c_i=\{1,1,1\}$ in (4), whereas Fig. 1c for $c_i=\{1,0,0\}$, i.e. only the R channel. This way we can amplify detection in selected channels, what will be also presented for more complex detections. Execution time was 0.3s (bc) and for larger scale 0.6s (Fig. 1d).

Fig. 2 depicts a 640×480 color image of a road intersection and its color channels (RGB and HSI). Fig. 2b-e contain binary masks outputted by the directional detectors L_1-L_4, respectively, as defined in (10)-(11). The combined output presents Fig. 2f where two silhouettes of road signs were detected. The three RGB+SI channels were employed, i.e. $c_i=\{1,1,1,0,1,1\}$ in this case. It shows that we have to examine a priori which channels are best for detection. In this case the H channel was not appropriate for the detection task. Execution takes 5.6 s (detectors L_1-L_4 worked in a series).

The detections for the "A9" road sign presents Fig. 3; Parameters $c_i=\{1,1,1,0,0,0\}$, the 5-tap directional filter (12) and the binomial smoothing were chosen. The latter filter is easier in implementation (especially for hardware) and results are comparable to the detection of the "A7" sign. Execution time was 5.1 s (serial detection).

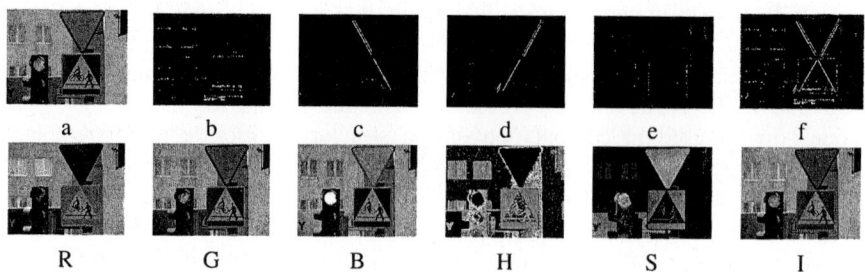

Fig. 2. The road sign "A7": original (a), binary masks after L_1-L_4 detectors (b-e), combined masks, RGB channels, HSI channels (second row)

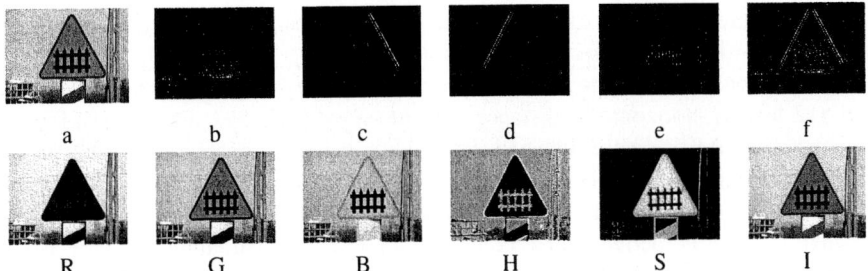

Fig. 3. The road sign "A9": original color image (a), binary masks after L_1-L_4 detectors (b-e), combined masks, RGB channels, HSI channels (second row)

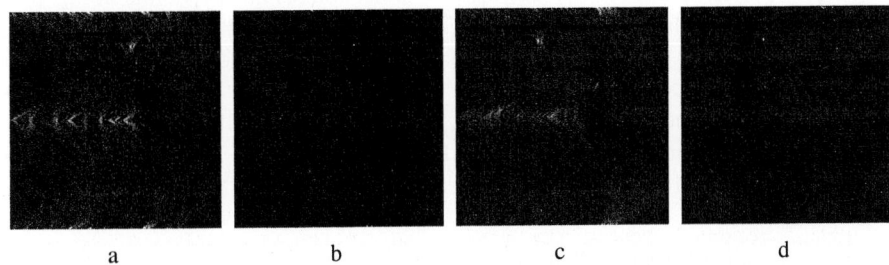

Fig. 4. The Hough space (vertical axis – angle 0-π, 512 discrete levels, horizontal – distance from origin, 512 discrete levels): for the "A7" sign (a, b-filtered), the "A9" sign (c, d-filtered)

Fig. 5. Detection of the "B20" (STOP) sign: color image (a), structural places (b), HSI representation of components T_{ij} (c), detected silhouettes for different sets of c_i (d-i)

Fig. 4 presents results of the Hough detector, operating in a tensor field, in accordance with (9), for detection of the signs "A7" (Fig. 2a) and "A9" (Fig. 3a). The Hough accumulators are shown with vertical axis containing angle φ (0-π, divided into 512 levels), horizontal – distance p from origin (also 512 discrete levels). The sought lines were correctly detected, although some inaccuracies are visible in non filtered spaces (Fig. 4a,c). However, this is caused by discrete values of the x and y coordinates in (9), rather than precision of detection with tensor. Execution time is 1.2 s, what is very attractive when compared to the classical algorithms of Hough computations.

For detection of other objects we need to define a proper detector. For example to detect the "B20" sign (Fig. 5a) we used the following grammar rule: $S_{B20} \rightarrow L_3L_4L_5L_6$, where parameters η_i (11) are: $\eta_5=1/4$, $\eta_6=3/4$. Detection results are visible in Fig. 5.

Fig. 5b depicts binary output of the segmentation detector that partitions an image into structural places (see [7][9] for details) – all further detections are restricted only to places with sufficient texture (depicted in white in Fig. 5b). Fig. 5c visualizes the three tensor components T_{xx}, T_{yy}, and T_{xy} from (2)-(6) as HSI channels. Detection results present Fig. 5d-i, for each channel RGB-HSI separately. The other parameters and execution time are similar to those already presented in Fig. 2 and Fig. 3.

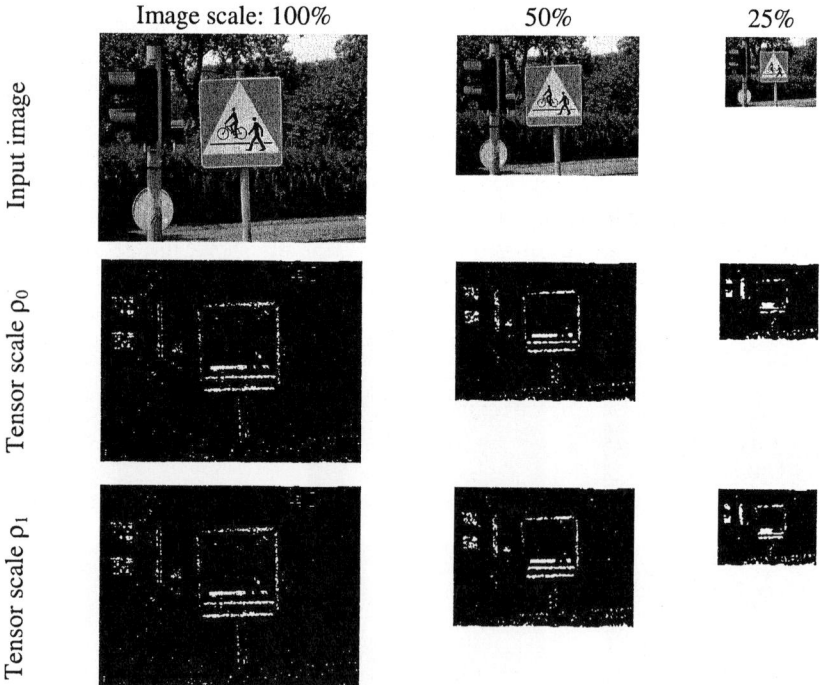

Fig. 6. Detection of the silhouette of the "D6b" road sign for different image scales and tensor scales. Six input channels: RGB and HSI. Parameters $c_i=\{1,1,1,0,0,0\}$.

Fig. 6 presents detection of the silhouette of the "D6b" sign for different image scales (from octave pyramid 1:1, 1:2, and 1:4) and tensor scales controlled by the parameter ρ from (6), which corresponds to the Gaussian smoothing with $\sigma=0.5$ and $\sigma=2$, respectively. The 6×640×480 (RGBHIS) channels constitute the input space. The detection rule is: $S_{D6b} \rightarrow L_3L_4$ (10). It is interesting to observe that application of the coarsest scale (smaller) images with coarser tensor scale allows for much faster image detection. This way of guided hierarchical detection in the finer scales can be used for precise detection of an already spotted object. However, since the time complexity of computation is proportional to the square of pixels in an image, then image reduction by factor of four allows for about order of magnitude speed improvement. This was verified in our realisation where execution times were: 5.58 s (coarsest scale), 0.77 s, and 0.21 s (finest scale). For the directional detectors in (6) the $\xi=5$ tap filters (12) were employed.

5 Conclusions

This paper presents the unified framework for computation of the scale space structural tensor operating in a domain of multi-dimensional signals. It was shown that such representation allows for simultaneous and very efficient detection of local features such as lines, corners, structural places, etc. The presented method can be applied at different stages of feature detection in images – e.g. the tensor can be used for direct line detection or it can return supporting points for subsequent line search by the Hough method. Detection of more complex objects involves combination of many basic detectors, operating however on only once pre-computed tensor field what greatly shortens detection time. It was also presented that such a compound detector can be formally described by simple grammar productions. The presented techniques were applied to the task of road signs detection. The input came from color images and the sign silhouettes were described as syntactical productions operating on simple structure detectors. The experimental results show that this is a very versatile technique which can be quite fast and does not require cumbersome thresholds. Using only simple filters it can be implemented in hardware, as well.

This paper was supported by the grant no. 3T11C 045 26 of the Polish Committee of Scientific Research (KBN).

References

1. Amit, Y.: 2D Object Detection and Recognition, MIT Press (2002)
2. Aubert, G., Kornprobst, P., Mathematical Problems in Image Processing. Springer (2002)
3. Bigün, J., Granlund, G.H., Wiklund, J., Multidimensional Orientation Estimation with Applications to Texture Analysis and Optical Flow. IEEE PAMI 13(8), (1991) 775-790
4. Brox, T., Rousson, M., Deriche, R., Weickert, J.: Unsupervised Segmentation Incorporating Colour, Texture, and Motion. INRIA Technical Report No 4760 (2003)
5. Bunke, H.: Structural and Syntactic Pattern Recognition. Handbook of Pattern Recognition & Computer Vision, Chen C.H., et al., World Scientific (1993) 163-209

6. Carson, C., Belonge, S., Greenspan, H., Malik, J.: Blobworld: Image Segmentation Using Expectation-Maximization. IEEE PAMI 24(8), (2002) 1026-1038
7. Cyganek, B.: Novel Stereo Matching Method That Employs Tensor Representation of Local Neighborhood In Binary Images, Machine Graphics & Vision, (2001) 289-316
8. Cyganek, B.: Combined Detector of Locally-Oriented Structures and Corners in Images Based, in Springer LNCS 2658 (2003) 721-730
9. Cyganek, B.: Depth Recovery with an Area Based Version of the Stereo Matching Method with Scale-Space Tensor Representation, in LNCS 3037 (2004) 548-551
10. Di Zenzo S.: A note on the gradient of a multi-image. Computer Vision, Graphics and Image Processing, 33: (1986) 116-125
11. Farid, H., Simoncelli, E.P.: Differentiation of discrete multidimensional signals. IEEE Trans. Image Proc. 13(4) (2004) 496-508
12. Forsyth, D.A., Ponce, J.: Computer Vision. A Modern Approach, Prentice-Hall (2003)
13. Haußecker, H., Jähne, B.: A Tensor Approach for Local Structure Analysis in Multi-Dimensional Images. Technical Report, University of Heidelberg (1998)
14. Jähne, B.: Digital Image Processing, Springer-Verlag (1997)
15. Sochen, N., Kimmel, R., Malladi, R.: A General Framework for Low Level Vision. IEEE Transactions on Image Processing, 7(3) (1998) 310-318

Evaluating Minimum Spanning Tree Based Segmentation Algorithms*

Yll Haxhimusa, Adrian Ion, Walter G. Kropatsch, and Thomas Illetschko

Pattern Recognition and Image Processing Group 183/2,
Institute for Computer Aided Automation, Vienna University of Technology, Austria
{yll, ion, krw, illetsch}@prip.tuwien.ac.at

Abstract. Two segmentation methods based on the minimum spanning tree principle are evaluated with respect to each other. The hierarchical minimum spanning tree method is also evaluated with respect to human segmentations. Discrepancy measure is used as best suited to compute the segmentation error between the methods. The evaluation is done using gray value images. It is shown that the segmentation results of these methods have a considerable difference.

1 Introduction

In [8] it is suggested to bridge and not to eliminate the representational gap, and to focus efforts on *region segmentation, perceptual grouping*, and *image abstraction*. The segmentation process results in "homogeneous" regions with respect to the low-level cues using some similarity measures. Problems emerge because i) homogeneity of low-level cues will not map to the semantics [8] and ii) the degree of homogeneity of a region is in general quantified by threshold(s) for a given measure [2]. The union of regions forming the group is again a region with both internal and external properties and relations. The low-level coherence of brightness, color, texture or motion attributes should be used to come up sequentially with hierarchical partitions [12]. It is important that a grouping method has the following properties [1]: i) capture perceptually important groupings or regions, which reflect global aspects of the image, ii) be highly efficient, running in time linear in the number of pixels, and iii) creates hierarchical partitions [12].

Low-level cue image segmentation cannot produce a complete final "good" segmentation [11]. This lead researchers to look at the segmentation only in the context of a task, as well as the evaluation of the segmentation methods. However in [9] the segmentation is evaluated purely as segmentation by comparing the segmentation done by humans with those done by the normalized cuts method [12]. As can be seen in Fig. 1, there is a high degree of consistency of segmentation done by humans (already demonstrated empirically in [9]), even thought humans segment images at different granularity (refinement or coarsening). This refinement or coarsening could be thought of as a hierarchical structure on the image, i.e. the pyramid. Therefore in [9] a segmentation consistency measure that does

---

* Supported by the Austrian Science Fund under grant FSP-S9103-N04.

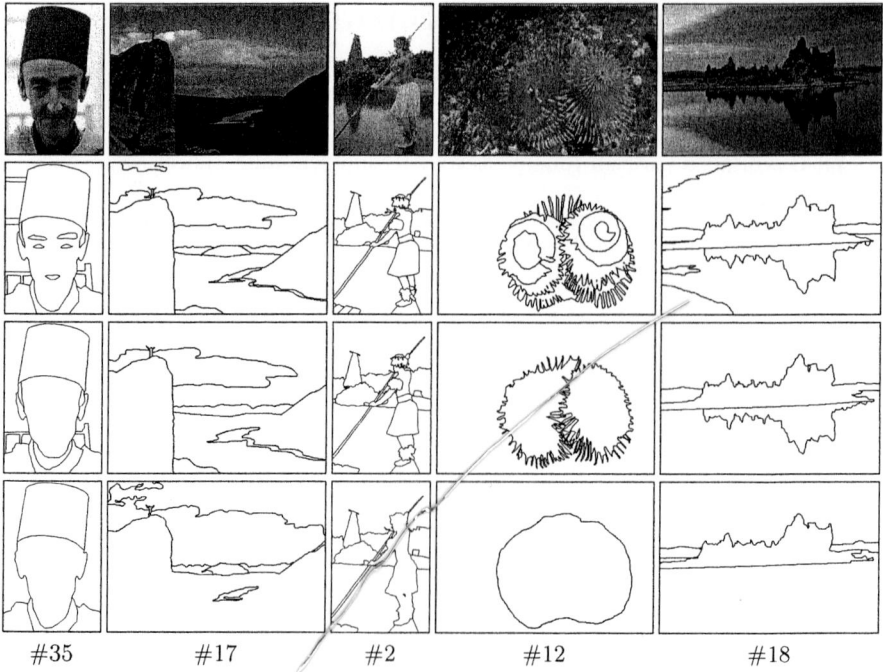

Fig. 1. Images from the Berkley image database with human segmentation [9]

not penalize this granularity difference is defined (see Sec. 4). Note that the segmented image #35 in row 2 can be coarsened to obtain the image in row 4 (and vice versa), this is called *simple refinement*; whereas to obtain image in row 3 from row 2 (or vice versa) we must coarsen in one part of the image and refine in the other (notice the chin of the man in row 3), this is called *mutual refinement*.

In this paper, we evaluate two segmentation methods based on the minimum spanning tree (MST) principle. The segmentation method based on Kruskal's algorithm [1](KrusSeg) and a parallel, hierarchical one, based on Borůvka's algorithm [6](BorůSeg) (Sec. 2). We compare these two methods following the framework of [9] i.e. comparing the segmentation results of these methods with each other. The BorůSeg is also evaluated with respect to the human segmentations. The results of the evaluation are reported in Sec. 4.

2 Segmentation Methods

A graph-theoretical clustering algorithm consists in searching for a certain combinatorial structure in the edge weighted graph, such as an MST [1,4], a minimum cut [14,12] and a search for a complete subgraph i.e. the maximal clique [10]. Early graph-based methods [15] use fixed thresholds and local measures in finding a segmentation, i.e MST is computed. The segmentation criterion is to break

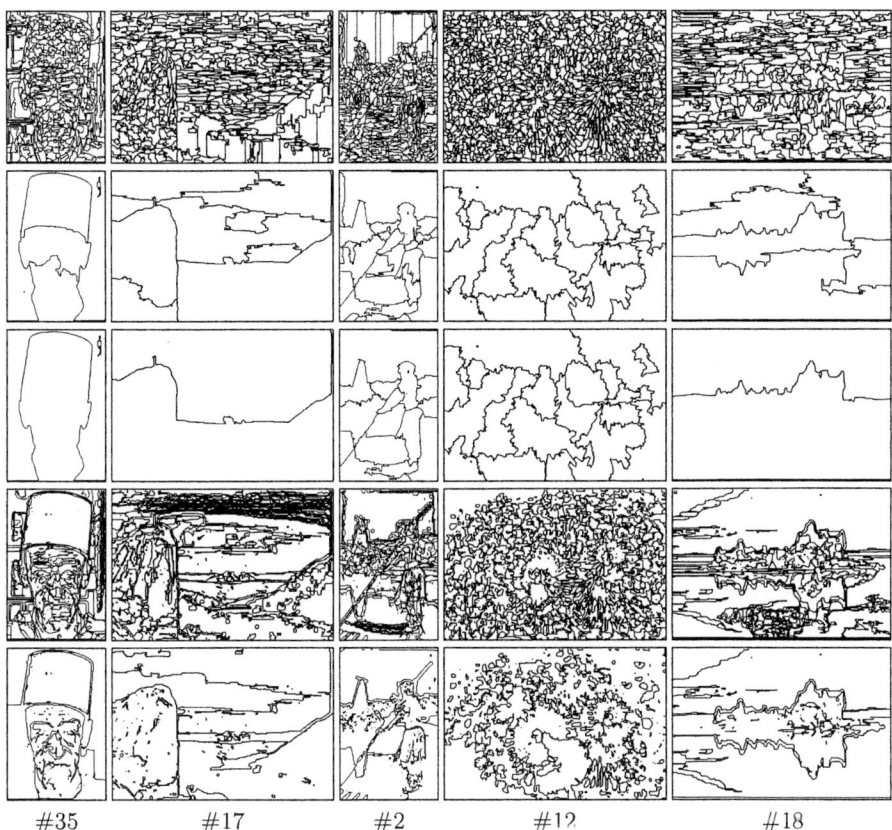

Fig. 2. Segmentation produces by BorůSeg($k = 300$) in row 1-3 (from coarser to finer segmentation), in row 4 KrusSeg($k = 300, \sigma = 1.5$) and in row 5 KrusSeg($k = 30000, \sigma = 1.5$)

the MST edges with the largest weight, which reflect the low-cost connection between two elements. To overcome the problem of a fixed threshold, Urquhart [13] normalizes the weight of an edge using the smallest weight incident on the vertices touching that edge. The methods in [1,4,6] use an adaptive criterion that depends on local properties rather than global ones.

We evaluate segmentations of the well known method [1] based on Kruskal's algorithm, with the one [6] based on Borůvka's algorithm. Since, for both methods there is a threshold dependent on the size of the connected component used ($k/|CC|$[1] see [1,6] for more details.) in the merging criteria, the segmentation inclusion trees are different, because of the way the data is processed, the first one does it in serial and the other one in parallel. Setting this threshold to zero

---

[1] $|CC|$ cardinality of the connected component.

both of the methods would produce the MST of the image, independent of the way the data is processed.

Some samples of the segmentation results, obtained by applying these methods to gray value images are shown in Fig. 2. The BorůSeg method is capable of producing a hierarchy of images, the pyramid (see the images in Fig. 2, where row 1 represent lower levels of the pyramid, row 2 the middle levels, and row 3 the higher levels). The methods use only local contrast based on pixel intensity values. We smoothed the images before segmenting them with the KrusSeg[2] method (Gaussian with parameter $\sigma = 1.5$), whereas BorůSeg worked with non smoothed images. As expected, and seen from Fig. 2, segmentation methods which are based only on low-level local cues can not create results as good as humans. The overall number of regions in rows 1 and 4 in each column of Fig. 2, are almost the same, and this condition is required in [9] to perform the evaluation in Sec. 4. Both of the methods are capable of segmenting the face of a man satisfactory (image #35). The BorůSeg method did not merge the statue on the top of the mountain with the sky (image #17), compared to humans which do segment this statue as a single region (see Fig. 1). Both methods have problems segmenting the sea creatures (image #12). Note that the segmentation done by humans on the image of rocks (image #18), contains the axis of symmetry, even thought there is no "big" local contrast, therefore both of the methods fail in this respect.

3 Evaluating Segmentations

There are two general methods used to evaluate segmentations: (i) qualitative and (ii) quantitative methods. Qualitative methods involve humans, meaning that different observers would give different evaluations about the segmentations (e.g. [7]). Quantitative methods are classified into analytic methods and empirical methods [16]. Analytical methods study the principles and properties of the algorithm, like processing complexity, efficiency and so on. For references on the analytic studies of methods based on minimum spanning tree see Sec. 2. The empirical methods study properties of the segmentations by measuring how "good" a segmentation is close to an "ideal" one, by determining this "goodness" with some function of parameters. Both of the approaches depend on the subjects, the first one, in coming up with the reference (perfect) segmentation[3] and the second one, in defining the "goodness" function. The difference between the segmented image and the (ideal) reference can be used to asses the performance of the algorithm [16]. The reference image could be a synthetic image or be manually segmented by humans. Higher value of the discrepancy means bigger error, signaling poor performance of the segmentation method. In [16], it is concluded that evaluation methods based on *"mis-segmented pixels should be more powerful than other methods using other measures"*. In [9] the error measures used for evaluating segmentation *counts* the mis-segmented pixels.

---

[2] The method is very sensitive to noise [1].
[3] Also called a gold standard [3].

In this paper we use the framework given in [9] to evaluate qualitatively the result of the KrusSeg [1] with BorůSeg [6] and of the BorůSeg with respect to humans using the discrepancy measures defined in the next section.

4 Benchmarking Segmentations

In [9] segmentations made by humans are used as a reference and basis for benchmarking segmentations produced by different methods. The concept behind this is the observation that even though different people produce different segmentations for the same image, the obtained segmentations differ, mostly, only in the local refinement of certain regions. This concept has been studied in [9] on a human segmentation database (see Fig. 1) and used as a basis for defining two error measures, which do not penalize a segmentation if it is coarser or more refined than the other. In this sense, in an image P a pixel error measure $E(S_1, S_2, p)$, between two segmentations S_1 and S_2 containing pixel $p \in P$, called the *local refinement error*, is defined as:

$$E(S_1, S_2, p) = \frac{|R(S_1,p) \setminus R(S_2,p)|}{|R(S_1,p)|} \quad (1)$$

where \ denotes set difference, $|x|$ the cardinality of a set x, and $R(S, p)$ is the set of pixels corresponding to the connected component in segmentation S that contains pixel p. Using the local refinement error $E(S_1, S_2, p)$ the following error measures are defined in [9]: the *Global Consistency Error* (GCE), which forces all local refinements to be in the same direction, and is defined as:

$$GCE(S_1, S_2) = \frac{1}{n} \min \left\{ \sum_{p \in P} E(S_1, S_2, p), \sum_{p \in P} E(S_2, S_1, p) \right\} \quad (2)$$

and the *Local Consistency Error* (LCE), allowing refinement in different directions in different parts of the image:

$$LCE(S_1, S_2) = \frac{1}{n} \sum_{p \in P} \min \left\{ E(S_1, S_2, p), E(S_2, S_1, p) \right\} \quad (3)$$

n is the number of pixels in the image. Notice that LCE $\leq$ GCE for any two segmentations. GCE is tougher measure than LCE, because GCE tolerates simple refinements, while LCE tolerates mutual refinement as well.

We have used the GCE and LCE measures presented above to evaluate the BorůSeg method [6] using the human segmented images from the Berkley humans segmented images database [9]. Also, the evaluation of BorůSeg with respect to KrusSeg is done.

4.1 Evaluation of Segmentations on the Berkley Image Database

As mentioned in [9] a segmentation consisting of a single region and a segmentation where each pixel is a region, is the coarsest and finest possible of any

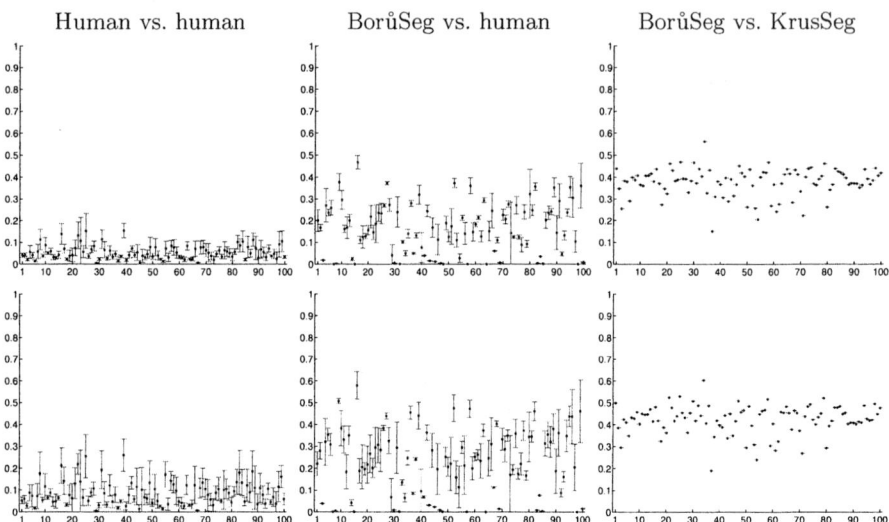

Fig. 3. The LCE (above) and GCE (below), error measure results for 100 images

segmentation. In this sense, the LCE and GCE measures should not be used when the number of regions in the two segmentation differs a lot. So, taking into consideration that the BorůSeg produces a whole hierarchy of segmentations with different number of regions (from coarser to finer), we have selected for the evaluation two levels of this pyramid. In the first case, we have taken for each image the segmentation level produced by the BorůSeg with the number of regions closest to the average number of regions produced by the humans (for the same image). When evaluating the KrusSeg we have chosen for the BorůSeg the segmentation level that had the number of regions closest to the number of regions produced by the KrusSeg method. In all the cases this meant going lower in the pyramid and taking a level which is basically a refinement of the one used when comparing to the humans. Also, as recommended by Felzenszwalb etal [1], the images given to the KrusSeg method have been smoothed with a Gaussian filter (e.g. $\sigma = 1.5$). Because the KrusSeg still produced much more regions than the human segmentations in the database have, an evaluation of the KrusSeg vs. the humans would have been unfair.

As data for the experiments, we take 100 gray level images from the Berkley Image Database[4]. For each of the images in the test, we calculate the GCE and LCE using the results produced by the KrusSeg and the corresponding level from the hierarchy produced by BorůSeg, and the human segmentations for the same image together with the corresponding level from the BorůSeg pyramid. In the case of humans and BorůSeg, having more than one pair of GCE and LCE for each image, we calculate the mean and the standard deviation. The results are summarized in Fig. 3. As a reference point, in the same figure, you can see the

---

[4] http://www.cs.berkeley.edu/projects/vision/grouping/segbench/

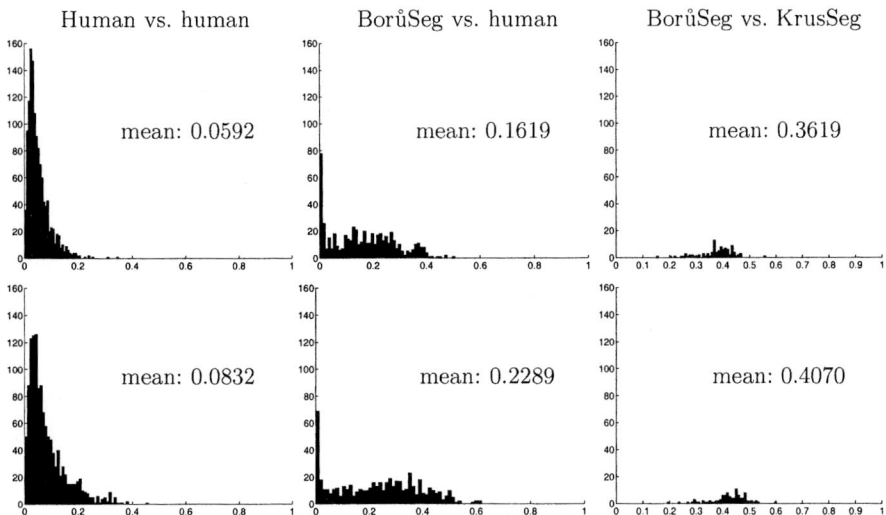

Fig. 4. Histograms of LCE (above) and GCE (below) discrepancy measure

results for calculating the GCE and LCE values for pairwise two segmentations made by humans, for the same image. We can see that the humans did very good and proved to be consistent when segmenting the same image, and that the BorůSeg produces segmentations that obtained higher values for the GCE and LCE error measures.

In Fig. 4 one can see the histograms of the GCE and LCE values obtained ([0...1], where zero means no error), humans vs. humans, BorůSeg vs. humans, and BorůSeg vs. KrusSeg. Notice that the humans are consistent in segmenting the images and the humans vs. humans histogram shows a peak very close to 0. Also, the results show that there is a considerable difference (GCE mean value 0.4) between the segmentations produced by the BorůSeg and KrusSeg methods.

5 Conclusion and Outlook

In this paper we have evaluated segmentation results of two methods based on the minimum spanning tree principle. The evaluation is done using discrepancy measures that do not penalize segmentations that are coarser or more refined in certain regions. We use gray scale images to evaluate the quality of results. In the case of BorůSeg, this evaluation can be used to find classes of images for which the algorithm has segmentation problems, corresponding to higher GCE and LCE values. We have observed that the results produced by the BorůSeg vs. KrusSeg methods have shown a considerable difference. We plan to use a larger image database to confirm the quality of the obtained results, and do the evaluation with additional low level cues (color and texture) as well as different statistical measures.

References

1. P. F. Felzenszwalb and D. P. Huttenlocher. Image Segmentation Using Local Variation. In *Proceedings of IEEE Conference on CVPR*, p:98–104, June 1998.
2. C.-S. Fu, W. Cho, S, and K. Essig. Hierarchical Color Image Region Segmentation for Content-based Image Retrieval System. *IEEE Transaction on Image Processing*, 9(1):156–162, 2000.
3. C. N. Graaf, A. S. E. Koster, K. L. Vincken, and M. A. Viergever. Validation of the Interleaved Pyramid for the Segmentation of $3d$ Vector Images. *Pattern Recognition Letters*, 15(5):469–475, 1994.
4. L. Guigues, L. M. Herve, and J.-P. Cocquerez. The Hierarchy of the Cocoons of a Graph and its Application to Image Segmentation. *Pattern Recognition Letters*, 24(8):1059–1066, 2003.
5. Y. Haxhimusa, A. Ion, W. G. Kropatsch, and L. Brun. Hierarchical Image Partitioning using Combinatorial Maps. *Joint Hungarian-Austrian Conference on Image Processing and Patt. Recog.*, p:179–186, 2005.
6. Y. Haxhimusa and W. G. Kropatsch. Segmentation Graph Hierarchies. In A. Fred, T. Caelli, R. P. Duin, A. Campilho, and D. de Ridder, editors, *Proceedings of Joint Inter. Work. on Struct., Synt., and Statis. Patt. Recog.*, LNCS 3138:343–351, 2004.
7. M. Heath, S. Sarkar, T. Sanocki, and K. Bowyer. A Robust Visual Methods for Assessing the Relative Performance of Edge-detection Algorithms. *IEEE Transactions on PAMI*, 19(12):1338–1359, 1997.
8. Y. Kesselman and S. Dickinson. Generic Model Abstraction from Examples. *IEEE Trans. on PAMI, issue on Synt. and Struct. Patt. Recog.*, 2005. to appear.
9. D. Martin, C. Fowlkes, D. Tal, and J. Malik. A Database of Human Segmented Natural Images and its Application to Evaluating Segmentation Algorithms and Measuring Ecological Statistics. In *Proc. 8th ICCV*, (2):416–423, July 2001.
10. M. Pavan and M. Pelillo. Dominant Sets and Hierarchical Clustering. In *ICCV03*, 2003.
11. B. S. Borra and S. Sarkar. A Framework for Performance Characterization of Intermediate-level Grouping Modules. *Pattern Recognition and Image Analysis*, 19(11):1306–1312, 1997.
12. J. Shi and J. Malik. Normalized Cuts and Image Segmentation. In *Proceedings IEEE Conference CVPR*, p:731–737, 1997.
13. R. Urquhart. Graph Theoretical Clustering Based on Limited Neighborhood Sets. *Pattern Recognition*, 13:3:173–187, 1982.
14. Z. Wu and R. Leahy. An Optimal Graph Theoretic Approach to Data Clustering: Theory and Its Application to Image Segmentation. *IEEE Transactions on PAMI*, 15(11):1101–1113, 1993.
15. C. Zahn. Graph-theoretical Methods for Detecting and describing Gestalt Clusters. In *IEEE Trans. Comput.*, Vol. 20:68–86, 1971.
16. Y. Zhang. A Survey on Evaluation Methods for Image Segmentation. *Pattern Recognition*, 29(8):1335–1346, 1996.

Feature Space Reduction for Face Recognition with Dual Linear Discriminant Analysis

Krzysztof Kucharski[1], Władysław Skarbek[1], and Mirosław Bober[2]

[1] Institute of Radioelectronics, Warsaw University of Technology, Poland
K.Z.Kucharski@elka.pw.edu.pl
[2] Visual Information Laboratory, Mitsubishi Electric, Guildford, UK

Abstract. Linear Discriminant Analysis (LDA) is widely known feature extraction technique that aims at creating a feature set of enhanced discriminatory power. It was addressed by many researchers and proved to be especially successful approach in face recognition. The authors introduced a novel approach Dual LDA (DLDA) and proposed an efficient SVD-based implementation controlled by two parameters. In this paper DLDA is analyzed from the feature space reduction point of view and the role of the parameters is explained. The comparative experiments conducted on facial database consisting of nearly 2000 individuals show superiority of this approach over class of feature selection methods that choose the features one by one relying on classic statistical measures.

1 Introduction

LDA in face recognition was inspired by the classic monographs on statistical pattern recognition [7] and [6], where different criteria of class separability were investigated given that elements x_j of the training set X are labelled. One of these measures was the ratio of between-class scatter matrix S_b determinant to within-class scatter matrix S_w determinant. As the determinants are calculated in an unknown linear subspace R^r, the problem of finding the transformation matrix W from an input space R^N, $N > r$ to that space was formulated assuming the separability criterion is maximized. Then columns of the solution matrix are eigenvectors of matrix $S_w^{-1} S_b$ corresponding to its greatest eigenvalues [6]:

$$S_w^{-1} S_b W' = W' \Lambda \Rightarrow W' = \arg\max_W \frac{|W^t S_b W|}{|W^t S_w W|} \qquad (1)$$

This result usually cannot be directly adopted to the face recognition area due to singularity of the matrix S_w, which is the case whenever dimension of the input space N is greater than number of face examples L in the training set. Therefore a good number of proposals was published on how to avoid this problem. In [12] and [1] a preliminary PCA was applied to the input data X to first reduce dimensionality to at least $N - J$ thus ensuring non-singularity S_w and then apply LDA to the reduced data. Here J stands for the overall number of classes.

In [5] authors reduce the dimensionality by pixel grouping technique but search for the solution within the S_w null space maximizing only the nominator of (1) by means of the conventional PCA. They use the result formulated in [9] that replacement of a denominator in (1) with the expression $|W^t S_T W|$, where S_T is the total scatter matrix, i.e. the input data covariance matrix, leads to the equivalent goal function. This approach is accelerated in [4], where the observation is proved that the orthogonal projection of every input vector belonging to the same class onto the S_w null space gives the same result. Hence the maximum of $|W^t S_b W|$ in the S_w null space can be sought among vectors arbitrarily selected from each class. These vectors are called the common vectors.

In [14] authors propose to invert the criterion (1) and search for its minimum point. In this approach the solution matrix W found by means of two eigenvalue decompositions diagonalizes both S_w and S_b whereas S_w is additionally whitened [7].

Alternatively to the criterion (1) in [16] the criterion based on within-class and between-class variances is addressed:

$$W' = \arg\max_W \frac{\text{tr}(W^t S_b W)}{\text{tr}(W^t S_w W)} \quad (2)$$

Its solution is also based on simultaneous diagonalization of S_w and S_b in the subspace orthogonal to the S_w null space assuming unit within-class variances in the output space. The complete theory justifying the optimality of the solution with respect to the criterion (2) is presented in [17], where also the minimization of the inverted criterion is introduced as the Dual LDA (DLDA) method. Both LDA and DLDA algorithms are parameterized in terms of subspace dimensions that result from the eigenvalue decompositions of matrices S_w and S_b respectively.

In section 2 of this paper, the DLDA approach is thoroughly investigated and the role of its parameters in face recognition is explained. The stress is put on the feature space reduction aspect that can be controlled by these parameters thus effectively supporting the feature extraction process. Section 3 contains comparative experiments as far as recognition performance and computational complexity is concerned, conducted on the base of above 10000 facial images belonging to nearly 2000 individuals. Section 5 summarizes the paper.

2   Dual Linear Discriminant Analysis

Dual Linear Discriminant Analysis (DLDA) finds a matrix W of linear transformation from R^N to R^r that separates the input data vectors $X = [x_1, \ldots, x_L]$ belonging to J different classes in terms of minimizing the within-class variance to the between-class variance ratio. More precisely, DLDA seeks for a optimal point W_{opt} of a goal function $f(W)$ defined as follows:

$$f(W) = \frac{\text{tr}(W^t S_w(X) W)}{\text{tr}(W^t S_b(X) W)} = \frac{\text{var}_w(W^t X)}{\text{var}_b(W^t X)} \quad (3)$$

It utilizes concepts of the within-class scatter matrix S_w and the between-class scatter matrix S_b defined below:

$$S_b(X) = \frac{1}{J-1} \sum_{j=1}^{J} L_j (\bar{x}^j - \bar{x})(\bar{x}^j - \bar{x})^t \tag{4}$$

$$S_w(X) = \frac{1}{L-J} \sum_{j=1}^{J} \frac{1}{L_j} \sum_{i \in I_j} (x_i - \bar{x}^j)(x_i - \bar{x}^j)^t \tag{5}$$

Here $L_1, \ldots, L_J$ stand for corresponding class populations whose index sets are denoted by $I_1, \ldots, I_J$ and $\bar{x}^j, \bar{x}$ are mean of j-th class and global mean, respectively.

Assuming lack of correlation in both, within and between class contexts as well as condition of unit within class variances searching for W_{opt} is a problem of quadratic constrained optimization:

$$W_{opt} \triangleq \arg \min_{W^t S_b W = I, W^t S_w W \text{ is diagonal}} tr(W^t S_w(X) W) \tag{6}$$

The solution is found using two subsequent Eigenvalue Decompositions (EVD):

$$W_{opt} = [w_1, \ldots, w_r] = [Av_{r_0}, \ldots, Av_{r_0-r+1}] \tag{7}$$

$$A \triangleq U_{q_0} \Lambda_{q_0}^{-1/2}, \quad S_b \stackrel{EVD}{=} U_{q_0} \Lambda_{q_0} U_{q_0}^t, \quad q_0 = \text{rank}(S_b) \tag{8}$$

$$A^t S_w A \stackrel{EVD}{=} V_{r_0} \Sigma_{r_0} V_{r_0}^t, \quad r_0 = \text{rank}(A^t S_w A), \quad 1 \leq r \leq r_0 \tag{9}$$

The scatter matrices S_b and S_w defined in (4) and (5) can be expressed as outer products of matrices X_b and X_w respectively:

$$S_b(X) = X_b X_b^t, \quad X_b \triangleq \left[\frac{\bar{x}^1 - \bar{x}}{\sqrt{J-1}}, \ldots, \frac{\bar{x}^J - \bar{x}}{\sqrt{J-1}} \right]^t \tag{10}$$

$$S_w(X) = X_w X_w^t, \quad X_w \triangleq \left[\frac{x_1 - \bar{x}^{j(1)}}{\sqrt{L-J}}, \ldots, \frac{x_L - \bar{x}^{j(L)}}{\sqrt{L-J}} \right]^t \tag{11}$$

Matrix X_b contains weighted between-class errors which may be expressed in alternative base formed by eigenvectors $u_1, \ldots, u_{q_0}$ of matrix S_b corresponding to its eigenvalues $\lambda_1, \ldots, \lambda_{q_0}$ sorted in non-descending order. The eigenvalues are, in fact, between-class variances in corresponding directions. The same reasoning cannot be strictly applied to variances of data vectors from X_b because of non-zero mean of these vectors. However, Fig. 1 shows that associating an interpretation of greatest X_b variance directions with subsequent vectors from U_{q_0} is reasonable in face recognition.

It follows from (9) and (11) that minimizing the expression $tr(V_{r_0}^t (A^t S_w A^t) V_{r_0})$ is equivalent to minimizing variance of data $A^t X_w$ after projection onto subspace spanned by columns of V_r, what may be perceived as inverted PCA problem. It is true, because mean of data vectors from X_w

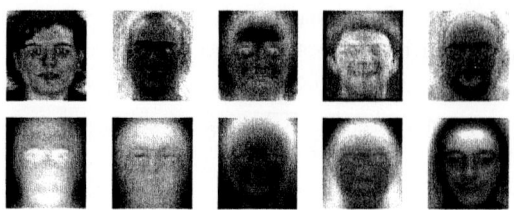

Fig. 1. Exemplary weighted between-class errors (upper row) and first five directions of greatest between-class variability (lower row)

is zero. Here, r is a parameter of the method that controls dimension of the output DLDA feature space. The data matrix $A^t X_w = \Lambda^{-1/2}(U_{q_0}^t X_w)$ contains weighted within-class errors that are first orthogonally projected onto subspace spanned by directions of greatest variance of weighted within class error, then whitened by diagonal matrix $U_{q_0}^{-1/2}$.

In DLDA, q_0 which is determined by the input data X is replaced with variable $q \leq q_0$, i.e. the parameter of the method. Therefore, weighted within-class errors from X_w are projected onto orthogonal subspace covering only part of the total variance of the weighted between-class errors. In Fig. 2 exemplary input and reconstructed facial vectors of such a projection for different values of q are presented.

Whitening matrix $\Lambda_{q_0}^{-1/2}$ ensures satisfying one of the imposed constraints i.e. data vectors from X have unit between-class variances after projection onto subspace spanned by columns of matrix A.

DLDA does not calculate matrices S_b and S_w but operates directly on weighted error matrices, between-class X_b and within-class X_w using a fact that for any matrix C EVD of CC^t can be performed through Singular Value Decomposition (SVD) of C [8]. Essential steps of the algorithm are as follows:

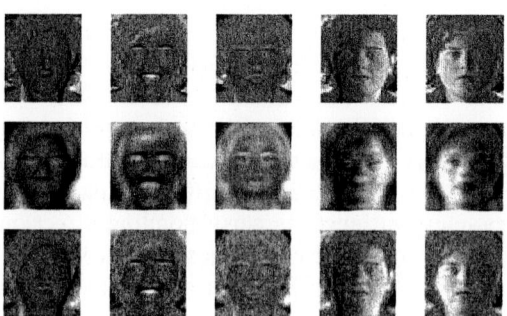

Fig. 2. The weighted within-class errors for one class (top row) and their reconstructions for the projection onto subspace of weighted between-class errors at $q = 50$ (middle row) and $q = 500$ (bottom row)

1. Calculate X_b and X_w due to formulas (10) and (11).
2. Perform SVD of X_b, obtaining left singular vectors U_{q_0} and singular values $\Lambda_{q_0}^{1/2}$.
3. Select first $q \leq q_0$ columns of U_{q_0} and $\Lambda_{q_0}^{-1/2}$ obtaining U_q and $\Lambda_q^{-1/2}$ respectively.
4. Perform a projection of vectors from X_w onto subspace spanned by columns of $A_q = U_q \Lambda_q^{-1/2}$.
5. Perform SVD of $A^t X_w$, obtaining left singular vectors V_{r_0} of matrix $(A^t X_w)(A^t X_w)^t$.
6. Select last $r \leq r_0$ columns of V_{r_0} thus obtaining V_r and return DLDA matrix $W = AV_r$.

The final number of selected features is controlled by parameter r in step 6 of the above algorithm but the results of this selection depends on reduction step 3 controlled by the parameter q as the second SVD works on the subspace whose dimension is q. Thus by allowing q to have values smaller than rank of the input between-class scatter matrix S_b an additional degree of freedom is introduced in the feature extraction process.

The time complexity of the DLDA algorithm evaluated as the number of floating-point multiplications is dominated by SVDs (steps 2 and 5) and matrix multiplications in steps 4, 5 and 6.

$$T_{\text{DLDA}} = O(J^3 + q^3 + qN + Lq^2 + qNr) = O(q^2(L+q) + J^3 + qNr) \quad (12)$$

3 Face Recognition Experiments

DLDA is compared here with Maximum Significant Difference and Independence algorithm (MSDI) [13]. MSDI represents a group of feature selection methods that choose a sub-optimal subset of the given feature set by choosing one by one members of the target set. The MSDI criterion of choice combines two factors, a significant difference (sd) that measures ability of the given feature to distinguish between different classes and independence (ind) of given feature from already selected features. The former is simply F-statistics whereas the latter is a transformation of the Pearson correlation coefficient.

To compare the ability of DLDA and MSDI methods to create a compact set of discriminative features for face recognition, the collection of five facial databases is used, namely Altkom, Extended MPEG-7, MPEG-7 testset in Xm2vts [10], MPEG-7 testset in Banca [3] and Feret [11]. The resulting base is the same as used during the MPEG-7 Video Group Core Experiment on face recognition descriptor [15], [2].

The base has 11845 images of 1937 persons in total. The images are normalized to the size 46x56 based on fixed eye centers positions that have been marked manually. The halves of Altkom, MPEG-7 and Xm2vts compose the training set consisting of 3655 images of 504 persons, the rest, i.e. 8190 images of 1433 persons having full bases Banca and Feret inside forms the testing set.

Every image from the training set is processed by some feature extraction algorithm, in extreme case pure pixel intensity values may be features. Then pre-processed training set $X \in R^{N \times L}$ is provided at the input of DLDA or MSDI algorithm to select an output set of such features. In case of DLDA it takes a form of matrix $W \in R^{N \times r}$ and in case of MSDI a subset of input feature indices $k_1, \ldots, k_r$ to be used. Finally, the descriptors $y_1, \ldots, y_L$ of all images from the testing set are calculated due to formulas $y = W^t x$ for DLDA and $y(1, \ldots, r) = x(k_1, \ldots, k_r)$ for MSDI respectively.

The recognition performance evaluation of a given method relies on a subsequent choice of an every descriptor from the testing set to become a query and excluding it from the testing set which forms a gallery. For each query descriptor the person identity corresponding to the nearest descriptor from the testing set is compared with the actual query identity. If they match a success is registered hence giving rise to Success Rate SR for each person $j = 1, \ldots, J$ and Average SR (ASR) performance measures:

$$\mathrm{SR}_j = \frac{\text{number of successes}}{L_j}, \quad \mathrm{ASR} = \frac{1}{J} \sum_{j=1}^{J} \mathrm{SR}_j \qquad (13)$$

First experiment (Fig. 3) illustrates the influence the parameters q and r has on the recognition performance in case of applying DLDA directly on the intensity images from the database. Two things are observed, firstly the best recognition performance is achieved for intermediate values of q parameter, namely 200 for $r = 20, 40$ and 400 for $r = 120$. Secondly, the more output features is taken into consideration the better recognition performance is, what is expected, but also a desired property of graph saturation for relatively small values of r may be noticed. For different but established q values relation between ASR and r behaves almost identically.

Fig. 4 presents the comparison between DLDA and MSDI when the input features are PCA coefficients. Regardless of number N of PCA features considered both algorithms select constant number of $r = 48$ output features.

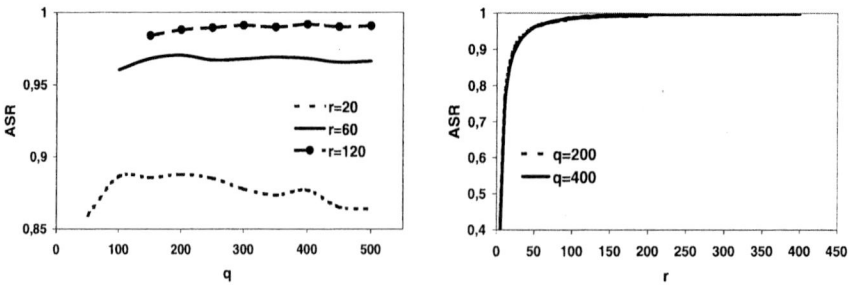

Fig. 3. Recognition performance's relation to DLDA algorithm parameters, q (left) and r (right)

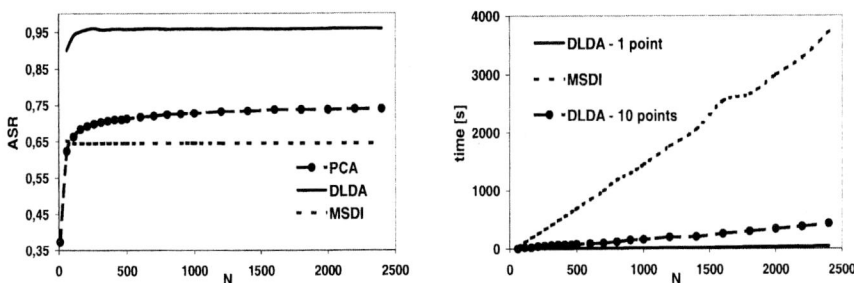

Fig. 4. DLDA and MSDI comparison for PCA N-dimensional input feature space and $r = 48$ in terms of ASR (left) and time complexity (right)

The best q value for DLDA algorithm is chosen in course of similar analysis as presented in Fig. 3, what means that the whole algorithm has to be run approximately ten times. Additionally, recognition performance for PCA feature vector consisting of N features is placed. The results show that MSDI is unable to benefit from increasing size of an input feature space because it effectively chooses the output features only from its small subset. Contrary to MSDI, DLDA, thanks to combining the reduction and extraction, utilizes all available information. In terms of time complexity, it turns out that DLDA, even applied ten times, outperforms MSDI too due to a high computational burden introduced by the independence step in the latter.

The result of changing the preliminary extraction method from PCA to Discrete Fourier Transform (DFT) or Discrete Cosine Transform (DCT) is shown in Fig. 5. Here, N indicates a number of frequency coefficients cut out from the whole spectrum. The quite large independence of DLDA method from the type of input feature space may be noticed whereas MSDI performance is better in case of DCT features.

In the last experiment (Fig. 6) MSDI is applied to the input feature set returned by DLDA algorithm operating on intensity images with $q = 400$ and $r = 120$ (cf. Fig. 3). Thus MSDI selecting r' out of $r = 120$ DLDA features

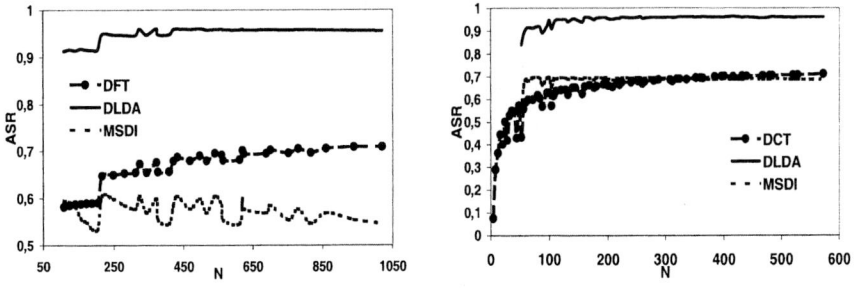

Fig. 5. DLDA and MSDI comparison for DFT (left) and DCT (right) N-dimensional input feature space and $r = 48$

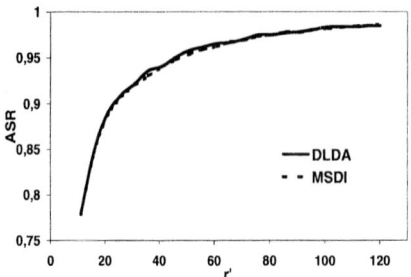

Fig. 6. DLDA and MSDI comparison for DLDA 120-dimensional input feature space

is compared with DLDA producing directly the set of r' output features. The results confirm that MSDI can hardly improve the selection performed by DLDA algorithm.

4 Conclusions

In this paper DLDA algorithm was presented as the method that can effectively incorporate the feature space reduction into the extraction process. The role of the parameters controlling DLDA algorithm was explained. It was shown how they affect the feature extraction process and how they can be adjusted to give the excellent face recognition performance at a relatively small number of the output features. The experiments conducted on a very challenging facial database proved the DLDA is stable against various types of input feature spaces. Additionally, the comparison with MSDI method that performs selection on extracted features set shown the superiority of DLDA both in terms of the recognition performance and the computational complexity.

References

1. Belheumeur, P. N., Hespahna, J. P., Kriegman, D.J.: Eigenfaces vs. Fisherfaces: Recognition Using Class Specific Linear Projection. IEEE Trans. on PAMI **19** (1997) 711–720
2. Bober, M.: Description of MPEG-7 Visual Core Experiments. ISO/IEC JTC1/SC29/WG11, report N749 (2002)
3. Bailly-Bailliere, E., Bengio, S., Bimbot, F., Hamouz, M., Kittler, J., Mariethoz, J., Matas, J., Messer, K., Popovici, V., Poree, F., Ruiz, B., Thiran, J. P.: The BANCA database and evaluation protocol. Audio- and Video-Based Biometric Person Authentication. Proc. 4th Int'l. Conf. AVBPA 2003, LNCS **2688** (2003) 625–638
4. Cevikalp, H., Neamtu, M., Wilkes, M., Barkana, A.: Discriminative Common Vectors for Face Recognition. IEEE Trans. on PAMI **27** (2005) 4–13
5. Chen, L.-F., Liao, H.-Y. M., Ko, M.-T., Lin, J.-C., Yu, G.-J.: A New LDA-based Face Recognition System Which Can Solve the Small Sample Size Problem. Pattern Recog. **33** (2000) 1713–1726

6. Devijver, P. A., Kittler, J.: Pattern Recognition: A Statistical Approach. Prentice Hall, Englewood Cliffs, N.J. (1982)
7. Fukunaga, K.: Introduction to Statistical Pattern Recognition. Academic Press (1972)
8. Golub, G. H., Van Loan, C. F.: Matrix Computations. The John Hopkins University Press (1993)
9. Liu, K., Yang, J.-Y., Liu, X.: An Efficient Algorithm for Foley-Sammon Optimal Set of Discriminant Vectors by Algebraic Method. Int'l. J. of Pattern Recog. and Artif. Intell. **6** (1992) 817–829
10. Messer, K., Matas, J., Kittler, J., Luettin, J., Maitre, G.: XM2VTSbd: The Extended M2VTS Database. Proc. 2nd Conf. on Audio and Video-base Biometric Personal Verification, Springer Verlag (1999)
11. Philips,P. J., Wechsler, H., Huang, J., Rauss, P.: The FERET database and evaluation procedure for face recognition algorithms. Image and Vision Computing J. **16** (1998) 295–306
12. Swets, D. L., Weng, J.: Using Discriminant Eigenfeatures for Image Retrieval. IEEE Trans. on PAMI **18** (1996) 831–837
13. Xu, Q., Kamel, M., Salama, M. M. A.: Significance Test for Feature Subset Selection on Image Recognition. Proc. Int'l Conf. on Image Analysis and Recognition, LNCS **3211** (2004) 244–252
14. Yu, H., Yang, J.: A Direct LDA Algorithm for High Dimensional Data - with Application to Face Recognition. Pattern Recog. **34** (2001) 2067–2070
15. Call for Proposals for Face Recognition Technology. ISO/IEC JTC1/SC29/WG11, report N3676 (2000)
16. Skarbek, W., Kucharski, K., Bober M.: Face Recognition by Fisher and Scatter Linear Discriminant Analysis. Proc. Int'l Conf. on Computer Analysis of Images and Patterns, LNCS **2756** (2003) 638–644
17. Skarbek, W., Kucharski, K., Bober M.: Dual LDA for Face Recognition. Fundamenta Informaticae **61** (2004) 303–334

On the Design of Reliable Graph Matching Techniques for Change Detection

Sidharta Gautama, Werner Goeman, and Johan D'Haeyer

TELIN, Ghent University, St.Pietersnieuwstraat 41, B-9000 Gent, Belgium
sidharta.gautama@ugent.be

Abstract. In this paper, we use inexact graph matching to detect changes between spatial features coming from different data sources, e.g. image derived information versus a GIS layer. Corresponding features in the data sources need to be matched taking into account outliers and spatial inaccuracy. We discuss the notion of consistency in inexact graph matching to be able to correctly determine the optimal solution of the matching problem. A condition based on the expected graph error is presented which allows to determine the bounds of error tolerance and in this way characterizes acceptable over inacceptable data inconsistencies.

1 Introduction

Graphs are a powerful data structure to represent objects and concepts in various domains. In geographic information systems (GIS), attributed graphs form a natural way to represent spatial objects together with its features and relationships to other objects. In our work, graph matching is used to find correspondences between the detected image information and the geospatial vector data, like digital road maps. The query process, based on attributed graph matching, is driven by the spatial relations between the features and takes into account different errors that can occur (e.g. spatial inaccuracy, data inconsistencies between image and vector data). Error-tolerant graph matching can be used to find correspondences between the detected image information and the vector data. Spatial constraints between objects are used to find a reliable object-to-object mapping. Spatial relations between objects prove to be more reliable for detecting change compared to local object features which cannot always be detected with high enough reliability. We derive an expression, based on the notion of consistency as introduced in [1], which characterizes the bounds where an image feature is identified as part of the object model or as a noise structure. This condition which maps a feature on the null label is a difficult constraint to model and has been traditionally set using heuristic rules-of-thumb. We show how the expected graph error of the object model can be used to determine this constraint.

The remainder of this paper is organized as follows. Section 2 introduces error-tolerant graph matching and derives the error bound to characterize acceptable over inacceptable inconsistencies. Section 3 gives experimental results on synthetic data which validate the derived bounds. Section 4 concludes the paper.

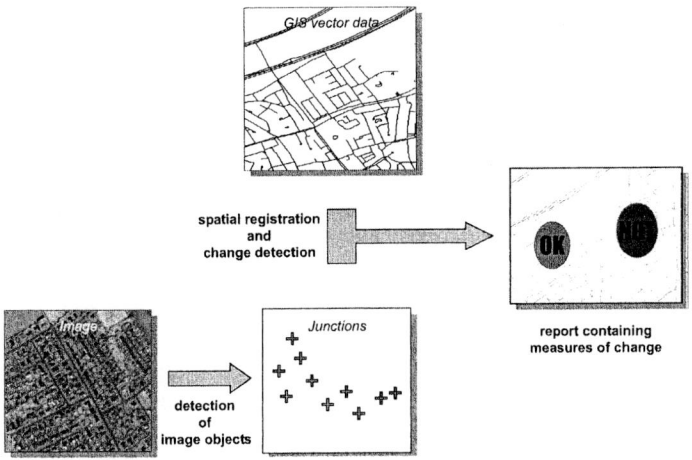

Fig. 1. Overview of the system for change detection

2 Error-Tolerant Graph Matching

The problem can be represented as finding the correspondence between two sets of features: one set originating from the geographic database and one set originating from the image. Given these features an abstract representation can be built as an attributed graph. The vertices of the graph represent image features and the vertex attributes can contain measurements on these features. The edges of the graph represent relations between features and the edge attributes can contain measurements on spatial relations. A similar graph can be built on the vector data, using data objects as vertices and relations between objects as edges. The problem of registration is represented as a graph matching problem, which seeks the correspondence of similar vertices between two attributed graphs.

2.1 Constraint Satisfaction Using Relaxation Labeling

The matching problem can be defined as a graph labeling problem, which consists out of the following elements:

1. a set of objects $i \in \Omega_i$, corresponding to image features;
2. a set of labels $\lambda \in \Omega_\lambda$, corresponding to GIS features;
3. a neighbour relationship over the objects;
4. constraints on possible labels between pairs of neighbouring objects.

Relaxation labeling techniques use an iterative process to determine the probabilities of each object. Different update rules have been proposed. In [1], the relation between different update rules is analytically shown. The problem of finding consistent solutions is shown to be equivalent to solving a variational inequality which is based on the mathematical concept of "consistency". This concept, which is defined below, is interesting because by using it, the labeling process can be redefined as a quadratic optimization process. This offers guidance in determining good compatibility coefficients.

To each object i a probability distribution $\{p_i(\lambda)\}_{\lambda \in \Omega_\lambda}$ is associated that expresses that object i has label λ:

$$0 \leq p_i(\lambda) \leq 1, \quad \sum_{\lambda \in \Omega_\lambda} p_i(\lambda) = 1 \qquad (1)$$

A labeling for the problem is specified by $\boldsymbol{p} = \{p_i(\lambda)\}_{i \in \Omega_i, \lambda \in \Omega_\lambda}$. For each pair of neighbouring objects i and j and for each pair of labels λ and λ', a compatibility coefficient $r_{ij}(\lambda, \lambda')$ is defined. These coefficients express the compatibility of assigning label λ to object i in combination with assigning label λ' to object j. Negative values express incompatibility, positive values compatibility. Given these quantities, the support of a label λ for the object i given by the correspondence $\boldsymbol{p}$ is defined as

$$s_i(\lambda) = s_i(\lambda, \boldsymbol{p}) = \sum_{j \in \Omega_i} \sum_{\lambda' \in \Omega_\lambda} r_{ij}(\lambda, \lambda') p_j(\lambda') \qquad (2)$$

Given a non-ambiguous solution $\boldsymbol{p}$ (i.e. $p_i(\lambda) = 0$ or 1), with $\lambda_1, ..., \lambda_n$ the labels which are given to the resp. object $i, ...n$, then $\boldsymbol{p}$ is a consistent solution iff

$$s_i(\lambda_i, \boldsymbol{p}) \geq s_i(\lambda, \boldsymbol{p}), \quad \forall \lambda, \quad i = 1...n \qquad (3)$$

For a non-ambiguous solution $\boldsymbol{p}$, this can be extended to the weighted sum of the support functions. $\boldsymbol{p}$ is a consistent solution iff

$$\sum_{\lambda \in \Omega_\lambda} p_i(\lambda) s_i(\lambda, \boldsymbol{p}) \geq \sum_{\lambda \in \Omega_\lambda} v_i(\lambda) s_i(\lambda, \boldsymbol{p}), \quad i = 1...n \qquad (4)$$

for all labelings $\boldsymbol{v}$.

Eq. 4 defines the solution $\boldsymbol{p}$ through a system of n inequalities. Hummel and Zucker have shown that if the compatibility matrix $r_{ij}(\lambda, \lambda')$ is symmetric, the solution can be calculated as maximizing the average local consistency, given by

$$A(\boldsymbol{p}) = \sum_{i \in \Omega_i} \sum_{\lambda \in \Omega_\lambda} p_i(\lambda) s_i(\lambda, \boldsymbol{p}) \qquad (5)$$

This is a quadratic function in the variables $p_i(\lambda)$, which can be optimized using a constrained gradient descent method taking into account the restrictions of Eq.(1).

2.2 Parameter Condition

To guarantee a good solution of the matching problem, the compatibility matrix $r_{ij}(\lambda, \lambda')$ needs to be determined correctly. In most applications, the value of these coefficients are determined using heuristics which basically impose a relative order on the constraints. Strong constraints receive a higher absolute value then weak constraints. The specific ratio between the constraints is usually determined through trial-and-error. For the null assignment it is however difficult to determine a correct value for the compatibility coefficient $r_{ij}(\lambda_\emptyset, \lambda')$. Since each object is a priori a possible null object, every assignment is consistent with the null assignment. The problem is to assess the relative importance of the null assignment with respect to the other constraints. It should be avoided that the null solution is the most consistent solution of the system. On the other hand, false correspondences of spurious points should be less consistent than the null assignment.

The definition of consistency can be used to determine the correct values. The definition not only determines the optimal solution of the labeling problem, it also determines what values the compatibility coefficients should take for an "ideal" solution to become the optimal solution of the system. The ideal solution is the matching we wish to find given the noise properties of the detection. For a correct null assignment, we need to determine when the errors, which occur in the neighbour structure of a node, are acceptable and when the number of errors becomes too large so that the null label should be assigned. To analyse this, we should look at the support of the different assignments. In the case of the null assignment, the support can be written as:

$$s_i(\lambda_\emptyset, p) = \sum_{j \in \Omega_i} \sum_{\lambda' \in \Omega_\lambda} r_{ij}(\lambda_\emptyset, \lambda') p_j(\lambda')$$
$$= w_\emptyset \sum_{j \in \Omega_i} \sum_{\lambda' \in \Omega_\lambda} p_j(\lambda') \qquad (6)$$
$$= w_\emptyset d(i)$$

with $d(i)$ the degree of node i (i.e. the number of neighbours). We have simplified $r_{ij}(\lambda_\emptyset, \lambda') = w_\emptyset$ if $j \in \Omega_i$ (else $r_{ij}(\lambda_\emptyset, \lambda') = 0$). The constant factor $w_\emptyset$ is reasonable in the absence of prior knowledge of assignments.

The support for a non-null label can be split up into three classes Ω_i^+, Ω_i^- and Ω_i^0, namely positive coefficients which express compatibility, negative coefficients which express incompatibility and negative coefficients which control the null assignment. If we consider the first two classes of coefficients constant (resp. w_+ and w_-) within the neighbourhood of node i then the support for λ_i can be simplified to

$$s_i(\lambda_i) = \sum_{j \in \Omega_i^+} r_{ij}^+(\lambda_i, \lambda_j) + \sum_{j \in \Omega_i^-} r_{ij}^-(\lambda_i, \lambda_j) + \sum_{j \in \Omega_i^0} r_i^0 \qquad (7)$$
$$= w_+ n_+ + w_- n_- + w_\emptyset n_0$$

Here n_+ is the number of compatible neighbours, n_- the number of incompatible neighbours and n_0 the number of null-neighbours, with $n_+ + n_- + n_0 = d(i)$.

Eq.(6) and (7) give the following condition which holds in the optimal solution:

$$w_+ n_+ + w_- n_- + w_\emptyset n_0 > w_\emptyset d(i) \qquad (8)$$

or equivalently

$$(1 - f^0) w_\emptyset < f^+ w_+ + f^- w_- \qquad (9)$$

where f^+, f^- and f^0 are the fraction of compatible, incompatible and null assignments in the neighbourhood of object i for the ideal mapping.

Eq. 9 can be used to determine the weights for the compatibility matrix given the expected relational graph error. It allows to make a distinction between points showing small distortions, which should find a correspondent in the other dataset, and points showing severe distortions, which should be assigned the null label. As previous research usually relied on rules-of-thumb to determine these weights (e.g. [4]), the importance of this equation is that it allows precise definition of the weights of the graph matching problem with respect to the expected graph error of the system.

3 Experimental Results

A set of experiments has been performed on images containing randomly scattered points. Each image is generated twice: one copy which serves as a reference and one copy which contains perturbations on the scattered points (e.g. noise on the position, added spurious points). The aim is to find the corresponding points between the two copies using graph matching while ignoring the spurious points in the data. The experiment is an abstraction of the correspondence problem between image and GIS data after features like road junctions have been detected in the image.

To apply the technique to matching sets of points, we need to introduce the constraints which define similarity. For road junctions several possibilities exist. However, the quality of detection of road junctions that can be achieved is not of sufficient quality to use object features, like number of incoming roads, as information for the correspondence process [3]. Fragmentation and false detections can frequently occur in the detected road network and are difficult to control. We therefore opt to use geometric invariants between subsets of corresponding junctions. The most simple constraints are binary relations like geometric relations (e.g. angle, distance) between a junction and its neighbours to find correspondences. These are much more stable features, given the detection quality which can realistically be expected from road detection. In these experiments we rely only on the relative angle between pairs of points. In mapping a pair of points i and j on λ and λ' the relative angle between the lines ij and $\lambda\lambda'$ does not exceed a given $\triangle \alpha$. (e.g. $\pi/4$). If this constraint is violated, the compatibility coefficient $r_{ij}(\lambda, \lambda')$ is assigned a negative weight w_-.

The graph representation of the data is of course not restricted to angles and can be readily generalized to incorporate other measurements like connectivity, distance or other topological relations. In our case, the angle between junctions was chosen because it could be reliably measured in the image. Other measurements like connectivity between junctions are more difficult to measure in the image due to the degree of fragmentation in road detection. Nevertheless, the graph matching technique is generic and applicable once image and GIS information are described in terms of attributed graphs. In the experiments, points

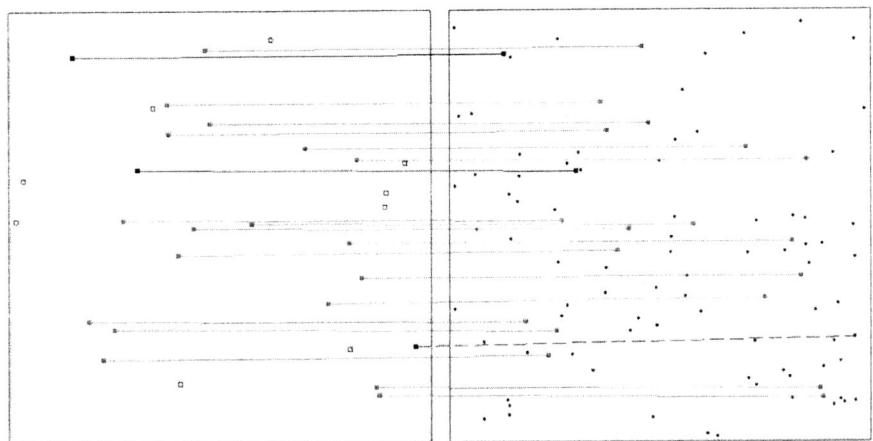

Fig. 2. Example of a 30-to-100 correspondence: (left) original set of points with white boxes showing spurious points, (right) points with added noise $\sigma = 4$ pixels. Correct matches are shown with grey lines; wrong matches with a black line; wrong spurious matches with a dashed line.

are randomly scattered within an image of 512 × 512 pixels. The first set of points contains 30 points and the second set contains 100 points. Both sets have 20 points in common with a perturbation on their position using gaussian noise with a standard deviation between one and eight pixels. The matching result needs to make a distinction between points which are common between the two datasets (so called "real" points) and spurious points. Figure 2 shows an example of this dataset with the first and second set displayed in resp. the left and right frame, and the correspondence computed with graph matching. In this example, the gaussian noise on the position has a standard deviation $\sigma_{noise} = 4$ pixels. The white rectangles in the left frame are added spurious points, which should be assigned the null label. The grey lines show the points which have been correctly associated. The black lines show points which have been incorrectly associated. The dashed black lines show spurious points which have been incorrectly associated.

To determine the optimal weights of the graph matching process, Eq. 9 is used. In these experiments, the parameters of RL have been set at $\triangle \alpha = \pi/16$ and $w_- = -0.5$. Compatible matches are not awarded, meaning that $w_+ = 0$. The data contains a ratio of 10:30 outlier points so that $f^0 = 1/3$. Eq. 9 can then be used to determine the weight $w_\emptyset$, which varies over the experiments since the graph label error f^- increases as more noise is added to the position. An added difficulty is that the label error f^- is a stochastic variable. To use Eq. 9, we need to determine the value of f^- which optimally makes the distinction between real distorted points and spurious points. This can be done by modeling the exhibited graph errors of real and spurious points as normal distributions with a certain mean and standard deviation, and taking the maximum likelihood estimate (MLE) as the optimal decision boundary f^-_{opt}. Label errors f^- below this threshold are then regarded as acceptable errors belonging to real points. Label errors f^- above this threshold are regarded as severe errors belonging to spurious points.

We measured the mean and standard deviation of the graph label error over a selection of 10 image pairs for a given amount of noise σ_{noise}. For real points, the ideal mapping is known and the graph label error for these points can be measured. Table 1 gives a summary of the label error statistics (m_1, σ_1) for the different amounts of noise. For spurious points, we selected the best matching corresponding point in the second dataset. Since this is a combinatorial problem, the match is approximated under the condition of a near ideal mapping, i.e. the real points are mapped on the correct correspondents, the other spurious points are mapped on the null label. Under these conditions, finding the best match for a point is a linear search. For this match, we measure the graph label error that would occur if a spurious point is mapped on his most likely candidate. Measured over the dataset, this gives an mean label error $m_n = 38.5\%$ with standard deviation $\sigma_n = 16\%$. Using MLE on these statistics, the threshold f^-_{opt} can be calculated and consequently $w_\emptyset^{opt}$ using Eq. 9.

Table 1 gives the calculated $w_\emptyset^{opt}$. These calculated weights are compared to the measured optimal weights $w_\emptyset^{meas}$. The weights $w_\emptyset^{meas}$ have been determined by plotting the "receiver operating characteristic" (ROC) curve by varying $w_\emptyset$. For this curve, sensitivity and specificity are defined as follows:

$$sensitivity = \frac{TP}{TP+FN}$$
$$specificity = \frac{TN}{TN+FP} \qquad (10)$$

where $\{TP, FP, TN, FN\}$ stands for true positive, false positive etc. If sensitivity is plotted along the X-axis and specificity along the Y-axis, the optimal performance is defined as the point on the ROC curve closest to the upper right corner $(1,1)$. The weight associated with this sample is taken as the optimal measured weight $w_\emptyset^{meas}$.

Table 1 shows a good correspondence between the predicted optimal weight $w_\emptyset^{opt}$ and the measured optimal weight $w_\emptyset^{meas}$. There is a slight overestimation with respect to the measured weight $w_\emptyset^{meas}$ which becomes more apparent at higher noise levels. This can be due to ambiguous points which are introduced by adding spatial noise. The ground truth which is used to determine true and false positives does not take into account the possibility of optimal

Table 1. Determining the null weight based on maximal likelihood with respect to the expected graph error. Noise statistics $m_n = 38.5\%$ and $\sigma_n = 16\%$

stdev [pix]	m_1	σ_1	$w_\emptyset^{opt}$	$w_\emptyset^{meas}$
1	0.5%	1.1%	0.05	0.05
2	2.3%	2.8%	0.09	0.07
4	7.8%	6.2%	0.19	0.15
8	21.7%	10.4%	0.32	0.25

point matches changing. Especially at high spatial noise levels this is possible in dense point clouds, since the spatial error can interchange the position of neighbouring points. For the constraint satisfaction problem, this interchange is not detected as the constraints will not be violated, but the ground truth will penalize the found match. Nevertheless, it remains relevant to use Eq. 9 to tune the graph matching process based on the expected graph error, as in many applications like road networks such interchanges do not occur often. If it does occur, a minimum point density should be applied to avoid this ambiguous mapping.

4 Conclusion

We have presented a condition based on the expected graph error which allows to determine the bounds of error tolerance in the matching process. The condition allows to characterize acceptable over inacceptable data inconsistencies. The derivation is based on the notion of consistency in inexact graph matching, and is useful to determine the optimal weights of the cost function given the expected graph label error. Experiments on synthetic point sets have shown the relevancy of this condition with respect to the specification of the null weight, which is typically been determined using rules-of-thumb. Although some problems still need to be solved concerning ambiguous points, the condition allows more control over the desired behaviour of the graph matching problem. This is essential for a reliable use of inexact graph matching in change detection applications.

References

1. Hummel, R., Zucker, S. 1983. On the foundations of relaxation labeling processes. IEEE Trans Pat. Anal. and Mach. Intel. 5(3), 742-776.
2. Christmas, W., Kittler, J., Petrou, M. 1995. Structural Matching in Computer Vision Using Probabilistic Relaxation. IEEE Trans Pat. Anal. and Mach. Intel. 17(8), 749-764.
3. Gautama, S., Borghgraef, A., Bruyland, I. 2002. Automatic registration of satellite images with GIS databases. In: Proc. Advanced Concepts for Intelligent Vision Systems (ACIVS 2002), Gent, Belgium. 7 pag (on CD-ROM).
4. Wilson R. 1995. Inexact Graph Matching Using Symbolic Constraints. Ph. D. thesis, Department of Computer Science, University of York.

Extraction of 3D Vascular Tree Skeletons Based on the Analysis of Connected Components Evolution

Juan F. Carrillo[1,2], Maciej Orkisz[1], and Marcela Hernández Hoyos[2]

[1] CREATIS, CNRS 5515 and INSERM U630 Research Unit, Lyon, France
[2] Grupo de Ingeniería Biomédica, Departamento de Ingeniería de Sistemas y Computación,
Universidad de los Andes, Bogota, Colombia

Abstract. The article is dealing with the automated extraction of branching structures in 3D medical images. A generic object-oriented programming framework is proposed, in which most existing iterative algorithms for centerline extraction in tubular objects can be efficiently implemented, and the bifurcations can be handled. New algorithms can thus easily be derived. We describe a simple algorithm for fast extraction of the 3D structure of the vascular tree, which has been implemented within this framework. The algorithm recursively tracks the branches and detects the bifurcations by analyzing the binary connected components on the surface of a sphere that moves along the vessels. It assumes that the vessels can locally be separated from the background by an appropriate adaptive threshold. The originality of the algorithm resides in the analysis of the evolution of the connected components during the sphere growth that allows it to cope with local abrupt changes of the vessel diameter and shape. It was successfully tested in 16 magnetic resonance angiography images. Its accuracy was assessed by comparing the resulting axes with those extracted by a reference algorithm. The distance between them was less than one voxel except in bifurcations, where the maximum distance was 3.8 voxels.

1 Introduction

Our work is dealing with the segmentation of 3D vascular images for computer-aided diagnosis, treatment planning and follow-up of arterial diseases. We are aiming at the segmentation of the local structure of the vascular tree, so that the segmented vessels can be used as input for the simulation of the blood flow patterns, to predict the outcome of surgical intervention. The first step towards this goal is the extraction of the vascular tree skeleton, i.e. of the axes of each branch and of the bifurcation points.

Many algorithms have been proposed to extract the vascular axes from 3D images (e.g. see overviews [1-4]). Most of them are based on a cylindrical model of the vascular segments and are designed to extract only one interactively selected segment, while ignoring its branches. Bifurcations are not handled by the axis-extraction process, but may be detected by an additional algorithm run along the previously extracted axis, or only at locations where the data do not fit the cylindrical model [5]. Alternatively, several interactively initialized branches can first be separately extracted, then appropriately connected, in order to recover the tree structure [6]. As the acquisition of the vascular images is usually based on physical processes that enhance the image intensity within the circulating blood lumen, the vessels can be seen as intensity ridges. In [7] all possible ridges are first detected in the image volume by an ordered region-growing algorithm, then connections between interactively selected endpoints are found. A powerful method has recently been proposed in [8], which uses a criterion based on the eigenvalues of the Hessian to assess the geometric flow and thus find the vascular pathways. However, like in the previously quoted method, the criterion is calculated in each point of the volume, which is computationally expensive. The remaining algorithms devised to directly handle the branching structures often use a threshold-based preprocessing, so that the actual axis extraction is carried out within a binary volume. In practice, the threshold is often set manually [9-11], although an adaptive histogram-based global threshold has also been used in this context [12]. The skeleton of the binary volume can be extracted by morphological thinning [9]. However, this approach is noise-sensitive and requires a careful pruning of spurious branches. Other authors preferred a step-by-step approach, which simulates a wave-front propagation [10] or moves along the vessels a small volume of interest (cell): a parallelepiped [12] or a sphere [11]. Consecutive points are recursively added to the axes, and the bifurcations are detected by counting the connected components of the wave-front or of the cell surface.

Our method falls within the latter category and uses a spherical cell both to detect the bifurcations and to predict the location of the next point of the current axis. Compared to [11, 12], two main differences are to be noted: 1) strategy of cell-size adaptation to abrupt diameter variations in pathologic segments, which is based on the analysis of the evolution of the connected components (CCs) on a growing spherical surface and 2) threshold-value determination, which is automatic and local. This adaptive strategy was devised for magnetic resonance angiography (MRA) images.

2 Method

Many axis-extraction algorithms (e.g. [5, 11-13]) can be modeled by an iterative process represented in Fig.1: 1) for each candidate point taken from a stack of points to be processed, the correction of its location is done if the point is not close enough to the center of the vessel axis defined as the center of the local cylindrical structure, 2) the point is added to a graph representing the vascular tree axis, 3) several (typically between zero and two) new candidate points are predicted and pushed into the stack to be processed later. The process begins with a user-selected point or an automatically detected seed, and finishes when there are no more points in the stack to be processed. This general structure can include the bifurcation handling. Various methods can be constructed by modifying some components of this structure, mainly the prediction and the correction. We therefore implemented this structure in an object-oriented programming framework, where each component can easily be replaced by deriving appropriate classes. In the sequel we describe one particular algorithm implemented within this framework. The correction and prediction processes based on the analysis of binary CCs is described in Section 2.1. The actual binarization scheme depends on the image acquisition technique. Section 2.2 describes the adaptive local thresholding strategy used in MRA images.

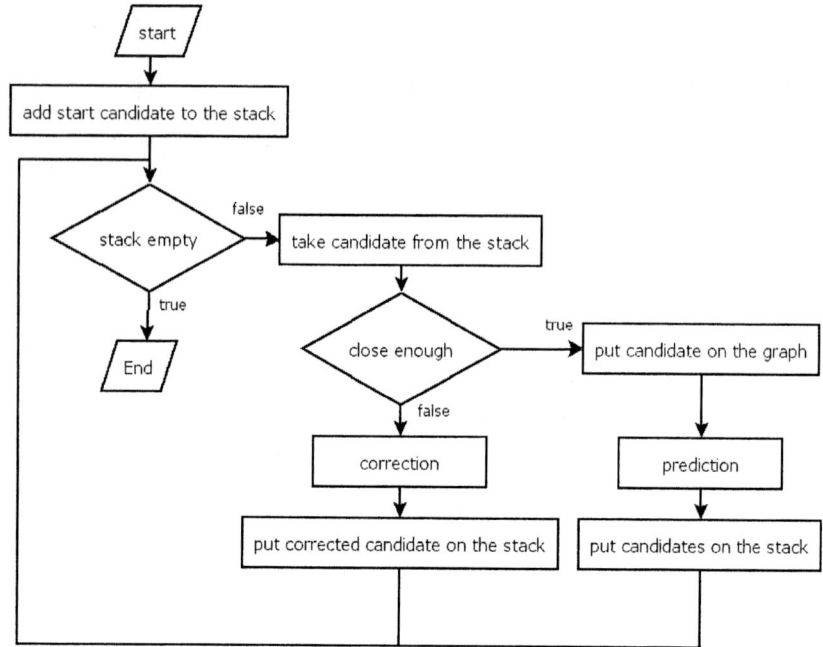

Fig. 1. General framework for recursive axis extraction

Fig. 2. Connected components: (*left*) volumetric, (*middle*) intersection sphere-surface/vessel ($N_V = 3$), (*right*) intersection sphere-surface/background ($N_B = 1$)

The sphere grows starting from a minimum radius that is a parameter of the algorithm. Only the volumetric component connected to the sphere center is kept: all its voxels are assigned the label "vessel", while the remaining ones receive the label "background", which eliminates the possible other objects contained in the sphere or intersecting it. The intersection between the vessel and the sphere surface is analyzed: the number of CCs of the vessel (N_V) and of the background (N_B) is calculated (Fig.2). During the growth of the sphere, each increase or decrease of N_V or of N_B can be interpreted as a change of the local position of the sphere surface with respect to the vessel boundary (inside or outside). This information is used to assess whether or not the sphere is correctly centered within the vessel, and to stop its growth.

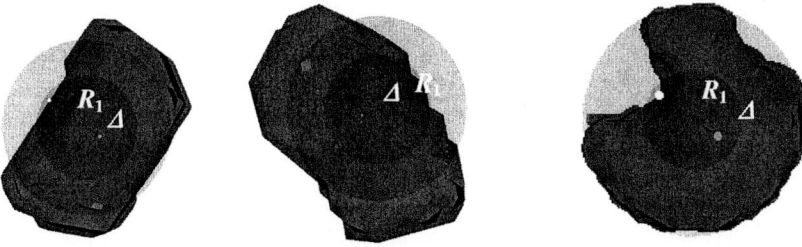

Fig. 3. Point correction in various configurations. In each case are represented: the small sphere that first reached the vessel boundary, its radius R_1, the larger sphere that subsequently reached the vessel boundary at the opposite side, and the correction Δ.

Fig. 4. Point prediction. (*left*) vessel end, $N_V = 1$, no point predicted, (*remainder*) bifurcation, $N_V = 3$, one point in already segmented vessel pathway, and two points predicted.

When the sphere is well centered (close enough to the center of the vessel axis), its surface simultaneously reaches the opposite boundaries of the vessels. Else, the sphere first reaches one boundary (its radius at this moment is called R_1), then it grows (radius R_2) and reaches another boundary. Bad centering is detected when the difference between the corresponding radii R_1 and R_2 is greater than the value used as radius increment. In this case, the center of the sphere, which is actually the current point of the axis, is corrected by moving it away from the vessel boundary reached at first. The point is moved by the amount $\Delta = \frac{1}{2}|R_2 - R_1|$ (see Fig.3).

At each change of the number of surface CCs a counter is reset which is used to stop the growth of the sphere. If no new change occurs before the counter reaches a fixed maximum value, the growth ceases. This maximum value is equal to the number of radius increments that occurred between the last two changes of the number of surface CCs. At that moment, if $N_V < 2$ the end of the current branch is detected and no new point is predicted (Fig.4 left). Otherwise the algorithm switches back to the smallest sphere having the same N_V, then the masses, and the centers of gravity of each one of the vessel CCs on that sphere surface are calculated. We need to make difference between the components that are located in the already segmented vessel pathway, and the remaining ones that correspond to the continuation of this vessel and to its branches, if any (Fig.4). To that purpose the track of the vessel segmented in the previous iterations is kept by constructing the union of the volumetric CCs (Fig.5). The gravity centers of the vessel CCs that do not remain inside this union are ordered by mass and pushed onto the stack of candidate points to be processed, so that the bigger vessels are then processed first.

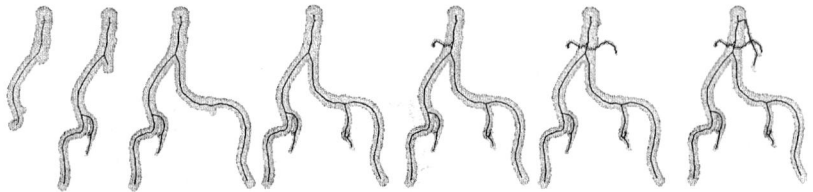

Fig. 5. Several iterations of vascular tree segmentation: axes and union of connected volumetric components

We assume that the local contrast between the vascular lumen and the background is sufficient so that a threshold value separating them can be found. Experimental studies showed that in MRA images this value can be estimated as a percentage of the local maximum intensity [14]. Namely, in gadolinium-enhanced MRA a good approximation of the vessel boundaries is located about half this local maximum [15]. In our algorithm, the threshold value is re-calculated for each radius of the sphere, as half the maximum intensity within the sphere.

3 Experiments

The algorithm was applied to 16 MRA 3D images from patients, representing the neck (carotid, vertebral, basilar arteries, etc.) and the aorto-iliac region (with renal, mesenteric arteries, etc.). This first qualitative evaluation aimed at verifying the algorithm's capability of extracting all the branches perceptible in the image volume, and of avoiding spurious detections. Additionally, to assess the efficiency of the local thresholding strategy in MRA images, we visually compared the unions of volumetric CCs with segmentations obtained by a global threshold equal to half the maximum intensity within the whole image. Furthermore, for each of these datasets the axis of the main arterial trunk was quantitatively compared to that extracted by a reference algorithm [13], the accuracy of which had already been clinically validated. This algorithm processes one vascular segment at a time. We calculated the distances between the axes extracted by the two algorithms.

3.1 Results

The algorithm detected all the principal branches of the vascular tree and the bifurcations in which the cross-sectional area of the secondary branch was at least 5% of that of the main branch. As expected, our method detects more arterial branches than global thresholding (Fig.6). However, this figure also shows that some branches were not extracted owing to a strong local signal drop in severe stenoses (see also Fig.7). The algorithm detected a few false bifurcations, where two vessels were very close to each other (Fig.7 right).

The mean distance (in 1000 points) between the axes extracted by our algorithm and by the reference one, was 0.76 mm, with a standard deviation of 0.46 mm and a maximum of 3.82 mm. The algorithm was tested on a Pentium 4 1.8GHz computer with 1GB RAM. It calculated on average 50 points every second, depending on the diameter of the vessels: the bigger the vessel the longer it takes.

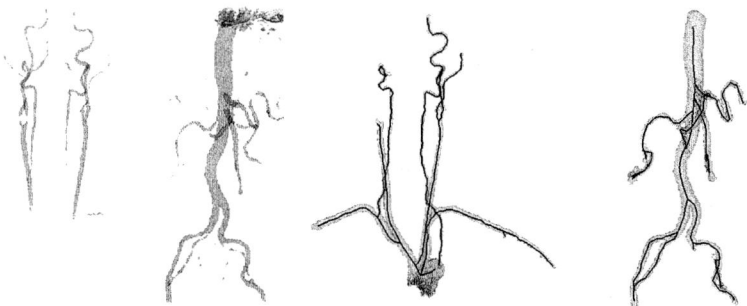

Fig. 6. Global vs. local thresholds: (*left*) arteries segmented using a threshold equal to half the global intensity maximum, (*right*) union of CCs extracted using a local threshold equal to half the maximum intensity within an adaptive moving sphere

Fig. 7. Failures of our algorithm: (*left*) missing connection in a severe stenosis, (*right*) false bifurcation

3.2 Discussion and Conclusions

Our algorithm was designed for quick approximate extraction of complex branching structures. The distance between the consecutive axis-points is always slightly larger than the local radius of the vessel, which determines both speed and precision. Compared to the reference algorithm, the largest distances between the axes were observed in bifurcations. However, the reference algorithm does not handle bifurcations, and actually should be used as reference only beyond the branching regions. Our algorithm cannot detect very small branches and the severely stenosed branches, *i.e.* vessels with a strong pathological narrowing, particularly when the stenosis is located near a bifurcation. In both cases the local intensity of the vessels falls below the adaptive threshold based on the maximum intensity of the main branch. Automated detection of low-intensity branches would require a lower threshold. This may be problematic if other structures are present near the vessel of interest. A pragmatic solution is to interactively add a seed point within the missing branch. False bifurcations were detected in regions where the initial assumptions did not hold, *i.e.* two neighboring vessels could not be separated by a threshold at half the local maximum of intensity. Although the local thresholding strategy may be improved, there will always remain images where thresholding is not sufficient to separate neighboring vessels closer than the image resolution. This problem may be solved by adding *a priori* knowledge to the segmentation of the contents of the spherical cell. As the vessels are expected to be globally cylindrical, a classification can be implemented combining photometric and geometric criteria. Moreover, our approach may be considered as a first step that can be subsequently refined according to the application. In our application, *i.e.* simulated flow-dynamics computation, the actual segmentation method can be devised using a deformable model initialized by the structure extracted with our simple algorithm. Other important applications in which our algorithm can be useful are: 1) measuring the length of vascular segments, 2) intra- and inter-patient registration of vascular trees, based on bifurcations as landmarks, 3) recognition and labeling of the vascular segments, 4) various visualization techniques such as 2D images perpendicular to the vessel axis, maximum intensity projection or volume rendering limited to the vicinity of the vascular axes, etc.

In conclusion, we presented a simple and fast algorithm capable of extracting the axes and the approximate shape of the vascular lumen of the vascular tree connected to a seed point. According to our first evaluation in MRA images, the algorithm efficiently detects and manages the bifurcations, provided that the branches are large enough to have the intensity larger than half the intensity of the main branch. An evaluation of this algorithm in computed tomography angiograms is ongoing, which uses the adaptive thresholding strategy described in [16].

Acknowledgements

This work was supported by C03S02 grant from ECOS-Nord program and by Colciencias project No. 12040416468.

References

1. Orkisz, M. & Hernández-Hoyos, M. Models for 3D vascular image analysis. *J Med Informatics Technol*, 2001; **2 part 1**: IP13-IP22.
2. Tizon, X. *Algorithms for the analysis of 3D Magnetic Resonance Angiography Images* Acta Universitatis Agriculturae Sueciae, Uppsala, Sweden, 2004 (ISBN 91-576-670-4).
3. Wink, O. *Vessel axis determination* Print Partner Ipskamp, Amsterdam, The Netherlands, 2004 (ISBN 90-393-3698-9).
4. Kirbas, C. & Quek, F. K. H. A review of vessel extraction techniques and algorithms. *ACM Comput. Surv.*, 2004; **36**(2): 81-121.
5. Toumoulin, C., Boldak, C., Dillenseger, J.-L., Coatrieux, J.-L. & Rolland, Y. Fast detection and characterization of vessels in very large data sets using geometrical moments. *IEEE Trans. Biomedical Engineering*, 2001; **48**(5): 604-606.
6. Bullitt, E. *et al.* Symbolic description of intracerebral vessels segmented from magnetic resonance angiograms and evaluation by comparison with X-ray angiograms. *Med Image Analysis*, 2001; **5**: 157-169.
7. Yim, P. J., Choyke, P. L. & Summers, R. M. Gray-scale skeletonization of small vessels in magnetic resonance angiography. *IEEE Trans Med Imaging.*, 2000; **19**(6): 568-576.
8. Descoteaux, M., Collins, L. & Siddiqi, K. Geometric flows for segmenting vasculature in MRI: theory and validation. In: *MICCAI'2004 - Med Image Computing and Computer-Assisted Intervention*, Springer Verlag, Saint-Malo, France, 2004; 500-507 .

9. Sauret, V., Goatman, K. A., Fleming, J. S. & Bailey, A. G. 3D topology and morphology of branching networks using computed tomography (CT) - application to the airway tree. In: *Medical Image Understanding and Analysis* Oxford (UK), 1999.
10. Zahlten, C., Jürgens, H. & Peitgen, H.-O. Reconstuction of branching blood vessel from CT data. In: *Visualization in Scient. Comput.* 1994; 41-52 .
11. Antiga, L., Ene-Iordache, B., Remuzzi, G. & Remuzzi, A. Automatic generation of glomerular capillary topological organization. *Microvascular Research*, 2001; **62**: 346-354.
12. Flasque, N., Desvignes, M., Constans, J.-M. & Revenu, M. Acquisition, segmentation and tracking of the cerebral vascular tree on 3D magnetic resonance angiography images. *Med Image Analysis*, 2001; **5**(3): 173-183.
13. Hernández-Hoyos, M. *et al.* Computer assisted analysis of three-dimensional MR angiograms. *RadioGraphics*, 2002; **22**: 421-436.
14. Hoogeveen, R. M., Bakker, C. J. G. & Viergever, M. A. Limits to the accuracy of vessel diameter measurement in MRA. *J Magn Reson Imaging*, 1998; **8**(6): 1228-1235.
15. Frangi, A. F., Niessen, W. J., Hoogeveen, R. M., van Walsum, T. & Viergever, M. A. Model-based quantitation of 3D magnetic resonance angiographic images. *IEEE Trans Med Imaging*, 1999; **18**(10): 946-956.
16. Flórez-Valencia, L., Vincent, F. & Orkisz, M. Fast 3D pre-segmentation of arteries in computed tomography angiograms. In: *Int Conf Comp Vision and Graphics* Kluwer, Warsaw (Poland), 2004.

Color-Contrast Landmark Detection and Encoding in Outdoor Images

Eduardo Todt[1] and Carme Torras[2]

[1] Faculty of Informatics, PUCRS, Av. Ipiranga, 6681,
90619-900 Porto Alegre, Brazil
`todt@ieee.org`
[2] Institut de Robòtica i Informàtica Industrial, CSIC-UPC, Llorens i Artigas 4-6,
08028 Barcelona, Spain
`torras@iri.upc.edu`

Abstract. This paper describes a system to extract salient regions from an outdoor image and match them against a database of previously acquired landmarks. Region saliency is based mainly on color contrast, although intensity and texture orientation are also taken into account. Remarkably, color constancy is embedded in the saliency detection process through a novel color-ratio algorithm that makes the system robust to illumination changes, so common in outdoor environments. A region is characterized by a combination of its saliency and its color distribution in chromaticity space. The newly acquired landmarks are compared with those already stored in a database, through a quadratic distance metric of their characterizations. Experimentation with a database containing 68 natural landmarks acquired with the system yielded good recognition results, in terms of both recall and rank indices. However, the discrimination between landmarks should be improved to avoid false positives, as suggested by the low precision index.

1 Introduction

The extraction of reliable visual landmarks in outdoor unstructured environments is still an open research problem. Our motivation for working on it comes from robot navigation, but the main issues concern also other fields, such as scene analysis and image indexing and retrieval from databases. Most existing feature extraction approaches are not adequate for this type of environments, since they rely on either structured information from non-deformable objects [3, 8], or a priori knowledge about the landmarks [1].

We have been pursuing a saliency-based approach to spot image regions with potential to represent good landmarks [13, 14], following biologically-inspired works on visual attention [7]. In [14], we introduced a way to embed color constancy within saliency computation, which showed to be faster and more stable than ensuring such constancy at a pre-processing stage. The present work builds on these previous studies to accomplish the next step, namely *landmark characterization to support subsequent recognition* under different illumination conditions and viewpoints.

2 Saliency Detection Based on Color Contrast

A region in an image is considered *salient* if it ranks high in a given feature and its surround ranks high in the opposite feature. The color features considered are based on the opponent colors proposed by Hering [9].

From the input image, Gaussian pyramids corresponding to intensity, orientation and color opponency images are constructed, each with eight spatial scales. A pixel at a fine scale corresponds to a center region, whereas the respective pixel at a coarser scale corresponds to its surround. This multiscale approach is advantageous in that it permits extracting landmarks of varied sizes.

Three sets of partial saliency maps are constructed, corresponding to the intensity, color and orientation features. The partial saliency maps should be combined to obtain one global saliency map. They cannot simply be added, because salient regions present in only a few maps can be masked by noise or less salient regions present in a larger number of maps. The process of combining the partial saliency maps is structured in two stages. In the first stage, the partial saliency maps are normalized by the maximum saliency value obtained at all center-surround scales. In the second stage, the maps are weighted by their information content. The information content of an image is based on their zero-order entropy [11]. Finally, the partial saliency maps are subject to exponentiation and added to compose the global saliency map.

The modifications introduced to the original visual saliency algorithm [7], to improve the color constancy properties, resulted in the *color-ratio visual saliency* algorithm [14], described next.

With the purpose of obtaining contour images with good color constancy properties, Gevers and Smeulders [5] developed a color space based on the color ratio between neighboring pixels. This differential version of color constancy gave us the idea of generalizing the concept of gradient between neighboring pixels to that of center-surround opposition. Thus, invariance of color gradients would turn into the desired invariance of center-surround oppositions. Under this approach, one pixel is replaced by the center region and the other pixel by the surround region. Moreover, the ratios no longer relate color bands, but color opponents, as follows:

$$RG = R_o^c G_o^s / G_o^c R_o^s \qquad (1)$$

$$GR = R_o^s G_o^c / G_o^s R_o^c \qquad (2)$$

where R_o^c and G_o^c are opponent red and green components at center regions and R_o^s and G_o^s are opponent red and green at surround regions. The same is valid for the yellow and blue components. According to the unichromatic reflection model, assuming that center and surround regions have a locally constant illuminant, the same surface normal and uniform albedo, and the use of narrow-band sensors, we have [14]:

$$C = m_b(\vec{n}, \vec{s}) e(\lambda_c) c_b(\lambda_c) \qquad (3)$$

where C is the light sensor response corresponding to a surface patch illuminated by an incident light $e(\lambda)$, λ is the light wavelength, m_b is the body geometric dependency, $\vec{n}$ is the surface normal, $\vec{s}$ is the direction of illumination source, and $c_b(\lambda)$ is the body spectral reflection property. Combining (3) and (1), we have:

$$RG = \frac{(m_b^c(\vec{n},\vec{s}) \; e^c(\lambda_R) \; c_b^c(\lambda_R))(m_b^s(\vec{n},\vec{s}) \; e^s(\lambda_G) \; c_b^s(\lambda_G))}{(m_b^s(\vec{n},\vec{s}) \; e^s(\lambda_R) \; c_b^s(\lambda_R))(m_b^c(\vec{n},\vec{s}) \; e^c(\lambda_G) \; c_b^c(\lambda_G))} = \frac{c_b^c(\lambda_R)c_b^s(\lambda_G)}{c_b^s(\lambda_R)c_b^c(\lambda_G)} \quad (4)$$

which is only dependent on the sensors and the surface albedo. The same can be done for Equation (2) and the blue-yellow components. A key feature of these color ratios is their invariance to both intensity and color normalizations, which makes them intrinsically invariant to lighting intensity and illumination color changes. The ratios have a local nature, avoiding the distorting effects possibly introduced by global normalizations. The logarithmic spaces (R_o/G_o) and (Y_o/B_o) permit the computation of the ratio opponencies by simple differences of logarithms across the scales.

3 Delimiting Landmark Regions

Since the extracted salient regions are not necessarily bounded by well-defined contours, nor associated to single elements in the scenes, a refinement step is necessary in the process of determining the boundaries of landmark candidates. As an initial approximation (Figure 1), a minimal rectangular bounding box (Figure 2) is computed for each segmented saliency spot. The objective of the next two processing steps is to get a better fitting of the bounding boxes to the salient features.

In the next step, the colors appearing in each saliency-selected region are identified, and a corresponding *backprojection map* is built, emphasizing where the same colors appear in the whole image. This is performed using histogram backprojection [12].

After this, the size and position of all bounding boxes are adjusted (Figure 2), taking into account the color feature spatial distribution and the respective visual saliency. This is achieved using the *continuously adaptive mean shift* algorithm [2]. This is a non-parametric technique that climbs the gradient of a probability distribution to find the nearest dominant mode, with the capability to adapt the window size. To increase the amount of information associated with the bounding boxes, their immediate surrounding region is also analyzed (Figure 2), giving additional context information to the recognition process.

4 Landmark Characterization

After the determination of the bounding boxes, region descriptors are extracted. These descriptors should be appropriate to characterize the bounding boxes as signatures of the landmarks and should make the comparison between them possible. Color has proven to be the most suitable of the considered low-level features for outdoor unstructured environments, where most objects have deformable shapes. The way color features are represented and color descriptions are compared using the adopted representation are described below.

The most common representation of color in image retrieval and recognition is the color histogram, which captures the global color distribution in an image or region [12, 6]. They are simple to compute and have the properties of invariance to translation, invariance to rotation about an axis perpendicular to the image, and they change smoothly with rotation about other axes, occlusion, and variations in scale. In

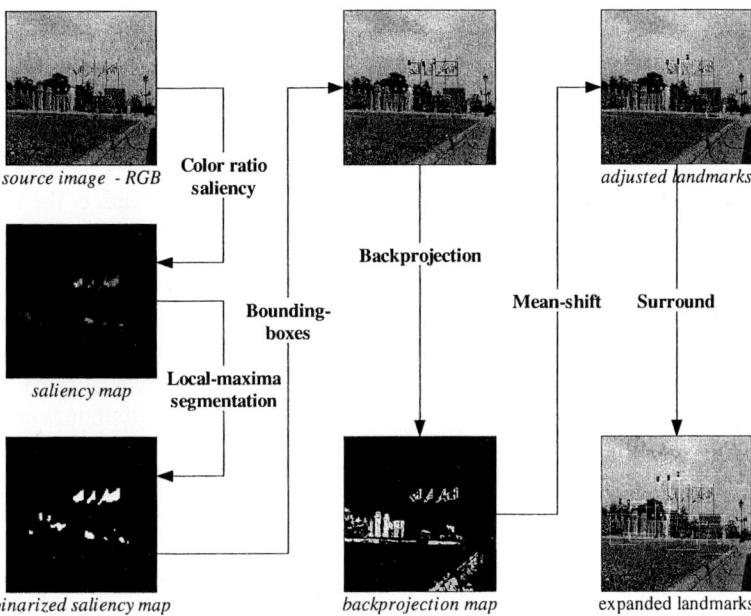

Fig. 1. The process of delimiting the landmark regions. From the source image a saliency map is computed, then this map is segmented, generating the seeds of the landmark regions. These seeds are enclosed by bounding boxes, which are adjusted to the salient elements in the image using color histogram backprojection and mean-shift algorithms. Finally, the landmark bounding boxes are expanded, encompassing the immediate surrounding regions.

Fig. 2. Initial (left), adjusted (center) and expanded (right) landmark bounding boxes

order to remove the dependency on the number of pixels that comprise the histogram by comparing histograms of images of different sizes, the histogram can be normalized by dividing each bin count by the total number of pixels. The normalized histogram corresponds to a color probability distribution function.

Taking this considerations into account, the following descriptors to characterize the landmarks were proposed:

1. Normalized chromaticity histogram of salient region inside bounding box.
2. Normalized chromaticity histogram of adjusted bounding box.
3. Normalized chromaticity histogram of expanded bounding box.

4. Normalized saliency histogram of adjusted bounding box
5. Mean saliency of adjusted bounding box

5 Landmark Matching

Once the feature representation has been defined as a histogram space, the similarity between two images or regions *i* and *j* is described as the distance between their corresponding points h_i and h_j in the histogram space [12].

There are several metrics to evaluate histogram distances. The most common are histogram intersection and Minkowski distances [12]. These distance metrics are quick to compute, but they only compare corresponding bins of the two histograms, disregarding any kind of similarity between colors. This characteristic makes these distance metrics strongly sensitive to slight changes in the distributions. In contrast with Minkowski and intersection distances, the quadratic form metric allows for similarity matching between different colors, and it is defined as follows [6]:

$$d^2_{hist}(h_1, h_2) = (h_1 - h_2)^T \mathbf{A} \, (h_1 - h_2) \qquad (5)$$

where h_1 and h_2 are *N*-dimensional color histograms, and $\mathbf{A}$ is the similarity matrix, whose elements a_{ij} denote similarity between bins *i* and *j*. The similarity of landmarks is evaluated with quadratic-form distance by combining the distances between each of the three color histograms stored in the landmark representation. The distances are combined using the root of the sum of the three squared distances.

6 Experimental Results

From eleven sample scenes in outdoors, 68 landmarks were extracted. To evaluate the retrieval performance of the system, each landmark was taken out of the database, and matched against all other landmarks. Then, the distances to all other landmarks were sorted in ascending order. In image retrieval systems, the quality of matching is usually qualified in terms of *recall* and *precision* figures [4]. Recall is defined as the ratio between the number of relevant images retrieved and the number of all relevant images in the database. Precision is defined as the ratio between the number of relevant images retrieved and the number of retrieved images.

$$Recall = C_K / M, \qquad Precision = C_K / K \qquad (6)$$

where *K* is the number of retrievals, C_K is the number of relevant matches among all the *K* retrievals, and *M* is the number of total number of relevant matches in the database. Another metrics used to quantify the performance of a retrieval system is the *success of target search* index (*STS*). It measures the rank of the first retrieved relevant image (target) in the database with respect to the query, defined as [10]:

$$STS = \left(1 - \frac{rank - 1}{N - 1}\right) \qquad (7)$$

where *rank* is the retrieval position of the first retrieved image, and *N* is the number of images in the database.

The *recall* score (Table 1) obtained was acceptable, considering that the recognition was based solely on color distribution information. This *recall* score indicates few false negative errors. Also the rank of the first (best) retrieved similar landmark was very significant, with the *STS* score near one. The *precision* score obtained is low, indicating the presence of false positives in the retrieval process. This occurs due to the similar color distributions of some detected salient features in different scenes, and since histograms do not provide spatial information about their arrangement, very different images can have similar color distributions, that could mislead into false evaluation of their dissimilarity.

The combined distance form (squared sum of the three region type distances) improves significantly the recall and precision metrics, because of the union of saliency-oriented information with surround information.

Table 1. Recall, STS and precision for the described landmark matching experiment. Resultant measures are shown for each region type individually, and then for a combined form of them.

	Recall	STS	Precision
Spot of saliency bounding box	0.62	0.98	0.24
Adjusted bounding box	0.60	0.99	0.21
Expanded bounding box	0.53	0.98	0.17
Combined histograms	0.70	0.99	0.26

The computational time of the main tasks (Table 2) were evaluated using a standard PC computer (Pentium III 900MHz, 256Mb DRAM, Microsoft Windows XP). It can be observed that the saliency detection is the task that demands more computational time, and that the histograms are computed very quickly. In the landmark comparison phase, although the quadratic-form histogram distances could take a lot of time to be computed, the small size of the histograms (16x16 bins) keeps computational time low for this task.

Table 2. Computational complexity and execution times of the main tasks related to landmark characterization and matching. N is the number of pixels in the input image and M is the number of bins in the histograms. Data is shown with two significant digits.

Task	Computational complexity	Seconds
Visual saliency with color ratios (512x512 pixels)	$O(N)$	0.81
256-bin histogram (16x16 bins)	$O(N)$	0.00015
Landmark characterization	$O(N+M)$	0.039
Quadratic-form histogram distance	$O(M)$	0.0085
Landmark matching	$O(M)$	0.028

7 Discussion

In a pioneering work on image indexing, Swain and Ballard [12] pointed out that, for real-time object recognition, color-based algorithms were especially promising, due to their fast performance and their capability to deal with viewpoint changes, object deformations, and inaccurate segmentation. They considered a challenging problem to identify the region from which to extract the histogram to be used as object signature for recognition purposes.

This is exactly the first contribution of the current research, proposing a novel saliency detection algorithm with embedded color constancy properties, and using this information to identify and delimit image regions that can be used as landmarks.

A second contribution is the landmark characterization that, going beyond the single histogram, combines saliency and chromaticity into a robust and stable signature, as confirmed by experimentation.

Indeed, the results show good recognition performance, in terms of both recall and rank indices. However, the discrimination between landmarks requires improvement to avoid false positive mistakes, i.e., retrieving landmarks from the database that do not correspond to the query landmark. This shortcoming is not a critical one in our application, since a rough knowledge of the robot trajectory can help to disambiguate between landmarks with similar appearance.

Acknowledgments

The authors would like to thank Enric Celaya and Pablo Jimenez for productive discussions about visual saliency and robot localization. This work is partially supported by the Spanish Council of Science and Technology under project "Vision-based reconfigurable navigation system for legged and wheeled robots in natural environments" (DPI 2003-5193).

References

[1] J. Batlle, A. Casals, J. Freixenet, and J. Martí, "A review on strategies for recognizing natural objects in colour images of outdoor scenes," *Image and Vision Computing*, vol. 18, pp. 515-530, 2000.
[2] G. R. Bradski, "Computer vision face tracking for use in a perceptual user interface," Fourth IEEE Workshop on Applications of Computer Vision, pp. 214-219, 1998.
[3] W. Burgard, A. Derr, D. Fox, and A. B. Cremers, "Integrating global position estimation and position tracking for mobile robots: the dynamic Markov localization approach," IEEE/RSJ Int. Conf. on Intelligent Robots and Systems (IROS '98), Canada, pp. 730-735, 1998.
[4] Y. Deng, B. S. Manjunath, C. Kenney, M. S. Moore, and H. Shin, "An efficient color representation for image retrieval," *IEEE Trans.on Image Processing*, vol. 10, pp. 140-147, 2001.
[5] T. Gevers and A. W. M. Smeulders, "Color-based object recognition," *Pattern Recognition*, vol. 32, pp. 453-464, 1999.
[6] J. Hafner, H. S. Sawhney, W. Equitz, M. Flickner, and W. Niblack, "Efficient color histogram indexing for quadratic form distance functions," *IEEE Transactions on Pattern Analysis and Machine Intelligence*, vol. 17, pp. 729-736, 1995.
[7] L. Itti, C. Koch, and E. Niebur, "A model of saliency-based visual attention for rapid scene analysis," *IEEE Trans. on Pattern Analysis and Machine Intelligence*, vol. 20, pp. 1254-1259, 1998.

[8] D. Lowe, "Distinctive image features from scale-invariant keypoints," *International Journal of Computer Vision*, vol. 60, pp. 91-110, 2004.
[9] S. J. Sangwine and R. E. N. Horne, *The color image processing handbook*, 1st ed. London: Chapman & Hall, 1998.
[10] R. Schettini, G. Ciocca, and S. Zuffi, "A survey of methods for colour image indexing and retrieval in image databases," in *Color Imaging Science: Exploiting Digital Media*, M. R. Luo and L. MacDonald, Eds., 1st ed: John Wiley & Sons, 2002, pp. 183-211.
[11] C. E. Shannon, "A mathematical theory of communication," *The Bell System Technical Journal*, vol. 27, pp. 379-423, 1948.
[12] M. J. Swain and D. H. Ballard, "Color indexing," *International Journal of Computer Vision*, vol. 7, pp. 11-32, 1991.
[13] E. Todt and C. Torras, "Detection of natural landmarks through multiscale opponent features," 15th International Conference on Pattern Recognition, Barcelona, Spain, pp. 976 - 979, 2000.
[14] E. Todt and C. Torras, "Detecting salient cues through illumination-invariant color ratios," *Robotics and Autonomous Systems*, vol. 48, pp. 111-130, 2004.

Global Color Image Features for Discrete Self–localization of an Indoor Vehicle

Włodzimierz Kasprzak, Wojciech Szynkiewicz, and Mikołaj Karolczak

Warsaw University of Technology, Institute of Control and Computation Eng.,
ul. Nowowiejska 15/19, 00-665 Warsaw, Poland
W.Kasprzak@ia.pw.edu.pl
http://www.ia.pw.edu.pl/

Abstract. In autonomous indoor navigation some number of localizations and orientations of the vehicle can be learned in advance. No artificial landmarks are required to exist. We describe and compare the detection of several global features of color images (sensor data). This constitutes the measurement process in a self-localization approach that is based on Bayes filtering of a Markov environment - the posterior probability density over possible discrete robot locations (the belief) is recursively computed. The approach was tested to provide robust results under varying scene brightness conditions and small measurement errors.

1 Introduction

The localization process of an autonomous robot takes as input a previously acquired map, an estimate of the robot's current pose, and a set of sensor data acquired in current pose, and it produces as output a new estimate of the robot's pose [1,5,7]. Obviously, any input data for the localization process may be incomplete and distorted by noise or errors. In generally, pose means the position and orientation of the robot in the world coordinates or global map.

The vision data is acquired by a passive sensor, i.e. a camera does not influences the environment by its measurement process. This kind of sensor is especially applicable for indoor navigation in environments, that are populated by humans, i.e. offices, hospitals, museums, etc. [3]. Additionally, image processing methods can rely on natural landmarks, whereas this case for the active sensor devices has started to be studied only recently [2]. The use of image analysis methods in robot navigation has been intensively studied over the past 30 years [8,9,10]. In this paper we focus on general image features, that could be relatively insensitive to changing lighting conditions, but at the same time, can be relatively easy computed, to be obtained in real-time by a simple processing unit.

In theoretical terms the localization process is equivalent to a Bayes filtering of a finite environment satisfying the Markov condition, i.e. past and future data are conditionally independent if one knows the current state. During the localization process the posterior probability density over possible discrete robot locations (the belief) is recursively computed. We describe a detailed algorithm for the discrete self-localization scheme and we propose and test different global features of monochromatic images (if the brightness of observed scene is constant or it can be compensated) and another (more robust) set of image features, based on color information and localization ques.

2 The Self-localization Algorithm

A typical state recursive estimation can be performed in terms of a Kalman Filter [11]. It can be shown that a normal distribution of the measurement error induces a Gaussian distribution of the state's pdf provided by the Kalman Filter. This is a unimodal distribution and as a direct consequence there is always one best state estimated. Hence KF is suitable for tracking a single hypothesis but not many possibly competitive hypotheses, unless we use many instances of the filter.

2.1 The Method of State Condensation

The general discrete self-localization scheme [13], based on Bayes filtering of a Markovian environment, is also called *state condensation* or *particle filtering* [6], [7]. It assumes, that the number of states can be limited to a finite number. Only then it is computationally feasible to estimate the probability distribution over states.

By *belief* we denote the pdf of states upon the condition of a sequence of observations (measurements m_t):

$$\forall s^k : Bel_t(s^k) = p(s_t^k | m_t, m_{t-1}, \ldots, m_{t-n}) \quad (1)$$

In the learning phase the system should acquire two a priori pdf's:

1. The a priori conditional pdf of measurement upon state, i.e. for each discrete state $s \in S$ and possible measurement vector m to determine the pdf: $p(m|s)$;
2. The a priori pdf of state transition

$$p(s_{t+1}^k | s_t^l, \ldots, s_0^i) = p(s^k | s^l) \quad (2)$$

where $s_t^l, \ldots, s_0^i$ is the history of past best belief states. In autonomous navigation the action performed by the vehicle or camera are usually known, due to the odometry. Hence, this knowledge can be incorporated into the state condensation scheme - for each pair of states s^k, s^j and each possible action a to determine the pdf of state transition with respect to action: $p(s^k | s^j, a)$.

The discrete self-localization algorithm consists of the initialization step and a main iterative belief "refinement" step with sub-steps of : *belief prediction, stochastic diffusion, measurement and modification of belief* (the reaction onto the measurement) [13].

2.2 The Algorithm of the Self–localization Process

1. Get the goal state.
2. Initialization of a default belief state at $t = 0$ (for example by a uniformly distributed pdf) $Bel_0(s^k) = p(s_0^k | H_0)$.
3. REPEAT until the goal state is not reached:
   (a) $t = t + 1$;
   (b) find the current best state: $s_{t-1}^* = \arg\max\ p(s_{t-1} | H_{t-1})$, where
   $H_{t-1} = (s_{t-1}, m_{t-1}, s_{t-2}, m_{t-2}, \ldots, s_0, m_0)$
   is the history of past belief states and measurements;
   (c) determine and perform the next action resulting from minimization of the distance between current best state and the goal state;
   (d) as the current action a_t and the a priori pdf $p(s_t | s_{t-1}, a_t)$ are known the predicted belief state at time t can be computed
   $\widehat{Bel_t}(s^k) = \sum_s [p(s_t^k | s_{t-1}, a_t) p(s_{t-1} | H_{t-1})]$
   (e) acquire the measurement m_t at new position.
   (f) with the a priori pdf $p(m_t | s_t)$ modify the belief state at time t:
   $Bel_t(s^k) = p(s_t^k | H_t) = c_t p(m_t | s_t) \widehat{Bel_t}(s)$,
   where c_t is the current normalization coefficient (the sum of belief state distribution should be equal to 1).

3 Global Image Features

Due to the iterative approach, exhibited by the self-localization procedure, individual image measurements need not to be unique for all states - they can be similar for many states. Hence, we expect that easy computable, general-nature image features that are combined with a Gaussian-like belief state filtering should already lead to robust navigation. We also expect that changes of the measurements between the learning phase and the active phase of self-navigation (due to change of scene illumination or inaccurate position of the vehicle) can be compensated by a longer belief state refinement sequence.

In this section we propose different color feature detection schemas, obtained in the RGB, HSV and YC_bC_r color spaces. A complete feature vector for a single image consists of features obtained for several sub-images. In this way we add some general feature localization information to a state's measurement vector.

3.1 Image Feature Detection Methods

The following global features are computed for every sub-image:

1. *Mean Var6* - the three mean and three standard deviation values of every color component (i.e. for H, S and V channels of the HSV color space);

$$m = [m_1, m_2, m_3, std_1^2, std_2^2, std_3^2].$$

2. *Hist6* - the three dominating color components in the image with their density values.
$$m = [I_{c1}, I_{c2}, I_{c3}, den(I_{c1}), den(I_{c2}), den(I_{c3})].$$
I_{ck} - the dominating value of the k-th color component, $den(I_{ck})$ - the number of pixels with color I_{ck} in relation to the total number of pixels.
3. *FFT6x2* - the modules of first 6 components of a Fourier transform of the image components H(hue) and S(saturation).
$$m = [|F_{(0,0)}|, |F_{(0,1)}|, |F_{(1,0)}|, |F_{(0,2)}|, |F_{(1,1)}|, |F_{(2,0)}|].$$

For a square image of size NN, the two-dimensional FFT is given as:
$$F_{(k,l)} = \frac{1}{N^2} \sum_{i=0}^{N-1} \sum_{j=0}^{N-1} I(i,j) e^{-i2\pi(ki/N + lj/N)},$$

where $I(i,j)$ is the image in the spatial domain; the exponential term is the basis function - one such function corresponds to one Fourier coefficient $F_{(k,l)}$. The first coefficient $F_{(0,0)}$ represents the DC-component of the image and the $F_{(N-1,N-1)}$ represents the highest frequency component.

Obviously above vectors *MeanVar6* and *Hist6* are sensitive to scene illumination changes. For the HSV and YC_bC_r schemas we perform a Y-driven normalization of the color (and we can omit the Y-components from further consideration). The RGB color scheme requires an other intensity normalization scheme - in this caase we scale the color components in such a way, that the sum of intensities of all pixels is equal to some fixed reference value.

3.2 Learning the a Priori Pdf

The a priori pdf $p(m|s)$ should be computed during the learning phase. But the number of possible measurement vectors is infinite, usually there are continuous-valued components of m. In practice this pdf can be made explicit only during the active work. In the learning phase we compute and store the feature vectors associated with each discrete state.

During the active work the feature vector of current view is detected (assuming a previous normalization of the scene illumination or camera contrast).

The a priori pdf $p(m_{k+1}|s)$ is implicitly defined, as we can compute for each state s^k the value of a Gaussian distributed pdf, with mid point equal to zero, for the distance of $w|m_{k+1} - m(s^k)|^2$ (where w is a weighting vector that adjusts the intervals of particular components to some common interval).

The a priori pdf $p(m_{k+1}|s)$ is defined according to the difference of both measurement vectors: the current measurement m_{k+1} at time $k+1$ and the stored measurement m_s for $\forall s \in s$. The conditional probability density is modelled by a 1–D Gaussian normal distribution, with its mid point corresponding to the zero value of a weighted difference $\sum_{i=1}^{N \times p} w_i |m_{k+1}^i - m_s^i|^2$ (where w is a weighting vector that scales the expected ranges of particular feature elements to some common level).

3.3 Test Scenes

In our experiments the camera was mounted on a mobile platform [14] (Fig. 1). The on-board processor with clock frequency of 900 MHz was able to process around 2 images per second. Three degrees of freedom of the vehicle were allowed: a translation along the X and Z axes by pre-defined unit steps and a rotation around its Y axis by an angle of $\pm 45°$. The "on-ground" locations of states and of possible directions in three test scenes are shown in Fig. 2 and 3.

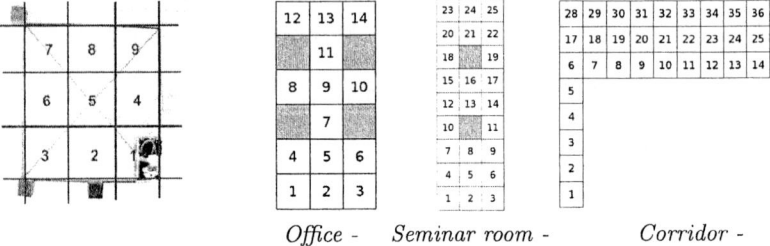

Fig. 1. An image is divided into 9 sub-images - a separate feature vector is computed for every sub-image

Office - 112 states.   *Seminar room - 200 states.*   *Corridor - 222 states.*

Fig. 2. The distribution of mobile platform positions during the learning phase for 3 test scenes

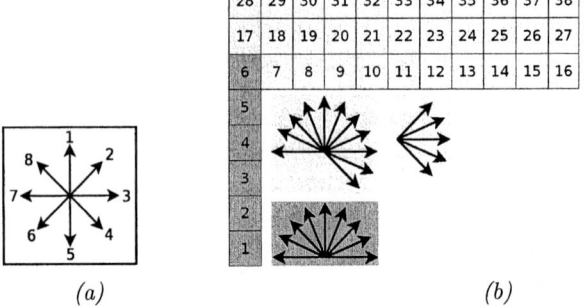

(a)   (b)

Fig. 3. The possible orientations: (a) for the *Office* and *Seminar room*, and (b) for the *Corridor*

Three scenes with different illumination conditions, spatial distributions and different colors were available for testing (Fig. 4). Obviously, we expect that the camera holds the white color balance properly both during learning and active localization work. As we measure intensity-normalized color coefficients, some changes in illumination are not significantly disturbing the data if only the color balance remains to be constant.

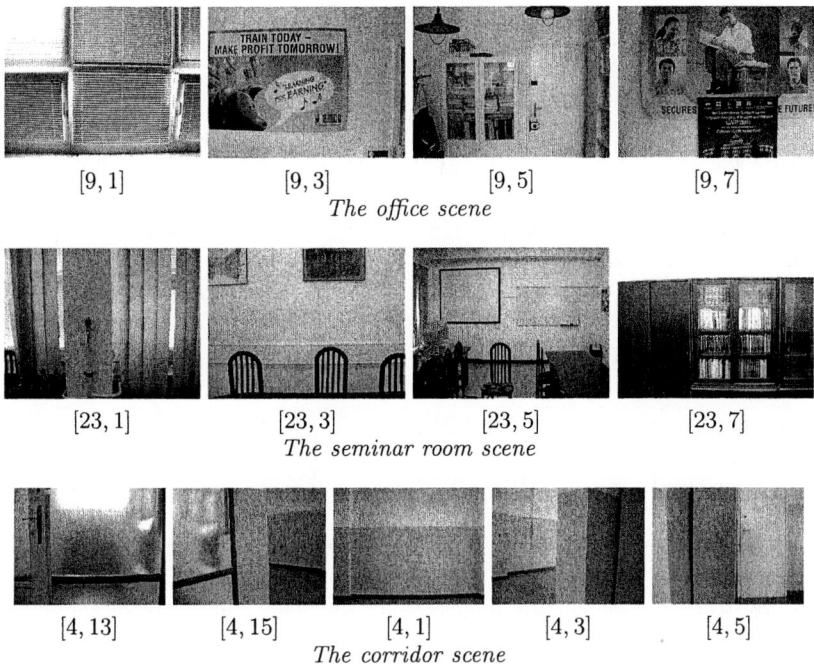

Fig. 4. Examples of images acquired in different states and scenes and states

4 Test Results

4.1 Statistics of Features

An exemplary distribution of features over states is shown in Fig. 5. It is visible that the particular feature values are very often the same for different states, i.e. a single use of feature can not fully differentiate between two states. Another question is, how much sensitive these features are with respect to errors in robot's position/orientation and to scene illumination changes. The *p-value* of two distributions expresses the correctness of a hypothesis, that both distributions are statistically equivalent. If the p-value is equal to zero, then the above hypothesis is wrong and both features can be treated as being different. We computed the *p-value* for all pairs of feature vectors, where the first element of the pair corresponded to the state of the original scene, and the second element - to the compatible state in the real scene. Usually, the compatible views are displaced by several pixels and their illumination conditions are also slightly different. The feature set FFT6x2 performed best of all, i.e. the other two sets were more more sensitive to changes in state positions.

4.2 Test Runs

For every test scene and for each measurement method we have run the self-localization process 100 times, with randomly chosen start and goal states. A 99-

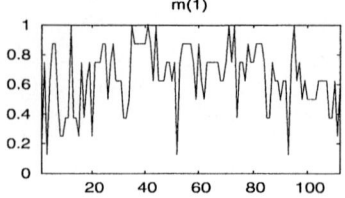 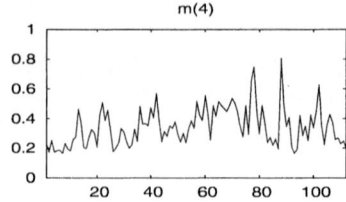

Fig. 5. The distribution of 2 measurement features over state from the *MeanVar6*-set of HSV color space for the *Office scene*

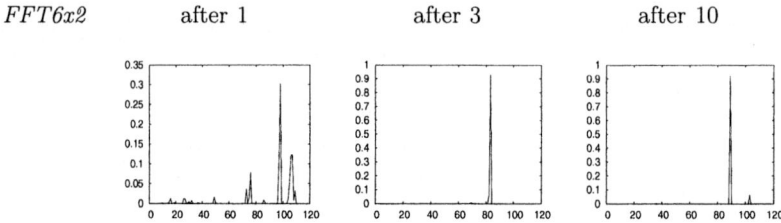

Fig. 6. Illustration of belief-state propagation - the belief state distribution after 1-st, 3-th and 10-th iteration

100 success rate appeared (i.e. the final goal state was reached) if color features expressed in the HSV and YC_rC_b color spaces were used. A particular self-localization process is illustrated on Fig. 6. At the start point the belief state distribution is an uniform distribution. After 3-4 steps the appropriate state, that corresponds to the real position, can already be selected as the belief value for such state dominates already the beliefs of remaining states. We assume that obstacles or moving persons in front of the vehicle will be detected by other sensors than vision. In order to limit their influence onto the measurement data we expect to "observe" higher wall sections instead of the floor.

5 Summary

Three different color image feature detection schemas were proposed and their use as the measurement step in a discrete self–localization process was experimentally verified. It was shown that even for natural scenes with changing illuminations and small perturbations of the odometry data, the use of even a small set of features, expressing only global information of a particular view, allows a robust and error-free self-localization (according to our test runs).

Acknowledgments

The authors would like to thank the Polish Ministry of Science and Information Society Technologies for supporting this work by the grant MNiI 4 T11A 003 25.

References

1. J. Borenstein, H. Everett, L. Feng, *Navigating Mobile Robots*. Wesley, Mass., 1996.
2. R.G. Brown, B.R. Donald, "Mobile Robot Self-Localization without Explicit Landmarks", *Algorithmica*, Springer Publ., vol. 26, pp. 515-559, 2000.
3. W. Burgard, A. Cremers, D. Fox, D. Hahnel, G.Lakemeyer, D. Schulz, W. Steiner, S. Thrun, "Experiences with an Interactive Museum Tour-Guide Robot", *Artificial Intelligence*, vol. 114, No. 1-2, pp. 3-55, 1999.
4. J. Denzler J., M. Zobel, "Automatische farbbasierte Extraktion naturlicher Landmarken und 3D-Positionsbestimmung. auf Basis visueller Information in indoor Umgebungen", V. Rehrmann (ed.), *Vierter Workshop Farbbildverarbeitung*, Fohringer-Vg., Koblenz, pp. 57-62, 1998.
5. D. Fox D., W. Burgard W., S. Thrun, "Markov Localization for Mobile Robots in Dynamic Environments", *Journal of Artificial Intelligence Research*, vol. 11, pp. 391-427, 1999.
6. D. Fox, S. Thrun, W. Burgard W., F. Dellaert, "Particle Filters for Mobile Robot Localization", In: Doucet A., DeFreitas N., Gordon N. (Eds), *Sequential Monte Carlo Methods in Practice*, Springer Publ., Berlin, etc., 2000.
7. M. Isard, A. Blake, "CONDENSATION - Conditional Density Propagation for Visual Tracking", *International Journal on Computer Vision*, vol. 29, No. 1, pp. 5-28, 1998.
8. W. Kasprzak, *Adaptive computation methods in image sequence analysis*, Prace Naukowe - Elektronika, No. 127, Warsaw Univ. of Technology Press, 2000.
9. C. Thorpe C. (ed.), *Vision and Navigation: The Carnegie Mellon Navlab*, Kluwer Academic Publ., Norwell, Mass., pp. 25-38, 1990.
10. I. Masaki, *Vision-based Vehicle Guidance*, Springer, New York etc., 1992.
11. Y. Bar-Shalom, T.E. Fortmann, *Tracking and Data Association*. Academic Press, 1988.
12. B. Heigl, J. Denzler, H. Niemann, "Combining Computer Graphics and Computer Vision for Probabilistic Visual Robot Navigation", *Proceedings of SPIE's 14th Annual International Symposium on Aerospace/Defense Sensing, Simulation and Controls*, Orlando, Florida, April 2000.
13. W. Kasprzak, W. Szynkiewicz, "Using color image features in discrete self-localization of a mobile robot", *9th IEEE International Conference on Methods and Models in Automation and Robotics* (August 2003, Miedzyzdroje, Poland), IEEE conference 8780, pp. 1101 - 1106, 2003.
14. B. Siemiatkowska, R. Chojecki, "Mobile Robot Navigation Based on Omnidirectional Sensor", *Proc. 1st European Conference on Mobile Robots ECMR'03*, EURON Conference, Radziejowice, Poland, September 2003, pp. 101-106, 2003.

Application of Automatic Image Registration in a Segmentation Framework of Pelvic CT Images*

Attila Tanács, Eörs Máté, and Attila Kuba

Department of Image Processing and Computer Graphics, University of Szeged,
H–6701 Szeged P.O.Box 652, Hungary
{tanacs, mate, kuba}@inf.u-szeged.hu

Abstract. In radiation treatment (RT) planning, clinicians must trace the outline of a few critical structures on a large number of images. Using automated image segmentation could save tremendous time and effort. Segmentation of the organs near the pubic bone (prostate and bladder) is an important and challenging task: Some of the neighboring organs have similar density values in the CT images and the border between the different organs is hardly visible.

In a segmentation framework, transforming a CT study to a common reference frame is used in two tasks: For statistical atlas (model) generation, and in the clinical application, establishing the voxel-to-voxel correspondence between the study and the model. In these cases precise alignment of all anatomical structures is not crucial, the focus is on proper alignment of the pubic bone area and fast execution. Our proposed method solves this by a new, two step process based on a voxel similarity-based registration algorithm.

1 Introduction

During clinical diagnosis, the patient's internal anatomy is imaged to determine how a disease has progressed. Several modalities are used to generate images of patient's anatomy or functionality, suitable for diagnostic purposes or radiotherapy treatment, or for surgical planning. In case of radiation treatment (RT) planning, CT imaging is generally used because image voxel gray values (Hounsfield Units) are in direct function of radiation dose calculation.

There are several regions of interest in radiation treatment planning either targets to radiation (e.g., tumor) or regions that should be avoided during radiation (e.g., healthy tissues and vital organs). Manually drawing the individual contours on a contiguous set of 2D slices then combining them is very time consuming and labor intensive. Using automated image segmentation could save tremendous time and effort that would otherwise be needed if using manual tracing. Also, automated segmentation could increase precision (intra-operator repeatability and inter-operator reproducibility) by eliminating subjectivity of the clinician.

Segmentation of prostate and bladder is an important and challenging task. E.g., the contour of the prostate in CT images is very poor and its interface with

---
* This work was supported by GE Medical Systems.

other structures, such as the bladder, seminal vesicles, rectum, and urethra is not always clearly defined. There are a few methods published about segmentation of pelvic organs. Philips already has a RT planning product containing model-based segmentation of pelvic organs [1] based on deformable models. Their model building process starts from a representative training set of segmented organs delineated by clinical experts. The surface of an organ is triangulated and aligned to the shapes in the remaining segmented datasets by rigid and nonrigid registration. A point distribution model is generated by computing the mean shape and the shape variation modes. The segmentation is performed by interactively positioning the model and then the deformable model is adapted to the image data using energy minimization.

In our proposed approach, the CT images of different patients are transformed to a common reference frame, thus besides the organ shapes, the variability of their positions in this frame can also be taken into account. The deformable model is described in this frame. In the clinical application, this model can be initialized automatically by applying the inverse of the transformation taking the study to be segmented to the reference frame. If necessary, this can be refined by the clinician interactively. By optimizing a cost function, the deformable model is adopted the image data. The scope of this paper is limited to the registration of the studies to a common reference frame and automatic initialization of the deformable segmentation process, which can be considered as a preprocessing step of a segmentation framework.

2 Methods

Registration of 3D medical data has been in focus of research for decades, several algorithms have been developed [2]. In our project manual and interactive registration algorithms are not convenient enough – the more automatic the method is the better. Fully automatic methods utilize geometric features, such as points, outlines or surfaces, or image intensities directly, computing statistical, information theory-based or correlation-based similarity of corresponding intensity values. Many of these methods can be used to register the pubic bone area. Methods based on voxel similarity measures provide fast and reliable results without any user interaction. Surface registration could also be used. The bone surface can be segmented automatically and the registration can be even faster than that of voxel based methods. Outliers (bone structures that can be found only in one of the studies) can cause problems though.

Another important part of the registration algorithm is the type of transformation to consider. Here the anatomy non-rigidly differs from patient to patient, the goal of registration is to bring the anatomic structures "close" to each other. Since an approximate result is satisfactory and fast execution is required, rigid-body or affine transformations can be utilized. Deformable registration can take too much time, and it is hard, if not impossible, to adequately model the anatomical differences between patients. Furthermore, since both organ position and shape are taken into account during model creation, too much deformation of the organs is not welcome at this point.

A previous work on pelvis registration focuses on precise bone alignment for bone atlas creation [3]. Such an application requires deformable registration due to the large differences between patient anatomies, since the size and shape of pelvises can vary widely. On the other hand, precise alignment of all bone structures is not crucial as a preliminary step in model-based segmentation of prostate and bladder, the focus is on acceptable alignment of the pubic bone. In addition, deformable registration requires more computing time, in our case fast registration is important. Furthermore, better bone alignment does not guarantee better soft tissue alignment.

In model-based segmentation, transforming the CT studies to a common reference frame is a useful step before two tasks. For model making, when the studies are registered, the assumption is that the anatomic regions of different studies can be found nearly in the same voxel regions. By transforming the hand-segmented ground truth segmentations of the organs of interest to this common reference frame together with the CT studies a deformable organ model can be calculated in the reference frame. In the clinical program, automatic alignment of the organ model to the patient study — via applying the inverse of the transformation that takes the study to the reference frame — can reduce the necessary user input to initialize the model-based segmentation.

Although the registration methods applied in these steps are almost the same, the requirements are different. The model generation is not part of the actual segmentation process thus the registration can be performed in "batch mode", i.e., one after the other without user interaction. More precise alignment is preferred to fast execution time. On the other hand, in the clinical program, the execution must be as fast as possible, even sacrificing some precision.

We propose an extension not addressed by previous algorithms. The idea is that after an affine transformation which gives global optimal alignment, a refinement step is performed. Global registration prefers alignment of body parts of big volume, like spine or pelvis causing slight or big differences in the pubic bone area (Fig. 1, top row). It is assumed that scale parameters are satisfactorily determined by this global part. During refinement, scale parameters are kept from the global part, then an optimal rigid-body transformation is searched in the pubic bone region only (Fig. 1, bottom row). Many methods could be extended this way [4]. In our actual implementation, we used a general registration method utilizing normalized mutual information [5].

3 Materials

Our test database consists of 33 pelvic CT images provided by General Electric Medical Systems Company. The chosen reference image has 83 2D slices of 512x512 voxels. The in-slice resolution is 0.936562 millimeters, while the slice distance is 3.00 millimeters. Most of the other studies have 60–100 slices, but in some extreme cases 33 or 189 slices are present. The spatial in-slice resolution is in the [0.60-0.98] interval, the slice distance is usually 2.5–3.00 mm. Studies are of varying quality, some are distorted by artificial (metallic) objects.

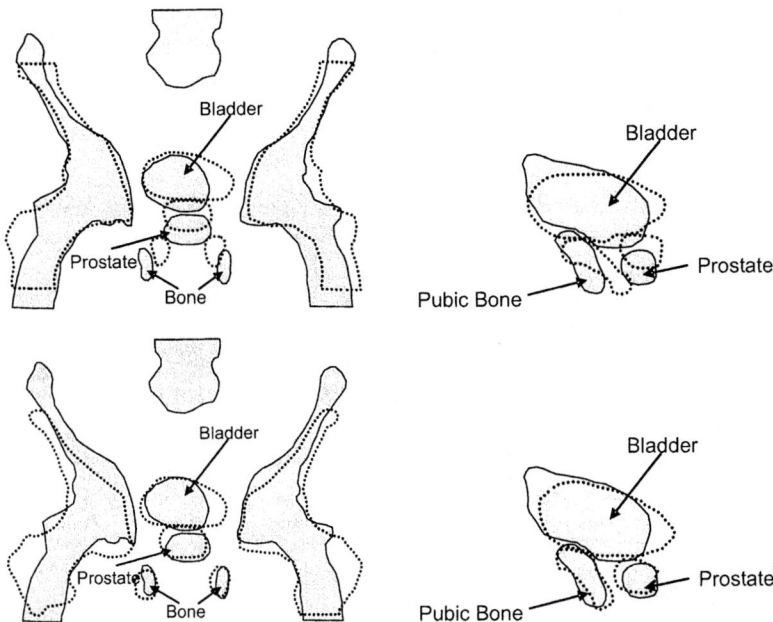

Fig. 1. Top row: The optimal global registration of a study (*dotted outline*) against the reference volume (*filled shape*) — a coronal (*left*) and a sagittal cross section (*right*). It is well visible that the organs of the two studies are close to each other, but the overlapping region e.g., of the prostate, is small. Bottom row: The optimal local rigid-body refinement following the global registration of a study against the reference volume — a coronal (*left*) and a sagittal cross section (*right*). The result of the registration provides a good starting point for a segmentation algorithm. The figures are derived from real data.

Three clinical experts manually segmented prostate in 26 and bladder in all the 33 studies independently. The experts visually checked the result of the majority vote segmentation (if a voxel was identified as the given organ by at least two experts) together, and accepted it or made some modifications. This final segmentation is used as the gold standard. After visual inspection of the registration results, three studies were omitted from the database because of unacceptable misregistrations. In one of these cases the patient orientation was wrong (a preprocessing step is necessary to solve this), in another case the bladder was filled with contrast material. Note that there are some more studies of this kind and even heavily distorted ones where the registration gave good results. Table 1 summarizes the properties of the studies we use in this paper.

Our proposed registration method requires the manual selection of the local neighborhood of the pubic bone in the reference study. This region of interest is used in the local refinement step of the algorithm. During local refinement, voxel intensity values inside this neighborhood only are taken into account. This region should contain the pubic bone, the lower part of ischium, and some soft

Table 1. Study database. The last three columns show the size of the gold standard prostates. The volume is given in pixels and cm^3, the last column shows the diameter if a perfect spherical prostate shape is assumed.

Study ID	Slices	Slice spacing (mm)	Slice Thick. (mm)	Prostate Gold Standard		
				(pixels)	(cm^3)	Sp. diam. (cm)
cd2pa2 (reference)	83	0.976562	3	7121	20.37	3.39
cd2pa3	70	0.976562	3	9927	28.40	3.79
cd2pa4	73	0.976562	3	6020	17.22	3.20
cd2pa5	68	0.976562	3	14267	40.82	4.27
cd2pa6	81	0.976562	3	11165	31.94	3.94
cd2pa7	64	0.976562	3	8936	25.57	3.66
cd1prostate1	86	0.9375	2.5	42501	93.39	5.63
cd1prostate2	149	0.820312	1.25	31181	26.23	3.69
cd1prostate3	81	0.9375	2.5	11269	24.76	3.62
cd3pa4st1se1	67	0.976562	2.5	13526	32.25	3.95
cd4pa5st1se1	112	0.976562	2.5	23520	56.08	4.75
cd4pa7st1se1	78	0.976562	2.5	8958	21.36	3.44
cd4pa8st1se1	83	0.976562	2.5	8402	20.03	3.37
cd4pa10st1se1	73	0.976562	2.5	15323	36.53	4.12
cd6pa5st1se2	84	0.976562	3	1570	4.49	2.05
cd6pa8st1se2	73	0.976562	3	15677	44.85	4.41
cd6pa9st1se2	55	0.976562	3	8642	24.72	3.61
cd6pa10st1se2	78	0.976562	3	13652	39.06	4.21
cd8pa8st1se1	39	0.9375	5	24620	108.19	5.91
cd8pa9st1se2	104	0.976562	2.5	33800	80.59	5.36
cd14anon10	49	0.98	5	5157	24.76	3.62
cd14anon14	46	0.976562	3	6362	18.20	3.26
cd14anon21	189	0.9375	5	8124	35.70	4.09

tissue region around them. This selection must be done only once and only for the reference study (Fig. 2).

4 Tests and Results

From the nature of the problem it is evident that ground truth information on the expected registration results is not available. What we have is the expert segmented gold standard database, and we expect that after spatial normalization, the organs will be "close" to each other. Since the sizes and shapes of the bladders vary too much and our database is too small to be able to select enough full, normal, and empty segmented bladders, only the prostate data is used for the evaluation of the global and local refinement methods.

We conducted three different tests to find out whether the method utilizing local refinement is significantly better, i.e., brings organs, in this case prostates, closer to each other than the method using global registration only.

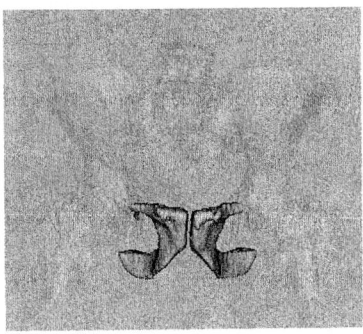
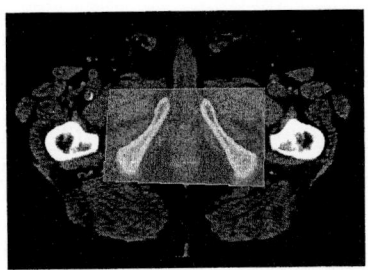

Fig. 2. Surface model (*left*) and manually selected neighborhood in a transaxial slice (*right*) of the pubic bone selected for local refinement

Let N denote the number of the studies and $PROST_i \subseteq Z^3 (1 \leq i \leq N)$ the voxel positions classified as prostate in the ith study after transforming to the common reference frame.

In the first test we assume that the prostates are spherical. For each study, the centroid of the prostate ($COG_i = \sum_{x \in PROST_i} x/|PROST_i|$) is computed. The centroid of this set of centroids (COG_{global}), and for each study the Euclidean distance between COG_i and COG_{global} are computed. The second and third columns of Table 2 show these.

The second and third tests utilize a so called probability atlas ($PROB$) which is defined as follows. By transforming the hand-segmented ground truth segmentations of the organs of interest to the common reference frame together with the CT studies for each voxel, the probability that the given voxel belongs to a specific organ can be assigned. E.g., the value is 0 if that voxel was not classified as part of the organ in any of the studies, 0.5 indicates that this happened in half of the studies.

The second test determines the average probability belonging to the voxels of the transformed gold standard prostates of each study,

$$prob_i^1 = \frac{\sum_{x \in PROST_i} PROB(x)}{|PROST_i|}.$$

The third test shows the summed probability of the prostate region of a study relative to the whole probability map,

$$prob_i^2 = \frac{\sum_{x \in PROST_i} PROB(x)}{\sum_x PROB(x)}.$$

For each method and test, statistical parameters (mean, standard deviation and paired two-tailed t-Test) were computed. Table 2 shows the results of the three tests for the global registration only and global registration followed by the local refinement, respectively.

Table 2. Results showing Euclidean distances of the centroids, and $prob_i^1$ and $prob_i^2$ values

Study ID	Centroid Test		Probability Test 1		Probability Test 2	
	Global	Refined	Global	Refined	Global	Refined
cd2pa3	8.08	2.92	0.5635	0.6790	0.3837	0.4588
cd2pa4	3.80	7.12	0.6439	0.6689	0.2970	0.3015
cd2pa5	9.81	7.14	0.4937	0.5685	0.4890	0.5400
cd2pa6	10.30	8.94	0.4853	0.5297	0.4143	0.4470
cd2pa7	4.75	4.95	0.5934	0.6263	0.4268	0.4466
cd1prostate1	9.90	11.19	0.3188	0.3290	0.7591	0.7819
cd1prostate2	3.73	5.51	0.5576	0.5995	0.4752	0.5229
cd1prostate3	3.64	6.64	0.6274	0.6400	0.4220	0.4157
cd3pa4st1se1	12.66	6.14	0.4028	0.6082	0.3012	0.4737
cd4pa5st1se1	11.40	14.82	0.3350	0.3160	0.5391	0.5020
cd4pa7st1se1	8.74	7.61	0.4867	0.5931	0.2622	0.3451
cd4pa8st1se1	22.95	18.07	0.1870	0.3049	0.1112	0.1805
cd4pa10st1se1	2.75	4.00	0.5299	0.5678	0.5515	0.5857
cd6pa5st1se2	8.77	8.18	0.6395	0.8404	0.0811	0.1077
cd6pa8st1se2	10.50	6.69	0.4588	0.5254	0.5451	0.6245
cd6pa9st1se2	17.95	8.65	0.3148	0.4205	0.4175	0.5553
cd6pa10st1se2	18.22	4.41	0.2792	0.4886	0.3284	0.5906
cd8pa8st1se1	22.49	18.99	0.2164	0.2501	0.6947	0.7987
cd8pa9st1se2	19.04	17.69	0.2661	0.4325	0.0165	0.0266
cd14anon10	2.57	3.39	0.6212	0.6734	0.4101	0.4652
cd14anon14	16.09	10.15	0.3897	0.6070	0.2036	0.3128
cd14anon21	13.19	7.04	0.4180	0.5325	0.4290	0.5514
Average	10.97	8.65	0.4468	0.5364	0.3890	0.4561
Std.Dev.	6.30	4.73	0.1435	0.1449	0.1836	0.1903
t-Test	0.0213		8.3513E-06		0.0001	

5 Discussion

The results in Table 2 indicates that after the refinement step the prostate regions are significantly ($P < 0.05$) closer to each other compared to the global registration. Registrations were performed on a 3Ghz Pentium IV desktop PC. The running time is about two minutes for a study. It is acceptable for the model creation process since this must be done only once. In the clinical application, fast execution is crucial especially since the registration is only a preprocessing step in the segmentation process which is time consuming by itself. Utilizing several optimizations (e.g., by using only the coarser levels of a hierarchical representation), the running time is currently between 20–40 seconds. It can be further reduced to nearly its half by reducing the number of voxels in the reference volume removing the unnecessary parts (e.g., using the bounding box of the patient data). Visual inspection and preliminary statistical results show that although the precision is slightly reduced, the result is acceptable in most cases.

6 Conclusions

In this paper we focused on a preprocessing step of a segmentation framework. Before model generation, transforming the studies of different patients to a common reference frame is useful. In the clinical application, initial organ model placement can be established automatically. Note that automatic registration does not guarantee acceptable results, so visual inspection is necessary. In our database the failure rate of registrations was low (three out of 26) even though the studies were "real-life", many of them distorted by metallic objects, or not satisfying the assumed protocol (e.g., wrong patient position, contrast agent is visible in the images).

Acknowledgements

This work has been supported and the image database was provided by GE Medical Systems. We thank our clinical experts, Dr. Katalin Gion, Dr. István Csenkey-Sinkó, and Dr. Endre Szabó from the Department of Radiology, University of Szeged for their indispensable work during the gold standard creation process.

References

1. Pekar, V., McNutt, T.R., Kaus, M.R.: Automated Model-based Organ Delineation for Radiotherapy Planning in Prostatic Region, Int. J. Radiation Oncology Biol. Phys. **60** No 3 (2004) 973–980
2. Maintz, J.B.A., Viergever, M.A.: A survey of medical image registration. Medical Image Analysis **2** (1998) 1–36
3. Yiqiang Zhan, Dinggang Shen, Russ Taylor: Deformable Registration of Male Pelvises in CT Images, IEEE International Symposium on Biomedical Imaging (ISBI), Arlington, VA, April 15-18, 2004.
4. West, J.B., Fitzpatrick, J.M., et al.: Retrospective Intermodality Registration Techniques for Images of the Head: Surface-Based Versus Volume-Based. IEEE Trans. on Medical Imaging **18** (1999) 144–150
5. Tanács, A., Kuba, A.: Evaluation of a Fully Automatic Medical Image Registration Algorithm Based on Mutual Information, Acta Cybernetica **16** (2003) 327–336

A New Snake Model Robust on Overlap and Bias Problems in Tracking a Moving Target

Youngjoon Han and Hernsoo Hahn

School of Electronic Engineering, Soongsil University, Seoul, Korea
{young, hahn}@ssu.ac.kr

Abstract. Performance of conventional snake models tends to decrease in the case where the target object is overlapped with other objects and where the bias between the initial snake and the target object is large. To solve these problems, this paper proposes an extended snake model including the energy dissipation function in the external energy, which is defined as a function of the variation rate of the target object' area and the target object's velocity obtained by the modified SSD algorithm. In the experiment, it is shown that the proposed snake model renders the mobile robot with a camera follow the moving target successfully even when it is occluded or overlapped temporarily by other objects.

1 Introduction

As the mobility of robots is improved, more intelligent functions are required for mobile robots to possess. One of them is the ability of tracking or following a moving target. In order for a mobile robot to follow a moving object, it is essential to detect the object in the input image and to measure its position first. Since both the target and the robot are moving, both the shape of the target and the background in the input image can be changed. In this case, the shape of a 3D moving object projected on a 2D image can be interpreted as a deformable 2D object depending on the viewing direction of the mobile robot[1,2].

For the purpose of detecting the target and determining its position, the snake, an active contour model has been widely used to extract the boundary of the target in the image[3,4]. However, when a target object is overlapped with other ones or when an input image is influenced by noise, the performance of the snake model is deteriorated. To solve this problem, Peterfreund[5] presented a Kalman-filter based snake model, where the velocity measurement which is not consistent with the estimated velocity is rejected during the update step of the system state. Since it discriminates the target object using the optical flow and edge-based potential field, it can detect the object boundary even when the target object is partially overlapped with other ones moving toward different directions. However, because the image flow is obtained with the background fixed, this approach is difficult to use for tracking the moving object while the camera moves too. Jiang et. al.[6] presented a modified snake model, which includes a new external force that makes the active contour be attracted to a shape similar to the one in the previous frame. It predicts the contour to be appeared in the next frame and uses the predicted contour as the reference. Although this approach prevents the contour from shrinking inside the object, it still does not provide a clear solution for the overlapped objects.

Another case where the snake model does not work well occurs when the positional difference, so called a bias between the object to be detected and the initial snake curve is large. To solve this problem, Kim[7] introduced a new snake model using image flow, which applies different algorithms depending on the amount of bias. It tracks the target in the rolling mode when the bias is small enough, otherwise in the jump mode. In the rolling mode, the snake approaches to the optimal shape as the conventional algorithm does. Instead, in the jump mode, the template found in the previous frame is discarded and the snake jumps to the new position reinitializing itself with the estimated radius of the object.

This paper proposes an extended snake model which can handle those problems mentioned above. The problem caused by the overlap of objects can be solved by introducing the momentum which will preserve the shape of the snake contour. The momentum added to the energy dissipation function which is used for damping the kinetic energy forbids the snake from fast expanding to neighboring objects while making the process robust to the image noise. For solving the large bias problem, the proposed new snake model takes the predicted velocity of the target into account to determine the position of the initial snake contour. The velocity of the target is estimated by the modified SSD (Sum of Square Difference) algorithm. So, even when the bias is somewhat large, the proposed snake model can stably track the target in a dynamic environment where both the camera and the target object move simultaneously.

2 New Snake Model with an Energy Dissipation Function

To exactly determine the match between the template and the detected object's contour, a modified SSD algorithm is provided. Once the target object is found in the next frame, then the velocity of the target object can also be estimated.

2.1 Prediction of the Moving Target's Velocity Using SSD Algorithm

SSD algorithm is used for finding the position of the best matching area in the (k)th frame corresponding to the given template, and returning the displacement of the object in the (k)th frame from the (k-1)th frame[8]. This algorithm is usually used for tracking a target in the case where its shape does not change in the images, thus it is modified in such a way that the template is updated in every frame as the shape of the target object found by using the snake model in the previous frame.

Let's assume that the template in the image represented by $\mathbf{p}_i(k-1)$ is a rectangle whose width and height are respectively M and N, and that its position in the (k-1)th frame is $(x_i(k-1), y_i(k-1))$. Then, the SSD algorithm finds the object $\mathbf{p}_i(k-1)$ in the searching range Ψ, which minimizes the dissimilarity measure given in Eq.(1).

$$Z(\mathbf{p}_i(k), \triangle \mathbf{x}) = \sum_{m \in M, n \in N} \Big[\mathbf{I}_{k-1}[x_i(k-1)+m, y_i(k-1)+n] \\ -\mathbf{I}_k[x_i(k-1)+m+u, y_i(k-1)+n+v]\Big]^2, \quad (1)$$

where $u, v \in \Psi$, and m and n represent the pixels inside the template. Also, $\mathbf{I}_k$ is the (k)th frame image and $(x_i(k-1), y_i(k-1))$ is the center of the template in the (k-1)th frame. Thus, in Eq. (1), represents the dissimilarity between $\mathbf{p}_i(k)$ and $\mathbf{p}_i(k-1)$ and they become more similar if its value gets smaller. Then the positional difference $\triangle \mathbf{x} = [u, v]^T$ between them is defined as the displacement of the target from (k-1)th frame to (k)th frame. Once the target object is found in the new frame, its displacement from the previous frame is approximated as the velocity of the object, $\mathbf{v}_t \equiv \frac{\partial \mathbf{x}}{\partial t}$, as follows, if the image sampling time is T.

$$\mathbf{v}_t^p \cong \lim_{T \to 0} \left[\frac{u}{T}, \frac{v}{T}\right]^T \quad (2)$$

2.2 Extended Snake Model with an Energy Dissipation Function

A snake can be expressed by the deformable closed curve $\mathbf{v}(s,t)$ where s is the spatial parameter and t is the time parameter, as given in the following equation(Eq.(3)). The length of the closed curve is normalized.

$$\mathbf{v}(s,t) = (x(s,t), y(s,t)) : s \in [0,1], t \in T \quad (3)$$

The potential energy of a snake $\mathbf{v}(s,t)$ is defined as the sum of the internal potential energy E_{int} and the external energy E_{ext} as shown in Eq.(4).

$$E_{snake}(\mathbf{v}) = \tfrac{1}{2} \oint \Big[E_{int}(\mathbf{v}) + E_{ext}(\mathbf{v})\Big] ds \quad (4)$$

The internal energy E_{int} constrains the bending and stretching force of the snake curve and expressed by Eq. (5).

$$E_{int}(\mathbf{v}) = \alpha |\mathbf{v}_s|^2 + \beta |\mathbf{v}_{ss}|^2, \quad (5)$$

where $\mathbf{v}_s = \partial \mathbf{v}/\partial s$ constrains the stretching of the snake like physical spring and $\mathbf{v}_{ss} = \partial^2 \mathbf{v}/\partial s^2$ constrains the bending of the snake like physical rod. The constant α and β are weights that control the tension and rigidity of the snake curve, respectively. The external energy E_{ext} is expressed in different ways depending on the applications of the snake, and it makes the points on a snake, called snaxels (snake elements), converge to the boundary of the object. The external potential function is usually defined as follows:

$$E_{ext}(\mathbf{v})(\equiv P(\mathbf{v},t)) = -|\nabla G_\sigma(\mathbf{x}) * I(\mathbf{x},t)|, \quad (6)$$

where $I(\mathbf{x},t)$ denotes the image intensity of the sample at time t, $G_\sigma(\mathbf{x})$ denotes Gaussian kernel with the standard deviation σ, and ∇ is the gradient operator. To find the optimal contour of the object, the snake changes its shape so that its potential energy E_{snake} can be minimized. For this purpose, the potential energy should be transformed into a kinetic energy in order to reach a new lower equilibrium. And the kinetic energy must be reduced by damping to reach the rest state ($\mathbf{v}_t = 0$). Since the motion of the snake curve to reach the rest state is generated using the potential energy of the snake curve itself, it can be interpreted as the movement of energy conservative system. This relationship is well expressed by Euler-Lagrangian equation, where Lagrangian L(v) is given by Eq. (7):

$$L(\mathbf{v}) = T(\mathbf{v}) - U(\mathbf{v}) \qquad (7)$$

where $T(\mathbf{v})$ and $U(\mathbf{v})$ denote the kinetic energy and potential energy of the snake curve $\mathbf{v}$, respectively. The kinetic energy is defined as follows:

$$T(\mathbf{v}) = \tfrac{1}{2} \oint \mu |\mathbf{v}_t|^2 ds, \qquad (8)$$

where $\mathbf{v}_t = \partial \mathbf{v}/\partial t$. Since the potential energy is expressed by Eq. (1), Lagrangian L(v) can be rewritten as Eq. (9):

$$L(\mathbf{v}) = \tfrac{1}{2} \oint \left[\mu |v_t|^2 - E_{int}(\mathbf{v}(s)) - E_{ext}(\mathbf{v}(s))\right] ds. \qquad (9)$$

To keep the conservative system at a rest state, the kinetic energy must be dissipated by damping only. That is, the motion of the snake curve must be described by a non-conservative system with an energy dissipation function. The dissipation function used here is represented by the following equation:

$$D(\mathbf{v}_t) = \tfrac{1}{2} \oint \gamma |\mathbf{v}_t|^2 ds. \qquad (10)$$

This function is generalized here considering the dynamic environment where both the camera and the target object move simultaneously. It considers the variation rate of the area enclosed by the snake curve and the difference between the snake velocity and the object velocity. Then Eq. (10) can be expressed by Eq. (11) as follows:

$$D(\mathbf{v}_s, \mathbf{v}_t, \mathbf{v}_t^p) = \tfrac{1}{2} \oint \left[\gamma |A(\mathbf{v}_t, \mathbf{v}_s)|^2 ds + \tfrac{1}{2} \oint \kappa |\mathbf{v}_t - \mathbf{v}_t^p|^2\right] ds \qquad (11)$$

where the constant γ and κ are the weight of the variation rate of the snake's area and that of the velocity difference, respectively. The first term dissipates the kinetic energy by generating the inner force that minimizes the time variation rate of the snake's area, where the snake's area is given by Green theorem in Eq. (12):

$$A(\mathbf{v}(s,t)) = \tfrac{1}{2} \oint \{x(s,t)y_s(s,t) - y(s,t)x_s(s,t)\} ds \qquad (12)$$

Then, the variation rate of snake's area is derived from the time derivative of Eq. (12) as follows:

$$A_t(\mathbf{v}_t, \mathbf{v}_s) = \frac{d}{dt} A(\mathbf{v}(s,t)) = \frac{1}{2} \oint \left\{ \begin{array}{c} -x_{st}(s,t)y(s,t) + x(s,t)y_{st}(s,t) \\ +y_{st}(s,t)x(s,t) - y(s,t)x_{st}(s,t) \end{array} \right\} ds$$
$$= \oint \left| \begin{array}{cc} x_t & x_s \\ y_t & y_s \end{array} \right| ds, \quad (13)$$

where $x_t = dx/dt$, $x_{st} = dx_t/ds$, $y_t = dy/dt$, and $y_{st} = dy_t/ds$.

As shown in Eq. (13), the variation rate of snake's area is the function of the temporal and spatial velocities of the snake. That is, minimization of the variation rate of snake's area will make the inner force conserve the shape of the snake contour, and cause the effect of frictional forces on the velocities of snaxels. The second term in Eq. (11) is the velocity difference between the snake contour and the object's velocities that should be minimized. Because the velocity of the target object is not exactly derived, here the velocity $\mathbf{v}_t^p$ defined in Eq. (2) and predicted by SSD algorithm is used. Incorporating these forces into Euler-Lagrange equation of motion, Eq. (14) is obtained as follows:

$$\frac{\partial L}{\partial \mathbf{x}} - \frac{\partial}{\partial t}\left(\frac{\partial L}{\partial \mathbf{x}_t}\right) - \frac{\partial}{\partial s}\left(\frac{\partial L}{\partial \mathbf{x}_s}\right) + \frac{\partial^2}{\partial s^2}\left(\frac{\partial L}{\partial \mathbf{x}_{ss}}\right) = -\gamma \mathbf{A}_t - \kappa(\mathbf{v}_t - \mathbf{v}_t^p). \quad (14)$$

By substituting Lagrangian given in Eq. (9) into Eq. (14), Euler-Lagrange equation of motion is finally written as Eq. (15):

$$\mu \mathbf{v}_{tt} + \gamma \mathbf{A}_t + \kappa(\mathbf{v}_t - \mathbf{v}_t^p) - \frac{\partial}{\partial s}(\alpha \mathbf{v}_s) - \frac{\partial^2}{\partial s^2}(\beta \mathbf{v}_{ss}) = -\nabla P(\mathbf{v}, t), \quad (15)$$

where $\mathbf{v}_{tt} = \partial^2 \mathbf{v}/\partial t^2$, $\mathbf{v}_s = \partial \mathbf{v}/\partial s$, $\mathbf{v}_{ss} = \partial^2 \mathbf{v}/\partial s^2$. Once the appropriate initial condition at t=0 and boundary conditions at the extremities of the interval Ω are given, the solutions of the above differential equation can be obtained. Compared to the conventional snake model, the proposed algorithm has a couple of major advantages in dynamic environment where both the camera and target object move. The first one is that the proposed one can track the moving target even if the part of the target is missed by overlapping or by noise, because it has the momentum to preserve the shape of snake contour. The second one is that the proposed one solves the bias problem by making the snake velocity converge to the predicted velocity $\mathbf{v}_t^p$ of the target object. Since the snake velocity can be slower than the target's velocity, the bias between the snake and the target object may increase a lot. This large bias will result in tracking the object located near the target object not the target object itself. The proposed one prevents this type of problem from occurring. These observations are proved by the experiments in the following section.

3 Experiments and Discussion

In the experiment, a monochrome CCD camera is mounted on a Nomad Scout Robot , and On-Air TV card is used to capture a 320 x 240 eight bit per pixel

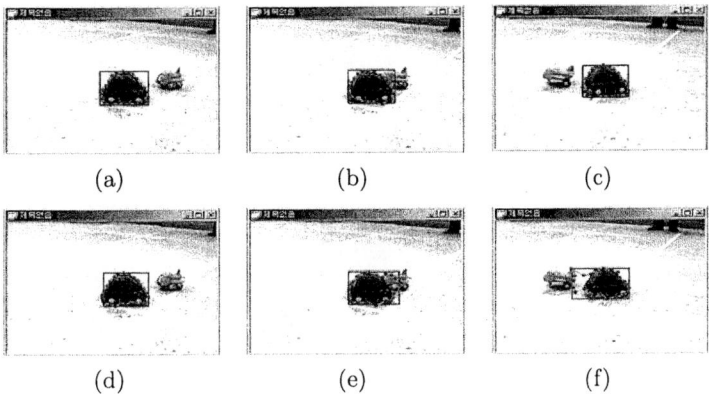

Fig. 1. The target object is overlapped with a moving object. The upper three pictures show the case of using the proposed snake model and the lower ones show the case of using the conventional one. A moving object is approaching in (a) and (d), overlapping in (b) and (e), leaving in (c) and (f).

image at 12 sampling frame rate. The algorithm has been implemented with Visual C++ 6.0 and installed in a PC with Pentium CPU (700MHz). A small car robot is used as the target object and a small airplane robot is used as an obstacle. The experiments have been performed to test whether the mobile robot follows the target with keeping the distance in 1m and keeps in around the center of the input image. The performance is compared with that of the conventional algorithm. To compare the performance of the proposed snake algorithm with that of the conventional one, two situations are considered. One is that the target object occludes temporarily another moving object, and the other one is that the target object is occluded by a man passing by the camera.

The results of the experiments for the case where the target is overlapped with the airplane robot are given in Fig. 1. A toy car is used as the target object, and a toy airplane is used as the overlapping object. In Fig. 1, (a) and (d) show the fifteenth frame where the moving object is approaching to the target object, (b) and (e) show the fifty-seventh frame where the moving object is passing behind the target object resulting in an overlapped input image, and (c) and (f) show the ninety-fourth frame where the moving object leaves the overlapping situation. Fig. 1(e) shows that the rectangle begins getting larger and (e) shows that the size of the rectangle is already out of the control, if the conventional algorithm is used. Instead, Fig. 1(b) and (c) show that the size of the rectangle is maintained stably in the case of using the proposed snake model. The results of the experiment in the case where the target object is occluded temporarily by a passing person are given in Fig. 2. When using the conventional algorithm, the contour shrinks abruptly as soon as the target object is completely occluded, as shown in (e). Above all, the snake is attracted by the neighboring shadow formed by noise after the target is appeared again, as shown in (f). However, when using the proposed snake model, the snake's contour is well preserved even when the

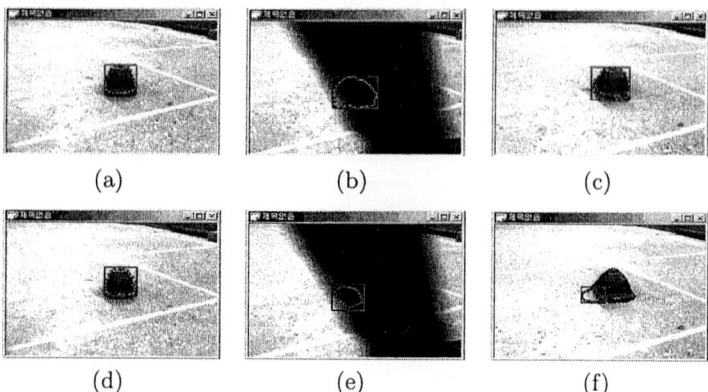

(a) (b) (c)

(d) (e) (f)

Fig. 2. The target object is completely occluded by a passing person. The upper three pictures show the case of using the proposed snake model and the lower ones show the case of using the conventional one. The target object moving in (a) and (c), occluded in (b) and (e), reappearing in (c) and (f).

Table 1. Performance comparison of the proposed algorithm with conventional one

Experiment Case		Variance of average error(pel^2)	Number of missed frames	Maximum Position Error(pels)
Case 1	Conventional	3.20	6.20	> 8.00
	Proposed	2.02	0	3.85
Case 2	Conventional	4.35	8.50	> 8.00
	Proposed	2.17	0	4.16

target is completely occluded and when the occluded target is appeared again, as shown in (a) and (c).

Table 1 summarizes the results of the experiments performed on the above two situations. For each situation, 5 tests are executed to acquire the statistical results. To tell the performance of the algorithm, three measures are used. The variance of average error shows the reliability and the number of missed frames shows how many images the algorithm could not find the contour among total 110 frames. The maximum position error shows the worst case performance. As can be found in the Table 1, the proposed algorithm never misses the target while the conventional algorithm does from time to time. It is because the maximum error between the desired and current position of the target object always exists in effective searching area. Table 1 also shows that the variances of average error in the situation 1 are larger than those in the situation 2. It is because the density of the car robot is similar to the density of background. And the reason why the variances of average error in situation 2 are larger than those in another situation is that the overlap between two objects is occurred.

4 Conclusion

This paper proposed a new extended snake model to solve the overlap and bias problems occurring in tracking a moving target with a mobile robot having a camera on it. The dissipation function of the snake model includes the variation rate of snake's area for generating the momentum to preserve the shape of snake's contour during the consecutive images, and the velocity error between the snake velocity and the predictive velocity from the SSD algorithm. The extended snake model also solves the large bias problem by making the snake velocity converge into the predictive velocity of the target. The comparative experiments have shown that it is able to stably track the moving target and robust to the image noise in the dynamic environment.

Acknowledgement. This work was supported by the Soongsil University Research Fund.

References

1. Lee, B. and Hahn, H.:Representation and recognition of polyhedral objects in a single 2-D image using the signature technique. Journal of the Korean Institute of Telematrics and Electronics **34S** (1997) 63-70
2. Fu,Y. et al.:Tracking Visible Boundary of Objects Using Occlusion Adaptive Motion Snake. IEEE Transaction on Image Processing **9** (2000) 2051-2060
3. Kass,M. et al.: Snakes: Active contour models. International Journal of Computer Vision **1** (1987) 321-331
4. Denzler,J., Niemann,H.: Combination of Simple Vision Modules for Robust Real-Time Motion Tracking. European Transactions on Telecommunications **5** (1995) 275-296
5. Peterfreund,N.: Robust Tracking of Position and Velocity With Kalman Snakes. IEEE Transactions on Pattern Analysis and Machine Intelligence. **21** (1999) 564-569
6. Jiang,J., Drew,M.: IA Predictive Contour Inertia Snake Model for General Video Tracking. International Conference on Image Processing (2002)
7. Kim,W. et al.: An Active Contour Model using Image Flow for Tracking a Moving Object. IEEE/RSJ International Conference on Intelligent Robots and Systems (1999) 216-221
8. Hager,G., Belhumeur,P.:Efficient Region Tracking With Parametric Models of Geometry and Illumination. IEEE Transactions on Pattern Analysis and Machine Intelligence **20** (1998) 1025-1039

Neighborhood Decomposition of 3D Convex Structuring Elements for Morphological Operations*

Syng-Yup Ohn

Hankook Aviation University,
Department of Computer and Information Engineering,
Seoul, Korea
syohn@hau.ac.kr

Abstract. Morphological operations with 3D images require a huge amount of computation. The decomposition of structuring elements used in the morphological operations such as dilation and erosion greatly reduces the amount of computation. This paper presents a new method for the decomposition of a 3D convex structuring element into a set of neighborhood structuring elements. A neighborhood structuring element is a convex structuring element consisting of a subset of a set consisting of the origin voxel and its 26 neighborhood voxels. First, we derive the set of decomposition conditions on the lengths of the original and the basis convex structuring elements, and then the decomposition problem is converted to linear integer optimization problem. The objective of the optimization is to minimize a cost function representing the optimal criterion for the implementation of morphological operations. Thus, our method can be used to obtain the different optimal decompositions minimizing the amount of computation in different cases.

Keywords: mathematical morphology, dilation, erosion, structuring element, decomposition, convex polyhedron.

1 Introduction

Mathematical morphology provides powerful tools in the fields of image processing and computer vision. The basic operations of mathematical morphology are dilation and erosion, which stem from Minkowski addition and subtraction. An image processing task can be achieved by arranging set operations as well as dilation and erosion operations suitably for the goal of the task. The structuring elements used in morphological operation play the important role of the probe to detect and extract the geometrical characteristics of an input image, and one should choose the structuring element with the size and the shape appropriate for the purpose of the operation[1], [2]. If a large structuring element is decomposed into a set of smaller structuring elements, the dilation of an image by the original structuring element can be achieved

---

* This research was supported by the Internet Information Retrieval Research Center(IRC) in Hankuk Aviation University. IRC is a Regional Research Center of Kyounggi Province, designated by ITEP and Ministry of Commerce, Industry and Energy.

by a sequence of the dilation operations by the set of smaller structuring elements[3]. Generally, such decomposition reduces the amount of computation required to perform dilation. Erosion can be benefited by decomposition similarly. In the rest of this paper, we discuss the decompositions for dilation only since an analogous discussion can be made for erosion.

The decomposition of 2D structuring elements was first investigated by Zhuang and Haralick[4]. Xu[8] and Park[9] developed the methods to decompose a 2D convex structuring element into a set of neighborhood structuring elements. However, their methods cannot be extended to decomposition of 3D structuring elements.

3D mathematical morphology is shown to be effective in the areas of medical image processing and shape analysis[10]. Also, numerous 3D parallel image processors have been proposed and implemented for fast processing of 3D images. As in the 2D case, it is desirable and often inevitable to decompose 3D structuring elements for effective and efficient computations of 3D morphological operations. Much research efforts are concentrated on the 2D decomposition problems. Furthermore, the amount of 3D image data is generally much larger than that of 2D image data, and the fast image operations are indispensable. However, 3D decomposition problems are yet to be explored.

In this paper, we present the conditions for decomposition of a digital convex polyhedron into a set of basis digital convex polyhedra and propose a new technique for the neighborhood decomposition of 3D convex structuring elements. The structuring elements in a neighborhood decomposition are neighborhood structuring elements, each of which is a subset of a set consisting of the origin voxel and its 26 neighborhood voxels. Convex structuring elements are often used in morphological image processing because of its good geometric characteristics[8].

The optimal decomposition of a structuring element depends on how a dilation operation is implemented. In case that there are many possible decompositions for a structuring element, one should choose the decomposition that not only provides a feasible implementation of dilation but also requires the minimum amount of computation on the implementation. In this paper, we defined cost function, which represents the total amount of computation or time required to perform a sequence of dilations by the structuring elements in a decomposition. By minimizing the cost functions representing the different optimal criteria for different implementations, the optimal decompositions for different cases can be obtained.

This paper is organized as follows. In Section 2, the terminologies and notations on 3D digital geometry are provided, and a digital convex polyhedron which is also a 3D convex structuring element is defined. In Section 3, we present the conditions for the decomposition of a digital convex polyhedron into the set of basis convex polyhedra. In Section 4, we propose the new technique for the neighborhood decomposition of 3D convex structuring element and show example decompositions. Finally, Section 5 presents our conclusion

2 Preliminaries

In this section, the geometrical terms on 3D Euclidean space are introduced, and their 3D digital counterparts are analogously defined. In the following, E^3 is the 3D Euclidean space, and Z^3 is the 3D digital space in which each component of the position vector of a point is an integer. Z^3 is the 3D image space in which an image is represented as a set of the voxels in the volume occupied by objects.

3D Euclidean hyperplane H normal to non-zero vector **d** and translation t is the set of points **x** such that $\mathbf{d}\,\mathbf{x} = t$. H divides the entire 3D Euclidean space into two half spaces. The set of points in H and the half space in the direction of -**d** forms the closed half space L with outward normal **d** and translation t. L is the set of points $\mathbf{x} \in E^3$ such that $\mathbf{d}\,\mathbf{x} \leq t$. If closed convex set $K \subset E^3$ exists only in L and $H \cap K \neq \emptyset$, then H is called a supporting hyperplane of K with outward normal **d**, and L is called the supporting half space of K with outward normal **d**. The closed bounded set K is called a convex polyhedron if it can be represented as the intersection of the set of closed half spaces.

The geometrical terms on 3D digital space is defined as follows. First, we define 26 principal directions, each of which is a non-zero 3D vector consisting of 3 components having the values of 1, -1, or 0, and they are denoted as $\mathbf{d}_i$, $i = 1, ..., 26$. Furthermore, the principal directions are categorized into type 1, 2, and 3 depending on the number of non-zero components in the vectors representing principal directions. For example, principal direction (1, 0, 0)/(1, 0, -1)/(1, 1, -1) is type 1/2/3.

The digital hyperplane normal to principal direction $\mathbf{d}_i$ and translation $t \in Z$ is the set of digital points in the analogous Euclidean hyperplane. The digital hyperplane is the set of points $\mathbf{x} \in Z^3$ such that $\mathbf{d}_i \mathbf{x} = t$. Note that a digital hyperplane sweeps the whole digital space while $t \in Z$ varies from minus infinity to plus infinity. Also, the digital half space with outward normal principal direction $\mathbf{d}_i$ and translation $t \in Z$ is the set of digital points in analogous Euclidean half space. Similarly, digital supporting half space and hyperplane are the sets of points in the analogous Euclidean counterparts.

3D chain code directions are defined on each of 26 hyperplanes with outward normal $\mathbf{d}_i$. 8/6/4 chain code directions are defined on type 1/2/3 hyperplanes, and they are ordered in clockwise sense by their orientations. The j th chain code directions on the hyperplane with outward normal $\mathbf{d}_i$ are denoted as $D_{(i,j)}$. See Fig. 1 for the examples of the chain code directions. The sets of the voxels covered by polygons A, B, and C forms the faces. The principal directions of the faces shown are $\mathbf{d}_1 = (0, 0, 1)$, $\mathbf{d}_{13} = (1, 0, -1)$, and $\mathbf{d}_{19} = (1, 1, 1)$. The face denoted as A/B/C is type 1/2/3 face. The set of arrows on each face represents the chain code directions on the face. The chain code directions are denoted as $D_{(i,1)}, D_{(i,2)},..., D_{(i,m)}$ in a clockwise sense starting with the directions marked with *. The number of chain code directions defined on type 1/2/3 face is 8/4/6.

The digital face of a set of points $S \subset Z^3$ with outward normal principal direction $\mathbf{d}_i$, denoted as $F(S, \mathbf{d}_i)$, is the set of the points shared by both S and the digital supporting hyperplane of S with outward normal $\mathbf{d}_i$. The digital half spaces, hyperplanes, and faces are also categorized into type 1, 2, and 3 depending on their outward normal principal directions.

The set of digital points $P \subset Z^3$ is called a digital convex polyhedron (DCPH), which is also a 3D convex structuring element, if P satisfies the following two conditions.

i) P is the intersection of 26 digital half spaces with outward normal principal direction $\mathbf{d}_i = 1, ..., 26$

ii) The boundary of each face of P, $F(P, \mathbf{d}_i)$, where $i = 1, ..., 26$, can be represented with a chain code in the form of

$$D^{l_1}_{(i,1)}D^{l_2}_{(i,2)}...D^{l_m}_{(i,m)}, \qquad (1)$$

where l_j represents the number of repetition of chain code $D_{(i,j)}$ and $m = 8/4/6$ for $\mathbf{d}_i$ of type 1/2/3 direction.

Fig. 1 shows an example of a DCPH. Since a DCPH is the intersection of 26 digital supporting half space, it is bounded by 26 digital supporting hyperplane and enclosed by 26 faces. The face with outward normal principal direction $\mathbf{d}_i$ of DCPH P, represented as F(P, $\mathbf{d}_i$), is a digital convex polygon on the supporting hyperplane of the DCPH with outward normal $\mathbf{d}_i$. A line segment or a vertex can be regarded as a degenerate form of a face.

The jth edge of the face with outward normal principal direction $\mathbf{d}_i$ on DCPH, denoted as E(P, $\mathbf{d}_i$, j), is the set of points corresponding to the chain code run of $D_{(i,j)}$ in the boundary chain code of the face including the starting and ending points of the chain code run. Furthermore, |E(P, $\mathbf{d}_i$, j)| denotes the length of digital edge E(P, $\mathbf{d}_i$, j). i.e. |E(P, $\mathbf{d}_i$, j)| = l_j, where $D^{l_1}_{(i,1)}D^{l_2}_{(i,2)}...D^{l_j}_{(i,j)}...D^{l_m}_{(i,m)}$ is the chain code representation of the boundary of P.

3 Decompositions of 3D Digital Convex Polyhedrons

In this section, decomposition condition of a DCPH is derived. First, the condition for a DCPH to be decomposed into two basis DCPH's is derived in terms of their faces, each of which in turn forms a digital convex polygon. Then the relationships of the faces are further converted into the relationships on the lengths of edges in each face. We ignore the positions of DCPH's in the discussion of decomposition and only consider the shapes of DCPH's. The considerations on the position will be added later.

Suppose $P = Q \oplus R$, where P, Q, and R are DCPH's. Consider the i th face of P and the i th faces of Q and R, where the i th face of DCPH A denotes the face of A outward normal $\mathbf{d}_i$. If we further suppose that the i th face of Q consists of the subset of the points on the hyperplane with outward normal principal direction $\mathbf{d}_i$ with translation t_q, then the points $\mathbf{u}$ on the face satisfies $\mathbf{d}_i \mathbf{u} = t_q$, where $\mathbf{u} = (x_u, y_u, z_u)$ denotes a digital point. Similarly, for the points $\mathbf{v}$ on the i th face of R, $\mathbf{d}_i \mathbf{v} = t_r$. Since the dilation of two sets are defined as the set of the vector sums between the elements from each sets, the dilation of the i th faces of Q and R consists of only the points $\mathbf{w}$ such that $\mathbf{d}_i \mathbf{w} = t_q + t_r$. Furthermore, $\mathbf{d}_i \mathbf{x} \leq t_q + t_r$ for the points $\mathbf{x} \in Q \oplus R$, and the dilation of the i th faces of Q and R is on the supporting hyperplane with outward normal principal direction $\mathbf{d}_i$ and translation $t_q + t_r$, Therefore, the i th face of $Q \oplus R$ is equivalent to the i th face of P, and

$$F(P, \mathbf{d}_i) = F(Q, \mathbf{d}_i) \oplus F(R, \mathbf{d}_i) \qquad (2)$$

for $i = 1, ..., 26$.

(2) is only a necessary condition for decomposition. It is not a sufficient condition since the dilations of some combinations of DCPH's result in the images shaped like a DCPH but with holes inside.

Since each face of a DCPH forms a digital convex polygon on a hyperplane, the condition for F(P, $\mathbf{d}_i$) to be decomposed into F(Q, $\mathbf{d}_i$) and F(R, $\mathbf{d}_i$) can be represented in terms of the lengths of the edges of the faces as follows.

$$|E(P, \mathbf{d}_i, j)| = |E(Q, \mathbf{d}_i, j)| + |E(R, \mathbf{d}_i, j)| \qquad (3)$$

for $j = 1, \ldots, m$ and $m = 8/4/6$ for $\mathbf{d}_i$ of type 1/2/3 direction. The decomposition condition for a convex polygon to be decomposed into two basis convex polygon can be proved similarly to the case of a convex polyhedron. In [8] and [9], such decomposition condition is exploited to decompose 2D convex structuring elements. In case of type 1 faces, the dilation of the two images shaped as diagonal line segments in different directions results in a rhombus-shaped image with holes inside and such an image is not a face of a DCPH. The condition to prevent the decomposition with such combinations of diagonal line segments is added in the case of type 1 faces.

4 Decomposition of Convex Structuring Element into Neighborhood Structuring Elements

The decomposition condition of a DCPH can be extended to a linear combination form. The condition for DCPH P to be decomposed into the combination of $a_1 Q_1$'s, $a_2 Q_2$'s, $\ldots$, $a_n Q_n$'s as

$$P = a_1 Q_1 \oplus a_2 Q_2 \oplus \ldots \oplus a_n Q_n, \qquad (4)$$

where P, $Q_1, Q_2, \ldots$, and Q_k are DCPH's, and $a_k Q_k$ represents a_k-fold dilation of Q_k, is

$$|E(P, \mathbf{d}_i, j)| = a_1 |E(Q_1, \mathbf{d}_i, j)| + a_2 |E(Q_2, \mathbf{d}_i, j)| + \ldots + a_n |E(Q_n, \mathbf{d}_i, j)| \qquad (5)$$

for $i = 1, \ldots, 26$, $j = 1, \ldots, m$, and $m = 8/4/6$ for $\mathbf{d}_i$ of type 1/2/3 direction. Also, in the case of type 1 principal directions, the condition to prevent the decomposition with the combination of only diagonal line segment shaped images in different orientations is added in the case of type 1 faces. The above condition is called boundary condition for decomposition.

However, the dilations of some combinations of DCPH's result in convex shaped volumes with holes inside. For example, the dilation of two DCPH's each consisting of the set of the points on a hyperplane with outward normal principal directions (1, 1, 1) and (1, -1, 1) does not results in a DCPH but a convex shaped volume with holes inside. To prevent such a combination in a decomposition, a condition on the connectivity of voxels is added as follows. First, a DCPH is defined to be f-connected if two of the voxels in the DCPH share a face. Then the connectivity condition is that at least one f-connected DCPH should be included in the decomposition of an f-connected DCPH. For an f-connected DCPH, the boundary condition along with the connectivity condition serves as necessary and sufficient conditions for the DCPH to be composed into a set of basis DCPH's. For a DCPH which is not f-connected, the connectivity condition is not necessary.

Finally, the positions of DCPH's in a decomposition is considered. Suppose A, B, and C to be the sets of 3D digital points such that $C = A \oplus B$. Then $\min_x(C) = \min_x(A) + \min_x(B)$, where $\min_x(C)$ denotes the minimum x-coordinate of the volume occupied by C, and similarly for y- and z-coordinates. Thus, if $P = a_1 Q_1 \oplus a_2 Q_2 \oplus \ldots \oplus a_n Q_n$, then $\min_x(P) = a_1 \min_x(Q_1) + a_2 \min_x(Q_2) + \ldots + a_n \min_x(Q_n)$, and similarly for y- and z-coordinates.

Since the boundary, position, and edge conditions are the necessary and sufficient conditions for decomposition, the n-tuple $(a_1, a_2, ..., a_n)$ which satisfies the three conditions decides a decomposition of DCPH P into the set of bases $\{Q_1, Q_2, ..., Q_n\}$, and the solution space of the n-tuples satisfying the three conditions contains all the possible decompositions of P into the set of bases.

The decomposition conditions for DCPH presented in the above can be immediately applied to the decomposition of a 3D convex structuring element into a set of 3D neighborhood structuring elements. A neighborhood structuring element is a 3D convex structuring element which can be contained in the window of size 3×3×3 centered on the origin. There are altogether 16,678 neighborhood structuring elements (B_1, B_2..., B_{16678}).

A cost function which represents the total processing cost or time required to perform the sequence of dilation operations with structuring elements of a_1 Q_1's, a_2 Q_2's, ..., a_n Q_n's can be formulated as

$$\sum_{k=1}^{n} a_k c_k, \qquad (6)$$

where c_k is the processing cost to perform a dilation operation with structuring element Q_k with an input image. Generally, it is reasonable to assign a constant cost to each structuring element since the processing time for a dilation operation does not depend on the contents of an input image but on the size. A cost function can be used to represent the optimal criterion of decomposition for different implementation methods of dilation operation. The optimal decomposition for a particular implementation of dilation is the one that minimizes the computation time or cost to perform dilation by the implementation, and different optimal decompositions can be obtained for different implementation methods.

On a general-purpose computer with single CPU, dilation can be performed by ORing the set of translated input images. In this case, the cost to perform a dilation operation with a structuring element is proportional to the number of the OR operations required to perform the dilation operation, which is equal to the number of the origin voxel's 26 neighbors having value 1 in the structuring element. In case of parallel processing architectures, different optimal decomposition criteria can be obtained according to the modes of parallelism that the architectures exploit.

The solution n-tuple that minimizes a cost function and satisfies the three decomposition conditions at the same time can be found by linear integer programming technique[11]. The objective function to be minimized is a cost function representing the optimal criterion for an implementation method of dilation operation. The constraints of the linear integer programming are the set of linear integer equations generated by the three decomposition conditions involving the original structuring element and the set of bases.

The optimal decompositions of example convex structuring elements in Fig.1 and 2 for general-purpose computers are shown in Table 2. 3D neighborhood structuring elements in the decompositions are listed in Table 1. Also, in Table 2, the costs for performing dilations with the sequence of the structuring elements in the optimal neighborhood decompositions are compared to the costs with the original structuring elements.

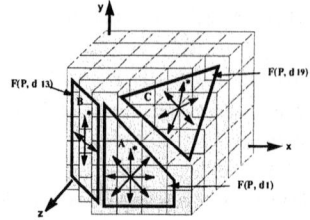

Fig. 1. Example DCPH P and chain code directions on some faces

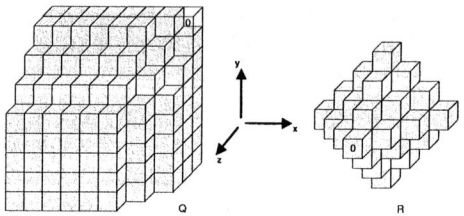

Fig. 2. Example DCPH Q and R. The arrows represent x, y, z directions and the voxels marked with 0 represent the origins.

Table 1. Neighborhood structuring elements used for the optimal neighborhood decomposition. Each matrix shows a slice of a structuring element on a plane $z = i$. The y/x-coordinate of the first row/column of each matrix is 1, the second 0, and the third -1.

	B_2	B_{30}	B_{34}	B_{42}	B_{190}	B_{281}	B_{294}	B_{480}	B_{931}	B_{1646}
plane $z = 1$	0 0 0 0 0 0 0 0 0	0 0 0 0 0 0 0 0 0	0 0 0 0 0 0 0 0 0	0 0 0 0 0 0 0 0 0	0 0 0 0 0 1 0 0 0	0 0 0 1 0 0 0 0 0	0 0 0 1 0 0 0 0 0	0 1 0 0 1 1 0 0 0	0 0 0 0 0 0 0 1 0	0 0 0 0 0 0 0 0 0
plane $z = 0$	0 0 0 0 0 0 0 1 0	0 0 0 0 1 0 0 1 0	0 1 0 0 1 0 0 0 0	0 0 0 1 1 0 0 0 0	0 0 0 0 1 1 0 0 0	0 0 0 1 1 0 0 0 0	1 0 0 1 1 0 0 0 0	0 1 1 0 1 1 0 0 0	0 0 0 0 1 0 0 1 0	0 0 0 0 1 0 0 0 0
plane $z = -1$	0 0 0 0 0 0 0 0 0	0 0 0 0 0 0 0 0 0	0 0 0 0 0 0 0 0 0	0 0 0 0 0 0 0 0 0	0 0 0 0 0 0 0 0 0	0 0 0 0 0 0 0 0 0	0 0 0 0 0 0 0 0 0	0 0 0 0 0 0 0 0 0	0 0 0 0 0 0 0 0 0	0 1 0 1 1 1 0 1 0

Table 2. Optimal neighborhood decompositions of P, Q, R and the comparison of the number of OR operations required to perform dilation

	Optimal Decomposition	Original	Decomposition
P	$2B_{34} \oplus 2B_{190} \oplus 3B_{480}$	124 ORs	24 ORs
Q	$3B_{1646} B_2 \oplus 4B_{30} \oplus 5B_{42} \oplus B_{281} \oplus B_{294} \oplus 2B_{931}$	258 ORs	19 ORs
R	$3B_{1646}$	43 ORs	15 ORs

5 Conclusion

In this paper, a new method to decompose 3D convex structuring element used in morphological operation is proposed. First, the decomposition condition for digital convex polyhedron is derived in terms of the length of edges of original and basis convex polyhedrons. The condition is applied to the decomposition of a convex structuring element into the set of neighborhood structuring elements. Furthermore, we defined cost function to represent the different optimal criteria on the decomposition for different implementations of morphological operations. The optimal decompositions which satisfy the decomposition condition and minimize the cost function at the same time can be found by linear integer programming. Thanks to the cost function, our method can be used to obtain different optimal neighborhood decompositions for different cases.

References

1. Serra, J.: Introduction to Mathematical Morphology. Computer Vision, Graphics and Image Processing 35 (1986) 285-305
2. Serra, J.: Image Analysis and Mathematical Morphology. Academic Press London(1982)
3. Haralick, R. M., Sternberg, S.R., Zhuang, X.: Image Analysis Using Mathematical Morphology. IEEE Trans. on PAMI 9 (1987) 532-550
4. Zhuang, X., Haralick, R. M.: Morphological Structuring Element Decomposition. Computer Vision, Graphics and Image Processing 35 (1986) 370-382
5. Dadda, L.; Parallel algorithms and architectures for CPUs and dedicated processors: development and trends Algorithms and Architectures for Parallel Processing ICAPP 95 vol. 2 (1995) 939 - 948
6. Svolos, A.I.; Konstantopoulos, C.G.; Kaklamanis, C.: Efficient Binary Morphological Algorithms on a Massively Parallel Processor. International Parallel and Distributed Processing Symposium 2000 Proceedings (2000) 281 - 286
7. York, G., Managuli, R., Kim, Y.: Fast Binary and Grayscale Mathematical Morphology on VLIW. Proc. Of SPIE: Real-Time Imaging IV (1999) 45–55
8. Levialdi, S.: Computer Architectures for Image Analysis. 9th International Conference on Pattern Recognition vol.2 (1988) 1148 - 1158
9. Xu, J.: Decomposition of Convex Polygonal Morphological Structuring Elements into Neighborhood Subsets. IEEE Trans. on PAMI 13 (1991) 153-162.
10. Park, H., Chin, R.T,: Optimal Decomposition of Convex Morphological Structuring Elements for 4-connected Parallel Array Processors. IEEE Trans. on PAMI 16 (1994) 304-313
11. Aykac, D., Hoffman, E.A., McLennan, G., Reinhardt, J.M.: Segmentation and analysis of the human airway tree from three-dimensional X-ray CT images., IEEE Transactions on Medical Imaging **22** (2003) 940 - 950
12. Syslo, M. M., Deo, N., Kowalik, J. S.: Discrete Optimization Algorithms. Prentice Hall Englewood Cliff (1983)

Domain Knowledge Extension with Pictorially Enriched Ontologies

M. Bertini[1], R. Cucchiara[2], A. Del Bimbo[1], and C. Torniai[1]

[1] D.S.I. - Università di Firenze - Italy
[2] D.I.I. - Università di Modena e Reggio Emilia - Italy

Abstract. Classifying video elements according to some pre-defined ontology of the video content is the typical way to perform video annotation. Ontologies are built by defining relationship between linguistic terms that describe domain concepts at different abstraction levels. Linguistic terms are appropriate to distinguish specific events and object categories but they are inadequate when they must describe video entities or specific patterns of events. In these cases visual prototypes can better express pattern specifications and the diversity of visual events. To support video annotation up to the level of pattern specification enriched ontologies, that include *visual concepts* together with linguistic keywords, are needed. This paper presents *Pictorially Enriched ontologies* and provides a solution for their implementation in the soccer video domain. The pictorially enriched ontology created is used both to directly assign multimedia objects to concepts, providing a more meaningful definition than the linguistics terms, and to extend the initial knowledge of the domain, adding subclasses of highlights or new highlight classes that were not defined in the linguistic ontology. Automatic annotation of soccer clips up to the pattern specification level using a pictorially enriched ontology is discussed.

1 Introduction

Semantic annotation of video content is performed by using appropriate domain-specific ontologies that model the video content domain. Ontologies are formal, explicit specifications of the knowledge domain: they consist of concepts, concept properties, and relationships between concepts. Ontologies typically represent concepts by linguistic terms. However, also multimedia ontologies can be created, that assign multimedia objects to concepts.

Standard description languages for the expression of concepts and relationships in domain ontologies have been defined, like Resource Description Framework (RDF) [1], Resource Description Framework Schema (RDFS) and the XML Schema in MPEG-7. In this way metadata can be tailored to specific domains and purposes, yet still remaining interoperable and capable of being accessed by standard tools and search systems.

Semantic annotation is either performed manually, by associating the terms of the ontology to the individual elements of the video, or, more recently and effectively, automatically, by exploiting results and developments in Pattern Recognition and image/video analysis. In this latter case, the terms of the ontology are put in correspondence with appropriate knowledge models that encode the spatio-temporal combination of low-intermediate level features. Once these models are checked, video entities are annotated with the concepts of the ontology; in this way, for example, in the soccer sport video domain, it is possible to classify highlight events in different classes, like *shot on goal*, *counterattack*, *corner kick*, etc.

Examples of automatic semantic annotation systems have been presented recently, most of them in the application domain of sports video. Among these, in [2] MPEG motion vectors, playfield shape and players position have been used with Hidden Markov Models to detect soccer highlights. In [3], Ekin et al. have assumed that the presence of soccer highlights can be inferred from the occurrence of one or several slow motion shots and from the presence of shots where the referee and/or the goal post is framed. In [4] Finite State Machines have been employed to detect the principal soccer highlights, such as shot on goal, placed kick, forward launch and turnover, from a few visual cues. The ball trajectory has been used by Yu et al. [5] in order to detect the main actions like touching and passing and compute ball possession by each team; a Kalman filter is used to check whether a detected trajectory can be recognized as a ball trajectory. In all these systems model based event classification is not associated with any ontology-based representation of the domain. Domain specific linguistic ontology with multilingual lexicons, and possibility of cross document merging has instead been presented in [6]. In this paper, the annotation engine makes use of reasoning algorithms to automatically create a semantic annotation of soccer video sources. In [7], a hierarchy of ontologies has been defined for the representation of the results of video segmentation. Concepts are expressed in keywords and are mapped in an *object ontology*, a *shot ontology* and a *semantic ontology*. However, although linguistic terms are appropriate to distinguish event and object categories, they are inadequate when they must describe specific patterns of events or video entities. Consider for example the many different patterns in which an attack action can occur in soccer. We can easily distinguish several different subclasses that differ each other by the playfield zone, the number of players involved, the player's motion direction, the speed. Each of these subclasses specifies a specific pattern of attack action that could be expressed in linguistic terms only with a complex sentence, explaining the way in which the event has developed. Despite of the difficulty of including pattern specifications into linguistic ontologies, classification at the pattern description level is mandatory, in many real operating contexts. Think for example, in the soccer domain, of a coach that is interested in the analysis of the ways in which the attack actions of his team have developed. In this case, it is important that the highlight patterns that share similar spatio-temporal behaviours are clustered and described with one single concept that is a specialization of the attack action term in the video ontology. These requirements motivate the possibility that events that share the same patterns are represented by *visual concepts*, instead of linguistic concepts, that capture the essence of the event spatio-temporal development. In this case, high level concepts, expressed through linguistic terms, and pattern specifications represented instead through visual concepts, can be both organized into new extended ontologies, that will be referred to as *pictorially enriched ontologies*. The basic idea behind pictorially enriched ontologies is that the concepts and categories defined in a traditional ontology are not rich enough to fully describe the diversity of the plethora of visual events that normally are grouped in a same class and cannot support video annotation up to the level of detail of pattern specification. To a broader extent the idea of pictorially enriched ontologies can be extended to *multimedia enriched ontologies* where concepts that cannot be expressed in linguistic terms are represented by prototypes of different media like video, audio, etc. Visual concepts of pictorially enriched ontologies, like linguistic concepts, can be expressed in RDF, and therefore used in a search engine to perform content based retrieval from video databases or to provide video summaries. This paper discusses pictorially enriched ontologies and provide a solution for their implementation for soccer video automatic annotation of highlight patterns. The highlights detected by the annotation engine define the initial linguistic ontology. In order to distinguish specific patterns of the principal highlighs additional visual features are added to the ontology. A clustering algorithm is used to create new subclasses of highlights representing specific patterns of the event and to group the clips within highlights subclasses according to their visual features. The visual concepts of the patterns of recognized highlights are automatically obtained as the centers of the clusters in which the video clip instances of the highlight are grouped. Once detected, visual concepts are added as prototypes in the ontology, to represent visually the appearance of the pattern category and integrate the semantics described by the linguistic terms. The ontology created is used both to directly assign multimedia objects to concepts and to extend the initial knowledge of the domain, adding subclasses of highlights or new highlight classes that were not defined in the linguistic ontology. Pictorially enriched ontologies are then used to support video annotation up to very specialized levels of pattern specification. The possibility of extending linguistic ontologies with multimedia ontologies, although with a different idea, has also been suggested in [8] to support video understanding. Differently from our contribution, the authors suggest to use *modal keywords*, i.e. keywords that represent perceptual concepts in the several categories, such as visual, aural, etc. A method is presented to automatically classify keywords from speech recognition, queries or related text into these categories. Multimedia ontologies are constructed manually ([9]): text information available in videos and visual features are extracted and manually assigned to concepts, properties, or relationships in the ontology. In [10] new methods for extracting semantic knowledge from annotated images is presented. Perceptual knowledge is discovered grouping images into clusters based on their visual and text features and semantic knowledge is extracted by disambiguating the senses of words in annotations using WordNet and image clusters. In [11] a Visual Descriptors Ontology and a Multimedia Structure Ontology, based on

MPEG-7 Visual Descriptors and MPEG-7 MDS respectively, are used together with domain ontology in order to support content annotation. Visual prototypes instances are linked to the domain ontology. In this paper an improvement to this approach is proposed, including visual features in the domain ontology and using a clustering algorithm that extends the domain ontology through visual features analysis. The paper is organized as follows: in Sect. 2 we present a prototype system for automatic semantic video annotation and discuss visual feature extraction. Creation of pictorially enriched ontologies for the representation of highlight patterns are discussed in Sect. 3. In Sect. 4 we discuss the preliminary results of the proposed system applied to soccer videos. Finally in Sect. 5 we provide conclusions and some future works.

2 Soccer Highlight Automatic Video Annotation

The annotation system performs semantic annotation of MPEG videos, by detecting attack actions and placed kicks and whether or not they are terminated with a shot on goal. Highlights are detected by using a limited set of visual features that are extracted respectively: *i)* from the compressed domain: motion vectors (used to calculate indexes of camera motion direction and intensity); YUV color components (used to extract and evaluate the playfield shape that is framed); *ii)* from the uncompressed domain (uncompressed I and P frames): the ratio between the pixels of the players of the two teams (by exploiting the a-priori knowledge of team colors); the playfield lines filtered out on the basis of their length and orientation (used to recognize the playfield zone that is framed). Frames are classified as close-, medium- and long-view, depending on the image-playfield ratio; long-view frames are further distinguished into left, central and right part of the playfield. Evidences and inferences of highlights are computed for each MPEG GOP (typically 12 frames, about 1/2 second in PAL video standard). Four Bayes networks are used to predict highlights: two networks are used to predict (left, right) attack actions and two networks to predict (left, right)placed kicks. If the highlight is predicted, in the following 6 seconds (12 GOPs) the video is processed by two different Bayesian validation networks that check the presence of a shot on goal. Conditional probabilities are updated every 2 secs.

The system has been tested on MPEG-1 and MPEG-2 videos recorded at 25 frames per second (PAL standard) and with a resolution of 360 × 288 and 720 × 576, respectively. 268 case examples (∼ 90 min) collected from World Championship 2002 and European Championship 2004 have been used to test the annotation system; the test set was composed by:

- 172 highlights that have been concluded with a shot on goal (SOG): 134 attack actions (AA) and 38 Placed kicks (PK)
- 54 highlights that have not been concluded with a shot on goal (NSOG): 51 attack actions and 3 Placed kicks
- 42 Other Actions (OA)

Figures of precision and recall that have been measured over the test set are reported in Table 2.

Table 1. Performance figures of the highlight annotation engine for Attack Action (AA), Placed Kick (PK), Shot on Goal (SOG), Not Shot on Goal (NSOG) and Other action (OA)

Highlight	Precision	Recall
AA	0.98	0.88
PK	0.63	0.91
SOG	0.96	0.88
NSOG	0.74	0.80
OA	0.77	0.95

Table 2. Precision and recall of clip clustering

Cluster	Elements	Relevant	Non rel.	Precision	Recall
1	6 (15%)	5	1	0.83	0.83
2	4 (10%)	4	0	1	0.8
3	6 (15%)	5	1	0.83	0.83
4	11 (28%)	9	2	0.82	0.9
5	4 (10%)	4	0	1	0.8
6	2 (5%)	1	1	0.5	1
7	6 (15%)	5	1	0.83	1
8	1 (3%)	1	0	1	0.5

3 Pictorially Enriched Ontologies

The linguistic ontology (see Fig. 1) is composed by the video and clip classes, the actions class and its highlights subclasses and an object class with its related subclasses describing different objects within the clips. Highlights, players and playground objects that are recognized by the annotation engine are associated with the concepts of the linguistic ontology.

In order to distinguish the specific patterns of the principal highlights detected by the annotation engine we use 6 additional visual features that are not per se useful for highlight classification but have instead enough discriminatory power to distinguish highlight sub-classes:

- the playfield area;
- the number of players in the upper part of the playfield;
- the number of players lower part of the playfield;
- the motion intensity;
- the motion direction;
- the motion acceleration.

In more detail, the playfield area is divided in twelve zones, using playfield lines and shape (see [4]). The estimation of the number of players in the upper and lower portion of the playfield (according to the playfield area that is framed) is obtained by applying a template matching of players' blobs; motion

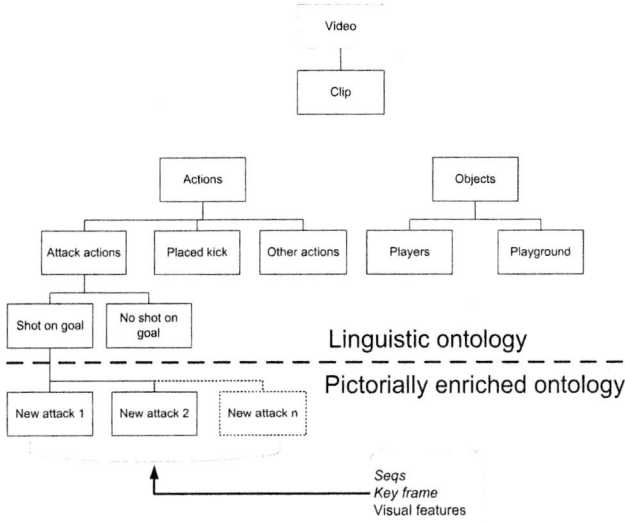

Fig. 1. Pictorially enriched ontology

intensity and direction are extracted as described in Sect. 2; camera acceleration is computed from motion data. For each clip we create a feature vector V of 6 distinct components, each of which is a vector U that contains the changes within the clip of one feature. The length of feature vectors U may be different in different clips, depending on the duration and content of the clips. Vectors U are quantized, and smoothed to eliminate possible outliers. Prototypes of the highlight patterns are obtained by clustering vectors V and taking the centers of the clusters as representatives of the patterns. They are regarded as visual concepts that visually represent the specific development pattern of the highlight. Pictorially enriched ontologies are hence created by adding the prototype clip as a specialization of the linguistic concept that describes the highlight. Visual concepts in the pictorially enriched ontology are *abstractions* of video elements and can be of different types:

- *Seqs*: the clip at the center of the cluster;
- keyframes: the key frame of the clip at the center of the cluster;
- *regions*: parts of the keyframe e.g. representing players;
- *visual features*: e.g. trajectories, motion fields, computed from image data...

Different visual concepts can be added, incrementally, as specializations of each highlight class so as to account for the visual diversity of the highlight patterns. As a new clip is presented to the annotation system, the clustering process determines whether it belongs to existing clusters or if a new cluster must be generated. We have employed the fuzzy c-means (FCM) clustering algorithm, [12], to take into account the fact that a clip could belong to a cluster, still being similar to clips of different clusters. The maximum number of clusters for each highlight has been heuristically set to 10. The distance between two different clip instances has been computed according to the Levenshtein edit distance between the U components of the feature vector V of the clips, to take into account the differences in the duration and the temporal changes of the feature values. The clustering process generates the pictorially enriched ontology providing the creation of subclasses for each highlight and the creation of new highlight classes that were not defined in the initial linguistic ontology as well as the visual concepts related to each class and subclass including the visual features in the ontology. At the same time annotation of clips up to the pattern specification level is achieved by grouping clips in highlight subclasses that represent a specific visual concept.

4 Experimental Results

We have performed experiments of automatic generation of pictorially enriched ontologies from video clips of soccer highlights that are automatically annotated. We have employed 40 video sequences taken from the latest Soccer World Championship. Each sequence contains number of clips variable from 3 to 8, for a total number of 258 clips. Each clip has been automatically annotated. We have focused on attack action highlights that can be terminated with a shot on goal, in that they present the largest variability of highlight patterns. Each time that a new clip is analyzed, according to the fuzzy C mean clustering algorithm, the system checks whether to assign it to an existing visual concept (the center of the clusters already detected) or if a new visual concept has to be added as a new subclass of the attack action highlight (a cluster splitting is needed).

The generation of visual concepts that represent prototypes of highlight patterns has been analyzed by comparing the results obtained with the manual classification of the same highlight patterns by three human testers. Precision and recall for each cluster are reported in Table 2 where clips are considered as non relevant if they have not been assigned to the cluster by human testers. Differences in the clustering between the system and human testers are in that cluster 6 contains 2 clips that should have been split instead into two classes of 1 clip each. Similarly, cluster 8 has only 1 clip instead of 2.

Average values of precision and recall calculated over all the clusters are 0.85 and 0.83, respectively. Fig. 2 shows an example of clip clustering. We have put into evidence the clip that has been chosen as the visual concept of the highlight pattern represented by the cluster (cluster 2 of table 2), two other clips of the cluster and one clip (enclosed in the rounded rectangle) that should have been associated with the cluster but was instead assigned to a different cluster.

5 Conclusions

This paper presents pictorially enriched ontologies as an extension of linguistic domain ontologies with visual features and provides a solution for their implementation in soccer video domain. A clustering algorithm has been proposed in

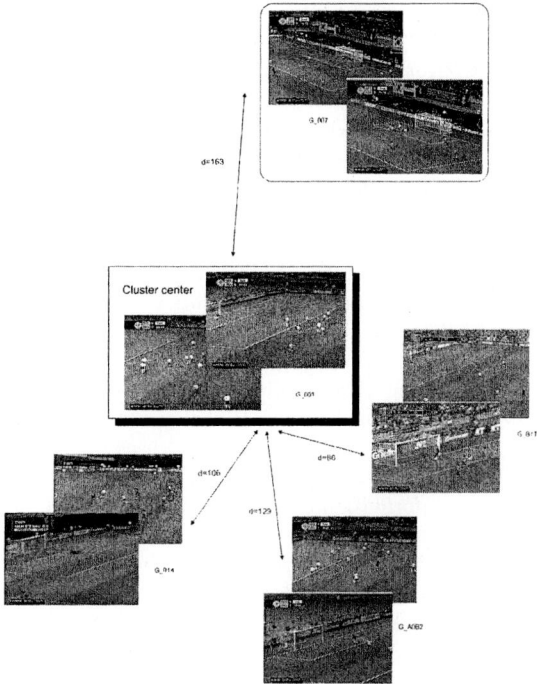

Fig. 2. Cluster 2 with its prototype clip (the cluster center), three clips of the cluster and one clip (enclosed in the rounded rectangle) that has been associated with a different cluster although it should belong to cluster 2. Distances w.r.t. the cluster center are indicated.

order to create new subclasses of highlights representing specific patterns of the events and to group the clips within highlights subclasses according to their visual features. Results for automatic generation of pictorially enriched ontologies have been presented in terms of precision and recall for each highlights subclasses generated by our prototype. Experiments have shown that with pictorially enriched ontologies it is possible to extend the initial knowledge of the domain, adding subclasses of highlights or new highlight classes that were not defined in the linguistic ontology, and support automatic clips annotation up to the level of detail of pattern specification. Directions for future works are improving visual features and metrics for clustering and introducing reasoning for subclass creation and ontology enrichment.

Acknowledgment. This work is partially supported by the Information Society Technologies (IST) Program of the European Commission as part of the DELOS Network of Excellence on Digital Libraries (Contract G038-507618).

References

1. World Wide Web Consortium, "Resource description framework (rdf)," Tech. Rep., W3C, http://www.w3.org/RDF/, Feb 2004.
2. R. Leonardi and P. Migliorati, "Semantic indexing of multimedia documents," *IEEE Multimedia*, vol. 9, no. 2, pp. 44–51, April-June 2002.
3. A. Ekin, A. Murat Tekalp, and R. Mehrotra, "Automatic soccer video analysis and summarization," *IEEE Transactions on Image Processing*, vol. 12, no. 7, pp. 796–807, July 2003.
4. J. Assfalg, M. Bertini, C. Colombo, A. Del Bimbo, and W. Nunziati, "Semantic annotation of soccer videos: automatic highlights identification," *Computer Vision and Image Understanding*, vol. 92, no. 2-3, pp. 285–305, November-December 2003.
5. X.Yu, C. Xu, H.W. Leung, Q. Tian, Q. Tang, and K. W. Wan, "Trajectory-based ball detection and tracking with applications to semantic analysis of broadcast soccer video," in *ACM Multimedia 2003*, Berkeley, CA (USA), 4-6 Nov. 2003 2003, vol. 3, pp. 11–20.
6. D. Reidsma, J. Kuper, T. Declerck, H. Saggion, and H. Cunningham, "Cross document ontology based information extraction for multimedia retrieval," in *Supplementary proceedings of the ICCS03*, Dresden, July 2003.
7. V. Mezaris, I. Kompatsiaris, N.V. Boulgouris, and M.G. Strintzis, "Real-time compressed-domain spatiotemporal segmentation and ontologies for video indexing and retrieval," *IEEE Transactions on Circuits and Systems for Video Technology*, vol. 14, no. 5, pp. 606–621, 2004.
8. A. Jaimes, B. Tseng, and J.R. Smith, "Modal keywords, ontologies, and reasoning for video understanding," in *International Conference on Image and Video Retrieval (CIVR 2003)*, July 2003.
9. A. Jaimes and J.R. Smith, "Semi-automatic, data-driven construction of multimedia ontologies," in *Proc. of IEEE Int'l Conference on Multimedia & Expo*, 2003.
10. Ana B. Benitez and Shih-Fu Chang "Automatic multimedia knowledge discovery, summarization and evaluation," *IEEE Transactions on Multimedia, Submitted*, 2003.
11. M. G. Strintzis S. Bloehdorn S. Handschuh S. Staab N. Simou V. Tzouvaras K. Petridis, I. Kompatsiaris and Y. Avrithis, "Knowledge representation for semantic multimedia content analysis and reasoning," in *European Workshop on the Integration of Knowledge, Semantics and Digital Media Technology*, November 2004.
12. J.C. Bezdek, *Pattern Recognition with Fuzzy Objective Function Algorithms*, Plenum Press, New York, 1981.

Segmentation via Graph-Spectral Methods and Riemannian Geometry

Antonio Robles-Kelly[1,2]

[1] NICTA, Locked Bag 8001, Canberra ACT 2601, Australia
[2] RSISE, Building 115, ANU, Canberra ACT 0200, Australia
[1]antonio.robles-kelly@nicta.com.au
[2]antonio.robles-kelly@anu.edu.au

Abstract. In this paper, we describe the use of graph-spectral techniques and their relationship to Riemannian geometry for the purposes of segmentation and grouping. We pose the problem of segmenting a set of tokens as that of partitioning the set of nodes in a graph whose edge weights are given by the geodesic distances between points in a manifold. To do this, we commence by explaining the relationship between the graph Laplacian, the incidence mapping of the graph and a Gram matrix of scalar products. This treatment permits the recovery of the embedding coordinates in a closed form and opens up the possibility of improving the segmentation results by modifying the metric of the space in which the manifold is defined. With the set of embedding coordinates at hand, we find the partition of the embedding space which maximises both, the inter-cluster distance and the intra-cluster affinity. The utility of the method for purposes of grouping is illustrated on a set of shape silhouettes.

1 Introduction

Many problems in computer vision can be posed as ones of pairwise clustering. That is to say, they involve grouping objects together based on their mutual similarity rather than their closeness to a cluster prototype. Such problems naturally lend themselves to a graph-theoretic treatment in which the objects to be clustered are represented using a weighted graph. Here the nodes represent the objects to be clustered and the edge-weights represent the strength of pairwise similarity relations between them.

One of the most elegant solutions to the pairwise clustering problem comes from spectral graph theory, i.e. the characterisation of the eigenpairs of the graph Laplacian and the adjacency matrix. Along these lines, some of the earliest work was done by Scott and Longuet-Higgins [11] who developed a method for refining the block-structure of the affinity matrix by relocating its eigenvectors. In a related development, Sarkar and Boyer [10] presented a spectral method which locates clusters that maximise the average association. Perona and Freeman [8] have a similar method which uses the second largest eigenvector of the affinity matrix. The method of Shi and Malik [12], on the other hand, uses the normalised cut, which balances the cut and the association.

Whereas eigenvectors have been traditionally viewed in combinatorial terms from the characteristic polynomial perspective, its relationship with eigenfunction expansions in differential geometry has been often overlooked for the purposes of segmentation and grouping. Nonetheless, there has recently been renewed interest in the use of manifold learning theory for the purposes of graph embedding [9, 6], classification [1] and visualisation [13].

In this paper, we draw on the field of mathematics known as spectral geometry, which aims to characterise the properties of operators on Riemannian manifolds using the eigenvalues and eigenvectors of the Laplacian matrix [3]. We commence by viewing the weight for the edge between each pair of nodes as a squared distance in a Euclidean space. Viewed in this way, the graph Laplacian can be related to a Gram matrix of scalar products. This, in turn, allows the use of matrix factorisation techniques to recover the coordinates for the embedding of the nodes in the graph into a metric space. With the embedding coordinates at hand, the clustering process is posed as a recursive partition of the space based upon a set of functions which bisect the embedding so as to minimise the distance between members of the same cluster and maximise the distance between elements of different clusters.

2 Clustering via Graph Embedding

We cast the problem of clustering into a graph-theoretic setting where the set of objects to be clustered are abstracted using a weighted graph. The problem is characterised by the set of nodes V that represent the objects and the set of edge weights, which are the affinities or "distances" between them. Viewed in this way, the goal of computation is then to partition the weighted graph $G = (V, E, W)$, with index-set V, edge-set $E = \{(v,w)|(v,w) \in V \times V, v \neq w\}$ and edge-weight function set $W : E \to [0, 1]$, into disjoint and disconnected subgraphs. Since the aim is to recover disconnected subgraphs, we can perform a recursive bipartition of the node-set V. In this section, we motivate the relationship between the graph Laplacian, the incidence mapping and the embedding of graphs into metric spaces. This treatment leads naturally to the clustering, as presented in the next section, via the sign of a vector of cluster membership functions.

To commence, we note that the weight matrix W is related to the normalised Laplacian $\mathcal{L} = \boldsymbol{D}^{-\frac{1}{2}}(\boldsymbol{D} - W)\boldsymbol{D}^{-\frac{1}{2}} = \boldsymbol{I} - \boldsymbol{D}^{-\frac{1}{2}}\mathcal{L}\boldsymbol{D}^{-\frac{1}{2}}$, where $\boldsymbol{D}$ is a diagonal matrix such that $\boldsymbol{D} = diag(deg(1), deg(2), \ldots, deg(|V|))$. Consider the mapping $\mathcal{I}$ of all functions over the set of vertices V to the functions $g(e)$ over the set of edges E. The incidence mapping $\mathcal{I}$ is then an operator such that $\mathcal{I}g(e) = f(e_+) - f(e_-)$, where the nodes $v = e_+$ and $w = e_-$ are the head and tail, respectively, of the edge $e \in E$. As a result, $\mathcal{I}$ is a $|V| \times |E|$ matrix which satisfies

$$\mathcal{L} = \mathcal{I}\mathcal{I}^T \tag{1}$$

The expression in Equation 1 opens-up the possibility of relating the graph Laplacian $\mathcal{L}$ to a matrix $\mathbf{H} = \mathbf{JJ}^T$, which can then be viewed as a matrix of scalar products. We view the scalar products as the sums of squared, geodesic pairwise distances on a manifold. Hence, the problem of embedding the graph reduces itself to that of finding the coordinates that satisfy, in an optimum manner, a set of known scalar products. We solve the problem in two stages. First, we find the matrix $\mathbf{H} = \mathbf{JJ}^T$, which is the matrix of pairwise sums of squares and scalar products. Second, we factorise it to find J.

With this in mind, we write the matrix H in terms of the graph Laplacian $\mathcal{L}$ as follows

$$\mathbf{H} = -\frac{1}{2}\mathbf{B}\mathcal{L}\mathbf{B} \qquad (2)$$

Further, by introducing the vector **c**, whose entries are the diagonal elements of $\mathbf{JJ}^T$, and the all-ones vector **e**, i.e. a vector whose coefficients are all unity, into the equation above, we can write

$$\mathbf{H} = -\frac{1}{2}\mathbf{B}\left[\mathbf{ce}^T + \mathbf{ec}^T - 2\mathbf{JJ}^T\right]\mathbf{B} \qquad (3)$$

Note that, in order to have $\mathbf{H} = \mathbf{JJ}^T$, the vectors $(\mathbf{e}^T\mathbf{B})^T$ and $\mathbf{Be}$ must be null and $\mathbf{BJJ}^T\mathbf{B} = \mathbf{JJ}^T$. If **B** is a centering matrix, this is the case and then the matrix **H** becomes the double-centered graph Laplacian. Double centering is a standard procedure in classical scaling [14, 5] which introduces a linear dependency over the columns of the matrix **H** [2]. As a result, the element indexed v, w of the matrix **H** is given by

$$\mathbf{H}(v,w) = -\frac{1}{2}[\mathcal{L}(v,w)^2 - \mathscr{A}^2 - \mathscr{B}^2 + \mathscr{C}^2], \qquad (4)$$

where

$$\mathscr{A} = \frac{1}{|\Upsilon_v|}\sum_{w\sim v}\mathcal{L}(v,w), \quad \mathscr{B} = \frac{1}{|\Upsilon_w|}\sum_{v\sim w}\mathcal{L}(v,w), \quad \mathscr{C} = \frac{1}{|V|^2}\sum_{w,v\in V}\mathcal{L}(v,w)$$

and Υ_v is the set of first-neighbours of the node $v \in V$. From the above equations, $\mathscr{A}f(v)$ can be regarded as the average value of the functions $\mathcal{I}g(e) = f(e_+) - f(e_-)$ over those nodes w adjacent to the node v. Similarly, $\mathscr{B}f(w)$ is the average value of the functions $-\mathcal{I}g(e) = f(e_-) - f(e_+)$ over those nodes $v \sim w$. The average value over the set of functions $\mathcal{I}g$ is given by $\mathscr{C}f$.

In order to obtain a matrix of embedding coordinates **J** from the matrix **H**, we perform an eigenvector analysis on **H**. The validity of this procedure is based upon the Young-Householder factorisation theorem [15]. The Young-Householder theorem states that if **J** is of the form $\mathbf{J} = [\psi_1 \mid \psi_2 \mid \ldots \mid \psi_k]$ for all $i = 1, 2, \ldots, k$, we have $(\mathbf{JJ}^T)\phi_i = \sqrt{\lambda_i}\psi_i$, where ψ_i is the eigenvector corresponding to the ith eigenvalue λ_i.

Let ϕ_i be the ith eigenvector scaled so its sum of squares is equal to λ_i (i.e. $\phi_i = \sqrt{\lambda_i}\psi_i$). Since $\mathbf{H}\phi_i = \lambda_i\phi_i$ and $(\mathbf{JJ}^T)\phi_i = \mathbf{H}\phi_i$, it follows that $\mathbf{H} = \mathbf{JJ}^T$. As a result, the vector of coordinates $\varphi(v)$ for the node $v \in V$ is given by $\varphi(v) = [\phi_1(v) \mid \phi_2(v) \mid \ldots \mid \phi_{|V|}(v)]^T$, where the eigenvalues λ_i of the matrix **H** are arranged according to their magnitude order so as to satisfy the condition $\mid\lambda_1\mid\geq\mid\lambda_2\mid\geq\cdots\geq\mid\lambda_{|V|}\mid> 0$.

3 Partitioning of the Embedding Space

There are a number of important consequences that result from both, the double-centering operation on the graph Laplacian, and the Young-Householder theorem itself. In this section, we use the properties of the embedding to recover the cluster membership functions $x(v) : v \in V \mapsto \Re$. The cluster membership functions are such that a pair or nodes v, w belong to the ith cluster ω_i if and only if $\text{sgn}(x(v)) = \text{sgn}(x(w))$, where $\text{sgn}(\cdot)$ is the sign function. We recover the cluster membership functions as follows. Firstly, we show that the leading eigenvector of the double-centered Laplacian **H** maximises the intra-cluster affinity. We then show that the leading eigenvector of the double-centered Laplacian also minimises the inter-cluster proximity. At this point, is also worth noting that, in order to be able to recover the set of membership functions $x(v) \; \forall \; v \in V$ in a closed form and, following Fiedler [4], we impose the constraints $\sum_{v \in V} x(v) = 0$ and $\sum_{v \in V} x(v)^2 = 1$ on the elements of the vector of cluster membership functions **x**.

3.1 Maximising Intra-cluster Affinity

Recall that, in the previous section, we commenced by relating the embedding coordinates to the graph Laplacian using the matrix of scalar products $\mathbf{H} = \mathbf{JJ}^T$. As a result, the scalar product between the vectors of coordinates for the nodes v and $w \in V$ is given by

$$\langle \varphi(v), \varphi(w) \rangle = \sum_{l=1}^{|V|} \lambda_l \phi_l(v) \phi_l(w) \tag{5}$$

whereas the squared distance between the same pair of nodes is

$$\| \varphi(v) - \varphi(w) \|^2 = \sum_{l=1}^{|V|} \lambda_l (\phi_l(v) - \phi_l(w))^2 = \mathbf{H}(v,v) + \mathbf{H}(w,w) - 2\mathbf{H}(v,w) \tag{6}$$

It is also worth noting that, from Equations 5 and 6, it follows that $\langle \varphi(v), \varphi(v) \rangle \equiv 0$ for any node $v \in V$. This, in turn, implies that $\mathbf{H}(v,v) \equiv 0$.

With these ingredients, the problem of finding the functions $x(v)$ such that the distances between members of the same cluster is minimum can be viewed as that of minimising the quantity

$$\epsilon = \sum_{w_i \in \Omega} \sum_{v,w \in w_i \subset V} \|x(v)\varphi(v) - x(w)\varphi(w)\|^2 \tag{7}$$

where Ω is the set of all clusters w_i. Thus, only pairwise distances corresponding to nodes in the same cluster contribute to the quantity ϵ. To take our analysis further, we use Equation 6 and, after some algebra, write

$$\epsilon = \sum_{v,w \in V} \left(x(v)^2 \mathbf{H}(v,v) + x(w)^2 \mathbf{H}(w,w) - 2x(v)x(w)\mathbf{H}(v,w) \right) \tag{8}$$

but, since $\mathbf{H}(v,v) \equiv 0$, the equation above can be rewritten, in matrix notation, as follows

$$\epsilon = -2\mathbf{xHx} \tag{9}$$

where **x** is the vector of order $|V|$ whose i^{th} element is given by $x(v)$. Thus, minimising ϵ is equivalent to maximising $\mathbf{xHx}$ and, therefore, **x** is given by the leading eigenvector of **H**, i.e. $\mathbf{x} = \phi_1$.

3.2 Minimising Inter-cluster Proximity

Having shown that the leading eigenvector of the double-centered Laplacian **H** is the maximiser of intra-cluster affinity, we now proceed to prove that it also minimises the inter-cluster proximity. We do this by making use of Lagrange multipliers to show that the distance between the centers of mass for the clusters ω_i and ω_j is maximised when the set of nodes in the graph are partitioned using the leading eigenvector of $\mathbf{H}$. We commence by noting that the squared distance between cluster mass centers is given by

$$\rho(\omega_i, \omega_j) = \left\| \frac{1}{|\omega_i|} \sum_{v \in \omega_i \subset V} \varphi(v) - \frac{1}{|\omega_j|} \sum_{w \in \omega_j \subset V} \varphi(w) \right\|^2 \tag{10}$$

At this point, we note that, as a consequence of the matrix $\mathbf{H}$ being double-centered, we have $\frac{1}{|V|} \sum_{v \in V} \varphi(v) \equiv 0$. In other words, the center of mass for the embedding is at the origin and, therefore, the squared distance $\rho(\omega_i, \omega_j)$ can be expressed in terms of the embedding coordinates as follows

$$\rho(\omega_i, \omega_j) = 2 \sum_{l=1}^{|V|} \left\{ \frac{\lambda_l}{|V|^2} \left(\sum_{v \in \omega_i \subset V} \phi_l(v) + \sum_{w \in \omega_j \subset V} \phi_l(w) \right)^2 \right\} \tag{11}$$

The importance of this observation resides in the fact that it enables us to make use of the cluster memberships to introduce the weighted squared distance

$$\varrho(\omega_i, \omega_j) = \tau \sum_{l=1}^{|V|} \left\{ \lambda_l \left(\sum_{v \in \omega_i \subset V} x(v)\phi_l(v) + \sum_{w \in \omega_j \subset V} x(w)\phi_l(w) \right)^2 \right\} \tag{12}$$

where $\tau = \frac{2}{|V|^2}$. The quantity above is the one we aim to maximise. Through the use of Lagrange multipliers, we can use the norm constraint $\|\mathbf{x}\|^2 = 1$ for the vector of cluster membership functions and write

$$\tau \frac{\partial \varrho(\omega_i, \omega_j)}{\partial x(w)} = \zeta \frac{\partial \|\mathbf{x}\|^2}{\partial x(w)} \tag{13}$$

where ζ is a Lagrange multiplier. After some algebra, it can be shown that the system of equations obtained in this manner can be cast as an eigenvalue problem of the form

$$\tau \mathbf{H} \mathbf{x} = \zeta \mathbf{x} \tag{14}$$

Therefore, the maximum of $\varrho(\omega_i, \omega_j)$ is reached when $\mathbf{x}$ corresponds to the leading eigenvector of the double-centered Laplacian $\mathbf{H}$.

4 Deforming the Embedding Space

In this section, we explore a means to improve the clustering results by modifying the intrinsic geometric properties of the embedding space $\mathcal{S}$ for the graph G. The goal of computation here is, therefore, to compute an improved matrix of edge weights $\hat{W}$ that is both, representative of the space in which the nodes of the graph G are to be embedded and, most importantly, better suited for the purposes of clustering. We do this by requiring the embedding space to have constant positive curvature. This approach hinges in the properties of spherical spaces. On a sphere, the optimum separation of the space corresponds to the hyperplane bisecting the sphere through the equator, i.e. the centers of mass for the clusters are at either opposite pole of the sphere.

To this end, we view the embedding space S as an n-dimensional Riemannian manifold M and express the weight $W(v, w)$ as the energy $\mathcal{E}(p_v, p_w)$ over the parametric geodesic curve $\gamma : t \in [\alpha, \beta] \mapsto M$ intersecting the pair of points $p_v, p_w \in M$. To establish a relationship between the energy $\mathcal{E}(p_v, p_w)$, the geodesic γ and the curvature tensor, we employ the theory of Jacobi vector fields [3]. A Jacobi field along γ is the differentiable vector field Y in the tangent space to M, orthogonal to γ', satisfying Jacobi's equation, i.e. $\nabla_t^2 Y + R(\gamma', Y)\gamma' = 0$. With these ingredients, we can obtain a bilinear form, i.e. the sectional curvature, from the curvature tensor $R(\gamma', Y)\gamma'$. The sectional curvature $\mathcal{K}(\gamma', Y)$ along γ is, hence, given by

$$\mathcal{K}(\gamma', Y) = \frac{\langle R(\gamma', Y)\gamma', Y \rangle}{|\gamma'|^2 |Y|^2 - \langle \gamma', Y \rangle} \tag{15}$$

Because Y is orthogonal to γ' and, due to the fact that Y is a Jacobi field, i.e. it satisfies the condition $\nabla_t^2 Y = -R(\gamma', Y)\gamma'$, we can write

$$\mathcal{K}(\gamma', Y) = \frac{\langle -\nabla_t^2 Y, Y \rangle}{\langle Y, Y \rangle} \tag{16}$$

where we have set $|\gamma'| = 1$.

This suggests a way of formulating the energy over the geodesic $\gamma \in M$ connecting the pair of points corresponding to the nodes indexed v and w. Consider the geodesic γ subject to the Jacobi field Y. The energy over the geodesic γ can be expressed making use of the following equation

$$\mathcal{E}(p_v, p_w) = \int_\gamma |\gamma' + \nabla_t^2 Y|^2 \, dt = \int_\gamma |\gamma' - \mathcal{K}(\gamma', Y)Y|^2 \, dt \tag{17}$$

In practice, as stated at the beginning of the section, we will confine our attention to the problem of embedding the nodes into a manifold of constant sectional curvature. For such a manifold, the sectional curvature is constant i.e. $\mathcal{K}(\gamma', Y) \equiv \kappa$. Under this restriction, the Jacobi field equation becomes $\nabla_t^2 Y = -\kappa Y$. With the boundary conditions $Y(0) = 0$ and $|\nabla_t Y(0)| = 1$, the solution is given by $Y(t) = \frac{\sin(\sqrt{\kappa}t)}{\sqrt{\kappa}}\eta$, where the vector η is in the tangent space of M at p_v and is orthogonal to γ' at the point indexed v, i.e. $\eta \in M_{p_v}$ and $\langle \eta, \gamma' |_{p_v} \rangle = 0$. Further, by rescaling the parameter t so that $|\gamma'| = a$, we can express the element of the improved weight matrix $\hat{W}$ a the energy over the geodesic connecting the points p_v and p_w as follows

$$\hat{W}(v, w) = \int_0^1 \left(a_{v,w}^2 + \kappa \left(\sin(\sqrt{\kappa} a_{v,w} t) \right)^2 \right) dt \tag{18}$$

where $a_{v,w} = W(v, w)$ is the Euclidean distance between each pair of nodes when they have been embedded into a "flat" space, i.e. $a_{v,w} = \| p_v - p_w \|$ for $\kappa = 0$.

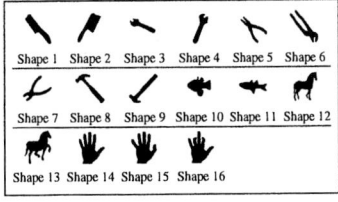 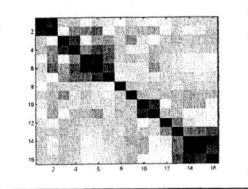 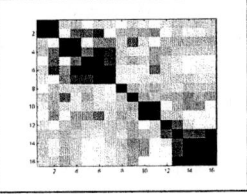

Fig. 1. From left-to-right: Set of silhouettes used in our experiments, matrix of raw similarities for the shapes in the left-hand panel and matrix $\hat{W}$ computed from the raw similarities

5 Experiments

In this section, we demonstrate the utility of the algorithm for purposes of unsupervised learning of shape-categories by means of grouping. This involves the abstraction of 2D binary shapes using shock-trees. Commencing from a data-base of silhouettes, the Hamilton-Jacobi skeleton is extracted and shocks, which correspond to singularities in the evolution of the object boundary under the eikonal equation, are located. The similarity of the shapes is then computed using the weighted tree edit distance developed by Luo et al. [7]. This is a structural method which hinges in augmenting the information given by the skeleton topology and the relative time of shock formation with a measure of feature importance based upon the rate of change of boundary length with respect to the overall distance along the skeleton. The problem of computing distances between pairs of shapes is then cast as that of finding the tree edit distance between the weighted graphs for their corresponding shock graphs.

In the left-hand panel of Figure 1, we show the shapes used in our experiments. The remaining two panels show the matrix of raw similarities, as computed using the algorithm of Luo et al. and the matrix $\hat{W}$ obtained by setting $\kappa = 5$. Here, the row and column indexes for both matrices have been set to those in the left-hand panel of Figure 1. The clusters recovered by the algorithm are the following

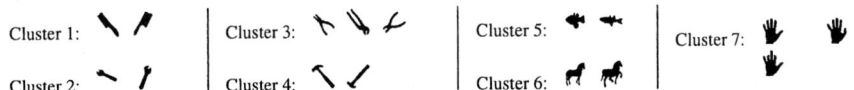

From the matrices in Figure 1, we can conclude that the block-diagonal structure of the matrix of raw shape similarities has been enhanced in the the matrix $\hat{W}$. Furthermore, the shape classes recovered by the algorithm are in good accordance with the silhouette categories in the database.

6 Conclusions

In this paper, we have cast the clustering problem in a graph theoretical setting. This opens up the possibility of embedding the objects to be clustered, abstracted as nodes in the graph, into a metric space. We have shown how the incidence mapping and the graph Laplacian can be used to pose the problem of embedding as that of recovering a Gram matrix of scalar products. Further, we have illustrated how the topology of the embedding space can be altered to improve the separation between clusters and, hence, the grouping results. We illustrated the utility of the method for purposes of grouping a set of shape silhouettes.

Acknowledgment

The author is indebted with Dr. Andrea Torsello (e-mail: **torsello@dsi.unive.it**) from the Univerità Ca' Foscari di Venezia, Italy, for facilitating him the shape silhouettes and similarities used in the experimental section of this paper.

References

[1] M. Belkin and P. Niyogi. Laplacian eigenmaps and spectral techniques for embedding and clustering. In *Neural Information Processing Systems*, number 14, pages 634–640, 2002.
[2] I. Borg and P. Groenen. *Modern Multidimensional Scaling, Theory and Applications*. Springer Series in Statistics. Springer, 1997.
[3] I. Chavel. *Riemannian Geometry: A Modern Introduction*. Cambridge University Press, 1995.
[4] M. Fiedler. A property of eigenvectors of nonnegative symmetric matrices and its application to graph theory. *Czech Math. Journal*, (25):619–633, 1975.
[5] J. C. Gower. Some distance properties of latent root and vector methods used in multivariate analysis. *Biometrika*, 53:325–328, 1966.
[6] J. Ham, D. D. Lee, S. Mika, and B. Scholkopf. A kernel view of the dimensionality reduction of manifolds. In *In Proc. Int. Conf. Machine Learning*, page 369376, 2004.
[7] B. Luo, A. Robles-Kelly, A. Torsello, R. C. Wilson, and E. R. Hancock. A probabilistic framework for graph clustering. In *EEE International Conference on Computer Vision and Pattern Recognition*, pages I:912–919, 2001.
[8] P. Perona and W. T. Freeman. Factorization approach to grouping. In *Proc. ECCV*, pages 655–670, 1998.
[9] S. T. Roweis and L. K. Saul. Nonlinear dimensionality reduction by locally linear embedding. *Science*, 290:2323–2326, 2000.
[10] S. Sarkar and K. L. Boyer. Quantitative measures of change based on feature organization: Eigenvalues and eigenvectors. *Computer Vision and Image Understanding*, 71(1):110–136, 1998.
[11] G. L. Scott and H. C. Longuet-Higgins. Feature grouping by relocalisation of eigenvectors of the proximity matrix. In *British Machine Vision Conference*, pages 103–108, 1990.
[12] J. Shi and J. Malik. Normalized cuts and image segmentations. In *Proc. of the IEEE Conf. on Comp. Vision and Pattern Recognition*, pages 731–737, 1997.
[13] J. B. Tenenbaum, V. de Silva, and J. C. Langford. A global geometric framework for nonlinear dimensionality reduction. *Science*, 290(5500):2319–2323, 2000.
[14] W. S. Torgerson. Multidimensional scaling I: Theory and method. *Psychometrika*, 17:401–419, 1952.
[15] G. Young and A. S. Householder. Discussion of a set of points in terms of their mutual distances. *Psychometrika*, 3:19–22, 1938.

A Practical Guide to Marker Based and Hybrid Visual Registration for AR Industrial Applications

Steve Bourgeois, Hanna Martinsson, Quoc-Cuong Pham, and Sylvie Naudet

CEA/LIST/SARC
{steve.bourgeois, hanna.martinsson, quoc-cuong.pham, sylvie.naudet}@cea.fr

Abstract. This paper presents two visual registration solutions for a mobile augmented reality system. The first one is a marker based solution whereas the second one is a hybrid approach. The hybrid method combines a coded marker technique for the initialization in the first frame, and a markerless registration in the next frames thanks to a 3-D model based tracking method. Because this mobile augmented reality system is designed for use in the industrial context of maintenance assistance for instance- robustness, accuracy, real-time and user comfort are the main concerns. For the different stages of the proposed solutions, various algorithms were evaluated to determine which one offers the best robustness and efficiency.

1 Introduction

The registration is a necessary step in any interactive augmented reality application. In the case of an optical see-through system, the operator looks, through glasses, at annotations and virtual models which must be correctly aligned with his view. A video see-through system mixes the real and virtual worlds in the video stream. Since there is relative motion between the camera and the object, the object must be temporally and accurately registered.

The main technical issues concern:

a) the required accuracy, essential for a correct alignment of the model with the object in the image,
b) the robustness: the registration system must be able to track objects with a high variability of appearance, with possible occlusions and changes in lighting conditions,
c) the real time constraint,
d) the high level of automation.

Finding a generic solution to these issues is still a challenge.

Popular approaches for solving the registration problem include marker based methods ([1], [2], [3] based on the ARToolKit, the cybercode described in [4]) and feature based methods ([5], [6], [7], [8]). In the first case, markers are well defined in order to facilitate their detection in the image and ensure speed, stability and robustness of the registration system independently of the environment. The main drawback of these approaches concerns the preliminary installation of markers which may not be an allowable constraint. The second type of methods consists in visually tracking object features. Since features change in appearance with the point of view, these techniques generally use high complexity algorithms. The speed versus robustness trade-off must be found. Moreover, these techniques are usually specific to a type of feature such as lines [9], textured objects [7] or geometric primitives [6]. The model based tracking methods are the most generic, as they only rely on the object model ([8], [6]). Another drawback of these approaches is the need a pose initialization, which is done manually in most of the cases.

In the context of an AR system for train maintenance, we have developed two registration solutions. The first one is a marker based method which addresses all the mentioned technical issues. The second one is a hybrid method combining the marker based solution to initialize the system and a model based tracking method.

2 Overview of the Registration Procedure

The main steps of the registration system are:

1. the object recognition: the algorithm automatically identifies the object in the image and selects the corresponding 3-D model,
2. the model-image correspondence: 2-D features are detected and matched to 3-D known features,
3. the camera pose estimation which outputs a 3-D rigid transform between the camera and the object coordinate systems. This transform is composed of rotation **R** and a translation **t**.

In the first proposed algorithm, we use feature points extracted from visual markers to compute the camera pose. The second algorithm starts with an initial pose estimation using a single marker, and then performs a markerless tracking of the object edges.

3 Marker Based Registration

Two type of markers were implemented: color coded markers and simple markers (white spots over a black background) as shown in Fig. 1.

The color coded markers enable to i) automatically identify the equipment from the code, ii) compute a first estimate of the camera pose by providing five feature points (the four corners and the center) and an orientation. The simpe markers are used to refine the pose parameters. These markers are easy to set up and can be efficiently detected in the image.

An overview of the algorithm is presented in fig. 2.

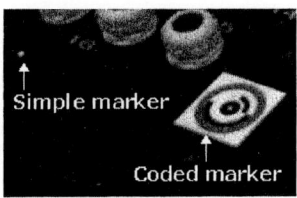

Fig. 1. Markers used in the registration process

3.1 Coded Marker Detection

The proposed marker system was originally developed for photogrammetry purposes (camera calibration and as-built reconstruction of plants). It was adapted to perform real time registration in AR applications.

A coded marker is characterized by a colored ring that can be detected by the connected component extraction algorithm proposed in [10] combined with a fast color classification method [11]. The candidates are then filtered with different shape criteria such as the elliptic variance. The efficiency and robustness of the detection process come from the association of color and shape information in cascade filters.

The corner points of a marker are then localized by computing the intersection of four lines interpolating high gradient points lying on the marker sides. The line determination is performed in a robust estimation framework [12].

The identification of the marker is straightforward, because it relies on a bar code like technique described in [13].

This new marker was compared to the ARToolkit marker system, which is widely used and considered as a reference in AR applications. The proposed system appeared to be more efficient, since the processing time of ARToolKit code identification is linearly dependent on the number of possible codes, whereas our system realizes this task in a constant time. Concerning the robustness, we observed a lower false-identification rate with our system than ARToolkit.

3.2 Iterative Pose Estimation

For each detected coded marker, five points are available to compute an initial estimate of the pose. If the coded markers are out of the field of view or temporarily occluded, a 0-order or a 1-order prediction gives an estimate of the current camera pose.

A more accurate value of the pose parameters can be obtained if additional points like the center of the detected simple markers are inputted to the pose estimation process. Thus it is possible to iteratively refine **R** and **t**, as more and more new simple targets can be detected. These markers are searched in small regions around the 2-D re-projection locations, using a fast multiresolution template matching technique.

The Fig.2 illustrates marker detection.

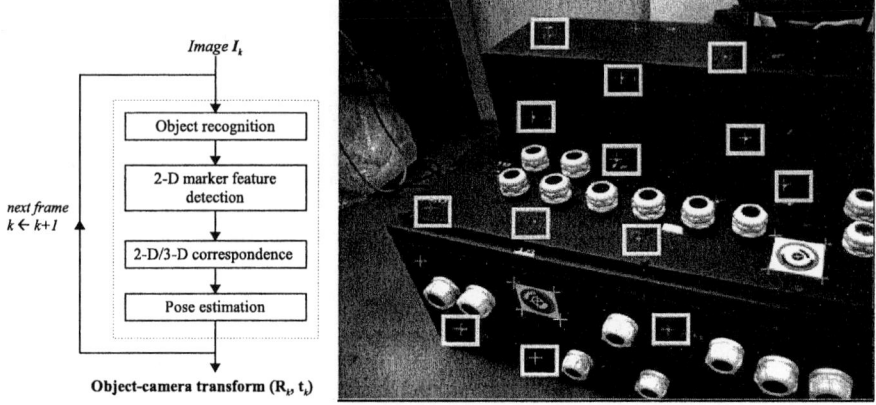

Fig. 2. Marker detection - *The coded marker feature points and the simple markers center points are denoted by crosses. The squares represent the search areas for the simple markers detection.*

Five camera pose estimation algorithms were evaluated in terms of robustness and efficiency. The two first algorithms are the linear method proposed by Quan et al [14] and POSIT [15]. The two next ones are extensions of the previous ones, where the pose is refined by a nonlinear minimization of the 2-D re-projection error upon the pose parameters. This nonlinear resection procedure is denoted NLR. The last tested algorithm implements POS [15] as an initialization step, followed by the NLR.

This comparative study was performed on synthetic scenes where the coded marker feature points were simulated with four coplanar points which are relatively close one to each other in the image coordinate system.

The simulation showed that in the specific geometry configuration mentioned:

– POSIT and the nonlinear algorithms outperform the linear pose method,

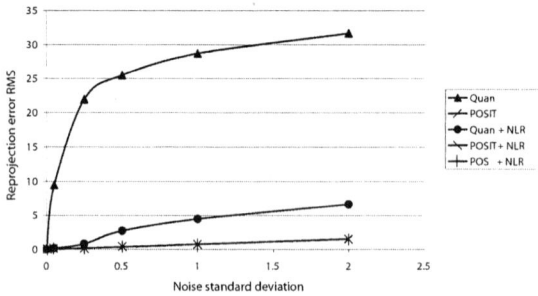

Fig. 3. Noise effect on reprojection error. *The pose used by reprojection error computation is evaluated on noised data. Reprojection error is evaluated on the four coplanar points.*

- POSIT, POS+NLR and POSIT+NLR performances are equivalent,
- POSIT is more efficient than all other linear and nonlinear algorithms.

Consequently, POSIT was selected for the pose estimation stage.

3.3 Using the 3-D Model Geometry to Improve Robustness

Depending on the point of view, all the markers are not always visible. The hidden markers must be identified because they can generate false detections and outliers for the pose estimation. Moreover, the registration will be faster because their detection can be avoided.

To determine which markers are visible or not at the actual pose, two point occlusion tests were considered: Z-buffer and space partition techniques. The Z-buffering method appeared to be more time consuming and was characterized by a poor precision. We thus chose a space partitioning method of the 3-D mesh in octrees to perform accurate point occlusion tests. In addition, because CAD models are usually locally complex (most of the data are localized in small regions), an octree decomposition enables to dramatically reduce the number of tests. The simplification of the mesh geometry can also significantly improve performances.

4 Feature Based Registration

This method combines the previously described coded marker method as an initial step to identify the object and compute the model-image correspondence in the first frame, and a feature based method to track the object edges. An overview of the algorithm is presented in Fig. 4.

The tracking technique is an adaptation of the method proposed by Drummond and Cipolla [8], based on a Lie group formalism. In each new image, the model is rendered in order to get the position of the visible edges according to the current estimate of object pose. The new position of an edge is searched in the direction of its normal. The result measurement vector corresponding to the 2-D motion, is then used to estimate the inter frame motion and retrieve the object pose.

Due to the hypothesis of small motion, tracking errors may arise when there are large inter frame motions. To overcome this difficulty, we propose a multiresolution implementation of the method.

5 Results

The Fig. 5 shows results obtained with the marker based registration. The required visual precision is achieved with a very good alignment of the 3-D model on the image.

The registration algorithm runs at about 30 frames per second on a Pentium IV 3.0 GHz with 1 Gb of memory.

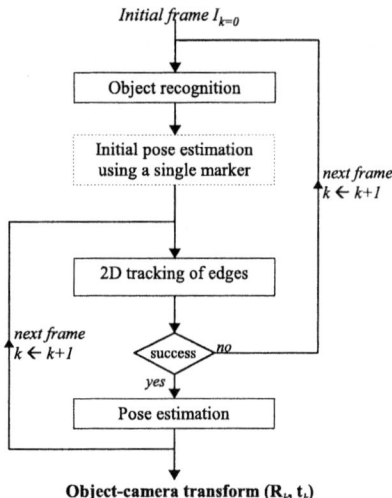

Fig. 4. Algorithm 2 - 2-D tracking in the registration process

Fig. 5. Results of the marker based registration. A simplified 3-D model is displayed in wireframe representation.

The Fig. 6 shows results obtained with the feature based registration in the table experiment. This method performs a robust tracking of the table. After a coarse initialization of the pose given by the marker based algorithm, the algorithm estimates the camera pose and projects the 3-D model onto the image successively throughout the sequence. Note that the marker that can be seen on top of the table in the images serves only for the initialization and not for the tracking that is based on the contours of the 3-D model. The introduced multiresolution approach significantly improves the performance of the tracking when the inter frame motion is large (Fig. 7).

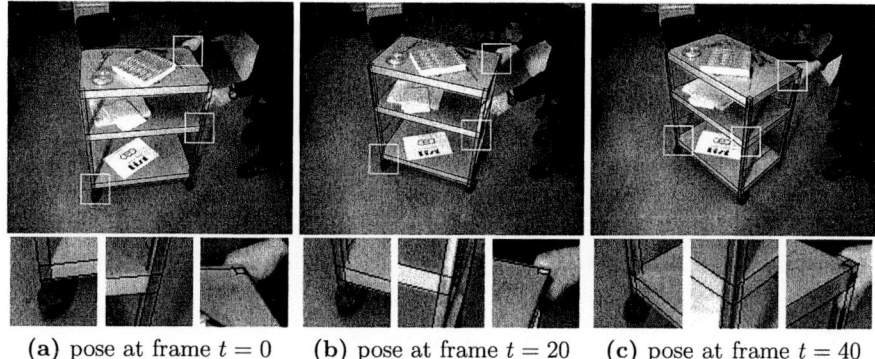

Fig. 6. Results of the feature based registration

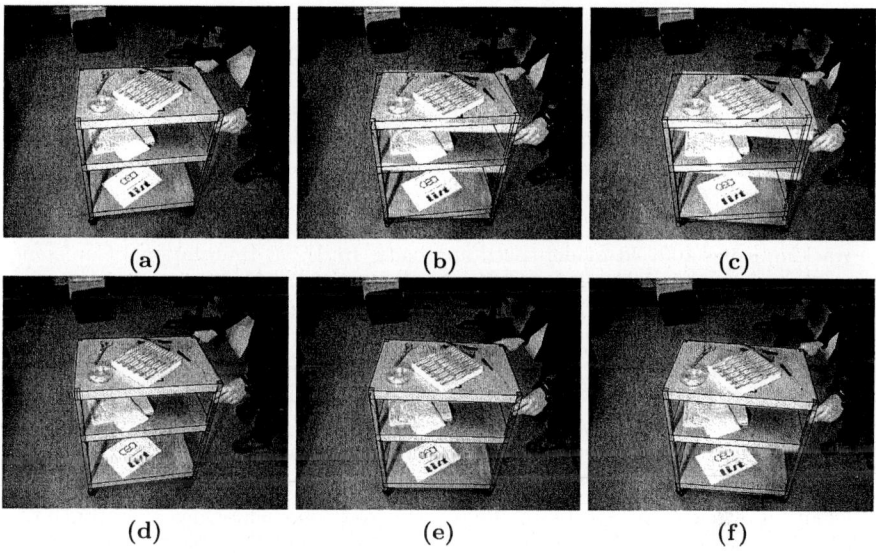

Fig. 7. Results of the tracking algorithm - *a,b,c : sequence without the multiresolution scheme. d,e,f : same sequence using the multiresolution approach*

6 Conclusion and Future Research Direction

The proposed solutions respect the robustness, accuracy and real-time requirements of common industrial context. Because the marker based system implies instrumentation of the environment, this approach is mainly dedicated to applications in a controlled environment. This solution was validated with a mobile augmented reality application for train maintenance training.

The hybrid approach is a first step toward a markerless system. The need of a unique marker offers a wider field of applications than the marker-based method.

In order to achieve a complete markerless augmented reality system, our current research concerns an initial step without marker. We are currently developing a markerless method based on CAD model knowledge to directly identify the object and its pose (image-model correspondence).

References

1. Zhang, X., Fronz, S., Navab, N.: Visual marker detection and decoding in ar systems: A comparative study. In: Proceedings of 2002 IEEE / ACM International Symposium on Mixed and Augmented Reality (ISMAR 2002). (2002) 97–106
2. Reiners, D., Stricker, D., Klinker, G., Muller, S.: Augmented reality for contruction task: Doorlock assembly. In: Proceedings 1st International Workshop on Augmented Reality (IWAR'98). (1998) 31–46
3. Billinghurst, M., Kato, H.: Collaborative augmented reality. Communications of the ACM **45** (2002) 64–70
4. Rekimoto, J., Ayatsuka, Y.: Cybercode: designing augmented reality environments with visual tags. In: DARE '00: Proceedings of DARE 2000 on Designing augmented reality environments, ACM Press (2000) 1–10
5. Ravela, S., Draper, B., Lim, J., Weiss, R.: Adaptive tracking and model registration across distinct aspects. In: Proc. IEEE/RSJ Conf. Intelligent Robots and Systems. (1995) 174–180
6. Marchand, E., Bouthemy, P., Chaumette, F., Moreau, V.: Robust real-time visual tracking using a 2d-3d model-based approach. In: IEEE International Conference on Computer Vision (ICCV). Volume 1., IEEE (1999) 262–268
7. Vacchetti, L., Lepetit, V., Fua, P.: Stable real-time 3d tracking using online and offline information. IEEE Trans. Pattern Analysis and Machine Intelligence **26** (2004) 1385–1391
8. Drummond, T., Cipolla, R.: Real-time visual tracking of complex structures. IEEE Transactions on Pattern Analysis and Machine Intelligence **15** (2002) 932–946
9. Ansar, A., Daniilidis, K.: Linear pose estimation from points or lines. IEEE Transactions on Pattern Analysis and Machine Intelligence **25** (2003) 578–589
10. Chang, F., Chen, C., Lu, C.: A linear-time component-labeling algorithm using contour tracing technique. Computer Vision and Image Understanding **93** (2004) 206–220
11. Bruce, J., Balch, T., Veloso, M.: Fast and inexpensive color image segmentation for interactive robots. In: Proceedings of the 2000 IEEE/RSJ International Conference on Intelligent Robots and Systems (IROS '00). Volume 3. (2000) 2061 – 2066
12. Fischler, M.A., Bolles, R.C.: Random sample consensus: a paradigm for model fitting with applications to image analysis and automated cartography. Commun. ACM **24** (1981) 381–395
13. Gaspard, F., Naudet, S., Noirfalise, E., Sayd, P.: Cibles codées et procédé de photogrammétrie utilisant de telles cibles. Patent (2002)
14. Quan, L., Lan, Z.: Linear n-point camera pose determination. IEEE Trans. Pattern Anal. Mach. Intell. **21** (1999) 774–780
15. Dementhon, D.F., Davis, L.S.: Model-based object pose in 25 lines of code. Int. J. Comput. Vision **15** (1995) 123–141

Pattern Selective Image Fusion for Multi-focus Image Reconstruction*

Vivek Maik, Jeongho Shin, and Joonki Paik

Image Processing and Intelligent Systems Laboratory,
Department of Image Engineering,
Graduate School of Advanced Imaging Science, Multimedia and Film
Chung-Ang University, Seoul 156-756, Korea
paikj@cau.ac.kr

Abstract. This paper presents a method for fusing multiple images of a static scene and shows how to apply the proposed method to extend depth of field. Pattern selective image fusion provides a mechanism for combining multiple monochromatic images through identifying salient features in the source images and combining those features in to a single fused image. The source images are first decomposed using *filter subtract decimate (FSD)* in laplacian domain. The *sum-modified-Laplacian (SML)* is used for obtaining the depth of focus in the source images. The selected images are then blended together using monotonically decreasing *soft decision blending (SDB)*, which enables smooth transitions across region boundaries. The resulting fused image utilizes focus information that is greater than that of the constituent images, while retaining a natural verisimilitude. Experimental results show the performance of the depth of focus extension using consumer video camera outputs.

1 Introduction

Recently, image fusion has become an important research topic in image analysis and computer vision [1, 2, 3]. Image fusion refers to the image processing techniques that produce a new, enhanced image by combining images from one or more sensors. The fused image is then made more suitable for human/machine perception, and for further image processing tasks such as segmentation, feature extraction and object recognition.

In this paper we propose a new pattern selective image fusion method that extends the depth of field of the sensor through the manipulation of multiple images at the same scene. An interesting observation motivating this approach is that, even though any single image may not have the entire scene in focus, the settings of the sensor and sensor optics can usually be adjusted so that at least some portion of the scene has the desired visual quality. The challenge, therefore, is to generate a set of images with varying apertures and focus settings, then to combine these images in to a single result where each scene feature has maximal focus.

---

*This work was supported by Korean Ministry of Science and Technology under the National Research Laboratory Project and by Korean Ministry of Information and Communication under the Chung-Ang University HNRC-ITRC program.

Prior work on the image fusion process has focused on operating on multiple intensity images based on wavelet and discrete cosine transformations [4, 5, 6] or use of a know camera point spread function (PSF) [5]. Other methods use pyramid based representation to decompose the source image in to different spatial scales and orientations [7]. Similar results, although with more artifacts and less visual stability can be achieved with the use of other basis functions [8]. Another technique similar to pyramid representation, have been based on wavelet transform as a means to decompose the image in to various sub bands [5, 6]. From the decomposed sub- bands the output is generated through selecting the sub bands that have maximum energy and reconstructing the fused sub-band. This representation, however, has an inherent limitation due to the sensitivity of the wavelet transform to translation and rotation and therefore is not particularly suitable for the fusion of images where, even after registration, residual motion is present.

Pattern selective image fusion method proposed in this paper is mainly composed of four step process: *pyramid construction, feature saliency computation, blending function, and reconstruction of the fused images*. This four-step process provides an overview of how images can be fused with maximum flexibility. The rest of the paper is organized as follows. Existing techniques and problem formulation are described in Section 2. The proposed pattern selective fusion algorithm is described in Section 3. Simulation results and comparisons are shown in Section 4. Finally, concluding remarks are outlined in Section 5.

2 Problem Formulation

The basic crux of the problem is deciding which portions of each image are in better focus than their respective counterparts in the associated frames and combining these regions to form the synthesized extended depth of focus image. In short, due to low pass filtering nature of the modified Bessel function present in the defocused images, the discrimination method of choice invariably involves quantification of high frequency content [1, 3].

Scenes containing large local changes in illumination and objects at greatly varying distances are impossible to image with high image quality throughout the scene [2, 4]. Known methods for adjusting a sensors integration time and aperture, including methods such as automatic gain control and automatic iris selection, are commonly used to adjust for overall illumination in a scene, but cannot compensate for large local variations in the scene brightness. Likewise, physical limitation in standard sensor optics result in finite depth of field, which enables features within the depth of field to be in focus while scene contents outside the depth of field suffer from progressively increased blurring as the features are further and further from the depth of focus [9].

Another optical phenomenon which presents a possible obstacle to the fusion of differently focused images is image misalignment due to magnification or misregistration. The former occurs when the sensor plane, is moved between frames, thereby changing the effective magnification of the imaged object. On a related note, misregistration can also occur as a result of slight camera movement between frames. In this paper we will focus on the fusion issue and the source images are assumed to be already registered.

3 Proposed Pattern Selective Fusion Algorithm

The problem is solved as follows: Given N images of a static scene obtained at different depth of focus using a stationary camera, it is required to combine the images in to a single image that has the maximum information content without producing details that are non-existent in the given images. The approach proposed here selects the most informative image for each local area and blends the selected images to create a new image. The foundation for combining multiple images into a single, enhanced result is the pattern selective fusion process itself. To simplify this discussion, we assume the fusion process is to generate a composite image C from a pair of source images denoted with A and B.

3.1 Pyramid Construction for Image Fusion

The pyramid representation can be used both for assessing the salience of the source image features, and for the reconstruction of the final image result. The following definitions for the pyramid are used. The fusion method described within this paper use a Laplacian pyramid representation. Laplacian pyramids are constructed for each image using the *filter subtract decimate (FSD)* method [8]. Thus the kth level of the FSD Laplacian pyramid, L_k, is constructed from the corresponding Gaussian pyramid level k based on the relationship.

$$L_k = G_k - wG_k = G_k(1-w), \qquad (1)$$

where w represents a standard binomial Gaussian filter, usually of 5×5 spatial pixels extent. When constructing the FSD Laplacian, due to the decimation process and the fact that w is not an ideal filter, a reconstruction of the original image based on the FSD Laplacian pyramid incurs some loss of information. To partially correct for this effect, an additional correction term is added to the Laplacian. This term is obtained by subtracting the filtered Laplacian from the original Laplacian, and results in the corrected FSD Laplacian given by,

$$\tilde{L}_k = L_k + (1-w)L_K = (2-w)(1-w)G_k. \qquad (2)$$

The addition of this term allows the reconstruction to restore some of the frequency information that would be otherwise lost. Throughout this paper, while referring to Laplacian representation of the image, the corrected FSD Laplacian defined above should be assumed.

3.2 Feature Saliency Computation

The feature saliency computation process, expresses a family of functions that operate on the pyramids of both images yielding saliency pyramids. In practice, these functions can operate on the individual pixels or on a local region of pixels within the given pyramid level. The saliency function captures the importance of what is to be fused. When combining images having different focus, for instance, a desirable saliency measure would provide a quantitative measure that increases when features are in better focus. Various such measures, including image variance, image gradients, have been employed and validated for related applications such as auto focusing [3, 4, 5]. The saliency function only selects the frequencies in the focused image that will be attenuated due to defocusing. Since defocusing is a low pass filtering process, its effects on the image are more pronounced and detectable if the image has strong high frequency content. One way to high pass filter an image is to determine its Laplacian or second derivative in our case.

$$\nabla^2 L_K = \frac{\partial^2 L_k}{\partial x^2} + \frac{\partial^2 L_k}{\partial y^2}, \qquad (3)$$

Also we know that in the case of Laplacian the second derivatives in the x and y directions can have opposite signs and tend to cancel each other. In the case of textured images, this phenomenon may occur frequently and the Laplacian at times may behave in an unstable manner. We overcome this problem by defining absolute Laplacian as

$$\nabla^2 L_K = \left| \frac{\partial^2 L_k}{\partial x^2} \right| + \left| \frac{\partial^2 L_k}{\partial y^2} \right|, \qquad (4)$$

Note that the modified Laplacian is always greater or equal in magnitude to the Laplacian. In order to accommodate for possible variations in the size of texture elements, we computer the partial derivative by using a variable spacing between the pixels used to compute the derivatives. Hence a discrete approximation to the modified Laplacian is given by,

$$ML(i, j) = |2I(i, j) - I(i-1, j) - I(i+1, j)| + |2I(i, j) - I(i, j-1) - I(i, j+1)|, \qquad (5)$$

Finally, the focus measure at a point (i, j) is computed as the sum of modified Laplacian values, in a small window around (i, j), that are greater than a threshold value.

$$F(i, j) = \sum_{x=i-N}^{i+N} \sum_{y=j-N}^{j+N} M_k(x, y) \, for M_k(x, y) \geq T_1. \qquad (6)$$

The parameter determines the window size used to compute the focus measure. In contrast to auto focusing methods, we typically use a small window of size, i.e. $N = 1$. The above equation can be referred to as *sum modified Laplacian (SML)*.

3.3 Soft Decision Blending and Reconstruction

The reconstruction process, operates on each level of the pyramid of the original images in conjunction with sum modified Laplacian to generate the composite image C.

The reconstruction process iteratively integrates information from the lowest to the highest level of the pyramid as follows:

$$L_{ck} = F_k . L_{Ak} + (1 - F_\kappa) L_{Bk}, \qquad (7)$$

$$C_k = L_{ck} + w[C_k + 1] \uparrow 2. \qquad (8)$$

Where C_k represents the reconstructed image from level N, the lowest level, to level k and $\uparrow 2$ refers to the expand process. The expansion process consists of doubling the width and height of the image by introducing columns and row in the original and then convolving the resulting image by the w filter. A typical problem that can occur with any type of image fusion is the appearance of unnatural borders between the decisions regions due to overlapping blur at focus boundaries. To combat this, *soft decision blending (SDF)* can be employed using smoothing or low pass filtering of the saliency parameter F_k. In this paper Gaussian smoothing has been used for obtaining the desired effect of blending. This creates weighted decision regions where a linear combination of pixels in the two images A and B are used to generate corresponding pixels in the fused image C. Then we have,

$$L_{ck} = \begin{cases} L_{Ak}, & \tilde{F}_k < l, \\ L_{Bk}, & \tilde{F}_k > h, \\ \tilde{F}_i . L_{AM} + (1 - \tilde{F}_K) L_{m}, & otherwise. \end{cases} \qquad (9)$$

where $\tilde{F}_k$ is now a smoothed version of its former self.

4 Experimental Results

In this section we experimentally demonstrate the effectiveness of the pattern selective fusion algorithm. Experiments were performed on a 256-level image of size 640x480. Here, each image contains multiple objects at different distances from the camera. Thus one or more objects naturally become out of focus when the image is taken. For example, the focus in on the clock in fig 1(a), while that in fig 1(b) is on the student.

Fig 1 and 2 shows the result of image fusion applied to two images having different depth of focus. The resulting composite merges the portions that are in focus from respective images. The result of salient focus measure is given in fig 1 (c), (d). The SML salient operator enhances the sharp edges and textures and makes them predominant for further selection and reconstruction. Fig 1(e) and 2(c) give the result of the patter selective fusion algorithm. The arbitrary threshold value in the range [0, 30], provides acceptable results in most cases. It can be seen the all objects are in focus in the final fused image and any undesired discontinuities at the region boundaries are prevented by soft decision blending function.

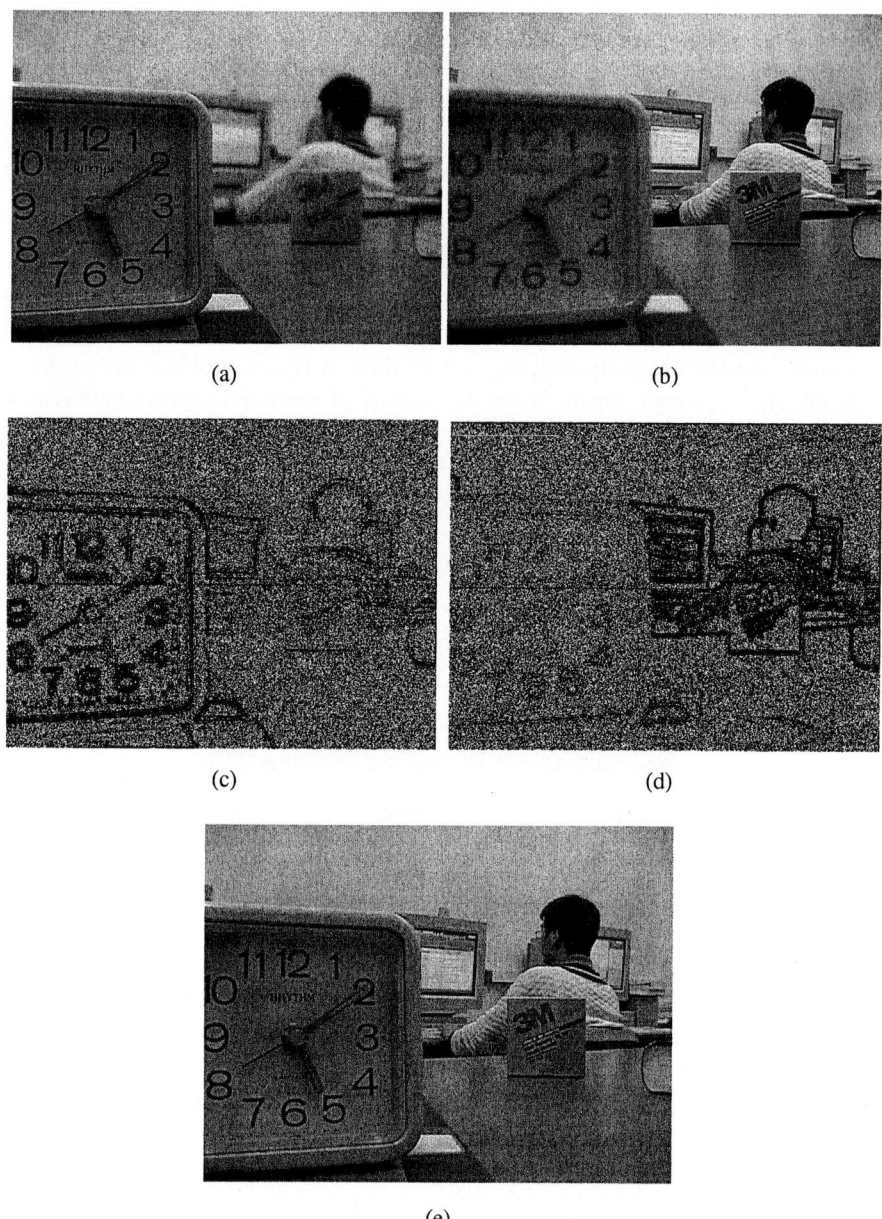

Fig. 1. The "Lab" source images and fusion results: (a) focus on the clock; (b) focus on the student; (c), (d) focus measure using *sum-modified-Laplacian*; (e) fused image with all objects in focus

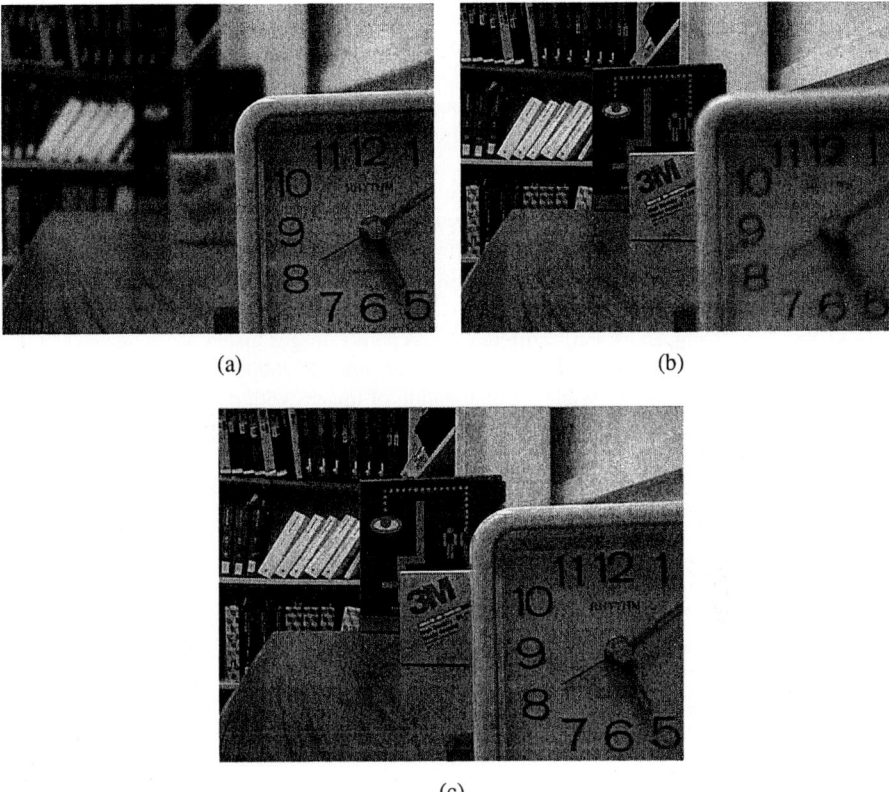

Fig. 2. The "Disk" source images and fusion results: (a) focus on the left; (b) focus on the right; (c) fused image

5 Conclusions

In this paper we proposed a pattern selective fusion algorithm for the synthesis of extended depth of focus imagery. The pyramid structure followed by sum-modified-Laplacian and soft decision blending make the algorithm effective and easy to implement. Also, no particular characteristics of the imaging is need to be known a priori; the main requirements are that underlying assumptions governing the fusion process. A natural extension to the work presented here will include the application of pattern selective fusion to image sequences and also for dynamic range enhancement.

References

[1] J. K. Aggarwal, Multisensor Fusion for Computer Vision, Springer, Berlin, 1993.
[2] A. Akerman, "Pyramid techiniques for multisensor fusion," Proc. SPIE, vol. 2828, pp. 124-131, 1992.

[3] Z. Zhang and R. S. Blum, "A categorization of multiscale-decomposition-based image fusion schemes with a performance study for a digital camera application," Proc. IEEE vol. 87(8), pp. 1315-1326, 1999.
[4] S. K. Kim, S. R. Park, and J. K. Paik, "Simultaneous out-of-focus blur estimation and restoration for digital AF system," IEEE Trans. Consumer Electronics, vol. 44, no. 3, pp. 1071-1075, August 1998.
[5] G. Ligthart and F. Groen, "A comparison of different autofocus algorithms," IEEE Int. Conf. Pattern Recognition, pp. 597-600, 1992.
[6] K. Aizawa, K. Kodama, and A. Kubota, "Producing object-based special effects by fusing multiple differently focused images," IEEE Trans. Circuits, Systems for Video Technology, vol. 10(2), pp. 323-330, 2000.
[7] X. Yang, W. Yang, and J. Pei, "Different focus points images fusion based on wavelet decomposition," Proc. Int. Conf. Information Fusion, pp. 3-8, 2000.
[8] S. Li, J. T. Kwok, and Y. Wang, "Combination of images with diverse focuses using the spatial frequency," Int. Journal, Information Fusion, vol. 2, no. 3, pp. 169-176, September 2001.
[9] W. B. Seales and S. Dutta, "Everywhere-in-focus image fusion using controllable cameras," Proc. SPIE, vol. 2905, pp. 227–234, 1996.

Fast Pixel Classification by SVM Using Vector Quantization, Tabu Search and Hybrid Color Space

G. Lebrun[1], C. Charrier[1], O. Lezoray[1], C. Meurie[1], and H. Cardot[2]

[1] LUSAC EA 2607, groupe Vision et Analyse d'Image, IUT Dept. SRC,
120 Rue de l'exode, Saint-Lô, F-50000, France
{gilles.lebrun, c.charrier, o.lezoray, cyril.meurie}@chbg.unicaen.fr
[2] Laboratoire Informatique (EA 2101), Université François-Rabelais de Tours,
64 Avenue Jean Portalis, Tours, F-37200, France
hubert.cardot@univ-tours.fr

Abstract. In this paper, a new learning method is proposed to build Support Vector Machines (SVM) Binary Decision Function (BDF) of reduced complexity, efficient generalization and using an adapted hybrid color space. The aim is to build a fast and efficient SVM classifier of pixels. The Vector Quantization (VQ) is used in our learning method to simplify the training set. This simplification step maps pixels of the training set to representative prototypes. A criterion is defined to evaluate the Decision Function Quality (DFQ) which blends recognition rate and complexity of a BDF. A model selection based on the selection of the simplification level, of a hybrid color space and of SVM hyperparameters is performed to optimize this DFQ. Search space for selecting the best model being huge. Our learning method uses Tabu Search (TS) metaheuritics to find a good sub-optimal model on tractable times. Experimental results show the efficiency of the method.

1 Introduction

Pixels classification is commonly used as an initial step in color image segmentation schemes [1,2] for the extraction of seeds. As for any classification problem, the choice of an inducer which produces efficient Decision Functions (DF) having good generalization performances is critical. Working with machine learning algorithm for pixel classification involves to take into account not only the recognition rate of the base inducer but also the processing time needed to perform a single pixel classification. In this paper, we are interested in SVMs and for those ones the processing time is only related to the complexity of the BDF. When a DF has an efficient recognition rate, but with a huge computing time per pixel, it cannot be directly used within the framework of pixel classification, expecially when processing time is critical. SVMs are powerful classifier having high generalization abilities [3]. However the BDF provided by SVM has a complexity which increases with the size of the training set [4,5]. Therefore using SVMs on a huge pixel set is not directly tractable for pixel classification. To this aim we propose a new learning method which makes it possible to use SVMs within the pixel classification framework. This method uses the VQ principle [6] to simplify the training set and thus permits to reduce the complexity of the BDFs built by SVMs. the DFQ for the pixel classification depends on two terms: the DF recognition rate and the DF complexity. For pixel classification the DF complexity depends on the color space used and the number of Support Vectors (SV) (cf. section 5). The classical color space representation of a pixel is denoted by its RGB values, however, depending on the application, another more adapted color space can be chosen (XYZ,$L^*a^*b^*$,$L^*u^*v^*$,...). This choice is difficult and subjective, therefore it is more reliable to define a hybrid color space [1] which will be more adapted to the definition of a proper DF. For this reason, it is essential that our learning method selects a hybrid color space adapted to each BDF produced by the SVM. This hybrid color space is built by selecting a set of color components which can belong to any of the different classical color spaces [1]. The mechanism used in our method for the selection of the color components is similar to that usually used within the features selection framework [7]. For each BDF produced by SVM, our learning method must thus choose the values of the SVM hypermarameters, the simplification level of the training set and the hybrid color space in order to optimize the DFQ. Exhaustive search for model selection is not tractable, so we decided for this model selection to use TS metaheuristic because of it efficiency [8]. The combination of SVM, a simplification step by using VQ, a hybrid color space, a new criterion for the DFQ and a TS metaheuristic enables us to define a new learning method which produces in tractable times a efficient BDF which have a reduced complexity.

2 Support Vector Machines

The SVMs were developed by Vapnik and al. They are based on the structural risk minimization principle from statistical learning theory [3]. SVMs express predictions in terms of a linear combination of kernel functions centered on a subset of the training data, known as support vectors. Given the training data (x_i, y_i), $i = \{1,...,m\}$, $x_i \in \mathcal{R}^n$, $y_i \in \{-1,+1\}$, SVM maps the input vector x into a high-dimensional feature space $\mathbf{H}$ through some mapping functions $\phi : \mathcal{R}^n \rightarrow \mathbf{H}$, and builds an optimal separating hyperplane in this space. The mapping $\phi(\cdot)$ is performed by a kernel function $K(\cdot,\cdot)$ which defines an inner product in $\mathbf{H}$. The separating hyperplane given by a SVM is: $w \cdot \phi(x) + b = 0$. The optimal hyperplane is characterized by the maximal distance to the closest training data. The margin is inversely proportional to the norm of w. Thus computing this hyperplane is equivalent to minimize the following optimization problem: $\mathcal{V}(w,b,\xi) = \frac{1}{2}\|w\|^2 + C\left(\sum_{i=1}^{m}\xi_i\right)$ where the constraint $\forall_{i=1}^{m} : y_i[w \cdot \phi(x_i) + b] \geq 1 - \xi_i$, $\xi_i \geq 0$ requires that all training examples are correctly classified up to some slack ξ and C is a parameter allowing trading-off between training errors and model complexity. This optimization is a convex quadratic programming problem. Its whole dual [3] is to maximize the following optimization problem: $W(\alpha) = \sum_{i=1}^{m} \alpha_i - \frac{1}{2}\sum_{i,j=1}^{m} \alpha_i \alpha_j y_i y_j K(x_i, x_j)$ subject to $\forall_{i=1}^{m} : 0 \leq \alpha_i \leq C$, $\sum_{i=1}^{m} y_i \alpha_i = 0$. The optimal solution α^* specifies the coefficients for the optimal hyperplane $w^* = \sum_{i=1}^{m} \alpha_i^* y_i \phi(x_i)$ and defines the subset SV of all SVs. An example x_i of the training set is a SV if $\alpha_i^* \geq 0$ in the optimal solution. The SVs subset gives the BDF h:

$$h(x) = \text{sign}(f(x)) \quad , \quad f(x) = \sum_{i \in SV} \alpha_i^* y_i K(x_i, x) + b^* \tag{1}$$

where the threshold b^* is computed via the unbounded SVs [3] (i.e. $0 < \alpha_i^* < C$). An efficient algorithm SMO [4] and many refinements [9,10] were proposed to solve dual problem. SVM being binary classifiers, several binary SVM classifiers are induced for a multi-class problem. A final decision is taken from the outputs of all binary SVM [11].

3 Vector Quantization

The VQ is a classification technique used in the compression field [6]. VQ maps a vector x to another vector x' that belongs to m' *prototypes* vectors which is named *codebook*. The *codebook* S' is built from a training set S_a of size m ($m >> m'$). The algorithm must produce a set S' of prototypes x' which minimizes the distorsion d' which is defined by: $d' = \frac{1}{m}\sum_{i=1}^{m} \min_{1 \leq j \leq m'} d(x_i, x_j)$ ($d(.,.)$ is a ℓ_2 norm). LBG is one of those algorithms [6] which can build this *codebook*. It is an iterative algorithm which produces 2^k prototypes after k iterates.

4 Hybrid Color Spaces

The pixels of a color image are digitized in (R, G, B) color space. However, this color space is not always the more appropriate for image processing problems and especially for pixel classification. There are many different color spaces and each one presents specific colorimetric, physical and physiological properties [1]. For our study, we have retained the most commonly used color spaces[1]: (X, Y, Z), (L^*, a^*, b^*), (L^*, u^*, v^*), (L_1, C, H_1), (Y_2, Ch_1, Ch_2), (I_1, I_2, I_3), (H_2, S, L_2), (Y_3, C_b, C_r). Moreover, in some experiments, it was shown that by combining color components from several color spaces, it is possible to build a hybrid color space more suitable than initial ones [1].
Let E be the space which regroups all n_E distinct color components from e different classical color spaces. By definition a hybrid color space H_E^β is composed of a set of n_β components from E and the vector β indicates which components from E are used (i.e. $i \in [1, \ldots, n_E]$, $\beta_i = 1$ if the ith color component of the space E is used in H_E^β and $\beta_i = 0$ in the other case). For our study, $e = 9$, $n_E = 25$ and $E = (R, G, B, X, Y_1, Z, L^*, a^*, b^*, u^*, v^*, C, H_1, Y_2, Ch_1, Ch_2, I_1, I_2, I_3, H_2, S, L_2, Y_3, C_b, C_r)$. Then, the objective of our method is to find a hybrid color space H_E^β (the value of β) which improves the DFQ produced by SVM.

---
[1] We have added indices for some color components to differentiate them when being denoted by the same letter but not being identically computed.

5 Decision Function Quality

The DFQ q for a given model θ depends on the recognition rate R_R but also on the complexity C_P of the DF h_θ when processing time is critical. The DFQ q can be modelled by: $q(h_\theta) = R_R(h_\theta) - C_P(h_\theta)$. When the DF is built by SVM with a fixed kernel, the complexity of this DF depends on n_{SV} and β (H_E^β). We chose to model $C_P(h_\theta)$ by: $C_P(h_\theta) = c_{p_1} \log(n_{SV}) + c_{p_2} \log(cost(\beta))$. Constants c_{p_1} and c_{p_2} are weighting coefficients which respectively represent the importance of the number of SVs and the choice of the hybrid color space ($cost(\beta)$) in the complexity of h_θ. The ith color components ($i > 3$) of a pixel are computed by linear or not linear transformation of the first three RGB components [1]. The time cost to compute a given color component is more or less expensive as regards the kind of transformation (linear or not, software or hardware). Let κ_i denote the transformation cost to compute the value of ith color components, the value of $cost(\beta)$ linked to the hybrid color space H_E^β is defined by: $cost(\beta) = \sum_{i=1}^{n_E} \beta_i \kappa_i$.

6 Tabu Search

TS is a metaheuristic for difficult optimization problems. The roots of tabu search go back to the 1970s; it was first presented in its actual form by Glover [12]. TS belongs to iterative neighbourhood search methods. The general step, at the it iteration, consists in searching from a current solution θ^{it} a next best solution θ^{it+1} in the neighbourhood. This new solution may be less efficient than the previous one, however it avoids local minimum trapping problems. That is why, TS uses short memory to avoid creating cycles. The use of this short memory is helpful to avoid moves which might led to recently visited solutions (*tabu* solutions). Although the basic idea of TS is straightforward, the choice of solutions coding, objective function, neighbourhood, tabu solutions definition depends on the application problem.

Our problem is to choose an optimal model (solution) θ which can be represented by a set of integer variables $\theta = (\theta_1, \ldots, \theta_{n'})$ with : $for all\, i \in [1, \ldots, n']$, $\theta_i \in [min(\theta_i), \ldots, max(\theta_i)]$ (*cf.* section 7). The objective function q to be optimized represents the quality of the BDF h_θ. One move in TS corresponds to adding $\Delta \in [-1, 1]$ to the value of θ_i, while preserving the constraints of the model which depends on it. From these constraints, the list of all possible neighboorhood solutions is computed. From these possible solutions the one which has the best DFQ and which is not *tabu* is chosen. The set of all Θ_{tabu}^{it} solutions θ which are *tabu* at the it iteration step of TS is defined as follow: $\Theta_{tabu}^{it} = \{\theta \in \Omega \mid \exists i, t' : t' \in \{1, \ldots, t\}, \theta_i = \theta_i^{it-t} \wedge \theta_i^{it-t} \neq \theta_i^{it-t+1}\}$ with Ω the set of all solutions and t an adjustable parameter for the short memory used by TS.

7 New Learning Method

When studying the SVM algorithm, one notices that processing time for SVM training quickly grows according to the size of the training base. For SMO algo-

Table 1. The Simplification algorithm (left) and the synopsis of SVM DFQ (right)

Simplification(S,k)	SVM-DFQ(θ,S_a)
$S' \Leftarrow \emptyset$	$(S_e, S_v) \Leftarrow \text{Split}(S_a)$
FOR $c = 1$ TO n_c	$S'_e \Leftarrow \text{Simplification}(S_e,k_\theta)$
| $T = \{x \mid (x,c) \in S\}$	$h_\theta \Leftarrow \text{TrainingSVM}(S'_e,K_{\beta_\theta},C_\theta,\lambda_\theta)$
| IF $2^k < \|T\|$ THEN $T' \Leftarrow \text{LBG}(T,k)$	$R_R \Leftarrow 1- \text{EmpiricalError}(h_\theta,S_v)$
| ELSE $T' \Leftarrow T$	$C_P \Leftarrow \text{Complexity}(h_\theta)$
| $S' \Leftarrow S' \cup \{(x,c) \mid x \in T'\}$	DFQ $\Leftarrow R_R - C_P$
RETURN S'	

rithms, it is between $O(m^{1,6})$ and $O(m^{2,1})$ [4]. Moreover the number of SVs used by the BDF increases with the problem size. As the objective of our learning method is to produce a BDF of optimal qualitie (section 5), the increase in the number of SVs is only interesting if it is linked to a significant improvement of the recognition rate. The idea of our method is to train a SVM from a small data set representative of the initial one, in order to reduce the complexity of the BDF and consequently training time. The LBG algorithm has been used to perform the simplification (reduction) of the initial data set. Algorithm in Tab. 1 gives the details of this simplification. As the level of simplification k cannot be easily fixed in an arbitrary way, a significant concept in our method is to regard k as variable. The optimization of SVM DFQ thus requires for a given kernel function K the choice of: the level of simplification k, the hybrid color space H_E^β, the constant of regularization C and the kernel parameters λ of K. The search of the values of these variables is called model search. Let θ be a model and k_θ, β_θ, C_θ, λ_θ be respectively the values of previous variables obtained from the model θ. The research of the exact value θ^* which optimizes the DFQ not being tractable, we decided to use tabu search as metaheuristic. To have a model θ easily usable by the TS, it must correspond to a vector of n' integer values. We have used the following equivalence: $(\theta_1,\ldots,\theta_{n'}) = (\beta_1,\ldots,\beta_{n_E},k,C',\lambda'_1,\ldots,\lambda'_{|\lambda|})$ with $C_\theta = 2^{C'}$, $C' \in [-5,\ldots,15]$ [9]. From this model θ, the function q which must be optimized by TS is $= q(h_\theta)$. The synopsis in Tab. 1 gives the details of the estimation of DFQ from a model θ and a training set S_a with $= q(h_\theta) = $ SVM-DFQ(θ, S_a). S_e, S_v which is produced by Split function ($|S_e| = \frac{2}{3}|S_a|$, $|S_v| = \frac{1}{3}|S_a|$) respectively indicates the base used for training SVM and the estimate of the recognition rate. This dissociation is essential to avoid the risk of overfitting when the empirical error is used for the estimate of R_R. The SVM training step is made by using a SMO algorithm version present in the library Torch [10]. The kernel functions K_β used for training SVM are defined from a distance d_β: $d_\beta(x_i,x_j) = \sqrt{\sum_{l=1}^{n_E} \beta_l(x_i^l - x_j^l)^2}$. It is identical to use ℓ_2 norm in the hybrid color space H_E^β for the design of BDF. For this study, only kernel: $K_\beta^L = d_\beta^2$ and $K_\beta^G = exp(-d_\beta^2/\lambda_1^2)$ are used (in TS model: $\lambda'_1 \in [-10,\ldots,10]$ and $\lambda_{1\theta} = 2^{\lambda'_1}$ [9]).

8 Experiments

We applied our learning method for pixel classification of microscopic images of bronchial tumors [2]. The training and testing set S_a and S_t are built from four ground-thruth microscopic color images (RGB, 574*752 pixels). For each image, a manual segmentation is made by an expert: background (class 1), cytoplasm (class 2), nucleus (class 3). As the number of pixels in each class is not balanced in the images (1: 89%, 2: 7%, 3: 4%), only a subset of the pixels of classes 1 and 2 was selected by random to build S_a and S_t, so that each class has the same number of examples ($\approx$ 60000 by class). Three training sets S_a^i (testing sets S_t^i) are built from the S_a (S_t) in order to produce binary decision problems (method *one against all* [11]). For each binary problem a model θ^i and BDF h_θ^i is built with our learning method. To avoid any biais for model selection the recognition rate of a BDF h_θ^i is evaluated from testing set S_t^i.

Figures 1(a) and 1(d) illustrate for each BDF h_θ^i with a kernel K_β^L (optimal value of C is searched) the evolution of the recognition rate and of the number of SVs according to the level of simplification k. That is done for all the classical color spaces retained. One can notice that improvement of R_R is obtained only for small values of k. Moreover, the choice of a color space which optimizes the DFQ depends to the trade-off between complexity and recognition rate. These remarks corroborate the choices which were made in the definition of our learning method.

Tables 3 illustrate results obtained with our learning method by using a kernel K_β^L and K_β^G. Table 2 gives the values of constants for all the configurations used. The column κ_i represents two cases: the first one is a microship transformation ($\kappa_i = 1$) and the second one is a software transformation ($\kappa_i = T_i/T$ with T_i the time to compute the color component i and $T = \sum_{i\in[1,...,n_E]} T_i$).

configuration	c_{p_1}	c_{p_2}	κ_i
A	0.0001	0.01	1
B	0.01	0.01	1
C	0.03	0.03	1
D	0.01	0.01	T_i/T

Table 2. Values of constants

In tables 3 HCS indicates hybrid color spaces used by the BDF, Δt the training time, and in column DF is mentioned after θ the configuration which is used. These results show that our learning method produces BDF with reduced complexity and efficient in generalization. The choice of a specific hybrid color space for each BDF generally improves the recognition rate. The improvement with the use of kernel K_β^L is very significant ($\approx$ 5%) with h_θ^2. For this problem, the choice to use a kernel K_β^G in comparison with K_β^L does not improve the recognition but increases the BDF complexity. Indeed, $h(x) = d_\beta(x^*, x)^2 + b^*$ with $x^* = \sum_{i \in SV} \alpha_i^* y_i x_i$ when kernel K_β^L is used, then the number of SVs does not penalize the BDF complexity. However, although it seems logical to choose zero or very low values for c_{p_1}, results (Tab. 3: left, configuration A and B) show a significant increase in time for the selection of a model without significant improvement of the recognition rate. Those results (Tab. 3: configuration B and D) also show that the uses of κ_i constants allow to select a hybrid color space according to its cost. In particular, in the case of software implementation the

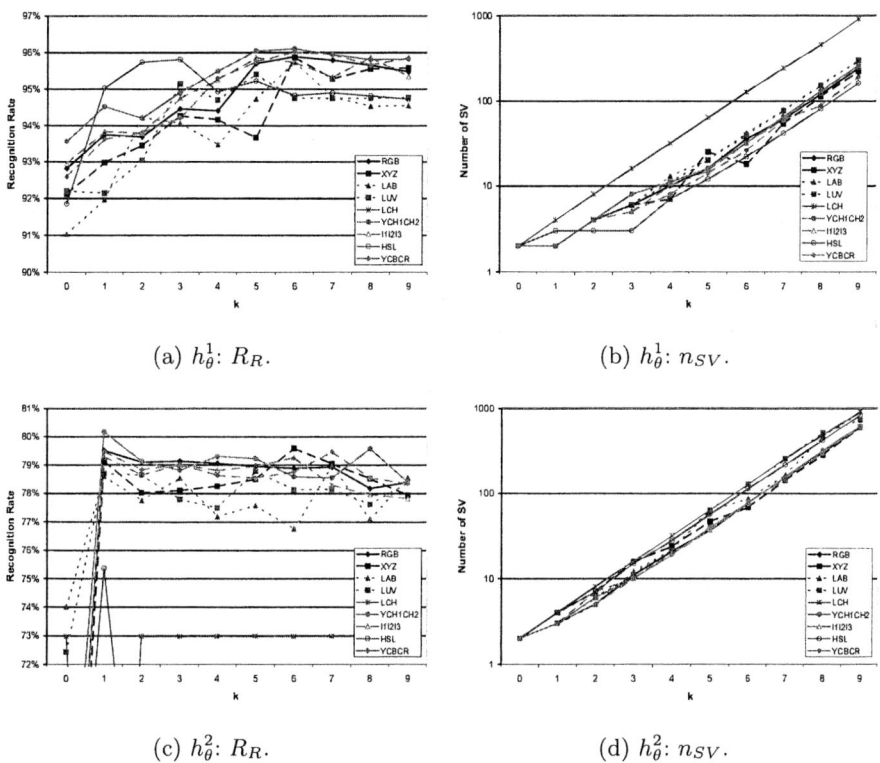

Fig. 1. Recognition rate and number of SVs in function of simplification level

Table 3. Results with a microscopic image pixels set by using a kernel K_β^L (left) or a kernel K_β^G (right)

DF	R_R	n_{SV}	HCS	k	Δt
$h_{\theta,A}^1$	96.44	2	ZC_r	2	144
$h_{\theta,A}^2$	85.99	48	$Bb^*L_2H_1CH_2SC_b$	5	26574
$h_{\theta,A}^3$	90.48	63	$Y_1L^*a^*u^*$	6	29540
$h_{\theta,B}^1$	96.50	2	C_r	2	140
$h_{\theta,B}^2$	84.98	18	$L^*b^*u^*CI_2S$	4	2352
$h_{\theta,B}^3$	89.79	2	Gu^*C_b	1	147
$h_{\theta,C}^1$	96.50	2	C_r	2	140
$h_{\theta,C}^2$	82.82	3	SC_r	1	179
$h_{\theta,C}^3$	89.73	2	v^*	1	140
$h_{\theta,D}^1$	95.66	2	R	2	151
$h_{\theta,D}^2$	83.53	2	$RBb^*SL_2C_r$	2	397
$h_{\theta,D}^3$	90.09	4	GB	2	197

DF	R_R	n_{SV}	HCS	k	Δt
$h_{\theta,B}^1$	96.08	5	RH_1	3	865
$h_{\theta,B}^2$	85.90	10	$RXa^*H_1Y_2Y_3$	3	1239
$h_{\theta,B}^3$	90.43	4	BYu^*v^*	2	708
$h_{\theta,C}^1$	95.66	2	R	1	482
$h_{\theta,C}^2$	85.17	10	$RH_1Y_2Y_3$	3	1223
$h_{\theta,C}^3$	89.47	2	b^*	0	434
$h_{\theta,D}^1$	95.66	2	R	1	440
$h_{\theta,D}^2$	85.78	10	$RY_1Ch_1Y_3C_r$	3	1174
$h_{\theta,D}^3$	90.45	5	GB	2	409

R, G, B components are mostly used and those requiring a nonlinear transformation lesser used, but the recognition rate still is as efficient.

As actually the whole process of microscopic images segmentation is software performed, then we have used the BDFs produced with the configuration D and a kernel K_β^L.

9 Conclusions

A new learning method is proposed to build SVM binary decision functions which are efficient for pixel classification. This learning method produces BDF whose advantages for pixel classification problems are threefold: high generalization ability, low complexities and definition of a adapted hybrid color space. Future works will have to test this method on other pixel classification problems. It will also have to check the influence of several combination schemes of BDF, especially when the number of classes is higher. Later, it will also have to quantify the influence of other simplification methods and to compare other metaheuristics for model selection.

References

1. Vandenbroucke, N., Macaire, L., Postaire, J.G.: Color image segmentation by pixel classification in an adapted hybrid color space: application to soccer image analysis. Comput. Vis. Image Underst. **90** (2003) 190–216
2. Meurie, C., Lebrun, G., Lezoray, O., Elmoataz, A.: A comparison of supervised pixels-based color image segmentation methods. application in cancerology. WSEAS Transactions on Computers **2** (2003) 739–744
3. Vapnik, V.N.: Statistical Learning Theory. Wiley edn. New York (1998)
4. Platt, J.: Fast Training of Support Vector Machines using Sequential Minimal Optimization, Advances in Kernel Methods-Support Vector Learning. MIT Press (1999)
5. Lebrun, G., Charrier, C., Cardot, H.: SVM training time reduction using vector quantization. In: ICPR. Volume 1. (2004) 160–163
6. Gersho, A., Gray, R.M.: Vector Quantization and Signal Compression. Kluwer Academic (1991)
7. Kudo, M., Sklansky, J.: Comparison of algorithms that select features for pattern classifiers. Pattern Recognition **33** (2000) 25–41
8. Hao, J.K., Galinier, P., Habib, M.: Métaheuristiques pour l'optimisation combinatoire et l'affectation sous contraintes. Revue d'Intelligence Artificielle **13** (1999) 283–324
9. Chang, C.C., Lin, C.J.: LIBSVM: a library for support vector machines. Sofware Available at http://www.csie.ntu.edu.tw/~cjlin/libsvm (2001)
10. Collobert, R., Bengio, S.: SVMTorch: Support vector machines for large-scale regression problems. Journal of Machine Learning Research **1** (2001) 143–160
11. Hsu, C.W., Lin, C.J.: A comparison of methods for multiclass support vector machines. IEEE Transactions in Neural Networks **13** (2002) 415–425
12. Glover, F., Laguna, M.: Tabu search. Kluwer Academic Publishers, Boston MA (1997)

CamShift-Based Tracking in Joint Color-Spatial Spaces

Bogdan Kwolek

Rzeszów University of Technology,
W. Pola 2, 35-959 Rzeszów, Poland
bkwolek@prz.rzeszow.pl

Abstract. This paper presents a visual tracking algorithm that is based on CamShift. Both the face and upper body are utilized simultaneously to perform tracking. They are first tracked independently by applying two separate CamShifts which continue tracking from the locations determined in the last time step and use only color probability images. Next, the candidate locations are subjected to CamShift which operates on distributions reflecting additionally geometrical relations between the face and the body. The aim of the CamShift-based searching in the joint color-spatial space is to find the mode. Experimental tracking results on meeting video recordings are presented. They demonstrate that this algorithm is superior over traditional CamShift. Furthermore, it is very simple and computationally fast.

1 Introduction

The goal of tracking is to establish a stable track for each object of interest in successive frames. It can be seen as a problem of assigning consistent identities to objects of interest. The tracking of people is very important component of many present and near-future applications of computer vision. A number of authors have previously considered the problem of tracking objects in video [1][2][3][8].

There are several computationally inexpensive visual techniques for face tracking. One of earliest attempts to track the face in live video sequences was made by Yang and Waibel [11]. They limited the number of CPU cycles needed for realization of efficient tracking by using color information to extract desirable skin-like regions. Bradski's CamShift is very interesting because it is very fast and requires minimal training. It can deal with irregular object motion arising due to perspective, uncalibrated lenses, image noise and so on. The major advantage of the algorithm is that it can work with cheap desktop cameras. The algorithm is representative of a group of algorithms that exploit the color cue to locate and subsequently track a human face in a video sequence. It is based on a robust non-parametric technique called Mean Shift to seek the nearest mode of probability distribution. A Mean Shift-based tracker by Comaniciu et al. [3] also exploits color distributions. The algorithm requires that the new target center remains within the kernel centered on the previous location of the target. A relatively computationally inexpensive tracker of Birchfield [1] simultaneously utilizes a gradient-based elliptical outline fitted to the oval shape of the head and the color distribution enclosed. The algorithm operates through a deterministic searching in 3D space. The particle filter-based tracker [9] utilizes color information. The filter performs a random seeking guided by a probabilistic motion model to estimate the posterior probability density distributions of general non-linear and non-Gaussian systems. The algorithm uses a multi-part color modeling to take into account a rough spatial layout. The discussed work demonstrates that splitting of considered entity into two parts with specific color models improves tracking performance.

In this work we present a CamShift-based tracking algorithm. The face and upper body are utilized simultaneously to improve the tracking performance. They are first tracked independently by applying two separate CamShifts to final positions determined in the last time step. The candidate locations of rectangles with the interior color distributions most similar to distributions of the color models of face and body are determined. The final face location is then computed by CamShift acting on joint color-spatial distributions. The algorithm has been tested using the PETS-ICVS-03 meeting recordings.

The paper is organized as follows. The next section contains a review of the CamShift algorithm. In section 3. we describe our algorithm and present some tracking results which were obtained on meetings recordings. Some conclusions are drawn in the last section.

2 Object Tracking Using CamShift

The Continuously Adaptive Mean-Shift (CamShift) algorithm has been developed to perform efficient tracking of head and face in a perceptual user interface [2]. The algorithm is a generalization of the Mean Shift algorithm [5], which can only deal with static distributions. The Mean Shift algorithm provides a way to find the density modes without estimating the density. The CamShift is designed for dynamically changing distributions. The size and location of the probability distribution changes during tracking due to object movement, changing illumination conditions, viewing angle, shadows, etc. The algorithm uses color information to generate a probability distribution which is utilized to locate and then to subsequently track an object in a video sequence. It finds the mean (mode) of the distribution by iterating in the direction of maximum increase in probability density. The probability density is recomputed in each frame on the basis of the histogram back-projection [10][2]. Each pixel in the probability image represents a probability that the color of the considered pixel from an input image belongs to the object of interest. Spatial moments are used during iterations towards the mode of the distribution. This differs the CamShift algorithm from the conventional Mean Shift where the target and the candidate distributions are used to iterate towards the mode.

A variety of parametric and non-parametric statistical methods can be utilized to represent color distributions of homogeneous colored areas. The histogram is the oldest and most widely applied non-parametric density estimator. It is computed by counting the number of pixels in a region of interest that have a given color. The colors are quantized into bins. This operation allows similar color values to be clustered as single bin. The quantization into bins reduces the memory and computational requirements. The unweighted histogram is computed in the following manner:

$$q_u = \sum_{i=1}^{n} \delta[c(x_i) - u] \quad (1)$$

where the function $c : \Re^2 \rightarrow \{1, ..., m\}$ associates the value of pixel at location x_i to the bin number, n is the number of pixels, and δ is the Kronecker delta function. Due to their statistical nature color histograms can only reflect the content of images in a limited way [10]. Therefore such characterization of an object is tolerant to the noise. Histogram-based techniques are effective only when the number of bins can be kept relatively low and where sufficient data amounts are available.

The color distribution of an object represents a feature that is relatively stable under object rotation and scaling. It is also robust to partial occlusions while edge-based methods are ineffective. The major drawback with modeling the color distribution with histograms is the lack of convergence to the true density if the data set is small. In certain applications the color histograms are invariant to object translations and rotations. They vary slowly under change of angle of view and with the change in scale.

The original implementation of the CamShift algorithm uses the HSV color space [2]. A shadow cast does not change significantly the hue color component. Shadow decreases mainly the illumination component and changes the saturation component. Since the algorithm is intended to spend the lowest number of CPU cycles as possible, the color model is created by taking only a 1-D histogram of the hue component. This algorithm may fail to track the object when hue alone cannot be sufficient to distinguish the targets from the background.

The probability density image $P(x, y)$ is extracted on the basis of the histogram back-projection. This operation replaces the pixel values of the input image with the value of corresponding bin of the histogram. The value of each pixel in the probability image represents the probability that the pixel belongs to the object of interest. In order to provide the range of probability values between 0 and 255 the histogram bin values are linearly rescaled according to the following formula:

$$p_u = \min\left(\frac{255}{q_{max}} q_u, 255\right), \quad u = 1, ..., m, \quad q_{max} = \{\max(q_u)\}_{u=1}^{m}. \quad (2)$$

The mean location of the distribution within the search window is computed using moments [6][2]. It is given by:

$$x_1 = \frac{\sum_x \sum_y x P(x, y)}{\sum_x \sum_y P(x, y)}, \quad y_1 = \frac{\sum_x \sum_y y P(x, y)}{\sum_x \sum_y P(x, y)} \quad (3)$$

where x, y range over the search window. The eigenvalues (major length and width) of the probability distribution are calculated as follows [6][2]:

$$l = 0.707\sqrt{(a+c) + \sqrt{b^2 + (a-c)^2}}, \quad w = 0.707\sqrt{(a+c) - \sqrt{b^2 + (a-c)^2}} \quad (4)$$

where

$a = \frac{M_{20}}{M_{00}} - x_1^2$, $b = 2\frac{M_{11}}{M_{00}} - x_1 y_1$, $c = \frac{M_{02}}{M_{00}} - y_1^2$, $M_{00} = \sum_x \sum_y P(x,y)$,
$M_{20} = \sum_x \sum_y x^2 P(x,y)$, $M_{02} = \sum_x \sum_y y^2 P(x,y)$.

The object orientation can be estimated as follows:

$$\theta = 0.5 * \arctan \frac{b}{a-c}. \quad (5)$$

The algorithm repeats the computation of the centroid and repositioning of the search window until the position difference converges to some predefined value, that is, changes less than some assumed value. Relying on the zero-th moment M_{00} the CamShift adjusts the search window size in the course of its operation. It requires the selection of the initial location and size of the search window. The algorithm outputs the position, dimensions, and orientation of an object undergoing tracking. It can be summarized in the following steps [2]:

1. Set the search window at the initial location (x_0, y_0).
2. Determine the mean location in the search window (x_1, y_1).
3. Center the search window at the mean location computed in Step 2, set the window size to zero-th moment M_{00}.
4. Repeat Steps 2 and 3 until convergence.

The CamShift algorithm has been tested using the PETS-ICVS-03 meeting recordings. For cameras 1 and 2 in scenario C there are maximum of 3 people sitting in front of each camera, see Fig. 1. The images of size 720x576 have been converted to size of 320x240 by subsampling (consisting in selecting odd pixels in only odd lines) and bicubic-based image scaling. The tracker has been initialized in frame #10949 with the number of bins m equals 30, Smin=10 and Vmin=10. In frames #11224, #11233, and #13669 we can observe how the window size is influenced by skin colored pixels from outside of the face. In frame #13670 the track was lost and the algorithm started tracking an other head which influenced the size and the location of the window.

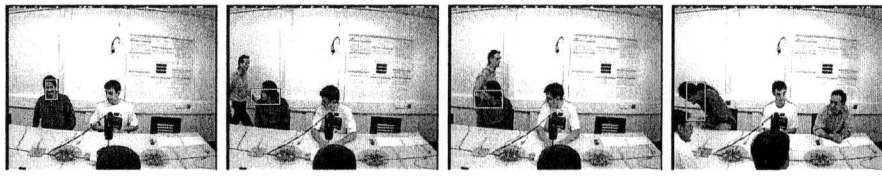

Fig. 1. Head tracking using CamShift. Frames #10969, #11224, #11233, #13669.

3 Tracking in Joint Color-Spatial Distributions

The tracking algorithm we present here follows the idea of person tracking through considering face-body relations, which has been presented in our previous paper [7]. The algorithm works by applying two probabilistic detectors of person's face and shirt colors. The probability images have been used to segment the candidates of person's face and shirt from the background. The ratio of areas, coordinates of gravity centers and geometrical relations between the labeled skin-like regions and shirt-like regions have been then used in extraction of the person from the background. The Kalman filter has been utilized to perform tracking the person within an image sequence.

In this work both the face and upper body are also utilized simultaneously to perform tracking. The face and body are first tracked independently by applying two separate CamShifts which continue tracking from the locations determined in the last time step. This operation finds the candidate locations of rectangles where the interior color distributions are most similar to distributions of the color models of face or body. A refined face location is then computed by CamShift which operates on distributions reflecting also geometrical relations between the face and the body.

Denote by $X_f = (x_f, y_f)$ and $X_b = (x_b, y_b)$ the position of the rectangles surrounding the face and body, respectively. The difference $X_f - X_b = (x_f - x_b, y_f - y_b) = (x_{fb}, y_{fb})$ reflects the configuration between face and body. The probability that $X_f - X_b$ represents the human H can be expressed by product of two Gaussians:

$$p(X_f - X_b \mid H) = G(x_f - x_b, \mu_x, \sigma_x) G(y_f - y_b, \mu_y, \sigma_y) \qquad (6)$$

where $\mu_x, \sigma_x, \mu_y, \sigma_y$ can be determined in advance from training samples.

Denote by $\rho(X_f)$ and $\rho(X_b)$ the similarity of the model color distributions of face and body to the candidate face or body color distributions, which are surrounded by rectangles at positions X_f and X_b, respectively. In order to compare two color distributions we need a metric of similarity or dissimilarity. In the discussed algorithm we have implemented the histogram intersection technique [10]. For a given pair of histograms I and M, each containing n values, the intersection of the histograms is defined as follows: $\rho = \sum_{i=1}^{N} \min(I_i, M_i)$. The terms I_i, M_i represent the number of pixels inside the i-th bin of the current and the model histogram, respectively, whereas N the total number of bins. The result of the intersection of two histograms is the number of pixels that have the same color in both histograms. To obtain a similarity measure with values between the zero and one the intersection has been normalized.

Bayes rule states that:

$$p(H \mid \rho(X_f), \rho(X_b), X_f - X_b) \propto p(\rho(X_f \mid H)) p(\rho(X_b \mid H)) p(X_f - X_b \mid H) p(H) \qquad(7)$$

The best location corresponding to the local maximum of the probability can be obtained through a time-consuming search in the 4D space $S = (X_f, X_b) = (x_f, y_f, x_b, y_b)$:

$$S^* = \arg\max_{S_i \in S} p(\rho(X_f \mid H)) p(\rho(X_b \mid H)) p(X_f - X_b \mid H). \qquad (8)$$

Instead of time consuming deterministic searching in the space S in order to find the extremum, we construct in each step a joint color-spatial distributions and apply the CamShift alternately to distributions in order to find two modes. The joint color-spatial distributions are created as the product of color probability images and Gaussian distributions reflecting the final face-body configuration in the last time step. The aim of CamShift iterations is to find such locations of two 2D Gaussians in the color probability images, where two successive locations of the face or body mode in joint color-space distribution differ less than some predefined value.

Having the candidate face location $X_f = (x_f, y_f)$ we can extract the product of corresponding raw probability image of the body P_b and a 2D Gaussian $G(\mu_b, \Sigma_b)$, where $\mu_b = (x_f - x_{fb}, y_f - y_{fb})$, $\Sigma_b = \begin{pmatrix} \sigma_x^2 & 0 \\ 0 & \sigma_y^2 \end{pmatrix}$, x_{fb} and y_{fb} are determined by face-body configuration from the last time step. Using such a modified body probability image we utilize CamShift in order to find the mode. Next, taking the location X_b corresponding to this mode we can extract the product of the raw probability image of the face P_f and a 2D Gaussian $G(\mu_f, \Sigma_f)$, where $\mu_f = (x_b + x_{fb}, y_b + y_{fb})$, $\Sigma_f = \begin{pmatrix} \sigma_x^2 & 0 \\ 0 & \sigma_y^2 \end{pmatrix}$. Finally, using the modified probability image of the face with joint color-spatial information we utilize CamShift to find the mode. At the end of each step we have a new candidate face location X_f which has been found by CamShift operating on joint color-spatial distributions. Using the raw probability images and the new face location X_f we repeat such recomputing of the raw probability images as well as CamShift-based searching until a distance between two successive face locations computed by CamShift converges to some predefined value.

Starting from the candidate body location $X_b = (x_b, y_b)$, which has been determined by one of the CamShifts working independently, a similar searching has been conducted. The upper images in Fig. 2. depict the locations of the face and body that were obtained with the searching initialized from X_f, whereas the images in the middle row show the locations which were obtained with the initialization at X_b. Having in disposal two face-body locations we computed the similarities of color distributions to the original face or body distributions and chosen the more similar face-body. The locations of face and body extracted in such a way estimate the locations S^* given by (8). The images which constitute the bottom row in the Fig. 2. demonstrate the locations of the rectangle surrounding the tracked face. The frames #11233 and #13669 demonstrate improved tracking capabilities of the proposed approach, see also Fig. 1.

To deal with situations where the evidence of one component of the face-body structure is weak or even missing, we generated additional Gaussian sub-distributions in the raw probability images. They have been constructed using information about the location of the corresponding face or body component as well as face-body geometrical configuration, which had been determined in the last frame. Due to such recovery parts in the distributions the algorithm can continue the tracking, even when the evidence of only one part of the face-body structure is relatively strong. Experiments demonstrated that such complementary distributions improve also the overall performance of tracking. The mentioned above operation has been realized before the computations in the joint color-spatial distributions.

Figure 3. depicts the number of iterations which were needed for convergence in each time step. Typically, the average number of iterations in each call of CamShift is less than four. The picture (a) reported in Fig. 4. demonstrates the candidate rectangles on the image with maximal number of iterations, whereas the picture (c) shows the candidate rectangles on the last image in the sequence. The locations of the rectangles have been then refined using CamShift operating

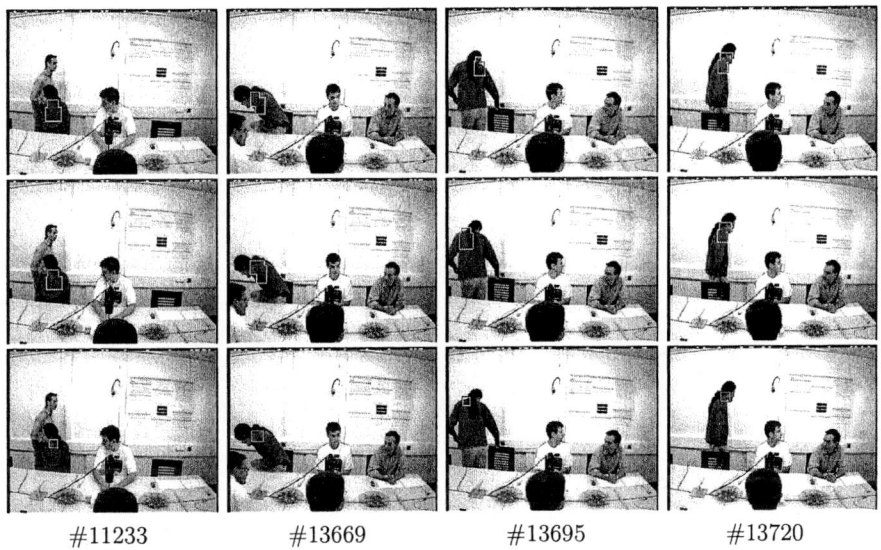

Fig. 2. Tracking using joint color-spatial distribution

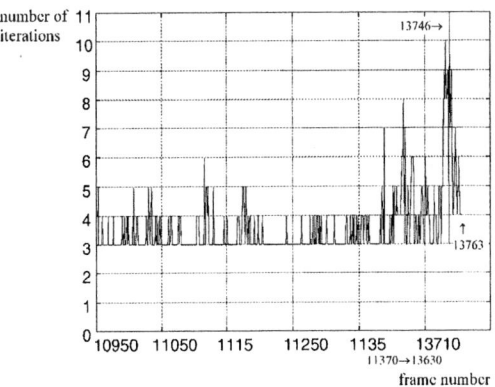

Fig. 3. Number of iterations versus frame number

Fig. 4. Convergence of the algorithm. Frame #13746 (a), (b). Frame #13763 (c), (d).

on joint color-spatial distributions, see pictures (b) and (d).The processing time is 100 msec on average for 320x240 images on an ordinary Pentium III PC.

4 Conclusion

The superiority of CamShift-based tracking using joint color-spatial distributions over the traditional CamShift tracking arises because the geometrical relations between face and body yield useful information. As a consequence we developed the modified CamShift tracking method. The method is computationally fast. Further improvements to the algorithm could be made through integrating the tracking algorithm with the background subtraction.

References

1. Birchfield, S.: Elliptical Head Tracking Using Intensity Gradients and Color Histograms, In Proc. of the IEEE Conf. on Comp. Vision and Pattern Recognition (1998) 232–237.
2. Bradski, G. R.: Computer Vision Face Tracking as a Component of a Perceptual User Interface, In Proc. of the IEEE Workshop on Applications of Comp. Vision, (1998) 214–219.
3. Comaniciu, D., Ramesh, V., Meer, P.: Real-Time Tracking of Non-Rigid Objects Using Mean Shift, In Proc. of the IEEE Conf. on Comp. Vision and Pattern Recognition (2000) 142–149.
4. Elgammal, A., Harwood, D., Davis, L.: Non-parametric Model for Background Subtraction, European Conf. on Computer Vision, vol. 2 (2000) 751–767.
5. Fukunaga, K.: Introduction to Statistical Pattern Recognition, sec. ed., Acad. Press (1990).
6. Horn, B. K. P.: Robot Vision, The MIT Press (1986).
7. Kwolek, B.: Color Vision Based Person Following with a Mobile Robot, In Proc. of the 3rd Int. Workshop on Robot Motion and Control (2002) 375–380.
8. Kwolek, B.: Stereovision-Based Head Tracking Using Color and Ellipse Fitting in a Particle Filter, 8th European Conf. on Computer Vision, LNCS, 3024 (2004) 192–204.
9. Perez, P., Hue, C., Vermaak, J., Gangnet, M.: Color-Based Probabilistic Tracking, European Conf. on Computer Vision (2002) 661–675.
10. Swain, M. J., Ballard, D. H.: Color Indexing, Int. Journal of Computer Vision, vol. 7, no. 1 (1991) 11–32.
11. Yang, J., Waibel, A.: A Real-Time Face Tracker. In Proc. of the IEEE Workshop on Applications of Comp. Vision (1996) 142–147.

A Robust Detector for Distorted Music Staves[*]

Mariusz Szwoch

Knowledge Engineering Department, Technical University of Gdansk,
80-952 Gdansk, Poland
szwoch@eti.pg.gda.pl

Abstract. In this paper an algorithm for music staves detection is presented. The algorithm bases on horizontal projections in local windows of a score image and farther processing of resulting histograms and their connections. Experiments carried out, proved high efficiency of presented algorithm and its robustness in case of non-ideal staff lines: skew and with barrel and pincushion distortions. The algorithm allows for usage of acquisition devices alternative to scanner such as digital cameras.

1 Introduction

Optical Music Recognition (OMR) is the process of converting digitized sheets of music into an electronic form that is suitable for further processing such as editing and performing by computer. More sophisticated areas of applications are automatic accompaniment, music transposing, extracting parts for individual instruments and musicological analysis of the music. The OMR systems are also the tools used for information retrieval process that takes place in creation of music digital libraries.

The OMR systems have already been developed for almost forty years that has lead to the state of high accuracy of music recognition process. Many researchers have reported the recognition efficiency over 90% of their systems [1-8]. Also several commercial systems are available on the market. In most cases, those systems operate properly only with well scanned documents of high quality. Using a scanner to digitize flat score pages assures that the only geometric distortion presented in a scanned image could be a small slant that is easily corrected by many of presented algorithms [1-10]. Only few attempts have been made to deal with scanned 3D score sources (like book pages) with non-linear bowing near the page edges [9] or with scores digitized with other optical devices [7].

The rapid growth of digital cameras' technology in last years caused that they can be considered as alternative devices for acquiring of digital images. Their essential advantages over popular scanners are high mobility and low destruction effects over digitized documents. Unfortunately, digital cameras have also several shortcomings preventing them from broad using in this domain. The main disadvantages of digital cameras are problems with picture exposure and non-linear distortions (*barrel* and/or *pincushion*) introduced to acquired images by their optics (Fig. 1).

---

[*] This paper is sponsored by the Polish Government's research funds for the years 2005-2008 as a research project No 3 T11C 027 28.

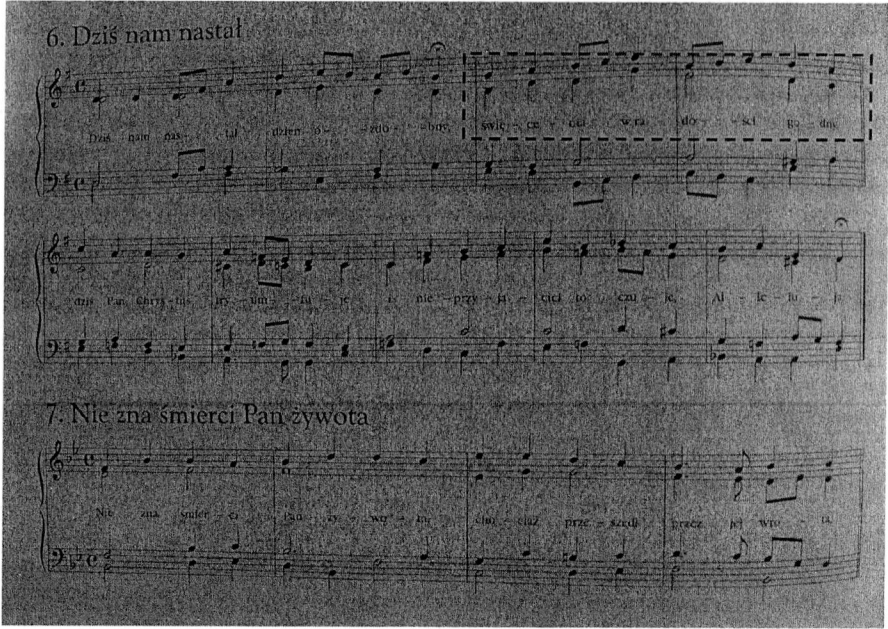

Fig. 1. Original score document taken by digital camera (5Mp) and converted to grayscale. Dotted rectangle marks the region shown as an example in Fig. 2 and 4.

In general, it is not possible to create an universal algorithm compensating geometrical distortions in images regardless of camera type and zoom settings. Fortunately, acquiring images with some regular patterns e.g. *squared* or with *staff lines*, gives a good opportunity for creation of algorithms that could detect their true shapes giving sufficient information for distortion removal. This paper concerns that aspect of *staves* detection in musical score images The presented algorithm enables to locate staff-lines with high precision giving all needed information for further image processing and recognition. The algorithm is fast and efficient for different kinds of distortions in analyzed score images.

2 Staves Location by Matching Local Histograms

The correct detection and processing of staves is fundamental to OMR process. The staff lines create a two dimensional coordinate system for interpretation of other musical symbols. The theoretically equal distance between any two subsequent lines within the same stave (and on the same page) gives the basic measure unit (called *Dist* in this paper) for other musical symbols within the same score. Finally, due to its regular linear shape, staff lines are also ideal determinant for any geometric distortions of digitized scores. Though, in most cases staff lines are removed from musical document's image, their positions are remembered for further usage during the recognition and interpretation processes.

Staves localization is not an easy task because of frequent disturbances and distortions of staff lines. Disturbances may be caused by low quality of original documents and also by other musical symbols coincident with determined lines. Geometric distortions of images are usually result of optical faults or not flat scanned surface (like books). Numerous tests proved that staff lines in digitized musical documents not always are parallel, horizontal, equidistant, of the same width or even straight!

In this section, the staves detection algorithm is presented. This algorithm bases on horizontal projections in narrow vertical strips and on farther analysis of created histograms. Many staves detection algorithms analyze *original image* searching for five equally spaced and sized run-lenghts of black pixels in [6,7,10] or straight lines using the Hough transform or mathematical morphology [4]. Unlike them, the presented algorithm operates on *histograms* what results in its low computational complexity. Additionally processing histograms of *local* projections gives it greater flexibility comparing with algorithm operating on *global* projections [1,2,5]. This flexibility allows to efficiently detect skew, bowed and spherically distorted staves.

Finally, the detected staff lines are approximated as piece-linear lines or by polynomial curves. These exact approximations allow for optional image unwarping and farther staves removal from analyzed image.

2.1 Local Horizontal Projections and Processing of Resulting Histograms

In the first stage, the analyzed image is vertically sliced into the narrow vertical strips VS_i of width equal to 2·*Dist*, numerated from 1 to N (Fig.2a). For each vertical strip VS_i, the horizontal projection's histogram H_i of black pixels is counted (Fig.2b). In the next step all histograms H_i are preprocessed in the following way:

1. Clearing histograms entries containing small values (region A in Fig. 2b-c).
2. Successive breaking of histogram columns that are wider then 1·*Dist*. Columns are broken near the local minimum values (region B in Fig. 2b-c).
3. Locating of distinct local maximum values (*peaks*) in histograms. Neighboring columns are cleared (region C in Fig. 2b-c).
4. All histograms are filtered in order to find five consecutive peaks within the distant of about 1·*Dist*. Unlike other stave filters (e.g. [6]), in this algorithm a greater level of tolerance is assumed allowing to detect lines lying in an average distance of *Dist*±1 pixel with variation of ±2 pixels for particular lines. After this stage all histograms contain mainly peaks representing pieces of proper staff lines (Fig. 2d).

2.2 Creating of Connection Arrays and Staves Detection

The next stage of the algorithm is creation of connections' arrays between histogram peaks HP_i^k and HP_{i+1}^l in every successive pair of histograms H_i and H_{i+1}, where k and l are vertical coordinates of histograms entries HP_i^k and HP_{i+1}^l (Fig.3). In each pair of histograms H_{i-1} and H_i, for each connection HP_{i-1}^j and HP_i^k, the linear approximation of predicted vertical position y_{pred} of the peak HP_{i+1}^l in the next histogram H_{i+1} is determined. Two histograms peaks HP_i^k and HP_{i+1}^l are then connected if their vertical distance $|l - y_{pred}| \leq 0.25 \cdot Dist$ (gray region (a) in Fig. 3). If no histogram peak is found in this range, y_{pred} coordination is replaced by the last vertical coordinate, i.e. k value (range b) in Fig. 3).

Fig. 2. Stages of histograms completing: part of original image (Fig. 1) sliced into vertical strips (a), local histograms H_i of horizontal projections (b), local histograms after preprocessing (c) and after final filtering (d)

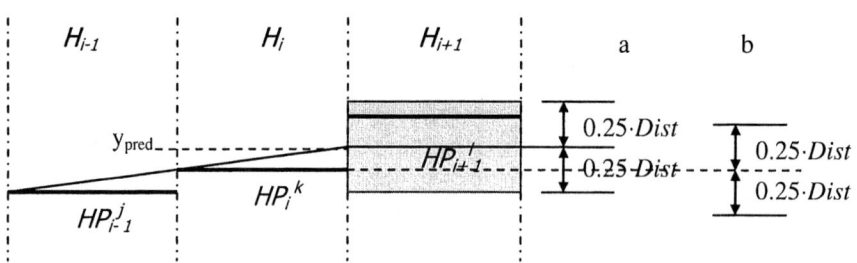

Fig. 3. Searching for connection between histograms peaks HP_i^k and HP_{i+1}^l using predicted vertical coordinate y_{pred} (a) or the last coordinate k (b) as a center for vertical range

Fig. 4. Stages of stave processing: determined connections (a), final staff lines (b) and image after staves removing

As a result, an initial piece-linear approximation of staff lines (and some other symbols) is achieved (Fig. 4 a). In the next step the array of connections is processed in order to remove redundant parallel connections and to link broken connections due to locally lower quality of image or some errors in histograms processing. Further processing covers removing of short lines, gathering staff lines into staves and removing of other lines. The final result is presented in Fig. 4b. Recognized staff lines can be farther approximated by polynomial curves. Staves removing algorithm uses line parameters to efficiently remove staff lines from the image (Fig. 4c).

3 Evaluation

To validate the results of stave detection by presented algorithm 30 full-page scores had been taken by digital camera[1]. The resulting 200DPI resolution of acquired images is sufficient[2] for OMR processing [8]. The main drawbacks are serious irregular barrel distortions near the corners of the images (Fig. 1). These distortions are well visualized as curvature of detected staff lines (Fig. 5).

The described algorithm was implemented in the *ScoreExplorer* OMR system [8]. All experiments carried out proved very high efficiency of staves detection algorithm (100%). Each staff line was properly localized and its run was properly routed that was confirmed by accurate staff lines removing and farther interpretation of

---

[1] For all tests the 5Mp Sony FX-717 camera was used, in full automatic exposure mode, with no flash light.
[2] A good measure of score image's quality is an average staff line width. For all tested images it was 3 pixels per line.

Fig. 5. Staff lines extracted from score image presented in Fig.1

recognized musical symbols (e.g. pitch of notes). The only drawback of the algorithm of stave detection is a problem with the ends of staff lines, which are too easily extended beyond staves limits, e.g. over an accolade. In fact this problem is solved later on in OMR process when vertical elements, such as bars, are located.

The algorithm based on local projections is characterized by low computational complexity due to processing rather histograms than pixels. The average staves detection time on 4.4Mp A4 image is about 0.3s including partial visualization of detection process[3]. The processing time is short enough not to influence the whole recognition process. The algorithm could obviously be sped up by several improvements including recoding it in assembler and using every second or even every third vertical strip. Some savings may also be achieved by setting the strips width to 8 or its even multiple (16, 32, ..).

Experiments with *ScoreExplorer* proved that, despite good staves localization, the overall system's recognition efficiency decreased from 95% (for scanned images) to about 80% (for distorted images). The obvious reason is lack of tolerance for image deformations in system's recognition algorithms. The detected staves (Fig.5) could be used to eliminate distortions present in score images possibly increasing the recognition rate. Unfortunately, at the moment only simple vertical-unwarping algorithm is implemented in the *ScoreExplorer*. It corrects only vertical positions of musical symbols whereas slight slant of vertical primitives still remains (Fig. 6).

Detected staff lines can be represented as piece-linear lines or as polynomial curves. The first representation is very exact but consumes a bit more memory for all vertical coordinates of nodes (about 70 for each staff line in tested images). Experiments carried out for *scanned* scores proved that quadratic polynomial approximation of lines is sufficient but it is not so in the case of images *acquired by digital camera*. In fact irregular distortions cause that it is impossible to exactly approximate staff

---

[3] All experiments were carried out on a PC with Athlon 2.2 GHz processor.

lines with cubic or greater degree polynomial curves. The problem usually arises near the ends of lines which curvature is usually stronger then in the middle parts. Fortunately, in most cases the approximations errors are perceptible at the very ends of lines and do not affect recognition of other musical symbols (Fig.7).

Fig. 6. The result of simple unwarping of the example image from Fig.1

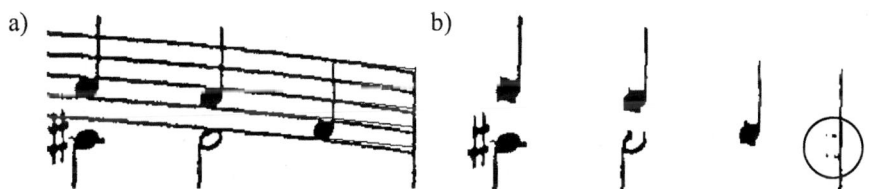

Fig. 7. An example of staff lines' approximation errors: a) part of original image with approximating cubic curves and b) staff lines removing errors (circled)

4 Summary

Incessant development of digital optical devices creates new possibilities of images acquiring for digital documents processing. These high-resolution devices cover not only digital cameras but in near future also Internet cameras, video cameras, handhelds and even phones. Though, the quality of their optics is generally not sufficient for pattern recognition it is possible to use them in some particular domains such as OMR.

The algorithm presented in this paper is fast and efficient for images scanned and taken by digital camera. It combines low computational complexity of histograms processing with flexibility of local methods allowing detection of straight, bowed and spherically distorted staff lines. By exactly determining the shapes of staff lines it is possible to efficiently remove them from score images enabling farther OMR processing and also to position on staves all recognized musical symbol. The experiments carried out proved that staff lines' approximation by polynomial curves is not sufficient in case of non-linear geometrical distortions of images. In that cases piece-linear approximation suits better.

Though, exact staves localization is a precondition for efficient recognition of musical documents it is not the sufficient condition in case of serious geometric distortions of source images. In that case, advanced de-bowing algorithms have to be used [9] or recognition algorithms have to be modified to take into account various deformations of recognized symbols. Developing of such algorithms will make possible to effectively use digital cameras in Optical Music Recognition.

References

1. Fujinaga I: Optical music recognition using projections, Master's thesis, McGill University, Montreal, CA, 1988.
2. Carter N.P., Bacon R.A.: Automatic Recognition of Printed Music, Structured Document Analysis, Springer-Verlag 1992, pp. 456-476.
3. Kato H., Inokuchi S.: A Recognition System for Printed Piano Music Using Musical Knowledge and Constraints, Structured Document Analysis, Springer-Verlag 1992.
4. Modayur B.R., et al.: MUSER: A prototype musical score recognition system using mathematical morphology, Machine vision and Applications, Springer-Verlag, 1993.
5. Roth M.: An Approach To Recognition Of Printed Music, Swiss Federal Institute of Technology Zurich January, 1994, Internet.
6. Reed K.T., Parker J.R.: Automatic Computer Recognition of Printed Music; Proceedings of ICPR'96, 803-807, 1996.
7. Matsushima T.: Automated high-speed recognition of printed music (WABOT-2 vision system). Proc. of the 1985 I.C. on Advances Robotics, JIRA, Tokyo, 1985.
8. Szwoch M., Meus G., Tutkaj P.: Score Explorer: A Musical Score Recognition System, In Proc. of GKPO, Warsaw 2000.
9. Wijaya K., Bainbridge D.: Staff Line Restoration, Image Processing and its Applications, Conference Publication No. 465, IEE 1999.
10. I. Leplumey, J. Camillerapp, G. Lorette: A robust detector for music staves, in Proc. of the ICDAR, pp. 902-905, Tsukuba Science City, Japan, 1993.

Illusory Surface Perception Using a Hierarchical Neural Network Model of the Visual Pathways*

Woobeom Lee and Wookhyun Kim

Department of Computer Engineering, Yeungnam University,
214-1 Dae-dong, Gyungsan-si, Gyungbuk 712-749, Republic of Korea
{beomlee, whkim}@yumail.ac.kr

Abstract. Illusory contours occurring in the various perceptual phenomena are essentially accompanied with illusory surfaces. Accordingly, we propose a novel approach for the perception of illusory surface arising from illusory contours. The proposed method uses a hierarchical neural network model. It is likely done in the visual cortex domain in a cascade manner, and uses the response properties of neuron cells found in the visual pathways. The stimuli for forming the illusory contours are induced by modelling the end-stopped cell, and the induced stimuli for the surface perception is then formed from the extracted illusory contours. Finally, the surface perception is completed by restoring surface successively from the induced contour stimuli. The proposed model was demonstrated on a variety of illusory contour figures, and experimental results showed that the perception of illusory surface is a very successful.

Keywords: illusory contours, illusory surface, visual cortex domain, induced stimuli, surface restoration

1 Introduction

An illusory contour variously called subjective contours, cognitive contours, ambiguous contours, anomalous contours, contours without gradients, and quasi-perceptive margins, is occurred in a wide variety of circumstances in nature. And, this illusory is an important cues in the various perceptual phenomena such as occlusion, transparency, depth sensations, brightness contrast and object recognition[1].

Object boundaries and surface discontinuities in the image exist as the physical changes generally such as intensity, wavelength, depth, and luminance. However, if the boundaries are not made explicit by the physical changes, illusory contours is very useful in that case, because it is seen when a stimulus configuration produces the perception of an edge in an area where there is no physical changes.

Many computational models have been proposed to describe the formation of illusory contours, including Ullman(1976), Brady and Grimson(1982), Grossberg

---

* This research was supported by the Yeungnam University research grants in 2004.

and Mingolla(1985), Nitzberg and Mumford(1990), Guy and Medioni(1992), Heitger and von der Heydt(1993), Grossberg(1994), Williams and Hanson(1994), Kellman and Shipley(1995), Williams and Jacobs(1995)[1]. However, it is still an open challenge to achieve the perception of an illusory contour and surface.

Accordingly, we propose a novel approach for the perception of illusory surface arising from illusory contours that uses a hierarchical neural network model. The proposed approach focuses on extracting the induced stimuli, such as similarity and proximity, concavities, closure, direction of line-endings, for perception of an illusory contour. Also, as these stimuli for the illusory contours are always accompanied with illusory surfaces essentially, the task of surface perception should be performed.

The proposed method is likely done in the visual cortex domain in a cascade manner, and uses the response properties of neuron cells found in the visual pathways. Thus, the stimuli for forming the illusory contours are induced by modelling the end-stopped cell, and the induced stimuli for surface perception is then extracted by applying the models of simple cell to the induced illusory contours. Finally, the surface perception is completed by restoring surface using a complex cell successively.

2 The Visual Pathways: Hubel and Wiesel's Hierarchical Hypothesis[2]

The mammalian visual system receives input in the form of visible light. Photoreceptors in the retina absorb this light, emitting neural signals on the process which, in turn, stimulates bipolar and retinal ganglion cells. The center-surround nature of these cells' receptive fields causes them to respond strongly to differential illumination. In the foveal region of the retina, where visual acuity is at its highest, there is a one-to-one correspondence between photoreceptors and retinal ganglion cells. Elsewhere, the outputs of many photoreceptors converge on single ganglion cells, significantly compressing the neural representation of our visual environment. Information from each retina passes along the optic nerves, though the optic chasm and into the LGN(: lateral geniculate nucleus). The cells within the LGN do not appear to exert any profound transformation upon the neural information they receive other than organizing retinal signals into right and left visual field components.

From the LGN, information is topographically mapped onto the visual cortex where it is further processed by simple, complex, and hypercomplex cells. The terms "simple", "complex" etc. refer to the types of stimuli that elicit responses from these cells. In a serial model of vision processing, the visual input required to activate a cell within the cortex becomes progressively more complicated further along the visual pathway.

The hypothesis made by Hubel and Wiesel was that information was processed by a cascade of cells: LGN to simple cells, simple cells to complex cells, complex cells to hypercomplex cells, and hypercomplex cells to another hypercomplex cells. Though there have been some different opinions to Hubel

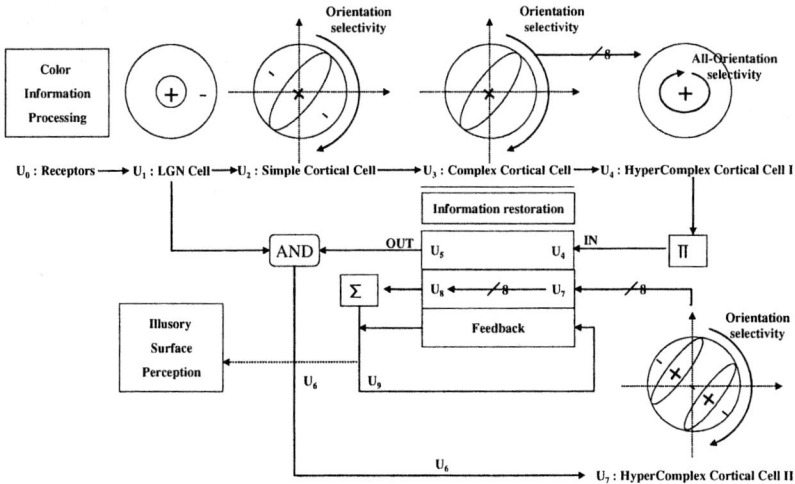

Fig. 1. A hierarchical Neural Network Model proposed in our approach

and Wiesel's serial model in the visual pathway, the architecture of the proposed model is still based on the ideas developed by Hubel and Wiesel.

Accordingly, as mentioned, a spatial filtering neural network in our approach is proposed according to the Hubel and Wiesel's hierarchical hypothesis. Each Layer in neural network refers to the response properties of neuron cells in the visual pathways. The receptive field corresponding to the response properties of those cells is then modeled as the spatial filters, which respond to the function of spatial features extraction from an image.

3 A Hierarchical Neural Network Model

As shown in Fig. 1, we propose a hierarchical neural network model for illusory surface perception. The proposed model is referring to the responses of cortical cells in the visual cortex domain, and consists of the following three stages: preprocessing, illusory contours perception, illusory surface restoration.

3.1 Preprocessing

U_0 **Image Acquisition Layer:** The mammalian visual system classifies color information, which is an important task in visual information processing. However, since the illusory contour figures, which is seen as lying on top of the remaining parts of patterns, is represented with white and the others usually are different colors, the color classification in illusory contour figures is not of great significance. Thus, for simplicity, we can remove the process of color classification by using a binary image.

U_1 **Contrast Extraction Layer:** In order to extract the contrast information from the binary image, a set of two dimensional circular symmetric DOG(: Difference Of two Gaussians) filters is used. This filter corresponds to an on-center and off-surround receptive field of ganglion cells found in mammal's retina[3], as follows:

$$d_1(x,y) = \frac{1}{2\pi\sigma_e^2}\exp\left(-\frac{r^2}{2\sigma_e^2}\right) - \frac{1}{2\pi\sigma_i^2}\exp\left(-\frac{r^2}{2\sigma_i^2}\right) \quad (1)$$

where r represents distance from the origin, σ_e and σ_i represent the space constants of excitatory and inhibitory regions, respectively, and the ratio of space constants $\sigma_e/\sigma_i = 1.6$. The ratio yields a good approximation to the ideal Laplacian operator[4]. The output $u_1(x,y)$ of layer U_1 can be expressed as following;

$$u_1(x,y) = \psi\left[\int\int_A d_1(\xi,\eta)u_0(x+\xi,y+\eta)d\xi d\eta - \theta_1\right] \quad (2)$$

where A denotes the area of receptive field (ξ,η), and θ_1 is the threshold value for a step function $\psi[\ ]$. U_1 layer of Eq. (2) is practically implemented as the discrete form for image convolution processing.

3.2 Illusory Contours Perception

An illusory surface arises from the perception of illusory contours. Thus, the induced stimuli for forming illusory contours must extract. This task is performed by detecting the end-stopped points in an image, and it refers to the response properties of hypercomplex cells in the visual cortex domain.

U_2 **Orientation Selectivity Information Extraction Layer:** Simple cells are excellent at detecting the presence of simple visual features, such as lines and edges of a particular orientation. In consideration of the orientation selectivity property of simple cells, a set of asymmetrical two dimensional DOG filters for eight preferred orientations is used. The filter with a preferred orientation ϕ is defined by

$$d_2(x',y',\phi) = \left(\exp(-\frac{x'^2}{2\sigma_e^2}) - \frac{\sigma_e}{\sigma_i}\exp(-\frac{x'^2}{2\sigma_i^2})\right) \cdot \exp(-\frac{y'^2}{2\sigma_{en}^2}) \quad (3)$$

$$u_2(x,y,\phi) = \psi\left[\int\int_A d_2(\xi,\eta,\phi)u_0(x+\xi,y+\eta)d\xi d\eta - \theta_1\right] \quad (4)$$

where $(x',y') = (x\cos\phi + y\sin\phi, -x\sin\phi + y\cos\phi)$ are rotated coordinates, and σ_{en} determines the sensitivity of preferred orientation of the filter. This filter corresponds to a simple cell receptive field found in mammal's visual cortex domain[3]. The output of layer U_2 can be expressed in the form of Eq. (4).

U_3 Orientation Selectivity Information Restoration Layer: An complex cell responds to stimuli such as lines and edges of a particular orientation. However, the exact location of the stimulus is of no concern to a complex cell, as long as it is within that cell's receptive field. Therefore, complex cells are very effective for restoring of the declined information. In order to apply a complex cell to the information restoration, a set of two dimensional Gaussian filters with a preferred orientation ϕ is used, as defined bellow:

$$d_3(x, y, \phi) = \exp(-\frac{x'^2}{2\sigma_x^2}) \cdot \exp(-\frac{y'^2}{2\sigma_{en}^2}) \tag{5}$$

This filter corresponds to a complex cell receptive field found in mammal's visual cortex domain[3]. The output of layer U_3 is likely to do that of layer U_2.

U_4 Induced Stimuli Extraction Layer for an Illusory Contour: The sorts of visual features that appear to elicit response from hypercomplex cells are light-dark stimuli containing corners, curves and broken lines. The hypothetical arrangement of complex cells can implement an end-stopped hypercomplex receptive field found in mammal's visual cortex domain[5].

Accordingly, an extracting of the induced stimuli is performed for the perception of an illusory contour in this layer, and then the induced stimuli correspond to end-stopped points in image. Consequently, the output of layer U_4 can be expressed in the form of Eq. (6).

$$u_4(x, y) = \prod_{\phi=0}^{7} u_3(x, y, \phi) \tag{6}$$

This layer corresponds to the synapse connection of complex cells that recover the information according to the orientation selectivity. This means that the common factor in all preferred orientation regards as end stopped points.

$U_{5,6}$ Information Restoration Layer: The role of layer U_5 is to recover the weaken or reduced stimuli while the induced stimuli is extracted. It is achieved by using a set of two dimensional circular symmetric Gaussian filters form of Eq. (5). However, The layer U_5 yields not only the information restoration, but also the unnecessary information. Thus, To remove unnecessary noises, the U_6 layer performs a boolean operation with the image u_1, as follows:

$$u_6(x, y) = u_5(x, y) \wedge u_1(x, y) \tag{7}$$

where $\wedge$ represents a logical AND operation in an image.

3.3 Surface Perception from Illusory Contours

After a completion of the illusory contours, the surface perception can be formed form illusory contours. This task consists of the extracting induced stimuli for surface perception, and the surface restoration from induced stimuli.

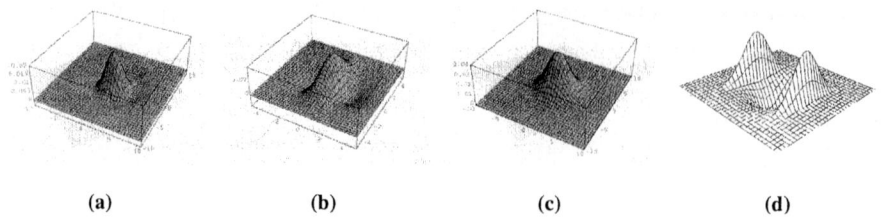

Fig. 2. 2D profile of spatial filter used in our approach (a) Ganglion cell, (b) Simple cell (c) Complex cell, (d) Hypercomplex cell

U_7 **Induced Stimuli Extraction Layer for Illusory Surface:** In order to perceive an illusory surface, this layer extracts the induced stimuli from responses between the induced stimuli of illusory contours. The spatial filter in this layer is a set of off-center even-symmetrical filter with eight preferred orientations. It is defined by using two dimensional three Gaussian function, as follows:

$$g(\sigma, x) = exp(-\frac{x^2}{2\sigma^2})$$

$$d_7(x', y', \phi) = \Big(g(\sigma_e, x' - l) - g(\sigma_i, x') + g(\sigma_e, x' + l)\Big) \cdot g(\sigma_{en}, y') \quad (8)$$

where l denotes the space constant between excitatory and inhibitory region, and as the distance between two positive peaks in this filter, corresponding to the interval of induced stimuli. The profile of this filter is similar to another type of simple cell receptive field found in mammal's visual cortex domain.[5]

U_8 **Information Restoration Layer:** As mentioned in layer U_3, U_5, this layer responds to recover the induced stimuli of a particular orientation. Thus, the filters used in this layer are the very same as the that of layer U_3, U_5.

U_9 **Illusory Surface Formation Layer:** The formation of illusory surface is achieved from the extracted stimuli using the boolean operation of image and the successive feedback process. However, although the surface perception is completed by the successive restoration of illusory surface, the results of restoration include an outer region of illusory contours. Thus, the surface restoration in this layer is restricted within the inner region of illusory contours.

The output of layer U_9 can be expressed as following:

$$u_9^{n+1}(x, y) = u_9^n(x, y) + \sum_{\phi=0}^{7} \psi\Big[\int\int_A d_3(\xi, \eta, \phi) u_9^n(x + \xi, y + \eta) d\xi d\eta - \theta_1\Big] \quad (9)$$

$$\text{where,} \quad u_9^0(x, y) = \Big(\sum_{\phi=0}^{7} u_8(x, y, \phi)\Big) + u_6(x, y)$$

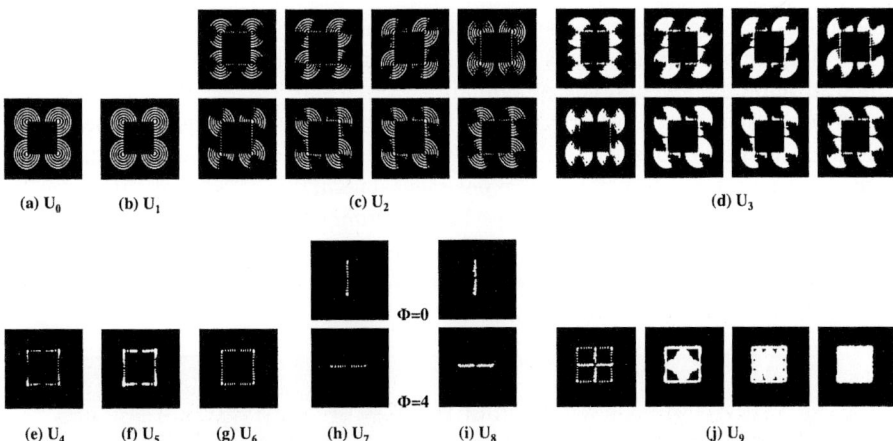

Fig. 3. Experimental Results in all Layers (a) U_0 Image acquisition layer, (b) U_1 Contrast extraction layer, (c) U_2 Orientation selectivity information extraction layer, (d) U_3 Orientation selectivity information restoration layer, (e) U_4 Induced stimuli extraction layer for an illusory contour, (f) and (g) $U_{5,6}$ Information restoration layer, (h) U_7 Induced stimuli extraction layer for illusory surface, (i) U_8 Information restoration layer for induced stimuli, (j) U_9 Illusory surface formation layer

where + represents a logical OR operation in an image. The feedback(fulfilling) processing in layer U_9 is performed successively until removing the gap between the induced stimuli and forming surface.

4 Experimental Results

In order to show the performance of the proposed model, experiments have been carried out using various Kanizsa-type illusory contour figures. The proposed neural network was implemented using the C language under the X-Window environment in a SUN SPARC workstation. It should be note that the color classification of layer U_0 is omitted for simplicity. Because the color classification in perceiving occluded surfaces from illusory contours is not of great significance, the binary image was merely used in experiment.

As a results, the proposed model was demonstrated on a variety of illusory contour figures, and experimental results showed that the proposed neural network model is a very successful and sufficiently general. Fig. 2 illustrates a 2D profile of the spatial filters corresponding to neuron cell receptive field implemented in the proposed neural network, and examples of the experimental result are shown in Fig. 3 and Fig. 4.

5 Conclusions

We propose a novel approach for the perception of illusory surface arising from illusory contours that uses a hierarchical neural network model. The focus of our modelling is to use the response properties of neuron cells in a cascade manner, and to implement spatial filters corresponding to a variety of cell receptive field found in mammal's visual cortex domain.

However, some problems remain for future works. It is an unsupervised problems such as the size of spatial filter, the interval of induced stimuli and threshold value determination. Nonetheless, experimental results showed that the proposed neural network model is a very successful and sufficiently general. Therefore, our approach has potential application in several other areas of vision, such as occluded surface perception, grouping, segmentation.

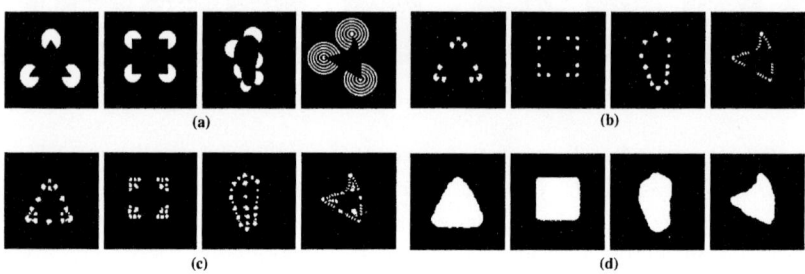

Fig. 4. Another Experimental Results (a) Some examples of illusory figure, (b) Induced stimuli for illusory contours perception, (c) Induced stimuli for illusory surface perception, (d) Surface perception results

References

1. K. Kumaran, D. Geiger and L. Gurvits, Illusory surface perception and visual organization, Computation in Neural Systems, **7** (1996) 33-60
2. D. Hubel, Eye, Brain, and Vision, http://neuro.med.harvard.edu (1995)
3. D. Marr, Vision: A Computational Investigation into the Human Representation and Processing of Visual Information, W. H. Freedom&Company, (1982)
4. D. Marr and E. Hildreth, A theory of edge detection, Proc. R. Soc. Lond. **B(207)** (1980) 187-217
5. Hubel D. H. and Wiesel T. N. Receptive fields binocular interaction and functional architecture in the cat's visual cortex", J Physiology, (1962) 106 -154
6. R. von der Heydt and E. Peterhans, Mechanisms of contour perception in monkey visual cortex. I. Lines of pattern discontinuity, J. of Neuroscience, **9** (1989) 1731-1748
7. K. Hukushima, S. Miyake, T. Ito, Neocognitron: A neural network model for a mechanism of visual pattern recognition, IEEE Trans. Syst., Man, Cybern. , **SMC-13** (1983) 826-832

A Robust Digital Watermarking Adopting 2D Barcode

Su-Young Han[1], Eui-Hyun Jung[1], and Seong-Yun Cho[2]

[1] Dept. of Computer Science, Anyang University,
Samseong-ri, Buleun-myeon, Ganghwa-gun, Incheon, 417-833, Korea
[2] Dept. of Digital Media, Anyang University,
708-113, Anyang 5-dong, Manan-Gu, Anyang City, Kyunggi-do, 430-714, Korea
{syhan, jung}@anyang.ac.kr, scho@aycc.anyang.ac.kr

Abstract. In this paper, a new watermarking algorithm using 2D barcode is proposed. The 2D barcode means 2-dimensional barcode that contains more information than conventional 1-dimensional barcodes. For error correction, 2D barcode allow the recognition of barcodes that are up 60% damaged. Therefore, the 2D barcode as watermark can be survived when it used in highly noisy environment. In this paper, a new wavelet based watermarking algorithm using 2D barcode as watermark is proposed. Dynamically generated 2D barcode is inserted as watermark in wavelet domain. From the experimental result, the proposed algorithm shows better invisibility and robustness comparing with the conventional methods using plain image as watermark.

1 Introduction

Digital watermark denotes information that is imperceptibly and robustly embedded within still images or moving pictures for protect copyrights[1]. So watermarking in the wavelet domain allows precisely to control the location of the watermark, it is very useful in the invisibility and robustness aspect. In the wavelet transform based watermark technique, the watermark is embedded in the subbands that except the lowest frequency band[2]. However, because the image compression is usually lossy compression that eliminates all the high frequency components, the studies that the watermark is embedded in the lowest frequency band have been preceded for high image compression. But this elastic change by the watermark embedding in the lowest frequency band causes damages of the original image.

To resolve this problem, wavelet based digital watermark algorithm using 2D barcode is suggested in this research. The 2D barcode means 2-dimensional barcode that contains more information than conventional 1- dimensional barcodes. Since a letter, numbers, text and actual bytes of data can be encoded in the 2D barcode, it can encode just about anything. For error correction, ECC200 supports advanced encoding and error checking with Reed Solomon error correction algorithms in 2D barcode[3]. These algorithms allow the recognition of barcodes that are up 60% damaged. Therefore, the 2D barcode as watermark can be survived when it used in highly noisy environment. In this paper, a new wavelet based watermarking algorithm using 2D barcode as watermark is proposed.

This paper is organized as follows; In section 2, a watermark creation using 2D barcode is explained. The watermark embedding and detection is described in section 3. The improvements of the proposed algorithm over the conventional algorithm are demonstrated by the experiment result in section 4. Finally section 5, the results are summarized, some technical issues are discussed, and some suggestions and further studies are discussed.

2 Watermark Creation

In general, a logo, seal or signature is used for watermark to prove copyright and these are presented as a binary image. A 2D barcode image is used for watermark in this research

2.1 Overview of 2D Barcode

The 2D barcode means 2-dimensional barcode that contains more information than conventional 1- dimensional barcodes. Conventional barcode gets wider as more data is encoded, but 2-dimenstioanl barcodes make use of the vertical dimension to pack in more data shown in Fig.2. DataMatrix is an efficient 2D barcode symbol that uses a unique square module perimeter pattern that helps the barcode scanner determine the cell locations Since a letter, numbers, text and actual bytes of data can be encoded in the 2D barcode, it can encode just about anything. It is commonly used to encode data from a few digits to several hundred digits. The symbol is square and can range from 0.001 inch per side up to 14 inches per side. For error correction, ECC200[3] is mainly used. It supports advanced encoding and error checking with Reed Solomon error correction algorithms. These algorithms allow the recognition of barcodes that are up 60% damaged. Therefore, the data encoded using DataMatrix can be survived when it used in highly noisy environment.

Fig. 1. Several kinds of 2D barcodes

2.2 Watermark Creation

Let $M_1 \times M_2$ be the 2D barcode image's size. For the prevention of deformation or detection of watermark, a watermark is scrambled using pseudo-random sequence that has deterministic random characteristics and statistical measurements such as Equation (1).

$$w = \{w(k), k = 1, 2, ..., N, N = M_1 \times M_2\}. \tag{1}$$

Where k is relocated by pseudo-random sequence and w is 2D barcode image sequence for watermark and N is the size of watermark sequence.

3 Watermark Embedding and Detection

3.1 Watermark Embedding

Early watermarks are embedded in the perceptually insignificant coefficient region for preventing recognition of their existence. But these watermarks are easily damaged or eliminated by image compressions or other image processing techniques. On that account, watermark has to be embedded in the perceptually significant coefficient region and the significant coefficient selecting process has to be concerned for watermark embedding. Moreover, this watermark has to be embedded over fullbands within the limit of original image quality for robustness. In the proposed algorithm in this research, watermark embedding process is composed as following sequences; the wavelet transform of original image, coefficient selection, watermark embedding and inverse wavelet transform (Fig. 2.).

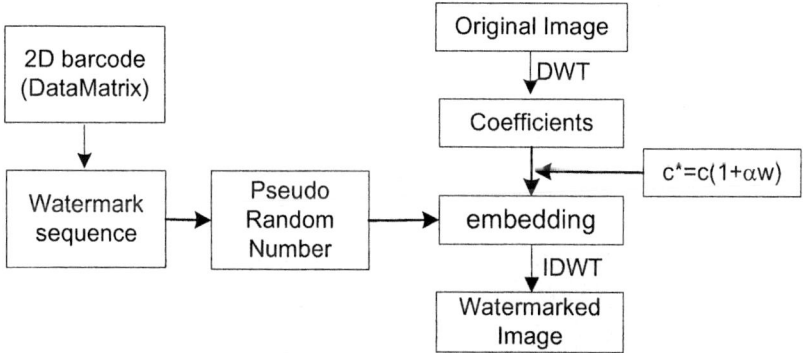

Fig. 2. Watermark embedding processing using wavelet transform and 2D barcode

First of all, input image is decomposed using the Haar wavelet filter by 2-level. The watermark is embedded in large coefficients of the high and middle frequency band (detail subbands). The LL subband does not carry any watermark information. Watermark is embedded to the wavelet coefficient using Equation (2).

$$c^* = c(1 + \alpha w) \tag{2}$$

$c*$ is the watermarked wavelet coefficient and is an embedding weight and a constant which controls the amplitude of the watermark signal. Equation (2) is used for embedding watermark adaptively based on the selected wavelet coefficient. That is, in case of large wavelet coefficients, a large α value is embedded and in case of small wavelet coefficients, a small α value is embedded. Watermark robustness generally increase with the watermark signal amplitude, α. As a next stage, after watermark embedded coefficient is transformed by inverse wavelet packet transform, watermark embedded image is accomplished[5].

4 Watermark Detection

Overall watermark detection is a reverse process of embedding process. That is, after watermarked audio signal is wavelet transformed, watermark information is analyzed and extracts watermark by pseudo-random sequence. The criterion of detection is defined by comparing similarity between watermark and extracted watermark such as Equation (3)[4].

$$Similarity(w, w*) = \frac{w \cdot w^*}{\sqrt{w^* \cdot w^*}} \qquad (3)$$

In the Equation (4), w is watermark sequence and w^* is extracted watermark. Especially, because a noise is not intensely inserted into logo or signature image as a watermark, after similarity between abstracted watermark and original watermark is smaller than 0.95, median filter is applied to abstracted watermark and recalculates similarity between two images

5 Experimental Results

In this section, experimental results for 512 x 512 aerial photograph images, Fresno (see Figure 3) and standard test image, Lena, sample-2 (see Figure 4) are summarized in Table 1 for comparing other result. Aerial photograph is collected from www.spaceimaging.com web site, which has supplied most advanced satellite and aerial images. These kind images are usually composed simplified and recursive geometrical structures such as rectangular, circles, lines and groups of points by high altitude view. A 2D barcode, as shown in Figure 5, is used for watermark image. This image includes the information such as IP, login user, and downloads time of the network server (Fig. 6.). This information is used for protecting the copyright from unauthorized copying. And two-dimensional Haar wavelet filters are used for wavelet decomposition. Invisibility and robustness of watermark is used for measurement of performance in this research. PSNR is used for performance of the invisibility after embedding watermark. Similarity using equation (3) is used for performance of the robustness. A plain image is used for comparing performance at the same condition with proposed algorithm (Fig. 6.).

Fig. 3. Satellite image (Fresno)   **Fig. 4.** Lena image

Fig. 5. 2D barcode image for watermark

5.1 Invisibility

Fig. 7 and Fig. 8 are watermark embedded images using the proposed algorithm. As shown in the two figures, it is impossible to distinguish in perceptually whether watermark is embedded in these images. After embedding watermark to original images, PSNR are calculated for observing image distortion as shown in Table 1. From PSNR in the Table 1, damages of image qualities are not recognized after applying the proposed algorithm for watermark.

Anyang Univ. Digital Media, 203.232.128.xx,
2005-03-12 at 09:12:42:21

Fig. 6. Plain image for watermark

Fig. 7. Watermark embedded image of Fresno

Fig. 8. Watermark embedded image of Lena

Table 1. PSNR of watermark embedded images

	2D barcode wateramrk	Plain image watermark
Fresno	44.2037	33.3349
Lena	50.7383	45.0139

5.2 Robustness

JPEG and conventional wavelet image compression are applied to proposed watermark-embedded image for robustness check against image compression. During compression, a preliminary work to obtain the information about the start position of watermarking was done. SPIHT is used for wavelet image compression in this experiment. Experimental result of robustness is shown in Table 2. As shown in Table 2, over 90% of watermark image is survived from high image compression. As represented in Table 2, the proposed watermarking algorithm demonstrates good robustness.

Table 2. similarity of JPEG/SPIHT lossy compression

JPEG	Fresno	Lena	SPIHT	Fresno	Lena
25%	0.952392	0.989231	25%	0.962561	0.983287
50%	0.975924	0.999431	50%	0.991024	0.997024
75%	0.996100	0.999911	75%	0.999325	1.00000

6 Conclusions

In this paper, a new watermarking algorithm using 2D barcode is proposed. The 2D barcode allow the recognition of barcodes that are up 60% damaged. Therefore, the 2D barcode as watermark can be survived when it used in highly noisy environment. In this paper, a new wavelet based watermarking algorithm using 2D barcode as watermark is proposed. Dynamically generated 2D barcode is inserted as watermark in wavelet domain. From the experimental result, the proposed algorithm shows better invisibility and robustness comparing with the conventional methods using plain image as watermark. Over 90% of watermark image is survived from high image compression. A new wavelet based watermark algorithm using 2D barcode is concerned for digital audio and moving picture as further study.

References

1. Christophe D., J. Delaigle, B. Macq: Invisibility and Application Functionalities in Perceptual Watermarking - An Overview. Proceedings of the IEEE, 90(1) (2002)
2. Xia X., C. Boncelet, G. Arce: A multiresolutional watermark for digital images. IEEE Int. Conf. on Image Processing, 1. (1997) 548–557
3. "Information technology - International symbology specification - Data Matrix," ISO/IEC 16022, Dec. (2004)
4. Cox I., J. Kilian, T. Leighton and T. Shamoon: Secure spread spectrum watermarking for multimedia. IEEE Trans. on Image Processing, 6(12) (1997) 1673–1687
5. Wang J., J. F. Doherty, R. E. Van Dyck: A wavelet-based watermarking algorithm for ownership verification of digital images. IEEE Trans. on Image Processing, 2(11) (2002) 77–88

4D Reconstruction of Coronary Arteries from Monoplane Angiograms

S. Bouattour, R. Arndt, and D. Paulus

Computational Visualistics, University of Koblenz-Landau, Germany
bouattour@uni-koblenz.de

Abstract. We describe a technique for 4D-reconstruction of coronary arteries from a sequence of *monoplane* X-ray angiograms. An initial 3D model of coronary centerlines is reconstructed from two *appropriate* views. A 3D-2D registration framework is formulated in which the model deforms in space to best fit the given angiograms. The 3D motion model is *hierarchical* and includes rigid, affine and B-spline transformations. The registration is guided by a sum of energy terms which measures the goodness of the 3D-2D mapping and constrains the deformation of the model. The method is tested on three sequences of patient data, each containing 248 frames. The registration time for one frame varies between one and four minutes.

1 Introduction

The early detection and correction of aberrations of coronary vessels is of highest medical importance. The 3D–reconstruction of the *moving* vessels of interest will lead to an improvement of the treatment. Image data of the beating heart are usually acquired with cardiac C-arm devices. Given a sequence of monoplane angiograms 3D-reconstruction is mostly reduced to the reconstruction from two views of the same electrocardiogram (ECG)-state. Including all views requires heart motion estimation and compensation [1,2]. Heart motion computation can be formulated as a registration problem. Shechter et al. [3] presented a method for 3D motion tracking of arteries over a sequence of *biplane* cienangiography images. At each acquisition time two simultaneous orthogonal views of the same heart state were available. We applied the Shechter's method to *monoplane* angiography sequences. We had to extend the method at several levels:

- 3D-model reconstruction: The ECG data was not used. We present several criteria that revealed to be sufficient to test the method on the monoplane sequences.
- 3D-2D-registration: we propose an approach to reduce the number of motion parameters and to optimize the search strategy
- performance: we reached a high decrease in application time (1-4 min/frame) which was not only due to the implementation of the method in C++.

Further details of the method are described in Section 2. Section 3 represents experiments on real patient data. Section 4 concludes and describes future work.

2 Method

The camera is part of a C-arm which is rotated around the patient with known motion parameters. The acquisition geometry is characterized by a projective mapping $\boldsymbol{P}_l \in \mathrm{I\!R}^{3\times 4}$ for the lth image f_l, where $l = 1 \ldots n_f$. The projection matrices are computed during a geometrical calibration step [4].

The method is based on three steps: preprocessing, 3D-model reconstruction out of two *appropriate* views and the 3D+t reconstruction. The goal of the *preprocessing*-step is to enhance the vessels from the background. We applied the method of Frangi et al. [5] to compute a multi-scale response map. Each filter response $r_l(x,y)$ for a pixel $(x,y)^{\mathrm{T}}$ is a value that describes how likely the current pixel belongs to an artery. The result of this step is illustrated in figure 1.

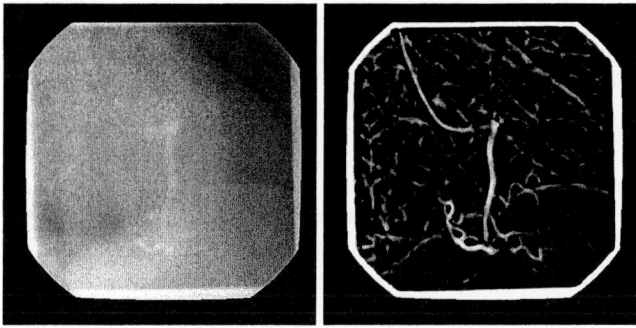

Fig. 1. Left: original X-ray image. Right: the corresponding response map. The vessels are clearly enhanced from the background.

2.1 3D-Model Reconstruction

In order to construct an anatomically correct 3D Model of arteries it is necessary to find two views of the same ECG state to apply epipolar geometry. In [3] this was not necessary because at each time two simultaneous orthogonal views were captured. The ECG data was not available in our case. So we propose to select two appropriate views m and n based on following criteria:

1. **Orthogonality**: the two C-arm positions of the views of interest should be orthogonal to assure a high numerical stability of the 3D-reconstruction. This criterium is formulated in terms of the known geometry of the C-arm:

$$\mathrm{null}(\boldsymbol{P}_m)\cdot\mathrm{null}(\boldsymbol{P}_n) \approx 0 \qquad (1)$$

2. **Position within the Sequence**: the reconstructed model is expected to have most similarity with the rest of the sequence if it is reconstructed out of two views in the middle of the sequence. This is formulated in eq. 2.

$$m \approx n_f - n \qquad (2)$$

3. **ECG-State**: if available, this information should necessarily be taken into consideration. Let η denotes the ECG-state, then

$$\eta_m \approx \eta_n \qquad (3)$$

Once two appropriate views are found, a semi-automatic graphical tool is developed to select corresponding points on the arteries of interest. For each selected point on the left frame, the epipolar line is drawn on the right one and vice versa. This should help the user to select points, which are consistent with the epipolar constraint. The path between two marked points in one frame is followed automatically based on the intensities of the response map and applying a hysteresis threshold similar approach. This results in centerlines having pixel-precision. The centerlines are represented by 2D B-splines [6]. A B-spline curve (BSC) $c(u)$ is defined in terms of three parameters: an order p, a set of n model control points (MCP) v_i and a knots vector $k = (k_1, k_2, \ldots, k_{n+p})$ of length $n + p$. The definition domain $\mathcal{D}$ of the curve is restricted by the knots vector. A location on a B-spline curve for a parameter $u \in \mathcal{D}$ is given by:

$$c(u) = \sum_{i=1}^{n} B_{i,p}(u \mid k)\, v_i \qquad (4)$$

where $B_{i,p}(u \mid k)$ is the DeBoor-recursion. In this paper we use third order B-splines ($p = 3$). We also use *uniform, open* knots vectors, i.e. the first and last p elements are equal, the knots values are equally spaced and $k_p \leq u \leq k_{n+1}$. We normalize the knots-values between 0 and 1 i.e $\mathcal{D} = [0, 1]$.

A B-spline curve $c^a(u)$ is associated to each vessel-branch a. Thereby it should be guaranteed that the curves have the same start and end points to ensure the continuity of the artery tree. This representation for the two 2D centerlines has two advantages. First the skeletons have *subpixel-precision*. Second since the arteries are acquired from different points of view, the projected physical length may be different. Matching points for the 3D-reconstruction becomes difficult. By using open, non-uniform B-spline representation, the length of the curves is unified by the knots vector to be in $[0, 1]$. Both advantages are crucial for the 3D-reconstruction.

Finally a 3D-model should be reconstructed out of two corresponding B-spline curves. We need to each point on the left curve to find a corresponding point on the right one. Our algorithm in a nutshell is described in table 1, where $L(c_m)$ is the length of the left curve, $\theta_{n_{3D}}$ is a threshold and $\bm{F}$ is the fundamental matrix determined by their projection matrices [7].

2.2 4D-Heart Reconstruction

This part is strongly based on the work of Shechter et al. [3]. In this section we will stress our changes and extensions. The temporal tracking of the 3D-model is formulated as a 3D-2D registration problem. The goal is to find for each frame l a *transformation* $\bm{T}^l : \mathbb{R}^3 \to \mathbb{R}^3$ that, when projected, *best fits* to the given angiograms. So the registration is realized as an optimization problem.

Table 1. Algorithm to reconstruct a 3D-B-spline out of two 2D-B-spline curves

compute number of 3D points to reconstruct $n_{3D} = \frac{L(c_m)}{\theta_{n_{3D}}}$
compute discretization step for sampling the knot vector of $c_m(u)$: $u_{3D} = \frac{1}{n_{3D}}$
FOR each point $c_m(u_{3D}), \ldots, c_m((n_{3D}-1)u_{3D})$
look for corresponding point on c_n that fulfills the epipolar constraint: $\|\tilde{c}_n(u_x)^T F \tilde{c}_m(x u_{3D})\| \approx 0$ with $1 \leq x \leq n_{3D} - 1$
reconstruct the 3D point using triangulation [7]
B-spline fitting: convert the discrete set of 3D points to a 3D B-spline curve[6]

A hierarchy of *transformation models* with increasing number of degrees of freedom (dof) is used. It contains a rigid transform T^l_R with 6 dof, an affine transform T^l_A with 12 dof and a B-spline transform T^l_B with much more dof allowing a non-rigid and local transformation of the 3D model. The transformation for each type is computed using eq. 5.

$$T^l_{R/A/B}[c(u)] = \sum_{i=1}^{n} B_{i,p}(u \mid k) T^l_{R/A/B}(v_i) \qquad (5)$$

B-splines are invariant to rigid and affine transform so the transformation is exact when the function is applied just on the MCP. However, the B-spline transform computed in this way is only an approximation of the real one. It is more efficient to compute and is more accurate the more control points are used.

A B-spline transform (BST) is defined in a similar way as the BSC. Each BST has an order p, a $n_x \times n_y \times n_z$ grid of 3D-control points (TCP) s_{ijk} and three knot-vectors: $k^x = (k^x_1, k^x_2, \ldots, k^x_{n_x+p})$, $k^y = (k^y_1, k^y_2, \ldots, k^y_{n_y+p})$ and $k^z = (k^z_1, k^z_2, \ldots, k^z_{n_z+p})$, which define a $(n_x+p) \times (n_y+p) \times (n_z+p)$ knot-grid. The transformation of a point $q = (q_x, q_y, q_z)^T$ is given by $q + b(q)$ where

$$b(q) = \sum_{i=1}^{n_x} \sum_{j=1}^{n_y} \sum_{k=1}^{n_z} B_{i,p}(q_x \mid k^x) B_{j,p}(q_y \mid k^y) B_{k,p}(q_z \mid k^z) s_{ijk}. \qquad (6)$$

The three DeBoor terms control the weighting of the control points. The sum of the weights of all TCP s_{ijk} is always 1. The parameters we are looking for during the registration are the coordinates of TCP. The rest of parameters must be set priorly. So we used third order BST with open knot vectors whose domains are set so that they cover the volume spanned by the bounding box of the 3D-model. The number of TCP is $8 \times 8 \times 8$. This leads to a search space of 1536-dimensions because each control point has three coordinates. Searching for T^l_B in such a space is almost infeasible We propose the following for parameter reduction:

C1 The motion of a TCP has influence just on the MCP lying within an $p \times p \times p$ area of the knot-grid. An *initial configuration* is computed using the 3D-model as reconstructed in section 2.1, more precisely its bounding box. The knots vectors are computed such that they cover the whole bounding box, and a grid of reference control points (RCP) r_{ijk} is placed around the model. This grid will serve as a *reference grid*; all transformations will take place with respect to it. Each RCP whose motion does not influence any of the MCP in this initial configuration is irrelevant and thus discarded.

C2 Since the sum of the weights of all TCP controlling one MCP is one, we can eliminate those which have a very small weight ($\leq \theta_{\text{influence}}$) because their contribution is minimal. These points are also chosen using the initial configuration.

C3 The resulting set of TCP will be split into groups, each controlling θ_{group} of MCP. This means that the transformation will be stepwise optimized. This requires many runs for the searching algorithms, but reduces enormously the number of parameters. Indeed, depending on the 3D-model segment, the search space ranges between 36 and 90 dimensions.

For each frame $\boldsymbol{T}_R^l$ is determined first. The best result is used to initialize $\boldsymbol{T}_A^l$. The best result is again used to initialize $\boldsymbol{T}_B^l$. To ensure temporal continuity $\boldsymbol{T}_R^{l+1}$ is initialized with the best $\boldsymbol{T}_B^l$. The registration is guided by a sum of energy terms that measures the goodness of the 3D-2D mapping and constrains the deformation of the Model.

$$e_{\text{total}}(\boldsymbol{T}^l) = -\omega_1 e_{\text{external}}(\boldsymbol{T}^l) + \omega_2 e_{\text{arteries}}(\boldsymbol{T}^l) + \omega_3 e_{\text{translate}}(\boldsymbol{T}^l). \quad (7)$$

The best transformation is

$$\hat{\boldsymbol{T}}^l = \underset{\boldsymbol{T}^l}{\text{argmin}}\; e_{\text{total}}(\boldsymbol{T}^l). \quad (8)$$

The external and arterial energy were defined in Shechter et al.[3]. The first measures the goodness of the backprojection of the transformed model on the 2D-frame. It is computed by integrating the values of the response map along the backprojected transformed model segment. The arterial energy prevents a big change in the length of the 3D-model by computing the difference of arc length before and after transformation. Shechter used in addition to that a B-solid energy which avoids strong changes in the TCP-grid. But this was here not necessary due to the optimization performed in **C3**. Instead we defined a translation energy which should avoid that the projections of MCP vary too much from the coordinates they had at the begin of the search. After initialization of $\boldsymbol{T}_R^l$ with $\boldsymbol{T}_B^{l-1}$ the 3D-model is transformed and projected with $\boldsymbol{P}_l$ on the l-th frame. Its 2D coordinates are denoted $\bar{\boldsymbol{g}}_i^a$ for each segment a. The translation energy is defined as the sum of Euclidian distances between the initial and the current projections of the 3D-model and is given by:

$$e_{\text{translate}}(\boldsymbol{T}^l) = \frac{1}{n_{\text{cp}}} \sum_{a=1}^{n_a} \sum_{i=1}^{n} \|\boldsymbol{g}_i^a - \bar{\boldsymbol{g}}_i^a\| \quad (9)$$

where n_{cp} is the number of all MCP and $\boldsymbol{g}_i^a$ (given by eq. 10) are the 2D-coordinates of the backprojected MCP of the a-th segment after transformation: $\hat{\boldsymbol{v}}_i^a = \boldsymbol{T}^l(\boldsymbol{v}_i^a)$.

$$g_i^a = \frac{\boldsymbol{P}_l \hat{\boldsymbol{v}}_i^a}{P_{l\,3,1}\hat{v}_i^{a\,x} + P_{l\,3,2}\hat{v}_i^{a\,y} + P_{l\,3,3}\hat{v}_i^{a\,z} + P_{l\,3,4}}. \tag{10}$$

3 Experiments

We applied the proposed approach on three monoplane sequences (seq1, seq2, seq3) captured by a Siemens AXIOM Artis system, each containing 248 views over an angular range of 200°. The angiograms were of low to very low quality. Despite the enhancement of the vessels, not all views were suitable for the 4D reconstruction. So we had to discard some of them manually. All 3D-models were reconstructed with $\theta_{n_{3D}} = 2$. The parameters of the registration were also the same for all sequences:$\theta_{\text{influence}} = 0.01$, $(\omega_1 = 1.0)$,$(\omega_2 = 0$ for $\boldsymbol{T}_R$, 0.5 for $\boldsymbol{T}_A$ and 0.01 for $\boldsymbol{T}_B$) and $(\omega_3 = 0.01$ for $\boldsymbol{T}_{R/A}$ and 0 for $\boldsymbol{T}_B$). We categorized the results *visually* in three classes: *very good* (vg) if the backprojected model fit to the vessels on the angiogram and followed their motion; *good* (g) if the backprojection fit just on some segments, but it followed the motion and *bad* (b) if the backprojected model neither fit the vessels nor correctly followed the motion. Figures 2, 3, 4 show some examples.

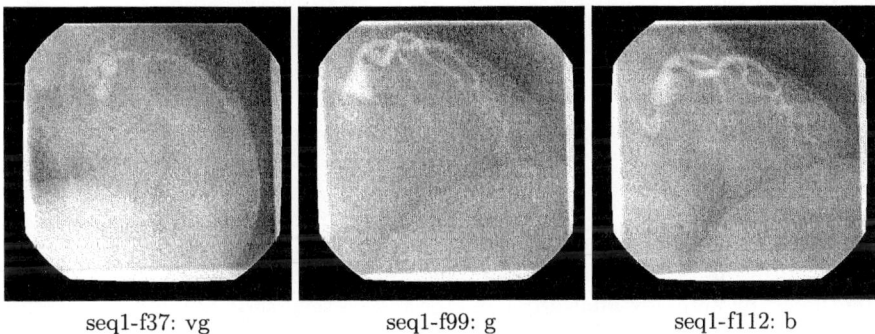

seq1-f37: vg   seq1-f99: g   seq1-f112: b

Fig. 2. Registration results from the first sequence. Both frame number and judgment of the frame are given.

Table 2 summarizes all results. It records the two reference views m and n, the average registration time per frame (artpf), the selected frames for 4D reconstruction and the visual evaluation.

Discussion: The results presented in table 2 show the effectiveness of the approach, especially for seq1 where we had a success rate of ca. 80% of good to very good registrations. However several factors influences the results negatively. First, frames which are far from the reference views were mostly badly registered. Problems arose especially in the middle of the sequences. This is due to the order we chose for registration. We start from each reference frame and go

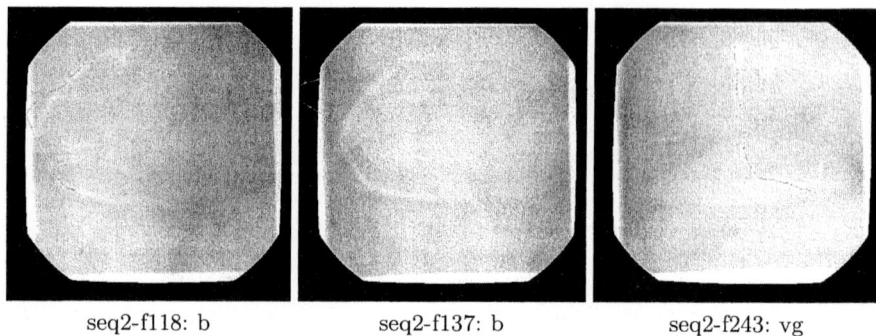

seq2-f118: b   seq2-f137: b   seq2-f243: vg

Fig. 3. Registration results for several frames from the second sequence

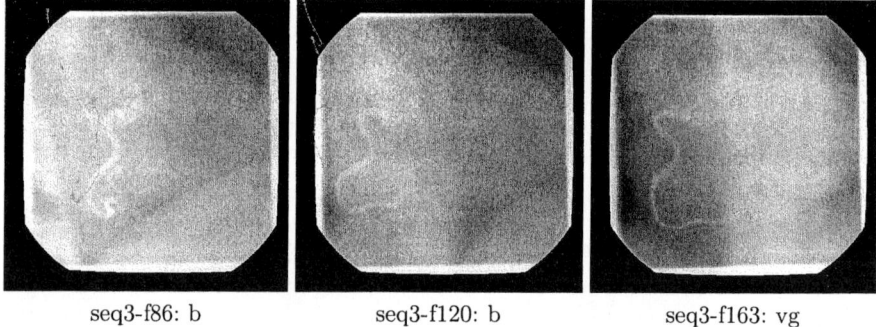

seq3-f86: b   seq3-f120: b   seq3-f163: vg

Fig. 4. Registration results for several frames from the third sequence

in two directions. Some frames in the middle are registered twice. The resulting 3D transforms are linearly interpolated before backprojection. The effect can be accentuated by complex anatomy like crossing vessels (seq1-f99 and seq1-f112). Second, vessels which were near the left *brighter* border were mostly lost during registration (seq2-f118). Border's response values after preprocessing were very high, so the algorithm stuck there and propagated the errors in the following frames (seq2-f137). Third, due to the lack of ECG data, the 3D model was not always conform to the anatomy even if this last was relatively simple (just one artery in seq3). This was due to the very fast beating heart in this sequence.

Table 2. Registration results for three sequences of real monoplane angiograms

	m,n	artpf (sec)	selected frames	vg (%)	g (%)	b (%)
seq1	57,161	232	29–198	64.12	16.47	19.41
seq2	85,214	53	35–247	51.17	0.0	48.43
seq3	63,179	173	67–179	15.04	12.39	75.22

The structure could be maintained for some views and just the motion was lost (seq3-f86). But both form and motion were lost in other frames (seq3-f120).

The rtpf (s. table 2) was measured on an AMD Athlon 1600+ with 512 MB RAM. It varies for each frame between 53 and 320 sec. The preprocessing step was *not* excluded. The estimation of $\boldsymbol{T}_R$ and $\boldsymbol{T}_A$ were not time consuming (5-10sec/frame). The rtpf depends on: First, the number of selected arteries. The more vessels were tracked the more computational time was need for computing the arc length for the arterial energy. The arc length is changing over time to adapt to the anatomy. Second, the arc length of the selected arteries. Depending on this data the number of MCP was determined. This number influences the optimization strategy **C3**. The more MCP are available the more optimization steps are necessary (compare artpf for seq1 and seq2). Third, the number of iterations needed for the downhill simplex. This number differs even from vessel to vessel and is constrained by a maximum number of iterations.

4 Conclusion

In this contribution we adapted the method of Shechter [3] for 4D heart reconstruction to monoplane angiograms with up to 248 frames per sequence. Presented results showed the effectiveness of the approach. Future work will concentrate on amelioration of the preprocessing step, usage of global optimization algorithms for the rigid and affine transform, better choice for the free parameters, accurate examination of the processing sequence and a more quantitative evaluation of the method.

Acknowledgment

We are thankful to Siemens Medical Solutions, Forchhcim, Germany to have provided us the heart sequences.

References

1. Mourgues, F., Devernay, F., Malandain, G., et. al: 3d+t modeling of coronary artery tree from standard non simultaneous angiograms. In: MICCAI. (2001)
2. Blondel, C., Vaillant, R., Malandain, G., et. al.: 3-d tomographic reconstruction of coronary arteries using a precomputed 4-d motion field. In: Fully3D Conf. (2003)
3. Shechter, G., Coste-Maniére, E., McVeigh, E.R., Devernay, F.: Temporal tracking of 3d coronary arteries in projection angiograms. In: SPIE- Medical Imaging. (2002)
4. Luong, Q.T., Faugeras, O.D.: The geometry of multiple images. MIT Press (2001)
5. Frangi, A.F., Niessen, W.J., Vincken, K.L., Viergever, M.A.: Multiscale vessel enhancement filtering. In: MICCAI. (1998)
6. Rogers, D.F.: An Introduction to Nurbs. Morgan Kaufmann Publishers, Inc (2000)
7. Hartley, R.I., Zisserman, A.: Multiple View Geometry in Computer Vision. Cambridge University Press (2000)

Temporal Video Indexing Based on Early Vision Using Laguerre Filters

Carlos Joel Rivero-Moreno and Stéphane Bres

LIRIS, UMR 5205 CNRS, Lab. d'InfoRmatique en Images et Systèmes d'information,
INSA de Lyon, Bât. Jules Verne, 17 av. Jean Capelle,
Villeurbanne Cedex, 69621 France
{carlos.rivero-moreno, stephane.bres}@liris.cnrs.fr

Abstract. Visual information of videos is based on spatial and temporal extents. However, most of video indexing techniques work in the spatial extent. Thus, spatial features are extracted from individual frames and then temporal information is introduced by their temporal evolution or tracking in order to construct motion vectors that serve as temporal features. In this paper we present a novel approach for video indexing based on temporal features extracted basically from the temporal extent. The approach is based on Laguerre filters of the Laguerre transform, which is a polynomial transform, that preserve the causality constraint in the temporal domain and model the early vision stages (V1 and MT) in the visual system for extraction and representation of visual motion (temporal events). The motion pathway is constructed by subsampling the spatial low-pass versions of frames (spatial integration) and by decomposing subsequently local temporal vectors at spatial positions. Results encourage our model for video indexing and retrieval.

1 Introduction

Video is a rich source of information that provides visual information about scenes. Visual information is one of the most important features that dominates and populates increasingly multimedia information systems and several of their applications. Since visual media require large amounts of memory and computing power for storage and processing, there is a need to efficiently index, store, and retrieve the visual information from multimedia databases. A digital video (video sequence) is a series of sequentially ordered (in time) images or frames, so it has both spatial and temporal extents. Hence a good video index should capture the spatio-temporal contents of the scene represented using spatial and/or temporal features.

Early vision, also known as preattentive vision, includes those mechanisms that subserve the first stages of visual processing for detecting the most basic visual features. In early vision, spatial features of images are related to colour, texture and shape content, whereas temporal features are mainly related to motion content due to independently moving objects in the scene (e.g., in the form of their trajectories) and/or camera operations within the set of images.

Visual motion perception has been the subject of extensive research in the fields of perceptual psychology, visual neurophysiology, and computational vision. It was argued [10] that the brain contains mechanisms specifically devoted to the processing of motion, which occur in a *motion pathway* consisting of at least two stages. The primary visual cortex (area V1), where main spatial attributes are processed, constitutes the first stage. Information passes from there to the middle temporal (MT or V5) visual area. [10] [11]. On the basis of these assumptions, some models of the early vision stages for extraction and representation of visual motion (temporal events) have been proposed [11] [4] [12]. Among these models, we focus on the Laguerre transform since it adheres to the causality condition of the temporal extent.

On the other hand, several content-based video retrieval (CBVR) techniques have been proposed in the literature. A survey and a review of these techniques can be found in [5] [6] [2]. In these approaches, the signatures (index terms) serve to encode the content of the sequence of images based on spatial and/or temporal features. However, most of the techniques proposed in the literature extract features in the spatial extent. This means that, in a first step, spatial features are extracted and then, in a second step, temporal information is introduced by the temporal evolution or tracking of spatial descriptors. Temporal descriptors are based on global and local motion vectors constructed from temporal tracking of objects defined by their spatial features (contours and/or regions).

In this paper we present a novel approach to construct video signatures for indexing and retrieval purposes. Unlike most of CBVR approaches, our approach consists on extracting temporal features from the temporal extent. The approach is based on Laguerre filters of the Laguerre transform [4], which is a polynomial transform [9]. In general, a polynomial transform decomposes locally a signal into a set of orthogonal polynomials with respect to the window used for localizing the signal. This process is equivalent to filtering the signal with the set of filters that arise in the analysis stage of the polynomial transform. These filters depend on the set of orthogonal polynomials time derivatives of the window. We only need the analysis part of such a transform since it encodes the required visual information. Moreover, Laguerre filters preserve the causality constraint in the temporal domain and model the early vision stages (V1 and MT) in the visual system, which allow extraction and representation of visual motion (temporal events). The motion pathway is constructed by subsampling the spatial low-pass versions of frames (spatial integration) and by decomposing subsequently local temporal vectors at spatial positions. Last but not least, we present the discrete representation of Laguerre filters, which corresponds to Meixner filters. Furthermore, we present their normalized recurrence relation, which is useful for their efficient implementation.

The paper is organized as follows. In section 2, we give the definition of Laguerre filters and their discrete representation: Meixner filters. In section 3, we present our approach for the construction of temporal video signatures, which is based on temporal feature extraction. Section 4 shows some results of our approach. Section 5 concludes the paper.

2 Laguerre and Meixner Filters

The Laguerre transform is a polynomial transform that uses a monomial-modulated exponential function as localization window. There is psychophysical evidence that the early visual processing of temporal stimuli in the human visual system (HVS) is described by this transform and channel responses resemble those of Laguerre filters [4]. Due to these properties, Laguerre filters will be used as a temporal feature extractor. Furthermore, an efficient implementation for video indexing purposes can be achieved by their discrete equivalent representation, i.e. Meixner filters.

Temporal and spatial processing differ essentially in that the temporal domain must adhere to the causality condition that stem from the nature of temporal signals. It means that we can only use what has occurred in the past or, equivalently, we cannot use future values of the signal such as in the case of real-time applications. Hence, characterizing temporal events up to a specified time, t_0, involves their integration over time from the past ($t \rightarrow -\infty$). This one naturally supposes, on the one hand, that events closer time t_0 should have more weight than past events (which tend to vanish), and on the other hand, variations of such events along time might be measured by time derivatives or, which is equivalent, to fit some oscillatory function with the same weight contribution. In such a way, these suppositions lead to a kind of event localization from the past up to present time t_0, i.e. a smoothing causal kernel or causal localization window is applied to the signal. As it was argued in [8], the only primitive scale-space kernels with one side support are the truncated exponential functions. However, we prefer to use here the term "exponential-*like*" since functions involving exponentials modulated by a time polynomial is a *generalized* case of such kernels.

2.1 Generalized Laguerre Filters

Generalized Laguerre filters $d_n(t)$ decompose a localized temporal signal $l_v(t-t_0) = v^2(t-t_0)\, l(t)$ by a gamma window (monomial-modulated exponential-like window) $v(t)$, with order of generalization $\alpha \geq 0$ and spread $\sigma > 0$, which is defined as [1]:

$$v(t) = \sqrt{\sigma}(-\sigma t)^{\alpha/2} e^{\sigma t/2} u(-t) \ . \tag{1}$$

where u is the Heaviside function ($u(t)=1$ for $t \geq 0$, $u(t)=0$ for $t<0$), into a set of generalized Laguerre orthogonal polynomials $L_n^{(\alpha)}(-\sigma t)$. Coefficients $l_n(t_0)$ at different times $t_0 \in R$ are then derived from the signal $l(t)$ by convolving with the generalized Laguerre filters. These filters are equal to time derivatives of the analysis window modulated by a monomial of order n, where n is the derivative order, for $n=0,\ldots,D$. Thus, the three parameters of generalized Laguerre filters are the maximum derivative order D (or polynomial degree), the scale σ, and the order of generalization α. Time-invariant filters, i.e. exponential decreasing filters, are obtained for $\alpha=0$. For $\alpha>0$, these filters have a non-symmetric bell-shaped envelope, i.e. a gamma-shaped window. It also implies that analyzed events correspond to those in a close past of t_0. In this case, temporal information is more on the basis of past events than on current ones. Besides, for large α the window $v(t)$ increasingly resembles a Gaussian window. These 1-D filters are then defined as:

$$d_n(t) = \left(\sqrt{n!/\Gamma(n+\alpha+1)}\right)\sigma(\sigma t)^{\alpha} e^{-\sigma t} L_n^{(\alpha)}(\sigma t) u(t) \ . \tag{2}$$

where Γ is the gamma function [1]. The generalized Laguerre polynomials $L_n^{(\alpha)}(t)$, which are orthogonal with respect to the weighting function $t^{\alpha} \cdot e^{-t}$, are defined by Rodrigues' formula [7] as:

$$L_n^{(\alpha)}(t) = \frac{t^{-\alpha}e^t}{n!} \frac{d^n}{dt^n}\left(t^{n+\alpha}e^{-t}\right). \qquad (3)$$

From (3) one can see that generalized Laguerre filters are related to time derivatives of the localizing window $v(t)$ defined in (1). Hence, filters of increasing order analyze successively higher frequencies or temporal variations in the signal.

2.2 Meixner Filters

Meixner filters are the discrete equivalent of generalized Laguerre filters [3]. They are equal to Meixner polynomials multiplied by a square window $v^2(x) = c^x(b)_x/x!$, which is the discrete counterpart of a gamma window and it behaves similarly to a Poisson kernel [8]. $(b)_x$ is the Pochhammer symbol defined by $(b)_0 = 1$ and $(b)_x = b(b+1)(b+2)\ldots(b+x-1)$, $x=1,2,\ldots$. Parameters b and c are equivalent to parameters of the generalized Laguerre filters α and σ, respectively. However, for the discrete case, $b>0$ and $0<c<1$. The equivalent time-invariant case ($\alpha=0$) arises for $b=1$. The Meixner polynomials are orthonormal with respect to this window and they are defined as [7]:

$$M_n(x) = \sqrt{\frac{c^n(1-c)^b}{n!(b)_n}} \sum_{\tau=0}^{n} C_n^\tau (b+\tau)_{n-\tau}(x-\tau+1)_\tau (1-1/c)^\tau. \qquad (4)$$

for $x=0,1,2,\ldots,\infty$ and $n=0,\ldots,D$. In general, one fixes the maximum value of x to N.

In order to achieve fast computations, we present a normalized recurrence relation of Meixner polynomials to compute these filters:

$$M_{n+1}(x) = \frac{1}{\sqrt{c(n+1)(n+b)}}\left[[(c-1)x+n+(n+b)c]M_n - \sqrt{nc(n+b-1)}M_{n-1}\right]. \qquad (5)$$

for $n \geq 0$, $M_n = M_n(x)$, and with initial conditions $M_{-1}(x)=0$, $M_0(x)=(1-c)^{b/2}$.

For the case in which the window length is set to a finite value N, important care then must be taken when selecting parameters b and c since they modify the orthogonality of polynomials. Fig. 1 shows two Meixner filter sets for different parameter values. One can then see that b controls the window shape and c the number of temporal samples involved in the analysis process. The larger c is the more past events are considered. A trade-off exists in choosing b and c since both of them shift the time t_0, found at the window's maximum, where the signal is estimated. Another parameter is the maximum order expansion, D, which defines the number of filters (primitives of the signal) for characterizing temporal events at time t_0 (last samples within the window). There will then be one (Laguerre) coefficient for each of the filters. Thus, there will be $(D+1)\cdot P$ coefficients, where P is the number of positions of the localizing window. Experiments have shown that a good signal interval reconstruction is achieved for $N=30$, $D=4$, $b=12$, and $c=0.4$ (fig. 1-(a)).

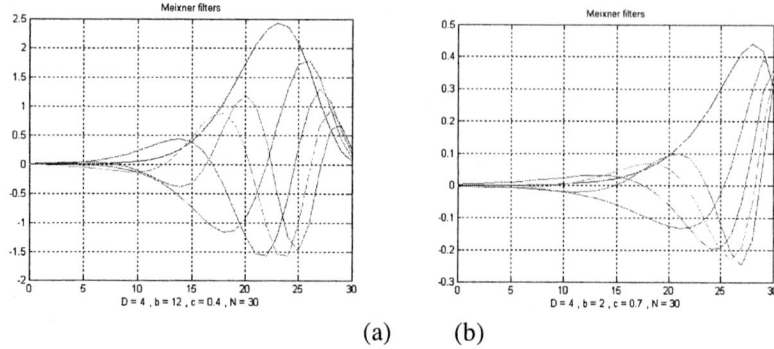

Fig. 1. Meixner (Laguerre) filters up to order $D=4$ and length $N=30$ (a) $b=12$, $c=0.4$ (b) $b=2$, $c=0.7$. Notice that b controls the shape of filter envelopes and c their time lag t_0 at their maxima.

3 Temporal Feature Extraction and Indexing

We use 1-D Meixner filters, by applying the equation (5) times the localizing discrete gamma window, to extract temporal events from a video sequence and used them as temporal descriptors. These descriptors, which correspond in such a way to motion trajectories of independent moving objects, serve to construct the signature necessary to index the video. For that doing, we construct a set of temporal vectors to which the Laguerre transform will be applied. There will then be as much temporal vectors as spatial positions in the analyzed frames and the length of each vector is equal to the length of the localizing discrete gamma window. We have set this length to $N=30$ samples according to the parameter values of Meixner filters. For a given spatial position, there will then be as much temporal vectors as temporal localizing positions (at the window's maximum) of the analysis window. Filtering is then performed by convolution between temporal vectors and Meixner filters. For each localized set of frames and for each filter there will be only one coefficient value.

In order to integrate spatial information, as area V1 does, the number of spatial positions is reduced to a fixed number K. It allows reducing the dimensionality of features and thereby the volume of descriptors used for the signature. This one is indeed a requirement of indexing systems. For our approach we have used $K=16\times12=192$ or $K=32\times24=768$ spatial positions. Each position is obtained by integrating spatial information within its neighborhood. This is achieved by low-pass-filtering (by a Guassian kernel) and subsampling at the desired positions. The size (scale) of the filter is selected so there is always a half spatial filter overlapping between two adjacent positions. Temporal information is integrated, as area MT does, by the Laguerre transform. As a result, the spatio-temporal signature consists of $(D+1) \cdot P \cdot K$ values, where D is the maximum degree decomposition, P is the number of temporal positions of the localizing window, and K is the number of spatial positions. Fig 2 shows samples of a localized video consisting of $N=30$ frames. Fig. 3 shows the temporal descriptors, which correspond to spatial regrouping of Laguerre coefficients. The signature is the set of all coefficients up to the order D.

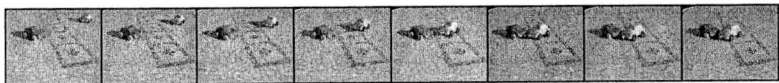

Fig. 2. Sample frames (one out of four) of a localized input image sequence of $N=30$ frames, containing a moving toy car and a still car (the sequence runs from left to right)

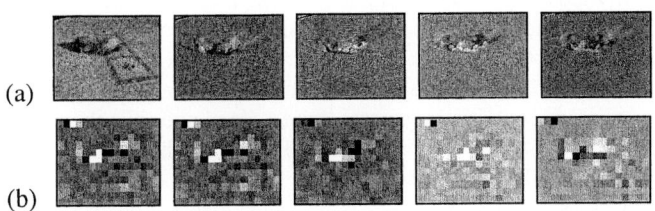

(a)

(b)

Fig. 3. Laguerre coefficients (temporal descriptors) up to order $D=4$ (from left to right) of the 30 frames of the sequence in fig. 2. They are regrouped according to the spatial position of their respective temporal vectors. Spatial positions correspond to (a) all pixel positions (b) 16×12 spatial neighborhoods, which result from low-pass filtering and subsampling of original frames.

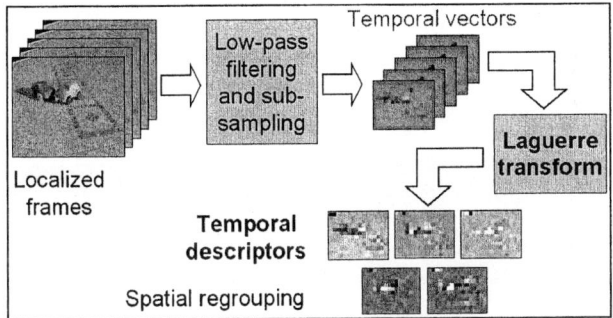

Fig. 4. Temporal descriptors extracted by applying the Laguerre transform to temporal vectors at each spatial position of the lower-pass filtered and subsampled version of input frames. Spatial regrouping of Laguerre coefficients yields the spatio-temporal signature.

Fig. 4 shows the framework of our feature extraction and indexing approach. Indexing is achieved by the construction of the video signature based on the extracted features and by introducing a similarity measure. We simply used a sigmoid function of the sum of the absolute value of the difference between two signatures p and q:

$$S_{SIG}(p,q) = \frac{1}{1+\exp\left(a \cdot \left(\sum |p_k - q_k| - \mu\right)\right)}. \quad (6)$$

where a and μ are positive parameters of the sigmoid function and $k=0,\ldots,(D+1)\cdot P\cdot K$. A video query could be any sub-sequence lasting one or more seconds.

4 Experimental Results

In this study, features are extracted from either gray-scale or luminance-based pixel values. Let Y be the luminance of an image frame, then it can be obtained from RGB components by the transformation $Y = 0.299R + 0.587G + 0.114B$. Images under consideration are previously adapted to match their central part to video format 4:3. For our experiments, we have constructed a video database by gathering some sportive videos such as broadcasted tennis matches or athletics meetings. We have then implemented in C/C++ and VirtualDub[1] the set of filters and the modules for the stages of feature extraction, signature construction, indexing, and similarity retrieval. We have extracted some video sequences from the whole videos. These sequences have been used as video queries and they correspond to simple sequences that have several very similar occurrences in the video database like special kinds of tennis points (serve-volley for example) or athletics movement (high jump, weight throw, etc). A fixed camera captures in general these scenes and thus the movement by itself is characteristic and not the camera motion. Fig. 5-(a) shows an example of query. It is a video sequence, lasting 4 seconds, that presents a serve-volley point. The best answer given by our indexing system is the query itself. The second best answer is a very similar sequence, presented on fig. 5-(b), which differs from the query only by the end of the movement (the player turns on the right and not on the left). The 7 next best answers are sequences of the same kind taken from different matches.

We obtained the same results with queries of weight throws and high jumps. At the moment, we examine by hand the whole database to establish a correct ground truth for different queries like the ones we tried already. We want to have a real statistic on the possible good sequences we miss (the first answers are correct answers). For instance, in the case of high jumps we obtained 75% of correct answers in the top ten answers representing the 1% of best similar answers for un hour of athletics video.

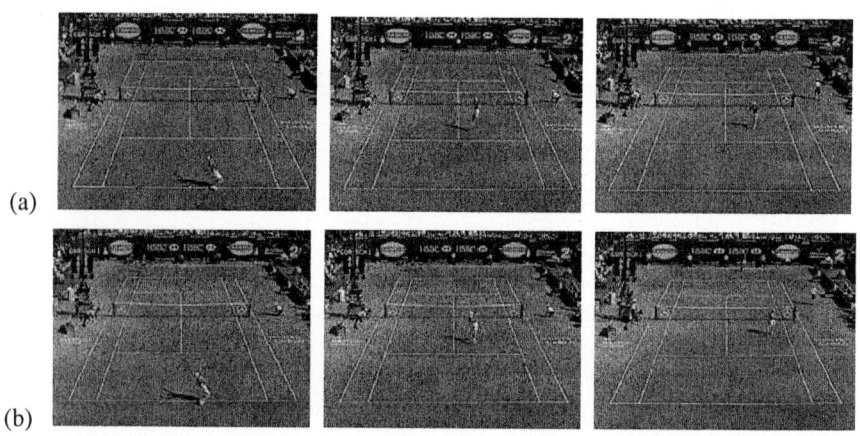

(a)

(b)

Fig. 5. (a) Example of a query sequence taken from a tennis match. This query last 4 seconds and represents a serve-volley point. It is itself the first best answer to the query. (b) Second best answer of our system to the preceding query.

5 Conclusion

We presented an approach for temporal early vision video indexing based on Laguerre (Meixner) filters. The motion pathway (V1 and MT areas) is modeled by the

---

[1] http://www.virtualdub.org/

way these filters extract temporal information from spatial information. *Temporal* (event) features are extracted by applying the Laguerre transform to time vectors at pixel or spatial region positions. *Spatial* information is then included by the spatial arrangement of such features. Dimensionality reduction is achieved by low-pass filtering and subsampling in the spatial domain and by integrating information through a localizing window in the time domain. The results we obtain are quite promising and validate the interest of our polynomial descriptors for signature computation and video indexing.

References

1. Abramowitz, M., Stegun, I.A.: Handbook of Mathematical Functions with Formulas, Graphs, and Mathematical Tables. 9th printing. Dover, New York. (1972)
2. Ahanger, G., Little, T.D.C.: A Survey of Technologies for Parsing and Indexing Digital Video. Journal Visual Communication Image Representation. Vol. 7 **1** (1996) 28-43
3. Belt, H.J.W., den Brinker, A.C.: Optimality Condition for Truncated Generalized Laguerre Networks. Int. Journal Circuit Theory and Applications. Vol. 23 (1995) 227-235
4. den Brinker, A.C., Roufs, J.A.J.: Evidence for a Generalized Laguerre Transform of Temporal Events by the Visual System. Biological Cybernetics. Vol. 67 (1992) 395-402
5. Del Bimbo, A.: Visual Information Retrieval. Morgan Kaufmann Publishers Inc., San Francisco. (1999)
6. Idris, F., Panchanathan, S.: Review of Image and Video Indexing Techniques. Journal Visual Communication Image Representation. Vol. 8 **2** (1997) 146-166
7. Koekoek, R., Swarttouw, R.F.: The Askey-scheme of Hypergeometric Orthogonal Polynomials and its q-Analogue. Delft University of Technology, Faculty of Information Technology and Systems, Department of Technical Mathematics and Informatics. Report 98-17 (1998)
8. Lindeberg, T., Fagerström, D.: Scale-Space with Causal Time Direction. In: Proc. European Conference on Computer Vision. Vol. 1064 (1996) 229-240
9. Martens, J.-B.: The Hermite Transform – Theory. IEEE Trans. Acoust. Speech Signal Processing. Vol. 38 **9** (1990) 1595-1606
10. Palmer, S.E.: Vision Science. Photons to Phenomenology. The MIT Press, Cambridge, Massachusetts. (1999)
11. Simoncelli, E.P., Heeger, D.J.: A Model of Neuronal Responses in Visual Area MT. Vision Research. Vol. 38 **5** (1998) 743-761
12. Young, R.A., Lesperance, R.M., Meyer, W.W.: The Gaussian Derivative Model for Spatial-Temporal Vision: I. Cortical Model. Spatial Vision. Vol. 14 **3,4** (2001) 261-319

Comparative Study of 3D Face Acquisition Techniques

Mark Chan, Patrice Delmas, Georgy Gimel'farb, and Philippe Leclercq

Department of Computer Science, University of Auckland, New Zealand
patrice@cs.auckland.ac.nz

Abstract. friendly–user interactivity while permanently eyeing towards 3D display technologies. As such, 3D face generation, modelling and animation techniques are in the frontline to design realistic animated 3D talking faces. Simple, reliable and economic, 2D image processing techniques have been widely used to reconstruct 3D faces. This paper focuses on the comparison of different 2D imaging techniques for 3D face generation. Stereo Vision techniques, using either automatic stereo correspondence algorithm or manual feature points location, Orthogonal Views and Photometric Stereo approaches are introduced and applied to acquire face 3D data. In addition, generated reconstruction results are compared qualitatively and quantitatively.

1 Introduction

Nowadays, research is actively conducted to create highly performant and reliable human-computer interface systems. As an essential component, face modelling has been a hot topic, recently receiving much attention [1]. Special characteristic face feature areas such as the eyes, mouth, nose, etc, are especially important as they carry most of the audiovisual information expressed by humans. Although many approaches (such as laser range scanner devices) may be used to generate 3D faces, 2D imaging techniques have been the most widely researched as they do not require extensive budget or special hardware equipment. For all these reasons, this paper solely focuses on the study of 2D imaging technologies for 3D face generation.

As widely acknowledged to provide satisfactory results while maintaining low complexity computation, Stereo Vision, Orthogonal Views, and Photometric Stereo methods are studied in this paper.

Stereo vision can be either automatic or interactive. Automatic stereo vision requires stereo images placed parallel in a line wise correspondent position (also called epipolar position). Corresponding pixels between both images are then searched automatically along the same lines in both images to generate a dense disparity map (or a depth map for display purpose) [2].

The interactive approach requires to manually (or automatically) chose a subset of corresponding pixels in the stereo images pair. If cameras are calibrated, the pixel 3D world coordinates are obtained using back-projection techniques to provide a sparse depth map of the stereo system common field of view.

Orthogonal views have already been used to detect facial features and infer their 3D positional values [3]. Using either one or two camera(s), two images are taken, one from the front and the other from the side of the face. The front-view image provides the X- and Y-coordinates, while the side-view provides the Z-coordinate of the pixel corresponding to the same feature in both images. This provides 3D information for all the pixels present in both front and side images.

Photometric stereo [4], is based on the way images of 3D objects are formed. Objects can be seen because they reflect light. The surface normal and other characteristics of the surface (e.g. depth) can be obtained using prior knowledge of the scenes' illumination geometry and the nature of surface reflection.

In this paper we test the above introduced 3D face techniques and compare their strengths and weaknesses introducing a new 3D surface comparison approach using Radial Basis Function (RBF) interpolation to normalize 3D faces.

In Section 2, four image-processing techniques are described in the context of 3D face generation. In section 3, 3D surface comparison and results are presented. The final section summarizes the paper and presents our future work.

2 Facial Reconstruction Techniques

In this section, Image processing techniques such as binocular stereo, orthogonal views and photometric stereo are discussed in detail.

2.1 Binocular Stereo Using Automatic Stereo Correspondence Algorithms

Binocular Stereo is the process of obtaining **dense** depth information from a pair of images. Often these two images (stereo images) are related by the epipolar geometry. First, stereo images are rectified to be placed in epipolar position [2]. Next, stereo matching finds the correspondence between stereo images (usually using Pixel to Pixel, correlation windows, surface constraint or Dynamic Programming matching techniques) and produces a dense disparity map.

Stereo Matching. Previous studies proved that for faces simpler stereo algorithms tend to produce marginally lesser results while being much faster than more complex algorithms in favour today [5]. For this reason, SAD has been used in this paper. SAD, is a correlation algorithm, which uses the sum of absolute difference to find the correspondences between stereo images. Correlation functions are evaluated over a 'window' of neighbouring pixels in each image. For each point on the reference image (left for instance), all correlations with a sliding window - for all disparity values - in the right image for the whole disparity range are computed and the best value is chosen, defining the matching pixels.

Experiment. Firstly, the stereo images are rectified. Then, image matching is performed using SAD. Studies of this stereo algorithms against noise [5] suggests that a window radius of 4 is most suitable. Since the disparity map is retrieved, a depth map can be generated using both the camera focal length obtained by the calibration technique, and the image pixel size.

2.2 Interactive Binocular Stereo

Here, three main steps are involved in this approach. First, the cameras are calibrated to attain the physical and optical properties of the acquisition system. Next, correspondence between a subset of the stereo-pair image pixels is achieved by finding similarities (usually by clicking on stereo corresponding pixels). The last step is to calculate the 3D coordinates of the corresponding points in the images by triangulation technique.

Calibration. Camera calibration is the process of estimating the intrinsic and extrinsic parameters of a camera. These coefficients allow a 3D point from the world reference frame to be transformed into its corresponding point in the image reference frame and vice versa. Extrinsic parameters, such as the rotation and translation coefficients, define the location and orientation of the camera axis with respect to a known world reference frame. Intrinsic parameters link the pixel coordinates of an image point with its corresponding points in the camera reference frame. In this project, Tsai's calibration algorithm is applied due to its simplicity and sufficient accuracy. Tsai's calibration is defined as a "two-step" calibration method [6] involving the direct computation of most of the calibration parameters while an iterative approach estimates the remaining parameters (namely the depth component of the translation vector, the focal length and the first order radial distortion parameter).

Two Sony EVI-D100P video cameras, a tripod with a horizontal bench and a calibration box are the main equipment used in this experiment. The video cameras are fixed on a tripod 20 centimetres apart. Two images of the calibration cube with 150 non-coplanar 3D reference points are taken simultaneously. Nine calibration parameters, namely six external (rotation angles and translation vectors) and three intrinsic (e.g. the focal length, the uncertainty scale factor and the radial distortion factor) coefficients, are then estimated [6].

In order to find the optimal distance between the cameras and the calibration object, tests on calibration accuracy at varying distance between the camera and the calibration object were performed. Experimental results indicate that given the current setup, calibration error is minimal at 115 cm.

Experimental results show that 86% of the reference points' calibration error is less than 1.2 mm with maximum error on average 2.2 mm.

Experiment. After both cameras are calibrated, a stereo pair of images is taken for each test subject.

Next, corresponding points between the images are found manually in this experiment as small white dots are put on test subject's face as markers. Once the camera calibration parameters are known, these 2D image points are back projected into real world and the real 3D coordinates are obtained by triangulation.

3D coordinates of the feature points are calculated and mapped to a generic 3D face model (1808 vertices) inspired from CANDIDE3 [7] (see Fig 1 first image). Its encapsulated MPEG-4 standard defines vertices according to the MPEG4 Face Feature Points(FFP)[1]. Second image of Fig 1 shows an example of the reconstruction result.

2.3 Photometric Stereo Method (PSM)

The theory of Photometric Stereo for Lambertian surfaces was developed by Woodham [4]. It calculates surface normal and other surface information by employing prior knowledge of the illumination geometry and the nature of surface reflection. For Lambertian surfaces, a surface normal can be determined if the considered surface point is illuminated from three or more light sources using the albedo-independent PSM method. Three consecutive images are taken with light sources being switched on from three different directions in our experiments (see left and middle left Figure 1) while a fourth one with all lights on is acquired for texture mapping.

A depth map or a 2.5-D model is then reconstructed by the Photometric Stereo method (See Figure 1). The reconstruction accuracy depends on the quality of the generation of the surface normal and the transformation from the surface normal to the depth map. Further details can be found in [8].

Experiment. In our experiment, Photometric Stereo has been developed by [8]. The experiment took place in a dark room where all external light sources were blocked as uncertain illumination can affect the experimental results. The equipment used for this experiment includes a JVC CCD camera, three halogen light bulbs used as light sources and a serial box, which connects all the hardware with the computer.

The first procedure of PSM is to calibrate the light source direction. A sphere has been chosen as the calibration object due to its reflecting properties as well as its concave shape. Three images of the test subject are then acquired and processed to reconstruct the face depth map. The application also allows the mapping of the test subjects' texture on to the depth map, which is then presented in VRML format. Fig 1 shows some of our reconstruction results obtained via PSM.

Fig. 1. From left to right: first 2 images: Interactive Binocular Stereo; Next 2 images: PSM results; last 2 images: Reconstruction results by Orthogonal Views

2.4 Orthogonal Views

To reconstruct a 3D face model from orthogonal view images, two images are required, the first from the front of the face, the other from the side. 3D coordinates of the face points, visible in both images, are then captured using the X,Y coordinates of the front view, while their Z values (depth) are attained from the side view.

Facial features such as the eyes, eyebrows, lips, nose and mouth can be extracted using image processing techniques [9]. These features are mapped to a 3D generic face model to reconstruct a 3D face. In our experiment, the frontal image is taken with test subject facing directly to the camera. Then, the camera is placed orthogonally (90 degree) and a side image of the face acquired. Fig 1 images show an example of orthogonal images for a test subject.

In this experiment, tiny white dots are placed on test subject's face as feature points. 29 facial feature points are extracted from the test subject's face manually. These points are then interpolated into the predefined face model.

3 3D Face Comparison

The goal of this project is to find the optimal 3D face reconstruction solution for 3D face analysis and synthesis. Therefore, it is necessary to determine which technique has the most accurate reconstruction. To do so, *3D Surface Comparison* is investigated in the following section.

3.1 3D Surface Comparison

3D Surface comparison allows finding the surface differences from individual reconstruction results by different image processing techniques. In addition, surface comparison can show the variances on areas between the reconstructed face surfaces. The overall surface differences for the whole test subject's population are computed. In order to find the optimal solution for 3D face analysis and synthesis in term of reconstruction accuracy, a surface comparison with the same vertices in surfaces generated by three image-processing techniques is performed.

There are a few factors that make the comparison extremely difficult in this experiment. Firstly, each system obtains results with different orientation and scaling. Secondly, benchmarks of each test subject are unavailable. In order to solve this problem, surface normalization is required, which involves rotation, scaling and translation of data. In this comparison approaches, we intend to apply RBF data interpolation technique to scale the 3D surfaces. After the normalization process, surface distances between reconstruction results are computed. In this experiment, we assumed the results from PSM as benchmark as it generates a complete face dense depth map and contains a large amount of vertices.

3D Surface Normalization. Research into 3D face comparisons from different systems is at an exploratory stage and no methodology has been defined for this particular type of comparison. Therefore, the approach applied in this experiment is a new idea and may not be the optimal method. In this project, depth maps of 3D faces generated from different systems are used for this comparison approach. Distances between the 3D surfaces are computed and compared. However, normalization is required for the 3D data, so that all 3D face meshes have the same orientation and scale.

Surface normalization is made up of three stages: rotation, scaling and translation. Rotation is for adjusting all the surfaces to face the same direction. Scaling adjust all the 3D surfaces with all primary facial features are located approximately the same area. The last procedure of normalization is to translate all the face surfaces to the minimum distance apart.

Rotation. The aim of this step is to have all the face surfaces sitting in the same coordinate setting and facing the same direction. Depth maps of face surfaces are used and the face should point upward. Figure 2 shows three 3D face surfaces after the rotation process. Each face dense map has the same size (500 x 500) and sits on the same coordinate system.

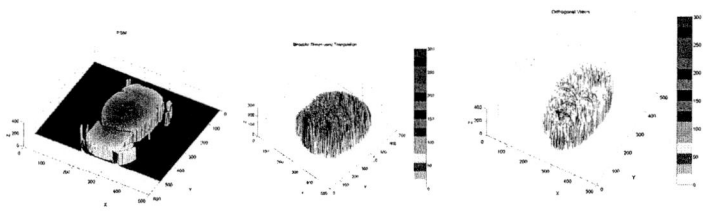

Fig. 2. Reconstruction Results after Rotation

Scaling. It is irrelevant to scale the whole face meshes by using just a few facial feature points. Ideally, all facial feature points should be used and these facial feature points should be distributed over the whole face surface. In this experiment, a new approach is investigated to scale 3D face surfaces. We intend to use Radial Basis Function (RBF), a data interpolation technique, for scaling 3D face surfaces. In this experiment, 18 points mostly located on the primary facial features are chosen in this normalization procedure. 3D data of these 18 points from the PSM result is extracted and interpolated into the Orthogonal Views' and Binocular Stereo with Triangulation's result. Since these 18 points are distributed over the whole 3D face, the whole face surfaces reconstructed by Orthogonal Views and Binocular Stereo with Triangulation technique is then deformed and scaled accordingly.

The Radial Basis Function (RBF) is a classical approximation function, defined as a weighted sum of translations of a radially symmetric basis function augmented by a polynomial term, and is widely used in surface reconstruction, image morphing, etc [10].

Translation. To simplify the comparison process, all these surfaces are translated as close as possible. In theory, the nose tip is the highest point among the whole face surface. In this normalization step, all the face surfaces are translated as the nose tips of all face surfaces are shifted to the centre of the depth map (250,250). Since all face surfaces are properly scaled, the location of facial features on each face surface such as the eyebrows, the eyes, nose and mouth should be located approximately in the same position. In addition, all the face surfaces are pulled to the same height. Again, the nose tip is used as the reference and all the face surfaces are translated until their nose tips are shifted to the same level.

Comparison Result. After all reconstructed 3D face surfaces are normalized, comparison can be made. All the face surfaces should have a uniform scaling, orientation and unit. The surface comparison is performed where the distances between the 3D surfaces are computed. Table 1 shows the depth map comparison result of the test population using the percentage of vertices having less than 5, between 5 and 10, between 10 and 15, and between 15 and 20 pixels variation between two surfaces. It indicates that 3D surface generated from Binocular stereo using Triangulation is closer to the 3D surface generated from PSM (benchmark) than any others. It has higher proportion of vertices (51.76% and 26.79%) with 5 and 10 pixels difference against PSM than Orthogonal Views.

Table 1. Overall Comparison Result on different 3D surfaces

	≤ 5	≤ 10	≤ 15	≤ 20	> 20	Max.	Mean	Variance	Std Dev.
PSM vs OV	49.3	26.1	13	4.7	6.8	80.9	9.2	111.5	26.3
PSM vs Tri	51.7	26.7	10.4	5.4	5.5	80.2	8.4	136.2	10.5
OV vs TRI	74	18	4.5	1.6	1.9	36.0	4.1	26.2	4.6

Table 1 also shows that the 3D faces generated by Orthogonal Views and Binocular Stereo using Triangulation are very similar. 74 % of the vertices are less than 5 pixels between these two face surfaces. This result was expected since both techniques interpolate the extracted 3D data from the test subjects into the same predefined face model.

In order to investigate which areas on the face surfaces has the biggest and smallest difference to the benchmark, we tend to display the pixel difference between two surfaces graphically. Result shows that there is much less vertex differences between Binocular Stereo using Triangulation and Orthogonal Views' results than others. However, further work is required to work out the vertices difference for particular areas on the 3D face surface for all test subjects. Areas to investigate would be mainly around primary facial features such as the eyebrows, eyes, nose and mouth.

4 Conclusion

In this paper, stereo vision, photometric stereo, and orthogonal views are compared for the purpose of 3D face analysis and synthesis. For sake of comparison, we assumed 3D faces generated by PSM as benchmarks since PSM generates denser depth map. 3D surface comparison indicates that results generated from Binocular Stereo using Triangulation are closest to PSM.

We are currently investigating a proper method to perform a face model comparison of accuracy using laser scan of a test subject as a benchmark. We are also investigating Binocular Stereo using Stereo Correspondence Algorithm with USB driven digital cameras. Currently we use PSM and Binocular stereo to generate animatable 3D faces for realistic expressions generation.

References

1. Wang, Q., Zhang, H., Riegeland, T., Hundt, E., Xu, G., Zhu, Z.: Creating animatable MPEG4 face. In: International Conference on Augmented Virtual Environments and Three Dimensional Imaging, Mykonos, Greece (2001)
2. Zhang, Z., Faugeras, O.: 3D Dynamic Scene Analysis: a stereo based approach. Springer Verlag (1992)
3. Kurihara, T., Arai, K.: A transformation method for modeling and animation of the human face from photographs. In: Proceedings of Computer Animation, Tokyo, Japan (1991) 45–58
4. Woodham, R.: Photometic method for determining surface orientation from multiple images. In: Optimal Engineering. Volume 19. (1980) 139–144
5. Leclercq, P., Morris, J.: Robustness to noise of stereo matching. In: International Conference on Image Analysis and Processing, Mantova, Italy (2003) 606–611
6. Tsai, R.: A versatile camera calibration technique for high-accuracy 3D machine vision metrology using off-the-shelf tv cameras and lenses. In: In IEEE Journal of Robotics and Automation. (1987) 323–344
7. Ahlberg, J.: Candide3 – an updated parameterized face. In: Report No.LiTH-ISY-R-2326, Department of Electrical Engineering, Linkoping University, Sweden (2001)
8. Ng, A., Schlöns, K.: Towards 3D model reconstruction from photometric stereo. In: Image and Vision Computing New Zealand, Auckland, New Zealand (1998)
9. Goto, T., Lee, W., Magnenat-Thalmann, N.: Facial feature extraction for quick 3D face modeling. In: Signal Processing: Image Communication. Volume 17. (2002) 243–259
10. Carr, J., Fright, W., Beatson, R.: Surface interpolation with radial basis functions for medical imaging. In: IEEE Transactions on Medical Imaging. Volume 16. (1997) 96–107

A Fuzzy Hierarchical Attributed Graph Approach for Handwritten Hieroglyphs Description

Denis Arrivault[1,2], Noël Richard[1], and Philippe Bouyer[2]

[1] Laboratoire SIC, CNRS - FRE 2731 - SP2MI, Boulevard Marie et Pierre Curie, F-86 962 Futuroscope Cedex
{denis.arrivault, noël.richard}@etu.univ-poitiers.fr
[2] RC-SOFT, Domaine de la Combe - BP39, F-16 710 Saint-Yriex
philippe.bouyer@rcsoft.fr

Abstract. For a complex writting as egyptian hieroglyphs, combining the works done in hierarchical modelizations and fuzzy grammar definitions seems natural. This paper introduce the hierarchical-fuzzy-attributed graph (FHAG), extended from fuzzy-attributed graph, which modelize attributes by fuzzy-tree grammar. We give a formal definition of FHAGs and explain the building process. Some results are given with a recognition system based on single models comparisons.

1 Introduction

The handwritten character recognition problem is studying since many decades [1]. In general, the character recognition systems consist of two steps : features extraction and classification of the feature vectors into a number of class. Then the classification can be done reffering to a learning base if such a base exists or reffering to single models if it does not. The models can furthermore come from an expert or from a clustering phase of prototypes (see [2] for exemple).

In this article, we are presenting a new approach for describing complex handwritten patterns as egyptian hieroglyphs. This work is integrated in a recognition system based on single models comparison. According to the complexity of egyptian hieroglyphs and the huge variations between models and characters to recognize (figure 1), a fuzzy structural description has been adopted.

As explained by L.A.Zadeh ([3],[4]), fuzzy logic is a very powerfull tool for describing uncertainty, ambiguity and vagueness. Moreover structural approaches for pattern recognition have improved pattern descriptions by introducing topological and contextual informations. That is why combining structural technics and fuzzy logic became natural. We can cite Chan & Cheung ([5]) who first used Fuzzy-Attributed Graphs (FAG) for chinese character recognition. An other very interesting work on character description by combining fuzzy and structural informations is the one made by Malaviya & Peters ([6], [7]). They built a complete fuzzy language for the syntactic description of on-line handwritten symbols. The characters are decomposed into semantic features and fuzzy logic techniques are used to describe their syntactic relations. The power of such a language lies in the possibility to fine tune uncertainty. Nevertheless such a description is limited to on-line writings (temporal aspects) or at least simple characters.

Our approach, presented in this article, is to consider an egyptian hieroglyph as a set of pattern primitives. Each primitive is described not only by classical fuzzy attributes but also, following the idea of Malaviya & Peters, by linguistic fuzzy trees. Then a FAG is built with primitives as vertices and relations between them as arcs.

This paper is structured as follows. At the beginning, a formal definition of Fuzzy Hierarchical Attributed Graphs (FHAG) is given. Then our character decompositions and primitive descriptions are explained in a second section. Finally we quikly explain the recognition process and give some results and conclusions.

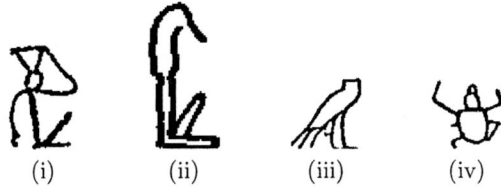

(i)   (ii)   (iii)   (iv)

Fig. 1. Handwritten Hieroglyphs

2 Fuzzy Hierarchical Attributed Graph

Attributed graph (AG) was introduced by Tsai and Fu for pattern analysis [8]. The vertices of the graph represent pattern primitives describing the pattern while the arcs are the relations between these primitives. A FAG can be defined as a generalization of the AG since a crisp set can always be represented as a special case of a fuzzy set ([5]). Starting from the FAG definition, our description introduces a hierarchy and the attributes become trees.

Let us take an example. In figure 2 (a) the primitive attribute "TYPE" of objects 1 and 2 can take values in $\tilde{A}_{S_1} = \{\text{circle,ellipse}\}$ or $\tilde{A}'_{S_1} = \{\text{circle, left\_ellipse, right\_ellipse}\}$. For an object comparison both value sets will give completly different results. Actually the first description will give objects 1 and 2 similar, but the second description will give them different. A more intuitive description can be given by a linguistic fuzzy tree as shown in figure 2 (b).

A linguistic fuzzy tree can be performed as a sample of a fuzzy tree grammar ([9],[10]).

Definition 1. *1. A tree t is a set of nodes satisfying :*
  (a) a unique node is called the root of tree t;
  (b) other nodes are divided into disadjoining sets $t_1, ..., t_n$ where t_i is called a subtree of tree t.
2. A fuzzy tree $\tilde{t}$ is $\tilde{t} = (t, \mu)$, where t is a tree and $\mu \in [0, 1]$.

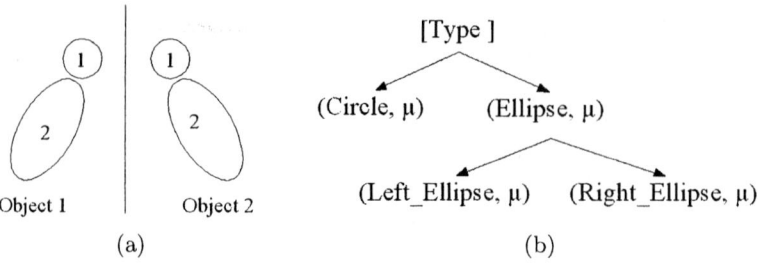

Fig. 2. Linguistic Fuzzy Tree Illustration

Definition 2. *1. A fuzzy tree grammar is a 4-tuple $G_t = (V_N, V_T, P, S)$, where*
  (a) V_N is a finite set of nonterminals;
  (b) V_T is a finite set of terminals;
  (c) P is a set of productions of the form : $t_i \xrightarrow{\mu} t_j$, where t_i, t_j are trees, $\mu \in [0, 1]$ is called the membership of the production.
  (d) $S \in V_N$ is a starting symbol.
2. The Language $L(G_t)$ generated by G_t is defined as $L(G_t) = \{(t, \mu) | S \xrightarrow{*} t\}$.

For a FHAG, each vertex may take hierarchical attributes from a set $\hat{Z} = \{\hat{z}_i | i = 1, ..., I\}$. For each hierachical attribute, $\hat{z}_i$ will have possible samples taken from a set $G_{v_i} = \{\hat{s_{ij}} | j = 1, ..., J_i\}$, where G_{v_i} is a fuzzy tree grammar and $\hat{s_{ij}}$ are linguistic fuzzy trees. $\hat{L}_v = \{(\hat{z}_i, \hat{s_{ij}}) | i = 1, ..., I; j = 1, ..., J_i\}$ denotes the set of possible attribute-linguistic_fuzzy_tree value pairs of vertices. A valid pattern primitive is just a subset of $\hat{L}_v$ in which each attribute appears only once, and $\hat{\Pi}$ is the set of all those valid pattern primitives. Thus each vertex will be represented by an element of $\hat{\Pi}$.

Similarly, we define $\hat{F} = \{\hat{f}_i | i = 1, ..., I'\}$, $G_{a_i} = \{\hat{t_{ij}} | j = 1, ..., J'_i\}$, $\hat{L}_a = \{(\hat{f}_i, \hat{t_{ij}}) | i = 1, ..., I'; j = 1, ..., J'_i\}$ and $\hat{\Theta}_i$ for the arcs. And finaly :

Definition 3. *A FHAG $\hat{G}$ over $\hat{L} = \{\hat{L}_v, \hat{L}_a\}$ with an underlaying graph structure $H = (N, E)$, is defined to be an ordered pair $(\hat{V}, \hat{A})$ where $\hat{V} = (N, \hat{\sigma})$ is called a hierarchical fuzzy vertex set and $\hat{A} = (E, \hat{\delta})$ is called a hierarchical fuzzy arc set. The mappings $\hat{\sigma} : N \to \hat{\Pi}$ and $\hat{\delta} : E \to \hat{\Theta}$ are called hierarchical fuzzy vertex and hierarchical fuzzy arc interpreters, respectively.*

3 Character Decomposition and FHAG Construction

The decomposition of a character into a FHAG is made in two steps. First the character is skeletonized and singular (intersections and end points) and inflexion points are extracted. Then the primitives are selected and the FHAG is built.

3.1 Skeletonization and Singular Points Extraction

A skeleton is a synthetic representation of a shape ([11]) set up with unit-thickness strokes. Among the numerous skeletonization and thinning methods

([12]), only the strictly 8-connected results are interesting for a fast and simple forward computing. We choosed the algorithm proposed by Zhang and Wang [13] because of its good properties and speed.

The singular points are extracted with simple morphological "hit or miss" transforms ([14]). Figure 3 ((1) is the skeleton, (2) is the skeleton and the singular points (grey and black)) illustrates those operations on the first character from figure 1.

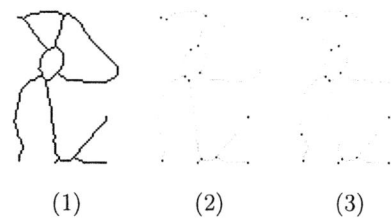

(1)   (2)   (3)

Fig. 3. Skeleton, singular points and inflexion points

3.2 Inflexion Points Detection

After singular points detection, the shape can be divided into a first set of primitives which are parts between two singular points. Then, for a better description, a second cut has to be made by extracting inflexion points.

The inflexion points calculation is made on each primitive of the first set. The principle is to parametrize the curve for a simple inflexion points detection where $D = (x'' \times y' - x' \times y'') = 0$.

This problem is easily solved by using a Bezier interpolation. The control points of the De Casteljo algorithm are calculated by a progressive Ramer polygonalization. The figure 4 depicted the process on a simple example :

- (a) is the orinal image,
- (b) is the skeleton (grey) with singular points (black),
- (c) is the skeleton (grey) with control points from the polygonalization phase (black),
- (d) is the skeleton (grey) with the sampled bezier curve (black),
- (e) is the skeleton (grey) with inflexion points calculated without the polygonalisation phase (black),
- (f) is the skeleton (grey) with inflexion points calculated with the polygonalisation phase (black).

The poligonalization phase for selecting the control points is in fact a smoothing operation of the bezier curve. The comparison between (e) and (f) in figure 4 attests the importance of such a smoothing. The FHAG is built from the final image of skeleton with singular and inflexion points (on figure 3-(3) there is only one inflexion point on the right arm). A primitive is delimited by two black points (which can be the same for a loop).

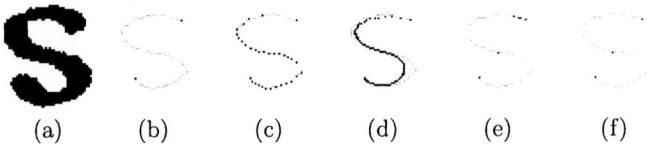

Fig. 4. Inflexion Points

3.3 FHAG Construction

Vertices Hierarchical Attributes Calculation. Each vertex of the FHAG stands for a primitive and is associated with two hierarchical attributes. The first one, called V_TYPE, details the type of the primitive. The second one, called V_LENGTH, details its length.

The fuzzy tree grammar of V_TYPE is outlined in figure 5, the terminals set $V_T = \{$Stroke (ST), Simple Curve (SC), Complex Curve (CC), Positive Stroke (PS), Negative Stroke (NS), Vertical Stroke (VS), Horizontal Stroke (HS), C-like Curve (C), D-like Curve (D), A-like Curve (A), U-like Curve (U), Loop(LOO), Others (OTH), Circle (CIR), Ellipse (ELL), Positive Ellipse (PE), Negative Ellipse (NE), Vertical Ellipse (VE), Horizontal Ellipse $(HE)\}$.

The μ_0^i are calculated with a fuzzification of arcness= $\sqrt{(1-d/l)}$, where d is the distance between the end points of the primitive and l is its length (figure 6-(a)). Then, the μ_1^i are obtained with a fuzzification of the slope function. For the μ_2^i, we use the slope of the stroke defined by the mean point of the curve and the middle of end points. The fuzzification is made on its slope (figure 6-(b) where θ is the angular slope). The μ_3^i come from a fuzzification of the correlation between the curve and its first order Fourier reconstruction. The μ_4^i are simply extracted from the fuzzyfication of the ratio between the big and the little axis of the shape. And finally, the fuzzification of the big axis slope gives the μ_4^i.

V_LENGTH is a 1-depth attribute which describes the $length/total\_length$ ratio

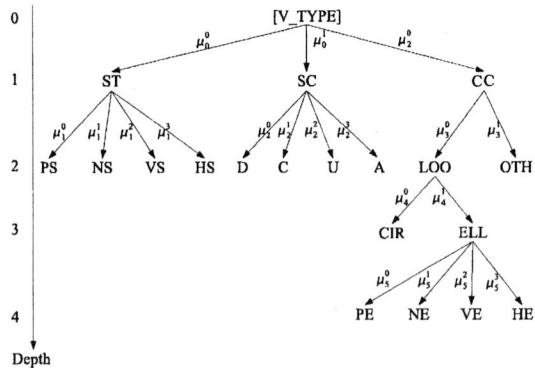

Fig. 5. V_TYPE representation

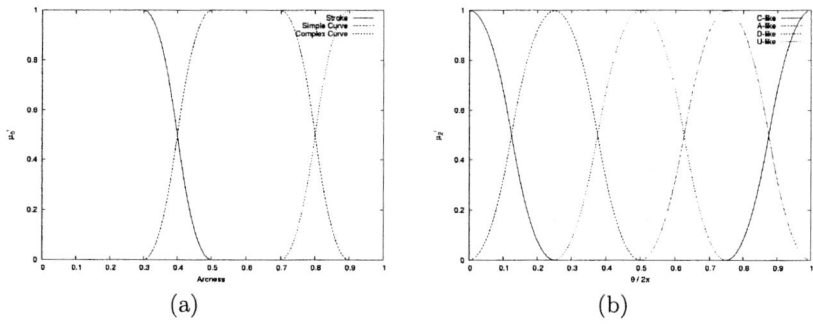

Fig. 6. (a) Fuzzification of the arcness; (b) Fuzzification of the simple curve type

where the total length is the sum of the lengths of all the primitives of the graph. The description is made by using the linguistic terms of Malaviya and Peters ([6]) and the terminals set $V_T = \{$ Zero Z, Very Very Low VVL, Very Low L, Low L, Medium M, High H, Very High VH, Very Very High VVH, Excellent $E\}$ (figure 7-(d)). Its tree representation is given in figure 7-(a).

Arcs Hierarchical Attributes Calculation. The arcs describe the relations between primitives. For a better topological representation, we use oriented arcs. As a matter of fact, the relation between two primitives is always described by a pair of arcs (a and a_b with opposite orientations). Then the graph underlaying from definition 3 is overwritten into $H' = (N, E')$ where $E' = E \times E_b$, E is the set of arcs from V_i to V_j, $i \leq j$, and E_b is the set of arcs from V_j to V_i. And finally AG, FAG and FHAG are called oriented AG, FAG and FHAG.

Two hierarchical attributes are associated to an arc. E_POS defines the relative position of the two primitives. E_PROX defines its proximity.

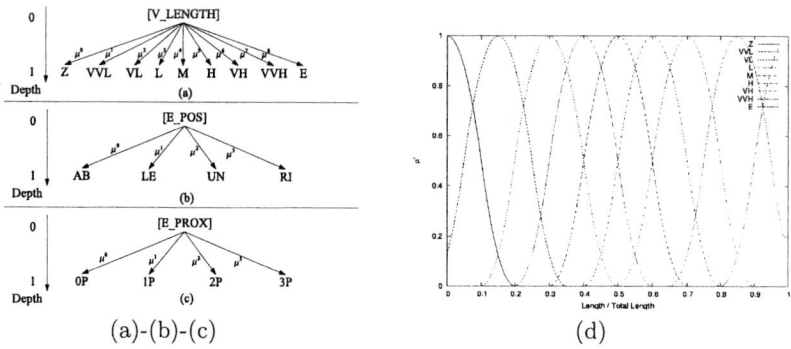

Fig. 7. (a) V_LENGTH; (b) E_POS; (c) E_PROX; (d) Fuzzification of $length/total\_length$

E_POS is a 1-depth attribute with $V_T = \{$ Above AB, On the left LE, Under UN, On the right $RI\}$. The tree representation is illustrated in figure 7-(b). The μ^i are calculated with the fuzzy relative position calculation of Bloch ([15]).

E_PROX is a 1-depth attribute with $V_T = \{$0-Proximity $0P$, 1-Proximity $1P$, 2-Proximity $2P$, 3-Proximity $3P\}$. The tree representation is illustrated in figure 7-(c). The proximity is the fuzzy connectivity of primitives. The μ^i are obtained by a fuzzification of the distances between end points of both primitives.

4 Results

The recognition process is based on a similarity measurement between the unknown hieroglyph and one model standing for a class. An inexact graph matching algorithm ([16]) gives the monomorphism between both graphs. Some tests have been computed with a model basis of 296 handwritten hieroglyphs. Figure 8 gives some examples of similarity measurements which illustrate the interest of our approach. The models were written by an egyptologist and the unknown characters were extracted from a handwritten document made by another egyptologist. The interest of our system is its capability to classify big families ("Man", "Calvary", "Bird" in figure 8).

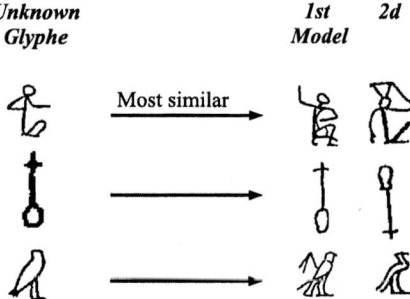

Fig. 8. Results of some queries. Unknown glyphe is on the left, the two most similar glyphes returned are on the right.

5 Conclusions

In this paper we propose an extension to the fuzzy-attribute graph by introducing a hierarchy on the attributes. The fuzzy-tree grammars give the possibility to modelize complex structures in a natural way. We explain the building process of FHAG for egytian hieroglyphs and introduce some encouraging results with a recognition system based on single models comparisons.

References

1. Plamondon, R., Srihari, S.: On-line and off-line handwriting recognition: A comprehensive survey. PAMI **22** (2000) 63–84
2. Bunke, H.: Recent advances in structural pattern recognition with applications to visual form analysis. In: VF01. (2001) 11 ff.

3. Zadeh, L.: Fuzzy sets. InfoControl **8** (1965) 338–353
4. Zadeh, L.: Fuzzy logic = computing with words. Fuzzy **4** (1996) 103–111
5. Chan, K., Cheung, Y.: Fuzzy-attribute graph with application to chinese character recognition. SMC **22** (1992) 402–410
6. Malaviya, A., Peters, L.: Fuzzy feature description of handwriting patterns. PR **30** (1997) 1591–1604
7. Malaviya, A., Peters, L.: Fuzzy handwriting description language: Fohdel. PR **33** (2000) 119–131
8. Tsai, W., Fu, K.: Subgraph error-correcting isomorphisms for syntatic pattern recognition. SMC **13** (1983) 48–62
9. Gonzalez, R., Thomason, M.: Syntactic Pattern Recognition: An Introduction. Addison-Wesley (1978)
10. Shu, L.: An inference method for fuzzy tree grammars. Fuzzy Sets Syst. **112** (2000) 173–176
11. Blum, H.: A transformation for extracting new descriptions of shape. In: Models for the Perception of Speech and Visual Form, MIT Press (1967) 362–380
12. Lam, L., Lee, S.W., Suen, C.Y.: Thinning methodologies - a comprehensive survey. PAMI **14** (1992) 869–885
13. Zhang, Y.Y., Wang, P.S.P.: A new parallel thinning methodology. PRAI **8** (1994) 999–1011
14. Serra, J., Soille, P.: Mathematical Morphology and Its Applications to Image Processing. Kluwer (1994)
15. Bloch, I.: Fuzzy relative position between objects in image processing : a morphological approach. PAMI **21** (1999) 657–664
16. Gold, S., Rangarajan, A.: A graduated assignment algorithm for graph matching. PAMI **18** (1996) 377–388

Adaptive Fuzzy Text Segmentation in Images with Complex Backgrounds Using Color and Texture *

Julinda Gllavata[1] and Bernd Freisleben[1,2]

[1] SFB/FK 615, University of Siegen, D-57068 Siegen, Germany
gllavata@fk615.uni-siegen.de
[2] Dept. of Math. and Comp. Science, University of Marburg, D-35032 Marburg, Germany
freisleb@informatik.uni-marburg.de

Abstract. Textual information present in images can help to achieve the aim of automatic content based annotation and retrieval of images. In this paper, we address the problem of text segmentation (TS) in images with complex background for recognition purposes. The proposed TS method takes as input the localized text and proceeds as follows: First, the number of initial clusters is determined by analyzing the colors of the image. Second, the image pixels are clustered using the number of clusters defined in the first step. The compactness of the clusters is evaluated in each step and improved iteratively to avoid possible oversegmentation of characters. Finally, an algorithm based on a rating scheme is proposed to determine the cluster where the text pixels are classified. The proposed method is evaluated on the basis of recognition results instead of visual segmentation results. Comparative experimental results using a test set of 2684 characters are reported.

1 Introduction

Text appearing in images can be classified into two groups: scene text and artificial text [12]. Scene text is part of the image (scene) and appears accidentally (e.g. traffic signs in an outdoor scene), whereas artificial text is laid over the image in a later stage (e.g. the name of somebody in an interview). Text embedded in images and video sequences, especially artificial text, provides important information about the content. Text extraction and recognition, which includes text detection, localization, segmentation, binarization and recognition, is an important component towards achieving automatic text-based image/video indexing. Often, text is superimposed over a complex background and its successful recognition by a commercial optical character recognition (OCR) engine is very difficult, although the text may be correctly localized. In this context, text segmentation methods which include the separation of the text from the background and the binarization of the text are crucial. Thus, the application of text segmentation methods on the localized text is the last step before before proceeding further with an OCR.

The idea of segmenting the localized text from complex background employing unsupervised learning methods was already presented in our previous work [9]. In this

---
* This work is financially supported by the Deutsche Forschungsgemeinschaft (SFB/FK 615, Teilprojekt MT).

paper, we further explore and extend this idea by introducing the following new aspects: I) a flexible number of clusters, which depends on the image colors; II) unsupervised fuzzy classification of image pixels using the number of clusters defined in the first step; III) evaluation of the compactness of the clusters and their iterative improvement; IV) determination of the cluster where the text pixels are classified and its binarization. All candidates are rated based on the geometric and spatial properties of their connected components. Finally, the image with the highest overall rating is identified as the correct binary text image. The character/word recognition rate is used to evaluate our method. The performance of our approach is demonstrated by presenting comparative experimental results for a dataset of 441 words or 2684 latin characters.

The paper is organized as follows. Section 2 gives a brief overview of related work in the field. Section 3 reviews the fuzzy c-means algorithm and introduces the individual steps of our text segmentation approach in detail. Section 4 describes our experimental results obtained for two sets of images and compares them to other text segmentation methods. Section 5 concludes the paper and outlines areas for future research.

2 Related Work

In [1], the average grayscale value of the pixel in the text box is considered as the optimal global threshold. In [13], a 16-bin normalized histogram of the grey level values is computed first. Then, by scanning the bins backward, bin k corresponding to the first valley in front of the first peak is located. Finally, a threshold with a value of $16 * (k - 1)$ is used to binarize the text image. Wu et al. [22] use a low pass Gaussian filter to first smooth the image and then compute an intensity histogram. The first peak from the left on the smoothed histogram is choosen as the optimal threshold for the binarization process. After enhancing the image using Shannon up-sampling, Li et al. [11] apply a local thresholding method to binarize the enhanced image. A block is marked as background only if its standard deviation is smaller than a fixed threshold. In [21], an adaptive local threshold based on a combination of proposals of Niblack [14] and Sauvola [19] is calculated for each block of the image to binarize it. Lienhart and Wernicke [12] first estimate the possible text and background color. After a geometrical analysis of the connected components, a binarization process follows where a global threshold is calculated as the mean of the estimated text and background color.

Odobez and Chen [15] have presented a multi-hypotheses approach based on a Markow random field (MRF) and on grayscale consistency constraints for text segmentation. The grey level distribution in text images is modeled as a mixture of Gaussian distributions. The assignment of each pixel to one of the Gaussian layers is based on prior contextual information, which is modeled by a MRF. Each layer is considered as a binary text image and is fed into the OCR system as one segmentation hypothesis. The text image which gives the best recognition performance is considered as the output of the system. Gllavata et al. [9] regard the text segmentation problem as a clustering process. As in [12], the possible text and background color is defined. Then, K-Means is employed to cluster the pixels into two clusters "text" and "background" based on their texture and color features. In [23], an unsupervised learning method is proposed. Samples of text pixels are extracted based on the heuristic that they lie between an edge couple. Then, a Gaussian Mixture Model (GMM) is used to model the intensity of text pixels and is trained with the extracted samples. Finally, text pixels are extracted from the background using the trained GMM and spatial connectivity properties of text. In [17], two histogram based clustering algorithms are presented for text extraction from color documents. The first is based on the RGB space while the second also uses the spatial information.

3 Adaptive Fuzzy Text Segmentation and Binarization

The proposed method is designed to segment text strings of arbitrary font, size and color. No assumption is made about the text color polarity in contrast to most of the existing text segmentation methods, which assume that the text has a specific color polarity (text color is always dark or light), finding thus limited application in segmenting real video texts that have various appearances and complex backgrounds. In this work it is assumed that the text string consists of a homogeneous color and aligns horizontally, which normally is the case for artificial text. The input of the method is the original image and the coordinates of the text bounding boxes, which can be generated using the algorithm in [7]. The excerpt shown in Figure 1 consisting of three images extracted from the test sets used in this paper illustrates various complex backgrounds where text is embedded. The proposed method overcomes the difficulties for finding the optimal global/local threshold [12,22,11,21] or the request for different training samples in [15,4] by applying unsupervised fuzzy clustering. In the following, a short review of the fuzzy c-means algorithm is given before proceeding further by explaining its application in our text segmentation technique.

Fig. 1. Example of the inputs of the proposed text segmentation algorithm

3.1 Fuzzy C-Means

Fuzzy c-means (FCM) is a data clustering technique where each data point belongs to a cluster to some degree, which is called a membership grade. Let $X = \{x_1, x_2, .., x_N\}$ be a data set of N elements in a d-dimensional Euclidian space R^d with a norm $\|*\|$ and let C be a positive integer larger than one. C shows the number of clusters in which the data set X should be partitioned. The FCM clustering is based on the minimization of the objective function: $J_m = \sum_{i=1}^{N} \sum_{j=1}^{C} u_{ij}^m \|x_i - c_j\|^2$, where m is the fuzzification constant, which can have influence on the clustering performance of FCM ($m = 2$), u_{ij} is the degree of membership of x_i in j^{th} cluster ($cluster_j$), x_i is the ith element in the data set X, c_j is the center of the $cluster_j$. Fuzzy partitioning is carried out through an iterative optimization of the objective function J_m, where the membership u_{ij} and the cluster centers c_j are updated using: $u_{ij} = \dfrac{1}{\sum_{k=1}^{C} (\frac{\|x_i - c_j\|}{\|x_i - c_k\|})^{\frac{2}{m-1}}}$ where $c_j = \dfrac{\sum_{i=1}^{N} u_{ij}^m * x_i}{\sum_{i=1}^{N} u_{ij}^m}$.

This iteration is stopped when $max_{ij}\{|u_{ij}^{k+1} - u_{ij}^k|\} < \epsilon$, where ϵ is a termination criterion between 0 and 1, whereas k are the iteration steps.

3.2 Resolution Enhancement

First, the image resolution is enhanced up to 300 dpi using a cubic interpolation. It has been demonstrated in [9] that the segmentation and the subsequent steps perform better on a higher resolution than on the original video frame resolution of 72 dpi. Furthermore, the segmentation algorithm performs better, if the text is not too small.

3.3 Feature Extraction

Several color and texture features are considered in order to find the best ones to classify pixels as text or background. The basic color features consist of the pixel color components. Generally, raw color data are expressed in the RGB color space. However, the RGB color space and its linear derivates do not constitute uniform color spaces. In contrast, the CIE L*a*b* color space [3] is perceptually an uniform color space, which means that the Euclidean distance between two color points in the CIE L*a*b* color space corresponds to the perceptual difference between the two colors by the human vision system. Therefore, color features are considered on both the RGB or CIE L*a*b* color space. Furthermore, to consider the texture of the pixels, the wavelet coefficients in the high frequency subbands (e.g. LH and HL) and their standard deviations are also included in the set of possible features. The standard deviation feature for a given pixel is calculated as the standard deviation of the wavelet coefficients in a small neighbourhood of the pixel. Before proceeding further, all feature components are scaled to the range [0, 1]. Additional details about the feature extraction process can be found in [9].

3.4 Adaptive Fuzzy Pixel Clustering

Due to the fact that color groups do not have hard boundaries and similarity measures between color data are relative, a fuzzy similarity measure is more appropriate than a hard one. Thus, fuzzy c-means is chosen to cluster the pixels of the text image. However, there are two major difficulties in applying the fuzzy clustering algorithm introduced in section 3.1: (1) the determination of the number of clusters C; (2) the initial fuzzy partition of objects into clusters (cluster centroids). Solutions are proposed for both of these problems in the following two paragraphs.

Determination of the Initial Number of Clusters. In contrast to the method presented in [9] where the number of clusters is fixed to two ("text" and "background" clusters), in this approach the number of clusters is defined at run time and is adaptive depending on the image that will be segmented. This solution is motivated by the fact that the background under the text is often multicolored and can show different texture properties from image to image. The number of clusters is defined using a heuristic approach which consists of the following steps: (1) a certain number of significant pixels from the input image is selected (e.g. the pixels that lie on the middle row); (2) then, the extracted pixels are divided into sets of pixels with similar colors. The Euclidean distance (in the selected color space) is used to measure the similarity between two different colors. If the difference between the colors of two pixels is below a threshold ($th_{similar}$), then the pixels are considered to be similar. The output of this stage are groups of pixels which have similar colors. It is assumed that the number of generated groups of colors is an indirect indicator about the possible different colors in the image. Thus, this number is used as the initial number of clusters C for the fuzzy c-means algorithm.

Initialization Method. There is no generally accepted approach for the initialization of the fuzzy clustering algorithm. The initialization step is important because different selections of the initial cluster centroids can potentially lead to different partitions. The proposed initialization method uses the groups of colors generated in the previous step. It works as follows: (1) a representative color is calculated for each group as the mean color of all colors that belong to the group. It is assumed that the set of estimated colors c_j for $j = 1..C$ composes the representative colors of the input image and are used as centers for the initial fuzzy partitioning during the next step. (2) the membership function of color u_{ij} between a color x_i and a center color c_j is defined as originally proposed in [10] using the formula 1:

$$u_{ij} = \begin{cases} 1.0 & \text{if } \delta(x_i, c_j) = 0, \\ 0.0 & \exists k \neq j \text{ fulfilling } \delta(x_i, c_k) = 0, \\ (\sum_{k=1}^{C} (\frac{\delta(x_i, c_j)}{\delta(x_i, c_k)})^\lambda)^{-1} & \text{otherwise} \end{cases} \quad (1)$$

where λ is a weighting parameter for the membership of x_i to c_j usually with the same value as the fuzziness parameter m ($m = \lambda = 2$) and $\delta(x_i, c_j)$ is the Euclidean distance between the colors x_i and c_j.

Adaptive Fuzzy Clustering (AFC). The FCM algorithm is applied to cluster the pixels of the text image into C clusters, where C and the initial membership matrix u are determined as in the previous paragraphs. The Euclidean distance is used to measure the similarity between the features that represent each pixel. After the clustering process has converged, the algorithm continues as follows: (1) the fuzzy membership is converted into a hard membership based on the maximum criterion, i.e. each pixel is classified to belong to the cluster with a maximum membership value; (2) the mean ($mean_j$) of the degrees of membership u_{ij} of the objects x_i in each $cluster_j$ is calculated using the equation: $mean_j = \frac{\sum_i u_{ij}}{|cluster_j|}, \forall i \mid x_i \in cluster_j$. As the membership degree u_{ij} provides a measure of the similarity between the point x_i and the center of the $cluster_j$, the value of $mean_j$ will offer an aproximate information how compact the $cluster_j$ is; (3) if the condition: "$mean_j >= th_{compact}, \forall cluster_j$" is not fulfilled, then the number of clusters is decremented: $C = C-1$. The two clusters with the lowest value of $mean_j$ are melted into one and a new center is calculated as the mean of the old centers. However, other criteria could be also considered, e.g. merging the cluster with the lowest value of $mean_j$ with its closest cluster in the color space. After the initialization with the new centers is done, the pixels are clustered again. The clustering process is repeated until the aforementioned condition is fulfilled or $C = 2$. In this way, possible oversegmentation of the text characters is avoided. In Figure 2, an example is shown how the segmentation result is improved when applying the presented AFC algorithm instead of a simple FCM.

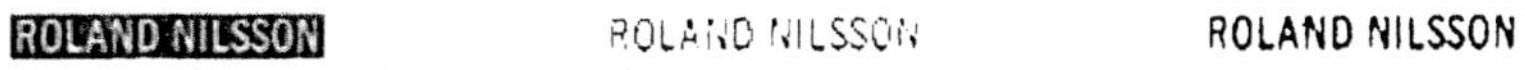

Fig. 2. The impact of AFC. From left to right: (a) the input image; the segmented image (b) without the AFC, the number of clusters $C = 6$; (c) with AFC, the number of clusters $C = 4$.

Fig. 3. The segmentation and OCR results for the images in Fig. 1. OCR results from left to right: (a) *Ricarda Stoller-Party-Service Offenbach*; (b) *Antires Martin Velasco*; (c) *ABDUL MAJEED*.

3.5 Binarization, Text Identification and Enhancement

After applying the steps explained above, C clusters of pixels are created. To proceed further, the correct cluster, i.e. the cluster containing text pixels should be found. For this purpose, a rating algorithm is proposed. It makes use of the fact that connected components (cc) and their bounding rectangles in the text image will show similar spatial and geometric properties compared to those of the other candidate images. A binary image, $bImage_j$ is generated for each $cluster_j$ marking all pixels which belong to the $cluster_j$ with black and the rest with white. After the extraction of cc (using the method in [5]) in each $bImage_j$, features that characterize their size distribution and spatial distribution are extracted. The same features are extracted even for their bounding rectangles (e.g. the standard deviation ($stDevYCC_j$) of the y coordinates of the lower right corner of the bounding rectangles). The density of blanks in the vertical projection ($densityBlank_j$) and the mean of the degrees of membership ($mean_j$) for each $bImage_j$ is also taken into consideration. First, all candidate images that do not fulfill the minimal criteria e.g. (($densityBlank_j > 0$) and ($densityBlank_j < 0.7$)). are excluded from further evaluations. Afterwards, an evaluation process consisting of several steps takes place, where each of the remaining candidates is rated based on the values of each of the extracted features. The maximum value for a feature rating is $max = C-1$, where C is the number of candidate images. Within an evaluation step, the candidate with the best feature value will be given the maximum feature rating, whereas the next best candidate will be given a feature rating of $max - 1$, and so on. For example, for the feature $stDevYCC_j$, the respective step of the rating algorithm will proceed as follows: the image which has the lowest standard deviation of the y will be given the maximum feature rating and the image which has the highest standard deviation of the y will be given the minimum feature rating. This is motivated with the fact that the cc (characters) in a text image often lie on a straight line. After each $bImage_j$ is rated for each of its features, the image with the highest overall rating is identified as the correct binary text image. Finally, an enhancement process takes place. All cc that: 1) are too small; or 2) lie on the boundaries of the text image and their bounding rectangles have an intersection with other bounding rectangles will be removed. The application of a morphological "open" operation for breaking the possible bridges across the characters concludes the operation.

4 Experimental Results

We have tested our text segmentation algorithm on two different test set of images. The first test set (TS1) is the public MPEG-7 test set [6] which consists of 45 images. There are 265 words or 1481 characters in this test set. The second test set (TS2) consists of 18 video frames with about 176 words or 1203 characters, which are chosen randomly from a set of video frames kindly provided to us by Lienhart [12]. Both test sets are selected in order to cover a wide variety of background complexity and different text color, font, size and polarity. In total, there are 441 words or 2684 latin characters. To evaluate the performance of the proposed text segmentation method (AFTS Method), character recognition experiments have been conducted. The recognition rate is used as an objective measure of the algorithm's segmentation performance. We have used a demo version of the commercial OCR software ABBYY FineReader 7.0 Professional [2] for recognition purposes. After segmentation, the segmented binary text image was fed manually into the OCR software and the correct recognized characters/words are counted. This evaluation is done on the OCR level in terms of character (word) recognition rate which are defined using the formula:
$WRR(CRR) = \frac{\#CorrectRecognizedWords(Chars)}{TotalNumberofWords(Chars)}$.

All the parameters used in the proposed method are evaluated experimentally, and the values that gave the best results on the average are used throughout these experiments. The following values of parameters are used during the text segmentation process: in the RGB color space $th_{similar} = 60$, $th_{compact} = 0.7$ and the sliding window size (in 3.3) was set to 3 x 3 pixels. The wavelet 5/3 filter bank evaluated in [20] was used with the low-pass filter coefficients -0.176777, 0.353535, 1.06066, 0.353535, -0.176777 and the high-pass filter coefficients 0.353535, -0.707107, 0.353535. In order to find the features which give the best results, different combinations were investigated:

- RGB or CIE La*b* Color Components;
- RGB or CIE La*b* Color Components + Wavelet Coefficients;
- RGB or CIE La*b* Color Comp. + Standard Deviation of Wavelet Coeff.;
- RGB or CIE La*b* Color Comp. + Wavelet Coeff. + Stand. Dev. of Wavelet Coeff.

The best results in terms of both CRR and WRR were achieved using the components of the RGB color space and the value of wavelet coefficients. Two groups of experiments are conducted in order to evaluate the proposed method. In the first group, the ground truth data are used as the input of the segmentation methods in order to avoid the impact of the localization algorithms on their accuracy, whereas in the second group the text boxes generated by the text localization method presented in [7] are used instead of the ground truths. For comparison purposes, two other methods, namely a thresholding-based [16] and an unsupervised text segmentation [9] method, were selected. For the second method, the same value of parameters as indicated in [9] are used.

The results obtained during the first group of experiments are listed in Tab. 1. The first number shows the WRR while the number in brackets shows the CRR. Our method has achieved an overall CRR of 90.4% and an overall WRR of 78% outperforming the

Table 1. Word (character) recognition performance comparison of three algorithms

Test Set	AFTS Method	K-means (k=2)[9]	Method in [16]
TS1	78.1 % (90.7 %)	65.7 % (78.1 %)	68.0 % (79.7 %)
TS2	78.0 % (90.0 %)	54.0 % (70.0 %)	52.0 % (70.0 %)
Overall	**78.0 % (90.4 %)**	**59.9 % (74.1 %)**	**60.0 % (74.9 %)**

other two methods. In Fig. 3, the segmentation and the OCR results for the images in Fig. 1 are shown. In the second group of experiments, evaluations were conducted only on TS1, and the text boxes generated by the text localization method presented in [7] are used as the input of the three different segmentation algorithms. The method in [7] has localized 88.88% of the text pixels present in TS1 (see [8]). The combination of [7] with the AFTS method using the OCR engine [2] has achieved an overall CRR of 77%. When the AFTS method is substituted by the Otsu method [16] (or k-means [9]), an overall CRR of 50% (or 41.4%) was obtained. Even in this case the proposed AFTS method has shown a better performance than the methods introduced in [16] and [9]. Fig. 4 shows an example of how the different text segmentation methods perform. We would like to point out that a performance measure such as CRR/WRR not only depends on the accuracy of the used segmentation methods but also on the quality of the OCR engine. During the experiments it was observed that in some cases, despite good segmentation results, the OCR fails to recognize the text image correctly.

The AFTS algorithm has a complexity of $O(NC^2k)$, since the maximum number of iterations for the AFTS is bounded by C, whereas the methods in [16] and in [9] have complexities of $O(N)$ and $O(NCk + N^{1/3})$ respectively. Considering that the initial number of clusters in [9] has a value of two and in AFTS it depends on the image colors, the AFTS algorithm is computationally more expensive. However, the AFTS method has shown a better performance than the methods in [9,16] in terms of CRR/WRR, and it usually takes place offline, since the purpose of this method is the text-based indexing of the images.

Fig. 4. The extraction results. From left to right: (a) the result of the localization alg. in [7]; the segmentation results (b) using Otsu [16]; (c) using k-means [9]; (d) using the proposed AFTS.

5 Conclusions

In this paper, an adaptive fuzzy algorithm (AFTS) for automatic text segmentation from complex images for recognition purposes has been proposed. Experimental results have shown the very good performance of the proposed method with an overall WRR of 78% and an overall CRR of 90.4% when using the ground truth data as input of the AFTS.

There are several areas for future work. For example, adapting the method for text strings that do not fulfill the assumption of having a homogeneous color will be our focus in the near future. The integration of a freely available OCR system will be also investigated to support the whole processing chain from the input image to the ASCII text in the end.

References

1. Agnihotri, L., Dimitrova, N.: Text Detection for Video Analysis. Proc. of Int'l Conf. on Multimedia Computing and Systems, Florence (1999) 109–113
2. ABBYY FineReader 7.0 Professional. http://www.abbyy.com
3. C. I. de LEclairage: Colorimetry. CIE Pub. 15.2 2nd ed. (1986)
4. Chen, D., Odobez, J.M.: Sequential Monte Carlo Video Text Segmentation, Proc. of IEEE Int'l Conf. on Image Processing, (2003) 21–24
5. Efford, N.: Digital Image Processing, a Practical Introduction using Java. Addison Wesley, (2000) 260–266
6. Hua, X.-S., Liu, W., Zhang, H. J.: Automatic Performance Evaluation for Video Text Detection. Proc. of IEEE Int'l Conf. on Document Analysis and Recognition, (2001) 545–550
7. Gllavata, J., Ewerth, R., Freisleben, B.: Text Detection in Images Based on Unsupervised Classification of High-Frequency Wavelet Coefficients. Proc. of Int'l Conf. on Pattern Recognition, Cambridge UK (2004) 425–428
8. Gllavata, J., Ewerth, R., Freisleben, B.: A Text Detection, Localization and Segmentation System for OCR in Images. Proc. IEEE Sixth Int'l Symposium on Multimedia Software Engineering, Miami, FL (2004) 310–317
9. Gllavata, J., Ewerth, R., Stefi, T., Freisleben, B.: Unsupervised Text Segmentation Using Color and Wavelet Features. Proc. of Int'l Conf. on Image and Video Retrieval, Dublin Ireland (2004) 216–224
10. Kim, D.W., Lee, K.H., Lee, D.: A Novel Initialization Scheme for the Fuzzy C-means Algorithm for Color Clustering. Pattern Recognition Letters 25, (2004) 227–237
11. Li, H., Kia, O., Doermann, D.: Text Enhancement in Digital Videos. SPIE Vol. 3651: Document Recognition and Retrieval VI, (1999) 2–9
12. Lienhart, R., Wernicke, A.: Localizing and Segmenting Text in Images and Videos. IEEE Transact. on Circuits and Systems for Video Technology, (2002) Vol. 12, Nr. 4, 256–258
13. Ngo, Ch. W., Chan, Ch. K.: Video Text Detection and Segmentation for Optical Character Recognition. ACM Multimedia Systems 10, (2005) 261-272
14. Niblack, W.: An Introduction to Digital Processing. Prentice Hall, (1986) 115–116
15. Odobez, J.M., Chen, D.: Robust Video Text Segmentation and Recognition with Multiple Hypotheses. Proc. of IEEE Int'l Conf. on Image Processing, Rochester NY (2002) Vol. II, 433–436
16. Otsu, N.: A Threshold Selection Method from Gray-Level Histograms. IEEE Transact. on Systems, Man and Cybernetics (1979) 9 (1) 62-66
17. Perroud, T., Sobottka, K. and Bunke, H., Hall, L.: Text Extraction from Color Documents-Clustering approaches in three and four dimensions. Proc. of IEEE Int'l Conf. on Document Analysis and Recognition, (2001) 937-941
18. Sato, T., Kanade, T., Huges, E.K., Smith, M.A., Satoh, S.: Video OCR: Indexing Digital News Libraries by Recognition of Superimposed Caption. ACM Multimedia Systems, Orlando, Florida (1999) Vol. 7, No. 5, 385–395

19. Sauvola, J., Seppänen, T., Haapakoski, S., Pietikäinen, M.: Adaptive Document Binarization. Proc. of Int'l Conf. on Document Binarization, (1997) Vol. 1, 147–152
20. Villasenor, J., Belzer, B., Liao, J.: Wavelet Filter Evaluation for Efficient Image Compression. IEEE Transactions on Image Processing, (1995) Vol. 4. 1053-1060
21. Wolf, C., Jolion, J.M., Chassaing, F.: Text Localization, Enhancement and Binarization in Multimedia Documents. Proc. of Int'l Conf. on Pattern Recognition, Quebec City Canada (2002) Vol. 4, 1037–1040
22. Wu, V., Manmatha, R., Riseman, E.M.: Textfinder: An Automatic System to Detect and Recognize Text in Images. IEEE Transact. on Pattern Analysis and Machine Intelligence, (1999) Vol. 21, Issue 11, 1224–1229
23. Ye, Q., Gao, W., Huang, Q.: Automatic Text Segmentation from Complex Background. Proc. of IEEE Int'l Conf. on Image Processing (2004)

Neighborhood Sequences and Their Applications in the Digital Image Processing

A. Fazekas, A. Hajdu, I. Sánta, and T. Tóth

Image Processing Group of Debrecen,
Faculty of Informatics,
University of Debrecen,
P.O.Box 12, H-4010 Debrecen, Hungary
Attila.Fazekas@inf.unideb.hu

Abstract. Digital distance functions and metrics based on neighborhood relations play important role in many applications in digital image processing. In this paper we summarize our results about the investigation of structural properties of neighborhood sequences and their possible applications in medial axis transformation.

1 Introduction

Motions in the digital space play an important role in several parts of discrete mathematics, including discrete geometry and digital image processing. The most important motions in $\mathbb{Z}^2$ are based upon the classical 4-neighborhood and 8-neighborhood relations. More detailed description about these neighborhood relations can be found in [13]. The alternate use of these neighborhood relations gives rise to the octagonal distance. These motions and the induced distance functions were systematically investigated in the classical paper of Rosenfeld and Pfaltz [18]. By allowing any periodic mixture of the 4- and 8-neighborhood relations, Das et al. [2] introduced the concept of periodic neighborhood sequences. They also extended this notion to $\mathbb{Z}^n$. Several papers are devoted to the description of the properties of such sequences, see e.g. [2]-[4] and the references given there. Later, Fazekas et al. (see [7]) extended the theory to the general case, i.e. when any (not necessary periodic) sequences are considered. The use of such sequences provide a more flexible tool than the previous ones. For example, A. Hajdu and L. Hajdu could obtain digital metrics on $\mathbb{Z}^2$ based upon such sequences, which yield the best approximation to the Euclidean distance [11].

In this paper we give a short overview on the main results of the investigation of neighborhood sequences based on classic neighboring relations and their applications in image processing. Section 2 generalizes the concept of neighborhood sequences (allowing not periodic sequences only). We overview the results of Das [4] and Fazekas [6] about ordering the set of periodic neighborhood sequences, and their extension to arbitrary dimension. Furthermore, we list the result about the structure of the set and some subsets of these generalized neighborhood sequences in $n\mathrm{D}$ under this ordering. Unfortunately, in several cases we obtain negative results: some of the structures considered do not have nice properties. Instead of this "natural" partial ordering we propose another relation, which is in close connection with the original one. More precisely, the "natural" ordering is a refinement of the relation introduced here. This ordering has nicer structural properties. The results related to this ordering can be found in Section 3, too. The proofs of the propositions can be found in [7], [9].

Digital distance measurement plays an important role in several branches of discrete mathematics, e.g. in discrete geometry or digital image processing. In Section 4 we perform an overall analysis on some properties of neighborhood sequences which induce metrics on $\mathbb{Z}^n$.

Section 5 demonstrates the dependency of medial axis transformation on the used distance function generated by a given neighborhood sequence. It is the first experimental results to show the selection the proper distance function based on neighborhood sequences in the applications can be important.

2 Basic Definition

In order to reach the aims formulated in the introduction, we give the basic definitions and notations in this chapter. From now on, n will denote an arbitrary positive integer.

Definition 1. *Let p and q be two points in $\mathbb{Z}^n$. The ith coordinate of the point p is indicated by $\Pr_i(p)$. Let m be an integer with $0 \leq m \leq n$. The points p and q are m-neighbors, if the following two conditions hold:*

- $|\Pr_i(p) - \Pr_i(q)| \leq 1$ *for $1 \leq i \leq n$,*
- $\sum_{i=1}^n |\Pr_i(p) - \Pr_i(q)| \leq m$.

Definition 2. *The infinite sequence $B = \{b(i) : i \in \mathbb{N} \text{ and } b(i) \in \{1, 2, \ldots, n\}\}$ is called a generalized nD-neighborhood sequence. If for some $l \in \mathbb{N}$, $b(i) = b(i+l)$ holds for every $i \in \mathbb{N}$, then B is called periodic, with a period l, or simply l-periodic. In this case we will use the abbreviation $B = \{b(1), \ldots, b(l)\}$.*

We note that the above concept of the generalized nD-neighborhood sequences is actually a generalization of the notion of neighborhood sequences introduced in [4].

Definition 3. *Let p and q be two points in $\mathbb{Z}^n$ and $B = \{b(i) : i \in \mathbb{N}\}$ a generalized nD-neighborhood sequence. The point sequence $\Pi(p, q; B)$ – which has the form $p = p_0, p_1, \ldots, p_m = q$, where p_{i-1} and p_i are $b(i)$-neighbors for $1 \leq i \leq m$ – is called a path from p to q determined by B. The length $|\Pi(p, q; B)|$ of the path $\Pi(p, q; B)$ is m.*

Definition 4. *Let p and q be two points in $\mathbb{Z}^n$ and B a generalized nD-neighborhood sequence. Clearly, there always exist paths from p to q, determined by B. The distance between p and q is defined as the common length of the shortest paths, and is denoted by $d(p, q; B)$.*

3 Neighborhood Sequences in nD

It is a natural question that what kind of relation exists between the distance functions generated by two given neighborhood sequences B_1 and B_2. The complexity of the problem can be characterized by the following 2D periodic example from [4]. Let $B_1 = \{1, 1, 2\}$, $B_2 = \{1, 1, 1, 2, 2, 2\}$. Choose the points $o = (0,0)$, $p = (3,1)$ and $q = (6,3)$. In this case we obtain that $d(o,p; B_1) = 3 < 4 = d(o,p; B_2)$, but $d(o,q; B_1) = 7 > 6 = d(o,q; B_2)$. So the distances generated by B_1 and B_2 cannot be compared.

Definition 5. *Let S_n, S'_n, $S'_n(l_\geq)$ and $S'_n(l)$ be the sets of generalized, periodic, at most l-periodic and l-periodic ($l \in \mathbb{N}$) nD-neighborhood sequences, respectively. For any $B_1, B_2 \in S_n$ we define the relation $\sqsupseteq^*$ in the following way:*

$$B_1 \sqsupseteq^* B_2 \quad \Leftrightarrow \quad d(p,q; B_1) \leq d(p,q; B_2).$$

It is evident that $\sqsupseteq^*$ is a partial ordering relation on S_n, hence also all on its subsets. Moreover, this relation $\sqsupseteq^*$ in 2D and 3D, is clearly identical to those introduced by Das [4] and Fazekas [6], respectively. Beside S_n, we investigate the structure of all those sets which were studied by Das [4] in the periodic case, like S'_n, $S'_n(l_\geq)$ and $S'_n(l)$ under $\sqsupseteq^*$. Unfortunately, in most cases the above sets with respect to this relation do not form nice structures. The only "positive" result in this direction is the following.

Proposition 1. *$(S_2, \sqsupseteq^*)$ is a complete distributive lattice.*

The above proposition does not hold in higher dimensions.

Proposition 2. *$(S_n, \sqsupseteq^*)$ is not a lattice for $n \geq 3$.*

Concerning some special sets of periodic sequences, we show that similar unkind properties of $\sqsupseteq^*$ also occur. In what follows we list these "negative" results.

Proposition 3. *$(S'_n, \sqsupseteq^*)$ is not a lattice for $n \geq 2$.*

In [4] Das proved that the set $S'_2(l)$ for any $l \geq 1$ forms a distributive lattice with respect to $\sqsupseteq^*$. However, this is not true for $S'_2(l_\geq)$, in general.

Proposition 4. *$(S'_2(l_\geq), \sqsupseteq^*)$ is not a lattice for any $l \geq 5$.*

Proposition 5. *$(S'_n(l_\geq), \sqsupseteq^*)$ and $(S'_n(l), \sqsupseteq^*)$ are not lattices for any $l \geq 2$, $n \geq 3$.*

The above results show that under the relation $\sqsupseteq^*$ we cannot obtain a nice structure neither in S_n, nor in various subsets of it. Now we introduce a new ordering relation, which is in close connection with $\sqsupseteq^*$. Moreover, S_n and its subsets considered above, will form much nicer structures under this new relation.

Definition 6. For any $B_1 = \{b^{(1)}(i) : i \in \mathbb{N}\}$, $B_2 = \{b^{(2)}(i) : i \in \mathbb{N}\} \in S_n$ we define the relation $\sqsupseteq$ in the following way:

$$B_1 \sqsupseteq B_2 \quad \Leftrightarrow \quad b^{(1)}(i) \geq b^{(2)}(i), \quad \text{for every } i \in \mathbb{N}.$$

It is clear that $\sqsupseteq^*$ is a proper refinement of $\sqsupseteq$ in S_n, S'_n, $S'_n(l_\geq)$ and $S'_n(l)$. We examine the structure of S_n, S'_n, $S'_n(l_\geq)$ and $S'_n(l)$ with respect to $\sqsupseteq$. As we will see, the structures we get will be much nicer than in the case of $\sqsupseteq^*$.

Proposition 6. $(S_n, \sqsupseteq)$ and $(S'_n, \sqsupseteq)$ are distributive lattice.

However, the ordering relation $\sqsupseteq$ has worse properties in S'_n than in S_n. This is shown by the following "negative" result.

Proposition 7. For $n \geq 2$, $(S'_n, \sqsupseteq)$ is not a complete lattice.

The forthcoming proposition shows that $S'_n(l_\geq)$ is not a "good" subset of S_n, in the sense that it does not form a nice structure even under $\sqsupseteq$. Of course, it is not surprising in view of the following observation: if A_1 and A_2 are in $S'_n(l_\geq)$, then $A_1 \vee A_2$ and $A_1 \wedge A_2$ defined in S_n, does not belong to $S'_n(l_\geq)$ in general.

Proposition 8. $(S'_n(l_\geq), \sqsupseteq)$ is not a lattice for $n, l \in \mathbb{N}$ with $n \geq 2$ and $l \geq 6$.

Proposition 9. $(S'_n(l), \sqsupseteq)$ is a distributive lattice for every $n, l \in \mathbb{N}$.

4 Lattices of Metrical Neighborhood Sequences

In this section we summarize the investigation of the structural behavior of the set of metrical neighborhood sequences with respect to both $\sqsupseteq^*$ and $\sqsupseteq$.

In [7] the authors introduced $\sqsupseteq$ to obtain better structural results for S_n than with $\sqsupseteq^*$. The following result shows the slightly surprising fact that M_n (set of nD-neighborhood sequences which generate metrics on $\mathbb{Z}^n$) does not form a nice structure under $\sqsupseteq$.

Proposition 10. $(M_n, \sqsupseteq)$ is not a lattice for $n \geq 2$.

The situation for $(M_n, \sqsupseteq^*)$ is similar to $(M_n, \sqsupseteq)$ at least when $n \geq 3$. However, this is not that surprising, since it was shown in [7] that $(S_n, \sqsupseteq^*)$ is also not a lattice in this case.

The following theorem shows that contrary to the higher dimensional case, metrical 2D-neighborhood sequences form a nice structure with respect to $\sqsupseteq^*$.

Proposition 11. $(M_2, \sqsupseteq^*)$ is a complete lattice.

5 Medial Axis Transformation

Distances have significant role in shape representation and analysis. In discrete spaces, distances are defined on selected neighborhoods. As it has been shown, they can be defined by neighborhood sequences as well.

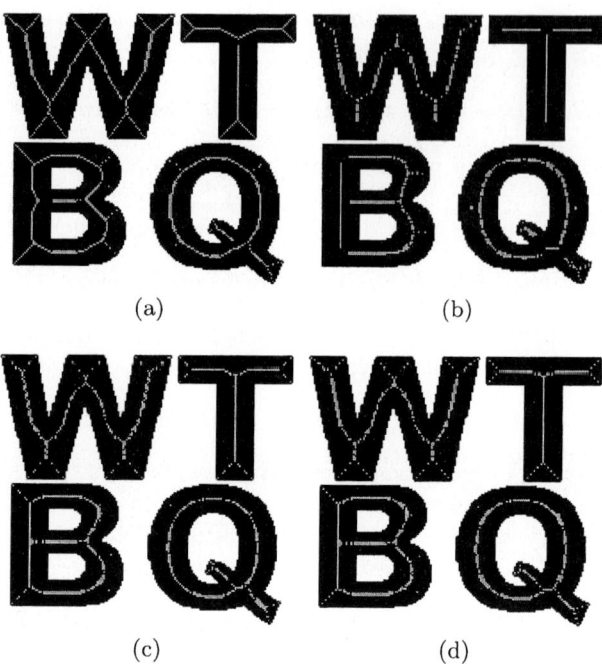

Fig. 1. Medial Axis Transformations. MAT_{B_1} (a), MAT_{B_2} (b), MAT_{B_3} (c), and MAT_{B_4} (d).

Medial Axis Transformation (MAT) [16], [17] is a special representation of a binary image. It contains the centres and radii of the maximal inner circles of the foreground. An inner circle is called maximal, if there is no such other inner circle that covers it entirely. An appropriate way for creating MAT is using the Distance Transformation of the image.

Distance Transformation (DT) of a shape of a binary image is a grey-scaled image, which assigns a value to each pixel of the shape representing its minimal distance from the boundary of this shape. Essentially, such a value is exactly the radius of the greatest inner circle with the given pixel as its centre. Thus, selecting the circles that are not covered by others, one can get actually the MAT of the shape.

Clearly, the DT and also the MAT of a shape can be created by using the distance function defined by a neighborhood sequence. It is easy to see, that these transformations differ from those derived from regular distances (e.g. 4-distance or 8-distance).

Let us define the following neighborhood sequences: $B_1 = \{1\}$ (4-distance), $B_2 = \{2\}$ (8-distance), $B_3 = \{1122\}, B_4 = \{1212\}, B_5 = \{211121211211\}$. Based on the definition of neighborhood sequences (see [7]), B_1 generates the 4-distance and B_2 the 8-distance.

One can select an l-period sequence B, which contains some 1's and some 2's. The MAT of an image created by using B is a transition from the MAT defined

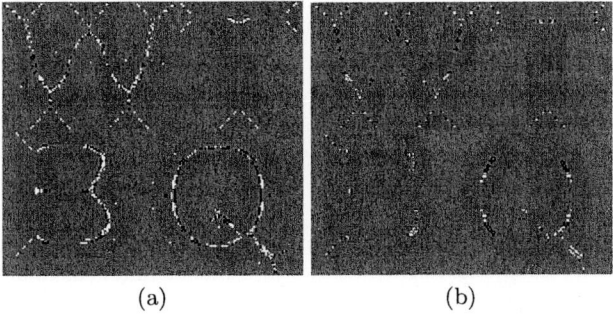

Fig. 2. Differences between MAT_{B_3} and MAT_{B_2} (a), MAT_{B_3} and MAT_{B_4} (b)

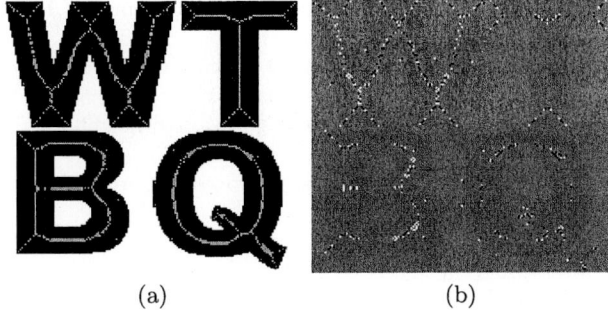

Fig. 3. The MAT defined by sequences B_5 (a), and the difference between MAT_{B_3} and MAT_{B_5} (b)

by 4-distance to that defined by 8-distance. Let MAT_{B_i} denote the MAT defined by the sequence B_i.

This first experiment shows the results of several image processing methods based on generated distance function can depent on selected neighborhood sequences. For example, to get the best approximation of the Euclidean distance we can apply the neighborhood sequence given in [11]. Our next step to continue the study of Medial Axis Transformation based on neighborhood sequences.

It can be seen on the figures, that the non-regular sequences give a better approximation of arcs of the shape than either the B_1 or B_2 sequence. In addition, they contain smaller splits than the 8-distance, and gives softer connections and less unnecessary branches than the 4-distance. The quality of MAT's depends on the sequences. The pixel-level differences between the MAT's can be seen in Figure 2 and Figure 3b. The white pixels in MAT are defined by the first and not by the second given sequence. The black pixels are on the contrary.

A. Hajdu and L. Hajdu gave a sequence, which is the best approximation of the Euclidean distance [11]. The MAT resulted from its 12-period prefix (i.e. B_5) is depicted in Figure 3a. The difference between the MAT defined by sequence B_3 and B_5 is shown in Figure 3b.

Acknowledgments

The research was supported in part by the János Bolyai Research Fellowship of the Hungarian Academy of Sciences and by the OTKA grant F043090.

References

1. M.R. Anderberg, Cluster analysis for application, Academic Press, New York, 1973.
2. P.P. Das, P.P. Chakrabarti, B.N. Chatterji, Distance functions in digital geometry, Information Sciences 42, 1987, 113-136.
3. P.P. Das, P.P. Chakrabarti, B.N. Chatterji, Generalised distances in digital geometry, Information Sciences 42, 1987, 51-67.
4. P.P. Das, Lattice of octagonal distances in digital geometry, Pattern Recognition Letters 11, 1990, 663-667.
5. P.P. Das, Best simple octagonal distances in digital geometry, J. Approx. Theory 68, 1992, 155-174.
6. A. Fazekas, Lattice of distances based on 3D-neighbourhood sequences, Acta Mathematica Academiae Pedagogicae Nyíregyháziensis 15, 1999, 55-60.
7. A. Fazekas, A. Hajdu, L. Hajdu, Lattice of generalized neighborhood sequences in nD and ∞D, Publ. Math. Debrecen 60, 2002, 405-427.
8. R.C. Gonzalez, R.E. Woods, Digital image processing, Addison-Wesley, Reading, MA, 1992.
9. A. Hajdu, Geometry of neighbourhood sequences, Pattern Recognition Letters 24, 2003, 2597-2606.
10. A. Hajdu, L. Hajdu, Velocity and distance of neighborhood sequences, Acta Cybernet. 16, 2003, 133-145.
11. A. Hajdu, L. Hajdu, Approximating the Euclidean distance by digital metrics, Discrete Math. 283, 2004, 101-111.
12. A. Hajdu, J. Kormos, B. Nagy, Z. Zörgő, Choosing appropriate distance measurement in digital image segmentation, Annales Univ.Sci. Budapest. Sect. Comp. 24, 2004, 193-208.
13. T.Y. Kong, A. Rosenfeld, Survey. Digital topology: Introduction and survey, Computer Vision, Graphics, and Image Processing 48, 1987, 357-393.
14. M.D. Levine, A.M. Nazif, Dynamic measurement of computer generated image segmentations, IEEE Trans. PAMI 7, 1985, 155-164.
15. J. Mukherjee, P.P. Das, M.A. Kumar, B.N. Chatterji, On approximating Euclidean metrics by digital distances in 2D and 3D, Pattern Recognition Letters 21, 2000, 573-582.
16. A. Rosenfeld, A.C. Kak, Digital picture processing. Vol. 2. Academic Press, New York, 1982.
17. A: Rosenfeld, J.L. Pfaltz, Sequential operations in digital picture processing, Journal of the ACM 13, 1966, 471-494.
18. A. Rosenfeld, J.L. Pfaltz, Distance functions on digital pictures, Pattern Recognition 1, 1968, 33-61.
19. M. Sonka, V. Hlavac, R. Boyle, Image processing, analysis, and machine vision, Brooks/Cole Publishing Company, Pacific Grove, CA, 1999.

Viseme Classification for Talking Head Application

Mariusz Leszczynski and Władysław Skarbek

Faculty of Electronics and Information Technology
Warsaw University of Technology
W.Skarbek@ire.pw.edu.pl

Abstract. Real time classification algorithms are presented for visual mouth appearances (visemes) which correspond to phonemes and their speech contexts. They are used at the design of *talking head application*. Two feature extraction procedures were verified. The first one is based on the normalized triangle mesh covering mouth area and the color image texture vector indexed by barycentric coordinates. The second procedure performs Discrete Fourier Transform on the image rectangle including mouth w.r.t. a small block of DFT coefficients. The classifier has been designed by the optimized LDA method which uses two singular subspace approach. Despite of higher computational complexity (about three milliseconds per video frame on Pentium IV 3.2GHz), the DFT+LDA approach has practical advantages over MESH+LDA classifier. Firstly, it is better in recognition rate more than two percent (97.2% versus 99.3%). Secondly, the automatic identification of the covering mouth rectangle is more robust than the automatic identification of the covering mouth triangle mesh.

1 Introduction

This research refers to a development of software tools supporting animation of human face models integrated with Polish speech generator.

With a gradual performance progress of computer systems w.r.t. computing and transmission speed the *talking head applications* show higher realism in speech and dynamic visual face appearance (viseme).

Except the performance of speech generator, the synchronization between the spoken content and facial *visual content,* is of high importance. The visual content should not only provide the time correspondence of face image and related sound but also respect the semantic context of the speech, and the internal emotions of the speaker.

One of the main tasks in *talking head system* is the design of a correspondence table between visemes and phonemes (CTVP table). This correspondence is of *one to many* relational type. We can convert this relation to a mapping if we consider a *speech context* for the particular phoneme. In practice to get a unique viseme to speech context, it is enough to take into account three phonemes for such context: the current phoneme, the previous one, and the next one.

Fig. 1. Representative images for six major viseme classes – the 16 minor classes are obtained by discrimination between small, medium, and high degree of mouth opening within the first five major classes

In case of Polish speech patterns stored in the CORPORA database [2], the design of *phoneme context to viseme mapping* requires recording of video and audio material lasting about 1000 seconds. Therefore we get more than 25000 visemes to be classified and assigned to recognized phonemes context. This amount excludes manual implementation. Both, an automatic viseme classifier and phoneme classifier are necessary to complete the design of CTVP table.

For the phoneme classifier we have used a speech recognition engine based on HTK toolkit (cf. [7]). As a side effect the speech recognition program produces the phoneme and diphone transcription labelled by time information. Having such timing we could segment the video sequence into phoneme related groups. From each group this video frame was selected for viseme classification which was closest in time to the middle of phoneme time interval, i.e. to the beginning of diphone interval. The recognized viseme class (cf. Fig.1) was joined to the phoneme context list. At the end, from each phoneme list the class id was selected using the majority rule.

This work explains how the viseme classifier had been designed to support the creation of CTVP table. To this goal the classification performance of 80% could be sufficient. However, we are going to use our viseme classifier to animate the human head model on the basis of live video. Therefore the real time and the high performance of the classifier are the main objectives of our research.

2 Image Normalization

The realistic visual speech can be achieved by integrating the person specific face model with mouth model optionally augmented with the model of chin and cheeks. Using a triangle mesh (cf. Fig.2), we can cover those speech sensitive areas and try to get the model for at least two goals: viseme classification and mouth animation.

Alternatively we can approximate the mouth area by a least rectangle touching lips from outside (cf. Fig.3 upper part). Obviously, the triangle mesh ap-

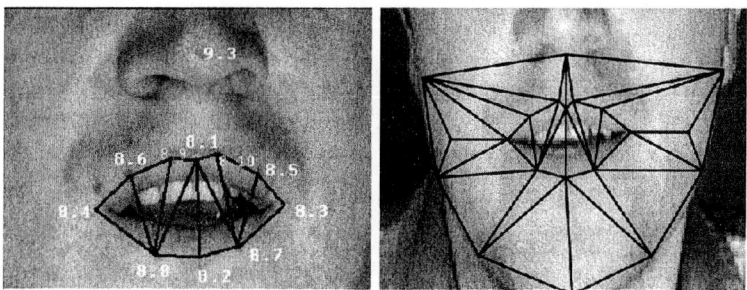

Fig. 2. Triangle mesh for mouth with MPEG-4 FAP points depicted (left), and its neighbourhood (right)

proximation of mouth area is more exact than rectangular one and therefore a texture vector built from the rectangle includes components hard for matching. In this case change to 2D Discrete Fourier Transform (DFT) domain enables correct matching of mouth images normalized to reference mouth rectangle. As the vertical variability of the mouth image dominates the horizontal one, we expect that out of three corner blocks (cf. Fig.3 lower part) in DFT domain (usually considered at DFT based feature extraction) only the one corresponding to the least frequencies (without conjugated part) will be important for classification. Our expectation has been confirmed by the experiments.

In mesh approach we deal with variations of the mesh shape and of the mesh texture (*appearance*). In order to make comparable two meshes we have to normalize them with respect to a reference mesh.

We perform the nonlinear normalization of the mesh by mapping each triangle in the current image onto the corresponding triangle in the reference im-

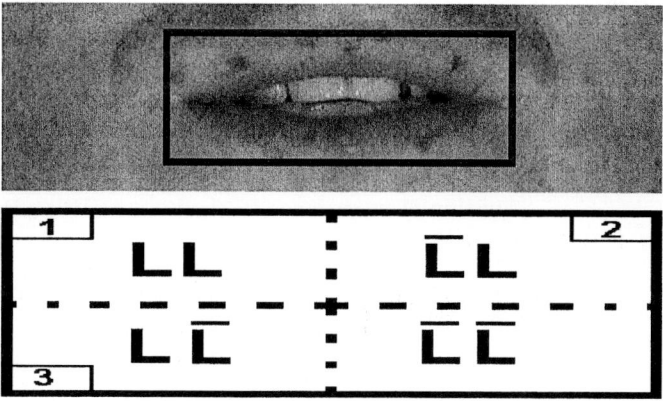

Fig. 3. The rectangle including mouth area (upper), and channel subdivision for 2D DFT (lower)

age. Each local mapping is affine, but globally we obtain the mapping which is piecewise affine.

Let the i-th triangle $\Delta_i(P_0, P_1, P_2)$ in the reference mesh $\mathcal{M}$ be mapped by the affine mapping $A_i(P) = B_i P + t_i$ onto the triangle $\Delta'_i(P'_0, P'_1, P'_2)$ in the current mesh $\mathcal{M}'$, where B_i is the square matrix, t_i is the vector, $P \in \Delta_i$, $P' \in \Delta'_i$, $i = 1, \ldots, K$. Then we have the following properties:

1. The piecewise affine mappings $A_1, \ldots, A_K$ are *continuous mappings* of $\mathcal{M}$ onto $\mathcal{M}'$ in geometric space
2. If $P = \alpha_0 P_0 + \alpha_1 P_1 + \alpha_2 P_2$ has the barycentric coordinates $\alpha_0, \alpha_1, \alpha_2$ w.r.t. the triangle $\Delta_i(P_0, P_1, P_2)$ then the point $A_i(P) = \alpha_0 P'_0 + \alpha_1 P'_1 + \alpha_2 P'_2$, i.e. it has *the same barycentric coordinates* with respect to the triangle $\Delta'_i(P'_0, P'_1, P'_2)$:

$$A_i(P) = B_i P + t_i = B_i(\alpha_0 P_0 + \alpha_1 P_1 + \alpha_2 P_2) + (\alpha_0 P_0 + \alpha_1 P_1 + \alpha_2)t$$
$$= \alpha_0(B_i P_0 + t) + \alpha_1(B_i P_1 + t) + \alpha_2(B_i P_2 + t) = \alpha_0 P'_0 + \alpha_1 P'_1 + \alpha_2 P'_2$$

3. If $f' : \Delta'_i(P'_0, P'_1, P'_2) \to \mathcal{C}_{RGB}$ is the texture mapping in the current mesh then the mapping $f : \Delta_i(P_0, P_1, P_2) \to \mathcal{C}_{RGB}$ is defined by the barycentric coordinates for $i = 1, \ldots, K$ as follows:

$$f(P) = f(\alpha_0 P_0 + \alpha_1 P_1 + \alpha_2 P_2) \triangleq f'(\alpha_0 P'_0 + \alpha_1 P'_1 + \alpha_2 P'_2) \qquad (1)$$

The above substitution transfers the texture from the current mesh onto the reference mesh with possible deformation of linear segments which intersect at least two triangles in the mesh.

3 LDA for Mouth Classification

The advantage of having all texture classes (in mesh case) or DFT coefficients classes (in rectangular case) in common space $\mathbb{R}^N$ allows us to use the Linear Discriminant Analysis (LDA) to design the extremely fast classifier of linear complexity $O(N)$.

Before we reached LDA feature vector of dimension five, the general Fisher LDA criterium (cf. [3,5,6]) had been used for K dimensional training feature vector $y_i = W^t x_i$, $x_i \in \mathbb{R}^N$, $i = 1, \ldots, L$, $y \in \mathbb{R}^K$, $W \in \mathbb{R}^{N \times K}$:

$$W_{opt} = \arg\max \frac{\text{between class variance for } \{y_i\}}{\text{within class variance for } \{y_i\}} = \frac{tr(W^t S_b W)}{tr(W^t S_w W)} \qquad (2)$$

where S_b, S_w are the between and within class scatter matrices.

The above criterium has points of singularity if W is arbitrary. Therefore Fisher imposed the following constraints on the domain of W:

$$W^t S_w W = I, \quad W \perp \ker(S_w) \qquad (3)$$

This leads us to the following steps to obtain the optimal W described in details as two singular subspace method in [1] with tuning parameters q equal to the dimension of the intra-class singular subspace (cf. [4]):

1. Class mean shifting of the training sequence: $X = [x_1, \ldots, x_L]$;
2. Grand mean shifting for class means: $M = [m_1, \ldots, m_C]$;
3. Singular Value Approximation for X with subspace dimension equal to q:

$$[U_q, \Sigma_q] := sva(X, q); \quad A_q = U_q \Sigma_q^{-1};$$

4. Whitening of columns in M : $M = A_q^t M$;
5. Singular Value Approximation for M with subspace dimension equal to r:

$$V_r := sva(M, q); \quad W = A_q V_r;$$

6. Return W;

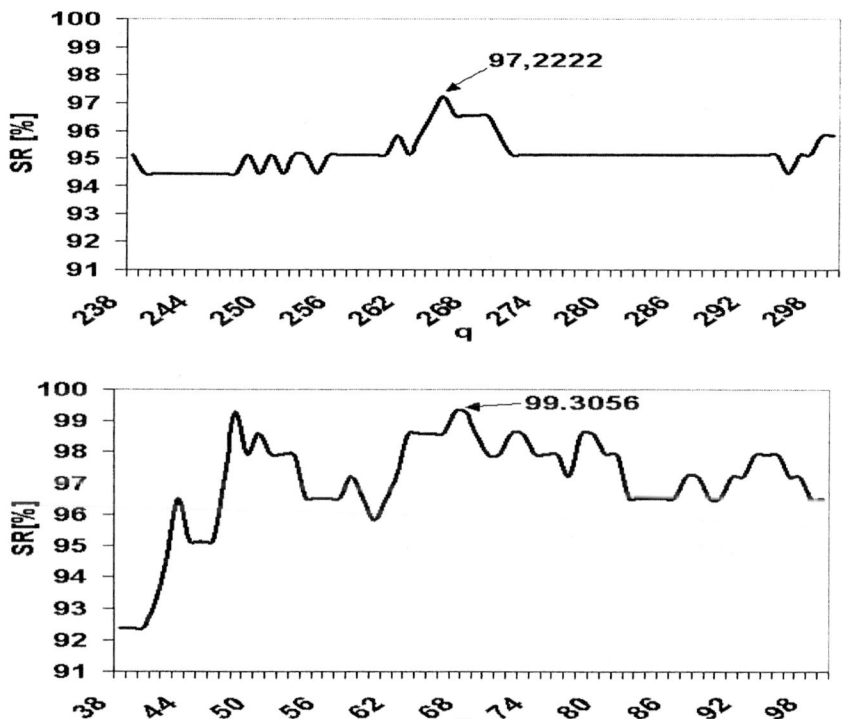

Fig. 4. Recognition rate versus LDA tuning parameter q when $r = 5$: for MESH+LDA (upper graph) and DFT+LDA (lower graph)

In case of mesh based feature vector (MESH+LDA) and DFT based feature vector (DFT+LDA), the Fig.4 shows the expected behavior of recognition rate versus the tuning parameter q.

The vector LDA features with maximum possible value $r = C - 1 = 5$ gives the best results.

The LDA feature $y = W^t x$ for the texture vector x is classified by the distance to LDA features $y_i = W^t x_i$ representing the mouth appearance classes $i = 1, \ldots, 6$:

$$i_{opt} = \arg \min_{1 \leq i \leq 6} \|y - y_i\|^2 \qquad (4)$$

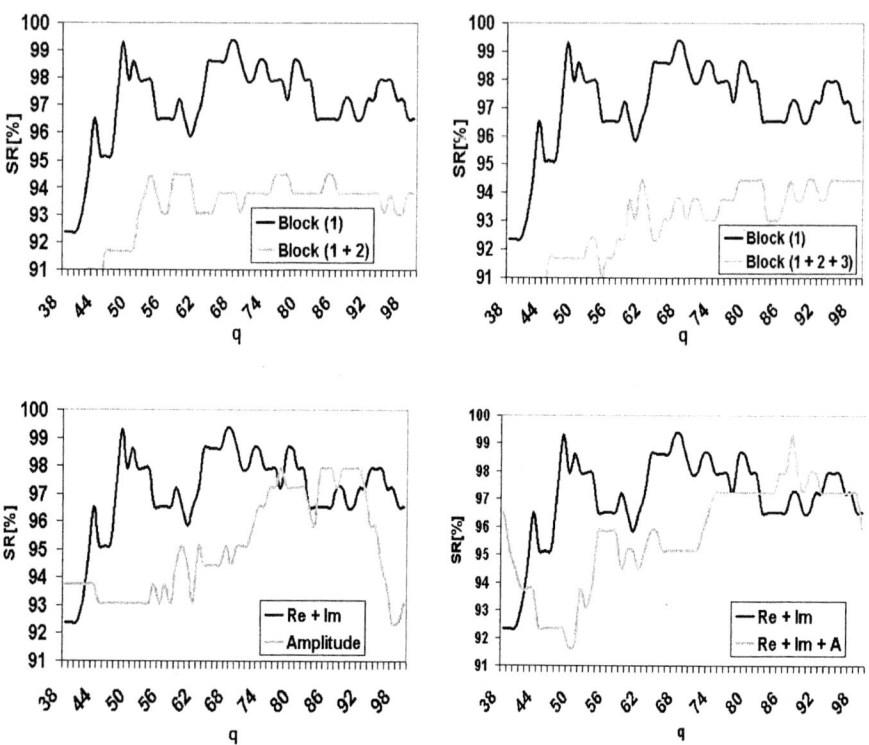

Fig. 5. Recognition rate versus LDA tuning parameter q when $r = 5$: for different choice of DFT channels (in upper graphs block 1 contains coefficients of LL frequencies, $2 - \bar{L}L$, $3 - L\bar{L}$) and different combinations of real, imaginary and amplitude parts in DFT (lower graphs)

4 Experimental Results

For the training of models for feature extraction, 497 mouth image were selected with unbalanced distribution in the classes what corresponds to the distribution in the whole recorded video sequence:

$$L_1 = 127, \ L_2 = 123, \ L_3 = 42, L_4 = 89, L_5 = 37, \ L_6 = 79$$

For the testing stage, 152 frames were selected independently of training frames.

In mesh texture case the best result (97.2% – cf. Fig.4 upper part) is achieved for lower resolution image with subsequent subsampling of texture vector. Since in case of LDA, the extraction time is independent of q, we accept higher values of q giving higher generalization of the classifier even if the recognition rate is slightly higher for lower values of q.

In rectangular DFT case the best recognition result (equal to 99.3%) is achieved for the following setup of parameters:

1. DFT block LL for horizontal frequencies $0-4$ and vertical frequencies $0-19$ (cf. Fig.3 at lower part and graphs of Fig.5 at upper part)
2. DC component is skipped
3. imaginary and real parts of all coefficients in blok LL are stacked in one vector of size 198 (contrary to the face classifier used in our system, the amplitude of DFT coefficients for mouth classifier has appeared to be insignificant – cf. graphs of Fig.5 at lower part)
4. intra-class singular subspace dimension equals to 67 (cf. Fig.4 lower part)
5. inter-class singular subspace dimension equals to 5

It appears that mouth images which were wrongly classified are only from the class of slightly opened mouth with visible upper teeth, without visible tongue. They were confused with opened mouth, visible upper teeth and visible tongue. However, by eye view (the important measure in talking head application) the difference between such two images is not annoying while watching the mouth animation.

5 Conclusion

Two real time algorithms MESH+LDA and DFT+LDA for visemes classification were compared.

Both algorithms benefit of optimization stage when the optimal first singular subspace dimension is selected in our LDA design. LDA matrix in mesh has about 30 times more elements than LDA matrix in DFT case. However this advantage at matrix computation is absorbed by dominating DFT computational time.

Preliminary feature extraction for MESH+LDA is slightly faster but less robust in case of automatic mesh identification.

DFT+LDA method is better than MESH+LDA in recognition rate more than two percent (97.2% versus 99.3%). Therefore for *talking head* applications, DFT+LDA technique is recommended.

Acknowledgments

The work presented was developed within VISNET, a European Network of Excellence (http://www.visnet-noe.org), funded under the European Commission IST FP6 programme.

References

1. Bober M., Kucharski K., and Skarbek W.: Face Recognition by Fisher and Scatter Linear Discriminant Analysis, in Computer Analysis of Images and Patterns, eds. Petkov N., Westenberg M., Springer LNCS 2756, 638:645, 2003
2. Grocholewski S.: CORPORA - Speech Database for Polish Diphones, 5th European Conference on Speech Communication and Technology EUROSPEECH '97 Rhodes, Greece, September 22-25, 1997
3. Fukunaga K.: Introduction to statistical pattern recognition (2nd ed). Academic Press, Boston, 1990
4. Golub G., Van Loan C.: Matrix Computations. Baltimore: Johns Hopkins University Press, 1996
5. Ripley B.D.: Pattern Recognition and Neural Networks. Cambridge University Press, 1996
6. Swets D.L., Weng J.: Using Discriminant Eigenfeatures for Image Retrieval, IEEE Trans. on PAMI, 18(8):831-837, August 1996
7. The Hidden Markov Model Toolkit (HTK) http://htk.eng.cam.ac.uk

New Algorithms for Example-Based Super-Resolution

László Czúni[1], Gergely Császár[1], Dae-Sung Cho[2], and Hyun Mun Kim[2]

[1] University of Veszprém, Dep. of Image Processing and Neurocomputing,
H-8200 Veszprém, Egyetem u. 10
czuni@almos.vein.hu
[2] Samsung Advanced Institute of Technology, Multimedia Lab, P.O. Box 111,
Suwon 440-600, Korea
{daescho,hyunmun27kim}@samsung.com

Abstract. This paper describes enhancements on example-based super-resolution. Example-based super resolution has the advantage that only one observation of the low-resolution image is required but reconstruction requires long processing time. We propose techniques to achieve faster operation and/or better quality by several modifications of previous techniques. We show some typical data as quantitative results also including video in electronic version.

1 Introduction and Previous Works

To generate high-resolution images from low-resolution observations there are several different approaches but basically three main groups can be defined:

- Special image filtering and zooming techniques e.g. [4,7,9]. These techniques are faster than those of the other two categories.
- Methods using several observations (i.e. video frames) to generate one enhanced frame e.g. [3].
- Methods using a learnt statistical database of high-frequency patches to enhance images [2,5].

[8] describes a method where image filtering is combined with example-based super-resolution. In our paper with deal with the example-based approach and our proposed algorithms can be applied also in the combined mode.

The main idea of example-based techniques is that the high- and medium-frequency representation of the patches of an image are statistically not independent from each other and adding high-frequency content to the medium frequency part of an image can be done on example bases (see Figure 1 for block schemes). In implementations of [2,5] each medium-frequency patch is a vector of length 3x7x7 = 147 (pixels of 3 color channels defined on patches of size 7x7). In [2] this dimensionality is reduced to 20 with PCA, and then a KD-tree [1,6] database is built up from medium and high-frequency image pairs with a technique to be able to run fast searches in it since training data comprises at least 200.000 patches taken from several training images. To enhance a low-resolution image for its medium-frequency patches high-frequency patches are looked up from the KD-tree. To get visually satisfactory results high-frequency patches need to overlap each other, to assure coherence, so choosing the optimal high-frequency patch requires a certain optimization. However, due to the very fast convergence of "belief propagation" algorithms a fast one-pass energy optimization algorithm is reported by [2,5] to be suitable for the task. This optimization considers two energy terms: the first term (E_1) is responsible to find a similar mid-frequency patch in the database the other (E_2) is to assure that the high-frequency patch, to be inserted, fits well its neighbors (spatial coherence by overlapping):

$$E = E_1 + E_2 \text{ where } E_1 = \frac{1}{NN}\sum_{i=1}^{N}\sum_{j=1}^{N}(LRP_{Query}(i,j) - LRP_{DB}(i,j))^2 \text{ and}$$

$$E_2 = \alpha \frac{1}{2N-1}\sum_{i=1}^{2N-1}(HRI_{REC}(i) - HRP_{DB}(i))^2$$

where the following notations are used: LRP_{Query}: low-resolution query patch; LRP_{DB}: low-resolution patch in the database; HRI_{REC}: already reconstructed neighboring edge pixels; HRP_{DB}: edge pixels of a high-resolution patch in the database (pair of LRP_{DB}); α is a design parameter (typically around 0.1), N is the size of a patch on the reconstruction frame.

In [2] the extension for video sequences can be found. Major differences are introduced because the original still image version leads to strong flickering when applied to consecutive image frames. To reduce this flickering effect two new energy terms are added to the cost function to evaluate a high-frequency patch candidate: one additional term increases the probability that at an image location the same high-frequency patch is chosen as in the previous frame; the other new term considers adaptive new dictionaries (set of medium/high-frequency image pairs) over moving image areas. Example videos of Bishop's method can be downloaded from [10].

Finding and optimal solution for the reconstruction problem would need a lengthy algorithm, which would consider both all neighbors of a patch for local consistency and all data stored in the database to find the most similar example. MRF (Markov

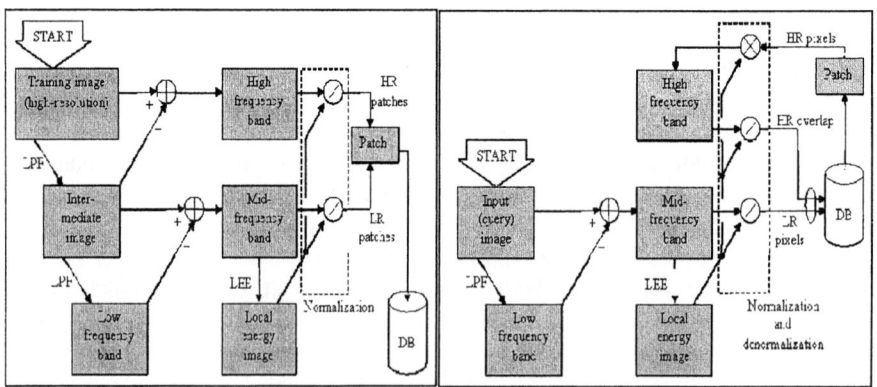

Fig. 1. Learning mid- and high-frequency patch pattern pairs (left) and reconstruction of an image (right). LPF: Low Pass Filtering.

Random Field) solutions with iterative relaxation algorithms can solve the first requirement while exhaustive search the second. However, Freeman reported that a one-pass, raster scan order repainting of the image is visually satisfactory and spares much computation time. Searching for appropriate patterns in the database still requires a long time since the database typically stores 200.000-1.000.000 records. To reduce retrieval time non-exhaustive (sub-optimal) searching methods are used to obtain good approximations. Freeman and Bishop both use KD-tree for indexing the learnt patterns. KD-trees arrange the data in a special tree-like structure and thus lead to faster query algorithms [1,6]. If we are satisfied with close-to-optimum searches then best-branch search can be applied as proposed by Freeman. Best-branch search runs down directly to the leaves of the tree always moving to the most probable branch direction. Bishop proposes an alternative technique to find the best candidates by indexing only the mid image band and so evaluating only E_1 during the tree search. A so-called candidate list is maintained (based only on E_1) during the tree search storing only some (typically 100-200) best candidates found. Those branches of the tree are not visited which contain patches with larger E_1 than the worst element in the candidate list already found. Then only the elements of this candidate list are evaluated by the fitting of the high-resolution candidate to the already rendered left and upper neighbor (E_2). This technique shortens the searching time. In our implementation we follow Bishop's solution by maintaining a candidate list and by evaluating E_2 only on the elements of this list when the tree search is finished.

2 Enhancements

2.1 Purpose of Enhancements

The purpose of our research is to investigate the use and behavior of the previously proposed techniques and to make the reconstruction faster and also to develop techniques which give better quality at the same cost or result in similar quality at lower cost (where cost can be measured by speed and by the database size). Unfortunately, neither [2] nor [5] gives objective comparisons with conventional interpolation. In this paper we give some objective and subjective comparisons either.

2.2 Modified Overlapping of Mid Band Images

Methods proposed in [2,5] all uses overlapping patches of size 7x7 defined on the mid-frequency band. In case of color images (with 3 channels) this means data vectors of size 7x7x3 to be indexed in the KD-tree data structure. The indexing and usage of databases of such high dimension is usually very slow, that is why in [2] PCA (Principal Component Analysis) was used to reduce the vector size or in [5] only best-branch search is run within respectable time. We tested three types of patches on the down-sampled mid band as illustrated on the left of Figure 2 (from left to right) and in Table 1: proposal of Freeman and Bishop (Type 1); 1 pixel overlapping in three colors (Type 2); 1 pixel overlapping only in gray channel (Type 3); no-overlapping (Type 4). The advantage of using non-overlapping patches of size 2x2 defined on the down-sampled mid band is that it leads to much smaller dimension (2x2x3 in case of color images) with minimal or no quality loss. Down-sampling reduces the number of components and basically loses no important information since the mid-frequency band is the difference of smooth images. Smaller dimension means smaller database and faster searching process. Typical data for the effect of different patch models are in Table 1.

Table 1. Typical data for different overlapping to enhance (2x zoom) the Bush (400x400) image with a database of 460.000 records

Type	Down-sampl.	Overlapping	Dimension	Size [MB] (example)	Reconstruction time [sec] [1]	PSNR [dB][2]
1.[2,5]	No	Yes (Color)	3(ch.)x7x7=147	NA	NA	NA
2.	Yes	Yes (Color)	3(ch.)x4x4=48	550+100	571/7; 3700/19	30.24/29.84; 30.33/30.08
3.	Yes	Yes (Gray)	3(ch.)x2x2 +1(ch.)x12=24	550+50	270/6; 1740/16	30.35/30.14; 30.39/30.27
4.	Yes	No	3(ch.)x2x2=12	285+27	29/6; 85/14	30.29/30.2; 30.3/30.29

2.3 Transforming Query Blocks for Finding Better Matches and Simultaneous Search for Transformed Queries

A straightforward way to increase the possibility of finding better matches in the example database for a query patch without increasing the number of stored samples is to rotate and mirror the query patch itself and to search for all these new variations either. This step is based on the general fact that the degradation process, from a high-resolution image into a low-resolution image, is isotropic and acts the same way on mirrored and rotated images. That is if we don't find good examples for a query patch we can easily generate 7 new alternatives by rotating and mirroring as shown in Figure 2. Naturally, we should apply the inverse geometrical transformation when inserting the high-frequency patch. Typical improvement (0.01-0.5dB) depends on the database size: greater improvement can be achieved when the database contains less data. In the example of Table 1 the improvement ranges from 0.01dB to 0.13dB. Basically, looking for transformed queries increases the searching time by 8 times but we propose a method to avoid such amount of computation overhead with the help of maintaining only 1 candidate list for all variations. In our mechanism we take each geometrical variation, circulating one after the other in a predefined order, and search similar patterns simultaneously: We take Query No.1, start at the root of the KD-tree then go one step down and make the decision: which branch to enter first or which branch to enter at all. Then we take Query No.2 (transformed version of Query No.1) and make also one step from the root on the tree independently of the other query patterns. In each step we update the shared candidate list. Since the candidate list contains the already found best matches of all 8 queries it makes the different queries to race with each other to fill the shared candidate list. The shared list has a strong effect in making a decision whether to enter a new branch of the tree or not. As in this case 8 variations are racing some variations have much less chance to wander most of

---

[1] Reconstruction (searching) time (on 3.2GHz P4 with 2GB RAM): full/best branch search without geometrical transforms and full/best search with 8 transforms.
[2] PSNR is the difference of the original high-resolution and the downscaled then reconstructed image.

the KD-tree branches since other variations already found better candidates than those being on the unexplored branches. Finally, by racing all variations on one shared candidate list leads to less movement in the tree saving time considerably: at least 40% time reduction is experienced in different experiments.

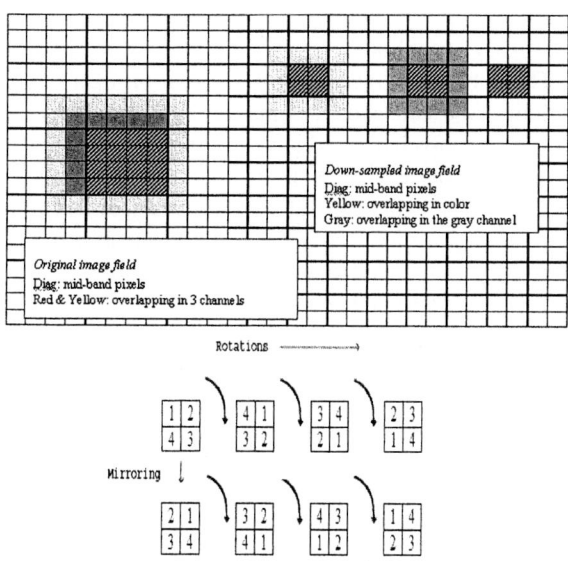

Fig. 2. Different overlapping and 1 non-overlapping sampling of the mid-band (left); generation of rotated and mirrored versions of a 2x2 patch (right). Pixel cells are numbered.

2.4 New Searching Method for Balancing Between Best-Branch Search and Full Search

Since example-based super-resolution techniques are far from real-time operation it is a question how to find faster reconstruction methods. Freeman used the best-branch search technique, which is far from finding an optimal solution but can be 10-100 times faster than exhaustive search. We propose a balancing technique, called "tolerance search", to enable a search between exhaustive (optimal but very slow) and best-branch (fast but not optimal) modes. By a simple parameter (epsilon) we can tune our algorithm to find a solution between the two extreme cases. Epsilon (epsilon ≥ 0) defines a range around the vector components of the query vector: a hypercube around the query. In tolerance search, we investigate the KD-tree branches in the following manner:

1. if there is no intersection of the space spanned by the branch and the space defined by the query hypercube then we go to the closer branch;
2. if there is intersection we enter the branch.

If epsilon is 0 then we get the fastest best-branch search algorithm but as we increase epsilon more and more branches are investigated, due to having more intersections, and finally we reach the full search mode. According to our tests we can reach about

95% of the quality of exhaustive search with at least 50% speed up with the rough setting of epsilon.

2.5 Filtering of the High-Frequency Band for Reducing Artifacts

Applying different smoothing kernels on the high-frequency band it is possible to balance between strong visual sharpness of the reconstructed image and strict high fidelity results. The subjective and objective evaluation of a reconstructed image is not always the same. We can generate images which look sharper for the human observer but in real contain noise reducing the image quality measured in PSNR, especially when the database size is limited around 200.000 patterns or below. Moreover, previous works with general databases contain strong artifacts on test images [2,5]. We found that these artifacts can be reduced or removed by smoothing the high-frequency image band (before reconstruction). By applying different smoothing kernels we can balance between stronger visual sharpness and high fidelity (see Figure 3 for illustration). Since the high-frequency image band is the difference of an image and its smoothed version it contains positive and negative values located close to each other. Statistically, by strong smoothing this difference image moves toward a zero plain (in extreme case, by applying a very strong smoothing operation, we get no resolution enhancement at all since a zero image is to be added). We found that slightly smoothing the high-frequency image band can reduce the reconstruction error and increases PSNR (between 0.01-0.2dB). Typical smoothing kernels giving the best results in PSNR are given below:

0.05	0.1	0.05		1/9	1/9	1/9
0.1	0.4	0.1		1/9	1/9	1/9
0.05	0.1	0.05		1/9	1/9	1/9

gives a sharper reconstruction　　　　results in a less sharp image.

Fig. 3. (from left to right) Bi-cubic interpolation, SR with stronger high-band smoothing, SR with weaker high-band smoothing. While the 3rd image seems a bit sharper it contains artifacts around the left ear on the blue background.

3 Still and Video Examples

Due to the limited length of the paper only two test images are given (see Figure 4 and Figure 5). Please, refer to [11] for electronic test images and video. We applied our method also to Bishop's test video, downloadable from the Internet [10], for comparison. Without using "motion prior", proposed by Bishop, and also without knowing the degradation model (no original ground truth is known for us for teaching the SR algorithm with other similarly degraded images) we produced visually better results with a simpler and more effective algorithm (see [11]).

Fig. 4. Bi-cubic interpolation (29.85dB) and super-resolution enhancement (30.12dB) of half-sized Boat image

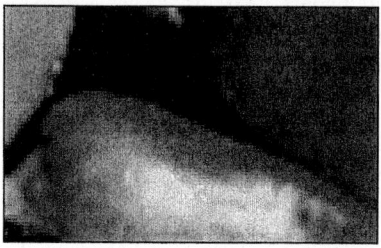 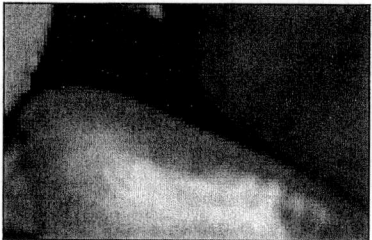

Fig. 5. Part of the Peppers image with bicubic interpolation (left, 31.93dB) and example-based SR (right, 32.34dB)

4 Conclusion and Future Work

In this paper we proposed improvements of example-based reconstruction methods. Example-based reconstruction can be useful when an image degradation process is difficult to be modeled or to be estimated by conventional methods and is known only by image examples or when only one observation is available. All proposed modifications resulted in improvement of PSNR (0.1-0.5dB), subjective visual quality or reconstruction time (typically 50% speedup). After all, example based methods are still too slow for real-time applications. In [8] 36 classes of image primitives were used as a first step of pattern classification when looking up high-frequency patterns. In our latest experiments we tested pre-classification of patches using the following 2x2 convolution kernels:

$$\begin{bmatrix} 0 & 1 \\ -1 & 0 \end{bmatrix}; \begin{bmatrix} 0 & -1 \\ 1 & 0 \end{bmatrix}; \begin{bmatrix} 1 & 0 \\ 0 & -1 \end{bmatrix}; \begin{bmatrix} -1 & 0 \\ 0 & 1 \end{bmatrix}$$

corresponding to diagonal edges (4 classes). Horizontal and vertical edges (4 classes altogether) are detected if two neighboring diagonal filters respond with similar values. If none of the filters responded above a given value then we classified the patch into the 9th group otherwise the filters acts as compass filters. This pre-classification resulted in approximately 40% time speedup (with no quality loss) when exhaustive search was carried out, however further research is needed to build up statistics of 2x2 image patterns and to get better results. The application of Maximum Likelyhood super-resolution for those areas, not having strong responses to edge filters, is also promising.

References

[1] J. L. Bentley: Multidimensional Divide and Conquer. Communications of the ACM, 23(4):214-229, 1980.
[2] Christopher M. Bishop, Andrew Blake, Bhaskara Marthi: Super-resolution Enhancement of Video, 9th Int. Conf. on AI and Statistics, 2003
[3] Sean Borman, Robert L. Stevenson: Super-Resolution from Image Sequences - A Review, Midwest Symposium on Circuits and Systems, 1998
[4] Sergio Carrato and Livio Tenze: A high quality 2x image interpolator, Signal Processing Letters, vol. 7, pp. 132-134, June 2000.
[5] William T. Freeman, Thouis R. Jones, and Egon C. Pasztor: Example-Based Super-Resolution, IEEE Computer Graphics and Applications, March/April 2002
[6] J. H. Friedman, J. L. Bentley and R. A. Finkel: An Algorithm for Finding Best Matches in Logarithmic Expected Time, ACM Trans. on Mathematical Software, 3(3):209-226, Sept. 1977.
[7] B. Morse and D. Schwartzwald: Image Magnification Using Levelset Reconstruction, Proc. of the International Conference on Computer Vision (ICCV), pp.333-341, 2001
[8] Jian Sun et al: Image Hallucination with Primal Sketch Priors, Proc. Int. Conf. on Computer Vision, CVPR'03, pp. II 729-736, 2003.
[9] B. Triggs: Empirical Filter Estimation for Subpixel Interpolation and Matching, Proc. of the International Conference on Computer Vision, pp.550-557, 2001
[10] http://research.microsoft.com/conferences/AIStats2003/proceedings/152/152.htm
[11] http://www.knt.vein.hu/~czuni/caip2005demo/

Determination of Fabric Viscosity Parameters Using Iterative Minimization

Hatem Charfi, André Gagalowicz, and Rémi Brun

INRIA Rocquencourt, Domaine de Voluceau, Rocquencourt - B.P. 105,
78153 Le Chesnay Cedex - France
Hatem.Charfi@inria.fr
Andre.Gagalowicz@inria.fr

Abstract. In this paper, we present an experimental work using a MOCAP system and an iterative minimization technique to compute damping parameters and to measure their contribution for the simulation of cloth in free fall movement.

Energy damping is an important phenomenon to consider for the 3D simulation of warp and weft materials, since it has a great influence on the animation realism.

This phenomenon can be generated either by friction between moving cloth and air, or by friction between the warp and the weft threads of the fabric.

The contribution of this paper is to determine viscous parameters of cloth using precise trajectory data of a real cloth.

1 Introduction

A great deal of work on simulating the motion of cloth, and generally of fabric, has already been done [1][2][3] and several cloth simulators have been developed [4][5][6].

The motion of fabric is determined by its resistance to bending, stretching, shearing, by aerodynamic effects such as friction and collisions [7].

Realism of a simulation is usually used as a criterion to evaluate the accuracy of simulation and energy damping plays an important role in this search of realism [8].However, the viscous model parameters used in previously developed cloth simulators have not been estimated experimentally.

Authors mentioned the use of damping models but do not present the method to compute these parameters. [8] has developed an algorithm based on perceptually motivated metric, to estimate cloth damping parameters from video. However, [8] also estimates cloth parameters from video which is a less precise method than using a MOCAP sytem.

2 Fabric and Damping Model

We model fabric (limited to warp/weft textile materials) using the mass-spring system developed by Provot [9] and improved by Baraff & Witkin [4].The springs have to be fed with correct parameters to meet the realism that we look for simulation. We use the Kawabata Evaluation System [10] to get the parameters to fed the springs with. The damping model used is the Rayleigh damping model. Its mathematical formula is :

$$[C] = \alpha[M] + \beta[K] \tag{1}$$

where $[C]$ is the damping matrix (n x n), $[M]$ is the mass diagonal matrix (n x n), $[K]$ is the stiffness matrix (n x n), α and β are the damping constants, and n is the total number of masses used to model the fabric.

However, our mechanical model uses 3 different types of springs. So, the stiffness matrix $[K]$ is decomposed as the sum of 3 stiffness matrices modeling bending, shear and tensile :

$$[K] = [K_b] + [K_{sh}] + [K_t]$$

Equation (1) becomes :

$$[C] = \alpha[M] + \beta_b[K_b] + \beta_{sh}[K_{sh}] + \beta_t[K_t] \tag{2}$$

The linearity of Rayleigh's model makes it possible to derive the equation above. The total damping force is :

$$F_{damp} = [C]V \tag{3}$$

where V is the velocity vector of all masses.

3 Experimental Setup

The experiment consists in dropping a piece of fabric in free fall and measuring its trajectory using a motion capture system (MOCAP).(see figure 1) The viscous parameters are then obtained by the adjustment of the simulated trajectory of this fabric computed by our simulator, to the real trajectory. A sample of 50cm by 50cm of a fabric (woven in warp/weft) with reflective round markers stuck on its both sides is thrown in a free fall and the MOCAP system starts recording the successive positions of the markers.

4 Damping Parameters Identification

Given the data collected by the MOCAP, it is possible to compute the speed of each mass i and its acceleration (by finite differences). The fundamental principle of dynamics (F.P.D) is then written for each mass

$$\forall i, m_i A_i = F_i$$

where F_i is the sum of external forces applied on mass i.

Fig. 1. 12 cameras of the Motion Capture System (MOCAP)

4.1 Global Minimization

We use global minimization in order to compute the best damping parameters that fit our data.

$$\text{Let } F_{error} = [M]A - [M]g - F_{springs} - F_{damp} \quad (4)$$

where $F_{springs}$ is the springs total force on masses. Damping parameters are obtained by minimizing the norm of F_{error}.

$$\Phi(\alpha, \beta_b, \beta_s, \beta_t) = F_{error}^T . F_{error} \quad (5)$$

$\Phi(\alpha, \beta_b, \beta_s, \beta_t)$ is a definite positive quadratic form, so we can find its minimum by computing its partial derivatives and making them equal to zero. We obtain a linear system.

$$M \begin{pmatrix} \alpha \\ \beta_b \\ \beta_s \\ \beta_t \end{pmatrix} = b \quad (6)$$

We could compute the conditioning number of matrix M to evaluate the solution stability using :

$$\kappa(M) = \| M \| . \| M^{-1} \| \quad (7)$$

$\kappa(M)$ can also be computed as the ratio between the greatest eigenvalue and the smallest one, since M is symmetric definite positive.

The diagonal terms of M are "proportional" to the square of the damping forces corresponding to air viscosity, bending, shear and tension which have sequentially values with an order of magnitude greater than the previous one. So, M is a largely diagonal dominant matrix and its determinant can be approximated by the product of its diagonal elements. So :

$$\kappa(M) \geq \frac{\frac{trace(M)}{4}}{\sqrt[4]{det(M)}} \gg 1 \qquad (8)$$

We notice that the conditioning is very large, so the system is ill-conditioned and the solution will not be stable. Thus, we propose to compute damping parameters using iterative minimization.

4.2 Iterative Minimization

The aspect of M suggests us to estimate α first, then β_b, β_s and finally β_t as the corresponding damping forces increase in this order.

Identification of the Parameter of Viscous Damping with the Air. In order to make this identification, all springs are omitted. In fact, the viscous damping force between fabric and air is applied only on masses (springs have a null weight).

Writing the F.P.D for each mass i, we obtain the following equation :

$$m_i A_i = m_i g + F_{damp}^{air}$$

where g is the gravity and F_{damp}^{air} the viscous damping force of the air.

$$F_{damp}^{air} = \alpha_i m_i V_i$$

Let $F_{error}^{air} = m_i A_i - m_i g$. We have to compute the α that minimizes

$$\Phi(\alpha) = \| F_{error}^{air} - F_{damp}^{air} \|^2$$

$$\alpha_i = \frac{(F_{error}^{air} . V_i)}{m_i \| V_i \|^2} \qquad (9)$$

So, for each mass and for each frame, we obtain an α_i. As the textile material is homogeneous, all α_i are equal and do not depend on the speed. So, we compute α_f for each frame as the mean of the α_i of this frame and then, we compute α as the mean of the α_f in the *viscous* part of the movement.

In fact, let's analyze the example shown in figure 2. The part of the movement between the frames 0 and 40 corresponds to the beginning of the free fall movement. The speed of the fabric is still very low and the movement of the fabric is still polluted by the launch (very noisy data).

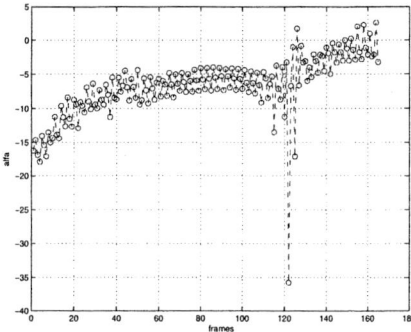 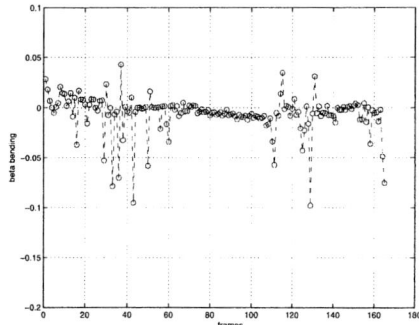

Fig. 2. Viscous damping parameter of the air per frame

Fig. 3. Viscous damping parameter of bending springs

Beyond frame 100, the fabric has a chaotic turbulent movement and the interaction type between the air and the fabric can no longer be modeled using the Rayleigh model.

So, we compute α as the mean of the α_f in the *viscous* part of the movement, ie between the frames 40 and 100.

Indeed, in this part of the movement, the fabric has already acquired a minimum speed that enables us to measure more reliably a force of viscous friction with the air (since this force is proportional to the speed of the masses).

In addition, we observe that the movement of the fabric on the video is slowed down in this part without having turbulent or chaotic movements, and we know that α_f does not depend on the frame, so we have to restrict the computation to the horizontal part of figure 2.

Identification of the Parameter of Viscous Damping of Bending Springs.

After computing the viscous friction parameter α between the fabric and the air, we include the bending springs in the simulation. Hence, the model evolves and allows to take into account forces between two adjacent facets.

A bending spring connects 2 adjacent facets (4 masses) and models the reaction of fabric to bending. Bending forces are very weak compared to tension forces or shearing forces, so errors induced by bending springs are much smaller as well. That is why we have added these springs first to the model (and omit shearing and tensile springs).

We write the F.P.D for each mass i:

$$m_i A_i = m_i g + \alpha m_i V_i + F_i^b + F_{damp}^b(i)$$

where $F_{damp}^b(i)$ is the viscous damping force of the bending springs.

$$F_{damp}^b(i) = \beta_i^b (K_b V)(i) \qquad (10)$$

where $K_b = \frac{dF^b}{dP}$, F^b is the vector of forces produced on masses by the bending springs and P is the position vector of all masses.

Let $F^b(P_i)$ be the vector of forces produced on mass i by the bending springs. $F^b = \sum_i F^b(P_i)$ and $F^b(P_i) = \sum_r F_r^b(P_i)$ where $F_r^b(P_i)$ is the vector of forces produced on mass i by the bending springs r connected to mass i.

$$F_r^b(P_i) = \mathcal{M}_r^{Kaw} \frac{d\theta}{dP_i}$$

where $\mathcal{M}_r^{Kaw}$ is the torque intensity produced by the spring, given by $Kawabata$ and θ is the angle between the two facets of the bending spring r. So, K_b is a 3n by 3n matrix whose (i,j) bloc (3 by 3) is:

$$\frac{dF^b(P_i)}{dP_j} = \sum_r \frac{dF_r^b(P_i)}{dP_j} \tag{11}$$

where

$$\frac{dF_r^b(P_i)}{dP_j} = \mathcal{M}_r^{Kaw} \frac{\partial^2 \theta}{\partial P_i \partial P_j} + \frac{\partial \mathcal{M}_r^{Kaw}}{\partial \theta} \left(\frac{d\theta}{dP_i}\right)\left(\frac{d\theta}{dP_j}\right)^T \tag{12}$$

Equation (10) shows that the computation of the damping force of a bending spring on a mass i uses properties of other masses (its neighbors). Thus, we will directly search for a β^b for each frame.

Let $F_{error}^b = MA - Mg - \alpha MV - \beta^b K_b V - F^b$ where F^b is the bending force vector.

We search for β^b that minimizes $\Phi(\beta) = \| F_{error}^b - F_{damp}^b \|^2$

$$\beta^b = \frac{(F_{error}.K_b V)}{\| K_b V \|^2} \tag{13}$$

Figure 3 shows the β^b value found for each frame. β^b is computed as before, as the mean of β^b in the *viscous* part of the movement, ie between frames 40 and 100. (see figure 3)

Identification of the Parameter of Viscous Damping of Shearing Springs. we use the already determined parameters α and β^b to compute the air and bending springs damping forces. We include the shearing springs in the fabric model. We write the F.P.D for each mass i:

$$m_i A_i = m_i g + \alpha m_i V_i + F_i^b + \beta^b (K_b V)(i) + F_i^{sh} + F_{damp}(i)$$

where $F_{damp}(i)^{sh}$ is the viscous damping force of the shearing springs.

$$F_{damp}^{sh}(i) = \beta_i^{sh}(K_{sh}V)(i) \tag{14}$$

where $K_{sh} = \frac{dF^{sh}}{dP}$, F^{sh} is the vector of forces produced on masses by the shearing springs and P is the position vector of all masses.

Let $F^{sh}(P_i)$ be the vector of forces produced on mass i by the shearing springs. $F^{sh} = \sum_i F^{sh}(P_i)$ and $F^{sh}(P_i) = \sum_r F_r^{sh}(P_i)$ where $F_r^{sh}(P_i)$ is the vector of forces produced on mass i by the shearing springs r connected to mass i.

$$F_r^{sh}(P_i) = F_r^{Kaw} \frac{ds}{dP_i}$$

where F_r^{Kaw} is the spring force intensity given by *Kawabata* and s is the stretch of the spring r. So, K_{sh} is a 3n by 3n matrix whose (i,j) bloc (3 by 3) is:

$$\frac{dF^{sh}(P_i)}{dP_j} = \sum_r \frac{dF_r^{sh}(P_i)}{dP_j} \quad (15)$$

$$\frac{dF_r^{sh}(P_i)}{dP_j} = F_r^{Kaw} \frac{\partial^2 s}{\partial P_i \partial P_j} + \frac{\partial F_r^{Kaw}}{\partial s} \left(\frac{ds}{dP_i}\right) \left(\frac{ds}{dP_j}\right)^T \quad (16)$$

We will use the same approach as that one used for computing β^b. We start by computing a β^{sh} for each frame.

Let $F_{error}^{sh} = F_{error}^b - \beta^{sh} K_{sh} V - F^{sh}$. We search for the β^{sh} that minimizes $\Phi(\beta) = \| F_{error} - F_{damp} \|^2$

$$\beta^{sh} = \frac{(F_{error}^{sh}.K_{sh}V)}{\| K_{sh}V \|^2} \quad (17)$$

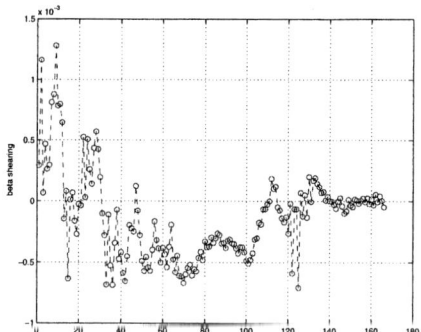 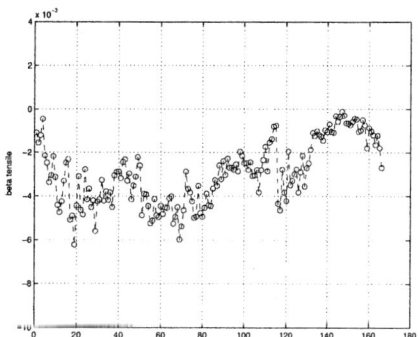

Fig. 4. Viscous damping parameter of shearing springs

Fig. 5. Viscous damping parameter of tensile springs

Figure 4 shows the β^{sh} value found for each frame. We compute β^{sh} as the mean of β^{sh} in the *viscous* part of the movement, i.e. between frames 40 and 100.

Identification of the Parameter of Viscous Damping of Tensile Springs.
We use the same approach as that one used for computing β^{sh}

$$\beta^t = \frac{(F_{error}^t.K_tV)}{\| K_tV \|^2} \quad (18)$$

Figure 5 shows the β^t value found for each frame. As for the shearing part, we compute β^t as the mean of β^t in the *viscous* part of the movement, i.e. between frames 40 and 100.

5 Results

Using the optimized parameters found, we can evaluate the improvement of the simulation. We can compute the error force without taking into account damping $F_{error}^{without-damp}$ at each step of the identification, and compare it with $F_{error}^{with-damp}$. All results are summed up in tables 1 and 2 (fabric 11).

5.1 Air Damping

Results shows that the norm of $F_{error}^{with-damp}$ is smaller than the norm of $F_{error}^{without-damp}$, which validates our work. We notice that damping due to viscous friction with the air allows to decrease the error by about 50% on average for this example.

5.2 Bending Spring Damping

We use the already determined parameter α. We compute the error force taking into account the bending spring damping and compare it with the error force without damping. The difference between the two error forces is very small. So, we can neglect the bending springs viscous damping while simulating the fabric movement in order to decrease the simulation time.

5.3 Shearing Spring Damping

On average the $F_{error}^{with-damp}$ norm is smaller than $F_{error}^{without-damp}$ norm. Shearing spring viscous damping decreases the error by 3%.

5.4 Tensile Spring Damping

Results show that tensile spring viscous damping decreases the error almost for each frame between frames 40 and 100.

The error decrease is most important between frames 50 and 90. On average, tensile spring viscous damping decreases the error by 9%.

5.5 Other Results Summary

The same experiments have been done with other types of fabrics. The results are summed up in tables 1 and 2.

5.6 Simulation

We have used the damping parameters found for our study fabric, and we have simulated a free fall movement using a cloth simulator. Then we have compared the position of the simulated piece of fabric with the real one.

We observe that in the viscous part of the movement, the simulated cloth follows faithfully the trajectory of the real cloth.

Table 1. Damping parameters

	α		β^{bend}		β^{shear}		$\beta^{tensile}$	
	mean	std	mean	std	mean	std	mean	std
fabric 11	-7.0	1.9	-6.8e-3	2.0e-2	-3.1e-4	2.9e-4	-3.9e-6	4.2e-6
fabric 12	-5.9	2.4	-5.2e-3	1.5e-2	-4.0e-4	4.0e-4	-2.7e-6	3.0e-6
fabric 13	-7.2	2.2	-3.1e-4	2.0e-3	-1.8e-4	4.6e-4	-4.0e-6	5.3e-6
fabric 21	-7.2	2.3	-2.0e-4	5.7e-4	-4.3e-4	6.7e-4	-4.6e-7	5.7e-7
fabric 31	-7.4	1.1	-8.4e-4	3.1e-3	-1.1e-3	6.1e-4	-2.2e-8	6.0e-8

Table 2. Error decrease using optimized parameters

	α	β^{bend}	β^{shear}	$\beta^{tensile}$
	error decrease	error decrease	error decrease	error decrease
fabric 11	50%	0.3%	3%	9%
fabric 12	45%	0.3%	1.1%	6%
fabric 13	51%	0.1%	1.4%	3.3%
fabric 21	48%	0%	2.3%	0.5%
fabric 31	72%	0.2%	36%	0.8%

6 Discussion

This paper describes experiments allowing the measurement of damping parameters for cloth simulation, in the case of warp and weft materials. We captured the behavior of pieces of fabric in a free fall movement using a MOCAP system. Then an optimization framework was used in order to compute damping parameters of the fabric. The validation of these measurements was performed by comparing real and simulated fabric free falls.

1. **Air damping:** results obtained for the damping parameter α of the fabric with the air show that we can use an average value equal to -7. When using an optimal α, we can decrease the error (numerical error made by ignoring air damping) by 50%.
   So, air damping has an important influence on the realism of cloth simulation.
2. **Bending damping:** results obtained for bending damping parameter β^{bend} show that bending damping does not decrease the error. So, there is no difference if we add bending damping or not in the simulation. Thus, we will ignore bending damping in future cloth simulation which allows some gain in computing time.
3. **Shear and Tensile damping:** These parameters model an inner phenomenon in the fabric, so they depend on the mechanical properties of the fabric. Fabric 11, 12 and 13 in tables 1 and 2 are three experiments with the same fabric. We notice, that the computed (β^{shear}) and ($\beta^{tensile}$) have almost the same value.

Shear and tensile damping decrease the error force, so they add some realism to coth simulation. However, the amount of error decrease depends on the experiment.

References

1. D. Terzopoulos, J. Platt, A. Barr, and K. Fleischer, "Elastically deformable models," in *Computer Graphics (Proceedings of ACM SIGGRAPH 87)*, 1987.
2. J. Eischen and R. Bigliani, "Continuum versus particle representations," in *Cloth Modeling and Animation*. A.K. Peters, 2000.
3. P. Volino, M. Courchesne, and N. Magnenat-Thalmann, "Versatile and efficient techniques for simulating cloth and other deformable objects," in *Proceedings of ACM SIGGRAPH 95*, 1995.
4. D. Baraff and A. P. Witkin, "Large steps in cloth simulation," in *Proceedings of SIGGRAPH 98, Computer Graphics Proceedings*, 1998.
5. D. Breen, D. House, and M. Wozny, "Predicting the drape of woven cloth using interacting particles," in *Proceedings of SIGGRAPH 94, Computer Graphics Proceedings*, 1994.
6. K.-J. Choi and H.-S. Ko, "Stable but responsive cloth," *ACM Transactions on Graphics (ACM SIGGRAPH 2002)*, 2002.
7. R. Bridson, R. Fedkiw, and J. Anderson, "Robust treatment of collisions, contact and friction for cloth animation," *ACM Transactions on Graphics (ACM SIGGRAPH 2002)*, 2002.
8. K. Bhat, C. Twigg, J. Hodgins, P. Khosla, Z. Popović, and S. Seitz, "Estimating cloth simulation parameters from video," in *Proceedings of ACM SIGGRAPH/Eurographics Symposium on Computer Animation (SCA 2003)*, 2003.
9. X. Provot, "Deformation constraints in a mass-spring model to describe rigid cloth behavior," in *Graphics Interface*, 1995.
10. S. Kawabata, *The standardization and analysis of hand evaluation*, The Textile Machinery Society of Japan, 1980.

Efficient Off-Line Verification and Identification of Signatures by Multiclass Support Vector Machines

Emre Özgündüz, Tülin Şentürk, and M. Elif Karslıgil

Computer Engineering Department, Yıldız Technical University,
Yıldız , Istanbul, Turkey
emre_ozgunduz@yahoo.com, tulinsenturk@hotmail.com
elif@ce.yildiz.edu.tr

Abstract. In this paper we present a novel and efficient approach for off-line signature verification and identification using Support Vector Machine. The global, directional and grid features of the signatures were used. In verification, one-against-all strategy is used. The true acceptance rate is 98% and true rejection rate is 81%. As the identification of signatures represent a multi-class problem, Support Vector Machine's one-against-all and one-against-one strategies were applied and their performance were compared. Our experiments indicate that one-against-one with 97% true recognition rate performs better than one-against-all by 3%.

1 Introduction

Handwritten signature recognition is a behavioral biometric technique for personal identification. Signatures are usually composed of special characters and picture-like patterns. In contrast to the unique and stable biometric features such as fingerprint and iris, even the sequentially signed signatures of a person can vary. Nevertheless as signatures are the primary mechanism both for authentication and authorization in legal transactions, the need of efficient automated solutions for signatute recognition is important.

In biometric applications, there are two types of identity recognition methods: verification (authentication) and identification. For the signature recognition, verificiation is the decision about whether the signature is genuine or forgery and identification is finding the owner of the signature. In the decision phase, the forgery images can be classified as random, simple and skilled [1]. In random forgeries, the signatures are signed without knowledge about the name and genuine signature of the owner. Simple forgeries define the signatures where the name of the signature owner is known and finally in skilled forgeries the aim is to make an almost exact copy of the genuine signature by using an existing sample.

Signature Recognition systems are categorized as on-line and off-line systems according to their applications. In the off-line systems, signature images are obtained by a scanner and usually shape characteristics are examined for the recognition. In the online systems data are obtained by a digitizing tablet. In addition to shape of the signature dynamic features as speed, stroke, pen pressure and signing duration are also analyzed.

There are several implementations for signature recognition and verification. Justino, Bortolozzi and Sabourin proposed an off-line signature verification system using Hidden Markov Model [2]. Zhang, Fu and Yan (1998) proposed handwritten signature verification system based on Neural 'Gas' based Vector Quantization [3]. Vélez, Sánchez and Moreno proposed robust off-line signature verification system using compression networks and positional cuttings [4]. Arif and Vincent (2003) concerned data fusion and its methods for an off-line signature verification problem which are Dempster-Shafer evidence theory, Possibility theory and Borda count method [5]. Chalechale and Mertins used line segment distribution of sketches for Persian signature recognition [6]. Sansone and Vento (2000) increased performance of signature verification system by a serial three stage multi-expert system [1].

In this paper a novel approach to off-line signature verification and identification using Support Vector Machine(SVM) is proposed. Support Vector Machine is a new learning method introduced by V.Vapnik and his co-workers [7] [8]. With a set of training examples belonging to two classes, Support Vector Machines finds the optimal separating hyperplane, which maximizes the minimum distance from either class to the hyperplane. Therefore the misclassification error of unseen data is minimized. The training points on the border are support vectors. Even with many features present, only support vectors are used for classification. In practice, the data may not be linearly separable. In this case, data map into a higher dimensional feature space by a kernel function and construct an optimal hyperplane in this space [9]. The commonly used kernel functions are polynomial, radial basis, and sigmoidal.

2 Preprocessing

The operations in preprocessing phase make signatures normalized and ready for feature extraction. The preprocessing steps are binarization, noise reduction, width normalization and skeletonization. An example of preprocessing is shown in Fig. 2.

Binarization: The signatures are scanned in gray level. To separate signatures from background, p-tile thresholding is applied. The pixels belonging to signature are changed to black and background is changed to white.

Noise Reduction: The small noises in the image is eliminated by a simple noise reduction filter. For each black pixel, if the the number of neighbors in white is more than number of neighbors in black, the pixel color is changed to white.

Width Normalization: Signature size may have interpersonal and intrapersonal differences. To compare two signatures their length must be the same. To provide this, the signature width is set to a default value and the height is changed with respect to height-to-width ratio[10].

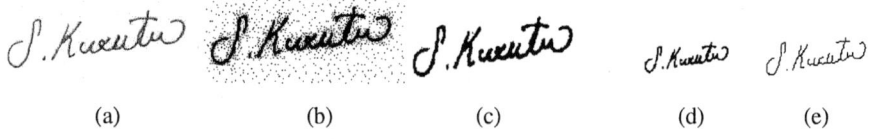

(a)   (b)   (c)   (d)   (e)

Fig. 2. Preprocessing steps: (a) scanning, (b) background elimination, (c) noise reduction, (d) width normalization, (e) skeletonization applied signature

Skeletonization: The thickness of the signature is irrelevant for recognition. To reduce thickness into single pixel thickness and have base shape of the signature, Hilditch's skeletoniziation algorithm is applied to the binary image [11].

3 The Feature Extraction Phase

The features in this system are global features, mask features and grid features. Global features provide information about specific cases of the signature shape. Mask features provide information about directions of the lines of the signatures. Grid features provide overall signature appearance information. The feature extraction steps of an example signature are shown in Fig. 3.

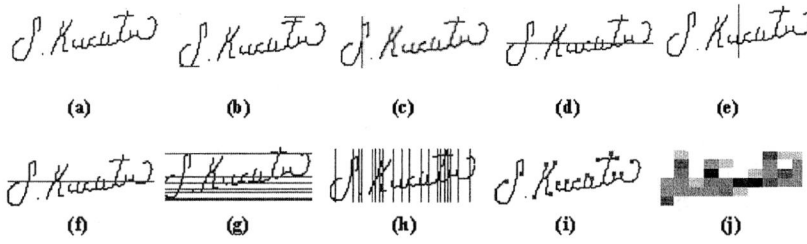

Fig. 3. Feature extraction steps: (a) preprocessed signature and (b) height, (c) maximum vertical histogram, (d) maximum horizontal histogram, (e) horizontal center, (f) vertical center, (g) horizontal local maxima numbers, (h) vertical local maxima numbers, (i) edge points, (j) grid features of the signature

3.1 Global Features

The following global features were used in the proposed system : 1) signature area, 2) signature height-to-width ratio, 3) maximum horizontal projection and maximum vertical projection, 4) horizontal and vertical center of the signature, 5) local maxima numbers of the signature 6) edge point numbers of the signature.

Signature area is the number of black pixels belonging to the signature. Height to width ratios of signatures belonging to the same person are approximately equal. The horizontal projection of the row with the highest value defines the maximum horizontal projection and analogously the vertical projection of the column with the highest value gives the maximum vertical projection. Horizontal and vertical centers of the signature are calculated using the formulas in[10]. The number of local maxima of the vertical and horizontal projections correspond to local maxima numbers of the signature. Finally the number of signature pixels having only one neighboring pixel in a 3x3 neihborhood matrix give the edge point numbers of the signature.

3.2 Mask Features

Mask features provide information about directions of the lines in the signatures. The angles of the signatures have interpersonal differences. The 8 direction masks used in this system are given in Figure 4. Each mask is applied all around the signatures and the number of 3x3 parts of the signature, which are same as the mask, is calculated.

1	0	0
0	1	0
0	0	1

0	0	1
0	1	0
1	0	0

0	1	0
0	1	0
0	1	0

0	0	0
1	1	1
0	0	0

0	0	1
0	1	0
0	0	1

1	0	0
0	1	0
1	0	0

1	0	1
0	1	0
0	0	0

0	0	0
0	1	0
1	0	1

Fig. 4. The direction masks used in this system

3.3 Grid Features

Grid features are used for finding the densities of signature parts [10]. In this system, 60 grid features are used. Each signature is divided into 60 equal parts and the image area in each divided part is calculated.

4 Constructing the SVM Classifiers

Off-line signature recognition systems are generally preffered for authentication. In this paper, both verifiaction and identification with SVM are discussed.

4.1 Verification

Verification is a two class problem. One class is for person to ask for authentication and the other class is for the rest of the people. To implement this we used one-against-all approach of SVM. The features are labeled as +1 for the one class and -1 for the other class. For n different person in signature database, n different SVM classifiers are needed. In authentication, query image is only compared to the claimed SVM classifier. If the comparing result is positive, the authentication is successful.

In Figure 5, A1 shows the positive class which consists of the signatures of a person, A2 shows the signatures of the other persons in the signature database.

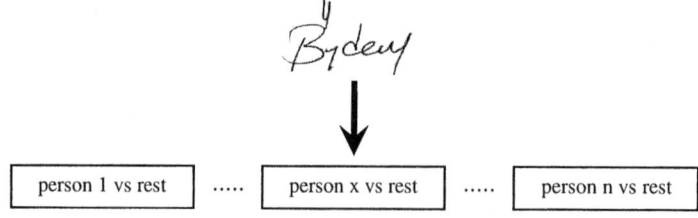

Fig. 5. An example verification

4.2 Identification

Signature identification is a multi-class problem. The query image must be checked with the all of the signatures in the database. We examined two different algorithms, one-against-all and one-agaist-one (pairwise) for multiclass recognition in SVM.

For identification with one-against-rest approach, the training strategy of the SVM classifier is the same as in the verification system. For n different classes, each classifier trained with one class vs the other classes in the database. But in testing phase, the query signature is compared with all of the classifiers instead of the claimed one. The positive class which has the greatest vote is the owner of the signature.

In one-against-one approach, each SVM classifier is constructed by a pair of persons signature. If there are n classes for n people, n*(n-1)/2 SVM classifiers are needed. Suppose there are 8 classes as in Fig. 7., the query image is first compared with 1-2, 3-4, 5-6 and 7-8 SVM classifiers. For each comparison the class with positive result is the winner. In the second stage the query image is compared with these winner class pairs. In this case, the winners are 1,4,5 and 7. At the last step there is only one positive class which is the owner of the queried signature.

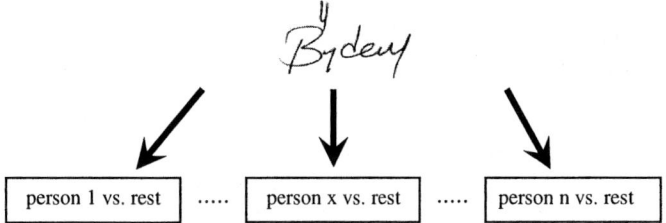

Fig. 6. An example of the one-against-all identification

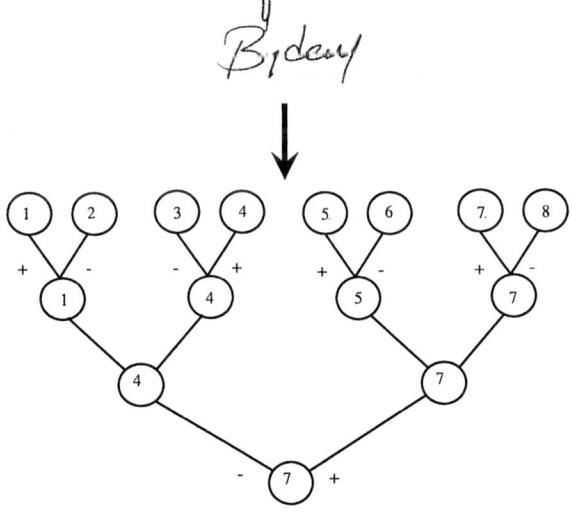

the owner is the 7th person

Fig. 7. An example of the one-against-one identification method used in this system

6 Experimental Results

To train and test the proposed signature verification and identification system, a signature database consisting of 1120 signature from 70 distinct person is constructed. Signatures from 70 person were used to train the system, where each of these 40 persons signed 8 genuine signatures whereas the other 30 persons were asked to imitate and forge the genuine signatures. For each person 4 forgery signatures were signed, thus the training set consisted of 480 signatures. For each person 16 test sihnatures are used and totally (16 x 40) 640 test signatures are used..Each example has 9 global, 8 mask and 60 grid features which are normalized to [0,1] interval.

Learning in one-against-all approach, we constructed 40 SVM classifiers using 40 persons from the signature database. In each classifier, we choose 8 genuine signature for the positive class. For the negative class we used 78 (39x2) signatures of other persons and 4 skilled signatures of the person in the positive class.

Learning in one-against–one approach, only genuine signatures were used. For each classifier 8 positive and 8 negative example were used.

Linear, polynomial, sigmoid and radial basis functions were experimented as SVM kernel functions. The best result was obtained with the radial basis function.

Table 1 shows the verification performance of proposed system. The possible cases in verification are true acceptation (TA), false rejection (FR), true rejection (TR), false acceptation (FA). Table 2 shows the identification performance of the system. One-against-one approach outperforms one-against-all approach.

Table 1. Verification results of proposed system

TAR	FRR	TRR	FAR
0.98	0.02	0.89	0.11

Table 2. Comparing the recognition results

	True Recognition Ratio	True Recognition Number	False Recognition Ratio	False Recognition Number
one-against-one	0.98	627	0.02	13
one-against-all	0.95	608	0.05	32

7 Conclusion

This paper proposes a novel off-line signature verification and identification approach using Support Vector Machine. The performance of the system is promising. In verification, the system is trained by one-against-all strategy whereas identification both one-against-all and one-against-one strategies are used and their performances are compared. In a database consisting n persons, one-against-all approach needs n classifiers, while one-against-one approach needs n*(n-1)/2 classifiers for training. Although training in one-against-one approach is slower, the recognition performance is better than one-against-all.

References

1. Sansone and Vento, "Signature Verification: Increasing Performance by a Multi-Stage System", Pattern Analysis & Applications, vol. 3, pp. 169–181, 2000.
2. E. J. R. Justino, F. Bortolozzi and R. Sabourin, "Off-line Signature Verification Using HMM for Random, Simple and Skilled Forgeries", ICDAR 2001, International Conference on Document Analysis and Recognition, vol. 1, pp. 105--110. 2001
3. B. Zhang, M. Fu and H. Yan, "Handwritten Signature Verification based on Neural 'Gas' Based Vector Quantization", IEEE International Joint Conference on Neural Networks, pp. 1862-1864, May 1998.
4. J. F. Vélez, Á. Sánchez, and A. B. Moreno, "Robust Off-Line Signature Verification Using Compression Networks And Positional Cuttings", Proc. 2003 IEEE Workshop on Neural Networks for Signal Processing, vol. 1, pp. 627-636, 2003.
5. M. Arif and N. Vincent, "Comparison of Three Data Fusion Methods For An Off-Line Signature Verification Problem", Laboratoire d'Informatique, Université de François Rabelais, 2003
6. Chalechale and A. Mertins, "Line Segment Distribution of Sketches for Persian Signature Recognition", IEEE Proc. TENCON, vol. 1, pp. 11–15, Oct. 2003
7. V.N.Vapnik, "The Nature of Statistical Learning Theory", Springer, 1995
8. V.N.Vapnik, "Statistical Learning Theory", Wiley, 1998.
9. K. Müller, S. Mika et al. "An Introduction to Kernel-Based Learning Algorithms", IEEE Transactions on Neural Networks, Vol. 12, pp.181-202, March 2001.
10. H.Baltzakis and N. Papamarkos, "A new signature verification technique based on a two-stage neural network classifier", Pergamon, pp. 95-103, 2001.
11. C.J. Hilditch, "Linear skeletons from Square Cupboards", Machine Intelligence 4, University Press Edinburgh, pp. 404-420, 1969
12. H. Gómez-moreno, P. Gil-jiménez, S. Lafuente-arroyo, R. Vicen-bueno and R. Sánchez-montero, "Color images segmentation using the Support Vector Machines", 2003.

Motion-Based Hierarchical Active Contour Model for Deformable Object Tracking*

Jeongho Shin, Hyunjong Ki, and Joonki Paik

Image Processing and Intelligent Systems Lab., Department of Image Engineering,
Graduate School of Advanced Imaging Science, Multimedia, and Film,
Chung-Ang University,
221 Huksuk-Dong, Tongjak-Ku, Seoul 156-756, Korea
paikj@cau.ac.kr, http://ipis.cau.ac.kr

Abstract. This paper proposed a novel scheme for combined contour extraction and deformable object tracking. In order to track fast moving objects, we first add the motion estimation term to the energy function of the conventional snake. Then, a hierarchical approach using wavelet analysis is applied. Although the proposed wavelet-based method can track objects with large motion, the proposed method requires less computational load than the conventional one. By using a training procedure, the proposed method overcomes occlusion problems and local minima due to strong edges in the background. The proposed algorithm has been tested for various images including a sequence of human motion to demonstrate the improved performance of object tracking.

1 Introduction

Recently, many researchers have developed various algorithms for non-rigid object tracking. Among various approaches, active contour models known as snakes, have been extensively used as an edge-based segmentation method. Snake is an active contour model for representing image contours. An energy functional of the snake is defined as

$$E = \int [\alpha(s)E_{continuity} + \beta(s)E_{curvature} + \gamma(s)E_{image}]ds, \qquad (1)$$

where the parameters α, β and γ control the relative influence of the corresponding energy term. The energy function is computed at v_i, which represents the i-th point of the contour (called snaxel), and its eight neighbors. Two points adjacent to v_i on the contour are used in computing the continuity constraints. The E_{image} continuity force $E_{continuity} = |\overline{d} - |v_i - v_{i-1}||$ tends to distribute the

---

* This work was supported by Korean Ministry of Science and Technology under the National Research Laboratory Project, by Korean Ministry of Information and Communication under the Chung-Ang University HNRC-ITRC program, and by the Korea Research Foundation Grant funded by Korean Government (MOEHRD)(R08-2004-000-10626-0).

points on the contour evenly spaced, where $\bar{d}$ represents the average distance between points. The curvature force $E_{curvature} = |v_{i-1} - 2v_i - v_{i+1}|^2$ gives a reasonable, quick estimate of the curvature. The location having the smallest E_{image} is chosen as the new position of v_i. At the end of each iteration, the curvature at each point on the new contour is determined. The snake algorithm performs iteration until when a certain percentage of the snaxels do not change. At the end of each iteration, the curvature at each point on the new contour is determined.

After the original snake model [1] was proposed, a greedy algorithm that searches local neighborhoods instead of performing global optimization was developed to reduce the computational complexity of the snake model [2]. Generally, the active contour model for object tracking suffers from three major problems: (i) it may fail when the motion between frames is large because the energy function of the snake model does not include the motion information of objects, (ii) it is vulnerable to glitches such as occlusion with other objects or strong edges in the background, and (iii) it relatively take a long time to converge because of the iterative minimization process. Therefore, it is not easy to track deformable objects in real-time.

In order to improve the performance of the snake, we propose a novel scheme that combines contour extraction and tracking. Compared with conventional snakes, the proposed algorithm has three technical improvements: (i) We add the motion estimation term to the energy minimization process of the conventional snake for improving the performance of fast moving object tracking. (ii) The hierarchical approach using wavelet analysis is adapted for tracking fast moving objects and low computational complexity. (iii) By using a training procedure, the proposed method overcomes occlusion problems and local minima due to strong edges in the background.

The rest of this paper is organized as follows. In section 2, we propose a modified snake model for object tracking with motion estimation. Section 3 describes model fitting using the PCA algorithm. In section 4, we propose the hierarchical approach based on wavelet transform. Finally, we present the experiment results and conclusions in sections 5 and 6, respectively.

2 Modified Snake Model with Motion Estimation

In the conventional snake-based tracking, accurate, stable tracking cannot be ensured when the size of object motion between two consecutive frames is large. Therefore, the energy function of the conventional snake algorithm should be modified by considering inter-frame information such as motion. The modified method finds a node (x, y) in the image at $t = t_1$ which is most similar to the snaxel (x', y') in the image at $t = t_1$. Using correlation between two blocks, minimum distance measure is obtained as

$$E_{motion} = \sum_{i=-n}^{n} \sum_{i=-n}^{n} [I(i + x', j + y', t_2) - I(i + x, j + y, t_1)]^2, \qquad (2)$$

where n represents the block size, I the intensity, (x', y') the position of the next image at $t = t_2$, and (x, y) the position of the previous image at $t = t_1$.

Adding the minimum distance measure, given in (2), to the original snake energy function in (1) significantly improves the accuracy and stability of tracking. More specifically the distance measure term enables smooth, robust tracking of fast moving object and environment. The modified snake energy function contains the addition motion energy term as

$$E = \int [\alpha(s)E_{continuity} + \beta(s)E_{curvature} + \gamma(s)E_{image} + \lambda(s)E_{motion}]ds, \quad (3)$$

where constraint λ can be chosen depending on the existence of the temporally differential image, which can be calculated as

$$D_{t_1,t_2}(x, y) = \begin{cases} 1, & \text{if } I(x, y, t_1) - I(x, y, t_2) > T \\ 0, & \text{otherwise} \end{cases}. \quad (4)$$

D_{t_1,t_2} represents the existence of object's movement. If we add a motion term to the snake energy function, where no object movement exist, the corresponding snake's node may fall into the local minima in the direction of motion to the new positions of the target object in the next image. So, the constraint λ should be set to zero when $D_{t_1,t_2}(x, y)$ is zero.

3 Hierarchical Approach Using Wavelet Transform

In this section, we deal with the hierarchical extension of the active contour model using wavelet transform. The discrete wavelet transform used in this paper is identical to a hierarchical subband system, where the subbands are logarithmically spaced in frequency and represent an octave-band decomposition. To begin the decomposition, the image is divided into four subbands and critically subsampled. Each coefficient represents a spatial area corresponding to $0 < |\omega| < \pi/2$, whereas the high frequencies represent the band from $\pi/2 < |\omega| < \pi$. The four subbands arise from separable application of vertical, horizontal and diagonal filters. The subbands labeled LH_1, HL_1, HH_1 represent the finest scale wavelet coefficients. To obtain the next coarser scale of wavelet coefficients, the subband LL_1 is further decomposed and critically subsampled as shown in Fig. 1. The process continues until the pre-specified final scale is reached. In order to achieve both hierarchical search and the use of the gradient direction information, we propose a hierarchical subband system using the wavelet transform. The input image frame is decomposed by the Daubechies 9/7 wavelet transform. Energy of each wavelet transform coefficients are used as image force in the snake energy function. The idea of the hierarchical method is to calculate the snake in a coarse image and then the result of the snake is used as an initial contour to fit the finer snake. This fine-tuning process is repeated until the highest level is reached. This method is a process that tracks the best solution from coarse to finer in a scale-space representation of an image. The search stated at the lowest resolution

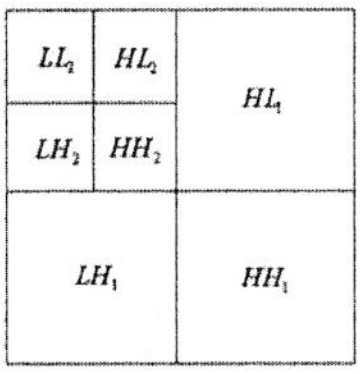

Fig. 1. A two-scale wavelet decomposition: Each coefficient in the subbands LL_2, LH_2, HL_2, HH_2 represents a spatial area corresponding to approximately a 4×4 area of the original picture

is then initiated one level below using the search output of the previous level. Such coarse-to-fine updates repeat until the original image level is reached. In order to perform the search in each level, we should be equipped with information about the gray level image in each level. This requires the application of each wavelet subband coefficient to image force in the snake's energy function according to each snaxel's orientation. For example, if the normal orientation of a snaxel is in the horizontal direction in level n, we perform the snake calculation with the wavelet coefficient of the HL_n subband. In the same manner, vertical and diagonal snaxels' are fit in LH_n, and HH_n, respectively, as shown in Fig. 1.

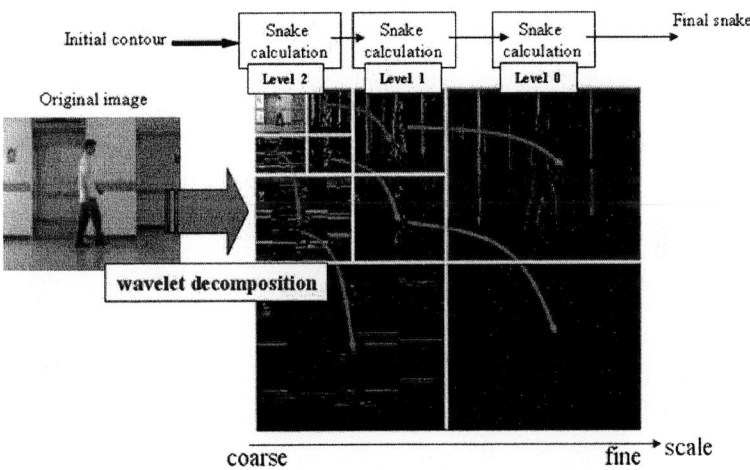

Fig. 2. Flow chart of the wavelet-based active contour model for object tracking

The criterion to change the search level in wavelet decomposition is as follows. Move to a lower level when a certain percentage of the snaxels do not change considerably, for example when 95 % of the snaxels move only within the central 50 % of the search mask size.

4 Model Fitting by the PCA Algorithm

There are two major problems in the snake-based tracking. First, the existence of strong edges outside the target object results in tracking failure because tracking error is propagated to the consecutive frame. Second problem is occlusions, which is one of the main reasons to lose the object being tracked. To solve the occlusion problem, we applied model fitting procedure to the snake algorithm as shown in Fig. 3.

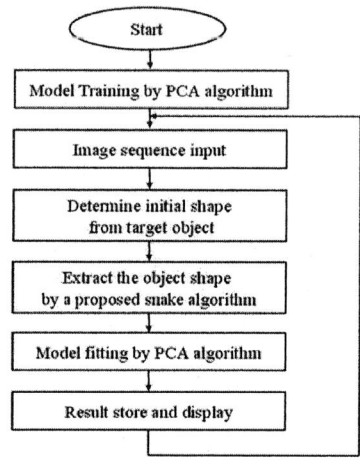

Fig. 3. Flow chart of a proposed PCA-based snake fitting algorithm

4.1 Model Training by PCA Algorithm

Suppose we have m shapes in the training set. A set of n snake's nodes, which is a member of the training set, represents the shape of an object as a 2D outline. Instead of using all nodes in a member of the training set, the PCA technique helps to model the shape of the object using a reduced number of parameters. Suppose there are m members in the training set and x_i, $i = 1, ...m$, represents each member. Given a set of feature points, the input shape can be modeled by using PCA as summarized in [5,6].

4.2 Model Fitting

The best set of parameters that represents the optimal location and the shape of the object can be obtained by matching the shape of models in the training set to the real object in the image. The matching is performed by minimizing the error function as

$$E = (y - Mx)^T W(y - Mx), \qquad (5)$$

where x represents the coordinate of the model, y represents the coordinate of the real object. W is a diagonal matrix whose diagonal elements are the weight for each landmark points. M is a matrix for the geometrical transform which consists of rotation θ, transition t, and scaling factor S. The weight decides the distance between the previous and new feature points.

The geometrical transformation matrix for a point $(x_0, y_0)^T$ can be represented as

$$M \begin{bmatrix} x_0 \\ y_0 \end{bmatrix} = s \begin{bmatrix} \cos\theta & \sin\theta \\ -\sin\theta & \cos\theta \end{bmatrix} \begin{bmatrix} x_0 \\ y_0 \end{bmatrix} + \begin{bmatrix} t_x \\ t_y \end{bmatrix}. \tag{6}$$

Once the set of geometrical parameters (θ, t, s) is determined, the projection of y to the frame of model parameters is given as

$$x_p = M^{-1} y. \tag{7}$$

5 Experiment Results

In this section, we present some experimental results to demonstrate the performance of the proposed algorithm for object tracking. We used a SONY 3-CCD DCR-TRV900 video camera to capture the set of input experimental images with the size of 320 × 240 pixels. A discrete Snake contour consists of 42 nodes, and 56 shapes were used as the training set for PCA. Motion estimation in the modified snake algorithm is based on block matching algorithm, with size 7 × 7 and search range 15 × 15.

The contour of the first frame is manually located near the boundary of the object as shown in Fig. 4(a). Figs. 4(b) and 4(b) respectively show modeling result of the conventional algorithm and the proposed algorithm for the first sequence. We can see that conventional snake algorithm has local minima in the region of the pedestrian's leg and the head part due to strong edges on the background. On the other hand, the proposed algorithm avoids local minima in tracking non-rigid object due to the successive model fitting by the PCA algorithm. Experimental results for the successive frames are shown in Fig. 5. In case of the conventional snake, contour error by strong edge in background accumulates every frame because error correction and motion information are not considered. However, the proposed snake algorithm successively tracks fast moving objects because of the additional motion estimation term in the snake energy function and model fitting by the PCA algorithm.

Fig. 6 shows the plot of total snake energy as a function of the number of iterations. Conventional snakes need a number of iteration for convergence as shown in Fig. 6(a). However, in the proposed snake, the number of iterations significantly decreased at finer scales. Therefore, the proposed wavelet-based hierarchical approach reduces the computations by decreased iteration number.

Another important reason to use model fitting by the PCA algorithm for tracking is to follow the shape of an occluded object. In Fig. 7, the proposed tracking scheme showed almost perfect reconstruction in occluded area. One property of the training-based method is that only small shape variations are

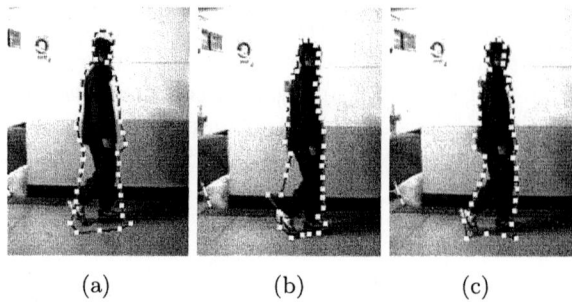

(a)   (b)   (c)

Fig. 4. Modeling results of the first frame; (a) initial contour, (b) conventional snake algorithm, and (c) the proposed algorithm

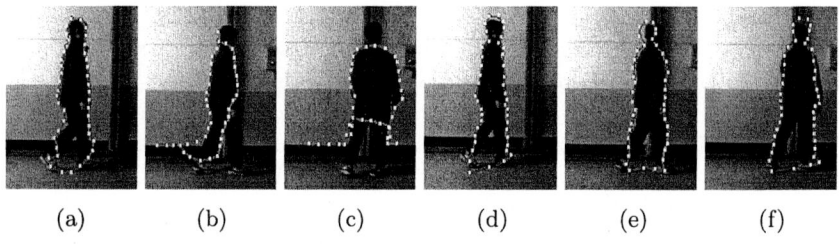

(a)   (b)   (c)   (d)   (e)   (f)

Fig. 5. Tracking results for the successive frames using the conventional snake ((a) 15th, (b) 31st, and (c) 52nd frames) and the proposed snake ((d) 15th, (e) 31st, and (f) 52nd frames)

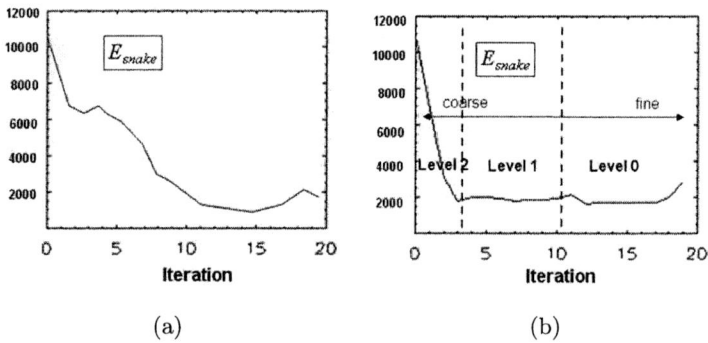

(a)   (b)

Fig. 6. The plot of E_{snake} as a function of iteration; (a) the conventional snake and (b) the proposed snake

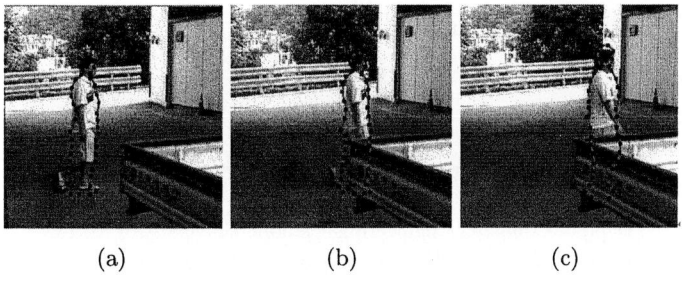

(a)　　　　　　　(b)　　　　　　　(c)

Fig. 7. Tracking results with a partially occluded object

allowed. Thus, the shape will not be distorted significantly although some parts of the tracked object are occluded.

6 Conclusions

We have proposed a framework for a wavelet-based active contour model. This framework has two main parts: wavelet-based hierarchical active contour model and model fitting by the PCA algorithm. The modified active contour model enables robust tracking of fast moving objects. Model fitting by the PCA algorithm can track the object's shape more robustly under occlusion. Experimental results using video sequences show that the proposed method successfully tracks deformable objects with large motion and partial occlusions.

References

1. Kass, M., Witkin, A., Terzopoulos, D.: Snake : Active contour models, International Journal of Computer Vision **1** (1998) 321-331
2. Williams, D., Shah, M.: A fast algorithm for active contours and curvature estimation, Computer Vision, Graphics, and Image Processing: Image Understanding **55** (1992) 14-26
3. Leymarie, F., Levine, M. D.: Tracking deformable objects in the plane using an active contour model, IEEE Trans. Pattern. Analysis, Machine Intelligence **10** (1988) 617-634
4. Xu, C., Prince, J. L.: Snakes, shapes, and gradient vector flow, IEEE Trans. Image Processing **7** (1998) 359-369
5. Koschan, A., Kang, S., Paik, J.K., Abidi, B.R., Abidi, M. A.: Color active shape models for tracking non-rigid objects, Pattern Recognition Letters **24** (2003) 1751-1765
6. Cootes, T.J., Taylor, C.J., Cooper, D.H., Gragam, J.: Training models of shape form sets of examples, Proc. British Machine Vision Conference (1992) 9-18

Multi-modal Face Tracking in Multi-camera Environments

Hang-Bong Kang and Sang-Hyun Cho

Dept. of Computer Engineering, Catholic University of Korea,
#43-1 Yokkok 2-dong Wonmi-Gu, Puchon City Kyonggi-Do, Korea
hbkang@catholic.ac.kr

Abstract. Reliable tracking has been an active research field in the computer vision. This paper presents a probabilistic face tracking method that uses multiple ingredients and integrates tracking from multiple cameras to increase reliability and overcome the occlusion cases. Color and edge ingredients are fused using Bayesian Network and context factors are used to represent the significance of each modality in fusion. We extend our multi-modal tracking method to multi-camera environments where it is possible to track the face of interest well even though the faces are severely occluded or lost due to handoff in some camera views. Desirable tracking results are obtained when compared to those of other tracking method.

1 Introduction

Face tracking is of interest for a variety of applications such as video surveillance and monitoring systems. The tracking system should cope with the changing object appearances and occlusions associated with both static and dynamic occluding objects. To increase reliability, it is desirable to fuse multiple cues because no single cue is generally robust enough to deal with complex environments. To overcome the occlusion cases, it is essential to combine tracking results from multiple overlapping field of view cameras.

Various researchers have attempted to develop face tracking methods. Birchfield [1] used intensity gradient around ellipse's perimeter and color information in ellipse's interior for elliptical head tracking. Toyama and Horvitz [2] proposed Bayesian network based multi-modal fusion method. Color, motion and background subtraction modalities are fused together for real-time head tracking. Liu et al. [3] suggests a multi-modal face tracking method using Bayesian network. It integrates color, edge and face appearance likelihood models into Bayesian networks for robust tracking. Nummiaro et al. [4] proposed a face tracking system in multi-camera environments. They showed that best view would be selected automatically for a virtual classroom application.

In this paper, we reformulate particle filtering into flexible Bayesian network for multi-modal fusion. Bayesian networks provide such a framework which enable multi-modal fusion to be considered in a consistent and probabilistic manner. We also extend this scheme in multiple overlapping field of view camera environments. The novelty of the proposed approach mainly lies in its adaptation of complex environments and occlusions.

The paper is organized as follows. Section 2 discusses multi-modal face tracking in multi-camera environments using Bayesian network. Section 3 presents learning method for context factors. Section 4 shows experimental results of our proposed method.

2 Multi-modal Face Tracking in Multi-camera Environments

2.1 Multi-camera Environments

To solve occlusion problems in face tracking, we use multiple cameras. Each camera has limited field of views (FOV) and the FOVs are overlapped. Fig. 1 shows multiple camera environments. In this paper, we use three cameras (left, center, right).

If a face is detected in one camera, we try to find corresponding object in other cameras using epipolar geometry. We compute epipolar lines between cameras and corresponding object's position is estimated along the epipolar lines.

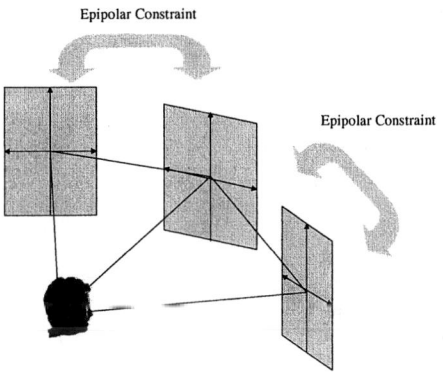

Fig. 1. Multi-camera environments

2.2 Bayesian Modality Fusion

In this paper, we present a particle filter-based face tracker that fuses two cues such as color and edge. We use color distributions because they achieve robustness against non-rigidity, rotation and partial occlusion. Since the shape of objects to be tracked is known a priori in face tracker, edge information is also important. Fig. 2 shows color and edge information.

Bayesian network allows a probabilistic way to determine a target object state in each frame by fusing modalities such as the prior model of reference state, color and edge likelihoods. Fig. 3 shows the Bayesian network structure in multi-camera environments. The target object candidates ($O_{t1} \sim O_{tn}$) are generated from previous object state O_{t-1}. Observations C_t and E_t represent color and edge likelihoods, respectively.

The posterior probability for each object candidate is evaluated through the integration of multiple cues using Bayesian Network. In other words, the posterior probability of the candidate is evaluated as

$$P(O_t \mid C, E, O_{t-1}) \qquad (1)$$

where O_t and O_{t-1} are the target object state and previous object state, respectively. C and E are the color and edge measurements, respectively. The posterior probability is interpreted as

$$P(O_t \mid C, E, O_{t-1}) \propto P(C \mid O_t) P(E \mid O_t) P(O_t \mid O_{t-1}) \qquad (2)$$

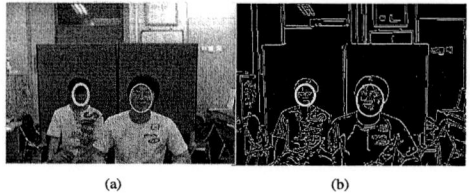

(a) (b)

Fig. 2. Color and edge information.(a) color, (b) edge.

2.3 Likelihood Models

The color likelihood $\log P(C \mid O_t)$ is defined as

$$\log P(C \mid O_t) = \left(\frac{1}{\sqrt{2\pi}\sigma} e^{ -\frac{1 - (\sum_{u=1}^{m} \sqrt{p_i^{(u)} q^{(u)}})}{2\sigma^2} } \right) \qquad (3)$$

where $p_i^{(u)}$ is the ith object candidate's color distribution and $q^{(u)}$ is color distribution of target object.

We use the edge likelihood as the one proposed by Nishihara [5]. The edge likelihood is computed as

$$\log P(E \mid O_t) = \left(\frac{1}{N_p} \sum_j \left| n(j) \cdot g(j) \right| \right) \qquad (4)$$

where $\{n(i)\}_{i=1,\ldots,N_p}$ is the unit vector normal to the ellipse (object) at pixel j and $\{g(i)\}_{i=1,\ldots,N_p}$ is the intensity gradient at perimeter pixel j of the ellipse, and N_p is the number of pixels on the perimeter of an ellipse.

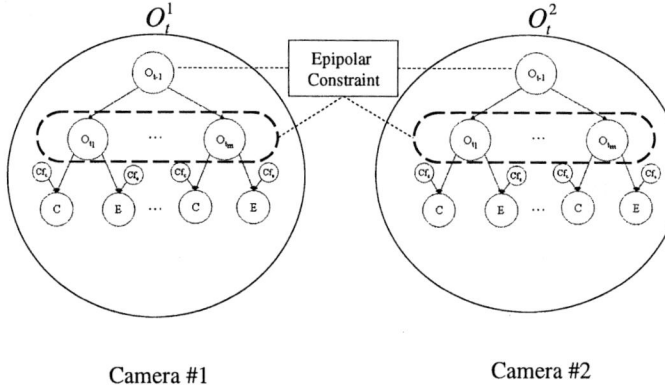

Fig. 3. Bayesian Networks in Multi-camera Environments

2.4 Estimation of Target Object

The prior model for target object state is computed from $P(O_t | O_{t-1})$ where O_{t-1} is the previous object state. It describes how the state evolves over time. In this paper, we only consider a first-order Markov process. Here, we define sample state vector O as

$$O = \{a, b, l_a, l_b, k\} \quad (5)$$

where a, b designate the location of the ellipse, l_a, l_b the length of the half axes and k the corresponding scale change. The dynamic model can be represented as

$$O_t = AO_{t-1} + r_{t-1} \quad (6)$$

where A defines the deterministic component of the model and r_{t-1} is a multivariate Gaussian random variables.

The significance of each modality is not the same in every frame. When the tracked object's color distribution is similar to the background color distribution, we increase the importance weight of edge information. Otherwise, it is desirable to increase the importance weight of color information. So, we use the context factor to deal with the significance of each modality.

Given the context factors cf_e and cf_c, the candidate evaluation is computed as follows:

$$P(O_t | C, E, O_{t-1}, cf_c, cf_e) \propto \\ P(C | O_t, cf_c) P(E | O_t, cf_e) \quad (5)$$

As in [3], we assumed that Eq. (5) can be written as

$$P(C | O_t, cf_c) P(E | O_t, cf_e) \propto \\ P(C | O_t)^{cf_c} P(E | O_t)^{cf_e} \quad (6)$$

The log posterior is

$$\log P(O_t | C, E, O_{t-1}, cf_c, cf_e) \propto \\ cf_c \log P(C|O_t) + cf_e \log P(E|O_t) + P(O_t|O_{t-1})$$ (7)

Our proposed tracker is based on the particle filtering method [6]. In other words, it selects the samples from the sample distribution of the previous frame, and predicts new sample positions in the current frame. After that, it measures the observation weights of the predicted samples. The weights are computed from color and edge likelihoods like Eq.(3) and Eq.(4), respectively. The estimated target object state is computed by

$$E(O_t) = \sum_{i=1}^{N} (cf_c P(C_i | O_t^i) + cf_e p(e_i | x_t^i)) x_t^i$$ (8)

3 Learning Context Factors

We classify the context of the frame into four classes as shown in Fig. 4. To classify frames into four classes, we use a cascade Support Vector Machines (SVM). To classify the frames into four classes, we compute another measures such as edge density (ED) and uniformity of edge density (UED) because the edge likelihood cannot show whether the background is cluttered or not. To measure it, we compute the edge density. The edge density is computed as

$$ED = \frac{1}{M \bullet N_S} \sum_{x,y} |E(x,y)|$$ (9)

where M is the maximum intensity value, N_s is the number of pixels in search area, and E(x,y) is the edge intensity value at (x,y).

If the edge density is low but distributed only on a small area, the value of edge context factor decreases because edge information is not reliable. So, in the case of low edge density, it is desirable to compute the uniformity of edge density. To compute the uniformity of edge density in the search window, we divide the search window into 4 sub-windows. So, we define another measure *UED* to calculate the uniformity of edge density. It is computed as

$$UED = \frac{1}{4} \sum_{i=1}^{4} (\frac{1}{M \bullet N_{bi}} \sum_{x,y} E_i(x,y) - \frac{1}{M \bullet N_{bk}} \sum_{x,y} E_k(x,y))^2$$ (10)

where $E_k(x,y)$ is the maximum edge density among four sub-windows, N_{bk} is the number of pixels in the maximum edge density sub-window. To detect color similarity between object and background, we compute color similarity as

$$CS = \frac{1}{\alpha} \sum_u \sqrt{q_u b_u}$$ (11)

where α represents normalizing factor, q_u is the object's color distribution, b_u is the color distribution of background.

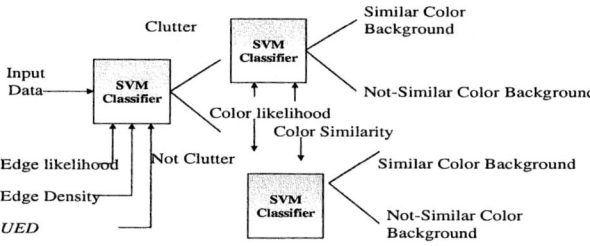

Fig. 4. Context Classification

At the first stage in Fig. 4, edge likelihood, *UED* and edge density are used to determine whether the frame is cluttered or not. Then, we classify the cluttered and non-cluttered frames into two cases using color similarity and color likelihood: similar color background frame and non-similar color background color. The training samples that are used in learning cascade SVMs are collected from the various sequences. From classified frames, we can learn context factors for each case using Perceptron algorithm. Four sets of context factors are obtained. The learned context factor is important in computing log posterior like Eq. (7).

4 Experimental Results

We made several experiments in a variety of environments to show the robustness of our proposed method. The camera topology is shown in Fig. 1. Three cameras (left, center, and right) have limited overlapping FOVs. For face tracking, we detect faces from each camera input using Viola and John's method [7]. Color and edge likelihoods for face object are computed. To learn context factors, we first classified frames into four cases as stated in Section 3 using cascade SVM. The SVM is trained with 5 sequences and tested with other sequences. When the kernel function is radial basis function, the best classified accuracy like 97.2 is obtained. Then, context factors are learned from the classified frames. In the multi-camera environments, if a face is detected in one camera, we try to find corresponding object in other cameras using epipolar geometry. We compute epipolar lines between cameras and corresponding object's position is estimated along the epipolar lines. If more than one face is detected in more than one camera, we determine whether these faces are the same face or not by intersecting epipolar lines.

Two sequences are used. One sequence is that one person is sitting in the chair and turn around in his office. He occludes his face by waving his hands. In Fig. 5, our proposed face tracking shows good performance in comparison with particle filter method regardless of waving hands in front of face because our method uses multi-modal features. In left camera, virtual face position is estimated from the intersection of epipolar lines during occlusion. Another sequence is that one person's face is occluded by another person. The result of proposed tracker is promising as shown in Fig. 6. The error result is shown in Fig. 7.

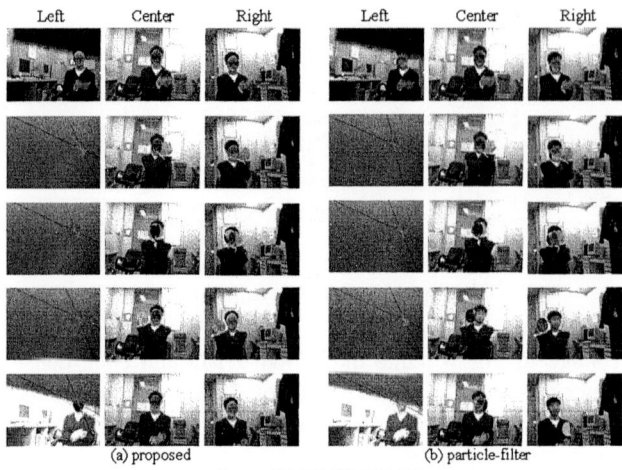

Fig. 5. Experimental Result of Sequence 1. (a)proposed, (b) particle filter.

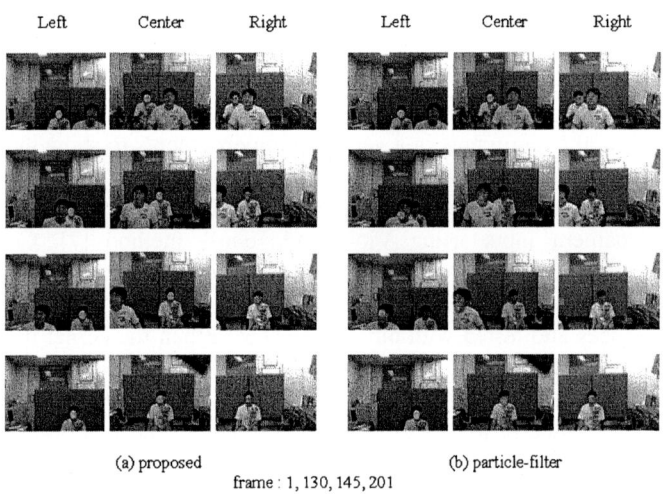

Fig. 6. Experimental Result of sequence 2. (a) proposed, (b) particle-filter.

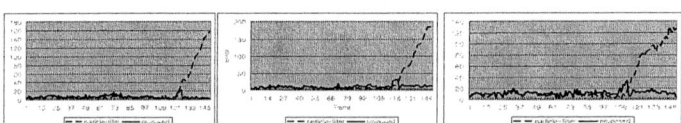

Fig. 7. Error Result of sequence 2 (proposed method- solid line, particle filter-dotted line)

5 Conclusions

In this paper, we proposed a multi-modal face tracking method that integrates color and edge cues in multiple camera environments. The proposed method used a Bayesian network that embeds context factors. The incorporation of context factors into the tracker enables the tracker to adapt itself to different situations. We have presented results on realistic scenarios to show the validity of the proposed approach. Compared with other algorithms, our proposed system shows a better and more robust tracking performance.

References

1. Birchfield, S.: Elliptical Head Tracking using Intensity Gradients and Color Histogram, Proc. CVPR, (1998) 232-237
2. Toyama, K. and Horvitz, E.: Bayesian modality fusion: Probabilistic integration of multiple vision algrorithms for head tracking. Proc. ACCV, (2000)
3. Liu, F., Lin, X., Li, S. and Shi, Y.: Multi-Modal Face Tracking Using Bayesian Network, IEEE Workshop, AMFG 2003, Oct. (2003) 135-142
4. Nummiaro, K., Koller-Meier, E., Svoboda, T.: Color-Based Object Tracking in Multi-Camera Environments, LNCS 2781, (2003) 591-599
5. Nishihara, H., Thomas, H. and Huber, E.: Real-time tracking of People using stereo and motion, Proc. SPIE, vol. 2183 (1994) 266-273
6. Nummiaro, K., Koller-Meier, E. and Van Gool, L.: A Color-Based Particle Filter, First International Workshop on Generative-Model-Based Vision (2002) 53-60
7. Viola, P., Jones, M.: Rapid Object Detection using a Boosted Cascade of Simple Features", Proc. CVPR '01 (2001)

Facial Features Detection by Coefficient Distribution Map

Daidi Zhong and Irek Defée

Institute of Signal Processing, Tampere University of Technology,
P.O.Box 553, FIN-33101 Tampere, Finland
{daidi.zhong, irek.defee}@tut.fi

Abstract. The Images and video are currently predominantly handled in compressed form. Block-based compression standards are by far the most widespread. It is thus important to devise information processing methods operating directly in compressed domain. In this paper we investigate this possibility on the example of simple facial feature extraction method based on the H.264 AC Transformed blocks. According to our experiments, most horizontal information of face images is mainly distributed over some key features. After applying block transform and quantization to the face images, such significant information become compact and obvious. Therefore, by evaluating the energy of the specific coefficients which are representing the horizontal information, we can locate the key features on the face. The approach is tested on FERET database of face images and good results is provided despite its simplicity.

1 Introduction

Facial features detection is nowadays a classical area with a huge amount of knowledge which has been collected over the years. It is defined as the process of locating specific points or contours in a given facial image. Human face and its feature detection is much significant in various applications as human face identification, virtual human face synthesis, and MPEG-4 based human face model coding [1]. Many research works have been conducted over this topic. [2], [3], [4]

The features detection is a highly overdimensioned problem which is seen easily if one would try to consider images as matrices in NxN space. Only extremely limited sets of such matrices carry useful information. Therefore, it is advisable to extract the key features by highly effective preprocessing to limit the amount of input information in the first place.

Currently great majority of pictures and video are available in compressed form with compression based on block transform. Compression has a goal of minimizing the amount of information while preserving perceptual properties. This goal is fully compatible with and desirable for pattern recognition and feature extraction. The problem is – how to utilize the efficiency from compression to benefit the feature extraction task, in order to achieve best extraction results? Indeed one could think that elimination of perceptually redundant information should be very beneficial for the efficiency of feature extraction process. In addition, this topic is also related to our parallel research about extracting the feature information from DCT domain [5].

In this paper, a novel features detection method based on information extracted from compressed domain is proposed. First, the 4x4 transform from H.264 standard [6] is utilized to remove the redundancy. Second, the quantization and luminance normalization are performed to further control the precision of the information extraction. Third, the most significant coefficients are selected and thresholded in specific bin positions. Finally, some detection procedures are performed with some prior geographical knowledge about the features on the human faces. The example results are shown based on some face images from the well-known public face recognition database – FERET [7]. The proposed methods can achieve a good result with low computation complexity.

2   4X4 H.264 AC Transform and Quantization

The transform we used in this research is introduced from the H.264 standard. This transform is a 4x4 integer transform, which is originally used to encode the coefficients of inter blocks. Overall, this transform performs in a similar way with the widely-used DCT. They can both make the information compact, which greatly facilitates the information extraction. Different from DCT, the integer transform used here allows rapid process.

The first uppermost coefficient after transform is called DC and it corresponds to average light intensity level of a block. Other coefficients are called AC coefficients; they correspond to components of different frequencies. The AC coefficients provide us some useful information about the texture detail of this block. Such information is essential for the following feature detection.

The forward transform matrix of H264 AC Transform is B_f and the inverse transform matrix is B_i.

$$B_f = \frac{1}{2}\begin{bmatrix} 1 & 1 & 1 & 1 \\ 2 & 1 & -1 & -2 \\ 1 & -1 & -1 & 1 \\ 1 & -2 & 2 & -1 \end{bmatrix} \quad B_i = \frac{1}{2}\begin{bmatrix} 1 & 1 & 1 & 1 \\ 1 & 0.5 & -0.5 & -1 \\ 1 & -1 & -1 & 1 \\ 0.5 & -1 & 1 & -0.5 \end{bmatrix}$$

For simplicity, here we removed the '1/2' in the matrix. The 4x4 pixel block P is forward transformed to block H using (1), and block R is subsequently reconstructed from H using (2). The 'T' means linear algebraic transpose here.

$$H = B_f \times P \times B_f^T \tag{1}$$

$$R = B_i^T \times H \times B_i \tag{2}$$

We perform 4x4 H.264 block transforms over more than thousand different blocks, and the results are further averaged. After applying the transform, one could see from Fig. 1(a) that the main energy is distributed around the DC coefficient. Since there are big differences between the values of different coefficients, the natural logarithm is used here to express the data.

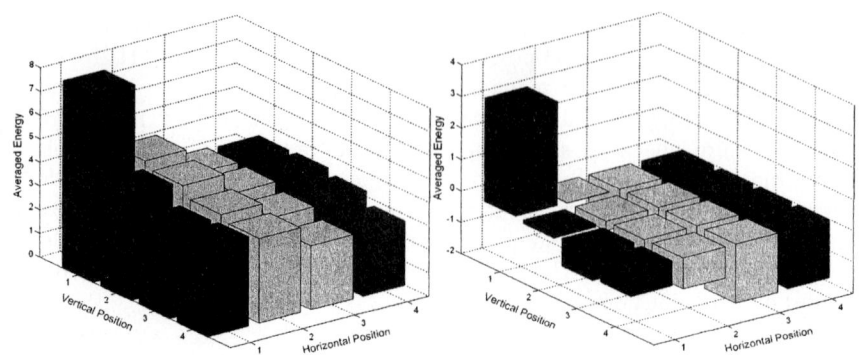

Fig. 1. (a) Natural logarithm of averaged distribution of energy after transform (b) Natural logarithm of averaged distribution of energy after quantization (QF=100)

However, from the feature detection point of view, using the whole AC information seems to be redundant. Therefore, a quantization factor (QF) is used to scale down each coefficient during the subsequent quantization process. As the energy is mostly presented at the upper-left corner, quantization can make most of the high-frequency coefficients to zero. This is shown by Fig. 1(b). After the quantization, the remaining high-frequency coefficients, which are non-zero, indicate the existence of a strong edge in this block area. Through this way, the redundant data is removed and the important data is preserved.

Furthermore, coefficients in different bin positions are representing different directional information. Given a 4x4 transformed block:

1. The AC coefficient in first line are corresponding to vertical information
2. The AC coefficient in first column are corresponding to horizontal information
3. The AC coefficient in diagonal direction are corresponding to diagonal information

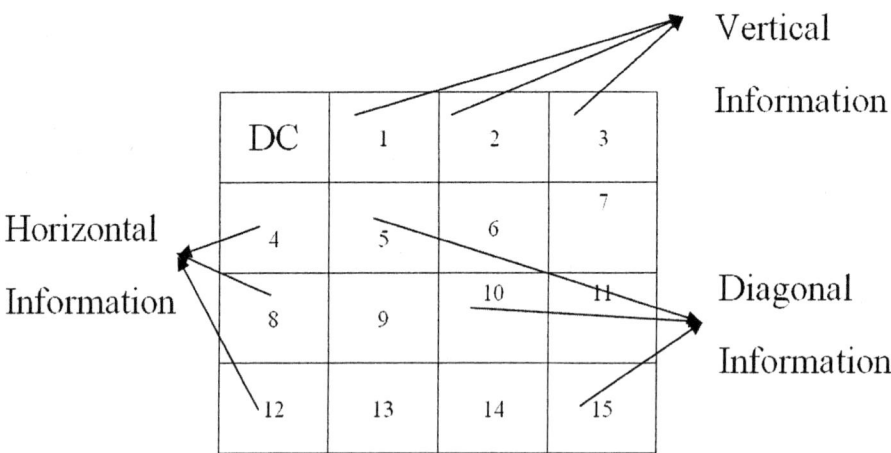

Fig. 2. Directional information represented by different coefficient

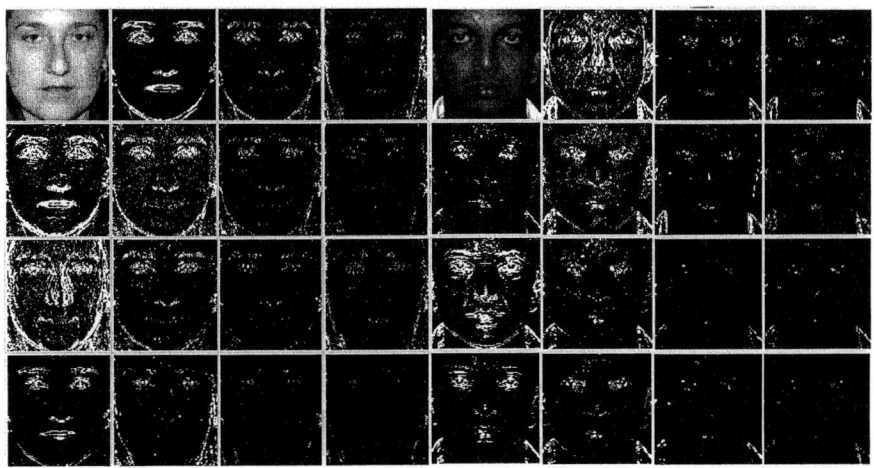

Fig. 3. Coefficient Distribution Map (QF=100)

This can be known from Fig. 3, which shows the energy distribution of these 15 AC coefficients (when the quantization factor is 100), from two example face images. We call it Coefficient Distribution Map (CDM). After quantization, all the coefficients are binarized into zero and non-zero. Non-zero points are the white points in Fig.3. As we can see, after quantization, some coefficients are mostly distributed and compact around key features, such as mouth, eyes and nose. A good example is the 12th coefficient according to the order in Fig. 2. Based on above observation; one may think to detect the facial features according to the distribution of these coefficients.

3 Luminance Normalization

The overall luminance condition has direct effect on the final detection performance. Same quantization will produce different coefficients from a scene taken at low luminance than from the same scene at higher luminance. To eliminate this impact, we normalize the luminance of images by rescaling the coefficients according to the average luminance level. The average luminance level is calculated based on the DC coefficients of the transformed blocks.

Assume there are N transformed blocks in an image j, and the DC value for each block is denoted by $DC_i(j)$, $1 \leq i \leq N$. From these DC values, we can calculate the mean DC value for this image

$$DC_{mean}(j) = \frac{1}{N} \sum_{i=1}^{N} DC_i(j) \quad (3)$$

Next, in similar way the average luminance DC_{all} of all images in a database is calculated based on (4). The ratio of luminance rescaling for image j is calculated through:

$$R = \frac{DC_{all}}{DC_{mean}(j)} \quad (4)$$

Next the, AC coefficients of a block are rescaled by

$$\overline{AC_{i,j}} = AC_{i,j} \times R, \quad 1 \leq i \leq N, \quad 1 \leq j \leq M \quad (5)$$

After normalization, all the coefficients are then quantized by the QF

$$\overline{\overline{AC_{i,j}}} = \frac{\overline{AC_{i,j}}}{QF}, \quad 1 \leq i \leq N, \quad 1 \leq j \leq M \quad (6)$$

We found that system performance is not sensitive to the exact value of rescaling so whenever images are of perceptually tolerable quality (not strongly under- or over-exposed) the rescaling works well.

4 Feature Detection

In order to detect these key features, a small block is moved on the binarized images and the sum of non-zero coefficients is calculated and displayed as a histogram. After that, the peak of histograms is detected which indicate the position of features. In order to keep the most important information, while removing the irrelevant information, the coefficients are binarized according to a threshold. On the other hand, different coefficients can be used to generate the CDM. Through our test, we found that the horizontal information is more robust than vertical information for detection, and the 12th AC coefficient is more robust than others.

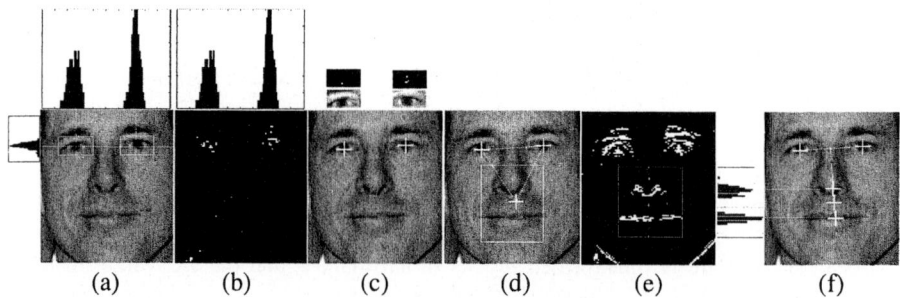

Fig. 4. Feature Detection Process

Fig. 4 is an example of using the 12th AC coefficient to detect the feature.

1. (b) is obtained by applying a larger threshold to the 12th AC coefficients. This threshold is set to 2/3 of the maximum value of 12th AC coefficients. The number of non-zero coefficients (after threshold) are summed, first horizontally, then vertically, as shown in (a) and (b). The rough locations of eyes are detected.

2. We evaluate the small block around these rough locations, using another threshold to keep the blocks with darkest DC values. The black color shows the locations of eyeballs. Finally, the location parameters are obtained from these black points. This process is shown in (c)
3. A rough location between nose and mouth can be obtained from the locations of left and right eye. They are forming an equilateral triangle. We will search the area arounding this point. The width of this searching window is the horizontal distance between the eyes. This area is shown in (d) and (e).
4. (e) is also obtained from the 12th AC coefficient, but the threshold is set to 1. This is because the eye areas usually contain the largest horizontal energy, while the nose and mouth areas contain smaller energy.
5. A similar way to step 1 is performed over (e) and the peaks of histograms indicate the vertical positions of nose and mouth. Presuming that the position of nose and mouth is in the middle of eyes, we can calculate the horizontal positions of them.

Above detection method is tested over 360 images from a public face recognition database – FERET. These images are the first 360 images of the FERET database, without glasses. They have different size, different light condition and other properties. They are quantized at QF=100. The correct detection rate is 91.4%. Some example results are shown as in Fig. 5.

Of course, since such detection is based on blocks, it is less precise than the detection result from pixel-domain. However, for some application which only require less precision, our method is still a good choice. It can also serve as a pre-process step for pixel-based detection. Furthermore, one should also notice that no color information is used here. One may also noticed that some faces with dense beard or exaggerated expression may are likely to have poor detection results, as well as the strongly rotated faces (e.g., Fig.5 (i)).

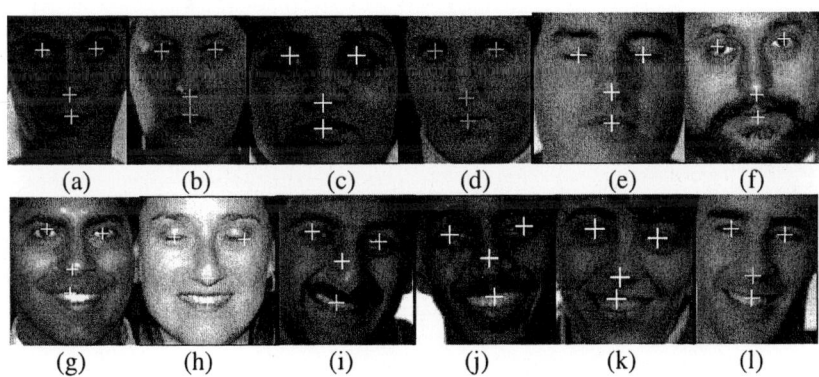

Fig. 5. Some Example Detection Results

5 Conclusions

In this paper, it is shown that facial feature detection using the Coefficients Distribution Map in compressed domain can provide a good performance. The 4x4 H.264 AC block transform is used to extract the energy which is representing the key features. Some prior geographical knowledge about the features on the human faces is used to evaluate the coefficients, in order to detect the positions of key features. Such method is carried directly in compressed-domain, which requires low computation. Furthermore, no color information is used in this process. In the future works, this method is expected to be used. Such structural information, combined with statistical information, is expected to provide good performance in the future works of face image retrieval in compressed-domain.

References

1. JTC1/SC29/WG11; MPEG-4, Final Draft of International Standard, Part 2 (Visual). Doc. No. N2502 of ISO 14496-1, (1998)
2. Jun, M., Wen, G., Yiqing C., Jie L.: Gravity-Center Template Based Human Face Feature Detection. ICMI'2000. Beijing, (2000) 207-214
3. Saman C., Noel O'C.: Facial Feature Extraction and Principal Component Analysis for Face Detection in Color Images. ICIAR, Lisbon, Portugal, (2004)
4. Jörgen A.: Facial Feature Extraction using Eigenspaces and Deformable Graphs. Workshop on Synthetic-Natural Hybrid Coding and Three Dimensional Imaging, (1999)
5. Daidi. Z., Defée. I.; Pattern recognition by grouping areas in DCT compressed images. Proceedings of the 6th Nordic Signal Processing Symposium, NORSIG 2004, Finland (2004)
6. Joint Video Team of ITU-T and ISO/IEC JTC 1; Draft ITU-T Recommendation and Final Draft International Standard of Joint Video Specification (ITU-T Rec. H.264 | ISO/IEC 14496-10 AVC), JVT-G050, (2003)
7. FERET Face Database. Available at: http://www.itl.nist.gov/iad/humanid/feret/.

Region Based Detection of Occluded People for the Tracking in Video Image Sequences

Yongtae Do

School of Electronic Engineering, Daegu University, Kyungsan-City,
Kyungpook, 712-714, Korea
ytdo@daegu.ac.kr

Abstract. This paper presents a framework to deal with occlusions when detecting people for the tracking in the image sequences of a stationary surveillance video camera. Unlike the cases of most existing techniques, people are in low-resolution and the detected foreground images are noisy. As the small sizes of target people make it difficult to build statistical shape or motion models, techniques proposed use simple features of the bounding boxes of target people such as position and size. Each foreground region in a bounding box is identified in independent, partially occluded, or completely occluded state, and the state is updated during tracking. Proposed technique is tested with an experiment of counting the number of pedestrians in a scene.

1 Introduction

Video surveillance (VS) is currently attracting a lot of attention in the computer vision community. In VS, people are important targets but difficult to process due to non-rigid shape and motion. Detection, tracking, and activity analysis are three key issues in the research of VS targeting people. Collins et al [1] claimed that the activity analysis is the most important area of future research. However, activity analysis is heavily depends on the other two processes and there are a number of difficult problems in practical people detection and tracking. The most obvious problem that is often encountered is occlusion. Occlusions occur by fixed objects in a scene such as trees and construction. This situation can be predicted by registering the fixed objects in advance. Occlusions among people in motion, however, are difficult to be tackled.

In recent years, plenty of new techniques have been proposed for detecting and tracking people in video image sequences. Pfinder [2] is a real-time system for tracking a single indoor person. Body parts of a person are represented by blobs characterized by position and color. The system proposed by Khan and Shah [3] also used position and color cues for indoor tracking. But, unlike Pfinder, multiple people could be detected and tracked dealing with occlusions among them. When occlusions occur and a person is no longer visible, the statistics of pixels belong to the person occluded are retained while statistics of other pixels are updated. Upon re-appearance of the occluded region, pixels belong to the region get back to their original identity as it maximizes the likelihood if the position and color of the region has not changed significantly during the occlusion. W^4 [4] was developed to track body parts of multiple people in the outdoor scenes of monocular grayscale image sequences. It used a combination of shape analysis and template matching for the tracking. W^4 is capable of tracking people who re-appear after occlusion using two-step matching, view-based first and, if it fails, intensity-based. The indoor people tracking system of Sindhu and Morris [5] finds occlusion when multiple people are predicted to be located within the same segmented region in the new frame. When de-occlusion event occurs, the color values are compared for restoring the identification. All techniques discussed so far use relatively high-resolution images. However, if a VS camera is fixed at a far distance from the scene monitored to cover a large area, the image resolution is low and detailed information of the target people is not available. Sizes of detected target people are too small to build a reliable statistical model and many of above techniques are difficult to be applied.

In this paper, we address a framework to deal with occlusions among people in motion. The scope includes detection and tracking issues but does not reach activity recognition [6]. The video images are taken in far distance and the image resolution is quite low. Thus people detected as foreground are noisy and their sizes are small. Fig 1 shows an example. A minimum bounding box is found for each independent target detected. When two people are in partial occlusion and in the same box, they are segmented into each independent person by analyzing the shape of the foreground in the box. Each box is then assumed in the one of three states, Independent Person (IP), Partial Occlusion (PO), and Complete Occlusion (CO). The transition of states is identified by monitoring the features of bounding boxes.

(a)   (b)

Fig. 1. Target people in a low-resolution image: (a) Original image, (b) Foreground detection

2 Segmentation of Partially Occluded People by Draping

When two or more people are in close distance, even if they are not actually overlap one another, a partial occlusion occurs in the detected foreground as shown in Fig. 2(a) and (b). In [5], when people merged into the same bounding box, the box was given all the labels of constituent people but segmentation of the box was not tried. In

[3], the partially occluded people were segmented by using a pixel-level model of statistics. On the other hand, people images in this paper are in low-resolution and the number of pixels belong to people detected are not large enough to build a statistical model.

Our technique for the vertical segmentation of people bounded in a box is based on the following assumption and observation:

- People in the scene are in roughly upright postures. This assumption is acceptable in most practical situations if the camera angles are set properly and people walk in normal way,
- The upper parts (head and torso) of a person have less variation than the lower parts (legs) in image sequences. This observation hints that processing with the information given from upper body parts may be more reliable than that from lower parts.

For a foreground binary image region within a bounding box, top pixels of columns are connected resulting in a line – we name it 'draping line'. As shown in Fig. 2(c), the draping line is different from contour. The foreground region is vertically segmented at the local minima of the draping line as shown in Fig. 2(d).

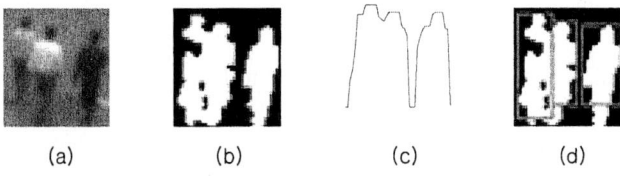

(a)   (b)   (c)   (d)

Fig. 2. Dividing a group of people into individuals by draping: (a) Original image, (b) Detected binary foreground, (c) Draping line, (d) Division at the local minima of the draping line

3 Analysis of Occlusions

One of following three states is assigned to each region detected as foreground and Fig. 3 shows examples:

- IP (Independent Person) if a single person is believed within a bounding box,
- PO (Partial Occlusion) if two or more people are believed within a bounding box but they can be separated by a method like that using draping line,
- CO (Complete Occlusion) if two or more people are believed within a bounding box but they cannot be separated. This occurs not only when actually one is behind the other but also when people are in close distance one another in very low-resolution images.

In our program, features of each region inside a bounding box of current image frame is registered in the variables of C_rect while those of a region of the previous image frame is registered in the variables of P_rect like

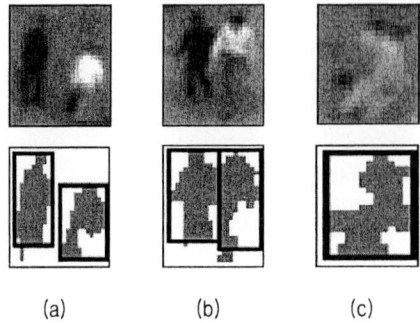

Fig. 3. States assigned to bounding boxes: (a) IP, (b) PO, (c) CO

```
P_rect or C_rect
    .coor = box coordinates
    .connect = 1 if connected to an adjacent box
    .state = IP, PO, or CO
    .pat = identity of parents box for tracking
    .num = estimated number of people within the box
```

For the initial image frame, a box is assigned to IP or PO depending on the value of C_rect.connect. Specifically, C_rect.state=IP if C_rect.connect=0, otherwise C_rect.state=PO. From the second frame, three cases are considered. First, if the number of boxes in current image frame is the same to that of previous image frame, the state assignment is done by the procedure of Fig. 4. Boxes in the previous image frame and current image frame is paired by comparing the positions and widths of boxes. Heights of boxes are used only for finding boxes wrongly drawn. In the figure, #(·) is used to mean 'the number of (·)'. If fewer boxes are found in current image frame than those of previous image frame, the procedure of Fig. 5 is used for state assignment. To detect the merging of two boxes, i.e. complete occlusion, the width of a box in current image frame, CW, and that in previous image frame, PW, are compared to a threshold th_M like Eq. (1). If more boxes are found in current frame, the procedure of Fig. 6 is used. The re-appearance of a box is detected by Eq. (2) for a threshold th_D.

$$fn\_mrg(i) = \sqrt{[PW(i)+PW(i+1)-CW(i)]^2} < th\_M \quad (1)$$

where $1 \leq i \leq \#(C\_rect)$,

$$fn\_div(i) = \sqrt{[PW(i)-CW(i)-CW(i+1)]^2} < th\_D \quad (2)$$

where $1 \leq i \leq \#(P\_rect)$. The threshold th_D is initially set to a small value and increased until the number of total segmented regions equals to $(\#(C\_rect)-\#(P\_rect))$.

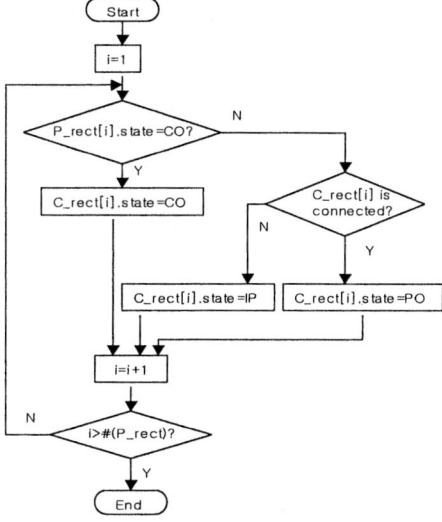

Fig. 4. Identifying the states of regions when the numbers of regions in previous and current image frames are the same

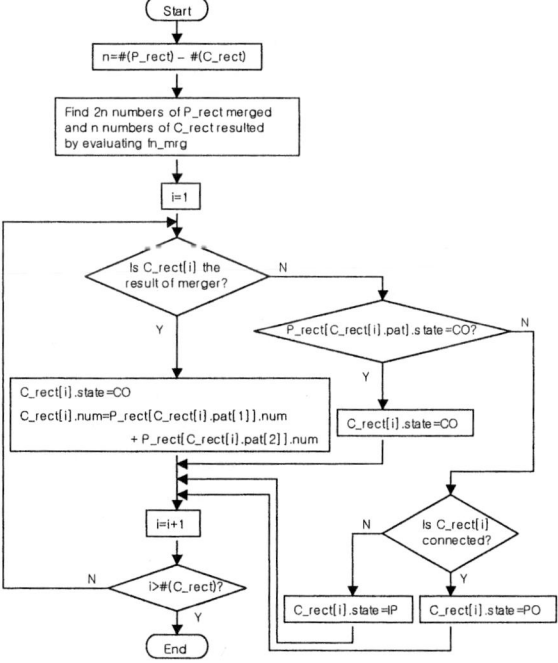

Fig. 5. Identifying the states of regions when the number of regions of current image frames is less than that of previous image frame

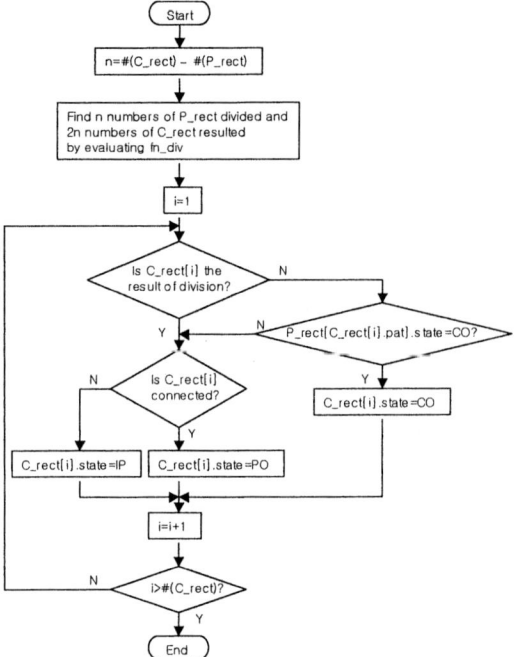

Fig. 6. Identifying the states of regions when the number of regions of current image frame is more than that of previous image frame

4 Experiments

We applied the proposed framework to the experiment of counting people in a scene. Finding the number of pedestrians passing an outdoor area is often required for traffic monitoring but currently done manually in most cases. A computer vision technique was proposed for automating this task using Quasi-Topological Codes (QTC) [7] but hard to be used for the low-resolution people images of this paper.

We processed video image sequences in the size of 240 × 320 pixels. First, the foreground image was detected by the adaptive background subtraction technique proposed by Fujiyoshi and Lipton [8]. Then, each detected region is bounded by a box. If a box is smaller than a predefined size, it is regarded as a wrong segmentation and ignored. The threshold we used in the experiment was 19 × 6 pixels. For the remaining boxes of foreground regions after size checking, the occlusion analysis framework proposed was applied to the tracking of the state transitions of people regions. Experiments were done for four video sequences and the results are summarized in Table 1. Basic processes such as foreground detection, draping, and drawing bounding boxes were done on-line and the results were stored. The interval between processed image frames was thus rather long and irregular depending particularly on the number of people in the image frame. The occlusion analysis and people counting were done later with the stored images and data. In all cases shown in the table, we could get correct counting. Note that, in the video of 5 people, 47 of 49 image frames contained complete occlusions but we could get a correct counting. Fig. 7 shows example images of this case. A group of people walked away and they occluded severely in smaller resolution in later image frames. However, our program kept the correct counting resulted from initial two frames.

Table 1. Results of experimental people counting

	Real #(people)	2	3	4	5
	Result of counting	2	3	4	5
	#(Total image frames)	38	45	32	49
Segmentation using draping lines	#(Excessively segmented images)	8	0	1	0
	#(Insufficiently segmented images)	0	13	12	47
	#(Exactly segmented images)	30	32	19	2
Size of a person	Maximum	33×16	51×29	42×21	47×22
	Minimum	19×7	22×7	20×7	19×6

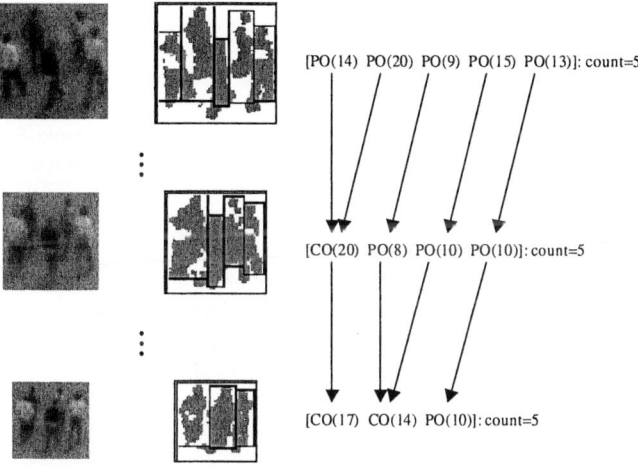

Fig. 7. Counting people by tracking state transition of occlusions. The number in parenthesis indicates the width of each bounding box.

5 Conclusions

A framework has been presented for dealing with the occlusion problem in people tracking. Work of this paper is different from most existing techniques in three important aspects: First, target people are in low-resolution. It is thus difficult to build statistical shape and motion models. Detected binary foreground image is quite noisy. Secondly, occlusions are identified and tracked in image sequences using simple features of the bounding boxes of detected targets such as position and width. Thirdly, a draping line is used as a simple and quick way to partition a box of people in partial occlusion.

We tested the proposed framework in a people counting experiment, which is often needed for traffic monitoring. The image resolution of people was too low to use any existing techniques. The proposed system, however, could successfully track the transitions of occlusion states in image sequences and counted the exact number of people in the scene. We believe that this technique can be useful for many practical VS camera applications where the image resolution is sacrificed for a large field of view.

References

1. Collins, R. T., Lipton, A. J., Kanade, T.: Introduction to the Special Section on Video Surveillance. IEEE Trans. Pattern Analysis and Machine Intelligence, Vol. 22, No. 8 (2000) 745-746
2. Wren, C. R., Azarbayejani, A., Darrell, T., Pentland, A. P.: Pfinder: Real-Time Tracking of the Human Body. IEEE Trans. Pattern Analysis and Machine Intelligence, Vol. 19, No. 7 (1997) 780-785
3. Khan, S., Shah, M.: Tracking People in Presence of Occlusion. In: Proc. Asian Conf. Computer Vision (2000)
4. Haritaoglu, I., Harwood, D., Davis, L. S.: W4 Who? When? Where? What? A Real Time System for Detecting and Tracking People. In: Proc. Conf. Face and Gesture Recognition (1998) 222-227
5. Sindhu, A. J., Morris, T.: A Region Based Approach to Tracking People Before, During, and After Occlusions. In: Proc. IASTED Conf. Visualization, Imaging and Image Processing (2004)
6. Efros, A. A., Berg, A. C., Mori, G., Malik, J.: Recognizing Action at a Distance, In: Proc. IEEE Int. Conf. Computer Vision (2003) 726-733
7. Heikkila, J., Silven, O.: A Real-Time System for Monitoring of Cyclists and Pedestrians. In Proc. IEEE Workshop on Visual Surveillance (1999) 74-81
8. Fujiyoshi, H., Lipton, A.: Real-time Human Motion Analysis by Skeletonization. In: Proc. IEEE Workshop on Application of Computer Vision (1998) 15-21

Virtual Garment Pre-positioning

Tung Le Thanh and André Gagalowicz

Mirages, INRIA, Rocquencourt, France
Tung.lethanh@inria.fr

Abstract. In this paper, we present an easy method for automatic 3D garment pre-positioning. Given a digital 3D mannequin and a set of 2D patterns, the problem consists in sewing automatically the patterns around the mannequin and give an initial position of the garment that the mannequin has to wear. Our method is based upon the use of a figurine. A figurine of a virtual garment, which is always present in the garment design, is associated to the 2D patterns used for producing the garment. This figurine is a 2D drawing which gives the flavor and the style of the future garment. The figurine is the key element of the technique presented in this paper. It can be stored in a 2D CAD file with the 2D patterns of garments or in a database. In this method, we use two figurines, corresponding to the front and the back view of the future garment and a standard silhouette. The designer just needs to work once on the garment construction to allow the automatic pre-positioning. Once the designer has specified the links between the 2D garments and the figurine, he has just to take some simple actions on the figurine to complete the pre-positioning. Our method provides a mapping algorithm from the standard silhouette to a silhouette of a future client, which is the starting point of the pre-positioning. When finalized the automatic pre-positioning will help the designer to see directly the garment he invented on a "real" body.

1 Introduction

In most recent years, many papers in the area of virtual garment design have been published, from simplified cloth models, [5], [11], to more accurate ones, [2], [4], some surveys and comparisons of recent researches are available in [7], [9]. Virtual garment is normally represented by its two-dimensional patterns. It can be used for sewing machines in cloth industry (CAD systems), or produced by a fashion designer. More information is needed to be added to the 2D patterns in order to produce garments. The automatic garment pre-positioning is a very difficult and challenging problem as we have to sew the different pieces correctly and the garment must be worn by a virtual human. This is equivalent to the problem we are faced to every morning when we have to dress up. Some approaches for dressmaking have been proposed. We could think of sewing the garment together and form a virtual garment, and then put it onto the virtual human by simulating the real human behavior, but that seems to be very difficult. Another approach has been introduced in the literature [1], [8], [10]. In this approach, 2D patterns are positioned by hand around the body and then, sewing is performed automatically. Depending on how the garments are treated in the pre-positioning, we can classify them into three main methods: 2D manipulation, 3D manipulation and hybrid: 2D-3D manipulation.

The method in [8] uses 2D manipulation. The authors place the 2D patterns directly onto the front plane or the back plane. The sewing lines are adjusted to tell to the simulator how to sew these 2D patterns together. In their method, the user has to make sure that the sewing lines do not pass through the body. This technique is normally found in animation systems, where clothes are very simple and the precision of the garments is not required ([3], [6]), else it can take a long computing time with a complex cloth. In [10], they propose a 3D manipulation method. The patterns are manipulated interactively. Some points are clipped on both the patterns and their destination locations on the puppet and bending directions are specified on the patterns in order to allow them to be wrapped around the puppet body. The user stitches each garment interactively directly onto the respective positions on the human body. This method is normally used for applications when the cloth is very special, However it is not easy to use and has the drawback to be interactive. The technique described in [1] seems to be the most advanced. Only one point is specified interactively on the front pattern and in the location where it has to appear on the mannequin. The front pattern is positioned in front of the mannequin first and then connected patterns are sewed apart from it and are simultaneously bent around the body with no lateral deformations. This method works well with different types of clothes, but for some complex clothes, it becomes difficult to keep the patterns around the body due to the "rigidity" constraint.

We want to develop a virtual dressing system which can be used easily by a normal user who can try garments using some very simple actions. In this paper, we will present a 2D manipulation method which will be coupled in the future to a 3D mapping technique allowing to reach the final pre-positioning required.

The main idea of the proposed technique is to assign an interaction part to the designer, but to produce a completely automatic pre-positioning for the client. Nowadays, designers already manipulate 2D patterns numerically and use a figurine which produces a 2D outlook of the future garment. The new contribution of the designer will be to assign interactively all 2D patterns to they final position in the figurine. It we be a simple 2D manipulation as the designer knows perfectly the design of the garment and this interaction will be done only once, for a given size, for each type of garment. Then, the designer will have to place the figurine on a generic 2D silhouette to indicate how the garment will be placed on the generic 2D silhouette. When this operation will be done, the result will be transferred to a data base for a final automatic 3D pre-positioning.

Our system starts with a generic 2D silhouette model that is to be dressed. The two figurines (showing the front view and the back view) of the future garment are either provided by the garment designer or will be selected from a database. The use of the generic silhouette and the figurines allows the designer to specify naturally in 2D how the various patterns will appear on the front and the back of the puppet when the garment will be on the puppet. The figurines have to be placed over the generic silhouette. After specifying the sewing informations on the figurines interactively, the designer will have finished his work which will be done only once for a specific garment. We have also to create an easy-to-use interaction software to provide to the designer. The remaining task will consist in deriving these informations when we replace the generic silhouette by the silhouette of a future client. This task will have to be automatic and will give the future front view and back view of the client wearing the garment.

In this article, we introduce our data definitions in section 2. In section 3, we describe how we do the transformation between a generic and a real silhouette model. Finally, we present our results in section 4 where we detail the designer work on the generic silhouette and we show how the equivalent one will be automatically performed on the silhouette of a future client before discussing some of our future works.

2 Preliminaries

2.1 Human Model

Our system starts with a 3D human model. An acceptable model has two extended arms. The angles between these extended arms and the body should be large enough so that there will be no collision when the garment will be added to the silhouette. In our work, we start with a normalized 3D human model which will serve as a generic silhouette for the designer.

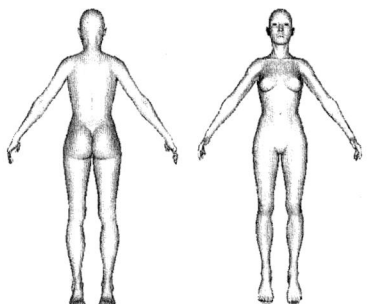

Fig. 1. 3D Human model

2.2 Garments

Fig. 2a presents a real very simple garment imported from a DXF file. It contains some holes corresponding to garment darts. In order to simplify the digitization, we

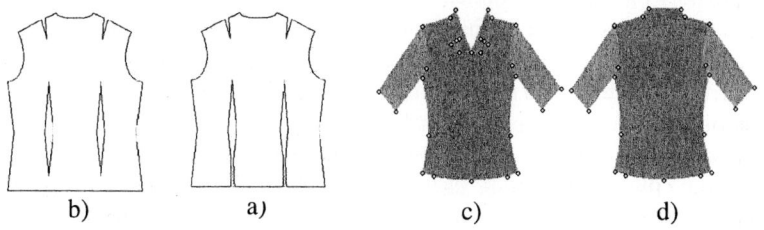

Fig. 2. Cloth garments (a,b). Front and back figurines (c,d) and base points defining their contours.

need to suppress the holes. This can be done by simply creating two virtual cuts (we do not see them) from the hole to the garment bound. The line cutting direction is selected by the user (fig. 2b).

The sewing information of the 2D patterns is provided by the designer, who will specify how two patterns are sewn together (sewing type, direction ...).

2.3 The Figurine

2D figurines (front and back) are used as key element in our method (fig. 2c, 2d). The figurines should be provided with the garments or be selected from a database.
In general, some clothes can use the same figurine, if they are from the same kind and design type (shirt, trousers or skirt of various sizes...).

2.4 Figurine Manipulation

First, the figurines are placed over the generic silhouette. They can be edited to always be "larger" than the silhouette. Next, a mapping between the garment patterns and the points in the figurine is done to initiate the pre-positioning.

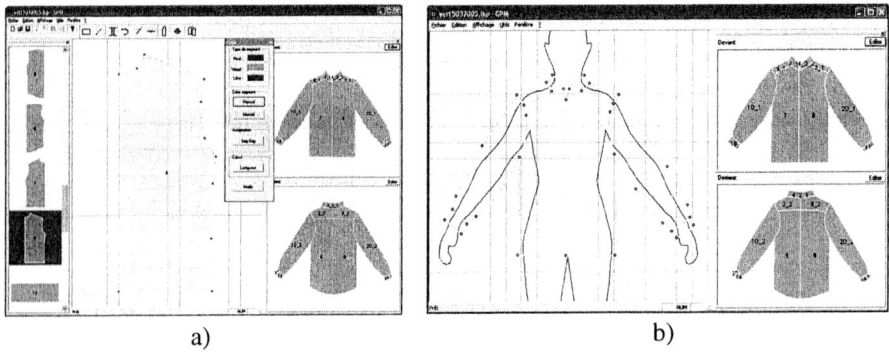

Fig. 3. Designer interface of Virtual Garment Pre-positioning program, a) editing a patron; b) editing a figurine

We developed software to do the pre-positioning. Fig 3a shows how the program works. We can see a list of 2D patterns in the left panel. Each 2D pattern has its own name (number by default or named by the designer).

The 2D pattern selected by the user is shown in work space. After an editing stage (correcting the contour, dividing 2D pattern to create new virtual 2D patterns ...), the 2D pattern will be assigned to the correspond one in the figurine (front or/and back).

In addition, we set a specific color for a segment type (green for a virtual, red for a real and purple for a free segment). Fig 3b shows how to edit a figurine to adapt it to the generic silhouette. In this case, the segments of the figurine are marked as assigned (yellow). The designer moves segments or/and control points to perform this task.

3 2D Pre-positioning

3.1 The Silhouette

Firstly, the input client model is projected into the front plane to obtain its silhouette. Since the figurines are placed over a generic silhouette, we need an automatic transformation to place the figurines over the real silhouette as well.

3.2 Silhouette Mapping

A figurine can be represented by some closed splines shapes. The figurine can be modified by changing the control points of its spline representation. On the other hand, the figurine may be created by a set of control points and knots. We define the base points *{Pi} (i=1...N (see figure 2c, 2d)*.

Editing a figurine is to change the position of its base points *{Pi}* in order to match it to the generic silhouette. The input human models come with different poses and sizes e.g. from fat to thin, tall to short. Our transformations have to ensure that the base points of the real and standard silhouette correspond.

To perform the task, we use a local region mapping. A silhouette is divided into basic regions, so that corresponding parts are consistent and stable.

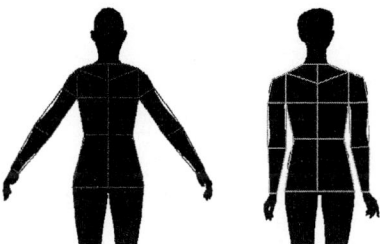

Fig. 4. Regions (in red) on the standard silhouette are mapped on the real one (in green)

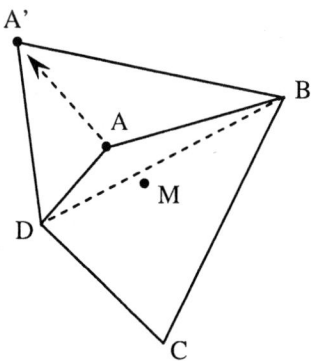

Fig. 5. Triangular mapping

There are some feature points in the silhouette that our system can identify automatically. These feature points can be located at e.g. the hip, waist ...etc. The local regions are created from the feature points. A region is normally a quadrangle (fig. 4). There are many ways to do these mappings. The simplest way is to map triangles to triangles. However, for our application, using triangle mapping is not enough.

Let us consider the region ABCD which contains two triangles ABD and CBD that are used for mapping (fig. 5). When the point A is transformed to the point A', all the points in ADB will be mapped to A'DB. But a point M on the triangle CBD will not be transformed correctly onto the surface of the region ABCD, which is not what we want. To overcome this problem, we choose to use quadrangle mappings

For quadrangle mappings, we want to find for any point M in the quadrangle ABCD its correspond M' in the quadrangle A'B'C'D'. We may represent our mapping using projective plane transformation.
In matrix form:

$$\begin{bmatrix} x'_1 \\ x'_2 \\ x'_3 \end{bmatrix} = \begin{bmatrix} h_{11} & h_{12} & h_{13} \\ h_{21} & h_{22} & h_{23} \\ h_{31} & h_{32} & h_{33} \end{bmatrix} \begin{bmatrix} x_1 \\ x_2 \\ x_3 \end{bmatrix} \tag{1}$$

or $x' = Hx$, where H is 3x3 non-singular homogeneous matrix.

$$x' = \frac{x'_1}{x'_3} = \frac{h_{11}x + h_{12}y + h_{13}}{h_{31}x + h_{32}y + h_{33}} \tag{2}$$

and:

$$y' = \frac{x'_2}{x'_3} = \frac{h_{21}x + h_{22}y + h_{23}}{h_{31}x + h_{32}y + h_{33}} \tag{3}$$

Each point of ABCD and A'B'C'D' generates two linear equations from (2) and (3):

$$x'(h_{31}x + h_{32}y + h_{33}) = h_{11}x + h_{12}y + h_{13}$$
$$y'(h_{31}x + h_{32}y + h_{33}) = h_{21}x + h_{22}y + h_{23} \tag{4}$$

Therefore, H can be determined by the equation:

$$\begin{bmatrix} x_A & y_A & 1 & 0 & 0 & 0 & -x'_A x_A & -x'_A y_A & x'_A \\ 0 & 0 & 0 & x_A & y_A & 1 & -y'_A x_A & -y'_A y_A & y'_A \\ & & & & \cdots & & & & \\ x_D & y_D & 1 & 0 & 0 & 0 & -x'_D x_D & -x'_D y_D & x'_D \\ 0 & 0 & 0 & x_D & y_D & 1 & -y'_D x_D & -y'_D x_D & y'_D \end{bmatrix} \begin{bmatrix} h_{11} \\ h_{12} \\ \vdots \\ h_{32} \\ h_{33} \end{bmatrix} = \begin{bmatrix} 0 \\ 0 \\ \vdots \\ 0 \\ 0 \end{bmatrix} \tag{5}$$

The equation can be rewritten in the form: $TH = 0$ and we can solve it using any least-square minimization method such as the SVD [12].

3.3 Figurine Mapping Algorithm

From the former section, we dispose of the mapping from each quadrangle of the generic silhouette to its corresponding one of the real client silhouette.

For each point p_i of the generic figurine P we compute what is the quadrangle of the generic silhouette which is the closest to p_i, then we transform p_i into its corresponding one p'_i by using the mapping applied to this quadrangle. We denote by G_s the set of quadrangles of the generic silhouette and by G_r, its corresponding one on the client silhouette.

The algorithm is summarized as follows:

```
for each p_i ∈ P do
    min_distance ← MAX_DISTANCE ;
    for each r_j ∈ G_s do
        if  p_i in r_j  then
            min_id ← j ;
            break ;
        end if ;
        distance ← d(p_i, r_j) ;
        if distance < min_distance then
            min_distance ← distance ;
            min_id ← j ;
        end if
    end for
    /* find mapped point p'_i of p_i on real region
       r_min_id ∈ G_r corresponding to the g_min_id ∈ G_s */

    p'_i = map( p_i, r_min_id , g_min_id ) ;
end for
return P' ;
```

3.4 Collisions

A point p'_i of the obtained client figurine may be located inside the client silhouette which produces a collision. This occurs when the angles between the arms and the

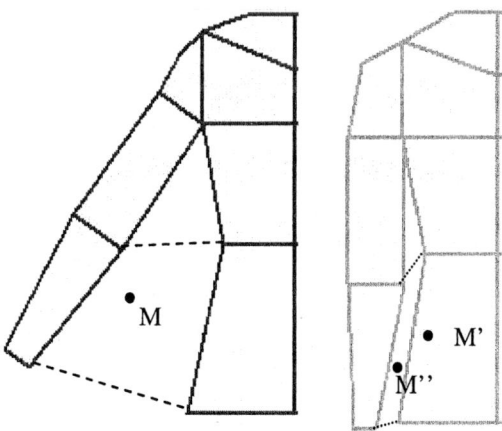

Fig. 6. Collision processing by adding regions. M: initial point (may be a figurine location). M': collision point M'': correct point by adding regions between the arms and the body.

body or the legs are too small, especially when there is a large shape and size differences between the generic and actual silhouette.

When two regions share a common edge, collision cannot happen. In order to avoid collision, we create additional regions for the silhouette models (fig.6): between the arms and body, and between the legs.

4 Implementation and Results

Our garment pre-positioning algorithm is implemented in C++ on a Windows environment. Computing is done in real-time.

Fig. 7 shows the result of using quadrangle mapping from the generic to the real silhouette. The green curve represents the generic silhouette, the red curve comes From the points mapped onto the real silhouette and the blue curves show the differences between

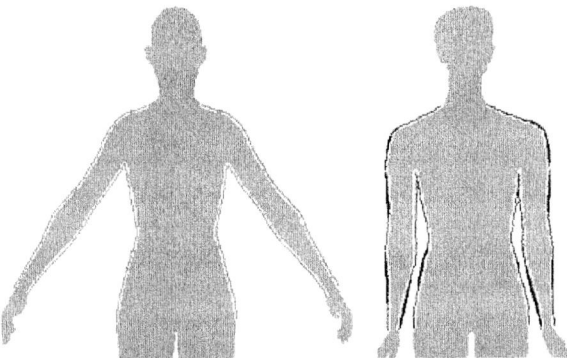

Fig. 7. Mapping result a) Standard silhouette. b) Real silhouette.

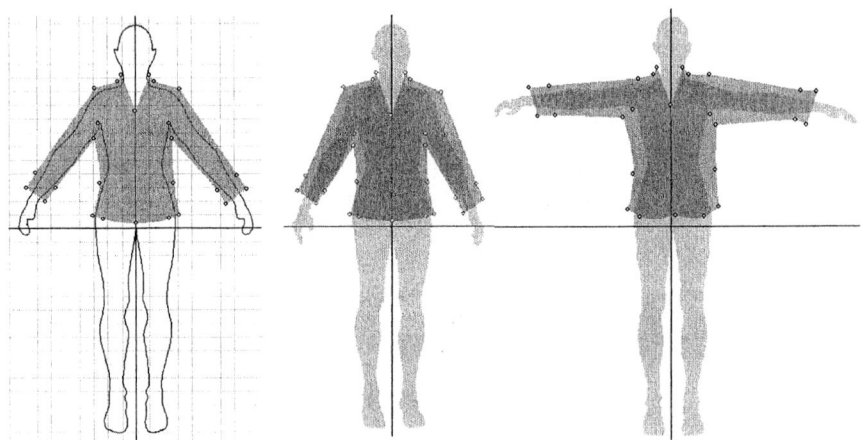

Fig. 8. Various examples of the mapping with different poses

the mapped points and the real ones. From this result, we can show that quadrangle mapping can be used.

Fig. 8 shows some examples of our final garment pre-position results. With different poses, the figurine is automatically positioned onto the model.

5 Conclusion and Future Work

In this paper, we presented a method for pre-positioning of a virtual garment. It is simple to implement and easy to use. All the computations are done in 2D so the program runs very quickly. We have still to transform the figurine from the real silhouette to the final 3D reconstruction around the 3D mannequin. It has the potential to be used for e-commerce or also in fashion software, where a user-friendly interaction can be furnished for garment virtual prototyping.

Our future work will focus on the transformation of the figurine onto the real 3D human puppet which is the continuation of the mapping step from generic silhouette to a specific one. The virtual garments will be digitized and placed close around the real model. This will reduce the computation time for our garment simulator.

References

1. Clemens Groß, Arnulph Fuhrmann and Volker Luckas. Automatic Pre-Positioning Of Virtual Clothing. In Proceedings of the 19th spring conference on Computer graphic, Pages 99 – 108 (2003).
2. David Baraff and Andrew Witkin. Large steps in cloth simulation. In Michael Cohen, editor, SIGGRAPH 98 Conference Proceedings, Annual Conference Series, pages 43–54, Orlando, FL, USA, (1998)
3. Discreet 3Dsmax software: http://www4.discreet.com/3dsmax/
4. Kwang-Jin Choi and Hyeong-Seok Ko. Stable but responsive cloth. In ACM Transactions on Graphics (SIGGRAPH 2002), volume 21, (2002).
5. Mark Meyer, Gilles Debunne, Mathieu Desbrun, and Alan H. Barr. Interactive animation of cloth-like objects for virtual reality. The Journal of Visualization and Computer Animation, 12:1–12, (2001)
6. Maya. http://www.alias.com/
7. H. N. Ng and R. L. Grimsdale. Computer graphics techniques for modelling cloth. IEEE Computer Graphics and Applications, 16(5):52–60 (1996).
8. P. Volino and N. Magnenat-Thalmann. Developing simulation techniques for an interactive clothing system. In Proceedings of Virtual Systems and MultiMedia'97, pages 109 – 118, (1997)
9. P. Volino and N. Magnenat-Thalmann. Comparing efficiency of integrationmethods for cloth animation. In Proceedings of Computer Graphics International 2001 (2001).
10. Takeo Igarashi, John F. Hughes. Clothing Manipulation. 15th Annual Symposium on User Interface Software and Technology, pages 91-100, ACM UIST'02 (2002).
11. Young-Min Kang and Hwan-Gue Cho. Bilayered aproximate integration for rapid and plausible animation of virtual cloth with realistic wrinkles. In Computer Animation 2002, page 203, (2002).
12. William H. Press, William T. Vetterling, Saul A. Teukolsky, Brian P. Flannery. Numerical Recipes in C : The art of scientific Computing, Cambridge University press (1992).

Real-Time Topology Modification for Finite Element Models with Haptic Feedback

Dan C. Popescu, Bhautik Joshi, and Sébastien Ourselin

BioMedIA Lab, Autonomous System Laboratory,
CSIRO ICT Centre, Marsfield NSW 2121, Australia
Dan.Popescu@csiro.au
http://www.ict.csiro.au/BioMedIA

Abstract. We propose a real-time procedure for performing topology modifications on finite element models of objects with linear elastic behaviour. For a 3D tetrahedral model, it requires the inversion of a 6×6 matrix and the weighted multiplication of a thin matrix with its transpose. We exemplify with an implementation in our surgical simulator, where we impose the tight computational constraints of haptic feedback. Our experimental results show that we can obtain response times of under one second for objects represented by tetrahedral meshes with more than 2000 nodes.

1 Introduction

Haptic Virtual Environments are complex, multisensory simulators, which enhance the virtual experience by adding a feeling of touch to the visual interaction. The addition of tactile component comes with computational challenges of its own: typically, haptic devices need to be updated at rates in the range of 300 to over 1000 Hz, otherwise they might provide degraded mechanical experience, such as bumpy motion or unpleasant vibrations.

The realism of the interaction with virtual objects depends on the type of models used to describe them. Non-physical models are simpler representations and therefore easier to update in real-time, but provide less realistic simulations. Physically-based models are more complex representations, allowing for simulations of increased realism, but involve more sophisticated computation. They are generally derived directly from the physical equations governing the evolution of the modelled system. The degree of fidelity needed in a simulation is generally dependent on the application. If a high level of fidelity is necessary – like in a surgical simulator to be used for training medical students and practitioners – the design has to address the challenge of a critically tight balance imposed by real-time response and computational complexity. In such situations, Finite Element (FE) models can provide an optimal solution.

Bro-Nielsen and Cotin [2] have described the explicit construction of the FE models based on tetrahedral meshes with linear elasticity and used them in the context of surgical simulation. Typically, a static FE deformable model is described by a stiffness matrix K, which encompasses the geometrical and physical properties of the object.

The interaction is governed by the equilibrium relation between forces and displacements: $K\mathbf{u} = \mathbf{f}$, where $\mathbf{u}$ and $\mathbf{f}$ are the vectors of displacements and forces at the (discrete) set of nodes of the object. In early versions of simulators, this equation was rewritten as $K^{-1}\mathbf{f} = \mathbf{u}$ and used for driving the simulation of the deformation, based on the assumption that the field of external forces acting on the object was known.

With the arrival of haptic devices, it was noticed that none of the above forms for the equilibrium equation can be used to drive an accurate, realistic simulation. In most realistic simulation scenarios, neither the forces acting on touched nodes, nor the global vector of deformations can be known. A good paradigm of interaction is to drive the simulation by the values of the *imposed displacements* on the *touched nodes* [5], [7]. From these displacements, both the forces on the touched nodes (needed for haptic feedback) and the other displacements on the non-touched nodes (needed for the global deformation) can be found. The basic idea is to block-partition the inverse stiffness matrix K^{-1}, according to the touched and untouched nodes, and rewrite the equilibrium equation as:

$$K^{-1}\mathbf{f} = \begin{bmatrix} A & B \\ C & D \end{bmatrix} \begin{bmatrix} f_t \\ 0 \end{bmatrix} = \begin{bmatrix} u_t \\ u_g \end{bmatrix} = \mathbf{u}. \qquad (1)$$

Because K^{-1} is positive definite, the central matrix A is always non-singular, so one finds $f_t = A^{-1}u_t$. If the size of the touched area is small, which is typically the case, this is a low cost operation. Then, knowing the force vector, one easily finds the displacement vector needed to update the deformation.

The above mechanism is accurate (within the limits of linear elasticity) and efficient. The main issue is that it requires the inverse of the stiffness matrix, K^{-1}. For objects represented by larger meshes (of more than 1000 nodes) the inversion of the matrix K, even using fast iterative methods, requires execution times of minutes or even hours [3]. This is not a problem as long as it is a once-only operation: if no topology change is required, the inverse of the stiffness matrix can be precalculated. However, when topology change is needed, like simulating cuts for a surgical procedure, any algorithm relying on the inversion of the stiffness matrix is unsuitable for real-time simulation. A paradigm shift towards a dynamical system can avoid the calculation of the inverse matrix altogether, but introduces new problems related to the stability of real-time numerical integration [6].

A better alternative to direct computation of the inverse stiffness matrix is to update the already recalculated inverse matrix K^{-1}. The core idea, based on the Sherman-Morrison-Woodbury formula [4], is that if the matrix K is modified by a "small" amount such that it remains nonsingular, then a lower complexity modification is needed to update the inverse matrix. Bro-Nielsen has suggested such an update based on a non-symmetric decomposition of the local stiffness matrix to be removed, and the inversion of a 12×12 matrix [1]. Update times for larger meshes (1000 or more nodes) using this method were around 1 minute.

Based on a similar formulation, Zhong et al. [8] have proposed a fast method of cumulative topology update. However, their method requires the external forces as primary input for updating the deformation and cannot be used in the context of haptic feedback.

In this paper, we present a topology update procedure based on a symmetric decomposition of local stiffness matrices and requiring the inversion of a 6 × 6 matrix. We show that the procedure can achieve acceptable update times (under one second) for meshes of sizes in the range of 2000 nodes.

2 The Update Procedure

We consider the case of a 3D tetrahedral mesh of n nodes, made up of tetrahedra indexed by an index spanning the set $\mathcal{I}$. The local stiffness matrix corresponding to tetrahedron i is:

$$K_i = v_i B_i^T C_i B_i \qquad (2)$$

where v_i is the volume of the tetrahedron i, B_i is a 6 × 12 matrix depending only on the geometry of the tetrahedron, and C_i is a 6 × 6 matrix describing the physical attributes of the tetrahedron. For details on the construction of the matrix B_i, see [2]. The matrix C_i is defined as:

$$C_i = \begin{bmatrix} \lambda_i + 2\mu_i & \lambda_i & \lambda_i & 0 & 0 & 0 \\ \lambda_i & \lambda_i + 2\mu_i & \lambda_i & 0 & 0 & 0 \\ \lambda_i & \lambda_i & \lambda_i + 2\mu_i & 0 & 0 & 0 \\ 0 & 0 & 0 & \mu_i & 0 & 0 \\ 0 & 0 & 0 & 0 & \mu_i & 0 \\ 0 & 0 & 0 & 0 & 0 & \mu_i \end{bmatrix} \qquad (3)$$

where λ_i and μ_i are the two local Lamé parameters.

A global $3n \times 3n$ stiffness matrix K' for an object is obtained by adding the globalised versions of the local stiffness matrices:

$$K' = \sum_{i \in \mathcal{I}} G_i^T K_i G_i = \sum_{i \in \mathcal{I}} \bar{K}_i. \qquad (4)$$

We have denoted by $\bar{K}_i$ the global version of matrix K_i. Here G_i is a "globalisation" matrix of size $12 \times 3n$: $G_i(u, v) = 1$ if the coordinate corresponding to position u in the local matrix K_i corresponds to position v in the global set of coordinates, and equals 0 otherwise. The matrix K' is singular; a typical procedure to remove the singularity is to fix, or "anchor" some of the mesh nodes. This is equivalent to obtaining a slightly smaller nonsingular stiffness matrix K, by removing the rows and columns corresponding to the fixed nodes. In what follows we shall always refer to this reduced matrix K and its inverse K^{-1}.

It is easy to check that we can extract a "symmetric square root" from the matrix C_i, that is, find a 6 × 6 matrix Γ_i such that $\Gamma_i^2 = C_i$ and $\Gamma_i = \Gamma_i^T$ if we define:

$$\Gamma_i = \begin{bmatrix} a_i & b_i & b_i & 0 & 0 & 0 \\ b_i & a_i & b_i & 0 & 0 & 0 \\ b_i & b_i & a_i & 0 & 0 & 0 \\ 0 & 0 & 0 & c_i & 0 & 0 \\ 0 & 0 & 0 & 0 & c_i & 0 \\ 0 & 0 & 0 & 0 & 0 & c_i \end{bmatrix} \quad (5)$$

with $a_i = \frac{1}{3}(\sqrt{3\lambda_i + 2\mu_i} + 2\sqrt{2\mu_i})$, $b_i = \frac{1}{3}(\sqrt{3\lambda_i + 2\mu_i} - \sqrt{2\mu_i})$ and $c_i = \sqrt{\mu_i}$.

If we denote by U_i the 6×12 matrix $U_i = \sqrt{v_i}\Gamma_i B_i$, from Eq. (4) we get for a global $\bar{K}_i$:

$$\bar{K}_i = G_i^T U_i^T U_i G_i. \quad (6)$$

We now wish to perform an incision into the object, by removing one of the constituent tetrahedra. We use a particular form of the Sherman-Morrison-Woodbury formula for updating the inverse of a matrix, for the case when the subtracted low-rank matrix is positive semidefinite, i.e. can be written in the form $V^T V$:

$$(K - V^T V)^{-1} = K^{-1} + K^{-1} V^T (I - V K^{-1} V^T)^{-1} V K^{-1} \quad (7)$$

The second term from the right side of Eq. (7) is the "update" that needs to be performed on the inverse matrix. If we wish to remove the effect of $\bar{K}_i$ from the global K^{-1}, according to Eq. (6) we substitute $V = U_i G_i$ and find the update matrix to be:

$$M = K^{-1} G_i^T U_i^T (I - U_i G_i K^{-1} G_i^T U_i^T)^{-1} U_i G_i K^{-1}$$
$$= K^{-1} G_i^T U_i^T A^{-1} U_i G_i K^{-1}. \quad (8)$$

with $A = I - U_i G_i K^{-1} G_i^T U_i^T$ a symmetric matrix of size 6×6. We remark that in practice all multiplications with the G_i or G_i^T are not actually performed; multiplications with globalisation matrices only involve the extraction of the rows or columns corresponding to the subset represented by the G-matrix. For example, in order to compute the matrix A, one extracts from K^{-1} the 12×12 matrix situated at the intersection of the rows and columns corresponding to the nodes in tetrahedron i. This is then multiplied to the left with the precomputed U_i and to the right with U_i^T and finally subtracted from the 6×6 identity matrix.

Because A is symmetric, it can be decomposed as $A = R^T \Lambda R$ with Λ the diagonal matrix of the eigenvalues, and R a rotation matrix ($R^T = R^{-1}$) formed with the eigenvectors of A. It can be shown that A and $K - \bar{K}_i$ are simultaneously singular or nonsingular, that is, testing the eigenvalues of A is sufficient to assess if the object remains stable after cutting, e.g. there is no piece that falls off. If A is non-singular, then the update matrix M of Eq. (8) becomes:

$$M = K^{-1} G_i^T U_i^T R^T \Lambda^{-1} R U_i G_i K^{-1} = W^T \Lambda^{-1} W. \quad (9)$$

The computation of $W = R U_i G_i K^{-1}$ requires the extraction of 12 rows corresponding to tetrahedron i from K^{-1} and the multiplication by the 6×12 matrix

RG_i. It results in a "thin", $6 \times 3n$ matrix W. The update M of Eq. (9) now requires the multiplication of W^T and W, weighted through the 6 inverses of the eigenvalues. Obviously, because of the symmetry, the actual computation of the lower-diagonal values is unnecessary. Our procedure improves on the state-of-the art found in the literature, by reducing the size of the matrix to be inverted to 6×6 from 12×12, and by requiring only one 6-thin matrix at the last multiplication step.

3 Simulator Structure

The cutting procedure described in the previous section has been integrated into our surgical simulator, which is a prototype system for evaluating and testing simulation algorithms. Fig. 1 shows a diagram of the system. The real-time execution runs two interactive and asynchronous loops: a graphics loop for rendering deformable virtual organs at 30 Hz, and a haptics loop, at 1 kHz, for rendering force feedback.

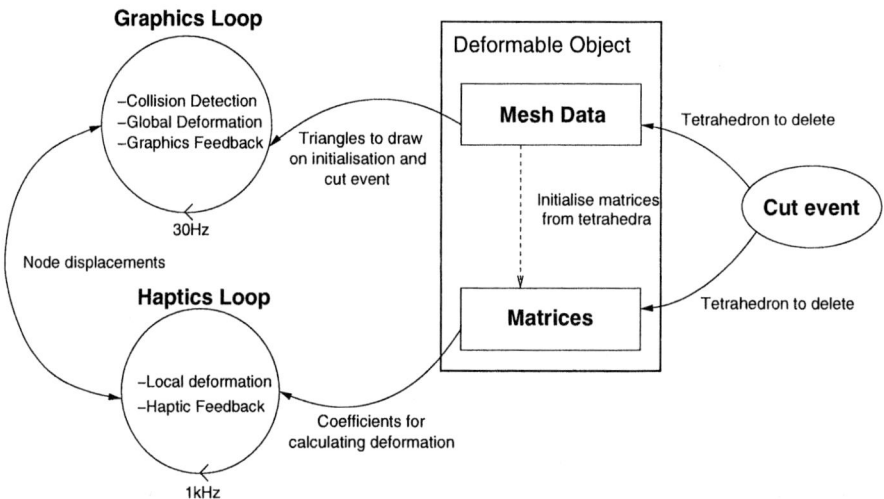

Fig. 1. Structure of our surgical simulator based on two asynchrounous loops

3.1 Interactive Modules

Indentations on the touched nodes are used as input for the simulation. The haptics loop calculates haptic feedback at 1kHz based on data from the inverse of the stiffness matrices. This loop communicates with the graphics loop at 30Hz; on each iteration of the graphics loop, the more expensive global node displacements of the mesh are calculated, as well as the collision detection.

3.2 Data Structures

The tetrahedral mesh is stored using a custom mesh data structure. A key part of this structure is that every face in the mesh stores a current list of its parent tetrahedra. The outer surface hull of the mesh can be determined by extracting the faces which have only one parent tetrahedron. The graphics loop can then be quickly updated when there are changes in topology occurring from tetrahedron removal.

The individual matrices U_i defined in Section 2 are cached in memory alongside K^{-1} when the matrices are initialised from the mesh data. On a cut event, they are used to construct an update matrix M, as shown in Eqs. (8) and (9), which is then added to K^{-1}. Simultaneously, the surface model is recomputed, and sent to the graphics loop for display.

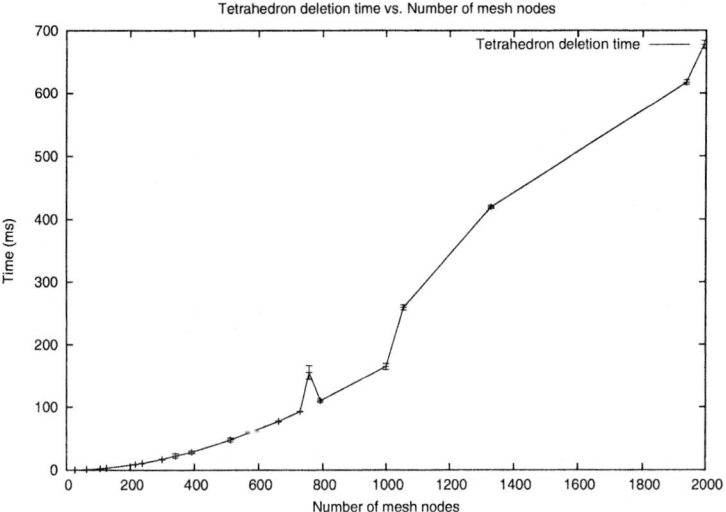

Fig. 2. Time necessary to delete a tetrahedron from a mesh, on a 3Ghz AMD64 running a 2.6 series Linux kernel

4 Results

The deletion time of a tetrahedron from a mesh was recorded and repeated 30 times for meshes of varying complexity, as shown in Fig. 2. This time scales quadratically with respect to the number of mesh nodes and is independent of topological complexity (i.e number of faces and tetrahedra). The quadratic nature of the timing graph is explained by the $O(N^2)$ calculation in Eq. (9).

The simulator is written in C++, is built on top of VTK and makes use of the CVMlib and ATLAS libraries for the linear algebra routines. Experiments for timing the algorithm were run on a 3 GHz AMD64 machine, running a 2.6 Linux kernel. The multi-threaded code was compiled and optimised with GCC 3.3. We expect better results when the matrix and graphics update routines are separated into individual threads and run on a multi-processor machine.

Fig. 3 demonstrates a simple surgical tool interacting and cutting a deformable model of a liver.

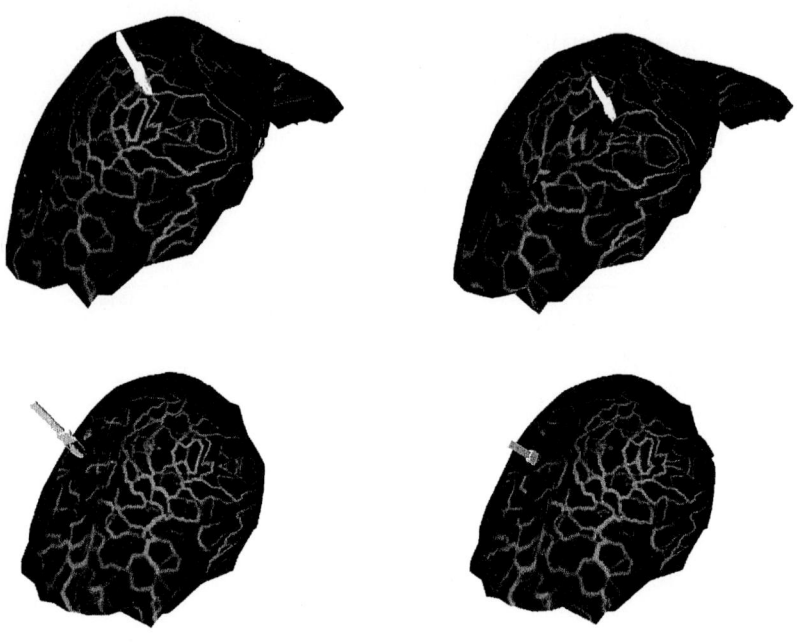

Fig. 3. Top row: Tool next to a deformable organ (left); Tool touching a deformable organ (right). Bottom row: Tool cutting a deformable organ (left); tool peeling aside tissue in a deformable organ (right).

5 Conclusion

We have presented a procedure for real-time topology modification of virtual deformable elastic objects, which can be used in the context of simulators with haptic feedback. The update procedure of the inverse of the stiffness matrix is based a symmetric version of Sherman-Morrison-Woodbury formula. It requires the inversion of a 6 × 6 symmetric matrix and the weighted multiplication of a 6-thin matrix with its transpose. Our procedure still displays an $O(N^2)$ computational complexity. However, we have demonstrated that cutting in real-time is feasible for medium complexity linear elastic meshes; the experimental results in our simulator show that update times of under 1 second can be obtained for object meshes with more than 2000 nodes.

References

1. Bro-Nielsen M.: Finite Element Modeling in Surgery Simulation. In *Proceedings of the IEEE*, vol. 86, no. 3, pp. 490-503, 1998.
2. Bro-Nielsen M. and Cotin S.: Real-time Volumetric Deformable Models for Surgery Simulation using Finite Elements and Condensation. In *Proceedings of Eurographics '96*, vol. 15, no. 3, pp. 57-66, 1996.
3. Cotin S., Delingette H. and Ayache N.: Real-Time Elastic Deformations of Soft Tissues for Surgery Simulation. *IEEE Transaction on Visualization and Computer Graphics*, vol. 5, no. 1, pp. 62-73, 1999.
4. Hager W.: Updating the inverse of a matrix. In *SIAM Review*, vol. 31, pp. 221-239, 1989.
5. Picinbono G.: Geometrical and Physical Models for Surgery Simulation *Phd Thesis, University of Nice-Sophia Antipolis*, 2001.
6. Picinbono G., Lombardo J., Delingette H., Ayache N.: Improving Realism of a Surgery simulator: Linear Anisotropic Elasticity, Complex Interactions and Force Extrapolation. *Journal of Visualization and Computer Animation*, 13:147–167, 2002.
7. Popescu D.C. and Compton M.: A Method for Efficient and Accurate Interaction with Elastic Objects in Haptic Virtual Environments. In *Proceedings of Graphite 2003*, pages 245-249, ACM Press 2003.
8. Zhong, H., Wachowiak M.P. and Peters T.M.: Adaptive Finite Element Technique for Cutting in Surgical Simulation. In *Proceeding of SPIE 2005*, SPIE Press 2005.

A Hierarchical Face Behavior Model for a 3D Face Tracking Without Markers

Richard Roussel and Andre Gagalowicz

INRIA Rocquencourt, France

Abstract. In the context of post-production for the movie industry, localization of a 3D face in an image sequence is a topic, with a growing interest. Its not only a face detection (already done!), but an accurate 3D face localization, an accurate face expression recognition, coupled with the localization, allowing to track a real "living" faces (with speech and emotion). To obtain a faithful tracking, the 3D face model has to be very accurate, and the deformation of the face (the behavior model) has to be realistic. In this paper, we present a new easy-to-use face behavior model, and a tracking system based upon image analysis/synthesis collaboration. This tracking algorithm is computing, for each image of a sequence, the 6 parameters of the 3D face model position and rotation, and the 14 behavior parameters (the amount of each behavior in the behavior space). The result is a moving face, in 3D, with speech and emotions which is not discriminable from the image sequence from which it was extracted.

1 Introduction

One of the greatest challenges in the field of post-production and special effects generation, is the 3D rotoscopy of real objects in an image sequence. In order to manipulate them, they should be located precisely. Previously manual, this search or tracking is more and more automated. Several tracking techniques of rigid and deformable object exist. Some are based only on information resulting from images, such as 2D contours or snakes. Others use 2D or 3D models to guide the tracking algorithms. The technique presented here enters into the framework of 3D model-based tracking. We use a 3D textured face as a tracking tool; this 3D face is projected in the image to compute, and the difference between the pixels of this synthetic image and the pixels of the real image is computed. This matching error drives a minimization algorithm with respect to the degrees of freedom of the system (6 for the position and rotation of the 3D model and 14 for its behavior parameters). We experienced that the 3D model needs to be very realistic and accurate in order for the tracking to be effective. Thats why, the face model has to be ani-mated like a real face in order to be really close to the face to track.

2 State of the Art

In the field of tracking of deformable and/or articulated objects, many publications are available. One can quote the seminal articles of Terzopoulos and Witkin[DTK88], of Pentland[APS91], and the reference work of Blake[BI98]. We are interested in techniques allowing to accurately locate a 3D deformable object in an image.Coarse localization has already been largerly studied problem (see for example work by Gee and Cipolla [GC96]) or Mr. Malciu, F Preteux, V Buzuloiu[MM]), but tracking of expressive faces with strong rotations / deformations is still an open problem. Precision is required for 3D rotoscopy The use of explicit 3D models already exists in the rigid case of objects (see Lowe[Low92], P. Gerard[PG99] or Drummond[DC99]), but the articulated or deformable case remains a problem. Current approaches, containing not very robust scattered primitives (points, contours) or differential computing, are not very reliable in complex environments, a fortiori on classes of objects with strong variability of aspect like faces. The current operational solutions require the use of easily detectable markers[Vtr], who allow to recover the trajectories of some points of interest of the face (like the movement of the lips). It still remains to the user the difficult task of matching these animated elements with those on a 3D synthesis face. Our approach clearly aims at tracking the face in only one stage, and without preliminary marking, thanks to an analysis/synthesis approach proposed by A. Gagalowicz in the past and which already proved its reliability on other applications[Gag94].

3 Dynamic Model of the Face

The tracking algorithm (the minimizer) has to easily control a deformation model of the face. We first use the MPEG-4 points defined over the face to create local deformations. Then, this deformation may be interpolated on the whole face. This set of points created for the animation of face in 3D, allows credible animations of avatars, and makes it possible to be coded with quite few animation parameters and to be sent at low cost through the network. On the other hand, the lack of control between these deformation points does not ensure the possibility to create precise face deformations due to its sparsity. Indeed, it is not possible, given only this set of points, and a very well known interpolation tool like the RBFs, to recreate accurate realistic facial expressions, compared with the real expressions of a speaking actor.

3.1 Hierarchical Deformation Model

Biology of the Face. In the realization of a model of facial deformations, it is obvious that the study of the muscles of the face is of primary importance. We can thus determine which muscles really are activated during the speech and producing the facial expressions, starting from boards of anatomies and especially thanks to works such as those of Parke and Waters[PW96] in their reference book, which lists the muscles that create emotions. These muscles have very different characteristics.

- Their attach points can be, as for the majority of the muscles, on the bone structure for one of their ends and be connected to the skin at the other end. For example, zygomatic muscles acting on the width of the mouth and the height of the lips, or even the forehead muscles, which raise the eyebrows.
- Some are connected exclusively to the skin, as the sphincter muscles of the mouth.

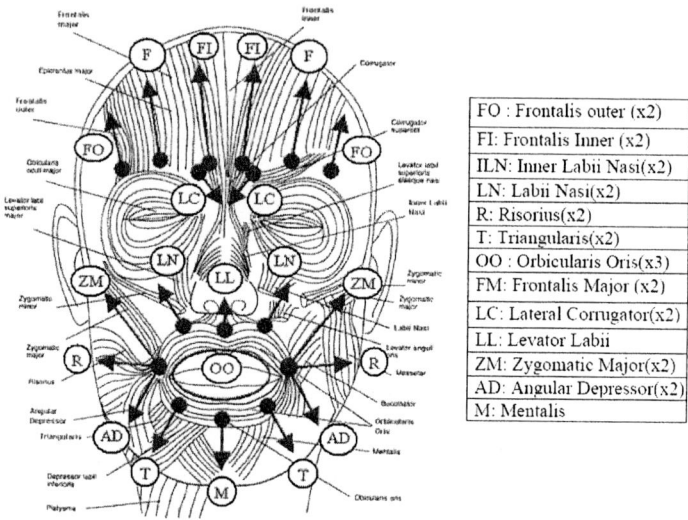

Fig. 1. Anatomical board showing the activated muscles (and their direction), during facial expressions

In all cases, these muscles have visible actions, like Ekman and Friesen[PW78] studied with the FACS. Thus, on the anatomical board of figure1, while taking as a starting point the work of[GBP01], we add, the visual action generated and, moreover, the direction of the action of the muscle, and its principal attach point on the skin.

Hierarchical Model. We thus combined this information, with the MPEG4 model, enabling us to create a complete model of de-formation. This model comprises 4 levels.

Level 1: the low-level deformers At this level, the deformations are applied to the 3D mesh. We thus choose the deformation tool based upon RBFs [JS01], which makes it possible to diffuse the de-formations that are applied only to some deformation centers on all the mesh. This deformation tool is well-known for its very smoothness, and well controlled interpolations. Duchon[Duc77], which

Fig. 2. MPEG-4 Subset point used by our deformation model

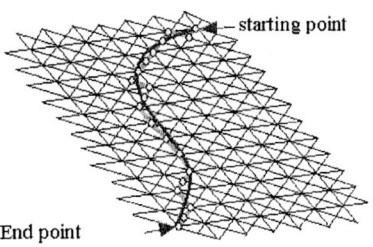

Fig. 3. Choice of the centers of deformation of RBFs (in yellow) among the points of the grid, along the Bzier curve (in red)

studied several types of Radial Basis Functions, showed that the choice of the function of interpolation makes it possible to control the locality of the effect, (its attenuation with the distance). In order to get a very smooth interpolation, distributed uniformly between the various centers of deformation, we choose the LINEAR Radial Basis Function.

Level 2: The high-level deformers We have defined two types of high level deformers on the face :

The "*Point deformers:*" are a sub-set of the MPEG-4 point set. (figure 2). the "*Curve deformers:*" are defined on the surface of the face, which allows, thanks to the control which they induce with their tangents, an increased flexibility for the creation of the deformations (figure 3).

These two types of deformers, "point" and "curve", will both control a low level deformer. In the specific case of the point deformers, it is obvious that they control one low level deformer. For the curves, it is different. A low level deformer will be defined in each point of the mesh close to the curve, in the direction of the curve, as indicated on figure 5. The idea is to represent the maximum of deformations, with less curves as possible. Thus, we have three great groups of curves: eyes, forehead and chin-mouth zone. Finally, we have a 3d model on which was placed two types of deformers, (see figure 4). These deformers must follow the deformation laws imposed by the behaviors. This is described at the next hierarchical level.

Level 3: The behaviors We defined, at the preceding hierarchical level, two types of deformers, points and curves. We define now, on the third level controllers, which are producing behaviors (we give the names of behaviors to these controllers); they are acting simultaneously on a subset of the deformers of the second level. Each deformer receives a basic deformation from the controller which will depend on the type of action that the controller wants to produce (i.e. its behavior).

To allow the 3D model to create phonemes with its mouth and to produce many facial expressions, we defined 14 behaviors which must, at this level of

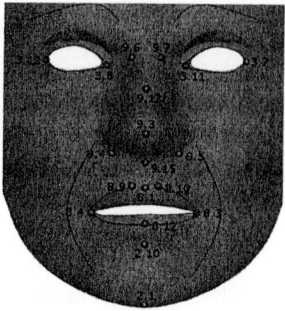

Fig. 4. The complete deforming model including curve deformers

the hierarchy, remain very basic. i.e., each behavior should carry out only one action, as for the FACS. For example, to raise or lower the corners of the lips, or to lower an eyelid. The 14 behaviors we have designed are the following:

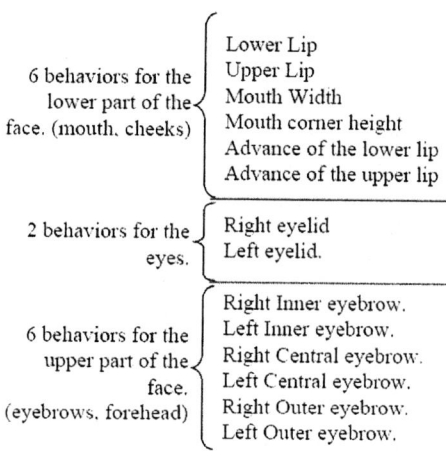

In order to be used in a very easy way by a minimization algorithm, each behavior will be associated to a value standardized between -1 and 1, representing its level of deformation.

Level 4: Expressions The last hierarchical level is the space in which we will find combinations of the 14 behaviors. This space is open to any type of expressions, but must at least contain the 6 universal expressions, that we generated on figure 5 by acting on the various behaviors. The tracking algorithm minimizes an error image where the degrees of freedom are precisely these 14 behaviors. In fact, the tracking algorithm finds, for each frame, the vector of behaviors producing the best expression of the filmed actor with respect to our criterion. We will see, now how the tracking algorithm works.

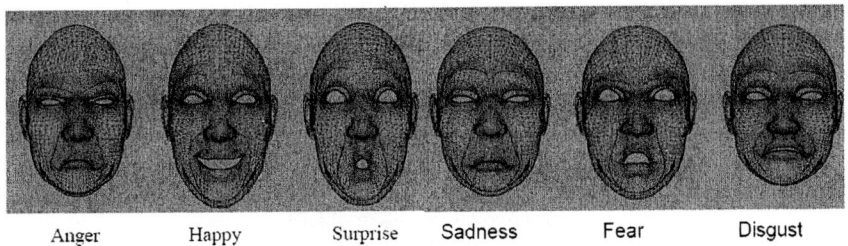

| Anger | Happy | Surprise | Sadness | Fear | Disgust |

Fig. 5. The 6 universal expressions

4 3d Tracking

The global idea of the tracking is to use a 3d textured model as a tool in order to locate very accurately the face in the consecutive images. The 3d model is projected in the image to compute, with a given pose, and a given expression. The objective of the tracking is to find, for each image of the sequence, the optimal parameters of the system, in order to minimize the error between the projected model in the image and the part of the image cut by the model (figure 6).

4.1 Initialization of the System

In the initialization phase, we need to texture the model first. To do it properly, the 3D model must be placed by hand on the first image to compute, not only with the correct camera calibration, but also with the correct facial expression. This task is largely facilitated by the use of POSIT, which calibrates a camera when at least five 3D points and their 2D projection are known, and with our behavior parameters edition window, for the initialization of the initial facial expression.

4.2 Texturing the Mesh

The 3D model being positioned on an image, each 3D vertex is then projected in the image. We can thus compute the texture coordinates (u,v) of each 3D vertex. This texture is carried out with each change of image, thus limiting to the maximum, the nuisances depending on the changes of illumination, or the appearance of new 3D facets, for a rotation of the 3D mesh, for example. Once the mesh is textured with the image N, we can move to the N+1 image, and compute the new location and the new expression automatically.

4.3 Minimization Tool

The minimization uses the matching error between the projected pixels of the textured 3D mesh, and the pixels of the real image. The system consists of 20 degrees of freedom: 6 degrees of freedom for the position and rotation of the 3D mesh of face and 14 others corresponding to the 14 behaviors defined for the face. In order not to be wedged in local minima, we utilize a simulated annealing that drives a simplex. It was applied success-fully in very similar cases for rigid tracking based upon a loop of analysis/synthesis identical to our approach[PG99]. The minimization has a problem common to a lot of minimization tools: it can not optimize, in reasonable time, more than 8 parameters simultaneously. This is why, we cut out the minimization task in 4 independent tasks: Rigid tracking, Mouth tracking, eye (eyelids) tracking and Forehead (eyebrows) tracking.

This is justified by the fact that these parts are rather independent in the face (except the rigid transform that has to be minimized first!) The first tracking locates the face in position and rotation, in the image. Once the face is positioned in an optimal way in the image, we act on the various groups of behaviors separately to find the real expression. Also, it should be noted that, on top of avoiding gigantic computing time, separating DOFs in small groups allows the algorithm minimization to be less sensitive to local minima traps, and thus allows to converge towards the global minimum corresponding to the real image. New DOFs calculated are then injected again into the system with the N+1 image, as an initialization state.

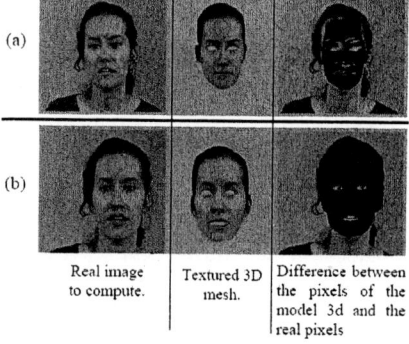

(a)

(b)

Real image to compute. | Textured 3D mesh. | Difference between the pixels of the model 3d and the real pixels

Fig. 6. On (a), the 3D mesh is badly placed. The difference between the real pixels and those of the model is significant and visible. On (b), the 3D face is well positioned, and the error in image is close to 0.

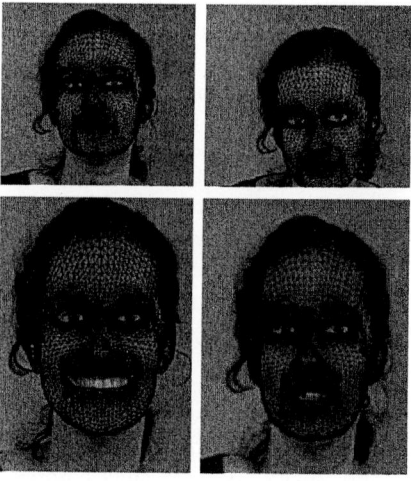

Fig. 7. Tracking resulst on a talking andsmiling head

5 Results

This algorithm was tested on different faces, in many conditions. In all cases, the results were very convincing. We tested scenes of speaking heads, but also of very expressive faces, such as for example the big smile of figure 7. The computation time of our algorithm is about 15 minutes for the 3D model building, and the tracking time is close to 1 minute by frame.

References

[APS91] B.Horowitz A. Pentland and S. Sclaroff, *Non-rigid motion and structure from contour*, In Proceedings of IEEE Conference on Computer Vision and Pattern Recognition, 1991, pp. 288–293.

[BI98] A. Blake and M. Isard, *Active contours*, Springer London, 1998.

[DC99] T. Drummond and R. Cipolla, *Real-time tracking of complex structures for visual servoing*, British Machine Vision Conference, Nottingham, 1999, pp. 574–583.

[DTK88] A. Witkin D. Terzopoulos and Mickael Kass, *Constraints on deformable models: Recovering 3d shape and nonrigid motion*, no. 1, 91–123.

[Duc77] J. Duchon, *Splines minimizing rotation invariant semi-norms in sobolev spaces*, Constructive Theory of Functions of Several Variables, 1977, pp. 85–100.

[Gag94] A. Gagalowicz, *Modeling complex indoor scenes using an analysis/synthesis framework*, Scientific Visualisation advances and Challenges, 1994.

[GBP01] C. Bouville G. Breton and D. Pel, *Face engine; a 3d facial animation engine for real time applications*, Proceedings of 6th International Conference on 3D Web Technology, 2001, pp. 15–22.

[GC96] A.H. Gee and R. Cipolla, *Fast visual tracking by temporal consensus*, Image and Vision Computing, 1996, pp. 105–114.

[JS01] Xianguyang Ju and Paul Siebert, *Conforming generic animatable models to 3d scanned data*, Conference on Human Modeling, Paris, 2001.

[Low92] David G. Lowe, *Robust model-based motion tracking through the integration of search and estimation*, International Journal of Computer Vision **8** (1992), no. 2, 113–122.

[MM] V. Buzuloiu M. Malciu, F. Preteux, *3d global head pose estimation : A robust approach*, Proceedings International Workshop on Synthetic-Natural Hybrid Coding and Three Dimensional Imaging (IWSNHC3DI'99), Santorini, Greece.

[PG99] A. Gagalowicz P. Grard, J.M. Vzien, *Three dimensional model-based tracking using texture learning and matching*, proceedings of SCIA'99 conference (Kanger-lussaq, Groenland), 1999.

[PW78] P.Ekman and W.Friesen, *Facial action coding system*, Facial Action Coding System, 1978.

[PW96] Frederic I. Parke and Keith Waters, *Computer facial animation*, A. K. Peters, 1996.

[Vtr] Vtracker, *http://www.famoustech.com/3d/products/profacevideo.html*.

Author Index

Alegre, Enrique 88
Alhalabi, Firas 197
Amin, Adnan 65, 73
Arndt, R. 724
Arrivault, Denis 748
Atkinson, Gary 162

Baek, Jae-Yeon 546
Baek, Nakhoon 464
Bai, Li 423
Balogh, Emese 456
Barnich, Olivier 280
Batouche, Mohamed 248
Battulga 449
Bauckhage, Christian 347
Baumann, Damien 562
Becker, Susanne 112
Bennamoun, M. 57
Bertini, M. 652
Bober, Mirosław 587
Bors, Adrian G. 213, 222
Bouattour, S. 724
Boukhriss, Isameddine 145
Bourgeois, Steve 669
Bouyer, Philippe 748
Bres, Stéphane 732
Brun, Rémi 789
Buchowicz, Andrzej 514

Cardot, H. 685
Carrillo, Juan F. 604
Chan, Mark 740
Charfi, Hatem 789
Charrier, C. 685
Cherifi, Hocine 205
Chetverikov, Dmitry 240
Cho, Dae-Sung 781
Cho, Sang-Hyun 814
Cho, Seong-Yun 717
Chon, Tae-Soo 546
Császár, Gergely 781
Cucchiara, R. 652
Cyganek, Bogusław 570
Czúni, László 781

Dana, J.M. 171
Defée, Irek 822
Del Bimbo, Alberto 433, 652
Delmas, Patrice 740
Demirel, Hasan 498
D'Haeyer, Johan 596
Distante, Arcangelo 398
Do, Yongtae 829
D'Orazio, Tiziana 398
Doshi, Ashish 222
Droogenbroeck, Marc Van 280

Ejima, Toshiaki 390
Enokida, Shuichi 390

Fazekas, A. 766
Feng, David 522
Fidrich, Márta 456
Flusser, Jan 9, 415
Franc, Vojtěch 407
Freisleben, Bernd 756

Gagalowicz, André 379, 789, 837, 854
García, I. 171
Gautama, Sidharta 596
Gimel'farb, Georgy 112, 740
Gllavata, Julinda 756
Goeman, Werner 596
Grest, Daniel 480
Guha, Sumanta 338
Güneş, Salih 81

Hahn, Hernsoo 636
Hajdu, A. 766
Han, Man-Wi 546
Han, Su-Young 717
Han, Youngjoon 636
Hanbury, Allan 441
Hancock, Edwin R. 96, 128, 153, 162, 179, 272
Haxhimusa, Yll 579
He, Lei 41
Hlaváč, Václav 407
Hong, Manpyo 464
Horáček, Ondřej 415

Hoyos, Marcela Hernández 604
Huang, Hai 304

Illetschko, Thomas 579
Imiya, Atsushi 104, 296, 355
Ion, Adrian 579
Iwanowski, Marcin 530, 538

Jaffré, Gaël 472, 489
Jankó, Zsolt 240
Jiang, Chunyan 264
Jiang, Xiaoyue 288
Joly, Philippe 472, 489
Joshi, Bhautik 846
Jung, Eui-Hyun 717
Jung, Ho Gi 231

Kamenický, Jan 415
Kang, Hang-Bong 814
Kanyó, Judit 456
Karolczak, Mikołaj 620
Karslıgil, M. Elif 799
Kasprzak, Włodzimierz 620
Khánh, Kiêu Trọng 338
Ki, Hyunjong 806
Kim, Dong Suk 231
Kim, Hyun Mun 781
Kim, HyungJun 256
Kim, Jai Hie 231
Kim, Jeehoon 546
Kim, Ku-Jin 464
Kim, Seung-Jin 120
Kim, Sungshin 546
Kim, Tae-Su 120
Kim, WonHa 256
Kim, Wookhyun 709
Klette, Reinhard 41, 321
Koch, Reinhard 480
Kodaz, Halife 81
Kropatsch, Walter G. 579
Kuba, Attila 456, 628
Kucharski, Krzysztof 587
Kühnapfel, Thorsten 49
Kumar, Ritwik K. 313
Kurzynski, Marek 330
Kwolek, Bogdan 693

Landucci, Lea 433
Le Thanh, Tung 837
Lebrun, G. 685

Leclercq, Philippe 740
Lee, Kuhn-Il 120
Lee, Sengtai 546
Lee, Woobeom 709
Leo, Marco 398
Leszczynski, Mariusz 773
Lezoray, O. 685
Li, Chengjun 363
Li, Fajie 321
Li, Si-Kun 188
Li, Tie-Jun 188
Lie, Agus Santoso 390
Lim, Fee-Lee 49
López, M.F. 171
Lu, Sijun 522
Lukac, Rastislav 137

Maik, Vivek 677
Makay, Géza 456
Martinsson, Hanna 669
Máté, Eörs 456, 628
Megson, Graham 554
Meinel, Christoph 264
Meurie, C. 685
Mičušík, Branislav 441
Miguet, Serge 145, 205
Mitra, Suman K. 313
Mochizuki, Yoshihiko 104

Nam, Mi Young 449
Nasios, Nikolaos 213
Naudet, Sylvie 669
Navara, Mirko 407
Nguyen, Trung 17
Nini, Brahim 248
Nyúl, László G. 456

Ohn, Syng-Yup 644
Orkisz, Maciej 604
Ortiz, J.P. 171
Ourselin, Sébastien 846
Özgündüz, Emre 799
Özkaramanlı, Hüseyin 498

Paik, Joonki 677, 806
Park, Jihun 1
Park, Kang Ryoung 33
Paulus, D. 724
Petkov, Nicolai 88
Pham, Quoc-Cuong 669
Pietrowcew, Adam 514

Plataniotis, Konstantinos N.   137
Polat, Kemal   81
Popescu, Dan C.   846

Qiu, Huaijun   128, 272
Quah, Chee Kwang   379

Reulke, Ralf   112
Rhee, Phill Kyu   449
Richard, Noël   748
Rital, Soufiane   205
Rivero-Moreno, Carlos Joel   732
Robles-Kelly, Antonio   661
Rodríguez, S.G.   171
Rosenhahn, Bodo   41
Roussel, Richard   379, 854
Ruiz, V.G.   171

Şahan, Seral   81
Sánchez, Lidia   88
Sánta, I.   766
Sas, Jerzy   330
Sato, Kosuke   296
Seah, Hock Soon   379
Şentrük, Tülin   799
Shah, Shishir   506
Shen, Cheng-Dong   188
Shen, Linlin   423
Shin, Jeongho   677, 806
Skarbek, Władysław   514, 587, 773
Smith, William A.P.   153
Soille, Pierre   530, 538
Soyel, Hamit   498
Spagnolo, Paolo   398
Sugaya, Hironobu   104
Suk, Tomáš   9
Sun, Xianfang   96
Szwoch, Mariusz   701
Szynkiewicz, Wojciech   620

Tan, Tele   49
Tanács, Attila   628
Tinembart, Jacques   562

Todt, Eduardo   612
Torii, Akihiko   104, 355
Torniai, C.   652
Torras, Carme   612
Tóth, T.   766
Tougne, Laure   145, 197
Tsotsos, John K.   347

Uyguroğlu, Mustafa   498

Valli, Alessandro   433
Varoğlu, Ekrem   498

Wada, Tomohito   390
Wang, Guoping   363
Wang, Zhizhong   304
Wilson, Richard C.   371
Wongso, Amelyn   49
Wu, Yunsong   554

Xiao, Rong   288
Xie, Hongbo   304
Xu, Tianmin   363

Yager, Neil   65, 73
Yang, Jie   26
Yin, Dali   363
Yoon, Pal Joo   231
Yu, Hang   179
Yu, Hongchuan   57
Yue, Weining   363
Yurtkan, Kamil   498

Zhang, Fan   272
Zhang, Jian   522
Zhang, Xinhua   264
Zhao, Jianmin   26
Zhao, Rongchun   288
Zhao, Tuo   288
Zheng, Zhonglong   26
Zhong, Daidi   822
Zhu, Ping   371

Lecture Notes in Computer Science

For information about Vols. 1–3597

please contact your bookseller or Springer

Vol. 3728: V. Paliouras, J. Vounckx, D. Verkest (Eds.), Integrated Circuit and System Design. XV, 753 pages. 2005.

Vol. 3718: V.G. Ganzha, E.W. Mayr, E.V. Vorozhtsov (Eds.), Computer Algebra in Scientific Computing. XII, 502 pages. 2005.

Vol. 3714: H. Obbink, K. Pohl (Eds.), Software Product Lines. XIII, 235 pages. 2005.

Vol. 3710: M. Barni, I. Cox, T. Kalker, H.J. Kim (Eds.), Digital Watermarking. XII, 485 pages. 2005.

Vol. 3703: F. Fages, S. Soliman (Eds.), Principles and Practice of Semantic Web Reasoning. VIII, 163 pages. 2005.

Vol. 3702: B. Beckert (Ed.), Automated Reasoning with Analytic Tableaux and Related Methods. XIII, 343 pages. 2005. (Subseries LNAI).

Vol. 3698: U. Furbach (Ed.), KI 2005: Advances in Artificial Intelligence. XIII, 409 pages. 2005. (Subseries LNAI).

Vol. 3697: W. Duch, J. Kacprzyk, E. Oja, S. Zadrożny (Eds.), Artificial Neural Networks: Formal Models and Their Applications - ICANN 2005, Part II. XXXII, 1045 pages. 2005.

Vol. 3696: W. Duch, J. Kacprzyk, E. Oja, S. Zadrożny (Eds.), Artificial Neural Networks: Biological Inspirations - ICANN 2005, Part I. XXXI, 703 pages. 2005.

Vol. 3691: A. Gagalowicz, W. Philips (Eds.), Computer Analysis of Images and Patterns. XIX, 865 pages. 2005.

Vol. 3690: M. Pěchouček, P. Petta, L.Z. Varga (Eds.), Multi-Agent Systems and Applications IV. XVII, 667 pages. 2005. (Subseries LNAI).

Vol. 3687: S. Singh, M. Singh, C. Apte, P. Perner (Eds.), Pattern Recognition and Image Analysis, Part II. XXV, 809 pages. 2005.

Vol. 3686: S. Singh, M. Singh, C. Apte, P. Perner (Eds.), Pattern Recognition and Data Mining, Part I. XXVI, 689 pages. 2005.

Vol. 3684: R. Khosla, R.J. Howlett, L.C. Jain (Eds.), Knowledge-Based Intelligent Information and Engineering Systems, Part IV. LXXIX, 933 pages. 2005. (Subseries LNAI).

Vol. 3683: R. Khosla, R.J. Howlett, L.C. Jain (Eds.), Knowledge-Based Intelligent Information and Engineering Systems, Part III. LXXX, 1397 pages. 2005. (Subseries LNAI).

Vol. 3682: R. Khosla, R.J. Howlett, L.C. Jain (Eds.), Knowledge-Based Intelligent Information and Engineering Systems, Part II. LXXIX, 1371 pages. 2005. (Subseries LNAI).

Vol. 3681: R. Khosla, R.J. Howlett, L.C. Jain (Eds.), Knowledge-Based Intelligent Information and Engineering Systems, Part I. LXXX, 1319 pages. 2005. (Subseries LNAI).

Vol. 3679: S.d.C. di Vimercati, P. Syverson, D. Gollmann (Eds.), Computer Security – ESORICS 2005. XI, 509 pages. 2005.

Vol. 3678: A. McLysaght, D.H. Huson (Eds.), Comparative Genomics. VIII, 167 pages. 2005. (Subseries LNBI).

Vol. 3677: J. Dittmann, S. Katzenbeisser, A. Uhl (Eds.), Communications and Multimedia Security. XIII, 360 pages. 2005.

Vol. 3675: Y. Luo (Ed.), Cooperative Design, Visualization, and Engineering. XI, 264 pages. 2005.

Vol. 3674: W. Jonker, M. Petković (Eds.), Secure Data Management. X, 241 pages. 2005.

Vol. 3672: C. Hankin, I. Siveroni (Eds.), Static Analysis. X, 369 pages. 2005.

Vol. 3671: S. Bressan, S. Ceri, E. Hunt, Z.G. Ives, Z. Bellahsène, M. Rys, R. Unland (Eds.), Database and XML Technologies. X, 239 pages. 2005.

Vol. 3670: M. Bravetti, L. Kloul, G. Zavattaro (Eds.), Formal Techniques for Computer Systems and Business Processes. XIII, 349 pages. 2005.

Vol. 3666: B.D. Martino, D. Kranzlmüller, J. Dongarra (Eds.), Recent Advances in Parallel Virtual Machine and Message Passing Interface. XVII, 546 pages. 2005.

Vol. 3665: K. S. Candan, A. Celentano (Eds.), Advances in Multimedia Information Systems. X, 221 pages. 2005.

Vol. 3664: C. Türker, M. Agosti, H.-J. Schek (Eds.), Peer-to-Peer, Grid, and Service-Orientation in Digital Library Architectures. X, 261 pages. 2005.

Vol. 3663: W.G. Kropatsch, R. Sablatnig, A. Hanbury (Eds.), Pattern Recognition. XIV, 512 pages. 2005.

Vol. 3662: C. Baral, G. Greco, N. Leone, G. Terracina (Eds.), Logic Programming and Nonmonotonic Reasoning. XIII, 454 pages. 2005. (Subseries LNAI).

Vol. 3661: T. Panayiotopoulos, J. Gratch, R. Aylett, D. Ballin, P. Olivier, T. Rist (Eds.), Intelligent Virtual Agents. XIII, 506 pages. 2005. (Subseries LNAI).

Vol. 3660: M. Beigl, S. Intille, J. Rekimoto, H. Tokuda (Eds.), UbiComp 2005: Ubiquitous Computing. XVII, 394 pages. 2005.

Vol. 3659: J.R. Rao, B. Sunar (Eds.), Cryptographic Hardware and Embedded Systems – CHES 2005. XIV, 458 pages. 2005.

Vol. 3658: V. Matoušek, P. Mautner, T. Pavelka (Eds.), Text, Speech and Dialogue. XV, 460 pages. 2005. (Subseries LNAI).

Vol. 3655: A. Aldini, R. Gorrieri, F. Martinelli (Eds.), Foundations of Security Analysis and Design III. VII, 273 pages. 2005.

Vol. 3654: S. Jajodia, D. Wijesekera (Eds.), Data and Applications Security XIX. X, 353 pages. 2005.

Vol. 3653: M. Abadi, L. de Alfaro (Eds.), CONCUR 2005 – Concurrency Theory. XIV, 578 pages. 2005.

Vol. 3652: A. Rauber, S. Christodoulakis, A M. Tjoa (Eds.), Research and Advanced Technology for Digital Libraries. XVIII, 545 pages. 2005.

Vol. 3649: W.M.P. van der Aalst, B. Benatallah, F. Casati, F. Curbera (Eds.), Business Process Management. XII, 472 pages. 2005.

Vol. 3648: J.C. Cunha, P.D. Medeiros (Eds.), Euro-Par 2005 Parallel Processing. XXXVI, 1299 pages. 2005.

Vol. 3646: A. F. Famili, J.N. Kok, J.M. Peña, A. Siebes, A. Feelders (Eds.), Advances in Intelligent Data Analysis VI. XIV, 522 pages. 2005.

Vol. 3645: D.-S. Huang, X.-P. Zhang, G.-B. Huang (Eds.), Advances in Intelligent Computing, Part II. XIII, 1010 pages. 2005.

Vol. 3644: D.-S. Huang, X.-P. Zhang, G.-B. Huang (Eds.), Advances in Intelligent Computing, Part I. XXVII, 1101 pages. 2005.

Vol. 3642: D. Ślezak, J. Yao, J.F. Peters, W. Ziarko, X. Hu (Eds.), Rough Sets, Fuzzy Sets, Data Mining, and Granular Computing, Part II. XXIII, 738 pages. 2005. (Subseries LNAI).

Vol. 3641: D. Ślezak, G. Wang, M. Szczuka, I. Düntsch, Y. Yao (Eds.), Rough Sets, Fuzzy Sets, Data Mining, and Granular Computing, Part I. XXIV, 742 pages. 2005. (Subseries LNAI).

Vol. 3639: P. Godefroid (Ed.), Model Checking Software. XI, 289 pages. 2005.

Vol. 3638: A. Butz, B. Fisher, A. Krüger, P. Olivier (Eds.), Smart Graphics. XI, 269 pages. 2005.

Vol. 3637: J. M. Moreno, J. Madrenas, J. Cosp (Eds.), Evolvable Systems: From Biology to Hardware. XI, 227 pages. 2005.

Vol. 3636: M.J. Blesa, C. Blum, A. Roli, M. Sampels (Eds.), Hybrid Metaheuristics. XII, 155 pages. 2005.

Vol. 3634: L. Ong (Ed.), Computer Science Logic. XI, 567 pages. 2005.

Vol. 3633: C. Bauzer Medeiros, M. Egenhofer, E. Bertino (Eds.), Advances in Spatial and Temporal Databases. XIII, 433 pages. 2005.

Vol. 3632: R. Nieuwenhuis (Ed.), Automated Deduction – CADE-20. XIII, 459 pages. 2005. (Subseries LNAI).

Vol. 3631: J. Eder, H.-M. Haav, A. Kalja, J. Penjam (Eds.), Advances in Databases and Information Systems. XIII, 393 pages. 2005.

Vol. 3630: M.S. Capcarrere, A.A. Freitas, P.J. Bentley, C.G. Johnson, J. Timmis (Eds.), Advances in Artificial Life. XIX, 949 pages. 2005. (Subseries LNAI).

Vol. 3629: J.L. Fiadeiro, N. Harman, M. Roggenbach, J. Rutten (Eds.), Algebra and Coalgebra in Computer Science. XI, 457 pages. 2005.

Vol. 3628: T. Gschwind, U. Aßmann, O. Nierstrasz (Eds.), Software Composition. X, 199 pages. 2005.

Vol. 3627: C. Jacob, M.L. Pilat, P.J. Bentley, J. Timmis (Eds.), Artificial Immune Systems. XII, 500 pages. 2005.

Vol. 3626: B. Ganter, G. Stumme, R. Wille (Eds.), Formal Concept Analysis. X, 349 pages. 2005. (Subseries LNAI).

Vol. 3625: S. Kramer, B. Pfahringer (Eds.), Inductive Logic Programming. XIII, 427 pages. 2005. (Subseries LNAI).

Vol. 3624: C. Chekuri, K. Jansen, J.D.P. Rolim, L. Trevisan (Eds.), Approximation, Randomization and Combinatorial Optimization. XI, 495 pages. 2005.

Vol. 3623: M. Liśkiewicz, R. Reischuk (Eds.), Fundamentals of Computation Theory. XV, 576 pages. 2005.

Vol. 3622: V. Vene, T. Uustalu (Eds.), Advanced Functional Programming. IX, 359 pages. 2005.

Vol. 3621: V. Shoup (Ed.), Advances in Cryptology – CRYPTO 2005. XI, 568 pages. 2005.

Vol. 3620: H. Muñoz-Avila, F. Ricci (Eds.), Case-Based Reasoning Research and Development. XV, 654 pages. 2005. (Subseries LNAI).

Vol. 3619: X. Lu, W. Zhao (Eds.), Networking and Mobile Computing. XXIV, 1299 pages. 2005.

Vol. 3618: J. Jedrzejowicz, A. Szepietowski (Eds.), Mathematical Foundations of Computer Science 2005. XVI, 814 pages. 2005.

Vol. 3617: F. Roli, S. Vitulano (Eds.), Image Analysis and Processing – ICIAP 2005. XXIV, 1219 pages. 2005.

Vol. 3615: B. Ludäscher, L. Raschid (Eds.), Data Integration in the Life Sciences. XII, 344 pages. 2005. (Subseries LNBI).

Vol. 3614: L. Wang, Y. Jin (Eds.), Fuzzy Systems and Knowledge Discovery, Part II. XLI, 1314 pages. 2005. (Subseries LNAI).

Vol. 3613: L. Wang, Y. Jin (Eds.), Fuzzy Systems and Knowledge Discovery, Part I. XLI, 1334 pages. 2005. (Subseries LNAI).

Vol. 3612: L. Wang, K. Chen, Y. S. Ong (Eds.), Advances in Natural Computation, Part III. LXI, 1326 pages. 2005.

Vol. 3611: L. Wang, K. Chen, Y. S. Ong (Eds.), Advances in Natural Computation, Part II. LXI, 1292 pages. 2005.

Vol. 3610: L. Wang, K. Chen, Y. S. Ong (Eds.), Advances in Natural Computation, Part I. LXI, 1302 pages. 2005.

Vol. 3608: F. Dehne, A. López-Ortiz, J.-R. Sack (Eds.), Algorithms and Data Structures. XIV, 446 pages. 2005.

Vol. 3607: J.-D. Zucker, L. Saitta (Eds.), Abstraction, Reformulation and Approximation. XII, 376 pages. 2005. (Subseries LNAI).

Vol. 3606: V. Malyshkin (Ed.), Parallel Computing Technologies. XII, 470 pages. 2005.

Vol. 3605: Z. Wu, M. Guo, C. Chen, J. Bu (Eds.), Embedded Software and Systems. XIX, 610 pages. 2005.

Vol. 3604: R. Martin, H. Bez, M. Sabin (Eds.), Mathematics of Surfaces XI. IX, 473 pages. 2005.

Vol. 3603: J. Hurd, T. Melham (Eds.), Theorem Proving in Higher Order Logics. IX, 409 pages. 2005.

Vol. 3602: R. Eigenmann, Z. Li, S.P. Midkiff (Eds.), Languages and Compilers for High Performance Computing. IX, 486 pages. 2005.

Vol. 3599: U. Aßmann, M. Aksit, A. Rensink (Eds.), Model Driven Architecture. X, 235 pages. 2005.

Vol. 3598: H. Murakami, H. Nakashima, H. Tokuda, M. Yasumura, Ubiquitous Computing Systems. XIII, 275 pages. 2005.